MACROECONOMICS

MACROECONOMICS

Andrew B. Abel
THE WHARTON SCHOOL OF THE UNIVERSITY OF PENNSYLVANIA

Ben S. Bernanke
PRINCETON UNIVERSITY

 ADDISON-WESLEY PUBLISHING COMPANY

READING, MASSACHUSETTS   MENLO PARK, CALIFORNIA   NEW YORK
DON MILLS, ONTARIO   WOKINGHAM, ENGLAND   AMSTERDAM   BONN
SYDNEY   SINGAPORE   TOKYO   MADRID   SAN JUAN   MILAN   PARIS

Sponsoring Editor: Barbara Rifkind
Development Editor: Jane Tufts
Senior Production Supervisor: Kazia Navas
Managing Editor: Mary Clare McEwing
Editorial-Production Service: Woodstock Publishers' Services
Copyeditor: Carol Beal
Design Director: Marshall Henrichs
Text Designer: Gary Fujiwara
Cover Designer: Peter Blaiwas
Technical Art Consultant: Dick Morton
Layout Artist: Woodstock Publishers' Services
Permissions Editor: Mary Dyer
Senior Marketing Manager: Dave Theisen
Production Services Manager: Sarah McCracken
Manufacturing Supervisor: Roy Logan
Compositor: Compset, Inc.
Separator: Color Associates, Inc.
Printer: R. R. Donnelley & Sons

Library of Congress Cataloging-in-Publication Data

Abel, Andrew B.
    Macroeconomics / Andrew B. Abel, Ben S. Bernanke.
        p.   cm.
    Includes bibliographical references and index.
    ISBN 0-201-50428-6
    1. Macroeconomics.   I. Bernanke, Ben.   II. Title.
HB172.5.A24   1991
    339—dc20   91-27447
                                                            CIP

ISBN 0-201-50428-6
1 2 3 4 5 6 7 8 9 10-DO-9594939291

Andrew B. Abel
The Wharton School of the University of Pennsylvania

Robert Morris Professor of Finance at The Wharton School and professor of economics at the University of Pennsylvania, Andrew Abel received his A.B. *summa cum laude* from Princeton University and, like coauthor Ben Bernanke, his Ph.D. from the Massachusetts Institute of Technology.

While working toward his Ph.D., Abel was the recipient of a three-year fellowship from the National Science Foundation. Since then he has been awarded numerous honors—including the John Kenneth Galbraith Award for excellence in teaching, an Alfred P. Sloan Research Fellowship, and grants from the U.S. Department of Energy and the National Science Foundation. He is also a research associate of the National Bureau of Economic Research.

Since his appointment to The Wharton School in 1986, Abel has held the Ronald O. Perelman and the Amoco Foundation Professorships. He began his teaching career at the University of Chicago and Harvard University, and has held visiting appointments at both Tel-Aviv University and The Hebrew University of Jeruslaem.

A prolific researcher, Abel has published extensively on fiscal policy, capital formation, monetary policy, asset pricing, and social security—as well as serving on the editorial board of numerous journals.

Ben S. Bernanke
Woodrow Wilson School of Public and International Affairs, Princeton University

Professor of economics and public affairs at Princeton University, Ben Bernanke received his B.A. in economics from Harvard University, *summa cum laude*—capturing both the Allyn Young Prize for best Harvard undergraduate economics thesis and the John H. Williams prize for outstanding senior in the economics department. Like coauthor Abel, he holds a Ph.D. from the Massachusetts Institute of Technology.

Bernanke began his career at the Stanford Graduate School of Business in 1979, moving to Princeton University in 1985. He has twice been visiting professor at M.I.T. and has taught in undergraduate, M.B.A., M.P.A., and Ph.D. programs. He has authored more than 35 publications in macroeconomics, macroeconomic history, and finance.

Bernanke has served as a visiting scholar for the Federal Reserve System in Philadelphia, Boston, and New York, as well as an associate editor of both the *Quarterly Journal of Economics* and the *Journal of Financial Intermediation*. He has been variously honored as an Alfred P. Sloan Research Fellow, a Hoover Institution National Fellow, a National Science Foundation Graduate Fellow, and a research associate of the National Bureau of Economic Research.

Preface

Our students come to the study of macroeconomics both curious and skeptical. They hear the facts and figures on the nightly news or echoed by friends and family; they read about economic policy controversies in the paper. They expect their macroeconomics course to help them make sense of all this information. But once the course is underway, in our experience, students discover that the world of economics is more complex than they had thought from their first encounter with macroeconomic principles. They see the difficulty of giving easy answers to questions such as "How will America's economic future be affected by its persistent trade and budget deficits?" and "What will labor market conditions be like when it's time for me to find a job?" And they learn that such answers cannot be found by carelessly applying supply and demand analyses or by superficially examining the conflicting pronouncements of experts or politicians.

So are students' expectations about the usefulness of their macroeconomics class unfounded and unrealistic? We don't think so; we believe that it is perfectly reasonable for students of intermediate macroeconomics to expect to learn how to think critically and coherently about the issues on today's macroeconomic agenda. Although this is a perfectly reasonable expectation, it presents a challenge for both instructors and students. Our goal in writing this textbook is to meet this challenge for the 1990s.

COVERAGE: THE CONTEMPORARY AGENDA

The first step toward meeting this challenge is defining the macroeconomic problems and issues that concern today's students. Increasingly, our students ask us about the future—not just about the macroeconomic prognosis for the next six months, but about the economic and social prospects for the twenty-first century.

Two long-term economic developments with exceedingly important implications for the future are the worldwide slowing of economic growth and the increasing integration of the world economy. Both of these developments receive expanded coverage in our book.

The importance we assign to long-term economic performance is reflected in our coverage of long-run questions *before* the chapters dealing with short-run analysis. Among the long-run issues discussed in detail in this book are the causes of low U.S. saving and investment rates, the effects on the economy of the government budget deficit and the trade deficit, and the causes and implications of the long-term decline in U.S. productivity growth.

Our coverage of international topics features two chapters, Chapters 7 and 13, that tightly integrate the open-economy themes with the rest of the analysis. Chapter 7 discusses trade balances and international lending from a saving-investment perspective; Chapter 13 gives a detailed treatment of the role of exchange rates and the trade balance in short-run economic performance and policymaking.

Although long-term issues are important, of course, students continue to care about the fluctuations of today's macroeconomy—which have an immediate impact on them and their families—and about the controversies surrounding short-run economic policy. Our book includes a modernized treatment of business cycle analysis and stabilization policy, using insights from both the classical and Keynesian perspectives. We also discuss a wide variety of other current policy issues, including, for example, the macroeconomic implications of financial instability and financial reform, incentive effects and distortionary impacts of taxes as a factor in fiscal policy, and the role of predetermined rules in the conduct of monetary policy.

A UNIFIED MACROECONOMIC MODEL

The issues that interest today's students also engage today's professional macroeconomists. Our goal has been to present the best that contemporary macroeconomics offers in both its agenda and its methods. To achieve this goal without confusing students with a host of conflicting theories and ideas was a real challenge. We chose to develop a unified model that encompasses all of the macroeconomic analyses in our book: long-run and short-run, open economy and closed economy, classical and Keynesian. To make communication easier, we have expressed our model in the conventional *IS-LM, AD-AS* format. However, our approach to macroeconomics is in fact quite different from that of many other texts. Instead of beginning with the traditional income-expenditure analysis, we start (in Chapters 3 and 4) with the classical full-employment version of the macro model, giving equal attention to aggregate supply (the production function, the labor market) and to aggregate demand (consumption, investment, money demand).

Beginning with the full-employment model has several important advantages:

1. It allows you to ground the macroeconomic analysis, easily and naturally, in terms of the economic choices made by consumers, workers, and firms. Because our model is based on the assumption of rational economic behavior, it directly reflects contemporary research in macroeconomics, which almost universally adopts that assumption. Further, the analysis required to understand the microeconomic underpinnings (as we present them) is well within the grasp of the average undergraduate.

2. In just a couple of chapters the full-employment model is sufficiently developed so that students can study long-run topics—such as the determinants of saving, investment, and growth—for which the assumption of full employment is

not controversial. Thus if you choose to cover the long-run topics first (as we do), you quickly have in hand a complete and versatile macroeconomic model.

3. If instead you choose to cover short-run issues early, the classical full-employment model provides you with the needed foundation on which to build modern theories of business cycles (Chapters 9–13), both classical and—with the addition to the model of sticky wages and prices—Keynesian. Using this framework, we are able to give the classical and Keynesian approaches a truly integrated and balanced treatment in our text: We don't treat either approach as a sidelight, nor do we look at them through a "history of thought" lens that ignores the substantial overlap between the two approaches and their cross-fertilization in contemporary research.

PUTTING MACROECONOMICS TO WORK

In sum, our framework is designed to give your students a consistent way of approaching the full range of contemporary macroeconomic issues. We know, though, that students need lots of help in seeing how formal models can be used to explain the real-world economy. We have dedicated a significant portion of each chapter, therefore, to showing the application of the theory to real events and issues and in helping the student learn how to "think like an economist."

The numerous *Application* sections in each chapter show the student how the theory can be used to understand an important episode or issue, such as the impact of tax reform, the causes and effects of the LDC debt crisis, the long-run viability of U.S. manufacturing in the face of foreign competition, or the 1990 credit crunch.

Boxes provide interesting additional information or sidelights, usually drawn from current research, about the theoretical or empirical issue under study. Among the topics covered in boxes are the relationship between the business cycle and the seasonal cycle, the treatment of natural resources and the environment in the national income accounts, and the degree to which recessions represent permanent declines in output.

It's valuable for students to see applications already constructed, but our goal is even more ambitious: We ask students to create their own connections between the model and reality, so that they will take the economic way of thinking with them after they leave the course. One important component of thinking like an economist is being knowledgeable about macroeconomic data—what's available, its strengths and shortcomings. To put students *In Touch with the Macroeconomy*, we introduce a series of boxes that show them where to find important macroeconomic data—such as the index of leading indicators, balance of payments data, and labor market data—and how to interpret them.

In our experience students are especially eager to ask questions about policy options discussed in the news. We have included a feature, *The Policy Debate*, that applies macroeconomic analysis to controversial policy issues, such as whether the United States should adopt a constitutional amendment requiring a balanced Federal budget, or whether we should have an "industrial policy" that promotes high-tech industries. These features lay out the background information, statements of the pro and con positions, an economic analysis, and a summary of the empirical evidence. The goal of these boxes is not to give firm conclusions on specific debates but, instead, to help students learn the steps needed to perform their own economic evaluations of current and future policy issues.

In talking about economic policy, our students frequently note the discrepancy between the recommendations of economists (assuming they even agree!) and the decisions that politicians or government institutions make. We address this discrepancy in boxes that highlight *The Political Environment*. Discussing the political aspects of macroeconomics (such as the link between the state of the economy and presidential elections or the relationship between political instability and national saving rates) reminds students that a complete macroeconomic analysis often demands looking at the political or institutional context.

OUTLINE OF THE BOOK

With our unified theoretical approach and our coverage of real-world events, institutions, and data, we present students with a comprehensive and balanced picture of the macroeconomy and macroeconomics as they are today. Here is a general description of the contents of the book.

Part I. Introduction (Chapters 1–2)

The first part of the book introduces the subject of macroeconomics and the problems of macroeconomic measurement. Chapter 1 includes discussions of what professional macroeconomists do and of the methods of macroeconomic research. Chapter 2 goes beyond standard national income accounting to discuss issues such as the link between national saving and national wealth and the interrelationship of the nominal interest rate, the real interest rate, and the inflation rate.

Part II. A Basic Framework for Macroeconomic Analysis: The Classical *IS-LM* Model (Chapters 3–4)

Part II develops the baseline full-employment macro model, including the goods market, the labor market, and the asset market. The production function and aggregate supply, which are ignored in the early chapters of many texts, receive a full discussion in Chapter 3. Chapter 4 covers basic monetary theory and provides the tools for studying the causes of inflation. Applications in these chapters include the effects of supply shocks, the impact of wars on the economy, and the link between money growth and inflation.

Part III. Saving, Investment, and Growth (Chapters 5–8)

Part III uses the full-employment model to analyze a variety of long-run issues, including international trade and lending and the determinants of saving and investment. The theme of this part is the trade-off between current and future consumption, as expressed in saving decisions by consumers and investment decisions by firms. For example, trade deficits are explained in Chapter 7 as resulting from a level of desired investment that exceeds desired national saving, and the growth chapter (Chapter 8) focuses on the role of capital formation (as well as productivity growth).

Part IV. Business Cycles (Chapters 9–13)

Part IV examines business cycles and short-run economic performance and policy, and it may be covered directly after Part II. In Chapter 9 we define the business cycle and set out a list of empirical findings about the cycle that we call the "business cycle facts." In the next chapters we explicitly compare the ability of the classical and Keynesian models to explain these facts. The classical and Keynesian theories are analyzed by using the *IS-LM* framework of Part II, differing only in the assumptions made about the speed of wage and price adjustment. Thus we emphasize the point that although the modern classical and Keynesian approaches differ, particularly in policy recommendations, they also have much in common. Our discussion of the classical and Keynesian approaches reflects current research, including (for example) sections on the real business cycle approach (Chapter 11) and on efficiency wages and menu costs (Chapter 12).

This part of the book also contains a detailed treatment of the labor market (Chapter 10), which discusses issues such as the effects of marginal and average tax changes on labor supply. The open-economy aspects of cyclical fluctuations and macro policy are discussed in Chapter 13.

Part V. Macroeconomic Policy: A Deeper Look (Chapters 14–17)

Macroeconomic policy is a major focus of the entire text but is particularly emphasized in Part V. This part discusses various policy trade-offs and debates and looks in more detail at policy institutions, such as the Federal Reserve and the Federal government's budget process. Among the issues discussed are the question of whether the Phillips curve reflects a usable policy trade-off (Chapter 14), the importance of Fed credibility (Chapter 15), and Ricardian equivalence and the burden of the debt (Chapter 16). A chapter that is unique to our text, Chapter 17, discusses the role of the financial system in the macroeconomy, including the question of how instability in the banking system or the stock market is related to macroeconomic instability.

FLEXIBILITY

The sequence of topics just outlined represents our own preferred way of teaching the material, but we recognize that instructors have differing preferences and constraints. To accommodate other course sequences, we have built maximum flexibility into the text, so that it is not necessary to cover the chapters in sequence. In particular, instructors who prefer to emphasize short-run issues can move directly from Part II to Part IV with no loss of continuity. Other options are to place less or greater emphasis on the international economy, or to put primary emphasis on either the classical or Keynesian approach. The *Instructor's Manual* provides more ideas on how to use the text to suit your needs best.

LEARNING FEATURES

Textbooks need to help students build understanding by encouraging them to develop good study and problem-solving skills. Our text contains many features aimed at this goal.

Detailed, Full-Color Graphs

Our analyses are liberally illustrated with both data graphs and analytical graphs. Data graphs continually emphasize the empirical relevance of the theory; and the large number of analytical graphs guide students through the development of model and theory in a well-paced, step-by-step manner. Both types of graphs include descriptive captions that summarize the details of events (in the world or in the model) shown on the graph.

In the analytical graphs color is used to highlight the important points or events in each graph, such as equilibrium points or curve shifts. For example, to expand students' understanding of what lies behind curve shifts, we show, on the graphs themselves, descriptions of the shock hitting the system (highlighted in orange) and of the effects of the shock on the elements of the graph (highlighted in blue).

Key Diagrams

Key diagrams, a unique study feature found at the end of selected chapters, are self-contained descriptions of the eleven most important analytical graphs in the book. On two facing pages we present the graph (the production function or the *AD-AS* diagram, for example) and define and describe its elements in words and equations. We then present an analysis of what the graph reveals and discuss the factors that shift the curves in the graph. Taken together, the key diagrams help students comprehend the steps we used in building our macroeconomic model and summarize our analytical framework.

Summary Tables

Summary tables are used throughout the book to bring the main results of an analysis together in one place. For example, Table 3.5 in Chapter 3 (p. 98) lists the factors identified as shifting the *IS* curve. Summary tables reduce the time the student must spend writing and memorizing results, allowing a greater concentration on understanding and applying these results.

End-of-Chapter Problems

In addition to supplying standard end-of-chapter review aids (summary, list of key terms, an annotated list of key equations, and review questions), we have provided an extensive set of interesting problems to help students understand and apply the theory.

Numerical problems have explicit numerical solutions and are especially useful for practice and for checking students' understanding of basic relationships and concepts.

Analytical problems ask the student to use or extend the theory in a qualitative way. These problems are a valuable way to teach students to apply macroeconomic models to situations beyond those presented in the chapters themselves.

Review of Useful Analytical Tools

Although we use no mathematics beyond high school algebra, some students will find it handy to have a review of the main analytical tools used in the book. Appendix A (at the end of the text) succinctly discusses functions of one and several variables, graphs, slopes, exponents, and formulas for finding the growth rates of products and ratios.

Glossary

The Glossary at the end of the text includes definitions of all key terms (boldfaced within the chapter and also listed at the end of each chapter) and refers the student to the page on which the term is fully defined and discussed.

Supplementary Materials

The *Study Guide* provides a review of each chapter, as well as multiple-choice and short-answer problems (and answers) so that students can practice and test their understanding.

The *Instructor's Manual and Test Item File* provides guidance for instructors on using the text in their course, solutions to all end-of-chapter problems in the textbook, and 1000 multiple-choice test questions.

Computerized testing makes the test items available on IBM-PC disks, so that instructors can add, delete, or edit questions and prepare their own tests.

Software includes a detailed macroeconomic data base and additional data-oriented problems for hands-on applications. It is available for IBM-PC.

MacNeil-Lehrer Business Reports Video Library includes three video segments excerpted from current "MacNeil-Lehrer Business Reports," narrated by Paul Solman.

The Economist Annual Yearbook Concise Edition is an annual country-by-country compilation of developments in economics; the annual educational edition is a useful tool for term projects.

ACKNOWLEDGMENTS

These days a textbook is not the lonely venture of its author or coauthors but is the joint project of dozens of skilled and dedicated people. We extend special thanks to Barbara Rifkind, our editor who brilliantly managed the whole project; Jane Tufts, our superb development editor, who contributed substance as well as style to the manuscript; Kazia Navas, who maximized the value that book production technology can have in addressing the needs of students and instructors; and Barbara Gracia, Dick Morton, Kari Heen, and many others at Addison-Wesley for their painstaking effort, care, and craft.

We also thank the reviewers and colleagues who offered valuable comments on succeeding drafts of the book.

Richard G. Anderson, *Federal Reserve Board, Washington, D.C., Division of Monetary Affairs*

Valerie R. Bencivenga, *Cornell University*

Bruce R. Bolnick, *Northeastern University*

Maureen Burton, *California State Polytechnic University-Pomona*

John Campbell, *Princeton University*

J. Lon Carlson, *Illinois State University*

Wayne Carroll, *University of Wisconsin-Eau Claire*

A. Edward Day, *University of Central Florida*

Johan Deprez, *Texas Tech University*

Donald H. Dutkowsky, *Syracuse University*

Alejandra Cox Edwards, *California State University-Long Beach*

Sharon J. Erenburg, *Eastern Michigan University*

Steven Fazzari, *Washington University-St. Louis*

Thomas J. Finn, *Wayne State University*

Charles C. Fischer, *Pittsburg State University*

Charles B. Garrison, *University of Tennessee-Knoxville*

John C. Haltiwanger, *University of Maryland-College Park*

James D. Hamilton, *University of Virginia*

E. Philip Howrey, *University of Michigan-Ann Arbor*

Charles W. Johnston, *University of Michigan-Flint*

Patrick R. Kelso, *West Texas State University*

John S. Lapp, *North Carolina State University*

Michael B. McElroy, *North Carolina State University*

Stephen A. O'Connell, *Swarthmore College*

Andrew J. Policano, *State University of New York-Stony Brook*

Richard Pollock, *University of Hawaii-Manòa*

Jay B. Prag, *Claremont McKenna College*

Charles F. Revier, *Colorado State University*

Scott P. Simkins, *University of North Carolina-Greensboro*

David E. Spencer, *Brigham Young University*

Bryan Taylor, *California State University-Los Angeles*

Stephen J. Turnovsky, *University of Washington*

David D. VanHoose, *University of Alabama*

Mark E. Wohar, *University of Nebraska-Omaha*

We are grateful to Mark Gertler (New York University), Ken Rogoff (University of California at Berkeley), Michael Woodford (University of Chicago), and Stephen Zeldes (University of Pennsylvania), who taught from the manuscript and provided us with invaluable feedback; and to Rick Mishkin (Columbia University), who made some extremely important suggestions. We are also grateful to several cohorts of students at the University of Pennsylvania and Princeton University who—not entirely of their own free will but nonetheless very graciously—assisted us in the development of this textbook.

Last and most important, we thank our families for their patience and support for husbands or dads who weren't home enough and were preoccupied when they were home. We dedicate this book to them.

Philadelphia, PA   A.B.A.
Princeton, NJ   B.S.B.

Brief Contents

Contents

FEDERAL RESERVE   598**

15.1 Principles of Money Supply Determination   599
      The Money Supply in an All-Currency
          Economy   599
      The Money Supply Under Fractional Reserve
          Banking   600
      Bank Runs   604
      The Money Supply with Both Public Holdings
          of Currency and Fractional Reserve
          Banking   604
      Open-Market Operations   606

      **Application: The Money Multiplier During the
          Great Depression   608**

15.2 Monetary Control in the United States   609
      The Federal Reserve System   609
      The Federal Reserve's Balance Sheet   612

      **The Political Environment:
          Reliability of Fed Governors   614**

      Other Means of Controlling the Money
          Supply   615
      Intermediate Targets   618

      **In Touch with the Macroeconomy:
          Decoding the Policy Directives of the
          FOMC   620**

15.3 The Conduct of Monetary Policy: By Rules or
          Discretion?   621
      The Monetarist Case for Rules   622
      Rules and Central Bank Credibility   624

      **Application: Monetary Targeting in West Germany,
          Japan, and the United States   631**

15.4 Chapter Summary   637

      Key Terms   639
      Key Equations   639
      Review Questions   639
      Numerical Problems   640
      Analytical Problems   641

**CHAPTER 16   GOVERNMENT SPENDING AND ITS
FINANCING   642**

16.1 The Government Budget: Some Facts and
          Figures   642
      Government Outlays   642
      Taxes   645
      The Composition of Outlays and Taxes: The
          Federal Government Versus State and Local
          Governments   646
      Deficits   648
16.2 Government Spending, Taxes, and the
          Macroeconomy   649
      Fiscal Policy and Aggregate Demand   649

      Box 16.1: The Federal Budget Process   652

      Government Capital Formation   653
      Incentive Effects of Fiscal Policy   654

      **Application: Does the Federal Government
          Smooth Tax Rates?   656**

16.3 Government Deficits and Debt   657
      The Government Debt   657
      Can the Government Roll Over Its Debt
          Forever?   660

      **Box 16.2: The Social Security Surplus and the
          Federal Deficit   662**

16.4 The Burden of the Government Debt on Future
          Generations   663

      **The Political Environment:
          Logrolling and the Tax Reform Act of
          1986   664**

      Deficits and National Saving: Ricardian
          Equivalence Again   665
      Departures from Ricardian Equivalence   668
16.5 Deficits and Inflation   669
      The Deficit and the Money Supply   669

      **The Policy Debate:
          A Balanced-Budget Amendment?   670**

      Real Seignorage Collection and Inflation   673

      **Application: Seignorage and the Budget Deficit in
          the German Hyperinflation of 1922–1923   677**

16.6 Chapter Summary   678

      Key Terms   680
      Key Equations   680
      Review Questions   680
      Numerical Problems   681
      Analytical Problems   682
      Appendix 16.A The Path of the Debt-GNP
          Ratio   683

MACROECONOMICS

INTRODUCTION

1
Introduction to Macroeconomics

WHAT MACROECONOMICS IS ABOUT

Macroeconomics is the study of the structure and performance of national economies and of the policies that governments use to try to affect economic performance. The questions that macroeconomists try to answer include the following:

- Why do some nations' economies grow quickly, providing their citizens with rapidly improving living standards, while other nations' economies stay relatively stagnant?

- Why do economies sometimes experience sharp short-run fluctuations, lurching between periods of prosperity and periods of hard times?

- Why is it that unemployment sometimes reaches very high levels? Why is it that even during good times a significant fraction of the work force is unemployed?

- What causes inflation, and what can be done about it?

- How do economic links between nations, such as international trade and borrowing, affect the performance of individual economies and of the world economy as a whole?

- How do national economic policies, such as government taxation and spending policies, affect the behavior of the overall economy? How should economic policy be conducted in order to keep the economy as prosperous and stable as possible?

You can see that the subject matter of macroeconomics includes questions that are of great practical importance and that are constantly debated by politicians, the press, and the public. In the rest of this section we look at these key macroeconomic issues in more detail.

Long-Run Economic Growth

If you have ever traveled in a developing country, you could not have helped but observe the difference in living standards relative to those of countries like the United States. The problems of inadequate food, shelter, and health care experi-

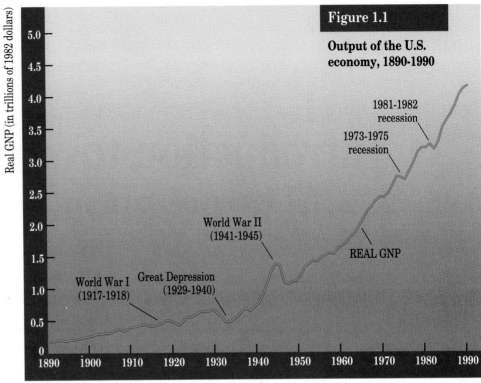

In this graph the measure of output is real gross national product (GNP), with goods and services valued at their 1982 prices (see Chapter 2). Notice the strong upward trend over time, as well as sharp fluctuations during the Great Depression (1929–1940), World War II (1941–1945), and the recessions of 1973–1975 and 1981–1982.

Sources: Pre-1939—*Historical Statistics of the United States*; 1940–1990—*Economic Report of the President.*

enced by the very poorest citizens of rich nations often represent the average or norm for the people of a developing country. From a macroeconomic perspective, the difference between the rich nations and the developing nations can be summarized by saying that the rich nations have at some point in their history experienced extended periods of rapid economic growth, but the poorer nations have either never experienced sustained growth or have had periods of growth offset by periods of economic decline.

The American growth record is summarized by Fig. 1.1, which shows how the output of the U.S. economy has risen over the past century.[1] The record is an impressive one: Over the past hundred years, the rate at which Americans produce goods and services has increased by a factor of 24. The performance of the U.S. economy is not unique, however; other industrial nations have had similar and in some cases higher rates of growth over the past hundred years. This massive increase in the output of industrial economies is one of the central facts of modern history and has had enormous political, military, social, and even cultural implications.

---

[1]The measure of output shown in Fig. 1.1 is called real gross national product (real GNP). We discuss real GNP in detail in Chapter 2.

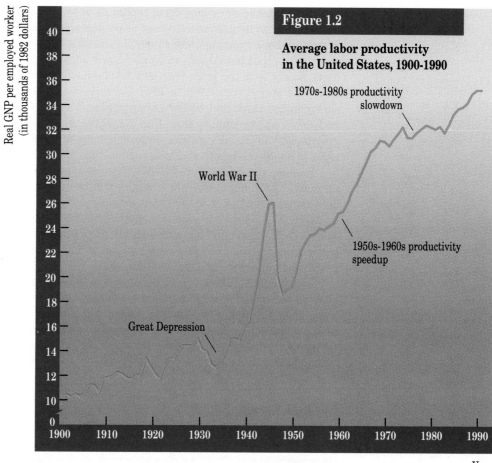

Figure 1.2

Average labor productivity in the United States, 1900-1990

Average labor productivity (output per employed worker over age sixteen) has risen over time, with a peak during World War II reflecting increased wartime production. Productivity growth was particularly strong in the 1950s and 1960s but slowed in the 1970s and 1980s. For the calculation of productivity, output is measured as real GNP with goods and services valued at 1982 prices.

Sources: 1900–1947—*Historical Statistics of the United States*; 1948–1990—*Economic Report of the President*. Annual employment data prior to 1900 were not available.

In part, the long-term growth of the American economy is the result of a rising population, which has meant a steady increase in the number of available workers. But another very significant factor is the increase over time in the amount of output that can be produced with any given amount of labor. The amount of output produced per unit of labor input—for example, per worker or per hour of work— is called **average labor productivity**. Figure 1.2 shows how average labor productivity, defined in this case as output per employed worker over age sixteen, has changed since 1900. In 1990 the average American worker produced about four times as much output as did her counterpart ninety years earlier, despite working significantly fewer hours over the course of the year. Because today the typical worker is so much more productive, she can support herself and her family at a significantly higher standard of living than would have been possible earlier in the century.

Although the very long-term record of productivity growth in the American economy is excellent, in more recent years average labor productivity in the United States has been growing quite slowly. In the twenty-two year period between 1968 and 1990, output per American worker grew a total of only about 11%, which compares poorly with the more than 50% total improvement that occurred in the eighteen-year period from 1950 to 1968. As a result, living standards rose relatively slowly in the 1970s and 1980s. Labor productivity growth did pick up a bit in the mid-1980s, as you can see from Fig. 1.2. Still, the possibility that the productivity growth slowdown will continue underlies many of the concerns that have been expressed about the health and long-term future of the American economy.

Because the rates of growth of output and, particularly, of output per worker ultimately determine whether a nation will be rich or poor, understanding what determines growth is one of the most important goals of macroeconomics. Unfortunately, explaining why economies grow is not easy. Why, for example, did resource-poor Japan and Korea experience growth rates that transformed them in a generation or two from war-torn nations to industrial powers, whereas several resource-rich nations of Latin America have had erratic or even negative growth in recent years? Although macroeconomists have nothing close to a complete answer to the question of what determines rates of economic growth, they do have some ideas to offer. For example, as we will discuss in some detail in this book, most macroeconomists believe that rates of saving and investment are important for growth. Another key determinant of growth we will discuss is the rate at which technological change and other factors help increase the productivity of machines and workers.

Business Cycles

If you look at the history of U.S. output in Fig. 1.1, you will notice that the growth of output is not always smooth but has hills and valleys. Most striking is the period between 1929 and 1945, which contains the Great Depression and World War II. During the 1929–1933 economic collapse that marked the first major phase of the Great Depression, the output of the U.S. economy fell by nearly 30%. Over the period 1939–1944, as America entered the war and expanded production of armaments, output rose by more than 90%. No fluctuations in U.S. output since 1945 have been as severe as those of the 1929–1945 period. However, during the postwar era there have been periods of unusually rapid economic growth, such as during the 1960s, and times during which output has actually declined from one year to the next, as happened in 1973–1975 and 1981–1982.

Macroeconomists use the term business cycle to describe short-run, but sometimes sharp, contractions and expansions in economic activity.[2] The downward phase of a business cycle, during which national output may be falling or perhaps growing only very slowly, is called a recession. Economically, for many people recessions are hard times. Recessions are also a major political concern, since almost every politician wants to be reelected and the chances of reelection are better if the nation's economy is expanding rather than declining. Macroeconomists put a lot of effort into trying to figure out what causes business cycles and into deciding what we can or should do about them. In this book we will describe a variety of

---

[2]A more exact definition is given in Chapter 9. Business cycles do not include fluctuations lasting only a few months, such as the increase in activity that occurs around Christmas.

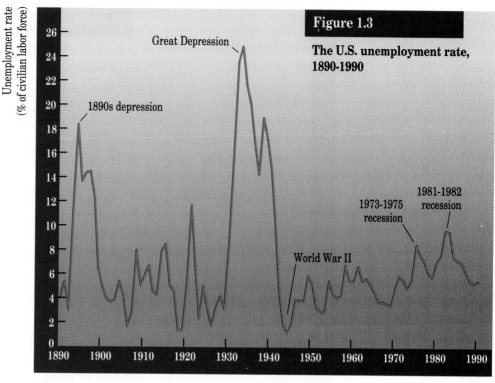

The figure shows the percentage of the civilian labor force (excluding people in the military) that was unemployed in each year since 1890. Unemployment peaked during the depression of the 1890s and the Great Depression of the 1930s and reached its low point during World War II. Since World War II, the highest unemployment rates occurred during the 1973–1975 and 1981–1982 recessions.

Sources: 1890–1970—*Historical Statistics of the United States*; 1971–1990—*Economic Report of the President*.

features of business cycles and compare alternative explanations for cyclical fluctuations.

Unemployment

One important aspect of recessions is that they are usually accompanied by an increase in **unemployment,** or the number of people who are available for work and are actively seeking work but cannot find jobs. Along with growth and business cycles, the problem of unemployment is a third major issue in macroeconomics.

The best-known measure of unemployment is the unemployment rate, equal to the total number of unemployed divided by the labor force, the number of people either working or seeking work. Figure 1.3 shows the unemployment rate in the United States over the past century. The highest and most prolonged period of unemployment occurred during the Great Depression of the 1930s. In 1933 the unemployment rate was 24.9%, indicating that about one out of every four potential workers was unable to find a job. In contrast, the tremendous increase in economic activity that occurred during World War II significantly reduced unemployment. In 1944, at the peak of the wartime boom, the unemployment rate was 1.2%.

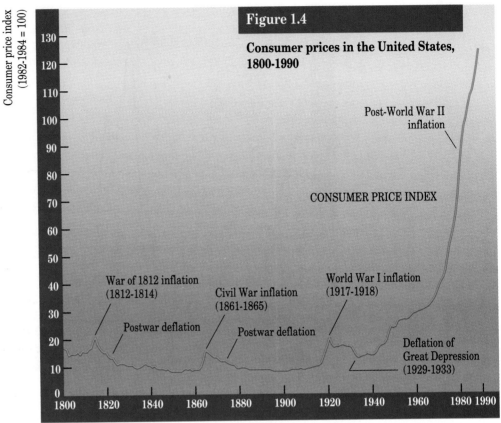

Figure 1.4

Consumer prices in the United States, 1800-1990

Consumer price index (1982-1984 = 100)

Year

Prior to World War II, the average level of prices faced by consumers remained at a relatively constant level, with periods of inflation (rising prices) offset by periods of deflation (falling prices). Since World War II, however, prices have risen more than sixfold. In the figure the average level of prices is measured by the consumer price index, or CPI (see Chapter 2). The CPI measures the cost of a fixed basket of consumer goods relative to the cost of the same basket in a base period, in this case 1982–1984. Thus a CPI of 124 in 1989 means that a basket of consumer goods that cost $100 in 1982–1984 would cost $124 in 1989.

Sources: Same as for Fig. 1.3.

Recessions have led to significant increases in unemployment in recent years as well. For example, during the 1981–1982 recession the U.S. unemployment rate reached 11.4%. As of early 1991, unemployment is again rising as the economy has fallen into a new recession. However, even during periods of economic expansion the unemployment rate remains well above zero, as you can see from Fig. 1.3. In early 1990, after eight years of economic growth with no recession, the unemployment rate remained above 5%. Why the unemployment rate can remain fairly high even when the economy as a whole is doing well is another important question in macroeconomics.

Inflation

When the prices of most goods and services are rising over time, the economy is said to be experiencing **inflation.** Figure 1.4 shows a measure of the average level of prices faced by consumers in the United States over the past two centuries.[3] Notice that prior to World War II inflation usually occurred only during wartime periods, such as during the War of 1812, the Civil War, and World War I. These wartime inflations were followed by periods of **deflation,** during which the prices of most goods and services fell. The result of these offsetting periods of inflation and deflation was that, over the very long run, the level of prices was fairly constant: For example, prices at the end of World War I stood at about the same level as in 1800, more than a century earlier.

However, the last significant deflation experienced in the United States was during 1929–1933, the initial phase of the Great Depression. Since that time inflation, without offsetting deflation, has become the normal state of affairs. Figure 1.4 shows that the level of consumer prices has risen significantly since World War II, with the measure of prices shown in Fig. 1.4 increasing more than sixfold during this period.

The percentage increase in the average level of prices over a year is called the inflation rate. If the inflation rate in consumer prices is 10%, for example, then on average the prices of items that consumers buy are rising by 10% a year. Rates of inflation may vary dramatically both over time and across countries, from a few percent a year in low-inflation countries like Switzerland to 1000% per year or more in countries (like Bolivia or Argentina in recent years) that are experiencing hyperinflations, or extreme inflations. When the inflation rate reaches a very high level, so that prices are being changed daily or hourly, the economy tends to function poorly. Imagine how difficult it is for consumers to find the best prices for the goods and services they want to buy when prices are changing continually! High inflation also means that the purchasing power of money erodes quickly, which forces people to scramble to spend their money almost as soon as they receive it.

The International Economy

Today every major economy is an **open economy,** one that has extensive trading and financial relationships with other national economies. (A **closed economy** does not interact economically with the rest of the world.) Macroeconomists study patterns of international trade and borrowing to better understand the links between national economies. For example, an important topic in macroeconomics is how international trade and borrowing relationships can help to transmit business cycles from country to country.

Another issue for which international considerations are central is trade imbalances. Figure 1.5 shows the historical behavior of the imports and exports of goods and services by the United States. U.S. imports are goods and services produced by foreigners that are purchased by Americans; U.S. exports are goods and services produced by American capital and labor that are sold to foreigners. In order to give you a sense of the relative importance of international trade, Fig. 1.5 expresses exports and imports as percentages of total U.S. output. Both exports and imports are currently larger fractions of U.S. output than they were during the 1950s and 1960s, reflecting both the recovery of trade from the disrup-

---

[3]This measure is called the consumer price index, or CPI, which is discussed in Chapter 2. Conceptually, the CPI is intended to measure the cost of buying a certain fixed set, or "basket," of consumer goods. However, the construction of a consumer price index over a period as long as two centuries involves many compromises. One is that the basket of goods priced by the CPI is not literally the same over the whole period shown in Figure 1.4 but is periodically changed to reflect the different mix of consumer goods available at different times.

The figure shows U.S. exports (*blue*) and U.S. imports (*red*), both expressed as a percentage of total output. Exports and imports need not be equal in each year: U.S. exports exceeded imports during much of the twentieth century, particularly during the two world wars. During the 1980s, however, U.S. exports fell relative to imports.

Sources: Same as for Fig. 1.3.

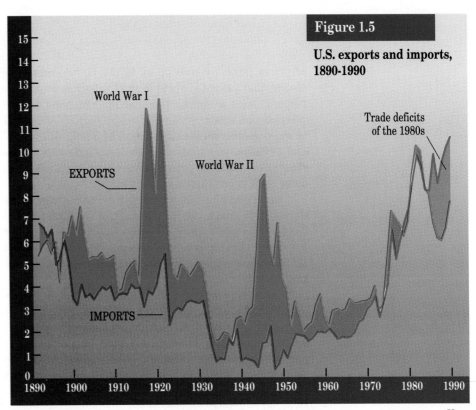

Figure 1.5

U.S. exports and imports, 1890-1990

Exports and imports (% of total output)

Year

tions of the Depression and World War II and the trend toward greater economic interdependence among nations. Notice, though, that a century ago exports and imports were already important relative to the size of the overall economy.

You can see from Fig. 1.5 that exports and imports need not be equal in each year. For example, during World War I and World War II, U.S. exports outstripped U.S. imports because the country was sending large quantities of supplies to its allies in Europe. U.S. exports exceeded imports in 1900–1910 and in the 1950s and 1960s as well. A situation in which exports exceeds imports is called a trade surplus. However, in the 1980s there was a striking decline in U.S. exports relative to imports, as you can see from Fig. 1.5. This recent excess of American imports over exports, or trade deficit, has received considerable attention from policymakers and the press. What causes these trade imbalances? Are they bad for the American economy or for the economies of America's trading partners? These are among the questions that macroeconomists try to answer.

Macroeconomic Policy

A nation's economic performance depends on many factors, including its natural and human resources, its capital stock (buildings and machines), its technology, and the economic choices made by its citizens, both individually and collectively. Another extremely important factor affecting economic performance is the set of macroeconomic policies chosen by the government.

Macroeconomic policies are policies that affect the performance of the economy as a whole. The two major types of macroeconomic policies are fiscal policy and monetary policy. **Fiscal policy,** which is determined both at the national and at the state and local level, concerns government spending and taxation. **Monetary policy** determines the rate of growth of the nation's money supply and is under the

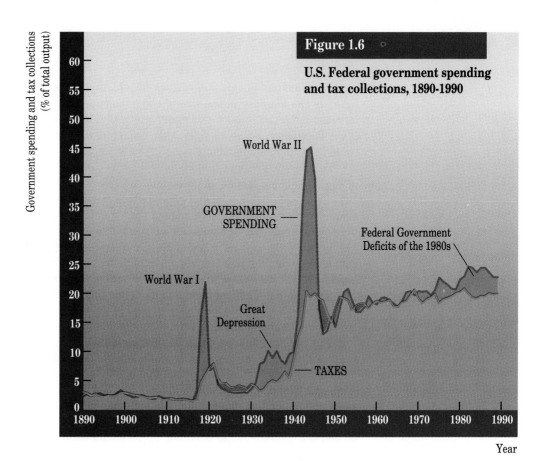

Figure 1.6

U.S. Federal government spending and tax collections, 1890-1990

Government spending and tax collections (% of total output)

Year

U.S. Federal government spending (*red*) and U.S. Federal government tax collections (*blue*) are shown as a percentage of total output. Deficits, or excesses of spending over tax collections, are shaded red, and surpluses (excess of taxes over spending) are shaded blue. The government sector's share of the economy has grown since World War II. Large deficits occurred during the two world wars, the Great Depression, and the 1980s.

Sources: 1890–1939—*Historical Statistics of the United States*; 1940–1990—*Economic Report of the President.*

control of a government institution known as the central bank. In the United States the central bank is called the Federal Reserve, or the Fed.

One of the biggest macroeconomic policy issues of recent years in the United States has been in the realm of fiscal policy. This issue concerns the potential effects on the economy of the Federal government's large budget deficit, the annual excess of government spending over tax collections. The recent deficit is put into a long-term perspective in Fig. 1.6, which presents data on Federal government spending and tax revenues for the past century.[4] Again, so that their importance relative to the economy as a whole is indicated, spending and tax collections are expressed as percentages of total output. Government budget deficits are shaded in red and government budget surpluses are shaded in blue in Fig. 1.6.

Obvious features of Fig. 1.6 are the two peaks in government spending and deficits resulting from military buildups in World War I and World War II. At its high point during World War II, government spending exceeded 45% of total output. Significant deficits also occurred during the Depression of the 1930s because the government increased its spending on various programs designed to help the

---

[4]Government spending includes both government purchases of goods and services, such as purchases of military equipment and the salaries of government officials, and government benefits paid to individuals, such as Social Security payments.

economy, such as government-financed jobs programs. Also shown clearly in the figure is the increase in the size of the government sector since World War II, an increase reflected in both the major upward shift in government spending and in tax collections relative to GNP that occurred around 1940 and the mild upward trend in both variables that has occurred since then.

The Federal budget deficits of the 1980s can be seen in the righthand portion of Fig. 1.6. These large and persistent deficits are historically unusual in that they have occurred during a period of peace and relative prosperity. Critics of the government's fiscal policies have argued that the deficits, which must be financed by borrowing from the public, soak up funds that might otherwise be put to more productive uses such as investment in modern equipment. Some critics also claim that there is a close link between the Federal budget deficits of the 1980s and the excess of U.S. imports over exports that occurred during the same period (see Fig. 1.5). Indeed, the Federal budget deficit and the trade imbalance have been called the "twin deficits." Are these claims true? If so, what can be done? These questions too fall under the heading of macroeconomics.

The possible link between the government's budget deficit and the trade imbalance illustrates an important aspect of macroeconomics: Macroeconomic issues and problems are frequently interconnected. For this reason it is generally not sufficient to study one macroeconomic question, such as the effects of the government budget deficit, in isolation. Instead, macroeconomists usually study the economy as a complete system, allowing for the possibility that changes in one sector or market may affect the behavior of the entire economy.

Aggregation

Macroeconomics is one of two broad areas within the field of economics, the other being microeconomics. Macroeconomics and microeconomics have in common many basic economic ideas and methods; the difference between them is the level at which the economy is studied. Microeconomics focuses on individual consumers, workers, firms, and markets; in microeconomic analysis the state of the national economy is usually taken as given. In contrast, macroeconomics studies the economy as a whole.

In order to study the economy from a macroeconomic, bird's-eye view, macroeconomists ignore the fine distinctions between the many different kinds of goods, firms, and markets that exist in the economy (that's left to microeconomics) and instead focus on national totals. For example, for the purposes of macroeconomic analysis we do not care whether consumers are buying VCRs or compact disc players, beef or chicken, Pepsi or Coke. Instead, we add consumer expenditures on all goods and services to get an overall total called aggregate consumption. The process of adding individual economic variables to obtain economywide totals is called **aggregation**. The use of aggregation and the emphasis on aggregate quantities such as aggregate consumption, aggregate investment, and aggregate output are the major factors that distinguish macroeconomics from microeconomics.

1.2   WHAT MACROECONOMISTS DO

How do professional macroeconomists use their skills? Besides teaching economics, macroeconomists engage in a wide variety of activities, including forecasting, macroeconomic analysis, basic research, and data development.

Macroeconomic Forecasting

We list forecasting first because of the popular image that economists spend most of their time trying to forecast the performance of the economy. In fact, except for a relatively small number of forecasting specialists, forecasting is a minor part of what macroeconomists do. One reason macroeconomists don't emphasize forecasting is that on the whole they are not terribly good at it! Forecasting is difficult not only because our understanding of how the economy works is imperfect but also because it is almost impossible to take into account all the factors—many of them not strictly economic—that might affect future economic trends. Here are some questions that a forecaster, in trying to project the course of the economy, might have to try to answer: How will events abroad affect congressional authorizations for military spending over the next few years? What oil price will OPEC (Organization of Petroleum Exporting Countries) decide on at its next meeting? Will there be a major drought in the agricultural regions with adverse effects on food quantities and prices? Will new technologies that are being developed ever come to market? Because answers to such questions can be known only with great uncertainty, macroeconomic forecasters rarely offer a single prediction. Instead, they usually combine their "most likely" forecast with "optimistic" and "pessimistic" alternative scenarios.

Does the fact that macroeconomics can't be used to make highly accurate forecasts of economic activity mean that it is a pointless field of study? Some people may think so, but that's really an unreasonable standard. Meteorology is an example of a field in which forecasting is difficult (will it *definitely* be nice this weekend?) but in which there is also a lot of useful knowledge (meteorologists helped discover the depletion of the earth's ozone layer and pointed out its dangers). Similarly, cardiologists can't usually predict if or when a patient will have a heart attack—they can only talk about probabilities. Like meteorologists and doctors, economists deal with a very complex system that makes gaining a thorough understanding difficult and forecasting the system's behavior even more difficult. Rather than predicting what will happen, most macroeconomists are engaged in analyzing and interpreting events as they happen (macroeconomic analysis) or in trying to understand the structure of the economy in general (macroeconomic research).

Macroeconomic Analysis

Macroeconomic analysts monitor the economy and think about the implications of current economic events. Many analysts are employed in the private sector, such as in banks or large corporations. Private sector analysts try to determine how general economic trends will affect their employers' financial investments, their opportunities for expansion, the demand for their products, and so on. There are also private firms that specialize in macroeconomic analysis and assist clients on a fee-for-service basis.

The public sector, which includes national and regional governments and international agencies such as the World Bank and the International Monetary Fund, also employs many macroeconomic analysts. The main function of public sector analysts is to assist in the policymaking process—for example, by writing reports that assess various macroeconomic problems and by identifying and evaluating possible policy options. Among American policymakers, the officials who set monetary policy can call on the aid of several hundred Ph.D. economists employed within the Federal Reserve System, and the President has the advice of the Council of

Economic Advisers and the professional staffs of numerous departments and agencies. For members of Congress a frequent source of macroeconomic analysis is the Congressional Budget Office. Economic policymakers also often go outside the government to seek the advice of macroeconomists from business or academia.

If a country has many well-trained macroeconomic analysts, as is true in the United States, does that mean that its macroeconomic policies will always be intelligent and farsighted? Unfortunately, no. Because of the complexity of the economy, macroeconomic policy analysis, like macroeconomic forecasting, is in many cases difficult and fraught with uncertainty. Perhaps even more importantly, though, *economic policy is usually made by politicians, not economists*. Politicians are typically less concerned with the abstract desirability of a policy than with the policy's immediate and visible effects on their constituents. Thus in late 1990 international talks intended to reduce trade barriers failed because European governments found it politically inadvisable to reduce high subsidy payments to their farmers—despite the nearly universal opposition of economists to both trade barriers and farm support payments. To reflect the importance of politics in economic policymaking, at various points in this book we include a feature called "The Political Environment," in which we discuss political aspects of macroeconomics.

Although the technical advice provided by macroeconomic analysts is not the sole basis upon which macroeconomic policy is made, such advice is probably necessary for making good policy decisions, especially if dramatic changes are being considered. In recent years, for example, a number of countries around the world—in Eastern Europe, Latin America, and elsewhere—have undertaken radical reforms of their economies. In most of these cases the countries' leaders have sought the technical advice of domestic and foreign economists, and this advice has been influential in policymaking. In the Soviet Union, economists have played an important role in the debate over restructuring and reform, in capacities both as technical specialists and as political advocates.

Macroeconomic Research

Macroeconomic research takes an amazing variety of forms, from abstract mathematical analysis to psychological experimentation to massive number-crunching projects in which supercomputers are used to process large amounts of economic data. Nevertheless, the goal of all macroeconomic research—which we will discuss further in the next section—is to make general statements about how the economy works. The general insights about the economy that flow from successful research form the basis for the analyses of specific economic problems, policies, or situations.

To see why research is important, imagine that you are an economist from the International Monetary Fund whose task is to help a small African country control its high rate of inflation. On what basis can you offer advice? It would help to know what policies for fighting inflation had been used by other countries in the past, what the results had been, how the results had depended on the characteristics of the country employing the policy, and so on. Particularly if the situation you are analyzing is not identical to any of the previous cases, it would also help to have some theoretical principles to help you identify and understand the main factors contributing to the inflation problem. Analyzing the historical cases and working out the theoretical principles by yourself from scratch might involve many years' effort. The value of ongoing research activities is that many of the results and ideas that you need would already be available, published in books or professional journals or circulated in unpublished form. Because it forms the basis for activities such as economic analysis and forecasting, in a very real sense macroeconomic research is the engine that pulls the whole enterprise of macroeconomics behind it.

Macroeconomic research takes place primarily in colleges and universities, in nonprofit institutions (such as the National Bureau of Economic Research, the Brookings Institution, and the American Enterprise Institute), and in the public sector (the government and international agencies). Particularly in the public sector, the line between economic analysis and macroeconomic research is much fuzzier than we have drawn it here, since many economists move back and forth between analysis of specific problems (such as the African country's inflation problem) and more basic macroeconomic research (such as the analysis of inflation as a general phenomenon).

Data Development

The collection of economic data is a vital part of macroeconomics, and many economists are involved in the data development process. In the United States as well as all other major countries, data on thousands of economic variables are collected and analyzed. We have already looked at some important macroeconomic data series, such as measures of output and the price level, and we will look at these and others in more detail in Chapter 2. Macroeconomists use economic data to assess the current state of the economy, make forecasts, analyze policy alternatives, and test macroeconomic theories.

Most economic data are collected and disseminated by the government—for example, by government agencies such as the Bureau of the Census, the Bureau of Labor Statistics, and the Bureau of Economic Analysis in the United States, and by central banks such as the Federal Reserve. However, to an increasing degree, these activities take place in the private sector as well. For example, marketing firms and private economic forecasting companies are important collectors, users, and sellers of economic data. In this book a feature called "In Touch with the Macroeconomy" will introduce you to major macroeconomic data series, telling you how they are collected and where to find them.

Much of the data collection and preparation process is routine. However, because providers of data want their numbers to be as useful as possible while keeping costs down, the organization of major data collection projects is typically the joint effort of many skilled professionals. Here are some of the questions providers of data must think about:

- What types of data should be collected—who will use them and how?
- How can measures of economic activity be constructed so that they best correspond to abstract concepts (such as "capital" and "labor") that are suggested by economic theory?
- How can accurate and timely data be collected at the least cost? For example, suppose that in order to do a study on productivity growth in manufacturing, an economist must obtain measures of capital investment by manufacturing firms. Is it sufficient just to survey big manufacturing firms about their investment spending, or must small firms be interviewed as well? Could the data be obtained instead from the firms that build capital equipment?
- If the data are collected by sampling a random group of households or firms,

as is usually the case, how can the results be statistically adjusted to give the best idea of what would have been found if all households or firms had been surveyed?

- How can confidentiality for firms and individuals that provide data about themselves be guaranteed?

In a large data-gathering organization, such as the Bureau of the Census, each of these questions is exhaustively analyzed by economists and statisticians before data collection begins.[5]

1.3   MACROECONOMIC RESEARCH: LEARNING ABOUT THE ECONOMY

In thinking about some specific economic policy or problem, a macroeconomist brings to bear knowledge about how the economy works that has been developed over years by many different people. As we have said, developing systematic knowledge about how the economy works is the goal of macroeconomic research.

How is macroeconomic research carried out? As in many other fields, macroeconomic research proceeds primarily through the formulation and testing of theories. An **economic theory** is a set of ideas about the economy that have been organized in a logical framework. Most economic theories are developed in terms of an **economic model,** which is a simplified description of some aspect of the economy, usually expressed in mathematical form. The testing of an economic theory or model is done by evaluating how well the theory or model can explain reality.

To see how economic theories and models are developed and tested, let's consider an illustrative example. Suppose I want to develop a theory that explains which routes people take when they commute from home to work and back. Such a theory would be useful to a traffic planner who is concerned about how a proposed housing development will affect traffic patterns, for example. To model this situation, I need some simple way of explaining how drivers choose their commuting routes. One possible description of driver behavior, which I might come up with by thinking about my own experience, is that drivers choose the route between home and work that minimizes the number of minutes spent driving. For the purposes of building a theory, let us *assume*, then, that drivers choose the quickest route available between home and work.

Why did I choose that particular assumption? It is certainly not totally realistic. Instead of minimizing driving time, some drivers may choose a route that is five minutes longer but passes by a beautiful lake, and lovers of variety may change routes every day. Probably numerous other factors—the desire to avoid a dangerous intersection or the need to pick up other people in the car pool—affect the choice of commuting route. But it is precisely because reality is so complicated that economic models, which are designed to be simplifications of reality, can be useful. The minimum–driving time assumption not only is simple and reasonable but also can be tested by **empirical analysis**—that is, by comparing its implications with actual data—as we will see. So, like any other assumption underlying an economic model, minimum driving time may be thought of as a *provisional* assumption; if it turns out not to describe real-world behavior very well, we can

---

[5]For a readable discussion of issues that face data collectors, see Janet L. Norwood, "Distinguished Lecture on Economics in Government: Data Quality and Public Policy," *Journal of Economic Perspectives,* Spring 1990, pp. 3–12.

always drop it and try another assumption (such as the assumption that commuters drive the shortest possible distance).

Given the minimum–driving time assumption, the next steps in the process are to work out the implications of that assumption for actual behavior and to compare the implications with reality. Suppose that I have access to a survey, conducted by the traffic-planning division, of a thousand randomly chosen drivers. The survey takers asked each driver to report home and job locations, the time of day of the commute, and the routes most commonly taken. Now to test my theory, all I need is a map of the city and some estimated driving times: For each driver I can figure out what the quickest route would be—the theory says that's the route he should take. Then I can compare what the theory says with what the drivers actually do. Doing this comparison is how I can tell if my theory is any good.[6]

What happens next? That depends on how well the theory worked empirically, that is, how well it explained what actually happened. If I find that, usually, people reported taking the minimum-time route, then the theory explains the data well and I can call it a success. I could then use this theory to try to figure out how a new housing development would affect traffic patterns. This would require some guesses about where the people who live in the development are likely to have jobs: Nearby manufacturing plants, shopping malls, and office complexes would be likely possibilities. By assuming that each commuter minimizes time driving to work, I could then work out the routes that residents of the housing complex would be likely to take. Knowing the routes would allow me to assess the effects on traffic flows of building the new development.

If the theory does a poor job of explaining commuters' route choices, however—say only 20% of the drivers chose the minimum-time route—then I'm back to the drawing board. In this case I have to think up a new model, with new assumptions, and see whether it fits the data any better.

If the theory does a fair job—say it explains the routes taken by half the drivers in the survey—then I have a decision to make. I probably don't want to throw out the minimum–driving time assumption, since it appears to be explaining part of what is going on. The issue is whether to complicate the model by adding more assumptions—for example, by assuming that people are willing to take a slightly longer route if it's more scenic. In the decision of whether to add more complexities of reality to the model, the trade-off is between tractability—simplicity and ease of use—on the one hand and realism on the other.

A summary of the main steps in developing and testing an economic theory or model is given in Box 1.1.

In the end, an economic model is judged by at least four criteria:

1. Are its assumptions reasonable and realistic?

2. Is it tractable enough to be understandable and useful for studying real problems?

3. Does it have implications that can be tested empirically by using real-world data?

---

[6]Wouldn't it have been easier just to ask the drivers why they took the route they did? Yes; in this particular situation that would probably be useful. But in more complicated situations—such as in choosing a career—people do things for a variety of reasons, and they can't always tell you which was most important. Or maybe they don't *want* to tell you why they do what they do. For these and other reasons economists like to compare their theories with what people do rather than with what they say.

The steps for developing and testing a theory given here are illustrated by the commuter example discussed in the text.

BOX *1.1:* DEVELOPING AND TESTING AN ECONOMIC THEORY

Step 1. State the research question.

Example: How will a new housing development affect traffic flows during the rush hours?

Step 2. Make assumptions that describe the economic setting and the behavior of the economic actors. These assumptions should be simple but should capture the most important aspects of the problem.

Example: The setting is described by the map of the city, marked with the surveyed commuters' home and work locations. The assumption about behavior is that commuters choose the routes that minimize driving time.

Step 3. Work out the implications of the theory.

Example: Using the map of the city, the home and work locations, and the estimated driving times, figure out the route each commuter would take to minimize driving time.

Step 4. Compare the implications of the theory with the data.

Example: See whether the routes predicted by the model are generally the same as those reported in the commuter survey.

Step 5. Evaluate the results of your comparisons.

If the theory fits the data well: Use the theory to predict what would happen if the economic setting or economic policies change.

Example: Using the minimum–driving time assumption, evaluate the traffic effects of a new housing development by figuring out which routes the residents of the development are likely to take.

If the theory fits the data poorly: Start from scratch with a new model. Repeat steps 3 through 5.

Example: Assume that commuters choose the route that minimizes the distance they must drive.

If the theory fits the data moderately well: Either make do with a partially successful theory, or complicate the model with additional assumptions and repeat steps 3 through 5.

Example: A possible modification of the minimum–driving time assumption is that commuters will choose more scenic over less scenic routes, if driving time is not increased by more than a certain number of minutes. To test the model with this modified assumption, you must determine which routes are more scenic (those that pass by a lake) and which are less scenic (those that pass by a dump).

---

4. Are those implications borne out empirically—that is, are they consistent with the data?

For a good theory or model—of any type, not just economic—the answer to each of these questions must be "yes." Unfortunately, though, economists may not always agree in their evaluation of a given model, which means that controversies about the best way to model a given economic situation sometimes persist.

The example of theory formulation and testing just described was about how individuals—in this case, commuters—behave. Building a theory based on individual behavior seems perfectly reasonable for a microeconomist; but can the same methods be used to study the behavior of entire economies, as macroeconomists want to do? Although care must be taken when doing so, most macroeconomists believe that individual-based theories can be usefully applied to the analysis of the economy as a whole. After all, the economy as a whole is made up of millions of individuals. So the hope is that explaining individual behavior will help us understand aggregate, or economywide, behavior as well. In Chapter 5, for example, we will analyze the decision of individuals to save part of their incomes; then we use the insights gained from this analysis to study national saving behavior.

Understanding individual economic behavior may not be all that is needed to explain macroeconomic behavior, however. As we have already mentioned, macroeconomic analysis also requires an understanding of the relationships among different parts of the economy. For example, we will show that a country's excess of imports over exports is equal to the difference between the country's total investment and its total saving. Using that relationship, and given models of investment and saving decisions based on individual behavior, we'll be able to analyze the determinants of trade imbalances.

Why Macroeconomists Disagree

Our discussion of macroeconomic research makes the field sound rather scientific, and indeed, the basic procedure for developing and testing economic theories is modeled on methods used in the natural sciences. This approach may make it seem as if disagreements about the economy should always be resolvable simply by doing further research. Yet no matter what the issue, it seems that the newspapers can find an economist to argue either side of it. Why do macroeconomists appear to disagree so much?[7]

To a certain extent, the amount of disagreement among macroeconomists is exaggerated by the tendency of the public and the media to focus on the most difficult and controversial issues. In addition, the very fact that economic policy and performance are of such broad interest and concern contributes to the intensity of debate: More than controversies in many other fields, debates in macroeconomics tend to be played out on the public stage, rather than in the seminar room or the laboratory. Although important disagreements among macroeconomists certainly exist, as we will discuss, there also are many areas of macroeconomics in which there is a substantial amount of agreement.

We can gain insight into why macroeconomists disagree if we draw the important distinction between positive and normative analyses of economic policy. A **positive analysis** of an economic policy examines the economic consequences of a policy but doesn't address the question of whether those consequences are desirable. A **normative analysis** of policy tries to determine whether a certain policy *should* be used. For example, if an economist is asked to evaluate the effects on the economy of a 5% rise in the income tax, that is a positive analysis. But if he is asked whether he thinks the income tax *should* be raised 5%, his answer requires a normative analysis. This normative analysis will involve not only the economist's objective, scientific understanding of how the economy works but also his personal value judgments—for example, about the appropriate size of the government sector or the amount of income redistribution that is desirable.

It is possible for economists to agree on the positive analysis of a question and yet disagree on the normative part, because of differences in values. Value differences are common in fields besides economics: Physicists may be in perfect agreement on what would happen if a nuclear bomb were detonated (that's a positive

---

[7]Not only do macroeconomists seem often to disagree with each other, but they also are sometimes accused of not being able to agree with themselves. President Harry Truman expressed the frustration of many policymakers when he said he wanted a one-handed economist—one who wouldn't always say, "On the one hand, . . .; on the other hand. . . ."

analysis). But physicist "hawks" may disagree strongly with physicist "doves" about whether nuclear weapons should be deployed (that's a normative question).

It is also possible to have disagreement on positive issues, however, and these are important in economics. In macroeconomics there are today and always have been many schools of thought, each with a somewhat different perspective on how the economy works. Examples of schools of thought in macroeconomics are monetarism and supply-side economics, both of which we will discuss in this book. However, the most important—and the most enduring—disagreements on positive issues in macroeconomics arise between two schools of thought called the classical approach and the Keynesian approach.

Classicals Versus Keynesians

The classical approach and the Keynesian approach are the two major intellectual traditions in macroeconomics. We discuss the differences between the two approaches briefly here and in much greater detail later on in the book.

The Classical Approach   The origins of the classical approach go back more than two centuries, at least to the famous Scottish economist Adam Smith. In 1776 Smith published his classic *The Wealth of Nations*, in which he set forth the idea of the "invisible hand." The invisible-hand idea states that if there are free markets and each person conducts his economic affairs in his own best interest, then the overall economy will work well. As Smith put it, in a market economy it is as if individuals, while pursuing their own self-interest, were led by an invisible hand to maximize the general welfare of people in the economy.

It is important not to overstate what Smith was claiming: To say that there is an invisible hand at work does *not* mean that no one in a market economy will be hungry or dissatisfied, since free markets cannot insulate a nation from the effects of drought, war, or political instability. Nor does the invisible hand rule out the existence of great inequalities between the rich and the poor, since in Smith's analysis the initial distribution of wealth across people is taken as given. Rather, the invisible-hand idea says that *given* a country's resources (natural, human, and technological) and its initial distribution of wealth, the use of free markets will make people as economically well off as possible.

For the invisible-hand idea to be valid, a key assumption is that the various markets in the economy, including financial markets, labor markets, and markets for goods and services, must function smoothly and without impediments such as minimum wages and interest rate ceilings. In particular, it must be true that wages and prices adjust rapidly enough to keep quantities supplied and quantities demanded equal in all markets. In markets where the quantity demanded exceeds quantity supplied, prices must rise; and in markets where there's more of the good available than people want to buy, prices must fall.

Wage and price flexibility is critical to the invisible-hand idea, because in a free-market system changes in wages and prices are the signals that coordinate the actions of people in the economy. To illustrate, suppose that war abroad disrupts oil imports. This fall in supply will drive up the oil price. A higher oil price will make it profitable for domestic oil suppliers to pump more oil and to drill more wells. The higher price will also induce domestic consumers to conserve oil and to switch to alternative sources of energy. Increased demand for alternative energy sources will raise their prices and stimulate *their* production, and so on. Thus in the absence of impediments such as government price controls, the adjustment of prices helps the free-market economy respond in a constructive and coordinated way to the initial disruption of supplies.

The classical approach to macroeconomics builds on Smith's basic assumptions that people pursue their own economic self-interest and that prices adjust reasonably quickly to balance quantities supplied and demanded. With these two assumptions as a basis, followers of the classical approach attempt to construct models of the macroeconomy that are consistent with the data and that can be used to answer the questions raised at the beginning of this chapter.

The use of the classical approach carries with it some strong policy implications. Because the classical assumptions imply that the invisible hand works well, classical economists often argue (as a normative proposition) that the government should have *at most* a limited role in the economy. As a positive proposition, classical economists also often argue that government policies will be ineffective or counterproductive at achieving their stated goals. Thus, for example, most classicals believe that the government should not try actively to eliminate business cycles.

The Keynesian Approach   Compared with the classical approach, the Keynesian approach is relatively young. The book that got this approach started, *The General Theory of Employment, Interest, and Money*, by the British economist John Maynard Keynes, appeared in 1936—160 years after Adam Smith's *The Wealth of Nations*. The year 1936 was the middle of the Great Depression, and the world was looking for answers: Terribly high rates of unemployment had afflicted most of the world's economies for years, and the invisible hand of free markets seemed completely ineffective. In the spirit of our discussion of testing economic theories, we could say that, as of 1936, the classical theory appeared to be seriously inconsistent with the data, creating a need for a new macroeconomic theory. This theory was provided by Keynes.

In his book Keynes offered an explanation for persistently high unemployment.[8] This explanation was based on an assumption about wage and price adjustment that was fundamentally different from the classical assumption: Instead of assuming that wages and prices adjust rapidly to equate quantities supplied and demanded in each market, Keynes assumed that wages and prices adjust slowly. Slow wage and price adjustment meant that markets could be out of equilibrium—with quantities demanded not equal to quantities supplied—for long periods of time. In the Keynesian theory unemployment can persist because wages and prices don't adjust quickly enough to bring labor demanded up to the number of people who want to work.

Keynes's proposed solution to high unemployment was to have the government increase its purchases of goods and services, thus raising the demand for output. Keynes argued that this policy would reduce unemployment, since in order to meet the higher demands for their products, businesses would have to employ more workers. In addition, Keynes suggested, the workers newly hired by firms would have more income to spend, creating another source of demand for output that would raise employment further. More generally, in contrast to classicals, Keynesians are skeptical of the invisible hand and are thus more willing to advocate a role for the government in improving macroeconomic performance.

---

[8]Actually, Keynes discussed a number of explanations of unemployment in his book, and a debate continues on "what Keynes really meant." Our interpretation of what Keynes meant is the one adopted by his major followers.

The Evolution of the Classical-Keynesian Debate   Because the Depression so strongly shook the faith of economists in the classical approach, the Keynesian approach dominated macroeconomic theory and policy from World War II until around 1970. At the height of Keynesian influence, economists widely believed that through the use of skillful macroeconomic policies, the government could promote economic growth while avoiding inflation or recession. It appeared tnat the main problems of macroeconomics had been solved, with only some details to be filled in.

However, in the 1970s the United States suffered from both high unemployment and high inflation—"stagflation", it was called, or stagnation plus inflation. This experience shook economists' and policymakers' confidence in the Keynesian approach, much as the Depression had undermined the traditional classical approach. At about the same time, a number of new theoretical developments made classical macroeconomics look a lot more interesting again. Although it did not achieve the dominance that Keynesianism enjoyed in the early postwar years, starting in the early 1970s a modernized classical approach enjoyed a major resurgence among macroeconomic researchers.

In the past fifteen years both approaches have been extensively reworked to repair their weaknesses. Economists working in the classical tradition have improved their explanations of business cycles and unemployment, and Keynesian models can now accommodate stagflation. Excellent research is now being done using both approaches, and there is substantial communication and cross-fertilization between them.

1.4 MACROECONOMICS: A UNIFIED APPROACH

In writing this book, we needed a strategy to deal with the fact that there are two major macroeconomic schools of thought. One possible strategy would have been to emphasize one of the two schools of thought and to treat the other school only briefly. The problem with this strategy is that it would not expose you, the reader, to the full range of ideas and insights that make up modern macroeconomics. Alternatively, we might have presented the two approaches separately and then compared and contrasted their conclusions; but this would have missed the opportunity to explore the large common ground shared by the two schools.

Our choice was to take an approach to macroeconomics that is as unified as possible. In keeping with this unified approach, all of our analyses in this book— whether of economic growth, of business cycles, of inflation, or of policy, and whether classical or Keynesian in spirit—are based on a *single economic model*, or on components or extensions of the basic model. This economic model, which draws heavily from both the classical and Keynesian traditions, has the following characteristics:

1. *The model's macroeconomic analysis is built up from the analysis of individual behavior.* As in the example of commuter route choices discussed earlier, we take a "bottom-up" approach and focus our analysis at the level of individual decision making. The insights gained are then used for studying the economy as a whole.

2. *Individuals in the model are assumed to try to maximize their own economic satisfaction, given their needs, desires, and resources.* In economists' jargon an individual who acts to maximize his own (or his family's) economic satisfaction

is said to be economically rational. The assumption of economic rationality (which is similar in spirit to the minimum–driving time assumption used in the commuter example) is a standard one in all fields of economics and has proven to be a useful simplification of behavior in many different contexts. Although this assumption was first emphasized by the founder of classical economics, Adam Smith, it is generally accepted by Keynesians as well as classicals; and it is used in virtually all modern macroeconomic research.

3. *Individuals in the model must trade off current and future satisfaction.* At the heart of many economic decisions is a trade-off between the present and the future. For example, when deciding how much to save, an individual is effectively deciding how much consumption to sacrifice today in order to be able to enjoy greater consumption at some point in the future. Similarly, a firm manager deciding how much to invest must trade off the commitment of the firm's resources today against the possibility of increased production at some future time. Because intertemporal choices—choices that involve trade-offs between the present and the future—are central to the behavior of the economy over time, these choices are emphasized in the economic model of this book.

4. *Individuals, firms, and the government interact in goods markets, asset markets, and labor markets.* We have already discussed the need for aggregation in macroeconomics. In the economic model of this book we follow standard macroeconomic practice and aggregate all the markets in the economy into three major markets—the market for goods and services, the asset market (in which assets such as stocks, bonds, and real estate are traded), and the labor market. We will study how participants in the economy interact in each of these three markets and how these markets relate to each other and the economy as a whole.

5. *The model can be used with either the classical assumption that wages and prices are flexible or the Keynesian assumption that wages and prices are slow to adjust.* This aspect of the model allows us to compare classical and Keynesian conclusions and policy recommendations within a common theoretical framework.

1.5 CHAPTER SUMMARY

1. Macroeconomics is the study of the structure and performance of national economies and of the policies that governments use to try to affect economic performance. Important topics in macroeconomics include the determinants of long-run economic growth, business cycles, unemployment, inflation, international trade and lending, and macroeconomic policy.

2. Because macroeconomics studies the economy as a whole, macroeconomists ignore the fine distinctions among different kinds of goods, firms, or markets and focus on national totals such as aggregate consumption. The process of adding individual economic variables to obtain economywide totals is called aggregation.

3. The activities engaged in by macroeconomists include (in addition to teaching) forecasting, macroeconomic analysis, macroeconomic research, and data development.

4. The goal of macroeconomic research is to be able to make general statements about how the economy works. Macroeconomic research makes progress through a process of developing economic theories and testing them empirically—that is, by seeing whether they are consistent with the data. A good economic theory is based on reasonable and realistic assumptions, is easy to use (tractable),

has implications that can be tested in the data, and is consistent with the data and the observed behavior of the real-world economy.

5. A positive analysis of an economic policy examines the economic consequences of the policy but does not address the question of whether those consequences are desirable. A normative analysis of a policy tries to determine whether the policy *should* be used. Disagreements among macroeconomists may arise because of differences in normative conclusions, which are due to differences in personal values and beliefs, as well as differences in the positive analysis of a policy proposal.

6. The classical approach to macroeconomics is based on the assumptions that individuals and firms act in their own best interests and that wages and prices adjust quickly to balance quantities supplied and demanded in markets. Under these assumptions the invisible hand of the free-market economy works well, and there is only limited scope for government intervention in the economy.

7. The Keynesian approach to macroeconomics assumes that wages and prices do not adjust rapidly and thus the invisible hand may not work well. Keynesians argue that because of slow wage and price adjustment, unemployment may remain high for a protracted period. Keynesians are usually more inclined than classicals to believe that government intervention in the economy may help improve economic performance.

Key Terms

aggregation, p. 12	economic theory, p. 16	monetary policy, p. 10
average labor productivity, p. 5	empirical analysis, p. 16	normative analysis, p. 19
closed economy, p. 9	fiscal policy, p. 10	open economy, p. 9
deflation, p. 9	inflation, p. 8	positive analysis, p. 19
economic model, p. 16	macroeconomics, p. 3	unemployment, p. 7

Review Questions

1. How have total output and output per worker changed over time in the United States? How have these changes affected the lives of typical Americans?

2. What is a business cycle? How does the unemployment rate behave over the course of a business cycle? Does the unemployment rate ever reach zero?

3. Define *inflation* and *deflation*. Compare the behavior of consumer prices in the United States in the periods before and after World War II.

4. Define the government budget deficit. Historically, when has the U.S. Federal government been most likely to run deficits? What has been the recent experience?

5. What is meant by *aggregation*? Why is aggregation important for macroeconomic analysis?

6. List the principal professional activities of macroeconomists. What role does macroeconomic research play in each of these activities?

7. What are the steps in developing and testing an economic theory or model? What are the criteria for a good theory or model?

8. Is it possible that two economists would agree about the effects of a particular economic policy but would disagree about the desirability of implementing the policy? Explain your answer.

9. Compare classical and Keynesians views on the speed of wage and price adjustment. What are the important consequences of the differences in their views?

Numerical Problems

1. Here are some macroeconomic data for the country of Oz for the years 1990 and 1991.

	1990	**1991**
Output	12,000 tons of potatoes	14,300 tons of potatoes
Employment	1000 workers	1100 workers
Unemployed	100 workers	50 workers
Prices	2 shekels per ton of potatoes	2.5 shekels per ton of potatoes

As the data suggest, Oz produces only potatoes, and its monetary unit is the shekel. Calculate each of the following macroeconomic variables for Oz, being sure to give units.
  a. Average labor productivity in 1990 and 1991.
  b. The growth rate of average labor productivity between 1990 and 1991.
  c. The unemployment rate in 1990 and 1991.
  d. The inflation rate between 1990 and 1991.

2. In a recent issue of the *Survey of Current Business*, find the data section entitled "Selected NIPA Tables." In Table 1.1, "Gross National Product," find data on gross national product (a measure of total output), exports, and imports. In Table 3.2, "Federal Government Receipts and Expenditures," find data on the government's total receipts (taxes) and expenditures.
  a. Calculate the ratio of exports to GNP, the ratio of imports to GNP, and the ratio of the trade imbalance to GNP in the latest reported quarter. Compare the answers with the values reported for the previous two complete years.
  b. Calculate the ratio of Federal government receipts to GNP, the ratio of Federal government expenditures to GNP, and the ratio of the deficit to GNP, for the most recent quarter and for the previous two complete years.

Analytical Problems

1. Is it possible for average labor productivity to fall even though total output is rising? Is it possible for the unemployment rate to rise even though total output is rising?

2. Prices were much higher in the United States in 1990 than in 1890. Does this mean that people were economically better off in 1890? Why or why not?

3. Give a theory for why people vote Republican or Democratic that potentially could satisfy the criteria for a good theory given in the text. How would you go about testing your theory?

4. Which of the following statements are primarily positive in nature and which are normative?
  a. A tax cut will raise interest rates.
  b. A reduction in the payroll tax would primarily benefit poor and middle-class workers.
  c. Payroll taxes are too high.
  d. A cut in the payroll tax would improve the President's popularity ratings.
  e. Payroll taxes should not be cut unless capital gains taxes are cut also.

2

The Measurement and Structure of the National Economy

Measurement is a crucial part of scientific study. Accurate measurement is essential for making new discoveries, for evaluating competing theories, and for predicting future events or trends. During the first half of the twentieth century, painstaking research by economists like Nobel Prize winner Simon Kuznets (the first person to obtain comprehensive measures of national output) and the team of Arthur Burns and Wesley Mitchell (who performed detailed measurements of the stages of the business cycle) showed that careful economic measurement is not only possible but also necessary for any serious understanding of the economy. Their work, and the efforts of many other researchers, transformed economics from a field in which scholars relied on informal observations and broad generalizations to one in which numbers and statistical analysis play a crucial role.

In this chapter we will look at some of the conceptual and practical issues involved in measuring the macroeconomy. We focus on the national income accounts, a framework for measuring economic activity that is widely used by economic researchers and analysts. Learning about the national income accounts will make you more familiar with some important and useful economic data. In addition, because the national income accounts are set up in a logical way that mirrors the structure of the economy, working through these accounts is an important first step toward understanding how the macroeconomy works. When you finish this chapter, you will have a much clearer picture of the relationships that exist among key macroeconomic variables and among the different sectors of the economy.

2.1 NATIONAL INCOME ACCOUNTING: THE MEASUREMENT OF PRODUCTION, INCOME, AND EXPENDITURE

The **national income accounts** are an accounting framework used in measuring current economic activity. Almost all countries have some form of official national income accounts. (For background information on the U.S. national income accounts, see the box, "In Touch with the Macroeconomy," p. 29.) In this section we discuss the basic idea that underlies national income accounting. In sections that follow we will see how the national income accounts are used in measuring economic activity in the United States and other countries.

The national income accounts are based on the insight that the amount of economic activity that occurs during a period of time can be measured in three different ways:

1. In terms of the amount of output that firms produce, excluding output used up in intermediate stages of production (the product approach).
2. In terms of the incomes received by the producers of output (the income approach).
3. In terms of the amount of spending done by the ultimate purchasers of output (the expenditure approach).

The product approach, the income approach, and the expenditure approach each give a different perspective on the economy. However, the fundamental principle underlying national income accounting is that, for the purpose of measuring economic activity, the three approaches are equivalent. In other words, except for problems such as incomplete or misreported data, *the product approach, the income approach, and the expenditure approach give identical measurements of the amount of current economic activity.*

The three approaches and why they are equivalent can be illustrated by an example. Imagine that an independent fisherman named Harvey has the following expenses during a year.

Harvey's Expenses

Boat rental	$15,000
Crew's wages	20,000
Total expenses	$35,000

With his boat and crew Harvey catches 25,000 fish during the year. He sells all of the fish at a price of $2 each, so his total receipts are $50,000. Receipts of $50,000 and expenses of $35,000 leave Harvey with $15,000 profit. He then pays $5000 to the government in various taxes, leaving an after-tax profit of $10,000. Harvey's final profit statement looks like this:

Harvey's Profit Calculation

Receipts	$50,000
Less: Expenses	35,000
Equals: Before-tax profit	15,000
Less: Taxes	5,000
Equals: After-tax profit	$10,000

Suppose that our goal is to find the total value, measured in dollars, of the economic activity generated by Harvey's business. The product approach, income approach, and expenditure approach are three different ways of getting this number.

1. The **product approach** measures economic activity by adding the market values of goods and services produced, excluding any goods and services used up in intermediate stages of production. The value of output in this example is $50,000 (25,000 fish times $2 per fish), so the product approach measure of economic activity is $50,000. Although services were provided by the fishing boat and the crew, these were used up in producing the fish and so are not included in the measure of economic activity.

2. The **income approach** measures economic activity by adding all income received, including taxes (which we can think of as the government's income) and after-tax profits (the income of Harvey, the entrepreneur). The incomes generated by Harvey's business are shown next.

Incomes Received

Rental income (to owner of boat)	$15,000
Wage income (to crew)	20,000
Taxes (to government)	5,000
Harvey's profit	10,000
Total income	$50,000

The income approach concludes that the value of economic activity was $50,000, just as the product approach did.

3. Finally, the **expenditure approach** measures activity by adding the amount spent by all purchasers of the firm's output. In this case the fisherman's customers spent $50,000 to buy his fish, confirming the results of the product and income approaches. Harvey's purchases of services used in production—the services of the boat and crew—are not counted.

Why the Three Approaches Are Equivalent

It is no accident that the product approach, the income approach, and the expenditure approach all give the same answer in the fisherman example. The logic of these three approaches is such that they must *always* give the same answer.

To see why, first observe that the market value of goods and services produced in a given period is *by definition* equal to what buyers must spend to purchase those goods and services. Harvey's fish have a market value of $50,000 only because that is what people are willing to spend to buy them. Since the market value of a good or service and the spending on that good or service are always the same, the product approach (which measures market values) and the expenditure approach (which measures spending) must give exactly the same measure of economic activity.[1]

Next, observe that what the seller receives must equal what the buyers spend. In this example Harvey's total receipts of $50,000 equal the total spending of his customers. The seller's receipts in turn equal the total income generated by his or her economic activity, including the incomes paid to workers and suppliers, taxes paid to the government, and the seller's profits (whatever is left over). Thus total

---

[1]Our explanation implicitly assumes that everything that is produced is sold. What if a firm produces some goods that it can't sell? As we will see shortly, the national income accounts treat unsold goods as if they were purchased by the firm from itself, that is, accumulation of unsold goods in inventory is treated as part of expenditure. Thus expenditure and production remain equal even if some goods are unsold.

with the Macroeconomy

The National Income and Product Accounts

In the United States the national income accounts are officially called the National Income and Product Accounts, or NIPA. These accounts provide comprehensive measurements of production, income, and expenditure for the American economy. Developed in the 1930s and 1940s by the Department of Commerce, the U.S. national income accounts were used for economic planning during World War II. Official accounts have been constructed for the period back to 1929, and some official data are available from 1909.*

Currently, the accounts are constructed on a quarterly basis by government economists and statisticians in the Bureau of Economic Analysis (BEA), a part of the Department of Commerce. In constructing the accounts, the BEA relies heavily on data provided by other government agencies, such as the Census Bureau and the Bureau of Labor Statistics. The BEA also uses data from tax returns and from private sources, such as industry associations.

Initial estimates of economic activity during a given quarter are released three or four weeks after the end of the quarter. Revised estimates, which may differ significantly from the initial estimates, are released in each of the next two months. More detailed revisions are done on an annual basis.

Historical NIPA data can be obtained from numerous sources, including the *Survey of Current Business* (the BEA's monthly publication), *Business Statistics*, and the *Economic Report of the President*. The most up-to-date numbers are most easily found in the business press, which gives extensive coverage to the BEA's monthly releases. National income accounts data for other countries are available in *National Accounts*, a publication of the Organization for Economic Cooperation and Development (OECD), and in the United Nations' *National Accounts Statistics*.

---

*An interesting recent study of the pre-1929 data is Christina D. Romer, "World War I and the Post-War Depression: A Reinterpretation Based on Alternative Estimates of GNP," *Journal of Monetary Economics*, July 1988, pp. 91–115.

expenditure must equal total income generated, implying that the expenditure and income approaches must also produce the same answer. Finally, since both product and income equal expenditure, they must be equal to each other as well.

Because of the equivalence of the three approaches, it must be true that, over any specified time period,

$$\text{total production} = \text{total income} = \text{total expenditure}, \qquad (2.1)$$

where production, income, and expenditure are all measured in monetary terms (for example, in dollars). Equation (2.1) is true for every individual economic unit, such as the fisherman's operation, and thus for the economy as a whole as well.

Equation (2.1) is called the **fundamental identity of national income accounting.** An identity is an equation that is true by definition.

Equation (2.1) forms the basis for national income accounting. In the next section we will see how this fundamental identity is used in measuring current economic activity for the economy as a whole.

2.2 GROSS NATIONAL PRODUCT

The broadest measure of aggregate economic activity, as well as the best-known and most often used, is the **gross national product,** or GNP. As in the fisherman example of the previous section, a country's GNP can be measured in three different ways: by the product approach, the expenditure approach, or the income approach. Although the three approaches arrive at the same final value for GNP, the government statisticians employ all three because each approach looks at GNP from a different angle. Using all three approaches gives a more complete picture of the structure of the economy than any single approach used alone could.

The Product Approach to Measuring GNP

The product approach defines a nation's GNP during a fixed period of time as the *market value of final goods and services newly produced by domestically owned factors of production.* In working through the various parts of this definition, we will discuss some practical issues that arise in measuring GNP.

Market Value   Goods and services are counted in GNP at their market values, that is, at the prices at which they are sold in markets. The advantage of using market values is that it allows us to add the production of different goods and services. Imagine, for example, that we want to measure the total output of an economy that produces 7 cars and 100 pairs of shoes: It wouldn't make any sense to add the number of cars and the number of pairs of shoes to get a total output of 107, since cars and shoes are not of equal economic value. But suppose we know that each car sells for $10,000 and each pair of shoes sells for $60. Taking these market-determined prices as measures of relative economic values, we can calculate the value of cars produced as $70,000 (7 times $10,000) and the value of shoes produced as $6000 (100 times $60). The total market value of production, equal to GNP, is $70,000 + $6000 = $76,000. Since using market values takes into account differences in the relative economic importance of different goods and services, adding market values to get a measure of total production makes sense, but adding the quantities of different goods and services produced wouldn't.

A problem with using market values to measure GNP is that some useful goods and services are not sold in formal markets. Ideally, GNP should be adjusted upward to reflect the existence of these goods and services; but because of the difficulty of obtaining reliable measures, some nonmarket goods and services are simply ignored in the calculation of GNP.[2] Homemaking and child-rearing services performed within the family without pay, for example, are not included in GNP,

---

[2]Periodically, attempts have been made by private economists to devise measures of GNP that include nonmarket economic activity. See, for example, Robert Eisner, "The Total Incomes System of Accounts," *Survey of Current Business,* January 1985, pp. 24–48.

although homemaking and child care that are provided for pay (for example, by professional housecleaning or day-care services) *are* included. Similarly, because the benefits of clean air and water aren't bought and sold in markets, actions to reduce pollution or otherwise improve environmental quality are not usually reflected in GNP (see Box 2.1, p. 37).

Some nonmarket goods and services are at least partially incorporated in official GNP measures. An example is activities that take place in the so-called underground economy. The **underground economy** includes both legal activities hidden from government record keepers (in order to avoid paying taxes or conforming to regulatory requirements, for example) and illegal activities like drug dealing, prostitution, and (in some places) gambling. It might be argued that activities like drug dealing are "bads" rather than "goods" and shouldn't be included in GNP anyway—although a consistent application of this argument might rule out many goods and services currently included in GNP. Clearly, though, we would want to include in GNP the services of a housepainter who is paid in cash in order to avoid taxes. Government statisticians regularly adjust GNP figures to include estimates of the size of the underground economy. Since cash is the favored means of payment for off-the-books transactions, one clue used in estimating the size of the underground economy is the amount of cash in circulation.[3]

A particularly important component of economic activity that does not pass through markets is the services provided by the government, such as defense, public education, and the services of roads and bridges. The fact that most government services are not sold in markets implies that there are no market values to use when calculating the government's contribution to GNP. In this case the solution that has been adopted is to value government services at their cost of production. Thus the contribution of national defense to GNP equals the government's cost of providing the defense: the salaries of soldiers and sailors, the costs of building and maintaining weapons and bases, and so on. Similarly, the contribution of public education to GNP is measured by the cost of teachers' salaries, new schools and equipment, and so on.

Newly Produced Goods and Services   As a measure of current economic activity, GNP includes only goods or services that are newly produced within the period. GNP excludes purchases or sales of goods produced in previous periods. Thus the market price paid in the sale of a used house or a used car is not counted in GNP, although the value of the services of the real estate agent or the used-car dealer is part of GNP, since those services are provided in the current period. The market value of a new house or a new car built during the current period *is* counted in GNP.

Final Goods and Services   Goods and services produced during a period of time can be classified as either intermediate goods and services or final goods and services. **Intermediate goods and services** are those used up in the production of other goods and services *in the same period that they themselves were produced.*

---

[3]A detailed discussion of NIPA adjustments for the underground economy is given in "The Underground Economy: An Introduction" in the May and July 1984 issues of the *Survey of Current Business*. On the use of cash in circulation to estimate the size of the underground economy, see Vito Tanzi, "The Underground Economy in the United States: Annual Estimates, 1930–1980," *IMF Staff Papers*, June 1983, pp. 283–305.

For example, flour that is produced during a given year and then is used to make bread *in the same year* is an intermediate good. The trucking company that delivers the flour to the bakery provides an intermediate service.

Final goods and services are those goods and services that are not intermediate. Instead, final goods are the end products of the productive process. For example, bread produced by the bakery is a final good, and a shopper's bus ride from the bakery to home is a final service. Since the purpose of economic activity is the production of final goods and services, with intermediate goods being only a step along the way, only final goods and services are counted in GNP.

The distinction between intermediate goods and final goods is sometimes subtle. For example, is a new lathe sold to a furniture manufacturer an intermediate good or a final good? Although the lathe is used to produce other goods and services, it is not used up during the year. Hence it is not an intermediate good; it is a final good. In particular, the lathe is an example of a type of final good called a capital good. Other more general examples of capital goods include factory equipment, office equipment, and the factories and office buildings themselves. A **capital good** is a good that is itself produced[4] and is used to produce other goods but—unlike an intermediate good—is not used up in the same period that it is produced. The preparers of the national income accounts decided to classify capital goods as final goods and thus to include their production in GNP, on the grounds that the addition to productive capacity that new capital goods represent is an important purpose of economic activity.

Another subtle distinction between intermediate and final goods arises in the treatment of inventory investment. **Inventories** are stocks of unsold finished goods, goods in process, and production materials held by firms. Inventory investment is the amount that inventories are increased during the year.[5] As an example, suppose that a baker began the year with $1000 worth of flour in her storeroom, and at the end of the year she is holding $1100 worth of flour. The difference between her beginning and ending stocks, which is $100 worth of flour, equals the baker's inventory investment during the year. Now even though the ultimate purpose of the baker's flour is for making bread, her increase in inventory represents production of flour that is not used up during the year. Thus her inventory investment counts as a final good during that year. As in the case of capital goods, the reason for treating inventory investment as a final good and thus part of GNP is that increased inventories on hand imply greater productive capacity in the future.

Domestically Owned Factors of Production   If American capital or labor—also called factors of production—is used abroad, the portion of production attributable to the American capital and labor is part of the U.S. GNP. So, for example, the value of roads built by an American construction company in Saudi Arabia, as measured by what the construction company receives in fees from the Saudi Arabian government, is counted in U.S. GNP. Similarly, the portion of the value of Japanese cars built in the United States that is attributable to Japanese capital and management counts in Japanese GNP, not in U.S. GNP.

As an alternative to using GNP, many countries emphasize a measure of national production called gross domestic product, or GDP. **Gross domestic product** measures the value of production that takes place within a nation's borders, with-

---

[4]This rules out natural resources such as land.

[5]When inventories are decreased during the year, inventory investment is negative.

out regard to whether the production is done by domestic or foreign factors of production. Thus the roads built in Saudi Arabia by the American firm would be part of Saudi GDP and not part of American GDP. The full value of the Japanese cars produced in the United States would be part of American GDP and not part of Japanese GDP.

For most countries GNP and GDP are similar and it does not matter which is used. However, the distinction between GNP and GDP is important for countries such as Egypt and Turkey that have many citizens working abroad, since remittances sent home by workers abroad are part of the country's GNP but not its GDP. If the government of Egypt is interested in the total income of its citizens, it should look at GNP; but if the policy question concerns the level of economic development within Egypt's borders, GDP might be the better measure of activity.

The Expenditure Approach to Measuring GNP

A different perspective on the components of GNP is obtained by looking at the expenditure side of the national income accounts. The expenditure approach measures GNP by finding total spending on final goods and services produced by domestic factors of production during a given period of time. There are four major categories of spending that are added to get GNP: consumption, investment, government purchases of goods and services, and net exports of goods and services. In symbols, if we define

Y = total production = total income = total expenditure = GNP,
C = consumption,
I = investment,
G = government purchases of goods and services,
NX = net exports of goods and services,

then, under the expenditure approach, GNP can be expressed by the following equation:

$$Y = C + I + G + NX. \tag{2.2}$$

Equation (2.2), like Eq. (2.1), is one of the most basic relationships in macroeconomics. Equation (2.2) is called the **income-expenditure identity,** since it states that income Y must equal total expenditure $C + I + G + NX$. Recent U.S. data for the four categories of spending, along with some major subcategories, are given in Table 2.1. As you read the rest of this section, you should look over Table 2.1 to get some feel for the relative sizes of different components of spending in the U.S. economy.

Consumption **Consumption** is spending by domestic households on final goods and services, including both those produced at home and those produced abroad.[6] Consumption is the largest component of expenditure, usually accounting for a bit less than two thirds of GNP in the United States. Consumption expenditures are broken down into three major categories:

1. *Consumer durables,* which are long-lived consumer items, like cars, televisions, furniture, and major appliances (but not houses, which are classified under investment).

---

[6]Later, we will subtract imports to get total spending on the production by domestic factors only.

Table 2.1 Expenditure Approach to Measuring GNP United States, 1990

	Billions of Dollars	Percent of GNP
Personal consumption expenditures	**3657**	**67**
Durable goods	480	9
Nondurable goods	1194	22
Services	1983	36
Gross private domestic investment	**741**	**14**
Business fixed investment		
Nonresidential structures	147	3
Producers' durable equipment	377	7
Residential Investment	222	4
Inventory investment	−5	0
Government purchases of goods and services	**1098**	**20**
Federal		
National defense	314	6
Nondefense	110	2
State and local	674	12
Net exports	**−31**	**−1**
Exports	673	12
Imports	−704	−13
Total (equal to GNP)	**5465**	

Source: *Survey of Current Business*, Table 1.1. Figures may not add owing to rounding.

2. *Nondurable goods*, which are shorter-lived goods like food, clothing, and fuel.

3. *Services*, such as education, health care, financial services, and transportation.

Investment Investment includes both spending for new capital goods, called fixed investment, and increases in firms' inventory holdings, called inventory investment. Fixed investment in turn has two major components:

1. *Business fixed investment*, which is spending by businesses on structures (factories, warehouses, office buildings, and so on) and equipment (machines, vehicles, furniture, and so on).

2. *Residential investment*, which is spending on the construction of new houses and apartment buildings. Houses and apartment buildings are treated as a form of capital good because they provide a service (shelter) over a long period.

Like consumption, investment includes spending on foreign-produced goods. Overall, fixed investment in the United States is usually around one sixth of GNP.

All increases in inventories are included in investment spending; this is true no matter why inventories rose. *In particular, if a firm produces goods that it cannot sell, which causes the firm's inventories to rise, this counts as investment by the firm. For the purposes of national income accounting, it is as if the firm purchased the unsold goods from itself.* This accounting rule is useful because it guarantees that production and expenditure will always be equal in the national income accounts. Anything that is produced must by definition either be bought by a customer or "purchased" by the firm itself.

Government Purchases of Goods and Services **Government purchases** of goods and services, which include any expenditure by the government on a currently produced good or service, foreign or domestic, is the third major component of spending. Government purchases in the United States have recently been around one fifth of GNP. Notice from Table 2.1 that in the United States the majority of government purchases are made by state and local governments rather than the Federal government. Since most Federal purchases are defense expenditures, the comparison between state and local purchases and Federal purchases is particularly striking if we look only at nondefense items such as education and transportation: In 1990, 86% of nondefense government purchases in the United States were made by state and local governments.

Not all of the checks written by the government are for government purchases of goods and services. **Transfers,** which include items such as Social Security and Medicare benefits, unemployment insurance, and welfare payments, are payments by the government that are not made in exchange for current goods or services. Because transfers do not reflect payment for current goods and services, they are excluded from the government purchases category and are not counted in GNP as calculated by the expenditure approach. Similarly, interest payments on the national debt are not counted as part of government purchases.

Net Exports **Net exports** are exports minus imports. As discussed in Chapter 1, exports are the goods and services produced by the residents of a country that are purchased by foreigners; imports are the goods and services that a country's residents buy from foreigners. Net exports are positive if exports are greater than imports and negative if imports exceed exports.

Exports are added to total spending because they represent foreigners' spending on final goods and services produced by domestic factors of production. Imports are subtracted from total spending because consumption, investment, and government purchases are defined to include imported goods and services. Subtracting imports ensures that total spending $C + I + G + NX$ will measure spending only on output produced by domestic factors of production. For example, an increase in imports may mean that Americans are buying Japanese cars instead of American cars. For fixed total spending by domestic residents, therefore, an increase in imports lowers spending on domestic production.

The Income Approach to Measuring GNP

The third and final way to measure GNP is the income approach. The income approach calculates GNP by adding the incomes received by producers, including profits, and taxes paid to the government. A standard breakdown reported in the national income accounts divides income into the following seven categories (see Table 2.2 for recent U.S. data).

1. *Depreciation.* A portion of the capital stock wears out, or depreciates, in the process of production, and businesses must earmark some of their revenues to replace this capital. **Depreciation** is the amount of capital that wears out during a given period of time, as estimated by the preparers of the national income accounts. Equivalently, depreciation may be thought of as the amount of compensation paid to owners of capital for using up their factories and machines. Depreciation appears in the national income accounts under the name "Capital Consumption Allowances," and it is usually about 11% of GNP.

Table 2.2 Income Approach to Measuring GNP United States, 1990

	Billions of Dollars
Gross national product	5465
Less: Capital consumption allowances	−576
Equals: Net national product	4890
Less: Indirect business taxes (and other small items)	−472
Equals: National income	4418

	Billions of Dollars	Percent of National Income
Components of national income		
Compensation of employees	3244	73
Proprietors' income	403	9
Rental income of persons	7	0
Net interest	467	11
Corporate profits	298	7
Total (equal to national income)	4418	

Source: *Survey of Current Business*, Tables 1.9 and 1.14. Figures may not add owing to rounding.

Incidentally, gross national product is called *gross* because it measures the nation's total production of goods and services without making any adjustment for depreciation. **Net national product,** or NNP, equals GNP minus depreciation. Written out for reference, the equation is

$$\text{NNP} = \text{GNP} - \text{depreciation.}$$

NNP measures aggregate output net of the quantity of goods required to replace capital that wears out during the year.

2. *Indirect business taxes.* Indirect business taxes, such as sales and excise taxes, are paid by businesses to Federal, state, and local governments.

Net national product less indirect business taxes (and some other minor items) is **national income:**

$$\text{national income} = \text{NNP} - \text{indirect business taxes.}$$

National income is the amount of income available to distribute among producers, after allowance for depreciation and indirect business taxes. The components of national income are the five types of income received by producers, items 3 through 7 that follow.

3. *Compensation of employees.* Compensation of employees is the income of workers (excluding the self-employed) and encompasses wages, salaries, employee benefits (including contributions by employers to pension plans), and employer contributions to Social Security. As you can see from Table 2.2, compensation of employees is the largest component of national income, comprising 73% of national income in 1990.

The compensation-of-employees income category overstates the take-home income of workers, since, as in each of the other measures of individual income on this list, part of this income must be paid to the government as personal taxes,

Much of our economic well-being flows from natural, rather than human-made, assets—our land, our rivers and oceans, our natural resources (such as oil and timber), and indeed the air that we breathe. Ideally, for the purposes of economic and environmental planning, the use and misuse of natural resources and the environment should be appropriately measured in the national income accounts. Unfortunately, they are not. There are at least two important conceptual problems with the way the national income accounts currently handle the economic use of natural resources and the environment:

1. *Natural resource depletion.* If a firm produces some output but in the process wears out a portion of its plant and equipment, the firm's output is counted as part of gross national product (GNP), but the depreciation of capital is subtracted in the calculation of net national product (NNP). Thus NNP is a measure of the net production of the economy, after a deduction for used-up capital. In contrast, when an oil driller drains oil from an underground field, the value of the oil produced is counted as part of the nation's GNP; but no offsetting deduction to NNP is made to account for the fact that nonrenewable resources have been used up. In principle, the draining of the oil field should be thought of as a type of depreciation, and the net product of the oil company should be accordingly reduced. The same point applies to any other natural resource that is depleted in the process of production.

2. *The costs and benefits of pollution control.* Imagine that a company has the following choices: It can produce $100 million worth of output and in the process pollute the local river by dumping its wastes. Alternatively, by using 10% of its workers to dispose properly of its wastes, it can avoid polluting but will only get $90 million of output. Under current national income accounting rules, if the firm chooses to pollute

BOX *2.1:* NATURAL RESOURCES, THE ENVIRONMENT, AND THE NATIONAL INCOME ACCOUNTS

rather than not to pollute, its contribution to GNP will be larger ($100 million rather than $90 million), because the national income accounts attach no explicit value to a clean river. In an ideal accounting system the economic costs of environmental degradation would be subtracted in the calculation of a firm's contribution to GNP, and activities that improve the environment—because they provide real economic benefits—would be added to GNP.

Discussing the national income accounting implications of resource depletion and pollution may seem to trivialize these important problems; but in fact, since GNP and related statistics are used continually in policy analyses, abstract questions of measurement may often turn out to have significant real effects. For example, economic development experts have expressed concern that some poor countries, in attempting to raise measured GNP as quickly as possible, have done so in part by overexploiting their natural resources and impairing the environment. Conceivably, if "hidden" resource and environmental costs were explicitly incorporated into official measures of economic growth, these policies might be modified. Similarly, in industrialized countries political debates about the environment have sometimes emphasized the impact on conventionally measured GNP of proposed pollution control measures, rather than the impact on overall economic welfare. Better accounting for environmental quality might serve to refocus these debates to the more relevant question of whether, for any given environmental proposal, the benefits (economic and noneconomic) exceed the costs.

Source: Jonathan Levin, "The Economy and the Environment: Revising the National Accounts," *IMF Survey*, 4 June 1990.

such as income taxes and Social Security taxes. This division of income between the government and the rest of the economy is discussed later.

4. *Proprietors' income.* Proprietors' income is the income of the nonincorporated self-employed. Since many of the self-employed own some capital (examples are a farmer's tractor or a dentist's X-ray machine), proprietors' income includes both labor income and capital income. Proprietors' income was 9% of national income in 1990.

5. *Rental income of persons.* Rental income of persons, a small item, is the income earned by individuals who own land or structures that they rent to others. Some miscellaneous types of income, such as royalty income, are also included in this category. Rental income of persons was less than 0.2% of national income in 1990.

6. *Net interest.* Net interest is interest earned by individuals from businesses and foreign sources minus interest paid by individuals. In 1990 net interest was 11% of national income, up from less than 5% of national income in the early 1970s. The increase in net interest reflects both greater use of debt by corporations and generally higher interest rates.

7. *Corporate profits.* Corporate profits are the profits earned by domestically owned corporations and represent what remains of corporate revenue after wages, interest, rents, and other costs have been paid. Corporate profits are used to pay taxes levied on corporations, such as the corporate income tax, and to pay dividends to shareholders. The remainder of corporate profits after taxes and dividends, which is called retained earnings, is kept within the corporation.

Corporate profits are generally a modest fraction of national income (7% of national income in 1990), but the amount of profits earned by corporations may change dramatically from year to year or even from quarter to quarter.

The Circular Flow of Product, Expenditure, and Income

The links among the three approaches to constructing GNP can be illustrated by a diagram called the circular flow diagram, shown in Fig. 2.1. In this diagram the economy is divided into four major sectors:

1. The *household sector,* made up of domestic households.
2. The *business sector,* made up of domestically owned businesses.
3. The *government sector,* which consists of Federal, state, and local governments.
4. The *foreign sector,* comprising foreign households, businesses, and governments.

Together, the household sector and the business sector form the **private sector.** The government sector is sometimes referred to as the public sector. The different sectors are indicated by the boxes in Fig. 2.1. Notice that the household and business sectors are grouped together as the private sector.

The product approach measures GNP as the value of currently produced output. To construct the circular flow diagram, it is easiest to assume that all output is produced in the business sector. So, for example, we ignore the distinction between government services produced by government employees and government services purchased from private firms (such as trash disposal companies) and sim-

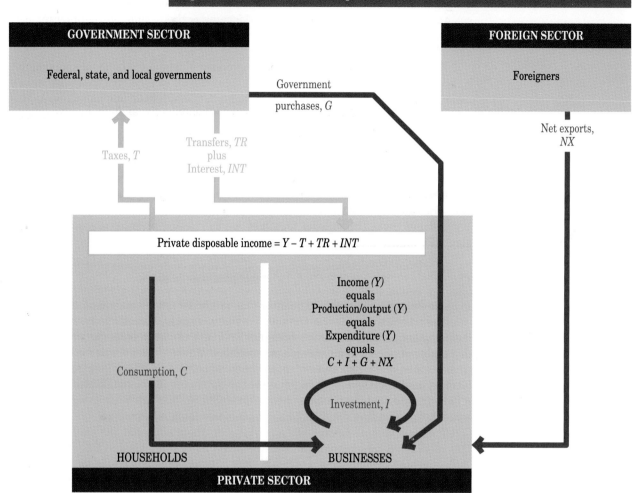

Figure 2.1   Income and Expenditure Flows

This diagram shows the flows of income and expenditure among the major sectors of the economy. Expenditure flows are shown by red arrows. Each sector purchases output from the business sector, where all production takes place. Income flows are shown by blue arrows. Private disposable income, the income of the private sector, equals the total spending on business sector output Y, minus taxes paid to the government T, plus transfers and interest received from the government TR + INT. The government has income equal to taxes T and outlays equal to the sum of government purchases G and transfers and interest TR + INT.

ply assume that all government services are purchased from the business sector. Figure 2.1 shows total production, equal to Y, occurring within the business sector.

Expenditure flows are shown in Fig. 2.1 by red arrows between the boxes indicating the different sectors. Consumption expenditures C are made by households, investment expenditures I are made by businesses, government purchases G are made by the government sector, and the expenditure of the foreign sector is net exports NX. All expenditures flow to the business sector, which produces what each of the sectors buys. Total expenditure $C + I + G + NX$ equals Y, the total value of production.

Income flows are shown in Fig. 2.1 by blue arrows. The largest single component of income is **private disposable income,** which is the income of the private sector (households and businesses taken together). As you can see in Fig. 2.1, there are three principal flows in and out of private disposable income, which are described next.

First, the business sector receives revenues $Y,$ equal to the total spending on its output, or GNP. Ignoring taxes for a moment, all of these revenues are either retained within the business sector or paid out to households as wages, rents, interest, or dividends. Thus the business sector's receipts Y are a flow *into* private disposable income.

Second, the private sector pays taxes to the government sector. Tax payments, denoted $T,$ are a flow *out* of private disposable income.

Finally, the private sector receives transfers from the government as well as interest on government debt. Transfers TR and interest on the government debt INT are flows *into* private disposable income.

Putting these three flows together, we can define private disposable income algebraically as

$$\text{private disposable income} = \text{GNP} - \text{taxes} + \text{transfers} + \text{interest} \quad (2.3)$$
$$= Y - T + TR + INT.$$

Private disposable income is the after-tax income of the entire private sector.

The national income accounts also define **personal disposable income,** which is the after-tax income of the household portion of the private sector. Personal disposable income equals the income received directly by households—including wages and salaries; proprietors' income; and household receipts of rents, dividends, interest, and transfers—minus personal tax payments. Personal disposable income differs from private disposable income in excluding the after-tax gross income of businesses, including depreciation and after-tax retained earnings.

Personal income figures are often cited in the media, but the distinction that this measure draws between income received by households and income received by businesses is somewhat artificial, since ultimately all domestic businesses are owned and controlled by members of the household sector. For example, except for tax considerations, it should make little difference to a small-business owner whether her company's profits are paid out to her personal bank account or are kept in the company's bank account. For this reason we will emphasize private disposable income rather than personal disposable income in our economic analysis.

Figure 2.1 also shows income flows in and out of the public sector. The government receives taxes T from the private sector and pays out transfers TR and interest on the government debt INT to the private sector. In actuality, the government also makes transfer and interest payments to the foreign sector.[7] To keep things simple, for now we ignore government payments to the foreign sector; they will be discussed in Chapter 7.

Using these public sector income flows, we can define some basic measures of the government's fiscal policy. First, **government outlays,** also called government expenditures, equal the government's purchases of goods and services G plus its transfers and interest payments:

$$\text{government outlays} = \text{government purchases} + \text{transfers} + \text{interest}$$
$$= G + TR + INT.$$

---

[7]Transfer payments to the foreign sector include foreign aid and payments to Americans living abroad.

Second, when the government's tax receipts minus its outlays is a positive number, the government has a **budget surplus;** if the number is negative, there is a **budget deficit:**

$$\text{taxes} - \text{government outlays} = T - (G + TR + INT) \tag{2.4}$$
$$= + (\text{budget surplus}) = - (\text{budget deficit}).$$

Figure 2.1 does not show any income flowing to the foreign sector because GNP is defined to include only those goods and services produced by domestically owned factors of production. Income received by foreigners is part of their own country's GNP. Thus in a given country's national income accounts, the income of the foreign sector is zero.[8]

Putting all the elements of Fig. 2.1 together, we can see why this diagram is called the circular flow diagram. There is a circular flow of expenditure and income, in which the spending of each sector on goods and services becomes the income of the private sector. Part of the private sector's income, equal to taxes less transfers and interest on the government debt, is transferred to the government sector. These income flows in turn finance spending on goods and services.

However, there is an important sense in which the circular flow shown in Fig. 2.1 is incomplete: Although *total* income and *total* spending are the same in the figure (both are equal to Y), it is not necessarily the case that *each sector's* income is the same as its spending. For example, if the government runs a deficit, its total outlays exceed its tax collections during the period. Similarly, if net exports are positive, the foreign sector is spending more on the domestic country's exports than it can pay for with the receipts from the domestic country's imports. As we will see in the next section, for a complete circular flow sectors whose spending exceeds their income must borrow from sectors with income greater than spending. So, for example, if the government is running a deficit, it must make up the difference by borrowing from the other sectors.

2.3 SAVING AND WEALTH

If we wanted to assess the economic situation of an individual or a family, the current income of the individual or of family members would be an important piece of information. However, it is not necessarily true that someone with a high current income is better off economically than someone with a low current income. For example, a retired tycoon who has no current earnings but owns $10 million worth of stocks and bonds may be better off than a newly graduated doctor with a high salary but heavy debts left over from medical school. Thus besides knowing current income, we also need to know what the individual or family owns (their assets) and owes (their liabilities). The difference between assets and liabilities is called *wealth*.

What is true for an individual or family is also true for a whole economy. Like an individual's current income, gross national product measures the economy's total income during the current quarter or year. However, as for an individual, the long-run economic well-being of a country depends not only on its income but also on its wealth. The wealth of an entire nation is called *national wealth*.

---

[8]This statement ignores the fact that foreigners receive government transfers and interest on government debt from the domestic country. Remember that for the time being we assume that these government payments to foreigners are zero.

An important determinant of wealth is the rate of saving: A family that puts aside a quarter of its income each month will accumulate wealth much more quickly than a family that spends nearly all the income that it receives. Similarly, the rate at which national wealth increases depends on the rate at which individuals, businesses, and governments in the economy choose to save. Thus rates of saving and wealth accumulation are closely related.

In this section we define some concepts of aggregate saving and wealth and examine the relationships among them. Our main interest here is in measurement. Questions such as what determines the rate of saving in a given country are covered in later chapters.

Measures of Aggregate Saving

In general, the **saving** of any economic unit is the unit's current income minus its spending on current needs. The saving *rate* of an economic unit is its saving divided by its income. From a macroeconomic perspective, three important measures of saving are private saving, government saving, and national saving. Each of these is discussed below; see Table 2.3 for summary definitions.

Private Saving   **Private saving** is the saving of the private sector, that is, of the household and business sectors combined. Private saving equals private disposable income (the income of the private sector) minus consumption. Consumption is subtracted from private disposable income to obtain private saving because consumption represents the private sector's spending on current needs. Investment, which is part of private sector spending, is not subtracted from private disposable income when we calculate private saving. It is not subtracted because capital goods bought by firms are not used up during the year, as are consumption goods, but are available for use in future production.

Table 2.3 Summary
Measures of Aggregate Saving

Saving Measure	Definition/Formula
Private saving	Private disposable income less consumption $S_{private} = (Y - T + TR + INT) - C$
Government saving	Tax collections less government outlays $S_{government} = T - (G + TR + INT)$
National saving	Private saving plus government saving; also, GNP less consumption and government purchases $S = S_{private} + S_{government}$ $= Y - C - G$

Since private disposable income equals income minus taxes plus transfers and interest (Eq. 2.3), we can write the definition of private saving as

$$S_{\text{private}} = \text{private disposable income} - \text{consumption} \tag{2.5}$$
$$= (Y - T + TR + INT) - C,$$

where S_{private} stands for private saving. The private saving *rate* is private saving divided by private disposable income.

A measure of aggregate saving that you may hear reported and discussed is personal saving, the saving of the household portion of the private sector. **Personal saving** equals personal disposable income (the after-tax income of households) minus consumption. The personal saving rate in the United States is notoriously low. However, the same point that we made in comparing private and personal disposable income applies here: Because businesses are owned and controlled by households, it makes little economic sense to distinguish between the portion of private saving done within households and the portion done within businesses. Thus we will focus on private rather than personal saving.

Government Saving   **Government saving** equals the government's tax collections T minus its outlays (government purchases G, transfers TR, and interest payments INT):

$$S_{\text{government}} = \text{taxes} - \text{government outlays} \tag{2.6}$$
$$= T - (G + TR + INT).$$

The definition of government saving $S_{\text{government}}$ fits the general definition of saving if we think of taxes as the government's income and outlays as the government's spending on current needs. In practice, however, a problem with this definition is that not all current government outlays are devoted to current needs. For example, some government purchases—such as roads and bridges—are not used up during the year and thus are available to satisfy future needs. Ideally, when we measure government saving, these longer-lived government purchases would not be subtracted. However, unlike those of some countries, the national income accounts of the United States do not distinguish these longer-lived government purchases from others. For simplicity we follow U.S. practice and subtract all government purchases when defining government saving.[9] This way of measuring government saving does, however, tend to underestimate the true amount of saving that the public sector does.

Comparing Eq. (2.6) with Eq. (2.4), you can see that *government saving is identical to the government budget surplus.* Thus when the government sector runs a surplus, so that its tax collections exceed its outlays, government saving equals the amount of the surplus. When the government runs a deficit, with taxes less than outlays, government saving is negative by the amount of the deficit.

National Saving   **National saving,** the saving of the economy as a whole, equals private saving plus government saving. Letting S stand for national saving and

---

[9]A similar argument would suggest that expenditures on cars and other consumer durables should not be subtracted from disposable income in the calculation of private saving, although in practice they are subtracted.

using the definitions of private and government saving, Eq. (2.5) and (2.6), we have

$$
\begin{aligned}
S &= S_{\text{private}} + S_{\text{government}} \\
&= (Y - T + TR + INT - C) + (T - TR - INT - G) \qquad (2.7) \\
&= Y - C - G.
\end{aligned}
$$

Equation (2.7) shows that national saving equals the income of the whole economy Y minus the spending that is used to satisfy current needs: consumption C and government purchases G.

The Uses of Private Saving

In discussing the circular flow diagram (Fig. 2.1), we noted that sectors for which expenditure exceeds income, such as the government sector in recent years, must borrow to make up the difference. An important source of funds for the government and other deficit sectors is private saving. In this section we show how an economy's pool of private saving is used.

The relationship between private saving and its uses can be illustrated by putting together some of the equations we have developed so far. Start by writing once again the definition of private saving (Eq. 2.5):

$$
S_{\text{private}} = Y - T + TR + INT - C.
$$

Next, using the income-expenditure identity $Y = C + I + G + NX$ (Eq. 2.2) to substitute for Y, we get

$$
S_{\text{private}} = (C + I + G + NX) - T + TR + INT - C.
$$

Finally, canceling the plus and minus C's on the right-hand side of the equation and rearranging terms gives us

$$
\begin{aligned}
S_{\text{private}} &= \text{investment} + \text{government deficit} + \text{net exports} \qquad (2.8) \\
&= I + (G + TR + INT - T) + NX.
\end{aligned}
$$

Equation (2.8) is another important macroeconomic identity, called the **uses-of-saving identity.** The uses-of-saving identity (illustrated in Fig. 2.2) says that an economy's private saving is used in the following three ways:

1. *Investment.* Firms borrow from private savers to finance the construction and purchase of new capital (including residential capital) and inventory investment.

2. *The government budget deficit.* When the government runs a budget deficit, it must borrow from private savers to cover the difference between expenditures and receipts.

3. *Net exports.* When American net exports are positive, so that exports exceed imports, foreigners' receipts from the goods and services they sell to the United States are not sufficient to cover the cost of the U.S. exports they buy. To make up the difference, foreigners must either borrow from American private savers or sell American savers some of their assets, such as land, factories, stocks, and bonds. Thus financing net exports is a use of a country's private saving.

In contrast, when American net exports are negative, as was true for most of the 1980s, the United States is importing more than it is exporting. To pay for the extra imports, Americans must borrow from foreigners or sell foreigners U.S. as-

Figure 2.2   The Uses of Private Saving

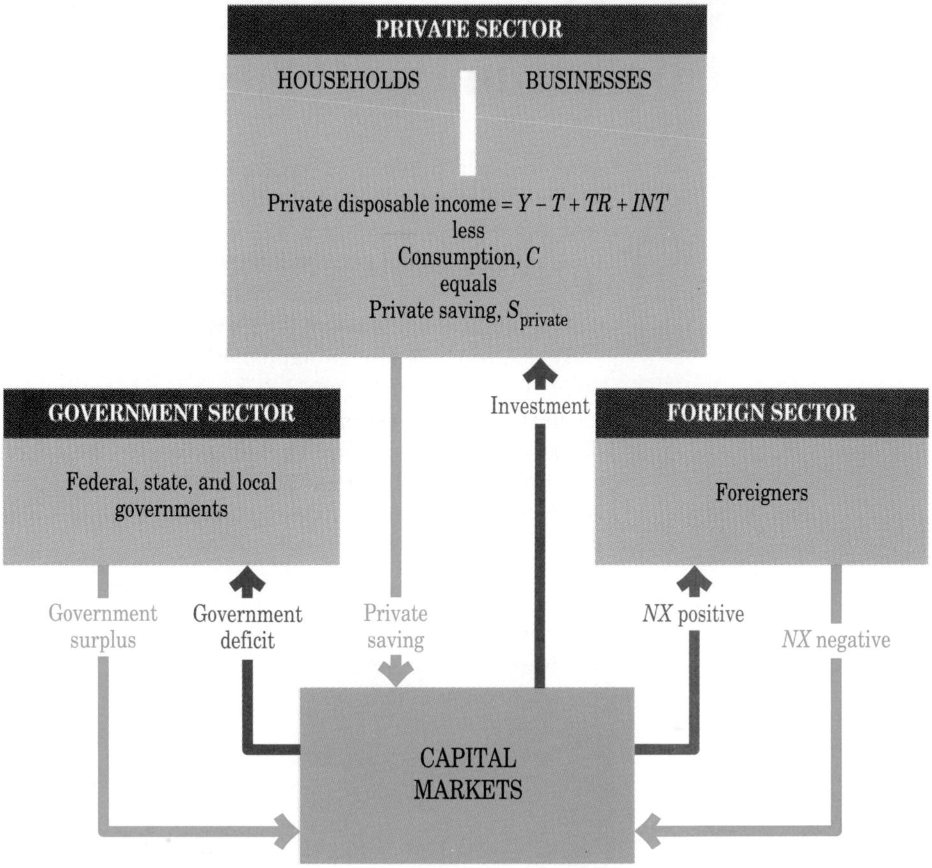

PRIVATE SECTOR

HOUSEHOLDS   BUSINESSES

Private disposable income = $Y - T + TR + INT$
less
Consumption, C
equals
Private saving, $S_{private}$

GOVERNMENT SECTOR

Federal, state, and local
governments

Investment

FOREIGN SECTOR

Foreigners

Government
surplus

Government
deficit

Private
saving

NX positive

NX negative

**CAPITAL
MARKETS**

Private saving equals private disposable income less consumption. Private saving (blue arrow) is lent to the capital markets, such as the bond and stock markets. Private saving has three uses (red arrows). It is used to finance investment by businesses and the government's budget deficit. When net exports are positive, so that foreigners sell less to the domestic country than they buy from it, private saving is also used to lend

foreigners the difference or to acquire foreign assets. When the government has a surplus, it provides additional funds to the capital markets (blue arrow). Similarly, when net exports are negative, foreigners are lending to domestic residents or acquiring domestic assets, which supplies funds to the capital markets (blue arrow).

sets. In this case foreigners use their saving to lend to the United States or to acquire American assets.[10]

In summary, the uses-of-saving identity shows how the circular flow of income and expenditure is completed. According to this identity, the difference between the private sector's saving and investment is used to finance the deficits of the public and foreign sectors. Because sectors with more income than spending are able to lend to sectors with more spending than income, in any given sector spending and income need not be equal in each period.

---

[10]International trade and borrowing are taken up in detail in Chapter 7.

The Uses of Saving and the Government Budget Deficit in the 1980s

Understanding the uses-of-saving identity is a helpful first step for understanding some complicated macroeconomic issues. For example, there are many debates about the effects of government budget deficits on the economy. Equation (2.8) shows that if the government budget deficit increases, at least one of the following three things, or a combination of them, *must* happen: (1) Private saving must rise, (2) investment must fall, and/or (3) net exports must fall.

Which of these things happened when U.S. government budget deficits rose sharply in the 1980s? Figure 2.3 shows the behavior of private saving and its three uses in the United States during this period, all measured as a percentage of GNP. You can see from the figure that in the early 1980s the increase in the government budget deficit was offset by a fall in investment relative to private saving. In the mid-1980s investment was nearly equal to private saving, so the large government

The figure illustrates the uses-of-saving identity—which says that private saving equals the sum of investment, the government deficit, and net exports—for the 1980s in the United States. In the early 1980s the increased government deficit was offset by declining investment, and in the middle 1980s the government deficit was offset by a fall in net exports. Recent declines in the government deficit were accompanied by increases in net exports. Here all variables are measured as a percentage of GNP, and the government deficit is the combined deficit of Federal, state, and local governments.

Source: Economic Report of the President, Feb. 1991, Tables B–1, and B–79.

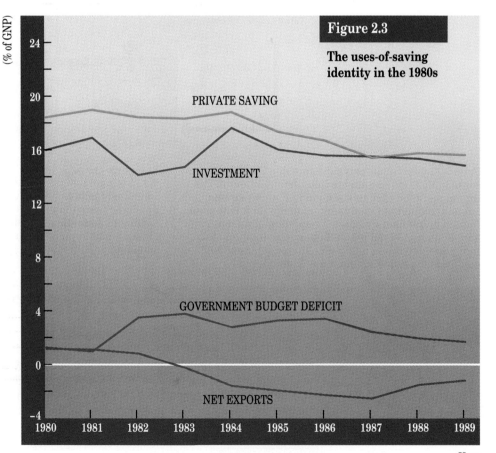

Figure 2.3

The uses-of-saving identity in the 1980s

Year

deficit was offset by negative net exports. More recently, a decline in the budget deficit has been accompanied by a rise in net exports.

Relating Saving and Wealth

Saving is a key economic variable because it is closely related to the rate of wealth accumulation. In the rest of the section we discuss the relationship of saving and wealth. However, we must first introduce the concept of stocks versus flows.

Stocks and Flows The economic variables we have discussed so far in this chapter—such as GNP and the various types of expenditure, income, and saving—are measured *per unit of time*, such as per quarter or per year. For example, annual GNP figures measure the economy's production per year. Variables that are measured per unit of time are called **flow variables.**

In contrast, some economic variables, called **stock variables,** are defined *at a point in time*. Examples of stock variables are the amount of money in your bank account on September 15 of this year and the total value of all houses in the United States on January 1, 1992.

In many applications flow variables are the rate of change of stock variables. A classic example is a bathtub with water flowing in from a faucet. The amount of water in the tub at any moment is a stock variable. Notice that the units of a stock variable (gallons, in this example) do not have a time dimension. The rate at which water enters the tub is a flow variable; its units (gallons per minute) have a time dimension. In this case the flow is equal to the rate of change of the stock.

Wealth and Saving as Stock and Flow Saving and wealth are related to each other in much the same way that the flow and stock of water in a bathtub are related. The **wealth** of any economic unit, also called net worth, is its assets (the things that it owns, including IOUs from other economic units) minus its liabilities (what it owes to other units). Wealth is measured in dollars at a point in time and is a stock variable. Saving is measured in dollars per unit time and is a flow variable. Since saving takes the form of an accumulation of assets or a reduction in liabilities (for example, if saving is used to pay off debts), saving adds to wealth just as the flow of water into the bathtub adds to the stock of water.

National Wealth **National wealth** is the total wealth of the residents of a country. National wealth consists of two parts: (1) the country's domestic physical assets, such as its stock of capital goods and land,[11] and (2) its net foreign assets. The **net foreign assets** of a country equal the country's foreign assets (for example, foreign stocks, bonds, and factories owned by domestic residents) minus its foreign liabilities (domestic physical and financial assets owned by foreigners). Net foreign assets are part of national wealth because they represent claims on foreigners that are not offset by foreigners' claims on the domestic economy.

Domestic financial assets held by domestic residents are not part of national wealth since the value of any domestic financial asset is offset by an equal-sized domestic financial liability. For example, a checking account held by an American in a U.S. bank is an asset for the depositor but an equal-sized liability for the bank;

---

[11]In principle, national wealth should also include the value of the skills and training of the country's residents—what economists call *human capital*. In practice, because of measurement problems, human capital is not usually included in measures of national wealth.

it thus does not represent wealth for the economy taken as a whole. In contrast, an American's checking account in a foreign bank has no corresponding domestic liability (it is a liability of a foreigner) and so is part of American national wealth.

There are two ways that national wealth can change over time. First, the value of the existing assets or liabilities that make up national wealth may change. So, for example, an increase in the value of American farmland raises U.S. national wealth, as does an increase in the value of foreign stocks held by Americans. The wearing out or depreciation of physical assets, which corresponds to a fall in the value of those assets, reduces national wealth.

The second way that national wealth can change is through national saving. Over any given period of time, holding constant the value of existing assets and liabilities, each extra dollar of national saving adds a dollar to national wealth. To illustrate this point precisely, recall the uses-of-saving identity (Eq. 2.8):

$$S_{\text{private}} = I + (G + TR + INT - T) + NX.$$

Adding to this equation the definition of government saving (Eq. 2.6), and recognizing that national saving S is the sum of private saving and government saving, we get[12]

$$S = I + NX \tag{2.9}$$

Equation (2.9) shows that national saving has two uses: to increase the stock of domestic physical capital through investment (I) and to increase the nation's stock of net foreign assets by financing net exports (NX). But each dollar by which domestic physical assets or net foreign assets are increased is a dollar by which national wealth is increased. Thus, as we claimed, increases in national saving increase national wealth dollar for dollar. As in the example of water flowing into a bathtub, the more rapid the flow of national saving, the more quickly the stock of national wealth will rise.

Application

An International Comparison of National Saving and Investment Rates

How do national saving and investment in the United States compare with saving and investment in other developed countries? A recent study by the Organization for Economic Cooperation and Development (OECD), an organization of twenty-two industrialized nations, examined saving and investment trends in each of its member countries. The results for 1960–1988 for the seven largest OECD members and for all OECD countries taken together are shown in Fig. 2.4. For each country national saving as a percentage of GNP is shown in blue, and investment as a percentage of GNP is shown in red. From the relationship $S = I + NX$, (Eq. 2.9), we know also that the excess of national saving over investment, $S - I$, for each country equals the country's net exports NX.

---

[12]Another way to get Eq. (2.9) is to start with the definition of national saving, $S = Y - C - G$. From the income-expenditure identity, $Y = C + I + G + NX$, we can see that $Y - C - G = I + NX$. Thus $S = I + NX$, as in Eq. (2.9).

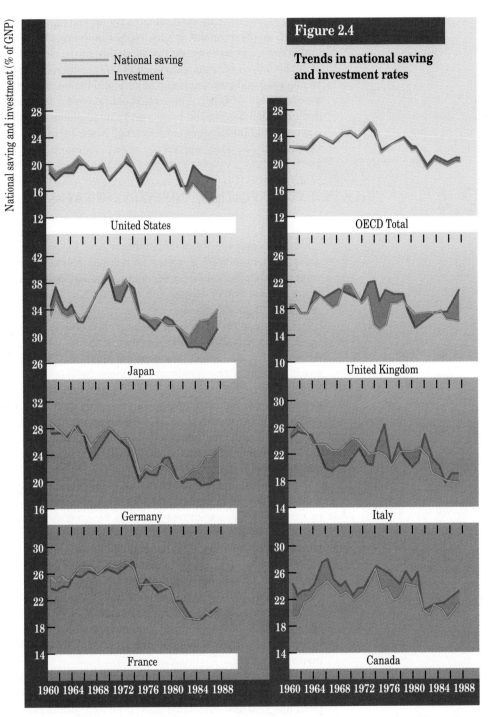

National saving and investment (% of GNP)

National saving
Investment

Figure 2.4

Trends in national saving and investment rates

United States

OECD Total

Japan

United Kingdom

Germany

Italy

France

Canada

1960 1964 1968 1972 1976 1980 1984 1988   1960 1964 1968 1972 1976 1980 1984 1988

National saving (*blue*) and investment (*red*) as a percentage of GNP are shown for 1960–1988 for seven OECD countries and for all twenty-two OECD countries taken together. The shaded areas indicate the country's net exports, the excess of national saving over investment. Blue indicates positive net exports (national saving greater than investment); red indicates negative net exports (investment greater than national saving).

Source: Andrew Dean, Martine Durand, John Fallon, and Peter Hoeller, "Saving Trends and Behaviour in OECD Countries," *OECD Economic Studies*, Spring 1990, Chart A (p. 11).

Figure 2.4 shows that the United States is a low-saving country, with the lowest national saving rate of any major OECD country. As a percentage of GNP, investment in the United States is also fairly low.

Two other points can be drawn from Fig. 2.4. First, there has been some tendency for national saving rates to fall over time. For example, Japan and France have had rather steep declines in national saving over the past twenty years, although Japan's saving rate remains by far the highest of any of the major countries studied. A second point is that within individual OECD countries national saving and investment have generally tended to move closely together. This point implies that the net exports of individual OECD countries, which equal the difference between each country's national saving and investment, have typically been small as a percentage of GNP. The exception has been the period since the early 1980s, during which the United States and Canada have had sharply negative net exports (an excess of investment over saving) while Japan and Germany have had positive net exports (an excess of saving over investment).

2.4 PRICE INDEXES, INFLATION, AND INTEREST RATES

All of the key macroeconomic variables we have discussed so far in this chapter— GNP, the components of expenditure and income, national wealth and saving— have been measured in terms of current market values. Variables measured in terms of current market values are called **nominal variables.** The advantage of using market values to measure economic activity is that it allows us to add different types of goods and services.

There is a problem with measuring economic activity in nominal terms, however, that arises if we want to compare the values of an economic variable—GNP, for example—at two different points in time. The problem is that if the current market value of the goods and services included in GNP changes over time, we can't tell whether this change is due to changes in the quantities of goods and services produced or to changes in the prices of goods and services. So, for example, a large increase in the current market value of GNP might mean that a country has greatly expanded its production of goods and services, or it just might mean that the country has experienced inflation, which has raised the prices of goods and services.

Economists have devised methods for breaking down changes in nominal variables into the part due to changes in physical quantities and the part due to changes in prices. To illustrate these methods by means of a numerical example, consider Table 2.4, which gives production and price data for the Outasite Golf Ball Company. Five years ago the nominal value of Outasite's production was $200,000 (60,000 superenergized golf balls worth $3.00 each plus 40,000 tees at $0.50 each). This year the nominal value of Outasite's production is $480,000 (80,000 balls at $5.00 plus 80,000 tees at $1.00). Although the nominal value of Outasite's production has increased by 140% over the past five years, this increase does not reflect either a 140% increase in physical output or a 140% increase in the prices of golf balls and tees. Instead, as you can see from Table 2.4, both physical quantities and prices have risen.

Suppose we are interested primarily in the growth of Outasite's physical output, perhaps because we want to study how the productivity of the company's work force has changed over time. Then the key question is, How much of the increase in the nominal value of Outasite's production is due only to changes in the quantity of balls and tees produced, rather than to changes in prices? A standard way to eliminate the influence of price changes is to measure the value of production in each period by using the prices that prevailed in some fixed base period. For this example, suppose we choose the year five years prior to the current year as the base year. Valuing Outasite's current production of 80,000 balls at $3.00 per ball

Table 2.4 Production and Price Data for Outasite Golf Ball Company

	Five Years Ago (Base Year)	This Year (Current Year)	Change from Five Years Ago
Balls	60,000 balls	80,000 balls	+20,000 balls
Tees	40,000 tees	80,000 tees	+40,000 tees
Prices			
Balls	$3.00 per ball	$5.00 per ball	+$2.00 per ball
Tees	$0.50 per tee	$1.00 per tee	+$0.50 per tee
Value of Production			
Balls	$180,000	$400,000	+$220,000
Tees	$20,000	$80,000	+$60,000
Total	$200,000	$480,000	+$280,000

(the price of balls five years ago) and its current production of 80,000 tees at $0.50 per tee (the price of tees five years ago), we find a value for Outasite's production this year of $280,000. This calculation is summarized in Table 2.5, step 1.

In general, an economic variable that is measured by using the prices of a fixed base year is called a **real variable.** Thus $280,000 is the real value of Outasite's current production. Real economic variables measure the physical volume of economic activity.

What was Outasite's real production five years ago? To find real production of five years ago, we multiply Outasite's production of balls and tees from five years ago times the prices of balls and tees in the base year, which is also five years ago. This calculation gives us (60,000 balls × $3.00 per ball) + (40,000 tees × $0.50 per tee) = $200,000. This is the same value we got for Outasite's nominal production of five years ago. This result is a general one: *Because current and base-year prices are the same in the base year, real and nominal quantities are also the same in the base year.*

Comparing Outasite's current real production of $280,000 with its real production of $200,000 five years ago, we find that the company's real production has risen by 40% over the five years. It is reasonable to interpret the change in real production as a measure of the change in Outasite's physical output, since when we calculate real production, prices are held constant at their base-year levels. Notice that the estimated increase in real production of 40% lies between the increase in physical production of balls of 33% and the increase in production of tees of 100%. The overall increase in production is estimated to be closer to 33% than 100% because the value of ball production is much greater than the value of tee production, so the increase in ball production is given a heavier weight in the overall growth rate.

Real Versus Nominal GNP

Just as the production of an individual firm can be expressed in nominal terms or in real terms, the output of an entire economy can also be expressed in both nominal and real terms. **Nominal GNP,** also called current-dollar GNP, is the market value of an economy's final output using current market prices. **Real GNP,** also

Table 2.5 Calculation of Real Output and the Price Level for Outasite Golf Ball Company

1. Calculation of the real value of current output

Real value of current output =

	current quantities	×	base-year prices	
Balls	80,000		$3.00	= $240,000
Tees	80,000		$0.50	= $40,000
			Total	= $280,000

2. Calculation of the price level (variable-weight index)

$$\text{Price level} = \frac{\text{value of current output at current prices}}{\text{value of current output at base-year prices}}$$

Value of current output at current prices =

	current quantities	×	current prices	
Balls	80,000		$5.00	= $400,000
Tees	80,000		$1.00	= $80,000
			Total	= $480,000

Value of current output at base-year prices =

	current quantities	×	base-year prices	
Balls	80,000		$3.00	= $240,000
Tees	80,000		$0.50	= $40,000
			Total	= $280,000

$$\text{Price level (variable-weight)} = \frac{\$480,000}{\$280,000} = 1.71$$

3. Calculation of the price level (fixed-weight index)

$$\text{Price level} = \frac{\text{value of base-year output at current prices}}{\text{value of base-year output at base-year prices}}$$

Value of base-year output at current prices =

	base-year quantities	×	current prices	
Balls	60,000		$5.00	= $300,000
Tees	40,000		$1.00	= $40,000
			Total	= $340,000

Value of base-year output at base-year prices =

	base-year quantities	×	base-year prices	
Balls	60,000		$3.00	= $180,000
Tees	40,000		$0.50	= $20,000
			Total	= $200,000

$$\text{Price level (fixed-weight)} = \frac{\$340,000}{\$200,000} = 1.70$$

called constant-dollar GNP, measures the market value of an economy's final output using prices that prevailed during some fixed base period. Real rather than nominal GNP should always be used when one is interested in how an economy's physical production has changed over time.

Currently, the base year that is used for calculating real GNP in the United States is 1982. Thus real GNP for (say) 1990 is calculated by multiplying the quantities of goods and services produced in 1990 times the prices for those goods and services that prevailed in 1982. In contrast, nominal GNP for 1990 is calculated by multiplying the quantities of goods and services produced in 1990 times their 1990 prices. Nominal GNP in 1990 of $5465 billion exceeded real GNP in 1990 of $4157 billion because prices rose on average between 1982 and 1990. In contrast, real and nominal GNP were equal at $3166 billion in 1982, because current and base-year prices were the same in 1982.

Not only GNP but also all the other macroeconomic variables discussed in this chapter—such as consumption, investment, saving, wealth, and so on—can be expressed in real terms. Because they measure physical quantities, real variables are better indicators than nominal variables of how a country's living standards and productive capacity are changing over time. In most of this book we focus on the real determinants of economic well-being. Therefore from now on, unless otherwise stated, *when we refer to output (Y), consumption (C), investment (I), and so on, we will be referring to these variables measured in real rather than nominal terms.*

Price Indexes and Inflation

By measuring GNP in real terms, we eliminate the effects of price changes from our measure of national output. Sometimes, however, as when studying the determinants of inflation, we want to see how much prices have changed over a period of time. A measure of the average level of prices for some specified set of goods and services, relative to the prices of a specified base period, is called a **price index.**

The simplest type of price index is an index for one good, say hamburgers. Suppose hamburgers cost $1.50 each in the base year, say 1982, and cost $2.25 each today. Then the price index for hamburgers, which measures the price of hamburgers today relative to 1982, is $2.25/$1.50 = 1.50. This price index tells us that hamburger prices have risen 50% since 1982.

Usually, however, we want to know how prices have changed not just for one good but for a larger set of goods and services, perhaps all the goods and services produced in the economy. So we must somehow combine the prices of many goods into a single index. Two basic types of price indexes, called variable-weight indexes and fixed-weight indexes, are used to measure average price change for a set of goods and services.

A **variable-weight price index** starts with the set of goods and services produced in the current period and then compares the cost of those goods and services today with what they would have cost in the base year. More precisely:

$$\text{variable-weight price index} = \frac{\text{value of current output at current prices}}{\text{value of current output at base-year prices}}$$

If the goods and services produced today are much more costly today than in the base year, the variable-weight price index will take on a high value.

Table 2.5, step 2, shows how to calculate a variable-weight price index for the Outasite example. Outasite's current output is worth $480,000 in today's prices and $280,000 at the prices of five years ago. Thus the price index for Outasite for the current year is $480,000/$280,000 = 1.71. This figure means that on average Outasite's prices are 71% higher in the current year than in the base year, five years earlier.

An often-used variable-weight price index, which is constructed as part of the national income accounts, is the GNP deflator. In any given period, the **GNP deflator** is the ratio of current nominal GNP to current real GNP:

$$\text{GNP deflator} = \frac{\text{nominal GNP}}{\text{real GNP}}$$

The GNP deflator is the variable-weight deflator that results when the set of goods and services being used covers all final goods and services in the economy. In that case the value of current output in current prices is the same as nominal GNP, and the value of current output in base-year prices equals real GNP. Thus the definition of the GNP deflator fits the general form of a variable-weight price index.[13]

The second type of price index is a fixed-weight index. A **fixed-weight price index** measures how much a fixed basket of goods costs in each year, relative to a base period:

$$\text{fixed-weight price index} = \frac{\text{value of fixed basket at current prices}}{\text{value of fixed basket at base-year prices}}$$

The fixed-weight price index for Outasite is calculated in Table 2.5, step 3, assuming that the fixed basket equals Outasite's base-year production. As the table shows, the value of Outasite's base-year output in current prices is \$340,000, and the value of its base-year output in base-year prices is \$200,000; so the fixed-weight price index is \$340,000/\$200,000 = 1.70—not very different from the value of 1.71 obtained for the variable-weight index.

The most-used fixed-weight price index is the **consumer price index,** or CPI. The Bureau of Labor Statistics constructs the CPI by sending out people each month to find the current prices of a fixed list, or basket, of consumer items, including many specific items of food, clothing, fuel, and so on. The CPI for that month is then calculated as the current cost of the basket of consumer items divided by the cost of the basket in the base period.[14]

Variable-weight and fixed-weight indexes of the price level have different advantages. The advantage of variable-weight indexes is that they reflect the prices of the basket of goods that people actually purchased in the current year, rather than the basket they purchased in the base year. The disadvantage of variable-weight indexes is that the current basket may contain many goods that did not exist or were of different quality in the base year. For such goods economic statisticians must estimate what a new or improved good would have cost had it existed in the base year, which certainly introduces a source of error.[15]

An important variable that is measured by using price indexes is the rate of inflation. The rate of inflation equals the percentage rate of increase in the price index per period. Thus if the CPI rises from 100 in one year to 105 the next, the rate of inflation between the two years is (105 − 100)/100 = 5/100 = 5% per year. If in the third year the CPI is 112, the rate of inflation between the second and third years is (112 − 105)/105 = 7/105 = 0.0667 = 6.67% per year. More generally, if we let P_t stand for the price level in period t and P_{t+1} stand for the price level in period $t + 1$, the rate of inflation between t and $t + 1$, which we denote π_{t+1}, is given by

$$\pi_{t+1} = \frac{P_{t+1} - P_t}{P_t} = \frac{\Delta P_{t+1}}{P_t},$$

where ΔP_{t+1}, equal to $P_{t+1} - P_t$, stands for the change in P_t.

---

[13]Published values of the GNP deflator and other price indexes are often multiplied by 100 to get rid of the decimal point. In this case you will see a notation like (1982 = 100), which means that the index is set equal to 100 (rather than 1.00) in the base year, 1982.

[14]Like the GNP deflator, the CPI is often multiplied by 100, so base-year prices are set equal to 100 rather than 1.00.

[15]Base years are also periodically changed, so as not to be too far in the past. Updating the base year reduces the problem of having current goods that are very different from the goods that existed in the base year.

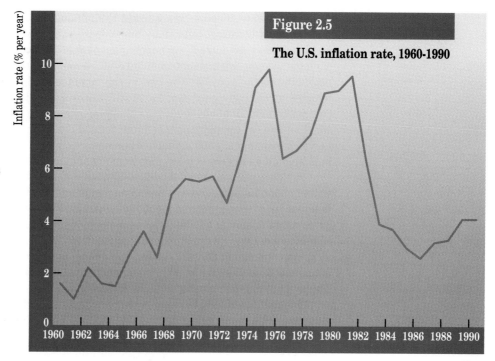

Figure 2.5

The U.S. inflation rate, 1960-1990

In this figure inflation is measured as the annual percentage change in the GNP deflator. Inflation rose during the 1960s, was high during the 1970s, and was brought down in the early 1980s.

Source: 1960–1989 from *Survey of Current Business*, Sept. 1990, Table 3, p. 24; 1990 from *Survey of Current Business*, Feb. 1991, Table 8.1, p. 20.

Figure 2.5 shows the U.S. inflation rate for 1960–1990, using the GNP deflator as the measure of the price level. Inflation rose during the 1960s, peaked during the 1970s, and was brought down sharply in the early 1980s.

Interest Rates

Interest rates are another important type of economic variable, a type familiar in everyday experience. An **interest rate** is a contractually specified rate of return promised by a borrower to a lender. If, for example, the interest rate on a $100, one-year loan is 8%, then the borrower has promised to repay the lender $108 one year from now, or $8 interest plus repayment of the $100 borrowed.

As we discuss in more detail in Chapter 6, there are many different interest rates in the economy. Interest rates vary according to who is doing the borrowing, how long the funds are borrowed for, and other factors. There are also many assets in the economy, such as shares of corporate stock, that do not pay a contractually specified interest rate but do pay their holders a return; for stock the return comes in the form of dividends and capital gains (increases in the stock's market price). The existence of so many different assets, each with its own rate of return, has the potential to greatly complicate our study of the economy. Fortunately, however, most interest rates and other rates of return in the economy tend to move up and down together. For purposes of macroeconomic analysis we will usually speak of "the" interest rate, as if there were only one. If we say that a certain policy change causes "the" interest rate to rise, for example, we mean that interest rates and rates of return in general are likely to rise.

Real Versus Nominal Interest Rates   As a measure of the economy, interest rates and other rates of return share a problem with nominal GNP, in the following sense:

An interest rate tells us how quickly the nominal or dollar value of an interest-bearing asset increases over time, but it does not tell us how much the value of the asset has changed in real, or purchasing-power, terms. Consider, for example, a savings account with an interest rate of 5% per year that has $300 in it at the beginning of the year. At the end of the year the savings account is worth $315, which is a relatively good deal for the depositor if inflation is zero; with no inflation the price level is unchanged over the year, and $315 buys 5% more goods and services in real terms than the initial $300 did a year earlier. If inflation is 5%, however, what cost $300 a year earlier now costs $315, and in real terms the savings account is worth no more today than it was a year ago.

To distinguish changes in the real value of assets from changes in nominal value, economists frequently use the concept of the real interest rate. The **real interest rate** (or real rate of return) on an asset is the rate at which the real value or purchasing power of the asset increases over time. To distinguish them from real interest rates, we will refer to conventionally measured interest rates, such as those reported in the newspaper, as nominal interest rates. The **nominal interest rate** tells us the rate at which the nominal value of an asset increases over time. The symbol for the nominal interest rate is i.

The real interest rate can be related to the nominal interest rate and the inflation rate. The relationship is

$$\text{real interest rate} = \text{nominal interest rate} - \text{inflation rate} \qquad (2.10)$$
$$= i - \pi.$$

This relationship is derived and discussed further in Appendix A, Section A.7.[16] As an example, consider the savings account paying 5% interest that was just discussed. If the inflation rate is zero, then the real interest rate on that savings account is the 5% nominal interest rate minus the 0% inflation rate, or 5%. A 5% real interest rate on the account means that the depositor will be able to buy 5% more goods and services at the end of the year than at the beginning. If inflation is 5%, on the other hand, the real interest rate on the saving account is the 5% nominal interest rate minus the 5% inflation rate, or 0%. In this case the purchasing power of the account is no greater at the end of the year than at the beginning.

The real interest rate for the United States for 1960–1990 is shown in Fig. 2.6. The real interest rate was unusually low in the mid-1970s, and then it rose to record highs in the early 1980s before returning to a more normal level in recent years.

The Expected Real Interest Rate   When you borrow, lend, or make a bank deposit, the nominal interest rate is specified in advance by the terms of the contract. But what about the real interest rate? For a given nominal interest rate Eq. (2.10) tells us that the real interest rate that is received depends on the rate of inflation over the period of the loan or deposit, say a year. However, the rate of inflation during the year can generally not be known until the year is over. Thus at the time that a loan or deposit is made, the real rate of interest that will be received is not known with certainty.

Because borrowers, lenders, and depositors do not know what the actual real interest rate will be, they must make their decisions about how much to borrow, lend, or deposit on the basis of the real interest rate they *expect* to receive. Since

---

[16]Equation (2.10) is an approximation, rather than an exact relationship. This approximation holds most closely when interest rates and inflation rates are not too high. See Appendix A, Section A.7.

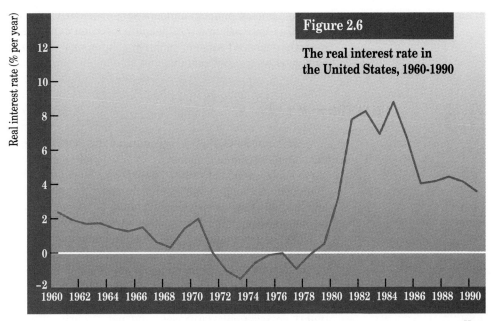

Figure 2.6

The real interest rate in the United States, 1960-1990

The real interest rate was unusually low in the 1970s and unusually high in the early 1980s. It has returned to something closer to a normal level in recent years. In this figure the real interest rate is measured as the nominal interest rate on three-year Treasury debt minus the average inflation rate (using the GNP deflator) over the current and subsequent two years. It is assumed that inflation in 1991 and 1992 will be 5%.

Sources: Interest rate from *Economic Report of the President*, Feb. 1991, Table B–71. Inflation rate from source in Fig. 2.5.

the nominal interest rate is known in advance, the real interest rate that people expect depends on what they think inflation will be. We define the **expected real interest rate** to be the nominal interest rate minus the expected rate of inflation. In symbols, if

r = the expected real interest rate,
i = the nominal interest rate,
π^e = the expected rate of inflation over the life of the loan or deposit,

then the expected real interest rate is given by

$$r = i - \pi^e. \tag{2.11}$$

Comparing Eqs. (2.11) and (2.10), you can see that if people are correct in their expectations—so that expected inflation and actual inflation turn out to be the same—the expected real interest rate and the real interest rate actually received will be the same.

The expected real interest rate is the correct interest rate to use when one is studying most types of economic decisions, such as people's decisions about how much to borrow or lend. However, a problem in measuring the expected real interest rate is that we do not generally know exactly what the public's expected rate of inflation is. Economists use various means to measure expected inflation: One approach is to survey the public and simply ask what rate of inflation they expect. A second strategy is to assume that the public's expectations of inflation are the same as publicly announced government or private forecasts. Yet a third possibility is to assume that people's inflation expectations are an extrapolation of recently observed rates of inflation. Unfortunately, none of these methods is perfect, so the expected real interest rate is always measured with some error.

2.5   CHAPTER SUMMARY

1. The national income accounts are an accounting framework used in measuring current economic activity. The national income accounts measure activity in three ways, called the product approach, the expenditure approach, and the income approach. Although each approach gives the same measure of current economic activity, all three approaches are used because each gives a different perspective on the economy.

2. Gross national product (GNP) is the broadest measure of aggregate economic activity occurring during a specified period of time. The product approach measures GNP by adding the market values of final goods and services newly produced by domestically owned factors of production. The expenditure approach measures GNP by adding the four categories of spending: consumption, investment, government purchases, and net exports. The income approach measures GNP by adding all of the incomes, including taxes and profits, generated by economic activity.

3. The economy can be divided into a private sector (households and businesses), a government sector, and a foreign sector. Corresponding to each sector is a flow of spending and income.

The private sector makes consumption and investment expenditures. The private sector's income, called private disposable income, is total output less taxes paid plus transfers and interest received from the government.

The government sector makes government purchases. It also pays out transfers and interest and makes tax collections. The difference between the government's tax collections and its outlays (government purchases plus transfers plus interest) is the government's budget surplus.

The expenditures of the foreign sector equal net exports. Since GNP is defined to be the output of domestically owned factors of production only, foreign sector income in the national income accounts is zero.

4. Saving is the portion of an economic unit's current income that it does not spend on its current needs. The saving of the private sector, called private saving, equals private disposable income minus consumption. Government saving, which is the same as the government budget surplus, equals the government's tax collections less outlays. National saving, which is private saving plus government saving, equals GNP minus consumption and government purchases.

5. The uses-of-saving identity says that private saving equals the sum of investment, the government deficit, and net exports. Equivalently, national saving equals the sum of investment and net exports.

6. The national wealth of a country equals the country's physical assets, such as capital, plus its net foreign assets. National wealth increases in two ways: through changes in the value of existing assets and through national saving. National saving adds to national wealth because national saving is used either for investment, thus adding to physical capital, or for financing net exports, which increases the country's net foreign assets.

7. Nominal GNP is the value of an economy's final output measured by using current market prices. Real GNP measures the market value of the economy's final output by using prices that prevailed in some fixed base period. Because prices are held fixed in the calculation of real GNP, changes in real GNP over time capture changes in the physical volume of production. More generally, nominal variables measure current market values; real variables are intended to measure physical magnitudes.

8. A price index is a measure of the average level of prices in a given period, relative to a base year. A variable-weight price index, such as the GNP deflator, compares the cost of a set of goods and services produced in the current period with what they would have cost in the base year. A fixed-weight index, such as the consumer price index, measures how much a fixed basket of goods and services costs in each period, relative to what they cost in the base year. Inflation is the percentage rate of change of the price level, as measured by a price index such as the GNP deflator or the CPI.

9. An interest rate is a contractually specified rate of return promised by a borrower to a lender. Interest rates as conventionally measured are called nominal interest rates. The nominal interest rate is the rate at which the nominal value of an interest-bearing asset increases over time. The real interest rate, equal to the nominal interest rate minus the rate of inflation, is the rate at which the value of an asset grows in real, or purchasing-power, terms. Borrowing and lending decisions are based on the expected real interest rate, which is the nominal interest rate less the expected rate of inflation.

Key Terms

budget deficit, p. 41
budget surplus, p. 41
capital good, p. 32
consumer price index, p. 54
consumption, p. 33
depreciation, p. 35
expected real interest rate, p. 57
expenditure approach, p. 28
final goods and services, p. 32
fixed-weight price index, p. 54
flow variable, p. 47
fundamental identity of national income accounting, p. 30
GNP deflator, p. 53
government outlays, p. 40
government purchases, p. 35
government saving, p. 43

gross domestic product, p. 32
gross national product, p. 30
income approach, p. 28
income-expenditure identity, p. 33
interest rate, p. 55
intermediate goods and services, p. 31
inventories, p. 32
investment, p. 34
national income, p. 36
national income accounts, p. 26
national saving, p. 43
national wealth, p. 47
net exports, p. 35
net foreign assets, p. 47
net national product, p. 36
nominal GNP, p. 51

nominal interest rate, p. 56
nominal variable, p. 50
personal disposable income, p. 40
personal saving, p. 43
price index, p. 53
private disposable income, p. 40
private saving, p. 42
private sector, p. 38
product approach, p. 28
real GNP, p. 51
real interest rate, p. 56
real variable, p. 51
saving, p. 42
stock variable, p. 47
transfers, p. 35
underground economy, p. 31
uses-of-saving identity, p. 44
variable-weight price index, p. 53
wealth, p. 47

Key Equations

$$\text{total production} = \text{total income} \qquad (2.1)$$
$$= \text{total expenditure}$$

The *fundamental identity of national income accounting* says that the same measure of total economic activity is obtained whether activity is measured by the production of final goods and services, by the amount of income generated by the economic activity, or by the expenditure on final goods and services.

$$Y = C + I + G + NX \qquad (2.2)$$

According to the *income-expenditure identity*, total income or product Y equals the sum of the four types of expenditure: consumption C, investment I, government purchases G, and net exports NX.

$$S_{\text{private}} = (Y - T + TR + INT) - C \qquad (2.5)$$

Private saving, the saving of the private sector, equals private disposable income less consumption C. Private disposable income, the income of the private sector, equals total product Y, less taxes paid T, plus transfers TR and interest INT received from the government.

$$S_{\text{government}} = T - (G + TR + INT) \qquad (2.6)$$

The government's saving equals its tax revenues T less government outlays. Government outlays are the sum of government purchases G, transfers TR, and interest on the national debt INT. Government saving is the same as the government budget surplus and is the negative of the government budget deficit.

$$S = S_{\text{private}} + S_{\text{government}} = Y - C - G \qquad (2.7)$$

National saving S is the sum of private saving and government saving. Equivalently, national saving equals total product Y less consumption C and government purchases G.

$$S_{\text{private}} = I + (G + TR + INT - T) + NX \qquad (2.8)$$

According to the *uses-of-saving identity*, private saving is used to finance investment spending I, the government budget deficit $(G + TR + INT - T)$, and net exports NX.

$$S = I + NX \qquad (2.9)$$

National saving S has two uses, to finance investment I and to finance net exports NX. Net exports equals the increase in net foreign assets.

$$r = i - \pi^e \qquad (2.11)$$

The expected real interest rate r equals the nominal interest rate i minus expected inflation π^e.

Review Questions

1. What are the three approaches to measuring economic activity? Why do they give the same answer?

2. Why are goods and services counted in GNP at market value? Are there any disadvantages or problems in using market values to measure production?

3. What is the difference between intermediate and final goods and services? In which of these categories do capital goods, such as factories or machines, fall? Why is the distinction between intermediate and final goods important for measuring GNP?

4. List the four components of total spending. Why are imports subtracted when GNP is calculated by the expenditure approach?

5. What are the major sectors of the economy? Show how production, expenditure, and income are divided among the various sectors.

6. Define *private saving*. How is private saving used in the economy? What is the relationship between private saving and national saving?

7. What is national wealth, and why is it important? How is national wealth linked to national saving?

8. For the purposes of assessing an economy's growth performance, which is the more important statistic: real GNP or nominal GNP? Why?

9. Describe how the GNP deflator and the CPI are calculated. What are the basic differences between these two price indexes?

10. Explain the differences among the nominal interest rate, the real interest rate, and the expected real interest rate. Which interest rate concept is the most important for the decisions made by borrowers and lenders? Why?

Numerical Problems

1. Robinson Crusoe grows coconuts and catches fish. Last year he harvested 1000 coconuts and caught 500 fish. He values one fish as worth two coconuts. Robinson gave 200 coconuts to Friday in exchange for help in the harvest, and he gave Friday 100 fish in exchange for collecting worms for use in fishing. Robinson stored 100 of his coconuts in his hut for consumption at some future time. He also used 100 fish as fertilizer for the coconut trees, as he must every year to keep the trees producing. Friday consumed all his coconuts and fish.

What is the GNP of Crusoe's island, in terms of fish? What are consumption and investment? What are the incomes of Crusoe and Friday?

2. ABC Computer Company has a $20,000,000 factory in Silicon Valley. During the current year ABC builds $2,000,000 worth of computer components. ABC's costs are labor, $1,000,000; interest on debt, $100,000; and taxes, $200,000.

ABC sells all of its output to XYZ Supercomputer. Using ABC's components, XYZ builds four supercomputers at a cost of $800,000 each ($500,000 worth of components, $200,000 in labor costs, and $100,000 in taxes per computer). XYZ has a $30,000,000 factory.

XYZ sells three of the supercomputers for $1,000,000 each; but as of year's end, it had not sold the fourth. The unsold computer is carried on XYZ's books as a $800,000 increase in inventory,

a. Calculate the contributions to GNP of these transactions, showing that all three approaches give the same answer.

b. Repeat part a, but now assume that in addition to its other costs, ABC also paid $500,000 for imported computer chips.

3. For each of the following transactions, determine the contribution to the current year's GNP. Explain the effects on the product, income, and expenditure accounts.

a. On January 1 you purchase 10 gallons of gasoline at $1.40 per gallon. The gas station purchased the gasoline the previous week at a wholesale price (transportation included) of $1.30 per gallon.

b. Colonel Hogwash purchases a Civil War–era mansion for $1,000,000. The broker's fee is 6%.

c. A homemaker enters the work force, taking a job that will pay $20,000 over the year. The homemaker must pay $8000 over the year for professional child care services.

d. The Japanese build an auto plant in Tennessee for $100,000,000, using only local labor and materials. (*Hint:* The auto plant is a capital good produced by Americans and purchased by the Japanese.)

e. You are informed that you have won $3,000,000 in the New Jersey State Lottery, to be paid to you, in total, immediately.

f. The New Jersey state government pays you an additional $5000 fee to appear in a TV commercial publicizing the state lottery.

g. Hertz Rent-a-Car replaces its rental fleet by buying $100,000,000 of new cars from General Motors. It sells its old fleet to a consortium of used-car dealers for $40,000,000. The consortium resells the used cars to the public for a total of $60,000,000.

4. You are given the following data on an economy.

Gross national product	$1000
Government purchases of goods and services	$200
Government deficit	$50
National saving	$200
Investment	$150

Find the following.
a. Consumption
b. Private saving
c. Disposable income
d. Net exports

5. Consider an economy that produces only three types of fruit: apples, oranges, and bananas. In the base year (a few years ago), the production and price data were as given next.

Fruit	Quantity	Price
Apples	3000 bags	$2 per bag
Bananas	6000 bunches	$3 per bunch
Oranges	8000 bags	$4 per bag

In the current year the production and price data are as given next.

Fruit	Quantity	Price
Apples	4000 bags	$3 per bag
Bananas	14000 bunches	$2 per bunch
Oranges	32000 bags	$5 per bag

a. What are the values of nominal and real GNP in the base year and the current year?

   b. How much did nominal GNP grow between the base year and the current year?

   c. How much did real GNP grow between the base year and the current year?

   d. What was the percentage change in the price level between the base year and the current year, as measured by the GNP deflator? As measured by a fixed-weight price index that takes actual production in the base year as the fixed basket of goods?

6. The table gives values for the consumer price index for the period 1929–1933. Calculate the rate of inflation in each year from 1930 to 1933. What is unusual about this period, relative to recent experience?

Year	1929	1930	1931	1932	1933
CPI	51.3	50.0	45.6	40.9	38.8

7. Hy Marks buys a one-year government bond on January 1, 1991, for $500. He receives principal plus interest totaling $545 on January 1, 1992. We suppose that the CPI stood at 200 on January 1, 1991, and at 214 on January 1, 1992. This increase in prices is more than Hy anticipated; his guess was that the CPI would be at 210 by the beginning of 1992.

   Find the nominal interest rate, the inflation rate, the real interest rate, Hy's expected inflation rate, and Hy's expected real interest rate.

8. The GNP deflator in Econoland is 200 on January 1, 1990. The deflator rises to 242 by January 1, 1992 (two years later), and to 266.2 by January 1, 1993.

   a. What is the *annual* rate of inflation over the two-year period between January 1, 1990, and January 1, 1992? In other words, what constant yearly rate of inflation would lead to the price rise observed over those two years?

   b. What is the annual rate of inflation over the three-year period from January 1, 1990, to January 1, 1993?

   c. In general, if P_0 is the price level at the beginning of an n-year period, and P_n is the price level at the end of that period, show that the annual rate of inflation π over that period satisfies the equation $(1 + \pi)^n = (P_n/P_0)$.

Analytical Problems

1. A reputable study shows that a particular new workplace safety regulation will reduce the growth of real GNP. Is this an argument against implementing the regulation? Explain.

2. In centrally planned economies many prices are set by the government. The government-set prices are sometimes too low, in that more people want to buy the good at the fixed price than there are supplies available; or the price may be too high, so that large stocks of the good sit unsold on store shelves. What problem does this create for economists attempting to measure the GNP of centrally planned economies? Can you suggest a strategy for dealing with this problem?

3. In the NIPA section of a recent issue of the *Survey of Current Business*, find Table 5.1, "Gross Saving and Investment." Using the table, find private saving and national saving in the United States for the past two years. Show that private saving equals the sum of its three uses in each year. The table refers to private saving as gross private saving, to investment as gross private domestic investment, and to net exports as net foreign investment.

A BASIC FRAMEWORK FOR MACROECONOMIC ANALYSIS: THE CLASSICAL *IS-LM* MODEL

3

The Real Economy:
Output,
Employment,
and Investment

One of the main goals of macroeconomics is to gain an understanding of how the economy works. Unfortunately, because of the immense complexity and ever-changing nature of modern economies, this is not an easy task. As we discussed in Chapter 1, economists try to cut through the complexity of the real world by using economic models, which are simplified descriptions of the economy usually expressed in mathematical form. By concentrating on the main features of the economy while suppressing unnecessary details, economic models help us think about the economy in a logical, clear way. Of course, we must not forget that because models are simplifications—sometimes oversimplifications—of reality, they must be applied with care and judgment.

To provide a theoretical framework for studying the macroeconomy, in this chapter and in Chapter 4 we introduce an economic model called the *IS-LM* model.[1] The *IS-LM* model—along with its close cousin, the aggregate demand–aggregate supply (*AD-AS*) model, which we discuss later in the book—is the most frequently used tool of macroeconomic analysis. A major reason for the *IS-LM* model's popularity is its versatility: The *IS-LM* model and its various components can be used to analyze phenomena ranging from economic growth to business cycles to inflation, and to study the effects on the economy of the government's macroeconomic policies. Later, we will also use the *IS-LM* model to explore fully both classical and Keynesian views of the economy.

Although setting up the *IS-LM* model requires that we spend much of these two chapters on macroeconomic theory, we also use the theory to discuss some real-world economic issues, including the productivity of the American economy,

---

[1]Why the *IS-LM* model has that name will be clear by the end of the next chapter. In brief, *IS* and *LM* are short for two key conditions in the model: *IS* stands for "investment (*I*) equals saving (*S*)" and *LM* stands for "demand for money (*L*) equals the supply of money (*M*)".

the effects of an oil price shock, and the sources of inflation. In Chapter 3 we focus on issues related to real economic variables, such as output, employment, and investment. Chapter 4 takes up questions related to nominal variables such as the price level and inflation.

As you read Chapters 3 and 4, there are two points to keep in mind. First, our reason for presenting the *IS-LM* model right away is to give you a sense of the big picture and of where we are going in the rest of the book. Thus in this first pass we move quickly and concentrate on laying out the main elements of the model. As we explore various topics later in the book, we come back and examine more thoroughly the economic ideas underlying the *IS-LM* model as well as the variety of practical applications for which this model is useful.

The second point has to do with the controversy between classical and Keynesian macroeconomists, discussed in Chapter 1. The main difference between classicals and Keynesians, recall, is that classicals believe that wages and prices adjust rapidly to equate quantities supplied and demanded in each market; Keynesians argue that wages and prices may be slow to adjust. *In these two chapters we will study the IS-LM model using the classical assumption that wages and prices adjust rapidly to clear markets* (set quantities supplied equal to quantities demanded). Later in the book, when we study Keynesian business cycle analysis, we introduce slow-adjusting wages and prices into the *IS-LM* model.

Why do we adopt the classical assumption in these introductory chapters? One reason is that, even for someone who ultimately wants to use the Keynesian approach, we believe that it makes sense to first understand the classical version of the *IS-LM* model. To use an analogy, in a physics course the laws of motion are first explained by assuming that there is no friction; once the no-friction case is mastered, the more complex situation with friction is introduced. Slow wage and price adjustment can be thought of as a "friction" in the operation of the economy. To understand the effects of this friction, we begin with the case where the friction is absent.

Another reason for assuming here that wages and prices adjust to clear markets is that, for the most part, even Keynesians accept that full wage and price adjustment does occur *in the long run*. Thus whether one takes a classical or a Keynesian position about short-run economic behavior, both sides agree that the version of the model assuming full wage and price adjustment is appropriate for analyzing issues such as long-run economic growth and the long-run behavior of inflation. Since these long-run issues are extremely important, the classical version of the *IS-LM* model introduced here is useful even if one chooses not to use it for short-run analysis.

3.1   THE *IS-LM* MODEL: AN OVERVIEW

The *IS-LM* model of the macroeconomy, which we explore in these two chapters, was introduced more than fifty years ago by Nobel Prize winner Sir John Hicks.[2] The model became the standard framework for macroeconomic analysis and over the years has been used and developed by many eminent economists. Hicks based his original *IS-LM* model on his interpretation of the work of Keynes, and histor-

---

[2]Hicks set forth the *IS-LM* framework in an article entitled "Mr. Keynes and the Classics: A Suggested Interpretation," *Econometrica*, April 1937, pp. 147–59.

ically, this model has been employed most often by Keynesians. However, as we already mentioned, the *IS-LM* framework can be used for classical analysis just as conveniently as for Keynesian analysis, and we will use it in both ways in this book.

Like most macroeconomic models, the *IS-LM* model ignores the enormous diversity of goods and services in the economy and concentrates instead on the behavior of aggregate quantities, such as total output, total consumption, and total investment. To explain how these aggregate quantities are determined, the *IS-LM* model focuses on the behavior of three sets of economic actors: firms, households, and the government.

1. *Firms* produce and sell output (goods and services). In order to produce this output, firms must invest in capital goods and employ workers.

2. *Households* supply labor to firms and receive from firms both labor income (wages) and capital income (interest, rents, dividends). Households also purchase and consume part of firms' output. The portion of households' after-tax income that is not spent on consumption is saved.

3. The *government* makes government purchases and transfer payments, and it collects taxes from the private sector. The government also determines the amount of money in circulation.

Notice that the three sets of actors correspond to three of the four sectors of the economy discussed in Chapter 2. We will assume for the time being that the economy does not trade with other countries and so will ignore the fourth sector, the foreign sector. We add the foreign sector to the model in Chapter 7.

The three sets of actors in the *IS-LM* model are assumed to trade with each other in three markets: the goods market, the labor market, and the asset market.

1. The output produced by firms is traded in the market for goods and services, or the *goods market*, for short. Firms sell their output to households for consumption, to other firms for use as capital goods, and to the government as government purchases.

2. Labor is sold by workers and bought by firms in the *labor market*.

3. When consumers save, they must hold their savings in the form of some type of asset. Examples of assets that consumers can hold include financial assets (such as cash, checking accounts, government bonds, and shares of stock) and real assets (such as land or housing). Assets are traded in the *asset market*.

In this chapter we study the goods market and the labor market. In Chapter 4 we add the asset market to the model.

In analyzing the three markets of the *IS-LM* model, we often use the concept of equilibrium. In general, a market is in **equilibrium** when the quantities demanded and supplied in that market are equal. Thus when we say that the goods market is in equilibrium, we mean that the amount of output that households, firms, and the government want to buy equals the amount of output that firms want to produce and sell. Similarly, the labor market is in equilibrium when the amount of labor that firms want to employ equals the amount of labor that workers want to supply; and the asset market is in equilibrium when the amount of each asset that consumers want to hold equals the amount of that asset that is available. Market equilibrium is an important concept because in many situations powerful economic forces tend to drive markets toward equilibrium.

3.2   HOW MUCH DOES THE ECONOMY PRODUCE? THE PRODUCTION FUNCTION

The first of the three markets in the *IS-LM* model is the goods market, in which firms sell their output. The output of firms is purchased by households for consumption, by firms for investment (the creation of new capital goods), and by the government.

What determines the quantity of goods and services that the firms in an economy provide? At the most basic level the amount of output that firms produce depends on the quantity of inputs they use. Economists refer to inputs to the production process—such as capital goods, labor, raw materials, and energy—as **factors of production.** Not surprisingly, when firms use greater quantities of factors of production, they are able to produce more output.

Of the various factors of production, the two most important are capital (factories and machines, for example) and labor (workers).[3] Thus in discussing the supply of output, we focus on these two factors. However, output in modern economies does sometimes respond strongly to changes in the supplies of other factors, such as energy. The effects of a change in energy supplies are discussed as an application of the theory later in this chapter.

The quantity of capital and labor employed by firms does not completely determine the amount of output that firms supply. Equally important is how effectively these factors of production are used. For given stocks of capital and labor, an economy in which firms have superior technologies and management practices will be able to produce more output than an economy without those advantages.

The effectiveness with which an economy uses capital and labor is expressed mathematically by the production function. The **production function** tells us the amount of output that can be produced using any given quantities of capital and labor. A convenient way to write the production function relationship is as follows:

$$Y = AF(K, N), \tag{3.1}$$

where

Y = real output produced in a given period of time,
A = a number measuring overall productivity,
K = the quantity of capital used in the period,
N = the number of workers employed in the period,
F = a function relating output Y to capital K and labor N.

According to Eq. (3.1), the amount of output Y that the economy can produce during a fixed period of time depends on the size of the capital stock K and the number of workers N. The symbol A in Eq. (3.1), which multiplies the function $F(K, N)$, is a measure of the overall effectiveness with which the economy uses capital and labor. We will refer to A as total factor productivity, or simply **productivity.** Notice that, for any given values of capital and labor, an increase in productivity A of, say, 10% implies a 10% increase in the amount of output that can be produced. Thus we can think of increases in productivity A as corresponding to improvements in technology, better management techniques, or any other changes that allow capital and labor to be utilized more effectively.

---

[3]One indication of the importance of capital and labor is that these two factors earn the lion's share of national income.

Table 3.1 The Production Function of the United States, 1980–1989

Production function: $Y = AK^{0.3}N^{0.7}$

Year	(1) Real GNP, Y (Billions of 1982 Dollars)	(2) Capital, K (Billions of 1982 Dollars)	(3) Labor, N (Millions of Workers)	(4) Total Factor Productivity, A[a]	(5) Growth in Total Factor Productivity (% Change in A)
1980	3187	3138	99.3	11.39	—
1981	3249	3244	100.4	11.41	0.2
1982	3166	3307	99.5	11.12	−2.5
1983	3279	3357	100.8	11.36	2.2
1984	3501	3456	105.0	11.69	2.9
1985	3619	3577	107.2	11.79	0.8
1986	3718	3671	109.6	11.83	0.4
1987	3845	3752	112.4	11.94	0.9
1988	4017	3861	115.0	12.17	1.9
1989	4118	3960	117.3	12.21	0.3

Sources: Real GNP—"Summary National Income and Product Series: Annually, 1929–89, and Quarterly, 1961–89," *Survey of Current Business,* September 1990, Table 2; capital stock—"Summary Fixed Reproducible Tangible Wealth Series, 1925–89," *Survey of Current Business,* October 1990 (constant-cost net stock of fixed private nonresidential capital); employment—*Economic Report of the President,* February 1990, Table C-32 (civilian employment over age 16).

[a]Total factor productivity is calculated by the formula $A = Y/(K^{0.3}N^{0.7})$.

Application

The Production Function of the U.S. Economy and U.S. Productivity Growth

Empirical studies suggest that the relationship between output and inputs in the American economy can be described reasonably well by the following production function:[4]

$$Y = AK^{0.3}N^{0.7}. \tag{3.2}$$

The production function in Eq. (3.2) is a specific example of the general production function in Eq. (3.1), in which we have set the general function $F(K, N)$ equal to $K^{0.3}N^{0.7}$. (This production function uses exponents; if you need to review the properties of exponents, see Appendix A, Section A.6.)

Equation (3.2) shows how output Y is related to the use of factors of production, capital K and labor N, and to productivity A in the United States. Data on output, factors of production, and productivity for the U.S. economy in the 1980s are given in Table 3.1. Columns (1), (2), and (3) of the table show output (real GNP), the capital stock, and labor for each year. Real GNP and the capital stock

---

[4]This type of production function is called a Cobb-Douglas production function. Cobb-Douglas production functions take the form $Y = AK^aN^{1-a}$, where $0 < a < 1$.

are measured in billions of 1982 dollars,[5] and labor is measured in millions of employed workers. Column (4) shows productivity for each year.

Output, capital, and labor as reported in Table 3.1 are directly measured. For example, the Bureau of Labor Statistics bases its count of workers on reports submitted by employers. In contrast, we do not have any way of directly measuring productivity. Instead, the productivity index A is indirectly measured by assigning A whatever value is necessary to make Eq. (3.2) hold. Specifically, for each year A is determined by the formula $A = Y/(K^{0.3}N^{0.7})$, which is a way of rewriting Eq. (3.2). You should confirm that in any given year Eq. (3.2) is satisfied. For example, in 1989 Table 3.1 reports that $Y = 4118$, $K = 3960$, $N = 117.3$, and $A = 12.21$. Since $4118 = 12.21(3960)^{0.3}(117.3)^{0.7}$, Eq. (3.2) is satisfied for the 1989 data.

The fact that the production function (Eq. 3.2) holds in each year for the data in Table 3.1 is not in itself such an exciting discovery, since as we have said, the value of the productivity index A in each year was chosen so that Eq. (3.2) would be satisfied. What *is* interesting is the year-to-year *growth rate* of the productivity measure, as shown in column (5) of Table 3.1.[6] Two points stand out.

First, the table shows that productivity growth can vary sharply in the short run. Most strikingly, productivity in the United States fell 2.5% in 1982, a deep recession year, then rose 2.2% in 1983 and 2.9% in 1984, a period of economic recovery, before slowing down subsequently. It is normal for productivity to fall in recessions and rise in recoveries, but why it behaves this way over the business cycle is the subject of much controversy. We will return to this issue in the section of the book on business cycles.

Second, over the longer run, productivity in the United States has been growing relatively slowly. Over the 1980s, productivity growth in the United States averaged less than 0.8% per year. This result is better than the performance of the 1970s, when productivity growth was essentially zero, but noticeably less than the 1950–1970 period, when productivity growth exceeded 1.3% a year. U.S. productivity growth is also lower than in most other industrialized nations. These trends are disturbing: When productivity is growing, the amount of output that can be produced with given factors of production is expanding over time, which leads to rising standards of living. In contrast, when productivity is not growing, output can expand only to the extent that the capital stock is increased or more people join the work force. Stagnant productivity growth is thus usually associated with little or no improvement in the average person's standard of living. Chapter 8 discusses the relationship between productivity improvement and economic growth in greater detail.

The Shape of the Production Function

The production function can be shown graphically as well as in algebraic terms. The easiest way to graph the production function is to hold fixed one of the two factors of production, either capital or labor, and then graph the relationship be-

---

[5]Measurement of the capital stock in 1982 dollars means that capital goods are counted at their 1982 prices. Thus changes over time in the capital stock in Table 3.1 reflect changes in the real quantity of capital, not changes in the prices of capital goods.

[6]The calculated *level* of total factor productivity A, as opposed to the growth rate, is difficult to interpret because it is not a unit-free measure. For example, if we measured the number of workers in thousands instead of millions, the estimated value of A in each year would change.

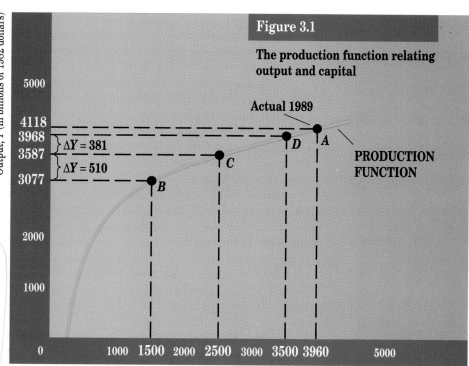

Figure 3.1

The production function relating output and capital

This production function shows how much output the U.S. economy could produce for each level of the U.S. capital stock, holding U.S. labor and productivity fixed at 1989 levels. Point *A* corresponds to the actual 1989 output and capital stock. The production function has diminishing marginal returns to capital: Raising the capital stock by $1000 billion in order to move from point *B* to point *C* would raise output by $510 billion, but adding another $1000 billion in capital to go from point *C* to point *D* would increase output by only $381 billion.

↑'s @ a slower rate

tween output and the other factor.[7] Suppose, for example, that we use the U.S. production function for the year 1989 and fix labor N at its actual 1989 value of 117.3 million workers (see Table 3.1). We also set A equal to its actual 1989 value of 12.21. Then the production function (Eq. 3.2) becomes

$$Y = AK^{0.3}N^{0.7} = (12.21)(K^{0.3})(117.3)^{0.7} = 342.9K^{0.3},$$

which is a relationship between output Y and capital K only.

This relationship is graphed in Fig. 3.1, with the capital stock K on the horizontal axis and output Y on the vertical axis. With labor and productivity held fixed at their 1989 values, the graph shows the amount of output that (hypothetically) could have been produced in that year for any given value of the capital stock. Point A on the graph shows the situation that actually occurred in 1989: Corresponding to point A is the actual 1989 value of the capital stock ($3960 billion), shown on the horizontal axis, and the actual 1989 value of real GNP ($4118 billion), shown on the vertical axis.

The U.S. production function graphed in Fig. 3.1 shares two properties with most production functions. The first property is that *the production function is upward sloping from left to right.* The upward slope of the production function tells us that as the capital stock gets larger, more output can be produced. So, for example, at point D in Figure 3.1 both the capital stock and the output that could be produced using that much capital are greater than at point B.

---

[7]To show the relationship between output and both factors of production simultaneously would require a three-dimensional graph.

The second property exhibited by most production functions is that *the slope of the production function becomes flatter as we move from left to right*. This property implies that although more capital always leads to more output, it does so at a decreasing rate.

For a numerical illustration of this second property, compare points B, C, and D in Fig. 3.1. If we start at point B, where the capital stock is $1500 billion, and add $1000 billion in capital, we arrive at point C, where the capital stock is $2500 billion. The difference in output between points B and C is $510 billion ($3587 billion output at point C minus $3077 billion output at point B). This extra $510 billion in output is the benefit from adding an extra $1000 billion in capital to an initial capital stock of $1500 billion.

Now suppose that starting at point C, we add another $1000 billion of capital, taking us to point D, where the capital stock is $3500 billion. The difference in output between points C and D is only $381 billion ($3968 billion output at point D minus $3587 billion output at point C), which is less than the $510 billion increase in output between points B and C. Thus although the second $1000 billion of extra capital raised total output, it did so by less than did the first $1000 billion of extra capital. This result confirms numerically that the production function rises less steeply between points C and D than between points B and C.

Diminishing Marginal Returns to Capital   The economist's term for the fact that the production function flattens as we move from left to right is diminishing marginal returns to capital. According to the principle of **diminishing marginal returns to capital,** the larger the capital stock already is, the less extra output can be gained by increasing the capital stock still further (holding constant the number of workers).

The economic reasons for diminishing marginal returns to capital can be explained by means of an example. Imagine a secretarial office in which three secretaries spend all of their time preparing letters and other documents, and three more secretaries spend most of their time filing but also do occasional letters. In this office the secretaries are the labor (the amount of labor is assumed fixed), and word-processing computers are the capital. The first three word processors purchased for this office, if made available to the secretaries who only prepare letters, would probably increase the total output of the office substantially, in comparison with a situation in which all secretaries use only manual typewriters. However, if word processors were also purchased for each of the three filing secretaries, who have much less occasion to use them, the resulting gain in the office's output would be smaller than when the first three word processors were brought in. Finally, if the office manager were to purchase a seventh, eighth, and ninth word processor— to be used only periodically as backups—the resulting gain in office output would be smaller still. In general, because firms will find it most profitable to allocate the first capital they buy to the most productive uses available, leaving only less productive uses for subsequent units of capital, we expect to observe diminishing marginal returns to capital.

The Marginal Product of Capital   Starting from some given capital stock K, suppose that we were to increase the capital stock by some amount ΔK, holding constant the number of workers. The increase in capital would cause output to increase by an amount ΔY. The **marginal product of capital** is the output produced per unit of the additional capital, or $\Delta Y / \Delta K$. For example, if capital is increased by one

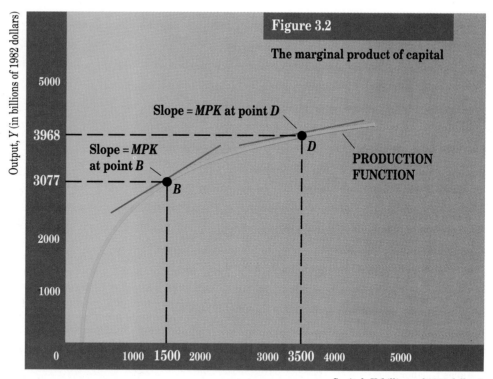

Figure 3.2

The marginal product of capital

The marginal product of capital (MPK) at any point can be measured as the slope of the line tangent to the production function at that point. Because the slope of the line tangent to the production function at point *B* is greater than the slope of the line tangent to the production function at point *D*, we know that the MPK is greater at *B* than at *D*. At higher levels of the capital stock, the MPK is lower, reflecting diminishing marginal returns to capital.

unit ($\Delta K = 1$), the marginal product of capital is just ΔY, or the extra output that is produced. The marginal product of capital is abbreviated MPK.

The marginal product of capital $\Delta Y/\Delta K$ is the change in the variable on the vertical axis of the production function graph (ΔY) divided by the change in the variable on the horizontal axis (ΔK), which you may recognize as a slope.[8] For small increases in the capital stock, the MPK can be measured by the slope of the line that is tangent to the production function. This way of measuring the MPK is illustrated in Fig. 3.2, which shows the same production function as in Fig. 3.1. In Fig. 3.2 the MPK when the capital stock is 1500 equals the slope of the line tangent to the production function at point *B;* the MPK when the capital stock is 3500 equals the slope of the line tangent to the production function at point *D*. Unless otherwise stated, in this book we will measure the MPK as the slope of the line tangent to the production function relating output and capital. We will also usually refer to the slope of the line tangent to the production function at a given point as simply the slope of the production function at that point, for short.

As you can see in Fig. 3.2, the MPK is larger (the slope of the production function is steeper) at point *B*, where the capital stock is relatively small, than it

---

[8]For definitions and a discussion of slopes of lines and curves, see Appendix A, Section A.2.

This production function shows how much output the U.S. economy could produce at each level of employment, holding productivity and the capital stock fixed at 1989 levels. Point A corresponds to actual 1989 output and employment. The marginal product of labor (MPN) at any point is measured as the slope of the line tangent to the production function at that point. The MPN is lower at higher levels of employment, reflecting diminishing marginal returns to labor.

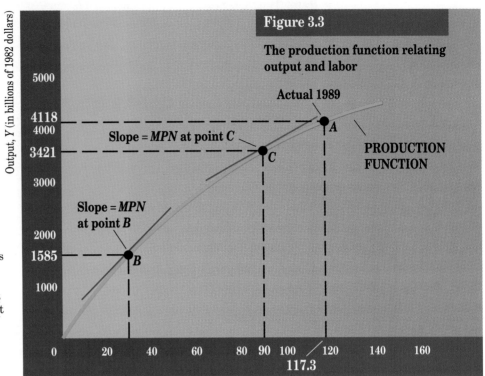

Figure 3.3

The production function relating output and labor

Labor, N (millions of workers)

is at point D, where the capital stock is larger. That is, the MPK falls as the capital stock gets larger. This is just another way of stating the principle of diminishing marginal returns to capital: The larger the capital stock already is, the less extra output is gained by expanding the capital stock further.

The Marginal Product of Labor In Figs. 3.1 and 3.2 we graphed the relationship between output and capital implied by the 1989 U.S. production function, holding constant the amount of labor. In the same way we can look at the relationship between output and labor, holding constant the quantity of capital. Suppose that we fix capital K at its actual 1989 value of $3960 billion and keep productivity A equal to its actual 1989 value of 12.21 (see Table 3.1). Then the production function (Eq. 3.2) becomes

$$Y = AK^{0.3}N^{0.7} = (12.21)(3960)^{0.3}(N^{0.7}) = 146.6N^{0.7},$$

which is a relationship between output Y and the number of workers N. This relationship is shown graphically in Fig. 3.3. Point A in the figure, where $N = 117.3$ million workers and $Y = \$4118$ billion, corresponds to the actual values that occurred in 1989.

The production function relating output and employment looks generally the same as the production function relating output and capital.[9] As in the case of capital, increases in the number of workers raise output but do so at a diminishing

---

[9]Because N is raised to the power of 0.7 but K is raised to the power of 0.3, the production function relating output and labor is not as sharply bowed as the production function relating output and capital.

rate. Thus the principle of diminishing marginal returns applies to labor as well: With the capital stock held constant, the greater the number of workers already employed, the less output is gained by adding another worker. The idea is that the first workers a firm employs will be set to work doing the most productive tasks or using the most efficient machines, which leaves less productive tasks for additional workers.

The **marginal product of labor,** abbreviated MPN, is defined in the same way as the marginal product of capital, as the output produced per unit of additional labor, $\Delta Y/\Delta N$. As in the case of capital, for small increases in employment the MPN can be measured as the slope of the line tangent to the production function relating output and employment. In Fig. 3.3 the MPN when employment is 30 million workers equals the slope of the line that touches the production function at point B, and the MPN when employment is 90 million workers is the slope of the line that touches the production function at point C. Because of diminishing marginal returns to labor, the MPN falls as employment rises; in graphical terms, the slope of the production function relating output and employment falls as we move from left to right.

Supply Shocks

The production function of an economy does not usually remain fixed over time. Economists use the term **supply shock**—or sometimes, productivity shock—to refer to a change in an economy's production function.[10] A positive, or beneficial, supply shock raises the amount of output that can be produced for given quantities of capital and labor. A negative, or adverse, supply shock lowers the amount of output that can be produced for each capital-labor combination.

Real-world examples of supply shocks include changes in the weather such as a drought or an unusually cold winter, inventions or innovations in management techniques that improve efficiency, and changes in government regulations (such as antipollution laws) that affect the technologies or production methods that firms are allowed to use. We also include in the category of supply shocks changes in the supplies of factors of production *other than capital and labor* that affect the amount that can be produced. For example, if flooding makes the best agricultural lands unusable, forcing farmers to use less fertile fields, then more capital and labor will be required to produce a bushel of corn after the flooding than were required before the flooding. Thus flooding of the best lands can be thought of as a negative supply shock in the corn industry.

Figure 3.4 shows the effects of an adverse supply shock on the production function relating output and labor. The negative supply shock *shifts the production function down,* so that less output can be produced for any given quantity of inputs. The shifting down of the production function is the essential feature of a negative supply shock. In addition, the supply shock shown in Fig. 3.4 *reduces the slope* of the production function, so that the output gains from adding a worker (the marginal product of labor) are lower at every level of employment.[11] Although, logically, an adverse supply shock need not always reduce marginal products (for example, the production function could make a parallel downward shift), it seems

---

[10]The term *shock* is a slight misnomer, since not all changes in the production function are sharp or unpredictable, although many are.

[11]A shift of the production function like that shown in Fig. 3.4 would occur if there were a decline in total factor productivity A, for example.

An adverse supply shock is a downward shift of the production function. At any given level of labor the amount of output that can be produced is now less than before. In addition, as drawn in the figure, the adverse shock reduces the slope of the production function (the production function becomes flatter), which is the same as reducing the marginal product of labor (MPN). The effect of an adverse supply shock on a production function relating output and capital would look similar.

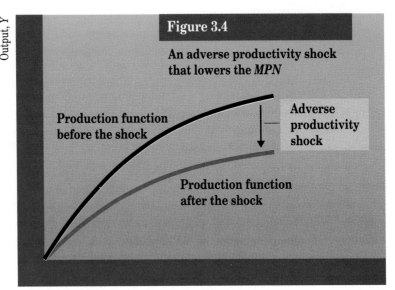

Output, Y

Figure 3.4

An adverse productivity shock that lowers the _MPN_

Production function before the shock

Adverse productivity shock

Production function after the shock

Labor, _N_

reasonable to think of an adverse supply shock reducing marginal products as being the normal case. Similarly, a beneficial supply shock shifts the production function up and (most likely) increases marginal products at any given level of employment.

3.3 DETERMINING OUTPUT AND EMPLOYMENT: THE LABOR MARKET

The production function tells us that, given the level of productivity, the amount of output that firms supply depends on the amount of capital and labor that they use. But how do firms choose how much capital and labor to employ?

The rate at which the capital stock changes depends on how much firms invest. If the quantity of new capital goods purchased by firms exceeds the quantity of capital that wears out or is scrapped, the capital stock will grow over time. However, because the amount invested each year is small relative to the total size of the capital stock, changes in the total capital stock occur relatively slowly. Thus for analyses spanning a few quarters or years, economists typically treat the economy's capital stock as fixed at the level determined by past investments. In this chapter we assume a fixed capital stock. When we study long-term economic growth in Chapter 8, however, we drop the assumption of a fixed capital stock and show how the capital stock evolves over time.

In comparison with the amount of capital, the amount of labor that firms employ can change quickly. For example, a firm can lay off workers or ask them to work overtime on fairly short notice. Workers can also quit or decide to enter the work force without long delays. Thus short-term changes in the output supplied by firms can often be traced to changes in employment.

To understand why employment changes and thereby to complete our analysis of output supply, in this section we discuss the labor market. At this point we cover the labor market only briefly, deferring details to Chapter 10.

As with the other markets of the _IS-LM_ model, to analyze market equilibrium in the labor market, we first need to introduce demand and supply.

Labor Demand

The demand for labor *ND* is the number of workers that firms choose to employ. In studying the behavior of firms, economists usually assume that firm managers attempt to maximize profits. Under this assumption firms' demand for labor will be the level of employment that firm managers expect to be the most profitable.

Two factors affect the profitability of employing workers: the marginal product of labor and the real wage.

The Marginal Product of Labor   Firms make their profits by producing and selling output. The more output an extra worker can produce, given the firm's available capital and technology, the more profitable it will be to hire that worker. In the terminology of the previous section, when the marginal product of labor at any given level of employment is higher, firms will want to employ more workers, everything else being equal. For example, if a new technology is introduced that makes workers in a given industry much more productive, that industry is likely to expand, drawing workers away from less productive sectors of the economy. Similarly, if improvements in education make the typical worker more skilled, firms will want to employ more workers, all else being equal.

The Real Wage   The amount that firms pay their workers each period, measured in real terms, is called the **real wage.** If *W* stands for the nominal wage (say the number of dollars a typical worker receives per hour) and *P* is the average price level, the real wage can be measured by the ratio *W/P*. To find the units of the real wage, note that the nominal wage is measured in dollars per hour and the price level is measured as dollars per good; therefore the units of the real wage *W/P* are (dollars per hour)/(dollars per good), or goods per hour. The real wage *W/P* tells us how many goods the worker can buy with her hourly wage. We let *w* stand for the real wage:

$$w = \frac{W}{P} = \text{real wage, in goods per hour.}$$

The real wage measures the real cost to the firm (that is, in terms of goods) of employing a worker. The higher the real wage, the less profitable it is to employ any given number of workers. Thus the higher the real wage, the lower will be the quantity of labor demanded by firms.

Labor Supply

Labor supply *NS* is the number of people who would like to be working. Labor supply is affected by demographic factors (that is, by the size and makeup of the population) and by the real wage.[12]

Demographic Factors   Population factors are the most basic determinants of a nation's labor supply. Obviously, the more people a country has of working age, the larger its labor supply will be, all else being equal. Thus a country with a high birth rate or a high immigration rate can expect its labor supply to grow quickly over time. Factors such as the official retirement age and the number of women working outside the home similarly affect a nation's labor supply.

---

[12]Additional factors affecting labor supply are discussed in Chapter 10.

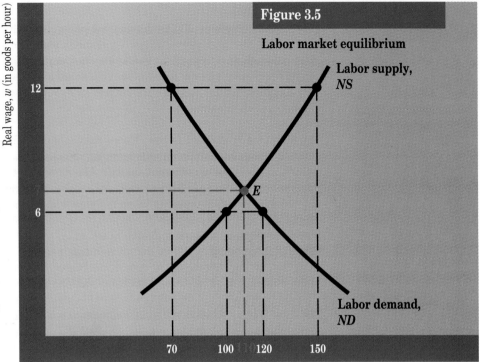

Figure 3.5

Labor market equilibrium

Labor market equilibrium occurs when the quantity of labor demanded equals the quantity of labor supplied. At a real wage of 6 goods per hour, labor demanded (120) exceeds labor supplied (100). At a wage of 12 goods per hour, labor demanded (70) is less than labor supplied (150). Only when the real wage is 7 goods per hour are the quantities of labor demanded and supplied equal, at 110.

The Real Wage   The real wage measures the economic benefit that people derive from working. When the current real wage rises, working becomes a more attractive option: If hamburger flipping pays very little in real terms—barely enough to cover uniforms and medication for grease burns—a student may prefer hanging out at the beach to taking a summer job at the Burger Barn. But if the Burger Barn pays a high real wage—high enough, say, to allow the student to buy a used car by the beginning of the fall term—the student may choose to work instead. Thus increases in the current real wage should raise the quantity of labor supplied.

Labor Market Equilibrium

Figure 3.5 shows supply and demand in the labor market. In the figure labor or employment N is measured on the horizontal axis and the real wage w is measured on the vertical axis. We express the real wage in goods per hour, to remind you that it is a real rather than a nominal quantity.

The relationship between the quantity of labor demanded by firms and the real wage is described by the labor demand curve, marked ND. The downward slope of the labor demand curve captures the idea that when the real wage rises, the amount of labor that firms find it profitable to employ falls. So, for example, when the real wage takes the relatively low value of 6 goods per hour, the figure shows that firms want to hire 120 workers; but when the real wage is 12 goods per hour, the amount of labor demanded by firms drops to 70 workers.

The relationship between the real wage and the quantity of labor supplied by workers is expressed by the labor supply curve, shown as NS in Fig. 3.5. The labor supply curve is upward sloping, since when the current real wage rises, more people choose to work. For example, the figure shows that 150 people want to be employed when the real wage is 12 goods per hour, but only 100 people want jobs when the real wage is 6 goods per hour.

The labor market is in equilibrium when the quantity of labor demanded equals the quantity of labor supplied. In Fig. 3.5 equilibrium in the labor market is at point E, where the labor demand curve and the labor supply curve cross. Corresponding to point E is a real wage of 7 goods per hour. In this example, when the real wage equals 7 goods per hour, the amount of labor demanded and the amount of labor supplied both equal 110 workers. We say that a real wage of 7 goods per hour clears this labor market, by which we mean that 7 goods per hour is the real wage at which the quantities of labor demanded and supplied are equal.

We said earlier that economic forces tend to push markets toward equilibrium. In the labor market it is the adjustment of the real wage that leads to equilibrium. Imagine, for example, that the real wage is initially 6 goods per hour, which is too low relative to the market-clearing wage of 7 goods per hour. When the wage is 6 goods per hour, firms want to hire 120 workers but only 100 people are interested in working at that wage. In order to attract workers in this "tight" labor market, firms will have to compete with each other by offering higher real wages, until eventually the real wage is bid up to 7 goods per hour and the market is in equilibrium. In a similar way, if the real wage is initially too high at 12 goods per hour, Fig. 3.5 shows that 150 people will want to work but only 70 jobs will be available. In this "slack" labor market competition of workers for scarce jobs will drive down the real wage to 7 goods per hour, where again the labor market is in equilibrium.

This simple picture of the labor market raises two questions that we will mention now but will not fully discuss until later in the book. The first question is, How quickly will real-wage adjustments lead to equilibrium? Classical economists argue that wage adjustments will be relatively rapid, and for the time being we will make that assumption. But as we have said, Keynesians are less confident that the real wage will adjust quickly and thus worry that the labor market may remain out of equilibrium for a long period of time.

The second question is, How do we explain the existence of unemployment? Our model of labor demand and labor supply implies that in equilibrium any worker who wants a job at the market-clearing wage can find one. In other words, in equilibrium unemployment is zero, which is obviously not true in reality. To explain unemployment, economists must extend the model; and as we will see, classicals and Keynesians extend it in different ways. Although the model as developed so far cannot explain unemployment, it *is* useful for studying employment and real wages; so for the time being we will focus on those two labor market variables.

Changes in the Real Wage and Employment   The labor demand curve shows how the quantity of labor demanded depends on the real wage, holding constant other factors that affect labor demand. A change in any factor that affects labor demand, *other than the real wage*, will cause the labor demand curve to shift. As a result, the equilibrium levels of the real wage and employment will change.

As an example, suppose that an adverse supply shock—such as a reduced supply of raw materials—lowers the marginal product of labor (MPN), as illustrated in Fig. 3.4. The effects of the adverse shock on the labor market are shown in Fig. 3.6. If the MPN falls, then at any given real wage firms will demand less labor. In

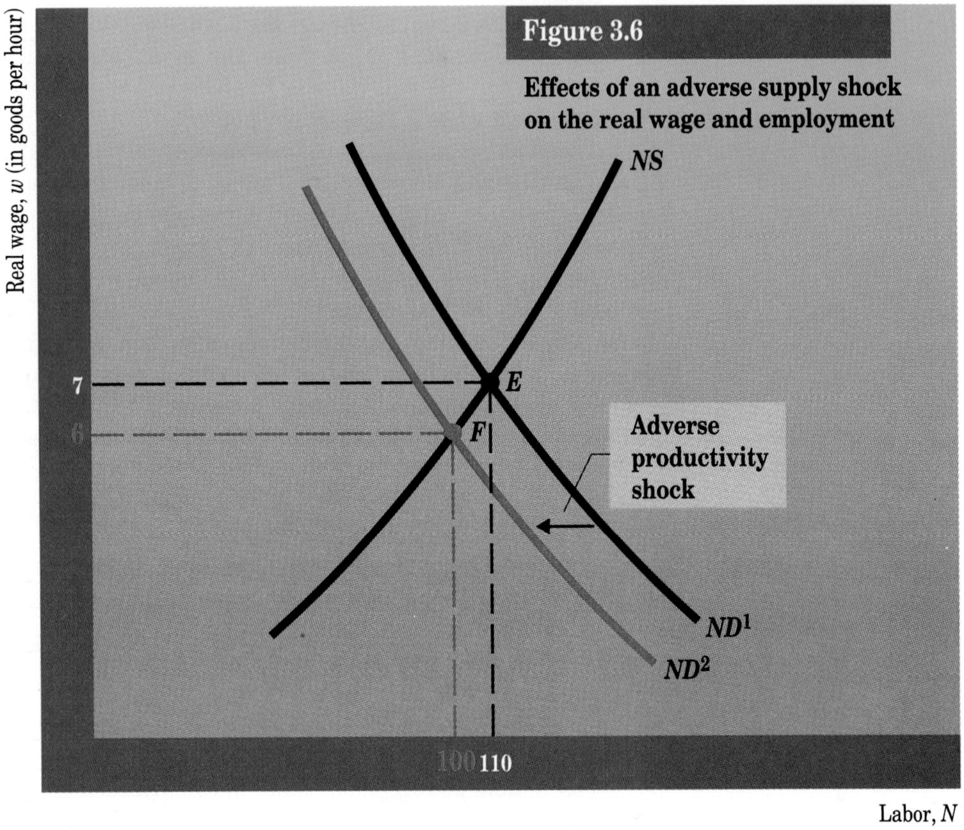

Figure 3.6

Effects of an adverse supply shock on the real wage and employment

An adverse supply shock that lowers the marginal product of labor (see Fig. 3.4) reduces the quantity of labor demanded at any given real wage. Thus the labor demand curve shifts left, from ND^1 to ND^2, and the labor market equilibrium moves from point E to point F. The adverse supply shock causes the real wage to fall, from 7 goods per hour to 6 goods per hour, and also lowers employment, from 110 workers to 100 workers.

turn, the labor demand curve will shift to the left, from ND^1 to ND^2 in Fig. 3.6. The labor market equilibrium changes from point E in the figure to point F. At the new equilibrium the real wage has fallen from 7 goods per hour to 6 goods per hour, and employment has fallen from 110 to 100 workers. The real wage is lower because, given the reduced supply of raw materials, the amount that an additional worker can produce has fallen; thus firms are not willing to pay so much for workers. Employment falls because the lower real wage discourages some people from looking for work.

In a similar way, a change in any factor that affects labor supply, *given the real wage*, will shift the labor supply curve. Figure 3.7 shows the effects of a baby boom that leads, after several decades, to an increase in labor supply. The increase in the number of people willing to work at any given real wage shifts the labor supply curve to the right, from NS^1 to NS^2, which in turn causes the labor market equilibrium point to move from E to G in the figure. The real wage falls, from 7 goods per hour to 6 goods per hour, and employment rises, from 110 workers to 120 workers. The real wage falls because competition among the baby boomers for available jobs bids the wage down.

Full-Employment Output By combining the labor market and the production function, we can determine how much output firms want to supply. The amount of output that firms want to supply is called full-employment output. More precisely, **full-employment output** is the level of output that firms supply when wages and prices in the economy have fully adjusted.

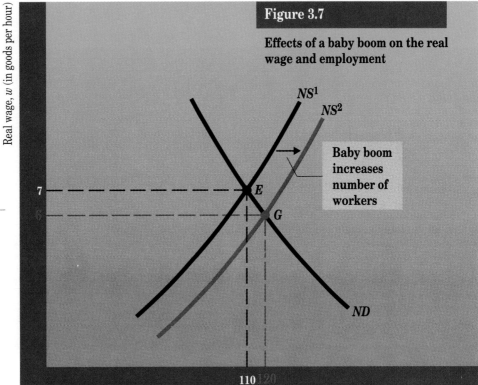

Figure 3.7

Effects of a baby boom on the real wage and employment

A baby boom that leads to an increase in labor supply causes the labor supply curve to shift right, from NS^1 to NS^2. The labor market equilibrium point moves from point E to point G. The increase in labor supply causes employment to rise, from 110 workers to 120 workers, but causes the real wage to fall, from 7 goods per hour to 6 goods per hour.

In the classical case that we are studying in this chapter, full wage and price adjustment implies that the quantities of labor supplied and demanded are equal. Thus in the classical case full-employment output is the output that firms supply when the labor market is in equilibrium. We use $\bar{Y}$ to stand for full-employment output and $\bar{N}$ to stand for the equilibrium level of employment in the labor market; then full-employment output is

$$\bar{Y} = AF(K, \bar{N}). \tag{3.3}$$

Equation (3.3) shows that, given the capital stock, full-employment output is determined by two general factors: the equilibrium level of employment and the production function relating employment to output.

Anything that changes either the equilibrium level of employment $\bar{N}$ or the production function will change full-employment output $\bar{Y}$. For example, the baby boom illustrated in Fig. 3.7 leads to a higher level of employment in labor market equilibrium and thus also raises full-employment output. The adverse supply shock that reduces the MPN, shown in Fig. 3.6, lowers full-employment output in two distinct ways: First, the adverse supply shock lowers output directly, by reducing the quantity of output that can be produced with any given amounts of capital and labor. Second, the adverse supply shock reduces the demand for labor and thus lowers equilibrium employment. The decline in the number of people working lowers full-employment output still further.

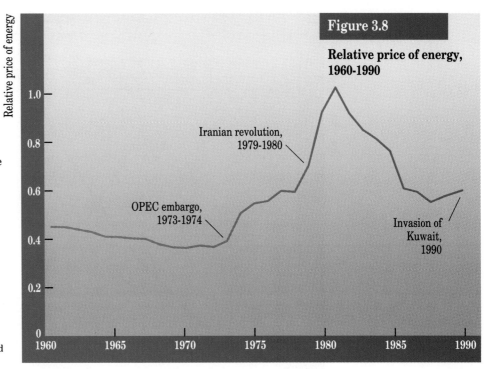

Figure 3.8

Relative price of energy, 1960-1990

The graph shows the producer price index of fuels and related products (an index of energy prices paid by producers) relative to the GNP deflator. The base period for both the producer price index and the GNP deflator is 1982, so that both indexes equal 100 and their ratio equals 1.00 in that year. Notice the impact of the 1973–1974 and 1979–1980 oil shocks, as well as the decline in energy prices in the first half of the 1980s.

Source: *Economic Report of the President*, 1990, Tables C-58 and C-65, with updates.

Year

Output, Employment, and the Real Wage During Oil Price Shocks

Among the most severe shocks hitting the American and world economies in the post–World War II period were sharp increases in the prices of oil and other energy products. Figure 3.8 shows how the price of energy paid by firms, measured relative to the GNP deflator, varied during the period 1960–1990. Two adverse oil price shocks stand out in the figure: one in 1973–1974, when the Organization of Petroleum Exporting Countries (OPEC) first imposed an oil embargo and then greatly increased crude oil prices; and a second in 1979–1980, after the Iranian revolution disrupted oil supplies. As you can see from Fig. 3.8, the 1979–1980 oil price shock was temporary; energy prices came back down in subsequent years. A third increase in oil prices followed Iraq's invasion of Kuwait in August 1990. Because the 1990 shock had less of an impact on overall energy prices than the previous two oil price shocks, and because it came relatively late in the year, the 1990 episode does not show up very strongly in Fig. 3.8.

When energy prices rise, firms cut back on their energy use, implying that less output can be produced for any given quantities of capital and labor. Thus we can think of an increase in energy prices as an adverse supply shock. How important were these supply shocks? In an empirical study of the 1979–1980 oil price

Table 3.2 Selected U.S. Macroeconomic Data, 1972–1986

Year	(1) Real GNP Growth	(2) Employment/ Population[a]	(3) Real Wage[b]	(4) Investment/GNP
1972	5.0%	57.0%	5.36	0.178
1973	5.2	57.8	5.38	0.189
1974	−0.5	57.8	5.21	0.176
1975	−1.3	56.1	5.10	0.142
1976	4.9	56.8	5.18	0.160
1977	4.7	57.9	5.25	0.176
1978	5.3	59.3	5.29	0.185
1979	2.5	59.9	5.14	0.180
1980	−0.2	59.2	4.89	0.160
1981	1.9	59.0	4.83	0.168
1982	−2.5	57.8	4.83	0.141
1983	3.6	57.9	4.89	0.154
1984	6.8	59.5	4.91	0.188
1985	3.4	60.1	4.88	0.176
1986	2.7	60.7	4.92	0.172

Source: *Economic Report of the President*, 1990, Tables C-1, C-2, C-38, C-44.

[a]The employment-to-population ratio is for civilian workers over 16 years.

[b]The real wage is total private average hourly earnings for nonsupervisory workers. The real wage is measured in 1977 dollars—that is, the nominal wage in each year is divided by a price index that is 1.00 in 1977.

shock, John A. Tatom[13] of the Federal Reserve Bank of St. Louis used postwar data to estimate a production function for the United States in which he allowed for effects of energy price changes. Tatom estimated that the increase in the relative price of energy that occurred in 1979–1980 reduced the amount of output that could be produced by given quantities of capital and labor by about 5.7%. Thus Tatom's results, if correct, suggest quite a large impact on supply from the oil price shocks, at least in the 1979–1980 case.

Our analysis predicts that an adverse supply shock will lower labor demand, reducing employment and the real wage, as well as reducing the supply of output. Data on output, employment, and the real wage for 1972–1986—a period that covers the major movements in the relative price of energy—are listed in columns (1)–(3) of Table 3.2. The table shows that the economy went into a recession following both the 1973–1974 and the 1979–1980 oil shocks, with negative real GNP growth in each case. The fraction of the adult population employed fell in both cases, and in both episodes the real wage fell substantially, by over 5% between 1973 and 1975 and by almost 9% between 1978 and 1981. Care must be taken in interpreting these results, since macroeconomic policies and other factors were changing at the same time; however, it does appear that the response of the economy to the two oil price shocks of the 1970s is as predicted by our model. The expansion of output and

---

[13]"Are the Macroeconomic Effects of Oil Price Changes Symmetric?" in K. Brunner and A. Meltzer, eds., *Carnegie-Rochester Conference Series on Public Policy*, Vol. 28, Spring 1988.

employment following the post-1980 decline in energy prices is also consistent with the model, although the failure of the real wage to rise after 1980 is not.

The U.S. economy showed a similar response to the smaller 1990 shock, with a recession beginning at about the same time the shock occurred and continuing into 1991.

3.4 GOODS MARKET EQUILIBRIUM: BALANCING SAVING AND INVESTMENT

In the previous two sections we have seen how the amount of output supplied by firms, or full-employment output, is determined. To get a complete picture of the operation of the goods market, we must also consider the demand for this output.

In an economy without foreign trade, the demand for goods (and services) consists of three components:

1. The quantity of goods that households want to consume, C^d (for "desired consumption").

2. The quantity of goods demanded by firms for investment purposes, I^d (for "desired investment").

3. The quantity of goods purchased by the government, G. We won't distinguish between actual and desired government purchases but will assume instead that the government's purchases always equal their desired level.

The goods market is in equilibrium when the quantity of goods supplied Y equals the quantity of goods demanded, $C^d + I^d + G$:

$$Y = C^d + I^d + G. \tag{3.4}$$

Equation (3.4) is called the goods market equilibrium condition.

The goods market equilibrium condition is different in an important way from the income-expenditure identity, $Y = C + I + G$.[14] The income-expenditure identity is a relationship between actual income (output) and actual spending that must always hold, by definition. The goods market equilibrium condition, Eq. (3.4), says not only that actual income and spending are equal but also that *actual* levels of consumption and investment must equal the levels of consumption and investment *desired* by consumers and firms, so that $C + I = C^d + I^d$.

There is a different—although exactly equivalent—way to write Eq. (3.4) that is very useful. If we subtract $C^d + G$ from both sides of that equation, we get

$$Y - C^d - G = I^d.$$

Recall from Chapter 2 that $Y - C - G$ equals national saving S. The left side of the equation here therefore equals what we will call desired national saving, S^d. Desired national saving is the level of national saving that occurs when consumption is at its desired level. Replacing the left side of the equation with desired national saving S^d gives us

$$S^d = I^d. \tag{3.5}$$

---

[14]See Eq. (2.2). Because we are assuming no foreign trade, we set net exports NX equal to zero in this identity.

Equation (3.5) is an alternative way of writing the goods market equilibrium condition; it says that the goods market is in equilibrium when desired national saving equals desired investment. Because we are often interested in how changes in the economy affect saving and investment, we will find this form of the equilibrium condition the more convenient one to work with. However, do not lose sight of the fact that Eq. (3.5) is just another way of stating the condition that the quantity of goods supplied must equal the quantity of goods demanded, Eq. (3.4).

To summarize, equilibrium in the goods market requires that desired national saving equal desired investment. In the rest of this section we discuss the most important factors that affect desired national saving and desired investment, as well as the forces that cause them to be equal and thus bring about goods market equilibrium.[15]

Determinants of Desired National Saving

Desired national saving S^d equals total output less desired consumption and government purchases, or $Y - C^d - G$. Thus, given output Y, desired national saving depends both on the decisions made by households about how much to consume and on the government's chosen level of purchases. We begin by discussing consumption and saving from the perspective of consumers; then we consider the government's role.

Why do individuals often choose to save part of their current income, instead of spending everything they earn on various forms of consumption? The reason is that most people care not only about the consumption they get to enjoy today but also about the consumption they hope to enjoy next week, next year, and twenty years from now. People save today so that they will be able to live better in the future or, at the least, have a reasonable standard of living in the future should their incomes fall or expenses rise. The basic insight that people save in order to provide for future consumption allows us to identify the principal factors affecting desired saving. These factors, discussed below, include current income, expected future income, and the expected real interest rate.

Current Income   If you received a bonus at work that raised your current income by $2000, what would you do with it? Probably you would spend part of the extra income on consumption goods, perhaps a vacation. The rest you might save—for example, by increasing the balance in your bank account or paying off some debts (a form of saving, since it reduces your liabilities and therefore increases your wealth). Thus the increase in your current income would raise both your total consumption and your total saving.

This response to an increase in current income makes good economic sense: When a person's current income rises, he feels better off and will thus want to consume more today. But as we have said, people value future consumption as well as current consumption. One benefit of a rise in current income is that, besides enjoying more consumption today, an individual can also plan for greater consumption in the future by saving part of his current increase in income.[16] Thus both consumption and saving should rise when current income rises.

---

[15]National saving and investment are discussed further in Chapters 5 and 6.

[16]We are assuming that the bonus leaves future income unchanged.

The same argument works in reverse if current income falls. Because a decline in income makes an individual worse off, he will respond both by consuming less today and by putting less aside in provision for future consumption. In response to a decline in current income, therefore, both total consumption and saving will fall.

From a macroeconomic perspective, a rise in current income corresponds to an increase in total output Y.[17] Our discussion suggests that when current output Y rises, desired current consumption C^d also rises but not by as much as the increase in output. Since desired consumption rises by less than output, desired national saving $Y - C^d - G$ also rises when output rises.

Expected Future Income   Suppose that, instead of receiving the $2000 bonus in your current paycheck, you are told that you will receive the bonus next year. This bonus is legally guaranteed and you have no doubt that you will receive it as promised. What will happen to your current (this year's) saving? Most likely, your current saving will fall: Since you know you will be receiving the bonus next year, you have less need to save for the future and can enjoy more current consumption instead. Similarly, a fall in expected future income—for example, if you learn that your employer is going out of business, which will cost you your job—should make you want to save more today.

In macroeconomic terms, a rise in expected future output raises today's desired consumption C^d. With today's output Y held constant, this rise then lowers desired national saving $Y - C^d - G$.

The Expected Real Interest Rate   An important aspect of saving is that the funds people put aside typically earn interest or some other form of return. We saw in Chapter 2 that the rate at which the real value of a financial investment is expected to grow over time is the expected real interest rate, or the nominal interest rate minus the expected rate of inflation.

Suppose that there is an increase in the real interest rate that people expect to earn on their saving. Thus the real value of any given amount of saving done today will grow more quickly. The question is, How will this higher real interest rate affect the amount of saving that people do?

Economists have pointed out that a higher real interest rate affects people's incentive to save in two opposite ways. On the one hand, a higher real interest rate means that any given amount of saving done today will have a larger payoff in the future, in terms of the goods and services the accumulated saving will be able to buy. This greater future reward for saving tends to make people more eager to save when the real interest rate rises.

On the other hand, a higher real interest rate means that less saving has to be done today to achieve any future savings target. Consider the doting parents of a future genius who know that they have to accumulate $100,000 (in 1990 dollars) by the year 2005 in order to pay college tuition and expenses. The higher the real interest rate, the faster their savings will grow, and the *less* they will have to put aside each month to achieve their long-run goal. Thus to the extent that some people are target savers, a higher real interest rate will depress saving.

Since theory does not tell us whether the positive or the negative effect on saving of a higher real interest rate is the stronger, we must rely on empirical

---

[17]If the government's tax collections T, transfers TR, and interest INT are held constant, an increase in Y also implies an equal increase in private disposable income.

Table 3.3 Summary		
		Determinants of Desired National Saving
An Increase in	**Causes Desired National Saving to**	**Reason**
Current output Y	Rise	Part of the extra income is saved to provide for future consumption
Expected future output	Fall	Anticipation of future income raises desired consumption today, lowering current saving
Expected real interest rate r	Probably rise	An increased return makes saving more attractive, probably outweighing the fact that less must be saved to reach a given savings target
Government purchases G	Fall	Higher government purchases directly lower desired national saving

studies (studies that examine this relationship by using actual data). Unfortunately, as Chapter 6 discusses in more detail, there is some dispute about how to interpret the empirical evidence, as well. The most widely accepted conclusion is that an increase in the real interest rate raises saving, but not by much.

Government Purchases   So far in discussing saving, we have focused on private saving decisions. However, the government can also affect desired national saving through its decisions about government purchases.

In general, an increase in current government purchases G that holds constant the government's planned purchases in future periods—in other words, a temporary increase in government purchases—will reduce desired national saving. To see why, let's return once more to the definition of desired national saving, $S^d = Y - C^d - G$. With output Y fixed, this definition tells us that a \$1 increase in government purchases G will lower desired national saving S^d, *as long as desired consumption C^d falls by less than \$1* in response to the increase in government purchases. Because consumers may fear that more government spending will lead to higher taxes and thus a lower disposable income for them, they may well reduce their consumption when government purchases increase. However, as we explain in later chapters, it is unlikely that consumers would reduce their current spending by the full amount of the increase in government purchases. We conclude that an increase in current government purchases lowers national saving.

The factors affecting desired national saving are summarized in Table 3.3.

Determinants of Desired Investment

From desired saving we turn to the other half of the goods market equilibrium condition, desired investment.

Investment, or the purchase of new capital goods, is done by firms. If firms maximize profits, as we assume, then firms' desired level of investment will be the amount that leads to the highest possible profits for the company. Factors that affect the profitability of using capital goods and thus the amount that firms want to invest include the expected future marginal product of capital, corporate taxes, and the real interest rate.

The Expected Future Marginal Product of Capital   For a given size of the work force, the more productive additional capital goods are, the more likely it is that the firm will find investing in new capital to be profitable. More precisely, the higher the marginal product of capital (MPK) at any given level of the capital stock, the more capital firms will want to use and the more they will invest.

In practice, important considerations in investment decisions are that new capital goods often take some time to build and install; and once acquired, they usually last for many years. These facts mean that when deciding how much to invest, firms are less interested in the current MPK than in what they *think* their MPK will be in the future. Because potential investors care primarily about the future productivity of capital, a supply shock that is expected to affect the MPK permanently—such as the introduction of a new technology—will have the strongest effect on desired investment. For example, purchases of computers were a major portion of U.S. investment during the 1980s, as companies acquired what they expected to be a highly productive new form of capital. In contrast, a temporary supply shock—such as a cold winter—does not affect the MPK over the long-term future and thus will have little or no effect on desired investment.

Corporate Taxes   Profits can be measured before or after payment of taxes. Since firm owners and managers care only about the profits they get to keep, it is after-tax profits that firms will try to maximize. Thus changes in the way corporations and other firms are taxed can affect managers' calculations about how much to invest. In general, tax breaks for investment—provisions allowing firms that invest more to pay less in taxes—will raise the profitability of investment and thus increase desired investment. Heavier taxes on the income earned by new capital will lower the profitability of holding capital goods and reduce desired investment.

The Expected Real Interest Rate   The expected real interest rate affects desired investment, just as it affects desired saving. However, although an increase in the expected real interest rate tends to raise desired saving, an increase in the expected real interest rate lowers desired investment.

One reason that a higher expected real interest rate lowers desired investment is that many firms must borrow in order to purchase new capital goods. The higher the expected real interest rate, the higher is firms' real costs of borrowing, and the less profitable new investment will be. When new capital projects appear to be less profitable, firms will desire to invest less.

Although the expected real interest rate can affect desired investment directly by affecting borrowing costs, even firms that do not have to borrow in order to invest will invest less when the expected real interest rate rises. Instead of pur-

Table 3.4 Summary		
Determinants of Desired Investment		
An Increase in	Causes Desired Investment to	Reason
Expected future marginal product of capital (MPK)	Rise	Higher future MPK means that additional capital is more productive
Corporate taxes	Fall	Higher taxes lower after-tax profitability of new investments
Expected real interest rate r	Fall	Higher real interest rate raises cost of financing new investments

chasing new capital goods, a firm always has the option of lending its funds to someone else (perhaps another firm or the government) and earning the real interest rate paid by those borrowers. The higher the expected real interest rate, the more attractive is this option of lending instead of making a capital investment. Thus a higher expected real interest rate reduces the desired investment of all firms, not just those that have to borrow.

Factors affecting desired investment are summarized in Table 3.4.

The Saving-Investment Diagram

For the goods market to be in equilibrium, desired saving must equal desired investment. We show in this section that adjustments of the expected real interest rate are what help to ensure that desired saving equals desired investment. For simplicity we now assume that expected inflation and actual inflation are equal, so that the expected real interest rate equals the real interest rate. We make this assumption so that we don't always have to refer to the expected real interest rate but can refer simply to the real interest rate.

The determination of goods market equilibrium can be shown graphically in what we will call the saving-investment diagram, illustrated in Fig. 3.9. In this diagram the real interest rate is measured along the vertical axis, and national saving and investment are measured along the horizontal axis. The curve marked S in Fig. 3.9, called the saving curve, shows the relationship between desired national saving and the real interest rate. The upward slope of the saving curve reflects the empirical finding that a higher real interest rate raises desired national saving. The curve marked I in the figure, the investment curve, shows the relationship between desired investment and the real interest rate. The downward slope of the investment curve captures the idea that a higher real interest rate reduces desired investment.

Goods market equilibrium occurs when desired national saving equals desired investment. In this figure equilibrium occurs when the real interest rate is 6% and both desired saving and investment equal 1000. If the real interest rate were 3%, for example, desired investment (1500) would not equal desired national saving (850), and the goods market would not be in equilibrium. Competition among borrowers for funds would then cause the real interest rate to rise until it reaches 6%.

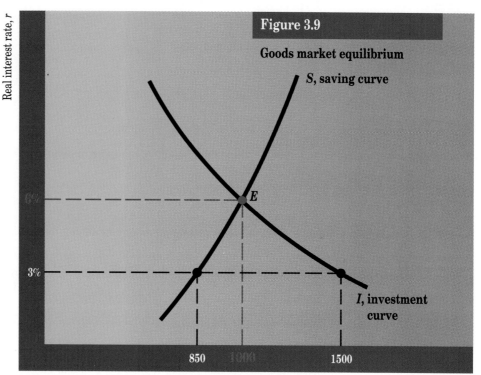

Figure 3.9

Goods market equilibrium

Desired national saving, S^d, and desired investment, I^d

Goods market equilibrium is represented by point E in Fig. 3.9. At point E desired national saving equals investment, as required by Eq. (3.5). The real interest rate corresponding to point E, 6% in this example, is the only real interest rate that clears the goods market. When the real interest rate is 6%, both desired national saving and desired investment equal 1000.

How does the goods market come to be in equilibrium? Much in the same way that adjustments of the real wage clear the labor market, changes in the real interest rate lead to a balancing of saving and investment in the goods market.

Suppose, for example, that the real interest rate happened to be 3% in Fig. 3.9, below the market-clearing rate of 6%. When the real interest rate is 3%, we can see from the investment curve that desired investment is 1500, and the saving curve tells us that desired national saving is 850. In an economy that does not trade with other nations, investors as a group must finance their purchases of capital by borrowing from their own country's savers. If the demand for investment funds exceeds the supply of saving, as in this example, competition among borrowers for funds will cause the real interest rate to rise. The real interest rate continues to rise until it reaches its market-clearing value 6%, at which point desired national saving and desired investment both equal 1000. Similarly, if the real interest rate is initially higher than 6%, the supply of saving will exceed the demand for investment funds, and competing lenders will bid down the real interest rate.

The saving and investment curves in the saving-investment diagram are not "nailed down". Changes in the economy can shift either or both of these curves, leading to changes in the goods market equilibrium.

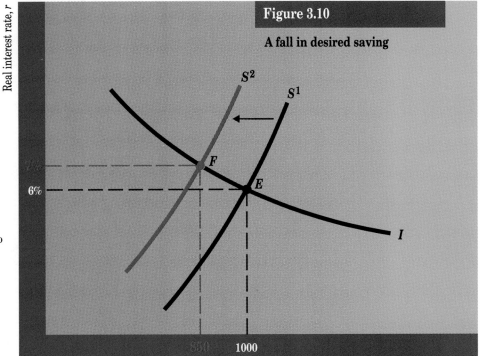

Figure 3.10

A fall in desired saving

Real interest rate, r

Desired national saving, S^d, and desired investment, I^d

An increase in, say, current government purchases will cause a fall in desired national saving, shifting the saving curve to the left, from S^1 to S^2. The goods market equilibrium point moves from E to F. The fall in desired saving raises the real interest rate, from 6% to 7%, and lowers saving and investment, from 1000 to 850.

Shifts of the Saving Curve   Any change in the economy that raises desired national saving *for a given value of the real interest rate* will shift the desired national saving curve to the right, and anything that reduces desired national saving for a given value of the real interest rate will shift the desired national saving curve to the left. See Table 3.3 for a list of factors affecting desired national saving.

A shift in the saving curve will lead to a new goods market equilibrium with a different real interest rate and different amounts of saving and investment. Figure 3.10 illustrates the effects of a decrease in desired national saving—resulting, for example, from an increase in current government purchases. The initial equilibrium point is point E, where (as in Fig. 3.9) the real interest rate is 6% and desired national saving and desired investment both equal 1000. When current government purchases increase, the resulting decrease in desired national saving causes the saving curve to shift leftward, from S^1 to S^2. At the new equilibrium point, point F, the real interest rate has risen from 6% to 7%. The real interest rate rises because at the initial real interest rate of 6% the supply of saving is less than the demand for funds by investors. Competition among borrowers for scarce funds pushes the real interest rate up.

The decrease in desired saving also causes the total amounts of saving and investment to fall, from 1000 to 850. Saving falls because of the initial decrease in desired saving, which is only partially offset by the increase in the real interest rate. Investment falls because the higher real interest rate makes investment less profitable for firms.

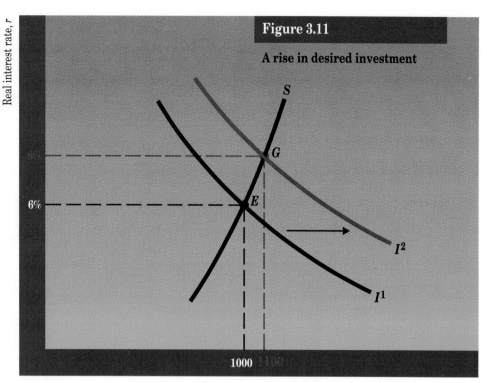

Desired national saving, S^d, and desired investment, I^d

Desired investment may rise when an invention, say, raises the future MPK. As a result, the investment curve shifts to the right, from I^1 to I^2, and the goods market equilibrium point moves from E to G. The real interest rate rises, from 6% to 8%, and saving and investment rise as well, from 1000 to 1100.

Shifts of the Investment Curve   In the same way that changes in factors affecting desired saving shift the saving curve, changes in factors affecting desired investment will cause the investment curve to move. In general, changes that raise desired investment, *given the real interest rate*, will shift the investment curve to the right; and changes that lower desired investment, given the real interest rate, will shift the investment curve to the left. The two investment curve shifters we have discussed are the expected future MPK and corporate taxes (see Table 3.4).

The effects on goods market equilibrium of an increase in desired investment—due, for example, to an invention that raises the future marginal product of capital—are shown in Fig. 3.11. As shown in the figure, the increase in desired investment shifts the investment curve to the right, from I^1 to I^2, changing the goods market equilibrium point from point E to point F. The real interest rate rises from 6% to 8%, since the increased demand for investment funds causes the real interest rate to be bid up. Saving and investment also increase, from 1000 to 1100, with the higher saving reflecting the willingness of savers to save more when the real interest rate rises.

The Effect of Wars on Investment and the Real Interest Rate

As an application of the saving-investment diagram, we can analyze the effects of wars on a country's investment and the real interest rate.

From an economic perspective an important aspect of wartime periods and of military buildups in general is that government purchases rise sharply as expenditures for military equipment and soldiers' pay increase. Also, to a greater degree than other types of increases in government purchases, increases due to military buildups are temporary, since military expenditures tend to return to lower peacetime levels after the war. Thus it is reasonable to think of a war as an increase in current government purchases that holds constant the government's future spending plans. This was the case we examined earlier when we discussed the effects of government purchases on saving.

The effects of an increase in current government purchases on the goods market were shown in Fig. 3.10. According to the saving-investment diagram, an increase in current government purchases lowers national saving, resulting in a higher real interest rate and a reduction, or "crowding out," of private investment.

How well do the predictions of this analysis hold up in the data? Historically, wars (especially large ones) have often had negative effects on investment. Figure 3.12 shows U.S. real investment spending and real government purchases, mea-

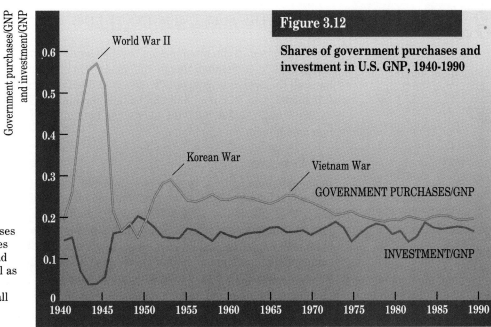

The graph shows the portions of U.S. GNP devoted to government purchases and to investment since 1940. Notice the sharp increases in government purchases during World War II and the Korean War, as well as the tendency for investment's share to fall during those military buildups.

Figure 3.12

Shares of government purchases and investment in U.S. GNP, 1940-1990

Year

sured relative to real GNP, for the period 1940–1990. You can see that during World War II a sharp increase in government purchases was mirrored by a large decline in private investment spending. A similar pattern can be seen in the Korean War of the early 1950s. Interestingly, the military buildups of the Vietnam era and the early 1980s did not change total government purchases enough to show up clearly in the figure.

Besides predicting that military buildups will crowd out investment, our analysis also implies that real interest rates will be higher during wars. The behavior of real interest rates during wars has been studied by Robert Barro[18] of Harvard University. Barro found that this prediction of the model does not fit the data very well for the United States: Although real interest rates were a bit above normal during the Korean and Vietnam wars, they were below normal in the United States during the Civil War, World War I, and World War II.

For the U.S. case, especially during the two world wars, government price controls, rationing, and control of production decisions may have prevented the private economy from functioning normally. As an alternative test of the theory, Barro used British data for the period 1730–1913. The British fought many wars, both large and small, during that period; and they rarely used price or production controls. Thus the British data should provide a good test of the theory.

Barro found evidence in the British data that real interest rates do rise during wars. Long-term nominal interest rates (which, since inflation was essentially zero over this period, were about the same as real rates) were normally about 3.5% in Britain for this time span. During the American Revolution, however, British rates rose to about 5.5%, and they reached 6% during the Napoleonic Wars. This effect is not huge, but it is statistically quite reliable. For the British case, at least, Barro's evidence is consistent with the prediction that wars raise real interest rates.

3.5   THE *IS* CURVE AND THE FULL-EMPLOYMENT LINE

As we stressed in the introduction to this chapter, a main goal of this early portion of the book is to develop the *IS-LM* model of the macroeconomy. At this point we have all the economic concepts we need to derive two major components of the *IS-LM* model, the *IS* curve and the full-employment (*FE*) line. Taken together, the *IS* curve and the *FE* line summarize the behavior of the goods and labor markets in a useful form.

The *IS* Curve

In the previous section we showed how to put together desired national saving and desired investment to find the real interest rate that clears the goods market. One factor that affects the market-clearing real interest rate is output: A rise in output Y, for example, leads to an increase in desired national saving, which in turn causes the market-clearing real interest rate to be bid down as relatively abundant lenders compete with each other to find borrowers. Thus a higher value of output reduces the real interest rate that clears the goods market.

[18]"The Neoclassical Approach to Fiscal Policy," in Robert Barro, ed., *Modern Business Cycle Theory*, Cambridge, Mass.: Harvard University Press, 1989.

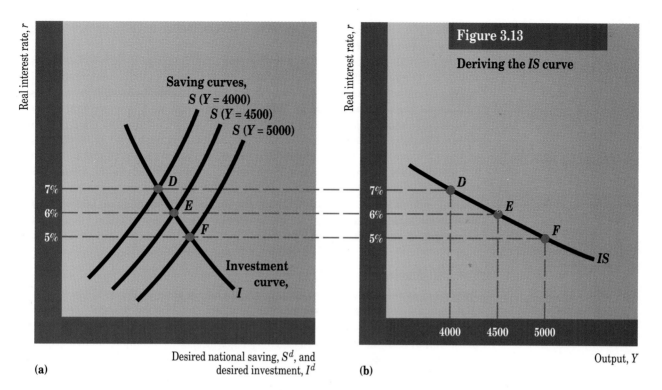

Figure 3.13

Deriving the *IS* curve

(a) The graph shows the goods market equilibrium for three different values of output: 4000, 4500, 5000 (the value of output corresponding to each saving curve is indicated in parentheses next to the curve). Higher values of output increase desired national saving and shift the saving curve to the right. When output is 4000, the real interest rate that clears the goods market is 7% (point *D*). When output is 4500, the market-clearing rate is 6% (point *E*); and when output is 5000, the market-clearing rate is 5% (point *F*).

(b) The graph is the *IS* curve. For each level of output the *IS* curve shows the corresponding real interest rate that clears the goods market. Thus each point on the *IS* curve corresponds to an equilibrium point in the goods market. Because higher output raises saving and leads to a lower market-clearing interest rate, the *IS* curve is downward sloping.

For any given value of output Y, the **IS curve** tells us what value of the real interest rate r clears the goods market. Equivalently, the *IS* curve shows the combinations of output Y and the real interest rate r for which the goods market is in equilibrium. The *IS* curve's name comes from the fact that at all points on the *IS* curve desired investment (I) equals desired saving (S).

The derivation of the *IS* curve is shown in Fig. 3.13. Figure 3.13(a) shows the saving-investment diagram, drawn for three different values of output: 4000, 4500, and 5000. Corresponding to each of the three values of output is a saving curve, and the value of output is indicated in parentheses next to each saving curve. Because an increase in current output (income) leads to more desired saving, the saving curve S ($Y = 4500$) is further to the right than the saving curve S ($Y = 4000$), and the saving curve S ($Y = 5000$) is further to the right than the saving curve S ($Y = 4500$).

As you can see from the figure, each of the three values of output implies a different market-clearing real interest rate. When output is 4000, goods market equilibrium is at point D and the market-clearing real interest rate is 7%. If output is 4500, the equilibrium is at point E and the real interest rate that clears the goods market is 6%. Finally, if output is 5000, the equilibrium is at F and the market-clearing real interest rate is 5%.

Figure 3.13(b) shows the IS curve for this economy. The IS curve diagram has output on the horizontal axis and the real interest rate on the vertical axis. For each value of output on the horizontal axis, the IS curve shows the real interest rate that clears the goods market. When output is 4000, we have seen that the real interest rate that clears the goods market is 7%. Thus the point where output equals 4000 and the real interest rate is 7%, marked point D in Fig. 3.13(b), lies on the IS curve. (Notice that point D in Fig. 3.13b corresponds to point D in Fig. 3.13a.) Similarly, at point E on the IS curve output is 4500 and the market-clearing real interest rate is 6%; at point F output is 5000 and the corresponding market-clearing real interest rate is 5%. *In general, because a higher output increases desired saving, leading to a lower real interest rate to clear the goods market, the IS curve is downward sloping.*

The Full-Employment (FE) Line

For any given level of current output, the IS curve tells us the real interest rate that clears the goods market. However, by itself the IS curve cannot tell us what the current level of output will be. Current output depends on how much output firms in the economy want to supply—that is, on what full-employment output is.

Recall that full-employment output $\bar{Y}$ is the level of output supplied by firms when wages and prices have adjusted fully. In the classical model this level is the same as the level of output supplied when the labor market is in equilibrium. Algebraically, if $\bar{N}$ is equilibrium employment, then full-employment output $\bar{Y}$ equals $AF(K, \bar{N})$; see Eq. (3.3).

In a diagram like the one for the IS curve, with output on the horizontal axis and the real interest rate on the vertical axis, full-employment output $\bar{Y}$ is shown by the **full-employment line,** marked FE in Fig. 3.14. Because full-employment output does not depend on the real interest rate but only on the current levels of productivity, capital, and labor, the FE line is vertical.[19]

Equilibrium in the Goods and Labor Markets

All points on the IS curve are points of goods market equilibrium. Similarly, because full-employment output is the level of output corresponding to labor market equilibrium, all points on the FE line are points of labor market equilibrium. By putting together the IS curve and the FE line in one diagram, we can study the equilibria of the goods market and the labor market simultaneously.

The two curves are shown together in Fig. 3.14. As you might guess, the crucial point in the figure is point E, where the IS curve and the FE line intersect. At point E both the goods market and the labor market are in equilibrium: Because point E is on the FE line, at that point output supplied (4500 in this example) equals full-employment output, or the level of output supplied when the labor market is in equilibrium. Point E is also on the IS curve. Therefore the real interest rate corresponding to point E (6% in this example) is the real interest rate that

---

[19]The real interest rate affects investment and thus the amount of capital that firms will have in the future, but it does not affect the current capital stock.

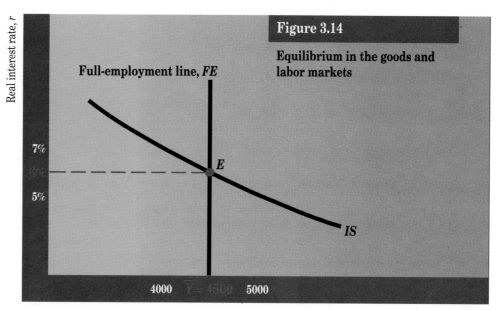

Figure 3.14

Equilibrium in the goods and labor markets

At point E, where the IS curve and the full-employment (FE) line intersect, both the goods market and the labor market are in equilibrium. At all points on the FE line labor supply equals labor demand, and firms are supplying output according to the production function. At all points on the IS curve the real interest rate takes the value that clears the goods market, given the level of output.

clears the goods market, given that output equals full-employment output (4500). Thus both the goods market and the labor market are in equilibrium at point E. If adjustments of the real interest rate and the real wage act to clear the goods market and the labor market, then from any starting point the economy will tend to move toward point E.

As in our previous analyses, the economic equilibrium may change, if changes in the factors influencing the IS curve or FE line cause one or the other to shift.

Factors that Shift the *IS* Curve   In drawing the IS curve, we held constant those factors other than output that affect the real interest rate that clears the goods market. If any of these other factors changes, the IS curve will shift. More precisely, *given output, any change that reduces desired saving relative to desired investment increases the real interest rate that clears the goods market and shifts the IS curve upward.* Similarly, given output, changes that increase desired saving relative to desired investment, thus reducing the market-clearing real interest rate, shift the IS curve downward. A list of all the potential IS curve shifters discussed so far is given in Table 3.5.

As an example, consider an increase in current government purchases. Given output, an increase in government purchases lowers desired national saving and raises the real interest rate that clears the goods market. Thus an increase in government purchases shifts the IS curve up and to the right.

	Table 3.5 Summary	
	Factors That Shift the *IS* Curve	
An Increase in	**Shifts the IS Curve**	**Reason**
Expected future output	Up	Reduces desired saving and raises the real interest rate that clears the goods market
Government purchases G	Up	Reduces desired saving and raises the real interest rate that clears the goods market
Expected future marginal product of capital (MPK)	Up	Increases desired investment and raises the real interest rate that clears the goods market
Corporate taxes	Down	Reduces desired investment and lowers the real interest rate that clears the goods market

Figure 3.15 develops this example further. Figure 3.15(a) shows the saving-investment diagram; Fig. 3.15(b) shows the corresponding *IS* curve and *FE* line.

Suppose that, initially, government purchases are 1000 and that output is fixed at its full-employment value of 4500. The saving curve when government purchases are 1000 and output is 4500 is shown in the saving-investment diagram of Fig. 3.15(a) as S ($Y = 4500$, $G = 1000$). In this case the goods market equilibrium is at point E and the market-clearing real interest rate is 6%. The *IS* curve corresponding to this initial situation is marked *IS* ($G = 1000$) in Fig. 3.15(b). When output is 4500 and government purchases are 1000, this initial *IS* curve tells us that the market-clearing real interest rate is 6%, as was found in the saving-investment diagram in Fig. 3.15(a).

Suppose now that current government purchases are raised from 1000 to 1100. With output constant, an increase in current government purchases lowers desired saving. This result is shown in Fig. 3.15(a) as a leftward shift in the saving curve, from S ($Y = 4500$, $G = 1000$) to S ($Y = 4500$, $G = 1100$), and as a change in the equilibrium from point E to point H. Because of the fall in desired saving, the real interest rate that clears the goods market rises from 6% to 7%. We see that with output held constant at 4500, the increase in government purchases raises the market-clearing real interest rate.

The effect of the increased government purchases on the *IS* curve is drawn in Fig. 3.15(b). Given output of 4500, the increase in government purchases has caused the real interest rate that clears the goods market to rise from 6% to 7%. Thus point H in Fig. 3.15(b), at which output is 4500 and the real interest rate is 7%, must lie on the new *IS* curve. Point H lies above the corresponding point on the old *IS* curve, point E. Indeed, for any given level of output, an increase in government purchases will raise the market-clearing real interest rate. Thus an increase in government purchases causes the whole *IS* curve to move upward. The *IS* curve following the increase in government purchases is shown in Fig. 3.15(b) as *IS* ($G = 1100$).

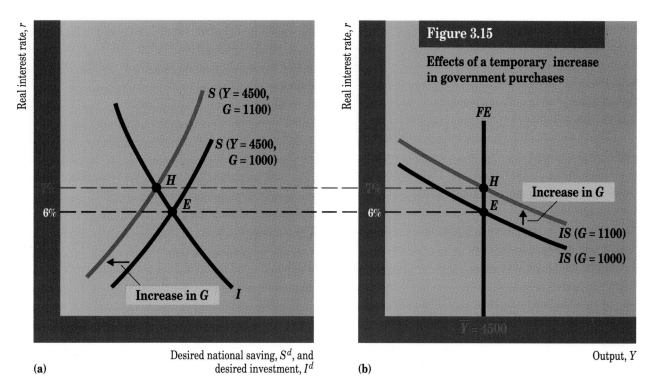

(a)

Desired national saving, S^d, and
desired investment, I^d

(b)

Output, Y

Figure 3.15

Effects of a temporary increase in government purchases

(a) The saving-investment diagram shows the effects of a temporary increase in government purchases G, holding output Y constant at 4500. The increase in G from 1000 to 1100 reduces desired national saving and shifts the saving curve to the left. The goods market equilibrium point moves from point E to point H, and the real interest rate rises from 6% to 7%.

(b) The increase in G raises the real interest rate that clears the goods market for any given level of output. Thus the IS curve shifts upward. Now when output is at its full-employment level of 4500, the real interest rate is 7% (point H) rather than 6% (point E).

Equilibrium in both the goods market and the labor market occurs at the intersection of the *IS* curve and the *FE* line. Initially, this equilibrium point was at point E in Fig. 3.15(b), with output equal to its full-employment value of 4500 and a real interest rate of 6%. The upward shift of the *IS* curve leads to a new equilibrium point, point H, where output remains at 4500 but the real interest rate has risen to 7%. Thus the overall effect of the increase in government purchases is to raise the real interest rate but to leave output unchanged.

The saving-investment diagram and the diagram with the *IS* curve and the *FE* line provide two different frameworks for analyzing the effects of an increase in government purchases. Although the two analyses look different, they are equivalent; for example, using either diagram, we found that an increase in current government purchases raises the real interest rate. Each way of doing the analysis has its own advantages: The advantage of using the saving-investment diagram is that it helps us to see that this increase in the real interest rate lowers investment, an effect that is hidden in the *IS* curve–*FE* line diagram. In general, the advantage of the *IS* curve–*FE* line diagram is that it shows more directly the effects of economic shocks or policy changes on output, since output rather than investment is on the horizontal axis of this diagram. However, in this example, as we have said, the increase in government purchases is found to have no effect on output, since output stays fixed at 4500.

Table 3.6 Summary

Factors that Shift the Full-Employment (*FE*) Line

FE Curve Shifter	Shifts the *FE* line	Reason
Beneficial supply shock	Right	1. More output can be produced for given capital and labor 2. If the MPN rises, an increase in labor demand raises employment Both raise full-employment output
An increase in labor supply (owing, for example, to immigration)	Right	Equilibrium employment rises, raising full-employment output

The result that increased government purchases have no effect on output is actually not very satisfactory from an empirical perspective, since we know, for example, that output tends to rise during wars when government military expenditures increase. In later chapters we will extend the model to allow for links between government purchases and output.

Factors That Shift the *FE* Line   Because the *FE* line is vertical at full-employment output $\bar{Y}$, any change that affects the full-employment level of output will cause the *FE* line to shift. As we discussed earlier, full-employment output $\bar{Y}$ increases when there is an increase in equilibrium employment $\bar{N}$ (resulting, for example, from an increase in labor supply) or when there is a beneficial supply shock. Thus either an increase in labor supply or a beneficial supply shock shifts the *FE* line to the right; and a fall in labor supply or an adverse supply shock shifts the *FE* line to the left. These two factors are summarized in Table 3.6.

Figure 3.16 analyzes the effects of an adverse supply shock due to, say, an increase in oil prices. It is easier to assume that the oil shock is temporary, so that although the shock lowers the current productivity of capital and labor, productivity is expected to return to normal in the future. Analytical Problem 5 in this chapter asks you to work out the case of a permanent rise in oil prices.

The initial equilibrium, prior to the supply shock, is shown in Fig. 3.16 as point E, where the initial *FE* line, marked FE^1, intersects the *IS* curve. At point E full-employment output is 4500 and the real interest rate that clears the goods market is 6%.

As we saw earlier in the chapter, an adverse supply shock reduces the output that firms want to supply (full-employment output) for two reasons: First, the supply shock (higher energy prices and less energy use) directly reduces the amount of output that can be produced for any combination of capital and labor. Second, if the shock reduces the marginal product of labor, labor demand and thus equilibrium employment $\bar{N}$ will fall (see Fig. 3.6). Lower employment means an additional

A temporary adverse supply shock, such as an oil price shock, lowers full-employment output from 4500 to 4000 and shifts the *FE* line left, from FE^1 to FE^2. The *IS* curve is unaffected (a change in current output is a movement along the *IS* curve, not a shift of the curve). The equilibria of the goods market and the labor market shift from point *E* to point *J*, where output is lower and the real interest rate is higher.

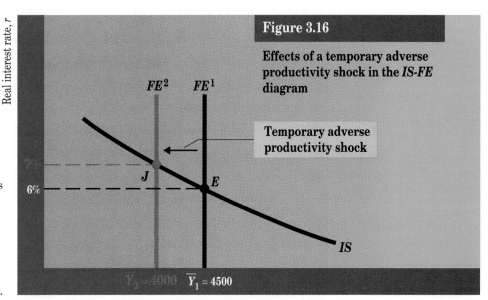

Figure 3.16

Effects of a temporary adverse productivity shock in the *IS-FE* diagram

fall in output. In this example we assume that the supply shock reduces full-employment output from $\bar{Y}_1 = 4500$ to $\bar{Y}_2 = 4000$, so that the *FE* line shifts left from FE^1 to FE^2.

The *IS* curve is not shifted by the supply shock. Since we assume that the shock is temporary (and that people in the economy know that), firms' expectations about the future marginal product of capital and thus their desired investment should be unaffected. Similarly, we assume that consumers' expectations of future income are not affected. Thus no *IS* shifter changes and the *IS* curve does not move. It is true that current output changes, which changes the real interest rate that clears the goods market; however, a change in current output is reflected as a movement *along* the *IS* curve, not a shift of the curve.[20]

Since the *FE* line shifts from FE^1 to FE^2 and the *IS* curve does not move, the new equilibrium is given by point *J* in Fig. 3.16. The oil shock causes output to fall from 4500 to 4000 and raises the real interest rate from 6% to 7%.

The real interest rate rises during the oil shock because the fall in output reduces desired saving. To see this result, look at the saving-investment diagram in Fig. 3.17. Two saving curves are drawn in the figure, one for income *Y* of 4500 and one for income of 4000. Since a fall in current income lowers saving, of the two saving curves the saving curve drawn for *Y* = 4000 is further to the left. The initial equilibrium is at point *E* in Fig. 3.17, which corresponds to point *E* in Fig. 3.16. After the oil shock lowers income, the equilibrium is at point *J*, which corresponds to point *J* in Fig. 3.16. At point *J* the real interest rate has risen to 7%, reflecting the fall in desired saving. The quantity of investment undertaken by firms is lower at point *J*, as a result of the increase in the real interest rate.

To summarize, the model predicts that a temporary adverse supply shock lowers output, national saving, and investment, while raising the real interest rate.

---

[20]A useful general rule is that changes in variables on the axes of a diagram do not shift curves in the diagram.

102

Here is a closer look at the effects of a supply shock on the goods market. A fall in output from 4500 to 4000 shifts the saving curve left and moves the equilibrium point from E to J. At the new equilibrium the real interest rate has risen from 6% to 7%, and national saving and investment have fallen. Since the shift in the saving curve is due to a change in current output, it corresponds to a movement along the IS curve, not a shift of the IS curve itself (see Fig. 3.16).

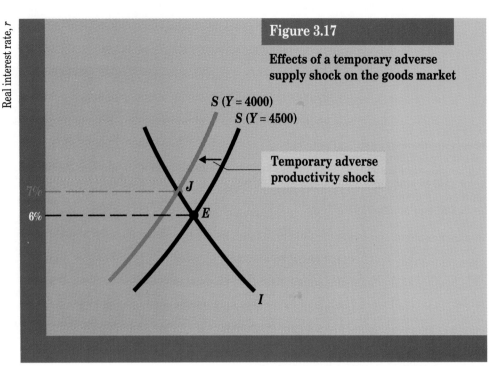

Figure 3.17

Effects of a temporary adverse supply shock on the goods market

Desired national saving, S^d, and desired investment, I^d

Oil Price Shocks and Investment

Earlier in the chapter we looked at the effects of oil price shocks on output, employment, and the real wage. The data confirmed the model's prediction that all three of those variables are reduced by an increase in energy prices.

The analysis we have just done provides an additional important implication, that an oil price shock will depress investment spending. Table 3.2 on p. 83 contains data on investment as a percentage of GNP over the 1972–1986 period (column 4). You can see that investment did indeed fall sharply following both the 1973–1974 and the 1979–1980 oil price shocks.

Our analysis also implied that an oil shock should cause the real interest rate to rise. However, this result turns out to depend very strongly on the assumption we made that people expect the oil price shock to be temporary. In Analytical Problem 5 in this chapter, in which you are asked to work out the effects of a permanent adverse supply shock, you will find that investment falls in the case of a permanent shock, but the real interest rate may not rise. Given that we cannot be sure what people expected about the duration of the two major oil price shocks, it is hard to say confidently what effect such a shock should have on the real interest rate. As it turns out, the real interest rate rose during the 1979–1980 shock but not during the 1973–1974 shock (see Fig. 2.6, p. 57). On the basis of only these data, our model would suggest that people expected the 1973–1974 oil shock to be permanent and the 1979–1980 shock to be temporary. It is interesting that those expectations turned out to be essentially correct; looking at Fig. 3.8 on p. 82, you can see that the oil price increase of 1979–1980 was reversed relatively quickly, but the price increase of 1973–1974 was not.

3.6   CHAPTER SUMMARY

1. The *IS-LM* model is a basic tool of macroeconomic analysis. The model studies the behavior of three types of economic factors (firms, households, and the government) who trade with each other in the goods market, the labor market, and the asset market.

2. The production function tells us the amount of output that can be produced with any given quantities of capital and labor. The production function can be graphed as a relationship between output and capital, holding labor fixed, or as a relationship between output and labor, holding capital fixed. In either case the production function is upward sloping, which implies that greater use of capital or labor leads to more output. A shift in the production function, which indicates a change in the amount of output that can be produced with given amounts of capital and labor, is called a supply shock.

3. The output that can be produced per unit of additional capital, holding labor fixed, is called the marginal product of capital (MPK). In a graph of the production function relating output to capital, the MPK can be measured as the slope of the production function. The MPK falls as the capital stock increases, reflecting diminishing marginal returns to capital. The marginal product of labor (MPN), analogously, is the amount of output that can be produced per unit of additional labor, holding capital fixed. The MPN can be measured as the slope of the production function relating output to labor. The MPN falls as employment rises, reflecting diminishing marginal returns to labor.

4. Labor demand, which is the number of workers firms want to employ, depends on the marginal product of labor and the real wage. Labor supply, the number of people who would like to have jobs, depends on demographic factors and the real wage. The labor market is in equilibrium when the quantity of labor demanded equals the quantity of labor supplied. Adjustments of the real wage bring the labor market into equilibrium.

5. The amount of output that firms supply when wages and prices have fully adjusted—so that in the classical case the labor market is in equilibrium—is called full-employment output. Increases in equilibrium employment or beneficial supply shocks raise full-employment output.

6. The goods market is in equilibrium when desired national saving equals desired investment. The goods market is brought into equilibrium by changes in the real interest rate. Factors that raise desired national saving relative to desired investment at any given real interest rate lead to a lower real interest rate in equilibrium.

7. For any given value of output, the *IS* curve tells us what value of the real interest rate clears the goods market. The *IS* curve is downward sloping, since higher output leads to more desired saving and thus a lower market-clearing real interest rate. Given output, any change that reduces desired saving relative to desired investment increases the real interest rate that clears the goods market and shifts the *IS* curve upward. Similarly, given output, changes that increase desired saving relative to desired investment shift the *IS* curve downward.

8. The full-employment (*FE*) line is vertical at full-employment output. Factors that raise full-employment output shift the *FE* line to the right, and factors that reduce full-employment output shift the *FE* line left. In the classical model both the goods market and the labor market are in equilibrium at the intersection of the *IS* curve and the *FE* line.

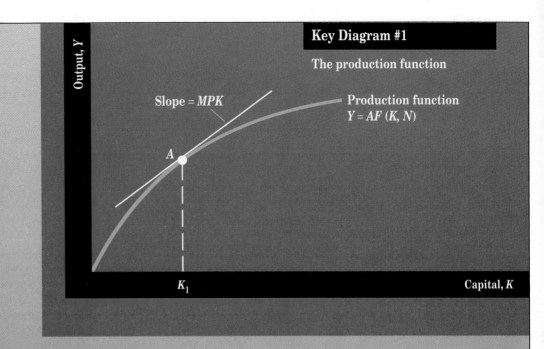

The production function tells how much output can be produced using any given quantities of capital and labor.

Diagram Elements

- The production function graphed here has the amount of output produced Y on the vertical axis and the quantity of capital used K on the horizontal axis.

- The production function can be drawn (as it is here) as a relationship between capital K and the amount of output produced Y, with labor N held constant. Alternatively, it can be drawn as a relationship between output and labor, with capital held constant. The production function relating output to labor looks similar to the one shown here.

- The equation for the production function is $Y = AF(K, N)$, where A is called total factor productivity, or simply productivity. The term A is a measure of how effectively the economy uses capital and labor.

Analysis

- The production function is upward sloping, reflecting the fact that an increase in the quantity of capital will allow more output to be produced.

- The production function becomes flatter as we move from left to right, implying that the larger the capital stock already is, the less extra output is gained by adding another unit of capital. The fact that extra capital becomes less productive as the capital stock grows is called diminishing marginal returns to capital.

- With labor held constant, if an increase in capital of ΔK leads to an increase in output of ΔY, then $\Delta Y/\Delta K$ is called the marginal product of capital, or MPK. The MPK is measured graphically by the slope of the line tangent to the production function. For example, in the diagram the MPK when the capital stock is K_1 equals the slope of the line tangent to the production function at point A.

Factors That Shift the Production Function

Any change that allows more output to be produced for given quantities of capital and labor—a beneficial supply shock—shifts the production function upward. Any change that reduces the amount of output that can be produced for given capital and labor—an adverse supply shock—shifts the production function downward. Examples of beneficial supply shocks include new inventions or improved management techniques. Examples of adverse supply shocks include bad weather or the depletion of natural resources.

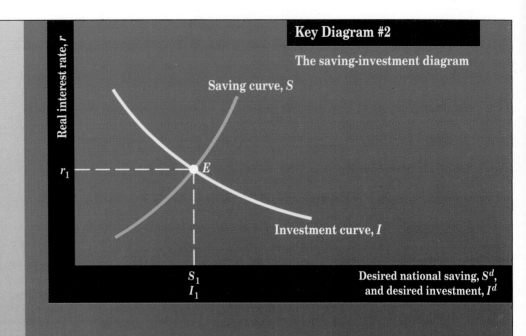

Key Diagram #2

The saving-investment diagram

In an economy with no foreign trade the goods market is in equilibrium when desired national saving equals desired investment. Equivalently, the goods market is in equilibrium when the supply of output equals the demand for output.

Diagram Elements

- The real interest rate r is on the vertical axis; desired national saving S^d and desired investment I^d are on the horizontal axis.

- The *saving curve,* marked S, shows the level of desired national saving at each real interest rate. The saving curve is upward sloping, because a higher real interest rate increases the reward for saving and causes households to save more. Desired national saving is defined by $S^d = Y - C^d - G$, where Y is output, C^d is desired consumption, and G is government purchases.

- The *investment curve,* marked I, shows the amount that firms want to invest in new capital goods at each real interest rate. The investment curve is downward sloping, because a higher real interest rate raises the cost of financing investment, which reduces the profitability of investing and thus lowers desired investment.

Analysis

- Goods market equilibrium requires that desired national saving equal desired investment, or $S^d = I^d$.

- Goods market equilibrium occurs in the diagram at point E, where the saving curve and investment curve intersect. At point E desired national saving equals S_1, desired investment equals I_1, and $S_1 = I_1$. The real interest rate corresponding to point E, shown as r_1 in the diagram, is the real interest rate that clears the goods market.

- An alternative way of writing the goods market equilibrium condition is as follows: The supply of goods Y equals the demands for goods by households C^d, firms I^d, and the government G, or $Y = C^d + I^d + G$. From the fact that $S^d = Y - C^d + G$, this condition can be shown to be equivalent to the condition that $S^d = I^d$.

Factors That Shift the Curves

- Any factor that raises desired national saving at a given real interest rate shifts the saving curve to the right; similarly, any factor that lowers desired national saving shifts the saving curve to the left. Any factor that raises desired investment at a given real interest rate shifts the investment curve to the right, and factors lowering desired investment shift the curve to the left. Shifts of either curve change the goods market equilibrium point and thus change national saving, investment, and the real interest rate.

- With the real interest rate held constant, any of the following factors raises desired saving and shifts the saving curve to the right (see Table 3.3):

  An increase in current output Y

  A decrease in expected future output

  A decrease in current government purchases G

- With the real interest rate held constant, any of the following factors raises desired investment and shifts the investment curve to the right (see Table 3.4):

  An increase in the expected future marginal product of capital, MPK.

  A decrease in corporate taxes that raises the profitability of investment.

Key Terms

diminishing marginal
  returns to capital,
  p. 72
equilibrium, p. 67
factors of production,
  p. 68
full-employment line,
  p. 96

full-employment output,
  p. 80
IS curve, p. 95
marginal product of
  capital (MPK), p. 72
marginal product of
  labor (MPN), p. 75

production function,
  p. 68
productivity, p. 68
real wage, p. 77
supply shock, p. 75

Key Equations

$$Y = AF(K, N) \qquad (3.1)$$

The *production function* tells us how much output Y can be produced for given quantities of capital K and labor N and for a given level of total factor productivity A.

$$\bar{Y} = AF(K, \bar{N}) \qquad (3.3)$$

Full-employment output $\bar{Y}$ is the quantity of output supplied by firms when wages and prices have fully adjusted. Equivalently, in the classical model $\bar{Y}$ is the amount of output produced when employment equals its equilibrium value $\bar{N}$.

$$Y = C^d + I^d + G \qquad (3.4)$$

The *goods market equilibrium condition* says that the goods market is in equilibrium when the aggregate supply of goods Y equals the aggregate demand for goods, $C^d + I^d + G$.

$$S^d = I^d \qquad (3.5)$$

Another way of stating the goods market equilibrium condition is that desired national saving S^d must equal desired investment I^d. This equation is equivalent to Eq. (3.4).

Review Questions

1. List the three types of economic actors and the three types of markets in the *IS-LM* model. Who trades and what is bought and sold in each market?

2. Define *production function*. What are some factors that can cause a nation's production function to shift over time? What do you have to know besides an economy's production function to know how much output the economy can produce?

3. The production function is upward sloping, but its slope declines as we move from left to right in the graph. Give an economic interpretation of each of these properties of the production function.

4. Define *marginal product of capital*, or MPK. What is the MPK if the capital stock is increased by one unit? How can the MPK be shown graphically?

5. What are the principal factors affecting labor demand? Labor supply? What economic forces cause the labor market to tend toward equilibrium?

6. What is full-employment output? How is full-employment output affected by an increase in labor supply? By a beneficial supply shock?

7. Give two equivalent ways of describing equilibrium in the goods market. Use a diagram to show how goods market equilibrium is attained.

8. What is the basic motivation for saving? List and explain three factors that affect saving.

9. What relationship is captured by the *IS* curve? Give two examples of changes in the economy that would cause the *IS* curve to shift downward and to the left.

Numerical Problems

1. The data give real GNP (Y), capital (K), and labor (N) for the U.S. economy in various years.

Year	Y	K	N
1950	1204	1024	58.9
1960	1665	1458	65.8
1970	2416	2212	78.7
1980	3187	3138	99.3

Units and sources are the same as in Table 3.1. Assume the production function is $Y = AK^{0.3}N^{0.7}$.

   a. How much did U.S. total factor productivity grow between 1950 and 1960? Between 1960 and 1970? Between 1970 and 1980?

   b. What happened to the marginal product of labor between 1950 and 1980? Calculate the marginal product numerically as the extra output gained by adding 1 million workers in each of the two years. (The data for employment N is measured in millions of workers, so an increase of one million workers is an increase of 1.0.)

2. An economy has the production function

$$Y = 0.2 (K + \sqrt{N}).$$

In the current period $K = 100$ and $N = 100$.

   a. Graph the relationship between output and capital, holding labor constant at its current value. What is the MPK? Are there diminishing marginal returns to capital?

   b. Graph the relationship between output and labor, holding capital constant at its current value. Find the MPN for an increase of labor from 100 to 110. Compare this result with the MPN for an increase in labor between 110 and 120. Are there diminishing marginal returns to labor?

3. An economy has full-employment output of 6000. Government purchases are 1200. Desired consumption and desired investment are given by

$$C^d = 3600 - 2000r + 0.10Y,$$
$$I^d = 1200 - 4000r,$$

where Y is output and r is the real interest rate.

   a. Find an equation relating desired national saving S^d to r and Y.

   b. Using both versions of the goods market equilibrium condition, Eqs. (3.4) and (3.5), find the real interest rate that clears the goods market. Assume output equals full-employment output.

   c. Government purchases rise to 1320. How does this rise change the equation describing desired national saving? Show the change graphically. What happens to the market-clearing real interest rate?

   d. Full-employment output rises to 6400 while government purchases return to their original level of 1200. Show how this change affects the equation for national saving and the value of the market-clearing real interest rate.

4. In a certain economy government purchases G are 800. Desired national saving and desired investment are given by

$$S^d = 200 + 4000r + 0.10Y - 0.10G,$$
$$I^d = 1000 - 6000r.$$

The equation for desired national saving S^d says that, given the real interest rate, higher output raises desired saving and increased government purchases lower desired saving.

   a. Find the real interest rate that clears the goods market when $Y = 4800$, $Y = 5000$, and $Y = 4600$. Graph the IS curve.

   b. Government purchases rise to 1000. Repeat part a.

Analytical Problems

1. a. A technological breakthrough raises a country's total factor productivity A by 10%. Show how this change affects the graphs of both the production function relating output to capital and the production function relating output to labor.

   b. Show that a 10% increase in A also increases the MPK and the MPN by 10% at any level of capital and labor. (*Hint:* What happens to ΔY for any given increase in capital ΔK or for any given increase in labor ΔN?)

   c. Is it possible to have a beneficial supply shock that leaves the MPK and MPN unaffected? Show graphically.

2. How would each of the following affect the current level of full-employment output? Explain.
   a. A large number of immigrants enter the country.
   b. Energy supplies become depleted.
   c. New teaching techniques improve the educational performance of high school seniors.
   d. A new law mandates the shutdown of some unsafe forms of capital.
   e. An increase in the expected future MPK stimulates investment spending.

3. A country loses much of its capital stock to a war.
   a. What effects should this event have on the country's current employment, output, and real wage?
   b. What effect will the loss of capital have on desired investment?
   c. The effects on desired national saving of the wartime losses are ambiguous. Give one reason why desired saving should rise and one why it should fall.
   d. Assuming that desired saving does not change, what effect does the loss of capital have on the country's real interest rate and the quantity of investment?

4. During the 1980s the average rate of unemployment in Europe was quite high. Some economists claimed that this high rate was in part due to "real-wage rigidity," a situation in which unions kept real wages above their market-clearing levels.
   a. Accepting for the sake of argument that real wages were too high in Europe in the 1980s, show how this would lead to unemployment (a situation where people who would like to work at the going wage cannot find jobs).
   b. What is the effect of real-wage rigidity on the output actually supplied by firms, relative to the output they would supply if there were no real-wage rigidity?

5. Analyze the effects of a permanent increase in the price of oil (a permanent adverse supply shock) on current output, employment, the real wage, national saving, investment, and the real interest rate. Show that in this case, unlike the case of a temporary supply shock, the real interest rate need not rise. (*Hint:* A permanent adverse supply shock lowers the current productivity of capital and labor, just as a temporary supply shock does. In addition, a permanent supply shock lowers the expected future MPK and lowers households' expected future income.)

4

The Asset Market, Money, and Prices

Chapter 3 discussed two of the markets included in the *IS-LM* model, the goods market and the labor market. In this chapter we add the third market of the *IS-LM* model, the asset market. By the *asset market* we mean to refer to the whole set of markets in which people buy and sell real and financial assets, including, for example, gold, houses, stocks, and bonds.

A type of asset that has long been believed to have special macroeconomic significance is money. Money is the economist's term for assets that can be used in making payments, such as cash and checking accounts. One reason that money is important is that most prices are expressed in units of money, such as dollars, yen, or francs. Because prices are measured in money terms, we need to understand the role of money in the economy in order to study issues related to the price level, such as inflation and its causes. In addition, as we will discuss in detail later in the book, many economists believe that the amount of money in the economy can affect real economic variables, such as output and employment.

Because money is such an important asset, it will be the focus of our discussion of the asset market. The first part of the chapter explains what money is and why people choose to hold it. We will see that people's decision about how much money to hold—their demand for money—is part of a bigger decision they must make about the forms in which they hold their wealth. The second part of the chapter completes the *IS-LM* framework by adding money (the asset market) to our model of the macroeconomy. Using the complete macro model, we then study how the economy's price level and rate of inflation are determined.

4.1 WHAT IS MONEY?

Money is an example of a term whose meaning in economics differs from its meaning in everyday speech. People often use *money* when they mean "income" or "wealth," as in "That job pays good money" or "Her family has a lot of money." In economics, however, **money** refers specifically to assets that are widely used and accepted as payment. Historically, there have been many forms of money, ranging from beads and shells to gold and silver, and even to cigarettes (see Box 4.1, p. 112). In modern economies the most familiar forms of money are coins and paper money, or currency. Another common form of money is checkable deposits, bank accounts on which checks can be written for making payments.

BOX 4.1: MONEY IN A PRISONER-OF-WAR CAMP

Among the Allied soldiers liberated from German prisoner-of-war (POW) camps at the end of World War II was a young man named R. A. Radford. Radford had training in economics, and shortly after his return home he published an article entitled "The Economic Organisation of a POW Camp."* This article, a minor classic in the economics literature, is a fascinating account of the daily lives of soldiers in several POW camps. It focuses particularly on the primitive "economies" that grew up spontaneously in the camps.

One might suppose that the scope for economic behavior in a POW camp would be severely limited, and to a degree this is right. There was little production of goods within the camps, although there was some trade in services, such as laundry or tailoring services and even portraiture. However, prisoners were allowed to move around freely within the compound, and they engaged in very active trading of goods obtained from the Red Cross, the Germans, and other sources. Among the commodities exchanged were tinned milk, jam, butter, biscuits, chocolate, sugar, clothing, and toilet articles. In one particular camp, which had at various times up to fifty thousand prisoners of many nationalities, there was a set of active trading centers run entirely by the prisoners.

A key practical issue was how to organize the trading. At first, the camp economies used barter, but this proved to be a slow and inefficient way to trade. Then the prisoners hit upon the idea of using cigarettes as money. Soon prices of all goods were quoted in terms of cigarettes, and cigarettes were ac-

cepted as payment for any good or service. Even non-smoking prisoners would happily accept cigarettes as payment, since they knew that they could easily trade the cigarettes for other things they wanted. The use of cigarette money greatly simplified the problem of making trades and helped the camp economy function much more smoothly.

Why were cigarettes, rather than some other commodity, used as money by the POWs? Cigarettes satisfied a number of criteria for a good money: A cigarette is a fairly standardized commodity whose value was easy for both buyers and sellers to ascertain. An individual cigarette is low enough in value that making "change" was not a problem. Cigarettes are portable, are easily passed from hand to hand, and do not spoil quickly.

A drawback was that as a commodity money (a form of money with an alternative use), cigarette money had a resource cost: Cigarettes that were being used as money could not simultaneously be smoked. In the same way, the traditional use of gold and silver as money was costly, in that it diverted these metals—and the labor and capital used to locate and mine them—away from alternative uses.

Cigarette money is not dead. It is reported that just before the collapse of communism in Eastern Europe, cigarette money was used in Romania and other countries in place of the nearly worthless official money.

*Economica, November 1945, pp. 189–201. This article is quite readable and is recommended.

The Functions of Money

Since the earliest times almost all societies—from the most primitive to the most sophisticated, both capitalist and Communist—have used money. Money has three useful functions in an economy: It is a medium of exchange, it is the unit of account, and it is a store of value.

Medium of Exchange In an economy with no money trading would have to take the form of barter, the direct exchange of goods for other goods. Even today some people belong to barter clubs, in which members swap goods and services among themselves. Generally, though, barter is an inefficient way to make trades, because it is difficult and time-consuming to find someone who both has the particular item that you want and is willing to give up that item in exchange for something you happen to have. So, for example, in a barter system, if one of the authors of this book wanted a restaurant meal, he would first have to find a restaurateur willing to trade his blue-plate special for an economics lecture. This might not be easy.

The existence of money makes searching for the perfect trading partner unnecessary. In an economy with money the economics professor does not have to find a restaurant owner who is hungry for knowledge. Instead, he can first sell his economics lecture to students in exchange for money and then use the money to buy the restaurant meal. In functioning as a **medium of exchange,** or a device for making transactions, money permits people to make trades at a lower cost in time and effort. In addition, having a medium of exchange raises productivity by allowing people to specialize in those economic activities at which they are most skilled; in an economy with money these specialized producers have no problem trading their goods or services for the things they need. In a barter economy, in contrast, the difficulty of making trades would leave people no choice but to produce most of their own food, clothing, and shelter. Thus in a barter economy the opportunity to specialize would be greatly reduced.

Unit of Account As the **unit of account,** money provides the basic unit for measuring economic value. In the United States, for example, virtually all prices, wages, asset values, and debts are expressed in terms of dollars and cents. Having a single, uniform measure of value is convenient. For example, because all goods in the United States are priced in dollars—instead of some goods being priced in yen, some in gold, and some in General Motors shares—comparison of the prices of different goods is much easier.

The medium-of-exchange and unit-of-account functions of money are closely linked. It is because goods and services are most often exchanged for money (the medium-of-exchange function) that it is natural to express economic values in money terms (the unit-of-account function). Otherwise, we could just as well express economic values in terms of, say, bushels of wheat. Interestingly, though, the medium of exchange and the unit of account are not invariably the same. In countries with high and erratic inflation, for example, the fluctuating value of the currency makes it a poor unit of account, because prices must be changed frequently. In such cases economic values are commonly stated in terms of a more stable unit of account, such as dollars or ounces of gold, even though transactions may continue to be carried out in the local currency.

Store of Value As a **store of value,** money is a way of holding wealth. An extreme example is a miser who keeps his life's savings in cash under the mattress. But even someone who spends her cash wages fifteen minutes after receiving them is using money as a store of value for that short period.

Although in most cases only money functions as a medium of exchange or a unit of account, any asset—for example, stocks, bonds, or real estate—can be a store of value. Since these other types of assets normally pay the holder a higher return than money does, why would anyone use money as a store of value? As we explain later in the chapter, the answer is that money's usefulness as a medium of exchange makes it worthwhile to hold, even though its return is relatively low.

Measuring Money: The Monetary Aggregates

Money is defined as those assets that are widely used and accepted in payment. This definition seems to suggest that there is a hard-and-fast line between those assets that should be counted as money and those that should not. However, in practice, the distinction between monetary assets and nonmonetary assets is not so clear.

Consider, for example, money market mutual funds (MMMFs), which first became popular in the late 1970s. MMMFs are organizations that sell shares to the public and invest the proceeds in short-term government and corporate debt. A principal goal of MMMFs is to earn a good return for their shareholders. At the same time, MMMFs typically allow their shareholders to write a small number of checks each month against their accounts, perhaps for a fee. Thus, although MMMF shares can be used to make payments, they are not as convenient as cash or regular checking accounts for this purpose. Should MMMF shares be counted as money or not? No definite answer can be given.

Because assets differ in their "moneyness," no single measure of the amount of money in the economy—or the money stock, as it is often called—is likely to be completely satisfactory. For this reason, in most countries economists and policymakers employ several different measures of the money stock. The official measures of the money stock are known as the **monetary aggregates.** The various monetary aggregates differ in how narrowly they define the concept of money. In the United States the two most widely used monetary aggregates are called M1 and M2. Summary definitions and data for these two aggregates are given in Table 4.1. Information about where to find data on the monetary aggregates is given in the box "In Touch with the Macroeconomy," (p. 117).

M1   The monetary aggregate **M1,** the most narrowly defined official money measure, is made up primarily of currency and balances held in checking accounts. More precisely, M1 consists of currency and travelers' checks held by the public, demand deposits (non–interest-bearing checking accounts) at commercial banks, and other checkable deposits. The category "other checkable deposits" includes

Table 4.1 The U.S. Monetary Aggregates (August 1990)

M1	**$814.2 billion**
Currency	$239.2 billion
Travelers' checks	$8.9 billion
Demand deposits	$276.7 billion
Other checkable deposits	$289.4 billion
M2	**$3302.1 billion**
Components of M1	$814.2 billion
Savings deposits	$417.3 billion
Small-denomination time deposits	$1151.1 billion
Money market mutual funds	$332.8 billion
Money market deposit accounts	$504.1 billion
Overnight repurchase agreements (RPs) and Eurodollars	$82.7 billion

Source: *Federal Reserve Bulletin*, November 1990, Table 1.21. Data are not seasonally adjusted. M1 is the sum of lines 29 to 32 in the table. M2 is M1 plus the sum of lines 35, 36, 37, 39, 40, 41, 43, and 45.

deposits at thrift institutions, such as savings and loans and credit unions. Also part of the "other checkable deposits" category are interest-bearing checkable deposits offered by banks, such as NOW (negotiated order of withdrawal) accounts and ATS (automatic transfer service) accounts. M1 is perhaps the closest counterpart of the theoretical definition of money, since all components of M1 are actively used and widely accepted for making payments.

M2   The monetary aggregate **M2** includes everything in M1 plus a number of other assets that are somewhat less "moneylike." The principal additional assets that are part of M2 include savings deposits, small-denomination (under $100,000) time deposits, noninstitutional[1] holdings of money market mutual funds (MMMFs), and money market deposit accounts (MMDAs). Time deposits are interest-bearing deposits with a fixed term (early withdrawal usually involves a penalty). As we have mentioned, MMMFs invest their shareholders' funds in short-term securities, pay market-based interest rates, and allow holders to write checks. MMDAs are like MMMFs, except they are offered by banks or thrifts.

Additional small components of M2 are overnight repurchase (RP) agreements and overnight Eurodollars issued to U.S. residents. In an RP agreement a bank borrows overnight from a nonbank customer by selling a security, such as a government bond, to the customer and promising to buy the security back the next day. Overnight Eurodollars are short-term deposits held in foreign branches of U.S. banks.

Other Monetary Aggregates   Two additional monetary aggregates, generally less well known and less used than M1 and M2, are called M3 and L. M3 contains everything in M2 plus a number of other assets, such as large-denomination (over $100,000) time deposits and MMMFs held by institutions. The aggregate L is broader still: It includes everything in M3 plus assets such as short-term Treasury debt, commercial paper (short-term debt of large corporations), and savings bonds.

Many of the assets that are included in M3 or L (as well as some that are in M2) are not money in the strict sense of being directly acceptable in payment. For example, assets such as Treasury bills or commercial paper, which are part of the broadest monetary aggregate L, cannot be used directly for making purchases. However, because these assets can be quickly and cheaply converted into monetary form, economists find it useful to include them in their broader measures of money.

Weighted Monetary Aggregates   The monetary aggregates are constructed by simply adding the amounts outstanding of a number of different assets, so that a dollar of currency contributes no more to the measured money stock than does a dollar of savings deposits. This standard way of measuring the money stock ignores the fact that some assets, such as currency, are more moneylike than others. Recently, some economists have experimented with what are called weighted monetary aggregates. In a weighted monetary aggregate a dollar of a very moneylike asset such as currency is given a greater weight in the total than a dollar of a less moneylike asset such as a savings deposit. Several studies have concluded that weighted monetary aggregates are more useful measures of money than are the

---

[1]Holdings of MMMFs by institutions, such as pension funds, are included in the broader monetary aggregate M3, which is discussed briefly in the section that follows.

standard aggregates.[2] There remain disagreements about the best way to weight the various monetary assets, however, and so far this approach has not been officially adopted.

The Money Supply

The **money supply** is the amount of money available in an economy.[3] In modern economies the money supply is determined by a government institution called the central bank. The central bank of the United States is called the Federal Reserve.

A detailed explanation of how the central bank controls the money supply raises a number of issues that would take us too far off the track at this point, so we defer this discussion to Chapter 15. To illustrate the basic idea, however, consider the simple hypothetical case in which the only form of money is currency. In this case to increase the money supply the central bank only needs to increase the amount of currency in circulation. How can the central bank accomplish this?

One way—which is close to what happens in practice—is for the central bank to take newly minted currency and use it to buy financial assets, such as government bonds, from the public. In making this swap, the public increases its holdings of money, and the amount of money in circulation rises. When the central bank uses money to purchase government bonds from the public, thus raising the money supply, it is said to have conducted an open-market purchase.

To reduce the money supply, the central bank can do this trade in reverse, selling government bonds that it holds to the public in exchange for currency. After the currency the central bank receives from the public has been retired from circulation, the money supply is lower. When the central bank sells government bonds to the public in order to reduce the money supply, the transaction is called an open-market sale. Open-market purchases and sales together are called **open-market operations.**

Besides buying government bonds from the public, the central bank can also increase the money supply by buying newly issued government bonds directly from the government itself. For example, if the treasury of a country needs $1 billion to pay for some new fighter planes, it might do so by giving an IOU for $1 billion (government bonds) to the central bank in exchange for $1 billion in newly minted currency. The treasury then gives the $1 billion of currency to the manufacturer of the fighter planes. Once the treasury has distributed the currency, the amount of money in circulation—the money supply—will be higher by $1 billion.

Effectively, this second way of increasing the money supply amounts to the government financing its expenditures by printing money.[4] The practice of governments' paying for their expenditures by printing money is most common in poor countries or in countries wracked by war or natural disaster, in which government spending often greatly exceeds what can be raised through taxes.[5]

---

[2]For a recent technical discussion of weighted aggregates, see Paul A. Spindt, "Money Is What Money Does: Monetary Aggregation and the Equation of Exchange," *Journal of Political Economy*, February 1985, pp. 175–204.

[3]The terms *money supply* and *money stock* are used interchangeably.

[4]In Chapter 2 we said that the portion of government outlays not covered by taxes had to be borrowed from the private sector. Is this still true when the government has the option of paying for its outlays by printing money? Yes; for national income accounting purposes, the Federal Reserve is treated as part of the private sector. So when the Treasury sells government bonds to the Federal Reserve in exchange for currency, it is still technically borrowing from the private sector.

[5]The financing of government spending through money creation is discussed further in Chapter 16.

with the Macroeconomy

The Monetary Aggregates

The official monetary aggregates*—currently known as M1, M2, M3, and L—are compiled and reported by the Board of Governors of the Federal Reserve System in Washington. Only data for M1 were reported until 1971, when the Fed introduced M2 and M3. Since then the list of monetary aggregates and their definitions has changed several times, reflecting the evolution of the financial system.

The Fed reports estimates of the aggregates both weekly and monthly, using data supplied by banks, the Treasury, money market mutual funds, foreign central banks, and other sources. Each Thursday at 4:30 P.M. the Fed announces figures for M1, M2, and M3 for the week ending the Monday of the previous week. These announcements are regularly reported by the business press; see, for example, the "Federal Reserve Data" column that appears on Fridays in the *Wall Street Journal*.

Historical data are available in the *Federal Reserve Bulletin*, the Federal Reserve's *Annual Statistical Digest*, the *Economic Report of the President*, and in numerous other sources. Monetary data are frequently revised, reflecting the receipt of new data by the Federal Reserve or changes in the definitions of monetary aggregates.

Publication of the monetary aggregates helps keep the public and Congress informed about how the Fed is changing the nation's money supply. In addition, twice a year the Federal Reserve must report to Congress its plans for the future growth of the monetary aggregates. These semiannual reports provide a useful opportunity for public discussion and review of current monetary policy.

*For more details on the monetary aggregates, see John R. Walter, "Monetary Aggregates," in Roy H. Webb, ed., *Macroeconomic Data: A User's Guide*, Federal Reserve Bank of Richmond, 1990.

For the rest of this chapter we will assume that the economy has a money supply of M dollars, which is determined by the central bank. The term M can be thought of as standing for M1, M2, or some other measure of money. For the purpose of developing the theoretical model, it does not matter much which measure of money M refers to.

4.2 PORTFOLIO ALLOCATION AND THE DEMAND FOR ASSETS

Now that we have defined money, our next goal is to understand what determines the amount of money that people choose to hold. We begin by considering the broader question of how people allocate their wealth among the many different assets that are available, of which money is only one example.

A consumer, a business, a pension fund, a university, or any other wealth holder must decide how to distribute its wealth among the many possible types of assets. The set of assets that a wealth holder chooses to own is called a *portfolio*.

The decision about which assets and how much of each asset to hold is called the **portfolio allocation decision.**

The portfolio allocation decision can be complex. Hundreds of thousands of people make their living by giving financial advice to wealth holders, and a major subfield of economics, called financial economics, is devoted in large part to the study of the portfolio allocation decision. Nevertheless, fundamentally, there are just three characteristics of assets that matter for the portfolio allocation decision: expected return, risk, and liquidity.

Expected Return

The *rate of return* to an asset is the rate of increase in its value per unit of time. For example, the return on a bank account is the interest rate on the account. The return to a share of stock is the dividend paid by the stock plus any increase in the stock's price. Clearly, a high return is a desirable feature for an asset to have: All else being equal, the higher the return on a wealth holder's portfolio, the more consumption she can enjoy in the future for any given amount of saving done today.

Of course, one does not always know in advance what return an asset will have. Stock prices can go up or down, for example. Thus wealth holders must base their portfolio allocation decision on **expected returns,** their best guesses about what asset returns will be. Everything else being equal, the higher an asset's expected return (after subtracting taxes and fees such as brokers' commissions), the more desirable the asset is and the more of it wealth holders will want to own.[6]

Risk

The fact that the return an asset will earn cannot be known with certainty in advance relates to the second important characteristic of assets, which is riskiness. An asset or a portfolio of assets is said to have high **risk** if there is a significant chance that the actual return received will be very different from the expected return. An example of a risky asset is a share in a start-up gene-splicing company that will be worthless if the company fails but will triple in value if the company succeeds. Because most people don't like risk, they will be willing to hold risky assets only if they have a higher expected return than relatively safe assets such as government bonds.

Liquidity

Besides risk and return there is a third characteristic, called liquidity, that affects the desirability of assets. The **liquidity** of an asset is the ease and quickness with which the asset can be exchanged for goods, services, or other assets. Because it is accepted directly in payment, money is a highly liquid asset. An example of a very illiquid asset is one's automobile: It takes time and effort to exchange a used car for other goods and services, since someone interested in buying the car must be found and legal transfer of ownership must be arranged. Between liquid money and illiquid autos there are many assets of intermediate liquidity, such as stocks and bonds. A share of stock, for example, could not be used directly to pay for groceries in the grocery store, as cash could; but stock can be transformed into cash with a short delay and at the cost of a broker's fee.

---

[6]For the purpose of comparing expected returns among assets, it does not matter whether returns are expressed in real or nominal terms. Given expected inflation, if asset A's nominal return is 1% higher than asset B's nominal return, then asset A's expected real return (its nominal return minus expected inflation) will also be 1% higher than asset B's expected real return.

Besides making transactions easier and cheaper, liquidity gives the wealth holder flexibility. A liquid asset can easily be disposed of if there is an emergency need for funds or if an unexpectedly good financial investment opportunity arises. Thus, everything else being equal, the more liquid an asset is, the more attractive it will be to wealth holders.

Asset Demands

To summarize, there are three characteristics that make an asset desirable: a high expected return, safety (low risk), and liquidity. Typically, there is a trade-off among these desirable characteristics. For example, an asset that is very safe and liquid, such as a checking account, is also likely to have a low expected return. The essence of the portfolio allocation decision is determining which set of assets, taken together, achieves the wealth holder's most preferred combination of expected return, safety, and liquidity.

The amount of each particular asset that a wealth holder desires to include in her portfolio is called her demand for that asset. Since all of an individual's or an institution's wealth must be held as some type of asset, the sum of a wealth holder's asset demands must equal her total wealth. For example, suppose that I have wealth of $10,000 and I decide to hold $5000 in stock, $4000 in bonds, and $1000 in cash. Then the sum of my three asset demands—$5000 of stock, $4000 of bonds, $1000 of cash—must equal my total wealth of $10,000.

4.3 THE DEMAND FOR MONEY

The **demand for money** is the quantity of monetary assets, such as cash and checking accounts, that people choose to hold in their portfolios. Choosing how much money to demand is thus a part of the broader portfolio allocation decision. In general, the demand for money—like the demand for any other asset—will depend on the expected return, risk, and liquidity of money and of other assets.

In practice, there are two features of money that are particularly important to wealth holders. First, money is the most liquid asset. This liquidity is the major benefit to a wealth holder of holding money.[7] Second, money pays a low return (indeed, currency pays a zero nominal return). The low return earned by money, relative to other assets, is the major cost of holding money. People's demand for money is determined by how they trade off their need for liquidity against the cost of a lower return.

In this section we look at how some key macroeconomic variables affect the demand for money. Although we primarily consider the aggregate, or total, demand for money, the same economic arguments apply to individual money demands as well. This is to be expected, since the aggregate demand for money is just the sum of all the individual money demands.

The macroeconomic variables that economists believe to have the most important effects on money demand are the price level, real income, and interest rates. We will see that higher prices or incomes increase people's need for liquidity and thus raise the demand for money. Interest rates affect money demand through the expected return channel: The higher the interest rate on money, the more money people will demand; however, the higher the interest rate paid on alternative as-

---

[7]Money also has low risk, but there are many alternative assets (such as short-term government bonds) that are no riskier than money and pay a higher return.

sets to money, the more people will want to switch out of money into those alternative assets.

The Price Level

The higher the general level of prices, the more dollars are needed to perform a given set of transactions, and thus the more dollars people will want to hold. For example, sixty years ago the price level in the United States was about one tenth of what it is today; as your grandfather will tell you, in 1930 a good restaurant meal could be had for a dollar. Because less money was needed for transactions, the number of dollars your grandfather held in the form of currency or checking accounts—his nominal demand for money—was probably much smaller than the amount of money you hold today. The general conclusion is that a higher price level, by raising the need for liquidity, increases the nominal demand for money. Indeed, we can make an even stronger statement: Because prices are ten times higher today than they were in 1930, it takes ten times as many dollars today as it would have in 1930 to perform the identical transactions. Thus, everything else being equal, the nominal demand for money is *proportional* to the price level.

Real Income

The more transactions individuals or businesses perform, the more liquidity they need and the greater is their demand for money. An important factor determining the number of transactions performed is real income. For example, a large, high-volume supermarket has to deal with a larger number of customers and suppliers and pay more employees than does a corner grocery. Similarly, a high-income individual makes more and larger purchases than a low-income individual. Since higher real income means more transactions and a greater need for liquidity, the amount of money demanded should increase when real income increases.

Unlike the response of money demand to changes in the price level, the increase in money demand need not be proportional to the increase in real income. Empirically, the percentage growth in money demand is usually less than the percentage growth in real income. One reason that money demand grows more slowly than income is that higher-income individuals and firms typically can be more efficient in their use of money. For example, a high-income individual may find it worthwhile to open a special cash management account in which money not needed for current transactions is automatically invested in nonmonetary assets paying a higher return. Because of minimum-balance requirements and fees, such an account might not be cost-effective for a lower-income individual.

Another reason that money demand grows more slowly than income is that nations' financial sophistication tends to increase as national income grows. In poor countries people may hold much of their saving in the form of money, for lack of anything better; in richer countries wealth holders have many attractive alternatives to money. Money substitutes such as credit cards also become more common as a country becomes richer, again leading to aggregate money demand's growing more slowly than income.

Interest Rates

The theory of portfolio allocation implies that, with risk and liquidity held constant, the demand for money depends on the expected returns of both money and alternative, nonmonetary assets. An increase in the expected return on money increases the demand for money, and an increase in the expected return on alternative assets causes wealth holders to switch out of money and into the higher-return alternatives, thus lowering the demand for money.

For example, suppose that of my total wealth of $10,000, I have $8000 in government bonds earning 10% interest and $2000 in a NOW account (an interest-bearing checking account) earning 5%. I am willing to hold the NOW account at a lower return because of the liquidity it provides. But if the interest rate on bonds rises to 12%, and the NOW account interest rate remains unchanged, I may decide to switch $1000 from the NOW account into bonds. In making this switch, I have reduced my holding of money (my money demand) from $2000 to $1000. Effectively, I have chosen to give up some of my liquidity in order to earn the higher return offered by bonds.

Similarly, if the interest rate paid on money rises, wealth holders will choose to hold more wealth in the form of money. In the example, if the NOW account begins paying 7% instead of 5%, with bonds still at 10%, I may sell $1000 of my bonds, lowering my holdings of bonds to $7000 and increasing my NOW account to $3000. Since the sacrifice in return associated with holding money is less than before, I find it worthwhile to increase my NOW account balance and enjoy the flexibility and other benefits of extra liquidity. Thus higher interest on money makes the demand for money rise.

There are many alternative assets to money, and in principle, the interest rate on each of them should affect money demand. However, the many interest rates in the economy generally tend to move up and down together. For the purposes of macroeconomic analysis, therefore, it is simpler and not too misleading to assume that there is just one nominal interest rate, i, which measures the nominal return on nonmonetary assets. The nominal interest rate i minus the expected inflation rate π^e gives the expected real interest rate r that is relevant to saving and investment decisions, as discussed in Chapter 3.

In reality, there are also a number of different interest rates paid on money. For example, currency pays zero interest; different kinds of checkable accounts pay varying rates. Again for simplicity, we will assume that there is just one nominal interest rate for money, denoted i^m. Our key results, then, are that an increase in the interest rate on alternative assets i reduces the amount of money demanded, and an increase in the interest rate on money i^m raises the amount of money demanded.

The Money Demand Function

The effects of the price level, real income, and interest rates on money demand can be summarized by the following equation:

$$M^d = PL(Y, i, i^m), \tag{4.1}$$

where

M^d = the aggregate demand for money, in nominal terms,
P = the price level,
Y = real income or output,
i = the nominal interest rate earned by alternative, nonmonetary assets,
i^m = the nominal interest rate on money,
L = a function relating money demand to real income, the nominal interest rate, and the nominal interest rate on money.

Equation (4.1) says that nominal money demand M^d is proportional to the price level P. So, for example, if the price level P doubles (and real income and interest rates do not change), nominal money demand M^d will double as well. Equation (4.1) also tells us that given the price level P, money demand depends (through the function L) on real income Y and the interest rates i and i^m. An increase in real income Y raises the demand for liquidity and thus increases money demand. An increase in the nominal interest rate i makes nonmonetary assets more attractive, which reduces money demand; an increase in the nominal interest rate paid on money i^m makes people want to hold more money. These effects are summarized in Table 4.2.

Nominal money demand M^d measures the demand for money in terms of dollars (or lire, or francs). It is sometimes more convenient to measure money demand in real terms. If we divide both sides of Eq. (4.1) by the price level P, we get

$$\frac{M^d}{P} = L(Y,\, i,\, i^m). \tag{4.2}$$

The expression on the left side of Eq. (4.2), M^d/P, is called real money demand or, sometimes, the demand for real balances. Real money demand is the amount of money demanded measured in terms of the number of goods the money can buy. Equation (4.2) says that real money demand M^d/P depends on real income (or output) Y and on the interest rates i and i^m. The function L that relates real money demand to output and interest rates in Eq. (4.2) is called the **money demand function**.

Table 4.2 Summary

Macroeconomic Determinants of the Demand for Money

An Increase in	Causes Money Demand to	Reason
Price level P	Rise proportionally	A doubling of the price level doubles the number of dollars needed for transactions
Real income Y	Rise less than proportionally	Higher real income implies more transactions and thus a greater demand for liquidity
Nominal interest rate i	Fall	A higher return on alternative assets causes people to switch out of money
Nominal interest rate on money i^m	Rise	A higher return on money makes people more willing to hold money

Other Factors Affecting Money Demand

The money demand function shown in Eq. (4.2) captures the main macroeconomic determinants of money demand. There are, however, other factors that affect money demand that should be mentioned. These factors include wealth, risk, liquidity of alternative assets, and payment technologies.

Wealth When wealth increases, part of the extra wealth may be held in the form of money, increasing total money demand. However, with income and the level of transactions held constant, a wealth holder has little incentive to hold extra wealth in the form of money rather than in higher-return alternative assets. Thus the effect of an increase in wealth on money demand is likely to be small, and for simplicity we ignore it in our macroeconomic analyses.

Risk We have seen that risk is an important factor influencing asset demands. Since money usually pays a fixed nominal interest rate (zero in the case of cash), holding money itself is usually not very risky. However, if the risk of alternative assets such as stocks and real estate becomes very high, then people may increase their demand for safer assets, including money. Thus increased riskiness in the economy may increase money demand.[8]

On the other hand, it is not always true that money has low risk. In a period of erratic inflation, even if the nominal return to money is fixed, the real return to money (the nominal return minus inflation) may become quite uncertain, making money risky. In such a situation money demand will go down as people switch to inflation hedges (assets whose real returns are less likely to be affected in times of erratic inflation) such as gold, consumer durables, and real estate.

The Liquidity of Alternative Assets The more quickly and easily one can convert alternative assets into cash, the less need there is to hold money. In recent years the joint impact of deregulation, competition, and innovation in financial markets has made alternative assets to money more liquid. For example, with a home equity line of credit a family can now write checks that are backed by the value of its home (for more on home equity lines, see the application in Chapter 5, Section 5.4). We have mentioned individual cash management accounts, whose introduction made it easy for an individual to switch wealth between high-return assets such as stocks and more liquid forms. As alternative assets become more liquid, the demand for money will fall.

Payment Technologies A last factor affecting money demand is the nature of the technologies available for making and receiving payments. For example, the introduction of credit cards gave people a way of making transactions without money—at least until the end of the month, when a check must be written to pay the credit card bill. Automatic teller machines have probably reduced the demand for cash, since people know that they can obtain cash quickly whenever they need it. In the future we can expect that more innovations in payment technologies will help people find ways to operate with less and less money.

---

[8]For some evidence that this effect occurred in the early 1980s, see James M. McGibany and Farrokh Nourzad, "Interest Rate Volatility and the Demand for Money," *Quarterly Review of Economics and Business*, Autumn 1986, pp. 73–83.

Financial Innovation and the "Case of the Missing Money"

The theory of portfolio allocation has helped economists identify a number of factors that should affect the aggregate demand for money. However, for many purposes—such as forecasting and quantitative analyses of the economy—economists must know not just which factors affect money demand but also how strong the various effects are. This can be determined only through statistical analysis of the data.

As of the early 1970s, economists prided themselves on what they believed to be precise and reliable measurements of money demand and its determinants. For example, in a famous 1973 paper Stephen Goldfeld[9] of Princeton University showed that a money demand function for M1 in a form similar to Eq. (4.2) fit the data up to that time very well. Goldfeld's results confirmed empirically that money demand is proportional to the price level, that it increases less than proportionally when real income rises, and that it falls when the interest rates paid on alternative assets increase.

Shortly after Goldfeld's paper appeared, however, problems arose. Between late 1974 and early 1976 the demand for M1 was much lower than the prediction of Goldfeld's equation—a puzzle that Goldfeld referred to in a later paper as the "case of the missing money."[10] After getting back on track in the late 1970s, demand for M1 went the other way in the early 1980s, coming in higher than predicted by money demand equations. Thus the relationship between money demand and its principal macroeconomic determinants—the price level, income, and interest rates—seems to have shifted erratically.

Numerous explanations have been offered for the surprising instability of money demand. One factor thought by many economists to have been important was the upsurge in financial innovation during the 1970s and 1980s. Spurred on by deregulation and intense international competition during this period, banks and other financial institutions provided the public with a menu of new financial assets to choose from, as well as a variety of new portfolio management techniques. Some of these innovations reduced the demand for narrowly defined money (M1); others increased it.

During the 1970s some of the most important innovations tended to reduce the demand for M1. New liquid and interest-bearing assets were introduced that provided attractive alternatives to the assets in M1, which paid no interest at the time. Examples of these new assets were money market mutual funds (utilized by consumers) and overnight repurchase agreements (utilized by firms), now both included in M2. As interest rates reached new peaks in the 1970s, these alternatives to M1 became widely used, reducing the demand for M1 (and increasing the demand for M2).

---

[9]"The Demand for Money Revisited," *Brookings Papers on Economic Activity*, 1973:4, pp. 577–638.

[10]Goldfeld, "The Case of the Missing Money," *Brookings Papers on Economic Activity*, 1976:3, pp. 683–730.

During the 1980s, on the other hand, financial innovations on net may have increased M1 money demand. Holdings of new interest-bearing checking accounts, such as NOW accounts, grew rapidly in the early eighties. Since these accounts are included in M1, the increased use of these accounts increased overall holdings of M1. Indeed, holdings of interest-bearing checkable accounts increased from 4% of M1 in November 1979 to 21% of M1 by December 1982.[11]

Financial innovation remains an important force today. Regulatory changes are likely to have a large impact on the structure of the banking system in coming years, while technological changes will continue to transform the nature of banking services. However, although financial innovation is good for the economy in general, changes in the financial system may continue to make money demand hard to predict.

Velocity

A concept related to money demand, which is sometimes used in discussions of monetary policy, is velocity. **Velocity,** which is supposed to measure how often the money stock turns over each period, is nominal GNP (equal to the price level P times real output Y) divided by the nominal money supply M. If we let V stand for velocity, the definition is

$$\longrightarrow \quad V = \frac{\text{nominal GNP}}{\text{nominal money supply}} = \frac{PY}{M}. \tag{4.3}$$

Figure 4.1 shows M1 velocity for the United States over the period 1959–1990.

The concept of velocity is a holdover from one of the earliest theories of money demand, the quantity theory of money.[12] The **quantity theory of money** asserted that nominal money demand is proportional to nominal GNP. In symbols, the money demand function under the quantity theory is

$$\longrightarrow \quad M^d = kPY,$$

where M^d is nominal money demand, PY equals nominal GNP, and k is a constant number. Alternatively, if we divide both sides of the equation by P, real money demand under the quantity theory can be written as

$$\longrightarrow \quad \frac{M^d}{P} = kY. \tag{4.4}$$

In Eq. (4.4) the real money demand function $L(Y, i, i^m)$ takes the simple form kY. This way of writing money demand makes the strong assumption that velocity is a constant, equal to $1/k$, and does not depend on income or interest rates.

Empirically, velocity certainly is not constant, as a glance at Fig. 4.1 will show. However, until the 1980s M1 velocity grew along a fairly stable trend line, with only a small break around 1973, just prior to the 1974–1976 "missing money" period. This apparent stability led some economists to suggest that the quantity

---

[11]This figure is cited in James L. Pierce, "Did Financial Innovation Hurt the Great Monetarist Experiment?" *American Economic Review*, May 1984, pp. 392–396. This article contains additional discussion and references on the topic of the effects of financial innovation.

[12]The quantity theory of money was developed by a number of classical economists, notably Irving Fisher, in the late nineteenth and early twentieth centuries. A famous statement of the theory is contained in Fisher's book *The Purchasing Power of Money* (New York: Macmillan, 1911).

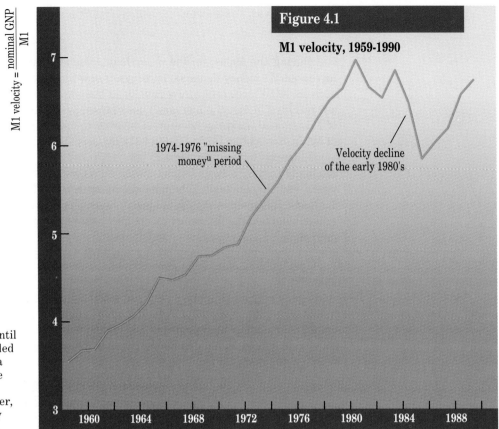

Figure 4.1

M1 velocity, 1959-1990

M1 velocity = $\dfrac{\text{nominal GNP}}{\text{M1}}$

1974-1976 "missing money" period

Velocity decline of the early 1980's

Year

M1 velocity is nominal GNP divided by M1. Until 1981, M1 velocity trended steadily upward, with a small break prior to the 1974–1976 "missing money" period. However, M1 velocity fell sharply during the early 1980s.

theory, with allowances for a trend in velocity, might be a good way to model the relationship between money and income.

Unfortunately, as with the conventional money demand equation, the stable trend of M1 velocity broke down in the 1980s (see Fig. 4.1), with velocity falling sharply. Financial innovations played a role in the 1980s' velocity decline: As we have discussed, the popularity of new interest-bearing checking accounts during this period raised money demand at any given level of GNP, thereby lowering velocity. But in addition, the quantity theory's assumption that interest rates don't affect money demand—an assumption contradicted by most empirical studies—probably also contributed to that theory's misprediction in the 1980s. Interest rates on nonmonetary assets fell sharply in the early 1980s. This fall in interest rates raised money demand at any given level of GNP, adding to the fall in velocity.[13]

ASSET MARKET EQUILIBRIUM AND THE *LM* CURVE

As we have said, the asset market is really a set of markets, in which real and financial assets are traded. The demand for any asset, say government bonds, is the quantity of the asset that wealth holders want to hold in their portfolios. The demand for each asset depends on the expected return, risk, and liquidity of that asset relative to other assets. The supply of each asset is the quantity of that asset that is available. At any given time the supplies of individual assets are typically

---

[13]M2 velocity has been somewhat more stable in the long run than M1 velocity, but it too has suffered sharp fluctuations in the short run.

fixed (for example, there is a fixed quantity of government bonds outstanding at any given time), although over time asset supplies can change (the government can issue more bonds, more gold can be mined, and so on).

The asset market is in equilibrium when the quantity of each asset that wealth holders demand equals the fixed available supply of that asset. In the rest of this chapter we study asset market equilibrium and show how it fits into the *IS-LM* model of the macroeconomy.

Asset Market Equilibrium: An Aggregation Assumption

In analyzing the labor market and the goods market in Chapter 3, we relied heavily on aggregation to keep things manageable. That is, instead of looking at the supply and demand for each of the many different types of labor and many different types of goods that exist, we studied the supply and demand for labor in general and goods in general. Aggregating in this way allowed us to analyze the behavior of the economy as a whole without getting lost in the details.

Since in reality there are many different types of assets, aggregation is equally necessary for studying the asset market. To keep things manageable, we adopt an aggregation assumption for the asset market that economists usually make when doing macroeconomic analysis. This assumption is that all assets can be grouped into two categories, money and nonmonetary assets. Remember that money includes assets that can be used in payment, such as currency and checking accounts. In the category of nonmonetary assets we lump together all assets other than money, such as stocks, bonds, land, and so on. All money is assumed to have the same risk and liquidity and to pay a nominal interest rate of i^m; nonmonetary assets are assumed all to have the same risk and liquidity and to pay a nominal interest rate of i. The fixed nominal supply of money is M, and the fixed nominal supply of nonmonetary assets is NM.

Although the assumption that assets can be aggregated into two groups greatly simplifies the reality, it has proved to be a very useful assumption. One immediate benefit of making this assumption is that if we allow for only two types of assets, *asset market equilibrium reduces to the condition that the quantity of money supplied equals the quantity of money demanded.*

To demonstrate this important point, let's look at the portfolio allocation decision of an individual named Ed. Ed has a fixed amount of wealth that he has to allocate between money and nonmonetary assets. If m^d is the nominal amount of money and nm^d is the nominal amount of nonmonetary assets that Ed wants to hold, then the sum of Ed's desired money holdings and his desired holdings of nonmonetary assets must be his total wealth:

$$m^d + nm^d = \text{Ed's total nominal wealth.}$$

This equation has to be true for every wealth holder in the economy.

Suppose we add this equation across all wealth holders in the economy: The sum of all individual money demands m^d equals the aggregate demand for money M^d. The sum of all individual demands for nonmonetary assets is the aggregate demand for nonmonetary assets, NM^d. Finally, adding nominal wealth for all wealth holders gives us the aggregate nominal wealth of the economy:

$$M^d + NM^d = \text{aggregate nominal wealth.} \tag{4.5}$$

Equation (4.5) says that the total demand for money in the economy plus the total demand for nonmonetary assets must equal the economy's total nominal wealth.

Next, we relate the total supplies of money and nonmonetary assets to aggregate wealth. Because money and nonmonetary assets are the only assets in the economy, aggregate nominal wealth equals the supply of money M plus the supply of nonmonetary assets NM:

$$M + NM = \text{aggregate nominal wealth.} \qquad (4.6)$$

Finally, subtracting Eq. (4.6) from Eq. (4.5) we obtain

$$(M^d - M) + (NM^d - NM) = 0. \qquad (4.7)$$

The term $M^d - M$ in Eq. (4.7) is the excess demand for money, or the amount by which the total amount of money demanded exceeds the money supply. Similarly, the term $NM^d - NM$ in Eq. (4.7) is the excess demand for nonmonetary assets.

Now suppose that the demand for money M^d equals the money supply M, so that the excess demand for money $M^d - M$ is zero. Equation (4.7) shows us that if $M^d - M$ is zero, $NM^d - NM$ must also equal zero; in words, if the amounts of money demanded and supplied are equal, then the amounts of nonmonetary assets demanded and supplied must be equal as well. But by definition, if quantities demanded and supplied are equal for each type of asset, then the asset market is in equilibrium.

We conclude that if we make the simplifying assumption that assets can be lumped into monetary and nonmonetary categories, then the asset market is in equilibrium if and only if the quantity of money demanded equals the quantity of money supplied. This result is convenient, because it means that we only have to study the supply and demand for money and can ignore other assets. As long as the amounts of money supplied and demanded are equal, the entire asset market will be in equilibrium as well.

The *LM* Curve: Money Supplied Equals Money Demanded

Equilibrium in the asset market occurs when the quantity of money supplied equals the quantity of money demanded. This is true whether money supply and demand are expressed in nominal terms or real terms. We will work with this condition in real terms. In real terms the condition that money supplied and demanded are equal is

$$\frac{M}{P} = L(Y, i, i^m). \qquad (4.8)$$

The left side of Eq. (4.8) is the nominal supply of money M divided by the price level P, which is the supply of money measured in real terms. The right side of the equation is the same as the real demand for money M^d/P, as you can see from Eq. (4.2). Equation (4.8), which says that the real quantity of money supplied equals the real quantity of money demanded, is called the asset market equilibrium condition.

The money demand function in Eq. (4.8) reminds us that real money demand depends on output Y, the nominal interest rate i, and the interest rate on money i^m. We can also relate real money demand to the expected real interest rate r: Remember that the nominal interest rate i equals $r + \pi^e$, where π^e is the expected rate of inflation (Eq. 2.11). Substituting $r + \pi^e$ for i in Eq. (4.8) gives us

$$\frac{M}{P} = L(Y, r + \pi^e, i^m). \qquad (4.9)$$

With the expected rate of inflation π^e held constant, an increase in the (expected) real interest r is the same as an increase in the nominal interest rate i, since $i = r + \pi^e$. Since an increase in the nominal interest rate lowers the amount of money demanded, we can conclude that an increase in the real interest rate also lowers the amount of money demanded. In general, higher interest rates lower the real quantity of money demanded by making alternative nonmonetary assets look relatively more attractive to wealth holders.

A graphical depiction of asset market equilibrium is given in Fig. 4.2(a), using what we will refer to as the money supply–money demand diagram. That diagram has the real interest rate on the vertical axis and money, measured in real terms, on the horizontal axis. The line marked *MS* shows the economy's real money supply, *M/P*. Because the nominal money supply *M* is set by the central bank, taking the price level *P* as given, the real money supply *M/P* is a fixed number and the *MS* line is vertical. For illustration, suppose that $M = 2000$ and $P = 2$; then the *MS* line is vertical at $M/P = 1000$.

Real money demand at two different levels of income *Y* is shown by the two curves marked *MD* in Fig. 4.2(a). Because a higher real interest rate r causes

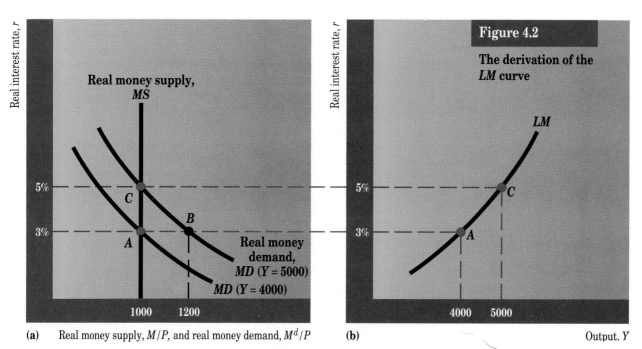

(a) Real money supply, M/P, and real money demand, M^d/P

(b) Output. *Y*

Figure 4.2

The derivation of the *LM* curve

(a) The curves show real money demand and real money supply. Real money supply is fixed at 1000. When output is 4000, the real money demand curve is *MD* ($Y = 4000$); and the real interest rate that clears the asset market is 3% (point *A*). When output is 5000, more money is demanded, so the real money demand curve shifts right to *MD* ($Y = 5000$). In this case the real interest rate that clears the asset market is 5% (point *C*).

(b) The graph shows the corresponding *LM* curve. For each level of output the *LM* curve shows the real interest rate that clears the asset market. Thus when output is 4000, the *LM* curve shows that the real interest rate that clears the asset market is 3% (point *A*). And when output is 5000, the *LM* curve shows a market-clearing interest rate of 5% (point *C*). Because higher output raises money demand, and thus raises the real interest rate that clears the asset market, the *LM* curve is upward sloping.

wealth holders to demand less money, the money demand curves are downward sloping. The money demand curve marked MD (Y = 4000) shows the real demand for money when output is 4000; similarly, the curve MD (Y = 5000) shows the real demand for money when output is 5000. Because the demand for money rises with income, the money demand curve for Y = 5000 is further to the right than the money demand curve for Y = 4000.

Graphically, asset market equilibrium occurs at the intersection of the money supply and money demand curves, where the real quantities of money supplied and demanded are equal. For example, when output is 4000, so that the money demand curve is given by MD (Y = 4000), the money demand and money supply curves intersect at point A in Fig. 4.2(a). The real interest rate at point A is 3%. Thus in this example, when output is 4000, the real interest rate that clears the asset market (sets the quantity of money supplied equal to the quantity of money demanded) is 3%. At a real interest rate of 3% and output of 4000, the real quantity of money demanded by wealth holders is 1000, which equals the available real money supply.

What happens to the asset market equilibrium in this example if the level of output rises from 4000 to 5000? When output rises to 5000, real money demand rises, and the money demand curve shifts right to MD (Y = 5000) in Fig. 4.2(a). If the real interest rate were to remain at 3%, then the real quantity of money demanded would exceed the real money supply: At point B in Fig. 4.2(a) the real quantity of money demanded is 1200, which is greater than the real money supply of 1000. To restore equilibrium, the real interest rate has to rise; a higher real interest rate makes alternative nonmonetary assets more attractive and thus brings the amount of real money demanded back down to the available supply. The new asset market equilibrium occurs at point C, where the money supply curve MS intersects the new money demand curve MD (Y = 5000). At point C the real interest rate has risen to 5%.

The example just given shows that when output rises, increasing real money demand, a higher real interest rate is needed to maintain equilibrium in the asset market. In general, the relationship between output and the real interest rate that clears the asset market is expressed graphically by what is called the LM curve. For any given level of output, the **LM curve** tells us the real interest rate for which the quantity of money supplied equals the quantity of money demanded. The term LM comes from the asset market equilibrium condition that the real quantity of money demanded, as determined by the real money demand function L, must equal the real money supply M/P.

The LM curve corresponding to our numerical example is shown in Fig. 4.2(b), with the real interest rate r on the vertical axis and output Y on the horizontal axis. Two points that lie on the LM curve are points A and C. At point A, which corresponds to point A in the money supply–money demand diagram of Fig. 4.2(a), output Y is 4000 and the real interest rate r is 3%. The fact that point A lies on the LM curve tells us that in this example when output is 4000, the real interest rate that clears the asset market is 3%. Similarly, the fact that point C in Fig. 4.2(b) is on the LM curve tells us that when output is 5000, the real interest rate that sets money supplied equal to money demanded is 5%; this output–real interest rate combination is the same as the asset market equilibrium point C in Fig. 4.2(a).

As the LM curve passes through points A and C in Fig. 4.2(b), it is upward sloping from left to right. The LM curves always slope upward, reflecting the fact that as output rises, so does the real interest rate needed to clear the asset market.

Table 4.3 Summary

Factors That Shift the *LM* Curve

An Increase in	Shifts the *LM* Curve	Reason
Nominal money supply M	Down	Raises the real supply of money and lowers the real interest rate that clears the asset market
Price level P	Up	Lowers the real supply of money and raises the real interest rate that clears the asset market
Interest rate on money i^m	Up	Raises real money demand and raises the real interest rate that clears the asset market
Expected inflation rate π^e	Down	Lowers real money demand and lowers the real interest rate that clears the asset market
Efficiency of the financial sector, arising from financial innovations or regulatory changes	Up, if money demand rises Down, if money demand falls	Increases in real money demand raise the asset-market-clearing real interest rate; decreases in real money demand lower it

Shifts of the *LM* Curve

In drawing the *LM* curve, we held constant factors other than output that affect the real interest rate that clears the asset market. Changes in any of these other factors will cause the *LM* curve to shift. In particular, *given output, any change that reduces money supply relative to money demand will increase the real interest rate that clears the asset market and cause the LM curve to shift upward.* Similarly, given output, anything that raises money supply relative to money demand will reduce the real interest rate that clears the asset market and shift the *LM* curve downward. In this section we discuss the most important *LM* curve shifters; for a list of *LM* shifters, see Table 4.3.

Changes in the Real Money Supply An increase in the real money supply M/P will reduce the real interest rate that clears the asset market and shift the *LM* curve downward. This shift is illustrated in Fig. 4.3, which extends our previous numerical example.

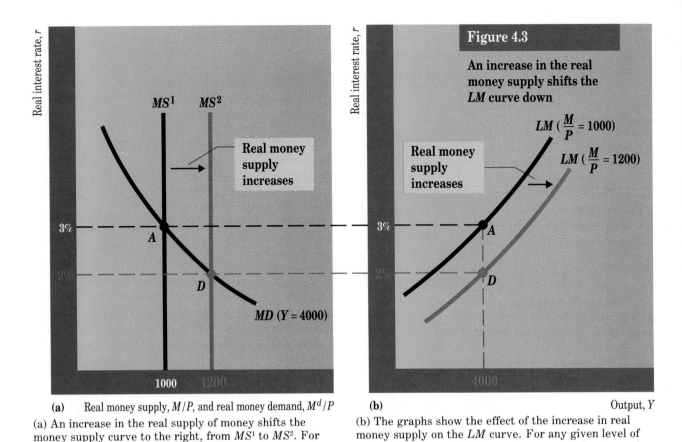

(a)   Real money supply, M/P, and real money demand, M^d/P

(a) An increase in the real supply of money shifts the money supply curve to the right, from MS^1 to MS^2. For a given level of output, the real interest rate that clears the asset market falls. If output is fixed at 4000, for example, the real interest rate that clears the asset market falls from 3% (point A) to 2% (point D).

(b)   Output, Y

(b) The graphs show the effect of the increase in real money supply on the LM curve. For any given level of output, the increase in the real money supply causes the real interest rate that clears the asset market to fall. So, for example, when output is 4000, the increase in the real money supply causes the real interest rate that clears the asset market to fall from 3% (point A) to 2% (point D). Thus the LM curve shifts downward, from LM ($M/P = 1000$) to LM ($M/P = 1200$).

Look first at Fig. 4.3(a), which contains the money supply–money demand diagram. Initially, suppose that the real money supply M/P is 1000 and output is 4000, so the money demand curve is given by MD ($Y = 4000$). Then equilibrium in the asset market occurs at point A in Fig. 4.3(a), with a market-clearing real interest rate of 3%. The LM curve corresponding to this initial situation, in which the real money supply is 1000, is shown as LM ($M/P = 1000$) in the Fig. 4.3(b). At point A on this LM curve, just as at point A in the money supply–money demand diagram in Fig. 4.3(a), output is 4000 and the real interest rate is 3%. The fact that point A lies on the initial LM curve tells us that when output is 4000 and the money supply is at its initial value of 1000, the real interest rate that clears the asset market is 3%.

Now suppose that, with output held constant at 4000, the real money supply rises from 1000 to 1200. This increase in the real money supply causes the vertical money supply curve to shift to the right, from MS^1 to MS^2 in Fig. 4.3(a). The asset market equilibrium point is now point D, where, with output remaining at 4000, the market-clearing real interest rate has fallen to 2%. Why has the real interest rate that clears the asset market fallen? At the initial real interest rate of 3%, wealth holders would not be willing to hold the extra real money supply in their portfolios, and there would be an excess supply of money. Given output, a fall in the real interest rate is needed to induce wealth holders to increase the amount of money that they demand.

The effect of the increase in real money supply on the *LM* curve is depicted in Fig. 4.3(b). With output held constant at 4000, the increase in the real money supply lowers the real interest rate that clears the asset market, from 3% to 2%. Thus point *D*, where $Y = 4000$ and $r = 2\%$, is now a point of asset market equilibrium, and point *A* no longer is. More generally, for any given level of output, an increase in the real money supply lowers the real interest rate that clears the asset market. Therefore the entire *LM* curve shifts downward. The new *LM* curve, designated *LM* ($M/P = 1200$), passes through the new equilibrium point *D* and lies below the old *LM* curve, *LM* ($M/P = 1000$).

Given output, an increase in the real money supply lowers the real interest rate that clears the asset market and causes the *LM* curve to shift downward; similarly, a fall in the real money supply causes the *LM* curve to shift upward. But what causes the real money supply to increase? Since the real money supply equals M/P, an increase in the real money supply will come about whenever the nominal money supply *M*, which is controlled by the central bank, grows more quickly than the price level *P*. We discuss changes in the real money supply in greater detail in the next section.

Changes in Real Money Demand A change in any variable that affects real money demand, other than output or the real interest rate, will also shift the *LM* curve. More specifically, with output held constant, an increase in real money demand raises the real interest rate that clears the asset market and thus shifts the *LM* curve upward. Similarly, a fall in real money demand lowers the real interest rate that clears the asset market and shifts the *LM* curve downward.

Figure 4.4 shows a graphical analysis of an increase in money demand similar to the analysis of a change in money supply shown in Fig. 4.3. As before, the money supply–money demand diagram is shown on the left, Fig. 4.4(a). Output is held constant at 4000, and the real money supply is once again 1000. The initial money demand curve is shown as MD^1. The initial asset market equilibrium point is at point *A*, where the money demand curve MD^1 and the money supply curve *MS* intersect. At the initial equilibrium point *A* the real interest rate that clears the asset market is 3%.

Now suppose that a change in some factor other than output or the real interest rate causes an increase in real money demand. For example, real money demand would be raised by an increase in the interest rate paid on money i^m. The increase in money demand shifts the money demand curve right, from MD^1 to MD^2. At the initial real interest rate of 3% the real quantity of money demanded is 1300, which exceeds the available supply of 1000. The real interest rate must rise to reduce the amount of money that people want to hold. In the example the real interest rate rises from its initial value of 3% at point *A* to 6% at point *G*.

Figure 4.4(b) shows the effect of the increase in money demand on the *LM* curve. The initial *LM* curve, designated LM^1, passes through point *A*, showing that when output is 4000, the real interest rate that clears the asset market is 3%. (Point *A* in Fig. 4.4b corresponds to point *A* in Fig. 4.4a.) Following the increase in money demand, with output held fixed at 4000, the market-clearing real interest rate rises to 6%. Thus the new *LM* curve must pass through point *G* (corresponding to point *G* in Fig. 4.4a), where $Y = 4000$ and $r = 6\%$. The new *LM* curve, shown as LM^2, is higher than LM^1, because the real interest rate that clears the asset market is now higher for any given level of output.

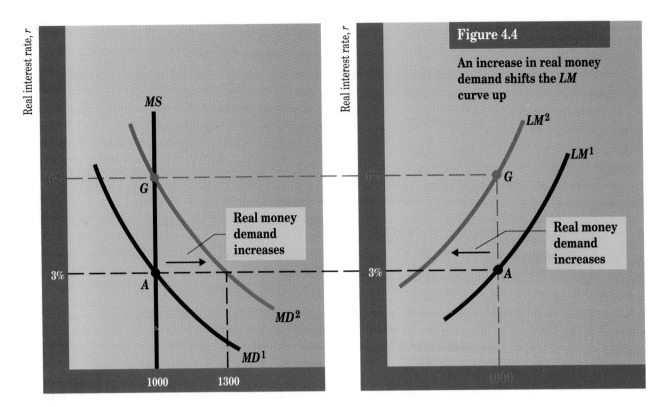

Figure 4.4

An increase in real money demand shifts the *LM* curve up

(a) With output held constant at 4000 and the real money supply at 1000, an increase in the interest rate paid on money raises real money demand. The money demand curve shifts upward from MD^1 to MD^2, and the real interest rate that clears the asset market rises from 3% (point *A*) to 6% (point *G*).

(b) The graph shows the effect of the increase in real money demand on the *LM* curve. When output is 4000, the increase in real money demand raises the real interest rate that clears the asset market from 3% (point *A*) to 6% (point *G*). More generally, for any given level of output, the increase in real money demand raises the real interest rate that clears the asset market. Thus the *LM* curve shifts upward, from LM^1 to LM^2.

Given output and the real interest rate, three factors might affect real money demand and thus shift the *LM* curve.

1. As mentioned in our example, an *increase in the interest rate paid on money* i^m makes money more attractive to hold and raises money demand. Thus an increase in the interest rate paid on money shifts the *LM* curve upward, and a decrease shifts the *LM* curve downward. An example of a change in the interest rate paid on money is the introduction of interest-bearing NOW accounts by banks, which raised the interest rate on NOW accounts from zero to a higher number set by the banks.

2. Given the real interest rate, a *fall in expected inflation* π^e lowers the nominal interest rate i (remember that $i = r + \pi^e$), raising money demand and shifting the *LM* curve upward. A rise π^e shifts the *LM* curve downward.

3. *Financial innovations or regulatory changes* can also affect money demand. For example, the introduction of new types of checking accounts that offer special services—such as automatic bill paying and overdraft protection—should increase the demand for money and shift the *LM* curve upward. Expanded use of credit cards or automatic teller machines would be likely to reduce the demand for money, shifting the *LM* curve downward.

4.5 MONEY AND PRICES IN THE COMPLETE *IS-LM* MODEL

As we discussed in Chapter 3, the *IS-LM* model of the macroeconomy examines the behavior of economic factors in three major markets: the labor market, the goods market, and the asset market. Now that we have looked at each of these markets, we can put everything together to create the complete *IS-LM* model. The bonus from adding the asset market to the model of Chapter 3 is that we will be able to use the model to analyze nominal variables, such as the price level and the rate of inflation, as well as real variables, such as employment and output.

Figure 4.5 is a diagrammatic representation of the complete *IS-LM* model. Shown in the figure are (1) the *IS* curve, along which the goods market is in equilibrium; (2) the full-employment (*FE*) line, along which the labor market is in equilibrium; and (3) the *LM* curve, along which the asset market is in equilibrium. The three curves are drawn intersecting at point *E* in Fig. 4.5. Since point *E* is the only point that lies on all three curves, *E* is the only point at which all three markets are in equilibrium. A situation in which all markets in an economy are simultaneously in equilibrium is called a **general equilibrium**. Point *E* in Fig. 4.5 is called the general equilibrium point.

Although it is easy to see that point *E* is a general equilibrium point, it is not immediately clear what forces, if any, will act to bring the economy to this point. To put it another way, although the *IS* curve and *FE* line must intersect somewhere, we have not given any reason why the *LM* curve must pass through that point of intersection. An important result of this section is that under the classical assumption that prices can change quickly, adjustment of the price level moves the *LM* curve to the intersection point and helps the economy reach general equilibrium. To illustrate this process of adjustment in the context of a specific application, we use the complete *IS-LM* model to consider what happens to the economy if there is an increase in the nominal money supply.

The economy is in general equilibrium when quantities supplied equal quantities demanded in every market. The general equilibrium point *E* lies on the *IS* curve, the *LM* curve, and the *FE* line. Thus at point *E*, and only at point *E*, the goods market, the asset market, and the labor market are simultaneously in equilibrium.

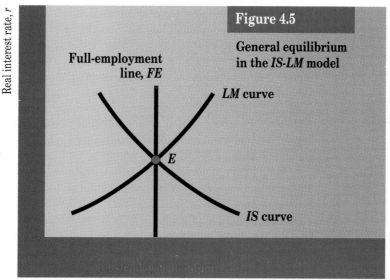

Figure 4.5

General equilibrium in the *IS-LM* model

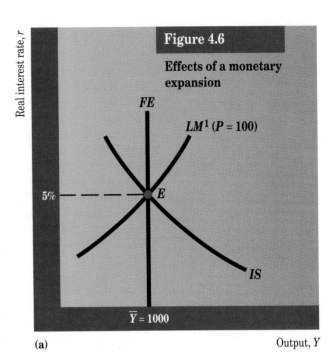

Figure 4.6

Effects of a monetary expansion

(a)

(a) The economy is in general equilibrium at point E. Output equals the full-employment level of 1000, the real interest rate is 5%, and the price level P is 100.

(b) A 10% increase in the nominal money supply shifts the LM curve down, from LM^1 to LM^2. At point F, the intersection of the IS and LM curves, the goods market and the asset market are in equilibrium but the labor market is not in equilibrium. At point F aggregate demand, equal to 1200, exceeds full-employment output of 1000.

(c) Because aggregate demand exceeds full-employment output, prices begin to rise. A 10% rise in the price level P, from 100 to 110, restores the real money supply to its original level and shifts the LM curve back to its original position at $LM.^1$ This returns the economy to point E, where output is again at its full-employment level of 1000, but the price level P has risen 10%, from 100 to 110.

The Effects of a Monetary Expansion

Suppose the central bank decides to raise the nominal money supply M by 10%. For the moment we hold the price level P constant, so that the real money supply M/P increases by 10% as well. What effects will this monetary expansion have on the economy? Figure 4.6 analyzes this question, using the complete IS-LM model.

The three panels of Fig. 4.6 show the sequence of events, starting with Fig. 4.6(a). For simplicity, suppose that the economy is initially in general equilibrium, so that in Fig. 4.6(a) the IS curve, the FE line, and the initial LM curve (LM^1) all pass through the general equilibrium point E. At point E output equals its full-employment value of 1000, and the real interest rate is 5%. Since both the IS curve and the LM curve pass through point E, we know that 5% is the market-clearing real interest rate in both the goods market and the asset market.

The 10% increase in the real supply of money M/P does not shift the IS curve or the FE line because, given output and the real interest rate, a change in M/P does not affect desired saving, desired investment, labor demand, or labor supply. However, as we saw in the previous section, an increase in the real money supply does shift the LM curve downward. This is shown as a shift of the LM curve from LM^1 to LM^2 in Fig. 4.6(b). The LM curve shifts downward because at any given level of output the increase in the money supply lowers the real interest rate that clears the asset market.

Notice that after the LM curve has shifted down to LM^2, there is no point in Fig. 4.6(b) at which all three curves intersect. In other words, there is no longer any point at which the goods market, the labor market, and the asset market are simultaneously in equilibrium. To help us think about what happens next, we must make some assumption about how the economy behaves when it is not in general equilibrium.

Of the three markets in the IS-LM model, the asset market (represented by the LM curve) undoubtedly adjusts the most quickly, since financial markets can

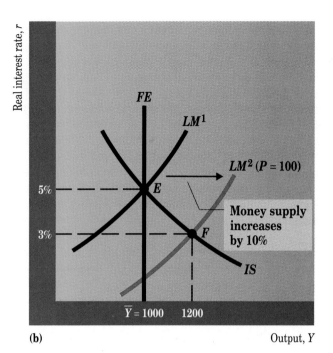

(b)   Output, Y

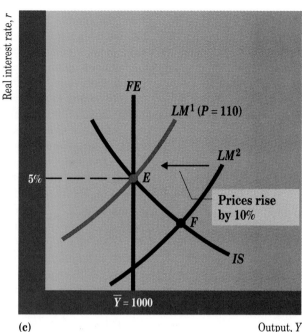

(c)   Output, Y

respond within minutes to changes in economic conditions. The labor market (the *FE* curve) is probably the slowest to adjust, because the process of finding a job takes time and wages may be renegotiated only periodically. The adjustment speed of the goods market (*IS* curve) is probably somewhere in the middle. For the sake of illustration, let us assume that when the economy is not in general equilibrium, it is the labor market in which supply and demand are not equal.[14] In terms of Fig. 4.6(b), this assumption means that after the shift of the *LM* curve from LM^1 to LM^2, the economy will be at point *F*, the intersection of the *IS* and *LM* curves. At point *F* both the goods market and the asset market are in equilibrium, but— because *F* does not lie on the *FE* line—the labor market is not in equilibrium.

At point *F* in Fig. 4.6(b), output is 1200 and the real interest rate is 3%. Recall from Chapter 3 (Eq. 3.4) that when the goods market is in equilibrium, output Y equals the aggregate demand for goods, $C^d + I^d + G$. Since the goods market is in equilibrium at point *F*, the level of output 1200 is therefore also the economy's aggregate demand for goods, or simply aggregate demand. *In general, we will always refer to the level of output at the intersection of the IS and LM curves as the level of aggregate demand.* However, since point *F* is not on the *FE* line, 1200 is not the amount of output that firms want to supply; what firms want to supply is the full-employment level of output, 1000 in this example. To produce output of 1200 and thus satisfy aggregate demand, firms must call upon their workers to work harder and longer than they prefer to at the given real wage. It is because workers are supplying more labor than is implied by their labor supply curve at point *F* that we say that the labor market is in disequilibrium at that point.

So far we have simply taken the price level P as given. Now we are ready to understand how adjustment of the price level can restore this economy to a general equilibrium. At point *F* in Fig. 4.6(b) the aggregate demand of 1200 exceeds the

---

[14]This is the assumption made in the Keynesian version of the *IS-LM* model that we study in Chapter 12.

full-employment level of output, 1000. If firms find that the demand for their output exceeds what they desire to produce, they will raise their prices, causing the price level P to rise as well.

How does an increase in the price level P affect the *IS-LM* diagram? Given the nominal money supply M as set by the central bank, an increase in the price level P lowers the real money supply M/P. A decline in the real money supply, in turn, causes the *LM* curve to shift upward. Indeed, as long as aggregate demand exceeds what firms want to supply, prices will keep rising. Thus the *LM* curve will keep shifting upward and to the left until aggregate demand equals full-employment output, 1000 in this example. Aggregate demand equals full-employment output only when the *LM* curve has returned all the way to its initial position, shown as LM^1 in Fig. 4.6(c), where it passes through the original general equilibrium point E. At point E all three markets of the economy, including the labor market, are once again in equilibrium.

Comparing Fig. 4.6(c) with the initial situation in Fig. 4.6(a), you can see that after the adjustment of the price level, the 10% increase in the nominal money supply has had no effect on output or the real interest rate. Employment is also unchanged from its initial value, since the economy has returned to its original level of output. However, as a result of the 10% increase in the nominal money supply, the price level is 10% higher. How do we know? To return the *LM* curve to its original position, the increase in the price level had to return the real money supply M/P to its original value. Since the nominal money supply M was raised by 10%, to return M/P to its original value, the price level P had to rise by 10% as well. Thus the change in the nominal money supply causes the price level to change in the same proportion.[15]

We went through this analysis in some detail because it helps us understand two central issues in macroeconomics: (1) the question of how the economy reaches general equilibrium and (2) the effects of monetary policy on the economy.

Price Adjustment and the Self-Correcting Economy   Earlier, we raised the question of how the economy comes to be in general equilibrium. We have shown that *the economy is brought into general equilibrium by adjustment of the price level P*. In graphical terms, if the intersection of the *IS-LM* curve is to the right of the *FE* line, so that aggregate demand exceeds full-employment output, as in Fig. 4.6(b), the price level will rise. The increase in P shifts the *LM* curve upward, reducing aggregate demand, until all three curves intersect at the general equilibrium point, as in Fig. 4.6(c). In a similar way, if the *IS-LM* intersection is to the left of the full-employment line, so that aggregate demand is less than aggregate supply, firms will cut prices. A falling price level raises the real money supply and shifts the *LM* curve downward, until once again all three curves intersect and the economy is returned to general equilibrium.

The speed at which the economy returns to general equilibrium is a much-debated issue in macroeconomics. Under the classical assumptions that we have used in Chapters 3 and 4, prices are flexible and the adjustment process is rapid. When prices are flexible, the economy is effectively self-correcting, automatically returning to full employment after a shock moves it away from general equilib-

---

[15]Although the increase in money supply raises the current price level P, for simplicity we hold fixed the expected rate of inflation, the percentage amount by which future prices are expected to be higher than current prices. In Analytical Problem 4 you are asked to find the effects on the current price level and other variables of a change in expected future inflation.

rium.[16] Indeed, if firms respond to increased demand by raising prices rather than by temporarily producing more, the adjustment process would be essentially immediate. According to the opposing Keynesian view, however, sluggish adjustment of prices might prevent general equilibrium from happening for a considerable period, perhaps even years. The issue of whether and how fast the economy self-corrects is at the heart of the classical-Keynesian debate, as we will explore in more detail later.

Monetary Neutrality   The second issue is the one that our analysis addressed directly, which is how a change in the nominal money supply affects the economy. We found that after the return of the economy to general equilibrium, the 10% increase in the nominal money supply had no effect on real variables such as output, employment, or the real interest rate, but it did raise the price level by 10%. Economists say that there is **monetary neutrality,** or simply that money is neutral, if a change in the nominal money supply changes the price level proportionally but has no effect on real variables. Our analysis shows that after the adjustment of prices, money is neutral in the *IS-LM* model.

The practical relevance of the result that money is neutral is also much debated by classicals and Keynesians. The basic issue is once again the speed of price adjustment. In the classical view a monetary expansion is rapidly transmitted into prices and has, at most, a transitory effect on real variables; that is, the economy moves quickly from the situation in Fig. 4.6(a) to the situation in Fig. 4.6(c), spending little time in the position of Fig. 4.6(b). Keynesians agree that money is neutral after prices adjust but believe that, because of slow price adjustment, the economy may spend a protracted period in a disequilibrium situation as in Fig. 4.6(b). During this disequilibrium period the monetary expansion causes output and employment to rise and the real interest rate to fall (compare Fig. 4.6b with Fig. 4.6a). In brief, Keynesians believe in monetary neutrality in the long run (after prices adjust) but not in the short run. Classicals are more accepting of the view that money is neutral even in the relatively short run.

Trend Money Growth and Inflation   In the previous example we analyzed the effects of a one-time increase in the nominal money supply, followed by a one-time adjustment in the price level. In reality, in most countries the money supply and the price level are growing continuously over time. This fact can easily be handled in our framework. Suppose, for example, that in some country both the nominal money supply M and the price level P are growing steadily at 7% per year, which implies that the real money supply M/P is constant. Since the *LM* curve depends on the real money supply M/P, in this situation the *LM* curve will not be shifting, even though the nominal money supply and prices are rising.

Now suppose that for one year the money supply of this country is increased an additional 3%—for a total of 10%—while prices keep growing at 7% per year. Then the real money supply M/P rises by 3% (10% minus 7%) and the *LM* curve shifts downward. Similarly, if for one year the nominal money supply were to increase by only 4%, with inflation still at 7% per year, the *LM* curve would shift upward, reflecting the fact that the real money supply has fallen by 3% ($-3\% = 4\% - 7\%$).

---

[16]The proposition that a free-market economy with flexible prices is automatically self-correcting is consistent with Adam Smith's invisible-hand idea, discussed in Chapter 1.

The main point of this example is that changes in M or P *relative to the expected or trend rate of growth of money and inflation* (7% in this example) are what shift the *LM* curve. Thus in this book when we analyze the effects of "an increase in the money supply," we will have in mind an increase in the money supply relative to the expected or trend rate of growth of money (for example, a rise from 7% to 10% growth for one year); by a "decrease in the money supply," we will mean a fall relative to trend (such as a decline from 7% to 4% growth in money). Similarly, if we say something like "the price level falls to restore general equilibrium," we do not mean necessarily that the price level literally falls but only that it rises by less than its trend or expected rate of growth would suggest.

Table 4.4 Inflation in Low-Money-Growth and High-Money-Growth Countries, 1986–1989

Low–Money-Growth Countries		
Country	Money Growth Rate (% per year)	Inflation Rate (% per year)
1. Chad	−2.1	−2.7
2. Niger	−0.3	−3.5
3. Cote D'Ivoire	−0.2	3.9
4. Switzerland	4.1	1.8
5. Rwanda	4.8	1.7
6. Belgium	5.0	1.8
7. Senegal	5.3	0.1
8. France	5.5	3.0
9. Burundi	5.7	6.2
10. United States	7.0	3.6

High–Money-Growth Countries		
Country	Money Growth Rate (% per year)	Inflation Rate (% per year)
1. Peru	425.9	545.7
2. Yugoslavia	358.5	305.3
3. Zaire	78.2	79.6
4. Mexico	71.3	81.9
5. Turkey	53.6	53.5
6. Ghana	49.3	30.1
7. Poland	46.6	68.8
8. Malawi	27.2	21.1
9. Madagascar	22.2	16.1
10. Nepal	19.9	11.8

Source: International Monetary Fund, *International Financial Statistics*, November 1990.

Note: Countries were chosen from those with complete data and populations of 5 million or more.

Application

Inflation in Low-Money-Growth and High-Money-Growth Countries

Classicals and Keynesians agree that in the long run increases in the nominal money supply will be associated with similar increases in the price level. It follows that countries with high money growth rates over a period of time should also experience high rates of price growth—that is, high inflation.

Evidence on this point is provided in Table 4.4. Starting with International Monetary Fund data for 1986–1989 for more than 140 countries, we eliminated very small countries (population under 5 million) and countries with any missing data. Of the remaining countries, the table lists 10 with among the lowest average rates of money growth over 1986–1989 and 10 with among the highest average rates of money growth over the period. Also given is each country's inflation rate (as measured by the rate of change of the consumer price index) over the same period. You can see that there is a close link between money growth rates and inflation. Countries such as Peru and Yugoslavia, with triple-digit money growth rates, also had triple-digit inflation rates over this period.

Figure 4.7 graphs the relationship between money growth and inflation for eighteen of the twenty countries (Peru and Yugoslavia are omitted from the graph for readability). Again the close relationship between money growth rates and inflation is apparent.

Money growth and inflation for 1986–1989 are plotted for the countries listed in Table 4.4, excluding Peru and Yugoslavia for readability. There is a strong relationship between money growth rates and inflation rates, with low-money-growth countries having low inflation and high-money-growth countries experiencing high inflation.

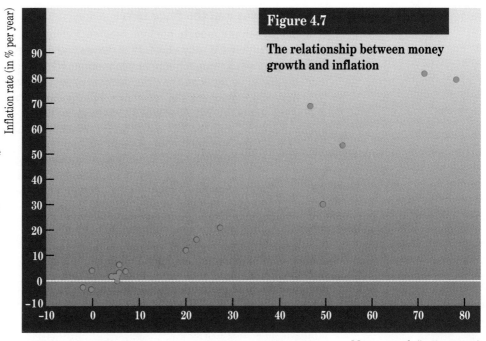

Figure 4.7

The relationship between money growth and inflation

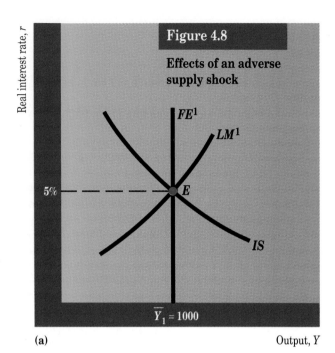

Figure 4.8

Effects of an adverse supply shock

(a) The economy is in general equilibrium at point E, with output at its full-employment level of 1000.

(a)

If rapid money growth causes inflation, why do countries allow their money supplies to grow so quickly? As we discussed earlier, governments sometimes find that printing money (borrowing from the central bank) is the only way that they can finance their expenditures; this is most likely to occur in poor countries or countries suffering from war or natural disaster. Unfortunately, the cost of financing government expenditures in this way is increased inflation.

Supply Shocks and the Price Level

The money supply is an important factor affecting the price level, but it is not the only one. In general, any shock that drives the economy away from general equilibrium may set a price adjustment in motion. Historically, a type of shock that has had significant effects on the price level is an adverse supply shock.

Figure 4.8 analyzes the effects of a temporary adverse supply shock. In Fig. 4.8(a) the economy is in general equilibrium, with the IS curve, the full-employment (FE) line, and the LM curve all intersecting at point E. Output is at its full-employment level of 1000, and the real interest rate is 5%.

As we saw in Chapter 3, a temporary adverse supply shock reduces both employment and the amount of output that can be produced by any given quantities of capital and labor. The resulting fall in full-employment output $\bar{Y}$ is shown in Fig. 4.8(b) as a shift of the FE line to the left, from $\bar{Y}_1 = 1000$ to $\bar{Y}_2 = 900$. With the price level held fixed, Fig. 4.8(b) shows an economy in disequilibrium: Full-employment output has dropped to 900, but aggregate demand (which is determined by the intersection of the IS curve and the LM curve) remains at 1000.

Since aggregate demand exceeds full-employment output, prices will begin to rise. A rise in the price level lowers the real money supply M/P, shifting the LM curve upward. The LM curve will shift upward until general equilibrium is restored, at point F in Fig. 4.8(c). Comparing point F with point E, we see that the adverse supply shock has reduced output and employment and raised the real in-

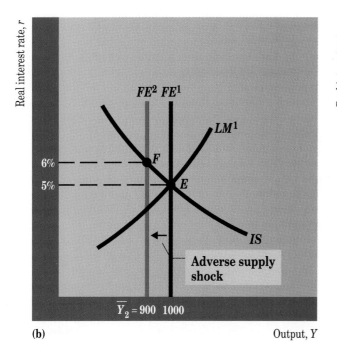

(b)   Output, *Y*

(b) A temporary adverse supply shock reduces full-employment output from 1000 to 900 and shifts the full-employment line to the left, from FE^1 to FE^2. At point *E*, the intersection of the *IS* and *LM* curves, aggregate demand of 1000 exceeds the new level of full-employment output, 900. Thus prices begin to rise.

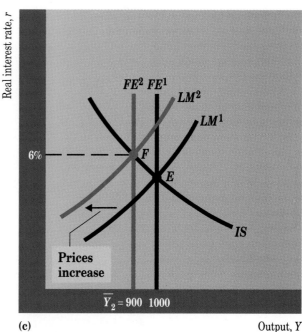

(c)   Output, *Y*

(c) The increase in the price level lowers the real money supply and shifts the *LM* curve upward, from LM^1 to LM^2. The *LM* curve shifts upward until it passes through the new general equilibrium point *F*. At point *F* output is lower, the real interest rate is higher, and the price level is higher than at the original general equilibrium point *E*.

terest rate. This is precisely the same result we obtained by using only the *IS* curve and the *FE* line in Chapter 3. In addition, however, we find that the supply shock has raised the price level *P*.

What is the effect of a temporary supply shock on the inflation rate, as distinct from the price level? Since the inflation rate is the rate of growth of the price level, during the period in which prices are rising to their new, higher level, there will be a burst of inflation. However, once the price level has stabilized at its higher value (and is no longer rising), inflation subsides. This observation suggests that a supply shock should cause a temporary rather than a permanent increase in the rate of inflation.

Application

Oil Price Shocks and Inflation

In Chapter 3 we compared the effects of the oil price shocks of the 1970s on real variables, such as output, employment, and investment, with the predictions of our macro model. Now we have one more prediction—that a temporary adverse supply shock will raise the price level and cause a burst of inflation.

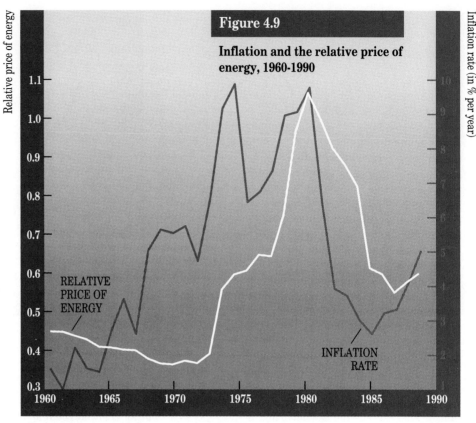

Figure 4.9

Inflation and the relative price of energy, 1960-1990

The figure shows the relative price of energy (as in Fig. 3.8) and the inflation rate for the period 1960–1990. The inflation rate is the rate of change of the GNP deflator. Notice that the inflation rate spiked following each of the two major oil price shocks, in 1973–1974 and 1979–1980, and both inflation and the relative price of energy fell subsequent to 1981.

Source: Relative price of energy, same as Fig. 3.8; GNP deflator, *Economic Report of the President*, February 1991, Table B–3.

Figure 4.9 graphs the relative price of energy (as was also shown in Fig. 3.8) and the rate of inflation, as measured by the rate of change of the GNP deflator, for the United States over the period 1960–1990.[17] The units of the relative price of energy are shown on the left vertical axis of Fig. 4.9, and the units of the inflation rate are shown on the right vertical axis. You can see that the first major surge of inflation during this period, which began in the late 1960s, was unrelated to energy prices. However, the two major oil price shocks of 1973–1974 and 1979–1980 were followed by spikes in the inflation rate during 1974–1975 and 1979–1981, and the decline in energy prices after 1981 corresponded to a fall in inflation. (The fall in inflation after 1981 also reflected reductions in the growth rate of the nominal money supply, as we discuss later.) These responses of inflation to oil price shocks are consistent with the model's predictions.

---

[17]Notice that in putting the relative price of energy and inflation on the same graph, we are comparing a variable measured in levels with one measured as a rate of change.

4.6

CHAPTER SUMMARY

1. Money is the set of assets that are widely used and accepted as payment, such as currency and checking accounts. Money functions as a medium of exchange, a unit of account, and a store of value.

2. The supply of money is set by the central bank, which is the Federal Reserve in the United States. The central bank's official measures of money are called the monetary aggregates. M1, which is made up primarily of currency and checking accounts, and M2, which includes a broader set of monetary assets, are the monetary aggregates that are most widely watched.

3. The portfolio allocation decision is the decision made by a wealth holder about which assets and how much of each asset to hold. The three characteristics of assets that most affect their desirability are expected return, risk, and liquidity.

4. Money demand is the total amount of money assets that financial investors choose to hold in their portfolios. The principal macroeconomic variables that affect money demand are price level, real income, and interest rates. Nominal money demand is proportional to the price level. Higher real income increases the number of transactions and thus raises real money demand. A higher interest rate on alternative nonmonetary assets lowers real money demand by making the alternative assets more attractive than money; a higher interest rate on money raises real money demand. The money demand function measures the relationship between real money demand and these macro variables.

5. Velocity is the ratio of nominal GNP to the nominal money supply. The quantity theory of money is based on the idea that velocity is constant. In practice, much like the money demand function itself, velocity has been unstable since the mid-1970s. Innovation and change in the financial system are important causes of this instability.

6. Under the simplifying assumption that assets can be grouped into two categories, money and nonmonetary assets, the asset market is in equilibrium if and only if the quantity of money supplied equals the quantity of money demanded.

7. For any given level of output, the *LM* curve tells us the real interest rate that sets equal the quantities of money supplied and demanded and thus clears the asset market. The *LM* curve is upward sloping, because an increase in output raises money demand, implying that a higher real interest rate is needed to clear the asset market. Given output, any change that reduces money supply relative to money demand increases the real interest rate that clears the asset market and causes the *LM* curve to shift upward. Changes that raise money supply relative to money demand lower the real interest rate that clears the asset market and cause the *LM* curve to shift downward.

8. General equilibrium in the macroeconomy occurs when all markets are in equilibrium. Graphically, the general equilibrium point is the point where the *IS* curve, the *FE* line, and the *LM* curve intersect. Adjustments of the price level push the economy toward general equilibrium.

9. A change in the money supply is neutral if it leads to a proportional change in the price level but does not affect real variables. In the *IS-LM* model money is neutral after prices have adjusted.

10. Important factors affecting the price level include money supply and supply shocks. Either an increase in the nominal money supply or an adverse supply shock raises the price level.

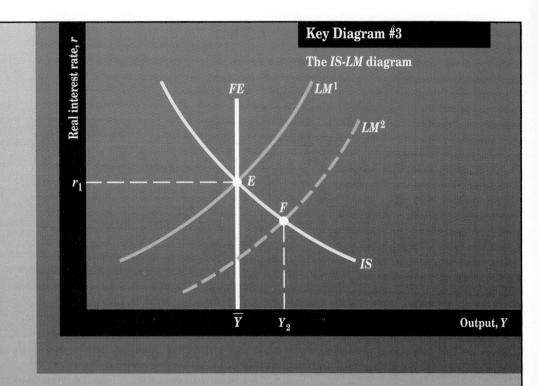

The *IS-LM* diagram shows general equilibrium in the goods, asset, and labor markets. It can be used to analyze the effects of economic shocks on output, the real interest rate, and the price level.

Diagram Elements

- The real interest rate r is on the vertical axis, and output Y is on the horizontal axis.

- The *full-employment line FE* is vertical at full-employment output. Full-employment output $\bar{Y}$ is the level of output that firms supply when wages and prices have fully adjusted. The equation for full-employment output is $\bar{Y} = AF(K, \bar{N})$, where $\bar{N}$ is the level of employment that occurs when wages and prices have fully adjusted.

- For any given level of output Y, the *IS curve* gives the real interest rate r that clears the goods market—or, in other words, that sets desired national saving equal to desired investment. Because higher output raises saving and lowers the real interest rate that clears the goods market, the *IS* curve is downward sloping. The equation for the *IS* curve is the goods market equilibrium condition $S^d = I^d$, or desired saving equals desired investment. Equivalently, the equation for the *IS* curve can be written $Y = C^d + I^d + G$, or the aggregate supply of goods equals the aggregate demand for goods.

- For any given level of output Y, the *LM curve* gives the real interest rate r that clears the asset market, or sets the quantity of money supplied equal to the quantity of money demanded. Because an increase in income raises real money demand, which raises the real interest rate that clears the asset market, the *LM* curve is upward sloping. The equation for the *LM* curve is $M/P = L(Y, r + \pi^e, i^m)$, or real money supplied equals real money demanded.

Factors That Shift the Curves

- Any factor that raises full-employment output $\bar{Y}$ shifts the full-employment line *FE* to the right. See Table 3.6, p. 100.

- Given output, any change that reduces desired national saving relative to desired investment increases the real interest rate that clears the goods market and shifts the *IS* curve upward. See Table 3.5, p. 98.

- Given output, any change that reduces money supply relative to money demand increases the real interest rate that clears the asset market and shifts the *LM* curve upward. See Table 4.3, p. 131.

Analysis

- If we assume that the *LM* curve is LM^1, the economy is in general equilibrium at point E, which lies on all three curves. At point E the labor market (*FE*), the goods market (*IS*), and the asset market (*LM*) are all in equilibrium. At point E output equals full-employment output $\bar{Y}$; and the real interest rate, shown as r_1 in the diagram, clears both the goods market and the asset market.

- The level of output corresponding to the intersection of the *IS* curve and the *LM* curve is called aggregate demand. In general equilibrium, when all three curves intersect as at point E, aggregate demand equals full-employment output $\bar{Y}$. If the economy is out of general equilibrium, as when the *LM* curve is LM^2, then aggregate demand Y_2 does not equal full-employment output $\bar{Y}$.

- If prices adjust quickly, as classical economists assume, then changes in the price level keep the economy in general equilibrium. For example, if aggregate demand exceeds full-employment output, as it does when the *LM* curve is LM^2 and aggregate demand is Y_2, prices rise. An increase in the price level P lowers the real money supply M/P and shifts the *LM* curve upward, until general equilibrium is reached at point E. At point E aggregate demand again equals full-employment output $\bar{Y}$.

Key Terms

Key Equations

$$\frac{M^d}{P} = L(Y, i, i^m) \qquad (4.2)$$

The *money demand function* says that the real quantity of money demanded, M^d/P, depends positively on output Y, negatively on the nominal interest rate on alternative assets i, and positively on the interest rate paid on money i^m. Equation (4.2) can also be written with

the real interest rate plus the expected inflation rate, $r + \pi^e$, substituted for i, as in Eq. (4.9).

$$V = \frac{\text{nominal GNP}}{\text{nominal money supply}} = \frac{PY}{M} \qquad (4.3)$$

Velocity V is defined to be nominal GNP, or P times Y, divided by the money stock M.

Review Questions

1. Define *money*. How is the economist's use of this term different from its meaning in everyday speech?

2. What are the three functions of money? How does each of these functions contribute to a better-functioning economy?

3. Who determines the nation's money supply? Explain how the money supply could be expanded or reduced in an economy in which all money is in the form of currency.

4. What are the three characteristics of assets that are most important to wealth holders? How does money compare with other assets on each of these three characteristics?

5. List and discuss the macroeconomic variables that affect the aggregate demand for money.

6. Define *velocity*. Give two reasons why velocity fell sharply in the early 1980s.

7. What relationship is captured by the *LM* curve? Show graphically why the *LM* curve slopes the way that it does.

8. Holding output and the real interest rate constant, give an example of a change in the economy that raises the real money supply and an example of one that raises real money demand. How does each of these changes affect the position of the *LM* curve?

9. Define *general equilibrium* and show the general equilibrium point in the *IS-LM* diagram. If the economy is initially not in general equilibrium, what economic forces act to bring it there?

10. Define *monetary neutrality*. Show that if prices adjust rapidly, money is neutral in the *IS-LM* model.

Numerical Problems

1. Money demand in an economy in which no interest is paid on money is

$$\frac{M^d}{P} = 500 + 0.2Y - 1000i.$$

  a. You are given $P = 100$, $Y = 1000$, $i = 0.10$. Find real money demand, nominal money demand, and velocity.

  b. The price level doubles from $P = 100$ to $P = 200$. Find real money demand, nominal money demand, and velocity.

  c. Starting from the values of the variables given in part a, and if the money demand function as written holds, how is velocity affected by an increase in real income? By an increase in the nominal interest rate? By an increase in the price level?

2. Mr. Midas has wealth of $100,000 that he invests entirely in money (a checking account) and government bonds. Mr. Midas instructs his accountant to invest $50,000 in bonds, plus $5000 more in bonds for every percentage point that the interest rate on bonds exceeds the interest rate on his checking account.

   a. Find an algebraic formula that gives Mr. Midas's demand for money as a function of bond and checking account interest rates.

   b. Find an algebraic formula that gives Mr. Midas's demand for bonds. What is the sum of his demand for money and his demand for bonds?

   c. Suppose that all wealth holders in the economy are identical to Mr. Midas. Fixed asset supplies per wealth holder are $80,000 of bonds and $20,000 of checking accounts. Checking accounts pay no interest. What is the interest rate on bonds in asset market equilibrium?

3. Assume that the quantity theory of money holds and velocity is constant at 5.0. Output is fixed at its full-employment value of 10,000, and the price level is 2.0.

   a. Find the real demand for money and the nominal demand for money.

   b. In this same economy the government fixes the nominal money supply at 5000. With output fixed at its full-employment level and with the assumption that prices are flexible, what will be the new value of the price level? What happens to the price level if the nominal money supply is raised to 6000?

4. In a particular economy the real money demand function is

$$\frac{M^d}{P} = 1000 + 0.2Y - 20{,}000(i - i^m).$$

Assume $M = 3000$, $P = 2.0$, $i^m = 0.05$, $\pi^e = 0.05$.

   a. What is the real interest rate r that clears the asset market when $Y = 5000$? When $Y = 6000$? Graph the LM curve.

   b. Repeat part a for $M = 3600$. How does the LM curve in this case compare with the LM curve in part a?

   c. Set $M = 3000$ again and repeat part a for $i^m = 0.06$. How does the LM curve in this case compare with the LM curve in part a?

   d. Finally, set $M = 3000$ and $i^m = 0.05$ again, and repeat part a for $\pi^e = 0.04$. Once again, compare the LM curve in this case with the one in part a.

Analytical Problems

1. All else being equal, how would each of the following affect the demand for M1? The demand for M2? Explain.

   a. The maximum number of checks per month that can be written on money market mutual funds and money market deposit accounts is raised from three to thirty.

   b. Home equity lines of credit that allow homeowners to write checks against the value of their home are introduced.

   c. The stock market crashes, and further sharp declines in the market are widely feared.

   d. Banks introduce overdraft protection, under which funds are automatically transferred from savings to checking as needed to cover checks.

   e. A crackdown reduces the illegal drug trade (which is carried out largely in currency).

2. As you can see from Fig. 4.1, prior to the 1980s M1 velocity was generally rising over time. Suggest some explanations for this upward trend.

3. The prisoner-of-war camp described by Radford (Box 4.1) periodically received large shipments of cigarettes from the Red Cross or other sources.

   a. How do you think cigarette shipments affected the price level (the prices of goods in terms of cigarettes) in the POW camp? Explain by using the IS-LM diagram.

   b. (More difficult) On some occasions the prisoners knew in advance when the cigarette shipments were to arrive. What do you think happened to the demand for cigarette money and the price level in the camp in the days prior to an anticipated shipment?

4. Assuming flexible prices, use the IS-LM diagram to evaluate the effects of each of the following on output, the real interest rate, and the current price level.

   a. A temporary increase in government purchases.

   b. A reduction in expected inflation.

   c. A temporary increase in labor supply.

   d. An increase in the interest rate paid on money.

5. In Analytical Problem 5 of Chapter 3, you were asked to analyze the effects of a permanent supply shock on the real economy. If you did that problem, now find, in addition, the effect of a permanent supply shock on the price level. (Be sure to look at the hint given in the Chapter 3 problem.) Compare this result with the effect of a temporary supply shock on the price level, and explain the difference.

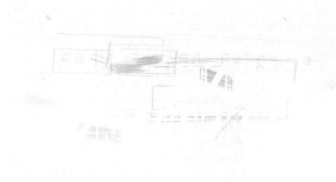

SAVING, INVESTMENT, AND GROWTH

5

Consumption and Saving: The Present Versus the Future

Many economic issues and debates concern the future rather than the present. Questions that policymakers and ordinary citizens ask include: What will the standard of living in the United States be like in the twenty-first century? When today's children are adults, will the nation be able to employ its workers, support its growing population of retirees, pay its domestic and foreign debts? Will the United States remain an international economic leader? It is important to think about and discuss these questions now, because actions that are taken today help determine what the future will be like.

Two important economic decisions that link the present and the future are saving and investment. Saving and investment are examples of what economists call intertemporal decisions, or decisions that trade off the present versus the future. For example, a consumer who saves part of his current income is effectively choosing to consume fewer goods and services today in order to be able to consume more in the future. Similarly, a firm that invests its current profits in building a new factory makes this commitment today in the hope of earning even greater profits in the future. From the perspective of society as a whole, saving and investment decisions represent choices about the extent that sacrifices should be made today in order to increase future national wealth and standards of living. For example, as we discussed in Chapter 2, countries with high rates of national saving enjoy less consumption in the present but accumulate national wealth more quickly than countries that do not save as much.

Part III of this book, Chapters 5 through 8, focuses on saving and investment and the role that these decisions play in the economy. We have two main goals in these chapters: The first goal is to understand better what determines the saving and investment decisions made by people in the economy. In this chapter and in the first part of Chapter 6, we examine the household's decision about how much to consume and how much to save, and in the remainder of Chapter 6 we discuss both the firm's investment decision and how government policies affect national saving and investment.

The second and more important goal of this part of the book is to use what we learn about saving and investment behavior to explore some major macroeconomic issues. These issues include *the factors that determine aggregate consumer spending* (Chapter 5); *the effects of government budget deficits on the economy* (Chapter 6); *the sources of trade imbalances* (Chapter 7); and *the determinants of long-run economic growth* (Chapter 8), among others. Although the links between these issues and saving and investment may not be obvious to you now, by the end of this part of the book you will see that saving and investment behavior are critical factors in each case.

How are these four chapters related to the *IS-LM* model developed in Chapters 3 and 4? Recall from Chapter 3 that desired national saving and desired investment are the two building blocks that determine goods market equilibrium and the position of the *IS* curve. Thus in studying the economics of saving and investment we improve our understanding of the broader *IS-LM* framework, particularly the *IS* curve. Further, the economic analyses done in this part of this book use and build on concepts introduced in Chapter 3, in which we developed the "real side" of the *IS-LM* model (the goods market and the labor market). Issues relating to the asset market (Chapter 4) are not discussed in this part of the book, but are deferred until we cover business cycles and short-run macroeconomic behavior in Part IV.

5.1   THE FORWARD-LOOKING CONSUMER

A large portion of a nation's saving is done by households (individuals and families), either directly in the form of personal saving, or indirectly in the form of saving done by businesses that households own. To study the determinants of saving, therefore, we begin by thinking about the household saving decision. In this chapter we focus on how that decision is affected by the household's income and wealth. Discussion of other factors affecting saving, such as the real interest rate, is left to Chapter 6.

An important point is that because an individual's or family's saving equals disposable (after-tax) income minus current consumption, *the decision about how much to save is the same as the decision about how much to consume*. For example, if a family with an annual disposable income of $40,000 decides to save $5000, then the family's consumption for the year is automatically determined to be $35,000 (their disposable income of $40,000 minus their saving of $5000). Alternatively, if the family decides to spend $35,000 on consumption goods and services, its saving is automatically determined to be $5000 ($40,000 in disposable income less $35,000 of consumption). Since saving and consumption decisions are two sides of the same coin, we can look at the household's decision from either perspective. It turns out to be a little easier to first determine how much the household wants to consume. Once we know how much consumption is desired, saving is found by subtracting the chosen level of consumption from disposable income.

Two principal factors affect how much an individual or family decides to consume in a given period of time. These factors are economic resources and preferences.

Important components of a household's *economic resources* are wealth and current income. Clearly, the wealthier an individual or a family is, or the higher its current income is, the more it will be able to consume, all else being equal. However, an additional important part of a household's total resources is the income that the individual or family *expects to receive in the future*. For example, a college basketball player who has just been made a first-round draft pick by a professional team knows that his future income will be high, and thus he will probably consume more and save less in the present than fellow students with the same wealth and current income. In general, a **forward-looking consumer** is one who thinks about his or her future economic circumstances—such as expected future income and expected future consumption needs. It is reasonable to believe that most saving is done by forward-looking people, so we assume forward-looking behavior throughout this chapter.

The second factor that affects consumption decisions is the household's *preferences*, specifically the preference for enjoying consumption today instead of in the future. For example, an individual who is impatient and inclined to live for the moment will consume more and save less in the present than someone who is future-oriented.

In this section we analyze how economic resources and preferences affect consumption and saving by using an economic model of consumer behavior. To illustrate how the model works, we follow the fortunes of an individual consumer named Prudence. Prudence, who we meet again later in the book, is a forward-looking consumer who thinks hard about her future circumstances and makes decisions that maximize her economic well-being. Although Prudence's meticulously careful analyses of her economic decisions may seem rather extreme, understanding the factors that influence her behavior will give us insights into the real economic choices that people make every day.

To study Prudence's consumption and saving decisions, we make three initial simplifying assumptions.

First, we assume that the time horizon over which Prudence makes her plans (her "lifetime") consists of only two periods, called the present or current period and the future period. You might think of the two periods as corresponding to Prudence's working years and her retirement years, for example. A two-period model is the simplest framework that captures the essential idea of a trade-off between the present and the future. Later in the chapter we discuss the case of consumption and saving decisions made over many periods.

Second, we assume that Prudence takes her current and future income and her wealth as given, ignoring the possibility that by working overtime or taking on a second job she might be able to increase her income. In Chapter 10 we consider what happens when, by varying the amount that she works, Prudence can change the amount of income that she receives.

Finally, we assume that Prudence can choose how much to borrow or save at a given real interest rate. Assuming that a consumer can borrow at the same interest rate at which she can save is not very realistic, since consumer borrowing rates typically exceed the rates that can be earned on saving. Perhaps more importantly, in practice, lenders may set limits on how far they will allow consumers to go into debt, which contradicts our assumption that Prudence can choose how much to borrow. In the last part of the chapter we consider how Prudence's behavior changes in the extreme case in which she is not allowed to borrow at all.

How Much Can the Consumer Afford? The Budget Constraint

To analyze Prudence's decision about how much to consume and save, we first examine how her economic resources determine the choices that are available to her. We then discuss how her preferences determine which choice she makes.

Remember that Prudence's planning horizon covers two periods, the present and the future. We suppose that she receives income in both periods and also starts out the first period with some initial wealth. To have some specific numbers to work with, suppose that Prudence receives a fixed nominal income of $32,000 in the current period and expects to receive a nominal income of $28,600 in the future period.[1] For now we assume there are no taxes, so that Prudence's before-tax and after-tax incomes are the same. In addition, she begins the current period with $4800 in a savings account.

Since Prudence's income and assets are expressed in dollar terms, the amount she can consume depends on the prices of consumption goods in each period. Since we don't want to focus here on Prudence's choices among different kinds of consumption goods, let us suppose that there is only one kind of consumption good, "hamburgers." Hamburgers cost $1.60 each in the current period and Prudence expects them to cost $2.60 each in the future period. Prudence's real income (that is, her income measured in terms of the consumption good) is therefore $32,000/ ($1.60 per hamburger) = 20,000 hamburgers in the current period and $28,600/ ($2.60 per hamburger) = 11,000 hamburgers in the future period. Her wealth at the beginning of the current period, measured in real terms, is $4800/($1.60 per hamburger) = 3000 hamburgers.

Listed next are the symbols we use in studying Prudence's decisions. Since we used capital letters as symbols for aggregate variables in Chapters 2 through 4, we use lowercase letters for an individual's variables.

y = Prudence's current real income (20,000 hamburgers),
y^f = Prudence's future real income (11,000 hamburgers),
a = Prudence's real wealth (assets) at the beginning of
　　the current period (3000 hamburgers),
a^f = Prudence's real wealth at the beginning of the future period
　　(not yet determined),
c = Prudence's current real consumption (not yet determined),
c^f = Prudence's future real consumption (not yet determined).

Given her economic resources, how much can Prudence consume in the present and in the future? Many different combinations of current and future consumption—that is, of c and c^f—are available to Prudence. Here is one possibility: In the current period she could consume all of her initial wealth a (3000 hamburgers) plus all of her current income y (20,000 hamburgers), for a total consumption of 23,000 hamburgers. If she did so, then in the future period Prudence would be able to consume 11,000 hamburgers, equal to her future income y^f. In summary, a possible consumption combination available to Prudence is

$$c = 23{,}000 \text{ hamburgers}, \qquad c^f = 11{,}000 \text{ hamburgers}.$$

If Prudence makes this particular consumption choice, then how much does she save in the first period? Saving s is current income minus current consumption, or, in symbols,

$$s = \text{saving} = y - c \tag{5.1}$$
$$= 20{,}000 - 23{,}000 = -3000.$$

Equation (5.1) reemphasizes the point that, given income, a choice of how much to consume in the current period automatically determines how much is

---

[1]It would be reasonable for Prudence to expect a lower income in the future period if the future period is her retirement years. In general, though, these numbers are just for illustration and are not intended to be realistic.

saved. In this particular example Prudence's saving (-3000 hamburgers) is negative; the term for negative saving is *dissaving*. Prudence dissaves in this example by spending her initial wealth as well as all of her current income. However, even with no initial wealth, Prudence could have consumed more than her income in the current period by borrowing the difference and repaying the loan in the future.

In general, any amount of current consumption c that Prudence chooses will determine the amount of future consumption c^f that she will be able to enjoy. To work out the relationship between Prudence's current consumption and her future consumption, note first that the funds that Prudence has on hand in the current period are her current income y and her initial wealth a. If her current consumption is c, then at the end of the current period she has $y + a - c$ left over. Prudence can put these leftover current resources in the bank to earn interest.

How much interest will Prudence earn? As in previous chapters, we let r stand for the real interest rate. A real interest rate of 10%, for example, means that for every "hamburger" (unit of real income) that Prudence deposits in the bank in the current period, she receives back 1.10 "hamburgers" (units of real income) in the future period. (Similarly, if Prudence decides to borrow from the bank in the current period, she must repay 1.10 hamburgers in the future period for every hamburger borrowed today.) So if Prudence deposits $y + a - c$ at the end of the current period, her bank account (principal plus interest) will be worth $(y + a - c)(1 + r)$ in the future period. The amount $(y + a - c)(1 + r)$ corresponds to a^f, Prudence's assets at the beginning of the future period.

In the future period the funds available to Prudence consist of her bank account plus the income she receives in the future period y^f, for a total of $(y + a - c)(1 + r) + y^f$. Because the future period is the last period of Prudence's "life" (and there is no one that she wants to leave an inheritance to), we suppose that in the future period she does not save but spends all her remaining resources on consumption. Then Prudence's future consumption c^f is

$$c^f = (y + a - c)(1 + r) + y^f. \tag{5.2}$$

Equation (5.2) is called the consumer's budget constraint. For any level of current consumption c, the **budget constraint** tells us how much future consumption c^f Prudence can afford, given her current and future income and initial wealth.[2]

Some sample calculations using the budget constraint are shown in Table 5.1. Column (1) of the table shows different values of current consumption c that Prudence might choose. Column (2) shows the implied level of current saving s, equal to current income y minus current consumption c. Column (3) of Table 5.1 gives the total amount of current resources left over $(y + a - c)$ after Prudence enjoys her current consumption. Since the leftover current resources can be deposited in the bank at interest rate r, Prudence's wealth at the beginning of period 2, a^f, equals leftover current resources times $1 + r$ [column (4) of the table].[3] Finally, future consumption, shown in column (5), equals Prudence's wealth at the beginning of the future period $(y + a - c)(1 + r)$, plus future income y^f.[4] This value

---

[2]In our derivation of (5.2), we assumed that Prudence's current consumption was less than her total current resources, so that she had some resources left over to deposit in the bank. However, the budget constraint equation (5.2) still works if Prudence's current consumption exceeds her total current resources, so that she must borrow from the bank. See Analytical Problem 3 at the end of the chapter.

[3]Negative values of future wealth a^f imply that Prudence enters the future period in debt.

[4]We do not include in future income y^f the interest that Prudence earns on her saving. Future income y^f includes only labor income or transfers received, such as Social Security payments.

Table 5.1 Consumption Combinations Available to Prudence

Current income $= y = 20{,}000$
Future income $= y^f = 11{,}000$
Initial wealth $= a = 3{,}000$
Real interest rate $= r = 10\%$

(1) Current Consumption, c	(2) Saving, $s = y - c$	(3) Leftover Current Resources, $y - c + a$	(4) Future Assets, $a^f = (y - c + a) \times (1 + r)$	(5) Future Consumption,[a] c^f	
0	20,000	23,000	25,300	36,300	A
5,000	15,000	18,000	19,800	30,800	B
10,000	10,000	13,000	14,300	25,300	C
15,000	5,000	8,000	8,800	19,800	D
20,000	0	3,000	3,300	14,300	E
23,000	−3,000	0	0	11,000	F
25,000	−5,000	−2,000	−2,200	8,800	G
30,000	−10,000	−7,000	−7,700	3,300	H
33,000	−13,000	−10,000	−11,000	0	J

[a]The letters in this column correspond to the lettered points in Fig. 5.1.

for future consumption could be directly calculated from the budget constraint (Eq. 5.2).

The Budget Line   The **budget line** is the graph of the consumer's budget constraint, Eq. (5.2); it shows the combinations of current and future consumption that Prudence can afford, given her current and future income and her initial level of wealth. Prudence's budget line is shown in Fig. 5.1, with Prudence's current consumption c on the horizontal axis and her future consumption c^f on the vertical axis. The possible consumption combinations calculated in Table 5.1 all appear as points on the budget line.

Figure 5.1 shows that the budget line slopes downward. The budget line's downward slope reflects the trade-off between current and future consumption: In particular, if Prudence increases current consumption by one hamburger, her future consumption will fall by $1 + r$ hamburgers. Why $1 + r$? If Prudence increases her current consumption by one hamburger, her saving falls by one hamburger. Because saving earns interest at rate r, a reduction in saving of one hamburger today means that Prudence's future wealth will be lower by $1 + r$ hamburgers, and thus her future consumption will be lower by $1 + r$ as well. Since an increase in current consumption by one unit lowers future consumption by $1 + r$ units, the slope of the budget line is $-(1 + r)$. In our numerical example the real interest rate is 10%, so the slope of the budget line in Fig. 5.1 is -1.10.

Present Values

In order to describe Prudence's budget constraint, we seemingly have to know four separate numbers: Prudence's current income y, her future income y^f, her initial wealth a, and the real interest rate r. It turns out, however, that by using a concept

The budget line shows the combinations of current and future consumption c and c′ that are available to Prudence, as outlined in Table 5.1. Each lettered point corresponds to a consumption combination in Table 5.1. The slope of the budget line is − (1 + r) = −1.10. The reason the slope equals − (1 + r) is that each extra unit of current consumption implies one less unit of saving. Because savings earn interest at rate r, each unit reduction in saving implies in turn a reduction of 1 + r units in Prudence's future consumption.

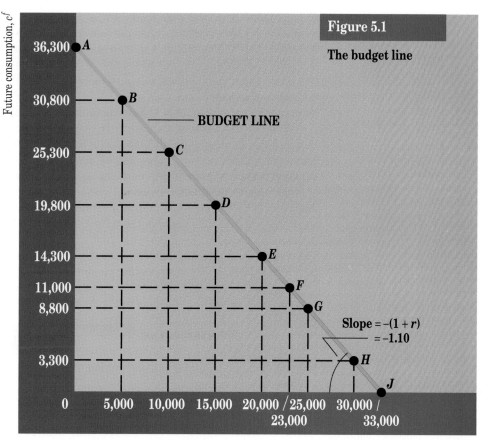

Figure 5.1

The budget line

Future consumption, c′

Current consumption, c

known as present value, we can conveniently summarize Prudence's economic resources, both current *and* future, with a single number. Because the concept of present value is useful for studying Prudence's problem—as well as for many other applications—we discuss it here.

Present value measures the value of payments to be made in the future in terms of today's dollars. To illustrate, suppose that I know that I must make a payment of $10,000 one year from now. I would like to deposit funds today that will be just sufficient to make that payment in one year. The present value of the $10,000 payment one year from now is the answer to the question: How much money do I have to deposit today in order to be able to make that future payment?

The answer to this question depends on the interest rate. Suppose that the current nominal interest rate i is 10% per year. In this case the present value of $10,000 to be paid one year from now is $9090.91. To see why, suppose that I deposit $9090.91 in the bank today. At a 10% interest rate, the interest this deposit will earn in one year is 10% of $9090.91, or $909.09. Adding the $909.09 interest to the initial $9090.91 yields exactly $10,000. So given an interest rate of 10%, having $10,000 one year from now is economically equivalent to having $9090.91 today.

More generally, if the nominal interest rate is i per year, each dollar that I put in the bank today is worth 1 + i dollars one year from now. To have $10,000 one year from now, I must deposit $10,000/(1 + i) today; thus the present value of

$10,000 to be paid one year from now is $10,000/(1 + i). So as we have already seen, if $i = 10\%$ per year, the present value of $10,000 one year from now is $10,000/1.10 = $9090.91. If $i = 20\%$ per year, then the present value of $10,000 one year in the future is $10,000/(1.20) = $8333.33. As you can see by comparing these two examples, an increase in the interest rate causes a decrease in the present value of a given future payment; the higher the interest rate is, the less must be put aside today to attain a given amount in the future.

What is the present value of $10,000 to be paid two years in the future? Suppose the interest rate both this year and the next is constant and equal to i. Then one dollar invested today will be worth $1 + i$ dollars in one year, and (assuming that principal and interest are reinvested) in two years it will be worth $(1 + i)(1 + i)$, or $(1 + i)^2$ dollars. In order to have $10,000 in two years, then, I must put aside $10,000/(1 + i)^2$ today. Thus $10,000/(1 + i)^2$ is the present value of a $10,000 payment two years in the future. Similarly, the present value of a $10,000 payment n years in the future, assuming a constant annual interest rate of i, is $10,000/(1 + i)^n$. Notice that for a fixed interest rate the further in the future a payment is (that is, the larger n is), the less the payment's present value is.

In general, with a constant interest rate of i per period, the present value of a payment to be made n periods in the future is

$$\text{present value} = \frac{\text{dollar amount of future payment}}{(1 + i)^n}. \tag{5.3}$$

Box 5.1 gives an example of a calculation of present values.

In this discussion we have measured future payments in nominal, or dollar, terms; in this case the appropriate interest rate for calculating present values is the nominal interest rate i. If the future payments had been measured in real terms (in "hamburgers" instead of dollars), then present values could have been calculated in exactly the same way, except that the real interest rate r rather than the nominal interest rate i would have been used. In analyzing Prudence's consumption-saving decision, we measure everything in real terms, so we use the real interest rate r to calculate the present values of Prudence's future income and consumption.

Present Value and the Budget Constraint

The concept of present value allows us to restate Prudence's budget constraint in a convenient form, using the concept of the present value of lifetime resources. The **present value of lifetime resources,** which we abbreviate $PVLR$, is the present value of the income the consumer expects to receive in current and future periods plus her initial wealth. In the two-period case we study here the present value of lifetime resources is

$$\text{present value of lifetime resources} = PVLR = y + \frac{y^f}{1 + r} + a, \tag{5.4}$$

which is the sum of Prudence's current income y,[5] the present value of her future income, $y^f/(1 + r)$, and her current wealth a. The $PVLR$ condenses into a single number the consumer's present and future purchasing power.

---

[5]Note that the present value of current income is just current income.

BOX *5.1:* THE WINNING TICKET IN A MILLION-DOLLAR LOTTERY

tickets that give them a very small chance to win a large amount of money. As you may know, however, large lottery prizes are not usually given out in one lump sum but are instead paid out over a period of time. For example, the winner of a million-dollar prize might actually receive only $50,000 immediately, then $50,000 per year for the subsequent nineteen years.

Assuming that the prize is tax-free (which, in practice, it usually is not), is this slow payout of the prize as good for the winner as receiving $1 million cash immediately? The answer is "no." The slow payout is not as good because if the winner were to receive $1 million today, she could save it and earn interest, ultimately enjoying more consumption than she could if she received the money spread out over time. Put another way, the present value of $1 million paid in installments over the future is less than $1 million.

Let's calculate the present value of the lottery winner's twenty payments of $50,000, assuming a constant interest rate of 5%. The current payment is received immediately, so it has a present value of $50,000. What is the present value of each of the nineteen future payments?

From Eq. (5.3), if the interest rate i is expected to remain fixed at 5% per year, then the present value of a $50,000 payment to be made n years from now is $\$50,000/(1.05)^n$. The second payment is received 1 year from now ($n = 1$), so it has a present value of $\$50,000/1.05 = \$47,619.04$. Similarly, the third $50,000 payment, received in 2 years ($n = 2$), has a present value of $\$50,000/(1.05)^2 = \$45,351.47$; and so on. The present value of the final $50,000 payment 19 years from now is $\$50,000/(1.05)^{19}$, which equals $19,786.70.

The present value of the whole series of payments of $50,000 equals the sum of the present values of the individual payments. Adding the present values of all twenty payments, we find that with a 5% interest rate the present value of the $1 million lottery prize is $654,266.

Using the concept of the *PVLR*, we can restate the budget constraint as follows:

> Any consumer's budget constraint requires that the present value of her consumption over her lifetime be equal to the present value of her lifetime resources (*PVLR*).[6]

Let's show that this restatement of the budget constraint holds true in our example. Recall that Prudence had $y = 20,000$ hamburgers, $y^f = 11,000$ hamburgers, and $a = 3000$ hamburgers. With a real interest rate r of 10%, Prudence's *PVLR* is $20,000 + 11,000/(1.10) + 3000$, or 33,000 hamburgers (see Eq. 5.4). According to the budget constraint, therefore, the present value of current and future consumption at any point available to Prudence should also be 33,000. At point F in Fig. 5.1, for example, $c = 23,000$ hamburgers and $c^f = 11,000$ hamburgers. (Data for Fig. 5.1 are also listed in Table 5.1.) The present value of c is 23,000 hamburgers and the present value of c^f is 11,000 hamburgers/1.10 = 10,000 hamburgers; so the present value of lifetime consumption at point F is 23,000 + 10,000 = 33,000 hamburgers, the same as Prudence's *PVLR*. Indeed, as you can check, the present value of lifetime consumption equals 33,000 hamburgers at *every* point along the budget line in Fig. 5.1.

---

[6]Remember that we are assuming that the consumer uses up all remaining resources in the future period. If we allowed the consumer to have some wealth left over at the end of the future period—as bequests to children, for example—the condition would be that the present value of consumption must be *no greater* than the *PVLR*.

The restatement of the budget constraint in terms of present values can be shown algebraically. First, divide both sides of Eq. (5.2) by $(1 + r)$; then add c to both sides, to get

$$c + \frac{c'}{1 + r} = y + \frac{y'}{1 + r} + a. \tag{5.5}$$

Equation (5.5), which is a rewriting of the budget constraint (Eq. 5.2), says that the present value of lifetime consumption, $c + c'/(1 + r)$, equals the present value of lifetime resources, $y + y'/(1 + r) + a$.

The *PVLR* also has a useful interpretation in terms of the budget line. Specifically, the *PVLR* is the value of current consumption c at which the budget line intersects the horizontal axis. To see this result, note from Eq. (5.5) that if future consumption c' is set equal to zero, then current consumption c equals the *PVLR*. Since along the budget line c' is zero only at the intersection with the horizontal axis, then c equals the *PVLR* at that point. In our numerical example the budget line's horizontal intercept (point J in Fig. 5.1) occurs at the point where $c = 33,000$. This value is the same as the value of Prudence's *PVLR* found earlier.

Shifting the Budget Line

We have seen that Prudence's economic resources—her current income, future income, and initial wealth—determine the combinations of consumption that she can afford and thus the position of her budget line. If Prudence's resources change, then the quantities of consumption she can afford will change and her budget line will shift.

An advantage of restating the budget constraint in the present value form of Eq. (5.5) is that it leads to a useful rule for finding the effects of income or wealth changes on the budget line. Here is the rule: With the real interest rate held constant, *any change in current income, expected future income, or initial wealth that raises the consumer's* PVLR *will cause the budget line to make a parallel shift to the right by the amount of the increase in the* PVLR. Similarly, a change in income or wealth that lowers the *PVLR* causes the budget line to make a parallel shift to the left by the amount that the *PVLR* decreases.

To illustrate the rule, suppose Prudence learns that her current real income will be higher than she thought, 24,000 instead of 20,000 hamburgers. Her initial wealth (3000 hamburgers), future income (11,000 hamburgers), and the real interest rate (10%) are unchanged. This increase in current income by 4000 hamburgers is also an increase of 4000 hamburgers in the present value of Prudence's lifetime resources. Thus, according to our rule, this increase in current income will cause Prudence's budget line to make a parallel shift to the right, by an amount equal to 4000 hamburgers. This shift is shown in Fig. 5.2 as a parallel shift from her original budget line BL^1 to a new budget line BL^2.

Why does the rule work? We know that the present value of lifetime consumption must equal the *PVLR* (Eq. 5.5). So if the *PVLR* increases by 4000, as in this example, the present value of lifetime consumption must increase by 4000 also. An increase of 4000 in the present value of consumption, $c + c'/(1 + r)$, implies in particular that for any fixed value of future consumption c', current consumption c can increase by 4000. An increase in c of 4000 for any given value of c' is represented by a parallel shift of the budget line to the right by 4000.

Equivalently, we have seen that the horizontal intercept of the budget line equals the *PVLR*. An increase in the *PVLR* of 4000 implies that the horizontal

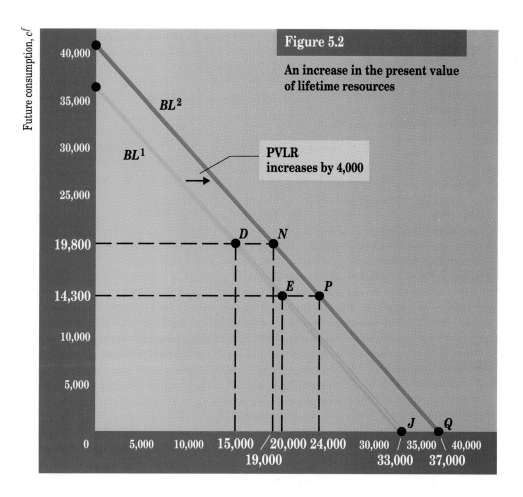

Figure 5.2

An increase in the present value of lifetime resources

An increase in the present value of lifetime resources (*PVLR*) of 4000—owing, for example, to an increase of 4000 in current income—causes the budget line to shift to the right, from *BL*¹ to *BL*². On the new budget line *BL*², for any given level of future consumption *c′*, the amount of current consumption *c* that Prudence can afford is higher by 4000. The budget line's horizontal intercept, which equals the *PVLR*, also increases by 4000 (compare point *J* with point *Q*). The slope of the budget line, equal to $-(1 + r)$, is unaffected by the change in the *PVLR*.

intercept, and thus the whole budget line, shifts right by 4000. The increase in the *PVLR* does not affect the slope of the budget line: The slope of the budget line, which is $-(1 + r)$, depends only on the real interest rate.

Choosing How Much to Consume and Save: The Consumer's Preferences

The budget constraint, represented graphically as the budget line, shows the combinations of current and future consumption available to Prudence, given her initial wealth and current and future income. However, although the budget constraint defines the consumer's opportunities, it doesn't tell us *which* of the many possible consumption combinations Prudence will choose. To answer this question, we have to say something about the consumer's preferences for current versus future consumption. Two important factors that influence most people's consumption and saving choices are their desire to have smooth (that is, stable) consumption over time and their degree of patience.

The Consumption-Smoothing Motive   According to Prudence's budget constraint, one option that she has is to save almost all of her current income, driving herself to the brink of starvation today but—because she has saved so much—being able to live quite well in the future. That is, she could pick a point like point A or point B on the budget line in Fig. 5.3, where c is low and c^f is high. (Figure 5.3 is a redrawing of Prudence's budget line shown in Fig. 5.1.) An alternative option for Prudence is to go heavily into debt in order to consume a lot in the present, while resigning herself to future poverty as she struggles to pay back what she has borrowed. This option corresponds to a point like point H or point J in Fig. 5.3, with a high c and a low c^f.

Neither of these extreme strategies seems very attractive. Most people would not voluntarily choose such a feast-or-famine pattern of consumption—primarily because of the extreme unpleasantness of the famine period—but would instead prefer a more steady pattern of consumption over time. The preference of most people for a relatively constant or stable pattern of consumption over time, as opposed to having very high consumption at some times and very low consumption at others, is called the **consumption-smoothing motive.** In terms of Fig. 5.3 the consumption-smoothing motive leads Prudence to choose a point in the middle portion of the budget line—say somewhere between points C and G, where both c and c^f have moderate values—rather than points like A, B, H, or J, with extreme values of consumption.

The fundamental reason for consumption smoothing is that people care about both their current consumption and their future consumption and so do not choose to spend most or all of their economic resources on one of these and little or none on the other.

The Degree of Patience   A second factor that influences the consumption-saving decision is the patience or future orientation of the individual. The more patient a person is, the more willing she will be to consume less today in order to consume more tomorrow.

The effect of the degree of patience on the consumption-saving decision is also shown in Fig. 5.3. Suppose that Prudence is trying to decide between the combination of current and future consumption represented by point D and the consumption combination represented by point E. Both points lie on the budget line and thus are available to Prudence, and both D and E are also in the middle portion of the budget line that is consistent with consumption smoothing. However, because point D is above and to the left of point E, at D current consumption is lower and future consumption is higher than at E. If Prudence were to choose point D instead of point E, we could conclude that she is relatively patient; that is, she is relatively willing to give up current consumption in exchange for future consumption. If, instead, she chooses point E, with higher current consumption and lower future consumption than at point D, we would say that Prudence is relatively less patient. More generally, a less patient consumer will choose a consumption combination that is further down and to the right on the budget line than the consumption combination that will be chosen by a more patient consumer.

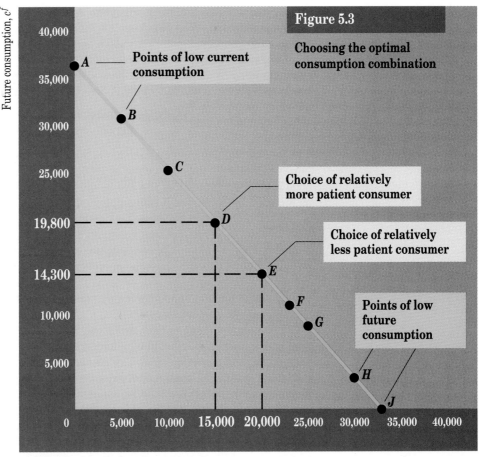

Figure 5.3

Choosing the optimal consumption combination

The budget line, which is the same as in Fig. 5.1, represents the combinations of current and future consumption available to Prudence. Prudence will pick the consumption combination on the budget line that makes her the happiest. The consumption-smoothing motive implies that Prudence will not pick a point like A, B, H, or J, at which consumption is very high in either the present or future period but very low in the other period. In addition, the more patient Prudence is, the further to the left on the budget line her consumption choice will be. For example, if she is relatively patient, she will pick point D rather than point E, because at point D current consumption is lower and saving is higher than at point E.

Depending on such factors as her degree of patience and her desire for smooth consumption, Prudence will pick the point on the budget line that makes her the happiest. For example, if she is relatively patient, she might pick point D on the budget line in Fig. 5.3. Corresponding to the point she chooses is what is called the optimal consumption combination, or the combination of current and future consumption among those available that makes her feel best off. We let c^* and c^{f*} stand for optimal current and future consumption. In the example, if Prudence picks point D, then $c^* = 15,000$ and $c^{f*} = 19,800$, which are the values of current and future consumption corresponding to point D.

Economists use the term **utility** to refer to an individual's economic satisfaction or well-being. Thus Prudence's optimal consumption combination, at point D in this example, is the one that makes her level of utility as high as possible.

Prudence's choice of an optimal consumption combination also determines her optimal saving or dissaving. Prudence's optimal saving s^* is the difference between her current income and her optimal current consumption:

$$s^* = y - c^*$$
$$= 20,000 - 15,000 = 5000.$$

In this example Prudence's decision to have current consumption of 15,000 hamburgers implies an optimal saving of 5000. You should check that if Prudence saves 5000 in the current period, she will be able to consume 19,800 in the future period, as required by her optimal consumption combination.

What if Prudence had been less patient, picking, for example, point E in Fig. 5.3? In this case her optimal consumption combination would have been $c^* = 20,000$ and $c^{f*} = 14,300$, the consumption combination represented by point E. Her optimal saving s^* would have been her current income of 20,000 less her current optimal consumption of 20,000, or zero. This example illustrates that, all else being equal, a less patient consumer enjoys more current consumption and saves less than a more patient consumer.

A well-known fact is that American households save less than households in many other countries. Should we therefore conclude that Americans are inherently less patient than other people? This interpretation may be correct; one sometimes hears, for example, that American culture emphasizes immediate gratification. However, although there may be some validity to cultural explanations of differences in national saving rates, this explanation also has weaknesses: First, cultural influences are hard to identify and measure, so that hypotheses about them are hard to prove or disprove. Second, because cultural factors presumably change slowly, it is difficult for such factors to explain the relatively large short-term changes in national saving rates that sometimes occur. (See, for example, the changes in Japanese and French saving rates shown in Fig. 2.4.) To explain such changes in saving, economists usually prefer to rely on changes in the economic environments that people face—for example, changes in income, wealth, interest rates, and tax rates. Using the model of the consumer developed here, we will be able to analyze the effects of these factors on saving.

Although economists are reluctant to rely on differences in patience to explain differences in national saving behavior, they do recognize that changes in a particular country's economic, social, or political environment can make the country's savers behave *as if* they were more patient or impatient; see the box "The Political Environment" (p. 168).

5.2 THE EFFECTS OF CHANGES IN INCOME AND WEALTH ON CONSUMPTION AND SAVING

Two of the most important factors that affect consumption and saving are the levels of income and wealth in an economy. In this section we use our model of the consumer to think about how changes in these two factors are likely to affect consumers' behavior.

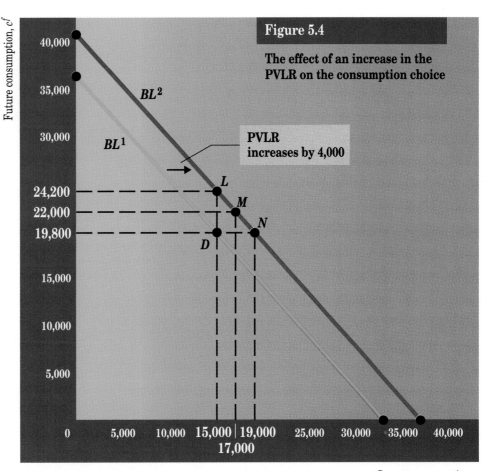

Figure 5.4

The effect of an increase in the PVLR on the consumption choice

An increase of 4000 in the present value of lifetime resources causes the budget line to make a parallel shift to the right by 4000, from BL^1 to BL^2. If Prudence's original plan was to consume at point D, she can move to point L by spending all of the increase in her resources on future consumption and none on current consumption; or she can move to point N by spending all the increase in her resources on current consumption and none on future consumption. However, if Prudence values both current *and* future consumption, she will use the increase in her resources to increase both current and future consumption, moving to a point like M.

The Effects of Changes in Income

For Prudence, a change in her income could mean either that her current income changes or that she changes her expectation of the amount of income she will receive in the future.

An Increase in Current Income   In Chapter 3 we used a bonus at work as an example of an increase in current income. Let's reconsider this case, using the example of Prudence. Suppose that Prudence receives a bonus of 4000 "hamburgers," raising her current real income from 20,000 hamburgers to 24,000 hamburgers. Her initial assets (3000), future income (11,000), and the real interest rate (10%) are unchanged; so the increase of 4000 in current income implies an equal-sized increase in Prudence's present value of lifetime resources, or *PVLR*. If she has not yet committed herself to her original consumption-saving plan, how can Prudence revise her plan in light of her increased current income?

We can use the graph in Fig. 5.4 to answer this question. In Fig. 5.4 BL^1 is Prudence's original budget line, and we suppose that point D, where $c = 15,000$ and $c^f = 19,800$, represents Prudence's original, prebonus consumption plan. The effect of the increase in Prudence's current income is to shift her budget line to the

CHAPTER 5 CONSUMPTION AND SAVING: THE PRESENT VERSUS THE FUTURE

The Political Environment

★ ★

Sociopolitical Instability and the Rate of Saving

Unfortunately, social and political instability are common in the world. What is the effect of instability on a country's saving rate? This question was investigated by Yiannis P. Venieris and Dipak K. Gupta* of San Diego State University.

The bulk of saving in most countries is done by middle-class or rich people. If a country has a revolution, the rich and middle class are likely to lose many of their accumulated assets. An increase in the probability of revolution may there-fore make the country's savers effectively more "impatient," that is, more focused on the present and less willing to save for the future. Thus saving rates should fall when instability increases.

To test this hypothesis, Venieris and Gupta studied forty-nine non-Communist countries, including both developing and industrialized countries. For each country they constructed a measure of sociopolitical instability. This measure depended on (1) the number of people participating in political protest demonstrations during the year, (2) the number of deaths attributable to political violence, and (3) the type of government—that is, whether or not the country was a democracy (democracies are more stable than nondemocracies). They then related this measure of instability to average private saving rates in each country.

As predicted by the theory, the researchers found a strong negative effect of instability on saving rates. At given levels of GNP, unstable countries saved about 18% less than countries of average sociopolitical stability, which in turn saved about 17% less than the most stable countries.

*"Income Distribution and Sociopolitical Instability as Determinants of Savings: A Cross-Sectional Model," *Journal of Political Economy*, August 1986, pp. 873–83.

right: As we saw earlier in the chapter (Fig. 5.2), an increase of 4000 in the *PVLR* causes the budget line to make a parallel shift to the right by that amount. This shift is shown in Fig. 5.4 as a shift of the budget line from BL^1 to BL^2.

Because Prudence's budget line has shifted, she now has the possibility of consuming more than before. Two consumption combinations that are now available to Prudence are represented by points L and N on the new budget line BL^2. At point L, which lies directly above point D, Prudence's current consumption is unchanged from what it was at point D, but her future consumption is higher by 4400. To reach point L, Prudence must save all of her bonus, using the bonus and the interest of 400 earned on it to increase future consumption. An alternative is represented by point N, where future consumption is unchanged from what it was at point D but current consumption has risen by 4000. To reach point N, Prudence must spend all of her bonus on current consumption, saving none of it for the future.

Both point L (save all of the bonus) and point N (save none of the bonus) represent extreme strategies for Prudence. Earlier, when we discussed consumption smoothing, we said that people value both current *and* future consumption. If Prudence prefers smooth consumption, she will use her bonus both to increase her current consumption and, by saving part of it, to increase future consumption. Thus we expect her to move from point D to a point like M in Fig. 5.4. At point M, which lies on the new budget line BL^2 between points L and N, both current consumption and future consumption are higher than at point D. Prudence's current saving is also higher at M than at D, since although her current consumption increases, it does so by less than the increase in her current income.

We conclude that an increase in current income should increase both current consumption and current saving. The basic idea, that the consumer will devote part of any increase in income to current consumption and part (by saving) to future consumption, is the same as in Chapter 3.

An Increase in Future Income   Now let's look at the effect of an increase in Prudence's future income. Suppose that Prudence doesn't get her bonus of 4000 in the current period (y remains at its initial value of 20,000). Instead, because of an improved company pension plan, she learns that her future income will increase by 4400 hamburgers, so y^f rises from 11,000 to 15,400. How will this change affect her current consumption and saving?

At a real interest rate of 10% the present value of Prudence's future income increases by 4400/1.10, or 4000. Thus, like the current bonus of 4000 discussed earlier, the improved pension plan raises Prudence's $PVLR$ by 4000 and shifts the budget line right by that amount.

Because the effects on the budget line of the future income increase of 4400 and the current income increase of 4000 are the same, we can once again use Fig. 5.4 to study the effects of the future income increase. The rightward shift of the budget line is shown in Fig. 5.4 as a movement from BL^1 to BL^2. If Prudence had chosen the consumption combination at point D before knowing of her future income increase, then, as in the previous case, she will move to point M when she learns of the increase. Thus the increase in expected future income of 4400 has exactly the same effect on current and future consumption as an increase in current income of 4000. The current and future increases in income have the same effects because the two increases have the same present value and thus raise Prudence's $PVLR$ by the same amount.

Although the increases in current income and future income have the same effects on current consumption, their effects on saving are different. Because the increase in future income raises current consumption but does not affect current income, it causes saving to fall (not rise, as in the case of an increase in current income). Intuitively, because Prudence knows she will be receiving more income in the future, she has less need to save today. The conclusion that an increase in future income raises current consumption and lowers saving is again the same as in Chapter 3.

A key result of this analysis is that Prudence should react today—by increasing her consumption and lowering her saving—to an increase in income that is not expected to occur until some time in the future. In other words, the theory says that a change in income should begin to affect consumption when the consumer first learns about it, not at the time that the income change actually occurs. So, for example, if I learn that my rich uncle has left $1 million in trust for me, to become mine in five years, then according to the model, I should begin consuming like a millionaire immediately—not when I actually receive the funds. Assuming that my income is currently low, I will have to go into debt, expecting to repay when I get access to the $1 million.

The prediction that I should start consuming today out of my future income may seem unrealistic. A problem with this implication of the theory is I may have difficulty finding someone willing to lend me a large amount of money today on the strength of my high future income. That is, I may face what economists call a borrowing constraint, or a limit on borrowing. We discuss the impact of borrowing constraints on consumption later in this chapter.

Consumers' Expectations and Consumer Confidence   The idea of the forward-looking consumer says that people think about their future incomes when making current consumption and saving decisions. Of course, nobody knows for sure what their future incomes will be; instead, people must make their plans on the basis of their best estimates of what the future will bring.

Because consumers' expectations about the future are an important factor affecting current economic behavior, economists have tried to measure those expectations. At least two major organizations regularly survey consumers about their expectations for the economy, reporting their results as measures of what they call "consumer confidence" or "consumer sentiment" (see the box "In Touch with the Macroeconomy," p. 171). The hope is that by providing an index of what consumers expect, measures of consumer confidence can help policymakers and forecasters anticipate consumer behavior and thus the course of the economy.

Permanent Versus Temporary Income Changes: The Permanent Income Theory

Some increases in income—winning money in a contest or getting a one-time bonus at work—are purely one-shot or temporary increases. Other increases in income, such as finding a new long-term job at a higher salary, are permanent. Our analysis implies that consumption and saving will react differently to these two different kinds of changes.

In terms of the model a temporary increase in income is an increase in current income y, with future income y^f held constant. A one-unit temporary increase in income increases the *PVLR* by one unit. In contrast, a permanent increase in income applies to future periods as well as to the current period; that is, a permanent increase in income of one unit increases *both* y and y^f by one unit. The effect of the permanent one-unit increase in income on the *PVLR* equals one unit for the effect on current income, plus $1/(1 + r)$ units associated with the future increase in income, for a total of $1 + 1/(1 + r)$ units. The impact of a permanent increase in income on the *PVLR* is thus greater than the impact of a temporary increase in income.

Since income changes affect consumption only by changing the *PVLR*, a permanent one-unit increase in income will raise current and future consumption more than a temporary one-unit increase in income will. Furthermore, because current consumption rises more when a given income increase is permanent, the amount that is saved from a permanent increase in income will be less than what is saved from a temporary increase in income.

This distinction between the effects of permanent and temporary income changes is emphasized in the **permanent income theory** of consumption and saving, first developed in the 1950s by Nobel laureate Milton Friedman. Friedman pointed out that income should affect consumption only through the *PVLR* in a many-period version of the model as well as in the two-period version. Thus permanent changes in income, because they last for many periods, can have much larger effects on consumption than temporary changes in income. As a result, temporary income increases should be mostly saved, and permanent income increases should be mostly spent.

In touch

with the Macroeconomy
The Index of Consumer Sentiment

The theory of consumer behavior tells us that current consumption and saving decisions should depend on consumers' expectations about the future of the economy. When consumers are generally optimistic about the future, they will consume more and save less than when they are pessimistic. Since consumption spending exceeds 60% of total expenditure, surveys that ask consumers how they feel about the future may be useful for assessing current trends in the economy.

There are a number of regular surveys of consumer attitudes. Two of the best-known include one by the Conference Board, which summarizes its results in a "consumer confidence index," and another by the Survey Research Center at the University of Michigan, which publishes an "index of consumer sentiment." Here we discuss the index of consumer sentiment.

The Survey Research Center has reported its index of consumer sentiment monthly since 1946. The index is based on the responses of about five hundred households to questions about their own current and future expected financial situation and about what they think the economy will do in the next one to five years. The index is measured relative to a value of 100 for 1966, with higher values corresponding to greater consumer optimism. The Survey Research Center publishes the index in a detailed monthly report called *Surveys of Con-*

sumer Attitudes. It is also available in the press and in the *Survey of Current Business*.

Historically, the index has been a sensitive indicator of recessions and other macroeconomic shocks. The accompanying figure shows the index of consumer sentiment for the period March 1987–December 1990. You can see that the stock market crash of October 1987 caused a drop in the index, but one that was quickly reversed. However, when Iraq invaded Kuwait in August 1990, the index of consumer sentiment took its sharpest decline ever, reflecting consumers' fears about the long-term implications of the invasion. Consumer spending also dropped sharply in the fourth quarter of 1990 as a recession began.

Source: *Survey of Current Business* and *Business Conditions Digest*, various issues. The Index of Consumer Sentiment is a copyrighted series published by the Surveys of Consumers, Survey Research Center, University of Michigan.

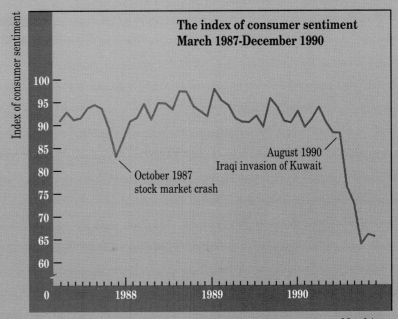

The index of consumer sentiment
March 1987-December 1990

Index of consumer sentiment

October 1987 stock market crash

August 1990 Iraqi invasion of Kuwait

Month/year

Friedman also provided some of the first empirical evidence for his theory. For example, he found that the consumption of farm families on average responded less to changes in income than did the consumption of nonfarm families. Friedman's explanation for this finding was that since farm incomes depend heavily on weather and crop prices, both of which are very volatile, changes in farm incomes are much more likely to be temporary than are changes in nonfarm incomes. Current changes in farm incomes thus have a smaller effect on the *PVLR* and therefore should have a smaller effect on current consumption.

The idea that permanent changes in income should affect consumption more strongly than temporary changes has generally held up well empirically. Box 5.2 (p. 174) describes a study that tested this proposition by examining the consumption of unemployed workers.

Application

Aggregate Consumption During Recessions

Recessions are periods during which real GNP declines (or grows very slowly), so that consumers' real incomes also decline. However, recessions are usually rather short-lived events, so that the falls in income suffered by consumers turn out to be at least to some degree temporary.[7] If the declines in GNP during recessions are at least partly temporary, then the permanent income theory predicts that aggregate consumption should fall less sharply than GNP falls when the economy turns down. More generally, if output fluctuations are partly temporary, the theory predicts that aggregate consumption should be "smoother" than real GNP, reflecting the consumption-smoothing motive of consumers.

Figure 5.5 shows the behavior of real GNP and real aggregate consumption, excluding spending on consumer durables, for the period 1970–1990. We exclude spending on consumer durables from the consumption measure because durable items such as cars or furniture are not completely consumed during the period in which they are purchased but, instead, are used up over many years. If we had included durables spending in the consumption measure of Fig. 5.5, we would have been erroneously counting all purchases of durables as current consumption, when in fact a durable good purchased today contributes both to current consumption and to future consumption.[8]

Figure 5.5 generally confirms the predictions of the permanent income theory that consumption is smoother than output and does not fall sharply in recessions. This is particularly clear in the 1981–1982 recession, in which GNP declined significantly but consumption remained relatively steady.

Consumption did fall somewhat more in the 1973–1975 recession than in the 1981–1982 recession. For this fall in consumption to be consistent with the permanent income theory, consumers would have had to expect the fall in GNP during

[7]Exactly how much of the decline in income in a recession is temporary and how much is permanent is controversial. Box 9.1 discusses the issue and reports the results of a study that found about 70% of the decline in income during a recession to be temporary.

[8]Although consumer durables contribute to both current and future consumption in an economic sense, expenditures on consumer durables nevertheless are counted as part of current consumption expenditures in the national income accounts.

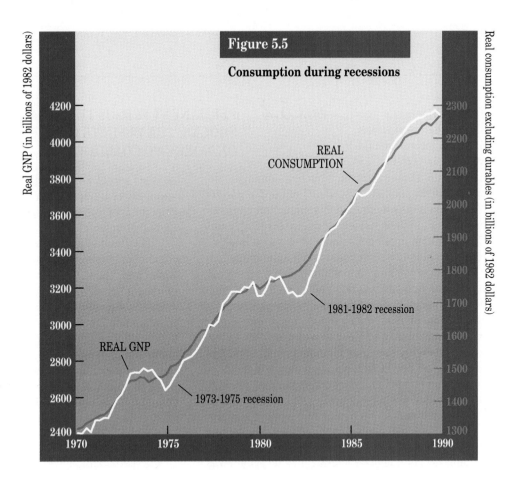

Figure 5.5

Consumption during recessions

Real GNP (in billions of 1982 dollars)

Real consumption excluding durables (in billions of 1982 dollars)

REAL CONSUMPTION

1981-1982 recession

REAL GNP

1973-1975 recession

The figure shows real GNP (*white*) and aggregate real consumption, excluding expenditures on consumer durables (*red*). As implied by the consumption-smoothing motive, the path of consumption is generally smoother than that of output, and consumption does not fall as sharply as output during recessions. The relative stability of consumption during a recession period is particularly clear for the 1981–1982 recession. Consumption fell somewhat more during the 1973–1975 recession, possibly because consumers thought that an unusually large part of the decline in output in that recession was permanent.

1973–1975 to be relatively more permanent than in the typical recession. Interestingly, there is evidence that the decline in output in 1973–1975, which followed on the heels of OPEC's quadrupling of oil prices and a slowdown in productivity growth, was considerably more permanent than is usually the case in recessions.

The Effects of Changes in Wealth

Changes in wealth as well as changes in income affect consumption and saving.[9] To illustrate, suppose that while rummaging through her attic, Prudence finds a passbook for a savings account that her grandmother had opened for her. Finding this passbook is a complete surprise; and when Prudence checks with the bank, she learns that the account has $6400 in it. At a current price level of $1.60 per hamburger, the real value of this increase in her wealth a is 4000 hamburgers. How will this unexpected increase in wealth affect Prudence's consumption and saving?

---

[9]Unlike the effects of current and future income, the effect of wealth on saving was not discussed in Chapter 3.

173

To test Friedman's hypothesis that permanent changes in income should have larger effects on consumption than temporary income changes do, Mark Dynarski and Steve Sheffrin* of the University of California at Davis studied the impact on workers' consumption of their becoming unemployed. Dynarski and Sheffrin divided a sample of workers into two categories: blue-collar workers (such as manufacturing production workers) and white-collar workers (office workers and managers). They found, first, that the probability of becoming unemployed during a given period of time was greater for a blue-collar worker than for a white-collar worker. This difference reflected the fact that manufacturing firms frequently lay off production workers during periods of slow demand but tend to keep office workers on. Second, blue-collar workers typically got quickly rehired when demand picked up again; but when firms had cut back and laid off white-collar workers, the layoffs were more likely to be permanent. Since it may be a long time before a laid-off white-collar worker found

BOX *5.2:* PERMANENT VERSUS TEMPORARY INCOME SHOCKS: THE EFFECTS OF UNEMPLOYMENT ON WORKERS' CONSUMPTION

another job of similar quality, the fall in income associated with becoming unemployed is more temporary for blue-collar workers than it is for white-collar workers.

The implication of the theory is that although becoming unemployed reduces the present value of income and thus should reduce consumption for all workers, the effect should be greater for white-collar workers, because the impact on their incomes is more permanent. Dynarski and Sheffrin found that, indeed, when workers became unemployed, the consumption of white-collar workers fell four times as much as that of blue-collar workers. This finding supports the implication of the permanent income theory that the more permanent a change in income is, the greater the effect on current consumption is.

*"Consumption and Unemployment," *Quarterly Journal of Economics,* May 1987, pp. 411–28.

We saw previously that changes in income affect consumption only to the extent that they affect the *PVLR*. The same is true for changes in wealth. An increase in current wealth of 4000 raises the *PVLR* by 4000; thus its effects on consumption must be the same as (for example) the effects of an increase in current income of 4000, which also raises the *PVLR* by 4000. Once again we can use Fig. 5.4 (p. 167): Prudence's increase in wealth raises her *PVLR* by 4000 and thus shifts the budget line to the right by 4000, from BL^1 to BL^2. As in the previous two cases, her optimal consumption choice goes from point *D* (before she finds the passbook) to point *M* (after her increase in wealth).

We conclude that the increase in wealth of 4000 raises both Prudence's current consumption and her future consumption, and by the same amounts as would a change in current or future income that increases her *PVLR* by 4000. Because the increase in wealth raises current consumption but leaves current income unchanged, it results in a decline in current saving. Being wealthier, Prudence doesn't have to save as much of her current income to provide for the future.

Income Effects

We have shown that changes in current income, future income, and initial wealth all lead to parallel shifts of the budget line, in each case by the amount of the change in the *PVLR*. Economists use the term *income effect* to describe the impact of any change that causes a parallel shift of the budget line. Because increases in current income, future income, or initial wealth raise current and future consumption, we say that the income effect on current and future consumption is positive.

Application

The 1987 Stock Market Crash and Consumer Spending

On October 19, 1987, stock prices took their biggest ever one-day plunge. The Standard and Poor's index of 500 stocks fell 20% in just one day; this fall came on top of a decline of 16% that had taken place since the market's peak in August. Although estimates differ, it appears that about $1 trillion of financial wealth (equal in value to nearly three months of GNP) was eliminated through declining stock values on October 19 alone.

According to our theory, how should a stock market crash affect consumption spending? There are two possible channels.

First, there is the direct effect of the crash on wealth. The crash lowered the *PVLR*s of stock market investors by $1 trillion and thus should have lowered their current consumption. The effect on current consumption, however, should have been much smaller than $1 trillion: Because consumers prefer smooth consumption, they should spread out the effects of their loss in wealth over a long period of time, reducing current consumption by much less than the full decline in wealth. To get a quick estimate of the effect of a $1 trillion fall in stock values on current consumption, suppose that consumers smooth their consumption over a twenty-five-year horizon. Assume also for simplicity that the real interest rate is zero. Then in response to a $1 trillion loss in wealth, consumers would plan to reduce their consumption in each of the next twenty-five years by 1/25 of $1 trillion, or $40 billion per year. This number is consistent with an estimate presented in the 1988 *Economic Report of the President* (p. 42) of the likely effects of a fall in stock values on current consumption.

The second way a crash could affect consumption is that it could reduce the consumption of people who don't own stock—for example, it may make them worry about what will happen to their future labor incomes. If workers fear that a market crash portends a recession, in which they may become unemployed, then they will probably expect their future income to be lower than previously thought, and they will reduce their current consumption. Surveys of consumer attitudes did find significant declines in consumer confidence in the months following the crash (see the box "In Touch with the Macroeconomy," p. 171). This effect appeared to be quite temporary, however, since consumer confidence had recovered strongly by early 1988.

What, then, was the actual effect of the October 19 crash on consumption? Consumption spending is affected by many factors and it is not easy to isolate the influence of any single one. However, C. Alan Garner[10] of the Kansas City Federal

---

[10]"Has the Stock Market Crash Reduced Consumer Spending?" *Economic Review*, Federal Reserve Bank of Kansas City, April 1988, pp. 3–16. Some of the other information in this application is also taken from this article.

Reserve Bank estimated that the crash led to a $7.5–$10 billion shortfall in consumption between October 1987 and January 1988, or $30–$40 billion at an annual rate. This range is in the ballpark for the direct impact of the change in wealth but leaves no room for an impact on expected future incomes. David Runkle[11] of the Minneapolis Federal Reserve Bank argued that, overall, the effect of the crash on the economy was surprisingly small, probably less than the $40 billion predicted.

The theory was correct, then, in predicting that the effect of the crash on consumption would be much smaller than the amount of wealth "lost" in the crash; but the effect on consumption appeared to be even smaller than the small effect predicted by the theory. Why? One possible explanation is connected with the unusually erratic behavior of stock prices during 1987. Despite the tremendous decline in stock prices after August 1987, the Standard and Poor index of stock prices actually stood at a higher level at the end of 1987 than at the end of 1986! This reflects the fact that the fall of stocks after August mirrored an equally impressive gain earlier in the year—39% between December 31, 1986, and August 25, 1987. Because the earlier increase of stock prices was so rapid, it is possible that by August 1987 stockholders had not yet fully adjusted their consumption to their higher level of wealth. Thus when the market fell, consumption did not have to decline by very much in order to fall back into line with wealth.

5.3 CONSUMPTION AND SAVING OVER MANY PERIODS: THE LIFE CYCLE MODEL

One useful interpretation of the two-period model studied in this chapter is to think of the first period as the working life and the future period as the retirement of the individual consumer. This interpretation captures the idea that much of saving is done to finance retirement. A problem with the two-period model, though, is that it cannot be used to describe some other important aspects of the consumer's lifetime income and consumption patterns. For example, the two-period model cannot capture the facts that income typically rises over most of the working life and that much saving is done for purposes other than retirement, such as for college tuitions or a home. The **life cycle model** of consumption and saving, developed in the 1950s by Nobel laureate Franco Modigliani and his associates, is a multiperiod version of the basic two-period model that focuses on the patterns of income, consumption, and saving over the various stages of an individual's life.

The essence of the life cycle model is shown in Fig. 5.6. The two lines in Fig. 5.6(a) graph the typical consumer's pattern of income and consumption against the consumer's age, from age twenty (the approximate age of economic independence) to age eighty (the approximate age of death). Two points about Fig. 5.6(a) are important.

First, as the figure shows, the average worker experiences a steadily rising real income over most of the working life. Income usually peaks when the worker is between the ages of fifty and sixty. After retirement, income (excluding interest earned from previous saving) drops fairly sharply.

---

[11]"Why No Crunch from the Crash?" *Quarterly Review*, Federal Reserve Bank of Minneapolis, Winter 1988, pp. 2–7. Interestingly, when the Japanese stock market fell sharply in the early part of 1990, the effect on consumption again appeared to be quite small.

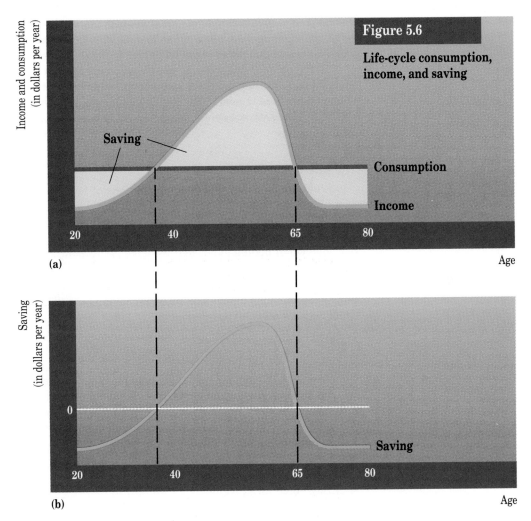

Figure 5.6

Life-cycle consumption, income, and saving

(a) Income and consumption are graphed against age. Income typically rises gradually throughout most of the working life and peaks shortly before retirement. The desire for a smooth pattern of consumption means that consumption shows much less variation over the life cycle than does income. We show consumption here as perfectly constant.

(b) Saving is the difference between income and consumption; the saving pattern is hump-shaped. Early in the working life consumption is larger than income, so saving is negative. In the middle years saving is positive; the excess of income over consumption is used to repay debts incurred earlier in life and to provide for retirement. During retirement consumers dissave.

Second, the lifetime pattern of consumption is much smoother over time than the pattern of income, which is consistent with idea of consumption smoothing discussed earlier. Because consumers value consumption in all periods, they will spread out their lifetime resources so as to maintain a fairly even standard of living. Although shown as perfectly flat in the figure, consumption, in reality, does vary some by age; for example, it will be higher during years of high child-rearing expenses.

The lifetime pattern of saving, shown in Fig. 5.6(b), is the difference between the income and consumption curves in Fig. 5.6(a). The overall pattern is hump-shaped: Saving is very low or even negative during the early working years, when income is low. Maximum saving occurs when the worker is between ages fifty and sixty, when income is highest. Finally, during retirement there is dissaving, as the worker uses accumulated wealth to meet living expenses.

An important implication of the hump-shaped pattern of saving is that national saving rates will depend on the age distribution of a country's population. Countries with unusually young or unusually old populations will have low saving rates, and countries with relatively more people in their middle years will have higher rates of saving.

The Life Cycle Model: An Example

Some additional insight into the implications of the life cycle model can be gained from a simple example. Imagine a consumer who is "young" for twenty years, "middle-aged" for twenty years, and "retired" for twenty years (after which he dies). He earns a salary of $20,000 per year when young, earns a salary of $60,000 per year when middle-aged, and receives retirement benefits of $10,000 per year when retired (all incomes are in real terms). He has no initial wealth.

Suppose that the real interest rate is zero, so that the present value of any future income just equals the future income itself. Then the consumer's *PVLR* simply equals total lifetime earnings:

$$PVLR = \text{total lifetime income}$$
$$= (20 \times \$20,000) + (20 \times \$60,000) + (20 \times \$10,000) = \$1,800,000.$$

Suppose also that the consumer is an extreme consumption smoother—that is, he tries to keep his annual real consumption at a constant level *c* for each of his sixty adult years. With a zero real interest rate, the present value of his consumption is 60 × *c*. The budget constraint, which states that the present value of consumption must equal the *PVLR*, is therefore

$$\text{present value of consumption} = 60 \times c = PVLR = \$1,800,000.$$

When we solve for *c*, we get

$$c = \$30,000.$$

If his consumption is $30,000 per year, what will the consumer's pattern of saving be in this example? When the consumer is young, earning $20,000 per year and consuming $30,000 per year, his saving will be −$10,000 per year (he will dissave, borrowing to do so). During middle age he will save $60,000 − $30,000 = $30,000 per year. Finally, during retirement the consumer will dissave at the rate of $20,000 per year (his saving will be $10,000 − $30,000 = −$20,000 per year). This example thus captures the life cycle model's prediction of a hump-shaped pattern of saving.

Bequests and Saving

In the two-period model discussed earlier, as well as in the example of the life cycle model just given, we assumed that the consumer plans to consume all his wealth and income during his lifetime, leaving nothing to heirs. Empirically, however, many people do leave bequests, or inheritances, to children, charities, and so on. What effect does a **bequest motive**, or a desire to leave inheritances, have on saving behavior?

In the life cycle example just given, for example, suppose that the consumer doesn't plan to consume all of his economic resources but wants to leave $120,000 to his heirs. Since the consumer's life spans sixty years, he can achieve this bequest by reducing his consumption and increasing his saving by $2000 in each year. (Remember that the real interest rate is zero.) We conclude that to the extent that consumers desire to leave bequests, they will save more relative to the situation in which they simply consume all of their resources during their lifetimes.

Application

Why Do the Japanese Save So Much?

The Japanese are known for their high saving rate, especially in comparison with the saving rate in the United States. To some extent, the perceived difference between Japan and the United States may be due to differences in accounting practices. For example, the Japanese count government investment projects, such as roads, as part of national saving, but the United States does not. Even with corrections, though, the Japanese saving rate seems to be significantly higher.

A number of possible explanations for high Japanese saving were examined by Fumio Hayashi of the University of Pennsylvania.[12] Several of these explanations were related to life cycle factors. The life-cycle explanations included the following:

1. *Population age structure.* The Japanese have among the world's highest life expectancies and thus long expected retirements. To finance these long retirements, they must save more during working years. The Japanese also had a postwar baby boom, followed by a population growth slowdown, which means that a relatively large proportion of the population is now middle-aged, the peak saving period.

2. *High income growth.* Because of Japan's rapid economic growth in the past forty years, current Japanese workers earn much higher real incomes than their now-retired parents did when they were working in the 1950s or 1960s. Thus current workers can plan to consume more when they retire than their parents did. This implies that current workers will save much more than current retirees are dissaving, leading to a high aggregate saving rate for the country as a whole.[13]

3. *High housing and land prices, plus high required down payments.* Despite recent decreases, Japanese housing prices are fantastically high. Although Japan is only about the size of California, the total market value of its land exceeds the market value of all the land in the United States by a considerable margin. Potential home buyers not only must face these high prices but also must make down payments that in percentage terms are much higher than in the United States. Thus young people frequently must save for years in order to buy a home.

---

[12]"Why Is Japan's Saving Rate So Apparently High?" in Stanley Fischer, ed., *NBER Macroeconomics Annual*, Cambridge, Mass.: MIT Press, 1986.

[13]Numerical Problem 5 further develops the relationship of income growth and saving.

4. *High bequests.* Japanese customarily leave large bequests, perhaps in reciprocity for the fact that many elderly Japanese live with their children. In order to be able to leave large bequests, the Japanese must save more during their working lives.

Hayashi's paper gives a detailed discussion of these factors. Although all the factors may make contributions, his tentative conclusion is that in recent years the desire to leave large bequests may be the single most important cause of high Japanese saving.

5.4   BORROWING CONSTRAINTS AND CONSUMPTION

In developing our two-period model of consumption and saving, we have assumed that consumers can borrow and lend as much as they choose at a single, given real interest rate. Borrowing is necessary to achieve the desired level of current consumption when that level of consumption exceeds the sum of the consumer's current income and initial assets.

Realistically, though, the ability of consumers to borrow against their future income is often limited.[14] There are good economic reasons for these limitations on borrowing. Consider the case of a starving business student who fully expects to be a millionaire corporate raider someday. According to the model, she should be borrowing against her future millions in order to enjoy champagne and caviar today. However, the loan officer at the bank—not knowing the student's plans, ability, and motivation as well as she does—may not be as sure as she is about her future success and thus will be uncertain about whether a loan, if made, will be paid back. The loan officer may also worry about the effects of a loan on the student's incentive to work: In the future, realizing that much of her earnings would have to go to making loan repayments anyway, the student may decide not to be a corporate raider but to default on the loan and become a beachcomber. For these reasons the bank will decline to make the loan in the first place. If she cannot get a loan against her future income, the business student will not be able to consume as much today as the basic two-period model predicts.

A restriction imposed by lenders on the amount that someone can borrow against future income is called a **borrowing constraint**. Borrowing constraints may modify the consumption-saving decision. In particular, as we will see, borrowing constraints may increase the degree to which current consumption responds to changes in current income.

To study the impact of borrowing constraints, let's suppose that Prudence is unable to borrow at all against future income. Prudence's inability to borrow implies that her current consumption c cannot be greater than her currently available resources, equal to her current income y plus her initial wealth a. In algebraic terms, the borrowing constraint implies

$$c \leq y + a. \tag{5.6}$$

Though she cannot borrow, we assume that Prudence can still save and earn interest at rate r.

---

[14]Most consumer borrowing is used to finance purchases of housing or consumer durables. In those cases the consumer has an asset—the house or the durable—that the bank can seize if payments are not made on time. In contrast, if borrowing is done to finance a level of current consumption that exceeds current income and assets, there may be no assets for the bank to take if the payments aren't made.

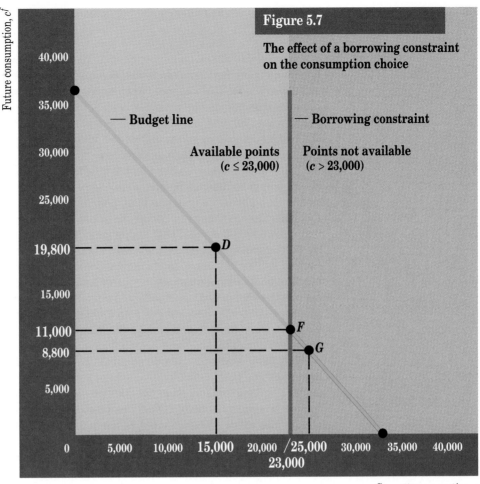

Figure 5.7

The effect of a borrowing constraint on the consumption choice

Future consumption, c^f

— **Budget line**

Available points
($c \leq 23,000$)

— **Borrowing constraint**

Points not available
($c > 23,000$)

Current consumption, c

If Prudence cannot borrow, then in the current period she cannot consume more than 23,000, the sum of her initial wealth and current income. Thus points to the right of the vertical line, for which $c > 23,000$, are unavailable to Prudence. If her favorite point on the entire budget line is point D, then she has no need to borrow; and the borrowing constraint does not affect her behavior. In this case the borrowing constraint is nonbinding. However, if her favorite point on the entire budget line is point G, which would require her to borrow, then the borrowing constraint is binding. Because the borrowing constraint prevents her from reaching point G, the best Prudence can do is to choose point F, at the intersection of the vertical line and the budget line. Point F, which requires that Prudence consume all her current income and wealth in the current period, is the point closest to point G that is available to Prudence.

The presence of a borrowing constraint does not affect Prudence's preferences for current and future consumption; it only affects the set of consumption combinations that are available to her. To see how this works in a numerical example, let's assume as before that Prudence's current real income y is 20,000 hamburgers, her future real income y^f is 11,000 hamburgers, her initial wealth a is 3000 hamburgers, and the real interest rate r she can earn on her saving is 10%. In this case, as before, Prudence's *PVLR* is 33,000 hamburgers. However, the borrowing constraint, Eq. (5.6), says that Prudence's current consumption must be less than the sum of her current income and initial wealth, or 23,000. To consume more than 23,000 in the current period, Prudence would have to borrow, which we assume is not allowed.

The effects of the borrowing constraint are shown in Fig. 5.7. The downward-sloping line is Prudence's budget line, just as in Fig. 5.1. Also shown in the figure is a vertical line at the point $c = 23,000$. The vertical line captures the effect of the borrowing constraint: Points to the right of the vertical line, at which $c > 23,000$, are not available to Prudence, even though they lie on the budget line. They are not available because in order for her current consumption to exceed 23,000, Prudence would have to borrow, which she is not allowed to do. However, points on the budget line on or to the left of the vertical line, for which $c \leq 23,000$, do not require borrowing and thus are available to Prudence as before.

How does the borrowing constraint affect Prudence's consumption-saving decision? Suppose that, as before, Prudence's most preferred consumption combination on the entire budget line is at point D, where $c = 15,000$ and $c^f = 19,800$. Prudence does not have to borrow to get to point D (it is to the left of the vertical line). Since D is the point that maximizes Prudence's utility and it is not ruled out by the borrowing constraint, she will choose it; and her consumption and saving choices will be the same as if there were no borrowing constraint at all. A **nonbinding borrowing constraint** occurs when a consumer would not want to borrow even in the absence of a borrowing constraint. *A nonbinding borrowing constraint has no effect on the consumer's consumption or saving behavior.* Since Prudence wouldn't want to borrow anyway, the fact that she is not allowed to borrow does not affect her decisions.[15]

Suppose, however, that Prudence's most preferred point on the budget line happens to be point G in Fig. 5.7, where $c = 25,000$ and $c^f = 8800$. At point G the level of current consumption (25,000) exceeds the total of Prudence's current income and wealth (23,000). If there were no borrowing constraints, Prudence could borrow the extra 2000 hamburgers needed to reach consumption of 25,000 in the current period. However, if borrowing is not allowed, Prudence cannot obtain the consumption combination at point G. In terms of the diagram point G is to the right of the vertical line that defines the borrowing constraint and therefore is not available to Prudence.

Given that she cannot reach her favorite point G, what will Prudence do? If Prudence's most preferred consumption combination is at point G, where current consumption is very high and future consumption is very low, then she must be very impatient, strongly preferring current to future consumption. To satisfy her preference for current consumption, Prudence will enjoy as much current consumption as the borrowing constraint allows. The most current consumption she can obtain without borrowing is 23,000, which is the sum of her current income and initial wealth. If Prudence consumes all of her current income and wealth, she will have no resources left to carry over to the future period, and her future consumption will equal her future income of 11,000.

Prudence's choice of current consumption of 23,000 and future consumption of 11,000 corresponds to point F in Fig. 5.7. Point F is the point where the vertical line defining the borrowing constraint intersects the budget line. Prudence picks point F because it is the point among those available to her that is closest to her most preferred consumption combination at point G.

When a consumer would like to borrow but is prevented from doing so, we say that there is a **binding borrowing constraint.** Our example shows that *if there is a binding borrowing constraint, the consumer will spend all available current*

---

[15]Technical note: This statement is precisely true only in a two-period model. In a multiperiod model, if Prudence is concerned that she might face a binding borrowing constraint at some time in the future, she might decide to increase her saving today in order to have less need to borrow in the future.

income and wealth on current consumption. The consumer consumes all her current resources in order to come as close as possible to the consumption combination she would have chosen in the absence of borrowing constraints.

In the basic model with no borrowing constraints, we saw that an increase in current income raises current consumption only to the extent that the income increase raises the *PVLR*. Thus, for example, a temporary increase in current income has less of an effect on current consumption than a permanent increase. The result in the borrowing-constrained case is different: Because a consumer facing a binding borrowing constraint spends all her current income and wealth on current consumption, she consumes *all* of any increase in current income, irrespective of whether the increase is temporary or permanent.[16] Since an unconstrained consumer saves part of an increase in current income, the effect of a current income increase on current consumption is greater for a borrowing-constrained consumer than for an unconstrained consumer. From a macroeconomic perspective this result implies that—if a significant number of consumers face binding borrowing constraints—the response of aggregate consumption to an increase in aggregate income (output) will be greater than is implied by the basic theory without borrowing constraints.

Empirically, how prevalent are borrowing constraints in the U.S. economy? This is a controversial question. However, several studies have estimated that during any given year somewhere between 20% and 50% of U.S. consumers face binding borrowing constraints.[17]

Application

Home Equity Lines and Household Saving

One of the many innovations in U.S. financial markets during the past dozen years has been the increased availability of home equity lines of credit (HELs). Home equity lines (technically a form of second mortgage, usually offered by a bank or savings and loan association) allow homeowners to borrow against the value of the equity in their house, often just by writing a check when funds are needed.[18] This contrasts with earlier periods, when borrowing against one's home at any time other than the initial purchase date was typically a complex and costly process.

The increased use of HELs during the 1980s coincided with a period of unusually low household saving in the United States. Could these two phenomena have been related? Possibly they were, if the increasing availability of HELs reduced the number of consumers facing borrowing constraints. The theory says that if a

---

[16]This statement assumes that after the increase in income the consumer still faces a binding borrowing constraint.

[17]See, for example, John Y. Campbell and N. Gregory Mankiw, "Consumption, Income, and Interest Rates: Reinterpreting the Time Series Evidence," in O. Blanchard and S. Fischer, eds., *NBER Macroeconomics Annual*, Cambridge, Mass.: MIT Press, 1989; and Robert E. Hall and Frederic S. Mishkin, "The Sensitivity of Consumption to Transitory Income: Estimates from Panel Data on Households," *Econometrica*, March 1982, pp. 461–81.

[18]A homeowner's equity in her house is the value of the house minus the value of any mortgage she owes against the house. Consumer use of home equity lines was particularly stimulated by tax law changes in 1986, which eliminated the tax deductibility of interest on most types of consumer debt but *not* on home equity lines and other mortgages. However, growth in this type of borrowing had been strong even before 1986.

borrowing-constrained consumer is suddenly told that he will now be able to borrow (because HELs have become available), he will do so in order to increase his consumption. Higher consumption by users of HELs implies lower aggregate saving. On the other hand, to the extent that people borrow against their homes to pay off other debts, to make financial investments, or to make purchases they would have made anyway, increased home equity borrowing need not lead to lower saving.

The empirical evidence provides modest support for the view that increased availability of HELs reduced saving in the United States. In a study of individual families[19] Joyce Manchester of Dartmouth and James Poterba of the Massachusetts Institute of Technology found that with family characteristics held constant, each extra dollar of second-mortgage borrowing was associated with about 75 cents less total saving by the family. This finding is at least consistent with the view that use of HELs has depressed saving. If each extra dollar of HEL borrowing did indeed cause a 75-cent reduction in saving, then the expansion of HELs would explain about a third of the drop in U.S. household saving in the 1980s.

The international evidence also seems consistent with the view that HELs reduce saving. Because of differences in regulation and banking practices, countries differ widely in the amount that consumers are allowed to borrow against their home. For example, in Italy and Japan consumers are required to make down payments equal to 40% of the value of a home they want to purchase; the percentage is 10%–25% in the United States. In those countries it is also difficult for people who already own homes to borrow against them. These restrictions on homeowner borrowing tend to be associated with higher national saving rates. In particular, Italy and Japan are both high-saving countries.[20]

5.5   CHAPTER SUMMARY

1. The amount that an individual or family consumes in the present and in the future depends on both economic resources and preferences. Economic resources, including wealth, current income, and income that is expected to be received in the future, determine the combinations of current consumption and future consumption that are available. The individual's or family's preferences determine which of the available combinations of current and future consumption is chosen. Saving equals current income minus the chosen level of current consumption.

2. For any possible level of current consumption, the budget constraint shows how much future consumption an individual can afford, given the individual's economic resources. The graph of the budget constraint, in a diagram with current consumption on the horizontal axis and future consumption on the vertical axis, is called the budget line. The budget line is downward sloping, because an increase in current consumption implies less saving and thus less consumption in the future.

---

[19]"Second Mortgages and Household Saving," *Regional Science and Urban Economics*, May 1989, pp. 325–46.

[20]See Tullio Jappelli and Marco Pagano, "Consumption and Capital Market Imperfections: An International Comparison," *American Economic Review*, December 1989, pp. 1088–1105, for international evidence on the link between consumer credit markets and consumption behavior.

3. Present values measure the value of payments to be made in the future in terms of today's dollars. The budget constraint can be expressed in terms of present values: The present value of an individual's consumption equals her present value of lifetime resources (*PVLR*). Thus a change in income or wealth affects an individual's consumption opportunities only to the extent that it changes her *PVLR*. A change in income or wealth that increases the *PVLR* causes the budget line to make a parallel shift to the right by the amount of the increase in the *PVLR*.

4. Two factors that influence people's consumption and saving choices are the consumption-smoothing motive and their degree of patience. The consumption-smoothing motive implies that people prefer a steady path of consumption over time to a consumption path that involves some periods of very high consumption and other periods of very low consumption. The more patient a consumer is, the more willing she is to accept lower consumption today in order to save more for the future.

5. An increase in current income, expected future income, or initial wealth raises the *PVLR* and shifts the budget line to the right, leading to increases in both current and future consumption. An increase in current income raises saving, but increases in future income or initial wealth—because they increase current consumption without raising current income—reduce saving. The effects of any parallel shift in the budget line are called income effects.

6. Friedman's permanent income theory of consumption and saving predicts that permanent increases in income, because they have a larger effect on the individual's *PVLR*, should have a larger effect on current consumption than temporary increases in income.

7. Modigliani's life cycle model of consumption and saving focuses on patterns of income, consumption, and saving over the stages of an individual's life. Because income is highest in an individual's middle years and because, owing to the consumption-smoothing motive, consumption is relatively constant over time, the life cycle model predicts that middle-aged people will have high saving and people in their early working years or in retirement will have low or negative saving.

8. A limit that lenders impose on the amount a consumer can borrow is called a borrowing constraint. Borrowing constraints do not affect the consumption of people who would not want to borrow anyway, but they reduce the current consumption of consumers who would like to borrow. For a consumer who would like to borrow but is unable to, current consumption equals current income plus wealth. If a borrowing-constrained consumer receives an increase in current income, he spends all of it on current consumption.

Key Terms

bequest motive, p. 178
binding borrowing
  constraint, p. 182
borrowing constraint,
  p. 180
budget constraint,
  p. 157
budget line, p. 158

consumption-smoothing
  motive, p. 164
forward-looking
  consumer, p. 155
life cycle model, p. 176
nonbinding borrowing
  constraint, p. 182

permanent income
  theory, p. 170
present value of lifetime
  resources (*PVLR*),
  p. 160
present value, p. 159
utility, p. 166

Key Equations

$$c^f = (y + a - c)(1 + r) + y^f \qquad (5.2)$$

For any possible level of current consumption c, the *budget constraint* shows how much future consumption c^f the consumer can afford, given current income y, future income y^f, and initial wealth a.

$$\text{present value} = \frac{\text{dollar amount of future payment}}{(1 + i)^n} \qquad (5.3)$$

The equation gives the formula for the present value of a nominal payment to be made n years in the future, assuming a constant nominal interest rate i.

$$c + \frac{c^f}{1 + r} = y + \frac{y^f}{1 + r} + a \qquad (5.5)$$

An alternative way to state the budget constraint, Eq. (5.2), is that the present value of lifetime consumption, $c + c^f/(1 + r)$, equals the present value of lifetime resources (*PVLR*), $y + y^f/(1 + r) + a$.

Review Questions

1. Explain why the consumer's consumption and saving decisions are really the same decision. What two general factors affect an individual's decision about how much to consume in the present and in the future?

2. Without using numbers or equations, sketch a consumer's budget line, labeling the axes of the graph. What can be said about points that lie on the budget line? Why does the budget line have the slope it does? If the budget line you have drawn were to shift to the left, would the consumer be better off or worse off? Why?

3. How is the present value of a given future payment affected if the interest rate rises? If the time until the payment is to be received increases? In words, how can the consumer's budget constraint be expressed in terms of present values?

4. How do the consumption-smoothing motive and the degree of patience affect the consumer's choice of current and future consumption?

5. What are the effects on current consumption and saving of an increase in current income? An increase in expected future income? An increase in wealth? Explain.

6. Compare the effects of a $1000 permanent increase in income on current consumption, future consumption, and saving with the effects of a $1000 temporary increase in income. Explain your answer by using the concept of the *PVLR*.

7. According to the life cycle model, when during a consumer's life is saving likely to be high? When is saving likely to be low? Explain.

8. Define *borrowing constraint*, and distinguish between binding and nonbinding borrowing constraints. Does your answer to Review Question 6 change if there is a binding borrowing constraint? If there is a nonbinding borrowing constraint?

Numerical Problems

1. A consumer has real initial wealth of 50, current real income of 100, and future real income of 132. The real interest rate is 10% per period.

a. Find the *PVLR*.

b. Write the equation for the consumer's budget constraint, and graph the budget line.

Suppose that the consumer's goal is to smooth consumption completely. That is, he wants to have the same level of consumption in the current and future periods.

c. How much will he save and consume in the current period?

d. How will his current saving and consumption be affected by an increase of 11 in current income?

e. How will his current saving and consumption be affected by an increase of 11 in future income?

f. How will his current saving and consumption be affected by an increase of 11 in his initial wealth?

2. You are taking out a $100,000 mortgage. You are offered two options: First, you can repay $10,000 at the end of each of the first four years after you get the loan, then repay $110,000 at the end of the fifth year. Or second, you can repay $12,000 at the end of each of the first four years, then repay $100,000 at the end of the fifth year. At a 10% constant annual interest rate, which option is the better deal in present value terms?

3. In a particular town there are 2000 people, each of whom makes consumption and saving plans over a current period and a future period. All of the people desire to smooth consumption completely (that is, set current and future consumption equal), if possible. For 1000 of the people current income is 120 and future income is 100. For the remaining 1000 people current income is 100 and future income is 120. There is no initial wealth. The real interest rate is zero (and is unaffected by decisions made by people in the town). People can freely borrow from and lend to people in other towns at the fixed real interest rate.

a. What is the town's aggregate consumption in the current period?

b. What is the effect on aggregate consumption if all consumers receive a temporary $10 increase in current income?

c. What is the effect on aggregate consumption if all consumers receive a permanent $10 increase in income?

Suppose that consumers are not allowed to borrow, but they may save if they want.

d. What is the value of the town's aggregate consumption in the current period?

e. What is the effect on aggregate consumption if all consumers receive a temporary $10 increase in current income?

f. What is the effect on aggregate consumption if all consumers receive a permanent $10 increase in income?

4. A consumer lives three periods, called the learning period, the working period, and the retirement period. Her income is 200 during the learning period, 800 during the working period, and 200 again during the retirement period. The consumer's initial assets are 300. The real interest rate is zero. The consumer desires perfectly smooth consumption over her lifetime.

a. What are consumption and saving in each period, assuming no borrowing constraints? What happens if the consumer faces a borrowing constraint?

b. Assume that the consumer's initial wealth is zero instead of 300. Repeat part a. Does being borrowing-constrained mean that consumption is lower in all periods of life than it would be if there were no borrowing constraints?

5. This problem discusses the relationship between the rate of income growth in a country and its rate of saving. (See item 2 in the application "Why Do the Japanese Save So Much?" p. 179.)

An economy lasts three periods. One hundred people called "parents" live during the first and second periods. Each parent earns a real income of 10,000 in the first period and earns nothing (is retired) in the second period. Parents desire to have equal consumption in their working life and in retirement. The real interest rate is zero in all periods.

One hundred people called "children" live during the second and third periods. Children each earn a real income of $(1 + g)$ times 10,000 in the second period, where g is the real growth rate of the economy. Children earn no income (are retired) in the third period. Children also desire perfectly even consumption over their lives.

Calculate total saving (adding the saving of parents and children) during the second period, assuming a growth rate $g = 0$. (*Hint:* Remember that parents dissave during retirement.) What happens if $g = 0.10$? If $g = 0.50$? How is saving in the second period related in general to the growth rate of the economy?

Analytical Problems

1. During the period in which Congress was passing legislation to bail out the savings and loan industry, estimates of $500 billion for the total cost of the cleanup were often cited by the press. This estimate was calculated by adding actual bailout costs plus associated interest costs over a period of many years.

    This question is intended to get you to think about the reasonableness of this way of estimating the cost of the savings and loan bailout. For concreteness, imagine that it costs $1 billion this year to completely pay off the depositors of a particular savings and loan. Congress finances this $1 billion payment by using $100 million from tax revenues and borrowing the remaining $900 million from the public. Assuming that the interest rate is 10%, this borrowing leads to $90 million in interest costs in each of the next five years. At the end of the fifth year the $900 million principal is paid off from tax revenues. The media report the total cost of this operation as $1.450 billion: $100 million in initial payouts, $450 million in interest payments ($90 million per year for five years), plus the final $900 million payment. What is the problem with the media's cost estimate? (*Hint:* Use the idea of present value.)

2. If you are a forward-looking consumer with no borrowing constraints, how would each of the following affect your current consumption and saving?

   a. You are informed that a long-lost relative has left you a large bequest. However, the bequest is to be kept in a trust, and you will not be able to withdraw any of the money for ten years.

   b. Your doctor tells you that you have an amazingly healthy constitution and you should easily live to age ninety. This prediction does not change your plan to retire at age sixty-five in order to perfect your fishing skills.

   c. You are a taxpayer, and you read in the paper that your state government's deficit is much worse than thought. A tax increase next year now seems inevitable.

   d. You work in the auto industry and read in the newspaper that a serious recession and tough foreign competition are predicted to drive down car sales.

   e. Your son's dentist tells you that in three or four years he will need a very expensive set of braces.

   f. After several years of litigation you receive an insurance award compensating you for losses incurred in a fire. Though fairly large, the award is less than what you had been expecting.

3. To derive the budget constraint (Eq. 5.2), we assumed that Prudence's current consumption was less than her current resources, so that she had some leftover resources to put into the bank until the future period. Show that the budget constraint (Eq. 5.2) still holds if Prudence's current consumption exceeds her current resources. (*Hint:* In this case Prudence must borrow an amount equal to the difference between her consumption and her resources in the current period and then repay this amount with interest in the future period. Her future consumption then equals her future income less her loan repayment.)

4. Many taxpayers have more income withheld from their paychecks than they owe in taxes, with the result that after filing their tax returns, they receive refund checks from the Internal Revenue Service. In early 1985 the installation of a new computer system at the IRS delayed the processing of individual income tax returns. During February and March, a period in which many refund checks are usually mailed out, relatively few got processed. However, as the new computer came on line, the IRS moved to catch up: Refunds were above normal in April and much higher than normal in May. By June nearly all refunds had been mailed out, as is usually the case. The upshot was that the aggregate income of U.S. consumers, including tax refunds, was noticeably below normal in February and March and higher than normal in April, May, and June.

    Some economic forecasters predicted that the IRS's computer problems would lead to a weakening in February and March consumer purchases. Discuss this prediction. Is it consistent with the permanent income theory? What happens if many consumers have binding borrowing constraints?[21]

---

[21]This problem is based on David W. Wilcox, "Income Tax Refunds and the Timing of Consumption Expenditure," Board of Governors of the Federal Reserve System, revised May 1990. Wilcox found that, empirically, the delay in making refunds did not affect the timing of consumer purchases.

6
Saving, Investment, and the Real Interest Rate

The saving decisions of households and the investment decisions of firms are among the most important decisions made in the economy. The rate of saving helps determine how quickly national wealth accumulates and the level to which living standards can rise. The rate of investment determines the amount of capital that workers have to use and thus has a significant impact on how much output the nation can produce. Because it is a large and volatile component of total spending, investment also plays an important role in business cycle fluctuations.

Saving and investment decisions are closely interrelated. Both are intertemporal decisions, or decisions that involve a trade-off between the present and the future. More fundamentally, the saving and investment decisions made in an economy must be consistent with each other. As we saw in Chapter 3, when the goods market is in equilibrium, desired national saving and desired investment are equal. The economic variable that adjusts to ensure that desired saving and investment are equal is the expected real interest rate.

In this chapter we continue our study of saving and investment, paying particular attention to the links between these decisions and the real interest rate. Building on our analysis of consumer behavior in Chapter 5, in the first part of the chapter we consider how changes in the real interest rate available to savers influence the amount that they consume and save. One reason to study the link between the real interest rate and saving is that, in practice, many government policies attempt to influence saving behavior by affecting the real rate of interest that savers receive. For example, Individual Retirement Accounts (IRAs), which the U.S. government introduced in the hope of stimulating saving, increase the rate of return earned by savers. We use our analysis of the relationship between saving and the real interest rate to discuss the effects of IRAs and similar types of policies.

Next, we look at how a firm decides how much to invest. The amount of investment that firms do depends on the profitability of adding new capital goods, which in turn depends on factors such as the productivity of capital, interest rates, and taxes. We apply the concepts developed in this section to the analysis of several issues concerning investment, including the question of why a smaller portion of GNP is devoted to investment in the United States than in countries such as Germany and Japan.

Once we have outlined the basic factors that influence saving and investment, we look more closely at one factor that has potentially important effects on a nation's saving and investment: the government's fiscal policy (its taxing and spending decisions). Specifically, we discuss how the size of the government's budget deficit affects the economy's national saving, investment, and the real interest rate. The question of how the deficit affects the economy is as controversial as it is important, and thus we focus as much on clarifying the issues in the debate as on trying to give a final answer.

6.1   THE REAL INTEREST RATE AND THE SAVING DECISION

In Chapter 5 we focused on the effects of changes in income and wealth on consumption and saving, holding constant the real interest rate. Now we consider what happens to consumption and saving when the real interest rate changes.

In public discussion (for example, of tax policies to promote saving) it is often assumed that a higher real rate of return, because it raises the reward to saving, will cause people to save more. But as we mentioned in Chapter 3, this assumption is not necessarily true. Because a change in the real interest rate has two offsetting effects on saving, it is possible that a higher real interest rate could increase or reduce saving. The evidence suggests that a higher real interest rate raises saving, but by how much is uncertain.

The Real Interest Rate and Saving in the Two-Period Model: Prudence Again

To see what economic theory has to say about the effects of a change in the real interest rate on consumption and saving, let's bring back Prudence and the two-period model and work out a numerical example. As in the example of Chapter 5, we assume that for Prudence

$$y = \text{current income} = 20{,}000,$$
$$y^f = \text{future income} = 11{,}000,$$
$$a = \text{initial wealth} = 3000,$$
$$r = \text{real interest rate} = 10\%,$$

where wealth and incomes are measured in real terms (hamburgers).

As we showed in Chapter 5, Prudence's present value of lifetime resources $(PVLR)$ in this example is 33,000: 20,000 in current income, plus 11,000/1.10 = 10,000 in present value of future income, plus 3000 in initial wealth. Prudence's budget line, which is the same as in Fig. 5.1, is shown in Fig. 6.1 as the line BL^1.

The budget line describes the combinations of current and future consumption that are available to Prudence. Because the real interest rate that Prudence earns on her saving or pays on her borrowing affects how much she will be able to consume in the future, a change in the real interest rate will change the position of Prudence's budget line. To illustrate, we consider what happens if the real interest rate makes the very large increase from 10% to 60%.

The Real Interest Rate and the Budget Line   To see how Prudence's budget line is affected when the real interest rate rises, let's first consider point F on the budget line in Fig. 6.1, where current consumption is 23,000 and future consumption is 11,000. If she chooses this consumption combination, Prudence neither borrows nor

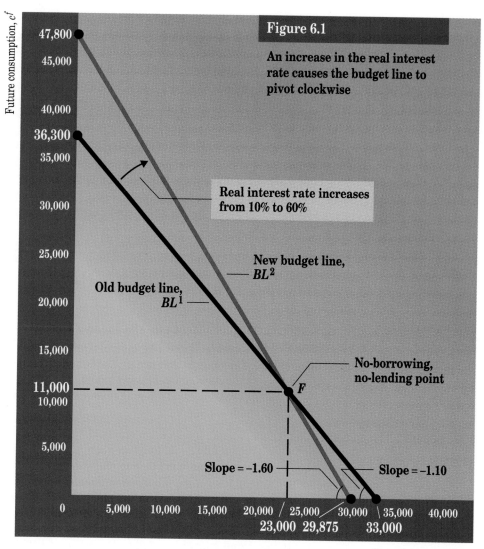

Figure 6.1

An increase in the real interest rate causes the budget line to pivot clockwise

Real interest rate increases from 10% to 60%

New budget line, BL^2

Old budget line, BL^1

No-borrowing, no-lending point

F

Slope = −1.60

Slope = −1.10

Current consumption, c

The figure shows the effect on Prudence's budget line of an increase in the real interest rate r from 10% to 60%. Because the slope of a budget line is $-(1 + r)$ and the initial real interest is 10%, the slope of Prudence's initial budget line BL^1 is −1.10. The initial budget line BL^1 also passes through the no-borrowing, no-lending point F, the consumption point that Prudence obtains by spending all current income and wealth on current consumption. Since point F can still be obtained when the real interest rate rises, that point also lies on the new budget line BL^2. However, the slope of BL^2 is −1.60, reflecting the rise in the real interest rate to 60%. Thus the higher real interest rate causes the budget line to pivot clockwise around the no-borrowing, no-lending point.

has any leftover current resources to deposit in (lend to) the bank. Thus point F is the no-borrowing, no-lending point. To confirm this result, note that the sum of Prudence's initial wealth (3000) and current income (20,000) is 23,000; so if her first-period consumption also equals 23,000, Prudence consumes all of her current resources and carries over neither debts nor wealth to the second period.

Because point F in Fig. 6.1 involves neither borrowing nor lending, the consumption combination represented by point F will be available to Prudence no matter what the real interest rate is. By consuming all her current income and wealth, Prudence was able to obtain point F when the real interest rate was 10%; by using the same strategy, she is still able to obtain the consumption combination at point F when the real interest rate is 60%. Thus *the no-borrowing, no-lending point* F *remains on the budget line when the real interest rate changes.*

The next step in figuring out how Prudence's budget line changes when the real interest rate rises is to recall from Chapter 5 that the slope of the budget line equals $-(1 + r)$. When the real interest rate r rises from 10% to 60%, the slope of the budget line therefore changes from -1.10 to -1.60; that is, the new budget line is steeper. Knowing one point on the new budget line (point F) and the slope of the new budget line (-1.60) is enough information to draw the complete new budget line, shown as BL^2 in Fig. 6.1. Comparing BL^2 with the old budget line BL^1, you can see that *an increase in the real interest rate causes a clockwise pivot of the budget line around the no-borrowing, no-lending point*, point F. Similarly, a fall in the real interest rate would cause a counterclockwise pivot of the budget line around point F.

The Substitution Effect and the Income Effect

Because an increase in the real interest rate changes the combinations of current and future consumption that are available to Prudence, it may cause her to change the amounts that she consumes and saves. There are two ways in which a change in the real interest rate can affect the consumption-saving decision: the substitution effect and the income effect.

The Substitution Effect If Prudence consumes one hamburger less today, increasing her saving by one hamburger, she will be able to consume $1 + r$ additional hamburgers in the future. Thus when the real interest rate r increases, the amount of future consumption that can be obtained in exchange for giving up a unit of current consumption rises. Effectively, a higher real interest rate makes future consumption cheaper, relative to current consumption.

In the same way that a fall in the price of coffee relative to the price of tea leads consumers to buy more coffee and less tea, a fall in the price of future consumption relative to current consumption leads consumers to switch from current consumption toward future consumption—that is, they save more. The tendency of consumers to save more in response to a higher reward for saving is called the **substitution effect,** because a higher real interest rate causes savers to substitute future consumption for current consumption. It is the substitution effect that people have in mind when they argue that a higher real interest rate raises saving by increasing the reward to saving.

The substitution effect is illustrated graphically in Fig. 6.2. The original budget line, BL^1, is the budget line when the real interest rate is 10%. We imagine that Prudence had initially chosen to consume at the no-borrowing, no-lending point F, which lies on the original budget line. When the real interest rate rises from 10% to 60%, the budget line pivots clockwise. The new budget line is shown as BL^2, just as in Fig. 6.1.

How will the pivot of the budget line affect Prudence's consumption-saving choice? Because Prudence's original consumption point, the no-borrowing, no-lend-

We assume that initially Prudence consumes at the no-borrowing, no-lending point F, which lies on her original budget line BL^1. An increase in the real interest rate from 10% to 60% causes the budget line to pivot clockwise from BL^1 to the new budget line BL^2. Point F lies on BL^2 and thus is still available to Prudence. However, because the higher real interest rate increases the reward to saving, Prudence changes her consumption from point F to point V on the new budget line BL^2. The fall in current consumption and the increase in saving between point F and point V represents the substitution effect of the increase in the real interest rate.

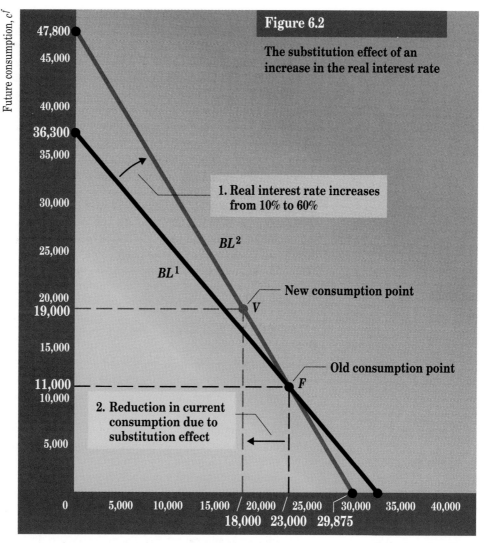

Figure 6.2

The substitution effect of an increase in the real interest rate

1. **Real interest rate increases from 10% to 60%**

2. **Reduction in current consumption due to substitution effect**

New consumption point

Old consumption point

Current consumption, c

ing point F, also lies on the new budget line BL^2, she has the option of remaining at point F and enjoying the same combination of current and future consumption as before. However, because the budget line is now steeper (reflecting the higher real interest rate), any additional saving that Prudence does will bring her a higher reward in terms of extra future consumption. In response to this increased incentive to save, we assume that Prudence reduces her current consumption and moves from point F to point V on BL^2. The reduction in current consumption and the increase in saving between points F and V reflect the substitution effect of a higher real interest rate on Prudence's saving.

The Income Effect   When the real interest rate rises, savers earn a higher return, which makes them better off. More precisely, as we will see, an increase in the real interest rate increases the amount of current and future consumption that a saver can enjoy. Since a saver is effectively made richer by an increase in the real interest rate, she will on this account tend to increase her current consumption and reduce her saving! The tendency of consumers to save less in response to being economically better off is called the **income effect** of an increase in the real interest rate.[1] Because the income effect of a higher real interest rate acts to reduce saving, it works in the opposite direction as the substitution effect.

The full impact of an increase in the real interest rate on Prudence's saving, including both the substitution effect and the income effect, is shown in Fig. 6.3. As before, Prudence's original budget line is BL^1. However, we assume now that Prudence's plan before the increase in the real interest rate was to consume at point D on BL^1, where current consumption is 15,000 and future consumption is 19,800. Since Prudence's current income is 20,000, her choice of point D implies that she originally planned to save 5000.

The increase in the real interest rate from 10% to 60% causes Prudence's budget line to pivot clockwise through the no-borrowing, no-lending point F, ending up at BL^2 as before. To separate the substitution and income effects of the increase in the real interest rate, it is useful to think of the movement of the budget line from BL^1 to BL^2 as taking place in two steps.

First, imagine that the original budget line BL^1 pivots clockwise around Prudence's original consumption combination, point D, until it is parallel with the new budget line BL^2 (that is, its slope is -1.60). The resulting intermediate budget line is shown as the dashed line BL^{int} in Fig. 6.3.

As the second step, imagine that the intermediate budget line BL^{int} makes a parallel shift rightward to the final budget line BL^2. Thus the movement of the budget line from its original position at BL^1 to its new position at BL^2 can be broken down into a pivot around the original consumption point plus a parallel rightward shift.

Corresponding to the two steps of the shift of the budget line, the response of Prudence's saving and current consumption to the increase in the real interest rate can also be broken down into two parts. First, consider her response to the pivot of her budget line through point D, from BL^1 to BL^{int}. If this were the only change in Prudence's budget line, then because point D lies on BL^{int}, she could continue to consume at point D if she wished. However, because the budget line BL^{int} is steeper than the original budget line BL^1, reflecting the higher real interest rate, any additional saving that Prudence decides to do will now bring an increased reward in terms of additional future consumption. In response to this increased reward to saving, Prudence would move from point D to a point such as W on the intermediate budget line BL^{int}, saving more and enjoying less current consumption than at point D. The increase in saving between point D and point W, similar to Prudence's shift from point F to point V in Fig. 6.2, measures the substitution effect on Prudence's saving of the increase in the real interest rate.

However, Prudence's response to the pivot of her budget line is not her complete response to the increase in the real interest rate. We must also consider the effect of the parallel shift of the budget line from BL^{int} to its final position at BL^2. We saw in Chapter 5 that a parallel shift of the budget line to the right, corresponding to an increase in the present value of lifetime resources, causes Prudence to

---

[1]In Chapter 3 we explained what we are now calling the income effect in terms of "target saving" behavior. The two ideas are basically the same: When the real interest rate rises, someone who is saving toward a target, such as a fixed sum for college tuition, can consume more and save less today and still reach the target. Thus the higher real interest rate makes the saver richer and able to consume more than before.

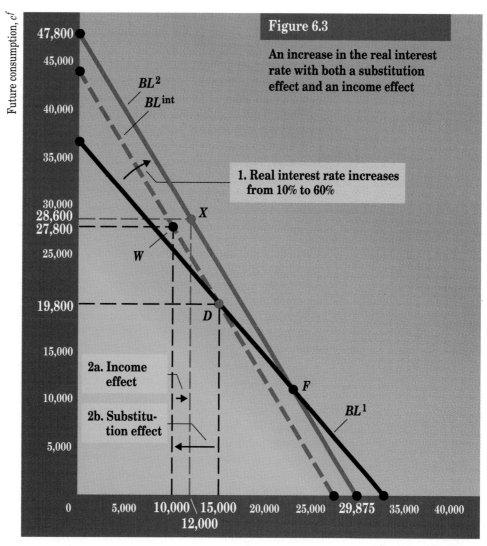

Figure 6.3

An increase in the real interest rate with both a substitution effect and an income effect

1. Real interest rate increases from 10% to 60%

2a. Income effect

2b. Substitution effect

We assume that initially Prudence consumes at point D on the original budget line BL^1. An increase in the real interest rate from 10% to 60% causes the budget line to pivot clockwise from BL^1 to the new budget line BL^2. We break the overall shift of the budget line into two parts: (1) a pivot around the original consumption point D to yield an intermediate budget line, the dashed line BL^{int}; and (2) a parallel shift from BL^{int} to the final

budget line BL^2. The substitution effect is measured by the movement from the original consumption point D to point W on the intermediate budget line BL^{int}, and the income effect is measured by the movement from point W to point X on the final budget line BL^2. As drawn, the substitution effect is larger than the income effect, so overall current consumption falls and saving rises.

consume more both in the present and in the future. Thus, starting from point W on the intermediate budget line BL^{int}, in response to the parallel shift from BL^{int} to BL^2, Prudence will move to a point like point X on the final budget line BL^2. At point X current and future consumption are higher, and saving is lower, than at point W. The decrease in saving and the increase in current consumption between point W and point X measures the income effect of the increase in the real interest rate. You can see now why this effect is called an income effect: As we discussed in Chapter 5, an income effect is the impact of any change that causes a parallel shift of the budget line. The income effect of an increase in the real interest rate is the part of the overall effect due to a parallel shift of the budget line.[2]

The overall effect on Prudence's saving of the rise in the real interest rate is shown in Fig. 6.3 as the change in saving between point D and point X. This overall effect is the sum of the substitution effect, measured by the increase in saving between point D and point W, and the income effect, measured by the decline in saving between point W and point X. As the figure is drawn, current consumption is lower and saving is higher at the final point X than at the original point D. However, the figure could just as well have been drawn so that saving at the final point X is less than at the initial point D (so that the income effect is greater than the substitution effect). Since the substitution effect of an increase in the real interest rate acts to raise Prudence's saving while the income effect tends to lower her saving, the overall effect cannot be determined by the theory.

Borrowing and the Real Interest Rate   In the example we have just worked out, the opposing impacts of the substitution and income effects made the overall response of Prudence's saving to an interest rate change uncertain. Although this theoretical ambiguity is a general problem, there is one case in which the substitution and income effects of an interest rate change work in the same direction: the case of someone who must borrow in order to achieve his optimal level of consumption.

Consider the situation (Fig. 6.4) of Prudence's twin brother Clement. Clement's current income, future income, and initial wealth are the same as his sister's, so his initial budget line BL^1 and his budget line after the increase in the real interest rate, BL^2, are the same as they were for Prudence (compare Fig. 6.4 with Fig. 6.3). However, Clement is more impatient than Prudence, so his initial consumption point is point G on the original budget line BL^1. At point G current consumption is 25,000, which exceeds Clement's current income plus initial wealth which total 23,000. Thus to reach point G, Clement must borrow 2000 (consumption of 25,000 less current resources of 23,000) and dissave by 5000 (current income of 20,000 minus current consumption of 25,000 equals saving of -5000).[3]

What happens to Clement's consumption and saving if the real interest rate rises, causing the budget line to pivot from BL^1 to BL^2? To analyze Clement's response, again we break down the shift of the budget line from BL^1 to BL^2 into two steps: (1) a pivot through Clement's initial consumption point G, which moves the budget line from BL^1 to the intermediate budget line marked BL^{int} in Fig. 6.4; and (2) a parallel shift from the intermediate budget line BL^{int} to the final budget line BL^2.

Remember that Clement's initial plan was to consume at point G. In response to the pivot of the budget line from BL^1 to BL^{int} in Fig. 6.4, Clement moves from point G to point Y on the intermediate budget line BL^{int}. The movement from point G to point Y, which measures the substitution effect of the increase in the real interest rate, reduces Clement's current consumption and raises his saving (or more precisely, reduces his borrowing and dissaving). Clement consumes less and saves more because the higher real interest rate raises the real cost of borrowing,

---

[2]Note that the income effect is absent if the consumer's original consumption point is the no-borrowing, no-lending point. For this reason we assumed that Prudence began at point F when we illustrated the substitution effect in Fig. 6.2.

[3]We assume in this example that there are no borrowing constraints.

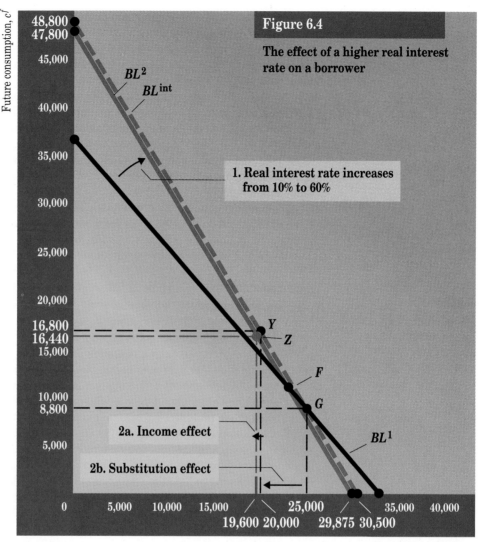

Figure 6.4

The effect of a higher real interest rate on a borrower

1. Real interest rate increases from 10% to 60%

2a. Income effect

2b. Substitution effect

Future consumption, c^f

Current consumption, c

We assume that initially Prudence's brother Clement consumes at point G on the initial budget line BL^1. At point G current consumption (25,000) exceeds current income plus initial wealth (23,000), so Clement must borrow. An increase in the real interest rate from 10% to 60% causes the budget line to pivot clockwise from BL^1 to BL^2. Again, we break the overall change in the budget line into two parts: (1) a pivot around the original consumption point G to yield an intermediate

budget line BL^{int}; and (2) a parallel shift from BL^{int} to the final budget line BL^2. The substitution effect is measured by the movement from the original consumption point G to point Y on the intermediate budget line BL^{int}, and the income effect is measured by the movement from point Y to point Z on the final budget line BL^2. For a borrower both the substitution effect and the income effect reduce current consumption and increase saving.

making borrowing to increase consumption today less attractive. Thus as for Prudence, the substitution effect of the higher real interest rate causes Clement to increase his saving (reduce his dissaving).

In contrast to what happened to Prudence, however, the income effect of a higher real interest rate also causes Clement to save more. The higher real interest rate means that Clement will have to pay more to borrow. This makes him *poorer*, not richer, as it made Prudence. You can see that Clement is poorer by noting that his initial consumption point G is to the right of his new budget line BL^2, which means that he can no longer afford to consume at this point. Because he has been made poorer, Clement further reduces his current consumption. This income effect is shown in Fig. 6.4 as the movement from point Y on the intermediate budget line BL^{int} to the final consumption point, point Z on the final budget line BL^2. At point Z current consumption is lower and saving is higher than at point Y, reflecting the fact that the income effect of a higher real interest rate is to make a borrower worse off rather than better off (the parallel shift from BL^{int} to BL^2 is to the left rather than to the right, as in the case of Prudence). For a borrower, then, the income effect of an increase in the real interest rate leads to less current consumption and thus more saving.

We conclude that for a borrower the theory gives a clear result: A higher real interest rate leads to lower current consumption, less borrowing, and more saving. The theory is unambiguous in this case, because for a borrower the substitution and income effects work in the same direction.

Aggregate Saving and the Real Interest Rate: Evidence

Aggregate private saving is the sum of all the saving done by households and firms in the economy (with dissaving done by households or firms subtracted from the total). For purposes of both policymaking and economic analysis it would be useful to know how aggregate saving responds to a change in the expected real interest rate. The theory tells us that a higher real interest rate will reduce dissaving by borrowers, but because of conflicting income and substitution effects, it cannot tell us for sure how the saving of people who are not borrowers will respond. Thus the effect of a higher real interest rate on overall saving is ambiguous.

Because theory cannot tell us for sure which way aggregate saving will respond to a change in the real interest rate, the question must be left to empirical evidence. Unfortunately, analysis of the data does not fully resolve the issue either: Despite dozens of studies, the sensitivity of saving to the real interest rate remains "one of the most controversial parameters in empirical economics."[4]

Traditionally, the accepted view among economists has been that the income and substitution effects of a change in the real interest rate largely cancel out, implying that the responsiveness of saving to the real interest rate is small. This accepted view was recently supported in an influential study by Robert Hall[5] of Stanford University, who found little evidence in U.S. macroeconomic data that an increase in the real interest rate will stimulate saving. However, there are some prominent dissenters from the conclusion that the effect of real interest rate changes on saving is weak: For example, Michael Boskin of Stanford University, who became the chairman of the Council of Economic Advisers under President Bush, and Lawrence Summers of Harvard University, a leading adviser to the 1988 Democratic Presidential candidate Michael Dukakis, have both published articles that conclude that an increase in the real return to saving can substantially increase

---

[4]Jerry A. Hausman and James M. Poterba, "Household Behavior and the Tax Reform Act of 1986," *Journal of Economic Perspectives*, Summer 1987, pp. 101–119; quotation is from p. 111. Hausman and Poterba survey the literature on the sensitivity of saving to the interest rate and also discuss tax effects, which we take up in the next section.

[5]"Intertemporal Substitution in Consumption," *Journal of Political Economy*, April 1988, pp. 339–357.

with the Macroeconomy

Interest Rates

Although in our theoretical discussions we refer to "the" interest rate, as if there were only one, there are in fact many different interest rates, each of which depends on the identity of the borrower and the terms of the loan. Shown here are some interest rates that appeared in the daily "Key Rates" box in the business section of the *New York Times* on February 8, 1991.

	CURRENT	YEAR EARLIER
Prime rate	9.00%	10.50%
Federal funds	5.47	8.12
3-month Treasury bills	5.94	7.81
6-month Treasury bills	5.89	7.74
7-year Treasury notes	7.70	8.41
30-year Treasury bonds	8.05	8.48
Municipal bonds	7.19	7.43

In this list the prime rate is the basic rate that banks charge on loans to their best customers. The Federal funds rate is the rate at which banks make overnight loans to each other. Treasury bills, notes, and bonds are debts of the U.S. government, and municipal bonds are obligations of state and local governments. With the exception of the prime rate, these interest rates vary continuously as financial market conditions change. The prime rate is an average of lending rates set by major banks and changes less frequently.

You can see that the interest rates charged on these different types of loans need not be the same. For example, the prime rate is a good bit higher than the rates on government debt. One reason for this variation is differences in the risk of nonrepayment, or default. Federal government debt is believed to be free of default risk, but there is always a chance that a business, bank, or municipality may not be able to repay its borrowings. Lenders charge risky borrowers extra interest to compensate themselves for the risk of default. Thus the prime rate, the Federal funds rate, and the municipal bond rate are higher than they would be if there were no default risk.

A second factor affecting interest rates is the length of time for which the funds are borrowed. Comparing the different Treasury obligations, you can see that generally (although not always) lenders charge a higher interest rate on long-term loans than on short-term loans. Thus the interest rate on Treasury bills repayable in 3 months or 6 months was around 6% (at an annual rate) at this time, and interest rates on 7-year or 30-year loans to the government were around 8% per year. The Federal funds rate, the rate on overnight loans between banks, is the lowest of the interest rates in the list, even though this rate reflects some default risk.

A final factor affecting interest rates is tax status. Interest on municipal bonds is not taxable, which is the primary reason that lenders are willing to accept relatively low rates on these loans.

Although the levels of the various interest rates are quite different, interest rates tend to go up and down together. For example, all of the interest rates in the list had fallen over the previous year, although by differing amounts. Because interest rates tend to move together, it is reasonable to talk about a change in "the" interest rate in our economic analyses.

saving.[6] Also, as we discuss in the next section, some empirical studies have found that tax policies that increase the rate of return received by savers have been successful in raising saving.

A fair summary is that most economists believe that an increase in the real interest rate will raise saving, but not by much; a minority of economists argue for a stronger positive effect on saving. Although it is theoretically possible that an increase in the real interest rate could *reduce* desired saving (if income effects outweigh substitution effects), there is little evidence to suggest that this occurs in practice. In our macroeconomic analyses we follow the bulk of the evidence and assume that an increase in the real interest rate raises saving.

6.2

TAX INCENTIVES FOR SAVING

As we saw in Chapter 2, national saving is an important determinant of how quickly a country accumulates wealth. For this reason governments have often adopted policies aimed at stimulating saving. A common type of policy with this goal is to structure the tax laws in order to raise the real rate of return received by savers.

To see how taxes affect the returns received by savers, we introduce the concept of an after-tax rate of return. We will use i to stand for the nominal interest rate, and we suppose that the rate at which interest income is taxed is t, so that savers get to keep a fraction $(1 - t)$ of total interest received. Then the **nominal after-tax rate of return** is the nominal interest rate received after payment of taxes, or $i(1 - t)$. The **expected real after-tax rate of return** is the nominal after-tax rate of return minus the expected inflation rate π^e. In symbols,

$$\text{expected real after-tax rate of return} = i(1 - t) - \pi^e. \tag{6.1}$$

Table 6.1 shows numerically how to calculate the nominal after-tax rate of return and the expected real after-tax rate of return. The table also illustrates the point that, given the nominal interest rate and expected inflation, a reduction in the tax rate on interest income increases the nominal and real after-tax rates of return that a saver receives. This result makes sense: The less of her interest earnings Prudence has to pay to the government, the higher the return she gets to enjoy.

Of the two measures of the after-tax rate of return, nominal and real, the expected real after-tax rate of return is more important in that it measures the increase in the purchasing power of savings after payment of taxes. Thus the expected real after-tax rate of return is the appropriate interest rate for consumers to use in making consumption and saving decisions.[7] By lowering the tax rate on interest earnings, government policy can raise the expected real after-tax rate of return received by savers. If the substitution effect is stronger than the income effect, lowering the tax rate on interest income should increase desired saving.

---

[6]See Michael J. Boskin, "Taxation, Savings, and the Rate of Interest," *Journal of Political Economy*, April 1978, pp. S2–S27; and Lawrence H. Summers, "The After-Tax Rate of Return Affects Private Savings," *American Economic Review*, May 1984, pp. 249–253.

[7]If interest paid is tax-deductible, as it traditionally has been in the United States, then the real after-tax rate of return reflects the real cost of borrowing as well as the real return to saving. See the application to follow.

Table 6.1 Calculating After-Tax Rates of Return

i = nominal interest rate = 5% per year
π^e = expected inflation rate = 2% per year

Example 1.

t = tax rate on interest income = 30%
Nominal after-tax rate of return = $i(1 - t) = 5\%(1 - 0.30) = 3.5\%$
Expected real after-tax rate of return = $i(1 - t) - \pi^e = 5\%(1 - 0.30) - 2\% = 1.5\%$

Example 2.

t = tax rate on interest income = 20%
Nominal after-tax rate of return = $i(1 - t) = 5\%(1 - 0.20) = 4\%$
Expected real after-tax rate of return = $i(1 - t) - \pi^e = 5\%(1 - 0.20) - 2\% = 2\%$

Application

Tax Policy and the Divergence of Canadian and U.S. Private Saving

Because Canada and the United States have similar and closely integrated economies, you might expect private saving behavior in the two countries to be similar. However, a study by Chris Carroll of the Massachusetts Institute of Technology and Lawrence Summers of Harvard University[8] found that although private saving rates in the two countries moved in parallel over much of the postwar period, beginning around 1971 private saving behavior in the United States and Canada began to diverge sharply. Over the 1970s and early 1980s Canadian private saving surged, but U.S. private saving declined. By the mid-1980s the private saving rate in Canada was substantially above the U.S. rate.[9]

Carroll and Summers concluded that differences in general macroeconomic conditions could not explain the differences in saving behavior between Canada and the United States. Instead, they argued that Canadian tax policies have been more favorable toward saving than American policies. They focused on two differences in tax policy.

First, Canada has tax-favored saving plans (including employer-sponsored Registered Pension Plans, or RPPs, and individual Registered Retirement Savings Plans, or RRSPs), which were substantially expanded in the early 1970s. The Canadian plans allow a significant portion of interest income to go untaxed. As discussed in the box "The Policy Debate" (p. 204), the United States has had similar "tax-sheltered" saving plans, such as Individual Retirement Accounts (IRAs). However, these plans were not made widely available until 1981.

---

[8]"Why Have Private Savings Rates in the United States and Canada Diverged?" *Journal of Monetary Economics*, September 1987, pp. 249–279.

[9]The private saving measure used by Carroll and Summers is net private saving, or private saving less depreciation of capital, divided by GNP. Using this measure, they found that the private saving rate in Canada rose from 7.8% in the 1971–1975 period to 11.9% in the 1981–1985 period; between the same two periods the U.S. private saving rate fell from 8.7% to 6.2%.

Second, compared to the tax system of Canada, the American tax system is relatively favorable to borrowers, a situation which encourages borrowing and consumption and discourages saving in the United States. In contrast to Canada, which does not allow consumers who borrow the right to deduct their interest payments from their taxable incomes, in the United States prior to 1986 all consumer interest payments were tax-deductible.[10] To see the effect of this difference in tax laws, compare an American and a Canadian who have both borrowed $10,000 at a 10% rate of interest, and assume that the American is in a 30% tax bracket. Both borrowers pay $1000 each year in interest, but the American borrower gets to deduct the $1000 from his taxable income, which saves him $300 (30% of $1000) in taxes. After taxes, the American's interest cost is $700 ($1000 less $300 in reduced taxes), for an after-tax nominal interest rate of 7% ($700 divided by the principal of $10,000). The Canadian borrower gets no tax break, so the after-tax interest rate she pays on her loan equals her before-tax interest rate of 10%.

Since interest rates paid by consumers were similar in the United States and Canada during the 1970s and 1980s, this difference in tax rules implied that, after taxes, it was cheaper to borrow in the United States than in Canada. Furthermore, the advantage to the borrower of tax deductibility of interest increases when interest rates rise: As we have seen, when the interest rate is 10%, the American borrower faces a 7% interest rate after taxes, 3% lower than what the Canadian borrower must pay. But when the interest rate rises to 15%, the American borrower pays an after-tax interest rate of 10.5% (15% less 30% of 15%), 4.5% less than the 15% interest rate facing the Canadian. Since interest rates rose in both countries in the 1970s, the difference in after-tax interest rates paid by American and Canadian borrowers also rose.

The theory tells us that the higher is the after-tax real interest rate faced by borrowers, the less they will dissave and the greater will be aggregate saving. Because of differences in tax deductibility of interest, the after-tax nominal interest rate faced by Canadian borrowers exceeded the after-tax nominal interest rate faced by American borrowers in the 1970s and 1980s, a difference that increased as nominal interest rates rose. Since inflation rates were similar in the two countries, these differences in after-tax nominal interest rates translated into similar differences in after-tax real interest rates. As predicted by the theory, Canadians borrowed at a much slower pace than Americans, particularly after about 1976. Lower dissaving by borrowers contributed to higher aggregate saving in Canada.

6.3 THE REAL INTEREST RATE, THE USER COST OF CAPITAL, AND INVESTMENT

We have been focusing so far on one major type of intertemporal decision, the decision by consumers about how much to save. Now we turn to a second, equally important type of intertemporal decision, which is the decision by firms about how much to invest. Recall from Chapter 2 that investment refers to the purchase or construction of capital goods, including residential and nonresidential buildings,

---

[10]The U.S. Tax Reform Act of 1986 began a phaseout of some types of consumer interest deductions. However, mortgage interest is still deductible, as is interest paid on home equity lines of credit; see the application on home equity lines in Chapter 5.

machines and equipment used in production, and inventories. Investment is an intertemporal decision because by investing, a firm commits the resources necessary to purchase or build new capital today in the hope of being able to produce more output in the future.

From a macroeconomic perspective there are two major reasons to study investment behavior. First, more so than the other components of aggregate expenditure (consumption, government purchases, and net exports), investment spending fluctuates sharply over the business cycle, falling in recessions and rising in booms. Even though on average investment is only about 17% of GNP, in the typical recession half or more of the total decline in spending takes the form of reduced investment spending. Explaining the behavior of investment is thus important for understanding the business cycle.[11]

The second reason that studying investment behavior is important is that investment plays a crucial role in determining the long-run productive capacity of the economy. Since investment is the creation of new capital goods, a high rate of investment means that the capital stock is growing rapidly, which over a period of years results in a greater ability of the economy to produce goods and services. Policymakers have long recognized the importance of investment for increasing output and have often taken steps to try to increase the rate of investment.[12]

The Desired Capital Stock

Since investment is the creation of new capital, to understand investment, we must consider how firms decide how much capital they want. If firms maximize profit, as we assume, then a firm's **desired capital stock** is the amount of capital that allows the firm to earn the largest possible expected profit. How can a firm determine whether its planned capital stock is profit maximizing? Starting from any given level of capital, firm managers can answer this question by considering the costs and benefits of using an additional piece of capital—a new machine, for example. If the benefits of using another machine outweigh the costs, then expanding the capital stock will raise profits. On the other hand, if the costs of using additional capital outweigh the benefits, then the firm should not increase its planned capital stock and might want to reduce it.

In real terms, the benefit to a firm of adding a unit of capital is the extra output that the firm can produce with this capital, with the firm's work force and other factors of production held fixed. In Chapter 3 we defined the marginal product of capital, or *MPK*, to be the amount of extra output that could be produced each period by using an additional unit of capital. We also discussed the point that because of lags in obtaining and installing new capital, it is the *expected future* marginal product of capital that is the benefit from increasing investment today. If we let *MPK^f* stand for the expected future marginal product of capital, then the *MPK^f* is the benefit that a firm expects to receive in the future period if it increases its investment in the current period by one unit of capital.

On the other side of the investment decision from the expected future benefit of using an extra unit of capital is the expected cost of using that capital in the future, the user cost of capital.

---

[11]Part IV of the book studies the business cycle.

[12]Chapter 8 examines the role of capital accumulation in the growth process, as well as government policies to stimulate growth.

Background

The chronically low personal saving rate in the United States has prompted policymakers to introduce tax breaks of various kinds to try to stimulate saving. An important example occurred in 1981, when the Economic Recovery Tax Act made all workers eligible for tax-deductible Individual Retirement Accounts (IRAs). IRAs had previously been available only to workers without employer pension plans.*

IRA rules allowed workers to contribute up to a fixed limit ($2000 per year for an individual worker) to their accounts. Withdrawals could be made before retirement age, but only by paying a significant penalty. Income contributed to IRAs was free of income tax in the year the contributions were made. Interest earned by the assets in the IRA, unlike interest on non-IRA assets, was also to be free of tax. Withdrawals made at retirement were to be treated as ordinary income and subject to tax in the years the withdrawals were made. Overall, the after-tax rate of return on a dollar of IRA saving was normally much higher than the after-tax rate of return on a dollar of non-IRA saving (see Numerical Problem 1).

IRAs were very popular with consumers, and large quantities of funds flowed into these accounts. However, personal and private saving rates were even lower following the 1981 tax bill than in previous years. Partly for that reason, and also partly for the purpose of increasing government tax revenues, the number of people eligible to use IRAs was sharply scaled back by tax law changes that took effect in 1986.

THE POLICY
DEBATE

Should the Tax Code Permit Individual Retirement Accounts?

Pro

"One reason that Americans save so little is that saving is overtaxed. Indeed, real after-tax returns to saving were negative during much of the 1970s. IRAs eliminate this problem by leaving interest untaxed, restoring appropriate incentives for saving.

"It is not certain whether the effects of IRAs on saving are large or only modest. We do know that U.S. consumers were eager to use IRAs while they were available. In any case, when it comes to saving, surely every little bit helps."

Con

"IRAs cost the government revenue but do little to increase saving. The first problem is that because of conflicting income and substitution effects, higher after-tax returns to saving are of minimal value in stimulating saving. The second problem is reshuffling: Consumers who have existing financial assets can simply transfer these assets to their IRAs, collecting the tax benefits but not doing any additional saving."

Analysis

Con makes an important point concerning the "reshuffling" problem. Under IRA rules a person who simply transferred $2000 from a non-IRA asset (such as a saving account) into an IRA could get the full tax benefit, without doing any additional saving. Even with no non-IRA assets individuals could achieve the same result by borrowing in order to fund the IRA; since interest on borrowing was tax-deductible, and the interest earned on the IRA was tax-favored, this strategy also had tax benefits. The IRA scheme was thus conceptually flawed in that it permitted consumers to get the tax break without changing saving behavior. Thus the fact that many people opened IRAs doesn't in itself prove that these accounts led to increased saving.

However, there is a situation in which the reshuffling problem doesn't apply, which is when the consumer has no initial wealth and is not allowed to borrow against future income (a borrowing constraint). The effect of introducing an IRA law in this case is shown in the accompanying figure. Before the introduction of the IRA the budget line of the consumer is shown as BL^1, drawn in black in the figure. The slope of the initial budget line is $-(1 + r_1)$, where r_1 is the expected real after-tax rate of interest before the introduction of IRAs. The vertical line passing through point A in the figure shows the effect of the borrowing constraint (compare with Fig. 5.7): Because the consumer has no initial wealth and cannot borrow, points to the right of A, where current consumption c exceeds current income y, are not available to him.

We assume that the consumer's preferred consumption combination before the introduction of the IRA is at point C in the figure.**

Now suppose an IRA law is passed that allows consumers to earn an expected after-tax real rate of return of r_2, higher than the original real return of r_1, on their first $2000 of saving. This change causes the consumer's budget line to shift from BL^1 to the kinked budget line BL^2, drawn in red in the figure. To understand this shift, note first that point A, where saving is zero, is on both the old and the new budget lines; the consumer is still free to consume all his current income after the introduction of the IRA. However, starting from point A, should the consumer decide to save, he can now earn the higher rate of return r_2. Thus the slope of the new budget line BL^2 between points A and E, which equals $-(1 + r_2)$, is steeper than the slope of the old budget line BL^1, which is $-(1 + r_1)$. However, since the higher rate r_2 can be earned on only the first $2000 of saving, and any saving beyond $2000 earns only a return of r_1, the slope of the new budget line changes to $-(1 + r_1)$ between points D and E.

Starting from his initial consumption point at point C, how does the consumer respond to this change in his budget line? The situation is exactly that of a consumer facing a higher real interest rate, analyzed in Fig. 6.3. On the one hand, the higher real return offered by the IRA increases the reward to saving (the substitution effect). On the other hand, the higher real return makes the saver better off, reducing the desire to save (the income effect). Following the empirical evidence discussed in the text, in the figure we show the consumer moving from point C to point F, where current consumption is slightly lower and saving slightly higher. This analysis shows that an IRA law may increase saving.

Evidence

As we noted earlier, U.S. saving did not increase after the expansion of IRA eligibility. For example, the personal saving rate fell from about 8% during the 1970s to about 6% during 1981–1985. On the other hand, studies at the level of individual families have found that, with other factors held constant, IRAs increased saving, sometimes substantially.† Empirically, the reshuffling problem seems not to have been a major issue; either many families using IRAs had low assets and borrowing constraints (consistent with our analysis), or people did not fully understand that tax benefits could be obtained by reshuffling their assets.

If IRAs did increase saving, then why did aggregate saving fall? Other factors depressing saving may have offset the effects of the IRAs. For example, during the 1980s significant rises in the stock market and in the value of real estate increased consumer wealth. As discussed in Chapter 5, higher wealth reduces desired saving.

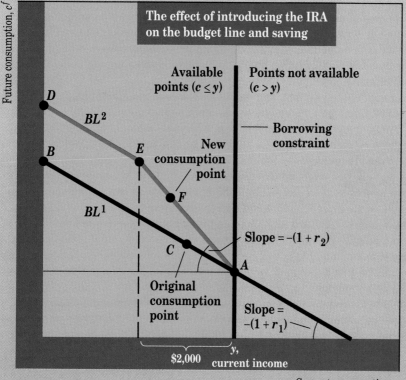

The effect of introducing the IRA on the budget line and saving

*Tax-favored retirement accounts for self-employed workers are called Keogh plans.

**Note that at point C the borrowing constraint is nonbinding. The borrowing constraint is needed in this analysis only to eliminate the possibility that the consumer borrows in order to fund his IRA.

†See R. Glenn Hubbard, "Do IRAs and Keoghs Increase Saving?" *National Tax Journal*, March 1984, pp. 43–54; Daniel Feenberg and Jonathan Skinner, "Sources of IRA Saving," NBER working paper no. 2845, February 1989; Steven F. Venti and David A. Wise, "Have IRAs Increased U.S. Saving? Evidence from Consumer Expenditure Surveys," *Quarterly Journal of Economics*, August 1990, pp. 661–698.

The User Cost of Capital   To make the discussion of the user cost of capital more concrete, we consider the case of Kyle's Bakery, Inc., a company that produces specialty cookies. Kyle, the bakery's owner-manager, is considering investing in a new state-of-the-art, solar-powered oven that will allow him to produce more cookies in the future. If he buys an oven, he must also decide how big an oven to buy. In making his decision, Kyle has the following three items of information:

1.   A new oven can be purchased in any size at a price of $100 per cubic foot, measured in real terms (that is, in base-year dollars).

2.   Because the oven is solar-powered, using it does not involve additional energy costs.[13] The oven also does not require maintenance expenditures. However, the oven becomes less efficient as it ages; with each year that passes, a given-sized oven can produce 10% fewer cookies. Because of this depreciation, the real value of an oven falls 10% per year. For example, after one year of use, the real value of an oven is $90 per cubic foot.

3.   Kyle can borrow or lend at the prevailing expected real interest rate of 8% per year.

Some useful notation, with values from the example of Kyle's Bakery, is defined below:

$$p_K = \text{real price of capital goods (\$100 per cubic foot),}$$
$$d = \text{rate at which capital depreciates (10\% per year),}$$
$$r = \text{expected real interest rate (8\% per year).}$$

The **user cost of capital** is the expected real cost of using a unit of capital for a specified period of time. As a convenient way of finding the user cost of capital in the example of Kyle's bakery, we consider what Kyle's expected costs would be if he purchased a new oven, used it for a year, then sold it on the used-oven market. We will see that the cost of using the oven has two components: the depreciation cost and the interest cost.

In general, the depreciation cost of using capital is the value lost as the building or machine wears out. After one year, because of depreciation, the oven that Kyle pays $100 per cubic foot for when new will be worth only $90 per cubic foot. The $10-per-cubic-foot loss that Kyle suffers over the year is the depreciation cost of using the oven. It is easiest to see that Kyle loses $10 per cubic foot if at the end of the year he sells the oven on the used-oven market, as we have assumed. But he bears the loss even if he doesn't sell the oven, since at the end of the year he will own an asset (the oven) with a 10% lower economic value.

The interest cost of using a piece of capital equals the expected real interest rate times the initial price of the capital. Since the expected real interest rate on a one-year government bond is 8%, Kyle's interest cost of using the oven for a year is 0.08 times $100 per cubic foot, or $8 per cubic foot. There are two equivalent ways of understanding why the interest cost is a cost of using capital: First, if Kyle must borrow the funds necessary to buy the oven (repaying the loan when the oven is sold at the end of the year), the interest cost is just the interest he pays on his loan.[14] Alternatively, suppose that Kyle did not borrow to buy the oven but used

---

[13]This assumption just serves to simplify the example. If there are operating costs, such as fuel costs, we may think of them as being subtracted from the expected future marginal product of capital when the benefit of using the machine is calculated.

[14]Recall that we assume that Kyle can earn the same real interest rate on his saving as he must pay to borrow.

profits from his business to make the purchase. By using his own funds to buy the oven, Kyle gave up the chance to use those funds to buy an interest-bearing asset, such as a government bond. If, for example, Kyle had bought one less cubic foot of oven capacity and used the $100 thus saved to buy a bond paying 8%, he could have earned $8 in interest. The $8 interest sacrificed by buying a cubic foot of capacity instead of the $100 bond is a cost that Kyle bears. Thus the interest cost is part of the true economic cost of using capital whether the capital's purchase is financed with borrowed funds or with the firm's own retained profits.

The user cost of capital is the sum of the depreciation cost and the interest cost. If

$$rp_K = \text{the interest cost}$$
$$dp_K = \text{the depreciation cost}$$
$$u = \text{the user cost of capital}$$

then the formula for the user cost of capital is

$$
\begin{aligned}
u = rp_K + dp_K &= (r + d)p_K \\
&= 0.08(\$100 \text{ per cubic foot}) + 0.10\,(\$100 \text{ per cubic foot}) \quad (6.2) \\
&= \$18 \text{ per cubic foot},
\end{aligned}
$$

Kyle's user cost, or the expected cost of using a cubic foot of oven capacity for a year, is $18. If Kyle borrows $100 to buy a cubic foot of oven capacity, at the end of the year he will owe $108. He receives $90 from selling the cubic foot of capacity, so his out-of-pocket cost is $18 per cubic foot. This $18 consists of an $8 interest cost and the $10 depreciation cost.

Determining the Desired Capital Stock   Using the concepts of the expected future marginal product of capital (which measures the expected future benefit of extra capital) and the user cost of capital (which measures the expected future cost of extra capital), we can figure out what level of the capital stock maximizes profit: The amount of capital that maximizes profits for a firm is the amount at which the expected future marginal product of capital MPK^f equals the user cost of capital u.

Figure 6.5 shows the determination of the desired capital stock for Kyle's Bakery. In this figure the capital stock K, expressed as the number of cubic feet of oven capacity, is measured along the horizontal axis. The MPK^f and the user cost of capital are both measured along the vertical axis. The downward-sloping curve shows the value of the MPK^f for different sizes of the capital stock. The MPK^f curve slopes downward because as the capital stock increases, the less additional output can be obtained by expanding the capital stock still further; this tendency of the MPK^f to fall as the capital stock rises is a result of the principle of diminishing marginal returns to capital (discussed in Chapter 3). The user cost of capital does not change as the amount of capital changes; in this example it equals $18 per cubic foot. Since the user cost of capital is constant, it is represented by a horizontal line in Fig. 6.5.

To find Kyle's desired capital stock, we assume arbitrarily that he is planning to purchase an oven of 4000 cubic feet and ask: "Should Kyle expand his planned capital stock even beyond 4000 cubic feet?" The answer depends on whether the expected future benefit of additional cubic feet of oven capacity exceeds the expected cost.

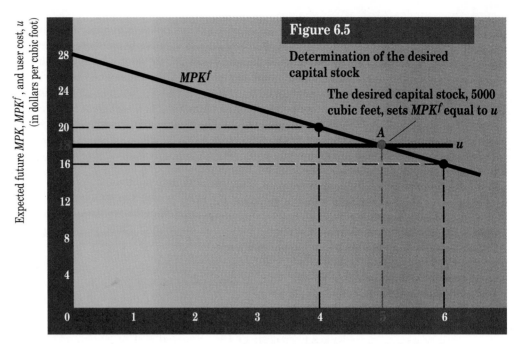

The desired capital stock (5000 cubic feet of oven capacity in this example) is the capital stock that maximizes profits. When the capital stock is 5000 cubic feet, the expected future marginal product of capital MPK^f is equal to the user cost of capital u. If MPK^f is larger than u, as it is when the capital stock is 4000 cubic feet, then the benefit of extra capital exceeds the cost, and the firm should increase its capital stock. If MPK^f is smaller than u, as it is at 6000 cubic feet, the cost of extra capital exceeds the benefit, and the firm should reduce its capital stock.

As we have said, the benefit of adding capital is MPK^f, or the extra future production that Kyle expects he would get, with his labor force held constant. Figure 6.5 shows that at a planned capacity of 4000 cubic feet the MPK^f of an additional cubic foot is $20 worth of cookies per year. This expected benefit exceeds the expected cost of the extra cubic foot of capacity, which is the user cost of $18. Starting from a planned capacity of 4000 cubic feet, if Kyle adds an extra cubic foot of capacity, he will gain an additional $20 worth of future output while incurring only $18 in expected future costs. It is thus profitable for Kyle to expand beyond 4000 cubic feet. In general, when a firm starts from any given planned capital stock, if the MPK^f exceeds the user cost of capital, the firm can increase its profits by raising its planned capital stock.

What if MPK^f is less than the user cost of capital? In this case in order to increase profits the firm should *reduce* the planned size of the capital stock. For example, Fig. 6.5 shows that when Kyle's planned capacity is 6000 cubic feet, the MPK^f is $16 per cubic foot, less than the user cost of $18 per cubic foot. Starting from a planned capital stock of 6000 cubic feet, if Kyle reduces his planned capacity by 1 cubic foot, he will lose cookie production worth $16 per year but will save user costs of $18 per year, raising annual profits by $2.

We have seen that if the MPK^f exceeds the user cost, Kyle raises his expected profits by expanding his planned oven capacity; but if the MPK^f is less than the user cost, Kyle increases expected profits by lowering planned capacity. Only when the MPK^f and the user cost of capital are equal can the firm be satisfied that its profits are as high as possible. Because the desired capital stock is the level of the capital stock that maximizes the firm's expected profits, *the firm's desired capital stock is the one at which the expected future marginal product of capital equals the user cost of capital*, or $MPK^f = u$. As you can see in Fig. 6.5, the desired capital stock for Kyle's Bakery is 5000 cubic feet of oven capacity.

Changes in the Desired Capital Stock

The capital stock that a firm chooses depends on economic conditions. In particular, any factor that shifts the MPK^f curve or changes the user cost of capital changes the firm's desired capital stock. For Kyle's Bakery suppose, for example, that the real interest rate decreases from 8% to 6%. If the real interest rate r is 0.06, and the depreciation rate d and the price of capital p_K remain at 0.10 and $100 per cubic foot, respectively, then the user cost of capital $(r + d)p_K$ now becomes $(0.06 + 0.10)$100$ per cubic foot, or $16 per cubic foot. Since $16 per cubic foot is lower than the original user cost of $18 per cubic foot, the fall in the real interest rate has reduced the user cost of capital.

This fall in the user cost is shown as a downward shift in the user cost line, from u^1 to u^2 in Fig. 6.6. As you can see in the figure, after the fall in the user cost the MPK^f at the original desired capital stock of 5000 cubic feet (point A), equal to $18 per cubic foot, exceeds the user cost of capital, now equal to $16 per cubic foot (point B). Kyle's Bakery can increase its profit by raising its planned oven capacity

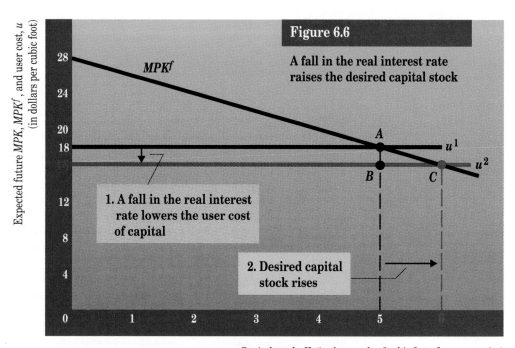

Figure 6.6

A fall in the real interest rate raises the desired capital stock

1. A fall in the real interest rate lowers the user cost of capital

2. Desired capital stock rises

Capital stock, K (in thousands of cubic feet of oven capacity)

In the example of Kyle's Bakery a reduction in the real interest rate from 8% to 6% reduces the user cost u of a cubic foot of oven capacity from $18 to $16 per cubic foot and shifts the user cost line down from u^1 to u^2. The desired capital stock rises from 5000 (point A) to 6000 (point C) cubic feet of oven capacity. At 6000 cubic feet the MPK^f and the user cost of capital are once again equal at $16 per cubic foot.

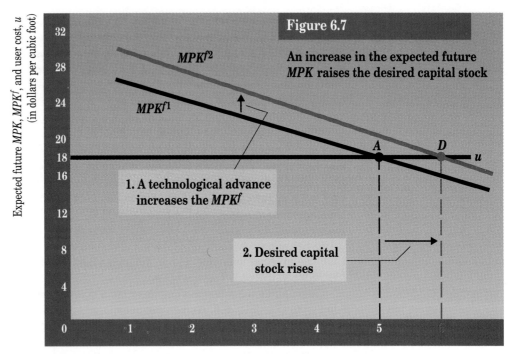

Here a technological advance raises the expected future marginal product of capital, MPK^f, shifting the MPK^f curve upward from MPK^{f1} to MPK^{f2}. The desired capital stock increases from 5000 (point A) to 6000 (point D) cubic feet of oven capacity. At 6000 cubic feet the MPK^f equals the user cost of capital u at \$18 per cubic foot.

to 6000 cubic feet, where the MPK^f equals the user cost of \$16 per cubic foot (point C). This example illustrates that a decrease in the expected real interest rate—or any other change that lowers the user cost of capital—increases the desired capital stock.

Technological changes that affect the MPK^f curve will also affect the desired stock of capital. Suppose that Kyle invents a new type of cookie dough that requires less baking time, allowing more cookies to be baked overall. We imagine that this technological advance causes the MPK^f curve for ovens to shift upward by 12.5% at each value of the capital stock. This effect is shown as a shift of the MPK^f curve from MPK^{f1} to MPK^{f2} in Fig. 6.7. If the user cost remains at \$18 per cubic foot, the figure shows that the technological advance causes Kyle's desired capital stock to rise from 5000 to 6000 cubic feet. At 6000 cubic feet (point D) the MPK^f once again equals the user cost of capital. In general, with the user cost of capital held constant, an increase in the expected future marginal product of capital at any given level of capital raises the desired capital stock.

Taxes and the Desired Capital Stock   So far we have ignored taxes. But since presumably it is the profit his firm gets to keep after paying taxes that Kyle is interested in maximizing, he must take account of taxes in evaluating the desirability of an additional unit of capital.

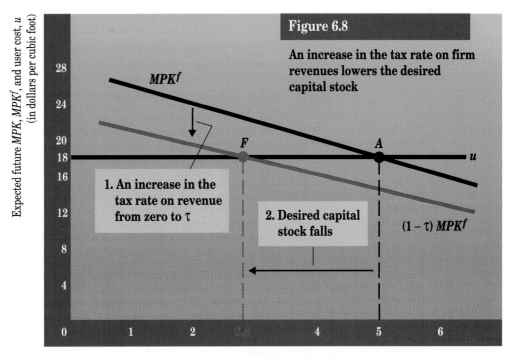

Figure 6.8

An increase in the tax rate on firm revenues lowers the desired capital stock

Capital stock, K (in thousands of cubic feet of oven capacity)

When firm revenues are taxed at rate τ, the desired capital stock is found at the point where the after-tax MPK^f, or $(1 - \tau)MPK^f$, equals the user cost. For example, a 20% tax rate on firm revenues reduces the after-tax marginal product of capital by 20% at every level of the capital stock, relative to the situation with no tax. In the example imposition of a 20% tax causes the desired capital stock to fall from 5000 (point A) to 2800 (point F) cubic feet of oven capacity.

Suppose, for example, that Kyle's Bakery pays taxes equal to 20% of its revenues. In this case extra oven capacity that increases the firm's future revenues by, say, $20 will raise Kyle's after-tax revenue by only $16, with $4 going to the government. To decide whether to add this extra capacity, Kyle should compare the after-tax MPK^f of $16—not the before-tax MPK^f of $20—with the user cost. In general, if τ is the tax rate on firm revenues, the after-tax future marginal product of capital is $(1 - \tau)MPK^f$. The desired capital stock is the one for which the after-tax future marginal product, $(1 - \tau)MPK^f$, equals the user cost.

Figure 6.8 shows the effects of a tax on firm revenues on the desired capital stock. The after-tax MPK^f curve, which graphs the value of $(1 - \tau)MPK^f$, lies below the original (before-tax) MPK^f curve. In this example we assume that the tax rate τ is 20%. At a tax rate of 20% the desired capital stock is 2800 cubic feet of oven capacity, since it is at 2800 cubic feet that the after-tax MPK^f equals the user cost of $18 per cubic foot. The figure also shows that increases in the tax rate on firm revenues reduce the desired capital stock. For example, in this case a rise in the tax rate from zero to 20% would reduce Kyle's desired capital stock from 5000 (point A) to 2800 (point F) cubic feet.

The condition that the after-tax marginal product, $(1 - \tau)MPK^f$, must equal the user cost u can also be written as

$$MPK^f = \frac{u}{1 - \tau} = \frac{(r + d)p_K}{1 - \tau,} \tag{6.3}$$

where we have divided through by $(1 - \tau)$. In Eq. (6.3), the term $u/(1 - \tau)$, is called the tax-adjusted user cost of capital. The **tax-adjusted user cost of capital** tells us how large the before-tax future marginal product of capital must be in order for the firm to make a profit from a proposed investment. An increase in the tax rate τ raises the tax-adjusted user cost and thus raises the "hurdle" (the required before-tax marginal product) that new capital projects must clear in order to be worth undertaking.

In our example we have considered the effects on desired capital of a proportional tax on corporate revenues. Although this example is useful for illustrating the effect of taxes on the desired capital stock, actual corporate taxes in the United States and other countries are much more complicated than in this simple case. Firms generally pay taxes on their profits rather than on their revenues, and the part of profit that is considered taxable may depend on how much the firm invests. For example, when a firm purchases some capital, it is allowed to deduct part of the purchase price of the capital from its taxable profit in both the year of purchase and in subsequent years. By reducing the amount of profit to be taxed, these deductions, known as depreciation allowances, allow the firm to reduce its total tax payment.

Another important tax provision, which has been used at various times although not at present in the United States, is the investment tax credit. An investment tax credit permits the firm to subtract a share of the purchase price of new capital directly from its tax bill. So, for example, if the investment tax credit is 10%, a firm that purchases a $10,000 piece of equipment can reduce its taxes by $1000 (10% of $10,000) in the year the equipment is purchased.

Economists have tried to summarize the many provisions of the tax code affecting investment into a single measure of the tax burden on capital called the **effective tax rate.** Essentially, the idea is to ask, "What tax rate τ on a firm's revenue would have the same effect on the desired capital stock as do the actual provisions of the tax code?" The hypothetical tax rate that answers this question is the effective tax rate. Changes in the tax law that (for example) raise the effective tax rate are equivalent to an increased tax on firm revenue and a rise in the tax-adjusted user cost of capital. Thus an increase in the effective tax rate lowers the desired capital stock.

Application

The Effective Tax Rates on Equipment and Structures

Does the effective tax rate on capital have an empirically important effect on investment patterns? Some evidence on this issue can be obtained by looking at spending on different types of capital that have different effective tax rates. In particular, in the United States, investment in equipment (such as furniture, computers, and automobiles) is treated differently by the tax law than investment in structures (such as factories, warehouses, and office buildings). Figure 6.9(a) shows the effective tax rates on equipment and structures as calculated in a study

(a) The effective tax rates on equipment investment and structures investment in the United States are shown for the period 1946–1980. Before 1962 equipment was taxed more heavily than structures, but since then, equipment has generally been more lightly taxed.

Source: Table 11 in Dale W. Jorgenson and Martin A. Sullivan, "Inflation and Corporate Capital Recovery," in Charles R. Hulten, ed., *Depreciation, Inflation, and the Taxation of Income from Capital*, Washington D.C.: The Urban Institute Press, 1981.

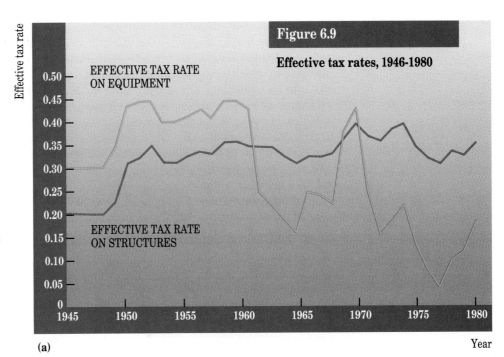

(a)

(b) Investment in equipment and investment in structures were about the same in the early 1960s, but since then, equipment investment has grown noticeably more quickly. One reason for the expansion of investment in equipment is a more favorable tax treatment since 1962, shown as a lower effective tax rate on equipment investment in part (a).

Source: *Economic Report of the President*, February 1991, Table B-1.

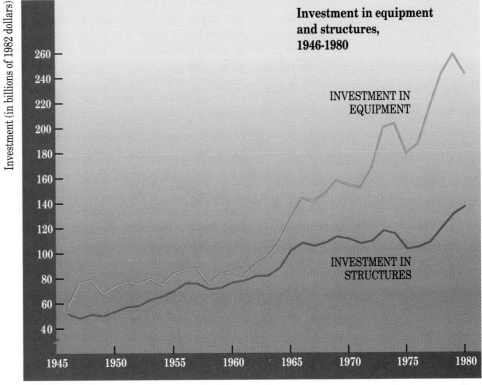

(b)

of the period 1946–1980.[15] In every year from 1946 to 1961, the effective tax rate on equipment was greater than the effective tax rate on structures. However, 1962 saw a major revision in the tax code that introduced an investment tax credit for equipment, which was repealed in 1969 and later reinstituted in 1971. The effective tax rate on equipment fell sharply from 0.428 in 1961 to 0.250 in 1962, while the effective tax rate on structures was virtually unchanged. Before 1962 equipment was more heavily taxed than structures, but after 1962 (except for 1969 and 1970) equipment was less heavily taxed than structures. Figure 6.9(b) shows that over the period 1962–1980 equipment investment grew much more quickly than did investment in structures (a trend that has continued since 1980). The change in the relative taxation of equipment and structures is no doubt a major reason for this shift in the composition of investment toward equipment.

From the Desired Capital Stock to Investment

We have seen how a profit-maximizing firm chooses its desired capital stock. Now let's look at the link between a firm's desired capital stock and the amount it invests.

There are two opposing channels through which the capital stock (of a firm or of a country) changes over time: First, the purchase or construction of new capital goods increases the capital stock. We have been calling the total purchase or construction of new capital goods that takes place each year "investment," but its precise name is **gross investment**. The second way that the capital stock changes is through the depreciation of existing capital, which reduces the capital stock.

Whether the capital stock increases or decreases over the course of a year depends on whether gross investment is greater or less than depreciation during the year; when gross investment exceeds depreciation, the capital stock grows. The change in the capital stock over the year—or, equivalently, the difference between gross investment and depreciation—is called **net investment.**

Useful algebraic symbols for these variables are as follows:

$$I_t = \text{gross investment during year } t,$$
$$K_t = \text{capital stock at the beginning of year } t,$$
$$K_{t+1} = \text{capital stock at the beginning of year } t + 1$$
$$\text{(equivalently, at the end of year } t).$$

Net investment, the change in the capital stock during period t, can be expressed as $K_{t+1} - K_t$. The amount of depreciation during year t is dK_t, where d is the fraction of capital that depreciates each year. Therefore the relationship between net and gross investment can be written as

$$\text{net investment} = \text{gross investment} - \text{depreciation}, \tag{6.4}$$
$$K_{t+1} - K_t = I_t - dK_t.$$

In most but not all years gross investment is larger than depreciation, so that net investment is positive and the capital stock increases. Figure 6.10 shows the behavior since 1940 of gross and net investment in the United States, expressed as percentages of GNP; the difference between gross and net investment is depreciation. Notice the occasional large swings in both gross and net investment and

---

[15]Dale W. Jorgenson and Martin A. Sullivan, "Inflation and Corporate Capital Recovery," in Charles R. Hulten, ed., *Depreciation, Inflation, and the Taxation of Income from Capital*, Washington, D.C.: The Urban Institute Press, 1981.

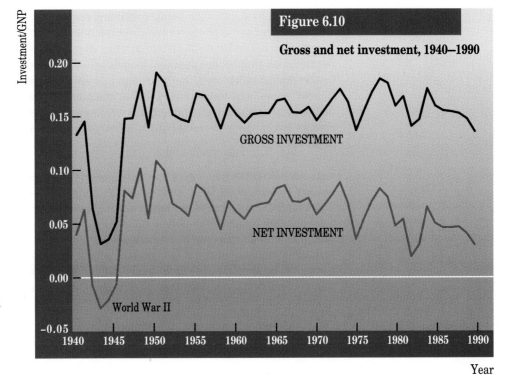

Investment/GNP

Figure 6.10

Gross and net investment, 1940–1990

GROSS INVESTMENT

NET INVESTMENT

World War II

Year

Gross and net investment in the United States since 1940 are measured as percentages of GNP. During some years of World War II net investment was negative. Net investment was also relatively weak in the 1980s, reflecting high rates of capital depreciation during that decade.

Source: *Economic Report of the President*, February 1991, Tables B-1 and B-16.

the negative rates of net investment that occurred in several years during World War II (1941–1945). Another observation to draw from Fig. 6.10 is that net investment was relatively weak during the 1980s, even though gross investment as a percentage of GNP was at about its normal level. The explanation for the divergence is that in recent years an increasingly high share of investment has been devoted to purchases of equipment (computers being a leading example) at the expense of structures, continuing the trend shown in Fig. 6.9(b). Because equipment depreciates more quickly than structures, depreciation in recent years has been high. Given gross investment, higher depreciation implies lower net investment.

We can use Eq. (6.4) to understand the relationship between the desired capital stock and investment. First, rewriting Eq. (6.4) gives us

$$I_t = K_{t+1} - K_t + dK_t.$$

This equation says that gross investment equals net investment plus depreciation.

Now suppose that, using information available at the beginning of year t about the expected future marginal product of capital and the user cost of capital, firms in the economy have determined the desired capital stock that they want by the end of year t (the beginning of year $t + 1$). Call this desired capital stock K^*. For the moment, suppose also that capital can be obtained fairly quickly, so that firms are able to set their actual capital stock at the end of year t, K_{t+1}, equal to their desired capital stock K^*. Substituting K^* for K_{t+1} in the previous equation yields

$$I_t = K^* - K_t + dK_t. \tag{6.5}$$

Equation (6.5) shows that firms' gross investment I_t during a year has two parts: (1) the desired net increase in the capital stock over the year, $K^* - K_t$; and (2) the investment needed to replace worn-out or depreciated capital, dK_t. The amount of depreciation that occurs during a year is given. However, the desired net increase in the capital stock over the year depends on the various factors—such as taxes, interest rates, and the expected future marginal product of capital—that affect the desired stock of capital. Indeed, Eq. (6.5) shows that any factor that leads to a change in the desired capital stock K^* results in an equal change in gross investment I_t.

Lags and Investment   The assumption just made, that firms can obtain capital quickly enough to set their actual capital stocks equal to desired levels in each year, is not realistic in all cases. Although most types of equipment are readily available, a skyscraper or a nuclear power plant may take years to construct. Thus in practice, a $1 million increase in a firm's desired capital stock may not translate into a $1 million increase in gross investment within the year; instead, the extra investment may be spread out over several years as the process of planning and construction is carried out. Despite this qualification, it is generally true that factors that increase firms' desired capital stocks also tend to increase the current rate of investment.

Investment in Inventories and Housing

In our discussion so far we have emphasized what is called business fixed investment, or investment by firms in structures (such as factories and office buildings) and equipment (such as machine tools or jetliners). There are two other components of investment spending, however—inventory investment and residential investment. As discussed in Chapter 2, inventory investment equals the increase in firms' inventories of unsold goods, unfinished goods, or raw materials; residential investment is the construction of housing, such as homes, condominiums, or apartment buildings.

Fortunately, the concepts of future marginal product and the user cost of capital, which we used to study business fixed investment, apply equally well to inventory investment and residential investment. Consider, for example, a new-car dealer trying to decide whether to increase the number of cars she normally keeps on her lot from 100 to 150—that is, to make an inventory investment of 50 cars. The benefit of having more cars to show is that potential car buyers will be able to see a variety of models and will be less likely to have to wait for delivery, so that the car dealer will sell more cars. The increase in sales commissions the car dealer expects to make, measured in real terms and with her sales force held constant, is the expected future marginal product of the increased inventory. The costs of holding more cars result from two factors: (1) Cars sitting on the lot lose value (depreciation); and (2) the car dealer must pay interest on the loan she took out to finance the higher inventory. The car dealer will make the inventory investment if the expected benefits of increasing her inventory, in terms of increased sales commissions, is at least as great as the interest and depreciation costs of adding the 50 extra cars. This principle is the same one that applies to business fixed investment.

Residential investment can also be analyzed by using this basic approach. The expected future marginal product of an apartment building, for example, is the real value of rents that can be collected from the tenants of the building, minus taxes and operating costs. The user cost of capital for an apartment building during a year is its depreciation, or loss of value due to wear and tear, plus the interest cost—as reflected in mortgage payments, for example. As for other types of capital, building an apartment house is profitable only if its expected future marginal product is at least as great as its user cost.

Application

Does the United States Overinvest in Housing?

In general, residential investment in the United States—particularly the construction of owner-occupied housing—is more lightly taxed than other types of investment. One important difference in tax treatment is that the "dwelling services" that homeowners receive from their homes are not counted as taxable income, but the returns to other types of capital—the output of a machine or the rents collected from an apartment building, for example—are taxed. Homes are also financed to a greater degree than other types of capital by debt (mortgages), the interest on which is tax-deductible. Because of these and other favorable tax rules that lower the tax-adjusted user cost of housing, there is more investment in housing in the United States than there otherwise would be.

To a large extent, tax breaks for housing result from policymakers' desire to encourage homeownership, which is a laudable social goal. Nevertheless, achieving this goal has a cost, which is that resources used for building houses are not available for creating other types of capital, such as factories. Thus in the long run the policy of favoring home construction probably reduces the amount of capital that businesses have to work with.

How large is the effect of tax breaks for housing on the composition of the U.S. capital stock? A study by Edwin Mills[16] of Northwestern University found that in 1983 housing accounted for 32% of the total capital stock in the United States. Mills calculated that if housing were not favored by the tax system, housing would have been only 24% of the capital stock. Thus the tax system increased the share of housing in the total capital stock by about one third.

The Saving-Investment Diagram

In this chapter and the previous one we have looked carefully at the consumer's saving decision and the firm's investment decision. Although we have analyzed saving and investment decisions separately, we saw in Chapter 3 that goods market equilibrium in an economy without foreign trade requires that desired national saving equal desired investment. This goods market equilibrium condition is illustrated by the saving-investment diagram, introduced in Chapter 3 and shown again as Fig. 6.11.

In the saving-investment diagram the saving curve (marked S) relates desired national saving to the expected real interest rate r, and the investment curve (I)

---

[16]"Has the U.S. Overinvested in Housing?" *Business Review*, Federal Reserve Bank of Philadelphia, March/April 1987, pp. 13–23.

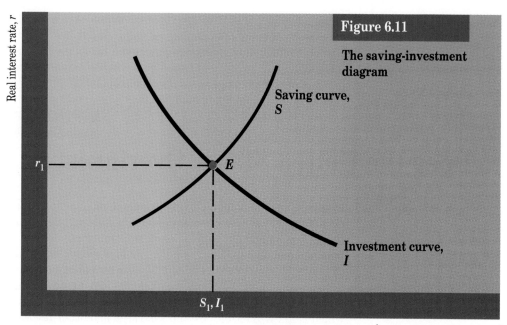

Figure 6.11

The saving-investment diagram

Desired national saving, S^d, and desired investment, I^d

The saving-investment diagram shows the determination of goods market equilibrium. The upward slope of the saving curve S reflects the finding that consumers desire to save more when the real interest rate rises. The investment curve I slopes downward because a lower real interest rate reduces the user cost of capital and increases the desired capital stock. Goods market equilibrium occurs at point E, where desired national saving equals desired investment. The real interest rate that clears the goods market is r_1, and the equilibrium values of national saving and investment are S_1 and I_1.

relates desired investment to the expected real interest rate. The analysis of this chapter clarifies why the two curves have the slopes they do:

- The saving curve slopes upward because even though the income and substitution effects on saving of a higher real interest rate work in opposite directions, the empirical evidence suggests that desired saving rises when the real interest rate rises.

- The investment curve slopes downward because a higher real interest rate r raises the tax-adjusted user cost of capital, equal to $(r + d)p_K/(1 - \tau)$. An increase in the user cost of capital reduces firms' desired capital stocks and thus the amount of investment they do.

Goods market equilibrium, represented by point E in Fig. 6.11, occurs when desired national saving equals desired investment and is brought about by adjustments in the expected real interest rate. In Fig. 6.11 the real interest rate that clears the goods market is shown as r_1, and the equilibrium values of national saving and investment are S_1 and I_1, respectively. As discussed in Chapter 3, changes in desired national saving or desired investment shift the curves and change the real interest rate that clears the goods market.

We saw in Chapter 3 that the saving-investment diagram is a component of the broader *IS-LM* model of the macroeconomy. Can the saving-investment diagram ever be used by itself for macroeconomic analysis, without the rest of the *IS-LM* model? Yes, it can, if two conditions are met: First, clearly, the issue being analyzed should center around saving and investment. For issues relating to, say, inflation or real wage behavior, other components of the *IS-LM* model are needed. Second, the saving-investment diagram takes output as given. Therefore this diagram should be used alone only in situations in which the assumption that output is given is appropriate. As we saw in Chapter 3, under the classical assumption that wages and prices are flexible, output always equals its full-employment level—as determined by the production function, the capital stock, and the supply of labor—and is not affected by current saving or investment decisions. Thus under the classical assumption of wage-price flexibility, output can be treated as given and the saving-investment diagram can be used alone for macroeconomic analysis.

Under the alternative Keynesian assumption of slowly adjusting wages and prices, output may not equal full-employment output in the short run but may depend on current saving and investment decisions, as we will see in Chapter 12. Thus, the saving-investment diagram should not be used alone for short-run analysis in a Keynesian framework. However, Keynesians accept that in the long run, after full wage and price adjustment, output will equal its full-employment level. Thus for the study of longer-run issues, using the saving-investment diagram alone is consistent with either the classical or Keynesian framework. We apply the saving-investment diagram in this way to discuss the effects of government deficits on the economy in the next section. In Chapter 7 we extend the saving-investment diagram to an open-economy context to analyze the sources of trade imbalances and foreign borrowing.

Application

International Differences in the User Cost of Capital

In recent years some economists, policymakers, and businesspeople have expressed the concern that the user cost of capital in the United States is higher, perhaps much higher, than in other leading industrial countries. If true, this problem is a serious one: A higher cost of capital in the United States would cause American firms to invest less than firms in other countries do, leading to relatively slow growth and less rapidly improving living standards.

It is true that investment rates in the United States are low compared with rates in some other industrial countries. Figure 6.12 shows that U.S. gross investment as a share of GNP is about the same as it is in the United Kingdom, but it is lower than investment shares in West Germany and Japan. Whether this lower investment is due to cross-country differences in the user cost of capital is not certain, however. One problem facing researchers is that international differences in tax laws, accounting practices, and financial systems can make comparisons of the user cost of capital difficult. Nevertheless, most studies have found that the cost of capital is higher in the United States than in Germany and Japan, particularly for longer-term projects.[17]

---

[17]See Robert N. McCauley and Steven A. Zimmer, "Explaining International Differences in the Cost of Capital," *Quarterly Review*, Federal Reserve Bank of New York, Summer 1989, pp. 7–28.

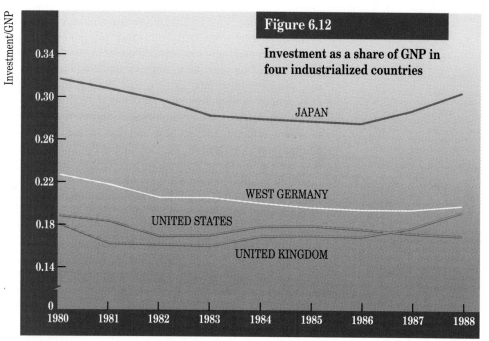

Figure 6.12

Investment as a share of GNP in four industrialized countries

Gross investment as a share of GNP is shown for Japan, West Germany, the United Kingdom, and the United States. As a share of GNP, gross investment in the United States has historically been similar to gross investment in the United Kingdom. Investment in both countries is lower than investment in Japan and West Germany.

What accounts for the difference in user costs? Two explanations for lower user costs in Germany and Japan are greater use of debt by German and Japanese firms and higher national saving rates in those countries. Relative to U.S. firms, German and Japanese firms finance their investments to a greater degree by borrowing from banks or issuing corporate bonds. Since interest on bank loans and corporate bonds is tax-deductible, heavy use of debt results in a lower effective tax rate and a lower tax-adjusted user cost for investment in Germany and Japan. These differences in the use of debt reflect historical differences in the banking systems of the three countries: Much more so than firms in the United States, firms in Germany and Japan have very close relationships with banks and find it easier to obtain bank loans to finance investment.

The second factor that may account for differences in the user cost of capital is the higher national saving rates in Germany and Japan. In the saving-investment diagram, if a country's saving curve is far to the right, then in goods market equilibrium the real interest rate will be low and investment high in that country. Thus high levels of saving potentially explain lower real interest rates and lower user costs in Germany and Japan.

If these two explanations for the U.S. user cost disadvantage are correct, then this disadvantage is likely to disappear soon, if it hasn't already. The use of debt in Germany and particularly in Japan has fallen in recent years as traditional firm-bank relationships have weakened and financial markets have been deregulated; meanwhile in the United States, use of debt by firms grew significantly in the 1980s. Furthermore, the internationalization of capital markets has made it easier for savers to lend across national borders in search of higher returns. As we discuss in Chapter 7, when funds are free to flow to wherever returns are highest, firms in high-saving countries who wish to borrow must pay the same real interest rate as firms in low-saving countries.

6.4   THE BUDGET DEFICIT, NATIONAL SAVING, AND THE REAL INTEREST RATE

Two striking features of the U.S. economy during the 1980s were high real interest rates and low rates of national saving. Real interest rates in the early part of the decade attained their highest values since the Great Depression, after being very low in the 1970s (see Fig. 2.6). At the same time, the U.S. national saving rate fell to unusually low levels (see Fig. 2.4).

The behavior of the real interest rate and of national saving no doubt had multiple causes, including, for example, the 1979–1980 oil price shock discussed in Chapter 3. However, one factor that has come in for a large share of the blame for high interest rates and low saving is the unusually large budget deficits run by the U.S. government in the 1980s. Many commentators argued that U.S. government borrowing drained funds from the capital markets and thus raised real interest rates. Furthermore, since national saving equals private saving minus the government deficit, they claimed that government deficits directly reduced national saving.

In evaluating these arguments, we should realize that the question of whether government deficits affect interest rates and the question of whether deficits affect national saving are essentially one and the same.[18] To make this point in terms of the saving-investment diagram (as in Fig. 6.11), let us suppose that the policies creating the deficit did not involve any change in the effective tax rate on capital. With no change in the tax rate on capital, the desired investment curve will not shift. If the desired investment curve does not shift, we know that the deficit-creating policies will raise the real interest rate if and only if they reduce desired national saving, thereby shifting the saving curve to the left. To answer the question of whether deficits affect the real interest rate, then, we need only answer the question of whether deficits affect desired national saving.

We discuss the link between the government budget deficit and national saving in the rest of this section. In doing so, we emphasize a point often missed in the public debate: that the effect of a budget deficit may depend on what caused the deficit in the first place. As we will explain, virtually all economists agree that a deficit caused by a temporary increase in government purchases will reduce national saving. However, whether a deficit caused by a cut in taxes will reduce national saving is much more controversial.

The Government Budget Constraint

In order to analyze the effects of fiscal policies, we must first discuss the relationship between government spending and revenues, called the government budget constraint. Analyses of fiscal policy sometimes treat the government's spending and taxation decisions as separate and unrelated. But in fact, just as a consumer's income and consumption must ultimately be consistent with each other, so must the government's tax revenues and spending. Like the consumer, the government faces a budget constraint.

To illustrate the government's budget constraint in the simplest possible framework, we assume that there are only two periods, the present and the future. As in our analysis of consumer behavior, the superscript f indicates future-period

---

[18]This statement is strictly true only for a closed economy. We discuss the open-economy case in the next chapter.

variables, and current-period variables have no superscript. We assume that the government collects tax revenue T in the current period and T^f in the future period, and it spends G to purchase goods and services in the current period and G^f to purchase goods and services in the future period. For simplicity we assume no transfers and that initially there is no government debt outstanding. Taxes and government purchases are measured in real terms.

Like a consumer, the government can borrow or save if its income (T) is different from its spending (G); and like a consumer, it must eventually repay its debts.[19] For the consumer the condition that debts must be repaid—the budget constraint—boils down to the condition that the present value of consumption must equal the present value of lifetime resources (Eq. 5.5). Similarly, the **government budget constraint** requires that the present value of the government's purchases, $G + G^f/(1 + r)$, be equal to the present value of its income from tax collection, $T + T^f/(1 + r)$. Writing this constraint out gives

$$G + \frac{G^f}{1 + r} = T + \frac{T^f}{1 + r} \tag{6.6}$$

The government budget constraint makes clear that in examining fiscal policy, we cannot consider a change in only one of the fiscal policy variables G, G^f, T, or T^f. If one of these fiscal policy variables changes, then at least one of the remaining three variables must also change, in order for the government budget constraint to continue to hold.

Suppose, for example, that starting from a budget that is balanced in both periods ($G = T$, $G^f = T^f$), the government raises current purchases G by one unit of real income, while keeping planned future purchases G^f unchanged. Then there are only two basic alternatives open to the government: First, current taxes T can be raised by one unit to pay for the increased purchases. Alternatively, the government can leave current taxes unchanged and borrow one unit from the private sector to pay for its increased purchases, for which it will have to promise to repay $1 + r$ units in the future period. In order to repay what it borrows plus accumulated interest in the future, the government will have to raise future taxes T^f by $1 + r$ units. You should check that if G rises by one unit, either a one-unit increase in T or a $(1 + r)$-unit increase in T^f will cause the government budget constraint, Eq. (6.6), to remain satisfied.

Keeping the government's budget constraint in mind, in the following subsections we ask how an increase in the budget deficit affects national saving and other variables.

A Deficit Due to Increased Government Purchases

Suppose that a military buildup raises current government purchases by $20 billion (in base-year dollars). The buildup is temporary, so future government purchases are unchanged. We assume that current taxes are not raised, so that the current government budget deficit $G - T$ (and hence government borrowing from the private sector) rises by $20 billion. If the real interest rate r is 10%, then future taxes will have to rise by 1.10 times $20 billion, or $22 billion, in order to repay the government's borrowings (with interest) and satisfy the government budget constraint.

---

[19]A difficult question is whether the government, by using new borrowings to repay old loans, can escape repaying at least part of its debt forever. We ignore this possibility here but discuss it in Chapter 16.

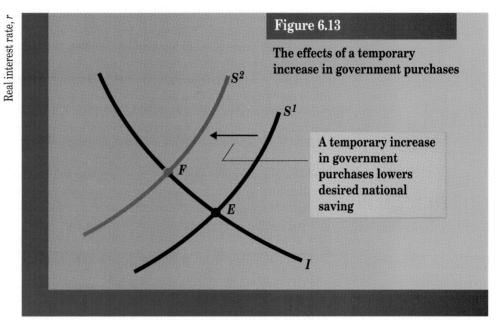

Figure 6.13

The effects of a temporary increase in government purchases

A temporary increase in government purchases lowers desired national saving

Desired national saving, S^d, and desired investment, I^d

A temporary increase in government purchases lowers desired national saving at every value of the real interest rate. The saving curve shifts left, from S^1 to S^2, and the goods market equilibrium point moves from point E to point F. The real interest rate rises and national saving and investment fall.

The effects on the economy of the temporary increase in government purchases are shown in the saving-investment diagram in Fig. 6.13. The initial saving and investment curves are marked S^1 and I, and the initial equilibrium is at point E. Assuming no change in the effective tax rate on capital, desired investment at any given level of the real interest rate is not changed by the increase in government purchases. Thus the investment curve does not shift.

However, the saving curve is shifted to the left, from S^1 to S^2, by the increase in government purchases. That is, desired national saving falls at every level of the real interest rate. Why? Remember that desired national saving equals $Y - C^d - G$, where C^d is desired consumption spending by individuals. We take output Y as given,[20] and G has risen by \$20 billion. To show that desired national saving $Y - C^d - G$ falls, therefore, we only need to show that in response to the increase in government purchases desired consumption C^d falls by less than \$20 billion.

Recall from Chapter 5 that the amount of current consumption households choose to enjoy depends on their present value of lifetime resources ($PVLR$). Households' $PVLR$s are affected by the fiscal policy change because the future taxes the private sector will have to pay are slated to rise by \$22 billion. At a real interest rate of 10%, a \$22 billion increase in future taxes lowers the present value of households' lifetime resources by \$22 billion/1.10, or \$20 billion.

[20]Recall from the classical *IS-LM* model of Chapter 3 that output Y is determined by the position of the full-employment (FE) line.

Since the prospect of higher taxes in the future has lowered households' *PVLRs* by $20 billion, consumers are poorer and will reduce their current consumption. But will current consumption fall by the full $20 billion? No, it will not; because consumers prefer smooth consumption, they will respond to the fall in their *PVLRs* by reducing both current and future consumption. Thus desired current consumption C^d falls, but by less than $20 billion. For example, if consumers reduce their current consumption by half the fall in their *PVLRs*, C^d will fall by $10 billion. If government purchases G rise by $20 billion and desired consumption C^d falls by $10 billion, then desired national saving $Y - C^d - G$ falls by $10 billion (at any given real interest rate). This analysis shows that the increase in government purchases shifts the saving curve to the left in Fig. 6.13.

In showing that the increase in government purchases lowers desired national saving, we assumed that households understand that their future taxes will have to rise. However, if households don't realize that future taxes will be going up and thus don't change their current consumption, the increase in G will reduce desired national saving $Y - C^d - G$ even more, by the full $20 billion of the increase in government purchases.

In Fig. 6.13, because the increase in government purchases shifts the saving curve from S^1 to S^2, the goods market equilibrium shifts from point E to point F. At point F national saving and investment have fallen, and the real interest rate has risen. We conclude that a deficit caused by a temporary increase in government purchases reduces national saving and investment and raises the real interest rate.

A Deficit Due to a Tax Cut: The Ricardian Equivalence Proposition

We have just examined the effects of a deficit caused by an increase in government purchases. Now suppose that, with current and future government purchases held constant, current taxes T are cut by $50 billion. We assume that the tax cut is a **lump-sum** tax cut, which means that the reduction in each taxpayer's taxes is a fixed amount that does not depend on her income, consumption, or other characteristics. Assuming a lump-sum tax cut simplifies the analysis by ensuring that there will be no changes in tax incentives to save and invest of the types discussed in Sections 6.2 and 6.3.

Since government spending is unchanged, the tax cut increases the current deficit by $50 billion. What effects will the increased deficit have on the economy?

We must not forget the government's budget constraint. The current tax cut lowers the present value of the government's tax revenues by $50 billion. Since purchases are unchanged, in order that the government budget constraint be satisfied, the present value of future taxes, $T^f/(1 + r)$, must increase by $50 billion (see Eq. 6.6). If, for example, the real interest rate is 10%, future taxes must increase by $55 billion to satisfy the government budget constraint. Thus the fiscal policy change we are considering must be not just a $50 billion reduction in current taxes T but a current tax cut combined with a $55 billion increase in future taxes T^f. The higher future taxes are required to repay the extra borrowing the government must do in the present when it cuts current taxes.

How will this shifting of taxes from the present to the future affect desired saving and investment? Assuming again that there is no change in the effective tax rate on capital, desired investment does not change. So once again the issue is whether the fiscal action affects desired national saving. Here we come to a surprising and important result: In the absence of borrowing constraints, *a change in the timing of taxes with no change in government purchases does not affect desired national saving.*

To see why this statement is true, recall once again that desired national saving is $Y - C^d - G$. Government purchases G are unchanged, by assumption. Furthermore, the shift in the timing of taxes does not affect desired consumption C^d either. Why? In Chapter 5 we saw that with no borrowing constraints current consumption choices depend only on the present value of lifetime resources and not on the period-by-period timing of income. The tax change we have described causes consumers' disposable income to rise by $50 billion (the amount of the tax cut) in the first period and fall by $55 billion (the amount of the future tax increase) in the second period. However, the tax change does not affect households' *PVLR*s, since at a real interest rate of 10% the $55 billion increase in future taxes reduces households' *PVLR*s by $55 billion/1.10, or $50 billion, which just offsets the $50 billion cut in current taxes. Because it does not change consumers' *PVLR*s, the tax cut has no impact on desired consumption C^d and thus has no effect on desired national saving, $Y - C^d - G$.

Because the tax cut does not affect desired national saving, the saving curve in the saving-investment diagram does not move. Since neither the national saving curve nor the investment curve is shifted by the tax cut, the equilibrium point is unchanged. We conclude that when there are no borrowing constraints, a reduction in current taxes accompanied by an offsetting increase in future taxes has no effect on national saving, investment, or the real interest rate. The result that a budget deficit caused entirely by a current tax cut has no effect on the economy is known as the **Ricardian equivalence proposition,** named after the nineteenth-century economist David Ricardo who first presented the argument.[21]

Ricardian Equivalence and Borrowing Constraints Whether the Ricardian equivalence proposition holds in the real economy is hotly disputed. Despite the logic we have presented, many economists still believe that a deficit created by a tax cut will reduce national saving and raise interest rates.

A possible reason why government budget deficits resulting from tax cuts might affect national saving after all is that some consumers may face binding borrowing constraints. As we saw in Chapter 5, a borrowing-constrained consumer spends all of her current income and wealth on current consumption. So if a borrowing-constrained consumer receives a reduction in her current taxes, even one that does not affect the present value of her lifetime resources, she will spend all of her tax cut on extra current consumption.

Suppose, for example, that half of the $50 billion current tax cut just discussed is received by borrowing-constrained consumers. If the borrowing-constrained consumers use their tax cuts to increase consumption, while the consumption of the unconstrained consumers is unchanged, total consumption will rise by $25 billion. As a result, desired national saving, $Y - C^d - G$, falls by $25 billion. Thus when there are binding borrowing constraints, a current tax cut lowers desired national saving.

---

[21]Although Ricardo first presented the argument, he had strong reservations about whether the irrelevance of tax cuts was true empirically. The strongest recent advocate of Ricardian equivalence is Robert Barro of Harvard. For a presentation of Barro's views, see "The Ricardian Approach to Budget Deficits," *Journal of Economic Perspectives*, Spring 1989, pp. 37–54.

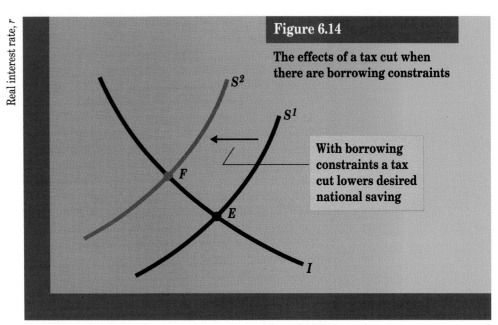

Figure 6.14

The effects of a tax cut when there are borrowing constraints

With borrowing constraints a tax cut lowers desired national saving

Real interest rate, r

Desired national saving, S^d, and desired investment, I^d

When there are borrowing constraints, a tax cut raises the consumption of borrowing-constrained consumers and thus lowers national saving. The national saving curve shifts left, from S^1 to S^2, and the goods market equilibrium point moves from point E to point F. The tax cut raises the real interest rate and lowers national saving and investment.

The effects of the tax cut on the economy when there are borrowing constraints are shown in Fig. 6.14. The initial equilibrium is at point E, at the intersection of the original saving curve S^1 and the investment curve I. Because it increases the current consumption of borrowing-constrained consumers, the tax cut reduces desired national saving and shifts the saving curve left, to S^2. The new equilibrium is at point F, where investment and national saving are lower and the real interest rate is higher. With borrowing constraints, then, the Ricardian equivalence proposition does not hold, and a budget deficit caused by a tax cut has real effects.

Although the existence of borrowing constraints provides a theoretical reason to doubt Ricardian equivalence, the quantitative importance of this and other objections to Ricardian equivalence is ultimately an empirical issue. We discuss Ricardian equivalence further in Chapter 16, where we conclude that budget deficits resulting from tax cuts probably do affect national saving, although by how much remains uncertain.

Whether or not Ricardian equivalence is empirically valid, underlying the concept is an important economic point: The basic measure of the cost of government is the real resources that the government uses, as measured by government purchases and not by the *current* amount of taxes that are collected. Even though government purchases can be funded in the short run through borrowing, we know from the government budget constraint that the government's use of resources must ultimately be reflected in tax collections.[22] This insight explains why knowl-

---

[22]This statement assumes that the government does not in some way default on its debt. Chapter 16 gives a more detailed discussion.

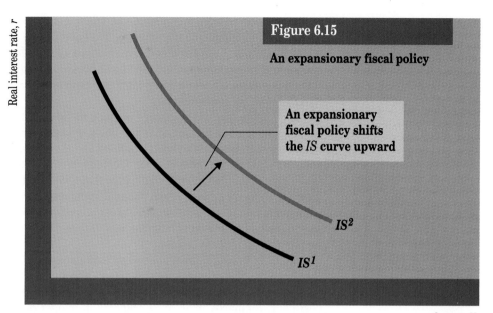

An expansionary fiscal policy lowers desired national saving relative to investment and causes the *IS* curve to shift upward. The two basic examples of expansionary fiscal policies are a temporary increase in government purchases and a lump-sum tax cut (assuming there are binding borrowing constraints).

edgeable taxpayers, who recognize that government expenditures must ultimately be paid for by taxes, concern themselves with the cost and effectiveness of government programs.[23]

Fiscal Policy and the *IS* Curve

Chapter 3 introduced the *IS* curve, which describes the combinations of output and the real interest rate for which the goods market is in equilibrium. We conclude this chapter by summarizing how various fiscal policies affect the *IS* curve.

Recall that, given the level of output, any change that lowers desired national saving relative to desired investment increases the real interest rate that clears the goods market and thus causes the *IS* curve to shift upward. Using this rule, we get the following results:

- An increase in current government purchases reduces desired national saving and thus shifts the *IS* curve upward.

- If Ricardian equivalence holds, a lump-sum reduction in current taxes (accompanied by an increase in future taxes and no change in government purchases) does not affect desired national saving and thus does not affect the *IS* curve.

- If Ricardian equivalence does not hold—say, because there are binding borrowing constraints—then a cut in current taxes reduces desired national saving and thus shifts the *IS* curve upward.

Fiscal policies that shift the *IS* curve upward are called **expansionary.** Figure 6.15 shows an expansionary fiscal policy shifting the *IS* curve from its original

---

[23]This concern may be particularly evident at the state and local level, where balanced-budget laws make the connection between government spending and tax collections especially clear to voters.

position at IS^1 to a higher position at IS^2. Fiscal policies that shift the IS curve downward are called **contractionary.** We have shown that an increase in government purchases is expansionary. By similar logic, a reduction in government purchases is contractionary. If Ricardian equivalence does not hold, a lump-sum tax cut is expansionary and a lump-sum tax increase (that assesses each taxpayer a fixed amount) is contractionary.

A complete list of IS shifters is given in Table 6.2. This table is like Table 3.5 (p. 98), but it adds factors affecting desired saving and investment that were introduced in Chapters 5 and 6. To understand the table, remember that, given output, factors that increase desired national saving relative to desired investment lower the real interest rate that clears the goods market and shift the IS curve downward; factors that reduce desired national saving relative to desired investment shift the IS curve upward. Table 6.2 also can be used as a summary of the factors, other than output and the real interest rate, that affect desired national saving and desired investment.

The link between fiscal policy and national saving is an important issue in macroeconomics. For example, to the extent that budget deficits reduce national saving, in a closed economy they will increase the real interest rate and reduce investment. Similarly, in an open economy, if budget deficits reduce national saving they may have important effects on a nation's trade balance, as we will see in the next chapter.

Table 6.2 Summary

Factors That Shift the IS Curve

An Increase In	Shifts the IS Curve	Reason
Expected future output	Up	Reduces desired national saving
Wealth	Up	Reduces desired national saving
Tax rate on interest income	Up	Reduces desired national saving
Government purchases G	Up	Reduces desired national saving
Lump-sum taxes T	Down	Increases desired national saving *if there are borrowing constraints*; otherwise, no effect
Expected future marginal product of capital MPK^f	Up	Increases desired investment
Effective tax rate on capital	Down	Reduces desired investment

6.5 CHAPTER SUMMARY

1. The effect of a higher real interest rate on saving is theoretically ambiguous. On the one hand, a higher real interest rate makes future consumption cheaper in terms of current consumption, which causes people to want to save more; this effect is called the substitution effect. On the other hand, being able to receive a higher rate of return makes savers feel richer, which causes them to save less and consume more; this effect is called the income effect. Because the income and substitution effects work in opposite directions, saving can either rise or fall when the real interest rate rises. Empirical evidence is not conclusive but suggests that saving rises slightly in response to a higher real interest rate.

2. Tax laws can affect the after-tax real rate of interest received by savers and thus may affect the rate of saving. There is some evidence that reduced taxation of interest, as in Individual Retirement Accounts, can help promote saving.

3. The user cost of capital is the expected real cost of using a unit of capital for a specified period of time. The user cost is the sum of the depreciation cost (the loss in value because the capital wears out) and the interest cost (the interest rate times the price of the capital good).

4. The desired capital stock is the level of capital that maximizes profits. At the desired capital stock the expected future marginal product of capital equals the user cost of capital. Any change that reduces the user cost of capital or increases the expected future marginal product of capital increases the desired capital stock. A reduction in the taxation of capital, as measured by the effective tax rate, also increases the desired capital stock.

5. Gross investment is the creation of new capital. Gross investment minus depreciation equals net investment, the change in the capital stock. When the desired capital stock increases, firms invest more.

6. The saving-investment diagram shows the determination of goods market equilibrium at the point that desired national saving equals desired investment. The saving curve slopes upward in the saving-investment diagram because empirical evidence suggests that, on net, a higher real interest rate raises desired saving. The investment curve slopes downward because a higher real interest rate raises the user cost of capital, which lowers firms' desired capital stocks and thus the amount of investment they do.

7. Like a consumer, the government faces a budget constraint. The government budget constraint requires that the present value of tax revenues equal the present value of government purchases.

8. The effects of budget deficits on national saving and the real interest rate depend on the source of the deficit. A deficit due to a temporary increase in government purchases reduces national saving and raises the real interest rate. According to the Ricardian equivalence proposition, a deficit due to a tax cut, with no change in current or future government purchases, does not affect national saving or the interest rate. However, Ricardian equivalence requires that there be no borrowing constraints. If there are binding borrowing constraints, a tax cut reduces national saving and raises the real interest rate.

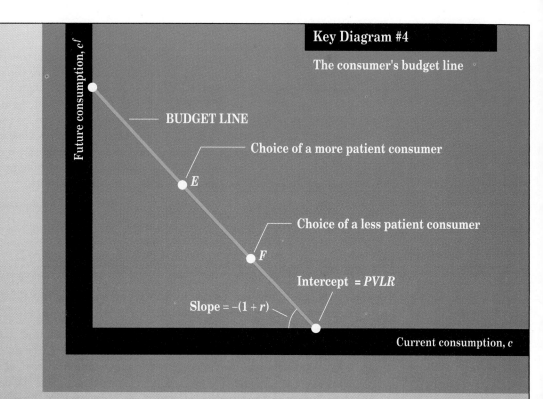

Key Diagram #4

The consumer's budget line

The budget line shows the combinations of current and future consumption that are available to the consumer, given current and future real income, initial wealth, and the real interest rate.

Diagram Elements

- Current consumption c is measured on the horizontal axis, and future consumption c^f is measured on the vertical axis.

- The budget line is the graph of the consumer's budget constraint, Eq. (5.2) or Eq. (5.5). Points on the budget line correspond to combinations of current and future consumption that are available to the consumer.

Analysis

- For each consumer, one point on the budget line is the no-borrowing, no-lending point: The no-borrowing, no-lending point is the point where current consumption equals current income plus initial wealth and future consumption equals future income.

- The slope of the budget line is $-(1 + r)$, where r is the real interest rate. An increase in current consumption by one unit reduces saving by one unit, which (because saving earns interest at rate r) implies a reduction in resources available for future consumption by $1 + r$ units. Thus the downward slope of the budget line captures the consumer's trade-off between current and future consumption.

- The position of the budget line depends only on the consumer's present value of lifetime resources, or *PVLR*. The *PVLR* equals $y + y^f/(1 + r) + a$, where y is current income, y^f is future income, and a is initial wealth. Because the *PVLR* is the amount of current consumption that could be enjoyed if future consumption were zero, the *PVLR* equals the horizontal intercept of the budget line.

- The point on the budget line that the consumer chooses depends on the consumer's degree of patience. A more patient consumer chooses a point like *E* in the figure, where future consumption is relatively high and current consumption is relatively low. A less patient consumer chooses a point like *F*, where current consumption is relatively high and future consumption is relatively low.

- If there is a borrowing constraint, so that borrowing is not allowed, the consumer's current consumption cannot exceed the sum of current income and initial wealth. If, in the absence of a borrowing constraint, the consumer would not have chosen to borrow, then the borrowing constraint has no effect on consumption (it is said to be nonbinding). However, if the consumer would have chosen to borrow in the absence of a borrowing constraint, the borrowing constraint is said to be binding. In this case current consumption is set equal to current income plus initial wealth.

- Saving is found as current income minus current consumption. Current income less than current consumption implies that there is dissaving.

Factors that Shift the Curve

- An increase in the *PVLR*, with the real interest rate held constant, causes the budget line to make a parallel shift to the right by the amount of the increase. In response to an increase in the *PVLR*, the consumer will increase both current and future consumption.

- An increase in the real interest rate causes the budget line to pivot clockwise through the individual consumer's no-borrowing, no-lending point. The slope of the new budget line is $-(1 + r_{new})$, where r_{new} is the new real interest rate.

- For someone who is not initially a borrower, the substitution effect of an increase in the real interest rate increases saving, and the income effect of an increase in the real interest rate reduces saving. The overall effect is uncertain (see Fig. 6.3). For a borrower both the substitution effect and the income effect of an increase in the real interest rate act to increase saving (see Fig. 6.4).

Key Terms

contractionary (fiscal policy), p. 225

desired capital stock, p. 203

effective tax rate, p. 212

expansionary (fiscal policy), p. 227

expected real after-tax rate of return, p. 200

government budget constraint, p. 222

gross investment, p. 214

income effect (of the real interest rate on saving), p. 194

lump-sum (tax change), p. 224

net investment, p. 214

nominal after-tax rate of return, p. 200

Ricardian equivalence proposition, p. 225

substitution effect (of the real interest rate on saving), p. 192

tax-adjusted user cost of capital, p. 212

user cost of capital, p. 206

Key Equations

$$\text{expected real after-tax rate of return} = i(1-t) - \pi^e \quad (6.1)$$

The expected real after-tax rate of return is the nominal after-tax rate of return, $i(1 - t)$, minus the expected inflation rate π^e.

$$u = rp_K + dp_K = (r + d)p_K \quad (6.2)$$

The user cost of capital u is the sum of the interest cost rp_K and the depreciation cost dp_K, where d is the depreciation rate and p_K is the price of a new capital good.

$$MPK^f = \frac{u}{1 - \tau} = \frac{(r + d)p_K}{1 - \tau} \quad (6.3)$$

The desired capital stock, or the capital stock that maximizes the firm's expected profits, is the capital stock for which the expected future marginal product of capital MPK^f equals the tax-adjusted user cost of capital, $u/(1 - \tau)$, where τ is the tax rate on firm revenues.

$$G + \frac{G^f}{1 + r} = T + \frac{T^f}{1 + r} \quad (6.6)$$

The *government budget constraint* says that the present value of government purchases must equal the present value of tax collections.

Review Questions

1. What are the two effects that an increase in the real interest rate has on desired saving? Describe each effect briefly. What is the overall effect of an increase in the real interest rate on saving?

2. How is the saving of someone who is initially a borrower affected by an increase in the real interest rate? Why is this case different from the case of someone who is not a borrower?

3. Define *expected real after-tax rate of return*, and give a numerical example. Why is this variable important to policymakers?

4. What are the two components of the user cost of capital? Explain why each is a cost of using a capital good for one period.

5. What is the desired capital stock? How does it depend on the expected future marginal product of capital,

the user cost of capital, and the effective tax rate?

6. What is the difference between gross investment and net investment? Is it possible for gross investment to be positive at the same time that net investment is negative?

7. Explain why the saving curve slopes upward and the investment curve slopes downward in the saving-investment diagram.

8. A government with an initially balanced budget begins to run a deficit. What is the effect on national saving? Discuss three cases: a deficit due to an increase in government purchases, a deficit due to a lump-sum tax cut (assuming no borrowing constraints), and a deficit due to a lump-sum tax cut (assuming there are borrowing constraints). In each case, what happens to the *IS* curve?

Numerical Problems

1. Joe wants to save $1000 of his current income. If Joe doesn't have an Individual Retirement Account (IRA), he must first pay taxes on the $1000 before he can deposit it in the bank, and he must then pay taxes each year on the interest earned in his account. However, no taxes are due when Joe withdraws. If Joe does have an IRA, he can deposit the full $1000 and accumulate interest without paying taxes until withdrawal, but he must pay taxes on the full amount withdrawn when he takes out his money at retirement. If Joe's tax bracket is 30%, the nominal interest rate is 10%, and Joe's retirement date is five years from the day he deposits the $1000, how much will he have on retirement if he uses the IRA (after all taxes are paid)? If he doesn't use the IRA?

2. Below are data for the Treasury bill interest rate and the GNP deflator for the 1970s. Treasury bills are short-term government bonds.

Year	Treasury Bill Rate	GNP Deflator
1970	—	42.0
1971	4.3%	44.0
1972	4.1	46.5
1973	7.0	49.5
1974	7.9	54.0
1975	5.8	59.3
1976	5.0	63.1
1977	5.3	67.3
1978	7.2	72.2
1979	10.0	78.6
1980	11.5	85.7

a. Calculate the real after-tax rate of return (the nominal after-tax rate of return minus actual inflation) for each year from 1971 to 1980, assuming a tax rate of 30%. For simplicity, assume (not quite accurately) that the interest rate in each year is the rate that could have been earned on a one-year investment made on January 1 of that year, and that the GNP deflator in each year gives the price level as of December 31 of that year.

b. As of December 31, 1980, what would have been the real value of $1000 saved on January 1, 1971, assuming that interest remaining after taxes is reinvested?

c. In part a you will find examples of a negative real after-tax return. If real after-tax returns are negative, is it better not to save at all? If you do save, is it better to hold your savings as cash in the mattress than to put it in the bank or to buy a Treasury bill?

3. Rudy has current real income of 12,000, has initial real wealth of 2000, and expects future real income of 12,000. The real interest rate between the present and the future periods is 20%.

a. Draw Rudy's budget line, and give numerical values for the budget line's horizontal intercept and its slope.

b. The real interest rate rises to 50%. Repeat part a.

c. Initially, Rudy's current consumption is 12,000. Show diagrammatically the substitution and income effects of the increase in the real interest rate on Rudy's saving. Do you have enough information to know whether his saving will increase or decrease?

d. Suppose that initially Rudy's current consumption is 16,000 rather than 12,000. Repeat part c.

4. Hula hoop fabricators cost $100 each. The Hi-Ho Hula Hoop Company is trying to decide how many of these machines to buy. The number of hoops that HHHHC expects to produce each year for each level of capital stock is given in the table.

Number of Fabricators	Total Number of Hoops Produced per Year
0	30
1	100
2	150
3	180
4	195
5	205
6	210

Hula hoops have a real value of $1 each. HHHHC has no other costs besides the cost of fabricators.

a. Find the expected future marginal product of capital (in terms of dollars) for each level of capital. The MPK^f for the third fabricator, for example, is the real value of the extra output obtained when the third fabricator is added.

b. If the real interest rate is 12% per year and the depreciation rate of capital is 20% per year, find the user cost of capital (in dollars per fabricator per year). How many fabricators should HHHHC buy?

c. Repeat part b for a real interest rate of 8% per year.

d. Repeat part b for the case in which there is a 40% tax on HHHHC's revenues from selling hula hoops.

e. A technical innovation doubles the total number of hoops any given number of fabricators can produce. How many fabricators should HHHHC buy when the real interest rate is 12% per year? 8% per year? Assume that there are no taxes and that the depreciation rate is still 20% per year.

5. You have just taken a new job that requires you to move to a new city. In relocating, you face the decision of whether to buy or rent a house. Here are the relevant data: A suitable house costs $200,000 and you have saved enough for the down payment. The (nominal) mortgage interest rate is 10% per year, and you can also earn 10% per year on your saving. Mortgage interest payments are tax-deductible, interest earnings on saving are taxable, and you are in a 30% tax bracket. Interest is paid or received, and taxes are paid, on the last day of the year. The expected inflation rate is 5% per year.

Maintenance expenses plus all other miscellaneous expenses are equal to 6% of the initial value of house. Assume that these expenses are also paid entirely on the last day of the year. If you incur all of the expenses, the house retains its full real value. There are no other relevant costs or expenses.

   a. What is the expected after-tax real interest rate on the home mortgage?
   b. What is the user cost of the house?
   c. If all you care about is minimizing your living ex-

penses, at what (annual) rent level would you be just indifferent between buying a house and renting a house of comparable quality? Rent is also paid on the last day of the year.

6. In a certain economy current output $Y = 1000$, current government purchases $G = 200$, and current taxes $T = 100$. In addition to any returns earned from saving, consumers expect future before-tax labor income of 600. Desired current consumption equals one half of the present value of consumers' lifetime resources, net of taxes paid to the government. Desired investment is fixed and equals 200. Initial wealth and future government purchases are zero. There are no borrowing constraints.

   a. Find the equilibrium real interest rate, current consumption, and national saving for this economy. (*Hint:* In finding the *PVLR* of consumers, use the government budget constraint to find the present value of the tax burden.)
   b. What are future taxes?
   c. Current taxes are raised to 200. What are the effects of this increase on the real interest rate, current consumption, and national saving? What happens to future taxes?
   d. With current taxes back to 100 current government purchases are raised to 250. Find the effects on the real interest rate, current consumption, national saving, and future taxes.

Analytical Problems

1. We mentioned in Chapter 5 that, in practice, consumers must pay a higher real interest rate to borrow than they receive on their saving. Draw a consumer's budget line under the assumption that the after-tax real rate of return earned on saving, r_s, is lower than the after-tax real interest rate paid to borrow, r_b. Assuming that initially interest income is taxed and interest paid is tax-deductible, how would the budget line you have drawn be affected by the elimination of tax deductibility of interest payments? How would the elimination of tax deductibility of interest payments be likely to affect aggregate saving?

2. Advocates of the "consumption tax" suggest that the government ought not to tax interest income but instead should levy a fixed-percentage sales tax on current and future consumption. Starting from an initial situation in which interest income is taxed and there is no sales tax on consumption, show the effects of implementing these

two measures on the consumer's budget line. Take the before-tax real interest rate as given and assume that total tax revenues are approximately unaffected by the policy change. Evaluate the claim that a consumption tax system would increase national saving.

3. Use the saving-investment diagram to analyze the effects of the following on national saving, investment, and the real interest rate.

   a. Consumers become more future-oriented and thus decide to save more.
   b. The government introduces an investment tax credit (this is offset by other types of taxes, so total tax collections are kept unchanged).
   c. The government introduces Individual Retirement Accounts, which increase the after-tax return earned by savers.

4. Economists often argue that a temporary increase in government purchases, say for military purposes, will crowd out private investment. Use the saving-investment diagram to illustrate this point. Assuming no borrowing constraints, does it matter whether the temporary increase in military spending is funded by taxes or by borrowing?

Alternatively, suppose that the temporary increase in government purchases is for "infrastru ture" (roads, sewers, bridges) rather than for military purposes. The government spending on infrastructure makes investment more productive, increasing the expected future *MPK* at each level of the capital stock. Using the saving-investment diagram, analyze the effects of government spending on infrastructure. What are the effects on consumption, national saving, investment, and the real interest rate? Does investment by private firms get crowded out by this kind of government investment? Assume that there is no change in current productivity or current output.

5. "A permanent increase in government purchases has a larger effect than a temporary increase of the same amount." Use the saving-investment diagram to evaluate this statement, focusing on the effects on consumption, investment, and the real interest rate. Model a permanent increase in government purchases as an equal increase in current and future government purchases. Assume no borrowing constraints.

7
Saving and Investment in the Open Economy

With virtually no exceptions, modern economies are open economies, which means that they engage in international trade and in international borrowing and lending. Economic openness is of tremendous benefit to the average person: Because the United States is an open economy, American consumers can enjoy products from around the world (Japanese videocassette recorders, Italian shoes, Irish woolens) and American businesses can find new markets abroad for their products (computers, beef, financial services). Similarly, the internationalization of financial markets means that American savers have the opportunity to purchase German government bonds or shares in Taiwanese companies as well as American assets, while American firms who want to finance investment projects can borrow in London or Tokyo as well as in New York.

Beyond the economic diversity and opportunity it creates, economic openness carries another important implication: In an open economy, *a country's spending need not equal its production in every period*, as would have to be the case in a closed economy with no foreign trade and no international borrowing and lending. In particular, by importing more than they export and borrowing from abroad to pay for the difference, the residents of an open economy can temporarily spend more than they produce.

The ability of an open economy to spend more than it produces is both an opportunity and a potential problem: For example, by borrowing abroad, the United States was able to finance a large excess of imports over exports during the 1980s. As a result, Americans enjoyed higher levels of consumption, investment, and government purchases than they could have otherwise, but at the same time they incurred increasing foreign debts that may be a future burden to the U.S. economy. Similarly, by means of heavy foreign borrowing during the 1970s, some less developed countries (LDCs) were able to avoid major reductions in domestic spending even though the two oil price shocks caused sharp declines in their output. During the 1980s, however, many LDC borrowers became unable to cope with the burden of their foreign debts—a situation that became known as the LDC debt crisis—and perhaps as a result suffered a severe reduction in economic growth.

Why is it that at certain times countries borrow abroad to pay for an excess of imports over exports, but at other times they export more than they import and lend the difference to other countries? Why doesn't each country just balance its books and import as much as it exports each year? This chapter explains why the fundamental determinants of a country's trade position are the country's saving and investment decisions.

To study how desired national saving and desired investment help determine patterns of international trade and lending, in this chapter we extend the idea of goods market equilibrium, as described by the saving-investment diagram, to include a foreign sector. We show that, unlike the situation in a closed economy, in an open economy desired national saving and desired investment do not have to be equal. Instead, we find that when a country's desired national saving exceeds its desired investment, the country will be a lender in the international capital market and its exports will exceed its imports. Similarly, when a country's desired national saving is less than desired investment, the country will be an international borrower and its imports will exceed its exports.

In its emphasis on saving and investment, this chapter fits well with the theme of this part of the book. However, in order to focus on the role of saving and investment, here we ignore some other factors that also influence international trade and lending. The most important of these factors is the exchange rate, or the rate at which domestic currency can be exchanged for foreign currency. Exchange rates and their role in the economy receive a full discussion in Chapter 13.

7.1   BALANCE OF PAYMENTS ACCOUNTING

In order to study the factors that affect international trade and lending, we first need to understand the basics of balance of payments accounting. The **balance of payments accounts,** which are part of the national income accounts discussed in Chapter 2, are the record of a country's international transactions. (The box "In Touch with the Macroeconomy," p. 241, contains information about how the balance of payments accounts are constructed and where these data can be found.) The balance of payments accounts consist of two separate accounts, called the current account and the capital account.

The Current Account

The **current account** of a given country measures the country's trade in currently produced goods or services. The goods and services that are included in the current account fall into three categories: merchandise, services, and income receipts from assets abroad.

Merchandise consists of currently produced goods, such as American soybeans, French perfume, Brazilian coffee, and Japanese cars. When an American buys a Japanese car, for example, the transaction is recorded as a merchandise import for the United States and a merchandise export for Japan. The difference between a country's merchandise exports and its merchandise imports is called the **merchandise trade balance,** or just the trade balance. The merchandise trade balance receives a lot of attention from the public and the press.[1] This attention does

---

[1]This attention may be due in part to the fact that the merchandise trade data are available monthly, whereas most balance of payments data are available only quarterly. See the box "In Touch with the Macroeconomy" (p. 241).

not seem entirely warranted, however, since merchandise trade is only one component of the current account.

Internationally traded services include transportation, tourism, insurance, education, and financial services, among others. When an American family spends a week's vacation in Mexico, the family's expenditures in Mexico on accommodations, food, entertainment, sight-seeing tours, and so on, are counted in the current account as an import of tourism services for the United States and as an export of tourism services for Mexico. When a foreign student attends college in the United States, her tuition payments are included as an export of services for the United States and an import of services for her home country.

Income receipts from assets abroad include interest payments, dividends, royalties, and other returns that residents of a country receive from assets (such as bonds, stocks, or patents) that they own outside their own country. Investment income received from abroad counts as an export for the home country. For example, the interest an American investor receives from a foreign government bond or the profits an American company receives from a foreign subsidiary count as exports for the United States (and imports for the foreign country). Income receipts from assets abroad are treated as exports because these receipts are payments from foreigners for the services of those assets. Indeed, until 1990 the income receipts category was lumped together with the services category in official tabulations of the current account.

In a given country's current account, exports are treated as credit (plus) items and imports are counted as debit (minus) items. Examples of credit items in the current account of the United States are the sale of an American-made jetliner to a European airline company (a merchandise export), payments to an American management consulting firm from a Canadian client (an export of services), and dividends received by an American stockholder in an Australian firm (income from assets abroad). Likewise, U.S. imports of oil from the Middle East, spending by U.S. tourists in Europe, and the payment of interest to a foreign holder of a U.S. Treasury bond are debit items in the U.S. current account. As an aid in keeping track of the distinction between credits and debits, remember that credit items in the U.S. current account involve a flow of funds *into* the United States (as when foreigners pay for a U.S. export or an American receives interest on a foreign investment), and debit items are those that involve a flow of funds *out of* the United States.

U.S. current account data for 1990 are given in the top portion of Table 7.1. Besides exports and imports of goods, services, and income from assets abroad, there is one additional item in the table, called net unilateral transfers. **Unilateral transfers** are payments made from one country to another that do not correspond to the purchase of any good, service, or asset. Examples are official foreign aid (a payment from one government to another) or a gift of money from a resident of one country to family members living in another country. When the United States makes a transfer to another country, the amount of the transfer is a debit or minus item in the U.S. current account. (Intuitively, the transfer causes funds to flow out of the country.) A country's net unilateral transfers equal unilateral transfers received by the country minus unilateral transfers flowing out of the country. As you can see from Table 7.1, the U.S. is a net donor to other countries, since the net unilateral transfers entry is negative. (Unusually, because of donations by foreign governments to help defray the cost of the war in the Persian Gulf, in the first quarter of 1991 the United States was a net recipient of unilateral transfers.)

Table 7.1 Balance of Payments Accounts of the United States, 1990 (in Billions of Dollars)

Current Account			
Exports of goods, services, and income		648.7	
Merchandise	389.3		
Services	130.6		
Income receipts from assets	128.8		
Imports of goods, services, and income		−727.0	
Merchandise	−498.0		
Services	−107.7		
Income payments on assets	−121.3		
Net unilateral transfers		−21.1	
Current account balance (CA)			−99.4
Capital Account			
Increase in U.S.-owned assets abroad (capital outflow)		−61.3	
U.S. official reserve assets	−2.2		
Other U.S. assets	−59.1		
Increase in foreign-owned assets in United States (capital inflow)		87.5	
Foreign official assets	30.8		
Other foreign assets	56.8		
Capital account balance (KA)			26.2
Statistical discrepancy			73.2
Addendum			
Official settlements balance = balance of payments = increase in U.S. official reserve assets − increase in foreign official assets = 2.2 − 30.8			−28.6

Source: *Survey of Current Business*, March 1991, p. 34. Data are preliminary.

Adding all of the credit items and subtracting all the debit items in the current account yields a number called the **current account balance.** If the current account balance is positive, with the value of credit items exceeding the value of debit items, the country is said to have a current account surplus. If the current account balance is negative, with the value of debit items exceeding the value of credit items, then the country has a current account deficit. Table 7.1 shows that the United States had a $99.4 billion current account deficit in 1990.

The current account balance is very similar to net exports NX, defined in Chapter 2 as exports minus imports. The only difference between the two concepts is that the current account balance includes net unilateral transfers but net exports do not. If we agree to ignore net unilateral transfers (it is a small item), then we can use the concepts of current account balance and net exports interchangeably. Ignoring net unilateral transfers, a current account surplus means the same thing as positive net exports, or exports greater than imports; and a current account deficit is the same as negative net exports, or imports greater than exports.

The Capital Account

Not all transactions with foreign countries are tallied in the current account. If a Japanese investor purchases a ten-year-old vacation house in Hawaii, for example, the purchase is not included in the current account of either the United States or

Japan. The reason is that the current account includes only the trade of currently produced goods and services. Since a ten-year-old house is an existing asset rather than a currently produced good or service, its sale is not part of the current account.

Trade between countries in existing assets, either real or financial, is recorded in the **capital account**. When the home country sells an asset to another country, the transaction is recorded as a **capital inflow** for the home country and as a credit item in the capital account. So, for example, if an American hotel is sold to Italian investors, the transaction is counted as a capital inflow to the United States and as a plus item in the U.S. capital account. When the home country buys an asset from abroad (say an American obtains a Swiss bank account), the transaction is a **capital outflow** from the home country (the United States in this example) and a minus item in the home country's capital account.

This terminology may seem puzzling: How can the sale of an asset from the home country represent an inflow of capital to the home country, and why is the sale of an asset treated as a credit in the capital account? As in the discussion of the current account, it is helpful to remember which way the funds are flowing. A capital *inflow* is called that because an asset sale generates an *inflow* of funds to the domestic economy. Thus when a Japanese investor buys a house in Hawaii, the transaction is recorded as a capital inflow for the United States and a capital outflow for Japan. Because a capital inflow implies that funds are flowing into the domestic economy, it is treated as a credit item in the capital account.

The **capital account balance** equals the value of capital inflows (credit items) minus the value of capital outflows (debit items). When residents of a given country sell more assets to foreigners than they buy from foreigners, the capital account balance is positive and there is said to be a capital account surplus. When residents of the home country purchase more assets from foreigners than they sell, the capital account balance is negative and there is a capital account deficit. Table 7.1 shows that in 1990 Americans increased their holdings of foreign assets by $61.3 billion, while foreigners increased their holdings of U.S. assets by $87.5 billion. Thus the United States had a capital account surplus (a net capital inflow) of $26.2 billion in 1990 ($87.5 billion minus $61.3 billion.)

The Official Settlements Balance   In Table 7.1 one set of capital account transactions, transactions in official reserve assets, has been broken out separately. These transactions differ from other capital market transactions in that they are conducted by central banks, which are the official institutions (such as the Federal Reserve in the United States) that control national money supplies. **Official reserve assets** are assets held by central banks, other than domestic money or securities, that can be used in making international payments. Historically, gold was the primary form of official reserve asset, but now the official reserves of central banks also include government securities of major industrialized economies, foreign bank deposits, and special assets created by the International Monetary Fund (an international agency set up to facilitate trade and financial relationships among countries).

Central banks can change the quantity of official reserve assets they hold by buying or selling reserve assets on open markets. According to Table 7.1, in 1990 official reserve assets held by the U.S. central bank increased by $2.2 billion (remember that the minus sign indicates a capital outflow, or a purchase of foreign

In touch

with the Macroeconomy

The Balance of Payments Accounts

The data on U.S. international transactions that make up the balance of payments accounts are produced quarterly by the Bureau of Economic Analysis (BEA) in the U.S. Department of Commerce. The BEA's data are released to the public about two and a half months after the end of the quarter to which they refer, and detailed figures appear in the March, June, September, and December issues of the *Survey of Current Business*. Summary data, much like those in Table 7.1, can be found in a number of publications, including the monthly *Federal Reserve Bulletin* and the *Economic Report of the President*, which appears each February. The *Economic Report* is also a good source of historical balance of payments data. Balance of payments data are revised each June to reflect more complete information, with revisions being made to data as much as four years old.

Although full information about the balance of payments accounts is available only quarterly, some components of the accounts are released monthly. The best-

known example is the merchandise trade balance, which equals exports of goods minus imports of goods. These data are initially tabulated by the Bureau of the Census (which then passes them on to the BEA) and are based primarily on information provided by the U.S. Customs Service, the government agency responsible for monitoring flows of goods in and out of the country. In recent years the Census Bureau has also negotiated with the data collection agencies of major U.S. trading partners to swap information about trade flows. The benefit of exchanging trade information is that it will allow the Census Bureau to find out if, for example, Canadian estimates of the imports they receive from the United States are similar to American estimates of U.S. exports shipped to Canada. In principle, of course, the two numbers should be the same.

For more information: Bureau of Economic Analysis, *The Balance of Payments of the United States: Concepts, Data Sources, and Estimating Procedures*, Washington, D.C.: U.S. Government Printing Office, 1990.

assets). In the same year foreign central banks accumulated $30.8 billion in dollar-denominated reserve assets (see the line "Foreign official assets"). The **official settlements balance**—also called the **balance of payments**—is the net increase (domestic less foreign) in a country's official reserve assets. A country that increases its net holdings of reserve assets during a year has a balance of payments surplus, and a country that reduces its net holdings of reserve assets has a balance of payments deficit. For the United States in 1990 the official settlements balance was $2.2 billion less $30.8 billion, or −$28.6 billion. Thus the United States had a balance of payments deficit of $28.6 billion in 1990.

The Relationship between the Current Account and the Capital Account

The logic of balance of payments accounting implies a close relationship between the current account and the capital account: Except for errors due to problems of measurement, in each period *the current account balance and the capital account balance must sum to zero*. In symbols, if

$$CA = \text{current account balance},$$
$$KA = \text{capital account balance},$$

then

$$CA + KA = 0. \tag{7.1}$$

The reason that Eq. (7.1) holds is that every international transaction involves a swap of goods, services, or assets between countries, and the two sides of the swap always have offsetting effects on the sum of the current and capital account balances, $CA + KA$. Thus the sum of the current and capital account balances must equal zero.

An example will help make the point clear (see Table 7.2 for a summary). Suppose that an American buys an imported British sweater, paying $75. This transaction is an import of goods to the United States and thus reduces the U.S. current account balance by $75. However, the British exporter who sold the sweater now holds $75. What will he do with it? There are several possibilities, any of which will offset the effect of the purchase of the sweater on the sum of the current and capital account balances.

For example, the Briton may use the $75 to buy an American product, say a computer game. This purchase is a $75 export for the United States. This U.S. export together with the original import of the sweater into the United States implies no net change in the U.S. current account balance CA. The U.S. capital account balance KA has not changed, since no assets have been traded. Thus there is no change in the sum of CA and KA.

A second possibility is that the Briton will use the $75 to buy a U.S. asset, say a bond issued by a U.S. corporation. The purchase of this bond is a capital inflow to the United States. So there is now a $75 surplus in the U.S. capital account offsetting the $75 deficit in the U.S. current account caused by the original import of the sweater. Again the sum of the current and capital account balances, $CA + KA$, is unaffected by the combination of transactions.

Finally, the Briton may decide to go to his bank and trade his dollars for British pounds. If the bank sells these dollars to another Briton for the purpose of buying American exports or American assets, or if it buys American assets itself, we are back in one of the previous two cases. Alternatively, the bank may sell the dollars to the Federal Reserve in exchange for pounds. But in giving up $75 worth of British pounds, the Federal Reserve reduces its holdings of official reserve assets by $75, which counts as a capital inflow. As in the previous case, the capital account balance rises by $75, offsetting the decline in the current account balance caused by the import of the sweater.[2]

This example shows why, conceptually, the current account balance and capital account balance must always sum to zero. In practice, problems in measuring international transactions prevent this relationship from holding exactly. The amount that would have to be added to the sum of the current and capital account balances for this sum to reach its theoretical value of zero is called the **statistical discrep-**

---

[2]In this case the balance of payments falls $75, reflecting the Fed's loss of official reserves. We did not consider the possibility that the Briton would just hold $75 in U.S. currency. Since dollars are an obligation of the United States (in particular, of the Fed), the Briton's acquisition of dollars would be a credit item in the U.S. capital account, which would offset the effect of the sweater import on the U.S. current account.

Table 7.2 Why the Current Account Balance and the Capital Account Balance Sum to Zero: An Example (Balance of Payments Data Refer to the United States)

Case I: United States Imports $75 Sweater from Britain; Britain Imports $75 Computer Game from United States

Current Account	
Exports	+ $75
Imports	− $75
Current account balance (*CA*)	0
Capital Account	
No transaction	
Capital account balance (*KA*)	0
Sum of current and capital account balances (*CA* + *KA*)	0

Case II: United States Imports $75 Sweater from Britain; Britain Buys $75 Bond From United States

Current Account	
Imports	− $75
Current account balance (*CA*)	− $75
Capital Account	
Capital inflow	+ $75
Capital account balance (*KA*)	+ $75
Sum of current and capital account balances (*CA* + *KA*)	0

Case III: United States Imports $75 Sweater from Britain; Federal Reserve Sells $75 of British Pounds to British Bank

Current Account	
Imports	− $75
Current account balance (*CA*)	− $75
Capital Account	
Capital inflow (reduction in U.S. official reserve assets)	+ $75
Capital account balance (*KA*)	+ $75
Sum of current and capital account balances (*CA* + *KA*)	0

Note: For a description of the example, see the text.

ancy. From Table 7.1 you can see that in 1990 the statistical discrepancy was about $73 billion. ($73 billion is an enormous "discrepancy"! Normally, the statistical discrepancy is much smaller. For a discussion of the discrepancy, see the *Survey of Current Business*, March 1991, p. 35.) Box 7.1 on p. 244 discusses a puzzle that arises because of statistical discrepancies in the balance of payments accounts.

Net Foreign Assets and the Balance of Payments Accounts

In Chapter 2 we defined the net foreign assets of a country as the foreign assets held by the country's residents (including, for example, foreign stocks, bonds, or real estate) minus the country's foreign liabilities (domestic physical and financial

---

The exports and imports of any individual country need not be equal in value. However, since every export is somebody else's import, for the world taken as a whole exports must equal imports and the current account surplus must be zero.

BOX 7.1: DOES MARS HAVE A CURRENT ACCOUNT SURPLUS?

Or must it? When official current account figures for all the world's nations are added up, the result is a current account deficit for the planet. This measured deficit increased sharply in the early 1980s, reaching $114 billion in 1982. Is the Earth a net importer, and does Mars have a current account surplus?

Since substantial extraterrestrial trade seems unlikely, the explanation of the Earth's current account deficit must be statistical and measurement problems. A study by the International Monetary Fund* concluded that the main problem is the misreporting of income from assets held abroad. For example, interest earned by an American on a foreign bank account should in principle be counted as a plus item in the U.S. current account and a minus item in the current account of the foreign country. However, if the American fails to report this interest income to the U.S. government, it may show up only as a debit to the foreign current account, leading to a measured Earth-wide current account deficit. The fact that the world's current account deficit rose in the early 1980s, at a time when interest rates were also rising, is consistent with this explanation.

*International Monetary Fund, *Report on the World Current Account Discrepancy*, September 1987.

---

assets owned by foreigners). Net foreign assets are part of a country's national wealth, along with the country's domestic physical assets, such as land and the capital stock.

The total value of a country's net foreign assets can change in two ways: First, the value of existing foreign assets and foreign liabilities can change, as when stock held by an American in a foreign corporation increases in value or the value of U.S. farmland owned by a foreigner declines. Second, the country can acquire new foreign assets or incur new foreign liabilities.

What determines the quantity of new foreign assets that a country can acquire? In any period *the net amount of new foreign assets that a country acquires equals its current account surplus*, which is the same as net exports, if we ignore unilateral transfers. For example, if a country exports $10 billion more in goods and services than it imports, thereby running a $10 billion current account surplus, it uses the $10 billion to acquire foreign assets or to reduce foreign liabilities. In this case we say that the country has done net foreign lending of $10 billion.

Similarly, if a country has a $10 billion current account deficit, it must cover this deficit either by selling assets to foreigners or borrowing from foreigners, which in either case reduces the country's net foreign assets by $10 billion. We describe this situation by saying that the country has done net foreign borrowing of $10 billion.

The link between the current account and the acquisition of foreign assets can also be shown by recalling that a country's current account balance CA and capital account balance KA must add up to zero (Eq. 7.1). Because the current account balance plus the capital account balance equals zero, if a country has a current account surplus, it must also have an equal-sized capital account deficit. A capital account deficit in turn implies that the country is experiencing capital outflows, or

| **Table 7.3 Summary** |
| Equivalent Measures of a Country's International Trade and Lending |
| **Each Item Describes the Same Situation** |
| Net exports of $10 billion[a] |
| A current account surplus of $10 billion |
| A capital account deficit of $10 billion |
| Net acquisition of foreign assets of $10 billion |
| Net foreign lending of $10 billion |

[a]Assuming no net unilateral transfers.

that on net it is acquiring foreign assets. Likewise, a current account deficit implies a capital account surplus and a decline in the country's net holdings of foreign assets.

Table 7.3 summarizes the relationships among net exports, the current and capital account balances, and a country's net acquisition of foreign assets.

read this ⟶ **Application**

Is the United States the World's Largest International Debtor?

From around World War I until the 1980s, the United States was a net creditor internationally, in that it had more foreign assets than liabilities. However, during the 1980s a string of large current account deficits—which had to be financed by equally large capital account surpluses—dramatically reduced the net holding of international assets by the United States. According to official statistics of the Bureau of Economic Analysis (BEA), the United States' foreign obligations drew even with its foreign assets in 1984, and by the late 1980s America was a net international debtor, with foreign liabilities exceeding foreign assets by about $500 billion. The implication of these numbers, that over the 1980s the United States had become the world's largest international debtor, was often cited as an indication of American economic decline.

It is certainly true that years of current account deficits have eroded America's net foreign assets. However, the claim that the United States is the world's largest debtor needs to be put in some perspective. First, the economic burden created by any debt depends not on the absolute size of the debt but on its size relative to the debtor's economic resources. If the $500 billion estimate for U.S. net foreign debt is correct, the debt represents less than 10% of American annual GNP—a much smaller share of GNP than the debt of countries such as Brazil or Mexico, although larger than the debt-to-GNP ratio of most other industrial countries.

Second, there are uncertainties about the $500 billion estimate of U.S. debt. Measuring the net foreign obligations of the United States is not an easy task, and the official BEA estimates have been criticized. The main point raised by critics is that many foreign assets and liabilities are valued by the BEA at their original cost, or book value, rather than at their current market value. So, for example, a company purchased for $10,000,000 ten years ago would still be valued at $10,000,000 in the BEA's calculation, even though inflation and economic growth might mean that the company's dollar value is much greater today. Since many American investments abroad were made some years ago, but many foreign investments in the United States were made relatively recently, the valuing of investments at original cost understates the value of American investments abroad more than it understates the value of foreign investments in the United States.[3]

Studies that have attempted to correct for measurement problems have generally obtained more optimistic results for the U.S. net foreign asset position. For example, Michael Ulan and William G. Dewald,[4] economists at the U.S. Department of State, estimated that as of 1987, the last year of their study, the United States was still a net international creditor. Another piece of evidence in favor of the view that the United States is not a large net debtor is that U.S. receipts from assets abroad remain about the same size as payments made to foreign holders of U.S. assets (see Table 7.1).

In evaluating the significance of a nation's foreign debt, we should also remember that net foreign assets are only one component of national wealth, the other being domestic physical assets. If national wealth is growing at a healthy rate overall, then there is not much reason to be concerned if one of its components is falling. For example, if a country were to incur large foreign debts in order to build up its capital stock, and if the new capital were highly productive, then the foreign debt would not be an economic burden. Unfortunately, this scenario does not seem to be applicable to the United States: Although measurement is again difficult, it appears that the national wealth of the United States has grown relatively slowly in real terms over the past two decades, reflecting low rates of national saving (see Fig. 2.4). This slow growth of total national wealth should be of much greater concern to policymakers than the behavior of net foreign assets viewed in isolation.

7.2   GOODS MARKET EQUILIBRIUM IN AN OPEN ECONOMY

In Chapter 3 we derived the goods market equilibrium condition for a closed economy. We saw that this condition can be expressed either as desired national saving equals desired investment or, equivalently, as the aggregate supply of goods equals the aggregate demand for goods. With a bit of modification these same two conditions can be used to describe goods market equilibrium in an open economy.

Let's begin with the open-economy version of the condition that desired national saving equals desired investment. In Chapter 2 we derived the following national income accounting identity (Eq. 2.9):

$$S = I + NX. \qquad (7.2)$$

[3]The BEA has acknowledged this problem. See Russell B. Scholl, "International Investment Position: Component Detail for 1989," *Survey of Current Business*, June 1990, pp. 54–65.

[4]"The U.S. Net International Investment Position: Misstated and Misunderstood," in James A. Dorn and William A. Niskanen, eds., *Dollars, Deficits, and Trade*, Boston: Kluwer Academic Publishers, 1989.

Equation (7.2) is a version of the uses-of-saving identity. It states that national saving S has two uses: (1) to increase the nation's stock of capital by funding investment I; and (2) to increase the nation's stock of net foreign assets by lending to foreigners the amount they need to purchase net exports NX. Equivalently, Eq. (7.2) says that net exports NX equal national saving S minus investment I.

Equation (7.2) is an identity and so must always hold. For the economy to be in goods market equilibrium, actual national saving and investment must also equal their desired levels. If actual and desired levels are equal, Eq. (7.2) becomes

$$S^d = I^d + NX, \tag{7.3}$$

where S^d and I^d stand for desired national saving and desired investment. Equation (7.3) is the goods market equilibrium condition for an open economy. Since net exports NX equals net lending to foreigners, or capital outflows, Eq. (7.3) can be interpreted as follows: *In goods market equilibrium in an open economy, the desired amount of national saving S^d must equal the desired amount of domestic investment I^d plus the amount lent abroad NX.* Note that the closed-economy equilibrium condition is a special case of Eq. (7.3) with NX set to zero.

The goods market equilibrium condition for the open economy can also be written in terms of the aggregate supply and aggregate demand for goods. In an open economy, where net exports NX are part of the aggregate demand for goods, this alternative condition for goods market equilibrium is

$$Y = C^d + I^d + G + NX, \tag{7.4}$$

where Y is output, C^d is desired consumption spending, and G is government purchases. This way of writing the goods market equilibrium condition is equivalent to the condition in Eq. (7.3).[5]

A bit of insight can be obtained by rewriting Eq. (7.4) once more as

$$NX = Y - (C^d + I^d + G). \tag{7.5}$$

Equation (7.5) says that in goods market equilibrium the amount of net exports a country sends abroad equals the country's total output Y less total desired spending by domestic residents, $C^d + I^d + G$. Total spending by domestic residents is called **absorption.** So Eq. (7.5) says that an economy in which output exceeds absorption will send goods abroad ($NX > 0$), and an economy that absorbs more than it produces will be a net importer ($NX < 0$).

7.3 SAVING AND INVESTMENT IN A SMALL OPEN ECONOMY

We now begin our analysis of saving and investment in an open economy and their relation to international trade and lending. We first consider the case of a small open economy. By a **small open economy** we mean an economy that is too small to affect the world real interest rate. The **world real interest rate** is the real interest rate that prevails in the international capital market, the market in which individuals, businesses, and governments borrow and lend across national borders. Because changes in saving and investment in the small open economy are not of a great enough magnitude to affect the world real interest rate, we can treat this interest rate as fixed in our analysis, which is a convenient simplification. Later in

---

[5]To see that Eq. (7.4) is equivalent to Eq. (7.3), subtract $C^d + G$ from both sides of Eq. (7.4) and note that $Y - C^d - G$ equals desired national saving.

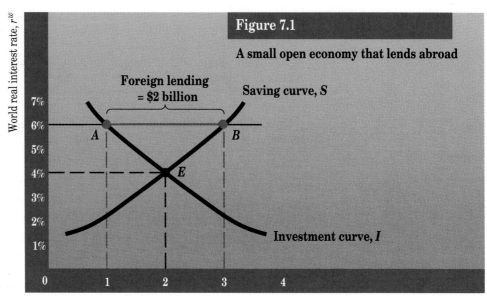

Figure 7.1

A small open economy that lends abroad

The graph shows the saving-investment diagram for a small open economy. The country faces a fixed world real interest rate of 6%. At this real interest rate national saving is $3 billion (point B) and investment is $1 billion (point A). The part of national saving that is not used for investment is lent abroad, so foreign lending is $2 billion (the distance AB).

this chapter we will consider the case of an open economy like the United States that is large enough to affect the world real interest rate.

As in the case of the closed economy, the goods market equilibrium in a small open economy can be studied by using the saving-investment diagram.[6] The key new assumption that we make is that residents of the economy can borrow or lend in the international capital market at the (expected) world real interest rate r^w, which for reasons just explained we assume is fixed. If the world real interest rate is r^w, then the domestic real interest rate must be r^w as well, since no domestic borrower with access to the international capital market would pay more than r^w to borrow, and no domestic saver with access to the international capital market would accept less than r^w to lend.[7]

Figure 7.1 shows the saving and investment curves for a small open economy. In a closed economy, goods market equilibrium would be represented by point E, the intersection of these curves. The equilibrium real interest rate in the closed economy would be 4% (per year), and national saving and investment would be $2 billion (per year). In an open economy, however, desired national saving need not be equal to desired investment. In Fig. 7.1 you can see that if the small open

---

[6]The saving-investment diagram can be used alone only when output is given (see Chapter 6, Section 6.3). We therefore assume in this chapter that output is always at its full-employment level, as determined by the production function, the capital stock, and the supply of labor. Since we are interested here in longer-run issues, and classicals and Keynesians agree that output equals its full-employment level in the long run, this assumption is a reasonable one.

[7]For simplicity, we ignore factors such as differences in risk or taxes that might cause the domestic real interest rate to differ from the world rate. We also assume that there are no capital controls—that is, there are no legal barriers to international borrowing and lending.

economy faces a fixed world real interest rate r^w that is higher than 4%, desired national saving will be greater than desired investment. For example, if r^w is 6%, desired national saving is $3 billion and desired investment is $1 billion, so desired national saving exceeds desired investment by $2 billion.

Can the economy be in equilibrium when desired national saving exceeds desired investment by $2 billion? In a closed economy it could not be: The excess saving would have no place to go, and the real interest rate would have to fall to bring desired saving and desired investment into balance. However, in the open economy the excess $2 billion of saving can be used to buy foreign assets. This capital outflow uses up the excess national saving, so that there is no disequilibrium. Instead, the goods market is in equilibrium with desired national saving equal to $3 billion, desired investment equal to $1 billion, and net foreign lending of $2 billion (see Eq. 7.3).

Alternatively, suppose that the world real interest rate r^w were 2% instead of 6%. As shown in Fig. 7.2, in this case desired national saving is $1 billion and desired investment is $3 billion, so that desired investment exceeds desired saving by $2 billion. Now firms desiring to invest will have to borrow $2 billion in the international capital market. Is this also a goods market equilibrium? Yes it is, since once again desired national saving ($1 billion) equals desired investment ($3 billion) plus net foreign lending (minus $2 billion). Indeed, a small open economy can achieve goods market equilibrium for *any* given value of the world real interest rate. All that is required is that, at the given world real interest rate, net foreign lending equal the difference between the country's desired national saving and its desired investment.

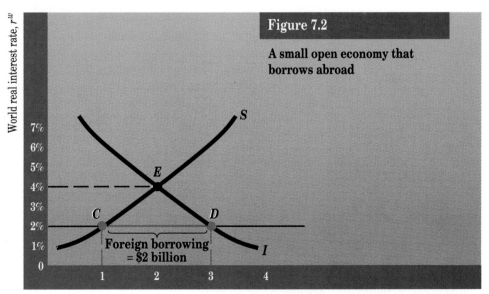

Figure 7.2

A small open economy that borrows abroad

World real interest rate, r^w

Foreign borrowing = $2 billion

Desired national saving, S^d, and desired investment, I^d
(in billions of dollars)

The same small open economy shown in Fig. 7.1 now faces a fixed world real interest rate of 2%. At this real interest rate national saving is $1 billion (point C) and investment is $3 billion (point D). Foreign borrowing of $2 billion (the distance CD) makes up the difference between what investors want to borrow and what domestic savers want to lend.

A numerical version of the example studied in Figs. 7.1 and 7.2 is given in Table 7.4. In this example we assume that output Y is fixed at its full-employment value of \$12 billion, and government purchases G are fixed at \$2 billion. In Table 7.4 column (1) gives three possible values for the world real interest rate r^w, and columns (2) and (3) give the values of desired national saving and desired investment corresponding to each level of the world real interest rate. These values are the same as those graphed in Figs. 7.1 and 7.2.

Column (4) of Table 7.4 shows how desired consumption C^d depends on the world real interest rate. To find desired consumption, remember that desired national saving S^d equals $Y - C^d - G$, or, solving for desired consumption,

$$C^d = Y - G - S^d. \tag{7.6}$$

Given that Y is fixed at \$12 billion and G is fixed at \$2 billion, for each value of desired national saving S^d shown in column (2) of Table 7.4, we can use Eq. (7.6) to calculate the corresponding value of desired consumption C^d in column (4). Note that since desired national saving falls as the world real interest rate falls, Eq. (7.6) implies that desired consumption rises when the world real interest rate falls.

As we have seen, the equilibrium in this example depends on the value of the world real interest rate r^w. Suppose, for example, that $r^w = 6\%$. Table 7.4 shows that in this case desired investment is \$1 billion and desired national saving is \$3 billion. Goods market equilibrium requires only that foreign lending, shown in column (5) of the table, equal the difference between desired national saving and desired investment, or \$2 billion. This value is the same result obtained from Fig. 7.1. Similarly, if $r^w = 2\%$, so that desired national saving is \$1 billion and desired investment is \$3 billion, column (5) of the table shows that foreign lending must be $-\$2$ billion—that is, there is foreign borrowing of \$2 billion.

An advantage of working through the numerical example in Table 7.4 is that it can be used to demonstrate how the goods market equilibrium, which we have been interpreting in terms of desired saving and investment, can also be interpreted in terms of output and absorption. Suppose again that $r^w = 6\%$. When r^w is 6%, column (4) of Table 7.4 shows that desired consumption C^d is \$7 billion, and column (3) shows that desired investment I^d is \$1 billion. Government purchases G are fixed at \$2 billion. Thus when r^w is 6%, desired absorption, or desired spending by domestic residents, $C^d + I^d + G$, totals \$10 billion, as shown in column (6).

Table 7.4 Goods Market Equilibrium in a Small Open Economy: An Example (in Billions of Dollars)

Output $= Y = 12$
Government purchases $= G = 2$

(1) World Real Interest Rate, r^w	(2) Desired National Saving, S^d	(3) Desired Investment, I^d	(4) Desired Consumption, $C^d = Y - G - S^d$	(5) Foreign Lending, $S^d - I^d$	(6) Desired Absorption, $C^d + I^d + G$	(7) Net Exports, $NX = Y - (C^d + I^d + G)$
6%	3	1	7	2	10	2
4%	2	2	8	0	12	0
2%	1	3	9	-2	14	-2

Net exports, the net quantity of goods and services that the economy sends abroad, are shown in column (7). Net exports equal output minus absorption (Eq. 7.5). In this example output is $12 billion and absorption is $10 billion. Thus in equilibrium this economy must be sending $2 billion in goods and services abroad, so NX equals $2 billion in equilibrium. Recall that when we considered the case of $r^w = 6\%$ from the saving–investment perspective, we found that equilibrium required that net foreign lending be $2 billion. Now looking at the same example from the output–absorption perspective, we see that equilibrium requires that net exports—or, equivalently, the current account surplus—be $2 billion. These two results are just opposite sides of the same coin: Because the capital account balance and the current account balance must sum to zero, $2 billion of net foreign lending can occur only if net exports are $2 billion, and vice versa.

What if the world real interest rate is 2%? Table 7.4 shows that when r^w is 2%, desired absorption $C^d + I^d + G$ equals $14 billion. In this case absorption exceeds output (which is $12 billion) by $2 billion, so that net exports NX equal $-\$2$ billion. This current account deficit of $2 billion corresponds exactly to our earlier result (see Fig. 7.2) that when the world real interest rate is 2%, this economy borrows $2 billion abroad (there is a $2 billion capital account surplus). Notice that the lower world real interest rate caused the small open economy's current account surplus to fall, actually becoming a current account deficit. The lower world real interest rate causes the small open economy's current account surplus (equal to $S - I$) to fall because it induces residents of the economy to save less and invest more.

Here are some key conclusions from this section. In goods market equilibrium in a small open economy:

- National saving and investment equal their desired levels at the given world real interest rate.

- Given the world real interest rate, net foreign lending, net exports, and the current account balance all equal national saving minus investment. Equivalently, net foreign lending, net exports, or the current account balance can be found as output minus absorption.

- An increase in the world real interest rate raises desired national saving and lowers desired investment. An increase in the world real interest rate therefore also increases the country's net foreign lending, net exports, and current account balance (which are equivalent).

The Effects of Economic Shocks in a Small Open Economy

The saving-investment diagram can be used to determine the effects of various types of economic disturbances in a small open economy. Briefly, any change that increases desired national saving relative to desired investment at a given world real interest rate will increase net foreign lending, net exports, and the current account balance; a fall in desired national saving relative to desired investment reduces those quantities. We look at two examples, both of which will be useful in the application that follows.

Example 1: A Temporary Adverse Supply Shock   Consider a small open economy that is hit with a severe drought—an adverse supply shock—that temporarily lowers output. The effects of the drought on the nation's saving, investment, and cur-

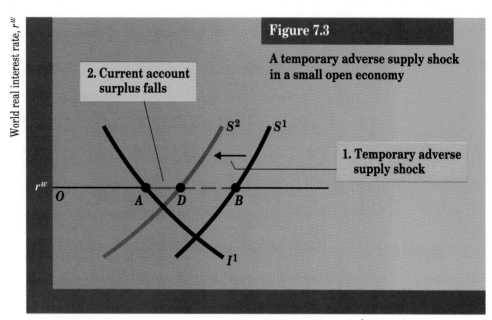

Desired national saving, S^d, and desired investment, I^d

Curve S^1 is the initial saving curve, and I^1 is the initial investment curve of a small open economy. With a fixed world real interest rate r^w, national saving equals the distance OB and investment equals the distance OA. The current account surplus (equivalently, net foreign lending) is the difference between national saving and investment, shown as the distance AB. A temporary adverse supply shock lowers current output and causes

consumers to save less at any given real interest rate, which shifts the saving curve left, from S^1 to S^2. National saving decreases to the distance OD, and the current account surplus decreases to the distance AD.

rent account are shown in Fig. 7.3. The initial saving and investment curves are shown as S^1 and I^1 in the figure. Given the world real interest rate r^w, initial net foreign lending (equivalently, net exports or the current account balance) is given by the length of the line segment AB.

The drought is a temporary decline in income. Since a fall in current income causes people to reduce their saving at any given real interest rate, the saving curve shifts left, from S^1 to S^2 in Fig. 7.3. If the supply shock is temporary, as we have assumed, then the expected future marginal product of capital is unchanged. As a result, desired investment at any given real interest rate is unchanged, and the investment curve does not shift. The world real interest rate is given and does not change.

In the new equilibrium net foreign lending and the current account have shrunk to the length of line segment AD. The current account shrinks because the country saves less and thus is not able to lend abroad as much as before.

In this example we assumed that the country started off with a current account surplus, which is reduced by the drought. If, instead, the country had begun with a current account deficit, the drought would have made the deficit larger. In either case the effect of the drought is to reduce (in the algebraic sense) net foreign lending and the current account balance.

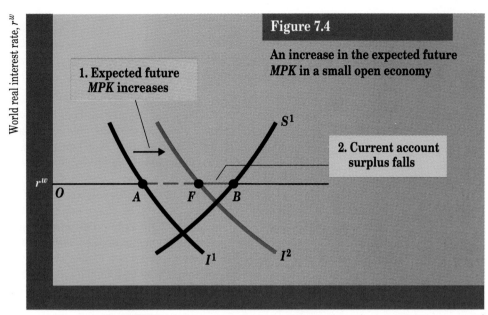

Figure 7.4

An increase in the expected future *MPK* in a small open economy

1. Expected future *MPK* increases

2. Current account surplus falls

Desired national saving, S^d, and desired investment, I^d

As in Fig. 7.3, the small open economy's initial national saving and investment curves are given by S^1 and I^1. At the fixed world real interest rate r^w, there is an initial current account surplus equal to the distance AB. An increase in the expected future marginal product of capital (MPK^f) shifts the investment curve right, from I^1 to I^2, causing investment to increase from distance OA to distance OF. The current account surplus, which is national saving minus investment, decreases from distance AB to distance FB.

Example 2: An Increase in the Expected Future Marginal Product of Capital Suppose that technological innovations increase the expected future marginal product (MPK^f) of current capital investments. The effects on a small open economy are shown in Fig. 7.4. Again, the initial national saving and investment curves are S^1 and I^1, so that the initial current account surplus equals the length of line segment AB.

An increase in the MPK^f raises the capital stock that domestic firms desire to hold, so that desired investment rises at every real interest rate. Thus the investment curve shifts to the right, from I^1 to I^2 in Fig. 7.4. The current account and net foreign lending shrink to the length of line segment FB. Why does the current account fall? Because building capital has become more profitable in the home country, more of the country's output is absorbed by domestic investment, leaving less to send abroad.[8]

_____

[8]A possibility that we have neglected so far is that the technological innovations also cause savers to expect a higher future income, which would reduce current saving at every level of the world real interest rate. A leftward shift of the saving curve would further reduce the current account balance. Since this effect would only reinforce the effect on the country's current account of the rightward shift of the investment curve, for simplicity we continue to ignore this potential change in desired saving.

The LDC Debt Crisis

The 1970s saw a large increase in international borrowing by less developed countries (LDCs). Table 7.5 presents data for a set of fifteen developing countries, ten of which are in Latin America, that had become heavily indebted by the early 1980s. Over the 1972–1981 period, as the table shows (column 1), these countries ran current account deficits averaging over 18% of their exports of goods and services. These current account deficits were financed by borrowing abroad, primarily from private commercial banks in the United States, Japan, and Europe. By 1982—the year in which the LDC debt crisis became generally recognized—foreign debt was 41% of the gross domestic product of the fifteen countries.

During 1982, for reasons that we discuss shortly, banks began to lose confidence that their LDC loans would be repaid as promised and refused to make new loans. Unable to obtain new credit to replace maturing loans or to make planned investments, dozens of countries came under intense financial pressure. Negotiations with the banks and with international agencies such as the International Monetary Fund resulted in some modest reductions in LDC debt outstanding, as did some unilateral decisions by debtor countries to reduce or delay payments to the banks. To a large extent, though, the debtors did not default on (refuse to repay) their debts and attempted to keep making interest payments.

In the years following the onset of the crisis, interest payments on international debt were a serious burden on LDC economies: Column (2) of Table 7.5 shows that for the fifteen heavily indebted countries interest payments during 1982–1989 were between a quarter and a third of total exports of goods and services. In the balance of payments accounts, payments of interest on debt are debit items in the current account. Since the LDCs could not get new loans (capital in-

Table 7.5 Macroeconomic Data for Fifteen Heavily Indebted Countries

Year	(1) Current Account Balance[a]	(2) Interest Payments on Debt[a]	(3) Balance on Merchandise Trade[a]	(4) Per Capita Real GDP Growth
1972–1981	−18.2%	—	—	2.2%
1982	−35.7	32.0%	3.1%	−2.6
1983	−11.3	30.3	21.1	−4.9
1984	−1.0	30.9	28.8	−0.3
1985	−0.1	30.2	27.9	1.6
1986	−13.3	31.1	16.2	1.9
1987	−6.4	26.8	18.9	0.4
1988	−5.6	26.0	19.3	−1.4
1989	−6.1	26.6	19.4	−0.7
1990 (est.)	−7.1	23.8	15.4	−0.7

Source: International Monetary Fund, *World Economic Outlook*, May 1990, Tables A6, A35, A39. The fifteen heavily indebted countries are Argentina, Bolivia, Brazil, Chile, Colombia, Cote d'Ivoire, Ecuador, Mexico, Morocco, Nigeria, Peru, the Philippines, Uruguay, Venezuela, and Yugoslavia.

[a]As a percentage of exports of goods and services.

flows) to make their interest payments, the debtor countries were forced to expand exports and cut imports of goods and services. In particular, merchandise exports for LDC debtors substantially exceeded merchandise imports throughout the decade (Table 7.5, column 3). Lower imports, especially reductions in imports of capital goods and intermediate goods, contributed to very poor growth performance during the 1980s (Table 7.5, column 4), with living standards in some countries falling sharply. By 1990 renegotiations and repayment had reduced LDC obligations to the commercial banks. Overall, however, the net foreign asset positions of the debtors had not improved; the current accounts of indebted LDCs (including interest payments) remained in deficit throughout the decade (Table 7.5, column 1).

The LDC debt crisis raises several important questions, which are addressed next.

Why Did the LDCs Borrow So Much in the First Place, and Why Were Lenders Willing to Lend?   There were two main causes of the increase in LDC debt, both of which can be conveniently analyzed by using our model of the small open economy. The first cause is that heavy foreign borrowing is a normal part of the process of economic development. The United States and Canada, for example, both piled up large international debts in their early growth phases. The reasons are illustrated in Fig. 7.5: In a developing economy the capital stock is low while other types of resources (labor, land, minerals) may be relatively abundant. As a result, the expected future marginal product of capital investments is potentially high. This high expected future MPK is reflected in Fig. 7.5 by a desired investment curve that is quite far to the right.

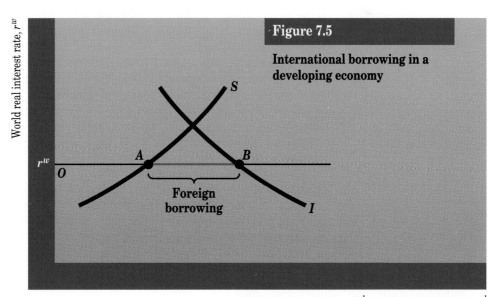

Figure 7.5

International borrowing in a developing economy

Desired national saving, S^d, and desired investment, I^d

In a small developing economy income and desired national saving are low, so the saving curve S is far to the left. Investment opportunities are good (the expected future MPK is high), so the investment curve I is far to the right. At the given world real interest rate r^w, investment (equal to distance OB) greatly exceeds national saving (equal to distance OA). To fund its desired investment, the country must borrow abroad. The distance AB is the developing country's foreign borrowing, or, equivalently, its current account deficit.

At the same time, at early stages of development a country's income is low, so desired national saving is low. Reflecting this low desired saving, in Fig. 7.5 the saving curve is far to the left.[9] The combination of high desired investment and low desired national saving at the given world real interest rate results in large capital inflows, or foreign borrowing, represented by the line segment AB in the figure. Corresponding to the capital inflows are current account deficits, which arise because the developing country is importing large quantities of capital goods and other supplies without yet producing much for export. Because in a growing LDC attractive investment opportunities exceed the domestic population's capacity to save, domestic investors find it profitable to borrow abroad and foreign lenders find it profitable to lend.

The second cause of the increase in LDC debt was specific to the 1970s. The oil shocks of 1973–1974 and 1979–1980 acted like productivity shocks, which sharply depressed income in non–oil-exporting LDCs. Presumably because they thought it likely that these shocks would be temporary, consumers in non–oil-exporting LDCs responded by reducing saving, so they would not have to reduce current consumption by as much as the current fall in output. Lower desired saving at given values of the world real interest rate led to increased current account deficits and foreign borrowing. This result is predicted by our analysis of a temporary adverse supply shock in Fig. 7.3.

A bit ironically, the ultimate source of a significant portion of the funds borrowed by LDCs was the oil-exporting countries themselves, which needed someplace to invest the huge increase in their oil revenues created by the higher prices. In practice, the oil exporters lent to banks in industrialized countries, who then re-lent the funds to LDCs in a process known as "recycling petro-dollars."

If the LDC Lending Was Justified, Why Did the Loans Go Bad?   With even the most careful research and analysis it is impossible to predict the future reliably. A number of adverse macroeconomic developments, not foreseen when most of the LDC loans were made, were major causes of the problems of the LDC debtors. Among these developments was a worldwide recession in 1979–1982 that lowered the demand for LDC exports. Reduced export sales made it difficult for LDC borrowers to achieve the large surplus on the merchandise and services portion of the current account that they needed to pay interest on their debts.[10] Another adverse macroeconomic development of the early 1980s was sharp increases in interest rates. Because most LDC debt was in the form of floating-rate loans, whose required interest payments rise automatically when current interest rates rise, the interest obligations of the LDC debtors were greatly increased.

Although the macroeconomic problems that arose had been generally unexpected, probably many of the loans made to the LDCs in the 1970s were not adequately researched by lenders and some borrowing firms and governments wasted or mismanaged the funds they received. The rapidity with which lending was expanded in the 1970s may have been one reason that careless lending and investment decisions were made.

---

[9]If the population expects the country to be richer in the future, that is another reason for current low saving. See footnote 8.

[10]The open-economy macroeconomic model used in this chapter is too simplified to explain the effects of a decline in demand for a country's exports. We incorporate this type of effect into the model in Chapter 13.

Why Has the LDC Debt Crisis Taken So Long to Be Resolved? Because the true economic value of LDC loans has fallen dramatically below their "paper" value, there is no alternative but that someone must bear large losses; the long delay in resolving the crisis is a result of continuing disagreement over how the losses should be shared. For their part, the borrowers could escape their debts by defaulting. However, default itself may impose sufficient economic and political costs on the borrowers to make it unattractive (see the box "The Political Environment," p. 258). The banks that made the LDC loans have little incentive to make concessions as long as there is hope that international agencies or industrialized countries' governments will provide assistance to help end the crisis. Industrialized countries' governments would like to see the crisis resolved for both political and economic reasons, but in a period of tight government budgets they are unwilling to commit the many billions of dollars of taxpayers' resources that would be required. Thus although several initiatives have been proposed for reducing LDC debt burdens, so far none has been sufficiently comprehensive to have had a major impact on the situation.

7.4 SAVING AND INVESTMENT IN LARGE OPEN ECONOMIES

Although the model of a small open economy facing a fixed real interest rate is appropriate for studying many of the countries in the world, it is not the right model to use for analyzing the world's major developed economies. The problem is that significant changes in the saving and investment patterns of a major economy can affect the world real interest rate, which violates the assumption made for the small open economy that the world real interest rate is fixed. Fortunately, the analysis of the small open economy can be readily adapted to the case of a **large open economy,** an economy large enough to affect the world real interest rate.

To study this case, we will think of the world as being composed of only two large economies: (1) the home or domestic economy and (2) the foreign economy, which may be thought of as representing the economies of the rest of the world combined. The saving-investment diagram that applies to this case is shown in Fig. 7.6. The saving curve S and the investment curve I of the home economy are shown in Fig. 7.6(a). Figure 7.6(b) displays the saving curve S_{FOR} and the investment curve I_{FOR} of the foreign economy. These saving and investment curves are the same as the saving and investment curves for the small open economy.

Instead of taking the world real interest rate as given, as we did in the model of a small open economy, for a large open economy we determine the world real interest rate within the model. What determines the value of the world real interest rate? Remember that for the closed economy, the real interest rate was set by the condition that the amount that savers want to lend must equal the amount that investors desire to borrow. Analogously, in the case of two large open economies, *the world real interest rate will be such that desired international lending by one country equals desired international borrowing by the other country.*

To illustrate the determination of the equilibrium world real interest rate, we return to Fig. 7.6. Suppose, arbitrarily, that the world real interest rate r^w is 6% (per year). Does this rate result in a goods market equilibrium? At a 6% real in-

The Political Environment

Default and Sovereign Debt

If an individual consumer defaults on a loan, his creditors have well-established legal means to try to force repayment. For example, they may be able to seize the consumer's assets, or a court may rule that part of the consumer's future wages may be taken in repayment. In contrast, when there is default on sovereign debt, or debt owed by an independent nation, the creditors' options may be much more limited. There is no international authority to enforce repayment of sovereign debts, and creditors can neither seize the debtors' domestic assets nor "attach" its income.

Given this lack of legal enforceability, why then do sovereign debtors usually try to repay what they owe, even when doing so imposes economic hardship at home? Some researchers have emphasized that defaulting countries may face significant economic costs. These potential costs include seizure of the country's assets held abroad, disruption of international trade (as creditors interfere with shipments or payments), and denial of future international loans.

Although the economic costs of default are part of the reason that international debtors usually repay, political considerations are equally important. Key political factors include:

1. *The importance or political power of creditors within their own country.* When there were widespread defaults on foreign bonds during the Great Depression, the American holders of the foreign bonds were politically unorganized and got little help from the U.S. government. In the 1980s, in contrast, concern about the health of the domestic banking system (which stood to suffer from LDC defaults) prompted the United States to put diplomatic and political pressures on the debtor countries to repay.

2. *Relations between creditor and debtor countries.* History has shown that debtors are more likely to repay when they value the political, economic, and military relations they have with creditors. A debt-laden Australia did not default during the Depression because it wanted good relations with its main creditor, Britain. At the opposite extreme, in 1990 Iraq "solved" its foreign debt problems by invading a principal creditor, Kuwait. Similarly, creditors are less likely to be tough when they value their relationships with the debtors: The United States has forgiven many of the war debts owed it by its military allies, for example.

3. *Relations among the debtor countries.* If many LDC debtors defaulted simultaneously, it would be much more difficult for the creditor countries to punish them. It is easier to enforce trade sanctions against one country than against thirty, for example. For this reason some LDC leaders have called for the formation of a "debtors' cartel," an organization of debtor countries that would negotiate with the creditors as a bloc. The feasibility of such debtor cooperation depends very much on the ability of the debtors to get along and cooperate politically. As of this writing, differing goals and animosities among debtors, plus political pressures from the creditor nations, have prevented the emergence of a debtors' cartel.

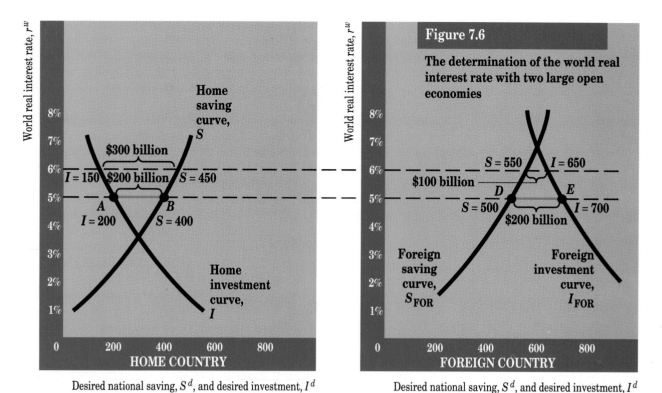

Figure 7.6

The determination of the world real interest rate with two large open economies

Desired national saving, S^d, and desired investment, I^d

(a)   (in billions of dollars)

Desired national saving, S^d, and desired investment, I^d

(b)   (in billions of dollars)

The equilibrium world real interest rate is the real interest rate at which desired international lending by one country equals desired international borrowing by the other country. In the figure, when the world real interest rate is 5%, desired international lending by the home country is $200 billion ($400 billion desired national saving less $200 billion desired investment, or distance AB), which equals the foreign country's desired international borrowing of $200 billion ($700 billion desired investment less $500 billion desired national

saving, or distance DE). Thus 5% is the equilibrium world real interest rate. Equivalently, when the interest rate is 5%, the current account surplus of the home country equals the current account deficit of the foreign country (both are $200 billion).

terest rate, you can see in Fig. 7.6(a) that in the home country desired national saving is $450 billion and desired investment is $150 billion. Because desired national saving exceeds desired investment by $300 billion, the amount that the home country would like to lend abroad is $300 billion.

To find how much the foreign country wants to borrow, we turn to Fig. 7.6(b). You can see that when the real interest rate is 6%, desired national saving is $550 billion and desired investment is $650 billion in the foreign country. Thus at a 6% real interest rate the foreign country wants to borrow $100 billion ($650 billion less $550 billion) in the international capital market. Since this amount is less than the $300 billion the home country wants to lend, 6% is *not* the real interest rate that is consistent with equilibrium in the international capital market.

Because at a real interest rate of 6% desired international lending exceeds desired international borrowing, the equilibrium world real interest rate must be less than 6%. Suppose we try 5%. At a real interest rate of 5% Fig. 7.6(a) shows that desired national saving is $400 billion and desired investment is $200 billion in the home country, so the home country wants to lend $200 billion abroad. From

Fig. 7.6(b), when the real interest rate is 5%, desired national saving in the foreign country is $500 billion and desired investment is $700 billion, so that the foreign country's desired international borrowing is $200 billion. Since at a 5% real interest rate desired international borrowing and desired international lending are equal (both are $200 billion), the equilibrium world real interest rate is 5% in this example.

Graphically, the home country's desired lending when r^w equals 5% is the length of the line segment AB in Fig. 7.6(a), and the foreign country's desired borrowing is the length of the line segment DE in Fig. 7.6(b). Because the length of segment AB equals the length of segment DE, desired international lending and borrowing are equal when the world real interest rate is 5%.

We have defined the international equilibrium in terms of desired international lending and borrowing. Equivalently, equilibrium can be defined in terms of international flows of goods and services. The amount the lending country desires to lend (distance AB in Fig. 7.6a) is the same as its current account surplus, or the excess of its exports over its imports. The amount the borrowing country wants to borrow (distance DE in Fig. 7.6b) equals its current account deficit, or the excess of its imports over its exports. Thus saying that desired international lending must equal desired international borrowing is the same as saying that the desired net outflow of goods and services from the lending country (its current account surplus) must equal the desired net inflow of goods and services to the borrowing country (its current account deficit).

To summarize, in the large open economy case the equilibrium world real interest rate is the rate at which the desired international lending by one country equals the desired international borrowing of the other country. Equivalently, it is the real interest rate at which the lending country's current account surplus equals the borrowing country's current account deficit.

Unlike the situation in small open economy, for large open economies the world real interest rate is not fixed but will change when desired national saving or desired investment changes in either country. Generally, any factor that increases desired international lending relative to desired international borrowing at the initial world real interest rate causes the world real interest rate to fall. Similarly, a change that reduces desired international lending relative to desired international borrowing at the initial world real interest rate will cause the world interest rate to rise. We illustrate this principle in an application.

Application

German Reunification and the World Real Interest Rate

The collapse of communism in Eastern Europe in 1989 revealed a legacy of economic decay. Factories and equipment were outmoded and in poor repair, infrastructure (such as roads and communications systems) was inadequate, and major environmental problems had to be addressed. Clearly, to give market-oriented reforms a chance to work, large infusions of capital were (and are) needed to modernize the Eastern European economies. As of this writing, the great uncertainties

As of this writing, we don't know whether these predictions will come to pass. No doubt developments yet unforeseen will affect the pace of investment in Eastern Europe, and many other types of shocks may affect international capital markets. Nevertheless, this analysis gives us a way to think about these questions; and indeed, our results are consistent with projections made by economists in both the private and the public sectors.[12]

Application

How Well Does the International Capital Market Operate?

In our analyses of this chapter we have assumed that international capital markets function well, in that domestic residents can lend to foreigners or borrow from foreigners as easily as they can lend or borrow domestically. Whether this assumption is reasonably accurate, or whether instead access to international capital markets is limited and costly so that most borrowing and lending must be done domestically, has been the subject of an interesting debate among economists.

Martin Feldstein and Charles Horioka[13] of Harvard University examined the question of how well the international capital market operates by studying the relationship between national saving and investment in many countries. They reasoned that if the international capital market did not operate at all, so that there could be no international borrowing or lending, then national saving would equal investment in each country, as we saw in our analysis of the closed economy. On the other hand, suppose that the international capital market operates perfectly, so that people in different countries face no barriers to borrowing or lending internationally. In this case, Feldstein and Horioka argued, there should be little relationship between the amount of saving and the amount of investment that takes place in any particular country, since savers in each country would lend to whatever country had the best investment opportunities and not necessarily to investors in their own country. Between these two extreme cases, saving and investment in each country might show some relation to each other. However, Feldstein and Horioka hypothesized that the less closely saving and investment in each country are related, the better the international capital market operates.

Figure 7.8 shows average national saving and investment for twenty-one countries examined by Feldstein and Horioka. National saving and investment are measured relative to GDP, and the years included in the study were 1960–1974. The figure shows that countries with high national saving rates also have high investment rates. A strong relationship between national saving and investment in each country is what one would expect if, owing to a poorly operating international capital market, most domestic saving ended up funding domestic investment rather than flowing abroad. From a study of these data Feldstein and Horioka concluded that there must be significant barriers to borrowing and lending between countries, so that the international capital market does not function well.

---

[12]See, for example, "Economic Reform in Eastern Europe and the U.S.S.R.," in International Monetary Fund, *World Economic Outlook*, May 1990, particularly the box on the effects of German reunification.

[13]"Domestic Saving and International Capital Flows," *Economic Journal*, June 1980, pp. 314–329.

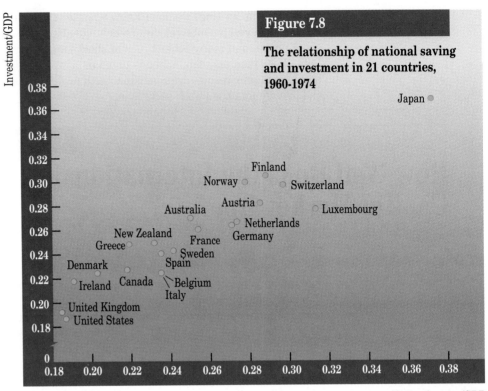

Figure 7.8

The relationship of national saving and investment in 21 countries, 1960-1974

For each of twenty-one countries studied by Feldstein and Horioka, the average (1960–1974) ratio of national saving to GDP is measured along the horizontal axis, and the average (1960–1974) ratio of investment to GDP is measured along the vertical axis. Note that countries with higher average ratios of national saving to GDP also have higher ratios of investment to GDP.

Maurice Obstfeld[14] of the University of California at Berkeley refined the test proposed by Feldstein and Horioka. Obstfeld analyzed national saving and investment in seven countries, using quarterly data up to the early 1980s. In Austria and Australia, two small open economies, Obstfeld found that quarterly movements in saving and investment were essentially independent of each other, a finding that differs from that of Feldstein and Horioka and suggests that the international capital market operates well. Obstfeld's data also showed that in Canada, Germany, and the United Kingdom, saving and investment tended to move together somewhat, and in the United States and Japan saving and investment were very strongly related to each other.

After analyzing his results, Obstfeld concluded that the international capital market was not operating well in the case of Japan. During much of the period he studied, Japan enforced a number of laws and regulations that limited the participation of Japanese savers and investors in the international capital market. However, Obstfeld warned against concluding from the U.S. data that the international capital market did not function well for the United States. Obstfeld argued that

---

[14]"Capital Mobility in the World Economy: Theory and Measurement," in K. Brunner and A. Meltzer, eds., *Carnegie-Rochester Conference Series on Public Policy*, vol. 24, Spring 1986.

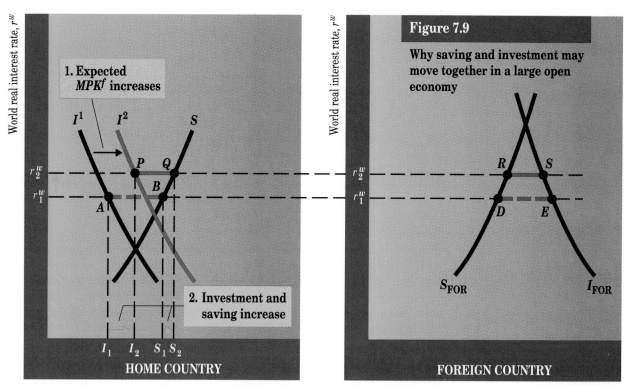

(a) Desired national saving, S^d, and desired investment, I^d

(b) Desired national saving, S^d, and desired investment, I^d

This example shows that in a large open economy an increase in investment may also cause national saving to rise. Initially, the saving and investment curves in the home economy are S and I^1. At the initial world real interest rate r_1^w, the current account surplus AB of the home country equals the current account deficit DE of the foreign country. An increase in the expected future MPK raises desired investment and shifts the home investment curve from I^1 to I^2. The new world real

interest rate is r_2^w, at which the current account surplus PQ of the home country equals the current account deficit RS of the foreign country. Investment in the home country has risen from I_1 to I_2 (see the horizontal axis), but saving in the home country has also risen, from S_1 to S_2. Saving in the home country rises because the world real interest rate has risen.

for a large open economy like that of the United States, national saving and investment might move together even if the international capital market functioned perfectly.

Figure 7.9 shows an example that illustrates Obstfeld's point. The figure shows once again the determination of the world real interest rate with two large open economies. Initially, the home economy's saving and investment curves are S and I^1 in Fig. 7.9(a); the saving and investment curves for the foreign economy are given by S_{FOR} and I_{FOR} in Fig. 7.9(b). The corresponding equilibrium world real interest rate is r_1^w; when the real interest rate is r_1^w, the current account surplus AB of the home country is equal to the current account deficit DE of the foreign country. In the initial equilibrium the home country's national saving is S_1 and its investment is I_1.

Now suppose, for example, that an increase in the expected future marginal product of capital raised desired investment in the home economy, shifting its investment curve to the right, from I^1 to I^2. At the original world real interest rate r_1^w this increase in desired investment causes the home country to reduce its foreign lending. Since desired international borrowing by the foreign country is unchanged, at the initial world real interest rate desired international borrowing exceeds desired international lending. For equilibrium to be restored in the international capital market, the world real interest rate must rise. The new world real interest rate is shown as r_2^w in Fig. 7.9. When the world real interest rate is r_2^w, the home country's desired lending equals the line segment PQ, and the foreign country's desired borrowing equals the line segment RS. Since at r_2^w desired foreign lending once again equals desired foreign borrowing (line segments PQ and RS are of equal length), r_2^w is the new equilibrium real interest rate.

In response to this shock to desired investment in the home country, how have national saving and investment in the home country changed? Investment in the home country has risen from a value of I_1 to a higher value I_2. This increase in investment reflects the rise in the expected future marginal product of capital and the resulting shift in the investment curve. Unlike the investment curve, the saving curve is not shifted by the increase in the expected future MPK. Nevertheless, the amount of national saving in the home country also rises, from S_1 to S_2. National saving rises in the home country in response to the increase in the world real interest rate, which itself was due to the increase in desired investment in the home country. This example shows that in a large open economy investment and saving may move in the same direction, even though the international capital market operates well.[15] The reason is that a shock to investment in a large open economy affects the world real interest rate, and the change in the world real interest rate in turn affects the amount of national saving the economy does. Similarly, a shock to saving in a large open economy can affect the world real interest rate and thus change the amount of investment that occurs.

Overall, Obstfeld concluded that the international capital market generally does function well and that, in fact, lending and borrowing across national borders have become increasingly easy over recent years.

7.5 FISCAL POLICY AND THE CURRENT ACCOUNT

The 1980s in the United States were characterized by large government budget deficits and large current account deficits. Were these two phenomena related? Many economists and other commentators argued that they were, suggesting that in fact the budget deficit was the primary cause of the current account deficit. Those supporting this view often used the phrase "twin deficits" to convey the idea that the government budget deficit and the current account deficit were closely linked. Not all economists agree with this interpretation, however; some argue that the two deficits were largely unrelated. In this section we briefly discuss what the theory has to say about this issue, and then we turn to the evidence.

The Critical Factor: The Response of National Saving

From a theoretical perspective, the issue of whether there is a link between the government budget deficit and the current account deficit boils down to the following observation: *An increase in the government budget deficit will raise the current account deficit if and only if the increase in the budget deficit reduces desired national saving.*

---

[15]See Analytical Problem 4. Note in Fig. 7.9 that although national saving increases along with investment, saving does not increase as much as investment does, since the current account surplus falls.

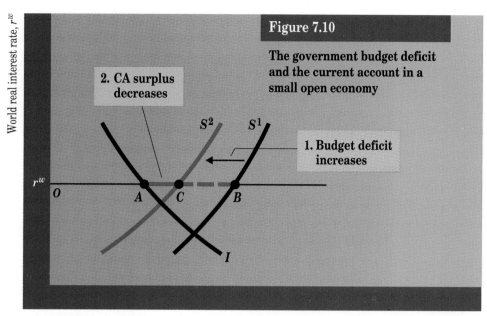

Figure 7.10

The government budget deficit and the current account in a small open economy

World real interest rate, r^w

2. CA surplus decreases

S^2 S^1

1. Budget deficit increases

r^w

O A C B

I

Desired national saving, S^d, and desired investment, I^d

An increase in the government budget deficit affects the current account only if the increased budget deficit reduces national saving. Initially, the saving curve is S^1 and the current account surplus equals the distance AB. If an increase in the government deficit reduces national saving, then the saving curve shifts left, from S^1 to S^2. Assuming no change in the effective tax rate on capital, the investment curve I does not move. Thus the increase in the budget deficit causes the current account surplus to decrease from distance AB to distance AC. In contrast, if the increase in the budget deficit has no effect on national saving, the current account is also unaffected and remains equal to distance AB.

Let's show first why the link to national saving is crucial. The case of the small open economy is shown in Fig. 7.10. The world real interest rate is fixed at r^w. We have drawn the initial saving and investment curves, S^1 and I, so that at the world real interest rate r^w the country is running a current account surplus, equal to the length of the line segment AB. Now suppose that there is an increase in the government deficit. For simplicity, we assume throughout this section that the change in fiscal policy does not affect the tax treatment of investment, so that the investment curve does not shift. If the investment curve does not move, we see immediately from Fig. 7.10 that the government deficit increase will change the current account balance only if it affects desired national saving.

The usual claim made by supporters of the twin-deficits idea is that an increase in the government budget deficit reduces desired national saving. If it does, then the increase in the government deficit shifts the desired national saving curve to the left, from S^1 to S^2 in Fig. 7.10. As we have drawn it, the country still has a current account surplus, now equal to the distance AC, but it is less than the original surplus AB.

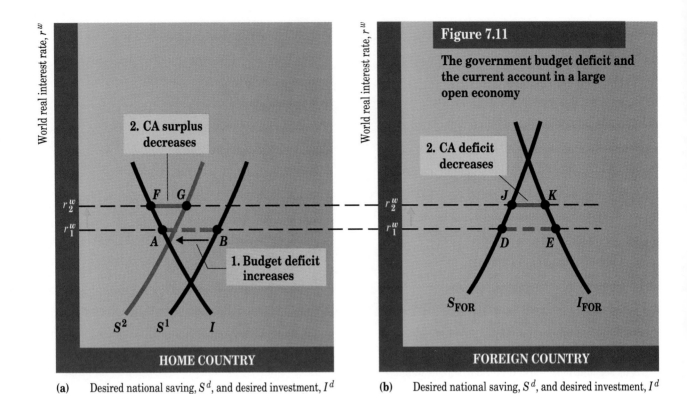

(a)   Desired national saving, S^d, and desired investment, I^d

(b)   Desired national saving, S^d, and desired investment, I^d

As in a small open economy, in a large open economy an increase in the budget deficit affects the current account only if it affects national saving. In the figure the home country's initial national saving curve is S^1. The initial equilibrium world real interest rate is r_1^w, at which the home country's current account surplus AB equals the foreign country's current account deficit DE. If an increase in the budget deficit does not affect national saving, then there is no change in the figure. If an increased budget deficit does reduce national saving, the

home country's national saving curves shifts left, from S^1 to S^2. The real interest rate rises to r_2^w, where the home country's current account surplus FG equals the foreign country's current account deficit JK. National saving, investment, and the current account surplus in the home country all fall.

We conclude that in a small open economy an increase in the government budget deficit reduces the current account balance by the same amount that it reduces desired national saving. By reducing saving, the increased budget deficit reduces the amount that domestic residents want to lend abroad at the world real interest rate, thus lowering capital outflows. Equivalently, reduced national saving means that a greater part of domestic output is absorbed at home; with less output to send abroad, the country's current account falls.

The point that the budget deficit affects the current account only if it changes national saving also holds in the case of a large open economy (Fig. 7.11). As the figure is drawn, at the initial world interest rate r_1^w, the home economy has a current account surplus marked AB, and the foreign economy has an equal-sized current account deficit DE. Now suppose an increased budget deficit shifts the saving curve of the home country left, from S^1 to S^2. At the initial real interest rate r_1^w, desired international lending is less than desired international borrowing, so the real interest rate must rise.

Figure 7.11 shows that in the new equilibrium the world real interest rate is r_2^w. The home country current account surplus has shrunk to the length of line segment FG, which equals the foreign country's current account deficit JK. Thus in a large open economy as well as in a small open economy, if an increased government budget deficit reduces national saving, it also reduces the current account balance. In addition, because the world real interest rate is higher, the increased budget deficit has "crowded out," or reduced, domestic investment.

Incidentally, this analysis illustrates a useful general point about the case of the large open economy: It can be thought of as a combination of the closed-economy and the small-open-economy cases. Recall, for example, that in a closed economy a reduction in desired national saving led to a higher real interest rate and less investment. In a small open economy the same reduction in desired saving did not affect the interest rate or investment but only reduced the current account balance. We have seen here that the analysis of the large open economy combines the results of the two cases: In the large open economy a reduction in desired saving raises the real interest rate and reduces investment (as in the closed economy) and reduces the current account balance (as in the small open economy). Thus for some purposes, both our closed-economy and small-open-economy analyses can be useful for thinking about an economy like that of the United States.

The Government Budget Deficit and National Saving

Having shown that the government budget deficit affects the current account only if it affects desired national saving, we now discuss the link between the budget deficit and saving. There are two cases to consider: a budget deficit arising from an increase in government purchases and a deficit rising from a cut in taxes.[16]

A Deficit Due to Increased Government Purchases Suppose that the source of the government budget deficit is a temporary increase in government purchases, perhaps due to a military buildup. In this case there is no controversy: As we saw in Chapter 3, with output Y held constant at its full-employment level, an increase in government purchases G directly reduces desired national saving $S^d = Y - C^d - G$.[17] Because economists agree that a deficit due to increased government purchases reduces desired national saving, they also agree that a deficit resulting from increased government purchases reduces the nation's current account balance.

A Deficit Due to a Tax Cut Suppose instead that the government budget deficit is the result of a cut in current taxes, with current and future government purchases unchanged. Since government purchases G are unchanged, and with output Y held constant at its full-employment level, the tax cut will cause desired national saving $S^d = Y - C^d - G$ to fall only if it causes desired consumption C^d to rise.

---

[16]Those who have covered Chapter 6 will recognize what follows as a summary of Chapter 6, Section 6.4.

[17]Because the increase in government purchases also means that taxes may be raised in the future, lowering consumers' expected future income, desired consumption C^d may fall. However, given that the increase in G is temporary so that the future tax increase need not be too large, this fall in C^d should not offset the effect of increased G on desired national saving.

Will a tax cut cause people to consume more? Some economists claim that it will not. After all, these economists argue, the government's current and future purchases, which must be paid for somehow, have not changed. If the government collects less taxes and thus borrows more in the present, in order to repay its current borrowing it will have to raise taxes in the future. Thus while the tax cut raises consumers' current after-tax incomes, because the tax cut creates the need for higher future taxes, it lowers consumers' expected future after-tax incomes. Overall, consumers are made no better off by the tax cut and thus will not increase their desired consumption. The idea that tax cuts will not affect desired consumption or desired national saving is called the Ricardian equivalence proposition.

If the Ricardian equivalence proposition is true, then a budget deficit due to a tax cut will have no effect on the current account, because it does not affect desired national saving. However, not all economists accept the idea of Ricardian equivalence but argue that in practice, for various reasons, consumers *will* respond to a current tax cut by consuming more. For example, it may be that consumers simply do not understand that a higher deficit makes higher taxes tomorrow more likely.[18] If for any reason consumers do respond to a tax cut by consuming more, then the deficit due to a tax cut will reduce national saving and the current account balance. Ultimately, the effects of a tax cut on desired consumption must be determined empirically, but until now no clear empirical conclusion has emerged.[19]

<hr/>

Application

The Twin Deficits of the 1980s

The relationship between the U.S. government budget deficit and the U.S. current account deficit—the twin deficits—is shown in Fig. 7.12 for the period 1970–1990. In Fig. 7.12 fiscal policy is measured by government purchases and by the government's net receipts (taxes less transfers and interest paid), in both cases relative to GNP and for combined Federal, state, and local governments. The difference between government purchases and net receipts is the government budget deficit. Also shown in Fig. 7.12 is the current account balance. Negative values of the current account balance indicate a current account deficit.

The key movements in the data occur in the early 1980s. Between 1981 and 1983 the government budget deficit increased from 1% of GNP to almost 4% of GNP. This increase was due mostly to a fall in net receipts (particularly important were tax cuts phased in following the Economic Recovery Tax Act of 1981), but there was also some increase in military spending. The current account, which was in surplus in 1981, fell between 1982 and 1984 to a deficit of almost 3% of GNP.

This correspondence in timing and magnitude is a bit of evidence in favor of the twin-deficits view—that the increase in the budget deficit was an important cause of the decline in the current account balance. Since the rise in the budget

<hr/>

[18]Chapter 6 discussed another possibility, that because of limits on borrowing against future income, some consumers will respond to any increase in current income by consuming more.

[19]Evidence on the validity of Ricardian equivalence is discussed in Chapters 6 and 16.

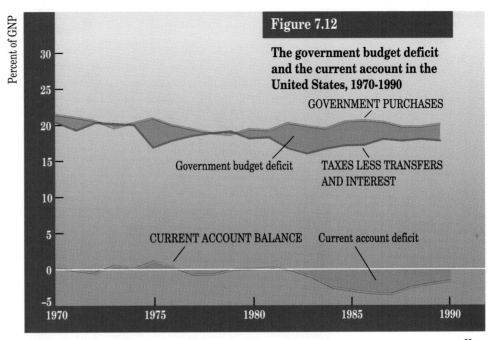

Figure 7.12

The government budget deficit and the current account in the United States, 1970-1990

Shown are government purchases, net government receipts (taxes less transfers and interest), and the current account balance for the United States for 1970–1990. Government data are for state, local, and Federal governments, and all series are measured as a percentage of GNP. The government deficit (*shaded*) is the difference between government purchases and net receipts. The expansion of both the government deficit and the current account deficit in the early 1980s is the twin-deficits phenomenon.

Source: *Economic Report of the President*, February 1991, Tables B-1, B-79, B-102.

deficit was due primarily to tax cuts rather than an increase in government purchases, this behavior of the two deficits seems also to contradict the Ricardian equivalence proposition, which says that tax cuts should have no effect on saving or the current account.

If the evidence is so clear, why do many economists still resist the idea that a budget deficit generated by tax cuts will reduce the current account balance? The problem is that, outside of the case of the United States in the 1980s, the evidence linking tax cuts and the current account seems to be much less decisive. Two examples will illustrate:

1. In 1975 in the United States, a one-time tax rebate contributed to the largest (relative to GNP) annual government budget deficit of the postwar period, exceeding 4% of GNP. And yet the U.S. current account balance rose noticeably in 1975, as you can see from Fig. 7.12.

2. Italy has one of the largest government budget deficits in the world, as a fraction of GNP. Between 1980 and 1983, at about the same time as the increase

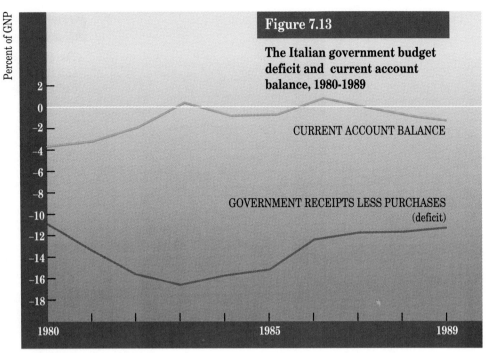

Figure 7.13

The Italian government budget deficit and current account balance, 1980-1989

Recent data are plotted for the Italian current account balance and government budget deficit, measured as a percentage of GNP. Negative values for government receipts less purchases imply a deficit. Note that the current account moved toward surplus in 1981–1983 even as the already large government budget deficit became larger.

Source: International Monetary Fund, *International Financial Statistics.*

in the U.S. government budget deficit, the Italian budget deficit increased from 11% of GNP to over 16% of GNP. Yet the Italian current account went from a deficit of over 3% of GNP in 1980 to a current account surplus in 1983. (Italian data are shown in Fig. 7.13.)

Because of this mixed evidence, we have no alternative but to be cautious in drawing conclusions about the relationship between a budget deficit caused by a tax cut and the current account deficit.[20]

7.6 CHAPTER SUMMARY

1. The balance of payments accounts consist of the current account and the capital account. The current account records trade in currently produced goods and services, as well as income receipts from assets held abroad and transfers made

---

[20]For a detailed study of the causes of the U.S. current account deficit in the 1980s, see Peter Hooper and Catherine L. Mann, "The Emergence and Persistence of the U.S. External Balance, 1980–87," *Princeton Studies in International Finance*, no. 65, October 1989. Hooper and Mann conclude that, at least in this particular episode, fiscal policy was an important cause of the decline in the current account balance.

between countries. The capital account records trade in existing assets, both real and financial.

2. In the current account, exports of goods or services, receipts of income from assets held abroad, and unilateral transfers received from abroad count as credit (plus) items. Imports of goods and services, payments to foreigners holding assets in the home country, and unilateral transfers sent abroad are debit (minus) items in the current account. The current account balance equals the value of credit items less debit items in the current account. If we ignore unilateral transfers, the current account balance equals net exports. The capital account balance is the value of assets sold to foreigners (capital inflows) minus the value of assets purchased from foreigners (capital outflows).

3. In each period, except for measurement errors, the current account balance and the capital account balance must add up to zero. This is because any international transaction amounts to a swap of goods, services, or assets between countries; and the two sides of the swap always have offsetting effects on the sum of the current account and capital account balances.

4. In an open economy, goods market equilibrium requires that the desired amount of national saving equal the desired amount of domestic investment plus the amount the country lends abroad. Equivalently, net exports must equal the country's output less desired total spending by domestic residents (absorption).

5. A small open economy faces a fixed real interest rate in the international capital market. In goods market equilibrium in a small open economy, national saving and investment equal their desired levels at the given world real interest rate; and foreign lending, net exports, and the current account all equal the excess of national saving over investment. Any factor that increases desired national saving or reduces desired investment at the given world real interest rate will increase the small open economy's foreign lending (equivalently, its net exports or current account).

6. A large open economy is one whose levels of saving and investment affect the world real interest rate. In a model of two large open economies, the equilibrium real interest rate in the international capital market is the one at which desired international lending by one country equals desired international borrowing by the other country. Equivalently, it is the rate at which the lending country's current account surplus equals the borrowing country's current account deficit.

7. In a large open economy any factor that increases desired national saving or reduces desired investment at the initial interest rate will increase the amount the large country wants to lend abroad. This increase in the supply of international loans relative to the demand for international loans will cause the world real interest rate to fall.

8. Assuming no change in the tax treatment of investment, an increase in the government budget deficit will raise the current account deficit if and only if the increase in the budget deficit reduces national saving. An increase in the budget deficit caused by a temporary increase in government purchases will reduce national saving, but whether an increase in the budget deficit caused by a tax cut reduces national saving is controversial.

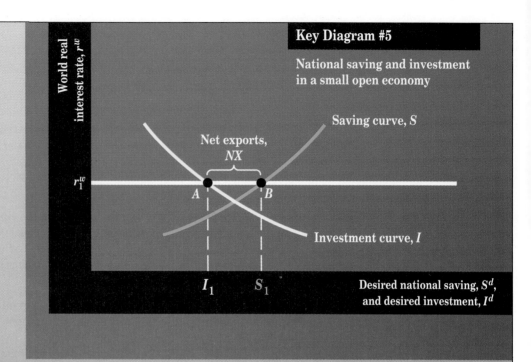

Key Diagram #5

National saving and investment in a small open economy

This open-economy version of the saving-investment diagram shows the determination of national saving, investment, and net exports in a small open economy that takes the world real interest rate as given.

Diagram Elements

- The world real interest rate is measured on the vertical axis, and the small economy's desired national saving S^d and desired investment I^d are on the horizontal axis.

- The world real interest rate r_1^w is fixed and indicated by the horizontal line.

- The saving curve S and the investment curve I are the same as in the closed-economy saving-investment diagram, Key Diagram #2 (p. 106).

Analysis

Goods market equilibrium in a small open economy requires that desired national saving equal desired investment plus net exports (Eq. 7.3). In the diagram when the world real interest rate equals r_1^w, desired national saving equals S_1 and desired investment equals I_1. The country's net exports NX, equal to $S_1 - I_1$, are then given by the length of the line segment AB. Equivalently, the length of the line segment AB, the excess of desired national saving over desired investment, gives the amount that the small open economy is lending abroad, its current account surplus, and its capital account deficit (see Table 7.3, p. 245).

Factors That Shift the Curves

- Anything that increases desired national saving in the small open economy, given the world real interest rate, shifts the saving curve to the right. Factors that shift the saving curve to the right include:

    An increase in current output Y

    A decrease in expected future output

    A decrease in current government purchases G

    An increase in current taxes T, if Ricardian equivalence does not hold and taxes affect saving

- Anything that increases desired investment at the given real interest rate shifts the investment curve to the right. Factors that shift the investment curve to the right include:

    An increase in the expected future marginal product of capital, MPK^f

    A decrease in corporate taxes that affect the profitability of investment

- An increase in desired national saving shifts the saving curve right and raises net exports, or national saving less investment. Equivalently, an increase in desired national saving raises the country's net foreign lending, current account surplus, and capital account deficit. Similarly, an increase in desired investment shifts the investment curve right and lowers net exports, net foreign lending, the current account surplus, and the capital account deficit.

- An increase in the world real interest rate r^w raises the horizontal line in the diagram. Because an increase in the world real interest rate increases national saving and reduces investment, it raises net exports, net foreign lending, the current account surplus, and the capital account deficit.

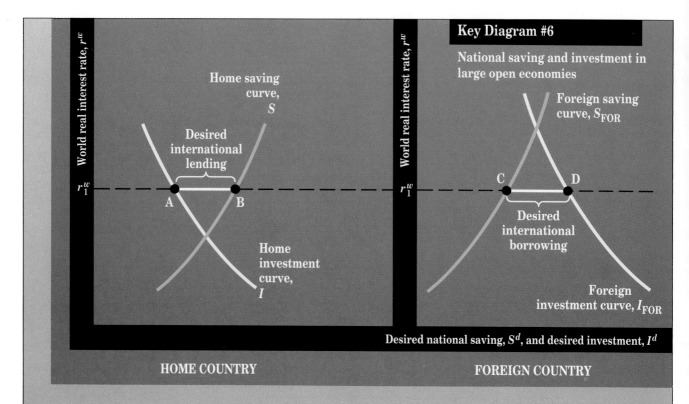

This diagram shows the determination of national saving, investment, and net exports in large open economies, economies large enough to affect the world real interest rate.

Diagram Elements

- The figure is made up of two saving-investment diagrams, one for the home country and one for the foreign country (representing the rest of the world).

- The world real interest rate r^w, measured on the vertical axis, is the real interest rate faced by both countries in the international capital market.

- The saving and investment curves in the home country (S and I) and in the foreign country (S_{FOR} and I_{FOR}) are the same as the saving and investment curves we have seen before (Key Diagram #2, p. 106, and Key Diagram #5, p. 274).

Analysis

- This case differs from the case of the small open economy (Key Diagram #5) in that the world real interest rate r^w is not given but is determined within the model.

- Goods market equilibrium for large open economies requires that the desired international lending of one country equal the desired international borrowing of the other. Equivalently, since a country's international lending must equal its net exports, goods market equilibrium requires that one country's excess of exports over imports equal the other country's excess of imports over exports.

- The world real interest rate adjusts to achieve goods market equilibrium. In the diagram r_1^w is the equilibrium world real interest rate, because at that interest rate the home country's desired international lending (its desired national saving less desired investment, the length of line segment AB) equals the foreign country's desired international borrowing (its desired investment less desired national saving, the length of line segment CD).

Factors That Shift the Curves

- The saving and investment curves in the two countries are shifted by the same factors as in Key Diagram #5 (p. 274).

- The world real interest rate is not fixed but will change when desired national saving or desired investment changes in either country. Any change that increases desired international lending relative to desired international borrowing at the initial world real interest rate will cause the world real interest rate to fall to restore equilibrium in the international capital market. Changes that increase desired international lending relative to desired international borrowing include an increase in desired national saving or a decrease in desired investment in either country. Similarly, a decrease in desired national saving or an increase in desired investment in either country reduces desired international lending relative to desired international borrowing and raises the world real interest rate.

Key Terms

absorption, p. 247
balance of payments,
    p. 241
balance of payments
    accounts, p. 237
capital account, p. 240
capital account balance,
    p. 240
capital inflow, p. 240

capital outflow, p. 240
current account, p. 237
current account balance,
    p. 239
large open economy,
    p. 257
merchandise trade
    balance, p. 237
official reserve assets,
    p. 240

official settlements
    balance, p. 241
small open economy,
    p. 247
statistical discrepancy,
    p. 242
unilateral transfers,
    p. 238
world real interest rate,
    p. 247

Key Equations

$$CA + KA = 0 \qquad (7.1)$$

Except for problems of measurement, the current account balance CA and the capital account balance KA always sum to zero. The reason is that every international transaction involves a swap of goods, services, or assets; and the two sides of the swap always have offsetting effects on $CA + KA$.

$$S^d = I^d + NX \qquad (7.3)$$

The *goods market equilibrium condition* in an open economy says that desired national saving S^d must equal desired investment I^d plus the amount lent abroad, where the amount lent abroad always equals net exports NX.

$$NX = Y - (C^d + I^d + G) \qquad (7.5)$$

An alternative way of writing the goods market equilibrium condition, Eq. (7.3), this equation says that net exports must equal the country's output Y less its desired absorption, $C^d + I^d + G$.

Review Questions

1. List the categories of credit items and debit items that appear in a country's current account. What is the current account balance? What is the relationship between the current account balance and net exports?

2. What is the key difference that determines whether an international transaction appears in the current account or the capital account?

3. An American publisher sells $200 worth of books to a resident of Brazil. By itself, this item is a credit item in the U.S. current account. Describe some of the types of offsetting transactions that might occur that would have the effect of ensuring that the U.S. current and capital account balances would continue to sum to zero.

4. How do a country's current and capital account balances affect its net foreign assets? If country A has greater net foreign assets per citizen than does country B, is country A necessarily better off than country B?

5. Explain why, in a small open economy, (a) national saving does not have to equal investment; and (b) output does not have to equal absorption.

6. Generally, what types of factors will cause a small open economy to run a large current account deficit and thus borrow abroad? More specifically, what two major factors contributed to heavy LDC borrowing in the 1970s?

7. In a world with two large open economies, what determines the world real interest rate? What relationship between the current accounts of the two countries is satisfied when the world real interest rate is at its equilibrium value?

8. How does an increase in desired national saving in a large open economy affect the world real interest rate? How does an increase in desired investment affect it?

Why do changes in desired saving or investment affect the world interest rate in large open economies but not in small open economies?

9. Under what circumstances will an increase in the government budget deficit affect the current account balance in a small open economy? In the cases in which the current account balance changes, by how much does it change?

10. What are the *twin deficits?* What is the connection between them?

Numerical Problems

1. Here are some balance of payments data (without pluses and minuses):

Merchandise exports	100
Merchandise imports	125
Service exports	90
Service imports	80
Income receipts from assets	110
Income payments on assets	140
Transfers from home country to other countries	10
Increase in home country assets abroad	160
Increase in foreign assets in home country	200
Increase in home reserve assets	30
Increase in foreign reserve assets	35

Find the merchandise trade balance, the current account balance, the capital account balance, the official settlements balance, and the statistical discrepancy.

2. In a small open economy output is $25 billion and government purchases are $6 billion. Desired consumption and desired investment are related to the world real interest rate as follows:

Real Interest Rate	Desired Consumption	Desired Investment
5%	$12 billion	$3 billion
4%	$13 billion	$4 billion
3%	$14 billion	$5 billion
2%	$15 billion	$6 billion

For each value of the world real interest rate, find national saving, foreign lending, and absorption. Calculate net exports as the difference between output and absorption. What is the relationship between net exports and foreign lending?

3. In a small open economy:

$$\text{desired national saving } S^d = \$10 \text{ billion } + (\$100 \text{ billion})r^w,$$
$$\text{desired investment } I^d = \$15 \text{ billion } - (\$100 \text{ billion})r^w,$$
$$\text{output } Y = \$50 \text{ billion},$$

government purchases $G = \$10$ billion,

world real interest rate $r^w = 0.03$.

a. Find the economy's national saving, investment, current account surplus, net exports, desired consumption, and absorption.

b. Owing to a technological innovation, the country's desired investment rises by $2 billion at each level of the world real interest rate. Repeat part a.

4. Consider two large economies, the home economy and the foreign economy. In the home country the following relationships hold:

$$\text{desired consumption } C^d = 320 + 0.4(Y - T) - 200r^w,$$
$$\text{desired investment } I^d = 150 - 200r^w,$$
$$\text{output } Y = 1000,$$
$$\text{taxes } T = 200, \quad 250$$
$$\text{government purchases } G = 275. \quad 325$$

In the foreign country the following relationships hold:

$$\text{desired consumption } C^d_{FOR} = 480 + 0.4(Y_{FOR} - T_{FOR}) - 300r^w,$$
$$\text{desired investment } I^d_{FOR} = 225 - 300r^w,$$
$$\text{output } Y_{FOR} = 1500,$$
$$\text{taxes } T_{FOR} = 300,$$

government purchases $G_{FOR} = 300$.

a. What is the equilibrium interest rate in the international capital market? What are the equilibrium values of consumption, national saving, investment, and the current account balance in each country?

b. Suppose that in the home country, government purchases G increase by 50 to 325. Taxes also increase by 50 to keep the deficit from growing. What is the new equilibrium interest rate in the international capital market? What are the new equilibrium values of consumption, national saving, investment, and the current account balance in each country?

5. A small island nation is endowed with indestructible coconut trees. These trees live forever and no new trees can be planted. Every year $1 million worth of coconuts fall off the trees and can be eaten locally or exported to other countries. In past years the island nation ran current account surpluses and capital account deficits, ac-quiring foreign bonds. It now owns $500,000 of foreign bonds. The interest rate on these bonds is 5% per year. The residents of the island nation consume $1,025,000 per year. What are the values of investment, national saving, the current account balance, the capital account balance, and GNP in this country?

Analytical Problems

1. Explain how each of the following transactions would enter the U.S. balance of payments accounts. Discuss only the transactions described. Do not be concerned with possible offsetting transactions.

  a. The U.S. government sells F-16 fighter planes to a foreign government.
  b. A London bank sells yen to, and buys dollars from, a Swiss bank.
  c. The Federal Reserve sells yen to, and buys dollars from, a Swiss bank.
  d. A New York bank receives the interest on its loans to Brazil.
  e. An American collector buys some ancient artifacts from an archaelogical dig in Egypt.
  f. An American oil company buys insurance from Lloyds of London to insure its oil rigs in the Gulf of Mexico.
  g. An American company borrows from a British bank.

2. For each transaction described in Analytical Problem 1 that by itself changes the sum of the U.S. current account balance (CA) and the U.S. capital account balance (KA), give an example of an offsetting transaction that would leave $CA + KA$ unchanged.

3. A large country imposes capital controls, which prohibit foreign borrowing and lending by domestic residents. Analyze the effects on the country's current account balance, national saving, and investment, and on domestic and world real interest rates. In answering this question, assume that before the capital controls were imposed, the large country was running a capital account surplus.

4. True or false: In a large open economy any change that raises either desired national saving or desired investment (as reflected by shifts in the saving or investment curve) will result ultimately in both higher levels of national saving and investment in the economy. How does your answer to this question bear on the debate about how well international capital markets operate?

5. How would each of the following affect national saving, investment, the current account balance, and the real interest rate in a large open economy?

  a. An increase in the domestic willingness to save (which raises desired national saving at any given real interest rate).
  b. An increase in the willingness of foreigners to save.
  c. An increase in foreign government purchases.
  d. An increase in foreign taxes (consider both the case in which Ricardian equivalence holds and the case in which it does not hold).

6. Analyze the effects on a large economy of a temporary adverse supply shock that hits only the foreign economy. Discuss the impact on the home country's national saving, investment, and current account balance, and on the world real interest rate. How does your answer differ if the adverse supply shock is worldwide?

8
Long-Run Economic Growth

A nation's ability to provide improving standards of living for its people depends crucially on its long-run rate of economic growth. Over a long period of time even an apparently small difference in the rate of economic growth can translate into a large difference in the income of the average citizen.

Compare, for example, the historical experiences of Australia and Japan. In 1870 real gross domestic product (GDP) per person was about five and a half times greater in Australia than in Japan. Indeed, of sixteen major economies considered by British economist Angus Maddison[1] in his important study of long-run growth, Australia was the richest and Japan the poorest in 1870. Australia's economy did not stand still after 1870: Over the next 109 years, according to Maddison's data, Australian real GDP per person grew by 1.1% per year, so that by 1979 the real income of the average Australian was approximately 3.2 times higher than it had been in 1870. However, during the same century-long period Japanese output per person grew at a rate of 2.7% per year, reaching a level in 1979 that was 17.6 times larger than it had been in 1870. The Japanese growth rate of 2.7% per year may not seem dramatically greater than the Australian growth rate of 1.1% per year. Yet by 1979 Japan, which had been far poorer than Australia a century earlier, had achieved essentially the same GDP per capita as Australia; and since 1979 Japan has taken the lead over its Pacific neighbor.

Although the Australia-Japan comparison is over a very long period, a change in the rate of economic growth can have important effects even over a decade or two. For example, since about 1973 the United States and other industrialized countries have experienced a sustained slowdown in their rates of growth: Between 1947 and 1973 real GNP in the United States grew by 3.7% per year, but between 1973 and 1989 America's real GNP grew by only 2.6% per year. To appreciate the significance of this slowdown, imagine that the 1947–1973 growth trend had continued—that is, suppose that real GNP in the United States had continued to grow at 3.7% per year instead of at the 2.6% per year rate actually achieved. Then in 1989 the U.S. real GNP would have been nearly a fifth higher than its actual value—a bonus of about $1 trillion, or $4000 per person (in 1989 dollars). Surely if this growth had happened, many of America's pressing economic problems would be far less severe.

---

[1]*Phases of Capitalist Development*, Oxford: Oxford University Press, 1982. See Table 1.4.

No one has a complete understanding of why economies grow, and no one has a magic formula for inducing rapid growth. Indeed, if such a formula existed, there would be no poor nations. Nevertheless, economists have obtained useful insights about the growth process. In this chapter we study the forces that determine the growth rate of an economy over long periods of time and examine various policies that governments can use to try to influence the rate of growth. As in the rest of this part of the book, saving and investment decisions play a central role in the analysis: Along with changes in productivity, the rates at which a nation saves and invests—and thus the rate at which it accumulates capital goods—are important factors in determining the standard of living that the nation's residents can attain.

8.1   THE SOURCES OF ECONOMIC GROWTH

An economy's output of goods and services depends on the quantities of available inputs, such as capital and labor, and on the productivity of those inputs. The relationship between output and inputs is described by the production function, introduced in Chapter 3:

$$Y = AF(K, N). \tag{8.1}$$

The production function in Eq. (8.1) relates total output Y to the economy's use of capital K and labor N and to productivity A.

If inputs and productivity are constant, then the production function tells us that output will also be constant—there will be no economic growth. For the quantity of output to grow, either the quantities of inputs must grow or productivity must improve, or both. The relationship between the rate of output growth and the rates of input growth and productivity growth is

$$\frac{\Delta Y}{Y} = \frac{\Delta A}{A} + a_K \frac{\Delta K}{K} + a_N \frac{\Delta N}{N}, \tag{8.2}$$

where

$$\frac{\Delta Y}{Y} = \text{rate of output growth,}$$

$$\frac{\Delta K}{K} = \text{rate of capital growth,}$$

$$\frac{\Delta N}{N} = \text{rate of labor growth,}$$

$$\frac{\Delta A}{A} = \text{rate of productivity growth,}$$

$$a_K = \text{elasticity of output with respect to capital,}$$

$$a_N = \text{elasticity of output with respect to labor.}$$

In Eq. (8.2) the elasticity of output with respect to capital a_K is the percentage increase in output resulting from a 1% increase in the capital stock, and the elasticity of output with respect to labor a_N is the percentage increase in output resulting from a 1% increase in the amount of labor used. The elasticities a_K and a_N are both numbers between 0 and 1 that must be estimated from historical data.[2]

Equation (8.2), called the **growth accounting equation**, is the production function in Eq. (8.1) written in growth rate form. Some examples will be helpful for understanding the growth accounting equation.

Suppose, first, that a new invention allows firms to produce 10% more output for any given amount of capital and labor. In terms of the production function in Eq. (8.1), for given capital and labor inputs a 10% increase in productivity A raises output Y by 10%. Similarly, from the growth accounting equation, Eq. (8.2), if productivity growth $\Delta A/A$ equals 10% while capital and labor growth are zero, output growth $\Delta Y/Y$ will be 10%. Thus the production function and the growth accounting equation give the same result, as they should.

As a second example, suppose that firms' investments cause the economy's capital stock to rise by 10% ($\Delta K/K = 10\%$), while labor input and productivity remain unchanged. What will happen to output? From the production function we know that if the capital stock grows, output will increase. However, because of diminishing marginal returns to capital (see Chapter 3), the extra capital will be less productive than the previously existing capital, so the increase in output will be less than 10%. Diminishing marginal returns to capital are the reason that the growth rate of capital, $\Delta K/K$, is multiplied by a factor less than 1 in the growth accounting equation. For the United States this factor a_K, the elasticity of output with respect to capital, has been estimated to be about 0.3. Thus the growth accounting equation, Eq. (8.2), tells us that a 10% increase in the capital stock, with labor and productivity held constant, will increase U.S. output by about 3% (0.3 times 10%).

Similarly, the elasticity of output with respect to labor a_N has been estimated to be about 0.7 in the United States. According to the growth accounting equation, therefore, a 10% increase in the amount of labor used ($\Delta N/N = 10\%$), with no change in capital or productivity, will raise U.S. output by about 7% (0.7 times 10%).[3]

Growth Accounting

According to the growth accounting equation, Eq. (8.2), output growth $\Delta Y/Y$ can be broken down into three parts:

1. The part due to productivity growth, $\Delta A/A$.

2. The part due to increased capital inputs, $a_K \Delta K/K$.

3. The part due to increased labor inputs, $a_N \Delta N/N$.

Growth accounting is a technique for measuring empirically the relative importance of these three sources of output growth.

---

[2]Elasticities and growth rate formulas like Eq. (8.2) are discussed further in Appendix A, Sections A.3 and A.7.

[3]Chapter 3 examined the production function for the U.S. economy, $Y = AK^{0.3}N^{0.7}$. In this production function, called a Cobb-Douglas production function, the exponent on the capital stock K, 0.3, equals the elasticity of output with respect to capital, and the exponent on the quantity of labor input N, 0.7, equals the elasticity of output with respect to labor. See Appendix A, Section A.7.

A typical growth accounting analysis involves the following four steps (see Table 8.1 for a summary and numerical example):

- *Step 1.* Obtain measures of the growth rates of output ($\Delta Y/Y$), capital ($\Delta K/K$), and labor ($\Delta N/N$) for the economy over a given period. In calculating growth rates of capital and labor, more sophisticated analyses make adjustments for changing quality as well as quantity of inputs. For example, to obtain a quality-adjusted measure of N an hour of work by a skilled worker is counted as more labor than an hour of work by an unskilled worker. Similarly, to obtain a quality-adjusted measure of K a machine that can turn fifty bolts a minute is treated as being more capital than a machine that can only turn thirty bolts a minute.

- *Step 2.* Estimate values for the elasticities a_K and a_N from historical data. As we have mentioned, estimates for the United States are around 0.3 for a_K and 0.7 for a_N.

- *Step 3.* Calculate the contribution of capital to economic growth as $a_K\,\Delta K/K$ and the contribution of labor to economic growth as $a_N\,\Delta N/N$.

- *Step 4.* The part of economic growth due to neither capital growth nor labor growth is attributed to improvements in total factor productivity. The rate of

Table 8.1 The Steps of Growth Accounting: A Numerical Example

Step 1. Obtain measures of output growth, capital growth, and labor growth over the period to be studied.
Example:

$$\text{Output growth} = \frac{\Delta Y}{Y} = 40\%$$

$$\text{Capital growth} = \frac{\Delta K}{K} = 20\%$$

$$\text{Labor growth} = \frac{\Delta N}{N} = 30\%$$

Step 2. Using historical data, obtain estimates of the elasticities of output with respect to capital and labor, a_K and a_N.
Example:

$$a_K = 0.3 \qquad a_N = 0.7$$

Step 3. Find the contributions to growth of capital and labor.
Example:

$$\begin{aligned}
\text{Contribution to output growth of growth in capital} &= a_K \frac{\Delta K}{K} = (0.3)(20\%) = 6\% \\
\text{Contribution to output growth of growth in labor} &= a_N \frac{\Delta N}{N} = (0.7)(30\%) = 21\%
\end{aligned}$$

Step 4. Find productivity growth as the residual (the part of output growth not explained by capital or labor).
Example:

$$\begin{aligned}
\text{Productivity growth} &= \frac{\Delta A}{A} = \frac{\Delta Y}{Y} - a_K \frac{\Delta K}{K} - a_N \frac{\Delta N}{N} \\
&= 40\% - 6\% - 21\% = 13\%
\end{aligned}$$

productivity change $\Delta A/A$ is calculated from the formula

$$\frac{\Delta A}{A} = \frac{\Delta Y}{Y} - a_K \frac{\Delta K}{K} - a_N \frac{\Delta N}{N}$$

which is the growth accounting equation, Eq. (8.2), rewritten with $\Delta A/A$ on the left-hand side. Thus the growth accounting technique treats productivity change as a residual, or the portion of growth not otherwise explained.[4]

Growth Accounting Estimates for the United States   What does growth accounting say about the sources of American economic growth? Among the best-known research that has been done using the growth accounting framework is that of Edward Denison, an economist at the Brookings Institution. Table 8.2 summarizes Denison's findings for the period 1929–1982.

The bottom entry in column (4) of Table 8.2 shows that over the 1929–1982 period output grew at an average rate of 2.92% per year in the United States. According to Denison's measurements (Table 8.2, column 4), the growth of labor accounted for output growth of 1.34% per year. The growth of labor in turn resulted primarily from rising population, an increase in the percentage of the population in the labor force, and higher educational levels, which had the effect of increasing workers' skills. (Offsetting these trends to a degree was a fall in the number of hours worked per person.) According to Denison, the growth of the capital stock accounted for output growth of 0.56% per year. So, together, labor and capital growth contributed 1.90% to the annual growth rate of output.

The difference between total growth (2.92%) and the amount of growth attributed to capital and labor growth (1.90%) is 1.02%. By the growth accounting method, this remaining 1.02% per year of growth is attributed to increases in productivity.

Table 8.2 Sources of Economic Growth in the United States (Denison) (in Percent per Year)

	(1) 1929–1948	(2) 1948–1973	(3) 1973–1982	(4) 1929–1982
Source of growth				
Labor growth	1.42	1.40	1.13	**1.34**
Capital growth	0.11	0.77	0.69	**0.56**
Total input growth	1.53	2.17	1.82	**1.90**
Productivity growth	1.01	1.53	−0.27	**1.02**
Total output growth	2.54	3.70	1.55	**2.92**

Source: Edward F. Denison, *Trends in American Economic Growth, 1929–1982*, Washington, D.C.: The Brookings Institution, 1985, Table 8.1, p. 111.

---

[4]The growth accounting method for calculating productivity growth is very similar to the method we used to find productivity growth in Chapter 3, Section 3.2, where we also determined productivity growth as the part of output growth not explained by increases in capital and labor. The differences are that growth accounting uses the growth accounting equation, which is the production function in growth rate form, instead of using the production function directly, as we did in Chapter 3; and growth accounting analyses usually adjust measures of capital and labor for changes in quality, which we did not do in Chapter 3.

Data for three shorter periods are given in columns (1)–(3) of Table 8.2. A striking finding is that during one of the periods, 1973–1982, estimated productivity growth was *negative*. In other words, Denison estimated that any given combination of capital and labor would have produced *less* output in 1982 than it could have in 1973! The application at the end of this section discusses the puzzle of the post-1973 productivity decline.

In summary, Denison found that in the United States the growth of labor input has regularly contributed more than 1% per year to the growth rate of output. The contribution of capital growth has been somewhat smaller and more variable than the contribution of labor growth. Finally, the contribution of productivity growth to the growth rate of output has varied substantially, being the most important source of growth in the 1948–1973 period but actually becoming negative in the period following 1973.

Some alternative and more recent estimates by another leader in the study of economic growth, Dale Jorgenson of Harvard University, are presented in Table 8.3. Jorgenson's estimates are for the postwar period only, 1947–1985. Comparison of Table 8.3 with Table 8.2 shows that Jorgenson and Denison obtain similar results for the contribution of labor to U.S. economic growth. Like Denison, Jorgenson also finds that productivity growth was negative in the period following 1973.

The main difference in results is that Jorgenson finds a significantly greater role for growth in the capital stock as a source of growth in output. Because productivity growth is measured as the unexplained residual, this finding of a greater role for capital implies that Jorgenson must attach less importance to productivity growth than Denison does. What explains this difference in findings? Recall that in measuring the growth of capital and labor inputs, growth accountants make adjustments for improvements in input quality. Jorgenson argues that Denison used methods that led him to seriously underestimate the rate of improvement in capital quality. By using methods that yield a more generous estimate of the rate at which the quality of the capital stock has improved over time, Jorgenson finds a larger role for capital growth and thus a smaller role for productivity growth.

There is a sense in which Denison's and Jorgenson's results are not really in disagreement. In general, a major source of increases in productivity is improvements in technology. Typically, the way that technological change is incorporated into the production process is through the introduction of new, more technologically

Table 8.3 Sources of Economic Growth in the United States (Jorgenson) (in Percent per Year)

	(1) 1973–1979	(2) 1979–1985	(3) 1947–1985
Source of growth			
Labor growth	1.39	0.89	1.12
Capital growth	1.40	0.98	1.45
Total input growth	2.79	1.87	2.57
Productivity growth	−0.67	0.34	0.71
Total output growth	2.12	2.22	3.28

Source: Dale W. Jorgenson, "Productivity and Economic Growth," Harvard Institute of Economic Research discussion paper no. 1487, June 1990, Table 1.

advanced capital goods. From a growth accounting perspective, should the benefits of a more technically sophisticated capital stock be attributed to increased productivity or to improvements in capital quality? One could argue the issue either way. How this type of economic change is classified is less important than simply appreciating that technological advance, as embodied in increasingly sophisticated capital goods, is a central element in the growth process.

Application

The Post-1973 Growth Slowdown

As we discussed in the introduction to this chapter, since around 1973 there has been a significant reduction in the rate of economic growth, both in the United States and in other countries. The consequences of this slowdown can hardly be overstated: For the United States there has been a major impact on both its role as a world economic leader and in its ability to solve domestic economic and social problems. Explaining this slowdown is obviously very important and has been the subject of a great deal of research.

What does growth accounting say about the slowdown? The main message from the work of both Denison (Table 8.2) and Jorgenson (Table 8.3) is that the slowdown in output growth is *not* due to a slowdown in the growth of capital or labor inputs. As you can see in Table 8.2, Denison finds that output growth slowed from 3.70% per year in 1948–1973 to 1.55% per year in 1973–1982, a drop of 2.15%; but between the same two periods the contribution of input growth slowed from 2.17% to 1.82%, a drop of only 0.35%. Thus most of the slowdown is the result of a tremendous drop in productivity growth, from 1.53% per year in 1948–1973 to −0.27% in 1973–1982. Similarly, Jorgenson's analysis, as reported in Table 8.3, attributes the entire difference between growth in 1973–1979 and growth for the whole 1947–1985 period to a sharp decline in productivity growth.

In finding that the post-1973 economic slowdown is due to a fall in productivity growth, however, we have only pushed the puzzle back one step. The obvious next question is, what caused productivity performance to deteriorate so sharply? We discuss a number of alternative explanations, including possible measurement problems, deterioration in the legal and human environment, reduced rates of technological innovation, and the effects of high oil prices.

Measurement   Interestingly, a few economists have suggested that the productivity slowdown is not a genuine economic problem at all. Instead, they argue, the slowdown is an illusion, the result of measurement problems that have overstated the extent of the decline.

As in the Denison-Jorgenson debate, the key issue is again whether the statistics adequately capture changes in quality. Consider the case of a firm producing air conditioners that, using unchanged quantities of capital and labor, makes the same number of air conditioners this year as last year. However, this year's air conditioners are of much higher quality than last year's, being more reliable and energy-efficient. Since the firm's output this year has a greater real economic value than last year's output, the true productivity of the firm's capital and labor has risen over the year, even though the firm produces the same *number* of air conditioners as before. However, if statisticians measuring the firm's output only counted the number of air conditioners produced and failed to adjust for quality change, this improvement in productivity would be missed. In fact, official output measures do try to take account of quality improvements—for example, by counting a more energy-efficient air conditioner as contributing more to output than a less efficient model. However, it is difficult to measure quality change, and to the extent that improvements are not fully accounted for in the data, productivity growth will be underestimated.

A careful study of the measurement issue has been done for the Brookings Institution by Martin N. Baily and Robert J. Gordon.[5] Baily and Gordon find that measurement problems may be important for explaining the productivity slowdown in some industries. A striking example is the construction industry. According to the official data, there was a 40% *decline* in productivity in the construction industry between 1967 and 1986. Baily and Gordon argue that this result is implausible and point to a number of quality improvements in residential construction (such as more frequent installation of central air-conditioning, more custom woodwork, better insulation and landscaping), which are not captured in official measures of construction output.

However, Baily and Gordon also point out that measurement problems are not new but existed before 1973 as well. For inadequate measurement to explain the post-1973 productivity decline, one must show not only that current measurement procedures understate productivity growth but also that recent productivity growth is understated by much more than was the case before 1973. Overall, Baily and Gordon conclude that measurement problems could at most explain a third of the reported post-1973 slowdown. Thus the productivity slowdown is not, for the most part, simply a figment of measurement.

The Legal and Human Environment In his growth accounting study cited previously, Edward Denison did not stop at reporting the decline in productivity growth but went on to try to develop some explanations for the decline. One explanation given by Denison for his finding of negative productivity growth in 1973–1982 is the change in what he called the legal and human environment. In this category Denison included a number of diverse factors. For example, since 1973 there has been increased emphasis on a cleaner environment and worker safety and health. To the extent that capital and labor resources are devoted to these goals, measured output and productivity will decline. (For further discussion, see Box 2.1.) Of course, the reduction in measured productivity caused by reducing pollution or increasing worker safety is not in any way an argument against pursuing these goals. The proper criterion for evaluating proposed environmental regulations, for example, is whether the benefits to society of the regulations, in terms of cleaner air or water, exceed the costs they will impose.

In addition to pollution control and worker safety, changes in the legal and human environment include factors that reduce productivity but do not yield any benefit to society. For example, Denison estimated that increased dishonesty and crime reduced the annual growth rate of output by 0.05% per year, because productive resources were diverted to protection against crime or were lost to theft, arson, or vandalism. A potentially more important problem under the heading of

---

[5]"The Productivity Slowdown, Measurement Issues, and the Explosion of Computer Power," *Brookings Papers on Economic Activity*, 1988:2, pp. 347–420.

legal and human environment was an apparent decline in educational quality during the 1970s, which led to slower improvement in workers' skills (see Box 8.1).

Technological Depletion and Slow Commercial Adaptation   The growth accounting findings discussed earlier are consistent with the view that technological advances, typically incorporated into the design of new and more efficient capital goods, are an important source of growth. Indeed, no one could deny that there are tremendous differences between fifty years ago and today in terms of the production processes that are used and in the products and services that are available. One possible explanation of the productivity slowdown is that the major technological advances of the past have now been largely exploited, but commercially significant new technologies have not arrived at a pace sufficient to maintain the accustomed rate of productivity growth. The idea that technological innovation has at least temporarily dried up is part of the "depletion hypothesis" suggested by William Nordhaus[6] of Yale University.

Why should the pace of technological innovation have slowed down since 1973? One argument is that the high rate of innovation in the decades following World War II was abnormal, reflecting a backlog of technological opportunities that were not exploited earlier because of the Depression and World War II. In this view we have in recent years returned to a more normal rate of innovation. Some economists also point out that there is no law of nature requiring that economically valuable inventions must arrive in a steady stream. Perhaps we have just been unlucky in that the major scientific developments of recent years, such as computerization and gene splicing, have not yet had the economic payoffs that were expected.

A variation of the technological depletion hypothesis holds that there is no shortage of breakthroughs in basic science. Instead, the problem is that American corporations have been slow or unable to adapt the most recent breakthroughs to commercial uses. In contrast, studies have found that Japanese firms do a much better job than American companies of maintaining communication and cooperation between the laboratory and the shop floor and of bringing new scientific results quickly into the marketplace—even when the original scientific breakthroughs occurred in other countries.[7]

The Oil Price Explanation   A popular explanation for the productivity slowdown is the large increase in energy prices that followed the OPEC oil embargo in 1973. The idea is that as companies responded to high energy prices by using less energy, the amount of output they could produce with a given amount of capital and labor declined, reducing productivity. What makes this explanation seem very plausible is not only that the timing is right—the productivity decline appears to have begun in earnest around 1973—but that, unlike several of the other explanations, the oil price story explains why all major industrial countries, not just the United States, experienced a slowdown.

---

[6]"Economic Policy in the Face of Declining Productivity Growth," *European Economic Review*, May/June 1982, pp. 131–158.

[7]See Edwin Mansfield, "Industrial R&D in Japan and the United States: A Comparative Study," *American Economic Review*, May 1988, pp. 223–228; Nathan Rosenberg and W. Edward Steinmueller, "Why Are Americans Such Poor Imitators?" *American Economic Review*, May 1988, pp. 229–234. The argument that the American problem is slow commercial adaptation of new scientific findings is also made by an influential MIT study; see MIT Commission on Industrial Productivity, *Made in America: Regaining the Productive Edge*, Cambridge, Mass.: MIT Press, 1989.

Has educational quality declined in the United States, and if so, is this decline a source of the productivity slowdown? A study of this question was done by John H. Bishop* of Cornell University. Bishop argued that educational quality is most directly reflected in the skills, abilities, and knowledge of the typical student—or in psychologist's language, in the student's general intellectual achievement (GIA). Although a student's GIA is intangible, it can be measured by standardized achievement tests such as the Iowa Test for Educational Development and the American College Test, and by aptitude tests such as the Armed Services Qualification Test and the Scholastic Aptitude Test (SAT). Bishop noted that after improving steadily for fifty years, the test scores of high school students started to decline in 1967. This decline continued for thirteen years, so that by 1980 the decline in test scores was equivalent to a reduction in academic achievement of about 1.25 grade levels. Then in 1980,

BOX 8.1: THE IMPACT ON PRODUCTIVITY OF THE DECLINE IN TEST SCORES

perhaps as a result of efforts to improve the quality of education, test scores once again started to rise.

What were the effects of this thirteen-year decline in GIA of high school students? Using statistical techniques, Bishop estimated the effect of an individual's GIA on his or her productivity and then used this result to calculate the overall effect on productivity of the drop in GIA. He found that if test scores had continued their upward trend after 1967, in 1987 worker productivity would have been 2.9% higher than what was actually observed.

Since people who were high school students during the period of declining test scores will remain in the work force for many more years, the effect on the economy of the measured decline in GIA is not yet over: According to Bishop, because of the decline in GIA in 1967–1980, U.S. GNP in the year 2010 will be 4.4% lower than it otherwise would have been.

*"Is the Test Score Decline Responsible for the Productivity Growth Decline?" *American Economic Review,* March 1989, pp. 178–197.

Pinning the blame for the productivity slowdown on oil price increases has not been easy, though. The fact is that for many industries energy costs are a relatively small part of total costs, which makes it hard to see why energy price increases should have had such dramatic effects. One answer, proposed by Martin N. Baily,[8] is that the rise in oil prices may have made many older, more energy-intensive machines and factories unprofitable to operate, thus effectively reducing the nation's capital stock. Such a fall in the "true" capital stock below the measured capital stock would show up in the data as a fall in productivity. If Baily's story were correct, however, then the prices of used capital goods should have dropped sharply when oil prices rose, reflecting their diminished economic value. Generally, though, the predicted decline in the prices of used capital goods was not observed.[9]

In his growth accounting analysis cited earlier, Dale Jorgenson argued that a large impact of oil prices can be found if one looks at productivity performance industry by industry. Some basic industries are very reliant on energy and were badly hurt by the oil price increases. According to Jorgenson, the effect of oil price increases on productivity is underestimated when one looks only at economywide data.

---

[8]"Productivity and the Services of Capital and Labor," *Brookings Papers on Economic Activity,* 1982:2, pp. 423–454.

[9]See Charles R. Hulten, James W. Robertson, and Frank C. Wykoff, "Energy, Obsolescence, and the Productivity Slowdown," NBER working paper no. 2404, October 1987.

Conclusion   Our problem in explaining the post-1973 slowdown in productivity growth may not be a lack of reasonable explanations but too many. We should not dismiss the possibility that there was no single cause of the slowdown but that many factors contributed to it. Unfortunately, from a policy perspective, if there are multiple explanations for the slowdown, then no single policy action is likely by itself to restart the productivity engine.

8.2   GROWTH DYNAMICS: THE SOLOW MODEL

Although growth accounting provides useful information about the sources of economic growth, it has some shortcomings. The main weakness of growth accounting is that it takes the economy's rates of input growth as given rather than explaining *why* capital and labor grow at the rate that they do. But the growth of the capital stock in particular is not simply given but is the result of the saving and investment decisions made by households and firms. By taking the growth of the capital stock as given, the growth accounting method leaves out an important part of the story.

In this section we take a closer look at the dynamics of economic growth, or how the growth process evolves over time. In doing so, we drop the assumption made in Chapter 3 that the capital stock is fixed and study the factors that cause the economy's stock of capital to grow. Our analysis is based on a famous model of economic growth developed in the late 1950s by Nobel laureate Robert Solow[10] of the Massachusetts Institute of Technology, a model that has become the basic framework for most subsequent research on growth. Besides clarifying how capital accumulation and economic growth are interrelated, the Solow model is useful for studying three other basic questions about growth:

1.   What is the relationship between a nation's long-run standard of living and fundamental factors such as its saving rate, its population growth rate, and its rate of technical progress?

2.   How does a nation's rate of economic growth evolve over time? Will economic growth stabilize, accelerate, or stop?

3.   Are there economic forces that will ultimately allow poorer countries to catch up with the richest countries in terms of living standards?

Setup of the Solow Model

The Solow model studies an economy as it evolves over time. So that we can analyze the effects of labor force growth as well as changes in capital, we assume that the population is growing and that at any given time a fixed share of the population is of working age. For any given year t, we let

$$N_t = \text{the number of workers available in year } t.$$

We suppose that the population and the work force both grow at a fixed rate n. So, for example, if $n = 0.05$, then the number of workers in a given year is 5% greater than in the previous year.

---

[10]The original article is Robert M. Solow, "A Contribution to the Theory of Economic Growth," *Quarterly Journal of Economics*, February 1956, pp. 65–94.

At the beginning of each year t the economy has available a capital stock K_t. (We will see shortly how this capital stock is determined.) During each year t capital K_t and labor N_t are used to produce the economy's total output Y_t. Part of the output produced in each year is invested in new capital or in replacing worn-out capital. We assume that the economy is closed and that there are no government purchases, so that the part of output that is not invested is consumed by the population. If we let

$$Y_t = \text{output produced in year } t,$$
$$I_t = \text{gross (total) investment in year } t,$$
$$C_t = \text{consumption in year } t,$$

then the relationship among consumption, output, and investment in each year is given by

$$C_t = Y_t - I_t. \tag{8.3}$$

Equation (8.3) says that the part of the economy's output that is not invested is consumed.

Because the population and the labor force are growing in this economy, it is convenient to focus on output, consumption, and the capital stock as measured *per worker*. Recalling that the labor force in year t is N_t, we use the following notation:

$$y_t = \frac{Y_t}{N_t} = \text{output per worker in year } t,$$

$$c_t = \frac{C_t}{N_t} = \text{consumption per worker in year } t,$$

$$k_t = \frac{K_t}{N_t} = \text{capital stock per worker in year } t.$$

The capital stock per worker k_t is also called the **capital-labor ratio.** An important goal of the model is to understand how output per worker, consumption per worker, and the capital-labor ratio change over time.[11]

The Per-Worker Production Function   In general, the amount of output that can be produced by given quantities of inputs is determined by the production function. Until now we have written the production function as a relationship between total output Y and the total quantities of capital and labor inputs, K and N. However, the production function can also be written in per-worker terms as

$$y_t = f(k_t). \tag{8.4}$$

The production function in Eq. (8.4) says that in each year t output per worker y_t depends on the amount of available capital per worker k_t.[12] Here we use a small f

---

[11]For purposes of analysis it is more convenient to discuss output and consumption per worker rather than output and consumption per member of the population as a whole. Nothing important is lost here, though, because under the assumption that the work force is a fixed fraction of the population, anything we say about the growth rate of output or consumption per worker will be true of the growth rate of output or consumption per member of the population as well.

[12]To write the production function in the form of Eq. (8.4) requires the assumption of constant returns to scale, which means that an equal percentage increase in both capital and labor inputs results in the same percentage increase in total output. So, for example, with constant returns to scale a 10% increase in *both* capital and labor raises output by 10%. In terms of the growth accounting equation, Eq. (8.2), constant returns to scale requires that $a_K + a_N = 1$. See Analytical Problem 6.

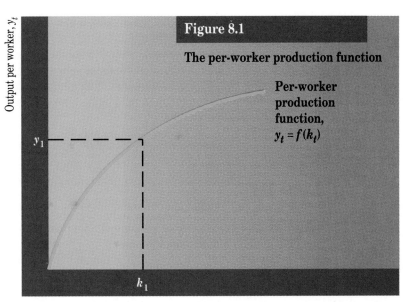

Figure 8.1

The per-worker production function

Per-worker production function, $y_t = f(k_t)$

The per-worker production function $y_t = f(k_t)$ relates the amount of output produced per worker y_t to the capital-labor ratio k_t. For example, when the capital-labor ratio is k_1, output per worker is y_1. The per-worker production function slopes upward from left to right because an increase in the capital-labor ratio raises the amount of output produced per worker. The bowed shape of the production function reflects diminishing marginal returns to capital.

instead of a capital F to stand for the production function to remind us that we are measuring output and capital in per-worker terms. In order to focus on the role of the capital stock in the growth process, for the time being we assume that there is no productivity growth and thus leave the productivity term out of the production function in Eq. (8.4).[13] We bring productivity growth back into the model later.

The per-worker production function is graphed in Fig. 8.1. The capital-labor ratio (the amount of capital per worker) k_t is measured on the horizontal axis of the figure, and output per worker y_t is measured on the vertical axis. The production function slopes upward from left to right because an increase in the amount of capital per worker allows each worker to produce more output. As with the standard production function, the bowed shape of the per-worker production function reflects diminishing marginal returns to capital: When the capital-labor ratio is already high, an increase in the capital-labor ratio has a relatively small effect on output per worker.

Steady States One of the most striking conclusions obtained from the Solow model is that in the absence of productivity growth the economy reaches a steady state in the long run. A **steady state** is a situation in which the economy's output per worker, consumption per worker, and capital stock per worker are constant—that is, in the steady state y_t, c_t, and k_t do not change over time.[14] To understand how the Solow model works, we first examine the characteristics of a steady state; then we discuss how the economy might reach such a situation.

First, let us see what investment will be in a steady state. In general, gross (total) investment in year t, I_t, can be broken into two parts: the part devoted to replacing worn-out or depreciated capital and the part used to expand the size of the capital stock. The amount by which the capital stock is increased is also called

[13]More precisely, we set the total factor productivity term A equal to 1.

[14]Note that if output, consumption, and capital per worker are constant, then *total* output, consumption, and capital are all growing at rate n, the rate of growth of the work force.

net investment. If d is the capital depreciation rate, or the fraction of capital that wears out in each year, then the total amount of depreciation in year t is dK_t. What is net investment in a steady state? Because capital *per worker*, K_t/N_t, is constant in a steady state, the *total* capital stock grows at the same rate as the labor force, that is, at rate n. Net investment is therefore nK_t in a steady state.[15]

Adding net investment nK_t and depreciation dK_t, we get an equation for steady-state investment:

$$I_t = (n + d)K_t \quad \text{in a steady state.} \tag{8.5}$$

Consumption in this economy is output less investment. To find steady-state consumption, we substitute Eq. (8.5) into Eq. (8.3) to get

$$C_t = Y_t - (n + d)K_t \quad \text{in a steady state.} \tag{8.6}$$

Equation (8.6) measures consumption, output, and capital as economywide totals, rather than in per-worker terms.

To put things in per-worker terms, we divide both sides of Eq. (8.6) by the number of workers N_t, remembering that $c_t = C_t/N_t$, $y_t = Y_t/N_t$, and $k_t = K_t/N_t$. Then we use the per-worker production function from Eq. (8.4) to replace y_t by $f(k_t)$. The result is

$$c = f(k) - (n + d)k \quad \text{in a steady state.} \tag{8.7}$$

Equation (8.7) shows the relationship between consumption per worker c and the capital-labor ratio k in the steady state. Because consumption per worker and the capital-labor ratio are constant in the steady state, we have dropped the time subscripts t in Eq. (8.7).

Equation (8.7) shows that an increase in the steady-state capital-labor ratio k has two opposing effects on steady-state consumption per worker c. First, an increase in the steady-state capital-labor ratio raises the amount of output each worker can produce, $f(k)$. Second, an increase in the steady-state capital-labor ratio also increases the amount of output per worker that must be devoted to investment, $(n + d)k$. More goods devoted to investment means fewer goods left over to consume.

The trade-off between these two effects is shown in Fig. 8.2. In Fig. 8.2(a) different possible values of the steady-state capital-labor ratio k are measured on the horizontal axis. The curve in Fig. 8.2(a) is the per-worker production function, $y = f(k)$, as in Fig. 8.1. The straight line shows investment per worker, $(n + d)k$, in the steady state. Equation (8.7) tells us that steady-state consumption per worker c equals the height of the curve $f(k)$ minus the height of the straight line $(n + d)k$. Thus consumption per worker is given by the height of the shaded area in Fig. 8.2(a).

The relationship between consumption per worker and the capital-labor ratio in the steady state is shown more explicitly in Fig. 8.2(b). For each value of the capital-labor ratio k steady-state consumption c is found as the difference between the production function and investment in Fig. 8.2(a). Notice that starting from low and medium values of k (values less than k_1 in Fig. 8.2b), increases in the steady-state capital-labor ratio lead to greater steady-state consumption per

---

[15]Algebraically, net investment in year t is $K_{t+1} - K_t$. If total capital grows at rate n, then $K_{t+1} = (1 + n)K_t$. Substituting for K_{t+1} in the definition of net investment, we find that net investment is nK_t in a steady state.

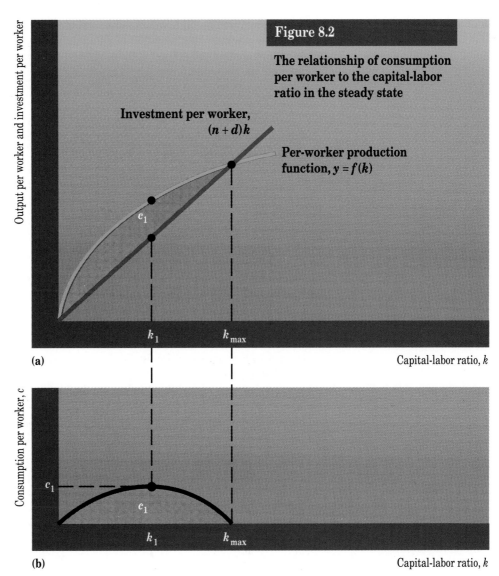

Figure 8.2

The relationship of consumption per worker to the capital-labor ratio in the steady state

(a)

(b)

(a) For each value of the capital-labor ratio k steady-state output per worker y is given by the per-worker production function $f(k)$. Steady-state investment per worker, $(n + d)k$, is shown as a straight line with slope $(n + d)$. Steady-state consumption per worker c is the difference between output per worker and investment per worker, shown as the shaded area. For example, if the capital-labor ratio is k_1, steady-state consumption per worker is c_1.

(b) For each value of the capital-labor ratio k steady-state consumption per worker c is derived in part (a) as the difference between output per worker and investment per worker. Thus the shaded area in part (b) corresponds to the shaded area in part (a). Notice that starting from a low value of the capital-labor ratio, an increase in the capital-labor ratio raises steady-state consumption per worker. However, starting from a capital-labor ratio greater than k_1 in the figure, an increase in the capital-labor ratio lowers consumption per worker. When the capital-labor ratio equals k_{max}, all output is devoted to investment, and steady-state consumption per worker is zero.

worker. However, for high values of k (values greater than k_1), increases in the steady-state capital-labor ratio can actually result in lower consumption per worker, because so much investment is needed to maintain the high level of capital per worker. In the extreme case, where $k = k_{max}$ in Fig. 8.2, all output has to be devoted to replacing and expanding the capital stock, with nothing left over to consume!

In this book we have made the point that increased saving and investment lead ultimately to higher levels of consumption; and indeed, policymakers have often tried to improve long-run living standards by means of policies aimed at stimulating saving and investment. Figure 8.2 shows that there are limits to this strategy: Although a country with a low amount of capital per worker may hope to improve long-run (steady-state) living standards substantially by increasing rates of saving and investment, a country that already has a high quantity of capital per worker may find that further increases in saving and investment do not raise steady-state consumption by very much. The fundamental reason for this outcome is diminishing marginal returns to capital (Chapter 3), which imply that the larger the capital stock already is, the smaller the benefit is to expanding the quantity of capital still further. Indeed, Fig. 8.2 shows that, theoretically, capital per worker can be so high that further increases will actually *lower* steady-state consumption per worker.

Is any economy in the world today in a situation where a higher capital stock might lead to less consumption in the long run? A recent study of seven advanced industrial countries concluded that the answer is "no": Even for high-saving Japan, further increases in capital per worker would lead to higher steady-state consumption per worker.[16] Thus in our analysis that follows, we will always assume that an increase in the steady-state capital-labor ratio raises consumption per worker.

Reaching the Steady State   Our discussion of steady states leaves two loose ends. First, we need to say something about why an economy like the one we study here eventually will reach a steady state, as we claimed earlier. Second, we have not yet shown *which* steady state the economy will reach; that is, we would like to know what steady-state levels of consumption per worker and the capital-labor ratio the economy will eventually attain.

To tie up these loose ends, we need one more piece of information: the rate at which people in the economy save. To keep things as simple as possible, suppose that saving in this economy is proportional to current income:

$$S_t = sY_t, \tag{8.8}$$

where S_t is national saving[17] in year t and s is the fixed average saving rate. We have seen that a \$1 increase in current income raises saving but by less than \$1. Therefore we assume that s is between 0 and 1. Equation (8.8) ignores some other determinants of saving discussed in earlier chapters, such as the real interest rate. However, since including these other factors would not change our basic conclusions, for simplicity we omit them.

---

[16]See Andrew B. Abel, N. Gregory Mankiw, Lawrence H. Summers, and Richard J. Zeckhauser, "Assessing Dynamic Efficiency: Theory and Evidence," *Review of Economic Studies*, January 1989, pp. 1–20.

[17]Since there is no government in this model, national saving and private saving are the same.

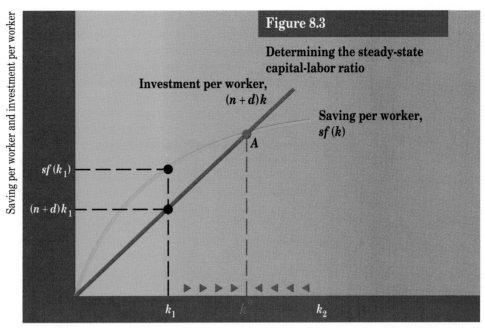

Figure 8.3

Determining the steady-state capital-labor ratio

The steady-state capital-labor ratio k^* is determined by the goods market equilibrium condition that saving per worker $sf(k)$ equal steady-state investment per worker $(n + d)k$. The steady-state capital-labor ratio k^* is the one corresponding to point A, where the saving curve and the investment line cross. From any starting point, eventually the capital-labor ratio reaches k^*: If the capital-labor ratio happens to be below k^*, say at k_1, then saving per worker $sf(k_1)$ exceeds the investment per worker $(n + d)k_1$ needed to maintain the capital-labor ratio at k_1. As this extra saving is converted into capital, the capital-labor ratio will rise, as indicated by the arrows. Similarly, if the capital-labor ratio is greater than k^*, say at k_2, then there is too little saving to maintain the capital-labor ratio, and the capital-labor ratio falls over time.

In every year goods market equilibrium requires that national saving S_t must equal investment I_t. In a steady state the saving-equal-investment condition is

$$sY_t = (n + d)K_t \qquad \text{in a steady state,} \qquad (8.9)$$

where the left side of Eq. (8.9) is saving (see Eq. 8.8) and the right side of Eq. (8.9) is steady-state investment (see Eq. 8.5).

Equation (8.9) shows the relation between total output Y_t and the total capital stock K_t that holds in the steady state. To determine steady-state capital per worker, we divide both sides of Eq. (8.9) by N_t; then we use the production function, Eq. (8.4), to replace y_t by $f(k_t)$. The result is

$$sf(k) = (n + d)k \qquad \text{in the steady state.} \qquad (8.10)$$

Equation (8.10) says that saving per worker $sf(k)$ equals investment per worker $(n + d)k$ in the steady state. Because the capital-labor ratio k is constant in the steady state, again we drop the time subscript in the equation.

With Eq. (8.10) we can now determine the steady-state capital-labor ratio that the economy will attain (see Fig. 8.3). In Fig. 8.3 the capital-labor ratio is measured along the horizontal axis. Saving per worker and investment per worker are measured on the vertical axis.

The bowed curve in Fig. 8.3 shows how the amount of saving per worker $sf(k)$ is related to the capital-labor ratio. This curve slopes upward because an increase in the capital-labor ratio implies higher output per worker and thus more saving per worker. The saving-per-worker curve has the same general shape as the per-worker production function, because saving per worker equals the per-worker production function $f(k)$ multiplied by the fixed saving rate s.

The line in Fig. 8.3 represents steady-state investment per worker $(n + d)k$. The investment line slopes upward because the higher the capital-labor ratio is, the more investment per worker is required to replace depreciating capital and to equip new workers with the same high level of capital.

According to Eq. (8.10), the steady-state capital-labor ratio must be such that saving per worker and investment per worker are equal. The one level of the capital-labor ratio for which this condition is satisfied is shown in Fig. 8.3 as k^*, which is the value of k at which the saving curve and the investment line cross. For any other value of k saving and investment will not be equal in the steady state. Thus k^* is the only possible steady-state capital-labor ratio for this economy.[18]

Given the unique steady-state capital-labor ratio k^*, we can also find steady-state output and consumption per worker. From the per-worker production function (Eq. 8.4), if the steady-state capital-labor ratio is k^*, then steady-state output per worker y^* is

$$y^* = f(k^*).$$

From Eq. (8.7) steady-state consumption per worker c^*, equals steady-state output per worker $f(k^*)$ minus steady-state investment per worker $(n + d)k^*$:

$$c^* = f(k^*) - (n + d)k^*.$$

As we mentioned earlier, in the empirically realistic case a higher value of the steady-state capital-labor ratio k^* implies greater steady-state consumption per worker c^*.

By imposing the goods market equilibrium condition that national saving must equal investment, we have found the steady-state capital-labor ratio k^*. When capital per worker is k^*, the amount that people choose to save will just equal the amount of investment necessary to keep capital per worker at k^*. Thus once the economy's capital-labor ratio reaches k^*, it will remain there forever.

But is there any reason to think that the capital-labor ratio will ever reach k^* if it starts at some other value? Yes, there is. Suppose that the capital-labor ratio happens to be less than k^*; for example, it equals k_1 in Fig. 8.3. When capital per worker is k_1, the amount of saving per worker $sf(k_1)$ is greater than the amount of investment needed to keep the capital-labor ratio constant, $(n + d)k_1$, as shown in the figure. When this extra saving is converted into capital, the capital-labor ratio will rise. As indicated by the arrows on the horizontal axis of Fig. 8.3, the capital-labor ratio will increase from k_1 toward k^*.

The time path of the capital-labor ratio, starting from an initial value of k_1, is shown in Fig. 8.4. As you can see, the capital-labor ratio rises gradually over time. Eventually, it equals k^*, its steady-state value, where it remains forever. Also shown in Fig. 8.4 is the path of output per worker. At each point in time output

---

[18]Actually, there is also a steady state at the point $k = 0$, at which the capital stock, output, and consumption are zero forever. However, as long as the economy starts out with a positive amount of capital, it will never reach the zero-capital steady state.

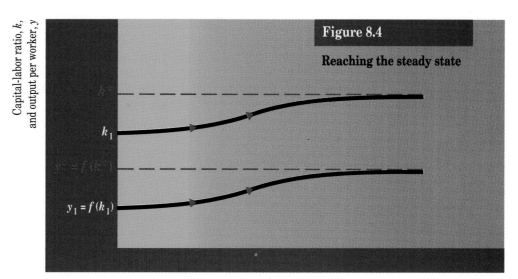

Figure 8.4

Reaching the steady state

The figure shows the time path of the capital-labor ratio k as well as the corresponding level of output per worker $y = f(k)$. Starting from a capital-labor ratio k_1 that is below the steady-state value of k^*, the capital-labor ratio rises steadily over time, eventually reaching (and remaining at) k^*. Similarly, over time, output per worker rises toward its steady-state value $y^* = f(k^*)$.

per worker is determined by the current value of the capital-labor ratio through the production function. That is, in each year t output per worker y_t equals $f(k_t)$. When the capital-labor ratio reaches its steady-state value k^*, output reaches its steady-state value $y^* = f(k^*)$, as well.

We have just considered the case where the initial capital-labor ratio is below k^*. If capital per worker is initially greater than k^*—for example, if k is equal to k_2 in Fig. 8.3—the argument is similar. If the capital-labor ratio exceeds k^*, the amount of saving will be less than the amount of investment that is necessary to keep the capital-labor ratio constant. (In Fig. 8.3 when k equals k_2, the investment-per-worker line is higher than the saving-per-worker curve.) Thus the capital-labor ratio will fall over time from k_2 toward k^*, as indicated by the arrows. Output will also fall until it reaches its steady-state value.

To summarize, we have shown that (under the assumption of no productivity growth) the economy must eventually reach a steady state. In this steady state the capital-labor ratio, output per worker, and consumption per worker remain constant over time. (However, *total* capital, output, and consumption grow at rate n, the rate of growth of the labor force.) This might be taken as a pretty gloomy conclusion, since it implies that living standards must eventually stop improving. However, this conclusion can be avoided if, in fact, productivity continually increases, as we will see.

The Fundamental Determinants of Long-Run Living Standards

What determines how well-off the average person in a given economy will be in the long run? If we measure long-run well-being by the steady-state level of consumption per worker, we can use the Solow model to answer this question. We discuss three factors that affect long-run living standards: the saving rate, the rate of population growth, and productivity growth. (See Table 8.4 for a summary.)

The Saving Rate   According to the Solow model, a higher saving rate implies higher living standards in the long run. This result is illustrated in Fig. 8.5. Suppose that initially the economy's saving rate is s_1, so that saving per worker is $s_1 f(k)$. The saving curve when the saving rate is s_1 is marked "Initial saving per worker" in Fig. 8.5. The initial steady-state capital-labor ratio k_1^* is determined in the figure as the capital-labor ratio at which the initial saving curve and the investment line cross (point A).

Suppose now that (because consumers become more patient, for example) the country's saving rate rises from its initial value of s_1 to a higher value of s_2. The increased saving rate raises saving at every level of the capital-labor ratio. Graphically, the saving curve shifts upward in Fig. 8.5, from $s_1 f(k)$ to $s_2 f(k)$. The new steady-state capital-labor ratio k_2^* corresponds to the intersection of the new saving curve and the investment line (point B in Fig. 8.5). Since k_2^* is larger than k_1^*, we see that the higher saving rate has increased the steady-state capital-labor ratio.

Table 8.4 Summary

The Fundamental Determinants of Long-Run Living Standards

An Increase in	Causes Long-Run Output, Consumption, and Capital per Worker to	Reason
The average saving rate s	Rise	Higher saving allows for more investment and a larger capital stock
The rate of population growth n	Fall	With higher population growth more output must be used to equip new workers with capital, leaving less output available to increase consumption or capital per worker
Productivity	Rise	Higher productivity directly increases output; by raising incomes, it also raises saving and the capital stock

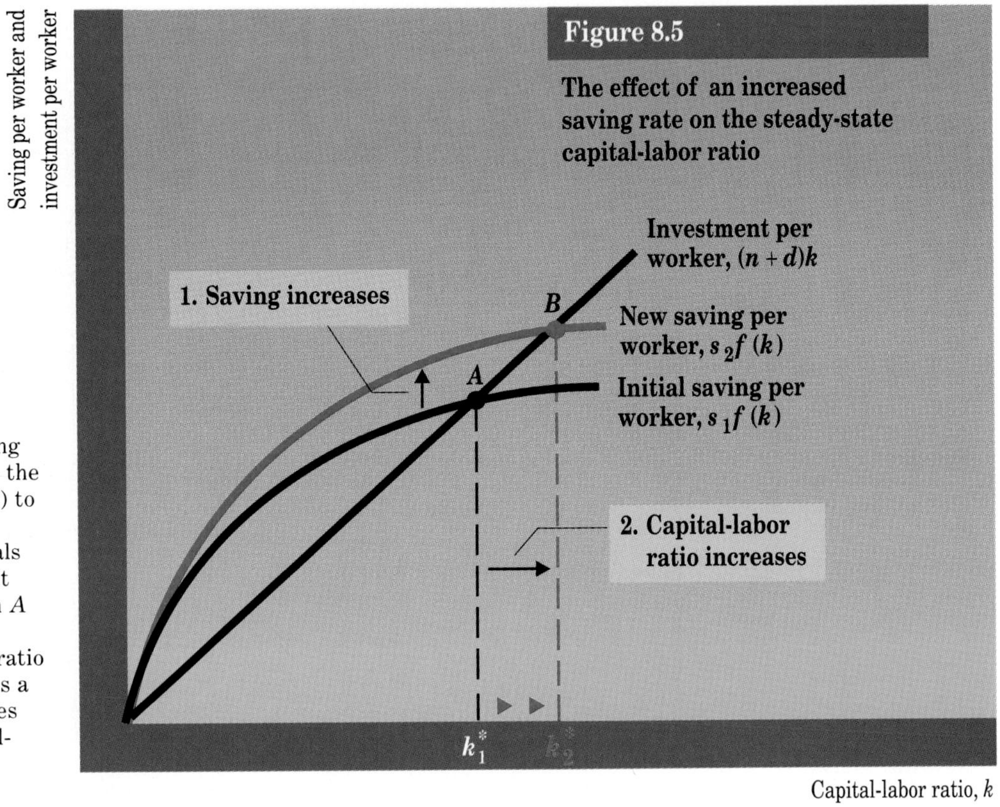

Figure 8.5

The effect of an increased saving rate on the steady-state capital-labor ratio

An increase in the saving rate from s_1 to s_2 raises the saving curve from $s_1f(k)$ to $s_2f(k)$. The point where saving per worker equals steady-state investment per worker moves from A to B, and the corresponding capital-labor ratio rises from k_1^* to k_2^*. Thus a higher saving rate raises the steady-state capital-labor ratio.

Gradually, over time, this economy will move to the higher steady-state capital-labor ratio, as indicated by the arrows on the horizontal axis of Fig. 8.5. In the new steady state output per worker and consumption per worker will be higher than in the original steady state.

Since the increased saving rate has led to higher output, consumption, and capital per worker in the long run, it may seem that the goal of policy should be to make the country's saving rate as high as possible. This conclusion is not necessarily correct. Although a higher saving rate raises consumption per worker in the long run, the initial effect of an increase in the saving rate is to cause consumption to fall. This fall occurs because at the initial level of output an increase in the amount that is saved and invested leaves less available for current consumption. Thus higher consumption in the future has a cost in terms of lost consumption in the present. The society's choice of a saving rate should take into account this trade-off between current and future consumption: Beyond a certain point the cost of reduced consumption today will outweigh the long-run benefits of a higher saving rate.

Population Growth In many developing countries a high rate of population growth is considered to be a major problem, and reducing the rate of population increase is a primary goal of policy. What is the relationship between population growth and a country's level of development, as measured by output, consumption, and capital per worker?

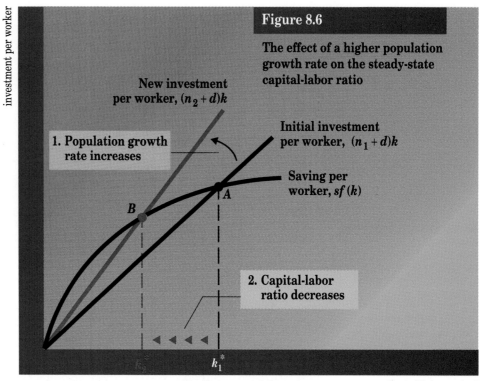

Figure 8.6

The effect of a higher population growth rate on the steady-state capital-labor ratio

New investment per worker, $(n_2 + d)k$

Initial investment per worker, $(n_1 + d)k$

1. Population growth rate increases

Saving per worker, $sf(k)$

B

A

2. Capital-labor ratio decreases

k_2^* k_1^*

Capital-labor ratio, k

An increase in the population growth rate from n_1 to n_2 increases the amount of required steady-state investment per worker from $(n_1 + d)k$ to $(n_2 + d)k$. The investment line pivots up and to the left as its slope rises from $(n_1 + d)$ to $(n_2 + d)$. The point where saving per worker equals steady-state investment per worker shifts from point A to point B, and the corresponding capital-labor ratio falls from k_1^* to k_2^*. A higher population growth rate therefore causes the steady-state capital-labor ratio to fall.

The Solow model's answer to this question is shown in Fig. 8.6. The diagram shows an initial steady-state capital-labor ratio k_1^*, which corresponds to the intersection of the investment line and the saving curve at point A. Now suppose that the rate of population growth, which is the same as the growth rate of the labor force, rises from an initial value of n_1 to a higher value n_2. What happens?

An increase in the population growth rate means that workers are entering the labor force more rapidly than before. These new workers must be equipped with capital. Thus to maintain a given steady-state capital-labor ratio, the amount of investment per current member of the work force must rise. Algebraically, the rise in n increases required investment per worker from $(n_1 + d)k$ to $(n_2 + d)k$. In Fig. 8.6 this increase in the population growth rate causes the investment line to pivot up and to the left, as its slope rises from $(n_1 + d)$ to $(n_2 + d)$.

After the pivot of the investment line, the new steady state is at point B in Fig. 8.6. The new steady-state capital-labor ratio is k_2^*, which is lower than the original capital-labor ratio k_1^*. Because the new steady-state capital-labor ratio is lower, the new steady-state values of output per worker and consumption per worker will be lower as well.

Thus the Solow model implies that increased population growth will lower living standards. The basic problem is that when the work force is growing very rapidly, a large part of current output must be devoted just to providing capital for the new workers to use. This result suggests that policies to control population growth will indeed improve living standards.

There are some counterarguments to the conclusion that policy should aim to reduce population growth. First, while a reduction in the rate of population growth n raises consumption per worker, it also reduces the growth rate of *total* output and consumption, which grow at rate n in the steady state. Having fewer people means that there is more for each person but also that there is less total productive capacity. For some purposes (military, political) a country may care about its total output as well as output per person. Thus, for example, some countries of Western Europe have been concerned by projections that their populations will actually shrink in the next century, possibly reducing their ability to defend themselves or influence world events.

Second, the Solow model assumes that the proportion of the total population that is of working age is fixed. When the population growth rate changes dramatically, this assumption may well be false. For example, declining birth rates in the United States imply that the ratio of working-age people to retirees will become unusually low in the early twenty-first century, a development that may cause problems for Social Security funding and in other areas such as health care.

Productivity Growth   A major result of the basic Solow model is that, ultimately, the economy reaches a steady state in which output per capita is constant. But in the introduction to this chapter we described how Japanese output per person grew by a factor of more than seventeen over the past century. How can the Solow model account for the sustained growth experienced by Japan? The key is a factor we have not yet incorporated into the analysis: productivity growth.

The effects of a productivity improvement—due, say, to an invention—are shown in Fig. 8.7 and Fig. 8.8. An improvement in productivity corresponds to an

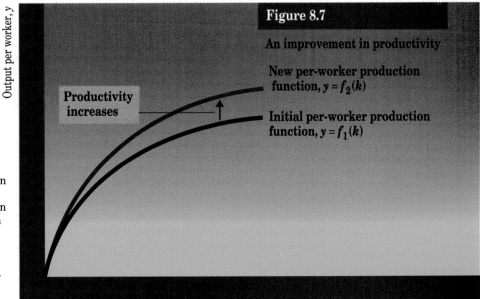

An improvement in productivity is shown as an upward shift of the per-worker production function from the initial production function $y = f_1(k)$ to the new production function $y = f_2(k)$. After the productivity improvement more output per worker y can be produced at any given capital-labor ratio k.

Figure 8.7

An improvement in productivity

New per-worker production function, $y = f_2(k)$

Initial per-worker production function, $y = f_1(k)$

Productivity increases

Output per worker, y

Capital-labor ratio, k

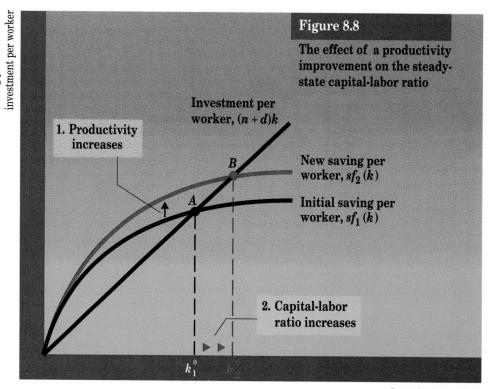

Saving per worker and investment per worker

Figure 8.8

The effect of a productivity improvement on the steady-state capital-labor ratio

1. Productivity increases

Investment per worker, $(n + d)k$

New saving per worker, $sf_2(k)$

Initial saving per worker, $sf_1(k)$

2. Capital-labor ratio increases

k_1^* k_2^*

Capital-labor ratio, k

A productivity improvement shifts the production function from $f_1(k)$ up to $f_2(k)$, raising output per worker at any given capital-labor ratio. Because saving is proportional to output, saving per worker also rises, from $sf_1(k)$ to $sf_2(k)$. The point where saving per worker equals steady-state investment per worker shifts from point A to point B, and the corresponding steady-state capital-labor ratio rises from k_1^* to k_2^*. Thus a productivity improvement raises the steady-state capital-labor ratio.

upward shift in the per-worker production function, since at any given capital-labor ratio each worker can produce more output. Figure 8.7 shows a shift from the original production function $y = f_1(k)$ to a "new, improved" production function $y = f_2(k)$. The productivity improvement corresponds to a beneficial supply shock, as in Fig. 3.4.

Figure 8.8 shows the effects of this productivity improvement in the Solow model. As before, the initial steady state is determined by the intersection of the saving curve and the investment line at point A; the corresponding steady-state capital-labor ratio is k_1^*. The productivity improvement raises output per worker at any given level of the capital-labor ratio. Since saving per worker is a fixed fraction s of output per worker, saving per worker also rises at any given capital-labor ratio. Graphically, the saving curve shifts upward from $sf_1(k)$ to $sf_2(k)$, now intersecting the investment line at point B. The new steady-state capital-labor ratio is k_2^*, which is higher than the original capital-labor ratio k_1^*.

Overall, a productivity improvement raises steady-state output and consumption per worker in two ways. First, it directly increases the amount that can be produced at any given capital-labor ratio. Second, as can be seen in Fig. 8.8, by raising the supply of saving, a productivity improvement also causes the long-run capital-labor ratio to rise. Thus a productivity improvement has a doubly beneficial impact on the standard of living.

Like a one-time increase in the saving rate or decrease in the population growth rate, a one-time productivity improvement only shifts the economy from one steady state to a higher one. Once the economy reaches the new steady state, consumption per head is once again constant. Is there some way to keep consumption per head growing indefinitely?

In practice, there are limits to how high the saving rate can rise (it certainly cannot exceed 100%!) or to how low the population growth rate can fall. Thus higher saving rates or slower population growth are unlikely to be sources of *continuing* betterment of living standards. However, since the Industrial Revolution, if not before, people have shown remarkable ingenuity in finding ways of becoming more and more productive. In the very long run, according to the Solow model, it is only these continuing increases in productivity that hold open the possibility of perpetually improving living standards. Thus we are led to the conclusion that, ultimately, *the rate of productivity improvement is the dominant factor determining how quickly living standards rise*.

Application

Do Economies Converge?

A wide gulf separates average living standards in the richest and the poorest nations of the world. Will this difference persist forever? Will, indeed, the "rich get richer and the poor get poorer"? Or will there ultimately be a **convergence,** or coming together, of national living standards? These are very important and very difficult questions.

The Solow model predicts that eventually living standards in different countries will converge. To see why, imagine that there are two countries that are fundamentally very similar, except that one has a high capital-labor ratio and thus a high standard of living, and the other has a low capital-labor ratio and a low standard of living. If the two countries have the same population growth rate and saving rate, and if they have access to the same production methods (in other words, they have the same production function), the Solow model predicts that they will reach the same steady state. As the two countries move toward the same steady state, ultimately the poorer country will catch up and achieve the same capital-labor ratio and standard of living as the richer country.

The argument just given assumes that the rich and the poor economies are both closed economies. According to the Solow model, convergence should occur even more quickly if economies are open and there is international borrowing and lending. Since the poor country has less capital per worker and thus a higher marginal product of capital than the rich country, savers in both countries will be able to earn a higher return by investing in the poor country. As a result, the capital stock in the poor country should grow rapidly. Even if the rate of saving in the poor country is low, investments by foreigners should cause the capital stock in the poor country to grow more quickly than in the rich country, ultimately causing output per worker to converge. However, although output per worker will converge in this case, consumption per worker will be lower in the poor country, since part of output must be used to repay the foreign investors.

What is the evidence on convergence? In a recent article William Baumol[19] of Princeton University and New York University found that over the past century there was substantial convergence in output per hour of work[20] among a group of sixteen major free-market industrial economies. The countries, from worst to best growth performers, were Australia, the United Kingdom, Switzerland, Belgium, the Netherlands, Canada, the United States, Denmark, Italy, Austria, Germany, Norway, France, Finland, Sweden, and Japan. Within this group those countries with high levels of output per hour in 1870 showed slower growth over the following century, and the countries with low output per hour in 1870 went on to experience the most rapid growth.

However, J. Bradford DeLong[21] of Harvard University pointed out that the countries Baumol studied were the richest countries as of 1980. In choosing this set of countries, DeLong argued, Baumol created a bias in favor of finding convergence, because countries that failed to converge to high levels of output per hour would not be included among the sample of currently rich countries. DeLong argued that as of 1870, Argentina, Chile, the area that until recently was East Germany, Ireland, New Zealand, Portugal, and Spain also looked like countries poised for rapid growth, but these countries failed to attain the living standards of the sixteen countries examined by Baumol. Including these additional seven countries and excluding Japan (which was a very poor country in 1870), DeLong found no evidence of convergence.

The results discussed so far are for relatively rich, industrialized countries. What about broader groups of countries? In the same research already mentioned, for a group of seventy-two countries, Baumol found no overall pattern of convergence over the period 1950–1980. Baumol then tried categorizing the seventy-two countries into four groups: (1) major free-market industrialized economies, including the sixteen countries discussed previously; (2) centrally planned economies; (3) middle-income market economies (such as Venezuela and Greece); and (4) poor economies (such as Ethiopia and Indonesia). Within groups (1), (2), and (3) Baumol found some evidence for convergence, although the criticism raised by DeLong may apply here also. However, within the group of poor countries, group (4), Baumol found no tendency toward convergence. In other words, there seems to be no tendency for the very poorest countries either to catch up with richer countries or even to converge among themselves.

Overall, then, the evidence for convergence seems rather weak. Where does the Solow model go wrong? Economists have pointed out a number of factors affecting the rate of economic growth, such as the availability of natural resources and political stability, which are left out of the basic Solow model. Possibly, taking account of such factors could help explain the failure of countries to converge.

In recent years there has been particular interest among growth researchers in the role of another factor excluded from the Solow model: **human capital,** which

---

[19]"Productivity Growth, Convergence, and Welfare: What the Long-Run Data Show," *American Economic Review*, December 1986, pp. 1072–1085. Baumol used data from the Maddison book cited in footnote 1.

[20]Baumol considered output per hour instead of output per worker, as in the Solow model. The results pertaining to convergence should be similar for the two measures.

[21]"Productivity Growth, Convergence and Welfare: Comment," *American Economic Review*, December 1988, pp. 1138–1154.

is the economist's term for the knowledge, skills, and training of individuals. Some economists have argued that the process of economic growth itself causes increases in human capital. For example, as the economy becomes richer, more people are able to go to college and more workers gain experience with modern production methods. This extra knowledge and skill in turn allows rich countries to maintain their lead over poor countries, who are less able to achieve improvements in productivity because they lack human capital.[22] Thus the greater development of human capital in rich countries, which in turn leads to higher rates of productivity growth in rich countries, may be the reason that poor countries don't catch up. A bit of evidence supporting the human capital explanation for growth is the rapid recovery of Germany and Japan from the destruction of World War II: Although Germany and Japan lost much of their capital stocks during the war, they retained highly educated and skilled populations who helped make these countries economic leaders again in little more than a generation.

8.3 GOVERNMENT POLICIES TO RAISE LONG-RUN LIVING STANDARDS

Increased growth and a higher average standard of living in the long run are often cited by political leaders as major objectives. Building on our analysis of the last section, we now take a closer look at policies that may be useful in raising a country's long-run standard of living. We consider policies to raise the saving rate and the rate of productivity growth and also discuss the role of political and economic institutions.

Policies to Affect the Saving Rate

The Solow model suggests that the rate of national saving is an important determinant of long-run living standards.[23] As we have already discussed, however, this conclusion does not necessarily mean that policymakers should try to force the saving rate upward, since more saving means less consumption in the short run. Indeed, if the "invisible hand" of free markets is working well, the saving rate freely chosen by individuals should be the one that optimally trades off current and future consumption.

Despite the argument that saving decisions are best left to private individuals and the free market, some people claim that Americans save too little and that U.S. policy should aim to raise the saving rate. One possible justification for this claim is that existing tax laws discriminate against saving by taxing away part of the returns to saving; a "pro-saving" policy is thus necessary (one could argue) to offset this bias. Some people hold the stronger view that Americans are just too shortsighted in their saving decisions and must be encouraged to save more.

What policies can be used to increase saving? If saving were highly responsive to the real interest rate, then tax breaks that increase the real return that savers receive (such as Individual Retirement Accounts; see the "Policy Debate" box in Chapter 6) would be effective. But as we have discussed, although saving does

---

[22]Evidence that lack of convergence arises for human capital reasons is presented in Robert Barro, "Economic Growth in a Cross Section of Countries," National Bureau of Economic Research working paper no. 3120, September 1989.

[23]Remember that although an increase in the saving rate raises the long-run standard of living, it cannot permanently raise the economic growth rate.

appear to increase when the expected real return available to savers rises, most studies do not find this response to be very large.

An alternative and perhaps more direct way to affect the national saving rate is by changing the total levels of government purchases or tax collections. For example, many economists have called on the U.S. government to reduce its government budget deficit as a way of stimulating national saving. Given output Y, if the deficit is reduced by a cut in government purchases G, national saving $Y - C - G$ will rise as long as the decline in government purchases is not offset by an increase in consumption C. Similarly, if the deficit is reduced through tax increases, national saving $Y - C - G$ will rise if in response to the tax increases consumers cut their spending C. Unfortunately, the amount by which a given reduction in the government deficit will increase national saving remains the subject of theoretical and empirical disputes.[24]

Policies to Raise the Rate of Productivity Growth

Of the factors affecting long-run living standards, the rate of productivity growth may well be the most important in that only ongoing productivity growth can lead to continuing improvement in output and consumption per worker. There are several ways government policy can attempt to increase productivity.

First, some research has suggested a significant link between productivity and the quality of a nation's infrastructure—its highways, bridges, dams, airports, and other publicly owned capital.[25] The construction of the interstate highway system in the United States, for example, significantly reduced the cost of transporting goods and stimulated tourism and other industries. In the past two decades U.S. government investment in infrastructure has taken place at a low rate, relative both to previous American experience and to rates of infrastructure investment in other developed countries. As a result of this low rate of infrastructure investment, many roads and bridges are in poor repair, and journalists and politicians speak of an "infrastructure crisis." Improvement of the nation's infrastructure might help achieve higher productivity.

Second, as we have mentioned, recent research has also found an important connection between productivity growth and human capital. The government affects human capital development through educational policies, programs that support worker training or relocation, social programs that improve the health of workers or potential workers, and in other ways. Although specific programs or initiatives should be examined carefully to see whether benefits exceed costs, to the extent that increased human capital leads to societywide productivity improvements, there may be a case for active government policies to support the creation of human capital.

One very important form of human capital, which we have not mentioned until now, is entrepreneurial skill. There is evidence that people with the ability to build a successful new business or to bring a new product to market play a key role in the process of economic growth. Productivity growth may increase if the government attempts to remove unnecessary barriers to entrepreneurial activity (such as

---

[24]Chapters 6 and 7 discussed the concept of Ricardian equivalence, which implies that lump-sum tax increases with no change in government purchases will have *no* effect on national saving. Chapters 6 and 16 also discuss objections to the Ricardian equivalence idea.

[25]See, for example, David A. Aschauer, "Rx for Productivity: Build Infrastructure," *Chicago Fed Letter*, Federal Reserve Bank of Chicago, September 1988.

excessive red tape) and to ensure that people with entrepreneurial skills have incentives to use those skills productively.[26]

The third general way government can stimulate productivity growth is by affecting rates of scientific and technical progress. The U.S. government directly supports much basic scientific research, through the National Science Foundation, for example. Most economists agree with this type of policy on the grounds that, like human capital development, scientific progress has benefits that are widespread throughout the economy. Basic scientific research may thus be a good investment from the society's point of view, even if no individual firm finds it profitable to fund such research. Some economists would go further and say that even more applied, commercially oriented research deserves government aid.

Perhaps the most aggressive approach that has been proposed for encouraging technological development is industrial policy. Generally, **industrial policy** is a growth strategy in which the government—using taxes, subsidies, or regulation—attempts to influence the nation's pattern of industrial development. More specifically, some advocates of industrial policy have argued that the government ought to subsidize and promote "high-tech" industries, in order to try to achieve or maintain national leadership in technologically dynamic areas. Industrial policy is discussed further in "The Policy Debate" box (p. 310).

The Institutional Framework: Market Versus Plan

Up to this point in this section we have discussed specific individual policies that the government can use to try to affect the rate of economic growth. Underlying this discussion, however, is a set of broader debates about what political and economic institutions provide the best framework for achieving a high rate of growth. For example, as discussed in "The Political Environment" box (p. 312), a longstanding question is whether democratic political institutions are consistent with rapid growth or whether, instead, citizens of poor countries must make a cruel choice between democratization and improved living standards.

Within the economic sphere the sharpest and most historically important debate of the twentieth century focused on whether market-based or centrally planned economic systems were most effective at generating growth. Under **central planning,** practiced until recently by most Communist countries, all aspects of economic activity—including production, pricing, distribution, and investment decisions—are determined by a detailed government plan. Under the plan each state-owned factory and farm is told at the beginning of the year (perhaps after some negotiation with the government) what and how much it is to produce. The responsibility for ensuring that firms' production plans are coordinated—so that, for example, each truck factory receives the quantities of tires and engine parts necessary to fulfill its production quotas—is left to the government planners.

There were two principal reasons that the creators of central planning thought that this approach would raise the rate of growth. First, they believed that a centrally planned economy could avoid the problem of high unemployment that periodically afflicts market economies simply by ensuring that all available labor was utilized under the plan. With zero or very low unemployment, they reasoned, output should be higher, more could be invested, and growth should be faster. Second,

---

[26]For a readable discussion of the importance of entrepreneurial activity and how it is affected by government policy and the social environment, see William J. Baumol, "Entrepreneurship: Productive, Unproductive, and Destructive," *Journal of Political Economy*, October 1990 (part 1), pp. 893–921.

THE POLICY
DEBATE

Should the United States Have a "High-Tech" Industrial Policy?

Background

The generally poor growth performance of the United States since the early 1970s has raised concerns that the United States is losing its ability to compete in the world economy. Some economists have argued that the United States is "de-industrializing," losing its manufacturing base and becoming primarily a low-productivity service economy. Of particular concern is the fading of U.S. supremacy in high-technology industries, in which Japan and other nations have achieved a growing market share. Advocates of the industrial policy approach call for a strategy of government targeting of high technology and other key industries. Targeted industries would be supported by subsidies and tax breaks until they achieve the ability to compete successfully in world markets.

Pro

"As in the past, economic growth in the future will be fueled by technological advance. But unlike advances in the past, technological advances in the future will not come from individual inventors working in their garages. Development of new generations of supercomputers, for example, requires huge capital investments and long lead times. It is unlikely that the private sector will be willing to undertake such large, complex, and risky projects without government assistance. Furthermore, we have to recognize that Japan and other countries are subsidizing *their* high-tech firms. If we in America don't do the same, we will be left behind."

Con

"Technological advance is certainly critical to growth. But there is no reason to believe that the government can do a better job of picking the most promising technologies and overseeing their development than the private sector can. Industrial policy would become just another wasteful government subsidy program."

Analysis

Economic theory and practice suggest that under normal circumstances the free market can do a good job of allocating resources without government assistance. Thus advocates of industrial policy must explain why the free market fails in the case of high technology. Two possible sources of market failure that have been suggested are *borrowing constraints* and *spillovers*.

Borrowing constraints are limits imposed by lenders on the amounts that individuals or small firms can borrow.* The possibility of borrowing constraints becomes important when, as suggested by PRO, high-technology projects involve large capital expenditures up front. Then it may be difficult for private companies, especially start-up firms, to obtain enough financing.

Spillovers occur when a given company's innovation—say the development of an improved memory chip—stimulates a rash of related innovations and technical improvements in other companies and indus-

---

*The behavior of a consumer who faces borrowing constraints was analyzed in Chapter 5.

tries. When spillovers are important, innovative companies enjoy only a portion of the total social benefit of their invention, while bearing the full development cost. Without a government subsidy, then, companies may not have a sufficiently strong incentive to innovate when their inventions have spillovers.

A third argument for industrial policy has less to do with market failure and more with nationalism. In some industries the efficient scale of operation is so large that there is room in the world market for only a few firms. From the point of view of the world as a whole, the most desirable outcome is that the few firms that do enter the market be the most efficient, lowest-cost producers. However, from the point of view of a given country, say the United States, it may be desirable that at least some of the firms in the market be American, so that the profits from the industry will accrue to the United States rather than other countries. Furthermore, having American firms in the market may enhance American prestige and possibly yield military advantages. These perceived benefits might lead the United States to subsidize its firms in that industry, helping them to compete with the firms of other

nations in the race to capture the world market. Of course, other nations may well retaliate by introducing or increasing subsidies to their own firms.

These theoretical arguments for government intervention all assume that the government is very skilled at picking "winning" technologies and that its decisions about which industries to subsidize would be free of purely political considerations. As CON suggests, both assumptions are open to question. A danger of industrial policy is that the favored industries would be the ones with the most powerful congressional representatives, rather than the ones with the most technological promise.

Evidence

The available evidence on the arguments for industrial policy has been surveyed by Gene Grossman* of Princeton University. Grossman concludes that, in general, industrial policy is not desirable because in choosing industries to target, governments have frequently "backed the wrong horse"; the costly attempt of European governments to develop the supersonic transport (SST) and

other new types of commercial airplanes is a case in point. Grossman also points out that there are alternative policies—such as a tax break for all research and development spending—that promote technology without requiring the government to target specific industries.

However, Grossman also concedes that there may be one situation in which targeted government intervention is desirable. This situation arises in the early development stages of technologically innovative products, such as computers and CAT scanners. Empirically, the potential for beneficial spillovers in these cases appears so large that government intervention may be justified, even though inevitably many projects the government chooses to support will not ultimately prove worthwhile.

*"Promoting New Industrial Activities: A Survey of Recent Arguments and Evidence," *OECD Economic Studies*, Spring 1990, pp. 87–125.

The Political Environment

★ ★

Economic Growth and Democracy

Economic growth is an important social goal, but it is certainly not the only one. Most people would also place a high value on political freedom and a democratic political process. An important question is, "Are these two goals conflicting or mutually supporting?" If the citizens of poor countries succeed in achieving democracy, as many did during the 1980s, can they expect as a result to enjoy faster economic growth as well? Or does increased political freedom involve economic sacrifice?

There are several reasons to believe that democracy may promote growth. Relative to dictatorships, democratic governments that command popular support might be expected to be more stable, to be less likely to start wars, and to have better relations with the advanced industrial nations, most of which are democracies. Constitutional protections of both human and property rights should increase the willingness of both foreigners and residents to invest in the country, and freedoms of speech and expression are probably essential for the full development of a nation's educational and scientific potential. On the other hand, the ability of a democratic government to undertake unpopular but necessary economic reforms or make other tough choices may be hampered by the pressures of interest groups or the fluctuations of public opinion. Similarly, a dictatorial government may be better able than a democratic one to enforce a high national saving rate and keep government spending under control.

What relationship between democracy and economic growth do we observe empirically? A simple fact is that, for the most part, the richest countries of the world are democratic, and the very poorest nations are nondemocratic. (There are exceptions: India is poor but is more democratic than wealthy Saudi Arabia or Singapore.) Not too much should be read into this fact, however, particularly since many wealthy nations that are currently democratic initially achieved economic leadership under the rule of kings, princes, or emperors.

A more relevant empirical test is to compare the current economic growth rates (rather than the current levels of output) of democratic and nondemocratic countries. Here the findings of recent research have been generally good news for democracy. In a study of 115 market economies over the period 1960–1980, Gerald Scully* of the University of Texas at Dallas found that "politically open" societies grew at an average of 2.7% per year, compared with only 0.9% per year for repressive societies. Most other researchers have found a somewhat smaller advantage for democracy or even a slight edge for nondemocratic economies. Importantly, though, there seems to be no support for the view that adopting democratic institutions imposes high costs in terms of lost economic growth.

*"The Institutional Framework and Economic Development," *Journal of Political Economy,* June 1988, pp. 652–662.

they believed that central planning was the most effective way to force poor countries away from traditional, small-scale modes of production toward large-scale heavy industry, a change that was perceived as the key to economic modernization. These arguments were sufficiently persuasive that even some non-Communist nations, primarily developing countries such as India, attempted to integrate elements of central planning into their economic systems.

The arguments for central planning were not completely wrong: Measured unemployment, at least, was generally lower in centrally planned economies than in market economies.[27] And countries such as the Soviet Union did develop substantial heavy industry. Overall, however, as a means of promoting economic growth and modernization, central planning must be judged a failure: In almost every case centrally planned economies have performed significantly worse than comparable market economies. For example, when the two Germanys united in 1990, output per person in centrally planned East Germany was only about one half that in West Germany. Similarly, centrally planned North Korea is far poorer than market-oriented South Korea. And the birthplace of central planning, the Soviet Union, has experienced very poor economic performance in recent years.

Why has central planning failed? Two major weaknesses of centrally planned economies, relative to market economies, are a *lack of incentives* for productive activity and *poor coordination* of different parts of the economy.

In a market economy the prospect of earning higher wages or more profits provides the incentive to work harder or more efficiently. In a centrally planned economy, in contrast, the manager of a plant may not be able to reward a good worker or fire a bad one, since wages and employment are determined by the plan. As a result, workers have little incentive to try hard and labor productivity is low. Neither does the manager have an incentive to look for ways to cut costs or to improve the quality of the product, since these activities will not increase her profits or salary, as they would in a market economy.

Besides providing good incentives, a market system also solves the problem of coordinating the activities of millions of producers and consumers. This coordination is achieved through the adjustment of prices. For example, in a free market when a good is in short supply, its price will rise. The higher price is a signal to consumers to consume less of the good and a signal to producers to produce more of it, thus relieving the shortage. In a planned economy prices are fixed by law and are not allowed to respond to supply-and-demand conditions; instead, the government tries to achieve coordination directly through the plan. But in a large economy the problem of coordination is just too complex to be solved by a central plan. Indeed, it may be all the government can do to gather basic information about the economy. There are many stories from centrally planned economies of, for example, tons of unwanted coal piling up in city A at the same time that lack of fuel is forcing factory shutdowns in city B. Such problems are much less frequent in market economies.

Lack of incentives and poor coordination are the source of most of the problems that plague centrally planned economies, including poor quality of goods,

---

[27]However, critics argue that planned economies suffer high rates of "disguised" unemployment—people who officially have jobs but are not actually working. For a discussion of unemployment in the Soviet Union, see Box 10.2.

BOX 8.2:   FROM PLAN TO MARKET IN EASTERN EUROPE

The year 1989 was one of stunning political changes in Europe. The Soviet Union, preoccupied with its own internal political and economic troubles, relaxed its grip on Eastern Europe. As a result, nations such as Poland, Czechoslovakia, and East Germany—disillusioned with what they perceived to be the failed promise of communism—seized the opportunity to try to adopt Western-style political and economic institutions.

Besides democratization, the most important aspect of Eastern Europe's break from communism was its stated intention to abandon central planning in favor of a free-market system, a change contemplated even by the Soviet Union itself. The motivation for switching to markets was clear enough: Any Pole or East German with access to a television set could see that living standards in the market economies of Western Europe were much higher than his own. Yet as desirable as a market system appeared, the problem of transition—how to get from a planned system to a market system—was a daunting one.

The roadblocks on the path to a free market are many. A major complication is the absence in the formerly Communist countries of important market institutions, such as financial markets, commercial banks, and laws governing matters such as bankruptcy and commercial contracts. Also lacking is experience with the market system: Managers are not accustomed to producing for profit, for example, instead of trying to meet a quota, and few people have entrepreneurial experience. Difficult technical questions are also raised by the transition process, including: What is the best way to "privatize" (that is, transfer to private owners) state-owned factories,

farms, and apartment buildings? And competition being essential for a well-functioning market system, how can large state-owned monopolies be transformed into smaller, competitive firms?

No matter how well the transition from plan to market is handled, economists generally agree that in the short run the switch will make many people worse off. For example, although improved economic performance in the long run requires that the most inefficient factories be shut down, in the near term this shutdown may cause unemployment to rise significantly. Similarly, although a market system must have prices that are freely determined by supply and demand, the removal of price controls and government subsidies for basic items such as food may cause hardships. A debate rages over the type of transition that will minimize the associated pain: Poland, for example, has opted for a "big bang" strategy in which the switch to the market is made as rapidly as possible; Czechoslovakia has so far used a "go slow" strategy in an attempt to reduce disruption of the economy.

East Germany may be the luckiest of the Eastern European countries. In its reunification with West Germany it has obtained a greater access to Western expertise, capital, and markets than is available to the other Eastern European nations.*

*For discussions of Eastern European and Soviet reforms, see David Lipton and Jeffrey Sachs, "Creating a Market Economy in Eastern Europe: The Case of Poland," and William D. Nordhaus, "Soviet Economic Reform: The Longest Road," both in *Brookings Papers on Economic Activity*, 1990:1, 75–133 and 287–308, respectively.

shortages, a slow rate of technical innovation, and low productivity. Although market-oriented economies are not free of these problems, there is now virtually universal agreement that over the long run the market performs better than the plan. Indeed, since 1989 the great majority of centrally planned economies have begun the process of converting to market systems (see Box 8.2).

8.4   CHAPTER SUMMARY

1. Economic growth is the principal source of improving standards of living over time. Over long periods even small differences in growth rates can have a large effect on nations' standards of living.

2. Growth accounting is a method for breaking down total output growth into the portions due to growth in capital inputs, growth in labor inputs, and growth in productivity. All three factors have contributed to long-run economic growth in the United States. However, the slowdown in U.S. output growth after 1973 reflects primarily a sharp decline in productivity growth. This decline in productivity growth in turn reflects a number of factors including problems in the legal and human environment, slower technical progress, and increased oil prices.

3. The Solow model of economic growth studies the interaction of growth, saving, and capital accumulation over time. The Solow model predicts that in the absence of productivity growth the economy will reach a steady state in which output, consumption, and capital per worker are constant.

4. According to the Solow model, each of the following leads to higher output, consumption, and capital per worker in the long run: an increase in the saving rate, a decline in the population growth rate, and an increase in productivity.

5. The Solow model also implies that living standards of different countries will tend to converge over time. However, the empirical evidence for convergence is weak. Differences in human capital—skills and training—across countries may explain the absence of convergence.

6. Government policies to raise long-run living standards include policies to raise the rate of saving and to increase productivity. More broadly, the evidence suggests that democratic, market-oriented economies provide a good framework for achieving economic growth.

Key Terms

capital-labor ratio, p. 292
central planning, p. 309
convergence, p. 305

growth accounting,
  p. 283
growth accounting
  equation, p. 283

human capital, p. 306
industrial policy, p. 309
steady state, p. 293

Key Equations

$$\frac{\Delta Y}{Y} = \frac{\Delta A}{A} + a_K \frac{\Delta K}{K} + a_N \frac{\Delta N}{N} \qquad (8.2)$$

The *growth accounting equation* says that output growth $\Delta Y/Y$ depends on the growth rate of productivity $\Delta A/A$, the growth rate of capital $\Delta K/K$, and the growth rate of labor $\Delta N/N$. The elasticity of output with respect to capital a_K gives the percentage increase in output that results when capital increases by 1%, and the elasticity of output with respect to labor a_N gives the percentage increase in output that results when labor increases by 1%.

$$y_t = f(k_t) \qquad (8.4)$$

For a given year t the *per-worker production function* relates output per worker y_t to capital per worker (also called the capital-labor ratio) k_t.

$$c = f(k) - (n + d)k \qquad (8.7)$$

Steady-state consumption per worker c equals steady-state output per worker $f(k)$ minus steady-state investment per worker, $(n + d)k$. Steady-state output per worker is determined by the per-worker production $f(k)$, where k is the steady-state capital-labor ratio. Steady-state investment per worker consists of two parts: the part used to equip new workers with the per-worker capital stock nk, and the part used to replace worn-out or depreciating capital dk.

$$sf(k) = (n + d)k \qquad (8.10)$$

The steady state is determined by the condition that saving per worker $sf(k)$ equals steady-state investment per worker $(n + d)k$. Saving per worker equals the average saving rate s times output $f(k)$.

Review Questions

1. According to the growth accounting approach, what are the three sources of economic growth? From what basic economic relationship is the growth accounting approach derived?

2. Of the three sources of growth identified by growth accounting, which one is primarily responsible for the slowdown in U.S. economic growth after 1973? What explanations have been given for the decline in this source of growth?

3. According to the Solow model of economic growth, if there is no productivity growth, what will happen to output per worker, consumption per worker, and capital per worker in the long run?

4. True or false? The higher the steady-state capital-labor ratio is, the more consumption each worker can enjoy in the long run. Explain your answer.

5. What effect should each of the following have on long-run living standards, according to the Solow model?
   a. An increase in the saving rate.
   b. An increase in the population growth rate.
   c. A one-time improvement in productivity.

6. What is *convergence?* What prediction does the Solow model make about convergence? What does the evidence say?

7. What are the major types of policies available to a government that wants to promote economic growth? For each type of policy you give, discuss how the policy is supposed to work, and list any costs or disadvantages that the policy has.

8. Why have centrally planned economies experienced relatively poor economic growth?

Numerical Problems

1. Two economies, Hare and Tortoise, each start out with a real GNP per person of $5000 in 1950. Real GNP per person grows 3% a year in Hare, 1% a year in Tortoise. In the year 2000, what will be real GNP per person in each economy? Make a guess first; then, use a calculator to find the answer.

2. Over the past twenty years an economy's total output has grown from 1000 to 1300. The capital stock has risen from 2500 to 3250. The labor force has increased from 500 to 575. All measurements are in real terms. Find the contributions to economic growth of growth in capital, labor, and productivity
   a. assuming $a_K = 0.3$ and $a_N = 0.7$.
   b. assuming $a_K = 0.5$ and $a_N = 0.5$.

3. For a particular economy, capital input K and labor input N in four different years were as follows:

Year	K	N
1	200	1000
2	250	1000
3	250	1250
4	300	1200

The production function in this economy is

where Y is total output.
   a. Find total output, the capital-labor ratio, and output per worker in each year. Compare year 1 with year 3 and year 2 with year 4. Can this production function be written in per-worker form? If so,

then write out algebraically the per-worker form of the production function.
   b. Repeat part a, assuming now that the production function is $Y = K^{0.3}N^{0.8}$.

4. An economy has the per-worker production function

$$y_t = 3k_t^{0.5},$$

where y_t is output per worker and k_t is the capital-labor ratio. The depreciation rate is 0.1, and the population growth rate is 0.05. The saving function is

$$S_t = 0.3Y_t,$$

where S_t is total national saving and Y_t is total output.
   a. What are the steady-state values of the capital-labor ratio, output per worker, and consumption per worker?
   The rest of the problem shows the effects of changes in the three fundamental determinants of long-run living standards.
   b. Repeat part a for the case in which the saving rate is 0.4 instead of 0.3.
   c. Repeat part a for the case in which the population growth rate rises to 0.06 (the saving rate is back to 0.3).
   d. Repeat part a for the case in which the production function becomes

$$y_t = 4k_t^{0.5},$$

and the saving rate and population growth rate take their original values.

Analytical Problems

1. According to the Solow model, how would each of the following affect consumption per worker in the long run (that is, in the steady state)? Explain.
   a. The destruction of a portion of the nation's capital stock in a war.
   b. A permanent increase in the rate of immigration (which raises the overall population growth rate).
   c. A permanent increase in energy prices.
   d. A temporary rise in the saving rate.
   e. A permanent increase in the fraction of the population in the labor force (the population growth rate is unchanged).

2. An economy is in a steady state with no productivity change. Because of an increase in acid rain, there is a

permanent rise in the rate of capital depreciation. Find the effects on steady-state capital per worker, output per worker, and consumption per worker. Is the long-run growth rate of the total capital stock affected?

3. This problem adds the government to the Solow model. Suppose that there is a government that purchases goods in the amount of g per worker every year; since there are N_t workers in year t, total government purchases in year t are gN_t. The government runs a balanced budget, so that its tax revenue in year t, T_t, equals total government purchases in year t. Total national saving S_t is given by

$$S_t = s(Y_t - T_t),$$

where Y_t is total output and s is the saving rate.

  a. Graphically show the steady state, given the initial level of government purchases per worker.

  b. Suppose that the government permanently increases its purchases per worker. What are the effects on the steady-state levels of capital per worker, output per worker, and consumption per worker? Does your result imply that the optimal level of government purchases is zero?

4. In a Solow-type economy total national saving S_t is given by

$$S_t = sY_t - hK_t.$$

The extra term, $-hK_t$, captures the idea that when wealth (as measured by the capital stock) is higher, saving is lower. (Wealthier people have less need to save for the future.)

  For this case, find the steady-state values of per-worker capital, output, and consumption. What is the effect on the steady state of an increase in h?

5. Two countries are identical in every way except that one country has a much higher capital-labor ratio than the other. According to the Solow model, which country's total output will grow more quickly? Does your answer depend on whether one country or the other is in a steady state? In general terms, how will your answer be affected if the two countries are allowed to trade with each other?

6. Suppose that total capital and labor both increase by the same percentage amount, so that the amount of capital per worker k is unchanged. In order for us to be able to write the production function in per-worker terms, $y = f(k)$, this increase in capital and labor must not change the amount of output produced per worker y. Using the growth accounting equation, show that equal percentage increases in capital and labor will leave output per worker unaffected only if $a_K + a_N = 1$.

BUSINESS CYCLES

PART IV

9
Business Cycles

Over the past several centuries the United States and other major industrialized countries have experienced tremendous economic growth, growth that has transformed their economies and greatly improved their citizens' living standards. Yet even in these prosperous countries economic expansion has been periodically interrupted by episodes of declining production, income, and spending, and rising unemployment. Sometimes—fortunately not very often—these episodes of economic weakness have been severe and prolonged. But whether brief or more protracted, almost invariably declines in economic activity have been followed by a resumption of economic growth.

This repeatedly observed sequence of economic expansion giving way to temporary economic decline, followed by recovery, is known as the business cycle. The business cycle is a topic of central concern in macroeconomics because business cycle fluctuations—the ups and downs in overall economic activity—are felt throughout the economy. When the economy is growing strongly, the prosperity is shared by most of the nation's industries and the workers and owners of capital in those industries. When the economy weakens, many sectors of the economy similarly experience declining sales, production, and employment. Because the effects of business cycles are so widespread, and because recessions or depressions can cause great hardship, economists have invested much effort in trying to find the causes of these episodes and to determine what, if anything, should be done to counteract them.

As we see in this chapter, there is a reasonable amount of agreement about the basic empirical business cycle facts. However, there remains a great deal of controversy about the causes of business cycles and the role that government policy should take in attempting to lessen the severity of cyclical fluctuations. Much of this controversy arises between the followers of the classical and Keynesian approaches to macroeconomics, introduced in Chapter 1. Classical economists view business cycles as generally representing the economy's best response to disturbances in production or spending. Thus classical economists do not see much, if any, need for the government to intervene to counteract these fluctuations. In contrast, Keynesian economists argue that because wages and prices adjust slowly, disturbances in production or spending may drive the economy away from its most desirable level of output and employment for protracted periods. According to the Keynesian view, there is scope for government intervention to mitigate business cycle fluctuations.

We discuss the classical-Keynesian controversy briefly in the last section of this chapter and explore it fully in Chapters 11 and 12. To provide background for this debate, most of this chapter presents the basic empirical features of the business cycle. We begin with a definition of the business cycle and an overview of the history of the business cycle in the United States. We then turn to a more detailed discussion of some of the general characteristics of business cycles, or "business cycle facts."

9.1 WHAT IS A BUSINESS CYCLE?

Fluctuations in overall economic activity have been experienced by countries since their earliest phases of industrialization and have been measured and studied by economists for well over a century. Marx and Engels referred to "commercial crises," an early term for business cycles, in their Communist Manifesto in 1848. In the United States business cycle research was pioneered by the National Bureau of Economic Research (NBER), a private nonprofit organization of economists founded in 1920. The NBER developed and continues to update the **business cycle chronology,** a detailed history of business cycles in the United States and other countries. The NBER has also sponsored many studies of the business cycle: An important early example was the 1946 book *Measuring Business Cycles*, by Arthur Burns (who became the Federal Reserve chairman from 1970 until 1978) and Wesley Mitchell (a principal founder of the NBER). This landmark work, which was among the first to document carefully and analyze the empirical facts about business cycles, begins with the following definition of business cycles:

> Business cycles are a type of fluctuation found in the aggregate economic activity of nations that organize their work mainly in business enterprises. A cycle consists of expansions occurring at about the same time in many economic activities, followed by similarly general recessions, contractions, and revivals which merge into the expansion phase of the next cycle; this sequence of changes is recurrent but not periodic; in duration business cycles vary from more than one year to ten or twelve years.[1]

Five points in this definition should be clarified and emphasized.

1. *Aggregate economic activity*. Business cycles are defined broadly as fluctuations of "aggregate economic activity" rather than as fluctuations in a single, specific economic variable such as real GNP. Although real GNP may be the single variable that most closely measures the concept of aggregate economic activity, Burns and Mitchell thought it important to look at other indicators of activity as well, such as employment and financial market variables.

2. *Expansions and contractions*. To explain what Burns and Mitchell meant by expansions and contractions, we show a diagram of a typical business cycle in Fig. 9.1. The dashed line in the figure shows the average, or normal, growth path of aggregate economic activity, and the solid curve shows the rises and falls of actual business activity. The period of time during which aggregate economy activity is falling is the **contraction** or the **recession.** If the recession is particularly severe, then it is called a **depression.** After reaching the low point of the contraction, called the **trough** (marked by a T in Fig. 9.1), economic activity begins to grow. The period of time during which aggregate economic activity grows is called

---

[1]Arthur F. Burns and Wesley C. Mitchell, *Measuring Business Cycles*, New York: National Bureau of Economic Research, 1946, p. 1.

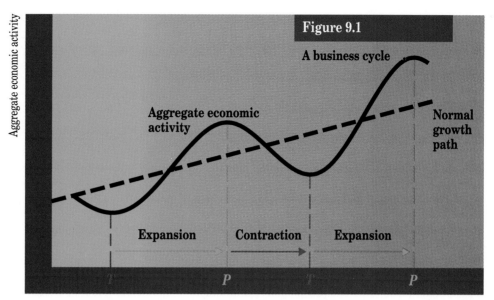

Figure 9.1

A business cycle

Aggregate economic activity

Normal growth path

Expansion Contraction Expansion

The solid curve graphs the behavior of aggregate economic activity over a typical business cycle. The dashed curve shows the economy's normal growth path. During a contraction aggregate economic activity falls until it reaches a trough, marked T. The trough is followed by an expansion during which economic activity grows until a peak (marked P) is reached. A complete cycle can be measured from peak to peak or trough to trough.

an **expansion** or a **boom.** After reaching the high point of the expansion, called the **peak** (marked by a P in the figure), aggregate economic activity begins to decline again. The entire sequence of decline followed by recovery, measured from peak to peak or from trough to trough, is called a **business cycle.**

Figure 9.1 suggests that business cycles are purely temporary deviations of output away from the economy's long-run growth path. This is an oversimplification, because part of the output losses and gains that occur during a business cycle may turn out to be permanent (see Box 9.1, p. 324).

Peaks and troughs in the business cycle are known collectively as **turning points.** One goal of business cycle research is to identify the dates at which turning points occurred. How are turning points identified? Since aggregate economic activity is not measured directly by any single variable, there is no simple formula that can be used to tell us when a peak or trough was reached.[2] In practice, the date at which the economy reaches a peak or trough is determined by a small group of economists that form the NBER's Business Cycle Dating Committee. This committee meets only when the members think a turning point may have occurred. From an examination of a variety of economic data the committee determines whether a peak or trough has been reached and, if so, in what month it happened. However, since the committee's announcements usually come well after the occurrence of the peak or trough, their judgments are used more for historical analysis of business cycles than as a guide to current policymaking.

---

[2]A conventional definition used by the media—that a recession has occurred when there are two consecutive quarters of negative real GNP growth—is not widely accepted by economists. The reason economists tend not to like this definition is that real GNP is only one of many possible indicators of economic activity.

BOX *9.1*:   TEMPORARY AND PERMANENT COMPONENTS
OF RECESSIONS

Until the 1980s economists generally believed that business cycles are temporary events. According to this view, once the economy has recovered from a recession, it returns to the level it would have reached had the recession not occurred. Thus although a recession creates short-run problems, it has no important long-run effects on a country's standard of living.

However, in a well-known 1982 article* Charles Nelson of the University of Washington and Charles Plosser of the University of Rochester showed that business cycles are not entirely temporary events. Instead, there is some permanent reduction in output associated with the typical recession. Nelson and Plosser examined many macroeconomic variables, including measures of output and employment. Using statistical techniques, they found that for every variable except the unemployment rate, part of a typical cyclical fluctuation represents a permanent change. Only in the unemployment rate were fluctuations found to be completely transitory.

The severe 1973–1975 recession illustrates the potential permanence of cyclical changes in output. The solid curve in the accompanying figure shows the actual path of real GNP in the United States over the period 1947–1990. The dashed curve in the figure shows the trend in real output, based on the period 1947–1973 and extended through 1990.† You can see that GNP in the 1980s remained well below the levels it would have reached on the basis of the earlier trend, suggesting that the 1973–1975 recession was associated with a permanent reduction in real GNP. Of course, we cannot conclude from the figure that

the 1973–1975 recession directly *caused* the subsequent slowdown: It may have been that external factors, such as OPEC's quadrupling of oil prices, caused both the recession *and* the subsequent slowdown. Alternatively, the slowdown of growth after 1973 may have been a pure coincidence, unrelated to the 1973–1975 recession. Whatever the reason, much of the fall in output that occurred in 1973–1975 turned out to be permanent.

In a typical recession, what fraction of the decline in output is permanent? Unfortunately, this is not an easy question to answer: One problem is that we cannot tell for sure whether a given decline in output will turn out to be temporary or permanent until a number of years have passed. Another problem is that all cyclical output changes may not be alike in their degree of permanence. For example, it is perhaps not so surprising that a portion of the output decline during the 1973–1975 recession turned out to be permanent, given that this recession was associated with a large and long-lasting change in the economy: a fourfold increase in the price of oil. Output declines in recessions not associated with long-lasting supply shocks, in contrast, may well be less permanent than the 1973–1975 decline.

*"Trends and Random Walks in Macroeconomic Time Series: Some Evidence and Implications," *Journal of Monetary Economics*, September 1982, pp. 139–162.
†The trend line in the figure curves up slightly because it is based on the assumption of a constant growth rate. A variable that grows by the same percentage in every year will follow a path that curves upward over time, rather than being a straight line.

3. *Comovement*. Business cycles do not occur in just a few sectors or in just a few economic variables. Instead, expansions or contractions "occur at about the same time in many economic activities." Thus, although some industries are more sensitive to the business cycle than others, output and employment in most industries tend to fall in recessions and rise in expansions. Many other economic variables in addition to output and employment, such as prices, productivity, investment, and government purchases, also have regular and predictable patterns of behavior over the course of the business cycle. The tendency of many economic variables to move together in a predictable way over the cycle is called **comovement**. We examine the comovements of key macroeconomic variables in Section 9.3.

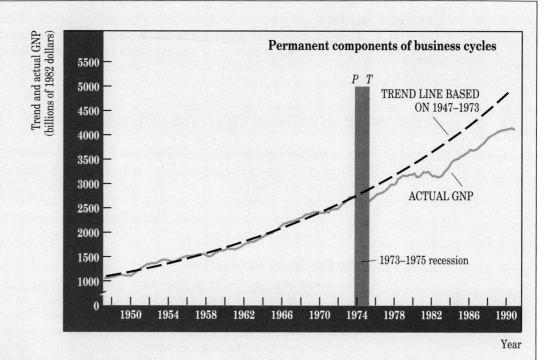

Permanent components of business cycles

Trend and actual GNP (billions of 1982 dollars)

TREND LINE BASED ON 1947–1973

ACTUAL GNP

1973–1975 recession

Year

The figure shows actual U.S. real GNP (measured quarterly) and a trend line based on real GNP growth from 1947 to 1973. The economy never returned to the earlier trend after the 1973 recession. In this sense, much of the output loss of the 1973 recession was permanent.

Source: *Survey of Current Business*, real GNP (billions of 1982 dollars).

One interesting attempt to measure the permanent and temporary components of cycles was carried out by George Evans,* now of the London School of Economics. Evans used the unemployment rate, which Nelson and Plosser found has only temporary fluctuations, as a measure of how far output is from its long-run or permanent level at any given time. Unusually high unemployment rates, for example, were used to indicate periods when output is well below its long-run level. Using this approach, Evans found that, on average, changes in real GNP are 30% permanent and 70% temporary in the postwar United States.

*"Output and Employment Dynamics in the United States: 1950–1985," Department of Economics, Stanford University, October 1986.

  → 4. *Recurrent but not periodic.* The business cycle is not periodic, in that it does not occur at regular, predictable intervals and does not last for a fixed or predetermined length of time. (Box 9.2 on p. 342 discusses the seasonal cycle—or economic fluctuations over the seasons of the year—which, unlike the business cycle, *is* periodic.) Although the business cycle is not periodic, it is recurrent, which means that the standard pattern of contraction-trough-expansion-peak has been observed to recur over and over again in industrial economies.

  → 5. *Persistence.* The duration of a complete business cycle can vary tremendously, from a year to over a decade, and is very hard to predict in advance. However, we do know that once a recession begins, the economy tends to keep contracting for a period of time, perhaps for a year or more. Similarly, an expansion once begun usually lasts a while. This tendency for declines in economic activity to be followed by further declines, and for growth in economic activity to be followed by more growth, is called **persistence.** Because movements in economic activity have some persistence, economic forecasters are always on the lookout for turning points, which are likely to indicate a change in the direction of economic activity in the future.

9.2 THE AMERICAN BUSINESS CYCLE: THE HISTORICAL RECORD

An overview of American business cycle history is provided by the NBER's monthly business cycle chronology,[3] shown in Table 9.1. The table gives the dates of the troughs and peaks of the thirty complete business cycles that the United States has experienced since 1854. Also shown are the number of months that each contraction and expansion lasted. Using Table 9.1 as a basis, we survey the evolution of the American business cycle over the past century and a half.

The Pre–World War I Period

The period between the Civil War (1861–1865) and World War I (1917–1918) saw rapid economic growth in the United States. Nevertheless, as you can see in Table 9.1, recessions were a serious problem during this time. Indeed, the longest contraction on record is the 65-month-long decline between October 1873 and March 1879, a contraction that was worldwide in scope and is referred to by economic historians as the Depression of the 1870s. Overall, during the 1854–1914 period the economy suffered 338 months of contraction, nearly as many as the 382 months of expansion. In contrast, from the end of World War II in 1945 through 1990, the number of months of expansion (449) outnumbered months of contraction (92) by about five to one.

The Great Depression and World War II

The worst economic contraction in the history of the United States was the Great Depression of the 1930s. After a prosperous decade in the 1920s aggregate economic activity reached a peak in August 1929, two months before the famous stock market crash in October 1929. Between the 1929 peak and the trough in the spring of 1933, real GNP fell by nearly 30%. During the same period the unemployment rate rose from about 3% to close to 25%, with many of those lucky enough to have jobs able to work only part-time. To appreciate how severe the Great Depression was, compare it with the two worst post–World War II recessions, in 1973–1975 and 1981–1982: In contrast to the 30% real GNP decline and 25% unemployment rate of the Depression, in the 1973–1975 recession real GNP fell by 4.3% and the unemployment rate rose from about 4% to about 9%; in the 1981–1982 recession real GNP fell by 3.2% and unemployment rose from about 7% to about 11% of the labor force.

Although no sector escaped the Depression, some were particularly hard hit. In the financial sector stock prices continued to collapse after the crash. Depositors withdrew their money from banks, and borrowers, unable to repay their bank

---

[3]For a detailed discussion of the NBER chronologies, see Geoffrey H. Moore and Victor Zarnowitz, "The NBER's Business Cycle Chronologies," in Robert J. Gordon, ed., *The American Business Cycle: Continuity and Change*, Chicago: University of Chicago Press, 1986.

Table 9.1 NBER Business Cycle Turning Points and Durations of Post-1854 Business Cycles

Trough	Expansion (Months from Trough to Peak)	Peak	Contraction (Months from Peak to Next Trough)
Dec. 1854	30	June 1857	18
Dec. 1858	22	Oct. 1860	8
June 1861	46	Apr. 1865	32
Dec. 1867	18	June 1869	18
Dec. 1870	34	Oct. 1873	65
Mar. 1879	36	Mar. 1882	38
May 1885	22	Mar. 1887	13
Apr. 1888	27	July 1890	10
May 1891	20	Jan. 1893	17
June 1894	18	Dec. 1895	18
June 1897	24	June 1899	18
Dec. 1900	21	Sep. 1902	23
Aug. 1904	33	May 1907	13
June 1908	19	Jan. 1910	24
Jan. 1912	12	Jan. 1913	23
Dec. 1914	44 (World War I)	Aug. 1918	7
Mar. 1919	10	Jan. 1920	18
July 1921	22	May 1923	14
July 1924	27	Oct. 1926	13
Nov. 1927	21	Aug. 1929	43 (Depression)
Mar. 1933	50	May 1937	13 (Depression)
June 1938	80 (World War II)	Feb. 1945	8
Oct. 1945	37	Nov. 1948	11
Oct. 1949	45 (Korean War)	July 1953	10
May 1954	39	Aug. 1957	8
Apr. 1958	24	Apr. 1960	10
Feb. 1961	106 (Vietnam War)	Dec. 1969	11
Nov. 1970	36	Nov. 1973	16
Mar. 1975	58	Jan. 1980	6
July 1980	12	July 1981	16
Nov. 1982	92	July 1990	

Source: *Survey of Current Business*, April 1991, page C-25: Business Cycle Expansions and Contractions.

loans, were forced to default; as a result, thousands of banks were forced to go out of business or to merge with other banks. In agriculture farmers were bankrupted by low crop prices, and a prolonged drought in the Midwest turned thousands of farm families into homeless migrants. Investment, both business and residential, fell to very low levels, and a "trade war"—in which countries competed in erecting barriers to imports—brought international trade to a virtual halt.

stopped reading here

Although we usually think of the Depression as a single episode, technically the Depression consisted of two business cycles, as you can see in Table 9.1. The contraction phase of the first cycle lasted forty-three months, from August 1929 to March 1933, and was the most precipitous economic decline in U.S. history. After Franklin Roosevelt took office as President in March 1933 and instituted a set of policies known collectively as the New Deal, a strong expansion began and continued for fifty months, from March 1933 to May 1937. By 1937 real GNP was almost back to its 1929 level, although at 14% the unemployment rate remained high. Unemployment remained high in 1937 despite the recovery of real GNP because the number of people of working age had grown since 1929 and because increases in productivity allowed employment to grow more slowly than output.

The second cycle of the Great Depression began in May 1937 with a contraction phase that lasted more than a year. Despite a new recovery that began in June 1938, the unemployment rate was still over 17% in 1939.

The Depression was ended in dramatic fashion by the advent of World War II. Even before the Japanese attack on Pearl Harbor brought America into the war in December 1941, the economy was gearing up for increased armaments production. After the shock of Pearl Harbor America prepared for total war. With the national productive capacity placed under the supervision of government planning boards and driven by the insatiable demands of the military for more guns, planes, and ships, real GNP rose by more than 90% between 1939 and 1944. The unemployment rate dropped sharply, averaging less than 2% in 1943–1945 and bottoming out at 1.2% in 1944.

Postwar U.S. Business Cycles

As the war ended in 1945, economists and policymakers were concerned that the economy would relapse into depression. One manifestation of this concern was the Employment Act of 1946, passed by Congress, which required the government to fight recessions and depressions with any measures at its disposal. But instead of falling into a new depression as was feared, the U.S. economy entered a period of strong growth.

The economic expansion of the early postwar period was interrupted only by a number of relatively brief and mild recessions. None of the five contractions that occurred between 1945 and 1970 lasted more than a year, whereas eighteen of the twenty-two previous cyclical contractions in the NBER's monthly chronology had lasted a year or more. The largest fall in real GNP between 1945 and 1970 was 3.5% in 1957–1958, and throughout this period unemployment never exceeded 8.1% of the work force. Again, unfortunately, there was a correlation between economic expansion and war: The 1949–1953 expansion corresponded closely to the time period of the Korean War, and the latter part of the strong 1961–1969 expansion occurred at the same time as the military buildup to fight the Vietnam War.

Because no serious recession occurred between 1945 and 1970, some economists suggested that the business cycle had been "tamed," or even that it was "dead." This view achieved its greatest popularity during the record 106-month expansion of 1961–1969, which was widely attributed not only to high rates of military spending during the Vietnam War but also to the macroeconomic policies of Presidents Kennedy and Johnson. Some argued that policymakers should stop worrying about recessions and focus their attention on inflation, which had been gradually increasing over the 1960s.

Unfortunately, reports of the business cycle's death proved premature. Shortly after the Organization of Petroleum Exporting Countries (OPEC) succeeded in quadrupling oil prices in the fall of 1973, the U.S. economy and the economies of many other nations fell into a severe recession. As we mentioned in the comparison with the Great Depression, in the 1973–1975 recession American real GNP fell by 4.3% and the unemployment rate reached 9%—not a depression but a serious downturn, nonetheless. Also disturbing was the fact that inflation, which in most previous cases had fallen during recessions, shot up to unprecedented double-digit levels. Inflation continued to be a problem for the rest of the 1970s, even as the economy recovered from the 1973–1975 recession.

More evidence that the business cycle was not dead came with the sharp 1981–1982 recession. This contraction lasted sixteen months, the same length of time as the 1973–1975 decline, and the unemployment rate reached 11%, a postwar high. Many economists claim that this recession was knowingly created by the Federal Reserve in order to reduce inflation, a claim we discuss in Chapters 14 and 15. Inflation did indeed come down substantially, falling from about 11% to less than 4% per year. The recovery from this recession was strong, however, and the expansion that ensued continued until the summer of 1990.

Have American Business Cycles Become Less Severe?

Until recently, the conventional macroeconomic wisdom was that over the long sweep of history business cycles have become generally less severe. Most obviously, no recession in the United States since World War II can begin to rival the severity of the Great Depression. Even putting aside the Great Depression, economists generally believed that business downturns before 1929 were longer and deeper than those since 1945. According to the NBER business cycle chronology (Table 9.1), for example, the average contraction before 1929 lasted nearly twenty-one months and the average expansion lasted a bit more than twenty-five months. Since 1945 contractions have shortened to an average of eleven months, and expansions have lengthened to an average of fifty months. Standard measures of economic fluctuations, such as real GNP growth and the unemployment rate, also show considerably less volatility since 1945, relative to data available for the pre-1929 era.

Since World War II a major goal of economic policy has been to reduce the size and frequency of recessions. If researchers found—contrary to the generally accepted view—that business cycles had *not* moderated in the postwar period, serious doubt would be cast on the ability of economic policymakers to achieve this stated goal. For this reason, although it may seem that the question of whether the business cycle has moderated over time is a matter of interest only to economic historians, this issue is in fact of great practical importance.

Thus a considerable controversy was started when Christina Romer, now at the University of California at Berkeley, wrote a series of articles denying the claim that the business cycle has moderated over time.[4] Romer's main point con-

---

[4]The articles included "Is the Stabilization of the Postwar Economy a Figment of the Data?" *American Economic Review*, June 1986, pp. 314–34; "The Prewar Business Cycle Reconsidered: New Estimates of Gross National Product, 1869–1908," *Journal of Political Economy*, February 1989, pp. 1–37; and "The Cyclical Behavior of Individual Production Series, 1889–1984," *Quarterly Journal of Economics*, February 1991, pp. 1–31.

cerned the dubious quality of the pre-1929 data. Unlike today, in earlier periods the government did not collect comprehensive data on economic variables such as GNP. Instead, historical measures of these variables had to be estimated by modern economic historians, using whatever fragmentary information they could find.

Romer argued that methods used for estimating historical data typically overstated the size of cyclical fluctuations in the earlier periods. For example, the widely accepted estimates of pre-1929 GNP compiled by Nobel laureate Simon Kuznets made heavy use of data, originally collected by William Shaw, on the economy's total output of "commodities" during those years. Shaw's commodity output data measured the output of the goods-producing sectors of the economy (agriculture, mining, manufacturing, and to some extent construction) but left out important components of GNP such as wholesale and retail distribution, transportation, and services. Since manufacturing and construction are among the most cyclically volatile components of the modern economy—and distribution, transportation, and services are much less volatile—Romer argued that basing GNP estimates only on commodity output would tend to overstate the size of business cycle fluctuations. She used statistical methods to create new estimates of GNP that showed much less volatility in the pre-Depression economy than was implied by Kuznets's work. Indeed, she concluded that pre-Depression business cycles were on average only 25% or so larger than post-1945 cycles, rather than being roughly twice as severe as implied by Kuznets's figures.

Since Romer raised the issue, much new research has been done, including work on the historical experience of other countries as well as the United States. Some of this research has supported Romer's view that cycles have not much moderated. For example, Matthew Shapiro[5] of the University of Michigan showed that the returns earned in the stock market—which are closely related to production and profitability and thus might be used as an indicator of cyclical conditions— were no more variable before the Depression than they are today. Steven Sheffrin[6] of the University of California at Davis looked at historical data for six European countries (United Kingdom, Denmark, Sweden, Italy, France, and Norway) and found that there was evidence for postwar moderation of the business cycle only in Sweden.

But the traditional view that the cycle has moderated has had effective defenders as well: In a comprehensive study of historical GNP Nathan Balke and Robert Gordon[7] employed previously unutilized data on transportation, communications, and construction for the period 1869–1928. Although these historical data had been available for more than twenty years, they had not been used in previous estimates of GNP. When Balke and Gordon combined these data with the Shaw-Kuznets data on commodity output to construct a new series for pre-Depression GNP, they found that the size of pre-1929 business cycle fluctuations was closer to what Kuznets had originally found than to Romer's revised estimate.

If Balke and Gordon turn out to be right, then Romer's challenge will have been answered; and the original belief that the business cycle has moderated over

---

[5]"The Stabilization of the United States Economy: Evidence from the Stock Market," *American Economic Review*, December 1988, pp. 1067–1079.

[6]"Have Economic Fluctuations Been Dampened? A Look at Evidence Outside the United States," *Journal of Monetary Economics*, January 1988, pp. 73–83.

[7]"The Estimation of Prewar Gross National Product: Methodology and New Evidence," *Journal of Political Economy*, February 1989, pp. 38–92.

time will be reconfirmed. Even if the traditional view is shown to be true, though, the debate has served the useful purpose of forcing a careful reexamination and improvement of the historical data. The improved data will help economists in the ongoing study of business cycles.

9.3   BUSINESS CYCLE FACTS   *started reading here.*

Although no two business cycles are exactly identical, there are features that all (or most) cycles have in common. This point has been put strongly by a leading business cycle theorist, Robert E. Lucas, Jr., of the University of Chicago, who has written:

> Though there is absolutely no theoretical reason to anticipate it, one is led by the facts to conclude that, with respect to the qualitative behavior of comovements among series [that is, economic variables], *business cycles are all alike.* To theoretically inclined economists, this conclusion should be attractive and challenging, for it suggests the possibility of a unified explanation of business cycles, grounded in the *general* laws governing market economies, rather than in political or institutional characteristics specific to particular countries or periods.[8]

Lucas's statement that business cycles are all alike (or more accurately, that they have many features in common) is based on researchers' examinations of the comovements among various economic variables over the business cycle. In this section, we study these comovements, which we call business cycle facts, for the postwar period in the United States. By knowing the business cycle facts, policymakers, managers, financial investors, and consumers can more effectively interpret announcements of economic data when evaluating the state of the economy. In addition, the business cycle facts provide guidance and discipline for developing economic theories of the business cycle. When we discuss alternative theories of the business cycle in Chapters 11 and 12, a principal means by which we evaluate the theories is by seeing how well they account for the major business cycle facts. To be completely successful, a theory of the business cycle should be able to explain not just the cyclical behavior of a few variables such as output and employment but also the cyclical patterns found in other important economic variables.

The Cyclical Behavior of Economic Variables: Direction and Timing

Two characteristics of the cyclical behavior of macroeconomic variables are important for our discussion of the business cycle facts. The first characteristic is the *direction* in which a macroeconomic variable moves, relative to the direction of aggregate economic activity. An economic variable that moves in the same direction as aggregate economic activity (up in expansions, down in contractions) is **procyclical.** A variable that moves in the opposite direction of aggregate economic activity (up in contractions, down in expansions) is **countercyclical.** Variables that do not appear to be sensitive to the business cycle are called **acyclical.**

---

[8]Robert E. Lucas, Jr., "Understanding Business Cycles," in K. Brunner and A. H. Meltzer, eds., *Carnegie-Rochester Conference Series on Public Policy*, vol. 5, Autumn, 1977, p. 10.

The <u>second</u> characteristic of cyclical behavior is the *timing* of the variable's turning points (peaks and troughs) relative to the turning points of the business cycle. An economic variable is said to be a **leading variable** if it tends to move in advance of aggregate economic activity. In other words, the peaks and troughs in a leading variable occur before the corresponding peaks and troughs in the business cycle. A **coincident variable** is one whose peaks and troughs occur at about the same time as the corresponding business cycle peaks and troughs. Finally, a **lagging variable** is one whose peaks and troughs tend to occur later than the corresponding peaks and troughs in the business cycle.

The fact that some economic variables consistently lead the business cycle suggests that they might be used to forecast the future course of the economy. This idea is behind the **index of leading indicators,** discussed in the "In Touch with the Macroeconomy" box (p. 346).

In some cases the cyclical timing of a variable is obvious when we look at a graph of its behavior over the course of several business cycles; in other cases elaborate statistical techniques are needed to determine timing. Conveniently, the Statistical Indicators Branch of the Bureau of Economic Analysis (BEA) has analyzed the timing of dozens of economic variables. This information is published monthly in the *Survey of Current Business*, along with the most recent data for these variables. For the most part, in this chapter we rely on the BEA's timing classifications.

Having defined direction and timing, we are ready to examine the cyclical behavior of a number of key macroeconomic variables. The historical behavior of many of these variables was already shown in the figures in Chapter 1. Those figures covered a long time period but were based on annual data. In order to provide a better view of short-run cyclical behavior, the figures we look at now present quarterly or monthly data. The direction and timing of the variables we consider are summarized in Table 9.2.

Production

Because the level of production is a basic indicator of aggregate economic activity, the peaks and troughs in production tend to occur at about the same time as peaks and troughs in aggregate economic activity. Thus production is a coincident and procyclical variable. Figure 9.2 shows the behavior of the industrial production index in the United States since 1960. The industrial production index is a broad measure of production in manufacturing, mining, and utilities. The vertical lines marked P and T in Fig. 9.2 and the figures to follow indicate the dates of business cycle peaks and troughs, as determined by the NBER. You can see that the turning points in industrial production are very close to the turning points of the cycle.

Although almost all types of production increase in expansions and fall in recessions, production in some sectors of the economy is more sensitive to the business cycle than in others. Industries that produce relatively durable, or long-lasting, output—such as houses, consumer durables (refrigerators, cars, washing machines), or capital goods (drill presses, computers, factories)—respond strongly to the business cycle, producing at high rates during expansions and much lower rates during recessions. In contrast, industries that produce relatively nondurable or short-lived goods (foods, paper products) or services (education, insurance) are less sensitive to the business cycle. Although the production of nondurable goods and services is procyclical, it increases less in booms and decreases less in recessions than the production of durable goods does.

Table 9.2 Summary

The Cyclical Behavior of Key Macroeconomic Variables (the Business Cycle Facts)

Variable	Direction	Timing
Production		
Industrial production	Procyclical	Coincident
Durable goods industries are more volatile than nondurable goods and services		
Expenditure		
Consumption	Procyclical	Coincident
Business fixed investment	Procyclical	Coincident
Residential investment	Procyclical	Leading
Inventory investment	Procyclical	Leading
Government purchases	Procyclical	—[a]
Investment is more volatile than consumption		
Labor Market Variables		
Employment	Procyclical	Coincident
Unemployment	Countercyclical	Unclassified[b]
Average labor productivity	Procyclical	Leading[a]
Real wage	Procyclical	—[a]
Money Growth and Inflation		
Money (M1)	Procyclical	Leading
Inflation	Procyclical	Lagging
Financial Variables		
Stock prices	Procyclical	Leading
Nominal interest rates	Procyclical	Lagging
Real interest rates	Acyclical	—[a]

Source: *Survey of Current Business*, December 1990. Official cyclical indicators in this table include industrial production—series 47 (total industrial production); consumption—series 57 (manufacturing and trade sales); business fixed investment—series 86 (gross private nonresidential fixed investment); residential investment—series 89 (gross private residential fixed investment); inventory investment—series 30 (change in business inventories); employment—series 41 (employees on nonagricultural payrolls); unemployment—series 43 (civilian unemployment rate); money supply—series 85 (percent change in money supply, M1); inflation—series 120 (CPI for services, change from previous month, smoothed); stock prices—series 19 (stock prices, 500 common stocks); nominal interest rates—series 119 (Federal funds rate), series 114 (discount rate on new issues of 91-day Treasury bills), series 109 (average prime rate charged by banks)

[a]Timing is not officially designated by the Bureau of Economic Analysis.

[b]Officially designated as "unclassified" by the Bureau of Economic Analysis.

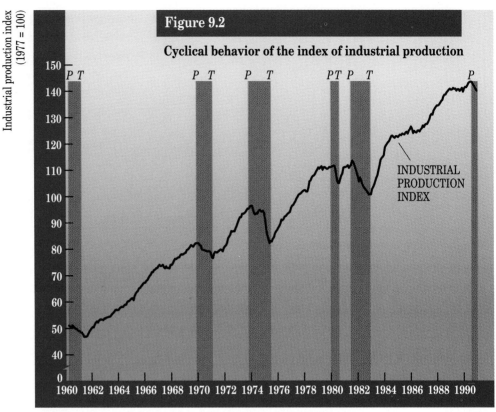

Figure 9.2

Cyclical behavior of the index of industrial production

Industrial production index (1977 = 100)

INDUSTRIAL
PRODUCTION
INDEX

Year

The index of industrial production, a broad measure of production in manufacturing, mining, and utilities, is procyclical and coincident. The peaks and troughs of the business cycle are shown by the vertical lines marked *P* and *T*. Thus the shaded areas represent recessions.

Source: *Business Conditions Digest* and *Survey of Current Business*, industrial production index, total.

Expenditure

For components of expenditure, as for types of production, durability is the key factor in determining sensitivity to the business cycle. Figure 9.3 shows the cyclical behavior of consumption spending and of fixed investment (both measured in real terms). Fixed investment, which consists of business fixed investment (structures, equipment) and residential investment, is made up primarily of spending on durable goods and is very strongly procyclical. However, consumption expenditures, which include expenditures on nondurable goods and services as well as consumer durables, are relatively smoother. A breakdown of consumption into its components would show that spending on consumer durables is strongly procyclical (sales of cars, furniture, and washing machines go up sharply in an economic expansion) but that consumption of nondurable goods and services is much less affected by the business cycle (see Fig. 5.5, p. 173). With respect to timing, consumption and investment are generally coincident with the business cycle, although individual components of fixed investment vary in their cyclical timing.[9]

---

[9]Table 9.2 shows that residential investment leads the cycle.

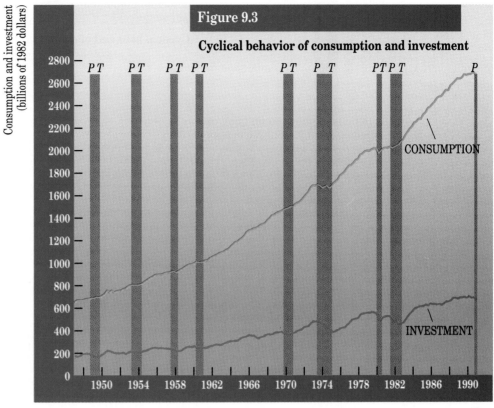

Figure 9.3

Cyclical behavior of consumption and investment

Both consumption and investment are procyclical. However, investment is more sensitive to the business cycle than consumption is, reflecting the fact that durable goods are a larger part of investment spending than of consumption spending.

Source: *Business Conditions Digest* and *Survey of Current Business*, consumption expenditures and fixed investment.

One component of spending that seems to follow its own rules is inventory investment, or changes in business inventories, shown in Fig. 9.4. Inventory investment is procyclical and leading. Even though goods kept in inventory need not be very durable, inventory investment is also very volatile. Although on average inventory investment is a small part (around 1%) of total spending, sharp declines in inventory investment have been a large part of the total decline in spending in some recessions, most notably the recessions of 1973–1975 and 1981–1982. The sense in which inventory investment follows its own rules is that it often displays large fluctuations that are not associated with business cycle peaks and troughs, as during the expansion that began in 1982.

Government purchases of goods and services (no figure shown) are generally procyclical. Rapid military buildups, such as occurred in World War II, the Korean War, and the Vietnam War, are usually associated with economic expansions.

Employment and Unemployment

The labor market is a part of the economy in which business cycles are strongly felt and in which the effects of downturns are of great concern. In a recession,

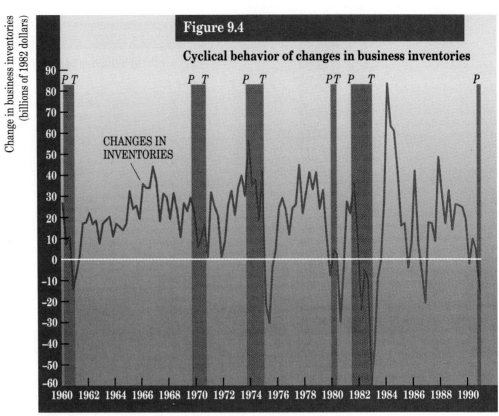

Figure 9.4

Cyclical behavior of changes in business inventories

Inventory investment, or changes in business inventories, is procyclical and leading but also extremely volatile. For example, between 1982 and 1990 inventory investment fluctuated sharply despite the fact that the economy was continuously in expansion.

Source: *Business Conditions Digest* and *Survey of Current Business*, inventory investment.

employment grows slowly or falls, many workers are laid off, and jobs become more difficult to find.

Figure 9.5 shows the number of civilians employed in the United States since 1960. Employment is clearly procyclical, as more people have jobs in booms than in recessions. Employment is also coincident with the cycle.

Figure 9.6 shows the civilian unemployment rate, which is the fraction of the civilian labor force (the number of people who are available for work and want to work) that is unemployed. The civilian unemployment rate is very strongly countercyclical, rising sharply in contractions and coming down somewhat more slowly in expansions. Although the BEA has studied the timing of unemployment, Table 9.2 reports that the timing of this variable is officially designated as "unclassified" owing to the absence of a clear pattern in the data.

Average Labor Productivity and the Real Wage

Besides employment and unemployment, two other important labor market variables are average labor productivity and the real wage.

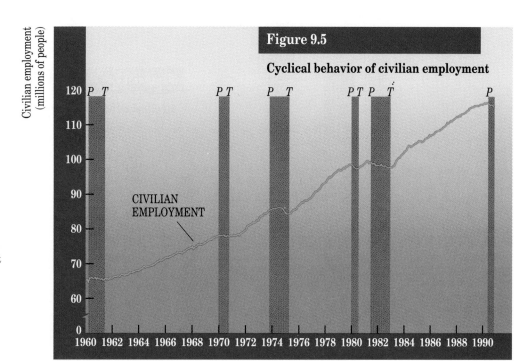

Figure 9.5

Cyclical behavior of civilian employment

CIVILIAN
EMPLOYMENT

Civilian employment
is procyclical and
coincident with the
cycle.

Source: *Business
Conditions Digest* and
*Survey of Current
Business*, civilian
employment.

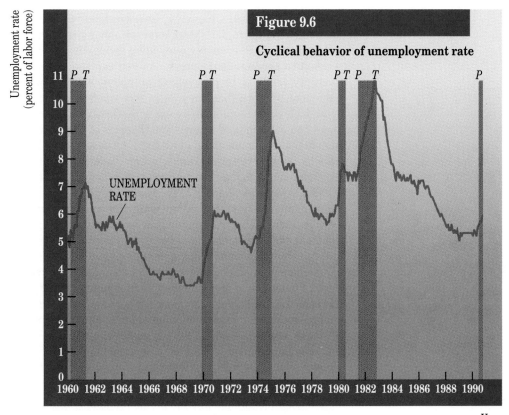

Figure 9.6

Cyclical behavior of unemployment rate

UNEMPLOYMENT
RATE

The unemployment
rate is
countercyclical and is
very sensitive to the
business cycle. Its
timing pattern
relative to the cycle
is unclassified,
meaning that there
is no definite
tendency for it to be
leading, coincident,
or lagging.

Source: *Business
Conditions Digest* and
*Survey of Current
Business*, civilian
unemployment rate.

337

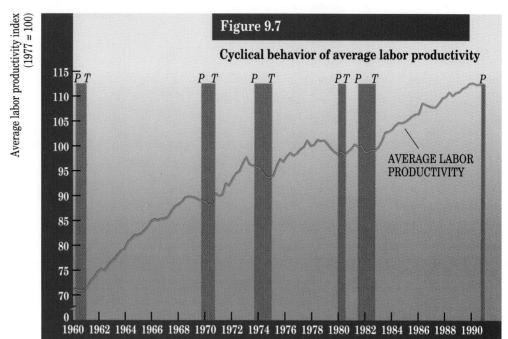

Figure 9.7

Cyclical behavior of average labor productivity

Average labor productivity, measured as real output per employee hour in the nonfarm business sector, is procyclical and leading.

Source: *Business Conditions Digest* and *Survey of Current Business*, index of output per hour, all persons, nonfarm business sector.

As discussed in Chapter 1, average labor productivity is output per unit of labor input. Figure 9.7 shows average labor productivity measured as total real output in the U.S. economy (excluding farms) divided by the total number of hours worked to produce that output. As you can see in the figure, average labor productivity tends to be procyclical. In booms workers produce more output during each hour of work than they do in recessions. For reasons explained in Chapters 11 and 12, procyclical average labor productivity is a challenge for macroeconomic theory to explain, and alternative theories of the business cycle give different explanations of this business cycle fact. Although the BEA does not officially designate the timing of this variable, other studies have found that average labor productivity tends to lead the business cycle.[10]

As we saw in Chapter 3, the real wage is the compensation received by workers per unit of time (such as an hour or a week) measured in real, or purchasing-power, terms. The real wage is an especially important variable in the study of business cycles because it is one of the main determinants of the amount of labor supplied by workers and demanded by firms.

Generally speaking, two types of studies have attempted to characterize the cyclical behavior of real wages. The first type examines the average real wage for the economy as a whole. In these studies the wage is usually measured as the total real compensation paid to all workers in the economy divided by the total number of hours worked. As Fig. 9.8 suggests, the average real wage measured in this way is mildly procyclical. (The most striking feature of Fig. 9.8 is how much the growth of the average real wage has slowed since around 1973.)

---

[10]See Robert J. Gordon, "The 'End of Expansion' Phenomenon in Short-Run Productivity Behavior," *Brookings Papers on Economic Activity*, 1979:2, pp. 447–461.

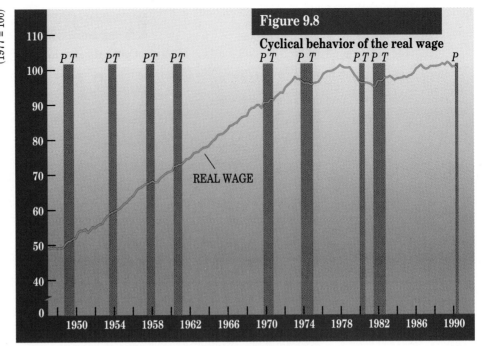

Figure 9.8

Cyclical behavior of the real wage

Real wage index (1977 = 100)

REAL WAGE

The economywide average real wage is mildly procyclical. Note how sharply real wage growth has slowed since 1973.

Source: *Business Conditions Digest* and *Survey of Current Business*, average hourly compensation, all employees, nonfarm business sector.

Year

However, many economists have argued that the economywide average real wage may not be a good indicator of the real wage received by the typical worker. An example illustrates the potential problem. Imagine that an economy consisted of two employed workers, each earning $9 per hour, and one unemployed worker. Clearly, the average wage paid to workers in this economy is $9 per hour. Now suppose that this economy expands, with the result that the two employed workers get raises to $10 per hour *and* the previously unemployed worker finds a job that pays $7 per hour. If all three workers work the same number of hours, then the economywide average wage is the same as before: ($10 + $10 + $7)/3, or $9 per hour. Thus although all three workers are earning more in the expansion than they did before, the economywide average wage has not changed. What has happened is that the increase in the employed individuals' wages has been offset by a change in the composition of the work force, which now includes a relatively low-wage worker who was not working before the expansion.

To eliminate effects of changing labor force composition on the measured real wage, a second type of study attempts to measure the cyclical behavior of the real wages of specific individual workers. Unfortunately, this type of study suffers from a lack of good data on individual wages and from a number of technical statistical problems. Because of these problems, the results of studies of individual wages range from the finding that real wages are acyclical to the finding that they are highly procyclical. However, a number of recent studies of individual wages agree with the finding of the aggregate studies of the average real wage—that the real wage is mildly procyclical.[11]

---

[11]See, for example, Michael Keane, Robert Moffitt, and David Runkle, "Real Wages Over the Business Cycle: Estimating the Impact of Heterogeneity with Micro Data," *Journal of Political Economy*, December 1988, pp. 1232–1266.

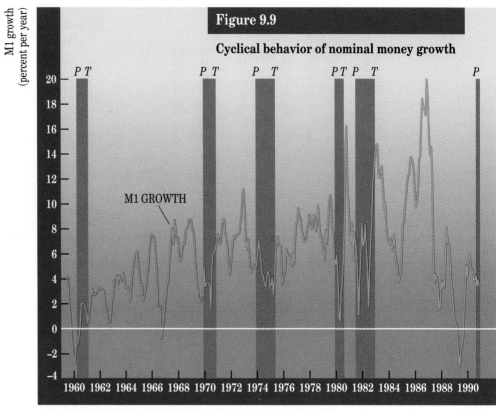

Figure 9.9

Cyclical behavior of nominal money growth

Nominal money growth, here measured as the average of monthly growth rates in M1 for the current and previous five months, is volatile. However, M1 growth has been found to be procyclical and leading.

Source: Federal Reserve Board, M1 money stock.

Overall, most evidence seems to point to the conclusion that real wages are mildly procyclical, but the range of results from the studies of individuals' wages cautions us that this conclusion is not definite.

Money Growth and Inflation

Another variable whose cyclical behavior is controversial is the money supply. Figure 9.9 shows the behavior since 1960 of the growth rate of the M1 measure of the money supply (see Table 4.1, p. 114, for a definition of M1).

The growth rate of the money supply can vary quite a bit from one month to the next, with the result that the underlying cyclical behavior of money growth may be obscured. To reduce the effect of month-to-month fluctuations, in Fig. 9.9 we report for each month the average monthly growth rate of the money supply over the current and previous five months, rather than the money growth rate over the current month only. As you can see, even after volatile month-to-month changes are averaged out, the money growth rate fluctuates a great deal (particularly since 1980!) and does not display an obvious cyclical pattern in the figure. Nevertheless, many statistical and historical studies—including a pathbreaking

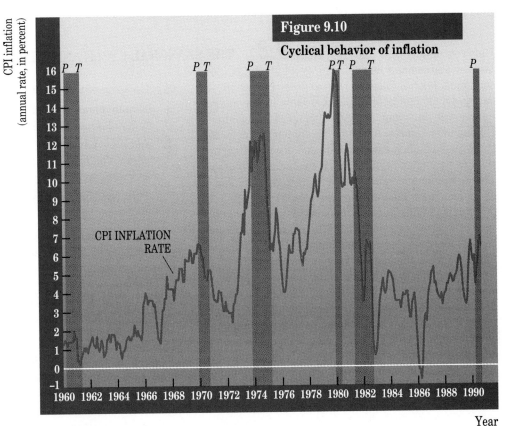

Figure 9.10

Cyclical behavior of inflation

CPI INFLATION RATE

Inflation, here measured as the average of monthly growth rates in the CPI for the current and previous five months, is procyclical and lags the cycle. A typical pattern is for inflation to build up during the expansion and then to fall after the cyclical peak.

Source: *Business Conditions Digest* and *Survey of Current Business*, consumer price index for all urban consumers.

work by Milton Friedman and Anna J. Schwartz[12] that used data back to 1867—have found that money growth is procyclical and leads the cycle. In particular, a slowdown in money growth often precedes the onset of a recession, a fact that can be seen in Fig. 9.9.

The cyclical behavior of inflation presents a somewhat clearer picture (Fig. 9.10). Inflation is procyclical with some lag. Inflation typically builds up during an economic expansion, peaks slightly after the business cycle peak, then falls until some time after the business cycle trough.

Financial Variables

Financial variables are another class of economic variables that are sensitive to the cycle. For example, stock prices (not shown in a figure) are generally procyclical (stock prices rise in good economic times) and leading (stock prices usually fall in advance of a recession).

---

[12]*A Monetary History of the United States, 1867–1960*, Princeton N.J.: Princeton University Press for NBER, 1963. This study will be discussed further in Chapter 11.

Did you know that the United States has a large

BOX 9.2: THE SEASONAL CYCLE AND THE BUSINESS CYCLE

economic boom, followed by a deep recession, in every year? The boom always occurs in the fourth quarter of the year (October through December). During this quarter GNP is 5% higher than in the third quarter (July–September) and about 8% higher than in the following first quarter (January–March). The first-quarter recession is fortunately always a short one, with GNP rising by almost 4% in the second quarter (April–June). This regular seasonal pattern of fluctuations, known as the seasonal cycle, actually accounts for more than 85% of the total fluctuations in the growth rate of real output!

Why don't large seasonal fluctuations appear in Figs. 9.2 through 9.12? Normally, macroeconomic data are seasonally adjusted, meaning that regularly recurring seasonal fluctuations are removed from the data. Seasonal adjustment allows users of economic data to ignore seasonal changes and focus on business cycle fluctuations and longer-term movements in the data. However, a study by Robert Barsky of the University of Michigan and Jeffrey Miron of Boston University* has argued that the practice of seasonally adjusting macroeconomic data may throw away information that could help us better understand the business cycle. Using data that had not been seasonally adjusted, Barsky and Miron found that the comovements of variables over the seasonal cycle are similar to their comovements over the business cycle. In particular, they found the following results:

1. Of the types of expenditure, expenditures on durables vary most over the seasonal cycle and expenditures on services vary least.

*"The Seasonal Cycle and the Business Cycle," *Journal of Political Economy*, June 1989, pp. 503–534.

2. Government spending is seasonally procyclical.

3. Employment is seasonally procyclical, and the unemployment rate is seasonally countercyclical.

4. Average labor productivity is seasonally procyclical. The real wage varies hardly at all over the seasonal cycle.

5. The nominal money stock is seasonally procyclical.

Each of these observations is true for the business cycle as well as the seasonal cycle. However, the seasonal fluctuations of inventory investment, the price level, and the nominal interest rate are much smaller than their fluctuations over the business cycle.

The seasonal cycle illustrates three potential sources of aggregate economic fluctuations: (1) changes in consumer demand, such as occur at Christmas; (2) changes in productivity, such as when construction workers become less productive because of winter weather in the first quarter; and (3) changes in labor supply, such as when people take summer vacations in the third quarter. Each of these three sources of fluctuations may contribute to the business cycle as well.

As we discuss in Section 9.4, classical economists believe that business cycles generally represent the economy's best response to changes in the economic environment, a response that macroeconomic policy need not try to eliminate. Although it does not necessarily confirm this view, the existence of the seasonal cycle shows that there can be large economic fluctuations that, as far as we can tell, are a desirable response to various factors (Christmas, the weather) and do not need to be offset by government policy.

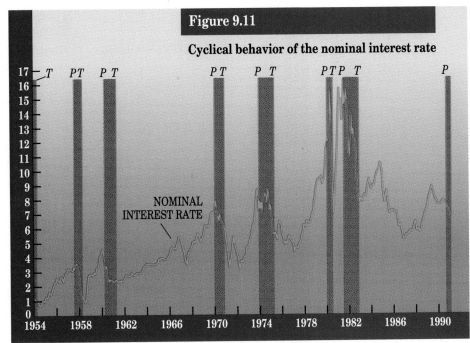

The nominal interest rate, here measured as the interest rate on three-month Treasury bills, is procyclical and lagging.

Source: *Business Conditions Digest* and *Survey of Current Business,* discount rate on new issues of 91-day Treasury bills.

interest rates include all types of interest rates?

Nominal interest rates (see Fig. 9.11) are procyclical and lagging. The nominal interest rate shown in Fig. 9.11 is the rate on three-month Treasury bills. However, other interest rates examined by the BEA, such as the prime rate (charged by banks to their best customers) and the Federal funds rate (the interest rate on overnight loans made from one bank to another) are also procyclical and lagging.

The real interest rate does not have an obvious cyclical pattern and hence we designate it as acyclical. For instance, the real interest rate was very low (indeed negative) during the 1973–1975 recession, but it was very high during the 1981–1982 recession. (Annual values of the real interest rate are shown in Fig. 2.6, p. 57.) The acyclicality of the real interest rate does not necessarily mean that movements of the real interest rate are unimportant over the business cycle. Instead, the lack of a stable cyclical pattern may arise because individual business cycles have different causes, and these different sources of cycles have varying effects on the real interest rate.

stopped reading

International Aspects of the Cycle

So far we have concentrated on business cycles in the United States. However, business cycles are by no means unique to the United States, having been regularly observed in all industrialized market economies. In most cases the cyclical behavior of key economic variables in these other economies is similar to what we have described for the United States.

There is another sense in which the business cycle is an international phenomenon: Frequently, the major industrial economies undergo recessions and expan-

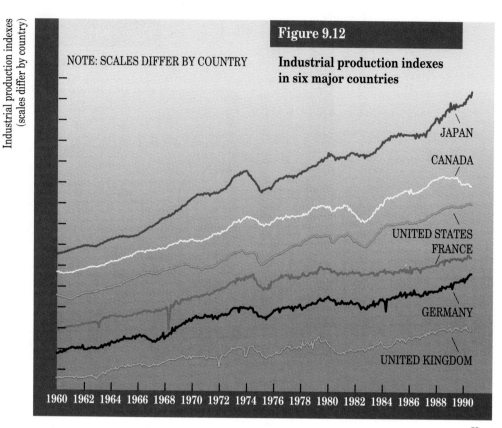

Industrial production indexes (scales differ by country)

NOTE: SCALES DIFFER BY COUNTRY

Figure 9.12

Industrial production indexes in six major countries

JAPAN

CANADA

UNITED STATES

FRANCE

GERMANY

UNITED KINGDOM

1960 1962 1964 1966 1968 1970 1972 1974 1976 1978 1980 1982 1984 1986 1988 1990

Year

The worldwide effect of business cycles can be seen in the similarity of the behavior of industrial production in each of six major countries. But individual countries also have fluctuations not shared with other countries. *Note:* The scales for the industrial production indexes differ by country, so for example the figure does not imply that Japan's total industrial production is the highest of the six countries.

Source: *Business Conditions Digest* and *Survey of Current Business*, industrial production indexes.

sions at about the same time, suggesting that they are sharing a common cycle. Figure 9.12 illustrates this common cycle by showing the index of industrial production since 1960 for each of six major industrial countries. Notice in particular the effects of worldwide recessions around 1975 and 1982. Figure 9.12 also shows that each economy experiences many small fluctuations not shared by the others.

9.4 CLASSICAL AND KEYNESIAN APPROACHES TO BUSINESS CYCLE ANALYSIS

started reading.

Chapter 1 introduced two leading schools of thought in macroeconomics, the classical approach and the Keynesian approach. In Chapters 5 through 8 we did not have to pay much attention to the differences between these alternative approaches, since those chapters focused on issues over which classicals and Keynesians do not have strong disagreements. For studying the business cycle, however, the differences between the two schools are central. In the chapters to come we will see that although classicals and Keynesians have many ideas and beliefs in common, they come to very different conclusions about the causes of business cycles and the appropriate role for government policy in attempting to moderate or eliminate them. As background for our comparison of the classical and Keynesian approaches to business cycle analysis, in this section we first briefly review the origins of these two approaches, already presented in Chapter 1. We then discuss in more detail recent developments in the debate between classicals and Keynesians over business cycle theory and policy.

The Early Classicals and the Keynesian Revolution

The classical approach, which began with Adam Smith's 1776 masterwork *The Wealth of Nations*, argues that free markets are a good way to organize the economy. In particular, Smith showed that if there are free markets and individuals pursue their own self-interest, then the economy can provide a desirable allocation of resources without extensive government intervention or central control. As we discussed in Chapter 1, the economic coordination achieved by free markets was dubbed "the invisible hand" by Smith.

Essential to the smooth operation of the invisible hand is that wages and prices adjust quickly in order to keep quantities demanded and quantities supplied equal in all markets. Rapid wage and price adjustment is essential because wages and prices provide the signals that coordinate the actions of people in the economy. For example, if a good is in short supply, its price will rise, signaling consumers to use less of the good and firms to produce more of it. Classical economists believe that wages and prices do in fact adjust relatively quickly, so that markets are virtually always in equilibrium with quantities supplied equal to quantities demanded. As a result, classicals argue that markets work well and that there is at most limited scope for government intervention in the economy.

In the early part of the twentieth century the classical approach dominated macroeconomics. With some exceptions the early classicals viewed business cycles in terms of supply and demand fluctuations—random changes in the supply and demand for labor, for example. Consistent with their philosophy of no government intervention, they saw little reason for the government to do anything about business cycles. In particular, the early classical economists believed that rapid wage adjustment would keep the labor market in equilibrium, thus keeping the economy at or near full employment.

Contrasting with the classical approach is the Keynesian approach. The roots of the Keynesian approach lie in John Maynard Keynes's famous book *The General Theory of Employment, Interest, and Money*. The *General Theory* appeared in 1936, a year in which the world economy remained mired in the Great Depression. Keynes observed that market economies had performed extremely poorly during the 1930s, and he presented a number of ideas about why the market mechanism seemed to have broken down. The main point that Keynes's followers distilled from his book was that, in practice, wages and prices appear to adjust too slowly to ensure that quantities supplied always equal quantities demanded in all markets. Slow adjustment of wages and prices is called wage-price rigidity, or sometimes wage-price stickiness.

The Keynesian idea of wage-price rigidity contradicts the classical assumption of rapid adjustment of wages and prices. If wages and prices are rigid, as Keynesians believe, then the economy can be out of equilibrium—with an imbalance between quantities supplied and demanded in many markets—for a protracted period

with the Macroeconomy

The Index of Leading Indicators

The index of leading indicators is a weighted average of eleven economic variables that each leads the business cycle. It is constructed for the purpose of forecasting future aggregate economic activity. The index was originally developed in 1938 at the National Bureau of Economic Research by Wesley Mitchell and Arthur Burns,* whose important early work on business cycles was mentioned earlier in the chapter. The index of leading indicators is currently updated by the Statistical Indicators Branch of the BEA, with results published monthly in the *Survey of Current Business*. (The index of leading indicators previously appeared in *Business Conditions Digest*, until this publication was discontinued in March 1990.)

The eleven variables that make up the index of leading indicators are listed in the accompanying table.

These variables were chosen because each has a tendency to predict (lead) economic activity and because data on these variables are frequently and promptly reported. This second characteristic is essential, since a variable cannot be of much help in forecasting if accurate data on the variable arrive only after a long delay.

Although the components of the index are something of a grab bag, as you can see in the table, there are good economic reasons why each component helps predict economic activity. For example, new orders for manufactured goods, new orders for plant and equipment, and new building permits are all direct measures of the amount of future production being planned in the economy. The index of stock prices reflects the optimism or

*Wesley C. Mitchell and Arthur F. Burns, *Statistical Indicators of Cyclical Revivals*, New York: NBER, 1938.

Components of the Index of Leading Indicators

1. Average weekly hours of production or nonsupervisory workers, manufacturing
2. Average weekly initial claims for unemployment insurance
3. Manufacturers' new orders in 1982 dollars, consumer goods and materials industries
4. Vendor performance, slower deliveries diffusion index (a measure of delays reported by purchasing agents in obtaining goods from suppliers)
5. Contracts and orders for plant and equipment in 1982 dollars
6. Index of new private housing units authorized by local building permits
7. Change in manufacturers' unfilled orders in 1982 dollars, durable goods industries
8. Change in prices of sensitive materials (raw industrial, crude, and intermediate materials)
9. Index of stock prices, 500 common stocks
10. Money supply M2 in 1982 dollars
11. Index of consumer expectations

pessimism of financial investors about the future course of the economy.

The percentage change in the index of leading indicators is reported monthly, with two or three consecutive monthly declines being regarded as the warning sign that a recession is on the way. The historical behavior since 1948 of the index of leading indicators is shown in the accompanying figure. Notice how the index tends to turn down in advance of cyclical peaks. On the whole, the index is a valuable and much-watched forecasting device, correctly predicting a large majority of economic turning points during the postwar period. However, the index is not without problems, including the following:

1. Despite the emphasis on the use of data that are promptly available, the data on the eleven components of the index and thus the index of leading indicators itself are usually revised during the first two months after their initial release. As a result, an early signal of recession or recovery can be reversed when the revised data become available.

2. As you can see in the figure, on several occasions the index has given false warnings, predicting a recession when in fact no recession occurred in the several months following the drop in the index.

3. Although it may forecast that a recession is coming, the index does not provide much information about how far in the future the recession is or how severe it will be when it arrives.

4. Changes in the structure of the economy over time may cause some variables to become better predictors of the economy and others to become worse. For this reason, the index of leading indicators must periodically be revised, either to change the list of component indicators or to change the weights with which the components are added.

Alternatives to the official index of leading indicators have recently been developed by James Stock of Harvard University and Mark Watson of Northwestern University,* working under the auspices of the NBER. Stock and Watson have proposed a new index of leading indicators, designed specifically to estimate the rate of economic growth over the next six months, that relies more heavily on financial market data than does the official index. An advantage of relying on financial market data is that these data are available very quickly and are rarely revised. A second index proposed by Stock and Watson, called the recession index, is intended to estimate the probability that the economy will be in recession six months in the future.

*"New Indexes of Coincident and Leading Economic Indicators," in Stanley Fischer and Olivier Blanchard, eds., *NBER Macroeconomics Annual*, Cambridge, Mass.: MIT Press, 1989.

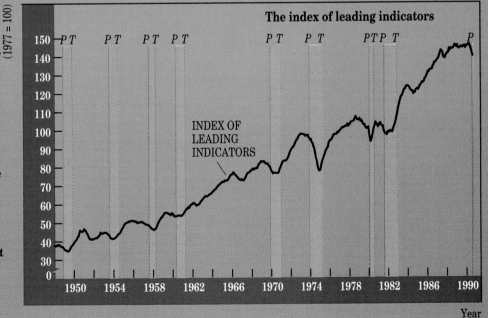

The index of leading indicators, used for forecasting, is an average of eleven economic variables that typically lead the business cycle. The index turns down in advance of business cycle peaks, signaling the onset of recession.

Source: *Business Conditions Digest* and *Survey of Current Business*, composite index of leading indicators.

of time. A possible example of such an imbalance of supply and demand is a situation of high unemployment (as in the Depression), in which the amount of labor workers want to supply exceeds the amount of labor that firms demand. A key implication of wage-price rigidity is that government policies may be necessary to keep the economy at full employment. For example, Keynes believed that higher government spending, by increasing the demand for firms' products and thus the number of workers employed, could help bring the economy out of a recession.

Keynes's work sparked what has been called the Keynesian revolution in macroeconomics. During the 1940s, 1950s, and 1960s, many outstanding young economists embraced Keynes's ideas, and the Keynesian approach dominated both macroeconomic theory and policy for a quarter of a century after World War II. The 1960s were the heyday of Keynesian macroeconomics, as many Keynesian economists participated actively in the formulation of national economic policies. With the country enjoying its longest-ever expansion during 1961–1969, Keynesians became increasingly confident that active use of macroeconomic policy—in particular, fiscal and monetary policy—could effectively eliminate the business cycle. As we discussed earlier in the chapter, about this time some economists were pronouncing the business cycle "dead."

The belief that the business cycle might no longer be a problem caused economists' interest in business cycle analysis to wane sharply. Why devise theories to explain the business cycle if cycles were a thing of the past? Instead, during this period macroeconomists focused their attention on studying **stabilization policy**, macroeconomic policies designed to promote steady economic growth without cyclical fluctuations or high inflation.

The classical approach was overshadowed during the 1945–1970 period by the apparently overwhelming success of Keynesianism, but this older approach was not eliminated. For example, many classical ideas were advocated by Nobel laureate Milton Friedman and his followers, a group called monetarists.[12] Clearly, though, during this period the classical approach was a minority view in the economics profession.

The New Classical Counterrevolution

Despite their successes, trouble was brewing for the Keynesians, both within the economics profession and in the economy. During the late 1960s and early 1970s many economists became dissatisfied with the Keynesian theory, which assumed that wages and prices were rigid without giving an adequate explanation of *why* they were rigid. Indeed, the assumptions of wage and price rigidity frequently seemed to contradict the idea, so fundamental to economics, that consumers and firms were rational in their economic behavior. For example, if a rigid wage was creating unemployment, what was to prevent unemployed workers and firms from getting together and reducing the wage? Simply assuming that they did not do so, as Keynesians did, seemed unsatisfactory.

The dissenters—under the leadership of Robert E. Lucas, Jr. (now at the University of Chicago), Thomas Sargent (now at Stanford University), Robert Barro (now at Harvard University), and others—set about systematically to "reconstruct" the microeconomic foundations of macroeconomic theory. These economists used the assumptions of rapid wage-price adjustment and market equilibrium fa-

---

[12]Monetarism is discussed in Chapter 15.

vored by the classical macroeconomists and became known as the "new classicals." Like the early classicals, they argued that active government intervention in the macroeconomy was unnecessary or undesirable—and probably ineffective, as well. However, the new classicals differed from the traditional classical school in their use of much more sophisticated and powerful mathematical techniques. These techniques helped the new classicals make important contributions to macroeconomic theory and empirical analysis, many of which were then adopted by Keynesians. Just as the best young economists of earlier decades were attracted to Keynesianism, a significant portion of the generation of economists trained in the 1970s embraced the new classical approach.

The cause of the new generation of classical economists was helped by developments in the economy. As we discussed earlier in this chapter, the belief of the 1960s that the business cycle had died turned out to be wrong: A moderate recession hit in 1969 and a serious downturn began in 1973. Besides witnessing a highly volatile economy, the 1970s saw both a disturbing increase in inflation and a slowdown in growth of output, productivity, and standards of living. Although it was not necessarily true that the new classicals had better explanations than the Keynesians for what was happening to the economy, these adverse developments caused a breakdown in confidence in the standard Keynesian macroeconomic policies and in the Keynesian theory.

During the 1970s the loss of confidence in Keynesian policies and the resurrection of the business cycle shifted the focus of macroeconomic research away from stabilization policy back toward the study of the business cycle. With the Keynesians in disarray, the new classicals launched a major research program of developing and testing business cycle theories. The classicals focused on developing models of the business cycle based on the assumptions that people are rational in their economic behavior, and that goods, services, assets, and labor are traded in markets with flexible prices and wages. By the 1980s this research program had made considerable progress and attracted much interest.

Despite its successes, the new classical counterrevolution was not as sweeping as the Keynesian revolution had been a generation earlier. Its greatest impact was in macroeconomic research, which was heavily influenced by the new classical ideas. However, many economists in the United States and especially in Europe continued to do research from a Keynesian perspective. On the policy side Keynesian influences ultimately remained important, perhaps even dominant: A major problem for the new classicals was that many policymakers viewed their recommendation of nonintervention in business cycles as being politically unacceptable. For example, even though political leaders such as President Reagan and Prime Minister Thatcher of Britain expressed disdain for the government interference advocated by Keynesianism, some observers have argued that these leaders nevertheless attempted to stabilize the economy by using policies that were, in effect, Keynesian.

Keynesians and Classicals Today

In the past decade there have been interesting developments in both the Keynesian and classical approaches. In response to the criticism by the new classicals, Keynesian theorists have developed economic models in which wage and price rigidity can be explained in terms of rational economic behavior on the part of consumers, workers, and firms. At the same time the new classicals have made considerable progress in refining their models of the business cycle to increase their realism and applicability. These two lines of research have not proceeded independently; rather, there has been considerable cooperation and communication, with good ideas flowing in both directions.

Despite the major differences between the classical and Keynesian theories of the business cycle, both approaches can be developed in terms of the *IS-LM* model that we introduced in Chapters 3 and 4. As we have seen, the fundamental difference between the two versions of the model is that prices and wages are assumed to adjust rapidly in the classical version of the *IS-LM* model but are assumed to be sticky in the Keynesian version.

We use the *IS-LM* model to study classical theories of the business cycle in Chapter 11 and Keynesian theories in Chapter 12. In judging these alternative theories, we will examine how well each theory can explain the business cycle facts presented in this chapter. However, an important task for any theory of the business cycle is to explain the large changes in employment and unemployment that occur over the cycle. We lay the groundwork for analyzing employment fluctuations by studying the labor market in the next chapter, Chapter 10.

9.5   CHAPTER SUMMARY

1. A business cycle consists of a period of declining aggregate economic activity (a contraction or recession) followed by a period of rising economic activity (an expansion or a boom). The low point of the contraction is called the trough, and the high point of the expansion is called the peak. Business cycles have been observed in market economies since the beginning of industrialization.

2. Many economic variables have regular and predictable patterns of behavior over the course of the cycle. The tendency of many economic variables to move together in a predictable way over the cycle is called comovement. We refer to the typical cyclical patterns of important macroeconomic variables as the "business cycle facts."

3. The fluctuations in aggregate economic activity that constitute business cycles are recurrent, having been observed over and over again in industrialized market economies, but they are not periodic, in that they do not occur at regular or predictable intervals. Business cycle fluctuations are also persistent, which means that once a recession or expansion begins, it usually lasts for a while.

4. The U.S. economy before 1929 is thought to have had longer recessions and more cyclical volatility than the post–World War II economy, although data problems make it hard to say precisely how much more cyclical the pre–World War I economy was. The Great Depression that began in 1929 and did not end until the onset of World War II was the most severe cyclical decline in U.S. history. Moderation of the business cycle after World War II led to premature pronouncements that the cycle was "dead." However, the U.S. economy suffered severe recessions in 1973–1975 and 1981–1982.

5. The direction of a variable relative to the business cycle can be procyclical, countercyclical, or acyclical. A procyclical variable moves in the same direction as aggregate economic activity, rising in booms and falling in recessions. A counter-

cyclical variable moves in the opposite direction of aggregate economic activity, falling in booms and rising in recessions. An acyclical variable has no clear cyclical pattern.

6. The timing of a variable relative to the business cycle can be coincident, leading, or lagging. A coincident variable has peaks and troughs occurring at about the same time as peaks and troughs in aggregate economic activity. Peaks and troughs in a leading variable come before, and peaks and troughs in a lagging variable come after, the corresponding peaks and troughs in aggregate economic activity.

7. The cyclical direction and timing of major macroeconomic variables—the business cycle facts—are summarized in Table 9.2 (p. 333). In brief, production, consumption, and investment are procyclical and coincident. Investment is much more volatile over the business cycle than consumption is. Employment is procyclical, but the unemployment rate is countercyclical. Average labor productivity and the real wage are procyclical, although the real wage is only mildly so. Money and stock prices are procyclical and lead the cycle. Inflation and nominal interest rates are procyclical and lagging. The real interest rate is acyclical.

8. The two main approaches to business cycle analysis are the classical approach and the Keynesian approach. Classicals believe that wages and prices adjust relatively quickly to balance quantities supplied and demanded; Keynesians think that wages and prices are more likely to be rigid or sticky. According to the classical approach, business cycles represent the best response of the economy to shocks in production or spending, implying that the government should not try to eliminate cycles. In contrast, Keynesians argue that because of the stickiness of wages and prices, the economy may be pushed away from full employment for a protracted period. Keynesians believe that the government can and should counteract business cycle fluctuations.

Key Terms

acyclical, p. 331
boom, p. 323
business cycle, p. 323
business cycle
    chronology, p. 322
coincident variable,
    p. 332
comovement, p. 324

contraction, p. 322
countercyclical, p. 331
depression, p. 322
expansion, p. 323
index of leading
    indicators, p. 332
lagging variable, p. 332
leading variable, p. 332

peak, p. 323
persistence, p. 326
procyclical, p. 331
recession, p. 322
stabilization policy,
    p. 348
trough, p. 322
turning point, p. 323

Review Questions

1. Draw a diagram showing the phases and turning points of a business cycle. Using the diagram, illustrate the concepts of recurrence and persistence.

2. What is *comovement?* How is comovement related to the business cycle facts presented in this chapter?

3. What is the evidence for the view that the American business cycle has become less severe over time? Why is the question of whether the cycle has moderated over time an important one?

4. What terms are used to describe the way a variable moves when economic activity is rising or falling? What terms are used to describe the timing of cyclical changes in economic variables?

5. If you knew that the economy was falling into a recession, what would you expect to be happening to production? To investment? To average labor productivity? The real wage? The unemployment rate?

6. How is the fact that some economic variables are known to lead the cycle used in macroeconomic forecasting?

7. What is the major difference in the assumptions that classicals and Keynesians make about the operation of the economy? What is the major difference in classical and Keynesian policy recommendations?

Analytical Problems

1. Expenditure on durable goods is much more sensitive to the business cycle than expenditure on nondurable goods and services. Why do you think it is?

2. Output, total hours worked, and average labor productivity are all procyclical. Which variable, output or total hours worked, increases by a larger percentage in expansions and falls by a larger percentage in recessions? (*Hint:* Average labor productivity = output ÷ total hours worked, so that the percentage change in average labor productivity equals the percentage change in output minus the percentage change in total hours worked.)

10
The Labor Market

Income earned in the labor market accounts for about three fourths of U.S. national income, or about three times as much as all other forms of income combined. For most families, wages and salaries are the primary source of income and are a major determinant of the standard of living that the family can afford.

The amount of income that workers earn, measured in real terms, depends on both the number of people employed and the average real wage that is paid. Because employment and the real wage are basic indicators of the well-being of workers, these two variables are closely watched and extensively studied by economists. Employment and wages are important to the macroeconomy even beyond their impact on the well-being of workers: For example, the level of employment, along with the capital stock and productivity, determines how much output the economy produces, and the real wage is a major factor determining the cost of that production.

Employment and the real wage are both examples of important macroeconomic variables that are determined in the labor market. Another important labor market variable is unemployment: Although the great majority of adults who want to work are able to find jobs, during even the best of times there are millions of unemployed workers in the United States. The burden of this unemployment is felt most directly by the unemployed workers and their families, of course, since they must bear the costs of lost income and uncertain economic prospects. But society as a whole also loses when there is high unemployment. For example, the slack labor market conditions associated with high unemployment typically lead to less job security and fewer promotion opportunities for those workers who remain employed. When unemployment is high, finding work is a long and difficult process, even for successful job seekers; and the job ultimately found is often less desirable than when unemployment is low. Finally, when there are fewer people working and paying taxes because of rising unemployment, the government's revenues go down at the same time that its obligations to pay unemployment insurance and other types of income support go up. Not surprisingly, unemployment is a politically sensitive issue, with the electoral fortunes of mayors, governors, or even the President often depending on the unemployment rate in their jurisdictions.

In our earlier discussions of saving, investment, international trade, and growth, we focused on equilibrium in the goods market and kept the labor market in the background. Now that we are discussing business cycles, however, fluctuations in employment and unemployment become key issues, and thus in this chapter the labor market moves to center stage. The first part of this chapter presents a more in-depth analysis of the classical model of the labor market that was introduced briefly in Chapter 3. Our focus is on the factors influencing the amount of labor that firms desire to employ (labor demand) and how much people want to work (labor supply), as well as the means by which quantities of labor demanded and supplied are made consistent with each other (labor market equilibrium). Using these concepts, we can analyze a variety of issues, such as minimum-wage policy and the effects of the 1980s tax cuts in the United States.

The simple classical model of the labor market is useful for studying the behavior of employment and the real wage and for many applications. However, this model cannot account for unemployment because it assumes that the quantities of labor demanded and supplied are always equal. In the latter part of the chapter we address the issue of unemployment by first looking at how unemployment is measured and then turning to the question of why, even in the best of times, there is always some unemployment in the economy.

10.1 THE DEMAND FOR LABOR: HOW MANY WORKERS SHOULD A FIRM HIRE?

We begin our analysis of the labor market by examining an individual firm's demand for labor. To keep things simple, we ignore differences in the skills, training, and other characteristics of workers. That is, rather than looking at the firm's separate demands for plumbers, accountants, computer programmers, and so on, we lump together all types of workers and consider only the total amount of labor that the firm wants to employ. Adding together different types of workers to obtain a single measure of labor is an example of aggregation, a procedure that we have already used a number of times in this book.

In studying labor demand, we focus on competitive firms, which view the wage as being determined by the labor market. Competitive firms therefore are not free to set the wage they must pay. For example, a competitive firm in Cleveland that wants to hire machinists knows it will have to pay the going local wage for machinists if it wants to attract qualified workers. Taking the wage as given, the firm must decide how many machinists to employ. We assume that in making this decision, the firm chooses to employ the number of machinists that enables it to earn the highest possible level of profit, just as we assumed in Chapter 6 that the firm picks the capital stock that maximizes its profit. In general, the amount of labor that maximizes the firm's profit is the firm's labor demand.

To find the amount of labor that maximizes profit, a firm compares the costs and benefits of employing additional labor. When a firm employs an additional unit of labor, it incurs a cost equal to the wage that it must pay, but it also gets the benefit of being able to sell the goods or services produced by that extra labor. As long as the benefits of an additional unit of labor (the value of the additional goods or services produced) exceed the cost of the additional labor (the wage the firm has to pay), the firm's profit will be increased by hiring the additional labor. The firm will continue to hire additional labor until the value of the extra goods or services produced by an additional unit of labor equals the wage.

The Marginal Product of Labor and Labor Demand: An Example

To make the discussion more concrete, we use the example of The Clip Joint, a small business that grooms dogs. The Clip Joint uses capital, such as clippers, tubs, and brushes, together with labor to produce its output of groomed dogs. As in

Table 10.1 The Clip Joint's Production Function

(1) Number of Dogs Groomed, Y	(2) Number of Workers, N	(3) Marginal Product of Labor, MPN	(4) **Marginal Revenue Product of Labor, $MRPN$** (when $P = \$10$ per grooming)
0	0	—	—
11	1	11	$110
20	2	9	$90
27	3	7	$70
32	4	5	$50
35	5	3	$30
36	6	1	$10

Chapter 3 (see Eq. 3.1), we assume that The Clip Joint has a production function of the form

$$Y = AF(K, N).$$

In general, the production function relates the amount of output produced Y to productivity A, the amount of capital K, and the amount of labor N. The specific production function that applies to The Clip Joint is given in Table 10.1: For given levels of productivity and the capital stock, Table 10.1 shows how The Clip Joint's daily output of groomed dogs (column 1) depends on the number of workers it employs (column 2). As you can see in the table, the more workers The Clip Joint has, the greater its daily output is.

Recall from Chapter 3 that the marginal product of labor, abbreviated MPN, is the amount of output produced per additional unit of labor, $\Delta Y/\Delta N$. The MPN of each worker at The Clip Joint is shown in column (3) of Table 10.1: Employing the first worker raises The Clip Joint's output from 0 to 11, so the MPN of the first worker is 11. Employing the second worker raises The Clip Joint's output from 11 to 20, an increase of 9, so the MPN of the second worker is 9; and so on.[1] Column (3) also shows that as the number of workers at The Clip Joint increases, the MPN falls, implying that The Clip Joint's production function has diminishing marginal returns to labor. The reason for diminishing marginal returns to labor at The Clip Joint is that the business owns a fixed number of tubs, clippers, and brushes (the capital stock is held fixed). The more workers there are on the job, the more they must share the fixed amount of equipment, and the less benefit there is to adding yet another worker.

The marginal product of labor measures the benefit of employing an additional worker in terms of the extra *output* produced. A related concept, the **marginal revenue product of labor,** abbreviated $MRPN$, measures the benefit of employing

---

[1]Here we are measuring the MPN as the extra product of an entire additional worker, and we assume that The Clip Joint must hire a whole number of workers. By considering part-time or overtime work, we could allow for fractional numbers of workers. This more general case is discussed shortly.

an additional worker in terms of the extra *revenue* produced. To calculate the *MRPN*, we need to know the price of the firm's output. If The Clip Joint receives $10 for each dog it grooms, the *MRPN* of the first worker is $110 per day (11 additional dogs groomed per day at $10 per grooming). The *MRPN* of the second worker is $90 per day (9 additional groomings per day at $10 per grooming). More generally, the marginal revenue product of an additional worker equals the price of the firm's output *P* times the extra output gained by adding the worker (the *MPN*):

$$MRPN = P \times MPN. \tag{10.1}$$

At The Clip Joint the price of output *P* is $10 per grooming, so the *MRPN* of each worker (Table 10.1, column 4) equals the *MPN* of the worker (Table 10.1, column 3) multiplied by $10.

    Now suppose that the nominal wage *W* that The Clip Joint must pay to attract qualified workers is $80 per day. How many workers should The Clip Joint employ in order to maximize its profits? To answer this question, The Clip Joint compares the benefits and costs of employing each additional worker. The benefit of employing an additional worker, in dollars per day, is the worker's marginal revenue product *MRPN*. The cost of an additional worker, in dollars per day, is the daily wage *W*.

    From Table 10.1 the *MRPN* of the first worker is $110 per day, which exceeds the daily wage of $80, so employing one worker is profitable for The Clip Joint. Adding a second worker increases The Clip Joint's profit as well, since the *MRPN* of the second worker ($90 per day) also exceeds the daily wage. However, employing a third worker is *not* profitable, because the third worker's *MRPN* of $70 per day is less than the $80 daily wage The Clip Joint would have to pay. Therefore, the profit-maximizing level of employment for The Clip Joint—equivalently, the quantity of labor demanded by The Clip Joint—is two workers.

    In finding the quantity of labor demanded by The Clip Joint, we measured the benefits and costs of adding an extra worker in nominal, or dollar, terms; but if we measured the benefits and costs of an extra worker in real terms, the results would be the same. In real terms the benefit to The Clip Joint of adding another worker is the number of extra groomings that the extra worker provides, which is the marginal product of labor (*MPN*). The real cost of adding another worker is the real wage *w*, which (recall from Chapter 3) is the nominal wage *W* divided by the price of output *P*.

    In this example the nominal wage *W* is $80 per day and the price of output *P* is $10 per grooming, so the real wage *w* equals ($80 per day) ÷ ($10 per grooming), or 8 groomings per day.[2] To find the profit-maximizing level of employment, The Clip Joint compares this real cost of an additional worker with the real benefit of an additional worker, the *MPN*. The *MPN* of the first worker is 11 groomings per day, which exceeds the real wage of 8 groomings per day, so employing this worker is profitable. The second worker also should be hired, since the second worker's *MPN* of 9 groomings per day also exceeds the real wage of 8 groomings per day. A third worker should not be hired, since the third worker's *MPN* of 7 groomings per day is less than the real wage. The quantity of labor demanded by The Clip

---

[2]Recall from Chapter 3 that the real wage is measured in units of goods per unit of labor.

Table 10.2 Summary		
Comparing the Benefits and Costs of Changing the Amount of Labor		
	To Maximize Profits, the Firm Should	
	Increase Use of Labor If	**Decrease Use of Labor If**
Real terms	$MPN > w$	$MPN < w$
Nominal terms	$MRPN > W$	$MRPN < W$

MPN = marginal product of labor
P = price of output
$MRPN$ = marginal revenue product of labor = $P \times MPN$
W = nominal wage
w = real wage = $\dfrac{W}{P}$

Joint is therefore two workers, which is the same result we got when we compared costs and benefits in nominal terms.

In this example we have shown that when the benefit of an additional worker exceeds the cost of an additional worker, the firm should increase employment in order to maximize profits. Similarly, if at the firm's current level of employment the benefit of the last worker employed is less than the cost of the worker, the firm should reduce employment. Table 10.2 summarizes the comparisons of benefits and costs of additional labor in both real and nominal terms. In the choice of the profit-maximizing level of employment, it does not matter whether benefits and costs are compared in real terms or nominal terms.

A Change in the Wage   The Clip Joint's decision to employ two workers was based on a nominal wage of $80 per day. Suppose that labor market conditions change in the city where The Clip Joint is located, so that the nominal wage needed to attract qualified workers drops to $60 per day. How will the reduction in the nominal wage affect the number of workers that The Clip Joint wants to employ?

To find the answer, we could compare costs and benefits in either nominal or real terms. Let us make the comparison in real terms: If the nominal wage drops to $60 per day while the price of groomings remains at $10, the real wage falls to ($60 per day) ÷ ($10 per grooming), or 6 groomings per day. From column (3) of Table 10.1 the MPN of the third worker is 7 groomings per day. Since the MPN for the third worker is now greater than the real wage, it is profitable for The Clip Joint to expand the quantity of labor it demands from two to three workers. However, the firm will not hire a fourth worker because the MPN of the fourth worker (5 groomings per day) is less than the real wage (6 groomings per day).

This example illustrates the general point that, all else being equal, *a decrease in the real wage raises the amount of labor demanded* by firms. Similarly, *an increase in the real wage decreases the amount of labor demanded*.

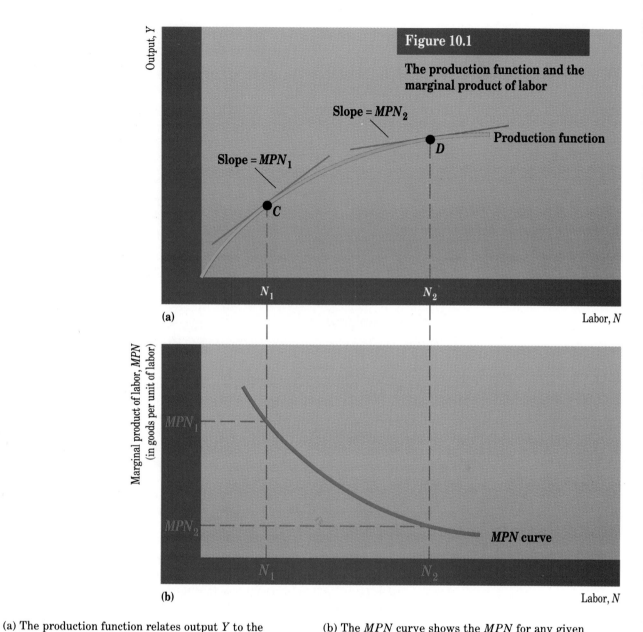

Figure 10.1

The production function and the marginal product of labor

(a) The production function relates output Y to the amount of labor employed N, with productivity and capital held constant. For any given amount of labor the MPN equals the slope of the line tangent to the production function at that amount of labor. For example, when labor equals N_1, the corresponding marginal product of labor MPN_1 is the slope of the line tangent to the production function at point C. When labor equals N_2, the marginal product of labor MPN_2 equals the slope of the line tangent to the production function at point D.

(b) The MPN curve shows the MPN for any given amount of labor. For example, when labor equals N_1, the marginal product of labor is MPN_1; and when labor equals N_2, the marginal product of labor is MPN_2, as in part (a). Because of diminishing marginal returns to labor, the MPN curve slopes downward.

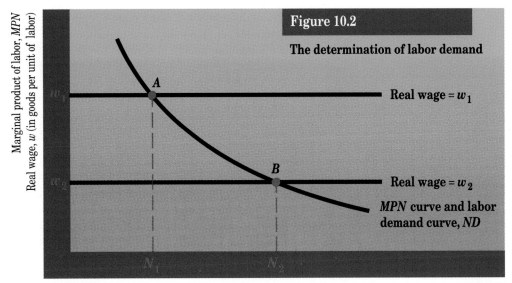

Figure 10.2

The determination of labor demand

To find the amount of labor a firm demands, locate the point at which the MPN curve intersects the real-wage line. At the amount of labor corresponding to the intersection point, the MPN equals the real wage, so that the firm's profit is maximized. For example, when the real wage is w_1, the amount of labor demanded by the firm is N_1; and when the real wage falls to w_2, the amount of labor demanded by the firm rises to N_2. The labor demand curve ND shows the amount of labor demanded at each level of the real wage; it is identical to the MPN curve.

The Marginal Product of Labor and the Labor Demand Curve

Using the example of The Clip Joint, we have shown that there is a negative relationship between the real wage and the quantity of labor that a firm demands. Figures 10.1 and 10.2 show in more general terms how the link between the real wage and the quantity of labor demanded is determined.

Figure 10.1(a) graphs a production function that relates the amount of output produced Y to the amount of labor N, with productivity A and capital K held constant. Recall from Chapter 3 that for any given level of labor N the marginal product of labor MPN can be measured as the slope of the production function at that point. Thus when N equals N_1 in Fig. 10.1(a), the marginal product of labor equals MPN_1, which is the slope of the line tangent to the production function at point C. When N equals the higher value N_2 in Fig. 10.1(a), the marginal product of labor equals MPN_2, the slope of the line tangent to the production function at point D. As we have seen before, because of diminishing marginal returns to labor, the higher labor input N is, the lower MPN is. Thus since N_2 is greater than N_1, MPN_2 is smaller than MPN_1.

Figure 10.1(b) graphs the relationship between labor N and the marginal product of labor MPN that is implied by the production function in Fig. 10.1(a). For example, we saw in Fig. 10.1(a) that when labor is N_1, the marginal product of labor is MPN_1. Thus in Fig. 10.1(b) when labor (measured on the horizontal axis) takes the value N_1, the marginal product of labor (measured on the vertical axis) equals MPN_1. Similarly, when labor equals N_2 in Fig. 10.1(b), the marginal product of labor equals MPN_2. We call the curve shown in Fig. 10.1(b) the MPN curve. Because of diminishing marginal returns to labor, which imply that MPN falls as the amount of labor N increases, the MPN curve slopes downward.

Figure 10.2 shows how to use the MPN curve to find the quantity of labor demanded, given the real wage. In this figure the amount of labor N is on the horizontal axis, and the MPN and the real wage, both of which are measured in goods per unit of labor, are on the vertical axis. The downward-sloping curve in Fig. 10.2 is the same MPN curve drawn in Fig. 10.1(b). The horizontal line in the figure represents the fixed real wage faced by firms. If we assume, for example, that the real wage has a value of w_1, then the horizontal line has height w_1.

Given that the real wage is w_1, the amount of labor that yields the firm the highest profit (and therefore the amount of labor that the firm demands) is determined at point A, the intersection of the real-wage line and the MPN curve. The amount of labor corresponding to point A in Fig. 10.2 is N_1. The firm's profit-maximizing level of labor input is N_1 because at values less than N_1, the marginal product of labor exceeds the real wage (the MPN curve lies above the real-wage line). Thus if the firm's employment is initially less than N_1, it can increase its profit by expanding the amount of labor it uses. Similarly, if the firm's employment is greater than N_1, then the marginal product of labor is less than the real wage and the firm should reduce employment.

If the real wage drops from w_1 to w_2, as shown in Fig. 10.2, the quantity of labor demanded rises from N_1 to N_2, since only when labor equals N_2 is the marginal product of labor equal to the new real wage w_2. In general, whatever the given real wage, the amount of labor demanded can be determined directly from the MPN curve: For any given real wage the amount of labor demanded corresponds to the point at which the MPN curve and the real-wage line intersect.

The graph of the relationship between the amount of labor demanded and the real wage is called the labor demand curve. Because the MPN curve also shows the amount of labor demanded at any given real wage, *the labor demand curve is the same as the MPN curve*, except that the vertical axis measures the real wage for the labor demand curve and measures the marginal product of labor for the MPN curve.[3] Like the MPN curve, the labor demand curve slopes downward, which shows that the amount of labor demanded falls as the real wage rises.

The labor demand curve that we have just derived is more general than the example of The Clip Joint in a couple of ways that are worth mentioning. First, we have referred to the demand for *labor* and not specifically to the demand for *workers*, as in The Clip Joint example. In general, labor N can be measured in various ways—for example, as total hours, weeks worked, or the number of employees, depending on the application. Second, although we assumed in the example that The Clip Joint had to hire a whole number of workers, the labor demand curve shown in Fig. 10.2 allows labor N to take any positive value, whole or fractional. Allowing N to take any value is sensible, since people can work fractions of an hour. In addition, in order to measure the MPN as the slope of the line tangent to

---

[3]Remember that the real wage and the MPN are measured in the same units, goods per unit of labor.

Table 10.3 The Clip Joint's Production Function After a Productivity Improvement

(1) Number of Dogs Groomed, Y	(2) Number of Workers, N	(3) Marginal Product of Labor, MPN	(4) Marginal Revenue Product of Labor, $MRPN$ (when $P = \$10$ per grooming)
0	0	—	—
22	1	22	$220
40	2	18	$180
54	3	14	$140
64	4	10	$100
70	5	6	$60
72	6	2	$20

the production function (as we did in Fig. 10.1), we must allow N to take fractional values, since this measure of the MPN is valid only for small changes in N.[4]

Factors That Shift the Labor Demand Curve

Since the labor demand curve shows the relation between the real wage and the amount of labor firms want to employ, changes in the real wage are represented as movements *along* the labor demand curve. Changes in the real wage do *not* cause the labor demand curve to shift. The labor demand curve shifts in response to factors that change the amount of labor that firms want to employ *at any given level of the real wage*. For example, supply shocks, which change the amount of output that can be produced with any given amount of capital and labor, will also cause the labor demand curve to shift if they affect the MPN. As we saw in Chapter 3, beneficial or positive supply shocks are likely to increase the MPN at all levels of labor input, and adverse or negative supply shocks reduce the MPN at all levels of labor input. Thus a beneficial supply shock shifts the MPN curve upward and to the right and raises the quantity of labor demanded at any given real wage; an adverse supply shock does the reverse.

To illustrate the effect of a supply shock on The Clip Joint's demand for labor, imagine that the proprietor of The Clip Joint discovers that playing New Age music soothes the dogs, makes them more cooperative, and doubles the number of groomings per day that can be produced by any given number of workers. This technological improvement gives The Clip Joint a new production function, described in Table 10.3. Notice that doubling total output doubles the MPN at any given level of employment.

The Clip Joint demanded two workers when faced with the original production function (Table 10.1) and a real wage of 8 groomings per day. From Table 10.3 you can see that the productivity improvement increases The Clip Joint's labor demand

---

[4]See Chapter 3, Section 3.2, or Appendix A, Section A.2.

A beneficial supply shock that raises the *MPN* at any amount of labor shifts the *MPN* curve (which is the same as the labor demand curve) upward and to the right (from ND^1 to ND^2). For any given real wage, after the beneficial supply shock firms will demand more labor.

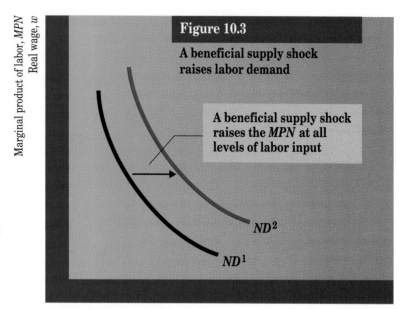

Figure 10.3

A beneficial supply shock raises labor demand

A beneficial supply shock raises the *MPN* at all levels of labor input

ND^2

ND^1

Marginal product of labor, *MPN*
Real wage, *w*

Labor, *N*

at the given real wage to four workers, because the *MPN* of the fourth worker (10 groomings per day) now exceeds the real wage but the *MPN* of the fifth worker (6 groomings per day) is less than the real wage.

The effect of a beneficial supply shock on a labor demand curve is shown in Fig. 10.3. The beneficial supply shock causes the *MPN* to increase at any level of labor, so the *MPN* curve shifts upward and to the right. But since the *MPN* curve and the labor demand curve are identical, the labor demand curve also shifts upward and to the right, from ND^1 to ND^2 in Fig. 10.3. When the labor demand curve is ND^2, the firm hires more workers at any given real wage than when the labor demand curve is ND^1.

Another factor that may affect labor demand is the size of the capital stock. Generally, we expect an increase in the capital stock K to raise the productivity of workers, increasing the *MPN* at any level of labor. In this case an increase in the capital stock will cause the labor demand curve to shift upward and to the right, raising the amount of labor that firms demand at any given real wage. However, an increase in the capital stock may *reduce* the demand for labor if the new capital substitutes for the use of labor. For example, the installation of automatic elevators reduced the marginal product of elevator operators and thus the demand for these workers.

Aggregate Labor Demand

We have so far been focusing on the demand for labor by an individual firm, such as The Clip Joint. For macroeconomic analysis, however, we usually work with the concept of the aggregate demand for labor. The aggregate demand for labor is the sum of the labor demands of all the firms in the economy.

Because the aggregate demand for labor is the sum of firms' labor demands, the factors that determine the aggregate demand for labor are the same as those that determine the demand for labor by individual firms. Thus the aggregate labor

Table 10.4 Summary		
Determinants of Aggregate Labor Demand		
An Increase in	Causes the Aggregate Quantity of Labor Demanded to	Reason
Marginal product of labor MPN	Rise	Higher MPN means that each extra unit of labor is more productive
Real wage w	Fall	Higher real wage raises the cost of each extra unit of labor
Capital stock K	Rise	A larger capital stock normally raises the marginal product of labor

demand curve looks the same as labor demand curve for an individual firm, shown in Fig. 10.2. Like the firm's labor demand curve, the aggregate labor demand curve slopes downward, showing that an increase in the economywide real wage reduces the total amount of labor that firms in the economy want to use. Similarly, the aggregate labor demand curve is shifted upward and to the right by a beneficial supply shock or an increase in the aggregate capital stock, and it is shifted downward and to the left by an adverse supply shock or a fall in the aggregate capital stock. The factors affecting aggregate labor demand are summarized in Table 10.4.

10.2 THE SUPPLY OF LABOR: THE INCOME-LEISURE TRADE-OFF

Although the demand for labor is determined by firms, the supply of labor is determined by individuals or, in some cases, by members of a family making a joint decision. Each person of working age must decide how much (if at all) to work in the wage-paying sector of the economy, as opposed to non–wage-paying alternatives such as looking after one's home and children, going to school, or being retired. The aggregate supply of labor equals the sum of the labor supplied by everyone in the economy.

Like many other economic decisions, the labor supply decision involves a balancing of benefits and costs. Aside from the psychological benefits gained from the interesting and enjoyable aspects of many jobs, the worker's principal economic benefit from working is the income that he or she earns—income that can be used to purchase goods and services for consumption or that will allow the worker to work less in the future. The worker's main cost of working is the time commitment: Hours spent at work are hours that are not available for other things the worker might like to do. The economist's term for all off-the-job activities, including eating, sleeping, working around the house, spending time with family and friends, and so on, is **leisure**.[5] The decision about how many hours of labor to supply thus boils down to a trade-off between income and leisure.

An Example: Prudence the Golf Pro

The basic elements of the labor supply decision can be illustrated by the example of a worker named Prudence.[6] Having played on the professional golf tour when she was younger, Prudence's best job opportunity is to work as a golf instructor. After paying taxes and job-related expenses, she finds that by giving golf lessons, she can earn a real income (measured in units of consumption) of 100 goods per day. Furthermore, by varying the number of students she allows to sign up for lessons, she can work anywhere from 0 to 365 days this year.

Prudence is reluctant to work too much, though, because every day she spends on the golf course means one less day available to devote to her real passion, skydiving. The decision Prudence faces is how many days to work this year—or, in other words, how much labor to supply.

Being a systematic person, Prudence approaches the question of how much to work by asking herself, "Economically speaking, what really makes me happy?" After a little reflection, she concludes that her happiness depends on the amount of goods and services she consumes (both in the present and in the future) and on the amount of leisure time she has available to jump out of airplanes (both in the present and in the future). Economists use the term *utility* to refer to an individual's economic satisfaction or well-being. Thus we can say that Prudence's utility depends on her current and future consumption and her current and future leisure. We can also recast her labor supply decision as the answer to the following question: How much should Prudence work this year in order to obtain the highest possible level of utility?

To find the level of labor supply that maximizes her utility, Prudence must compare the costs and benefits of working an extra day. The cost of an extra day of work is the loss of a day of leisure; this cost can be measured as the loss in utility that Prudence experiences when she has to work for a day instead of skydive. The benefit of working an extra day is that Prudence increases her real income by 100 goods. This increase in real income raises Prudence's utility in as many as three different ways: First, higher real income allows Prudence to consume more goods and services in the present. Second, since Prudence can save some of her earnings, she can also use the extra income to increase her consumption in the future. Finally, by earning more income today, Prudence may be able to afford to work less and thus enjoy more leisure in the future. The overall increase in utility resulting from the extra real income of 100 goods is the benefit of an extra day of work.

If the benefit of working an extra day (utility gained from extra income) exceeds the cost (utility lost by reducing leisure), then Prudence should work the extra day. In fact, she should continue to increase her time at work until the utility she receives from extra real income of 100 goods just equals the loss of utility

---

[5]In following the conventional practice of using the term *leisure* to refer to all off-the-job activities, we don't mean to imply that all of these activities (housework or schoolwork, for example) are "leisurely" in the usual sense.

[6]We saw Prudence in Chapters 5 and 6 where we studied how much of her given current income she would consume and how much she would save. In this chapter we allow her to vary her income by deciding how much to work for pay.

associated with missing a day jumping out of planes. Prudence's labor supply at that point is the one that maximizes her utility.[7]

Using the idea of labor supply as a trade-off between leisure and income, we can discuss factors influencing the amount of labor Prudence supplies.

The Effect of the Real Wage on Labor Supply

The real wage is the amount of real income that a worker receives in exchange for giving up a day (or an hour, or a week) of leisure in order to work. It is thus an important determinant of the quantity of labor that is supplied.

Generally, an increase in the real wage affects the labor supply decision in two ways: First, an increase in the real wage raises the reward (in terms of extra real income) that a worker receives for working an extra day. An increase in the benefit from working will tend to make the worker want to supply more labor. The tendency of workers to supply more labor in response to a higher reward to working is called the **substitution effect** of a higher real wage on the quantity of labor supplied.

Second, an increase in the real wage also makes workers effectively wealthier, since for any given amount of work they now earn a higher real income. Someone who is wealthier will feel less need to earn extra income and more able to afford extra leisure—and as a result, will supply less labor. The tendency of workers to supply less labor in response to being made wealthier is called the **income effect** of a higher real wage on the quantity of labor supplied. Notice that the substitution effect and the income effect of a higher real wage work in opposite directions, with the substitution effect tending to raise the quantity of labor supplied and the income effect tending to reduce it.[8]

A Pure Substitution Effect: A One-Day Rise in the Real Wage To illustrate the substitution effect, we return to the case of Prudence. Suppose that after due consideration Prudence decides to work six days per week, leaving every Wednesday free to go skydiving. She could work and earn 100 goods each Wednesday, but her highest utility is obtained by taking leisure on that day instead.

Now imagine that one Tuesday, an eccentric golf hacker calls Prudence and requests a golf lesson on Wednesday to help him prepare for a weekend amateur golf tournament. The eccentric hacker offers Prudence her regular wage of 100 goods per day, but Prudence declines, explaining that she is going skydiving on Wednesday. Not willing to take no for an answer, the hacker then offers to pay 1000 goods for an all-day lesson on Wednesday. When Prudence hears this offer to work for ten times her usual wage rate, she thinks, "I don't get offers like this every day. I'll go skydiving some other day, but this Wednesday, I'm going to work."

---

[7]Prudence's trade-off between leisure and income is conceptually similar to her trade-off between current consumption and future consumption, discussed in Chapter 5. However, because her labor supply decision actually involves a trade-off among four variables (current and future consumption, current and future leisure) rather than between two, as in Chapter 5, the labor supply decision is much more complicated to show graphically than is the saving decision. Thus we stick with an intuitive discussion.

[8]In Chapter 6 we discussed the substitution and income effects of a higher real interest rate on saving, which are very similar to the effects discussed here. As with an increase in the real wage, the substitution effect of a higher real interest rate works by increasing the reward (to saving, in that case) and the income effect works by making the saver wealthier.

Prudence's decision to work rather than skydive on this one Wednesday is a response to a very high reward, in terms of extra income, that the extra day of work will bring. Thus her decision to work the extra day is the result of the substitution effect. (This effect is called the substitution effect because it causes Prudence to substitute work for leisure.) Because receiving a very high wage for only one day does not make Prudence substantially wealthier, the income effect of the one-day wage increase is very small. Thus the effect of a one-day increase in the real wage on the quantity of labor supplied by Prudence is an almost pure example of a substitution effect.

A Pure Income Effect: A Gift   By the next week Prudence has forgotten all about the eccentric hacker. But then she hears that through a series of improbable events he managed to win his amateur tournament. Furthermore, in his gratitude he sends Prudence a check worth 30,000 goods, nearly a year's pay. Prudence's response is to reduce the amount she works from six days a week to five days a week.

Why did Prudence reduce the quantity of labor she supplied when she received the unexpected gift? As we have said, Prudence treasures the time she spends skydiving. She would spend all of her time jumping if she did not have to work in order to be able to afford food, clothes, rent, and skydiving trips. But given her circumstances, she skydives only on Wednesdays and works the rest of the time. However, when the large check arrives, suddenly she can afford to take more time off from work, and so she does. Because the gift made her wealthier, she reduces her labor supply. This is an example of a pure income effect.

The Substitution Effect and the Income Effect Together: A Long-Term Increase in the Real Wage   Some weeks following her windfall, Prudence receives a call from a country club across town offering her a long-term position as the resident golf pro. She will receive a wage of 200 goods per day, or twice her previous wage, and she will continue to be free to set the number of days she works. Prudence accepts the offer immediately.

Once she is at her new job, will Prudence work more days or fewer days than she did before? Now there are effects working in both directions. On the one hand, because the reward to working is greater, she will be tempted to work more than at her previous job. (If she earns enough, perhaps someday she can buy her own plane for skydiving.) This tendency to increase labor supply in response to a higher real wage is the substitution effect. On the other hand, at double her original wage Prudence can pay for food, rent, and skydiving expenses by working only three or four days a week, which inclines her to work less and spend more time skydiving. This tendency to reduce labor supply because she is wealthier is the income effect.

Which effect wins? One factor that will influence Prudence's decision is the length of time she expects her new, higher wage to last. The longer the higher wage is expected to last, the larger the impact is on Prudence's lifetime resources, and the stronger the income effect is. Thus if Prudence expects to hold the new job until she retires, the income effect is strong (she is effectively much wealthier) and she is more likely to reduce the amount she works. If Prudence thinks the job may not last very long, then the income effect is weak (the increase in her lifetime resources is small) and she may choose to work more in order to take advantage of the higher wage while she can. In general, the longer an increase in the real wage is expected to last, the larger the income effect is and the more likely it is that the quantity of labor supplied will be reduced.

Table 10.5 Effect of Real-Wage Changes on the Quantity of Labor Supplied

	Temporary Increase in the Real Wage	Permanent Increase in the Real Wage
Male labor supply	Small increase	Decrease
Female labor supply	Large increase	Increase
Aggregate labor supply	Small increase	Decrease

Empirical Evidence on Real Wages and Labor Supply Because of conflicting income and substitution effects, there is some ambiguity in how a given real-wage change will affect labor supply. Thus it is useful to know what the empirical evidence says about the relationship between the real wage and labor supply.

In his book on labor supply Mark Killingsworth[9] of Rutgers University surveyed the results of more than sixty studies of the labor supply decision in the United States, the United Kingdom, Canada, West Germany, Japan, and Taiwan. Although the studies differed on many dimensions and did not all yield the same findings, a few general conclusions are summarized in Table 10.5. This table presents empirical findings for men and women separately because important differences were found between male and female labor supply behavior. The results for aggregate labor supply combine the labor supplies of both men and women. The aggregate results look like the results for men rather than the results for women because in the countries studied more men than women supply labor in the wage-paying sector.

As shown in Table 10.5, the studies surveyed by Killingsworth generally found that the aggregate amount of labor supplied rises in response to a temporary increase in the real wage but falls in response to a permanent increase in the real wage. The finding that a temporary increase in the real wage raises the amount of labor supplied is an empirical confirmation of the substitution effect: If the reward to working rises for a short period, people will take advantage of the opportunity to work more. The result that a permanent increase in the real wage lowers the aggregate amount of labor supplied tells us that for very long-lived increases in the real wage the income effect outweighs the substitution effect: If higher wages cause workers to become permanently better off, they will choose to work less.

The differences between the labor supply responses of men and women shown in Table 10.5 reflect the fact that labor supply is often a family decision that depends on family circumstances. For example, although gender roles have changed dramatically in the past two decades, families in which the husband's job provides most of the family income and in which the wife works part-time or not at all in the wage-paying sector remain fairly common. In a family with this structure the husband will typically want to work full-time most of the time and will not be responsive to temporary wage changes—although he may reduce the amount of labor he supplies (for example, by retiring earlier) if the real wage rises permanently. These responses are consistent with the results for male labor supply in Table 10.5.

---

[9]*Labor Supply*, Cambridge, England: Cambridge University Press, 1983. See especially Tables 3.1 through 3.5 and 4.2 through 4.4.

In contrast, depending on factors like the ages of the children and economic necessity, the wife may have more flexibility to choose when she wants to be in the labor market. Presumably she will be more likely to choose to work outside the home when opportunities are good and real wages are high, so that the quantity of labor she supplies will be responsive to temporary changes in the real wage, as suggested by Table 10.5. The positive response of female labor supply to permanent increases in the real wage shown in the table suggests that as job opportunities for women improve, more women elect to pursue careers rather than stay at home.

An interesting additional finding, obtained in several studies, is that the typical person's labor supply falls when the wage of his or her spouse rises. This finding makes sense: When one spouse earns more, his or her partner can afford to spend more time at home or in other activities outside of the labor market.

Application

Weekly Hours of Work and the Wealth of Nations

In 1869 the typical worker in the U.S. manufacturing sector worked about 56 hours per week. However, as shown in Fig. 10.4, the average workweek in U.S. manufacturing declined steadily into the 1930s. Although various forces contributed to the shortening of the workweek before 1930, the major reason was sharply rising

The steady increase in the real wage in the United States during the late nineteenth and early twentieth centuries tended to reduce the average weekly hours of manufacturing workers because of the income effect on labor supply. Weekly hours fluctuated sharply during the Depression and World War II but stabilized in the postwar period. *Note:* Data were available only for selected years prior to 1919.

Source: Average weekly hours, production workers in manufacturing establishments: Bureau of Economic Analysis, *Long-Term Economic Growth 1860–1970*, June 1973, pp. 212–213; and *Employment and Earnings*, Table C-1, various issues.

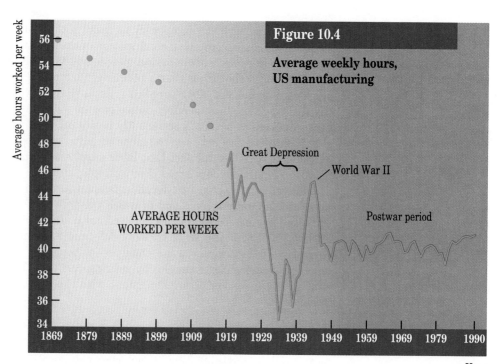

Figure 10.4

Average weekly hours, US manufacturing

Great Depression

World War II

AVERAGE HOURS WORKED PER WEEK

Postwar period

Year

The point corresponding to each country shows the country's real GDP per person in 1980 on the horizontal axis and the average number of hours worked per week in manufacturing on the vertical axis. Because of the income effect on labor supply, richer countries tend to have shorter workweeks.

Source: Average hours per week—*United Nations Statistical Yearbook*, 1985/86, p. 89; real GDP per capita (in 1975 dollars) Robert Summers and Alan Heston, "Improved International Comparisons of Real Product and its Components: 1950–1980," *Review of Income and Wealth*, June 1984, pp. 259–261.

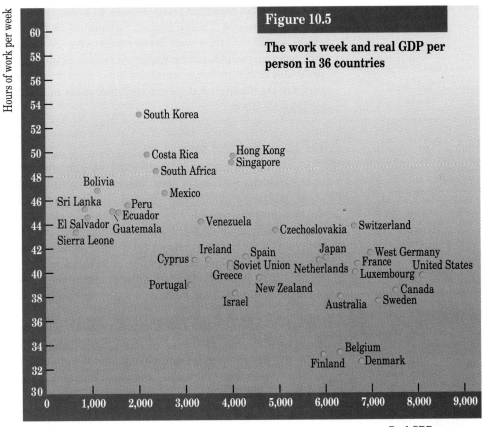

Figure 10.5

The work week and real GDP per person in 36 countries

real wages. Increases in real wages over the late nineteenth and early twentieth centuries in the United States were driven by technological innovation and increased productivity and thus were largely permanent. In response to permanent increases in the real wage, workers reduced the amount of labor they supplied.

The response of labor supply to increases in real wages does not explain all of the changes in weekly hours worked shown in Fig. 10.4. For example, the relatively low number of hours worked per week during the 1930s reflects primarily the general economic collapse that occurred during the Great Depression; and the sharp increase in weekly hours of work during the 1940s was due in part to the threat to national survival posed by World War II, which induced workers to work more hours per week. Since World War II the workweek in U.S. manufacturing has stabilized at around forty hours, with little decline despite increases in the real wage in the 1950s and 1960s. However, since World War II workers have reduced the quantities of labor supplied along other dimensions, notably by retiring earlier and taking more vacation time.

The historical data in Fig. 10.4 provide some evidence that in response to a permanent increase in the real wage, workers choose to have more leisure and to work fewer hours per week. Figure 10.5 presents additional evidence, drawn from thirty-six nations. Each point in the diagram represents a different country. The horizontal axis measures real gross domestic product (GDP) per person, and the vertical axis measures the average number of hours worked per week by production workers in manufacturing. Figure 10.5 shows that workers in richer countries with higher wages (United States, Canada) work fewer hours per week than workers in poorer countries with lower wage rates (South Korea, Bolivia). Because the differences in wages among countries reflect long-term differences in productivity, the result that high-wage countries have shorter workweeks provides further support for the finding that permanent increases in the real wage cause workers to supply less labor.

The Labor Supply Curve

The labor supply curve of an individual worker relates the amount of labor supplied to the *current* real wage, with other factors, including the expected future real wage, taken as given. Figure 10.6 graphs a typical labor supply curve. In the figure the current real wage is measured on the vertical axis, and the amount of labor supplied is measured on the horizontal axis. An increase in the current real wage with no change in the expected future real wage is the same thing as a temporary increase in the real wage. Both theory and empirical analysis confirm that, because of the substitution effect, a temporary increase in the real wage raises the quantity of labor supplied. Thus the labor supply curve slopes upward from left to right.

Factors That Shift the Labor Supply Curve

Any factor that changes the amount of labor supplied at a given current real wage shifts the labor supply curve. We discuss the effects on labor supply of changes in wealth, the future real wage, and fiscal variables such as government purchases and the income tax rate.

The labor supply curve of an individual worker shows the amount of labor that the worker will supply at any given current real wage. With the future real wage held constant, an increase in the current real wage increases the amount of labor supplied. Therefore the labor supply curve slopes upward.

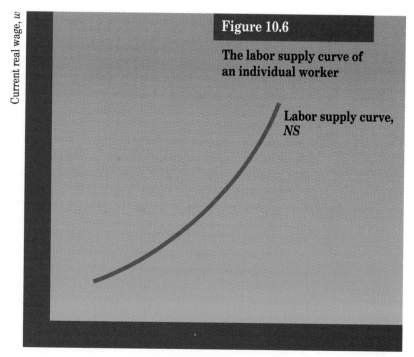

Current real wage, w

Figure 10.6

The labor supply curve of an individual worker

Labor supply curve, *NS*

Labor, N

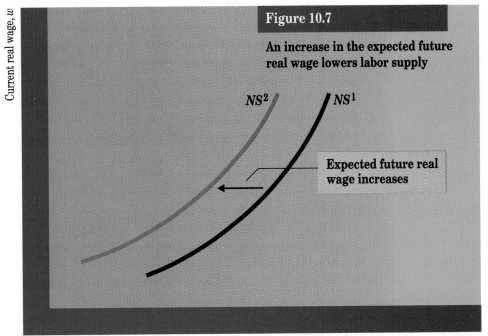

Figure 10.7

An increase in the expected future real wage lowers labor supply

NS^2 NS^1

Expected future real wage increases

Current real wage, w

Labor, N

An increase in the expected future real wage, with the current real wage constant, makes workers wealthier. The income effect on labor supply reduces the amount of labor supplied at any given value of the current real wage. Thus the labor supply curve shifts to the left, from NS^1 to NS^2.

Wealth   In the example of Prudence, recall that when she received the gift from the grateful amateur golfer, she decided to work less because of the income effect. In general, when the wealth of an individual rises, she can afford to earn less income and take more leisure. Thus an increase in wealth reduces labor supply at any given real wage and shifts the labor supply curve to the left.

The Expected Future Real Wage   An increase in the real wage that a worker expects to receive in the future makes her effectively wealthier[10] and thus has an income effect that reduces her labor supply. An increase in the future real wage does not affect the reward for working today and thus does not have a substitution effect on the current amount of labor supplied. Because there is only an income effect, the amount of labor currently supplied will decline at any given current real wage. Thus an increase in the expected future real wage causes the labor supply curve to shift to the left, as shown in Fig. 10.7.

Figure 10.8 illustrates the effect of a *permanent* increase in the real wage, which can be thought of as an increase in the current real wage *plus* an equal-sized increase in the future real wage. Suppose that, initially, the current and future real wage are equal to w_A and the amount of labor supplied is N_A, as represented by point A on the labor supply curve NS^1 in Fig. 10.8. If the real wage increases permanently to w_B, then both the current real wage and the future real wage increase to w_B. The increase in the future real wage causes the labor supply curve to shift left to NS^2, as in Fig. 10.7. The increase in the current real wage leads to a movement *upward along* the new labor supply curve to point B, where the current real wage is w_B and the amount of labor supplied is N_B. Thus the overall effect of

---

[10]If you covered Chapter 5, you recognize that an increase in expected future labor income raises the worker's present value of lifetime resources.

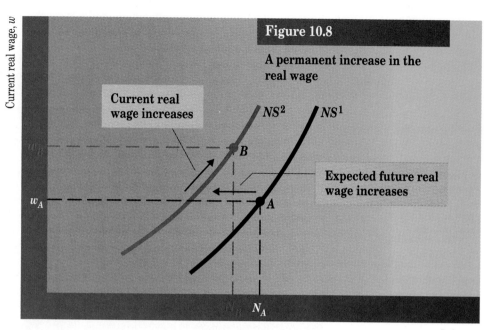

Figure 10.8

A permanent increase in the real wage

Initially, both the current and future real wage equal w_A, and the labor supply curve is NS^1. The amount of labor supplied is N_A. A permanent increase in the real wage increases both the current real wage and the future real wage to w_B. The increase in the future real wage shifts the labor supply curve to the left, from NS^1 to NS^2. The increase in the current real wage is represented as a movement upward along the new labor supply curve NS^2 to point B, where the current real wage is w_B and the amount of labor supplied is N_B. The overall effect of the permanent increase in the real wage is to reduce the amount of labor supplied from N_A to N_B.

the permanent increase in the real wage is to reduce the quantity of labor supplied from N_A to N_B.

The result shown in Fig. 10.8—that a permanent increase in the real wage lowers the quantity of labor supplied—is consistent with the empirical findings for men and for aggregate labor supply (Table 10.5). For women the empirical result is that a permanent increase in the real wage raises the quantity of labor supplied. Analytical Problem 4 asks you to redraw Fig. 10.8 to show the case in which a permanent increase in the real wage leads to an overall increase in the quantity of labor supplied.

Government Purchases Economists have claimed that increases in the level of government purchases will increase labor supply. The argument is somewhat subtle. To understand the idea, suppose that the government increases its current purchases while holding future purchases unchanged. These extra purchases must be paid for somehow, so suppose for simplicity that the government also imposes a current lump-sum tax increase equal to the increase in government purchases. A lump-sum tax increase is one in which each person's taxes are increased by a fixed amount that does not depend on the person's income, consumption, or other characteristics. We explain in a moment why the lump-sum assumption is important.

How will workers react to this fiscal package? Since workers are also taxpay-

**Table 10.6 Marginal and Average Tax Rates: An Example
(Total Tax = 25% of Income over $10,000)**

Income	Income − $10,000	Tax	Average Tax Rate	Marginal Tax Rate
$ 18,000	$ 8,000	$ 2,000	11.1%	25%
50,000	40,000	10,000	20.0%	25%
100,000	90,000	22,500	22.5%	25%

ers, they will find that they have been made poorer by the increase in government purchases and the associated increase in taxes. Thus there will be an income effect on labor supply: In response to the increase in government purchases, workers will supply more labor at any given current real wage, and the labor supply curve will shift to the right.

Our example raises two questions: First, what if, instead of raising current taxes, the government simply pays for its extra purchases by borrowing from the public? It turns out that borrowing by the government does not change the result that increased government purchases raise labor supply: The reason is that, ultimately, the government must repay what it borrows with interest, so borrowing today does not avoid a tax increase entirely but only puts it off until the future.[11] If the taxpayers recognize that their tax obligations have been deferred but not avoided, and that the debt of the government is ultimately theirs to repay, then they will still feel poorer when government purchases rise even if current taxes don't go up. Thus, again, the increase in government purchases will increase labor supply.

The second question raised by our example is, What if taxes are increased, but not in a lump-sum manner? If tax changes are not lump-sum changes, then the fiscal package may have a substitution effect as well as an income effect on labor supply. This point is discussed next.

Income Taxes   We have just seen that an increase in government purchases accompanied by a lump-sum tax increase shifts the labor supply curve to the right. However, most taxes are not lump-sum taxes but, instead, are levied as a percentage of income, sales, profits, and so on. We focus here on taxes levied on individuals' income.

In analyzing the effect of income taxes on labor supply, we must distinguish between average and marginal tax rates. The **average tax rate** is the total amount of taxes paid by a person divided by the person's income. The **marginal tax rate** is the fraction of an additional dollar of income that must be paid in taxes. To illustrate the distinction between average and marginal tax rates, suppose that no taxes are levied on the first $10,000 of income, and a 25% tax is levied on all income above $10,000. As shown in Table 10.6, under this income tax system a person with an income of $18,000 pays a tax of $2000. Thus her average tax rate is 11.1% ($2000 in taxes divided by $18,000 in before-tax income). However, this taxpayer's marginal tax rate is 25%, because a $1.00 increase in her income will increase her taxes

---

[11]This is the idea of the government budget constraint, discussed in Chapter 6.

by $0.25. In Table 10.6 you can see that everyone with an income higher than $10,000 faces the same marginal tax rate of 25%, but that the average tax rate increases with income.

We make the distinction between average and marginal tax rates because the effects on labor supply of changes in the two types of tax rates differ. Put briefly, *a change in the average tax rate, with the marginal tax rate held constant, has only an income effect on labor supply.* In contrast, *a change in the marginal tax rate, with the average tax rate held constant, has only a substitution effect on labor supply.*

To explain these points, we first consider the effects of a change in the average tax rate. Returning to our example in Table 10.6, imagine that the marginal tax rate stays at 25%, but now all income over $8000 (rather than all income over $10,000) is subject to a 25% tax. The taxpayer with income of $18,000 finds that her tax bill has risen from $2000 to $2500 (25% of $18,000 minus $8000), so her average tax rate has risen from 11.1% to 13.9% ($2500 divided by $18,000). How will the increase in the average tax rate affect the taxpayer's labor supply? There is a pure income effect: The taxpayer is $500 poorer (her taxes have risen from $2000 to $2500). Being poorer, the taxpayer will increase her labor supply, just as in the case of a lump-sum tax increase (which is equivalent to an increase in the average tax rate with no change in the marginal tax rate). As we claimed, with the marginal tax rate held constant, a change in the average tax rate has only an income effect on labor supply, with higher average taxes raising labor supply and lower average taxes reducing labor supply.

Now consider the effects of an increase in the marginal tax rate. Suppose that the marginal tax rate on income in our example is raised from 25% to 40%. From the viewpoint of the taxpayer this increase amounts to a reduction in the (after-tax) wage rate that she can earn. For example, when the marginal tax rate is 25%, a worker whose before-tax wage is $20 per hour gets to keep $15 for every extra hour that she works, with $5 (25% of $20) going to the government. When the marginal tax rate rises to 40%, the worker gets to keep only $12 for every extra hour that she works, with $8 (40% of $20) going to the government.

Since a change in the marginal tax rate affects the after-tax real wage earned by workers, we would expect it to have both a substitution effect and an income effect, just as any change in the wage does. However, suppose that the marginal tax rate change is accompanied by other changes in the tax law that keep the average tax rate—and thus the total amount of taxes paid by the typical taxpayer—unchanged. To illustrate, suppose that in our example of Table 10.6 the increase in the marginal tax rate from 25% to 40% is accompanied by an increase in the portion of income not subject to tax, from $10,000 to $13,000. Then for the taxpayer earning $18,000 total taxes are $2000 (40% of $18,000 minus $13,000), and the average tax rate of 11.1% ($2000 divided by $18,000) is the same as it was under the initial tax schedule shown in Table 10.6.

With the average tax rate unchanged, the taxpayer pays the same total taxes as before at the initial level of income, and thus the income effect is eliminated. Consequently, only a substitution effect is left for a marginal tax rate change. Thus, as we said, with the average tax rate held constant, a change in the marginal tax rate has only a substitution effect on labor supply. In particular, an increase in marginal tax rates with no change in average tax rates reduces the reward for working and thus reduces labor supply, and a cut in marginal tax rates with no change in average tax rates raises labor supply.

Table 10.7 Average Tax Rates in the United States, 1981–1988

Year	Federal Taxes		Federal, State, and Local Taxes	
	Real Tax Revenue (Billions of 1982 Dollars)	Average Tax Rate (% of GNP)	Real Tax Revenue (Billions of 1982 Dollars)	Average Tax Rate (% of GNP)
1981	680.3	20.9	1039.6	32.0
1982	635.3	20.1	1000.8	31.6
1983	635.1	19.4	1021.5	31.2
1984	674.1	19.2	1089.0	31.1
1985	711.2	19.6	1145.9	31.7
1986	727.5	19.6	1184.0	31.8
1987	776.3	20.1	1247.8	32.4
1988	801.6	19.9	1288.3	32.0

Application

Labor Supply and Tax Reform in the 1980s

Twice during the 1980s the U.S. Federal government passed major tax reform legislation that dramatically reduced marginal tax rates. At the beginning of the decade the highest marginal tax rate on any form of income was 70% and the highest marginal tax rate on labor income was 50%. The Economic Recovery Tax Act of 1981 (known as ERTA) reduced personal income tax rates in three stages, with a complete phasein by 1984.[12] The Tax Reform Act of 1986 further reduced personal tax rates. By the end of the 1980s the marginal tax rate on the highest levels of personal income had fallen to 28%.[13]

ERTA, the tax act passed in 1981, was championed by a group of economists, politicians, and journalists who favored an approach to economic policy called supply-side economics. The basic tenet of **supply-side economics** is that all aspects of economic behavior—such as labor supply, saving, and investment—respond to economic incentives, in particular, to incentives provided by the tax code. Although most economists agree with this idea, supporters of supply-side economics have gone further in claiming that the incentive effects of tax policy are much larger than economists have traditionally believed. In particular, the supply-siders argued that the amount of labor supplied would increase substantially as a result of the tax reductions in ERTA. (One strong implication of this supply-sider claim was that a cut in tax rates could conceivably lead to an increase in the tax revenues collected by the government; see Box 10.1, p. 377.)

To see what the theory of labor supply predicts about the response of labor supply to ERTA, we need to examine what happened to both marginal tax rates and average tax rates. We have already said that marginal tax rates were sharply reduced after 1981. As you can see in Table 10.7, the average tax rate also fell after

[12]For a description of ERTA, see the *Economic Report of the President*, February 1982.

[13]However, because of a quirk in the tax law, some people with relatively high income, but not those with the highest levels of income, faced a 33% marginal tax rate.

1981. Between 1981 and 1984 Federal taxes fell from 20.9% of GNP to 19.2% of GNP, and the taxes collected by all levels of government combined (Federal, state, and local governments) fell from 32.0% of GNP to 31.1% of GNP. Our theory suggests that the reduction in marginal tax rates should have increased labor supply, while the decline in average tax rates should have reduced labor supply, leading to an ambiguous and probably small effect overall.[14]

What actually happened to the amount of labor supplied after the 1981 tax change? One way that economists measure the amount of labor supplied is by the labor force participation rate, which is the fraction of adults who are working or actively searching for jobs. The labor force participation rate did not change noticeably after 1981, so it seems that any effect of ERTA on labor supply was small.

The 1986 Tax Reform Act also reduced the marginal tax rate on labor income, but unlike ERTA, it left the average tax rate essentially unchanged. To see the effect on the average tax rate, we compare the data for 1986 and 1988. (We skip 1987 because the tax changes did not become fully effective until 1988.) Table 10.7 shows that the average Federal tax rate rose slightly between 1986 and 1988, rather than falling as it did after ERTA. The average tax rate of Federal, state, and local governments combined also rose slightly.

Because the marginal tax rate was reduced and the average tax rate slightly increased by the 1986 Tax Reform Act, the result should have been an increase in labor supply. There is some evidence that this increase in labor supply occurred: For example, the labor force participation rate for men had been gradually decreasing since at least 1950. However, the labor force participation rate for men leveled off in 1988 and actually increased in 1989 for the first time in more than a decade.

Overall, the responses of labor supply to the revisions in the tax law that occurred in the 1980s are consistent with our analysis of the effects of average and marginal tax changes. However, we emphasize again that the changes in labor supply that occurred were small. For example, one study estimated that the Tax Reform Act of 1986 increased labor supply of men by 0.9%, and the 1981 ERTA increased the labor supply of men by only 0.4%.[15] This small response of labor supply contradicts the supply-siders' claim that the tax changes would have a dramatic effect on economic behavior.

Aggregate Labor Supply

As we mentioned earlier, the aggregate supply of labor is the total amount of labor supplied by everyone in the economy. The aggregate labor supply curve, which shows the relation between the aggregate amount of labor supplied and the current real wage, slopes upward, because an increase in the current real wage increases the total amount of labor supplied. Higher current real wages raise aggregate labor supply for two reasons: First, when the real wage rises, people who are already working may supply even more hours—for example, by offering to work overtime, by changing from part-time work to full-time work, or by taking on a second job. Second, a higher real wage may entice some people who are not currently working

---

[14]Technical note: Supporters of the Ricardian equivalence idea (Chapter 6), who point out that the real cost of government is measured by what the government actually spends rather than by current taxes, might argue that the average tax burden should be measured as the ratio of government purchases to GNP rather than the ratio of actual taxes collected to GNP. We ignore this complication here.

[15]Jerry A. Hausman and James M. Poterba, "Household Behavior and the Tax Reform Act of 1986," *Journal of Economic Perspectives*, Summer 1987, pp. 101–119. Cited results are from p. 106.

BOX *10.1:* THE LAFFER CURVE

When supply-side economists suggested reducing tax rates in the early 1980s, many economists worried that a tax cut would increase the Federal government's budget deficit. However, advocates of supply-side economics dismissed this worry by arguing that by stimulating labor supply, a tax cut might actually *increase* the government's tax revenue. Because tax revenue equals the (average) tax rate multiplied by the income that is taxed, a reduction in the tax rate could increase tax revenue if, in response to the tax cut, income earned rose by a sufficiently large amount.

The possibility that a cut in tax rates would increase tax revenue was popularized by Arthur Laffer, who first sketched the relation between the tax rate and tax revenue—the Laffer curve—on a cocktail napkin. The accompanying figure shows the Laffer curve: In the figure the income tax rate* t is measured along the horizontal axis and the amount of income tax revenue T is measured along the vertical axis. The tax rate $\hat{t}$, corresponding to the peak of the Laffer curve, is the maximum-revenue tax rate. For tax rates lower than $\hat{t}$ the Laffer curve slopes upward, indicating that higher tax rates lead to higher total tax revenue. However, for tax rates higher than $\hat{t}$ the Laffer curve slopes downward, implying that an increase in the tax rate leads to a *reduction* in tax revenue. (Equivalently, when the tax rate is initially above $\hat{t}$, a cut in the tax rate increases tax revenue.) The reason that increases in the tax rate above $\hat{t}$ reduce total revenue collected is that people respond to very high tax rates by working less (or working in the untaxed, "underground" sector; see Chapter 2). Thus although the tax rate is higher, there is less income to tax, and total tax collections fall. Note that according to the Laffer curve, when t equals 100%, no revenues at all are collected; with 100% tax rates no one would have any incentive to earn taxable income and so revenues would be zero.

Whether tax revenue rises or falls when the tax rate is reduced depends on whether the initial tax rate is higher or lower than the maximum-revenue tax rate $\hat{t}$. In a careful study of this question Don Fullerton* (now at the University of Virginia) calculated that $\hat{t}$ in the United States was about 79%, more than twice as high as the tax rate facing the average American in 1981. Because the actual tax rate was so much lower than $\hat{t}$, the economy was on the upward-sloping portion of the Laffer curve, and a decrease in the tax rate should have reduced tax revenue.

Our analysis of labor supply in this chapter also suggests that tax revenue will fall when the tax rate is reduced. In order for tax revenue to increase when the tax rate is reduced, labor supply would have to increase substantially in response to the increase in the after-tax real wage. However, the empirical evidence suggests a relatively weak response of the aggregate quantity of labor supplied to an increase in the real wage. Indeed, if the tax cut is permanent, so that the after-tax real wage is permanently increased, the amount of labor supplied might even fall in response to the tax cut, if the income effect outweighs the substitution effect.

Table 10.7 shows what actually happened to real Federal tax revenues after the tax cuts of 1981. Between 1981 and 1982 real Federal tax revenues fell by more than 6%, and they remained below their 1981 level in 1983 and 1984. Although real Federal tax revenue in 1985 exceeded its 1981 level, there is no evidence that actual Federal tax revenue in 1985 was higher than it would have been without the 1981 tax cut.

*"On the Possibility of an Inverse Relationship Between Tax Rates and Government Revenues," *Journal of Public Economics*, February 1982, pp. 3–22.

*For simplicity, we assume that taxes are proportional to income, so tax revenues T equal tY, where t is the tax rate and Y is income. In this case t is both the average tax rate and the marginal tax rate.

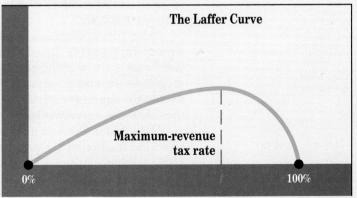

The Laffer Curve

Income tax revenue, T

Maximum-revenue tax rate

0% $\hat{t}$ 100%

Income tax rate, t

Table 10.8 Summary

Determinants of Aggregate Labor Supply

An Increase In	Causes the Aggregate Quantity of Labor Supplied to	Reason
Current real wage w	Rise	Higher current real wage increases the reward for working
Wealth	Fall	Higher wealth makes workers able to afford more leisure
Expected future real wage	Fall	Higher expected future real wage makes workers wealthier and able to work less
Government purchases G	Rise	Higher government purchases raise tax burdens and make workers poorer, inducing them to work more
Average tax rate	Rise	Higher average tax burdens make workers poorer, inducing them to work more
Marginal tax rate	Fall	Higher marginal tax rate reduces after-tax real wage, lowering the reward for working
Working-age population	Rise	More people are available to supply labor

to enter the labor force; that is, a higher real wage may lead to increased labor force participation.

Table 10.8 summarizes the determinants of aggregate labor supply. We have already discussed the first six factors in our analysis of individual labor supply. The last factor is the working-age population: An increase in a country's working-age population (occurring, perhaps, because of a higher birth rate or immigration) increases the aggregate amount of labor supplied at any given current real wage and thus shifts the aggregate labor supply curve to the right.

Not listed in Table 10.8 are a variety of other social and legal factors that may affect the fraction of the population working in the wage-paying sector. For example, evolving attitudes about the role of women in society contributed to a large increase in the number of women in the U.S. labor market during the 1970s and 1980s. Similarly, legislative restrictions on mandatory retirement policies may increase the labor supply of older people.

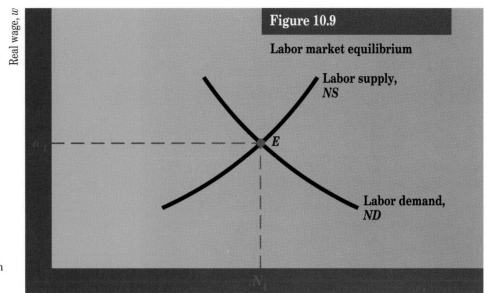

Figure 10.9

Labor market equilibrium

The figure graphs aggregate labor supply *NS* and aggregate labor demand *ND*. At the equilibrium real wage w_1 the quantity of labor demanded equals the quantity of labor supplied (point *E*). The equilibrium level of employment is shown as N_1.

10.3 LABOR MARKET EQUILIBRIUM

Labor demand and labor supply both depend on the current real wage, but what determines the current real wage? The classical answer to this question is that the real wage is determined by the forces of demand and supply in the labor market.

Figure 10.9 graphs the aggregate labor demand curve *ND* and the aggregate labor supply curve *NS* in the same diagram. The equilibrium (or market-clearing) real wage is the real wage at which the quantity of labor supplied equals the quantity of labor demanded. In Fig. 10.9 the equilibrium real wage is w_1, and the corresponding equilibrium level of employment[16] is N_1. As we discussed in Chapter 3, the labor market is driven toward equilibrium by the forces of competition: If the real wage is higher than w_1, the quantity of labor supplied exceeds the quantity of labor demanded, and competition among workers for available jobs will cause the real wage to fall. If the real wage is lower than w_1, the quantity of labor demanded exceeds the quantity supplied, and competition among firms to attract workers will bid up the real wage.

Factors that shift either the aggregate labor demand curve or the aggregate labor supply curve affect both the equilibrium real wage and the level of employment. An important example, which will play a major role in our discussion of classical business cycle theory, is a temporary adverse supply shock. (This case was studied in Chapter 3; see Fig. 3.6.) A temporary adverse supply shock—for example, owing to a spell of unusually bad weather—decreases the marginal product of labor at every level of employment. As shown in Fig. 10.10, this decrease causes the labor demand curve to shift to the left, from ND^1 to ND^2. Because the

---

[16]We refer to *N* as employment, but *N* could also stand for some other measure of labor input, such as total hours worked.

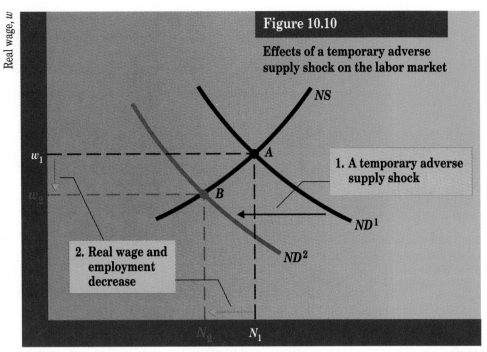

Real wage, w

Figure 10.10

Effects of a temporary adverse supply shock on the labor market

NS

w_1

A

1. A temporary adverse supply shock

B

w_2

ND^1

2. Real wage and employment decrease

ND^2

N_2 N_1

Labor, N

A temporary adverse supply shock reduces the marginal product of labor at every level of employment and causes the labor demand curve to shift downward and left, from ND^1 to ND^2. Because the supply shock is temporary, the expected future real wage does not change, and the labor supply curve does not shift. Labor market equilibrium moves from point A to point B. The real wage decreases from w_1 to w_2, and employment decreases from N_1 to N₂.

supply shock is temporary, it does not affect expected future real wages, so the labor supply curve does not shift. Equilibrium in the labor market moves from point A to point B in Fig. 10.10, with the real wage falling from w_1 to w_2 and employment falling from N_1 to N_2. A temporary adverse supply shock reduces the real wage by reducing worker productivity and thus the real wage that firms are willing to pay. Employment falls because at the lower current real wage fewer workers want to supply labor.

The classical supply-equals-demand model of the labor market has the virtue of simplicity and is useful for analyzing fluctuations in employment and the real wage. However, as we discussed in Chapter 3, a significant drawback of this model is that it cannot be used to study unemployment: Since this model assumes that any worker who wants to work at the equilibrium real wage can find a job, taken literally the model implies zero unemployment, which we never observe.

One way to get unemployment into the model is to drop the assumption that the real wage adjusts rapidly to equate supply and demand. The assumption that the real wage is slow to adjust underlies the Keynesian approach, discussed in Chapter 12. A variation on this theme, analyzed in "The Policy Debate" box (p. 384), is that a legislated minimum wage could prevent firms from paying workers the market-clearing wage rate, thereby causing unemployment.

An alternative way to extend the model of the labor market so that it can explain unemployment is to recognize that the process of matching unemployed workers with appropriate available jobs is not immediate but takes time. Because matching workers with jobs takes time, at any given moment there will be some workers without jobs. We discuss the matching process in the next section, after we look at some basic facts about unemployment.

10.4   UNEMPLOYMENT

Unemployment was one of the major macroeconomic issues introduced in Chapter 1. We are now ready to take our first look at this important problem. We begin by presenting the basic facts about unemployment, and then we discuss why there are always some people who are unemployed.

Measuring Unemployment

In order to estimate the unemployment rate in the United States, each month the Bureau of Labor Statistics (BLS) surveys about 60,000 households. Each person over sixteen in the surveyed households is assigned to one of three categories:

1. *Employed*, if the person worked full-time or part-time during the past week (or was on sick leave or vacation from a job).

2. *Unemployed*, if the person did not work during the past week but looked for work during the past four weeks.

3. *Not in the labor force*, if the person did not work during the past week and did not look for work during the past four weeks (examples are full-time students, homemakers, and retirees).

Table 10.9 shows the numbers of people in each category in the United States in August 1990. (A good source for these and other data about the labor market is

Table 10.9 Employment Status of Adult Population, August 1990

Category	Number	Share of Labor Force	Share of Adult Population
Employed workers	119.3 million	94.5%	62.8% (employment ratio)
Unemployed workers	7.0 million	5.5% (unemployment rate)	3.7%
Labor force (employed + unemployed workers)	126.3 million	100%	66.5% (participation rate)
Not in labor force	63.6 million		33.5%
Adult population (labor force + not in labor force)	189.9 million		100%

Source: Bureau of Labor Statistics, *The Employment Situation, August 1990*, Table A-1.

described in the "In Touch with the Macroeconomy" box, p. 387.) In that month there were 119.3 million employed workers and 7.0 million unemployed. The **labor force** consists of all employed and unemployed workers, so the labor force in August 1990 was 126.3 million workers (119.3 million employed plus 7.0 million unemployed). The adult population in August 1990 was 189.9 million, which leaves 63.6 million adults not in the labor force (total population of 189.9 million less 126.3 million in the labor force).

Some useful measures of the labor market are the unemployment rate, the participation rate, and the employment ratio. The **unemployment rate** is the fraction of the labor force that is unemployed. In August 1990 the unemployment rate was 5.5% (7.0 million unemployed divided by 126.3 million in the labor force). Figure 9.6 showed the behavior of the U.S. unemployment rate over the period 1960–1990.

The fraction of adults who are in the labor force is the **participation rate.** Of the 189.9 million adults in the United States, 126.3 million were in the labor force, so the participation rate was 66.5%.

The **employment ratio** is the fraction of the adult population that is employed. In August 1990 the employment ratio was 62.8% (119.3 million employed divided by adult population of 189.9 million). With an employment ratio equal to 62.8%, 37.2% of the adult population was not employed in August 1990. Of this 37.2%, 3.7% reflected unemployment and the remaining 33.5% reflected adults not in the labor force. Thus a large majority of adults who are not employed at any given time are usually not in the labor force rather than unemployed.

Changes in Employment Status

In order to understand the phenomenon of unemployment, we must recognize that the labor market is not static but is constantly changing. Even when the unemployment rate remains constant from one month to the next, during the month hundreds of thousands of U.S. workers become unemployed and hundreds of thousands become employed.

Figure 10.11 shows how workers change their employment status (that is, whether they are employed, unemployed, or not in the labor force) within a typical month. The arrow between each pair of boxes represents a change from one employment status to another, and the number on the arrow shows the fraction of the people in one status that switch to the other status in a typical month.[17] Thus, for example, the arrow from the "Employed" box to the "Unemployed" box has the number 1%, indicating that 1% of employed workers in a typical month will become unemployed by the following month.

What are the employment prospects of an unemployed worker? Figure 10.11 shows that 22% of the unemployed people in a typical month will be employed in the following month, and 13% of the unemployed people will be out of the labor force in the next month. The remaining 65% of the unemployed people will still be unemployed in the following month. Of the 13% of the unemployed who leave the labor force each month, some are **discouraged workers,** or people who have become so discouraged by lack of success at finding a job they stop searching. Other

---

[17]Figure 10.11 uses data on employed and unemployed people and people not in the labor force from Table 10.9. The flow rates are from John M. Abowd and Arnold Zellner, "Estimating Gross Labor-Force Flows," *Journal of Business and Economic Statistics*, July 1985, pp. 254–283. Abowd and Zellner calculated these figures from monthly data for the period January 1977–December 1982.

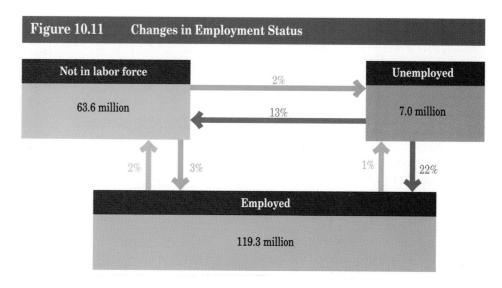

Figure 10.11   Changes in Employment Status

The figure shows the flow of workers between different categories of employment status that occurs in a typical month. The arrow between two boxes represents a change from one employment status to another, and the number on the arrow shows the percentage of people in one status that switch to the other status in a typical month. For example, the arrow from the "Unemployed" box to the "Employed" box indicates that 22% of unemployed workers become employed in the following month. The arrow from the "Employed" box to the "Unemployed" box indicates that 1% of employed workers become unemployed in the following month.

unemployed workers leave the labor force in order to engage in some activity outside the labor market, such as homemaking or going to school.

How Long Are People Unemployed?

We have seen that 65% of the people who are unemployed in a typical month are still unemployed in the following month. Some of these people remain unemployed for several months. The period of time that an individual is continuously unemployed is called an **unemployment spell.** The length of time that an unemployment spell lasts is called its **duration.**

The economic hardship suffered by an unemployed worker depends on the duration of the unemployment spell. For example, someone who works throughout the year except for a two-week spell of unemployment loses only about 4% of her income during the year, because she is unemployed for about 4% of the year. Thus very short spells of unemployment generally do not create much economic hardship. However, long spells of unemployment deprive a worker of income for a long period of time and often exhaust the worker's savings. Also, unemployed workers in the United States are eligible to collect unemployment insurance benefits for only a limited number of weeks. Thus long spells of unemployment can be economically devastating for unemployed workers and their families.

The duration of unemployment spells in the United States is characterized by two seemingly contradictory statements:

1. Most unemployment spells are short, about two months or less.

2. Most people who are unemployed on a given date are experiencing spells of unemployment with long duration.

Background

The United States has had a legal minimum wage since 1938, when the Fair Labor Standards Act introduced a minimum wage of $0.25 per hour (about $2.30 in 1990 dollars). The principal rationale for the minimum wage is to increase the incomes of poor families. To keep pace with general increases in prices and wages, Congress has periodically raised the minimum wage. The most recent minimum-wage legislation, signed by President Bush in November 1989, raised the minimum wage from $3.35 per hour to $3.80 per hour on April 1, 1990, and then to $4.25 per hour on April 1, 1991. This legislation was a compromise between those who wanted to raise the minimum wage even higher and those who resisted any increase in the minimum wage.

PRO

"An increase in the minimum wage will increase the wage income of unskilled workers and help some families to escape from poverty."

CON

"The minimum wage interferes with the free market and the invisible hand. An increase in the minimum wage will reduce the employment of unskilled workers and actually harm the workers it is designed to help. In addition, an increase in the minimum wage will raise costs and contribute to higher inflation."

THE POLICY DEBATE

Should the Minimum Wage Be Increased?

Analysis

The basic economics of the minimum wage is illustrated in Figure A, which shows the labor market for unskilled workers. The demand for unskilled workers is shown by the labor demand curve ND, and the supply of unskilled workers is shown by the labor supply curve NS. In the absence of a legislated minimum wage, the equilibrium is located at point E, with employment equal to N_1 and the real wage equal to w_1.

Now suppose that Congress sets a minimum wage of w_m, which is greater than w_1.* The figure shows that when the wage rate is w_m, the amount of labor supplied by unskilled workers (point H) is greater than the amount of labor demanded (point F). Because firms are legally required to increase the wage to w_m, they will cut back on their use of unskilled labor, so that employment of unskilled workers falls from N_1 to N_m. Hence a minimum wage above the market-clearing wage lowers employment of the unskilled.

*Minimum-wage legislation actually sets a minimum nominal wage W_m. But for a given price level P this minimum nominal wage implies a minimum real wage w_m equal to W_m/P.

Will a minimum wage raise the labor income of unskilled workers as a group? There are two opposing effects: The increase in the wage tends to increase labor income, but the resulting decrease in the number of workers employed (or, perhaps, in the hours that each worker is able to work) tends to reduce labor income. The overall impact of an increase in the minimum wage on the total labor income of the unskilled depends on which effect is stronger.

To analyze the effect on inflation that CON is worried about, we use the IS-LM-FE diagram from Chapters 3 and 4 (see Figure B). We suppose that, initially, there is no minimum wage, and the economy is in general equilibrium at point E. If a minimum wage above the market-clearing level is imposed, employment of the unskilled falls, as we have just seen. As a result of lower employment in the labor market, full-employment output falls from $\bar{Y}_1$ to $\bar{Y}_2$, and the FE line shifts to the left, from FE^1 to FE^2 in the figure. After the shift of the FE line, the aggregate demand for output (still at point E, the intersection of the IS and LM^1 curves) exceeds the amount of output that firms want to supply (shown by the new FE line, FE^2). Because the aggregate demand for output exceeds the aggregate supply, prices rise. As in Chapter 4, the rising price level reduces the real money supply M/P and causes the LM curve to shift to the left, until general equilibrium is restored at point F. Thus the increase in the minimum wage does increase the price level. However, because prices stop rising when the new general equilibrium point F is reached, the increase in the minimum wage does not lead to a sustained increase in the rate of inflation.

Evidence

Existing studies suggest that an increase in the minimum wage causes employment to fall by a much smaller percentage than the increase in the real wage. Therefore, the total labor income of unskilled workers does increase when the minimum wage rises.*

However, as a tool for reducing poverty, the minimum wage does have some problems: First, not all unskilled workers benefit from the increase in the minimum wage, because the unskilled workers who cannot get or hold jobs at the higher real wage do not share in the in-

*See Charles Brown, "Minimum Wage Laws: Are They Overrated?" *Journal of Economic Perspectives*, Summer 1988, pp. 133–145. This article contains a useful overview of the debate about minimum wages.

crease in income. Second, increases in the incomes of unskilled workers don't necessarily translate to increases in the incomes of poor families, because many unskilled and low-wage workers are not members of poor families. For example, only 10% of teenagers with low wages and 18% of adults with low wages were in low-income families in 1986.* Poor families not helped by a higher minimum wage include those in which no one is employed and those in which some family members earn a wage above the minimum when working but are unable to find steady work. Overall, taking these various effects into account, a recent study finds that raising the minimum wage from $3.35 per hour to $4.25 per hour could reduce the number of families in poverty by

*Ronald B. Mincey, "Raising the Minimum Wage: Effects on Family Poverty," *Monthly Labor Review*, July 1990, pp. 18–25.

about 6%, on balance a reasonably substantial effect.*

As for the effect on the overall price level, another recent study reports that a 10% increase in the minimum wage would increase the price level by about a fourth to a half of 1%.† Thus the inflationary effects of an increase in the minimum wage are relatively small. The effect is minor because only a small part of the labor force is affected by an increase in the minimum wage. As a result, an increase in the minimum wage has negligible effects on aggregate employment and output.

*Mincey, cited in the previous footnote, Table 4.
†Frederick Furlong and Marc Charney, "Minimum Wage Rate," *Weekly Letter*, Federal Reserve Bank of San Francisco, June 24, 1988.

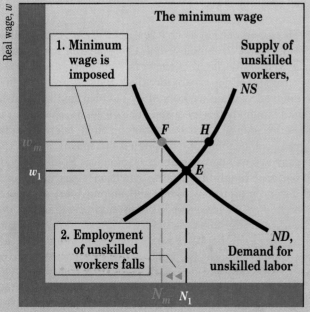

A — The minimum wage

Real wage, w

1. Minimum wage is imposed

Supply of unskilled workers, NS

w_m

w_1

F H

E

2. Employment of unskilled workers falls

ND, Demand for unskilled labor

N_m N_1

Labor, N

B — Macroeconomic effects of a minimum wage

Real interest rate, r

FE^2 FE^1

2. Price level increases

F

E

LM^2

LM^1

IS

1. Minimum wage increases

Y_2 $\overline{Y}_1$

Output, Y

To understand how both of these statements can be true, consider an economy with 100 people in the labor force. At the beginning of every month, suppose that two workers become unemployed and remain unemployed for one month before finding a new job. In addition, at the beginning of every year four workers become unemployed and remain unemployed for the entire year.

In this example there are twenty-eight spells of unemployment during a year: twenty-four spells that last one month, and four spells that last one year. Thus 86% of the spells last only one month, which is consistent with the first statement.

How many people are unemployed on a given day, for example, on May 15? There are six unemployed workers on May 15: two unemployed workers who began one-month spells of unemployment on May 1, and four unemployed workers who began one-year spells of unemployment on January 1. Thus 67% of the workers unemployed on May 15 are experiencing one-year spells of unemployment, which is consistent with the second statement.

Why There Are Always Unemployed People

The unemployment rate has two features that any theory of unemployment must explain: First, the unemployment rate is never zero. Second, unemployment rates are strongly countercyclical, rising in recessions and falling in expansions. In the rest of this chapter we discuss why the unemployment rate is always greater than zero. We delay our discussion of the cyclical behavior of unemployment until we have developed the alternative classical and Keynesian models of the business cycle.

The fact that the unemployment rate is never zero implies that even in the most prosperous economic times, there are always some people who are unemployed. Why is unemployment apparently a permanent feature of the economy? Here we discuss two types of unemployment, frictional unemployment and structural unemployment, that always exist in the labor market and thus prevent the unemployment rate from ever reaching zero.

Frictional Unemployment   The labor market is characterized by a great deal of searching by both workers and firms. Unemployed workers search for suitable jobs, and firms with vacancies search for suitable workers.

If all workers were identical and all jobs were identical, these searches would be short and easy. An unemployed worker would simply have to find some firm that had a vacancy and he would immediately be hired. The difficulty, of course, is that neither jobs nor workers are identical. Workers vary in their talents, skills, experience, goals, and geographical location (and willingness to move), and in the amount of time and energy they are willing to commit to their job. Similarly, jobs also vary in the skills and experience required, working conditions, location, hours, and pay. Because of the differences among workers and among jobs, an unemployed worker may search for several weeks or more before finding a suitable job. Similarly, a firm may search for a considerable time before hiring a suitable worker.

The difficulty in the search process is not necessarily that the number of vacant jobs is too small or too large compared with the number of unemployed workers. Rather, the problem is one of *matching* workers with the appropriate jobs. The unemployment that arises as workers search for suitable jobs and firms search for suitable workers is called **frictional unemployment.** Because the economy is dynamic, with jobs continually being created and destroyed and workers continually entering and exiting the labor force, there is always some frictional unemployment.

with the Macroeconomy

Labor Market Data

Government agencies collect and distribute a remarkable variety of data pertaining to the labor market. A useful summary of labor market data can be found in *The Employment Situation*, a monthly report issued by the Bureau of Labor Statistics. This report, which is usually released on the first Friday of the month, includes data for the previous month on employment, unemployment, average hours worked each week, and average weekly and hourly earnings. The data are presented for the aggregate U.S. economy, as well as for various categories of workers based on age, sex, race, occupation, and industry. Many of these data are later reprinted in a variety of sources, including *Employment and Earnings*, *Economic Indicators*, and the *Economic Report of the President*.

The data in *The Employment Situation* are obtained from two different surveys, a household survey and an establishment survey. The household survey is the monthly survey described in the text and is used to calculate employment and the unemployment rate. The establishment survey (also known as the payroll survey) is based on the responses of more than 300,000 business establishments about their employment, hours worked, and earnings of employees.

Both the household survey and the establishment survey provide information on employment, but they sometimes give conflicting signals about what happened to employment in the previous month. A major difference between the two surveys is that the establishment survey counts *jobs* but the household survey counts *people*. Thus a worker with two jobs would be counted twice in the establishment survey but only once in the household survey. The employment data from the establishment survey are more comprehensive and seem to be more closely related to GNP than are the employment data from the household survey.* On the other hand, the household survey provides information about unemployment and the establishment survey does not.

*See Roy Webb, ed., *Macroeconomic Data: A User's Guide*, Federal Reserve Bank of Richmond, pp. 22–23.

Although frictional unemployment imposes some costs, it is a necessary part of a well-functioning economy, because making good matches between workers and jobs is critical for economic efficiency. To become convinced of this point, you need only observe an economic system that does *not* provide for good matches. For example, on a visit to Beijing, China, one of the authors of this book had as a tour guide a young resident of Beijing who, it turned out, had an advanced degree in nuclear physics. According to the young man, during the month in which he had graduated there had been no openings for nuclear physicists; and so, because he spoke English, he was assigned to the Ministry of Tourism. That had been over five years earlier. Since then, he had been trying to no avail to be assigned to a job commensurate with his training. He was informed, however, that until the Ministry of Tourism could be convinced to release him from his job as a guide, he could not be reassigned.

This system of job assignment, even putting aside its infringement of personal freedoms, is economically disastrous. China is a developing country with a severe shortage of qualified scientists. Using someone with advanced scientific training as a tour guide reduces the country's capacity for economic growth.

China is a centrally planned economy in which jobs are assigned bureaucratically. In a market economy, in contrast, the process of matching jobs and workers is decentralized, as potential employees and firms with vacancies search for good matches. Since the most productive job-worker matches allow firms to offer a relatively high wage and still make a profit, these are the matches that tend to occur in a market economy. A trained physicist would not be likely to remain long as a tour guide because his productivity (and thus his wages)—as well as his personal satisfaction—would be higher in a job that used his special skills. Although this search process is desirable, it does lead to the existence of frictional unemployment.

Structural Unemployment   As we discussed earlier, most people who are unemployed on a given date are suffering long spells of unemployment. In addition, many people are chronically unemployed: Although their unemployment spells may be broken up by brief spells of employment or spells out of the labor force, workers who are **chronically unemployed** are unemployed a large fraction of the time. Long spells of unemployment and chronic unemployment cannot be attributed primarily to the matching process, because people in those situations do not seem to search for work very intensively and do not generally find stable employment. The long-term and chronic unemployment that exists even when the economy is not in a recession is called **structural unemployment.**

Structural unemployment arises from an imbalance between the number of workers with particular attributes and skills and the number of available jobs that require those attributes and skills. There are two major sources of this imbalance:

1.   Generally, the number of potential workers with low skill levels greatly exceeds the number of jobs requiring low skill levels.

2.   As the economy undergoes structural change, some sectors expand and others contract. Workers who lose their jobs in shrinking industries may have a hard time finding a new job.

To explain the first source of structural unemployment—the persistently high unemployment rate among unskilled workers—Peter Doeringer (now at Boston

BOX **10.2:**   **UNEMPLOYMENT IN THE SOVIET UNION**

The unemployment rate in the Soviet Union is not officially tabulated by the government because the official stance is that unemployment was "liquidated" during the early 1930s. Despite the official position that the unemployment rate is zero, there are always Soviet workers who are unemployed according to the U.S. definition described in the text.

Paul R. Gregory and Irwin L. Collier* of the University of Houston constructed estimates of the Soviet unemployment rate based on interviews of 2793 Soviet immigrants to the United States. The immigrants were asked about their labor market experiences during the five years immediately before they decided to emigrate (1974–1979, for most of the people interviewed). From these interviews Gregory and Collier estimated that the Soviet unemployment rate, as measured by the U.S. definition, was at least 1.2%.

Some features of Soviet unemployment are similar to U.S. unemployment, but in other ways Soviet and American unemployment are markedly different. For example, the unemployment rate for young Soviet workers (aged eighteen to twenty-four) was found to be almost triple the overall unemployment rate. The United States also has high unemployment rates among young workers.

However, in contrast to the situation in the United States, the unemployment rate among highly educated Soviet workers is higher than the overall Soviet unemployment rate. The high unemployment rate among educated workers seems to be a consequence of the Soviet system by which a bureaucracy assigns jobs to young workers. Because of needs for specific skills, graduates from universities are more likely to be assigned to jobs in remote areas away from where they were raised, whereas workers with less education are more likely to be assigned to jobs in their home towns. As a result, university graduates are more likely than less educated workers to find themselves dissatisfied with their initial jobs, and to endure some period of unemployment in order to search for jobs they like better.

The labor force participation of Soviet women differs from that of American women. American women tend to move in and out of the labor force more frequently than American men. In the Soviet Union women and men are equally strongly attached to the labor force. The strong labor force attachment of Soviet women results in part from "antiparasitism" laws that stipulate that even mothers of young children must work in the wage-paying sector.

*"Unemployment in the Soviet Union: Evidence from the Soviet Interview Project," *American Economic Review*, September 1988, pp. 613–632.

University) and Michael Piore (at the Massachusetts Institute of Technology)[18] developed the **dual labor market theory.** According to this theory, the labor markets of advanced industrialized countries are divided into two submarkets, the primary labor market and the secondary labor market.

The primary labor market, which is the larger part of the labor market in developed countries, is the market for desirable long-term jobs. These jobs may be either white-collar (managerial, professional) or blue-collar (production line). Primary-sector jobs are permanent jobs that pay well. Usually, they also offer opportunities for acquiring new skills and for advancement. Primary-sector jobs are "good" jobs.

In contrast, the secondary labor market consists of jobs with low skill requirements, little chance for training or advancement, and relatively low wages. Employment spells in secondary-market jobs are often short; after a few months the

[18]*Internal Labor Markets and Manpower Analysis*, Lexington, Mass.: D. C. Heath, 1971.

job may have ended, or the worker may have quit or been fired, to suffer another spell of unemployment. Secondary-sector jobs are "bad" jobs or "dead end" jobs. Ideally, secondary-sector jobs would serve as stepping-stones that allow individuals, after gaining some skills and experience, to attain primary-sector jobs. And many people do make the jump from secondary-sector jobs to primary-sector jobs. However, because of factors such as inadequate education, discrimination, and language barriers, some workers remain in the secondary labor market more or less indefinitely. According to the dual labor market theory, workers trapped in the secondary labor market account for most of the chronically unemployed workers.

Besides high unemployment among unskilled workers, the second source of structural unemployment is the sectoral reallocation of labor from shrinking industries and regions to growing industries and regions. When industries find that there is no longer a demand for their product (for example, buggy whip manufacturers) or that they are no longer sufficiently competitive (for example, U.S. producers of color televisions who lost much of the market to the Japanese), workers in these industries lose their jobs. At the same time, some industries will be growing (for example, service industries in the United States). Workers who lose jobs in declining industries need somehow to be matched with jobs in the growing industries. This matching may involve a lengthy period of unemployment, especially if workers need to be retrained or relocated to take a new job.

Because of the combination of frictional unemployment and structural unemployment, the unemployment rate is never zero. We have argued that frictional unemployment is probably not very costly, since it facilitates the matching process that is essential for economic efficiency. However, structural unemployment is in many cases a much more serious problem: Workers trapped for a long period in the secondary labor market or in a declining industry bear much higher costs than people who are frictionally unemployed. To the extent that the structurally unemployed are idle when they could be making productive contributions, society also loses from structural unemployment. The costs of unemployment are discussed in more detail in Chapter 14.

10.5   CHAPTER SUMMARY

1. The amount of labor demanded by a firm is the amount of labor that maximizes the firm's profit. The profit-maximizing amount of labor equates the marginal revenue product of labor ($MRPN$) with the nominal wage rate (W). Equivalently, it equates the marginal product of labor (MPN) with the real wage rate (w).

2. The labor demand curve is identical to the marginal product of labor (MPN) curve. Because an increase in the real wage causes firms to demand less labor, the labor demand curve slopes downward. Factors that increase the amount of labor demanded at any given real wage, such as a beneficial supply shock or an increase in the capital stock, shift the labor demand curve to the right.

3. The decision about how much labor to supply reflects a trade-off between income and leisure. Working an extra hour involves a sacrifice of leisure, which reduces the individual's utility. However, working an extra hour also raises income earned. Because income can be used to increase current consumption, future consumption, or future leisure, extra income leads to increased utility. Labor is sup-

plied to the point where the cost of working an extra hour (utility lost because of reduced leisure) equals the benefit of working an extra hour (utility gained because of increased income).

4. An increase in the real wage has competing substitution and income effects on the amount of labor supplied. The substitution effect of a higher real wage increases the amount of labor supplied, as the worker responds to the increased reward for working. The income effect reduces the amount of labor supplied, as the higher real wage makes the worker wealthier and thus able to afford a greater amount of leisure. The longer the increase in the real wage is expected to last, the stronger the income effect is. Thus permanent increases in the real wage may reduce the quantity of labor supplied.

5. The labor supply curve relates the amount of labor supplied to the current real wage. The labor supply curve slopes upward, indicating that a temporary increase in the real wage (an increase in the current real wage with the expected future real wage held constant) raises the amount of labor supplied. The labor supply curve shifts to the right in response to factors that increase the amount of labor supplied at a given current real wage.

6. An increase in the average tax rate, with the marginal tax rate held fixed, has only an income effect and increases the amount of labor supplied. An increase in the marginal tax rate, with the average tax rate held constant, has only a substitution effect and reduces the amount of labor supplied. The idea that labor supply and other economic decisions are very sensitive to incentives provided by the tax code is a basic tenet of supply-side economics.

7. In the classical model of the labor market the real wage adjusts to equalize the amount of labor demanded and the amount of labor supplied. Fluctuations in employment and the real wage are the result of factors that shift the labor supply curve or the labor demand curve.

8. Adults who are not employed are classified as unemployed if they looked for work in the previous four weeks and are classified as not in the labor force if they have not been looking for work. The labor force consists of all employed workers plus all unemployed workers. The unemployment rate is the fraction of the labor force that is unemployed.

9. The period of time that an individual is continuously unemployed is called an unemployment spell. Most unemployment spells are of short duration. However, on any given day most of the people who are unemployed are experiencing long spells of unemployment.

10. Frictional unemployment arises because it takes a while for potential workers to find suitable jobs and for firms with vacancies to find suitable workers. Structural unemployment arises because of an imbalance between the number of workers with particular skills and attributes and the number of vacant jobs requiring those skills and attributes. The existence of frictional and structural unemployment explains why the unemployment rate is never zero.

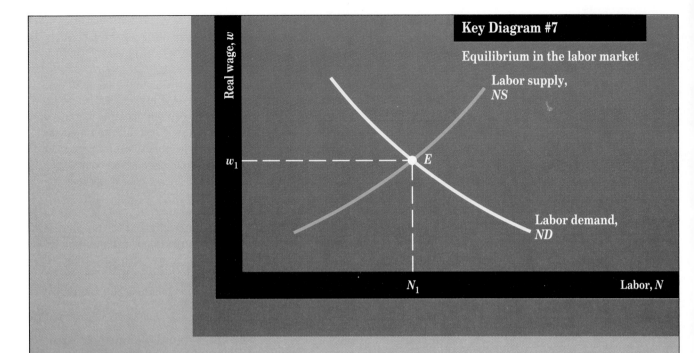

The level of employment and the real wage are determined in the labor market.

Diagram Elements

- The current real wage w is on the vertical axis, and the level of employment N is on the horizontal axis. The variable N can also stand for alternative measures of labor, such as total hours worked.

- The labor demand curve, marked ND, shows the amount of labor that firms want to employ at each current real wage. The labor demand curve slopes downward because firms find it profitable to hire more labor when the real wage falls.

- The labor supply curve, marked NS, shows the amount of labor that is offered by workers at each current real wage. Assuming that the substitution effect of an increase in the current real wage is larger than the income effect, workers will supply more labor when the current real wage increases. Thus, the labor supply curve slopes upward.

Analysis

Equilibrium in the labor market occurs when the quantity of labor demanded equals the quantity of labor supplied. In the figure equilibrium employment is N_1 and the equilibrium real wage is w_1.

Factors That Shift the Curves

•   Any factor that increases the amount of labor demanded at a given current real wage shifts the labor demand curve to the right. Factors that shift the labor demand curve to the right include an increase in the marginal product of labor at any given level of employment and an increase in the capital stock. See Table 10.4, p. 363.

•   Any factor that increases the amount of labor supplied at a given current real wage shifts the labor supply curve to the right. Factors that shift the labor supply curve to the right include a fall in wealth, a fall in the expected future real wage, a rise in government purchases, a rise in the average tax rate (with the marginal tax rate held constant), a fall in the marginal tax rate (with the average tax rate held constant), and a rise in the working-age population. See Table 10.8, p. 378.

Key Terms

average tax rate, p. 373

chronically unemployed, p. 388

discouraged workers, p. 382

dual labor market theory, p. 389

duration, p. 383

employment ratio, p. 382

frictional unemployment, p. 386

income effect (of the real wage on labor supply), p. 365

labor force, p. 382

leisure, p. 364

marginal revenue product of labor (*MPRN*), p. 355

marginal tax rate, p. 373

participation rate, p. 382

structural unemployment, p. 388

substitution effect (of the real wage on labor supply), p. 365

supply-side economics, p. 375

unemployment rate, p. 382

unemployment spell, p. 383

Key Equation

$$MRPN = P \times MPN \qquad (10.1)$$

The marginal revenue product of labor *MRPN* is the extra revenue the firm receives when it employs an additional unit of labor. The marginal revenue product of labor equals the price of output *P* times the marginal product of labor *MPN*.

Review Questions

1. Explain why the profit-maximizing level of employment occurs when the marginal revenue product of labor equals the nominal wage. How can this profit-maximizing condition be expressed in real terms?

2. What is the *MPN* curve? How is the *MPN* curve related to labor demand?

3. What two effects does a temporary increase in the real wage have on the amount of labor supplied? What determines which effect is the stronger?

4. Why does a temporary 15% rise in the real wage lead to a greater increase in labor supplied than a permanent 15% rise in the real wage does?

5. Discuss the effects of each of the following on aggregate labor supply: an increase in government purchases, an increase in the average tax rate, an increase in the marginal tax rate.

6. Why is the classical model of the labor market not very useful for studying unemployment?

7. Define the following: *labor force, unemployment rate, participation rate, employment ratio*.

8. Define *unemployment spell* and *duration*. What are the two seemingly contradictory facts about unemployment spells? Why are the two facts not actually contradictory?

9. What is frictional unemployment? Why is a certain amount of frictional unemployment probably necessary in a well-functioning economy?

10. What is structural unemployment? What are the two principal sources of structural unemployment?

Numerical Problems

1. Acme Widget, Inc., has the following production function.

Number of Workers	Number of Widgets Produced
1	8
2	15
3	21
4	26
5	30
6	33

  a. Find the MPN for each level of employment.
  b. Acme can get $5 for each widget it produces. How many workers will it hire if the nominal wage is $38? If it is $27? If it is $22?
  c. Graph the relationship between Acme's labor demand and the nominal wage. How is this graph different from a labor demand curve? Graph Acme's labor demand curve.
  d. With the nominal wage fixed at $38, the price of widgets doubles from $5 each to $10 each. What happens to Acme's labor demand and production?
  e. With the nominal wage fixed at $38 and the price of widgets fixed at $5, the introduction of a new automatic widget maker doubles the number of widgets that a given number of workers can produce. What happens to labor demand and production?
  f. Explain why, in general, a doubling of the price of a firm's product has the same effect on labor demand as does a doubling of worker productivity with the product price unchanged.

2. The marginal product of labor (measured in units of output) for a certain firm is given by

$$MPN = A(100 - N),$$

where A measures productivity and N is the number of labor hours used in production. The price of output is $2.00 per unit.

  a. If $A = 1.0$, what will be the demand for labor if the nominal wage is $10? If it is $20? Graph the demand curve for labor. What is the equilibrium real wage if the supply of labor is fixed at 95?
  b. Repeat part a for the case where $A = 2.0$.

3. Suppose the income tax law exempts income under $8000 from tax, taxes income between $8000 and $20,000 at a 25% rate, and taxes income over $20,000 at a 30% rate.

  a. Find the average tax rate and the marginal tax rate for someone earning $16,000 and for someone earning $30,000.
  b. The tax law is changed so that income under $6000 is untaxed, income from $6000 to $20,000 is taxed at 20%, and income over $20,000 continues to be taxed at 30%. Repeat part a.
  c. How will the tax law change in part b affect the labor supply of the person initially making $16,000? How will it affect the labor supply of the person making $30,000?

4. For an economy the MPN is given by

$$MPN = 500 - 0.5N,$$

where N is aggregate employment. The aggregate quantity of labor supplied is $400 + 8(1 - t)w$, where w is the real wage and t is the income tax rate. The expression for labor supply reflects the fact that workers care about their after-tax real wage, $(1 - t)w$, rather than their before-tax real wage w. There are no taxes on employers.

  a. Find the before-tax real wage and employment when $t = 0.50$.
  b. Find the before-tax real wage and employment when $t = 0.25$. Compare the result with part a. Explain why the cut in the income tax rate has the effect that it does on the labor market.

5. In this problem you are asked to find the effects of a legal minimum wage on the labor income of unskilled workers. Assume that the marginal product of labor for unskilled labor is given by

$$MPN = 100 - 0.2N.$$

The supply of unskilled labor is given by $80 + 2w$, where w is the real wage received by unskilled labor.

  a. Assuming that there is no minimum wage, find the equilibrium values of the real wage, employment, and labor income for unskilled workers.
  b. Now suppose that a minimum wage is instituted that sets the real wage equal to 70. What are the new levels of employment and total labor income for unskilled workers?
  c. Repeat parts a and b assuming $MPN = 100 - 0.9N$. How does the imposition of a minimum real wage of 70 affect labor income this time? How does the impact of a minimum wage on labor income depend on the sensitivity of labor demand to the real wage?

6. Consider an economy with 500 people in the labor force. At the beginning of every month 5 people lose their jobs and remain unemployed for exactly one month; one month later, they find new jobs and become employed. In addition, on January 1 of each year 20 people lose their jobs and remain unemployed for six months before finding new jobs. Finally, on July 1 of each year 20 people lose their jobs and remain unemployed for six months before finding new jobs.

    a. What is the unemployment rate in this economy in the typical month?

    b. What fraction of unemployment spells lasts for one month? What fraction lasts for six months?

    c. What is the average duration of an unemployment spell?

    d. On any given date, what fraction of the unemployed are suffering a long spell (six months) of unemployment?

7. Using the data in Fig. 10.11, calculate how many people become unemployed during a typical month. How many become employed? How many leave the labor force?

Analytical Problems

1. How would each of the following affect Helena Handbasket's supply of labor?

    a. The value of Helena's home triples in an unexpectedly hot real estate market.

    b. Originally an unskilled worker, Helena acquires skills that give her access to a higher-paying job. Assume that her preferences about leisure versus income are not affected by the change in jobs.

    c. A temporary income tax surcharge raises the percentage of her income that she must pay in taxes, for the current year only. (Taxes are proportional to income in Helena's country.)

    d. There is a large increase in government military spending, currently financed by government borrowing but ultimately expected to be paid for by higher lump-sum taxes.

    e. Helena's husband loses his job.

2. John Doe learns that the fixed percentage of his wages that he has to pay into the Social Security fund has been permanently raised.

    a. Suppose that John's expected Social Security benefits are not changed; instead, the increase in his Social Security tax is used to make up some unexpected shortfalls in the current Social Security program. John also does not expect his before-tax real wages in the future to be any different from what they would have been if the Social Security tax had not been changed. John is well below the Social Security "cap"; that is, none of his labor earnings is exempt from the Social Security tax.

What will be the effect of the increase in the Social Security tax on the amount of labor that John supplies?

    b. Repeat part a, but this time assume that John's extra Social Security taxes all go directly to increase his expected retirement benefits. Assume also that John will get the full increase in retirement benefits whether or not he keeps working at his present rate. What happens to John's labor supply now?

3. Suppose that under a new law all businesses must pay a tax equal to 6% of their sales revenue. Assume that this tax is not passed on to consumers. Instead, consumers pay the same prices after the tax is imposed as they did before the tax was imposed. What is the effect of this tax on labor demand? Assuming that labor supply is unchanged, what will be the effect of the tax on employment and the real wage?

4. Figure 10.8 shows a permanent increase in the real wage decreasing labor supply. Redraw the figure to show that if labor supply is very responsive to the current real wage, a permanent increase in the real wage can raise the amount of labor supplied. Discuss in terms of income and substitution effects.

5. Can the unemployment rate and the employment ratio rise during the same month? Can the participation rate fall at the same time that the employment ratio is rising? Explain.

11

Classical Business Cycle Analysis: Market-Clearing Macroeconomics

To understand the business cycle, we need both knowledge of the basic business cycle facts and a theory that can account for these facts. In Chapter 9 we described the most important business cycle facts, and in Chapter 10 we began the process of building a business cycle theory by studying the factors that underlie fluctuations in employment and unemployment. Now we are ready to develop and compare the major alternative theories of the business cycle.

A theory of the business cycle consists of two components. One component is a specification of the types of shocks or disturbances that are believed to be the most important in affecting the economy. Examples of economic disturbances that have been emphasized by various theories of the business cycle include supply shocks, fluctuations in money supply or money demand, changes in fiscal policy, and shocks to consumer spending. The second component of a theory of the business cycle is a model of the macroeconomy that describes how key variables, such as output, employment, and prices, respond to these economic shocks. As we have discussed, the two main macroeconomic models used in business cycle analysis are the classical model and the Keynesian model. In order to be useful, a theory of the business cycle must make predictions about the behavior of key macroeconomic variables that are consistent with what we observe. That is, the theory must fit the business cycle facts.

In this chapter we study theories of the business cycle that employ the classical model, and Chapter 12 examines theories based on the Keynesian model. We developed the basic classical model, which we called the classical *IS-LM* model, in Chapters 3 and 4. Combining the classical *IS-LM* model with an assumption about the sources of economic shocks gives us the classical theory of the business cycle. We see in this chapter that the classical theory of the cycle comes in several versions. One version, known as real business cycle theory, assumes that supply shocks (or as advocates of this theory call them, productivity shocks) are the primary source of cyclical fluctuations. A broader version of the classical theory accepts that some other types of shocks—including, for example, fiscal policy shocks—may also be important for explaining the business cycle.

In both this chapter and Chapter 12 we make extensive comparisons of the predictions of various business cycle theories and the business cycle facts that the theories are attempting to explain. Comparing the predictions of the business cycle theories with the facts is part of the process of developing and testing economic theories, discussed in Chapter 1. In general, each of the leading theories can account for a majority of the business cycle facts, but so far no theory clearly explains *all* the facts.

A particular business cycle fact that is a challenge for the classical theory to explain is the fact (discussed in Chapter 9) that changes in the money stock lead the cycle. As you may recall from Chapter 4, an implication of the classical assumption that wages and prices adjust quickly to clear markets is that money is neutral, so that changes in the money supply do not affect output, the real interest rate, or other real variables. However, many economists interpret the business cycle fact that money leads the cycle as evidence that money is *not* neutral in all situations. If money is not neutral, we must either modify the basic classical model to account for monetary nonneutrality or abandon the classical model in favor of a different approach. Toward the end of this chapter we take the first tack and show how the classical model can be extended to allow for monetary nonneutrality. In the next chapter we examine the explanation for nonneutrality offered by the major alternative to the classical model, the Keynesian model.

11.1   A REVIEW OF THE CLASSICAL *IS-LM* MODEL

Classical theories of the business cycle are based on the classical *IS-LM* model introduced in Chapters 3 and 4. We begin the chapter with a review of that model.

The classical *IS-LM* model assumes that wages and prices adjust rapidly, so that the economy is in general equilibrium with supply and demand equal in all markets. This general equilibrium is represented by the intersection of the *IS* curve, the *LM* curve, and the *FE* line.

The *IS* Curve: Goods Market Equilibrium

The goods market is in equilibrium when the quantity of goods and services supplied equals the quantity of goods and services demanded. In a closed economy with no net exports the demand for goods and services equals $C^d + I^d + G$, where C^d is desired consumption by households, I^d is desired investment by firms, and G is the government's purchase of goods and services. The total amount of goods and services produced by firms is represented by Y, so the goods market equilibrium condition is

$$Y = C^d + I^d + G.$$

An alternative way of expressing the goods market equilibrium condition is obtained by subtracting $C^d + G$ from both sides of the equation, which yields

$$S^d = I^d, \tag{11.1}$$

where S^d is desired national saving, $Y - C^d - G$. Equation (11.1) says that the

For any given value of output Y, the *IS* curve shows the real interest rate r that sets desired national saving equal to desired investment and thus clears the goods market. If we start from point A, an increase in output leads to an increase in desired saving. For the equality of desired saving and desired investment to be restored, the real interest rate must fall, increasing desired investment and reducing desired saving. The rise in output accompanied by the fall in the real interest rate is shown by the movement from point A to point B.

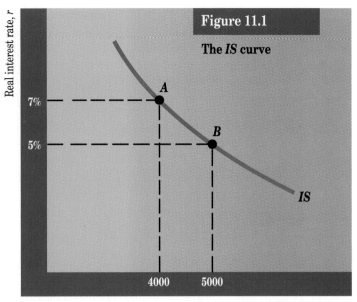

Figure 11.1

The *IS* curve

goods market is in equilibrium when desired national saving equals desired investment.

Equilibrium in the goods market is represented graphically by the *IS* curve, which is drawn in a diagram with output Y on the horizontal axis and the real interest rate r on the vertical axis. For any given value of output Y, the *IS* curve gives the value of the real interest rate r that sets desired saving equal to desired investment, and thus clears the goods market.

The *IS* curve slopes downward. The reason for this downward slope is illustrated in Fig. 11.1. Suppose that output equals 4000 goods and the real interest rate equals 7%, as at point A in Fig. 11.1. Because point A is on the *IS* curve, at that point the goods market is in equilibrium, and desired saving equals desired investment.

Now consider what happens if output increases to 5000 goods: An increase in output (equivalently, an increase in income) raises the desired amount of national saving at any given real interest rate. Following the increase in output, if the real interest rate were to remain equal to 7%, desired saving would exceed desired investment, and the goods market would no longer be in equilibrium. The excess of desired saving over desired investment can be eliminated by a fall in the real interest rate, which reduces the desired amount of saving and increases the desired amount of investment. If the real interest rate falls to 5%, as at point B in Fig. 11.1, then desired saving equals desired investment, and goods market equilibrium is restored. Because an increase in output raises desired saving and thus lowers the real interest rate needed to clear the goods market, the *IS* curve slopes downward.

Given the level of output, any change in the economy that reduces desired national saving relative to desired investment increases the real interest rate that clears the goods market and shifts the *IS* curve upward. For example, a temporary increase in government purchases reduces desired national saving at each level of

Table 11.1 Summary

Principal Factors Shifting the *IS* Curve, *LM* Curve, and *FE* Line (Classical *IS-LM* Model)

The *IS* Curve

An Increase in	Shifts the *IS* Curve
Expected future output	Up
Government purchases G	Up
Expected future marginal product of capital MPK^f	Up
Corporate taxes	Down

The *LM* Curve

An Increase in	Shifts the *LM* Curve
Nominal money supply M	Down
Price level P	Up
Interest rate on money i^m	Up
Expected inflation rate π^e	Down

The *FE* Line

An Increase in	Shifts the *FE* Line
Productivity	Right
Labor supply	Right
Government purchases G	Right

Note: Additional factors shifting the *IS* curve are listed in Table 6.2, p. 228.

output and thus shifts the *IS* curve upward. Other factors that shift the *IS* curve are listed in Table 11.1.

The *LM* Curve: Asset Market Equilibrium

Asset markets are in equilibrium when the demand for each asset equals the available supply of that asset. Asset demands are the result of portfolio allocation decisions in which people decide in what forms to hold their wealth. We have simplified the portfolio allocation decision by categorizing all assets into two groups: money (assets used in making payments, such as currency and checking accounts) and nonmonetary assets (bonds, stocks, real estate, and so on). With only two types of assets, the portfolio allocation decision boils down to deciding how much money to hold, since any wealth not held in the form of money must be held as a nonmonetary asset. Whenever the amount of money demanded equals the amount supplied, the quantities of nonmonetary assets demanded and supplied are also equal. Thus the asset market as a whole is in equilibrium whenever the market for money is in equilibrium.

Algebraically, the asset market equilibrium condition (Eq. 4.9) is

$$\frac{M}{P} = L(Y,\ r\ +\ \pi^e,\ i^m),$$

where M/P is the real money supply (the nominal money supply M divided by the price level P), and the money demand function L gives the real quantity of money that is demanded. The money demand function shows that the real quantity of money that is demanded depends on three factors: output Y, the nominal interest rate on nonmonetary assets i (equal to the expected real interest rate r plus the expected inflation rate π^e), and the nominal interest rate paid on money i^m. An increase in output increases the number of transactions that people want to make and thus raises the real amount of money demanded. A rise in the nominal interest rate on nonmonetary assets or a fall in the nominal interest rate paid on money increases the cost of holding money instead of holding nonmonetary assets and thus reduces the real amount of money demanded.

Equilibrium in the asset market is represented graphically by the *LM* curve. For any given level of output Y, the *LM* curve shows the real interest rate that sets the real quantity of money supplied equal to the real quantity of money demanded and thus clears the asset market.

The *LM* curve, shown in Fig. 11.2, slopes upward. To review why the *LM* curve slopes upward, suppose that when output Y is 4000, the real interest rate that clears the asset market is 3% (point A in Fig. 11.2). Now imagine that output increases to 5000. The increase in output raises the real quantity of money de-

For any given level of output Y, the *LM* curve shows the real interest rate r at which the real quantity of money demanded equals the real supply of money, so that the asset market is in equilibrium. If we start from point A, an increase in output increases the real quantity of money demanded. For asset market equilibrium to be restored, the real interest rate must rise to reduce the real quantity of money demanded back to its initial level. The rise in output accompanied by the rise in the real interest rate is shown by the movement from point A to point B.

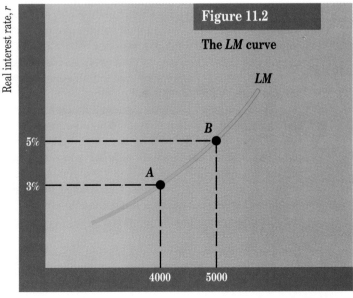

Figure 11.2

The *LM* curve

manded above the real money supply. For equilibrium in the asset market to be restored, the real interest rate must rise: An increase in the real interest rate, with the expected rate of inflation held constant, increases the nominal interest rate and thus brings the real quantity of money demanded back down to the available supply. In this example, following the rise in output to 5000, an increase in the real interest rate to 5% is needed to reduce the real quantity of money demanded to its initial level and restore asset market equilibrium (point B in Fig. 11.2). Because an increase in output raises the real quantity of money demanded and thus increases the real interest rate needed to clear the asset market, the LM curve slopes upward.

Given output, any change that reduces real money supply relative to real money demand increases the real interest rate that clears the asset market and shifts the LM curve upward. For example, a reduction in the real money supply M/P (arising from either a reduction in the nominal money supply M or an increase in the price level P) causes the real quantity of money demanded to exceed the real money supply at any given level of output. Thus at any given level of output, the real interest rate needed to clear the asset market rises, and the LM curve shifts upward. Other factors that shift the LM curve are listed in Table 11.1.

The Full-Employment Line

Full employment is the level of employment that prevails when all wages and prices have completely adjusted to their equilibrium values. In the classical model full employment refers to the level of employment $\bar{N}$ at which the labor demand curve and the labor supply curve cross. Keep in mind that even at full employment the unemployment rate is not zero, because there is frictional unemployment and structural unemployment.

Given the economy's capital stock K, which for the purposes of business cycle analysis we assume fixed, and given the full-employment level of employment $\bar{N}$, the full-employment level of output $\bar{Y}$ is determined by the production function:

$$\bar{Y} = AF(K, \bar{N}).$$

In the IS-LM diagram the full-employment (FE) line shows the full-employment level of output. Because at full employment the quantity of labor demanded equals the quantity of labor supplied, the FE line also represents equilibrium in the labor market. The FE line is a vertical line that meets the horizontal axis where output Y equals $\bar{Y}$, indicating that the full-employment level of output is $\bar{Y}$ for any value of the real interest rate.

Any factor that changes the market-clearing level of employment or that shifts the production function changes the full-employment level of output $\bar{Y}$ and shifts the FE line. For example, as we saw in Chapter 10, an increase in government purchases raises the amount of labor supplied at any given real wage and thus increases the equilibrium level of employment. Because it increases the full-employment level of employment, this change in fiscal policy also raises the full-employment level of output and shifts the FE line to the right. Other factors that shift the FE line are given in Table 11.1.

General Equilibrium in the Classical *IS-LM* Model

The economy is in general equilibrium when all markets—the goods market, the asset market, and the labor market—are in equilibrium, that is, at the intersection of the IS curve, the LM curve, and the FE line.

The *IS* curve, the *LM* curve LM^1, and the *FE* line do not have a common point of intersection, so the economy is not in general equilibrium. The aggregate demand for output is represented by the intersection of *IS* and LM^1 at point *A*. Because the aggregate demand for output Y_A is greater than $\bar{Y}$, the price level rises, which reduces the real money supply and shifts the *LM* curve upward and to the left. When the *LM* curve reaches LM^2, general equilibrium in the economy is restored at point *E*, with output equal to $\bar{Y}$.

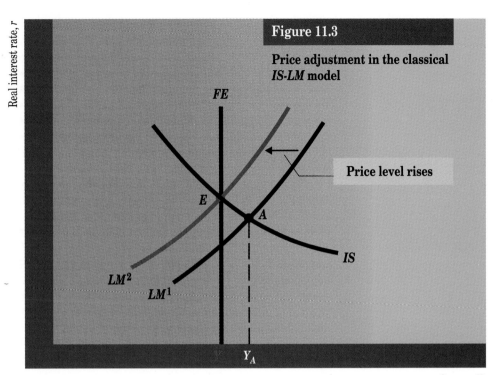

Figure 11.3

Price adjustment in the classical *IS-LM* model

General equilibrium is attained by the adjustment of the price level. If the *IS* curve, the *LM* curve, and the *FE* line do not intersect at a common point, the price level adjusts to shift the *LM* curve until it passes through the intersection of the *IS* curve and the *FE* line. This price adjustment process is illustrated in Fig. 11.3. In Fig. 11.3 the initial *LM* curve is LM^1, which does not pass through the intersection of the *IS* curve and the *FE* line. As in Chapter 4, to explain the adjustment of prices in a situation of disequilibrium, we imagine that the goods market and asset market are in equilibrium but the labor market is not. Under the assumption that the goods market and asset market are in equilibrium, the economy is at point *A* in Fig. 11.3, which lies on the *IS* curve and the *LM* curve but not on the *FE* line. At point *A* the aggregate demand for goods is Y_A, which is greater than the quantity of goods that firms desire to supply $\bar{Y}$. The excess demand for goods drives up the price level *P*, which reduces the real money supply *M/P* and shifts the *LM* curve upward until it passes through point *E*. At point *E* the new *LM* curve is LM^2, and the economy is in general equilibrium with all three markets clearing.

11.2 THE REAL BUSINESS CYCLE THEORY

The classical *IS-LM* model provides a useful framework for analyzing how major macroeconomic variables respond to various shocks that hit the economy. However, if we are to form a complete *business cycle theory*, the classical *IS-LM* model must be combined with a description of the major sources of shocks to the economy.

An influential group of classical macroeconomists, led by Edward Prescott of the University of Minnesota and Finn Kydland of Carnegie-Mellon University, has developed a theory that takes a strong stand on the sources of shocks that cause cyclical fluctuations. This theory, known as the **real business cycle theory** (or RBC theory, for short), argues that real shocks to the economy (hence the name of the approach) are the primary cause of business cycles. **Real shocks** are disturbances to the "real side" of the economy, such as shocks that affect the production function, the size of the labor force, the real quantity of government purchases, and the spending and saving decisions of consumers. Real shocks are contrasted with **nominal shocks,** which are shocks to money supply or money demand. In terms of the *IS-LM* model real shocks directly affect only the *IS* curve or the *FE* line, whereas nominal shocks directly affect only the *LM* curve.

Although in principle many types of real shocks could contribute to the business cycle, RBC theorists focus on shocks to the production function—what we have called supply shocks and what the RBC theorists usually refer to as **productivity shocks.** Productivity shocks include the development of new products or production methods, the introduction of new management techniques, changes in the quality of capital or labor, changes in the availability of raw materials or energy, unusually good or unusually bad weather, changes in government regulations affecting production, and any other factor affecting productivity. According to RBC theorists, economic booms result from beneficial productivity shocks, and recessions are caused by adverse productivity shocks.

The Recessionary Impact of an Adverse Productivity Shock

To show how productivity shocks can generate cyclical fluctuations, we imagine that because of a drought or a disruption of energy supplies, the economy becomes temporarily less productive. (RBC theorists consider permanent as well as temporary productivity shocks, but the temporary case is the easier.) Figure 11.4 shows the effects of an adverse productivity shock on the economy.[1] The initial general equilibrium is represented by point E in both parts of Fig. 11.4. The temporary productivity shock reduces the marginal product of labor and thus shifts the labor demand curve downward from ND^1 to ND^2 in Fig. 11.4(a). The labor supply curve is unaffected. At the new labor market equilibrium (point F in Fig. 11.4a), both the real wage and employment have fallen.

The adverse productivity shock reduces the full-employment amount of output $\bar{Y}$, both by reducing employment *and* by reducing the amount of output that can be produced at any level of employment. Thus the *FE* line shifts to the left, from FE^1 to FE^2 in Fig. 11.4(b). Because the productivity shock is temporary, future income and the expected future marginal product of capital (MPK^f) are unaffected; thus desired national saving and desired investment are unchanged at given levels of output, and the *IS* curve does not shift. Because neither money supply nor money demand are changed by the shock, there is also no direct effect on the *LM* curve.

As a result of the leftward shift of the *FE* line, the *IS-LM* intersection at point E lies to the right of the *FE* line in Fig. 11.4(b). Thus the aggregate demand for goods exceeds the amount of output that firms want to supply, which causes prices to rise. The increase in the price level reduces the real money supply, shifting the *LM* curve upward and to the left, from LM^1 to LM^2. The new general equilibrium

---

[1] We have seen this analysis before, when we studied the effects of an oil price shock in Chapters 3 and 4.

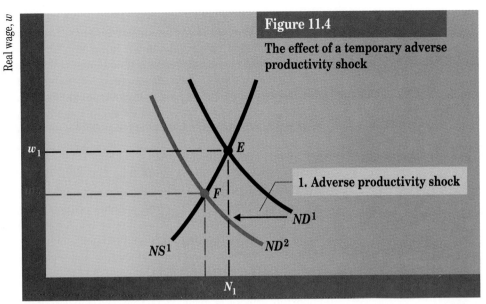

Figure 11.4

The effect of a temporary adverse productivity shock

(a) Labor market

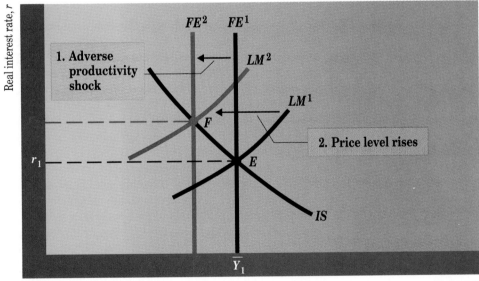

(b) General equilibrium

Initial equilibrium is represented by point E in both parts of the figure.

(a) A temporary decline in productivity reduces the marginal product of labor and shifts the labor demand curve downward, from ND^1 to ND^2. In the new labor market equilibrium, point F, the real wage and employment have fallen.

(b) The FE line shifts to the left, from FE^1 to FE^2, because the fall in employment and the fall in productivity both cause the full-employment level of output to fall. The IS-LM intersection at point E is to the right of the new FE line, indicating that the aggregate demand for output exceeds the new full-employment level of output, which puts upward pressure on the price level. The increase in the price level reduces the real money supply and shifts the LM curve upward and left to LM^2. In the new equilibrium, at point F, output has fallen to $\bar{Y}_2$ and the real interest rate has risen to r_2.

is represented by point F in Fig. 11.4(b), where IS, LM^2, and FE^2 intersect. In the new general equilibrium, output is lower, the real interest rate is higher, and the price level is higher than in the initial equilibrium at point E.

This analysis illustrates how an adverse productivity shock can cause a fall in output (a recession). The same exercise in reverse would show that a beneficial productivity shock leads to a rise in output (a boom). Although these analyses are simplifications of the real business cycle theory, they make the basic point that productivity shocks can lead to cyclical fluctuations in the economy.

Business Cycle Facts Explained by the Real Business Cycle Theory

Real business cycle theory has developed rapidly since research in this area began in the early 1980s, and new refinements of the theory are currently being developed. Thus it is somewhat premature to reach any definitive conclusions about the value of the RBC theory as a framework for understanding business cycles. Nevertheless, we can illustrate some strengths and weaknesses of the RBC approach by comparing the predictions of the simple version of the theory illustrated in Fig. 11.4 with the business cycle facts documented in Chapter 9. We first discuss some important business cycle facts that are consistent with the RBC theory. Later, when we list some objections to the RBC theory, we discuss some business cycle facts that are not well accounted for by this approach.

Business cycle fact: Employment is procyclical. As we saw in Fig. 11.4, the RBC theory predicts that a temporary fall in productivity causes a simultaneous reduction in employment and output. Similarly, the RBC theory predicts that a temporary increase in productivity causes a simultaneous increase in employment and output. Thus the RBC theory predicts that employment is procyclical, rising in expansions and falling in recessions. Under the assumption that the economy is constantly being subjected to random productivity shocks, the RBC theory can account for a recurrent business cycle in economic activity and employment.

Business cycle fact: Average labor productivity is procyclical. According to the RBC theory, economic booms are associated with beneficial productivity shocks and recessions are associated with adverse shocks. Productivity shocks have two effects on average labor productivity, which work in opposite directions: On the one hand, a beneficial productivity shock during a boom raises labor productivity directly by increasing the amount of output that can be produced with any given amount of capital and labor. On the other hand, a beneficial productivity shock also raises employment, which, because of the diminishing marginal productivity of labor, tends to reduce average labor productivity. In general, the direct positive effect on labor productivity of a beneficial productivity shock is the stronger of the two effects, so the RBC theory correctly predicts that average labor productivity is procyclical.

Business cycle fact: The real wage is mildly procyclical. Beneficial productivity shocks shift the labor demand curve upward, increasing employment and the real wage during expansions. Adverse productivity shocks shift the labor demand curve downward, reducing employment and the real wage during recessions. Therefore the RBC theory is consistent with the finding that the real wage is procyclical.

Business cycle fact: Investment is more volatile than consumption. The RBC theory implies that investment spending fluctuates more than consumption spending. To explain why, we again consider the case of a temporary productivity shock. By definition, temporary productivity shocks don't last very long, and so they have relatively little effect on consumers' lifetime resources. Because consumers have not been made significantly better or worse off by a temporary productivity shock, they will not change consumption much, implying that most of the change in income will be saved. In other words, saving will respond much more than consumption to a temporary productivity shock.

In a closed economy, investment equals national saving. Thus investment, like saving, must vary more sharply than consumption over the cycle. The implication of the RBC theory that in a closed economy fluctuations in investment will be much larger than fluctuations in consumption is consistent with the business cycle fact.[2]

As you can see, the simple version of the RBC theory we have presented can account for some important business cycle facts. Besides predicting the general direction in which key macroeconomic variables move over the course of the business cycle, the RBC theory can also account for the *sizes* of cyclical fluctuations in key macroeconomic variables, as we discuss in the following application.

Application

Calibrating the Business Cycle

Real business cycle theorists argue that a good theory of the business cycle should be quantitative as well as qualitative. In other words, as well as predicting in general terms how key macroeconomic variables move over the business cycle, a business cycle theory should give numerical predictions of the magnitudes of economic fluctuations and the strength of the relationships among different macroeconomic variables.

To study the quantitative implications of their theories, RBC theorists have developed a method called *calibration*. Basically, the idea of calibration is to work out a detailed numerical example of a more general theory. The first step in calibration is to write down a simple classical model of the aggregate economy—much like the version of the RBC model we illustrated in Fig. 11.4—except that in place of general functions specific functions are used. For example, instead of representing the production function in general terms as

$$Y = AF(K, N),$$

the person conducting the calibration exercise uses a specific algebraic form for the production function, such as[3]

$$Y = AK^a N^{1-a},$$

---

[2]In an open economy the RBC theory predicts that both investment and net exports will absorb fluctuations in national saving, but that consumption will still vary relatively little.

[3]This production function, which we saw in Chapter 3 and Chapter 8, is called a Cobb-Douglas production function. As we have noted, although the Cobb-Douglas production function is relatively simple, it fits U.S. data quite well.

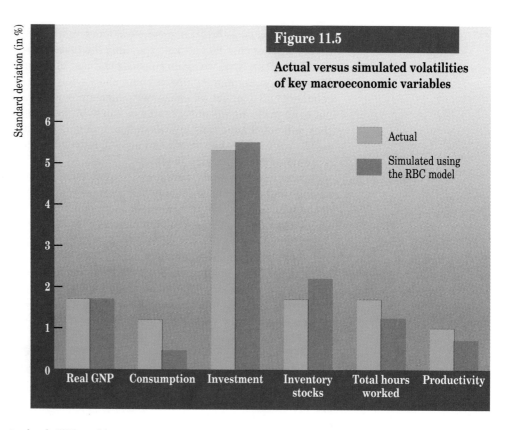

Figure 11.5

Actual versus simulated volatilities of key macroeconomic variables

The figure compares the actual volatilities of key macroeconomic variables observed in postwar U.S. data with the volatilities of the same variables predicted by computer simulations of Edward Prescott's calibrated RBC model. Prescott set the size of the random productivity shocks in his simulations so that the simulated volatility of GNP would match the actually observed volatility of GNP exactly. Given these random productivity shocks, the simulated volatilities of the other five macroeconomic variables (with the possible exception of consumption) match the observed volatilities fairly well.

where a is a number between 0 and 1. Similarly, specific functions are used to describe the behavior of consumers and workers.

Next, the specific functions chosen are made even more specific by expressing them in numerical terms. For example, if we set a in the production function just given equal to 0.3, the production function becomes

$$Y = AK^{0.3}N^{0.7}.$$

In the same way, specific numbers are assigned to the functions describing the behavior of consumers and workers. Where do these numbers come from? Generally, they are *not* estimated from macroeconomic data but are based on other sources. For example, the numbers assigned to the functions in the model may come from previous studies of the production function or of the saving behavior of individuals and families.

The third step, which must be carried out on a computer, is to see how the numerically specified model behaves when it is hit by random shocks, such as shocks to productivity. The shocks are created by the computer with a random number generator, with the size and persistence of the shocks (unlike the numbers

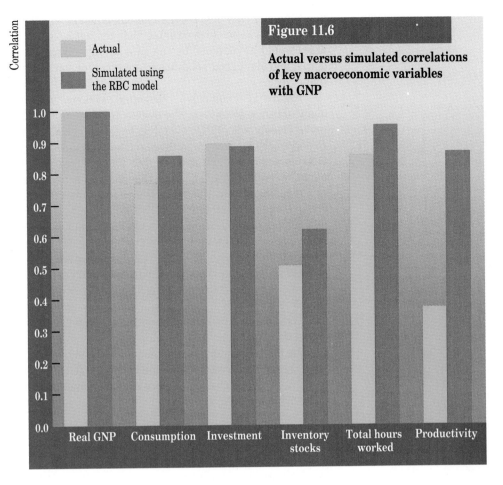

Figure 11.6

Actual versus simulated correlations of key macroeconomic variables with GNP

The degree to which a variable moves closely with GNP over the business cycle is measured by its correlation with GNP, with higher correlations implying a closer relationship. The figure compares the correlations of key variables with GNP that were actually observed in the postwar U.S. economy with the correlations predicted by computer simulations of Prescott's calibrated RBC model. Except for productivity, the simulations predict correlations of macroeconomic variables with GNP that closely resemble the actual correlations of these variables with GNP.

assigned to the specific functions) being chosen to fit the actual macroeconomic data. Given the shocks, the computer tracks the behavior of the model over many periods and reports the implied behavior of key macroeconomic variables such as output, employment, consumption, and investment. The results are then compared with the behavior of the actual economy to see how well the model captures reality.

An influential calibration exercise was performed by one of the developers of RBC theory, Edward Prescott[4] of the University of Minnesota. Prescott used a model very similar to the RBC model we have presented here, the main difference being that our version of the RBC model is a two-period model (the present and the future), and Prescott's model allowed for many periods. The results of Prescott's computer simulations are shown in Figs. 11.5 and 11.6.

Figure 11.5 compares the actually observed volatilities of six macroeconomic variables, as calculated from postwar U.S. data, with the volatilities predicted by Prescott's calibrated RBC model.[5] Prescott set the size of the random productivity shocks in his simulations so that the volatility of GNP in his model would match the actual volatility in U.S. GNP, which explains why the actual and simulated

---

[4]"Theory Ahead of Business Cycle Measurement," *Quarterly Review*, Federal Reserve Bank of Minneapolis, Fall 1986, pp. 9–22.

[5]The measure of volatility is called the *standard deviation*. The higher this measure is, the more volatile the variable being measured is.

volatilities of GNP are shown as being equal in Fig. 11.5. However, nothing in the calibration was set to guarantee that the actual volatilities of the other five variables would be matched by the simulation; and as you can see from Fig. 11.5, the actual and simulated volatilities for the other variables reported are in most cases quite close.

Figure 11.6 compares the actual economy with Prescott's calibrated model along another dimension, the degree to which important macroeconomic variables move closely with GNP over the business cycle. The statistical measure of how closely variables move together is called *correlation*. If a variable's correlation with GNP is positive, then the variable tends to move in the same direction as GNP over the business cycle (that is, the variable is procyclical). A correlation with GNP of 1.0 indicates that the variable's movements track the movements of GNP perfectly (thus the correlation of GNP with itself is 1.0), and a correlation with GNP of 0 indicates no relationship to GNP. Correlations with GNP between 0 and 1.0 reflect relationships with GNP of intermediate strength. Figure 11.6 shows that Prescott's model also accounts well for the strength of the relationships between some important macroeconomic variables and GNP, although the correlation of productivity and GNP predicted by Prescott's model is much larger than the actual correlation.

The degree to which relatively simple calibrated RBC models can match the actual data is impressive. In addition, the results of calibration exercises provide a guide to subsequent development of the model. For example, versions of the RBC model that followed the one discussed in this application have been modified to try to improve the match between the actual and predicted correlations of productivity with GNP.

Objections to the Real Business Cycle Theory

Although the real business cycle theory can account for several empirically observed features of business cycles, many economists have raised objections to this approach. In this section we discuss the major objections to the RBC theory as well as replies to these objections by RBC proponents.

Objection: It is difficult to measure or identify the productivity shocks that have caused business cycle fluctuations. Except for the oil price shocks of 1973, 1979, and 1990, which affected the productivity of capital and labor and contributed to subsequent recessions, it is hard to think of historical examples of economywide productivity shocks. Some technological innovations, such as railroads in the nineteenth century and computers in recent years, affect productivity in the whole economy; but the impact of most innovations is probably restricted to just a few industries. Box 11.1 on p. 417 illustrates the difficulties that economists have had in identifying and measuring productivity shocks.

Reply: Large cyclical movements are not necessarily caused by large, identifiable productivity shocks. Instead, business cycles can result from a series of small shocks. To illustrate the point that small shocks can cause large cycles, Fig. 11.7 shows the results of a computer simulation of productivity shocks and the associated behavior of output for a highly simplified RBC model. In this simple RBC model the change in output from one month to the next consists of two parts: (1) a fixed part that arises from normal technical progress or from a normal increase

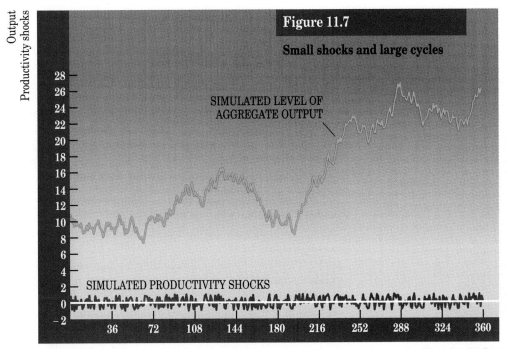

Figure 11.7

Small shocks and large cycles

A computer simulation of a simple RBC model is used to find the relationship between computer-generated, random productivity shocks and aggregate output. Even though all of the productivity shocks are small, the simulation predicts large cyclical fluctuations in aggregate output. Thus large productivity shocks are not necessary to generate large cyclical fluctuations.

in population and employment; and (2) an unpredictable part that reflects a shock to productivity during the current month.[6] The random, computer-generated productivity shocks are shown at the bottom of Fig. 11.7, and the implied behavior of output is displayed in the middle of the figure. Despite the fact that none of the shocks is large, you can see in Fig. 11.7 that the cumulative effect of the shocks is to cause large fluctuations in output that look something like business cycles. Since cyclical fluctuations can result from the effects of many small shocks, RBC theorists argue that it is not necessary to try to identify large productivity shocks corresponding to every major recession or boom.

Objection: According to RBC theory, changes in aggregate hours worked and the economywide real wage reflect movements of the aggregate labor demand curve along the aggregate labor supply curve. However, the aggregate labor supply curve is too steep for this theory to explain the large cyclical fluctuations in hours worked and the small cyclical fluctuations in the real wage that we observe. We

---

[6]Specifically, the model is $Y_t = Y_{t-1} + 0.01 + e_t$, where Y_t is output in month t, Y_{t-1} is output in the previous month (month $t - 1$), and e_t is the random productivity shock in month t. The productivity shocks are randomly chosen numbers between -1.0 and 1.0. A similar example is given in Numerical Problem 5.

saw in Fig. 11.4(a) that temporary productivity shocks shift the aggregate labor demand curve but do not affect the aggregate labor supply curve, implying that changes in the amount of labor used by firms and in the real wage over the cycle reflect movements along the labor supply curve. If the aggregate labor supply curve is flat, as shown in Fig. 11.8(a), then temporary productivity shocks that shift the labor demand curve cause large fluctuations in hours worked and small fluctuations in the real wage, which is consistent with what we observe. However, empirical studies have often found that the labor supply curve is relatively steep, as in Fig. 11.8(b). If the aggregate labor supply curve is steep, productivity shocks lead to large fluctuations in the real wage and small fluctuations in hours worked over the cycle, which is not consistent with the facts.

Reply: The aggregate labor supply curve may in fact be relatively flat, even though studies have found that individual workers have very steep labor supply curves. Although an increase in the real wage does not induce individual workers to supply many additional hours of work, a higher real wage may lead additional people to enter the labor force, thereby increasing substantially the total amount of labor supplied. Indeed, most of the year-to-year variation in total hours of work in the United States reflects changes in the number of people working rather than changes in the average number of hours worked by individual workers.[7] RBC theorists argue that studies of aggregate labor supply have focused too much on the hours supplied by individual workers and not enough on changes in the number of people working, which has caused these studies to conclude that the aggregate labor supply curve is steeper than it actually is. The question of how flat the aggregate labor supply curve is—and, in particular, whether it is flat enough to account for the cyclical behavior of hours worked and the real wage—remains controversial.

Objection: The RBC theory predicts that the price level will be countercyclical, but the business cycle fact is that the price level is procyclical. As we saw in our discussion of Fig. 11.4, the RBC theory predicts that an adverse productivity shock will both cause a recession and increase the general price level. In other words, the RBC theory predicts that the price level will be countercyclical. A few recessions have indeed been accompanied by inflation, notably the recessions following major oil price shocks, which is consistent with the RBC prediction. However, Chapter 9 reported the conventional finding that, more generally, inflation slows during or immediately after a recession.

Reply: As in the debate about the slope of the aggregate labor supply curve, there is controversy about what the business cycle facts really are. In a recent article RBC proponents Finn Kydland and Edward Prescott[8] argued that the U.S. price level has in fact been countercyclical since the 1950s, contrary to the generally accepted view. In their statistical study of the price level and real GNP during the period 1954–1989, Kydland and Prescott found that when GNP is above its long-run trend, the price level has tended to be below its long-run trend, and vice

---

[7]James J. Heckman, "Comments on the Ashenfelter and Kydland Papers," in K. Brunner and A. Meltzer, eds., *Carnegie-Rochester Conference Series on Public Policy* vol. 21, Autumn 1984.

[8]"Business Cycles: Real Facts and a Monetary Myth," *Quarterly Review*, Federal Reserve Bank of Minneapolis, Spring 1990, pp. 3–18.

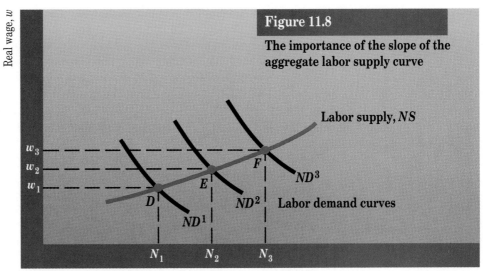

Figure 11.8

The importance of the slope of the aggregate labor supply curve

(a) Flat labor supply curve needed by the RBC theory

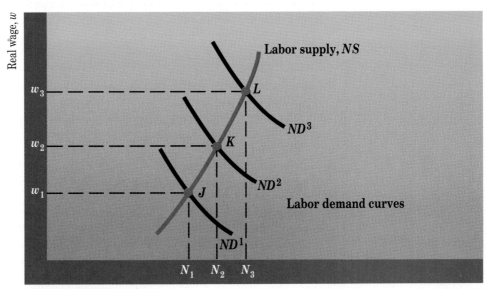

(b) Steep labor supply curve implied by empirical evidence

Temporary productivity shocks cause the labor demand curve ND to move back and forth along a fixed labor supply curve NS.

(a) If the aggregate labor supply curve were flat, then productivity shocks would lead to large fluctuations in total hours worked and small fluctuations in the real wage over the cycle, which is what we observe.

(b) However, empirical studies usually find that the aggregate labor supply curve is steep (as shown here) rather than flat. A steep aggregate labor supply curve implies that productivity shocks lead to small fluctuations in hours worked and large fluctuations in the real wage, which is inconsistent with the data. Critics of the RBC theory argue that this discrepancy is a problem for the RBC approach.

versa.[9] They interpret this result as showing that the price level is countercyclical. Kydland and Prescott also suggest that the standard view that the price level is procyclical is based mostly on the behavior of prices during the period between the two world wars (1918–1941), when the economy was different in structure and subject to a much different set of shocks than the modern economy.

11.3   FISCAL AND MONETARY POLICY IN THE CLASSICAL MODEL

Having discussed a particular classical theory of the business cycle, the real business cycle theory, we now examine what the classical model has to say about macroeconomic policy. There are several reasons for studying the role of macroeconomic policy in the classical model. First, although many classical economists are sympathetic to the real business cycle approach, some disagree with the RBC theorists' strong emphasis on productivity shocks as the dominant source of business cycles and argue that other types of shocks may also be important. Shocks to government policy are an additional potential source of economic fluctuations that many classical economists believe to be important in practice. Second, an important issue in macroeconomics is whether the government can or should try to use macroeconomic policies to offset or moderate the business cycle. To discuss this issue from a classical perspective, we must first understand how macroeconomic policies affect the economy in the classical model.

Fiscal Policy

Classical economists agree that changes in fiscal policy are at least potentially an important source of fluctuations in the economy. To illustrate the effects of a change in fiscal policy in the classical model, let's consider what happens when the government temporarily increases its purchases of goods, as it would, for example, when the country is at war.

Figure 11.9 illustrates the effects of a temporary increase in government purchases. Before the fiscal policy change the economy's general equilibrium is represented by point E in both parts of the figure. To see what happens once purchases rise, we start with the labor market as represented in Fig. 11.9(a). The change in fiscal policy does not affect the production function or the marginal product of labor (the MPN curve), so the labor demand curve does not shift. However, as we discussed in Chapter 10, higher government purchases must be paid for by higher taxes, either in the present or in the future, or both. Because workers know their taxes must rise, they feel poorer and supply more labor at any given real wage. Thus the labor supply curve shifts to the right, from NS^1 to NS^2. Since the increase in government purchases is only temporary, however, we assume that workers' wealth is not greatly affected, and so we show the shift of the labor supply curve as being relatively small.

Following the shift of the labor supply curve, the equilibrium in the labor market shifts from point E to point F in Fig. 11.9(a), with employment increasing and the real wage decreasing. Because equilibrium employment increases, full-employment output $\bar{Y}$ also increases. Thus the FE line shifts to the right, from FE^1 to

---

[9]Kydland and Prescott use a novel method for calculating trends, which may help explain why their results are different from conventional findings.

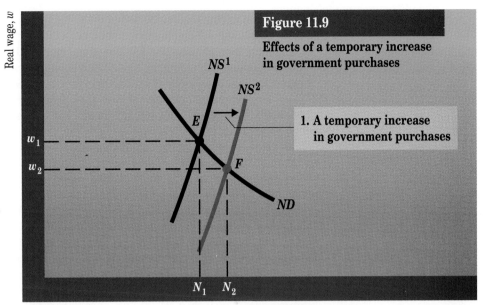

Figure 11.9

Effects of a temporary increase in government purchases

(a) Labor market

1. A temporary increase in government purchases

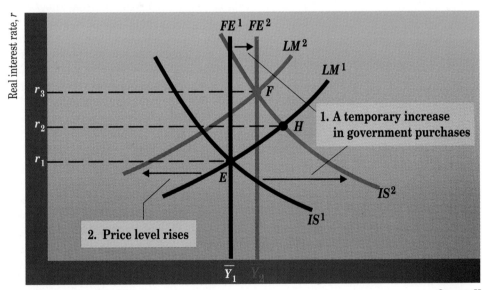

(b) General equilibrium

1. A temporary increase in government purchases

2. Price level rises

Initial equilibrium is at point E in both parts.

(a) A temporary increase in government purchases raises workers' current or future tax burdens. Since workers feel poorer, they supply more labor and the labor supply curve shifts right, from NS^1 to NS^2. The shift in the labor supply curve reduces the real wage and increases employment at point F.

(b) The increase in employment shifts the FE line to the right, from FE^1 to FE^2. The increase in government purchases also reduces desired national saving and shifts

the IS curve upward, from IS^1 to IS^2. Because the intersection of IS^2 and LM^1 is to the right of FE^2, the aggregate demand for goods is higher than the full-employment level of output $\bar{Y}_2$, so that the price level rises. The rise in the price level reduces the real money supply and shifts the LM curve upward, from LM^1 to LM^2, until the new general equilibrium is reached at point F. The effect of the increase in government purchases is to increase output, the real interest rate, and the price level.

FE^2 in Fig. 11.9(b). Under the assumption that labor supply increases only by a small amount, the FE line does not shift very far.

In addition to shifting the FE line to the right in Fig. 11.9(b), the fiscal policy change also causes the IS curve to shift. As we have seen before, at any given level of output a temporary increase in government purchases reduces desired national saving and raises the real interest rate that clears the goods market. Thus the IS curve shifts upward, from IS^1 to IS^2. Unlike the FE line and the IS curve, the LM curve is not directly affected by the change in fiscal policy.

The new IS curve (IS^2), the LM curve (LM^1), and the new FE line (FE^2) do not have a common point of intersection. For general equilibrium to be restored, prices must adjust, shifting the LM curve until it passes through the intersection of the new IS curve and the new FE line (point F in Fig. 11.9b). Will prices rise or fall? The answer to this question is potentially ambiguous, since the fiscal policy change has increased both the aggregate demand for goods (by reducing desired saving and shifting the IS curve upward) and the aggregate supply of goods (by increasing labor supply and shifting the FE line to the right). Since we have argued that the effect on aggregate supply is probably small (the FE line doesn't shift very far), it is most likely that after the fiscal policy change aggregate demand exceeds aggregate supply: In Fig. 11.9(b) we show aggregate demand (point H, at the intersection of IS^2 and LM^1) exceeding aggregate supply (full-employment output $\bar{Y}_2$). Thus the price level must rise, shifting the LM curve left and causing the economy to return to general equilibrium at point F. At point F both output and the real interest rate are higher than at the initial equilibrium, point E.

To summarize, the increase in government spending increases output, employment, the real interest rate, and the price level. Because the increase in employment is the result of an increase in labor supply rather than an increase in labor demand, real wages fall. The fall in the real wage and the rise in taxes make workers worse off, unless the benefits of the government's spending program outweigh the losses in workers' private resources. These results all apply to a temporary increase in government purchases. (Analytical Problem 3 asks you to work out what happens when government purchases rise permanently.)

Our analysis shows that changes in the government's fiscal policies can have real effects on the economy. Potentially, therefore, changes in fiscal policy could be used to stabilize output and employment. This brings us to the normative question of whether policymakers *should* try to use fiscal policy to smooth out business cycle fluctuations. As we have discussed, classical economists (which include the RBC theorists) generally answer "no" to this question, because of Adam Smith's invisible-hand argument that free markets produce efficient outcomes without government intervention. This does *not* mean that classical economists don't regard recessions as a serious problem. If an adverse productivity shock causes a recession, for example, real wages, employment, and consumption all fall, which means that many people are experiencing hardship. But would it help to offset the recession by increasing government purchases? According to the classical analysis, an increase in government purchases raises output and employment but nevertheless makes workers worse off, unless the direct benefits of the government program exceed the costs (in which case the program should be undertaken whether or not a recession is in progress).

Besides arguing that policies to smooth out the business cycle are undesirable in principle (a normative point), classical economists also frequently argue that, in practice, policy cannot be used successfully to smooth out the cycle anyway (a

An alternative to the RBC view that productivity shocks cause business cycles is the idea that cycles are caused by macroeconomic policy shocks, such as changes in government spending or the money supply. It would be interesting to know whether productivity shocks or macroeconomic policy shocks are more important empirically.

To try to answer this question, Alan Stockman* of the University of Rochester analyzed the behavior of production in each of ten industries in seven European countries and the United States (for a total of eighty industry-country combinations) for the period between 1964 and 1984. Stockman's idea was that it may be reasonable to think of productivity shocks as generally industry-specific rather than country-specific: For example, major improvements in technology in the paper industry should affect the paper industry in all countries, but these technological changes should have little impact on industries that are not producers or heavy users of paper. On the other hand, macroeconomic policy shocks are generally country-specific rather than industry-specific: An expansionary fiscal policy in France, for example, would affect production in all French industries but would not be likely to have strong effects on industries in other countries. Therefore, Stockman argued, if productivity shocks are the more important, production in the French paper industry should be more closely related to production in the paper industries of other countries than to the production of other industries in France. But if policy shocks are more important, production in the French paper industry should be more closely tied to the production of other French industries than to the rest of the world's paper industry.

Using a statistical model, Stockman found that the total variation in the production of the industries

BOX *11.1:* WHERE DO SHOCKS TO THE MACROECONOMY COME FROM?

he studied could be broken into three parts:

1. Industry-specific shocks unrelated to country-specific shocks caused 28% of the variation in industrial production. Stockman interpreted this part of the variation of production as arising purely from productivity shocks.

2. Country-specific shocks unrelated to industry-specific shocks caused 24% of the variation in industrial production. Stockman attributed this portion of the variation to national economic policy shocks and other country-specific factors unrelated to productivity.

3. The remaining 48% of the variation in production arose from industry-specific shocks and country-specific shocks that were related to each other.

Stockman's interpretation of his results, that only 28% of the variation in industrial production could be attributed purely to productivity shocks, casts doubt on the RBC view that productivity shocks are the dominant source of shocks. However, a possible RBC response to Stockman's findings is to question the assumption that productivity shocks are necessarily industry-specific rather than country-specific. For instance, a local drought, earthquake, or other natural disaster would be a productivity shock; but if confined to only one country, it would also be a country-specific shock. A change in educational standards is another example of a productivity shock that may be largely country-specific.

*"Sectoral and National Aggregate Disturbances to Industrial Output in Seven European Countries," *Journal of Monetary Economics,* March/May 1988, pp. 387–409.

positive point). According to classicals, our imperfect knowledge of the economy, political constraints on policy actions, and time lags between the onset of a recession and the implementation of effective countermeasures all make antirecessionary macroeconomic policies impractical. These issues are addressed in more detail in Part V of this book.

If fiscal policy should not be used to offset business cycle fluctuations, then how should the government choose its purchases and set taxes? Classical economists argue that the level of government purchases should be based solely on a comparison of the benefits and costs of new roads, schools, fighter planes, and so on. As for taxes, tax rates should be set to provide incentives for productive economic activity and to distribute the burden of paying for government activities fairly. Tax rates should also be kept approximately constant over time, to avoid uncertainties and inefficiencies that can be created by erratic changes in tax rates. We discuss these issues further in Chapter 16.

Monetary Policy

The effect of changes in the money supply in the classical *IS-LM* model were examined in Chapter 4. There we found that according to the classical model, changes in the money supply are *neutral:* A change in the nominal money supply M causes the price level P to change in the same proportion, but a change in the money supply has no effect on real variables, such as output, employment, or the real interest rate.

Figure 11.10 reviews why money is neutral in the classical model. Suppose that the initial general equilibrium is represented by point E in the figure, and suppose that the Federal Reserve reduces the money supply. The reduction in the money supply causes the LM curve to shift upward, from LM^1 to LM^2. The reduction in the money supply has no effect on either the IS curve or the FE line, since neither goods market equilibrium nor labor market equilibrium depends on the money supply.

In Fig. 11.10, after the fall in the money supply, the intersection of the IS curve and the new LM curve (point F) lies to the left of the FE line, so that the aggregate demand for goods is less than the aggregate supply. This excess supply of goods reduces the price level,[10] which in turn raises the real money supply and shifts the LM curve back to the right. The price level continues to fall until (1) the real money supply returns to its initial value, (2) the LM curve returns to its initial position at LM^1, and (3) the economy returns to its original general equilibrium at point E. The reduction in the nominal money supply has no real effects (money is neutral), although the fall in the nominal money supply does cause the price level to fall proportionally in order to keep the real money supply M/P unchanged. The nominal wage rate W must also fall in the same proportion as the price level, so that the real wage rate, $w = W/P$, can remain unchanged.

What does the classical model say about how monetary policy should be conducted? Because money is neutral in the classical model, monetary policy cannot be used to offset business cycle fluctuations, even if offsetting fluctuations were

---

[10]Recall from Chapter 4, Section 4.5, that the fall in the money supply and the price level should be thought of as being *relative to their trends*. For example, if the money supply and the price level initially were both growing at 5% per year, then a slowdown in nominal money growth to 3% for one year would be a reduction in the nominal money supply *relative to its trend*. As a result, the price level would rise by only 3%, which is a reduction in the price level *relative to its trend*.

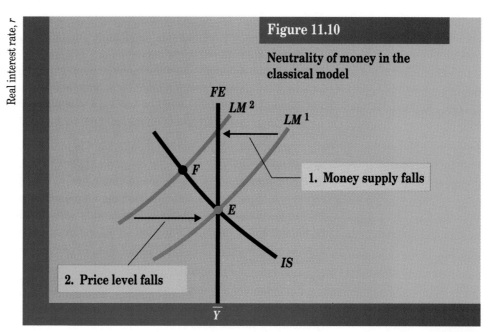

Figure 11.10

Neutrality of money in the classical model

1. **Money supply falls**

2. **Price level falls**

Initial equilibrium is at point E, and the Fed reduces the nominal money supply. The reduction in the money supply shifts the LM curve left to LM^2. The intersection of IS and LM^2 is to the left of the FE line, so that the aggregate demand for output is less than full-employment output $\bar{Y}$. Therefore the price level falls, increasing the real money supply and shifting the LM curve back to LM^1. When the price level has fallen by the same proportion as the money supply, the economy returns to its initial equilibrium at point E. The monetary contraction lowers the price level proportionally but does not affect any real variables such as output. Thus money is neutral in the basic classical model.

desirable. However, changes in the money supply do affect the price level. Thus classical economists suggest that the money supply should be increased slowly and steadily to maintain a low and stable rate of inflation.

Monetary Nonneutrality and Reverse Causation

The prediction that money is neutral is a striking result of the classical model, but it seems inconsistent with the business cycle fact that money is a leading, procyclical variable (Chapter 9). If an expansion of the money supply has no effect, why are expansions of the money supply typically followed by increased rates of economic activity?

The business cycle fact that increases in the money supply tend to precede expansions in output does not necessarily mean that economic expansions are *caused* by the increases in the money supply. After all, just because people put storm windows on their houses before winter begins does not mean that winter is caused by putting on storm windows. Instead, the causation runs in the opposite direction: People put storm windows on their houses *because* they know that winter is coming.

Many classical economists, including RBC theorists in particular, argue that the link between money growth and economic expansion is like the link between putting on storm windows and the onset of winter, a relationship they call reverse causation. Specifically, **reverse causation** means that expected future increases in output cause increases in the current money supply, and expected future decreases in output cause decreases in the current money supply. Reverse causation, if correct, explains how money could be a procyclical and leading variable even if changes in the money supply are neutral and have no real effects.[11]

To see how reverse causation might arise, suppose that the Federal Reserve wants to keep the aggregate price level stable. Imagine also that the Fed knows that an adverse productivity shock is causing or soon will cause a recession. We saw in the analysis of a temporary productivity shock (Fig. 11.4) that if the money supply is left unchanged, an adverse productivity shock will increase the price level as well as cause a recession. To avoid the increase in the price level, the Fed should reduce the money supply as soon as it knows that a recession is coming. This behavior by the Fed, in which it adjusts the money supply in response to the prospective macroeconomic situation, could explain why money growth slows down before a recession. This scenario is known as reverse causation because the prospective change in the macroeconomic situation causes the Fed to change the money supply, rather than the other way around. An alternative way that the prospect of a recession may cause the current money supply to fall is discussed in Analytical Problem 4.

It is undoubtedly true that reverse causation explains at least some of the tendency of money to lead output (see Box 11.2). However, this observation does not rule out the possibility that changes in the money supply also sometimes cause changes in output, so that money is nonneutral. That is, both reverse causation and monetary nonneutrality could potentially account for the procyclical behavior of money.

The Nonneutrality of Money: Additional Evidence

Because of reverse causation, the leading and procyclical behavior of money cannot by itself establish that money is nonneutral. To settle the issue of whether or not money is neutral, we need additional evidence. One useful source of additional evidence is the analysis of historical episodes of monetary policy. The classic study of the history of monetary policy in the United States is the landmark 1963 work by Milton Friedman and Anna J. Schwartz, *A Monetary History of the United States, 1867–1960*.[12] Using a variety of sources, including Federal Reserve policy statements and the journals and correspondence of monetary policymakers, the *Monetary History* presents careful descriptions and analyses of the causes of money supply fluctuations and the interrelation of money with other economic variables over a 93-year period. In their summing up Friedman and Schwartz concluded:

> Throughout the near-century examined in detail we have found that:
>
> 1. Changes in the behavior of the money stock have been closely associated with changes in economic activity, [nominal] income, and prices.
> 2. The interrelation between monetary and economic change has been highly stable.

---

[11]Robert G. King and Charles I. Plosser, "Money, Credit, and Prices in a Real Business Cycle Model," *American Economic Review*, June 1984, pp. 363–380, explain reverse causation in a real business cycle model and present supporting evidence.

[12]Princeton, N.J.: Princeton University Press for NBER, 1963.

According to the reverse causation argument, the association of higher-than-normal money growth with economic booms and lower-than-normal money growth with recessions occurs because money growth *responds* to changes in output, not because money growth *causes* changes in output. An example of reverse causation is provided by the behavior of money and economic activity at Christmas: In the United States both the money supply and retail sales grow faster in the fourth quarter of the year than in any other quarter, as shown in the accompanying table.* Clearly, the sharp increase in fourth-quarter retail sales (measured in real terms) results from Christmas gift buying and not from the fourth-quarter increase in the money supply. Thus at Christmastime higher economic activity must cause a higher money supply, rather than vice versa. Where does the extra money come from? The Federal Reserve regularly increases the money supply in the fourth quarter to meet the demands of merchants and shoppers for more money.

The existence of reverse causation from output to money around Christmas doesn't rule out monetary nonneutrality, but it does mean that we have to be cautious in interpreting the positive association

BOX 11.2: MONEY AND ECONOMIC ACTIVITY AT CHRISTMAS

between money and output over the course of the business cycle. This association could arise because of monetary nonneutrality, or because of reverse causation, or both. The relationship between money and economic activity around Christmas shows that reverse causation does in fact occur and can be empirically important.

Quarter	Growth of Money Supply	Growth of Real Retail Sales
Jan.–Mar.	− 0.72%	− 4.83%
Apr.–June	1.00	1.53
July–Sept.	0.52	− 1.44
Oct.–Dec.	1.55	7.90

*Growth rates are measured quarter to quarter. Sources: Money supply (M1, seasonally unadjusted)—Board of Governors of the Federal Reserve System, *Banking and Monetary Statistics, 1941–1970*, and Board of Governors of the Federal Reserve System, *Annual Statistical Digest*, various issues; retail sales, total (seasonally unadjusted) and deflator (CPI-U)—U.S. Department of Commerce, *Business Statistics, 1961–88*.

3. Monetary changes have often had an independent origin; they have not been simply a reflection of changes in economic activity. (p. 676)

The first two conclusions restate the basic business cycle fact that money is procyclical. The third conclusion says that reverse causation cannot explain all of the relationship between money and real income or real GNP. Friedman and Schwartz focused on a number of historical episodes in which changes in the supply of money were not (they argued) responses to macroeconomic conditions but instead resulted from other factors such as gold discoveries (which affect money supplies under the gold standard), changes in monetary institutions, or changes in the leadership of the Federal Reserve. In the majority of these cases "independent" changes in money growth were followed by changes in the same direction in real output. This evidence suggests that money is not neutral.

Recently, Christina Romer and David Romer,[13] both at the University of California at Berkeley, reviewed and updated the Friedman-Schwartz analysis. Al-

[13]"Does Monetary Policy Matter? A New Test in the Spirit of Friedman and Schwartz," in Olivier J. Blanchard and Stanley Fischer, eds., *Macroeconomics Annual*, Cambridge, Mass.: M.I.T. Press, 1989.

though they disputed the interpretations of some episodes given by Friedman and Schwartz, they generally agreed with the conclusion that money is not neutral. In particular, they argued that since 1960 (the year in which the study by Friedman and Schwartz stopped) there have been a half dozen additional episodes of monetary nonneutrality. Probably the most famous one occurred in 1979, when Federal Reserve Chairman Paul Volcker announced that money supply procedures would change and that the growth rate of money would be reduced in order to fight inflation. Volcker's change in monetary strategy was followed by a minor recession in 1980 and a severe one in 1981–1982. Relaxation of the Fed's anti-inflationary monetary policy in 1982 was followed by an economic boom.

Because of the Friedman-Schwartz evidence, and because of episodes like the 1979–1982 Volcker policy (and a similar experience in Britain at the same time), many—probably most—economists believe that money is not neutral. If we accept the evidence that money is not neutral, contrary to the prediction of the classical model, then we are left with two choices: Either we must adopt a new framework for macroeconomic analysis (such as the Keynesian framework discussed in the next chapter), or we must modify the classical model. In the next section we take the second approach and consider how monetary nonneutrality can be explained in a classical model.

11.4   AGGREGATE DEMAND, AGGREGATE SUPPLY, AND THE NONNEUTRALITY OF MONEY

To explore the issue of monetary neutrality more deeply, we introduce two new curves, called the aggregate demand (AD) curve and the aggregate supply (AS) curve. Although we have not seen these curves before, they are completely consistent with the classical IS-LM model; the AD and AS curves just represent a different way of describing general equilibrium in the economy. Unlike the IS curve, the LM curve, and the FE line, which relate the *real interest rate* to real output, the AD and AS curves relate the *price level* to real output.

The Aggregate Demand Curve

The **aggregate demand curve** shows the relation between the price level and the aggregate demand for goods and services. As we will see, the AD curve is a downward-sloping relation between the price level and the aggregate quantity of output demanded, just as the demand curve for a single product, apples for example, is a downward-sloping relation between the price of apples and the quantity of apples demanded. Despite the superficial similarity between the AD curve and the demand curve for a specific good, however, there is an important difference between these two types of curves. The demand curve for apples relates the demand for apples to the price of apples *relative to the prices of other goods*. In contrast, the AD curve relates the aggregate quantity of output demanded to the *general price level P*. If the prices of all goods increase by 10%, the price level P increases by 10% as well, even though all relative prices of goods remain unchanged. Nevertheless, as we will explain, the increase in the price level reduces the aggregate quantity of goods demanded.

The reason that an increase in the price level P reduces the aggregate quantity of goods demanded is that given the nominal money supply M, an increase in P reduces the real money supply M/P. A fall in the real money supply shifts the LM

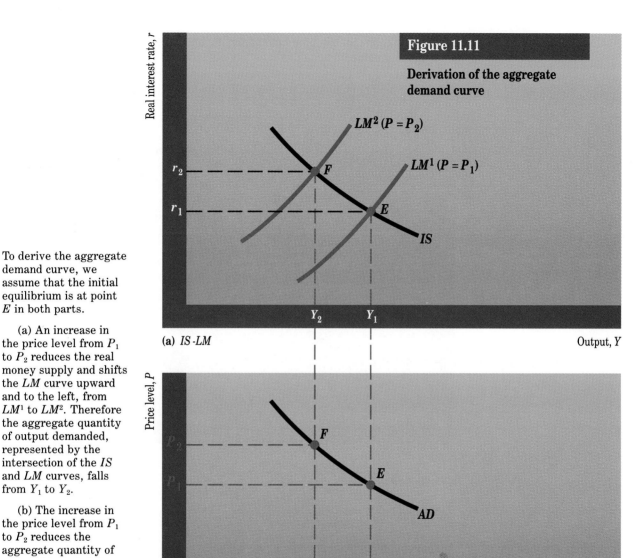

Figure 11.11

Derivation of the aggregate demand curve

To derive the aggregate demand curve, we assume that the initial equilibrium is at point E in both parts.

(a) An increase in the price level from P_1 to P_2 reduces the real money supply and shifts the LM curve upward and to the left, from LM^1 to LM^2. Therefore the aggregate quantity of output demanded, represented by the intersection of the IS and LM curves, falls from Y_1 to Y_2.

(b) The increase in the price level from P_1 to P_2 reduces the aggregate quantity of output demanded from Y_1 to Y_2, so the aggregate demand curve slopes downward.

curve upward and to the left and reduces the aggregate quantity of output demanded. This sequence is shown in Fig. 11.11. Suppose that the nominal money supply is M and the initial price level is P_1, so that the real money supply is M/P_1 and the LM curve is LM^1 in Fig. 11.11(a). Recall that the aggregate quantity of goods demanded is shown by the intersection of the IS and LM curves. The IS curve and the initial LM curve intersect at point E, so that when the price level is P_1, the aggregate amount of output demanded is Y_1.

Now suppose that the price level increases to P_2. This increase in the price level reduces the real money supply to M/P_2 and shifts the LM curve upward and to the left, to LM^2 in Fig. 11.11(a). The intersection of the IS curve and the new LM curve is at point F, where the aggregate quantity of output demanded is Y_2.

Thus the increase in the price level from P_1 to P_2 reduces the aggregate quantity of output demanded from Y_1 to Y_2. This negative relation between the price level and the aggregate quantity of output demanded is shown as the downward-sloping AD curve in Fig. 11.11(b). Points E and F in Fig. 11.11(b) correspond to points E and F in Fig. 11.11(a).

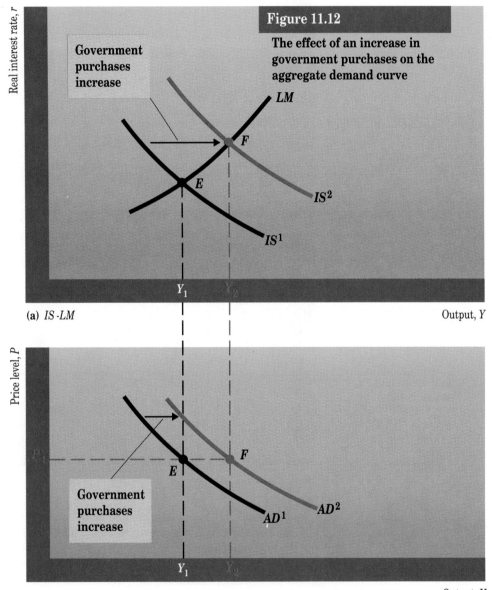

Figure 11.12

The effect of an increase in government purchases on the aggregate demand curve

(a) An increase in government purchases shifts the IS curve upward and to the right, from IS^1 to IS^2. At the initial price level the aggregate quantity of output demanded increases from Y_1 to Y_2, as shown by the shift of the IS-LM intersection from point E to point F.

(b) Because the aggregate quantity of output demanded rises at any given price level, the AD curve shifts to the right. Points E and F in part (b) correspond to points E and F in part (a).

Factors That Shift the *AD* Curve Given the price level, any factor that causes the intersection of the *IS* curve and the *LM* curve to shift to the right raises aggregate demand and causes the *AD* curve to shift to the right. Similarly, given the price level, any factor that causes the intersection of the *IS* and *LM* curves to shift to the left also shifts the *AD* curve to the left. An example of a factor that shifts the *AD* curve to the right is a temporary increase in government purchases (see Fig. 11.12). The initial *IS* curve, IS^1, intersects the *LM* curve at point *E* in Fig. 11.12(a), so that the initial aggregate quantity of output demanded is Y_1. An increase in government purchases shifts the *IS* curve right to IS^2. With the price level held constant at its initial value of P_1, the intersection of the *IS* and *LM* curves moves to point *F*, so that the aggregate quantity of output demanded increases to Y_2. The increase in the aggregate quantity of output demanded at the given price level P_1 is shown by the movement from point *E* to point *F* in Fig. 11.12(b). Thus as a result of the temporary increase in government purchases, the *AD* curve shifts right, from AD^1 to AD^2. Other factors that shift the *AD* curve are listed in Table 11.2.

Table 11.2 Summary

Factors That Shift the *AD* Curve

An Increase in	Shifts the *AD* Curve	Reason
Expected future output	Right	Reduces desires saving, raises desired consumption, and shifts the *IS* curve to the right
Government purchases *G*	Right	Reduces desired saving and shifts the *IS* curve to the right
Expected future *MPK*	Right	Increases desired investment and shifts the *IS* curve to the right
Corporate taxes	Left	Reduces desired investment and shifts the *IS* curve to the left
Nominal money supply *M*	Right	Raises the real money supply and shifts the *LM* curve to the right
Interest rate on money i^m	Left	Increases the demand for money and shifts the *LM* curve to the left
Expected inflation rate π^e	Right	Reduces the demand for money and shifts the *LM* curve to the right

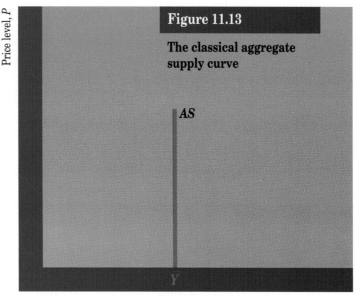

Figure 11.13

The classical aggregate supply curve

In the classical model the labor market clears, so that employment always equals its full-employment level. Therefore output equals its full-employment level $\bar{Y}$, regardless of the price level, and the aggregate supply curve is vertical.

The Aggregate Supply Curve

The **aggregate supply curve** shows the relation between the price level and the aggregate amount of output that firms supply. In equilibrium in the classical model the labor market clears at the full-employment level of employment $\bar{N}$ and firms supply the full-employment level of output $\bar{Y}$, regardless of the value of the price level. Because in the classical model the amount of output that firms supply is fixed at $\bar{Y}$ and does not depend on the price level, the AS curve is a vertical line at $Y = \bar{Y}$, as shown in Fig. 11.13.

Factors That Shift the AS Curve   Any factor that increases the full-employment level of output $\bar{Y}$ shifts the aggregate supply curve to the right, and any factor that reduces $\bar{Y}$ shifts the aggregate supply curve to the left. Thus any change that shifts the FE line to the right in the IS-LM diagram (see Table 11.1) also shifts the AS curve to the right. For instance, an increase in the labor force raises the full-employment levels of employment and output, thereby shifting the AS curve to the right.

General Equilibrium in the AD-AS Model

General equilibrium in the economy is represented by the intersection of the AD curve and the AS curve, as at point E in Fig. 11.14. At point E output equals its full-employment level $\bar{Y}$, and the price level equals P_1. In the classical model prices and wages are assumed to adjust quickly, so that the economy reaches its general equilibrium quickly. To see how the price level adjusts, suppose that the price level happened to be P_2, which is lower than the equilibrium level P_1. In this case, as shown in Fig. 11.14, the aggregate amount of output demanded is Y_2, which is greater than $\bar{Y}$. The excess demand for output causes the price level to be bid upward. The price level will continue to increase until it reaches P_1 and aggregate demand and aggregate supply are equal. Similarly, if the price level were higher

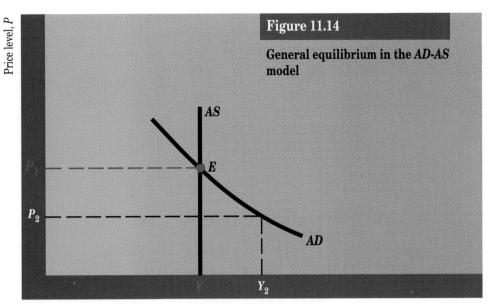

Figure 11.14

General equilibrium in the *AD-AS* model

The general equilibrium of the economy is located at the intersection of the *AD* and *AS* curves at point *E*, where output equals $\bar{Y}$ and the price level equals P_1. The general equilibrium is attained by the adjustment of the price level. If, for example, the price level is P_2, which is lower than P_1, the aggregate quantity of output demanded Y_2 exceeds the supply of output $\bar{Y}$. The excess demand for output causes the price level to be bid up until it reaches P_1. Similarly, if the price level is above P_1, the aggregate quantity of output demanded will be less than $\bar{Y}$, and prices will be bid downward to P_1.

than the equilibrium price level P_1, then the aggregate quantity of goods demanded would be smaller than the aggregate quantity of goods supplied, and the price level would be bid down until it reached P_1.

The results obtained so far with the *AD-AS* model are no different from the results found using the classical *IS-LM* model. The only difference is that with the *AD-AS* model we focus on the relationship between output and prices, rather than the relationship between output and the real interest rate, as in the *IS-LM* model.

Monetary Neutrality in the *AD-AS* Model

We can use the *AD* and *AS* curves to illustrate the neutrality of money in the classical model. Although we have already seen that money is neutral in the classical model, showing this result in terms of the *AD* and *AS* curves provides a useful warm-up for the next section, in which we use the *AD-AS* diagram to study an extension of the classical model that allows for monetary nonneutrality.

Suppose that the economy is initially in equilibrium at point *E* in Fig. 11.15, and then the money supply increases by 10%. In the *IS-LM* diagram we know that an increase in the money supply shifts the *LM* curve downward and to the right, raising the aggregate quantity of output demanded at any given price level. Thus an increase in the money supply also shifts the *AD* curve upward and to the right, from AD^1 to AD^2 in Fig. 11.15.

We can say even more about the effects of the increase in the money supply on the *AD* curve: *When the money supply rises by 10%, the AD curve shifts ver-*

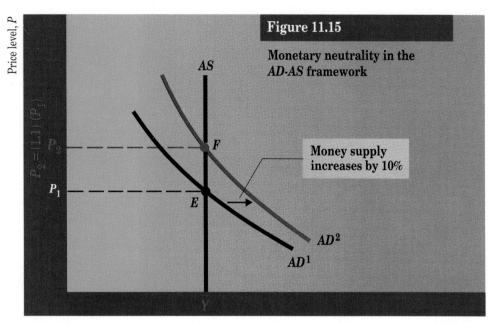

Figure 11.15

Monetary neutrality in the AD-AS framework

If we start from general equilibrium at point E, a 10% increase in the nominal money supply shifts the AD curve upward by 10% at each level of output, from AD^1 to AD^2. The AD curve shifts upward by 10% because at any given level of output, a 10% increase in the price level is needed to keep the real money supply, and thus the aggregate quantity of output demanded, unchanged. In the new equilibrium at point F output is unchanged at $\bar{Y}$, and the price level P_2 is 10% higher than the initial price level P_1. Because the increase in the money supply raises prices but does not affect real variables such as output, money is neutral in this framework.

tically upward by 10% at each level of output demanded. To see why, compare points E and F in Fig. 11.15. Because point F lies on AD^2 and point E lies on AD^1, the nominal money supply M is 10% higher at point F than at point E. However, the aggregate quantity of output demanded is the same (equal to $\bar{Y}$) at point F and point E. The aggregate quantity of output demanded can be the same at points F and E only if the real money supply M/P, which determines the position of the LM curve and hence the aggregate quantity of output demanded, is the same at point F as at point E. Since the nominal money supply M is 10% higher at point F, for the real money supply to be the same at the two points the price level at point F must be 10% higher than the price level at point E. Therefore P_2 is 10% higher than P_1. Indeed, for every level of output the price level is 10% higher on AD^2 than on AD^1.

The AS curve is not affected by the increase in the nominal money supply, because full-employment output does not depend on the money supply. Therefore, as a result of the increase in the money supply, the general equilibrium of the economy moves from point E to point F in Fig. 11.15, with the price level increasing by 10%. Because the price level rises by 10%, the real money supply M/P is unchanged between points E and F. Figure 11.15 also shows that output is unchanged. Thus, once again, we find that money is neutral in the classical model.

The neutrality of money illustrated in Fig. 11.15 depends crucially on the fact that the *AS* curve is vertical. An increase in the money supply shifts the *AD* curve upward, but because the *AS* curve in the classical model is vertical, there is no effect on the amount of output produced. In order for an increase in the money supply to change the equilibrium amount of output produced, the aggregate supply curve would have to be nonvertical. We now turn to an extension of the classical model that features an upward-sloping aggregate supply curve, with the important consequence that (at least sometimes) money is not neutral.

The Misperceptions Theory

This extension to the classical model is based on a theory that we call the misperceptions theory. This theory was originally put forth by Nobel laureate Milton Friedman and then was rigorously formulated by Robert E. Lucas, Jr., of the University of Chicago. According to the **misperceptions theory,** *the aggregate quantity of output supplied rises above the full-employment level $\bar{Y}$ when the aggregate price level P is higher than expected.* Thus given the expected price level, the aggregate supply curve relating the price level and the aggregate quantity of output supplied slopes upward.

If you took a course in principles of economics, you learned that supply curves generally slope upward, with higher prices leading to increased production. However, just as the demand curves for individual goods differ from the aggregate demand curve, there is an important distinction between the supply curves for individual goods and the aggregate supply curve. An ordinary supply curve relates the supply of some good to the price of that good *relative to other prices*. In contrast, the aggregate supply curve relates the aggregate amount of output produced to the *general price level*. Changes in the general price level can occur when there are no changes in the relative prices of individual goods.

To understand the misperceptions theory and why it implies an upward-sloping aggregate supply curve, let's think about an individual producer of a particular good, say bread. If a baker is maximizing his utility, then the amount of bread he produces depends on the relative price of bread. When the price of bread increases relative to other prices in the economy, including the prices of the goods and services that the baker wants to buy, then the amount of real income that the baker gets by producing and selling a loaf of bread—effectively, the baker's real wage—rises. In response to the higher return to bread baking, the baker increases the production of bread.[14] Similarly, when the price of bread falls relative to other prices in the economy, the baker's real benefit from bread baking declines, and he decreases his production of bread.

But how does an individual baker know whether the relative price of bread has changed? To calculate the relative price of bread, the baker needs to know both the nominal price of bread and the general price level. It is easy for the baker to know the nominal price of bread because he sells bread every day and observes the price directly. However, the baker is probably not as well informed about the general price level, because he observes the prices of the many goods and services he might want to buy less frequently than he observes the price of bread.

---

[14]We assume that the substitution effect of the baker's higher real wage outweighs the income effect.

To see how the baker's imprecise knowledge about the general price level affects his choice of how much bread to bake, suppose that the nominal price of bread, which is determined in a competitive market, increases by 10%. How does the baker react to this increase in the nominal price of bread? It depends on what he thinks has happened to the general price level. If he thinks the general price level remained constant, then the 10% increase in the nominal price of bread will be a 10% increase in the relative price of bread and the baker will increase his production. Alternatively, if he thinks the general price level also rose by 10%, then the 10% rise in the price of bread will just maintain the relative price of bread at its previous level, and the baker will not change the amount of bread produced. Thus the baker's reaction to a 10% increase in the nominal price of bread depends on his beliefs about what is happening to prices in general.

However, because the baker's knowledge of the current price level is imprecise, when he sees a 10% increase in the price of bread, he does not know for sure whether the price level has risen by 10% or by something less than 10%. Suppose that from past experience the baker knows that sometimes a 10% increase in the price of bread occurs when the general price level is unchanged, and sometimes it occurs when the general price level increases by 10%. Not knowing which situation applies to the current increase in the price of bread, the baker takes a sort of average of these experiences and estimates that the general price level has increased by, say, 5%. Because his estimate of the increase in the general price level (5%) is less than the increase in the price of bread (10%), the baker's best guess is that the relative price of bread has increased. Therefore the baker increases the amount of bread produced in response to the 10% increase in the nominal price of bread.

We have shown that when the nominal price of a particular good increases, suppliers of that good increase production. Now we consider the effect on *aggregate* production of an increase in the general price level. Suppose that the general price level increases by 10% and that the nominal prices of all goods and services increase by 10%. In this case the relative prices of all goods are unchanged. Nevertheless, aggregate output increases because each individual producer observes that the price of his own good increases by 10%. As in the case of the baker, when suppliers see the price of their own product increase by 10%, they guess that the general price level has increased by less than 10%. Every supplier is fooled into thinking that the relative price of his own good has increased, and hence the production of all goods increases. Thus the increase in the general nominal price level leads to an increase in aggregate output.

Producers' expectations about the price level are critical in determining how they react to a given change in the aggregate price level. Suppose that before he observes the current market price of bread, the baker expects an overall inflation rate of 5%. How will he react if he then observes that the price of bread increases by 5%? The baker reasons as follows: "I expected the overall rate of inflation to be 5%, and now I know that the price of bread has increased by 5%. This 5% increase in the price of bread is consistent with what I had expected. My best estimate is that all prices increased by 5%, and thus I think that the relative price of bread is unchanged. There is no reason to change my output." If all suppliers expected the nominal price level to increase by 5% and reason in the same way as the baker, then there is *no effect* on aggregate output of a 5% increase in the price level.

In order for a change in the nominal price of bread to affect the quantity of bread produced, the increase in the nominal price of bread must differ from the

The misperceptions theory says that for a given value of the expected price level P^e, an increase in the actual price level P fools producers into increasing output. This relationship between output and the price level is shown by the short-run aggregate supply curve $SRAS$. Along the $SRAS$ curve output equals $\bar{Y}$ when prices equal their expected level ($P = P^e$, at point E); output exceeds $\bar{Y}$ when the price level is higher than expected ($P > P^e$); and output is less than $\bar{Y}$ when the price level is lower than expected ($P < P^e$). In the long run the expected price level and the actual price level are equal, so that output equals $\bar{Y}$. Thus the long-run aggregate supply curve $LRAS$ is vertical at $Y = \bar{Y}$.

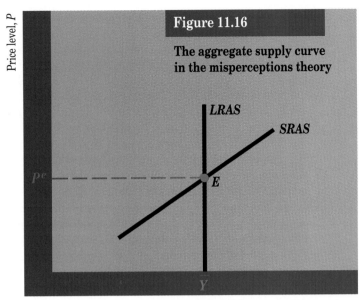

Figure 11.16

The aggregate supply curve in the misperceptions theory

expected increase in the general price level. For example, suppose that the baker expected the general price level to increase by 5% but then observes that the price of bread has risen by 8%. Upon observing that the price of bread has risen by more than he expected the general price level to rise, the baker estimates that the relative price of bread has increased. In response to the perceived increase in the relative price, he increases the production of bread.

Looking at the economy as a whole, we now suppose that everyone expects the general price level to increase by 5%, but instead it actually increases by 8%, with the prices of all goods increasing by 8%. In this case all producers will estimate that the relative price of the good they produce has increased, and hence the production of all goods will increase. Similarly, if the price level actually increases by only 2% when all producers expected a 5% increase, each producer will think that the relative price of his own good has declined. In response, all producers reduce their output.

To summarize our discussion so far: According to the misperceptions theory, the amount of output that producers choose to supply depends on the actual value of the general price level compared with the expected value of general price level. When the price level exceeds what was expected, producers increase their output; and when the price level is lower than expected, producers reduce their output. This relation between output and prices is captured by the following equation:

$$Y = \bar{Y} + b(P - P^e). \tag{11.2}$$

Equation (11.2) summarizes the misperceptions theory by saying that output Y exceeds full-employment $\bar{Y}$ when the price level P exceeds the expected price level P^e. In Eq. (11.2) b is a positive number that describes how strongly output responds when the price level exceeds the expected price level.

To obtain an aggregate supply curve from the misperceptions theory, we graph Eq. (11.2) in Fig. 11.16. For given values of full-employment output $\bar{Y}$ and the expected price level P^e, the aggregate supply curve is an upward-sloping relation between the amount of output supplied and the actual price level P. Point E in Fig. 11.16 is a useful point that helps us locate the aggregate supply curve: At point E the price level P equals the expected price level P^e, so that (as you can see from Eq. 11.2) the amount of output supplied equals full-employment output $\bar{Y}$. When the price level is higher than was expected ($P > P^e$), the aggregate supply curve in Fig. 11.16 shows that the amount of output supplied is greater than $\bar{Y}$; and when the price level is lower than expected ($P < P^e$), output is less than $\bar{Y}$.

The aggregate supply curve in Fig. 11.16 is called the **short-run aggregate supply curve**, $SRAS$, because it applies only over the short period of time in which the expected price level remains unchanged. In the long run people learn what is actually happening to prices, and the expected price level adjusts to equal the actual price level ($P = P^e$). When the actual price level and the expected price level are equal, there are no misperceptions anymore and producers supply the full-employment level of output. In terms of Eq. (11.2), in the long run P equals P^e, so that output Y equals full-employment output $\bar{Y}$. Thus the long-run aggregate supply curve, marked $LRAS$ in Fig. 11.16, is vertical at the point that output equals $\bar{Y}$. According to the **long-run aggregate supply curve,** in the long run the supply of output does not depend on the price level. The long-run aggregate supply curve is the same as the vertical aggregate supply curve in the basic classical model without misperceptions.

Monetary Policy and the Misperceptions Model

Now that we have developed the misperceptions theory and the upward-sloping $SRAS$ curve, we can reexamine the neutrality of money in an extended version of the classical model. In this framework it turns out that there is a distinction between changes in the money supply that are anticipated and changes that are unanticipated: Unanticipated changes in the nominal money suppply have real effects, but anticipated changes are neutral.

Unanticipated Changes in the Money Supply   Suppose that the economy is initially in general equilibrium at point E in Fig. 11.17, where AD^1 intersects $SRAS^1$. In the initial equilibrium, output equals the full-employment level $\bar{Y}$, and the price level and the expected price level are the same (both equal P_1). Suppose that everyone expects the money supply and the price level to remain constant, but that the Fed unexpectedly and without publicity increases the money supply by 10%. A 10% increase in the money supply shifts the AD curve upward to AD^2, increasing the price level at each level of output by 10%. Given the expected price level P_1, the $SRAS$ curve remains unchanged, still passing through point E.

The increase in aggregate demand bids up the price level to the new equilibrium level P_2, where AD^2 intersects $SRAS^1$ (point F in Fig. 11.17). In the new short-run equilibrium at point F, the price level exceeds the level that was expected and output exceeds $\bar{Y}$. Because the increase in the money supply has led to a rise in output, money is not neutral in this analysis.

The reason that the unanticipated increase in money is not neutral is that producers are fooled. Each producer mistakenly interprets the higher nominal price of his output as an increase in his relative price, rather than as an increase in the general price level. Although output increases in the short run, firms are not made

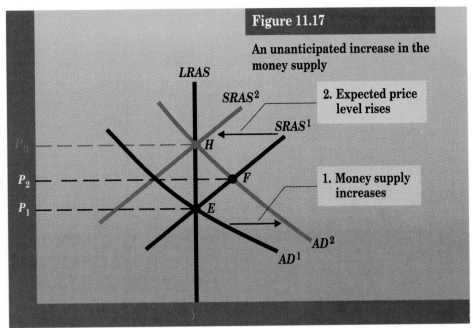

Figure 11.17

An unanticipated increase in the money supply

LRAS

*SRAS*²

*SRAS*¹

2. Expected price level rises

1. Money supply increases

H

F

E

P_3

P_2

P_1

*AD*²

*AD*¹

Output, *Y*

If we start from the initial equilibrium at point *E*, an unanticipated 10% increase in the money supply shifts the *AD* curve upward by 10% at each level of output, from *AD*¹ to *AD*². The short-run equilibrium is located at point *F*, the intersection of *AD*² and *SRAS*¹, where prices and output are both higher than at point *E*. Thus an unanticipated change in the money supply is not neutral in the short run. In the long run people learn the true price level, and the equilibrium shifts to point *H*, the intersection of *AD*² and the long-run aggregate

supply curve *LRAS*. In the long-run equilibrium at point *H*, the price level has risen by 10%, but output returns to its full-employment level $\bar{Y}$, so that money is neutral in the long run. As expectations of the price level rise from P_1 to P_3, the *SRAS* curve also shifts upward until it passes through point *H*.

better off. They end up producing more than they would have had they known the true relative price.

The economy cannot remain for long at the equilibrium represented by point *F*, because at point *F* the actual price level P_2 is higher than the expected price level P_1. Over time, people will obtain information about the true level of prices and will adjust their expectations accordingly. The only equilibrium that can be sustained in the long run is one in which people do not permanently underestimate or overestimate the price level, so that the expected price level and the actual price level are equal. Graphically, once people learn the true price level, the relevant aggregate supply curve is the long-run aggregate supply curve, *LRAS*, along which *P* always equals *P*ᵉ. In Fig. 11.17 the long-run equilibrium is located at point *H*, the intersection of *AD*² and *LRAS*. At point *H* output equals its full-employment level $\bar{Y}$, and the price level P_3 is 10% higher than the initial price level P_1. Because everyone now expects the price level to be P_3, there is also a new *SRAS* curve, *SRAS*², which passes through point *H*.

The conclusions to be drawn from Fig. 11.17 are that according to the misperceptions theory, an unanticipated increase in the money supply raises output and

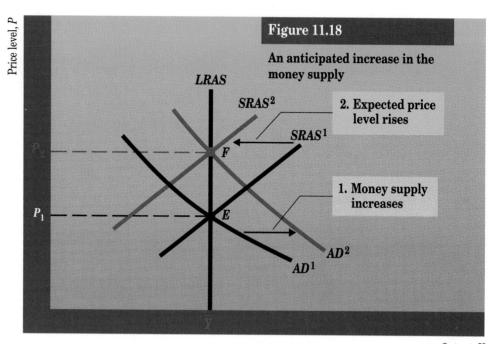

Figure 11.18

An anticipated increase in the money supply

2. Expected price level rises

1. Money supply increases

The initial equilibrium is at point E, and the Fed publicly announces a 10% increase in the money supply. When the money supply increases, the AD curve shifts upward by 10%, from AD^1 to AD^2. But in addition, because the increase in the money supply was anticipated by the public, the expected price level increases by 10%, from P_1 to P_2. Thus the short-run aggregate supply curve shifts upward from $SRAS^1$ to $SRAS^2$. The new short-run equilibrium, which is the same as the long-run equilibrium, is at point F. At point F output is unchanged at $\bar{Y}$, and the price level is 10% higher than in the initial equilibrium at point E. Thus an anticipated increase in the money supply is neutral in the short run as well as in the long run.

thus is not neutral *in the short run*. However, an unanticipated increase in the money supply *is* neutral in the long run, after people have learned the true price level.

Anticipated Changes in the Money Supply In the extended classical model based on the misperceptions theory, the effects of a money supply increase that is anticipated by the public are different from the effects of a surprise increase in the money supply. The effects of an anticipated increase in the money supply are examined in Fig. 11.18. Again we suppose that the initial general equilibrium point is point E, at which output equals its full-employment level and the actual price level and the expected price level both equal P_1. We assume that the Federal Reserve announces that it is going to increase the money supply by 10%, and that this announcement is heard and believed by the public.

As we have seen, a 10% increase in the money supply shifts the AD curve upward by 10% at each level of output, from AD^1 to AD^2. However, in this case the $SRAS$ curve also shifts upward. The reason the $SRAS$ curve shifts upward is that the public's expected price level rises as soon as they learn of the increase in the money supply. Suppose that people expect—correctly, it turns out—that the price level will also rise by 10%, so that P^e rises by 10%, from P_1 to P_2. Then the new SRAS curve, $SRAS^2$, passes through point F in Fig. 11.18, where Y equals $\bar{Y}$ and both the price level and the expected price level equal P_2. The new equilibrium is also at point F, where AD^2 and $SRAS^2$ intersect. At the new equilibrium, output equals its full-employment level, and prices are 10% higher than they were initially. The anticipated increase in the money supply has not affected output but has raised prices proportionally. Similarly, an anticipated fall in the money supply would lower prices but not affect output or other real variables. Thus *anticipated changes in the money supply are neutral in the short run as well as in the long run*. Anticipated increases in the money supply are neutral because if producers know that an increase in the nominal price of their product is the result of an increase in the money supply and does not reflect a change in the relative price, they will not be fooled into increasing their production when prices rise.

Rational Expectations and the Role of Monetary Policy

In the extended classical model based on the misperceptions theory, *unanticipated* changes in the money supply affect output, but *anticipated* changes in the money supply are neutral. Thus it would seem that if the Federal Reserve wanted to use monetary policy to affect output, it should use only unanticipated changes in the money supply. So, for example, when the economy is in recession, it would seem that the Fed should try to have surprise increases in the money supply in order to raise output; and when the economy is booming, the Fed should have surprise decreases in the money supply in order to slow down the economy.

A serious problem for this strategy is the existence of private economic forecasters and "Fed watchers" in financial markets. These people spend a good deal of time and effort trying to forecast macroeconomic variables such as the money supply and the price level, and their forecasts are well publicized. If the Fed began a pattern of raising the money supply in recessions and reducing it in booms, this fact would quickly be understood and reported by forecasters and Fed watchers. As a result, the Fed's manipulations of the money supply would no longer be unanticipated, and the changes in the money supply would have no effect other than possibly causing instability in the price level. More generally, according to the misperceptions theory, to achieve any systematic change in the behavior of output, the Fed must conduct monetary policy in a way that systematically fools the public. But there are strong incentives in the financial markets and elsewhere for people to try to figure out what the Fed is doing. Thus most economists believe that attempts by the Fed to surprise the public in a systematic way cannot be successful.

The idea that the Federal Reserve cannot systematically surprise the public is part of a larger hypothesis that the public has rational expectations. **Rational expectations** means that the public's forecasts of various economic variables, including the money supply, the price level, and GNP, are based upon reasoned and intelligent examination of available economic data. If the public has rational expectations, it will eventually understand the Federal Reserve's general pattern of behavior. If expectations are rational, purely random changes in the money supply may be unanticipated and thus nonneutral, but the Federal Reserve will not be able to surprise the public systematically and so cannot use monetary policy to stabilize output. Thus even if it were desirable to smooth out business cycles, according to the combination of the misperceptions theory and rational expectations, the Fed cannot systematically use monetary policy to do so.

Propagating the Effects of Unanticipated Changes in the Money Supply   The misperceptions theory implies that unanticipated changes in the money supply are nonneutral because individual producers are temporarily fooled about the price level. However, money supply data are available weekly and price level data come out monthly, suggesting that any misperceptions about monetary policy or the price level—and thus any real effects of money supply changes—should be quickly eliminated.

To explain how changes in the money supply can have real effects lasting more than a few weeks, classical economists stress the role of propagation mechanisms. A **propagation mechanism** is an aspect of the economy that allows short-lived shocks to have long-term effects on the economy.

An important example of a propagation mechanism operates through the behavior of inventories. To illustrate, consider a manufacturing firm that has a normal level of monthly production and a normal amount of finished goods in inventory that it tries to maintain. Suppose that there is an unanticipated increase in the money supply that raises aggregate demand. Because it is costly to increase the rate of production sharply in a short period, the manufacturing firm will respond to the increase in demand partly by producing more goods and partly by selling some finished goods out of inventory, thus depleting its inventory stocks below their normal level.

In the next month we suppose that everyone learns the true price level, so that the demand for the firm's product returns to its normal level. Despite the fact that the monetary shock has passed, however, the firm may continue to produce for a while at a higher-than-normal rate. The reason for the continued high level of production is that besides meeting its normal demand, the firm wants to replenish its stock of inventories that was depleted during the previous month. As a result of the firm's desire to rebuild its inventories, there may be higher-than-normal production beyond the length of time it takes to learn the general price level. The need to rebuild inventories illustrates a propagation mechanism that allows a short-lived shock (a monetary shock, in this case) to have a longer-term effect on the economy.

Anticipated and Unanticipated Changes in the Money Supply: Empirical Evidence

The misperceptions theory, together with the hypothesis of rational expectations, predicts that anticipated changes in the money supply are neutral but that unanticipated changes in the money supply are not neutral in the short run. This prediction is difficult to test empirically because we usually do not know whether a particular change in the money supply was anticipated, unanticipated, or partly anticipated by the public.

Any actual change in the money supply, ΔM, consists of two components: (1) the anticipated change in the money supply, ΔM^a, which is the amount that the public expected money supply to increase; and (2) the unanticipated change in the money supply, $\Delta M^u = \Delta M - \Delta M^a$, which is the difference between the actual increase in the money supply and the anticipated change in the money supply. The Federal Reserve regularly reports data on the nation's money supply (see "In Touch with the Macroeconomy," Chapter 4, p. 117), so one can easily calculate the actual changes in the money supply ΔM. The hard part is to break down ΔM into its anticipated and unanticipated parts, ΔM^a and ΔM^u.

In a well-known article Robert Barro[15] of Harvard University used a statistical forecasting model to estimate the changes in the money supply that were expected by the public (ΔM^a) for each year during the period 1941–1976. He then estimated the unanticipated changes in the money supply (ΔM^u) by subtracting the estimated anticipated changes (ΔM^a) from the actual changes (ΔM). Using these estimated values of ΔM^a and ΔM^u, Barro found that output (real GNP) was positively related to unanticipated changes in money, but he found no evidence of a link between anticipated changes in the money supply and the level of real GNP. These findings are consistent with the implications of the misperceptions theory combined with rational expectations.

Barro focused on output effects occurring within three years of a change in the money supply. In a reexamination of Barro's results, Frederic Mishkin[16] of Columbia University expanded the analysis to look for effects of changes in the money supply occurring over a longer period, up to as many as five years after the change in the money supply had taken place. Contrary to Barro's results, Mishkin found that anticipated changes in the money supply are at least as important as unanticipated changes in explaining changes in GNP. Mishkin's finding contradicts the proposition that anticipated changes in the money supply are neutral.

Robert Gordon[17] of Northwestern University also reexamined Barro's results. He pointed out that the neutrality of money requires that the price level move in proportion to the money supply, and then he tested this implication statistically. Like Mishkin, Gordon also found evidence against the neutrality of anticipated changes in the money supply.

Despite the findings by Mishkin and Gordon that anticipated changes in the money supply have real effects, there are delicate statistical issues that make it difficult to interpret these findings definitively. As we have said, we cannot directly measure the anticipated and unanticipated components of changes in the money supply, and so we must rely on statistical techniques to estimate them. Unfortunately, the estimates of the anticipated and unanticipated components of monetary changes may be flawed if the statistical model that the researcher uses does not accurately describe the expectations held by the public.

A second statistical problem is related to the issue of reverse causation discussed earlier. Because of the possibility of reverse causation, the findings of Mishkin and Gordon that there is a link between anticipated changes in the money supply and subsequent changes in output does not necessarily mean that the anticipated changes in the money supply *caused* the changes in output. Perhaps the changes in the money supply were caused by current or anticipated future

---

[15]"Unanticipated Money, Output, and the Price Level in the United States," *Journal of Political Economy*, August 1978, pp. 549–580.

[16]"Does Anticipated Monetary Policy Matter? An Econometric Evaluation," *Journal of Political Economy*, February 1982, pp. 22–51.

[17]"Price Inertia and Policy Ineffectiveness in the United States, 1890–1980," *Journal of Political Economy*, December 1982, pp. 1087–1117.

changes in output, as suggested by the reverse causation idea. If reverse causation is important, then the results reported by Mishkin and Gordon are not strong evidence against neutrality. Unfortunately, these statistical problems are not likely to be resolved soon.

11.5   CHAPTER SUMMARY

1. Classical business cycle analysis employs the classical *IS-LM* model. In this model the *IS* curve represents equilibrium in the goods market, the *LM* curve represents equilibrium in the asset market, and the *FE* line represents equilibrium in the labor market. The general equilibrium of the economy is located at the intersection of the *IS* curve, the *LM* curve, and the *FE* line. If these three curves do not have a common point of intersection, the price level adjusts to shift the *LM* curve until it passes through the intersection of the *IS* curve and the *FE* line.

2. The real business cycle (RBC) theory is a version of the classical theory that stresses productivity shocks (shocks to the production function) as the source of business cycle fluctuations. According to the classical *IS-LM* model, a temporary decrease in productivity reduces the real wage, employment, and output, while raising the real interest rate and the price level. Thus the RBC theory can account for the procyclical behavior of the real wage and employment. This approach can also explain the procyclical behavior of average labor productivity and the fact that investment is more volatile than consumption. However, to explain the large cyclical fluctuations in hours worked and the small cyclical fluctuations in the real wage that are observed, the RBC theory needs a flatter aggregate labor supply curve than has been found by most empirical studies.

3. According to the classical model, a temporary increase in government purchases raises employment, output, the real interest rate, and the price level. Although fiscal policy can affect employment and output, classical economists argue that fiscal policy should not be used to smooth out the business cycle because the invisible hand leads the economy to an efficient outcome without government interference. Instead, decisions about government purchases should be based on comparisons of costs and benefits.

4. In the basic classical theory, which includes RBC theory, money is neutral. If money is neutral, changes in the nominal money supply change the price level proportionally but do not affect real variables such as output, employment, and the real interest rate.

5. The basic classical model can account for the procyclical behavior of money if there is reverse causation, that is, if anticipated changes in output lead to changes in the money supply in the same direction. For instance, if the Fed wants to stabilize the price level and sees that a fall in output is imminent, it can reduce the money supply to prevent the price level from rising. In this case the Fed's anticipation of a fall in output causes the money supply to fall in advance of the fall in output.

6. Examination of historical episodes of monetary policy suggests that money is not neutral. Specifically, there are episodes in which the money supply changed for independent reasons, such as gold discoveries or changes in monetary institutions, and these changes in the money supply were followed by changes in output in the same direction.

7. The aggregate demand for output is the level of output given by the intersection of the IS curve and the LM curve. An increase in the price level reduces the real money supply and shifts the LM curve upward and to the left, which reduces the quantity of output demanded. The aggregate demand (AD) curve relates the aggregate quantity of output demanded to the price level. Because an increase in the price level reduces the aggregate quantity of goods demanded, the aggregate demand curve slopes downward.

8. The aggregate supply curve relates the quantity of output supplied by firms to the price level. In the basic version of the classical model, output supplied always equals full-employment output $\bar{Y}$ regardless of the price level, so the aggregate supply curve is a vertical line that intersects the horizontal axis at $Y = \bar{Y}$. With a vertical aggregate supply curve, money is neutral.

9. The misperceptions theory is based on the idea that producers have imprecise information about the current price level. According to the misperceptions theory, the amount of output supplied equals the full-employment level of output $\bar{Y}$ only if the price level equals the level that was expected. When the price level is higher than was expected, the quantity of output supplied exceeds $\bar{Y}$; and when the price level is lower than was expected, the quantity of output supplied is less than $\bar{Y}$. The short-run aggregate supply curve ($SRAS$), which is based on the misperceptions theory, is an upward-sloping relation between output and the actual price level, with the expected price level held constant. In the long run the price level equals the expected price level, so that output equals $\bar{Y}$. Thus the long-run aggregate supply curve ($LRAS$) is a vertical line at the point that output equals $\bar{Y}$.

10. With the upward-sloping $SRAS$ curve based on the misperceptions theory, an unanticipated increase in the money supply increases output in the short run, so that money is not neutral in the short run. However, because the long-run aggregate supply curve is vertical, an unanticipated increase in the money supply does not affect output in the long run, so that money is neutral in the long run. Because an anticipated increase in the money supply causes price expectations to adjust immediately and there are no misperceptions about the price level, an anticipated increase in the money supply is neutral in both the short run and the long run. Statistical evidence about the effects of anticipated and unanticipated changes in the money supply is inconclusive.

11. According to the extended classical model based on the misperceptions theory, only surprise changes in the money supply can affect output. If the public has rational expectations about macroeconomic variables, including the money supply, then the Fed cannot systematically surprise the public because the public will eventually learn the Fed's pattern of behavior. Thus under these assumptions the Fed cannot systematically use changes in the money supply to affect output.

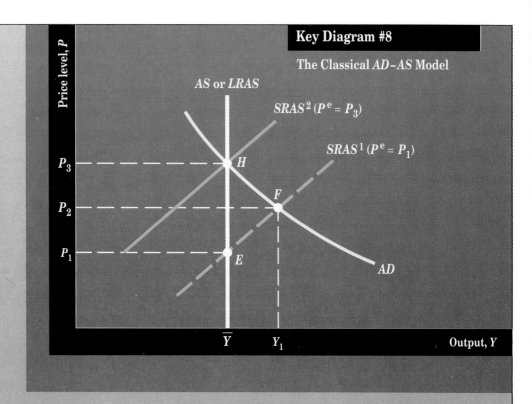

The classical *AD-AS* model shows how the aggregate demand for output and the aggregate supply of output interact to determine the price level and output in the classical model.

Diagram Elements

- The price level P is on the vertical axis, and the level of output Y is on the horizontal axis.

- The aggregate demand (*AD*) curve shows the amount of output demanded at each price level. The aggregate amount of output demanded is given by the intersection of the *IS* and *LM* curves (see Fig. 11.11), representing equilibrium in the goods market and the asset market. An increase in the price level P reduces the real money supply, shifting the *LM* curve upward and to the left and reducing the aggregate quantity of output demanded. Thus the *AD* curve slopes downward.

- The aggregate supply (*AS*) curve shows the amount of output supplied at each price level. In the basic classical model, in which producers correctly perceive the relative prices of their products, producers supply the full-employment level of output $\bar{Y}$ regardless of the price level. Thus in the basic classical model the *AS* curve is a vertical line at $Y = \bar{Y}$.

- The basic classical model is extended by adding the assumption that producers have imperfect information about the general price level and hence do not precisely know the relative prices of their products (the misperceptions theory). When producers misperceive the price level, an increase in the general price level above the price level that was expected fools each supplier into thinking that the relative price of her own output has increased, so that all suppliers increase output. The short-run aggregate supply curve $SRAS$ shows the amount of output supplied at each price level, with the expected price level held constant. Because an increase in the price level fools producers into supplying more output, in the extended classical model the short-run aggregate supply curve slopes upward, as shown by $SRAS^1$.

The short-run aggregate supply curve $SRAS^1$ is drawn under the assumption that the expected price level P^e equals P_1. When the price level equals the expected price level, producers are not fooled and so supply the full-employment level of output $\bar{Y}$. Therefore at point E, where the actual price level P_1 equals the expected price level P_1, the short-run AS curve $SRAS^1$ implies that producers supply $\bar{Y}$.

• In the long run producers learn about the price level and adjust their expectations until the actual price level and the expected price level are equal. When the actual price level and the expected price level are equal, producers supply the full-employment level of output $\bar{Y}$, regardless of the price level. Thus in the extended classical model the long-run aggregate supply curve $LRAS$ is vertical at $Y = \bar{Y}$. The $LRAS$ curve is the same as the AS curve in the basic classical model.

Factors That Shift the Curves

• The aggregate quantity of output demanded is determined by the intersection of the IS curve and the LM curve. Given the price level, any factor that shifts the IS-LM intersection to the right increases the aggregate quantity of goods demanded and thus also shifts the AD curve to the right. Factors that shift the AD curve are listed in Table 11.2, p. 425.

• In the basic classical model any factor that increases full-employment output $\bar{Y}$ shifts the (vertical) AS curve to the right. Factors that increase full-employment output include beneficial supply shocks or an increase in labor supply. An increase in government purchases, because it induces workers to supply more labor, also shifts the AS curve to the right.

• In the extended classical model with the misperceptions theory, any factor that increases full-employment output $\bar{Y}$ shifts both the short-run and the long-run aggregate supply curves to the right.

• In the extended classical model with the misperceptions theory, an increase in the expected price level shifts the short-run aggregate supply curve upward.

(Continued)

Analysis

- In the basic classical model the equilibrium of the economy is represented by the intersection of the *AD* curve and the (vertical) *AS* curve. There is no distinction between the short run and the long run, and output is always at its full-employment level $\bar{Y}$.

- In the extended classical model based on the misperceptions theory, the short-run equilibrium is located at the intersection of the *AD* curve and the *SRAS* curve. For example, if the expected price level is P_1, the *SRAS* curve is $SRAS^1$, and the short-run equilibrium is at point *F*. At point *F* output Y_1 is higher than the full-employment level $\bar{Y}$, and the price level P_2 is higher than the expected price level P_1. As producers obtain information about the price level, the expected price level is revised upward, which shifts the *SRAS* curve upward. The long-run equilibrium is at point *H*, where the long-run aggregate supply curve *LRAS* intersects the *AD* curve. In the long run, (1) output equals $\bar{Y}$ and (2) the price level equals the expected price level (both equal P_3). In the long run, when the expected price level has risen to P_3, the short-run aggregate supply curve $SRAS^2$ passes through point *H*.

Key Terms

aggregate demand curve,
  p. 422
aggregate supply curve,
  p. 426
long-run aggregate
  supply curve, p. 432
misperceptions theory,
  p. 429

nominal shocks, p. 404
productivity shocks,
  p. 404
propagation mechanism,
  p. 436
rational expectations,
  p. 435

real business cycle
  theory, p. 404
real shocks, p. 404
reverse causation, p. 420
short-run aggregate
  supply curve, p. 432

Key Equation

$$Y = \bar{Y} + b(P - P^e) \qquad (11.2)$$

The short-run aggregate supply curve, based on the misperceptions theory, says that the aggregate amount of output supplied Y equals full-employment output $\bar{Y}$ when the price level P equals the expected price level P^e. When the price level is higher than expected ($P > P^e$), output exceeds $\bar{Y}$; and when the price level is lower than expected ($P < P^e$), output is less than $\bar{Y}$.

Review Questions

1. What are the two main components of any theory of the business cycle? Describe these two components for the specific case of the real business cycle theory.

2. Define *real shock* and *nominal shock*. What type of real shock do real business cycle theorists consider the most important source of cyclical fluctuations?

3. What major business cycle facts does the RBC theory explain successfully? What business cycle facts does it have more difficulty explaining?

4. What effects does an increase in government purchases have on the labor market, according to the classical theory? When does an increase in government purchases make workers worse off, and when does it make workers better off? According to classical economists, should fiscal policy be used to smooth out the business cycle? Why or why not?

5. What is reverse causation? What business cycle fact is it intended to explain?

6. What two variables are related by the aggregate demand (*AD*) curve? Why does the *AD* curve slope downward? Give two factors that shift the *AD* curve to the right, and explain why the shift occurs.

7. According to the misperceptions theory, what effect does an increase in the price level have on the amount of output supplied by producers? Explain. Does it matter if the increase in the price level was expected?

8. What conclusion does the basic classical model draw about the neutrality or nonneutrality of money? In what ways is this conclusion modified by the extended classical model based on the misperceptions theory?

9. Define *rational expectations*. According to the classical model, what implications do rational expectations have for the ability of the central bank to use monetary policy to smooth out business cycles?

Numerical Problems

1. In a certain economy the marginal product of labor is

$$MPN = A(100 - N),$$

where A is productivity and N is total hours worked. Initially, $A = 1.0$, but a beneficial productivity shock raises A to 1.1.

a. The labor supply curve NS is

$$NS = 45 + 0.1w,$$

where w is the real wage. Find the equilibrium levels of hours worked and the real wage before and after the productivity shock. Recall from Chapter 10 that the MPN curve is the same as the labor demand curve with the real wage put in place of the MPN.

b. Repeat part a assuming that the labor supply curve is

$$NS = 10 + 0.8w.$$

c. Compare your answers to parts a and b. How do your results bear on the debate about whether the RBC theory can explain the cyclical behavior of hours worked and the real wage?

2. An economy is described by the following equations:

desired consumption C^d = $600 + 0.5(Y - T) - 50r$,
desired investment I^d = $450 - 50r$,
real money demand L = $0.5Y - 100i$,
full-employment output $\bar{Y} = 2210$,
expected inflation π^e = 0.05.

In this economy the government always runs a balanced budget, so $T = G$, where T is total taxes collected.

a. Suppose that $M = 4320$ and $G = 150$. Using the classical IS-LM model, find the equilibrium values of output, the real interest rate, the price level, consumption, and investment.

b. The money supply rises to 4752. Repeat part a. Is money neutral?

c. With the money supply back at 4320, government purchases and taxes rise to 190. Repeat part a. Assume that $\bar{Y}$ is fixed (unaffected by G). Is fiscal policy neutral?

3. Consider the following economy:

desired consumption C^d = $1275 + 0.5(Y - T) - 200r$,
desired investment I^d = $900 - 200r$,
real money demand L = $0.5Y - 200i$,

full-employment output $\bar{Y}$ = 4600,
expected inflation π^e = 0.

a. Suppose that $T = G = 450$ and $M = 9000$. Find an equation describing the IS curve. (*Hint:* Set desired national saving equal to desired investment, and solve for the relationship between r and Y.) Find an equation describing the LM curve. (*Hint:* Set real money supply equal to real money demand, and again solve for the relationship between r and Y, given P.) Finally, find an equation for the aggregate demand curve. (Use the IS and LM equations.) What are the equilibrium values of output, consumption, investment, the real interest rate, and the price level?

b. Suppose that $T = G = 450$ and $M = 4500$. What is the equation for the aggregate demand curve now? What are the equilibrium values of output, consumption, investment, the real interest rate, and the price level?

c. Repeat part b for the case where $T = G = 330$ and $M = 9000$. Note that we are assuming that $\bar{Y}$ is fixed.

4. An economy has the following AD curve and AS curve:

AD curve: $Y = 300 + 30\left(\dfrac{M}{P}\right),$

AS curve: $Y = \bar{Y} + 10(P - P^e),$

where $\bar{Y} = 500$ and $M = 400$.

a. Suppose that $P^e = 60$. What are the equilibrium values of the price level P and output Y? (*Hint:* The solutions for P in this part and part b are multiples of 10.)

b. There is an unanticipated increase in the money supply to $M = 700$. Because the increase in the money supply is unanticipated, P^e remains equal to 60. What are the equilibrium values of the price level P and output Y?

c. The Federal Reserve announces that the money supply will be increased to $M = 700$, an announcement that is heard and believed by the public. Now what are the equilibrium values of the price level P, the expected price level P^e, and output Y?

5. Try the following experiment: Flip a coin fifty times, keeping track of the results. Think of each "heads" as a small positive shock that increases output by one unit, and similarly, think of each "tails" as a small negative shock that reduces output by one unit. Let the initial value of output Y be 50 units, and graph the level of output over time as it is hit by the "positive" and "neg-ative" shocks (coin flips). So, for example, if your first four flips are three heads and a tail, output takes the values 51, 52, 53, 52. After fifty flips, have your small shocks produced any large cycles in output?

Analytical Problems

1. The discovery of a new technology increases the expected future marginal product of capital.
   a. Using the classical *IS-LM* model, determine the effect of the increase in the expected future *MPK* on current output, the real interest rate, employment, real wages, consumption, investment, and the price level. Assume that expected future real wages and expected future labor income are unaffected by the new technology. Assume also that current productivity is unaffected.
   b. Find the effects of the increase in the expected future *MPK* on current output and prices, using the *AD-AS* diagram based on the misperceptions theory. What accounts for the difference with part a?

2. Consider a business cycle theory that combines the classical *IS-LM* model with the assumption that temporary changes in government purchases are the main source of cyclical fluctuations. How would this theory do in explaining the observed cyclical behavior of each of the following variables? Explain.
   a. Employment
   b. The real wage
   c. Average labor productivity
   d. Investment
   e. The price level

3. The problem asks you to use the classical *IS-LM* model to analyze the effects of a permanent increase in government purchases of 100 goods per period. The increase in purchases is financed by a permanent increase in lump-sum taxes of 100 goods.
   a. Begin by finding the effects of the fiscal change in the labor market. How does the effect of the permanent increase in government purchases of 100 goods compare with the effect of a temporary increase in purchases of 100 goods?
   b. Because the tax increase is permanent, assume that at any given level of output and the real interest rate, consumers respond by reducing their consumption each period by the full amount of the tax increase. Under this assumption, how does the permanent increase in government purchases

affect desired national saving and the *IS* curve?
   c. Using the classical *IS-LM* model, find the effects of the permanent increase in government purchases and taxes on output, the real interest rate, and the price level in the current period. What happens if consumers reduce their current consumption by less than 100 goods at any given level of output and the real interest rate?

4. When firms expect to increase production in the future, they may need to increase their current transactions (for example, they may need to purchase raw materials, hire workers, and so on). Assume that, for this reason, current real money demand rises when expected future output rises.
   a. Under the assumption that real money demand depends on expected future output, use the classical *IS-LM* model to find the effects of an increase in expected future output on the current price level. For simplicity, assume that any effects of the increase in expected future output on the labor market or on desired saving and investment are small and can be ignored.
   b. Suppose that the Fed wants to stabilize the current price level. How will the Fed respond to the increase in expected future output? Explain why the Fed's response is an example of reverse causation.

5. Two countries called East and West agree to unify. The real value of full-employment output in East is 1 trillion widgets and in West is 2 trillion widgets. The combined full-employment output of the unified country is expected to be just the sum of the two full-employment outputs, or 3 trillion widgets.
   Real money demand in the West is 10% of West's real output and will remain so after reunification. In the East people do not have access to financial instruments, such as stocks and bonds, and so are forced to save in the form of money. As a result, real money demand in the East is 40% of East's real output. However, after unification Easterners will have access to a full range of financial assets, and thus their real money demand will drop to 10% of output.

The unified country will use only Western currency. As part of the unification plan, the West central bank has agreed to print new Western currency and trade it for Eastern currency, which will be destroyed. At the initial price levels the total real value of the Western currency received by Easterners equals the total real value of the Eastern currency they give up.

Using the classical *IS-LM* model, find the effects on postunification output and prices of the currency swap. Give a quantitative estimate of the effect on the price level (measured in the Western currency). Qualitatively, does your answer change if you use the *AD-AS* model based on the misperceptions theory? What can the West central bank do to offset the effects of the currency swap on the price level?

6. Starting from a situation with no government spending and no taxes, the government introduces a foreign aid program (in which domestically produced goods are shipped abroad) and pays for it with a temporary 10% tax on current wages. Future wages are untaxed.

a. What effects will the temporary wage tax have on labor supply? (*Hint:* From Chapter 10, recall the difference in the effects of temporary and permanent wage changes.) Using the classical *IS-LM* model, find the effects of the fiscal change on output, employment, the (before-tax) real wage, the real interest rate, and the price level.

b. Instead, suppose the government puts a 5% tax on both current and future wages (raising approximately the same total amount of revenue). What is the effect on first-period labor supply now? What are the effects on the macroeconomic variables listed in part a?

12
Keynesianism: The Macroeconomics of Wage and Price Rigidity

In the previous chapter we discussed the classical, or market-clearing, approach to macroeconomics. In the classical approach wages and prices are assumed to adjust quickly so that all markets are always in equilibrium, and business cycles are viewed as the free market's best response to economic disturbances such as productivity shocks. Since business cycles represent the economy's optimal response to disturbances, there is little reason for government policy to try to "smooth out" the cycle, according to the classical approach.

In contrast to the classicals, Keynesians are less optimistic about the ability of free-market economies to respond quickly and in a desirable way to shocks. One of the central ideas of Keynesianism is that wages and prices are "rigid" or "sticky" and do not adjust quickly to market-clearing levels. Wage and price rigidity implies that the economy can be pushed away from its general equilibrium for long periods of time. From the Keynesian perspective a deep recession is not an optimal response of the free market to outside shocks; rather, it is a disequilibrium situation in which a high unemployment rate reflects a supply of labor that is much greater than the demand. Keynesians believe that there is a need for the government to step in and try to eliminate these periods of low output and high unemployment.

Since wage and price rigidity is the critical factor underlying Keynesian theory and policy recommendations, we must understand the potential causes of rigidity. A major criticism that the classicals launched against the Keynesians in the early 1970s was that the Keynesians simply assumed that wages and prices are rigid, without giving a good economic explanation of why these rigidities occur. After all, argued the classicals, wages and prices are not simply "given" to the economy but are the results of decisions made by individuals and firms. If excessively high wages are causing unemployment, why don't unemployed workers offer to work for lower wages until firms are willing to hire them? If prices are not at the levels that set supplies of goods equal to the demands, why don't firms just change their prices? In effect, the classicals challenged the Keynesians to show how wage and price rigidity could be consistent with the idea—basic to almost all of economics—that individuals and firms are economically rational, that is, they do the best they can for themselves when making economic decisions.

Keynesian researchers took up the classical challenge and have made progress in developing explanations for wage and price rigidity that are consistent with economic rationality. In the first part of this chapter we discuss some leading Keynesian explanations for wage and price rigidity. We then show how slow adjustment of wages and prices can be incorporated into the *IS-LM* model, converting it from a classical model to a Keynesian model. Fortunately, bringing in wage and price rigidity does not involve much modification of the structure of the classical business cycle model developed in Chapter 11. However, the implications of the model with wage and price rigidity, especially for the role of macroeconomic policy, are quite different from those of the classical model.

Although we need to understand the theoretical differences between Keynesian and classical theories of the business cycle, the ultimate aim, of course, is to see which theory provides a better understanding of the real world. Unfortunately, given the divided state of the economics profession and the fact that the current classical and Keynesian theories are under intensive development, we cannot give a conclusive answer to that question. Instead, we continue to focus on the ability of basic versions of the two theories to explain the important business cycle facts that we outlined in Chapter 9. Since the theories we are evaluating are not "final products," however, this comparison is best viewed as indicating areas for future development of the classical and Keynesian models.

12.1   REAL-WAGE RIGIDITY

Although the classical model of Chapter 11 can explain some of the cyclical behavior of labor markets, such as the fact that employment and average labor productivity are both procyclical, it has some difficulty explaining the fact that real wages vary only slightly over the course of the business cycle. In order for the classical model to explain both the large cyclical movements in employment and hours worked on the one hand and the small cyclical movements in the real wage on the other, the aggregate labor supply curve must be relatively flat. However, from the available empirical evidence many economists believe that the aggregate labor supply curve is not flat enough for the classical theory to explain the small cyclical fluctuations in the real wage.

There is another way to state essentially the same criticism of the classical model. According to the classical model, declines in employment during a recession reflect voluntary decisions made by workers to work less in response to lower real wages. This conclusion follows directly from the market-clearing assumption that workers are always on their labor supply curves. However, much of the variation in employment over the cycle is the result of involuntary layoffs of workers in recessions and worker recalls in expansions, which are initiated by employers without any consultation with the affected workers. In an involuntary layoff workers are simply told that they have lost their jobs; they are not allowed to keep supplying their customary amount of labor even though they might be willing to do so at a lower wage. Furthermore, when firms demand less labor, they generally lay off some workers without lowering the wages of the workers that they retain. These observations are hard to explain with the basic market-clearing model. In that model decreases in employment *always* reflect voluntary reductions in the amount of labor supplied.

From the Keynesian perspective the fact that real wages apparently move "too little" over the cycle to keep the quantity of labor supplied equal to the quantity of labor demanded is called **real-wage rigidity**.

Some Reasons for Real-Wage Rigidity

Various explanations have been offered for the apparent rigidity of real wages over the cycle. One explanation is that there are legal and institutional barriers to cutting wages, such as the minimum-wage law and union contracts. However, since the majority of workers in the United States economy are neither union members nor minimum-wage earners, these barriers to wage cutting cannot be the main reason for real-wage rigidity. Furthermore, the minimum wage in the United States is specified in nominal terms, so that workers who are paid the minimum wage would have rigid nominal wages rather than rigid real wages.

A second explanation focuses on the fact that workers are not all the same. Instead, workers differ in many ways: in their innate abilities, their attachment to their current job, their drive and ambition, and so on. Because of these differences among workers, a firm that cuts wages in a recession and simply waits for some workers to quit would expose itself to the risk that the "wrong" workers would leave the firm. Probably the workers who would leave the firm would include the most talented employees, who would have relatively better alternatives outside the firm. The least talented employees would have fewer good outside alternatives and would be the ones most likely to stay. Thus instead of a simple cut in wages to reduce employment, a better alternative for the firm may be to leave wages alone and, instead, to choose directly which workers or groups of workers to lay off.

A third reason for real-wage rigidity involves the incentives of the employees who remain after a wage cut. Keynesians argue that wage reductions are likely to reduce the efficiency and effort of the workers who remain in the firm. By reducing productivity, lower real wages may end up reducing the firm's profits rather than increasing them! The idea that a worker's productivity depends on the real wage underlies the **efficiency wage model,** which we discuss next.

The Efficiency Wage Model

Why might a worker's productivity depend on the real wage? There are both "carrot" and "stick" aspects of the explanation. The "carrot" or positive incentive is based on the idea that workers who feel well treated will work harder and more efficiently. George Akerlof of the University of California at Berkeley has argued that workers who believe their employer is treating them "fairly"—say by paying higher wages than she has to in order to retain them and by not cutting wages in slack times—will in turn want to treat the employer "fairly" by doing a good job. Akerlof calls this motivation the *gift exchange motive*,[1] because the underlying psychology is similar to the one that leads people to exchange gifts. If high wages increase workers' productivity by enough, then it could be profitable for an employer to pay wages higher than the market-clearing level. In addition, paying high

---

[1]See George Akerlof, "Labor Contracts as Partial Gift Exchange," *Quarterly Journal of Economics*, November 1982, pp. 543–569.

wages may reduce the frequency with which workers quit, thereby saving the firm the costs of hiring and training new workers.

The "stick" or threat aspect of why a firm would pay a higher wage than necessary is analyzed in an economic model called the shirking model.[2] According to the *shirking model*, if a worker is paid only the minimum amount needed to attract him to a particular job, he will not be very concerned about the possibility of being fired from his job if he does not perform well. After all, if the job pays the minimum amount necessary to induce him to take the job, he is not much happier with the job than without the job. In this case the worker will be more inclined to take it easy at work and shirk his duties, and the employer will have to bear the cost of shirking or of paying supervisors to ensure that the work gets done. However, a worker receiving a higher wage will place a higher value on his job (it's not that easy to find another job as good) and will want to perform well in order to avoid being fired for shirking. By reducing shirking and cutting supervision costs, then, a relatively high real wage may increase the employer's profits.

The gift exchange idea and the shirking model both imply that workers' effort depends on the real wage they receive. Graphically, the relation between the real wage and the level of effort is known as the **effort curve,** shown in Fig. 12.1. In Fig. 12.1 the real wage w is measured along the horizontal axis, and the level of effort E is measured along the vertical axis. The effort curve passes through points 0, A, and B in this figure. When real wages are higher, workers choose to work harder, for either the "carrot" or "stick" reasons described above; therefore the effort curve is upward sloping. We assume that the effort curve is S-shaped: At very low levels of the real wage workers offer hardly any effort at all, and effort rises only slowly as the real wage is increased at low levels. At higher levels of the real wage effort rises sharply, as shown by the steeply rising portion of the effort curve. The effort curve flattens out at very high levels of the real wage because there is some maximum level of effort beyond which workers really cannot go no matter how motivated they are.

Wage Determination in the Efficiency Wage Model   The effort curve shows that effort depends on the real wage, but what determines the real wage? In order to be able to make as high a profit as possible, firms will choose the level of the real wage that gets the most effort from workers for each dollar of real wages paid. The amount of effort per dollar of real wages equals the amount of effort E divided by the real wage w. The ratio of E to w can be found graphically by using Fig. 12.1. Consider, for example, point A on the effort curve, at which the real wage w_A induces workers to supply effort E_A. The slope of the line from the origin to point A equals the height of the curve at point A, E_A, divided by the horizontal distance, w_A. Thus the slope of the line from the origin to point A equals the amount of effort per dollar of real wages at point A.

The real wage that achieves the highest effort per dollar of wages is represented by point B in Fig. 12.1. The slope of the line from the origin to point B, which is the amount of effort per dollar of real wage at point B, is greater than the slope of the line from the origin to any other point on the curve. In general, the way to locate the real wage that maximizes effort per dollar of real wage is to draw a line from the origin that is tangent to the effort curve; the real wage at the

[2]See Carl Shapiro and Joseph E. Stiglitz, "Equilibrium Unemployment as a Worker Discipline Device," *American Economic Review*, June 1984, pp. 433–444.

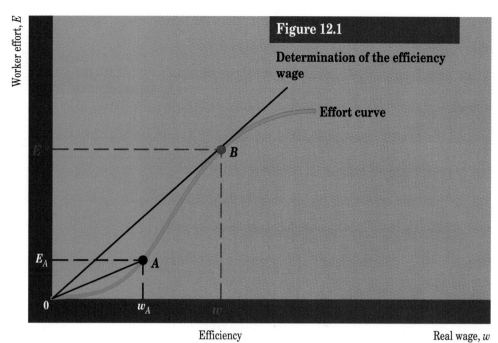

Figure 12.1

Determination of the efficiency wage

Effort curve

Worker effort, E

E_A — — — — — A

B

0 w_A w^*

Efficiency wage

Real wage, w

The effort curve shows the relation between worker effort E and the real wage workers receive w. A higher real wage leads to more effort, but above a certain point higher wages are not able to increase effort by very much, so that the effort curve is S-shaped. For any point on the curve the amount of effort per dollar of real wage is the slope of the line from the origin to that point. At point A effort per dollar of real wage is E_A/w_A. The highest level of effort per dollar of real wage is located at point B, where the line from the origin is tangent to the curve. The real wage rate at point B is the efficiency wage w^*, and the corresponding level of effort is E^*.

tangency point is the one that maximizes effort per dollar of real wage. We call the real wage that maximizes effort or efficiency per dollar of real wages the **efficiency wage.** In Fig. 12.1 the efficiency wage is w^*, and the corresponding level of effort is E^*. (A famous episode in labor history that can be interpreted in terms of the efficiency wage theory is given in Box 12.1, p. 455.)

The efficiency wage theory helps to explain real-wage rigidity. Because the employer chooses the real wage that maximizes effort received per dollar, as long as the effort curve shown in Fig. 12.1 does not change, the employer will not change the real wage. Therefore the theory implies that the real wage is permanently rigid and equals the efficiency wage.

Employment Determination in the Efficiency Wage Model In the classical model of the labor market employment depends on both the supply and the demand for labor. In contrast, in the efficiency wage model we will see that the level of employment depends only on labor demand. Provided that the quantity of labor supplied exceeds the quantity demanded at the efficiency wage w^*, the supply of labor will not affect the level of employment.

As we saw in Chapter 10, the amount of labor demanded by a firm depends on the marginal product of labor. To calculate the marginal product of labor in the

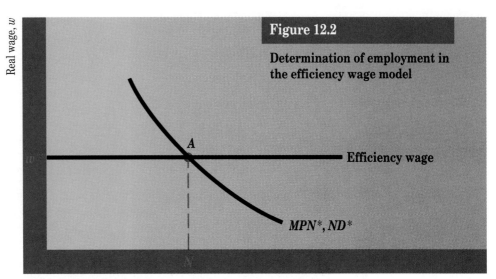

Real wage, w

Figure 12.2

Determination of employment in the efficiency wage model

A

Efficiency wage

MPN^*, ND^*

N

Labor, N (in hours)

MPN^* shows the marginal product of labor when worker effort is E^*. The labor demand curve ND^* is identical to the MPN^* curve. The amount of labor demanded is $\bar{N}$, which is the amount of labor for which the efficiency wage w^* equals the marginal product of labor MPN^* (point A).

efficiency wage model, we modify the firm's production function to reflect the assumption that output depends on the effort, or efficiency, of labor as well as on the number of labor hours used. More precisely, we suppose that output depends on the number of effort-hours, $E \times N$, the product of worker effort (E) and the number of labor hours (N). The production function in Eq. (12.1) shows that given capital K and productivity A, an increase in effort-hours, $E \times N$, leads to an increase in output:

$$Y = AF(K, E \times N). \tag{12.1}$$

Recalling that the firm chooses the efficiency wage w^* that elicits the effort level E^*, we define the marginal product of labor MPN^* to be the output produced by an additional hour of labor, with effort held fixed at E^*. Equivalently, MPN^* is the additional output produced by E^* additional effort-hours, because each additional hour of labor produces E^* additional effort-hours. Figure 12.2 shows the relation between MPN^* and the number of hours worked N. This curve slopes downward because of diminishing marginal returns to labor.

We saw in Chapter 10 that the labor demand curve and the marginal product of labor (MPN) curve are the same. Similarly, given the effort level E^*, the labor demand curve in the efficiency wage model $(ND^*$ in Fig. 12.2) is the same as the marginal product of labor curve (MPN^*) corresponding to effort of E^*. In the efficiency wage model the real wage equals the efficiency wage w^*, as indicated by the horizontal line in Fig. 12.2. The firm will employ the amount of labor $\bar{N}$ at which MPN^* equals the real wage w^* (point A in Fig. 12.2, where the horizontal line intersects ND^*). When employment equals $\bar{N}$, the cost to the firm of employing an additional hour of labor (w^*) just equals the benefit to the firm of the additional hour of labor (MPN^*).

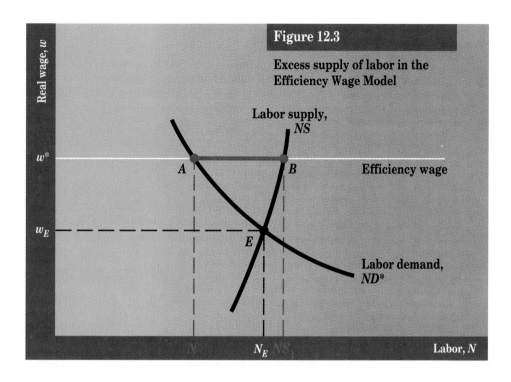

Figure 12.3

Excess supply of labor in the Efficiency Wage Model

When the efficiency wage w^* is paid, the firm's demand for labor is $\bar{N}$, represented by point A. However, the amount of labor that workers would like to supply at a real wage of w^* is NS_1, point B. There is an excess supply of labor equal to distance AB. We assume that the efficiency wage w^* is higher than the market-clearing wage w_E that would prevail if the supply of labor equaled the demand for labor at point E.

A complete picture of the labor market with an efficiency wage is shown in Fig. 12.3. The profit-maximizing efficiency wage w^* and the labor demand curve ND^* are the same as in Fig. 12.2. The standard labor supply curve, discussed in Chapter 10, is NS in the figure. Point A on the labor demand curve shows that when the real wage is w^*, firms would like to employ $\bar{N}$ hours of labor. Point B on the labor supply shows that when the real wage is w^*, workers would like to supply NS_1 hours of labor, which is greater than the amount demanded by firms. With the quantity of labor supplied greater than the quantity demanded, the level of employment is determined by the labor demand of firms and hence equals $\bar{N}$.

What is full employment in the efficiency wage model? Recall that full employment is defined to be the level of employment that is reached after wages and prices have completely adjusted to their equilibrium levels. In the classical model full employment occurs when the quantity of labor demanded equals the quantity supplied (point E in Fig. 12.3). However, in the efficiency wage model, as you can see in Fig. 12.3, the quantity of labor demanded is less than the quantity supplied even after complete adjustment of wages and prices. In the efficiency wage model in Fig. 12.3, full employment is $\bar{N}$, the quantity of labor employed by firms when the wage rate equals the efficiency wage. In contrast to the situation in the classical model, in the efficiency wage model when employment equals its full-employment level $\bar{N}$, there is an excess supply of labor. This excess supply of labor, $NS_1 - \bar{N}$, is equal to the distance AB in Fig. 12.3.

In the market-clearing model, if the real wage is higher than the market-clearing wage, so that there is an excess supply of labor, some unemployed workers offer to work for a lower wage. As a result, the real wage is bid down until the quantity of labor supplied equals the quantity of labor demanded, as at point E in Fig. 12.3. In contrast, in the efficiency wage model the real wage cannot be bid down by people offering to work at lower wages, because employers will not hire these workers. Employers know that workers working at lower wages will not put out as much effort per dollar of real wages as workers receiving the higher efficiency wage. Thus the excess supply of labor shown in Fig. 12.3 will persist indefinitely.[3]

Figure 12.3 embodies an assumption of the efficiency wage model that we have not yet discussed, which is that the efficiency wage w^* is higher than the real wage that would clear the labor market (w_E, corresponding to the market-clearing point E). If the efficiency wage were below the market-clearing real wage, the employer would be forced to pay the market-clearing wage; otherwise, she would get no workers. To keep things simple, we assume that the efficiency wage is always greater than the real wage that would clear the labor market.

If the effort curve in Fig. 12.1 remains fixed over time, then the efficiency wage w^* will be constant; and employment will vary only when there is a shift of the MPN^* curve. For example, an improvement in technology that increases productivity A will shift the MPN^* curve to the right and thus increase employment. In the version of the efficiency wage model we have developed here, however, an increase in productivity will *not* affect the real wage. The real wage in this model is determined only by the effort curve and hence does not change unless the effort curve shifts.

The Cyclical Behavior of the Labor Market   Now that we have seen how efficiency wages affect the real wage and employment in the labor market, we can discuss how the efficiency wage model addresses some of the objections raised to the market-clearing model of the labor market.

One objection to the market-clearing model is that real wages do not appear to fluctuate much over the cycle, and employment fluctuates relatively more. For the classical, market-clearing approach to explain these findings, the aggregate labor supply curve must be relatively flat, which conflicts with empirical studies that find that the aggregate labor supply curve is relatively steep. A steep slope of the aggregate labor supply curve poses no problem for the efficiency wage model, however, because the labor supply curve is *irrelevant* to the determination of wages and employment in this model. As long as labor supply exceeds labor demand at the efficiency wage, the real wage paid by firms will be fixed; and firms will be able to change the level of employment without changing real wages. Thus wages and employment in the efficiency wage model behave *as if* the aggregate supply curve were perfectly flat, even though in reality the labor supply curve may be steep.

The efficiency wage approach also provides an answer to the question of why firms choose to lay off workers against their will in recessions, rather than cutting

---

[3]Because the excess supply of labor persists indefinitely, it is part of structural unemployment, discussed in Chapter 10. Frictional unemployment does not show up in Fig. 12.3, just as it does not show up in the diagram in the classical model in which the quantities of labor supplied and demanded are equal. Keynesians also emphasize the importance of a third type of unemployment, cyclical unemployment, which arises when employment differs from its full-employment level $\bar{N}$. We discuss cyclical unemployment in Chapter 14.

BOX 12.1: HENRY FORD'S EFFICIENCY WAGE

Over the period 1908–1914 Henry Ford instituted at Ford Motor Company a radically new way of producing automobiles.* Prior to Ford's innovations, automobile components were not produced to uniform specifications. Instead, cars had to be assembled one by one by skilled craftsmen, who could make the parts fit together even if sizes or shapes were off by fractions of an inch. Ford introduced a system of assembly line production in which a standardized product, the Model T automobile, was produced from precisely made, interchangeable components. The production process was also broken down into a large number of small, simple steps, so that the skilled craftsmen who had built cars from start to finish were replaced by unskilled workers performing only a few operations over and over.

The high speed at which Ford ran the assembly line and the repetitiveness of the work were hard on the workers. As one laborer said, "If I keep putting on Nut No. 86 for about 86 more days, I will be Nut No. 86 in the Pontiac bughouse."† As a result, turnover of workers was high, with the typical worker lasting only a few months on the job. Absenteeism was also high, about 10% on any given day, and morale was low. There were cases of worker slowdowns and even sabotage.

In January 1914 Ford announced that the company would begin paying $5 a day to workers who met certain criteria, one of these being that the worker had been with the company at least six months. Five dollars a day was over double the normal wage for production workers at the time. Although the motivations for Ford's announcement have been debated, its effect was stunning: Thousands of workers lined up outside the plant, hoping for jobs. Within the plant the number of people quitting dropped 87%, absenteeism dropped 75%, and productivity rose by 30% or more. The productivity increases helped to increase Ford's profits, despite the higher wage bill and a cut in the price charged for a Model T.

The Ford $5 day seems to have had many results predicted by the efficiency wage model, including improved efficiency and higher profits. It is also interesting that as other auto firms introduced Ford's technological innovations, they also introduced his wage policies. By 1928, before unions were important in the industry, auto industry wages were almost 40% higher than in the rest of manufacturing.

*The source for this box is Daniel M. G. Raff and Lawrence H. Summers, "Did Henry Ford Pay Efficiency Wages?" *Journal of Labor Economics*, October 1987, pp. S57–S86.

†This quote is originally from Stephen Meyer, *The Five-Dollar Day: Labor Management and Social Control in the Ford Motor Company, 1908–1921*, Albany: State University of New York Press, 1981.

---

wages until enough workers decide to quit, as the classical model suggests would happen. According to the efficiency wage theory, firms realize that lower real wages reduce worker effort and productivity. Thus the more profitable way to reduce employment is to lay off workers directly and leave the real wage unchanged.

Despite the ability of the basic efficiency wage model to explain some aspects of labor market behavior, the model's result that real wages are literally fixed is too extreme, as real wages do vary a little over the cycle. An extension of the efficiency wage model that can account for the mildly procyclical behavior of real wages assumes that the amount of effort that workers provide depends on the unemployment rate as well as the real wage. According to this extended model, when there is a boom and the unemployment rate is low, it is easy for workers to find new jobs if they are fired for shirking. Hence in booms workers must be paid a relatively high real wage to induce them not to shirk. On the other hand, when a recession is in progress and the unemployment rate is high, it is difficult for

The *FE* line tells how much output firms would like to supply, which is the same as full-employment output $\bar{Y}$. The full-employment level of employment $\bar{N}$ is determined by the condition that the efficiency wage equals the marginal product of labor, and full-employment output $\bar{Y}$ is the amount that can be produced when employment is $\bar{N}$. Full-employment output does not depend on the real interest rate. Thus the *FE* line is a vertical line at $Y = \bar{Y}$.

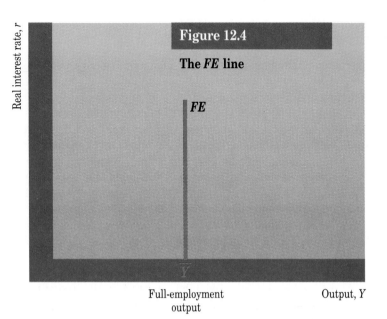

Figure 12.4

The *FE* line

workers to find new jobs. Thus in a recession workers are less likely to shirk, and a lower efficiency wage is sufficient to elicit effort from them.

Allowing effort to depend on the unemployment rate helps explain the procyclical behavior of real wages in a way consistent with the efficiency wage concept. However, for simplicity we ignore this extension and use the version of the efficiency wage model with a constant real wage for our macroeconomic analysis.

Efficiency Wages and the *FE* Line   Efficiency wages enter the Keynesian version of the macro model through the *FE* line, which shows the amount of output produced when employment is at the full-employment level $\bar{N}$. Using the production function (Eq. 12.1), we can write the full-employment level of output $\bar{Y}$ as

$$\bar{Y} = AF(K, E^* \times \bar{N}), \tag{12.2}$$

where E^* and $\bar{N}$ are the effort level and the employment level from the efficiency wage model. As in the classical model, the amount of output that firms want to supply is $\bar{Y}$, regardless of the value of the real interest rate. Thus the *FE* line is a vertical line at $Y = \bar{Y}$, as shown in Fig. 12.4.

As in the classical model, anything that changes full-employment output $\bar{Y}$ causes the *FE* line to shift. In the classical model we emphasized two factors that shift the *FE* line: changes in the supply of labor and changes in productivity. However, in the efficiency wage model labor supply does not affect employment, so *changes in labor supply do not affect the FE line in the Keynesian model.* A change in productivity *does* affect the *FE* line in the Keynesian model, as in the classical model. For example, a fall in productivity reduces full-employment output $\bar{Y}$ and shifts the *FE* line to the left, for two reasons: First, by reducing the marginal product of labor at any given level of employment, a fall in productivity lowers the demand for labor and thus reduces the full-employment level of employment $\bar{N}$. Because employment (and therefore effort-hours) is lower, firms supply less output. Second, a fall in productivity reduces the amount of output that can be produced with any given amount of capital and effort-hours.

12.2   PRICE STICKINESS

The rigidity created by efficiency wages is a *real* rigidity in that the real wage, rather than the nominal wage, remains fixed. Keynesian theories also emphasize *nominal* rigidities that occur when a price or wage is fixed in nominal, or dollar, terms and does not readily change in response to changes in supply or demand. In this section we discuss nominal rigidity in prices. Keynesians often refer to rigidity of nominal prices—a tendency of prices to adjust only slowly to changes in the economy—as **price stickiness.**

We saw in the previous section that real-wage rigidity addresses a problem of the basic market-clearing model, that the real wage appears to move less over the business cycle than is necessary to balance labor supply and labor demand. In a similar way, the assumption of price stickiness addresses what Keynesians believe is another important weakness of the basic classical model: the classical prediction that monetary policy is neutral.

The classical model assumes that wages and prices adjust quickly to equate supply and demand in all markets. In the basic classical model without mispercep-tions, the assumption that wages and prices adjust quickly implies that the aggregate supply curve is vertical and, therefore, that money is neutral. If money is neutral, a change in the money supply changes the price level by the same proportion but has no effect on real variables, such as output, employment, or the real interest rate.

Chapter 11 described empirical evidence that suggests that money is not neutral in the short run. Part of this evidence is that money is a leading procyclical variable, although this fact is also consistent with the interpretation that money is neutral and that the relationship between money and output arises from reverse causation. More convincing evidence that money is not neutral in the short run is presented in the analyses of historical episodes by Friedman and Schwartz and later by Romer and Romer, as discussed in Chapter 11.

To account for monetary nonneutrality, we can extend the classical model by assuming that producers have imperfect information about the current price level (the misperceptions theory). An alternative strategy for explaining monetary non-neutrality, favored by Keynesians, is to modify the classical assumption that prices adjust quickly. If, instead, prices are sticky, then the price level cannot adjust immediately to offset changes in the money supply, and money is not neutral. Thus for Keynesians price stickiness is important because it can help explain monetary nonneutrality.

Although we focus on nominal-price rigidity in this section, there is a long Keynesian tradition that emphasizes nominal-wage rigidity instead of nominal-price rigidity. An alternative version of the Keynesian model that assumes nomi-nal-wage rigidity is discussed in Appendix 12.A at the end of the chapter. This alternative model has similar implications to the Keynesian model with price rigid-ity. In particular, the alternative Keynesian model also reaches the conclusion that money is not neutral.

Sources of Price Stickiness: Monopolistic Competition and Menu Costs

To say that price stickiness gives rise to monetary nonneutrality does not com-pletely explain nonneutrality because it raises another question: Why are prices sticky? The Keynesian explanation for the existence of price rigidity relies on two main ideas: (1) Most firms actively set the prices of their products rather than taking the price of their output as given by the market; and (2) when a firm changes a price, it incurs a cost, known as a menu cost.

Monopolistic Competition   In a highly competitive, organized market like the market for corn or the stock exchange, it wouldn't make much sense to talk about price stickiness. In these markets prices adjust rapidly to reflect changes in supply or demand. Principal reasons for the flexibility of prices in these competitive, organized markets include the standardization of the product being traded (one bushel of corn, or one share of IBM stock, is pretty much like another) and the large number of actual or potential market participants. Standardization and a large number of participants make it worthwhile to organize a centralized market, such as the New York Stock Exchange, in which prices can react swiftly to changes in supply and demand. These same two factors also promote keen competition among buyers and sellers, which greatly reduces the ability of any individual to affect prices.

Most participants in the corn market or stock market think of themselves as **price takers.** A price taker is a market participant who takes the market price as given. For example, a small farmer correctly perceives the market price of corn as being out of his own control. In contrast, a **price setter** has some power to set prices.

Markets in which there are fewer participants and less standardized products than in the corn or stock markets may exhibit price-setting rather than price-taking behavior. As an example, consider the market for movies in a medium-sized city. This market may be fairly competitive, in that there are many different movie theaters, each trying to attract customers away from other theaters, home video stores, and so on. However, although the market for movies is competitive, it is not competitive to the same degree as the corn market. If a farmer tried to raise the price of his corn by 5¢ above the market price, he would sell no corn; but a movie theater that raised its ticket prices by 5¢ above its competitors' prices would not see its sales go to zero. Because the movie theater's product isn't completely standardized (it is showing a different movie than other theaters, its location is better for some people, it has different candy bars in the concession stand, a larger screen, or more comfortable seats), the theater has some discretion about what price to set. It is a price setter, not a price taker.

Generally, a situation in which all buyers and sellers are price takers (such as the market for corn) is called **perfect competition.** In contrast, a situation in which there is some competition, but in which a smaller number of sellers and imperfect standardization of the product allow individual producers to act as price setters, is called **monopolistic competition.**

Perfect competition is the model underlying the classical view of price determination, and as we have said, price rigidity would be very unlikely in a perfectly competitive market. Keynesians agree that price rigidity would not occur in a perfectly competitive market but point out that a relatively small part of the economy is perfectly competitive. Keynesians argue that it is possible, even likely, that price rigidity would occur in a monopolistically competitive market.

To illustrate the issues, let's return to the example of the competing movie theaters. If the market for movie tickets were perfectly competitive, how would tickets be priced? Presumably there would be some central meeting place where buyers and sellers of tickets would congregate. Market organizers would call out "bids" (prices at which they are willing to buy) and "asks" (prices at which they are willing to sell). Prices would fluctuate continuously as new information hit the market, causing supplies and demands to change. For example, a "two thumbs up" review by Siskel and Ebert would instantly drive up the price of tickets to that movie, but news of a prospective shortage of baby-sitters would cause all movie ticket prices to fall.

Obviously, though, this is not how movie tickets are priced. Actual pricing behavior by most theaters has the following three characteristics, which are also common to most price-setting markets:

1. Rather than accept the price of movies as completely determined by the market, a movie theater *sets* the price of tickets, in *nominal* terms, and maintains the nominal price for some period of time.[4]

2. At least within some range, the theater *meets the demand* that is forthcoming at the fixed nominal price. By "meets the demand" we mean that the theater will sell as many tickets as people want to buy at its fixed price, up to the point where it runs out of seats.

3. The theater readjusts its price from time to time, generally when costs of production or the level of demand change significantly.

Can this type of pricing behavior be profit maximizing? Keynesian theory suggests that it can, if there are small costs associated with changing nominal prices, and if the market is monopolistically competitive.

Menu Costs and Price Setting   The classic example of a cost of changing prices is the cost that a restaurant faces when it has to reprint its menu to show changes in the prices of its offerings. Hence the costs of changing prices are called **menu costs.** More general examples of menu costs (which can apply to any kind of firm) include costs of remarking merchandise, of reprinting price lists and catalogues, and of informing potential customers. Clearly, if firms incur costs when changing prices, they will change prices less often than they would otherwise, which creates a certain amount of price rigidity.

A potential problem with the menu cost explanation for price rigidity is that these costs do not seem to be very large. How, then, can they be responsible for an amount of nominal rigidity that could have macroeconomic significance?

Here is the first point at which the monopolistic competition assumption is important. For a firm in a perfectly competitive market, getting the price "a little bit wrong" has serious consequences: The farmer who prices his corn 5¢ a bushel above the market price sells no corn at all. Therefore the existence of a menu cost would not prevent the farmer from pricing his product at precisely the correct level. However, the demand for the output of a monopolistically competitive firm responds much less sensitively to changes in its price; the movie theater does not lose very many of its customers if its ticket price is 5¢ higher than its competitors'. Thus as long as the monopolistic competitor's price is in the right general range, the loss of profits from not getting the price exactly right is not too large. If the loss in profits is less than the cost of changing prices—the menu costs—the firm will not change price.

---

[4]This price may vary for different shows (for instance, there may be a "twilight" discount), and different people (such as senior citizens) may face different ticket prices. However, the whole schedule of ticket prices is changed relatively infrequently.

Over time, the production function and the demand curve facing a firm will undergo a variety of shocks so that eventually the profit-maximizing price for a firm will be significantly different from the pre-set price. When the profits lost by having the "wrong" price clearly exceed the cost of changing the price, the firm will change its nominal price. Thus movie theaters periodically raise their ticket and popcorn prices to reflect general inflation and other changes in market conditions.

Empirical Evidence on Price Stickiness   Several studies have examined the degree of rigidity or stickiness in actual prices. Using data first collected by Nobel laureate George Stigler and James Kindahl for the low-inflation period 1957–1966, Dennis Carlton[5] of the University of Chicago documented that industrial prices can be very sticky. Table 12.1, taken from Carlton's study, shows the average number of months between price changes for various industrial product groups. Notice that for three of eleven groups the average time between price changes exceeds a year. Using a statistical analysis, Carlton also found that prices were less rigid in relatively more competitive industries, a finding that is consistent with the theory.

There is also some evidence that prices of consumer goods can be sticky. Stephen Cecchetti[6] of Ohio State University studied the price changes of thirty-eight newsstand magazines over the period 1953–1979. He found that magazine prices are remarkably sticky. During the low-inflation period 1953–1965 magazines changed their prices on average only once every seven and a half years. Even during the inflationary 1970s, price changes occurred on average less than once every three years. This degree of stickiness is probably greater than can be explained by simple menu costs. The direct cost of changing a magazine's price is virtually zero (since a new cover that states the price must be printed for each issue anyway), nor is it very expensive to inform newsstands and subscribers of a price change. A possibility is that since most magazine revenue comes from advertisers and subscribers (who usually do not pay the newsstand price), publishers did not find it profitable to review their pricing policies frequently. Perhaps more likely, publishers may have feared that raising prices before their close competitors did would cause them to lose customers. Thus neither *Time* nor *Newsweek* may have been willing to move first to raise its price, until it was obvious to customers as well as newsstands that a price increase was appropriate.

In another study of price stickiness Anil Kashyap[7] of the Research Staff of the Federal Reserve Board examined the prices of twelve individual items listed in the catalogues of L.L. Bean, Orvis, and Recreational Equipment, Inc., over a thirty-five-year period. It is virtually costless to change the prices listed in a new catalogue, yet Kashyap found that the nominal prices of many goods remained fixed in successive issues of the catalogue. When nominal prices were changed, Kashyap found that sometimes the changes were large, but that sometimes the changes were quite small. He interpreted the presence of small price changes together with long periods of unchanged prices as evidence against menu costs. If menu costs are the reason that prices do not change frequently, then prices should be changed only when they are relatively far out of line, and the price changes should be large. The

---

[5]"The Rigidity of Prices," *American Economic Review*, September 1986, pp. 637–658.

[6]"The Frequency of Price Adjustment: A Study of the Newsstand Prices of Magazines," *Journal of Econometrics*, April 1986, pp. 255–274.

[7]"Sticky Prices: New Evidence from Retail Catalogs," Federal Reserve Board, FEDS Working Paper No. 112, February 1990.

Table 12.1 Average Times Between Price Changes for Various Industries

Product Group (Most to Least Rigid)	Average Time Between Price Changes (Months)
Cement	13.2
Steel	13.0
Chemicals	12.8
Glass	10.2
Paper	8.7
Rubber tires	8.1
Petroleum	5.9
Truck motors	5.4
Plywood	4.7
Nonferrous metals	4.3
Household appliances	3.6

Source: Dennis W. Carlton, "The Rigidity of Prices," *American Economic Review*, September 1986, pp. 637–658, Table 1.

fact that some changes are small seems to contradict this implication of menu costs. Even if menu costs are not the underlying cause of observed pricing behavior, however, Kashyap's study confirms the findings of Carlton and Cecchetti that there is substantial nominal-price rigidity in the economy.

Meeting the Demand at the Fixed Nominal Price When prices are sticky, firms react to changes in demand by changing the amount of production rather than by changing prices. According to Keynesians, why are firms willing to meet demand at a fixed nominal price? To answer this question, we again rely on the assumption of monopolistic competition. We have noted that a monopolistically competitive firm can raise its price at least a little without having to fear that it will lose all of its customers. The profit-maximizing strategy for a monopolistically competitive firm is to charge a price higher than its **marginal cost,** the cost of producing an additional unit of output. The excess of the price over the marginal cost is known as the **markup.** For example, if a firm charges a price 15% above its marginal cost, we say that the firm has a markup of 15%. More generally, if the firm charges a constant markup of η over marginal cost, its price can be described according to the following markup rule:

$$P = (1 + \eta) \times MC, \tag{12.3}$$

where P is the nominal price charged by the firm and MC is the nominal marginal cost.[8]

When the firm sets its price according to Eq. (12.3), it has an idea of how many units it will be able to sell. Now suppose that, to the firm's surprise, more customers come along and demand several more units than the firm expected to sell, at the price given in Eq. (12.3). Will it be profitable for the firm to meet the demand at this price?

[8]Technical note: For a monopolistically competitive firm that (1) faces a demand curve with a constant price elasticity and (2) has a constant marginal cost, the constant-markup rule in Eq. (12.3) will maximize profit. Also, in this case the labor demand curve is proportional to (rather than equal to) the marginal product of labor curve, a qualification that does not affect any conclusions of this chapter.

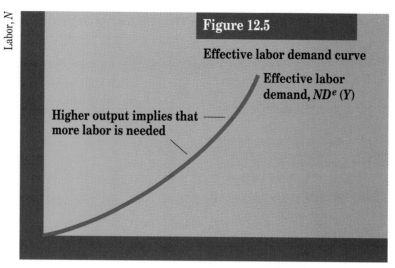

Figure 12.5

Effective labor demand curve

Effective labor demand, $ND^e(Y)$

Higher output implies that more labor is needed

Labor, N

Output, Y

When a firm meets the demand for its output, it employs just the amount of labor it needs to produce the quantity of output demanded. Because more labor is needed to produce more output, firms must employ more labor when the demand for output is high. This relation between the amount of output demanded and the amount of labor employed is the effective labor demand curve. The effective labor demand curve is the same as the production function relating output and labor, except that it is drawn with labor on the vertical axis and output on the horizontal axis.

The answer is "yes." Because the price the firm receives for each extra unit exceeds its cost of producing that extra unit (its marginal cost), the firm's profits increase when it sells additional units at the fixed price. Thus as long as the marginal cost remains below the fixed price of its product, the firm is happy to supply more units at this fixed price. Furthermore, if the firm is paying an efficiency wage, it will be easy to hire additional labor to produce the output needed to meet the demand, because there is an excess supply of labor.

The macroeconomic importance of firms' meeting the demand at the fixed nominal price is that the economy can produce an amount of output that is not on the full-employment line. Remember that the FE line shows the amount of output that firms would produce after complete adjustment of all wages and prices. However, with nominal-price stickiness the prices of goods do not adjust rapidly to their general equilibrium values. During the period in which prices have not yet completely adjusted, the amount of output produced need not be on the FE line. Instead, monopolistically competitive firms will meet the demand for their product, producing whatever amount is demanded.

Effective Labor Demand   When a firm meets the demand for its output at a given price, it may produce a different amount of output and employ a different amount of labor than it had planned. How much labor will a firm actually employ when it meets the demand? The answer is given by the effective labor demand curve, $ND^e(Y)$, shown in Fig. 12.5. For any given amount of output Y, the **effective labor demand curve** tells us how much labor is needed to produce that output, with productivity, the capital stock, and effort held constant.

We already have a concept that expresses the relationship between the amount of labor used and the amount of output produced; that concept is the production function. Indeed, the effective labor demand curve in Fig. 12.5 is simply a graph of the production function relating output and labor input, except that output Y is measured on the horizontal axis and labor N is measured on the vertical axis. (Flipping the axes in this way will be convenient later on.) The effective labor demand curve slopes upward from left to right because a firm needs more labor in order to produce more output.

The effective labor demand curve is used to determine the level of employment in the Keynesian macro model in the next section. When the economy is off the FE line, the level of employment is given by the effective labor demand curve.

12.3 MONETARY AND FISCAL POLICY IN THE KEYNESIAN MODEL

Having discussed the underlying Keynesian assumption of wage and price rigidity, we are ready to introduce the complete Keynesian model. Like the classical model of Chapter 11, the Keynesian model can be expressed in terms of the IS-LM-FE diagram, or alternatively, in terms of the AD-AS diagram. Rather than describe the Keynesian model in the abstract, we put it to work analyzing the effects of monetary and fiscal policy.

Monetary Policy

The primary motivation for introducing nominal-price stickiness into the Keynesian model was to provide an explanation of monetary nonneutrality. We examine the link between price stickiness and monetary nonneutrality first in the Keynesian IS-LM framework and then in the AD-AS version of the Keynesian model.

Monetary Policy in the Keynesian IS-LM Model   The Keynesian IS-LM model, which includes the FE line as well as the IS and LM curves, is similar in many respects to the classical IS-LM model discussed in Chapter 11. In particular, the IS curve and the LM curve are the same as in our earlier analyses of the classical model. The FE line in the Keynesian model is also similar to the classical case: As in the classical model, the Keynesian FE line is a vertical line that shows the full-employment level of output Y, which in turn depends on the full-employment level of employment determined in the labor market. There are two differences between the Keynesian FE line and the classical FE line, however: First, in the Keynesian model the full-employment level of employment is determined at the intersection of the labor demand curve and the efficiency wage line, not at the point where the quantity of labor demanded equals the quantity of labor supplied, as in the classical model. Second, because labor supply does not affect employment in the efficiency wage model, changes in labor supply do not affect the Keynesian FE line, although changes in labor supply do affect the classical FE line.

The most important difference between the Keynesian model and the classical model is that the price level P, which is flexible in the classical model, is fixed in the short run in the Keynesian model. This short-run price rigidity arises from the price-setting behavior of monopolistically competitive firms that face menu costs. Because of price stickiness, in the Keynesian model the economy does not have to be in general equilibrium in the short run. However, in the long run when prices adjust, the economy reaches its general equilibrium at the intersection of the *IS* curve, the *LM* curve, and the *FE* line, just as in the classical model.

According to Keynesians, what happens to the economy in the short run, if sticky prices prevent it from reaching general equilibrium? Keynesians assume that the asset market and the goods market adjust quickly, so that *the economy always lies on the intersection of the IS curve and the LM curve*. However, because monopolistically competitive firms are willing to meet the demand for goods at the fixed level of prices, output can differ from full-employment output and the economy can be off the *FE* line in the short run. When the economy is off the *FE* line, firms use just enough labor to produce the output they need to meet the demand. Because we have assumed that the efficiency wage is higher than the market-clearing real wage, there are always unemployed workers who would like to be working and firms are able to change employment as needed to meet the demand for output without changing the wage.

To show the Keynesian *IS-LM* model in action, Fig. 12.6 analyzes the effect of a decrease in the nominal money supply. We assume the economy starts at its general equilibrium point *E*. As we have seen before, a decrease in the money supply shifts the *LM* curve upward and to the left, from LM^1 to LM^2 in Fig. 12.6(a). Because a decrease in the money supply does not directly affect the goods market or the labor market, the *IS* curve and the *FE* line are unaffected. So far this is like the classical model.

Unlike the classical model, however, the Keynesian model assumes that (because of menu costs) prices are temporarily fixed, so that the general equilibrium at point *E* is not restored immediately. Instead, the short-run equilibrium of the economy—that is, the resting point of the economy, given the fixed price level—is located at the intersection of *IS* and LM^2 (point *F*), where output drops to Y_2 and the real interest rate rises to r_2.

Because the *IS-LM* intersection at point *F* is to the left of the *FE* line, the aggregate demand for output Y_2 is less than the full-employment level of output $\bar{Y}$. Monopolistically competitive firms facing menu costs do not cut their prices in the short run, as competitive firms would do, but instead cut their production to Y_2 in order to meet the lower level of demand. To reduce production, firms cut employment—for example, by laying off workers. The level of employment is given by the effective labor demand curve in Fig. 12.6(b). Because the level of output falls from $\bar{Y}$ to Y_2 in the short run, the level of employment falls from $\bar{N}$ to N_2. We refer to a monetary policy that shifts the *LM* curve upward and to the left—and thus reduces output and employment—as a contractionary monetary policy, or "tight" money. Analogously, an expansionary monetary policy, or "easy" money, is an increase in the money supply that shifts the *LM* curve downward and to the right, raising output and employment.

Why does tight money reduce output in the Keynesian model? Because in the Keynesian model prices are fixed in the short run, a reduction in the nominal money supply *M* is also a reduction in the real money supply *M/P*. To make wealth holders willing to hold a smaller real quantity of money and hold nonmonetary assets instead, the real interest rate must rise. The final link in the chain is that the higher real interest rate reduces both consumption spending (because saving rises) and investment spending. With less demand for their output, firms reduce production and lay off workers, taking the economy to point *F* in Fig. 12.6.

The rigidity of the price level is not permanent, however. Eventually, firms

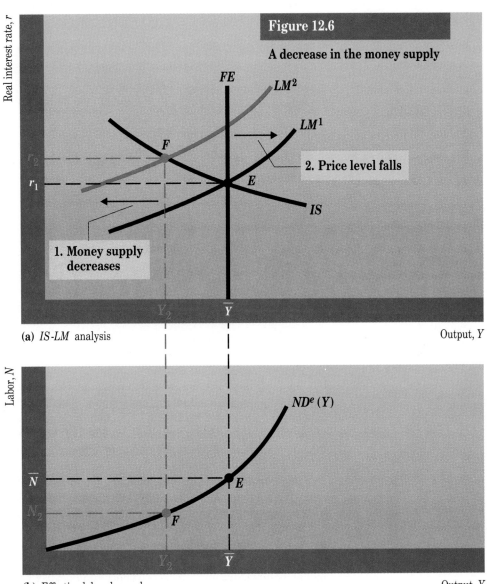

Figure 12.6

A decrease in the money supply

FE   *LM²*

LM¹

r_2 F

2. Price level falls

r_1 E

IS

1. Money supply decreases

Y_2 $\overline{Y}$

(a) *IS-LM* analysis   Output, *Y*

$NDᵉ(Y)$

$\overline{N}$ E

N_2 F

Y_2 $\overline{Y}$

(b) Effective labor demand   Output, *Y*

(a) If we start from an initial general equilibrium at point *E*, a decrease in the money supply shifts the *LM* curve upward and to the left, from *LM¹* to *LM²*; the *IS* curve and the *FE* line remain unchanged. Because prices are fixed and firms meet the demand in the short run, the economy moves to point *F*, which is to the left of the *FE* line. Output falls to Y_2, and the real interest rate rises.

(b) Because firms produce less output, employment falls to N_2, as shown by the effective labor demand curve.

In the long run the price level falls in the same proportion as the money supply, the real money supply returns to its initial level, and the *LM* curve shifts to its initial position, *LM¹* in part (a). The economy returns to point *E* in both parts, and money is neutral in the long run.

will review and readjust their prices, allowing the economy to reach its long-run equilibrium. In the case of the monetary contraction discussed here, firms find that the demand for their product in the short run is less than they had planned, so eventually they lower their prices. The decline of the price level increases the real money supply back to its initial level, which shifts the *LM* curve back to *LM¹* and restores the general equilibrium at point *E* in Fig. 12.6(a).

The aggregate demand (*AD*) curve slopes downward in the Keynesian model for the same reason that it slopes downward in the classical model: An increase in the price level reduces the real money supply, which shifts the *LM* curve upward and to the left and reduces the aggregate quantity of output demanded. The short-run aggregate supply (*SRAS*) curve is horizontal in the Keynesian model because firms meet the demand for their output at a fixed price. In the long run prices adjust completely, so that firms produce the full-employment level of output $\bar{Y}$ regardless of the price level. Thus the long-run aggregate supply (*LRAS*) curve is a vertical line at $Y = \bar{Y}$.

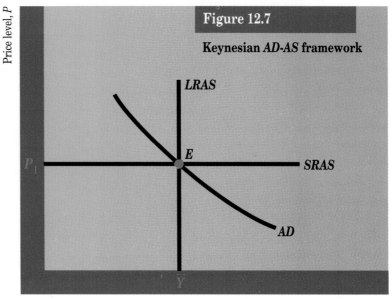

Figure 12.7

Keynesian *AD-AS* framework

In summary, the Keynesian model predicts that *money is not neutral in the short run but is neutral in the long run.* The important difference between the short run and the long run is that in the short run price stickiness prevents the economy from reaching its general equilibrium, but in the long run prices are flexible, so that general equilibrium can be attained.

The Keynesian conclusion that money is not neutral in the short run differs from the conclusion of the basic classical model that money is always neutral. However, the Keynesian results that money is nonneutral in the short run and neutral in the long run are the same as those we found by using the *extended* classical model based on the misperceptions theory. Although the Keynesian model and the extended classical model make the same predictions about monetary neutrality, these predictions are based on different mechanisms. In the extended classical model money is not neutral in the short run because changes in the price level fool producers into believing that the relative prices of their products have changed, which causes them to change their production. In the Keynesian model money is not neutral in the short run because monopolistically competitive firms facing menu costs find it profitable to respond to changes in aggregate demand by changing production rather than by changing prices. Although both the extended classical model and the Keynesian model predict that money is not neutral in the short run, Keynesians would argue that price stickiness lasts longer than any misperceptions that might occur. Thus the nonneutrality of money predicted by the Keynesian model might be expected to be longer lasting than the nonneutrality predicted by the extended classical model.

The Keynesian *AD-AS* Framework   Macroeconomic behavior in the Keynesian model can also be represented in terms of aggregate demand and aggregate supply. The aggregate demand (*AD*) curve in the Keynesian model is the same as in the classical model (Chapter 11). The *AD* curve (shown in Fig. 12.7) relates the aggregate quantity of output demanded to the price level. An increase in the price level

If we start from the full-employment general equilibrium at point E, a 10% reduction in the money supply shifts the AD curve downward by 10% at each level of output, from AD^1 to AD^2. In the short run the economy moves to point F, where the new aggregate demand curve AD^2 intersects the short-run aggregate supply curve $SRAS^1$. At point F output has fallen to Y_2. Because the aggregate demand for output is smaller than $\bar{Y}$, the price level falls. In the long run the economy returns to the full-employment general equilibrium at point H, where AD^2 intersects the vertical long-run aggregate supply curve, $LRAS$. Output returns to $\bar{Y}$, and the new price level P_2 is 10% lower than the initial price level P_1. Thus, again, money is neutral in the long run. As a result of the fall in the price level, the short-run aggregate supply curve shifts downward to $SRAS^2$.

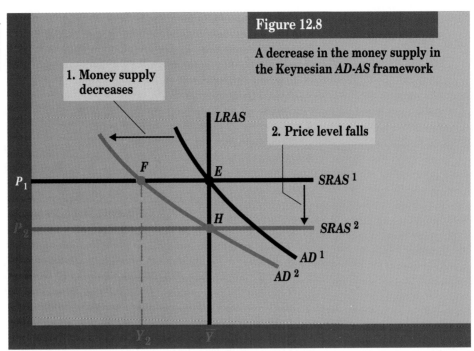

Figure 12.8

A decrease in the money supply in the Keynesian *AD-AS* framework

1. Money supply decreases

2. Price level falls

Output, Y

P reduces the real money supply M/P and shifts the LM curve upward and to the left (see Fig. 11.11, p. 423). Because the aggregate demand for goods corresponds to the intersection of the IS curve and the LM curve, the leftward shift of the LM curve reduces the aggregate quantity of output demanded. Since an increase in the price level reduces the aggregate quantity of output demanded, the AD curve slopes downward, as shown in Fig. 12.7.

In the Keynesian model the short-run aggregate supply curve, $SRAS$, is a horizontal line, as shown in Fig. 12.7. The Keynesian short-run aggregate supply curve is horizontal because with monopolistic competition and menu costs firms hold the price level P fixed in the short run and produce whatever level of output is needed to meet demand. Thus the $SRAS$ curve is horizontal at the historically given initial price level. However in the long run, after complete price adjustment, firms produce the full-employment level of output $\bar{Y}$ regardless of the price level P. Because the amount of output supplied by firms does not depend on the price level in the long run, the long-run aggregate supply curve, $LRAS$, is a vertical line at the point $Y = \bar{Y}$. The economy's long-run equilibrium is at the intersection of the aggregate demand (AD) curve and the long-run aggregate supply ($LRAS$) curve, point E in Fig. 12.7. At the long-run equilibrium point output equals its full-employment level, and the price level is such that the aggregate quantity of output demanded equals the aggregate quantity of output supplied.

To examine the issue of monetary neutrality in the Keynesian AD-AS framework, suppose that the economy is initially in long-run equilibrium at point E in Fig. 12.8, with output equal to $\bar{Y}$ and the price level equal to P_1, and that the Fed then reduces the money supply by 10%. As in the classical model, the reduction in the money supply shifts the AD curve downward by 10% at each level of output, from AD^1 to AD^2. The short-run equilibrium is at point F, where AD^2 intersects the short-run aggregate supply curve, $SRAS^1$. At point F the price level is unchanged from its initial value of P_1, and output equals the aggregate quantity of output demanded at that price level, Y_2. Point F in Fig. 12.8 is analogus to point F in the IS-LM diagram in Fig. 12.6, where it was also the case that the price level equaled its initial value and output equaled the quantity of output demanded at that price level.

The economy does not stay at point F forever. Because the quantity of output demanded Y_2 is smaller than the full-employment level of output $\bar{Y}$, firms eventually reduce their prices. The $SRAS$ curve gives the price level at which firms are willing to meet the demand; thus as the prices set by firms fall, the $SRAS$ curve moves downward. In the long run the price level falls by 10%, and the economy reaches general equilibrium at point H, where the aggregate demand curve AD^2 intersects the long-run aggregate supply curve $LRAS$. The fall in the price level shifts the short-run aggregate supply curve downward to $SRAS^2$, so that it too passes through point H in the long run.

The AD-AS framework is equivalent to the IS-LM model and thus leads to the same conclusions about monetary neutrality as the IS-LM model does. In the short run the Keynesian AD-AS framework implies that money is not neutral, as the reduction in money supply caused output to fall (point F in Fig. 12.8). However, as in the IS-LM model, in the long run in the AD-AS framework money is neutral: Changes in the money supply leave output unchanged and affect only the price level (point H in Fig. 12.8).

Fiscal Policy

The Keynesian model was initially developed during the Great Depression of the 1930s as economists struggled to explain the worldwide depression and to find policies to help the economy return to normalcy. One of the results stressed by early Keynesians was that fiscal policy, the government's decisions about government purchases and taxes, could be an important tool for raising output and employment. Keynesians believe that both increased government purchases and lower taxes can be used to raise output and employment, and so we discuss both cases.

The Effect of Increased Government Purchases   The Keynesian analysis of how a rise in the government's purchases affects the economy is shown in Fig. 12.9. Point E represents the initial equilibrium in both parts. As we have seen before, a (temporary) increase in government purchases reduces desired national saving at any level of the real interest rate, so that the IS curve shifts upward and to the right, from IS^1 to IS^2. In the short run, before prices can adjust, the economy moves to point F in Fig. 12.9(a), where the new IS curve IS^2 and LM^1 intersect. At point F output and the real interest rate both increase. Because firms meet the higher demand at the fixed price level, employment also rises, as shown by the movement from point E to point F along the effective labor demand curve in Fig. 12.9(b). A fiscal policy change, such as this one, that shifts the IS curve upward and to the right and raises output and employment is called an expansionary change (or "easy," or "loose," fiscal policy). Similarly, a fiscal policy (such as a reduction in government purchases) that shifts the IS curve downward and to the left and reduces output and employment is a contractionary or "tight" fiscal policy.

As we saw in Chapter 11, the classical IS-LM model also leads to the result that a temporary increase in government purchases increases output, but through a different mechanism. The classical analysis focuses on the fact that when govern-

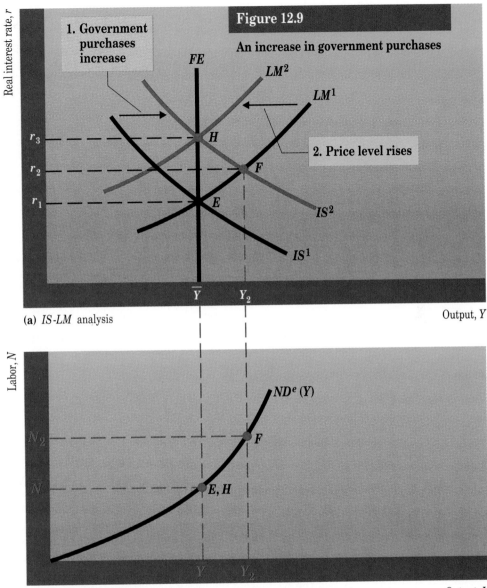

(a) *IS-LM* analysis

(b) Effective labor demand

(a) If we start from the general equilibrium at point E, an increase in government purchases reduces desired national saving and shifts the IS curve upward and to the right, from IS^1 to IS^2. The short-run equilibrium is at point F, with output increasing to Y_2 and the real interest rate rising to r_2.

(b) As firms increase production to meet the demand, employment increases from $\bar{N}$ to N_2, as shown by the effective labor demand curve.

However, the economy does not remain at point F: Because the aggregate demand for output exceeds $\bar{Y}$ in the short run, the price level increases, which reduces the real money supply and shifts the LM curve upward and to the left, from LM^1 to LM^2. In the long-run equilibrium at point H, output returns to $\bar{Y}$ and employment returns to $\bar{N}$, but the real interest rate rises further to r_3.

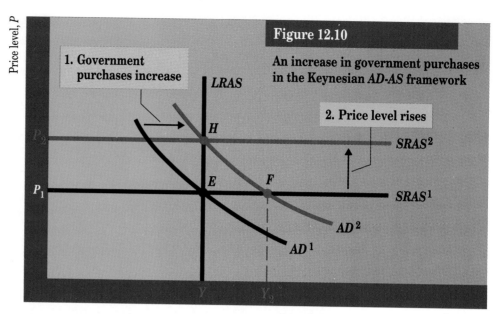

Price level, P

1. Government purchases increase

Figure 12.10

An increase in government purchases in the Keynesian *AD-AS* framework

2. Price level rises

LRAS

H

P_2 *SRAS*^{2}

P_1 E F *SRAS*^{1}

AD^2

AD^1

Y Y_2

Output, Y

An increase in government purchases raises the aggregate demand for output at any given price level (see Fig. 12.9). Thus the aggregate demand curve shifts to the right, from *AD*^{1} to *AD*^{2}. In the short run the increase in aggregate demand increases output to Y_2 (point F) but does not affect the price level, since prices are sticky in the short run. Because at point F the aggregate demand for output Y_2 exceeds $\bar{Y}$, eventually

firms raise their prices. The long-run equilibrium is at point H, where *AD*^{2} intersects the long-run aggregate supply curve *LRAS*. At point H output has returned to $\bar{Y}$ and the price level has risen from P_1 to P_2. Because the price level has risen, the short-run aggregate supply curve also rises, from *SRAS*^{1} to *SRAS*^{2}.

ment purchases increase, either current or future taxes must rise to pay for the extra spending. Higher taxes make workers (who are taxpayers) effectively poorer, which induces them to supply more labor. This increase in labor supply shifts the *FE* line to the right and causes output to rise in the classical model. In contrast, the *FE* line in the Keynesian model does not depend on labor supply (because of efficiency wages) and thus is unaffected by the increase in government purchases. Instead, the increase in government purchases has its effect on output in the Keynesian model by raising aggregate demand (that is, by shifting the *IS-LM* intersection to the right). Output increases above its full-employment level in the short run as firms meet the extra demand at the initial price level.

The effect of increased government purchases on output is transitory in the Keynesian model, lasting only as long as it takes the price level to adjust. (However, many Keynesians believe that price adjustment is sufficiently slow that "transitory" could mean several years.) In the long run, when firms adjust their prices, the *LM* curve moves upward and to the left, from *LM*^{1} to *LM*^{2} in Fig. 12.9(a), and the economy reaches general equilibrium at point H, with output again equal to $\bar{Y}$. Thus the increase in government purchases does not raise output in the long run.

The effects of the increase in government purchases can also be seen in the Keynesian *AD-AS* framework (Fig. 12.10). We have seen that increased government purchases shift the *IS* curve upward and to the right and raise the aggregate demand for output at any given price level. Thus as a result of the expansionary fiscal policy, the aggregate demand curve shifts to the right, from AD^1 to AD^2 in Fig. 12.10. The increase in aggregate demand raises output above $\bar{Y}$, as shown by the shift from the initial equilibrium at point E to the short-run equilibrium at point F. Because at point F the aggregate demand for output is greater than full-employment output, eventually firms raise their prices. In the long run the economy reaches the full-employment general equilibrium at point H, with output again equal to the $\bar{Y}$ and a higher price level. These results are identical to what we found using the Keynesian *IS-LM* framework.

The Effect of Lower Taxes   Keynesians generally believe that, like an increase in government purchases, a lump-sum reduction in current taxes is expansionary. In other words, Keynesians expect that a tax cut will shift the *IS* curve upward and to the right and raise output and employment in the short run. Similarly, a tax increase is expected to be contractionary, shifting the *IS* curve downward and to the left.

Why does a tax cut affect the *IS* curve, according to Keynesians? The argument is that if consumers receive a tax cut, they will spend part of it on increased consumption. Given output Y and government purchases G, an increase in desired consumption arising from a tax cut will lower desired national saving, $Y - C^d - G$, raising the real interest rate that clears the goods market and shifting the *IS* curve upward. Equivalently, the increase in desired consumption directly increases the aggregate demand for output, $C^d + I^d + G$, at any given price level.

The idea that a lump-sum tax cut will shift the *IS* curve upward, although accepted by most Keynesians, is somewhat controversial. In particular, many classicals maintain the view that lump-sum tax cuts will not affect desired consumption or the *IS* curve to any significant extent. The issues, which were discussed in detail in Chapter 6, are summarized in Appendix 12.B.

If a tax cut does raise desired consumption and shift the *IS* curve upward, as Keynesians claim, then the effects on the economy are very similar to the effects of increased government purchases (Figs. 12.9 and 12.10). In the short run a tax cut raises aggregate demand and thus output and employment at the initial price level. In the long run, after complete price adjustment, the economy returns to full employment with a higher real interest rate than in the initial general equilibrium. The only difference between the tax cut and the increase in government purchases is that instead of raising the portion of full-employment output devoted to government purchases, a tax cut raises the portion of full-employment output devoted to consumption.

Application

The Policy Mixes of the Early 1980s and the Early 1990s

The beginning of the 1980s saw significant shifts in both monetary and fiscal policy in the United States. The shift in monetary policy began in October 1979 with the announcement by Federal Reserve Chairman Paul Volcker that in order to bring down inflation, which was running at a rate of about 11% per year, monetary policy

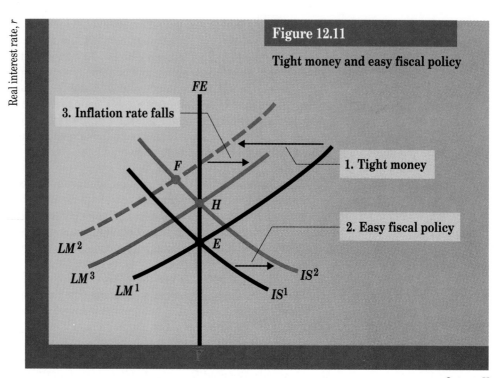

Figure 12.11

Tight money and easy fiscal policy

The U.S. economy was essentially at full employment in 1979 (point E), and late in the year the Fed tightened monetary growth in an attempt to reduce inflation. The reduction in monetary growth shifted the LM curve upward and to the left, from LM^1 to LM^2. Then in 1981 the Economic Recovery Tax Act reduced taxes. This tax cut combined with an increase in government purchases shifted the IS curve upward and to the right, from IS^1 to IS^2. With tight money and an easy fiscal policy, the economy moved to point F, with a high real interest rate. Point F is drawn to the left of the FE line, which assumes that the contractionary effects of tight money outweighed the expansionary effects of easy fiscal policy and caused a recession. The slowdown in monetary growth had the intended effect of reducing the rate of growth of prices relative to trend, so that the LM curve shifted downward and to the right to LM^3. At the long-run equilibrium at point H, full employment is restored and inflation has been slowed.

would be tightened. On the fiscal side, in 1981 Congress passed the Economic Recovery Tax Act (ERTA), which significantly reduced tax rates. As we discussed in Chapter 10, ERTA was supported by supply-side economists who argued that tax cuts would stimulate economic growth. An additional fiscal change was an increase in military expenditures by the Reagan administration. From a Keynesian perspective, tax cuts plus increased government purchases added up to a more expansionary fiscal policy.

The effects of the combination of tight money and easy fiscal policy are illustrated in Fig. 12.11. Because the economy was essentially at full employment in 1979 (unemployment was 5.8% of the labor force, close to its normal level, and the business cycle reached a peak in January 1980), the initial situation in 1979 is represented by the full-employment general equilibrium at point E. Following Volcker's announcement, money growth was reduced below its previous trend, causing the LM curve to shift upward and to the left, from LM^1 to LM^2. The easing of fiscal policy, arising both from the tax cut and from the increase in military spending, shifted the IS curve upward and to the right, from IS^1 to IS^2. As a result of the two policy changes, the economy shifted from point E to a short-run equilibrium at point F in Fig. 12.11.

What effects did this policy mix—the combination of tight money and expansionary fiscal policy—have on the economy? According to the Keynesian analysis of Fig. 12.11, an unambiguous impact of this combination of policies is to raise the real interest rate. In fact, following the policy shifts, the real interest rate in the United States soared to its highest level since the 1930s. (The real interest rate for the period 1960–1990 is shown in Fig. 2.6, p. 57.)

The effects on output of this policy mix are potentially ambiguous, since tight money tends to reduce output, and expansionary fiscal policy tends to increase output. In other words, it is not clear whether the short-run equilibrium point F should be drawn to the right or to the left of the FE line. The overall effect on output of the policy changes depends on when and how far the IS and LM curves shifted. Because the tightening of monetary policy preceded the fiscal policy expansion by more than a year, the initial effect should have been falling output, as the LM curve shifted upward and to the left, followed by a fall in inflation, as prices adjusted to the slowdown in money growth. Both the adjustment of prices, which raised the real money supply and shifted the LM curve back toward the general equilibrium point H, and the ensuing fiscal expansion should have caused output to rise, ultimately returning to its full-employment level.

According to this Keynesian analysis, the combination of tight money and loose fiscal policy accounts fairly well for three of the major aspects of macroeconomic behavior in the early 1980s: (1) the fall in output during the two recessions that occurred in 1980–1982 (output fell by 0.2% in 1980 and by 2.5% in 1982); (2) the sharp increase in the real interest rate, from less than 1% per year in 1979 to more than 8% per year in 1982; and (3) the dramatic slowdown in the rate of inflation (to less than 4% per year in 1983) that followed Volcker's monetary tightening.

As the 1990s began, the economy was once again at full employment (the business cycle reached a peak in July 1990), and once again it received doses of monetary and fiscal medicine. However, this time, the policy changes were in the opposite directions from those at the beginning of the 1980s. In the fall of 1990 Congress responded to a growing sense of urgency about the size of the Federal government's budget deficit by passing a deficit reduction bill. This bill increased taxes and cut Federal government expenditures, thus turning fiscal policy more contractionary. While this legislation was being debated in Congress, Federal Reserve Chairman Alan Greenspan promised to ease monetary policy to offset the contractionary effects of any deficit reduction package passed by Congress. Greenspan made good on this promise by easing monetary policy in late 1990 and early 1991. The Keynesian model predicts that this combination of fiscal restriction and monetary ease should reduce the real interest rate (the reverse of what happened in the early 1980s, when the policy mix was tight money and easy fiscal policy). Interest rates did fall: For example, between the spring of 1990 and the spring of 1991, the Treasury bill interest rate fell from about 8% to about 6%. Since inflation was stable, this fall in the nominal interest rate largely reflected a fall in the real interest rate.

As often happens, however, reality was more complicated than is suggested by these simple analyses. One important complication was that oil price shocks occurred both during 1979–1980 and in 1990.[9] Nevertheless, a Keynesian interpretation that focuses on the role of the policy mix seems to explain the behavior of the macroeconomy during these periods fairly well—especially the behavior of the real interest rate.

Macroeconomic Stabilization

In the classical model of the macroeconomy cyclical fluctuations are the best responses of the economy to various shocks. Although recessions may be hard times for people in the economy, there is no benefit to be had from government attempts to smooth out the business cycle. In the Keynesian model, however, business cycle expansions and contractions may be periods in which the economy is temporarily away from its general equilibrium at the *IS-LM-FE* intersection point. Recessions are particularly undesirable in the Keynesian view, because in a recession employment may be far below the amount of labor that workers would like to supply, which leads to hardships for the unemployed as well as to output that is "too low." Keynesians therefore argue that average economic well-being would be increased if governments tried to reduce cyclical fluctuations, especially recessions.

The Keynesian analysis of monetary and fiscal policies suggests that these policies could be used to smooth out the business cycle. To see how this might be done, consider Fig. 12.12. Suppose that the economy, initially in general equilibrium at point *E* in the figure, has been driven into recession at point *F*. Various types of shocks could have caused this recession: For example, a fall in consumer confidence about the future would increase current desired saving and shift the *IS* curve downward from *IS*¹ to *IS*². How might policymakers respond to this recession? We consider three policy scenarios: (1) no change in monetary or fiscal policy; (2) an increase in the money supply; and (3) an increase in government purchases.

Scenario 1: No change in macroeconomic policy. One option for policy in the face of the recession is to do nothing. With no government intervention at all, the economy will eventually correct itself: Because at point *F* the aggregate demand for output is below the full-employment level of output $\bar{Y}$, over time, prices will begin to fall, increasing the real money supply and shifting the *LM* curve downward and to the right. In the long run price declines shift the *LM* curve from *LM*¹ to *LM*², restoring the economy to general equilibrium at point *H*. However, a disadvantage of this strategy is that during the (possibly lengthy) price adjustment process, output and employment are below their full-employment levels.

Scenario 2: An increase in the money supply. Instead of waiting for the economy to reach general equilibrium through price adjustment, the Fed could increase the money supply, which also would shift the *LM* curve from *LM*¹ to *LM*² in Fig. 12.12. Assuming that the price adjustment process is relatively slow, this expansionary policy would move the economy to the general equilibrium point *H* more quickly than doing nothing.

[9]The effect of an oil price shock on the real interest rate was discussed in the context of the classical *IS-LM* model in Chapter 3.

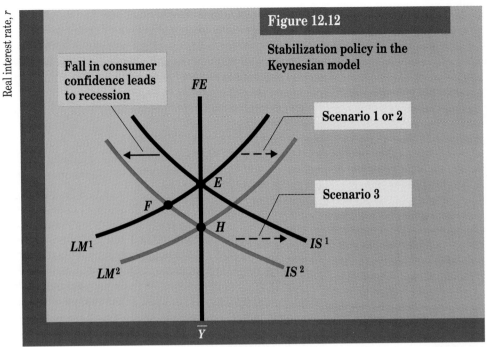

Figure 12.12

Stabilization policy in the Keynesian model

From point E the economy is driven into a recession at point F by a fall in consumer spending, which shifts the IS curve downward, from IS^1 to IS^2. If the government took no action, in the long run price adjustment would shift the LM curve from LM^1 to LM^2 and restore general equilibrium at point H (scenario 1). Alternatively, the government could try to offset the recession through stabilization policy: For example, the Fed could increase the money supply, which would shift the LM curve directly from LM^1 to LM^2, speeding up the recovery in output (scenario 2). Another possibility is a fiscal expansion, such as an increase in government purchases, which would shift the IS curve from IS^2 to IS^1, again restoring full employment but this time at point E (scenario 3). Expansionary monetary or fiscal policy helps the economy recover more quickly—but leads to a higher price level in the long run—than a strategy of doing nothing.

Scenario 3: An increase in government purchases. An alternative policy of raising government purchases will shift the IS curve upward and to the right, from IS^2 to IS^1. This policy also takes the economy to full employment, although at point E in Fig. 12.12 rather than at point H.

In all three scenarios the economy eventually returns to full employment. However, the use of monetary or fiscal policy to achieve full employment leads to two important differences from the scenario in which no policy action is taken. First, if the government uses monetary or fiscal expansion to end the recession, the economy is returned directly to full employment; but if policy is not changed, the economy remains in recession in the short run, returning to full employment only when prices have fully adjusted. Second, if there is no policy change (scenario 1), in the long run the price level falls relative to the nominal money supply. Indeed, it is the drop in the price level relative to the money supply that increases the real money supply, shifts the LM curve downward and to the right, and restores full employment at point H. In contrast, when monetary or fiscal policy is used to restore full employment (scenarios 2 and 3), the downward adjustment of the price level does not occur, since expansionary policy directly returns aggregate demand to the full-employment level. Thus according to the Keynesian analysis, using expansionary monetary or fiscal policy has the advantage of bringing the economy back to full employment more quickly but the disadvantage of leading to a higher price level than if no policy is undertaken.

Given that either monetary or fiscal policy can be used to bring the economy back to full employment, does it make any difference which policy is used? Yes, there is at least one important difference between the two policies, which is that monetary and fiscal policies have different effects on the composition of spending (the amount of output that is devoted to consumption, the amount to investment, and so on). In Fig. 12.12, although total output is the same at the alternative general equilibrium points E and H, at point E (which was reached by an increase in government purchases) government purchases are higher than at point H (which was reached by an increase in the money supply). Because government purchases are higher at point E, the remaining components of spending—in a closed economy, consumption and investment—must be lower at point E than at point H. Relative to a monetary expansion, an increase in government purchases crowds out consumption and investment by raising the real interest rate, which is higher at point E than at point H. In addition, the fact that increased government purchases imply higher current or future tax burdens also reduces consumption relative to what it would be under the monetary expansion.

Difficulties of Macroeconomic Stabilization   The use of monetary and fiscal policies to smooth out or moderate the business cycle is called **macroeconomic stabilization.** Using macroeconomic policies to try to smooth out the cycle is also sometimes called **aggregate demand management,** because monetary and fiscal policies shift the aggregate demand curve. Macroeconomic stabilization was a very popular concept in the heyday of Keynesian economics in the 1960s, and it still plays an important role in policy discussions. Unfortunately, even if we put aside the debates between classicals and Keynesians about whether smoothing out the business cycle is sensible in the first place, macroeconomic stabilization has been a lot harder to use successfully than the simple Keynesian theory suggests.

There are a number of technical problems associated with using macroeconomic stabilization, some of them already alluded to in the classical critique of stabilization policy in Chapter 11. First, because our ability to measure and analyze the economy is imperfect, it is difficult in practice to gauge how far the economy is from full employment at any given time. Second, we do not know precisely how much output will increase in response to a monetary or fiscal expansion. These uncertainties make it difficult to assess how much of a monetary or fiscal change is needed to restore full employment. Finally, even if we knew how large a policy change the economy needed at the current moment, we would still not have enough information: Because macroeconomic policies take time to implement and more time to affect the economy, their optimal use would require knowledge of where the economy will be six months or a year in the future. But such knowledge is, at best, very imprecise. Because of these problems, aggregate demand management has been likened to trying to hit a moving target in a heavy fog. These problems have not persuaded most Keynesians that stabilization policy should be abandoned; however, many Keynesians agree that policymakers should concentrate on fighting major recessions and not try to fine-tune the economy by smoothing out every bump and wiggle.

Beyond the technical problems associated with trying to find the right policies to stabilize the economy, economists also face the practical problem of convincing policymakers to take their advice. See the "Political Environment" box, p. 478, for a discussion of the role of the Council of Economic Advisers in formulating actual government policies.

12.4 THE KEYNESIAN MODEL AND THE BUSINESS CYCLE FACTS

To see how well the classical theory explained the business cycle facts, we had to make some assumptions about the types of shocks hitting the economy. In Chapter 11 we followed the real business cycle theorists in assuming that productivity shocks, which directly shift the FE line, were the most important type of shock. In a similar way, to see how well the Keynesian theory fits the business cycle facts, we have to specify the types of shocks hitting the economy.

Keynesians believe that aggregate demand shocks are the primary source of business cycle fluctuations. **Aggregate demand shocks** are shocks to the economy that shift the IS curve or the LM curve and thus affect the aggregate demand for output. Examples of aggregate demand shocks affecting the IS curve are changes in fiscal policy, changes in desired investment arising from changes in the expected future marginal product of capital,[10] and changes in consumers' patience or confidence about the future that affect desired saving. Examples of aggregate demand shocks to the LM curve are changes in the demand for money or in the money supply. The Keynesian model, combined with the hypothesis that most shocks are aggregate demand shocks, constitutes the Keynesian theory of business cycles.

Like real business cycle theory, the Keynesian theory of cycles can account for many of the business cycle facts. We list and discuss six business cycle facts explained by the Keynesian theory.

Business cycle fact: Employment is procyclical. In the Keynesian model aggregate demand shocks (shifts of the IS or LM curve) lead to fluctuations in output in the short run. Employment fluctuates in the same direction as output because firms employ just enough labor to produce the output needed to meet the demand. Thus employment is procyclical.

Business cycle fact: The real wage is mildly procyclical. In the basic efficiency wage model in which workers' effort depends only on the real wage, firms pay the real wage that maximizes effort per dollar. As a result, this model implies a constant real wage over the business cycle rather than a procyclical real wage. Recall, however, that if the efficiency wage model is extended to allow workers' effort to depend on the unemployment rate as well as the real wage, then an increase in the unemployment rate reduces the efficiency wage paid to workers. If the real wage falls in recessions when unemployment is high, then the real wage is procyclical.

---

[10]A change in the expected future MPK might also be thought of as a technological shock, because it involves a change in the future production function. However, since a change in the future MPK shifts the IS curve and does not affect the current FE line, Keynesians classify it as an aggregate demand shock.

The Political Environment

★ ★

The Role of the Council of Economic Advisers in Formulating Economic Policy

As World War II drew to an end in 1945, many people feared that the U.S. economy would lapse back into the depression that prevailed in the 1930s. This concern prompted Congress to pass the Employment Act of 1946 "to promote maximum employment, production, and purchasing power." A more concrete provision of the Employment Act of 1946 was the establishment of the three-person Council of Economic Advisers (the CEA). In addition to advising the President on a variety of economic issues, the CEA prepares the annual *Economic Report of the President* and works with other agencies of the Federal government to forge economic policy.

Most CEA members have been professional economists drawn from leading research universities and nonprofit institutions, and as such, they are often newcomers to the political establishment. Because they generally are at the frontier of economic research, CEA members are able to bring fresh ideas and perspectives to policy discussions. However, being usually inexperienced in the political arena, CEA members must also get a grasp of the political dimensions of policymaking and must develop a style for dealing with situations in which their views differ from those of others in the administration.

When President John F. Kennedy took office in 1961, he inherited a lackluster economy and promised to "start the country moving again."* Kennedy's newly appointed CEA, chaired by Walter Heller, recommended tax cuts to stimulate the economy, but the President's belief in "fiscal responsibility" initially made him reluctant to propose any policies that would create government budget deficits.† The opposition to fiscal stimulus was shared by other Administration officials, including Treasury Secretary Douglas Dillon and Commerce Secretary Luther Hodges. However,

*Arthur M. Okun, *The Political Economy of Prosperity*, Washington: The Brookings Institution, 1970, p. 24.
†The debate within the Kennedy administration about the tax cuts is documented in Michael G. Rukstad, "The Zenith of Keynesian Economics," *Macroeconomic Decision Making in the World Economy*, Chicago: The Dryden Press, 1986, Chapter 6.

Business cycle fact: Investment spending and other spending on durable goods are procyclical and very volatile. The strongly procyclical behavior of spending on durable goods can be explained by the Keynesian theory if shocks to the demand for durables are themselves an important source of cycles. The demand for durables would be a source of cyclical fluctuations if, for example, investors frequently reassessed their expectations of the future *MPK*. Keynes himself thought that waves of investor optimism and pessimism, which he called "animal spirits," were an important source of cyclical fluctuations. A rise in investment demand at any given real interest rate is expansionary, since it shifts the *IS* curve to the right.

Investment will also be procyclical in the Keynesian model whenever cycles are caused by fluctuations in the *LM* curve. For example, an increase in the money supply that shifts the *LM* curve downward and to the right both increases output and (by reducing the real interest rate) increases investment. Similarly, a monetary contraction reduces both output and investment.

Business cycle fact: Government purchases are procyclical. Our analysis of fiscal policy showed that an increase in government purchases raises output in the Keynesian model. Similarly, a reduction in government purchases reduces output.

by working effectively within the administration, the CEA was able to convince the President and his aides to support expansionary fiscal policies. The result was a fiscal stimulus that was implemented in two stages: The Revenue Act of 1962 provided tax incentives for investment, and a more comprehensive tax reduction was instituted by the Revenue Act of 1964. This fiscal package was followed by a strong economic expansion and was widely regarded as a successful experiment in Keynesian demand management.

Twenty years later, the CEA was again at odds with the President and the administration about fundamental aspects of fiscal policy. In the early 1980s President Ronald Reagan supported supply-side tax cuts (discussed in Chapter 10) while the chairman of the CEA, Martin Feldstein, urged fiscal restraint. Feldstein warned that tax cuts would lead to persistent government deficits, high real interest rates, and lower investment in the United States. When his warnings were repeatedly ignored by the Reagan administration, Feldstein made his views known to the public. Relations between the CEA and the administration then deteriorated to the point that the administration no longer relied on the CEA for economic advice, and the CEA temporarily lost its ability to influence economic policy. In testimony before Congress, Treasury Secretary Donald Regan recommended that the *Economic Report of the President* written by the CEA under Feldstein should be thrown in the trash.* In July 1984 Feldstein resigned from the CEA with his professional reputation intact and having earned a reputation for speaking his mind in the best interests of the country. However, the Reagan administration was so angered by the experience that for a while it considered trying to abolish the CEA or to minimize its role in policymaking.

Did Feldstein do the right thing? In looking back at this incident, William Nordhaus, a member of the CEA under President Jimmy Carter, argued that "by taking the dispute public, Feldstein lost the trust of the President and of the President's confidants, thereby losing the Council's unique power to affect economic policy by persuading the President in close personal contacts."† However, we will never know whether President Reagan and his close advisors could have been persuaded to change their policies by behind-the-scenes discussion and negotiation. If not, then the public interest may have been well served by Feldstein's public statements, which educated the Congress and the public about the potential risks of government budget deficits.

*William D. Nordhaus, "The Council of Economic Advisers: Conscience or Advocate?" in Karl Brunner and Allan Meltzer, eds., *Carnegie-Rochester Conference Series on Public Policy* vol. 25, Amsterdam: North-Holland, 1986, p. 272.
†*Ibid.*, p. 273.

Thus the Keynesian model predicts that government purchases will be procyclical.

Business cycle fact: Money is procyclical and leading. Because of price stickiness, increases in the money supply cause output to rise, and decreases in the money supply result in declines in output. This monetary nonneutrality is the Keynesian explanation of why money is procyclical and leads the cycle.

Business cycle fact: Inflation is procyclical and lagging. We have seen in our analyses of monetary and fiscal policy that when output rises above the full-employment level, there is upward pressure on the price level, which gives rise to inflation. In the Keynesian model an increase in aggregate demand initially causes output to rise, as firms increase their production to meet demand; but then the price level rises, so that there is inflation. Thus the Keynesian model predicts that inflation is procyclical and lagging.

Supply Shocks in the Keynesian Model

Until the 1970s the Keynesian business cycle theory focused almost exclusively on aggregate demand shocks as the source of business cycle fluctuations. Because

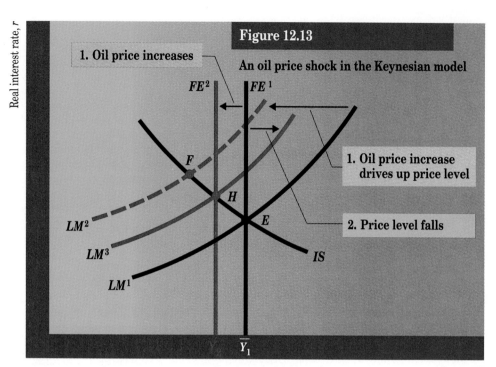

Figure 12.13

An oil price shock in the Keynesian model

An increase in the price of oil is an adverse supply shock that reduces full-employment output from $\bar{Y}_1$ to $\bar{Y}_2$ and thus shifts the FE line to the left. In addition, the increase in the price of oil increases prices in sectors that depend heavily on oil, while prices in other sectors remain fixed in the short run. Thus the average price level rises, which shifts the LM curve upward and to the left, from LM^1 to LM^2. In the short run the economy moves to point F, with output falling below the new, lower value of full-employment output and the real interest rate increasing. Because the demand for goods at point F is less than the full-employment level of output $\bar{Y}_2$, the price level falls, partially offsetting the initial increase in prices. The fall in the price level causes the LM curve to shift downward and to the right, from LM^2 to LM^3, moving the economy to the full-employment equilibrium at point H.

aggregate demand shocks lead to procyclical movements in inflation, however, the Keynesian theory had serious difficulty accounting for the stagflation—high inflation together with a recession—that hit the U.S. economy following the 1973–1975 oil price shock. Following this episode, Keynesians recast their theory to allow for supply shocks as well as demand shocks. Today Keynesians agree with real business cycle theorists that, at least sometimes, supply shocks can be a source of business cycle fluctuations.

Figure 12.13 shows a Keynesian analysis of the effects of a particular supply shock, a sharp temporary increase in the price of oil. As we saw in Chapter 3, if firms respond to an increase in the price of oil by using less energy, the amount of output that can be produced with a given amount of capital and labor falls. Thus the increase in the price of oil is an adverse supply shock, which reduces the full-employment level of output $\bar{Y}$ and shifts the FE line to the left, from FE^1 to FE^2 in Fig. 12.13. After complete wage and price adjustment, which occurs virtually immediately in the basic classical model but only in the long run in the Keynesian model, output falls to its new full-employment level $\bar{Y}_2$. Thus in the long run (after full wage and price adjustment), the Keynesian analysis and the classical analysis of a supply shock are the same.

The Keynesian analysis of the short-run effects of an oil price shock is a bit different from the classical analysis. To understand the short-term effects of the oil price shock in the Keynesian model, we must first think about the effects of the increase in the oil price on the general price level. Recall that firms facing menu costs will not change their prices if the "right" price is only a little different from the pre-set price. However, if the right price is substantially different from the pre-set price, so that firms would lose a lot of potential profit by maintaining the pre-set price, then they will change their prices. In the case of a large increase in the price of oil, firms whose costs are strongly affected by the price of oil—including gas stations, suppliers of home heating oil, and airlines, for example—will find that the right prices for their products are substantially higher than the pre-set prices. These oil-dependent firms will increase their prices quickly, while firms in other sectors will maintain their pre-set prices in the short run. Thus there is price stickiness in the sense that not all prices adjust to their equilibrium values, and yet the average price level rises in the short run.

Because a sharp increase in the price of oil raises the price level P in the short run, it also reduces the real money M/P. A fall in the real money supply shifts the LM curve to left, from LM^1 to LM^2 in Fig. 12.13. As we have drawn this figure, the LM curve shifts further to the left than the FE line shifts, though this does not need to be the case. The short-run equilibrium is at point F, where LM^2 intersects the IS curve. Because point F is to the left of the FE line, the economy is in a recession at point F, with output below the new value of full-employment output, $\bar{Y}_2$. In the short run the economy experiences stagflation, with both a drop in output below the full-employment level *and* a burst of inflation. The analysis also implies that the real interest rate will rise in the short run, which did occur following the 1979–1980 oil price shock but did not occur following the 1973–1975 increase in oil prices (see Fig. 2.6, p. 57).

As time passes, prices adjust throughout the economy. Because the aggregate demand for output at point F is less than full-employment output $\bar{Y}_2$, the price level falls (relative to the money supply). The fall in the price level raises the real money supply, shifting the LM curve downward and to the right, to LM^3. Eventually the economy returns to the general equilibrium point H, with a lower level of full-employment output $\bar{Y}_2$. Notice that although the adjustment of prices downward between point F and point H offsets some of the initial price shock, the price level at the final general equilibrium point H is higher than at the initial general equilibrium point E. We know this is true because the final LM curve, LM^3, is to the left of LM^1; thus the real money supply is lower and prices are higher at point H than at point E.

12.5   OBJECTIONS TO THE KEYNESIAN MODEL

Although like the real business cycle theory, the Keynesian theory can explain a number of the business cycle facts, there are some objections that can be raised against this theory. We discuss several of these objections and the Keynesian replies.

Objection: The Keynesian theory predicts that average labor productivity is countercyclical, but it is in fact procyclical. Keynesians assume that demand shocks rather than supply shocks cause most cyclical fluctuations. Supply shocks are shifts of the production function; therefore in assuming that supply shocks are usually unimportant, Keynesians are also assuming that the production function is fairly stable over the business cycle. If the production function is stable and is not shifted by supply shocks, then increases in employment during booms should reduce average labor productivity, because of diminishing marginal returns to labor. Thus the Keynesian model predicts that average labor productivity is countercyclical, contrary to the business cycle fact.

Reply: To explain the procyclical behavior of average labor productivity, Keynesians have modified their models to include labor hoarding. **Labor hoarding** occurs if, because of the costs of firing and hiring workers, firms continue to employ some workers in a recession that they would otherwise have laid off. The "redundant" workers that are retained during the recession are "hoarded labor." They are being kept on the payroll so that the firm will not have to incur the costs of firing them and then hiring and training new workers when the economy revives. The hoarded labor either works less hard during the recession (since there is less for them to do) or is set to work doing tasks, such as maintaining equipment, that are not measured as part of the output of the firm (see Box 12.2). When the economy revives, the hoarded labor goes back to working in the normal way. The presence of hoarded labor producing a reduced amount of measured output during recessions can explain why measured productivity is low during recessions and high during booms, even though the firm's production function is stable and exhibits diminishing returns.

Objection: Menu costs seem to be too small to generate enough price stickiness to be important at the macroeconomic level. The costs of changing price tags or informing customers about price changes is trivial for many products and would not seem to offer any substantial reason for price stickiness.

Reply: The actual cost of changing prices is larger than the costs of changing price tags and posted signs. In any case, small menu costs can imply significant price stickiness if firms perceive the benefits of changing prices as also being small. Beyond re-marking merchandise, costs of changing prices may include gathering and processing data, doing marketing surveys, and arranging meetings among several personnel within the company. Changing prices also risks angering longtime customers or starting a price war with competitors. These more comprehensive costs of changing prices may still be relatively small, but Keynesians also point out that if the "right" price is not very far from the pre-set price, the potential benefit from changing the price to the right price may also be very small. If this potential benefit is smaller than the cost of changing prices, then the firm will leave its price unchanged in the short run and, instead, meet the demand by varying its production.

Objection: If there are costs to changing prices, aren't there costs to changing quantities produced as well? If so, wouldn't firms be just as likely to respond to demand changes by changing prices and keeping output unchanged? This objec-

When a monopolistically competitive firm with menu costs faces a fall in demand during a recession, it responds by reducing its output rather than cutting prices. The reduction in output implies, in turn, that the firm can reduce its employment. Do firms cut employment to the minimum level needed to produce the lower level of output? Or do they "hoard" labor, as some Keynesians suggest? To answer these questions, Jon A. Fay and James L. Medoff* of Harvard University sent questionnaires to large manufacturing enterprises, asking about employment and production during the most recent downturn experienced at each plant.

Fay and Medoff found that during a downturn the average plant in their survey cut production by 31% and cut its total use of blue-collar hours to 23% below the normal level. Plant managers estimated that total hours could have been reduced by an addi-

BOX 12.2: HOW IMPORTANT IS LABOR HOARDING IN PRACTICE?

tional 6% of the normal level without further reducing output. Of this 6% of normal hours, about half (3% of normal hours) were typically assigned to various types of useful work, including maintenance and overhaul of equipment, painting, cleaning, reworking output, and training. The remaining 3% of normal hours were assigned to "make-work" and other unproductive activities. These numbers suggest that firms retain a fairly significant amount of redundant or hoarded labor during recessions, which helps Keynesians explain the business cycle fact that average labor productivity falls in recessions and rises in booms.

*"Labor and Output Over the Business Cycle," *American Economic Review*, September 1985, pp. 638–655.

tion to the Keynesian theory is potentially a serious one. For example, the Keynesian explanation of monetary nonneutrality rests on the stickiness of the price level in the face of changes in the money supply. If, instead, output remained fixed, and the price level changed in proportion to changes in the money supply, then money would be neutral. Classical economists argue that a cost of changing prices leading to price rigidity is no more plausible than a cost of changing output resulting in an "output rigidity," which would make money neutral and invalidate much Keynesian analysis.

Reply: Empirically, prices seem to be more rigid than output. The evidence discussed earlier in this chapter on the frequency of price adjustment suggests that firms are reluctant to change prices frequently, but production rates are changed often. This evidence implies that in fact the costs of changing prices are greater, though further research may be needed to provide a convincing description of these costs.

Objection: At the current time Keynesian models of the economy are less well developed than the current generation of classical models. For example, most modern Keynesian models attempt to capture macroeconomic behavior over only one or two periods. In contrast, real business cycle models have been developed that can be used to study the movement of the economy over many periods. Building multiperiod Keynesian models poses many difficult problems, including working out how firms will adjust their prices over time when there are menu costs and when other firms are also changing prices infrequently.

Reply: Keynesian models that try to explain wage and price rigidity rather than merely assume its existence are still in their infancy. Recently, Keynesians have made considerable progress accounting for wage and price rigidity in ways that are consistent with economic rationality. Improved theoretical explanations of wage-price rigidity have improved the new generation of Keynesian models and made communication between the Keynesian and classical schools easier. Still, as in the classical theory, much more remains to be done.

12.6   CHAPTER SUMMARY

1. Keynesians argue that real wages fluctuate too little over the business cycle to be consistent with the classical view that cyclical fluctuations in employment reflect movements along the labor supply curve. The apparent tendency of real wages to fluctuate too little to keep labor supplied equal to labor demanded is called real-wage rigidity by Keynesians.

2. One explanation for real-wage rigidity is based on the efficiency wage model, which assumes that workers work harder in response to an increase in the real wage. Firms can attain the highest level of profit by paying the real wage, known as the efficiency wage, that elicits the most effort per dollar of wages. If the effort curve relating effort provided by workers to the real wage does not change, then the efficiency wage, and hence the real wage actually paid, is rigid.

3. Given the efficiency wage, firms choose the level of employment $\bar{N}$ at which the marginal product of labor equals the efficiency wage. Provided that the efficiency wage is above the market-clearing real wage, the quantity of labor supplied exceeds labor demanded in the efficiency wage model. Therefore employment is determined by labor demand, and the supply of labor is irrelevant.

4. Full-employment output $\bar{Y}$ is determined by the production function and the number of workers employed at the efficiency wage $\bar{N}$. The *FE* line, which shows the amount of output that firms want to supply, is vertical at the point $Y = \bar{Y}$. In the Keynesian model full-employment output and the *FE* line are affected by productivity shocks but not by changes in labor supply, because labor supply is irrelevant in the efficiency wage model.

5. Keynesians interpret the results of empirical studies of monetary policy as evidence that monetary policy can affect output, so that money is not neutral. They attribute the nonneutrality of money to price stickiness, which means that some firms may not change their prices in the short run even though the demand for their product has changed. Price stickiness is contrary to the assumption of the basic classical model that prices and wages are completely flexible.

6. Price stickiness can arise from the profit-maximizing behavior of monopolistically competitive firms that face menu costs, or costs of changing prices. Such firms will not change their prices unless the profit-maximizing price and the existing price differ by enough to make it worthwhile to incur the menu cost to change the price. While holding their prices fixed, these firms adjust their production to meet the demand for their output.

7. In the Keynesian model with price rigidity, output is determined in the short run at the intersection of the *IS* and *LM* curves. The economy can be off the *FE* line in the short run because firms are willing to meet demand at the existing price. The level of employment in the short run is given by the effective labor demand curve, which shows the amount of labor needed to produce a given amount of output. In the long run, after prices and wages have completely adjusted, the *LM* curve will move to restore general equilibrium with full employment.

8. As in the classical model, the aggregate demand (*AD*) curve slopes downward in the Keynesian model. The reason for the downward slope is that an increase in the price level reduces the real money supply and shifts the *LM* curve upward and to the left, which reduces aggregate demand. The Keynesian short-run aggregate supply (*SRAS*) curve is horizontal, because in the short run the price level is fixed and firms supply whatever amount of output is demanded. In the long run, after complete wage and price adjustment, firms supply the full-employment level of output $\bar{Y}$, regardless of the price level; so the long-run aggregate supply (*LRAS*) curve is vertical.

9. In the Keynesian model an increase in the money supply shifts the *LM* curve downward and to the right, raising output and lowering the real interest rate in the short run. Thus money is not neutral in the short run. In the long run, however, when prices adjust, money is neutral: The monetary expansion raises the price level proportionally but has no real effects.

10. In the Keynesian model an increase in government purchases or a cut in taxes shifts the *IS* curve upward and to the right, raising output and the real interest rate in the short run. In the long run, after prices and wages fully adjust, output returns to the full-employment level but the real interest rate increases. Fiscal policy is not neutral in the long run because it affects the composition of output among consumption, investment, and government purchases.

11. Macroeconomic stabilization, also called aggregate demand management, is the use of monetary or fiscal policy to try to eliminate recessions and keep the economy at full employment. The Keynesian theory suggests that macroeconomic stabilization is both desirable and possible. However, there are problems in practice, including the difficulty of measuring and forecasting the state of the economy and of determining how much monetary and fiscal stimulus is needed at any given time. Keynesian antirecessionary policies also lead to a higher price level than would occur in the absence of policy changes.

12. Keynesian business cycle theory, which has traditionally emphasized the importance of aggregate demand shocks, can account for the procyclical behavior of employment, money, government purchases, and inflation. It can also explain the relatively small cyclical movement of real wages and the fact that investment is very volatile over the course of the business cycle. To account for stagflation, or high inflation during a recession, the Keynesian theory must be expanded to allow for supply shocks. In order to explain the procyclical behavior of average labor productivity, the Keynesian theory must include the additional assumption that firms hoard labor—that is, they employ more workers than necessary during recessions.

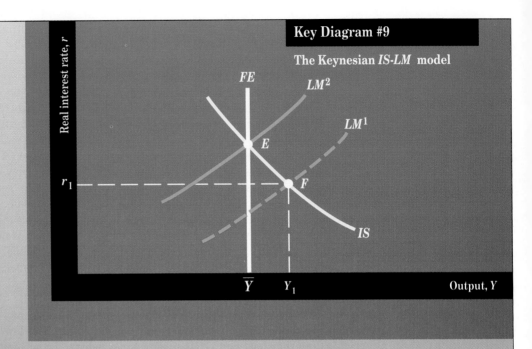

The Keynesian *IS-LM* model describes the behavior of the macroeconomy when the real wage is rigid and prices do not adjust quickly to keep the economy in general equilibrium.

Diagram Elements

- The real interest rate r is on the vertical axis, and output Y is on the horizontal axis.

- The *IS* curve, which represents equilibrium in the goods market, and the *LM* curve, which represents equilibrium in the asset market, are identical to the *IS* and *LM* curves in the classical *IS-LM* model (see Key Diagram #3, p. 146).

- The full-employment line *FE* is a vertical line at the full-employment level of output $\bar{Y}$, which is the amount of output that firms supply after prices and wages have completely adjusted to their equilibrium values. Full-employment output is determined by the production function equation $\bar{Y} = AF(K, E^* \times \bar{N})$, where E^* is the level of effort when workers are paid the efficiency wage, $\bar{N}$ is the amount of labor demanded by firms that pay the efficiency wage, A is productivity, and K is the fixed capital stock.

Factors That Shift the Curves

- Given output, any change that reduces desired national saving relative to desired investment increases the real interest rate that clears the goods market and shifts the *IS* curve upward. Factors shifting the *IS* curve in the classical model, which also shift the *IS* curve in the Keynesian model, are listed in Table 11.1 (p. 400). In addition, unlike classicals, Keynesians argue that lump-sum tax cuts, by increasing desired consumption and reducing desired saving, shift the *IS* curve upward.

- Given output, any change that reduces money supply relative to money demand shifts the *LM* curve upward. Factors shifting the *LM* curve in the Keynesian model are the same as those shifting the *LM* curve in the classical model; see Table 11.1.

- A beneficial supply shock increases full-employment output $\bar{Y}$ and shifts the *FE* line to the right. Changes in labor supply do *not* affect full-employment output or the *FE* line in the Keynesian model, as they do in the classical model.

Analysis

- In the Keynesian model prices are sticky in the short run but adjust fully in the long run.

- If there is no common point of intersection of the *IS* curve, the *LM* curve, and the *FE* line, the short-run behavior of the economy is represented by the intersection of the *IS* curve and the *LM* curve, where the goods market (*IS*) and asset market (*LM*) are in equilibrium but the labor market (*FE*) is not in equilibrium. For instance, if the *LM* curve is LM^1, the economy is at point *F* in the short run, with output equal to Y_1 and real interest rate equal to r_1. It is possible for the economy to be off the *FE* line in the short run, because in the short run monopolistically competitive firms are willing to meet the demand for their output at a fixed price. Employment at point *F* equals the amount of labor needed to produce Y_1, as determined by the effective labor demand curve (see Fig. 12.9, p. 469).

- In the long run price adjustment restores the economy to general equilibrium. For example, at point *F* aggregate demand Y_1 exceeds full-employment output $\bar{Y}$, so eventually firms raise their prices. Higher prices lower the real money supply M/P and shift the *LM* curve upward and to the left, from LM^1 to LM^2. In the long run the economy reaches general equilibrium at point *E*, where *IS*, LM^2, and *FE* intersect and output equals the full-employment level $\bar{Y}$.

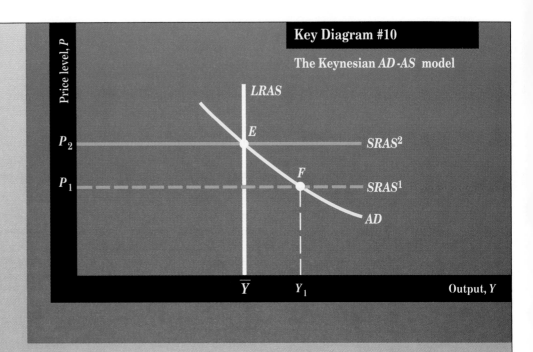

The Keynesian *AD-AS* framework shows how aggregate demand and aggregate supply interact to determine the price level and output in the Keynesian model.

Diagram Elements

- The price level *P* is on the vertical axis, and the level of output *Y* is on the horizontal axis.

- The aggregate demand (*AD*) curve, which shows the amount of output demanded at each price level, is identical to the *AD* curve in the classical model (Key Diagram #8, p. 440). An increase in the price level reduces the real money supply, shifts the *LM* curve upward and to the left, and reduces the aggregate quantity of output demanded. Thus the *AD* curve slopes downward.

- The aggregate supply curve shows the amount of output supplied at each price level. In the short run monopolistically competitive firms that face menu costs meet the demand for their output at a fixed price level. Thus the short-run aggregate supply curve *SRAS* is a horizontal line at the initial price level.

- In the long run, after complete adjustment of prices, firms supply the full-employment level of output $\bar{Y}$ regardless of the price level. Thus the long-run aggregate supply curve *LRAS* is vertical at $Y = \bar{Y}$.

Factors That Shift the Curves

- The aggregate demand for output is determined by the intersection of the *IS* curve and the *LM* curve. Given the price level, any factor that shifts the *IS-LM* intersection to the right increases the aggregate demand for output and thus also shifts the *AD* curve to the right. Factors that shift the *AD* curve in the classical model, which also shift the Keynesian *AD* curve, are listed in Table 11.2 (p. 425). In addition, in the Keynesian model a lump-sum tax cut increases aggregate demand and shifts the *AD* curve to the right.

- In the Keynesian model with monopolistic competition and menu costs, any factor that increases the price level in the short run, such as an increase in the price of oil, shifts the horizontal short-run aggregate supply (*SRAS*) curve upward by the amount of the increase in the price level.

- Any factor that increases full-employment output $\bar{Y}$, such as a beneficial supply shock, shifts the long-run aggregate supply (*LRAS*) curve to the right. Changes in labor supply do not affect full-employment output in the Keynesian model with efficiency wages and thus do not affect the *LRAS* curve.

Analysis

- In the short run the economy is located at the intersection of the *AD* curve and the initial *SRAS* curve, $SRAS^1$, at point *F* in the figure. At point *F* the price level remains at its initial level of P_1 and output is Y_1, which is greater than the full-employment level of output $\bar{Y}$. Output can exceed $\bar{Y}$ in the short run because monopolistically competitive firms facing menu costs are willing to meet the demand for their output at the initial price level.

- If output exceeds $\bar{Y}$ in the short run, as at point *F*, over time firms revise their prices upward. In the long run, after complete adjustment of prices, the economy reaches general equilibrium at point *E*, where the *AD* curve intersects the long-run aggregate supply curve *LRAS*. At point *E* the economy is at full employment, and the price level has risen from P_1 to P_2. Because the price level at which firms are willing to meet the demand has risen, the *SRAS* curve rises, from $SRAS^1$ to $SRAS^2$.

Key Terms

aggregate demand
   management, p. 476
aggregate demand
   shocks, p. 477
effective labor demand
   curve, p. 462
efficiency wage, p. 451
efficiency wage model,
   p. 449

effort curve, p. 450
labor hoarding, p. 482
macroeconomic
   stabilization, p. 476
marginal cost, p. 461
markup, p. 461
menu cost, p. 459

monopolistic
   competition, p. 458
perfect competition,
   p. 458
price setter, p. 458
price stickiness, p. 457
price taker, p. 458
real-wage rigidity, p. 449

Key Equations

$$Y = AF(K, E \times N) \qquad (12.1)$$

In the efficiency wage model the production function relates the amount of output produced Y to productivity A, capital K, and effort-hours, $E \times N$. Effort-hours equal the total number of hours worked N times the average level of worker effort E.

$$\bar{Y} = AF(K, E^* \times \bar{N}) \qquad (12.2)$$

Full-employment output $\bar{Y}$ is the amount of output supplied by firms when wages and prices have completely adjusted. In the Keynesian model with efficiency wages, full-employment output is also the amount of output produced when effort-hours equal $E^* \times \bar{N}$. The term E^* is the level of worker effort when firms pay the efficiency wage, and $\bar{N}$ (the full-employment level of employment) is the amount of employment when the marginal product of labor equals the efficiency wage.

Review Questions

1. Define *efficiency wage*. Why is the real wage constant over the business cycle in the efficiency wage model? What problems with the classical theory of the labor market is the efficiency wage model intended to address?

2. How is full-employment output $\bar{Y}$ determined in the Keynesian model with efficiency wages? In this model, how is full-employment output affected by changes in productivity (supply shocks)? How is it affected by changes in labor supply?

3. What is price stickiness? Why do Keynesians believe that it is important to allow for price stickiness in macroeconomic analysis?

4. Define *menu cost*. Why might menu costs lead to price stickiness in monopolistically competitive markets but not in perfectly competitive markets? Why is it profitable for a monopolistically competitive firm to meet the demand at its fixed price when demand turns out to be higher than the firm had planned?

5. What predictions does the Keynesian model make about monetary neutrality (both in the short run and in the long run)? Compare with the predictions about neutrality of the basic classical model and the extended classical model with misperceptions.

6. In the Keynesian model, what effects does an increase in government purchases have on output and the real interest rate in the short run? In the long run? How does an increase in government purchases affect the composition of output in the long run?

7. Describe three alternative responses that policymakers could choose from when the economy is in recession. What are the advantages and disadvantages of each strategy? Be sure to discuss the effects on employment, the price level, and the composition of output. Are there any practical difficulties in using macroeconomic stabilization policies to fight recessions?

8. Use the Keynesian model to explain the procyclical behavior of employment, money, government purchases, and investment.

9. What does the Keynesian model predict about the cyclical behavior of average labor productivity? How does the idea of labor hoarding help bring the prediction of the model into conformity with the business cycle facts?

Numerical Problems

1. A firm faces the following relationship between the real wage it pays and the effort exerted by its workers:

Real Wage	Effort
8	7
10	10
12	15
14	17
16	19
18	20

The marginal product of labor for this firm is given by

$$MPN = \frac{E(100 - N)}{15},$$

where E is the effort level and N is the number of workers employed. Assuming that the firm can pay only one of the six wage levels given, which wage will it choose? How many workers will it employ?

There are 200 workers in the town where the firm is located, all willing to work at a real wage of 8. Does this change your answer to the first part of this question?

2. An economy is described by the following equations:

desired consumption C^d = $130 + 0.5(Y - T) - 500r$,
desired investment I^d = $100 - 500r$,
government purchases G = 100,
taxes T = 100,
real money demand L = $0.5Y - 1000r$,
money supply M = 1320,
full-employment output $\bar{Y}$ = 500.

We assume that expected inflation is zero, so that money demand depends directly on the real interest rate.

a. What are the equations of the IS curve and the LM curve? (These equations express the relationship between r and Y when the goods market and the asset market are in equilibrium.)
b. Calculate the full-employment values of output, the real interest rate, the price level, consumption, and investment.
c. Now suppose that because of investor optimism about the future marginal product of capital, the investment function becomes

$$I^d = 200 - 500r.$$

What are the new values of output, the real interest rate, the price level, consumption, and investment in the short run? In the long run? Show your results graphically.

3. Consider the following economy:

desired consumption C^d = $325 + 0.5(Y - T) - 500r$,
desired investment I^d = $200 - 500r$,
government purchases G = 150,
taxes T = 150,
real money demand L = $0.5Y - 1000r$,
money supply M = 6000,
full-employment output $\bar{Y}$ = 1000.

a. Calculate the full-employment values of output, the real interest rate, the price level, consumption, and investment.
b. Now suppose that government purchases are increased to 250, with no change in taxes. (For the purposes of this problem you may ignore the government's budget constraint.) What are the new values of output, the real interest rate, the price level, consumption, and investment in the short run? In the long run?
c. Repeat part b for the case in which the money supply is increased to 7200. Assume that $G = 150$.

4. An economy is described by the following equations:

desired consumption C^d = $300 + 0.5(Y - T) - 300r$,
desired investment I^d = $100 - 100r$,
government purchases G = 100,
taxes T = 100,
real money demand L = $0.5Y - 200r$,
money supply M = 6300,
full-employment output $\bar{Y}$ = 700.

a. What is the equation of the aggregate demand curve? (*Hint:* Find the equations describing goods market equilibrium and asset market equilibrium. Use these two equations to substitute out the real interest rate. For any given price level the aggregate demand equation gives the level of output that satisfies both goods market equilibrium and asset market equilibrium.)

b. Suppose that $P = 15$. What are the short-run values of output, the real interest rate, consumption, and investment?

c. What are the long-run equilibrium values of output, the real interest rate, consumption, investment, and the price level?

5. (Appendix 12.A) Consider an economy in which all workers are covered by contracts that specify the nominal wage and give the employer the right to choose the amount of employment. The production function is

$$Y = 20\sqrt{N},$$

and the corresponding marginal product of labor is

$$MPN = \frac{10}{\sqrt{N}}.$$

Suppose that the nominal wage is $W = 20$.

a. What is the equation of the labor demand curve relating the real wage and the amount of employment demanded by firms?

b. Given the nominal wage of 20, what is the relation between the price level P and the amount of employment demanded by firms?

c. What is the relation between the price level and the amount of output supplied by firms? Graph this relation.

Now suppose that the IS and LM curves of the economy are as follows:

IS curve: $Y = 120 - 500r$,

LM curve: $\dfrac{M}{P} = 0.5Y - 500r$.

d. The money supply M is 300. Use the IS and LM equations to derive a relation between output Y and the price level P. This is the equation for the aggregate demand curve. Graph this relation on the same axis as the relation between the price level and the amount of output supplied by firms (the aggregate supply curve) from part c.

e. What are the equilibrium values of the price level, output, and the real interest rate?

f. Now suppose that the money supply M is 135. What are the equilibrium values of the price level, output, and the real interest rate?

Analytical Problems

1. According to the Keynesian *IS-LM* model, what is the effect of each of the following on output, the real interest rate, employment, and the price level? Distinguish between the short run and the long run.

a. Increased tax incentives for investment (the tax breaks for investment are offset by lump-sum tax increases that keep total current tax collections unchanged).

b. Increased tax incentives for saving (as in part a, lump-sum tax increases offset the effect on total current tax collections).

c. A wave of investor pessimism about the future profitability of capital investments.

d. An increase in consumer confidence, as consumers expect that their incomes will be higher in the future.

2. According to the Keynesian *IS-LM* model, what is the effect of each of the following on output, the real interest rate, employment, and the price level? Distinguish between the short run and the long run.

a. Financial deregulation allows banks to pay a higher interest rate on checking accounts.

b. The introduction of sophisticated credit cards greatly reduces the amount of money that people need for transactions.

c. A severe water shortage causes sharp declines in agricultural output and increases in food prices.

d. A temporary beneficial supply shock affects most of the economy, but no individual firm is sufficiently affected so that it changes its prices in the short run.

3. Suppose that the Federal Reserve has a policy of increasing the money supply when it observes that the economy is in recession. However, suppose that it takes an increase in the money supply about six months to affect aggregate demand, which is about the same amount of time that it takes firms to review and reset their prices. What effects will the Fed's policy have on output and price stability? Does your answer change if (a) the Fed has some ability to forecast recessions or (b) price adjustment takes longer than six months?

4. Classical economists argue that using fiscal policy to fight a recession does not make workers better off. Suppose, instead, that the Keynesian model is correct. Relative to a policy of doing nothing, does an increase in government purchases that brings the economy to full employment make workers better off? In answering the question, discuss the effects of the fiscal expansion on the real wage, employment, consumption, and current and future taxes. How does your answer depend on (a) the direct benefits of the government spending program and (b) the speed with which prices adjust in the absence of fiscal stimulus?

5. According to the dual labor market theory (Chapter 10), the labor market is divided into a primary sector, where good jobs are located, and a secondary sector, which has bad or dead-end jobs. Suppose we model the primary sector as a sector in which the marginal product of labor is high and (because effort is costly for firms to monitor) firms pay an efficiency wage. The secondary sector has a low marginal product of labor and no efficiency wage; instead, the real wage in the secondary sector adjusts so that the quantities of labor demanded and supplied are equal in that sector. Workers are alike, and all would prefer to work in the primary sector. However, workers who can't find jobs in the primary sector supply labor in the secondary sector.

What are the effects of each of the following on the real wage, employment, and output in both sectors?

a. Expansionary monetary policy increases the demand for primary-sector output.

b. Immigration increases the labor force.

c. The effort curve changes so that a higher real wage is needed to elicit the greatest effort per dollar in the primary sector.

d. There is a temporary productivity improvement in the primary sector.

e. There is a temporary productivity improvement in the secondary sector.

APPENDIX
12.A   LABOR CONTRACTS AND NOMINAL-WAGE RIGIDITY

In the Keynesian theory the nonneutrality of money is a consequence of nominal rigidity. In the text of this chapter we emphasized nominal-*price* rigidity. An alternative nominal rigidity that could account for the nonneutrality of money, and which is emphasized by many Keynesians, is nominal-*wage* rigidity. Nominal-wage rigidity could arise, for example, because of long-term labor contracts between firms and labor unions in which wages are set in nominal terms (the case we study here). In terms of the *AD-AS* framework the difference between nominal-price rigidity and nominal-wage rigidity is that nominal-price rigidity implies a flat short-run aggregate supply curve, whereas nominal-wage rigidity (as we see in this appendix) implies a short-run aggregate supply curve that slopes upward. However, this difference has no major effect on the results obtained from the Keynesian model. In particular, in the Keynesian model with nominal-wage rigidity, money remains nonneutral in the short run and neutral in the long run.

The Short-Run Aggregate Supply Curve with Labor Contracts

In the United States most labor contracts specify employment conditions and nominal wages for a period of three years. Although labor contracts specify the nominal wage rate, they usually do not specify the total amount of employment. Instead, employers unilaterally decide how many hours will be worked and whether workers will be laid off. These institutional facts imply that the short-run aggregate supply curve slopes upward, as we now explain.

To see why the short-run aggregate supply curve slopes upward when there are labor contracts that prespecify the nominal wage, let's see what happens when the price level increases. With the nominal wage W already determined by the contract, an increase in the price level P reduces the real wage, $w = W/P$. In response to the fall in the real wage, firms demand more labor. Because firms unilaterally choose the level of employment, the increase in the amount of labor demanded leads to an increase in employment and therefore an increase in output. Thus an increase in the price level leads to an increase in the amount of output supplied, as shown by $SRAS^1$ in Fig. 12.A.1.

Nonneutrality of Money

The version of the Keynesian model in which long-term labor contracts create nominal-wage rigidity is an alternative to the model based on efficiency wages and sticky prices, but both models predict that money is not neutral in the short run.

The nonneutrality of money in the model with long-term labor contracts is illustrated in Fig. 12.A.1. The initial general equilibrium is located at point E, where the initial aggregate demand curve AD^1 intersects the short-run aggregate supply curve $SRAS^1$. A 10% increase in the money supply shifts the AD curve upward to AD^2. (For any given level of output the price level is 10% higher on AD^2 than on AD^1.) In the short run the rise in the money supply increases the price level to P_2 and increases output to Y_2, as shown by point F. Output is higher than its full-employment level at point F because the rise in prices has lowered the real wage, which leads firms to employ more labor and produce more output.

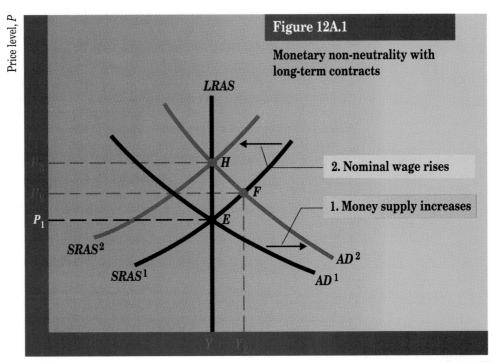

Figure 12A.1

Monetary non-neutrality with long-term contracts

With long-term labor contracts that fix the nominal wage in the short run, an increase in the price level lowers the real wage and induces firms to employ more labor and produce more output. Thus the short-run aggregate supply curve $SRAS^1$ slopes upward. When nominal wages are rigid, money is not neutral: From the initial equilibrium at point E a 10% increase in the money supply shifts the AD curve upward, from AD^1 to AD^2. In the short run both output and the price level increase, as shown by point F. Output increases at point F because the increase in the price level P has lowered the real wage W/P, leading firms to employ more labor and produce more. Over time, contracts are renegotiated and nominal wages rise to match the increase in prices. As wages rise, the short-run aggregate supply curve shifts upward, from $SRAS^1$ to $SRAS^2$, so that general equilibrium is restored at point H. At point H both the price level P and the nominal wage W have risen by 10%, so the real wage is the same as it was initially, and firms supply the full-employment level of output $\bar{Y}$.

At the short-run equilibrium at point F, however, workers will be dissatisfied because their real wages are lower than they had expected. Over time, as contracts are renewed or renegotiated, nominal wages will rise to offset the increase in prices. At any given price level a rise in the nominal wage also raises the real wage, inducing firms to employ less labor and produce less output. Thus rising nominal wages cause the short-run aggregate supply curve to shift upward, from $SRAS^1$ to $SRAS^2$ in Fig. 12.A.1. Eventually, general equilibrium is restored at point H.

In the long run at point H, the price level rises to P_3, which is 10% higher than its initial value P_1. At point H the nominal wage W has also increased by 10%, so that the real wage W/P has returned to its initial value. With the real wage back to its original value, firms employ the same amount of labor and produce the same of amount of output (equal to $\bar{Y}$) as they did at the initial equilibrium, point E. Thus, just as in the Keynesian model based on efficiency wages and price stickiness, in the Keynesian model with nominal-wage rigidity money is neutral in the long run but not in the short run.

Although nominal-wage rigidity arising from labor contracts can explain short-run monetary nonneutrality, there are some objections to this explanation. The first objection is the fact that only one sixth of the labor force in the United States is unionized and covered by long-term labor contracts. A possible reply to this objection is that many nonunion workers receive wages that behave similarly to those set in union contracts. For example, although most nonunion workers do not have formal wage contracts, they may have "implicit contracts" with their employers, or informal unwritten arrangements that set wages in a manner similar to the way that formal union contracts do.

A second objection is that many labor contracts contain cost-of-living adjustments (COLAs), which tie the nominal wage to the overall price level, as measured, for example, by the consumer price index. Contracts with *complete* indexation increase the nominal wage by the same percentage as the increase in the price level. If wages are completely indexed to the price level, then the short-run aggregate supply curve is vertical and money is neutral. To see why, suppose that the price level increases by 6%. If labor contracts are completely indexed, then nominal wages also increase by 6% and the real wage W/P remains unchanged. Since the real wage does not change, firms choose the same levels of employment and output. Since with complete indexation changes in the price level have no effect on employment or output, the aggregate supply curve is vertical in both the short run and the long run. A vertical aggregate supply curve implies that money is always neutral, as in the case of the basic classical model in Chapter 11.

A response to this objection is that most labor contracts in the United States do not have complete indexation of wages to prices. In recent years, fewer than half of the workers covered by major private industry bargaining agreements had any COLA provisions at all.[11] Furthermore, most contracts with COLA provisions have *partial* indexation rather than complete indexation. For example, under a contract that calls for 50% indexation, the nominal wage will increase by a percentage equal to 50% of the overall increase in prices. In this case, if the price level increases by 6%, the nominal wage increases by 3%. As a result, the real wage falls by 3% (a 3% increase in the nominal wage W minus a 6% increase in the price level P). The reduction in the real wage induces firms to increase employment and production. Thus with partial indexation the short-run aggregate supply curve is again upward sloping, and money is not neutral in the short run.

A third and final objection to the Keynesian theory based on labor contracts is that it predicts that real wages will be countercyclical, contrary to the business cycle fact that real wages are mildly procyclical. For example, at point F in Fig. 12.A.1 output is higher than the full-employment level, but the real wage is lower than at full employment (indeed, it is the low real wage that induces firms to produce the extra output). Thus the theory says that real wages will fall in booms—that is, the real wage is countercyclical—which is inconsistent with the evidence.

A possible reply to this last objection is that perhaps both supply shocks and aggregate demand shocks may affect real wages. We saw in studying the real business cycle theory in Chapter 11 that if productivity shocks cause cyclical fluctuations, the real wage should be procyclical, perhaps strongly so. A combination of supply shocks (which cause the real wage to move procyclically) and aggregate demand shocks (which, as in Fig. 12.A.1, cause the real wage to move counter-

---

[11]The Bureau of Labor Statistics in the U.S. Department of Labor summarizes features of recent contracts in its monthly publication, *Current Wage Developments*.

cyclically) might average out to an overall behavior of the real wage that is mildly procyclical. Some evidence for this view was provided in a recent study by Scott Sumner and Stephen Silver,[12] which concludes that, empirically, the real wage has been procyclical during periods dominated by supply shocks but has been counter-cyclical during periods in which aggregate demand shocks were more important.

APPENDIX
12.B   TAX CUTS AND THE *IS* CURVE

Keynesians generally believe that a lump-sum reduction in current taxes shifts the *IS* curve upward and to the right and is therefore expansionary. The reason that a tax cut shifts the *IS* curve, according to Keynesians, is that consumers will spend some part of any tax cut, so that desired consumption C^d rises and desired national saving $Y - C^d - G$ falls, given output Y and government purchases G. A fall in desired national saving raises the real interest rate that clears the goods market and thus shifts the *IS* curve upward.

An opposing view is given by the Ricardian equivalence proposition, accepted by many classical economists. (The Ricardian equivalence proposition is discussed in detail in Chapters 6 and 16 and is only summarized here.) According to the Ricardian equivalence proposition, a lump-sum reduction in current taxes that leaves current and future government purchases unchanged will *not* affect desired consumption and thus will not shift the *IS* curve. The basic argument for Ricardian equivalence is as follows: If the government cuts current taxes without cutting purchases, it must borrow more from the public today. Ultimately, the government's debts must be repaid with interest, which will require higher taxes in the future. Thus a tax cut doesn't really make consumers better off; it increases their current income (current taxes are lower) but reduces their future income (future taxes are higher). Since consumers are not better off in any long-run sense, they will not increase their consumption in response to the tax cut, and the *IS* curve will not shift.

Keynesians have several responses to this argument. One response is that consumers may not be sophisticated enough to understand that the debts of the government are ultimately their own debts; if consumers are shortsighted, they may spend part of their tax cut even if they are not really any better off in a long-run sense. Another response is that consumers may face borrowing constraints, or limits imposed by lenders on the amount that the consumer can borrow in order to consume more today. If consumers are prevented by borrowing constraints from consuming as much as they would like today, then they will treat a tax cut as a welcome opportunity to increase current consumption, and again consumption will be affected by the tax cut.

Empirical evidence on the effect of tax cuts on consumption is mixed. Consumption did increase in the United States following tax cuts passed in 1981. In some other cases, though, consumers have received tax cuts without substantially increasing consumption.

---

[12]"Real Wages, Employment and the Phillips Curve," *Journal of Political Economy*, June 1989, pp. 706–720.

13
Business Cycles and Macroeconomic Policy in the Open Economy

Major business cycle fluctuations are rarely limited to one or a few countries. Instead, when economic conditions change for better or worse, they tend to change in many countries at about the same time. For example, although the Great Depression of the 1930s affected some countries more seriously than others, it had a large impact on almost all of the world's capitalist economies. Similarly, in the first few decades following World War II a popular saying was that "when America sneezes, the rest of the world catches cold," meaning that cyclical downturns in the then-dominant U.S. economy had effects around the world. The United States no longer plays the central role in the world economy that it did in the 1950s and 1960s, but links among the economies of different nations have continued to strengthen. More so than ever before, we live in a highly interdependent world economic system.

One major aspect of worldwide economic integration since World War II is the steady increase in the volume of international trade. Today individual countries produce with an eye toward foreign as well as domestic markets, and they draw raw materials from distant as well as nearby sources. This expansion of trade has increased productivity by allowing countries to specialize in producing those goods and services for which their natural and human resources make them best suited. However, expanded trade relations also imply that national economies are more dependent on what happens in other countries. For example, because Japan sells so much of its output to the United States, if the United States goes into a recession, the resulting fall in American demand for Japanese exports may slow down the Japanese economy as well. The effect of an American recession on Japan would be much less significant if there were no trade between the two countries.

Besides expanding trade, a second dimension of worldwide economic integration is the increasingly tight interweaving of national financial markets into a world financial market. It is no longer the case, as it once was in many countries, that when a firm wants to build a new plant, it must obtain funds primarily from domestic savers. Instead, firms can use international financial markets to borrow from savers anywhere. Similarly, domestic savers are no longer restricted to lending domestically but can look for the most attractive lending opportunities either at home or abroad.

By allowing savings to flow to the highest-return uses regardless of where the savers and investors happen to reside, the integration of world financial markets increases worldwide productivity, just as the development of an integrated world trading system does. But financial market linkages, like trade linkages, increase the sensitivity of individual economies to developments abroad. For example, because of closely connected financial markets, macroeconomic policies that change the real interest rate in one country may affect real interest rates and economic activity in other countries as well.

Clearly, an understanding of short-run economic fluctuations in the modern world requires attention to international factors. In this chapter we broaden our macroeconomic model to allow for trading and financial relationships between the domestic economy and the economies of other countries. We begin our discussion by introducing two important new variables: the nominal exchange rate, which is the relative price of currency in two countries, and the real exchange rate, which is the relative price of goods in two countries. We are particularly interested in how macroeconomic disturbances and policy changes affect exchange rates, and how variations in exchange rates in turn feed back into the performance of the economy.

13.1   EXCHANGE RATES

In discussing exchange rates, we make an important distinction between nominal and real exchange rates. Briefly stated, the nominal exchange rate is the answer to the question, "How many units of a foreign *currency* can I get in exchange for one unit of my domestic *currency?*" The real exchange rate is the answer to the question, "How many units of the foreign *good* can I get in exchange for one unit of my domestic *good?*"

Nominal Exchange Rates

If you have ever visited a foreign country, then you probably had to deal with a different national currency. In order to pay your hotel bill or shop in the stores in a foreign country, you first had to trade your own country's money (dollars, for example) for that of the country you were visiting. The rate at which dollars could be traded for the local currency on that particular day was probably clearly posted in the bank, exchange office, or hotel where you changed your money.

The rate at which two currencies can be exchanged for each other in the market is the **nominal exchange rate** between those two currencies, or, as it is more commonly known, the **exchange rate.** For example, if the nominal exchange rate between the U.S. dollar and the Japanese yen is 125 yen per dollar, then a dollar can buy 125 yen in the **foreign exchange market,** the market for international currencies. Equivalently, 125 yen can buy \$1 in the foreign exchange market. We use the symbol e_{nom} to stand for the nominal exchange rate between two currencies. Specifically, e_{nom} is the number of units of foreign currency that can be purchased with one unit of the home currency. For residents of the United States the home (or domestic) currency is the U.S. dollar, and the nominal exchange rate between the U.S. dollar and the Japanese yen is expressed as $e_{\mathrm{nom}} = 125$ yen per dollar.

If you changed money more than once during your visit abroad, then you may have noticed that the exchange rate had changed during your stay. Such changes are a normal occurrence under a flexible exchange rate system, the type of system in which world's major currencies (such as the dollar or yen) are currently traded. In a **flexible exchange rate system,** also called a floating exchange rate system, exchange rates are not officially fixed but are determined by conditions of supply and demand in the foreign exchange market. Under a flexible exchange rate system exchange rates move continuously and respond quickly to any economic or political news that might influence the supplies and demands for various currencies. The "In Touch with the Macroeconomy" box, p. 501, discusses exchange rate data.

The values of currencies have not always been determined by a flexible exchange rate system. Historically, there has often been some type of **fixed exchange rate system** under which exchange rates were set at officially determined levels. These official rates were maintained by the commitment of nations' central banks to buy and sell their own currencies at the fixed exchange rate. For example, under the international gold standard, which prevailed in the latter part of the nineteenth century and the early part of the twentieth century, the central bank of each country maintained the value of its currency in terms of gold by agreeing to buy or sell gold in exchange for currency at the official exchange rate. The gold standard was suspended during World War I, was temporarily restored, and then collapsed during the economic and financial crises of the 1930s.

A more recent example of a fixed exchange rate system was the Bretton Woods system, named after the town in New Hampshire where the 1944 conference establishing the system was held. Under the Bretton Woods system the values of various currencies were fixed in terms of the U.S. dollar, and the value of the dollar was set in terms of gold at a price of $35 per ounce of gold. Countries that were members of the Bretton Woods system had the right to sell dollars to the Federal Reserve in exchange for gold at the official rate. The Bretton Woods system functioned until the early 1970s, when inflation in the United States made it virtually impossible to keep the price of gold from rising above $35 per ounce. Since the breakdown of the Bretton Woods system, the dollar has floated against other major currencies.

The world exchange rate system currently in effect is far from a pure flexible exchange rate system. Many individual countries, especially smaller ones, attempt to fix their exchange rates against a major currency. (For example, a number of African countries tie their currencies to the French franc.) By fixing their exchange rates against a major currency, these countries hope both to stabilize the value of their own currency and to reduce the sharp swings in import and export prices that may result from exchange rate fluctuations. There are also some groups of countries, called exchange rate unions, that have agreed to try to fix exchange rates among themselves while allowing their currencies to fluctuate against those of countries outside the union. An important example of an exchange rate union is the European Monetary System (EMS), which was founded in 1979 and whose members include the major Western European countries. The members of the EMS agreed to fix exchange rates among themselves in the hope of increasing the economic integration among the countries in the union.

with the Macroeconomy

Exchange Rates

Exchange rates are determined in foreign exchange markets, in which the currencies of different countries are traded. Major foreign exchange markets are located in New York, London, Tokyo, and other financial centers. Because the foreign exchange markets are in widely separated time zones, at least one of the markets is open at almost any time of the day, so that there is essentially around-the-clock trading in currencies.

Exchange rates among major currencies are often reported as part of the daily news broadcasts on radio and television, and daily quotations of exchange rates are available in major newspapers and financial dailies. The exchange rates in the accompanying list were reported in the "Money and Investing" section of the *Wall Street Journal* on March 1, 1991. The exchange rates were quoted as of 3 P.M. (Eastern time) on the previous day, February 28, 1991.

Notice that four exchange rates relative to the U.S. dollar are reported for each country, a spot rate and three forward rates. All of these exchange rates are expressed as units of foreign currency per U.S. dollar. The spot rate is the rate at which foreign currency can be traded immediately for U.S. dollars. For instance, the spot exchange rate for France, 5.1920, means that on

February 28, 1991, one U.S. dollar could buy 5.1920 francs for immediate delivery.

The forward exchange rates are prices at which you can agree now to buy foreign currency at a specified date in the future. For example, on February 28, 1991, you could have arranged to buy or sell German marks 30 days later at an exchange rate of 1.5288 marks per dollar. Notice that for each of the currencies listed, the 30-day forward exchange rate is higher than the spot exchange rate, and that forward exchange rates increase as we look at dates further in the future (90 days and 180 days). This pattern of rising exchange rates indicates that as of February 28, 1991, participants in the foreign exchange market expected the value of the dollar relative to the other currencies to increase over the 180 days following February 28, 1991. Sometimes, the forward exchange rates fall as we look at dates further in the future, which indicates that market participants expect the value of the dollar to fall relative to other currencies. Although forward rates would appear to help you forecast the future value of a currency, there is tremendous volatility in exchange rates; and the forward rates predict only a small part of the actual movements of exchange rates.

| | | EXCHANGE RATE AGAINST U.S. DOLLAR | | |
COUNTRY	SPOT	30-DAY FORWARD	90-DAY FORWARD	180-DAY FORWARD
Britain (pounds per U.S. dollar)	0.5234	0.5261	0.5309	0.5369
Canada (Canadian dollars per U.S. dollar)	1.1500	1.1528	1.1588	1.1665
France (francs per U.S. dollar)	5.1920	5.2031	5.2275	5.2625
Germany (marks per U.S. dollar)	1.5260	1.5288	1.5348	1.5433
Japan (yen per U.S. dollar)	133.05	133.22	133.47	133.67

In addition to those countries that officially maintain fixed exchange rates with one or more currencies, the central banks of countries with officially floating exchange rates occasionally attempt to influence their exchange rates by buying and selling their currencies in the foreign exchange market. Because of central banks' intervention in the foreign exchange market, such a system is described as a "managed float" or, sometimes, a "dirty float." Despite these departures from completely flexible exchange rates, however, exchange rates between the major currencies often experience large fluctuations. Because the current exchange rate system is closer to a completely flexible, rather than a fixed, exchange rate system, we assume that the exchange rate is completely flexible for the remainder of this chapter.

Real Exchange Rates

The nominal exchange rate doesn't tell us all we need to know about the purchasing power of a given currency. If you were told, for example, that the nominal exchange rate between the dollar and the Japanese yen is 125 yen per dollar, but you didn't know anything else about the American or Japanese economies, you might be tempted to conclude that it would be very cheap for someone from Kansas City to visit Tokyo. After all, 125 yen is a lot of yen to get for just $1. But even at 125 yen per dollar, Japan is an expensive place for Americans. The reason is that although $1 can buy a lot of yen, it also takes a lot of yen (thousands or hundreds of thousands) to buy everyday goods in Japan.

Suppose, for example, that we want to compare the price of a hamburger in Tokyo with the price in Kansas City. It doesn't help much just to know that the exchange rate is 125 yen per dollar. But if we also know that a hamburger costs $2 in Kansas City and 1000 yen in Tokyo, then we can compare the price of a hamburger in the two cities by asking how many dollars it takes to buy a hamburger in Japan. Because it takes 1000 yen to buy a hamburger in Tokyo, and 125 yen cost $1, the price of a Tokyo hamburger is $8 (calculated by dividing the price of a Japanese hamburger, 1000 yen, by 125 yen per dollar, to obtain $8 per hamburger). The price of an American hamburger relative to a Japanese hamburger is therefore ($2 per American hamburger)/($8 per Japanese hamburger) = 0.25 Japanese hamburger per American hamburger. The Japanese hamburger is expensive in the sense that giving up one American hamburger allows someone to buy only one fourth of a Japanese hamburger.

The price of domestic goods relative to foreign goods—equivalently, the number of foreign goods one gets in exchange for one domestic good—is called the **real exchange rate** or the **terms of trade.** In the hamburger example the real exchange rate between the United States and Japan is 0.25 Japanese hamburger per U.S. hamburger. In general, the real exchange rate is related to the nominal exchange and to prices in both countries. We can write this relation by using the following symbols:

$$e_{nom} = \text{the nominal exchange rate}$$
$$\text{(125 yen per dollar),}$$

$$P_{FOR} = \text{the price of foreign goods,}$$
$$\text{measured in the foreign currency}$$
$$\text{(1000 yen per Japanese hamburger),}$$

P = the price of domestic goods,
measured in the domestic currency
($2 per U.S. hamburger).

The real exchange rate e is the number of foreign goods (Japanese hamburgers) that can be obtained in exchange for one unit of the domestic good (U.S. hamburgers). The general formula for the real exchange rate is

$$e = \frac{e_{\text{nom}}P}{P_{\text{FOR}}}$$

$$= \frac{(125 \text{ yen per dollar})(\$2 \text{ per U.S. hamburger})}{1000 \text{ yen per Japanese hamburger}} \quad (13.1)$$

$$= 0.25 \text{ Japanese hamburger per U.S. hamburger}$$

When we discussed the open economy in Chapter 7, we implicitly assumed that all countries produce identical goods that could be used for all purposes (consumption, investment, and so on). This assumption caused no problems in Chapter 7, which focused on the intertemporal borrowing and lending aspects of international trade. However, if every country really did produce the same good, and if there were active trade among countries, the real exchange rate would always be equal to one foreign good per domestic good. If the real exchange rate were not equal to one, then one country or the other would be trading a unit of output for less than one unit of an identical good, which doesn't make sense.

Because in discussing the international transmission of business cycles, we must allow for changes in the real exchange rate, we can no longer assume that all countries produce the same good. At the same time we do not want to complicate the analysis any more than necessary. As a compromise, we assume in this chapter that each country produces a single good, but that different countries produce different goods. So, for example, think of Japan as producing only cameras and Saudi Arabia as producing only oil. Under this assumption P stands for the price of the single domestic good (measured in terms of the domestic currency), P_{FOR} stands for the price of the single foreign good (measured in terms of the foreign currency), and the real exchange rate e is the number of units of the foreign good that can be traded for one unit of the domestic good.

In practice, because each country produces many different goods, real exchange rates are calculated by using price indexes (such as the GNP deflator or the CPI) to measure P and P_{FOR}. Therefore in actuality the real exchange rate is not the rate of exchange between two specific goods, as we assume here. Instead, the real exchange rate is the rate of exchange between a typical basket of goods in one country and a typical basket of goods in the other country. Changes in the real exchange rate over time indicate that, on average, the goods of the country whose real exchange rate is rising are becoming more expensive relative to the goods of the other country.

Appreciation and Depreciation

When the nominal exchange rate e_{nom} falls so that, say, a dollar buys fewer units of foreign currency, we say that the dollar has undergone a **nominal depreciation.** This is the same as saying that the dollar has become "weaker." If the dollar's nominal exchange rate e_{nom} rises, then the dollar has had a **nominal appreciation.**

Table 13.1 Terminology for Changes in Exchange Rates

Type of Exchange Rate System	Exchange Rate Increases (Currency Strengthens)	Exchange Rate Decreases (Currency Weakens)
Flexible exchange rates	Appreciation	Depreciation
Fixed exchange rates	Revaluation	Devaluation

When the dollar appreciates, it can buy more units of foreign currency and thus has become "stronger."[1]

The terms *appreciation* and *depreciation* are associated with flexible exchange rates. Under a fixed exchange rate system, in which exchange rates are changed only by official government action, different terms are used: Instead of a depreciation, a weakening of the currency is called a **devaluation.** A strengthening of the currency under fixed exchange rates is called a **revaluation,** rather than an appreciation. These terms are summarized in Table 13.1.

An increase in the *real* exchange rate e is called a **real appreciation.** When there is a real appreciation, a given quantity of domestically produced output can be traded for more of the foreign good than before because e, the price of domestic goods relative to the price of foreign goods, has risen. A fall in the real exchange rate, which decreases the quantity of foreign goods that can be purchased with a given quantity of domestic output, is called a **real depreciation.**

Real Versus Nominal Exchange Rate Movements

Now that we have defined nominal and real exchange rates, let's look at how movements in these two types of exchange rate are related. We use the definition of the real exchange rate in Eq. (13.1), $e = e_{nom}P/P_{FOR}$, to calculate $\Delta e/e$, the percentage change in the real exchange rate. Because the real exchange rate is expressed as a ratio, its percentage change equals the percentage change in the numerator minus the percentage change in the denominator.[2] The percentage change in the numerator of the expression for the real exchange rate[3] is $\Delta e_{nom}/e_{nom} + \Delta P/P$, and the percentage change in the denominator is $\Delta P_{FOR}/P_{FOR}$. Thus the percentage change in the real exchange rate is

$$\frac{\Delta e}{e} = \frac{\Delta e_{nom}}{e_{nom}} + \frac{\Delta P}{P} - \frac{\Delta P_{FOR}}{P_{FOR}}. \tag{13.2}$$

In Eq. (13.2) the term $\Delta P/P$, the percentage change in the domestic price level, is the same as the domestic rate of inflation π, and the term $\Delta P_{FOR}/P_{FOR}$, the percentage change in the foreign price level, is the same as the foreign rate of inflation

---

[1]You will sometimes see the exchange rate defined as the number of units of domestic currency per unit of foreign currency, which is the reciprocal of how we have defined it. For example, the exchange rate between the British pound and the U.S. dollar is typically quoted in this form, such as $1.90 per pound. Under this alternative definition an appreciation of the dollar corresponds to a fall in the nominal exchange rate. The two ways of defining the exchange rate are equally valid, as long as consistency is maintained. We have chosen to define the exchange rate as the number of units of foreign currency per unit of home currency because it is easier to remember that an appreciation (when the value of the dollar goes *up*) is associated with a *rise* in the exchange rate.

[2]Appendix A, Section A.7, describes how to calculate growth rates of products and ratios.

[3]This result is obtained by using the rule that the percentage change in a product XY is the percentage change in X plus the percentage change in Y. See Appendix A, Section A.7.

π_{FOR}. Making these substitutions, we can rewrite Eq. (13.2) as

$$\text{or} \longrightarrow \quad \frac{\Delta e_{\text{nom}}}{e_{\text{nom}}} = \frac{\Delta e}{e} + \pi_{\text{FOR}} - \pi \tag{13.3}$$

Equation (13.3), which is purely definitional, tells us that the rate of nominal exchange rate appreciation $\Delta e_{\text{nom}}/e_{\text{nom}}$ equals the rate of real exchange rate appreciation $\Delta e/e$ plus the excess of foreign inflation over domestic inflation, $\pi_{\text{FOR}} - \pi$. Thus we see that two factors contribute to a strengthening currency (nominal appreciation): (1) an increase in the relative price of a country's exports (a real appreciation), which might occur if, for example, foreign demand for those exports rises; and (2) a rate of domestic inflation π that is lower than that of the country's trading partners π_{FOR}. It is possible for either of these two factors alone to create a nominal appreciation. For example, it is possible for a country to simultaneously have a nominal appreciation *and* a real depreciation, if domestic inflation is low enough relative to foreign inflation.

13.2 THE DETERMINANTS OF NET EXPORTS

The real exchange rate has its most important impact on the macroeconomy through its effects on net exports, which in turn may affect domestic levels of output and employment. In order to understand these links, in this section we examine how the real exchange rate and other factors determine how much a country imports and exports.

Measuring Real Net Exports

Recall from Chapter 2 that a country's real net exports are its exports minus its imports. When exports and imports are measured in the same physical units, as when they are the same type of good, then it is easy to calculate exports minus imports. Measuring net exports is more complicated, however, when exports and imports are different goods. It doesn't make sense to calculate Japan's net exports, for example, by subtracting the number of imported barrels of oil from the number of exported cameras, because a barrel of oil and a camera may not have the same value. Instead, we first ask, "How many cameras (the export good) would it take to equal the total value of Japan's imported oil?" The answer to this question is called the real value of Japan's imports. To get Japan's net exports, measured in terms of cameras, we subtract the real value of imports from the real value of exports.

In calculating net exports, we use the following symbols:

$$X = \text{the quantity of a country's exports}$$
$$\text{(for example, the number of cameras}$$
$$\text{sold abroad by Japan),}$$
$$X_{\text{FOR}} = \text{the quantity of imports by}$$
$$\text{that country (the number of barrels of}$$
$$\text{oil imported by Japan).}$$

The notation X_{FOR} reminds us that the imports of a given country must equal the exports of its trading partners.

To figure out the real value of imports (that is, the value of imports in terms of the good that the importing country produces), we use the real exchange rate.

Table 13.2 The Effect of a Real Depreciation on Net Exports: An Example

	Real Exchange Rate, e (Barrels per Camera)	Exports, X (Cameras)	Imports, X_{FOR} (Barrels)	Real Imports, X_{FOR}/e (Cameras)	Real Net Exports, $X - X_{\text{FOR}}/e$ (Cameras)
Initially	4	40	64	16	24
Case 1: Small response of imports and exports to a real depreciation (real net exports fall)	3	42	60	20	22
Case 2: Large response of imports and exports to a real depreciation (real net exports rise)	3	45	54	18	27

Remember that the real exchange rate is the number of units of the foreign good (barrels of oil, in the case of Japan) that can be exchanged for one unit of the home good (cameras). Dividing the number of imported barrels of oil X_{FOR} by the real exchange rate e gives the value of Japan's imports in terms of cameras. Thus X_{FOR}/e is the real value of Japan's imports. To find net exports NX, we subtract the real value of imports X_{FOR}/e from the real value of exports X:

$$NX = X - \frac{X_{\text{FOR}}}{e} \tag{13.4}$$

Table 13.2 shows how to use this equation to calculate real net exports in an example. Suppose, as in the first row of this table, that Japan exports 40 cameras and imports 64 barrels of oil and that the real exchange rate is 4 barrels per camera. In symbols we have $X = 40$ cameras, $X_{\text{FOR}} = 64$ barrels, and $e = 4$ barrels per camera. At a real exchange rate of 4 barrels per camera, the real value of the 64 barrels of imported oil is 16 cameras. Subtracting the real value of imports (16 cameras) from the real value of exports (40 cameras), we find in the example that real Japanese net exports NX equal 24 cameras.

The Effect of the Real Exchange Rate on Net Exports

Now that we have seen how to calculate a country's net exports, the next step is to discuss the factors that determine net exports. We initially focus on the real exchange rate and then consider other factors.

To make the discussion concrete, we continue the example in which Japan produces and exports cameras while importing oil. The only other country in the example is Saudi Arabia, which imports cameras from Japan and exports oil to Japan. Now imagine that for some reason the Japanese real exchange rate e falls. What effect will this real depreciation have on Japan's net exports?

The real depreciation of the yen means that oil becomes more expensive relative to cameras (one camera buys fewer barrels of oil). This change in relative prices affects both imports and exports by Japan. In response to the higher relative price for oil, Japan demands less oil, so that Japanese imports of oil (X_{FOR}) fall. In addition, because cameras are now cheaper relative to oil, the Saudis buy more cameras; so that Japanese exports of cameras (X) rise. Because the fall in the

Japanese real exchange rate causes the quantity of Japanese imports to fall and the quantity of Japanese exports to rise, it would seem that real Japanese net exports must rise. This conclusion is not necessarily correct, however. Working in the other direction is the fact that when the real exchange depreciates, imports become more expensive, so that the real value of imports may rise even though the quantity of imports falls. This point is illustrated by example in Table 13.2.

Suppose that before the real depreciation the real exchange rate is 4 barrels per camera and that Japan exports 40 cameras and imports 64 barrels of oil, as shown in the first row of Table 13.2. As we have already discussed, Japan's real net exports equal 24 cameras in this case. Now consider the effects on Japan's net exports when the real exchange rate depreciates to 3 barrels of oil per camera. The second row of the table (case 1) shows what happens when exports and imports respond only a little to the change in the exchange rate (exports rise from 40 to 42 cameras and imports drop from 64 to 60 barrels of oil). Despite the fact that Japan imports fewer barrels of oil than it did initially, because oil is now relatively more expensive, Japan spends more in terms of cameras to import oil. Specifically, when the real exchange rate falls to 3 barrels per camera, the 60 barrels of oil imported by Japan are worth 20 cameras. In this case Japan's net exports equal 22 cameras, as shown in the last column. Thus when the quantities of goods exported and imported change only a little in response to a change in the real exchange rate, the real depreciation reduces net exports.

Now let's see what happens to Japan's net exports if the quantities of goods exported and imported respond more strongly to the change in the exchange rate. The third row of Table 13.2 (case 2) assumes that in response to the real depreciation, Japan's exports increase from 40 to 45 cameras and its imports fall from 64 to 54 barrels of oil (worth 18 cameras at the real exchange rate of 3 barrels of oil per camera). In this case Japan's net exports equal 27 cameras, which is higher than the initial net exports of 24 cameras. Thus if a real depreciation causes large changes in the quantities of goods exported and imported, net exports will increase.

The example in Table 13.2 illustrates that a real depreciation can either decrease or increase net exports, depending on how much the quantities of imports and exports respond to the change in the real exchange rate. A technical condition related to this situation, known as the **Marshall-Lerner condition,**[4] says that a real depreciation will lead to an increase in net exports if exports and imports are sufficiently sensitive to changes in the real exchange rate.

Whether or not the Marshall-Lerner condition holds in practice generally depends on the time frame being considered. In the very short run, before consumers and firms have had a chance to adjust their spending patterns in response to the change in the real exchange rate, the quantities of imports and exports do not change much, and the Marshall-Lerner condition typically does not hold. Thus a fall in the real exchange rate tends to reduce net exports in the very short run, as in case 1 in Table 13.2. After consumers and firms have had more time to change the quantities of imports bought and exports sold, the Marshall-Lerner condition is more likely to hold, and a fall in the real exchange rate is likely to lead to increased net exports (case 2 of Table 13.2).

---

[4]This condition was formulated independently by Alfred Marshall and Abba Lerner in the first half of this century. Formally, the Marshall-Lerner condition requires that the elasticity of export demand with respect to the real exchange rate plus the elasticity of import demand with respect to the real exchange rate add, in absolute value, to a number greater than one. Elasticity is defined in Appendix A, Section A.3.

The J curve shows the time pattern of the response of net exports to a real depreciation. In the figure net exports are negative at time zero, when the real exchange rate depreciates. In the short run net exports become more negative as the fall in the real exchange rate makes the cost of imports higher. Over time, however, the quantity of exports increases, the quantity of imports decreases, and the net export balance improves.

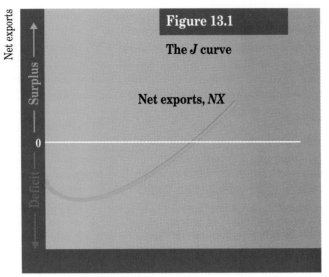

Figure 13.1

The *J* curve

Figure 13.1 shows the typical pattern of response of net exports to a real depreciation. The figure assumes the economy initially has negative net exports at the time that the real exchange rate depreciates. In the short run the real depreciation reduces net exports, because the fall in the real exchange rate forces the country to pay more for its imports. Over time, however, as quantities of exports rise and quantities of imports decline, net exports begin to rise. As shown in the figure, eventually there is an increase in the country's net exports relative to the initial situation. This typical time pattern of the response of net exports to a real depreciation is called the **J curve,** because the graph of net exports against time looks like the letter J lying on its back.

When we do macroeconomic analyses in this chapter, we assume that the time period is long enough so that the Marshall-Lerner condition holds. Thus we assume that an increase in the real exchange rate reduces net exports and a decrease in the real exchange rate increases net exports. Keep in mind, though, that this assumption may not be valid for shorter periods—and in some cases, even for several years—as the next application demonstrates.

Application

The Value of the Dollar and U.S. Net Exports in the 1970s and 1980s

Beginning in the early 1970s, the major countries of the world switched from fixed to flexible exchange rates. Figure 13.2 shows the U.S. real exchange rate (the "real value of the dollar") and the value of U.S. net exports since the exchange rate began to float. The real value of the dollar and U.S. net exports should move in opposite directions if the Marshall-Lerner condition is satisfied, and if changes in the real exchange rate are the primary source of changes in net exports. Figure

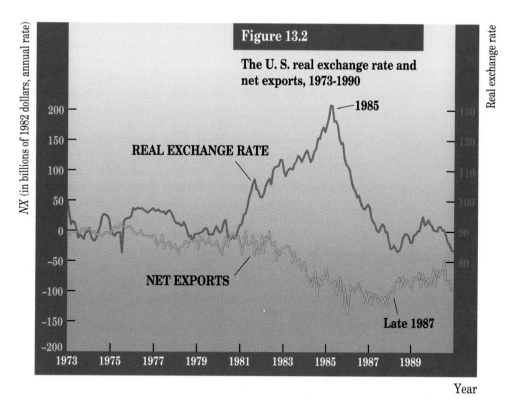

Figure 13.2

The U. S. real exchange rate and net exports, 1973-1990

U.S. net exports are measured along the left axis, and the real exchange rate of the dollar (1980–1982 average = 100) is measured along the right axis. If the Marshall-Lerner condition holds, net exports and the real exchange rate should move in opposite directions. Generally, this relationship has held, except that the fall in the real exchange rate beginning in March 1985 did not begin to increase net exports until late 1987.

Sources: Exchange rates—Morgan Guaranty Trust, *World Financial Markets*, various issues; net exports—U.S. Department of Commerce, *Business Statistics, 1961–1988*, updates from *Survey of Current Business*.

13.2 shows that over longer periods net exports and the real value of the dollar do tend to move in opposite directions. For example, the dollar appreciated in real terms in late 1975 and remained relatively high for about two years. Over this same two-year span real net exports declined from a positive value in late 1975 to a negative value in late 1977.

The dollar moved much more dramatically during the 1980s. Over the period from 1980 to 1985 the real value of the dollar increased by about 40%. This sharp increase in the value of the dollar was followed, with a delay of about a year and a half, by a large decline in U.S. net exports. The delayed reaction of net exports to the real appreciation of the dollar is consistent with the point that exports and imports respond less in the short run than in the long run, as we emphasized when discussing the J curve.

After peaking in March 1985, the real value of the dollar fell sharply for almost three years. Despite this precipitous decline in the dollar, U.S. net exports continued their downward trend until late in 1987, when finally they began to increase. During the two and a half years in which U.S. net exports continued to decline despite the rapid depreciation of the dollar, the public and policymakers expressed increasing skepticism about economists' predictions that the depreciation would lead to increased net exports. Initially, economists responded by saying that because of the J curve, there would be some delay between the depreciation of the dollar and the improvement in net exports. By 1987, however, even the strongest believers in the J curve had begun to wonder whether net exports would ever begin to rise.

Why did it take so long for U.S. net exports to begin to increase after the dollar began its decline? An explanation that has been suggested is that because the dollar was so very strong in the first half of the 1980s (which made American goods very expensive relative to foreign goods), American firms lost many of their foreign customers. Once these foreign customers were lost, it was difficult to regain them or to add new foreign customers, especially since many American exporters reduced production capacity and cut back foreign sales operations when the dollar was high. Similarly, the strong dollar gave foreign producers, including some who had not previously sold their output to the United States, a chance to make inroads into the U.S. domestic market. Having established sales networks and customer relationships in the United States, these foreign companies were better able than before to compete with U.S. firms when the dollar began its decline in 1985.

The idea that the strong dollar permanently increased the penetration of the U.S. market by foreign producers, while similarly reducing the capability of American firms to sell in foreign markets, has been called the "beachhead effect."[5] According to this view, if the effects of the strong-dollar period on U.S. net exports are to be undone, the real value of the dollar will have to fall back not just to its 1980 level, before the appreciation, but to a much lower level. Only with a very weak dollar will American firms be able to regain the markets they lost when the dollar was so unusually strong.

Other Determinants of Net Exports

Besides the real exchange rate, various other factors affect a country's net exports. Three of these factors, discussed next, are the country's domestic income, foreign income, and shifts in the demand for exported or imported goods. Factors affecting net exports are summarized in Table 13.3.

Domestic Income   An increase in domestic income (equivalently, output) leads domestic consumers to purchase more goods, including imported goods. Higher domestic income does *not*, however, increase exports; exports are purchased by foreigners and thus depend on foreign income. Because an increase in domestic income raises imports but does not affect exports, net exports decline when domestic income rises, assuming that other factors (including the real exchange rate) are held constant.

Foreign Income   The effect of an increase in foreign income is just the opposite of the effect of an increase in domestic income. An increase in foreign income (output) leads foreign consumers to increase their spending on all goods, including goods exported abroad by the domestic country. An increase in foreign income does not

---

[5]Empirical support for the beachhead effect is presented in Richard E. Baldwin, "Hysteresis in Import Prices: The Beachhead Effect," *American Economic Review*, September 1988, pp. 773–785.

Table 13.3 Summary		
Determinants of Net Exports		
An Increase in	**Causes Net Exports to**	**Reason**
Real exchange rate e	Fall	Higher real exchange rate makes domestic goods relatively more expensive compared with foreign goods
Domestic income (output) Y	Fall	Higher domestic income raises domestic demand for imports
Foreign income (output) Y_{FOR}	Rise	Higher foreign income raises foreign demand for the home country's exports
Demand for domestic goods relative to foreign goods	Rise	Shift in demand increases foreign demand for exports and reduces domestic demand for imports

affect the spending of domestic residents on imports. Thus, with other factors held constant, net exports rise when foreign income rises.

Shifts in Demand A shift in demand by foreigners toward goods exported by the home country, or a shift in demand by domestic residents away from imports and toward domestically produced goods, will raise the domestic country's net exports, other factors held constant. Demand shifts may arise from changes in tastes, as when the exports of a particular country come into fashion, or from changes in quality that make a given country's goods more or less desirable. A shift in demand may also result from government policy—for example, government import quotas that limit the amount of a particular good that can be imported.

13.3 THE INTERNATIONAL FLOW OF GOODS: INTERTEMPORAL EXTERNAL BALANCE

The real exchange rate, the quantity of foreign goods that can be acquired in exchange for one unit of the domestic good, is an important determinant of a country's net exports and therefore, as we find later in the chapter, of domestic production and employment. But what determines a country's real exchange rate? We will see that the real exchange rate is determined by two equilibrium conditions, each of which is economically significant in its own right. One of these conditions applies to the international market for goods and one applies to the international market for assets. We study the equilibrium condition in the international goods market in this section and the equilibrium condition in the international asset market in the next section.

As we discussed in Chapter 7, a country with positive net exports produces more goods than are purchased by its consumers, firms, and governments. The country's excess of output over spending equals its lending to other countries. In the future the country will be paid back what it has lent with interest, which will allow it to spend more than it produces and have negative net exports.

Similarly, a country with negative net exports produces less output than is bought by domestic consumers, firms, and governments and therefore must borrow from abroad an amount equal to the excess of its spending over its output. Ultimately, the country must repay with interest the funds that it borrows from other countries. In order to repay foreign loans, countries with negative net exports today must at some point in the future achieve positive net exports.

The requirement that countries that have positive net exports and lend today have negative net exports in the future—and similarly, that countries that have negative net exports and borrow today have positive net exports in the future—is known as **intertemporal external balance.** (*External* refers to the flows of goods across international borders, and *intertemporal* emphasizes that the flow of goods between countries need not balance in every period but must balance over time.) Put simply, intertemporal external balance—or external balance, for short—says that no country can borrow abroad indefinitely without repaying, and that no country would want to lend abroad indefinitely without being repaid.

To illustrate the concept of external balance, consider a numerical example with only two periods, the current period and the future period. Suppose that a country's current net exports NX are negative, equal to -100 home goods. To pay for this deficit, the country borrows in the international capital market at a real interest rate r of 8% per period. In the future period the country must repay its international borrowing with interest, for a total repayment of 108 goods. Where will the country get the 108 goods it needs to repay its foreign debt? To obtain the 108 goods it needs, in the future period the country must spend 108 goods less than it produces, so that its future net exports NX^f equal 108 goods.

In general, for a country to achieve external balance, its future net exports NX^f must equal $-(1 + r)NX$, where NX is current net exports and r is the real interest rate. (For simplicity, we continue to assume two periods.) In our example $NX = -100$ and $r = 0.08$, so $NX^f = 108$, as we found. Alternatively, suppose that the country's current net exports were positive and equal to 100 home goods. With net exports of 100 goods, the country lends 100 goods abroad today. If the real interest rate is 0.08, the country will be repaid 108 goods in the future, which means that it will be able to have future net exports of -108 goods. This result is once again as implied by the formula $NX^f = -(1 + r)NX$.

Formally, we write the intertemporal external balance (*IEB*) condition as

$$NX(e, \ldots) + \frac{NX^f(e^f, \ldots)}{1 + r} = 0, \tag{13.5}$$

which is a rearrangement of the condition that $NX^f = -(1 + r)NX$. In Eq. (13.5) e is the real exchange rate in the current period and e^f is the real exchange rate in the future period. The notations $NX(e, \ldots)$ and $NX^f(e^f, \ldots)$ emphasize that the country's net exports in each period depend on the real exchange rate in that period, as well as on other factors.[6]

---

[6]Those readers who covered Chapter 5 will recognize that Eq. (13.5) requires the present value of net exports to equal zero.

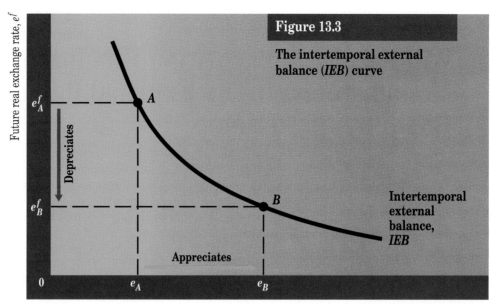

Figure 13.3

The intertemporal external balance (*IEB*) curve

The intertemporal external balance (*IEB*) condition requires that future net exports equal − (1 + r) times current net exports. If we start at point *A*, which satisfies the *IEB* condition, an increase in the current real exchange rate from e_A to e_B causes a fall in current net exports. To restore external balance, future net exports must increase, which is achieved by a depreciation of the future real exchange rate from e^f_A to e^f_B. Thus point *B* also satisfies the *IEB* condition. Since both point *A* and point *B* lie on the *IEB* curve, the *IEB* curve slopes downward.

The Intertemporal External Balance Curve

The intertemporal external balance curve *IEB* in Fig. 13.3 shows the combinations of the current real exchange rate e and the future real exchange rate e^f that satisfy the external balance condition, Eq. (13.5). To understand why this relation slopes downward, suppose the economy starts with the combination of current and future real exchange rates represented by point *A* in Fig. 13.3. The exchange rates at point *A*, e_A and e^f_A, lie on the *IEB* curve and thus satisfy the external balance condition. Now suppose that the current real exchange rate increases to e_B, a real appreciation. The real appreciation reduces the country's net exports in the current period. So that external balance is maintained and the country can repay foreign borrowings, lower net exports today must be offset by higher net exports in the future. This increase in future net exports can be achieved by real depreciation in the second period, or a decrease in the future real exchange rate to e^f_B. The new equilibrium combination of exchange rates, e_B and e^f_B, is represented by point *B* in Fig. 13.3. Since points *A* and *B* both satisfy external balance, the *IEB* curve slopes downward.

In general, external balance requires that an increase in the current real exchange rate be offset by a decline in the expected future real exchange rate. Intuitively, a high real exchange rate today causes negative net exports today, so a low real exchange rate in the future is needed to allow net exports to be positive in the future. Thus the *IEB* curve slopes downward, as shown in Fig. 13.3.

Application

Will Foreign Competition Eliminate U.S. Manufacturing?: The External Balance Condition in Action

During the 1980s U.S. imports of manufactured goods began to exceed exports of manufactured goods by a large margin. Many observers feared that the United States had lost its ability to compete with foreign manufacturers and that the U.S. manufacturing sector would be largely replaced by the service sector. In the long run a shrunken manufacturing sector would be unable to supply domestic demands for manufactured goods, and the United States would have to be a permanent net importer of manufactured goods.

However, Paul Krugman, of the Massachusetts Institute of Technology, and George Hatsopoulos, a businessman and a director of the Federal Reserve Bank of Boston,[7] have argued that U.S. manufacturing will not shrink dramatically. Instead, they believe that it is inevitable that the United States will become a net *exporter* of manufactured goods. The basis for this view is the ultimate necessity of intertemporal external balance: Because U.S. net exports were substantially negative throughout the 1980s, the United States greatly reduced its net foreign assets, by some measures becoming the world's largest international debtor.[8] External balance requires that the United States cannot borrow forever but eventually must have positive net exports, enabling it to repay the principal and interest it owes to other countries.

In what areas can the United States hope to generate the positive net exports it needs to repay its international debts? Putting aside income generated by existing foreign assets, total net exports can be broken down into three categories: net exports of manufactured goods, net exports of nonmanufactured goods, and net exports of services. At some point in the future these three categories of net exports must add to a positive number to enable the United States to pay what it owes. People who fear the destruction of U.S. manufacturing capacity are forecasting that the first item, net exports of manufactured goods, will be a large negative number indefinitely. However, this forecast implies that the remaining two items, net exports of nonmanufactured goods and services, must ultimately add to a large positive number.

Krugman and Hatsopoulos argue that there is no evidence that either nonmanufactured goods or services can generate large enough surpluses to repay U.S. foreign debts. They believe instead that in order for the sum of the three items to be large enough to pay future interest, a large surplus in manufactured goods will have to occur. Thus a revival in U.S. manufacturing is necessitated by the external balance condition.

---

[7]"The Problem of U.S. Competitiveness in Manufacturing," *New England Economic Review*, Federal Reserve Bank of Boston, January-February 1987, pp. 18–29.

[8]Chapter 7 discussed issues surrounding the question of whether the United States is in fact the world's largest international debtor.

It may be true that in order to satisfy external balance, the United States must ultimately achieve a large surplus in trade in manufactured goods; but how is such a surplus to be achieved? The answer given by Krugman and Hatsopoulos is that the U.S. real exchange rate will have to depreciate quite dramatically, so that manufactured goods in the United States will become cheaper relative to foreign manufactured goods. As U.S. manufactured goods become cheap, both foreigners and U.S. residents will switch from foreign manufactured goods to American manufactured goods, raising U.S. net exports. Indeed, as of 1991, this prediction looked pretty good, as a weak dollar contributed to a surge in U.S. exports of manufactured goods.

Factors That Shift the *IEB* Curve

The *IEB* curve shows the combinations of current and future real exchange rates that lead to external balance. Factors other than real exchange rates that affect current net exports or future net exports will shift the *IEB* curve. We discuss three important *IEB* curve shifters: a change in domestic income, a change in foreign income, and shifts in demand. Table 13.4 gives a summary of these shifters.

Domestic Income   Suppose that a country's current and future real exchange rates are represented by point E on the curve IEB^1 in Fig. 13.4, so that the country is initially in external balance. Now imagine that current income (output) increases. At the initial values of e and e^f the increase in income makes domestic consumers wealthier, leading them to spend more on all goods, including imported foreign

Table 13.4 Summary

Factors That Shift the *IEB* Curve

An Increase in	Shifts the *IEB* Curve	Reason
Domestic income (output) Y	Down	Higher domestic income raises import demand and reduces net exports, so real exchange rates must fall to restore external balance
Foreign income (output) Y_{FOR}	Up	Higher foreign income raises demand for domestic exports and increases net exports, so real exchange rates must rise to restore external balance
Demand for domestic goods relative to foreign goods	Up	Net exports increase, so exchange rates must rise to restore external balance

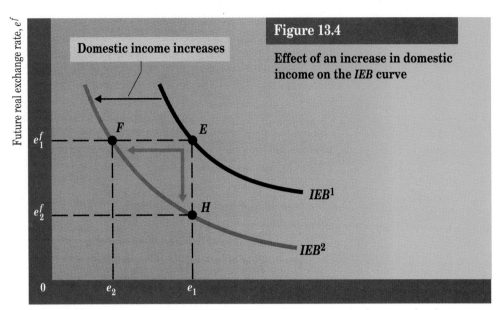

Figure 13.4

Effect of an increase in domestic income on the *IEB* curve

The initial equilibrium at point *E* on *IEB*^{1} satisfies the intertemporal external balance condition. An increase in domestic income increases the domestic demand for imported goods and reduces net exports. With the future real exchange rate held constant, a decrease in the current real exchange rate (point *F*) will raise current net exports and restore external balance. Alternatively, a decrease in the future real exchange rate, with the current real exchange rate held constant (point *H*), will raise future net exports and restore external balance. The new *IEB* curve, *IEB*^{2}, passes through points *F* and *H*. Thus an increase in domestic income shifts the *IEB* curve downward.

goods, in both the current and future periods. The increase in imports reduces net exports in both periods, so that the country is no longer in external balance. For external balance to be restored, real exchange rates must fall. For example, a depreciation of the current real exchange rate, with the future real exchange rate held constant—represented by the movement to point *F* in Fig. 13.4—would increase current net exports and restore external balance. Alternatively, future net exports could be increased by a depreciation of the future real exchange rate, with the current real exchange rate held constant—represented by the movement to point *H*. Thus the increase in domestic income causes the *IEB* curve to shift downward to *IEB*^{2}, which passes through points *F* and *H*.

Foreign Income   The effect of an increase in foreign income on the *IEB* curve is just the opposite of the effect of an increase in domestic income. Suppose that before the increase in foreign income the current and future real exchange rates are represented by point *E* on *IEB*^{1} in Fig. 13.5. Because foreign consumers are made wealthier by the increase in income, they will buy more of the goods produced by the home country in the current period and in the future, which increases net exports by the home country in both periods. An appreciation of the current real exchange rate, represented by the movement to point *F*, will reduce the net exports of the home country and restore external balance. Alternatively, an appreciation of the future real exchange rate, represented by the movement to point *H*,

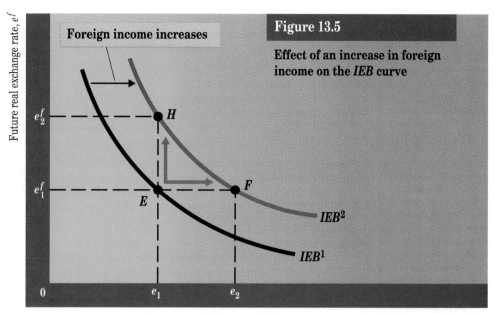

Figure 13.5

Effect of an increase in foreign income on the *IEB* curve

Current real exchange rate, *e*

The initial equilibrium at point *E* satisfies the intertemporal external balance (*IEB*) condition. An increase in foreign income raises the home country's current and future net exports at point *E*. An appreciation of the current real exchange rate, with the future real exchange rate held constant (point *F*), will reduce current net exports and restore external balance. Alternatively, an appreciation of the future real exchange rate, with the current real exchange rate held constant (point *H*), will reduce future net exports and restore external balance. The new *IEB* curve, *IEB²*, passes through points *F* and *H*. Thus an increase in foreign income shifts the *IEB* curve upward.

would restore external balance. Therefore the new *IEB* curve, *IEB²*, which passes through points *F* and *H*, lies above the original *IEB* curve, *IEB¹*.

Shifts in Demand A shift in demand away from foreign goods toward goods produced by the home country shifts the *IEB* curve upward, just as an increase in foreign income does. The reason is that, like an increase in foreign income, a shift in demand toward domestic goods increases both current and future net exports by the home country. For external balance to be restored, the current real exchange rate or the future real exchange must appreciate; so the *IEB* curve shifts upward.

13.4 THE INTERNATIONAL ASSET MARKET: INTEREST RATE PARITY

Besides affecting the international flow of goods, the real exchange rate also plays a key role in international asset markets. We will see in this section that there is a close link between the expected behavior of the exchange rate and the interest rates that are paid on assets in different countries.

Returns on Domestic and Foreign Assets

To illustrate the role of the real exchange rate in international asset markets, we again use a numerical example. Imagine that you want to invest $10,000 in a financial asset for one year, and suppose that you have limited your choice to either U.S. government bonds or German government bonds. U.S. government bonds are denominated in dollars and pay a nominal interest rate of 8% for one year (that is, $i = 0.08$). German government bonds, which are denominated in marks, pay a nominal interest rate of 6% for one year ($i_{FOR} = 0.06$). The two financial investments have comparable risk and liquidity. If you want to maximize your financial return, which bonds should you buy?

At first glance, the answer seems obvious: Buy the U.S. government bonds, because they offer a higher interest rate. But this answer may not be right. The correct answer depends on what you think is going to happen to the exchange rate between the U.S. dollar and the German mark over the next year.

We can compare the financial returns on the two assets by calculating the value in dollars one year from now of $10,000 invested in each asset. For the U.S. government bond the answer is easy. At a nominal interest rate of 8% per year, the bond will earn $800 in interest and will be worth $10,800 in one year. For the German bond, however, we must take into account that the $10,000 must first be converted into marks in order to buy the bond; then, when the German bond matures in one year, the principal and interest (which will be in marks) must be converted back into dollars.

Table 13.5 illustrates the calculation of the future dollar value of the German bond, assuming that (1) the current nominal exchange rate e_{nom} is 2.00 marks per dollar and that (2) the exchange rate is expected to depreciate by 3% over the coming year, so that the expected future nominal exchange rate e^f_{nom} equals 1.94 marks per dollar (1.94 is 97% of 2.00). Converting $10,000 to German marks at an exchange rate of 2 marks per dollar yields 20,000 marks (step 1 in Table 13.5), which are used to buy a German bond. At a 6% nominal interest rate the German bond earns 1200 marks interest and is worth 21,200 marks at the end of one year (step 2). Finally, converting 21,200 marks to dollars at 1.94 marks per dollar yields

Table 13.5 Calculating the Gross Nominal Rate of Return for a Foreign Asset

Example		
Today: e_{nom} = 2 marks per dollar	i_{FOR} = 0.06	*Future:* e^f_{nom} = 1.94 marks per dollar
Step 1	**Step 2**	**Step 3**
Convert home currency to foreign currency	Earn interest on foreign bond	Convert foreign currency to home currency
$10,000 → 20,000 marks	→ 21,200 marks	→ $10,928
General Case		
Today		*Future*
Step 1	**Step 2**	**Step 3**
Convert home currency to foreign currency	Earn interest on foreign bond	Convert foreign currency to home currency
1 unit of home currency → e_{nom} units of foreign currency	→ $(1 + i_{FOR})e_{nom}$ units of foreign currency	→ $[(1 + i_{FOR})e_{nom}]/e^f_{nom}$ units of home currency

$10,928 (step 3)—which is higher than the $10,800 that would be obtained from investing in a U.S. bond! Thus the German bonds have a higher expected rate of return in this case, even though they pay a lower nominal interest rate.

The German bonds have a higher rate of return in this example because, relative to the dollar asset, the German bonds have two sources of return. The first source is the nominal interest paid on the bonds ($i_{\text{FOR}} = 0.06$). The second source of return is the appreciation of the mark relative to the dollar. At the end of the year, when you convert your investment back into dollars, the value of a mark in terms of dollars is 3% higher than at the beginning of the year, when you converted your dollars into marks.

The gross nominal rate of return on an investment is the value at the end of the year (in terms of dollars) of one dollar invested at the beginning of the year. The gross nominal rate of return from investing in U.S. government bonds is $1 + i$, which is 1.08 in this example because each dollar invested in these bonds is worth $1.08 at the end of the year. The bottom section of Table 13.5 calculates the gross nominal rate of return on the German bond. One dollar will buy e_{nom} marks (step 1), which can be invested in a German bond at a nominal interest rate of i_{FOR} to yield $(1 + i_{\text{FOR}})e_{\text{nom}}$ marks at the end of a year (step 2). Converting the $(1 + i_{\text{FOR}})e_{\text{nom}}$ marks to dollars yields $(1 + i_{\text{FOR}})e_{\text{nom}}/e_{\text{nom}}^{f}$ dollars the end of the year (step 3). Thus the gross nominal rate of return from investing in the German government bond is

$$
\begin{aligned}
\text{gross nominal rate of} \atop \text{return on foreign bond} &= \frac{(1 + i_{\text{FOR}})e_{\text{nom}}}{e_{\text{nom}}^{f}} \\
&= \frac{(1.06)\ (2\ \text{marks per dollar})}{1.94\ \text{marks per dollar}} \qquad (13.6) \\
&= 1.0928.
\end{aligned}
$$

With a gross nominal rate of return equal to 1.0928, a $10,000 investment grows to a value of $10,928 at the end of one year, just as we calculated previously.

Equation (13.6) is an exact expression for the gross nominal rate of return. A simple approximation ($\approx$) to the gross nominal rate of return is

$$
\text{gross nominal rate of return on foreign bond} \approx 1 + i_{\text{FOR}} - \frac{\Delta e_{\text{nom}}}{e_{\text{nom}}}. \qquad (13.7)
$$

In our example of the German government bond with $i_{\text{FOR}} = 0.06$ and $\Delta e_{\text{nom}}/e_{\text{nom}} = -0.03$, Eq. (13.7) indicates that the gross nominal rate of return from investing in the German government bond is approximately 1.09, which is very close to the exact value of 1.0928. The approximation in Eq. (13.7) permits easy calculation of the gross nominal return, generally without using pencil and paper (or a calculator). The other virtue of this approximation is that it makes clear the two sources of return from holding the German government bond: the interest on the bond i_{FOR}, and the nominal appreciation of the mark relative to the dollar over the course of the year, $-\Delta e_{\text{nom}}/e_{\text{nom}}$.

Interest Rate Parity

In our example the gross nominal rate of return expected on the German government bond exceeded the gross nominal rate of return on the U.S. government bond. However, if both types of government bonds have the same risk and liquidity, this difference in rates of return would not persist for long. If savers are free to choose between German bonds and U.S. bonds, they will choose the German bonds as long as they offer a higher gross nominal rate of return than U.S. bonds. But if investors choose German bonds in preference to U.S. bonds, the rate of return on German bonds will fall and the rate of return on U.S. bonds will increase until the two rates of return are equal.

In general, when the international asset market is in equilibrium, the gross nominal rates of return to domestic and foreign assets of comparable risk and liquidity must be the same. This equilibrium condition can be written as

$$\left(\frac{e_{\text{nom}}}{e_{\text{nom}}^f}\right)(1 + i_{\text{FOR}}) = 1 + i, \tag{13.8}$$

where the left side is the gross nominal rate of return on the foreign bond (Eq. 13.6) and the right side is the gross nominal rate of return on the domestic bond. The equilibrium condition in Eq. (13.8) is the **nominal interest rate parity condition,** which says that the nominal returns on foreign and domestic financial investments with equal risk and liquidity, when measured in a common currency, must be the same.[9]

Interest rate parity can also be expressed in terms of real interest rates and real exchange rates as the **real interest rate parity condition:**

$$\left(\frac{e}{e^f}\right)(1 + r_{\text{FOR}}) = 1 + r, \tag{13.9}$$

where r_{FOR} is the foreign real interest rate, r is the domestic real interest rate, and e and e^f are the current and future real exchange rates. The real interest rate parity condition, Eq. (13.9), is identical to the nominal interest parity condition, Eq. (13.8), except that the nominal interest and exchange rates in Eq. (13.8) are replaced by real interest and exchange rates in Eq. (13.9). (In Analytical Problem 1 at the end of the chapter, you are asked to derive the real interest rate parity condition from the nominal interest rate parity condition.)

Notice that real interest rate parity does *not* require that the domestic real interest rate r and the foreign real interest rate r_{FOR} be equal. The two real interest rates are not directly comparable, since r is measured in terms of the domestic good and r_{FOR} is measured in terms of the foreign good. Instead, real interest rate parity requires that the real returns on domestic and foreign assets be equal when real returns are measured in terms of the same good.[10]

The Interest Rate Parity Line

Like the intertemporal external balance condition in the international goods market, the real interest rate parity condition in the international asset market can be shown graphically as a relationship between the current and future real exchange rates, e and e^f. To write the real interest rate parity condition in a form that is

---

[9]With the approximation in Eq. (13.7) the nominal interest rate parity condition can also be expressed more simply as

$$i_{\text{FOR}} - \frac{\Delta e_{\text{nom}}}{e_{\text{nom}}} \simeq i$$

According to this approximate formula for interest rate parity, the difference between nominal interest rates in two countries equals the rate at which the currency of the country with the higher nominal interest rate is expected to depreciate.

[10]If there is only one good, as we assumed in Chapter 7, then $e = e^f = 1$, and Eq. (13.9) reduces to $r_{\text{FOR}} = r$.

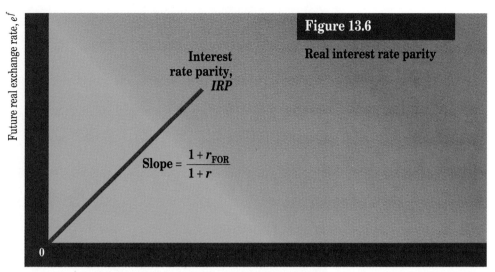

Figure 13.6

Real interest rate parity

According to the real interest rate parity (*IRP*) condition, the future real exchange rate is proportional to the current real exchange rate. Specifically, the future real exchange rate equals the current real exchange rate multiplied by $(1 + r_{\text{FOR}})/(1 + r)$, so that $(1 + r_{\text{FOR}})/(1 + r)$ is the slope of the *IRP* line.

easily graphed, we multiply both sides of Eq. (13.9) by e^f and then divide both sides by $1 + r$, to obtain

$$e^f = \left(\frac{1 + r_{\text{FOR}}}{1 + r} \right) e. \tag{13.10}$$

Equation (13.10) shows that the future real exchange rate e^f is proportional to the current real exchange rate e if the domestic and foreign real interest rates are held constant. Equation (13.10) also shows that if the foreign real interest rate is greater than the domestic real interest rate, then the future real exchange rate must exceed the current real exchange rate. The reason is that no financial investor will hold domestic assets paying a lower real return than is available on foreign assets unless a real appreciation of the domestic exchange rate is expected. Similarly, if the real return on foreign assets is lower than the real return on domestic assets, a real depreciation must be expected. An expected real depreciation implies that the future real exchange rate is lower than the current real exchange rate.

Figure 13.6 graphs the real interest rate parity (*IRP*) condition in Eq. (13.10). Given values of r and r_{FOR}, the *IRP* line relates the expected future real exchange rate e^f to the current real exchange rate e. Because the future real exchange rate e^f is proportional to the current real exchange rate e, the *IRP* line is a straight line through the origin.

Factors That Shift the *IRP* Line

The position of the *IRP* line depends on only two factors: the domestic real interest rate r and the foreign real interest rate r_{FOR}. As you can see in Eq. (13.10), the slope of the *IRP* line is $(1 + r_{\text{FOR}})/(1 + r)$. So if we are given the values of r and r_{FOR}, the *IRP* line is completely determined.

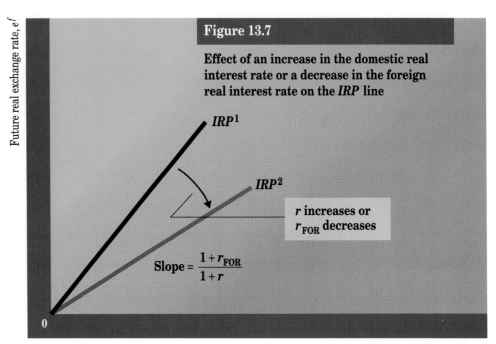

Future real exchange rate, e^f

Figure 13.7

Effect of an increase in the domestic real interest rate or a decrease in the foreign real interest rate on the *IRP* line

IRP^1

IRP^2

r increases or r_{FOR} decreases

$$\text{Slope} = \frac{1 + r_{FOR}}{1 + r}$$

0

Current real exchange rate, *e*

Either an increase in the domestic real interest rate *r* or a decrease in the foreign real interest rate r_{FOR} makes domestic bonds more attractive than foreign bonds. To be willing to hold foreign bonds, financial investors must expect the domestic real exchange rate to depreciate. For a given value of the current real exchange rate *e*, therefore, the future real exchange rate e^f must fall, and the *IRP* line pivots clockwise. Equivalently, an increase in the domestic real interest rate *r* or a decrease in the foreign real interest rate r_{FOR} reduces the slope of the *IRP* line, $(1 + r_{FOR})/(1 + r)$, resulting in the rotation of the *IRP* line from *IRP*^{1} to *IRP*^{2}.

A fall in the foreign real interest rate r_{FOR} or a rise in the domestic real interest rate *r* reduces the slope of the *IRP* line, $(1 + r_{FOR})/(1 + r)$, thus causing the *IRP* line to pivot clockwise (see Fig. 13.7). A decline in the real rate of return on the foreign asset relative to the domestic asset is possible only if financial investors expect the domestic real exchange rate to depreciate. Thus for any given current real exchange rate *e*, the future real exchange rate e^f must fall, which causes the *IRP* line to pivot clockwise. Similarly, a rise in the real return on foreign assets relative to the real return on domestic assets would increase the slope of the *IRP* line and cause it to pivot counterclockwise.

Table 13.6 summarizes the effects of domestic and foreign real interest rates on the *IRP* line.

13.5 THE DETERMINATION OF THE REAL EXCHANGE RATE

In the previous two sections we focused on the role of real exchange rates in the international markets for goods and assets. We derived and discussed two equilibrium conditions, the intertemporal external balance (*IEB*) condition in the goods market and the real interest rate parity (*IRP*) condition in the asset market. In this section we put these two conditions together to discuss the determinants of real exchange rates.

The determination of the current and future real exchange rates is shown in Fig. 13.8, which graphs both the intertemporal external balance (*IEB*) curve and the interest rate parity (*IRP*) line. As you can see in the figure, the only combi-

Table 13.6 Summary

Factors That Shift the *IRP* Line

An Increase in	Shifts the *IRP* Line	Reason
Domestic real interest rate r	Down (clockwise)	Increase in the domestic real interest rate requires an expected real depreciation, or a fall in the future real exchange rate for any given current real exchange rate
Foreign real interest rate r_{FOR}	Up (counterclockwise)	Increase in the foreign real interest rate requires an expected real appreciation, or a rise in the future real exchange rate for any given current real exchange rate

nation of e and e^f that simultaneously satisfies both the intertemporal external balance condition and the real interest rate parity condition is represented by point E, the intersection of the *IEB* curve and the *IRP* line. The values of the current and future real exchange rates that correspond to point E are the values that will occur in equilibrium.

Using the diagram in Fig. 13.8, we can examine the factors that influence real exchange rates. As an aid to intuition, it is helpful to keep in mind that the real value of a currency, say the dollar, depends on supplies and demands in the foreign

Equilibrium in the international market for goods requires that the *IEB* condition hold, and equilibrium in the international market for assets requires that the *IRP* condition hold. The only combination of current and future real exchange rates that satisfies both the *IEB* condition and the *IRP* condition is located at point E, the intersection of the *IEB* curve and the IRP line.

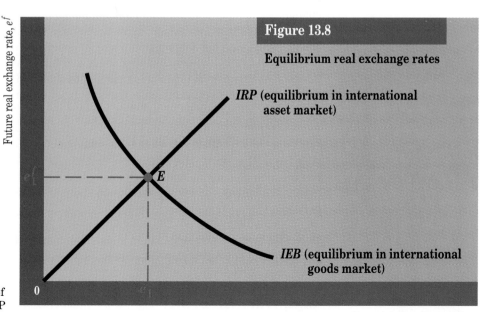

Figure 13.8

Equilibrium real exchange rates

IRP (equilibrium in international asset market)

IEB (equilibrium in international goods market)

Future real exchange rate, e^f

Current real exchange rate, e

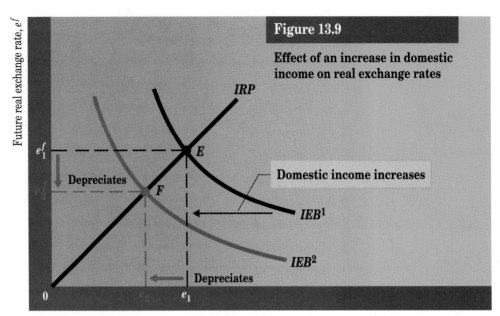

Figure 13.9

Effect of an increase in domestic income on real exchange rates

At the initial real exchange rates at point E, an increase in domestic income raises the domestic demand for imported goods and thus reduces current and future net exports. For external balance to be restored, real exchange rates must fall; so the IEB curve shifts downward, from IEB^1 to IEB^2. The interest rate parity (IRP) line is unaffected by the change in domestic income. Thus the increase in domestic income shifts the equilibrium from point E to point F. The current and future exchange rates both depreciate (from e_1 to e_2 and e_1^f to e_2^f, respectively).

exchange market. When foreigners want to buy American goods or assets, they must trade their own currency for dollars (they demand dollars in the foreign exchange market); and when Americans want to buy foreign goods or assets, they must trade dollars for foreign currencies (they supply dollars to the foreign exchange market). Thus factors that make American goods or assets more attractive to foreigners raise the demand for dollars and increase the real value of the dollar (the real exchange rate). Likewise, factors that make foreign goods or assets more attractive to Americans increase the supply of dollars and thus reduce the real value of the dollar.

Factors That Change the Real Exchange Rate

Any factor that shifts the IEB curve or the IRP line will change the equilibrium combination of current and future real exchange rates. Table 13.7 (p. 527) summarizes the effects of several factors on the real exchange rate, which we discuss below.

Domestic Income (Output)   An increase in domestic income raises the home country's demand for foreign goods. To buy foreign goods, domestic residents supply their own currency to the foreign exchange market, which—by the intuitive argument suggested a few moments ago—lowers the real exchange rate. In terms of the IEB-IRP diagram (Fig. 13.9), if we start from an initial equilibrium at point E, an increase in domestic income raises imports by the home country and causes

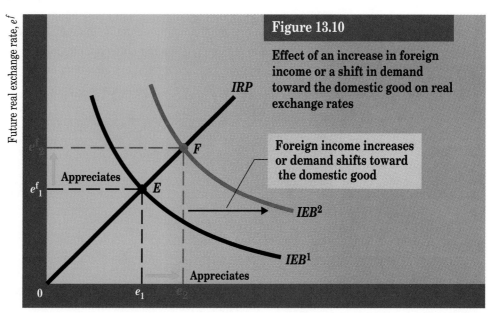

Figure 13.10

Effect of an increase in foreign income or a shift in demand toward the domestic good on real exchange rates

Foreign income increases or demand shifts toward the domestic good

Current real exchange rate, e

At the initial combination of real exchange rates at point E, either an increase in foreign income or a shift in demand toward the domestic good increases net exports. For net exports to be reduced and for external balance to be restored, real exchange rates must appreciate. Therefore the IEB curve shifts upward, from IEB^1 to IEB^2. The IRP line is unaffected by an increase in foreign income or a shift in demand toward the domestic good. Thus the current and future real exchange rates both appreciate (from e_1 to e_2 and e_1^f to e_2^f, respectively), as shown by the shift from point E to point F, where IEB^2 intersects IRP.

the IEB curve to shift downward, from IEB^1 to IEB^2 (see Table 13.4). The interest rate parity line is unaffected by the change in domestic income. At the new equilibrium, point F, both the current and the future real exchange rates have fallen. The fall in the current and future real exchange rates restores external balance while maintaining interest rate parity.

Foreign Income (Output)   An increase in foreign income has exactly the opposite effect of an increase in domestic income. Intuitively, higher foreign income increases the demand for home country exports, raises the demand for the home country's currency, and thus causes the real exchange rate to rise. In terms of Fig. 13.10, an increase in foreign income shifts the IEB curve upward, from IEB^1 to IEB^2 (see Table 13.4). The IRP line is not affected by the change in foreign income. At point F, the new equilibrium, the values of the current and future real exchange rates both increase. The higher real exchange rates restore external balance in a way that is consistent with interest rate parity. Again, notice that the effects of the increase in foreign income are just the opposite of the effects of an increase in the home country's income.

Shifts in Demand   A shift in demand toward the goods produced by the home country increases the demand for the home country's currency and thus raises the real exchange rate. In terms of the IEB-IRP diagram, a shift in demand toward the home country's exports causes the IEB curve to move upward (see Table 13.4).

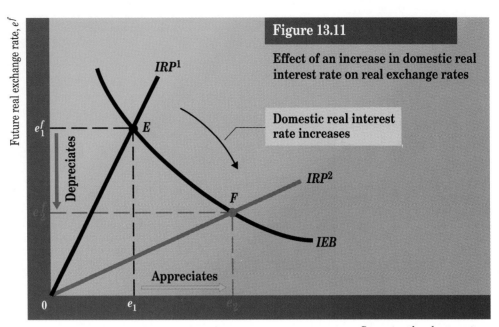

Figure 13.11

Effect of an increase in domestic real interest rate on real exchange rates

Domestic real interest rate increases

If we start from an initial equilibrium at point E, an increase in the domestic real interest rate makes domestic assets more attractive than foreign assets. As foreigners acquire domestic currency to buy domestic assets, the current real exchange rate appreciates. In the new international asset market equilibrium, the current real exchange rate has increased relative to the future real exchange rate, as shown by the clockwise

rotation of the IRP line from IRP^1 to IRP^2. The IEB curve is unaffected by the change in the real interest rate. At the new equilibrium at point F, the current real exchange rate has appreciated (from e_1 to e_2), and the future real exchange rate has depreciated (from e_1^f to e_2^f).

The IRP line is not affected by the shift in the demand for goods. Figure 13.10, which was introduced to illustrate the effects of an increase in foreign income, applies to the shift in demand toward home goods as well. As a result of the shift in demand toward the goods produced by the home country, both the current and future equilibrium values of the real exchange rate increase.

The Domestic Real Interest Rate   An increase in the domestic real interest rate makes domestic assets more attractive, which increases the demand for the home country's currency and thus causes the current real exchange rate to appreciate. Diagrammatically, an increase in the domestic real interest rate reduces the slope of the IRP line and causes it to pivot clockwise, from IRP^1 to IRP^2 in Fig. 13.11 (see Table 13.6). The IEB curve is unaffected by the change in the domestic real interest rate.[11] Therefore, the equilibrium moves from point E to point F, where IEB intersects IRP^2. The result of an increase in the domestic real interest rate is a rise in the current real exchange rate and a fall in the future real exchange rate,

[11]To say that the domestic real interest rate does not affect the IEB curve is not quite accurate, since the real interest rate r does appear in the external balance condition, Eq. (13.5). A change in r has no effect on the IEB curve at the point at which exports equal imports in both periods ($NX = NX^f = 0$), and the effect is small at points at which exports and imports in each period are close to being in balance. Since allowing for an effect of the domestic real interest on the IEB curve does not significantly affect our results, for simplicity we ignore this effect.

Table 13.7 Summary The Determination of Real Exchange Rates			
An Increase in	**Shifts**	**Current Real Exchange Rate**	**Future Real Exchange Rate**
Domestic income (output) Y	*IEB* down	Falls	Falls
Foreign income (output) Y_{FOR}	*IEB* up	Rises	Rises
Demand for domestic goods relative to foreign goods	*IEB* up	Rises	Rises
Domestic real interest rate r	*IRP* clockwise	Rises	Falls
Foreign real interest rate r_{FOR}	*IRP* counterclockwise	Falls	Rises

or a larger expected rate of exchange rate depreciation. Since the domestic real interest rate has increased, the larger expected depreciation is needed to make financial investors willing to hold foreign assets.

The Foreign Real Interest Rate An increase in the foreign real interest rate has the opposite effects of an increase in the domestic real interest rate. As you can verify, an increase in the foreign real interest rate (by rotating the *IRP* line counterclockwise and leaving the *IEB* curve unaffected) depreciates the current real exchange rate and appreciates the future real exchange rate. Intuitively, the fall in the current real exchange rate occurs because the rise in the foreign real interest rate makes foreign assets more attractive.

13.6 THE *IS-LM* MODEL FOR AN OPEN ECONOMY

In Chapters 11 and 12 we used the *IS-LM* model to analyze cyclical fluctuations and the effects of macroeconomic policy. However, the *IS-LM* model used in those chapters did not include a foreign sector and thus could not be used to analyze the international dimensions of the economy. Fortunately, given the work we have already done in this chapter, it is not difficult to extend the *IS-LM* model so that it can be used to study an open economy.

The components of the *IS-LM* model include the *IS* curve, which describes goods market equilibrium; the *LM* curve, which describes asset market equilibrium; and the *FE* line, which describes labor market equilibrium. Nothing we have discussed in this chapter substantially affects our analysis of the supply of money or the demand for money; so in developing the open-economy *IS-LM* model, we take the *LM* curve to be the same as in the closed-economy case. Similarly, the labor market and the production function are not directly affected by international factors, so the *FE* line is also unchanged.[12]

However, because net exports are part of the demand for goods, the *IS* curve has to be modified somewhat in order to describe the open economy. There are three main points to be made about the *IS* curve in the open economy:

1. Although the open-economy *IS* curve is derived a bit differently than the closed-economy *IS* curve, it is a downward-sloping relationship between output and the real interest rate, just as the closed-economy *IS* curve is.

2. Factors that shift the *IS* curve in the closed economy shift the *IS* curve in the open economy in the same way.

3. In addition, factors other than domestic output or the domestic real interest rate that raise a country's current net exports shift the open-economy *IS* curve upward; and factors that lower a country's net exports shift the *IS* curve downward.

We discuss each of these three points. We then use the open-economy *IS-LM* model to analyze the international transmission of business cycles and the operation of macroeconomic policies in an open economy.

The Open-Economy *IS* Curve

For any level of output the *IS* curve gives the real interest rate that clears the goods market. In a closed economy the goods market equilibrium condition is that desired national saving S^d must equal desired investment I^d, or $S^d - I^d = 0$. In an open economy, as we saw in Chapter 7, Section 7.2, the goods market equilibrium condition is that desired saving S^d must equal desired investment I^d plus net exports NX. Equivalently, the goods market equilibrium condition for an open economy is

$$S^d - I^d = NX. \tag{13.11}$$

In an open economy, for any given level of domestic output Y, the *IS* curve gives the domestic real interest rate r that makes Eq. (13.11) hold.

The derivation of the open-economy *IS* curve is shown graphically in Fig. 13.12. The horizontal axis measures desired saving minus desired investment, $S^d - I^d$, as well as net exports NX. Note that the horizontal axis is drawn to include both positive and negative values. The vertical axis, which intersects the horizontal axis at the origin, measures the real interest rate r.

Two curves are graphed in Fig. 13.12. The upward-sloping curve, $S^d - I^d$, gives the difference between desired national saving and desired investment for each value of the real interest rate r. This curve slopes upward because, with output held constant, an increase in the real interest rate raises desired national saving and reduces desired investment, thereby increasing the excess of desired saving over desired investment.

---

[12]A case in which the *FE* line does depend on international considerations is when some raw materials (such as oil) are imported. In this book we have modeled oil price shocks as productivity shocks, which captures the main domestic macroeconomic effects. Unfortunately, a full analysis that includes all of the international aspects of an oil price shock is quite complex, and so we do not present it here.

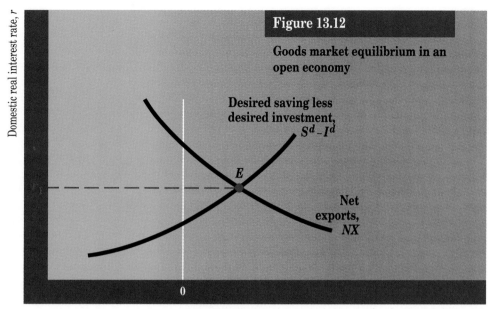

Figure 13.12

Goods market equilibrium in an open economy

Domestic real interest rate, r

Desired saving less desired investment, $S^d - I^d$

E

Net exports, NX

0

Desired saving less desired investment, $S^d - I^d$, and net exports, NX

The upward-sloping curve shows desired saving S^d less desired investment I^d. This curve slopes upward because a higher domestic real interest rate increases the excess of desired saving over desired investment. The NX curve relates net exports to the domestic real interest rate. This curve slopes downward because a higher domestic real interest rate causes the current real exchange rate to appreciate, which reduces net exports. Goods market equilibrium occurs at point E, where the excess of desired saving over desired investment equals net exports. The real interest rate that clears the goods market is r_1.

The downward-sloping curve in Fig. 13.12, NX, shows the relationship between the country's net exports and the domestic real interest rate. As Table 13.3 summarizes, a country's net exports depend *directly* on the real exchange rate and on domestic and foreign income. However, a country's net exports are *indirectly* related to the domestic real interest rate through the effect of the real interest rate on the current real exchange rate. As we have seen in using the *IEB-IRP* diagram, an increase in the domestic real interest rate makes domestic assets more attractive and increases the current real exchange rate (see Table 13.7). The current real appreciation makes domestic goods more expensive relative to foreign goods and reduces net exports by the domestic country. Therefore an increase in the domestic real interest rate reduces net exports, and the NX curve in Fig. 13.12 slopes downward.

In drawing both of the curves in Fig. 13.12, we hold constant the levels of domestic output Y, foreign output Y_{FOR}, and the foreign real interest rate r_{FOR}. However, as just explained for the case of the NX curve, we allow the real exchange rate to change when factors that affect it change.

Goods market equilibrium requires that the excess of desired saving over desired investment be equal to net exports (Eq. 13.11). This condition is satisfied at the intersection of the $S^d - I^d$ curve and the NX curve at point E in Fig. 13.12. Thus the domestic real interest rate that clears the goods market is the interest rate corresponding to point E, shown as r_1 in the figure.

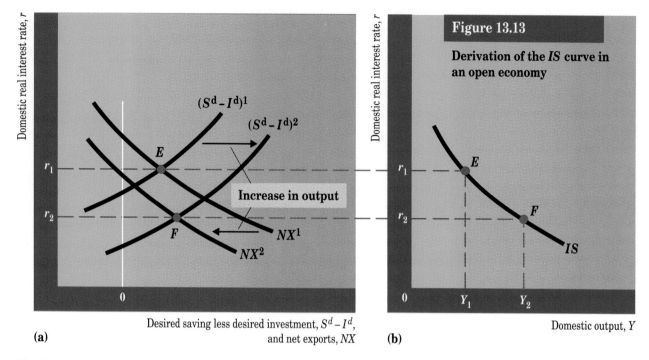

Figure 13.13

Derivation of the *IS* curve in an open economy

(a)

Desired saving less desired investment, $S^d - I^d$, and net exports, *NX*

(b)

Domestic output, *Y*

The initial equilibrium in the goods market is represented by point *E* in both parts of this figure.

(a) At point *E* domestic output is Y_1 and the domestic real interest rate is r_1. An increase in domestic output from Y_1 to Y_2 raises desired national saving at each real interest rate and does not affect desired investment. Therefore the curve describing desired saving less desired investment shifts right, from $(S^d - I^d)^1$ to $(S^d - I^d)^2$. The increase in output has two effects on net exports: It raises the demand for imported goods, which

reduces net exports; but it also causes the real exchange rate to depreciate, which increases net exports. We assume that the overall effect is to reduce net exports, so the *NX* curve shifts left, from NX^1 to NX^2. At the new equilibrium, point *F*, output is Y_2 and the real interest rate is r_2.

(b) Because an increase in output from Y_1 to Y_2 lowers the real interest rate that clears the goods market from r_1 to r_2, the *IS* curve slopes downward.

To derive the *IS* curve, we ask what happens to the real interest rate that clears the goods market when the current level of domestic output rises (see Figs. 13.13a and 13.13b). In the figure we suppose that domestic output initially equals Y_1, and goods market equilibrium is at point *E*, with the real interest rate equal to r_1. Now suppose that output rises to Y_2. An increase in current output raises desired national saving but does not affect desired investment, so the excess of desired saving over desired investment rises at any given real interest rate. Thus the curve measuring the excess of desired saving over desired investment shifts right, from $(S^d - I^d)^1$ to $(S^d - I^d)^2$ in Fig. 13.13(a).

What about the *NX* curve? An increase in domestic output has two opposing effects on a country's net exports. On the one hand, when domestic income is higher, domestic residents want to spend more on imported goods, which reduces net exports. On the other hand, through its effect on the country's external balance, the increase in income also causes the real exchange rate to depreciate. The lower real exchange rate makes imports relatively more expensive, which tends to make net exports rise. Thus the overall effect is potentially ambiguous. Empirically, the direct effect on net exports of an increase in output is probably stronger than the indirect effect working through the depreciation of the real exchange rate.

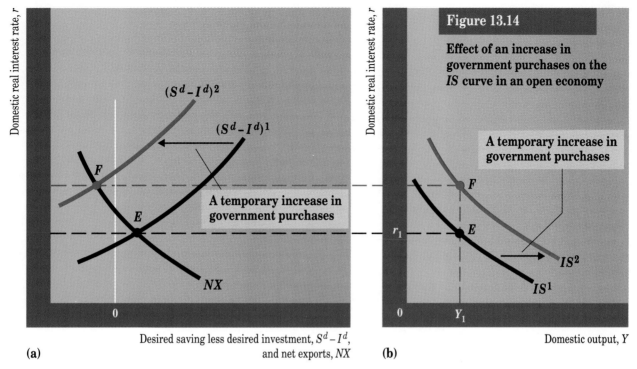

Figure 13.14

Effect of an increase in government purchases on the *IS* curve in an open economy

(a)

Desired saving less desired investment, $S^d - I^d$, and net exports, NX

(b)

Domestic output, Y

Initial equilibrium is at point E in both parts, where output is Y_1 and the real interest rate is r_1.

(a) A temporary increase in government purchases lowers desired national saving at every given level of output and the real interest rate. Thus the curve that shows the excess of desired saving over desired investment shifts left, from $(S^d - I^d)^1$ to $(S^d - I^d)^2$.

(b) Given the level of output Y_1, the real interest rate that clears the goods market is now r_2 (point F in both parts). Because the real interest rate that clears the goods market has risen, the *IS* curve shifts upward, from IS^1 to IS^2.

If we assume that the direct effect of the increase in output is the stronger, then, overall, an increase in output reduces net exports at any given level of the real interest rate. Thus when output rises from Y_1 to Y_2, the net export curve NX shifts left, from NX^1 to NX^2 in Fig. 13.13(a).

After the increase in output from Y_1 to Y_2, the new goods market equilibrium is at point F in Fig. 13.13(a), with the real interest rate equal to r_2. The *IS* curve, graphed in Fig. 13.13(b), shows that when output equals Y_1, the real interest rate that clears the goods market is r_1; and that when output equals Y_2, the real interest rate that clears the goods market is r_2. Since a rise in current output lowers the real interest rate that clears the goods market, the open-economy *IS* curve slopes downward, just as in a closed economy.

Factors That Shift the *IS* Curve   Just as in a closed economy, in an open economy any factor that raises the real interest rate that clears the goods market at a given level of output shifts the *IS* curve upward. In particular, as we mentioned, factors that shift the *IS* curve upward in a closed economy also shift the *IS* curve upward in the open economy.

The point is illustrated in Figs. 13.14(a) and 13.14(b), which show the effects on the open-economy *IS* curve of a temporary increase in government purchases.

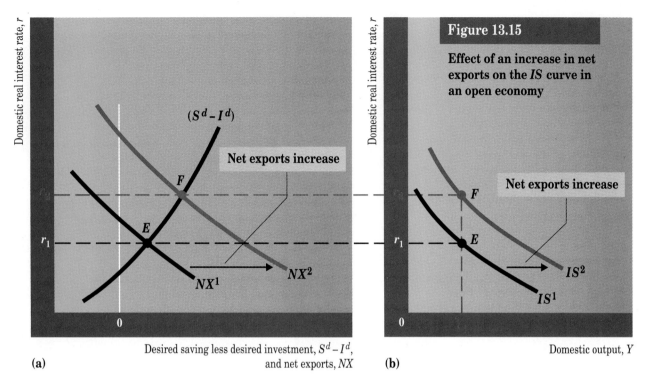

(a)

Desired saving less desired investment, $S^d - I^d$, and net exports, NX

(b)

Domestic output, Y

Figure 13.15

Effect of an increase in net exports on the IS curve in an open economy

At the initial equilibrium point E (in both parts), output is Y_1 and the real interest rate that clears the goods market is r_1.

(a) If some change occurs that raises the country's net exports at any given level of domestic output and the domestic real interest rate, then the NX curve shifts to the right, from NX^1 to NX^2.

(b) Given output of Y_1, the real interest rate that clears the goods market has risen from r_1 to r_2 (point F in both parts). Thus the IS curve shifts upward, from IS^1 to IS^2.

With output held constant at Y_1, the initial equilibrium is at point E, where the real interest rate equals r_1. A temporary increase in government purchases lowers desired national saving at every level of output and the real interest rate. Thus the curve that shows the excess of desired saving over investment shifts upward and to the left, from $(S^d - I^d)^1$ to $(S^d - I^d)^2$. The new goods market equilibrium is at point F, where the real interest rate takes the higher value r_2.

The effect on the IS curve is shown in Fig. 13.14(b). Given output Y_1, the increase in government purchases raises the real interest rate that clears the goods market from r_1 to r_2 and thus causes the IS curve to shift upward, from IS^1 to IS^2. In general, any factor that shifts the closed-economy IS curve upward—such as an increase in the expected future MPK—does so by reducing desired national saving relative to desired investment. Since a change that reduces desired national saving relative to desired investment shifts the $S^d - I^d$ curve to the left in a diagram like Fig. 13.14(a), such a change shifts the open-economy IS curve upward as well.

In addition to the standard IS curve shifters we have seen before, anything that raises current net exports, given domestic output and the domestic real interest rate, will shift the open-economy IS curve upward, as illustrated in Figs. 13.15(a) and 13.15(b). At the initial equilibrium at point E in both parts of Fig. 13.15, domestic output is Y_1 and the domestic real interest rate is r_1. Now suppose

Table 13.8 Summary		
International Factors That Shift the *IS* Curve		
An Increase in	**Shifts the *IS* Curve**	**Reason**
Foreign output Y_{FOR}	Up	Higher foreign output raises demand for home country exports
Foreign real interest rate r_{FOR}	Up	Higher foreign real interest rate depreciates the real exchange rate, raising net exports
Demand for domestic goods relative to foreign goods	Up	Higher demand for domestic goods raises net exports

that some change occurs that raises the country's net exports at any given level of domestic output and the domestic real interest rate: This increase in net exports is shown as a rightward shift of the *NX* curve in Fig. 13.15(a), from NX^1 to NX^2. At the new goods market equilibrium, point *F*, the real interest rate has risen to r_2. Since the real interest rate that clears the goods market has risen at any given level of output, the *IS* curve shifts upward, as shown in Fig. 13.15(b).

What factors might cause a country's net exports to rise, given domestic output and the domestic real interest rate? We have discussed three possibilities in this chapter: an increase in foreign output, an increase in the foreign real interest rate, and a shift in demand toward the home country's goods (see the summary in Table 13.8).

An *increase in foreign output* Y_{FOR} increases purchases of home country goods by foreigners, thus raising net exports (see Table 13.3). An increase in foreign output, through its effect on external balance, also causes the current real exchange to appreciate (see Table 13.7), which tends to reduce net exports. As we have mentioned, in practice, the first effect is probably the stronger, so that the overall effect of an increase in foreign output is to raise the home country's net exports.

An *increase in the foreign real interest rate* r_{FOR} makes foreign assets relatively more attractive and thus causes the real exchange rate to depreciate (see Table 13.7). A lower real exchange rate makes the domestic good relatively cheaper and causes net exports to rise.

A *shift in demand* toward the home country's goods raises net exports directly as foreigners purchase more of the home country's output (see Table 13.3). Such a shift in demand also causes the real exchange rate to appreciate (see Table 13.7). The higher real exchange rate tends to reduce net exports. Again the overall effect on net exports will be positive if the impact of the higher real exchange rate is not too strong.

The International Transmission of Business Cycles

In the introduction to this chapter we discussed how trade and financial links among countries cause cyclical fluctuations to be transmitted across borders. The analysis of this section shows that the principal means by which cycles are transmitted internationally is through the impact of foreign economic conditions on the real exchange rate and net exports.

As an example, consider the impact of a recession in the United States on the economies for which the United States is a major export market—Japan, for example. In terms of the *IS-LM* model a fall in U.S. output lowers Japanese net exports, which shifts the Japanese *IS* curve downward. In the Keynesian version of the model this downward shift of the *IS* curve throws Japan into a recession, with output below its full-employment level, until price adjustment restores full employment. In the classical version of the *IS-LM* model the *IS* shift does not affect Japanese output, although the Japanese real interest rate falls and the yen weakens as the result of the fall in foreign (U.S.) output.

Similarly, a country's domestic economy can be sensitive to shifts in the international demand for its exports. For example, a shift in demand away from Japanese goods—induced perhaps by trade restrictions against Japanese products— would shift the Japanese *IS* curve downward, with the same contractionary effects as the decrease in foreign (U.S.) output had.

13.7   MACROECONOMIC POLICY IN AN OPEN ECONOMY

A primary reason for developing the *IS-LM* model for the open economy is to see how economic openness affects the operation of fiscal and monetary policies. In examining this issue in this section, we find that the effects of macroeconomic policy on domestic variables such as output and the real interest rate are largely unchanged by the addition of a foreign sector. However, two additional questions that arise in the open economy are: (1) How do fiscal and monetary policy affect a country's real exchange rate and net exports? and (2) How do the macroeconomic policies of one country affect the economies of other countries? Using the open-economy *IS-LM* model, together with the *IEB-IRP* diagram, we can answer both of these questions.

As usual, in the open economy the predicted effects of policy changes depend on whether we make classical or Keynesian assumptions. Rather than examine all possible cases, in analyzing fiscal policy in an open economy, we focus on the classical version of the *IS-LM* model; and in studying monetary policy in an open economy, we emphasize the Keynesian version.

To examine the international effects of various policies, we proceed in three steps:

1. We use the *IS-LM* diagram for the domestic economy to determine the effects on domestic output and the domestic real interest rate. This step is the same as it was in our analyses of closed economies in Chapters 11 and 12.

2. We use the *IEB-IRP* diagram to determine the effects on the current and the future real exchange rates. Any change in domestic output from step 1 will shift the *IEB* curve, and any change in the domestic real interest rate from step 1 will shift the *IRP* line.

3. We use the *IS-LM* diagram for the foreign economy to determine the effects on foreign output and the foreign real interest rate. Changes in net exports at a given level of the foreign real interest rate will shift the foreign *IS* curve.

Fiscal Policy in an Open Economy

We focus our discussion of fiscal policy on a temporary increase in domestic government purchases. However, the analysis applies also to a cut in domestic (lump-sum) taxes, provided that Ricardian equivalence does not hold (see Appendix 12.B).

We work with the classical version of the model, and we suppose that the original equilibrium is represented by point E in the *IS-LM* and *IEB-IRP* diagrams in Fig. 13.16 (p. 536). The increase in government purchases shifts the domestic *IS* curve upward, from IS^1 to IS^2, as shown in Fig. 13.16(a). In addition, in the classical model the *FE* line shifts to the right, from FE^1 to FE^2. The *FE* line shifts because the increase in government purchases raises present or future tax burdens; since higher taxes make workers poorer, they increase their labor supply. The new equilibrium is represented by point F, the intersection of IS^2 and FE^2. The domestic price level rises, which shifts the domestic *LM* curve left, from LM^1 to LM^2, until it passes through point F. As you can see by comparing point F with point E, the increase in government purchases increases both output Y and the real interest rate r in the home country. So far the analysis is identical to that for a closed economy (Chapter 11).

Next, we use the *IEB-IRP* diagram to study the effects of the increases in domestic output and the domestic real interest rate on the real exchange rate and net exports. First, consider the effect of a higher Y: The increase in domestic output (income) raises residents' demands for imported goods, which reduces current and future net exports. For external balance to be restored, the current or future real exchange rate (or both) must depreciate. Therefore the *IEB* curve shifts downward, from IEB^1 to IEB^2 (see Table 13.4).

The increase in the domestic real interest rate r makes domestic assets more attractive than foreign assets and causes the current real exchange rate to appreciate relative to the future real exchange rate. Thus the *IRP* line rotates clockwise (see Table 13.6).

The new equilibrium in the international market for goods and assets is represented by point F in Fig. 13.16(b). As we have drawn the diagram, the current real exchange rate is unchanged, because the real depreciation caused by increased income is offset by the real appreciation induced by the increase in the domestic real interest rate. More generally, the current real exchange rate can either increase or decrease, but in any case the size of the change is likely to be small. Although the real exchange rate is unchanged, higher output causes domestic residents to increase their purchases of imports, so that net exports of the domestic country definitely decrease.

The effects of the domestic fiscal expansion on the rest of the world (represented by the foreign country *IS-LM* diagram in Fig. 13.16c) are transmitted through the change in net exports. The reduction in the domestic country's net exports is equivalent to an increase in the net exports of the foreign country, so that the foreign country's *IS* curve shifts upward, from IS^1_{FOR} to IS^2_{FOR} in Fig. 13.16(c). After adjustment of the price level shifts the *LM* curve to restore general equilibrium (the shift of the *LM* curve is not shown), the foreign economy ends up

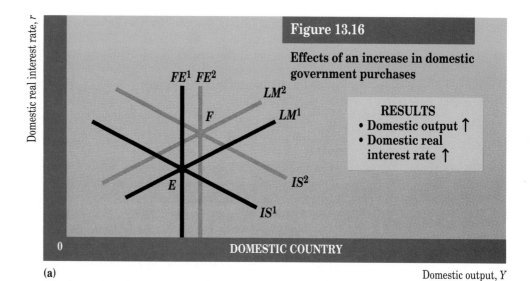

Figure 13.16

Effects of an increase in domestic government purchases

RESULTS
- Domestic output ↑
- Domestic real interest rate ↑

(a)

Domestic real interest rate, r

Domestic output, Y

DOMESTIC COUNTRY

RESULTS
- Current real exchange rate unchanged (ambiguous)
- Future real exchange rate ↓
- Current net exports by home country ↓

(b)

Future real exchange rate, e^f

Current real exchange rate, e

INTERNATIONAL MARKETS FOR GOODS AND ASSETS

RESULTS
- Foreign income unchanged in classical model, short-run rise in Keynesian model
- Foreign real interest rate ↑

(c)

Foreign real interest rate, r_{FOR}

Foreign output, Y_{FOR}

FOREIGN COUNTRY

at point F, with the real interest rate and the price level higher than they were initially.

Because of the assumption of rapid price adjustment, in the classical model the domestic fiscal expansion does not expand output in the foreign economy. If prices were sticky, as in the Keynesian model, the shift of the IS curve would lead the foreign economy to have temporarily higher output at the intersection of the IS and LM curves at point H in Fig. 13.16(c), with price adjustment ultimately bringing the economy to point F. Otherwise, the implications of the classical and Keynesian analyses are the same.

Beyond the principal effects of the fiscal expansion that we have just analyzed, there are two possible feedback, or repercussion, effects from the foreign country to the domestic country. We omit these feedback effects from the diagrams because they are small. The first effect is that because the foreign real interest rate r_{FOR} has increased, the slope of the IRP line in Fig. 13.16(b) will increase back toward its initial level. As long as the increase in the foreign interest rate is smaller than the increase in the domestic interest rate, the new IRP line (IRP^2) will remain less steep than the initial IRP line (IRP^1), as shown in Fig. 13.16(b). Because the foreign country represents the rest of the world, it is much larger than the domestic country; and thus its interest rate will probably not be much affected by the increase in domestic government purchases.

The second feedback effect applies only in the Keynesian case, in which foreign output rises. If foreign output rises, then the foreign demand for domestic goods will increase, which will shift the IEB curve upward toward its initial position. Attempts to measure this type of feedback effect have generally found it to be small.

To summarize, in the classical model the increase in domestic government purchases increases domestic income, the domestic real interest rate, and the domestic price level, as in a closed economy. In addition, net exports fall because of the increase in income; thus increased government purchases crowd out both investment and net exports. The real exchange rate is approximately unchanged. In the foreign economy the real interest rate and the price level rise. In the Keynesian version of the model foreign output rises as well.

◀ (a) In the classical IS-LM model an increase in domestic government purchases shifts the domestic IS curve right (from IS^1 to IS^2) and also shifts the domestic FE line right (from FE^1 to FE^2). Therefore domestic income and the domestic real interest rate both increase.

(b) The increase in domestic income shifts the IEB curve downward, from IEB^1 to IEB^2 (as in Fig. 13.4). The increase in the domestic real interest rate rotates the IRP line clockwise, from IRP^1 to IRP^2 (as in Fig. 13.7). The equilibrium point shifts from point E to point F. The current real exchange rate changes little or not at all from its initial value, and the future real exchange rate falls from its initial value. Because domestic income has risen and the current real exchange rate has not changed, net exports decrease.

(c) As a result of the decrease in net exports by the domestic country, the net exports of the foreign county increase. The increase in net exports shifts the foreign IS curve upward, from IS^1_{FOR} to IS^2_{FOR}. In the new equilibrium at point F the foreign real interest rate is higher, but foreign output is unchanged. In the Keynesian model price stickiness would cause a temporary increase in foreign output at point H.

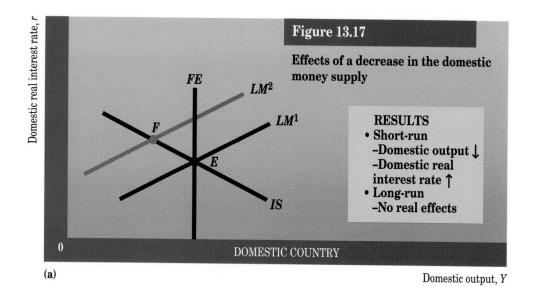

Figure 13.17

Effects of a decrease in the domestic money supply

RESULTS
- Short-run
  - Domestic output ↓
  - Domestic real interest rate ↑
- Long-run
  - No real effects

(a)
DOMESTIC COUNTRY

Domestic output, Y

RESULTS
- Current real exchange rate ↑
- Future real exchange rate unchanged (ambiguous)
- Current net exports by home country ↑

(b)
INTERNATIONAL MARKETS FOR GOODS AND ASSETS

Current real exchange rate, e

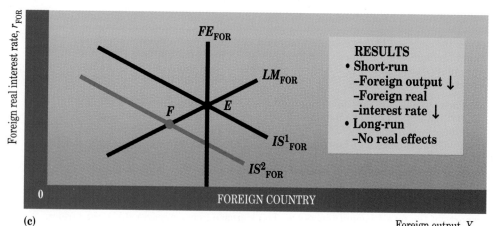

RESULTS
- Short-run
  - Foreign output ↓
  - Foreign real
  - interest rate ↓
- Long-run
  - No real effects

(c)
FOREIGN COUNTRY

Foreign output, Y_{FOR}

Monetary Policy in an Open Economy

We analyze the effects of monetary policy in the short run and in the long run using the Keynesian model. However, because the effects of monetary policy in the basic classical model are the same as in the long run in the Keynesian model, our discussion illustrates the classical results as well.

Short Run The effects of a monetary contraction are shown in Fig. 13.17. Suppose that the initial equilibrium is represented by point E, and a decrease in the money supply shifts the domestic LM curve upward and to the left, from LM^1 to LM^2 in Fig. 13.17(a). The price level is rigid in the short run in the Keynesian model, so the short-run equilibrium is represented by point F, the intersection of IS and LM^2. Comparing point F with point E, we see that in the short run domestic output falls and the domestic real interest rate rises. This is the same result we found for the closed economy in Chapter 12.

Following the monetary contraction the real exchange rate appreciates in the short run, for two reasons. First, the decrease in domestic income reduces the domestic demand for imports. As domestic consumers demand less foreign currency to buy imported goods, the domestic real exchange rate appreciates; diagrammatically, this effect is shown by the upward shift of the IEB curve from IEB^1 to IEB^2 (see Table 13.4). Second, the increase in the domestic real interest rate makes domestic assets more attractive than foreign assets at the initial values of the current and the future real exchange rates. As foreign investors demand more domestic currency to buy domestic assets, the current real exchange rate appreciates relative to the future real exchange rate, and the IRP line rotates clockwise, from IRP^1 to IRP^2 (see Table 13.6). The new values of e and e^f are represented by point F in Fig. 13.17(b), where IEB^2 intersects IRP^2. Comparing points E and F in Fig. 13.17(b), we see that the current real exchange rate appreciates, but the effect on the future real exchange rate is ambiguous, depending on the sizes of the shifts of the IEB curve and the IRP line.

There are two competing effects on net exports. The fall in domestic income reduces the domestic demand for foreign goods and thus tends to increase net ex-

(a) A decrease in the domestic money supply shifts the domestic LM curve upward, from LM^1 to LM^2. The short-run equilibrium in the Keynesian model is located at point F, the intersection of IS and LM^2. The reduction in the money supply reduces domestic output and increases the domestic real interest rate.

(b) In the international markets for goods and assets, the fall in domestic output shifts the IEB curve upward, from IEB^1 to IEB^2. The rise in the domestic real interest rate rotates the IRP line downward, from IRP^1 to IRP^2. In the new equilibrium at point F the current real exchange rate has increased, and the future real exchange rate changes only a very small amount or not at all. If we assume that the effect on net exports of the fall in domestic income is stronger than the effect of the appreciation of the exchange rate, then net exports increase as domestic residents demand fewer goods from abroad.

(c) Because the domestic country's net exports increase, the foreign country's net exports decrease, and the foreign IS curve shifts from IS^1_{FOR} to IS^2_{FOR}. Thus output and the real interest rate fall in the foreign country.

In the long run prices fall and both economies return to point E. Thus in the long run money is neutral.

ports. However, the appreciation of the current real exchange rate makes domestic goods more expensive relative to foreign goods and tends to reduce net exports. We cannot say for certain which way net exports will change; although if we accept as a rule of thumb that real exchange rate effects on net exports are weaker than income effects on net exports in the short run, then overall net exports will increase.

Figure 13.17(c) shows the effects on the foreign economy. Assuming that net exports by the domestic country increase, net exports by the foreign country decrease. Thus the IS curve of the foreign country shifts left, from IS^1_{FOR} to IS^2_{FOR}. The short-run equilibrium is at point F, where IS^2_{FOR} intersects LM_{FOR}. Output in the foreign country declines, and the foreign real interest rate falls. Under the assumption that domestic net exports increase, the domestic monetary contraction, by reducing the demand for foreign goods, also leads to a recession abroad.

Long Run After full adjustment of wages and prices, the domestic and foreign economies return to their original positions at point E. Thus money is neutral in the long run, and all real variables—including net exports and the real exchange rate—are unaffected by the monetary contraction. Although monetary neutrality holds in the long run in the Keynesian model, it holds immediately in the basic classical model. So, in particular, monetary policy changes have no effect on real exchange rates or trade flows in the basic classical model but only affect the price level.

Although money cannot affect the *real* exchange rate in the long run, it affects the *nominal* exchange rate by affecting the domestic price level. For instance, a 10% decrease in the domestic nominal money supply decreases the price of domestic goods by 10% and appreciates the nominal exchange rate by 10%. To see why a monetary contraction raises the nominal exchange rate, note from Eq. (13.1) that the nominal exchange rate e_{nom} equals eP_{FOR}/P, where e is the real exchange rate, P_{FOR} is the foreign price level, and P is the domestic price level. Since e and P_{FOR} are unchanged in the long run by a domestic monetary contraction, if the monetary contraction causes a 10% fall in P, it must also raise the nominal exchange rate e_{nom} by 10%.

Application

Why the Dollar Rose So High and Fell So Far in the 1980s

As we saw in Fig. 13.2, the U.S. dollar appreciated strongly during the first half of the 1980s. Then after reaching its peak in March 1985, the dollar fell precipitously for nearly three years. Associated with the rise in the dollar was a sharp decline in U.S. net exports, as we also saw in Fig. 13.2. What were the ultimate causes of these gyrations in the U.S. foreign sector?

To explain the fluctuations in the dollar and U.S. net exports in the 1980s, Keynesians focus on the effects of macroeconomic policies during that decade—

specifically, a policy mix that combined tight monetary policy and expansionary fiscal policy. As we discussed in Chapter 12, the tight-money policy began in October 1979; in that month Federal Reserve Chairman Paul Volcker announced that money growth rates would be reduced in order to fight inflation, which at the time was at worrisome levels. Contractionary monetary policy contributed to a short recession in 1980 and a deep recession in 1981–1982. Fiscal policy became expansionary around 1981, when the tax cuts mandated by the Economic Recovery Tax Act (ERTA) began to be phased in. Military expenditures by the government also increased in this period.

In the Keynesian analysis the effects on output of tight money and expansionary fiscal policy tend to cancel out, and indeed, by 1983 the economy had begun a strong recovery from the 1981–1982 recession. However, tight money and expansionary fiscal policy both lead to a higher real interest rate, and in the early 1980s the real interest rate in the United States had reached record levels (see Fig. 2.6, p. 57). We have seen that a high real interest rate in the United States makes U.S. assets attractive to foreign investors; as foreigners demanded dollar-denominated assets, the real value of the dollar rose sharply. Because the dollar was so strong, according to this story, U.S. net exports fell sharply in 1983 and 1984.

The Keynesian analysis, which attributes the dollar's rise to the high real interest rate induced by policy, can also explain the fall in the dollar after 1985. We saw in Fig. 13.11 that an increase in the domestic real interest rate, with output held constant, causes the *IRP* line to pivot clockwise. Thus although an increase in the domestic real interest rate increases the current real exchange rate, it also reduces the future real exchange rate. Intuitively, there are two reasons why, as of the mid-1980s, people should have expected the real value of the dollar to fall (as indeed it eventually did). First, because the U.S. real interest rate exceeded foreign real interest rates in the early 1980s, real interest rate parity required that financial investors expect a future real depreciation of the dollar. Second, since the high dollar led to a severe decline in U.S. net exports, the United States, to satisfy the external balance condition, had to move toward positive net exports in order to repay its foreign debts. For the U.S. net export position to improve, ultimately the dollar had to fall.

An alternative explanation of the dollar's rise has been offered by some classical economists. The explanation is based on the idea that during the early 1980s the United States became a relatively more attractive place to invest. The argument is based on both a "push" and a "pull." The "pull" came from the liberalization of U.S. tax laws pertaining to investment and the generally probusiness attitude of the Reagan administration, both of which acted to increase the profitability of investing in the United States. The "push" came from the failure of many developing countries to repay their international debts fully and on schedule (see Chapter 7). Investors in the United States, as well as abroad, began to shy away from investing in these countries, preferring instead the safe haven of the United States. According to the classical argument, the increased desirability of U.S. assets relative to foreign assets increased the demand for the dollar and raised the U.S. real exchange rate, which in turn reduced net exports. Again, however, the external balance condition and interest rate parity both imply that the rise in the dollar could only have been temporary. (You are asked to analyze the classical explanation of the dollar's rise in Analytical Problem 2.)

13.8 CHAPTER SUMMARY

1. The nominal exchange rate is the number of units of foreign currency that can be obtained in exchange for one unit of domestic currency. The real exchange rate is the number of units of foreign goods that can be obtained in exchange for one unit of the domestic good.

2. In a flexible exchange rate system a decrease in an exchange rate is called a depreciation, and an increase in an exchange rate is called an appreciation. The rate of appreciation of the nominal exchange rate equals the rate of appreciation of the real exchange rate plus the excess of the foreign rate of inflation over the domestic rate of inflation.

3. Net exports equal exports minus imports, with imports weighted by the relative price of imports (equal to 1 divided by the real exchange rate). A decline in the real exchange rate can reduce net exports in the short run because a fall in the real exchange rate raises the relative price of imports. In the longer run, when physical flows of exports and imports adjust, a fall in the real exchange rate is likely to raise net exports. The characteristic time pattern of the response of net exports to a fall in the real exchange rate—falling net exports in the short run but rising net exports in the long run—is called the J curve.

4. With the real exchange rate held constant, net exports increase in response to lower domestic income, higher foreign income, or a shift in demand away from foreign goods toward domestic goods.

5. The intertemporal external balance (*IEB*) condition requires that countries that have negative net exports and borrow abroad today have positive net exports in the future, so that they can repay their foreign loans. The *IEB* curve, the graph of the *IEB* condition, is a downward-sloping relation between the current real exchange rate and the future real exchange rate. Factors other than real exchange rates that change current and future net exports shift the *IEB* curve.

6. The interest rate parity (*IRP*) condition states that the returns to comparable foreign and domestic assets must be the same when measured in the same currency. An approximate version of interest rate parity is that the foreign interest rate plus the rate of depreciation of the domestic exchange rate must equal the domestic interest rate. Interest rate parity holds both for nominal interest rates and exchange rates and for real interest rates and exchange rates. The interest rate parity condition is represented graphically by the *IRP* line, which is an upward-sloping relation between the current and future real exchange rates. Changes in the domestic or foreign real interest rate cause the *IRP* line to pivot.

7. Current and future real exchange rates are determined in the international markets for goods and assets. These exchange rates must satisfy the intertemporal external balance (*IEB*) condition and real interest rate parity (*IRP*), represented by the intersection of the *IEB* curve and the *IRP* line. Factors that shift the *IEB* curve or the *IRP* line change current and future real exchange rates.

8. The *IS-LM* model for an open economy is similar to the model for the closed economy. The principal difference is that in the open-economy *IS-LM* model factors (other than output or the real interest rate) that increase a country's net exports cause the *IS* curve to shift upward. Economic shocks or policy changes are transmitted from one country to another through changes in net exports that lead to *IS* curve shifts.

9. A fiscal expansion in an open economy increases domestic output and the domestic real interest rate, just as in a closed economy. The effect on the current real exchange rate is ambiguous, since the increase in output raises the demand for imported goods, which weakens the exchange rate, but the higher real interest rate makes domestic assets more attractive, which strengthens the real exchange rate. Because increased output raises the demand for imports, net exports fall. The fiscal expansion is transmitted to the foreign country through the increase in demand for the foreign country's exports.

10. In an open economy, changes in the money supply are neutral in the basic classical model. Changes in the money supply are also neutral in the long run in the Keynesian model. In the short run in the Keynesian model, however, a decrease in the domestic money supply reduces domestic output and raises the domestic real interest rate, both of which cause the current real exchange rate to appreciate. Net exports by the domestic country increase, assuming that the effect of lower output (which reduces imports) is stronger than the impact on net exports of the rise in the real exchange rate. The monetary contraction is transmitted to the foreign country through the effect on the foreign country's net exports.

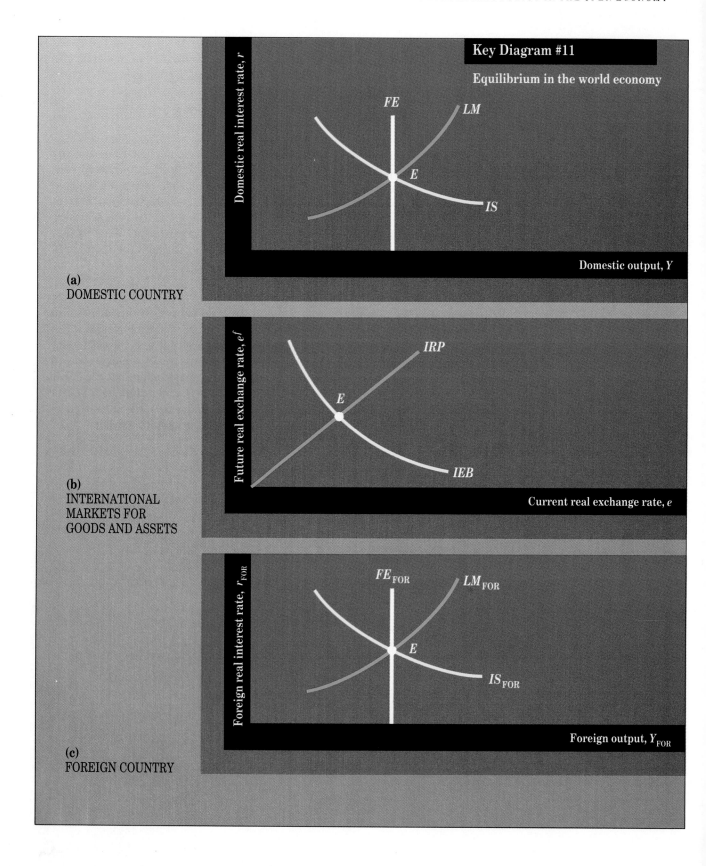

Key Diagram #11

Equilibrium in the world economy

(a)
DOMESTIC COUNTRY

(b)
INTERNATIONAL
MARKETS FOR
GOODS AND ASSETS

(c)
FOREIGN COUNTRY

Macroeconomic equilibrium in the world economy is shown by using three separate diagrams: (a) an *IS-LM* diagram for the domestic economy; (b) an *IEB-IRP* diagram illustrating equilibrium in the international markets for goods and assets; and (c) an *IS-LM* diagram for the foreign economy.

Diagram Elements

- The *IS-LM* diagrams for the domestic and foreign economies (parts a and c) are essentially the same as for closed economies. There is both a classical version of the *IS-LM* model (see Key Diagram #3, p. 146) and a Keynesian version (see Key Diagram #9, p. 486).

- The *IEB-IRP* diagram (part b) depicts equilibrium in the international markets for goods and assets. This diagram has the domestic country's current real exchange rate e on the horizontal axis and the domestic country's future real exchange rate e^f on the vertical axis.

- In the *IEB-IRP* diagram the *IEB* (intertemporal external balance) curve gives combinations of current and future real exchange rates such that any foreign borrowing (negative net exports) or lending (positive net exports) is ultimately repaid. The *IEB* curve slopes downward because an increase in the current real exchange rate reduces current net exports; for future net exports to rise and intertemporal external balance to be restored, the future real exchange rate must fall.

- In the *IEB-IRP* diagram the *IRP* (interest rate parity) line gives combinations of current and future real exchange rates such that the real interest rate parity condition is satisfied, which means that foreign and domestic assets of comparable risk and liquidity have the same real return measured in terms of the domestic good. Given the foreign real interest rate r_{FOR} and the domestic real interest rate r, real interest rate parity implies that the future real exchange rate is proportional to the current real exchange rate. Thus the *IRP* line is a straight line from the origin. The slope of the *IRP* line is $(1 + r_{FOR})/(1 + r)$.

Factors That Shift the Curves

- Factors that shift the *IS* curve, the *LM* curve, or the *FE* line in a closed economy have the same effect in an open economy (see Key Diagram #3, p. 146). In addition, given domestic output and the domestic real interest rate, any factor that increases the domestic country's net exports causes its *IS* curve to shift upward (see Table 13.8, p. 533). Similarly, the foreign *IS* curve shifts upward in response to any factor that increases the foreign country's net exports at given levels of foreign output and the foreign real interest rate.

- Given the current and future real exchange rates, any factor that reduces the domestic country's current and future net exports shifts the *IEB* curve downward (see Table 13.4, p. 515).

(Continued)

- Given the current and future real exchange rates, any factor that increases the domestic real interest rate relative to the foreign real interest rate causes the *IRP* line to rotate downward, or clockwise (Table 13.6, p. 523).

Analysis

- The general equilibrium in the world economy is represented by point *E* in all three diagrams: The intersection of the domestic country's *IS* curve, *LM* curve, and *FE* line in part (a) describes general equilibrium in the domestic economy. The intersection of the *IEB* curve and the *IRP* line in part (b) determines the values of the current and future real exchange rates. Finally, the intersection of the foreign country's *IS* curve, *LM* curve, and *FE* line in part (c) describes the general equilibrium in the foreign economy.

- To analyze any shock that originates in the domestic economy, start with the domestic *IS-LM* diagram and determine the effects of the shock on domestic output *Y* and the domestic real interest rate *r*.

- Next, use the *IEB-IRP* diagram to analyze the effects of the changes in *Y* and *r* on real exchange rates. If domestic output increases, then the *IEB* curve shifts downward in order to restore intertemporal external balance; if domestic output falls, the *IEB* curve shifts upward. If the domestic real interest rate increases, then because domestic assets have become more attractive relative to foreign assets, the *IRP* line rotates downward (clockwise); if the domestic real interest rate falls, the *IRP* line rotates upward. The new equilibrium values of the current and future real exchange rates are given by the intersection of the new *IEB* curve and the new *IRP* line.

- Net exports are increased by a fall in domestic output or a fall in the current real exchange rate, and they are decreased by a rise in output or the current real exchange rate. If output and the real exchange rate work in opposite directions, we normally assume that the output effect is the stronger.

- If net exports by the domestic country increase, then net exports by the foreign country decrease, and the foreign *IS* curve shifts downward. Similarly, a decrease in the home country's net exports raises the foreign country's net exports and shifts the foreign *IS* curve upward. Given the shift in the foreign country's *IS* curve, the effects of the shock on the foreign economy can be determined.

- In the short run in the classical model and in the long run in the Keynesian model, price adjustment returns both economies to full employment. In the long run money is neutral (that is, changes in the money supply have no effects on real variables) in both the classical and Keynesian models. However, changes in the money supply affect price levels and nominal exchange rates in the long run.

Key Terms

devaluation, p. 504
exchange rate, p. 499
fixed exchange rate
    system, p. 500
flexible exchange rate
    system, p. 500
foreign exchange
    market, p. 499
intertemporal external
    balance, p. 512

J curve, p. 508
Marshall-Lerner
    condition, p. 507
nominal appreciation,
    p. 503
nominal depreciation,
    p. 503
nominal exchange rate,
    p. 499

nominal interest rate
    parity condition, p. 520
real appreciation, p. 504
real depreciation, p. 504
real exchange rate,
    p. 502
real interest rate parity
    condition, p. 520
revaluation, p. 504
terms of trade, p. 502

Key Equations

$$e = \frac{e_{\text{nom}}P}{P_{\text{FOR}}} \qquad (13.1)$$

The real exchange rate e, the number of foreign goods that can be obtained in exchange for one domestic good, is defined in terms of the nominal exchange rate e_{nom} (the amount of foreign currency that can be obtained for one unit of domestic currency), the domestic price level P, and the foreign price level P_{FOR}.

$$\frac{\Delta e_{\text{nom}}}{e_{\text{nom}}} = \frac{\Delta e}{e} + \pi_{\text{FOR}} - \pi \qquad (13.3)$$

The percentage change in the nominal exchange rate $\Delta e_{\text{nom}}/e_{\text{nom}}$ equals the percentage change in the real exchange rate $\Delta e/e$ plus the excess of the foreign rate of inflation over the domestic rate of inflation, $\pi_{\text{FOR}} - \pi$.

$$NX = X - \frac{X_{\text{FOR}}}{e} \qquad (13.4)$$

Net exports NX, measured in units of the domestic good, equal exports X minus the real value of imports measured in terms of the domestic good X_{FOR}/e.

$$NX(e, \ldots) + \frac{NX'(e', \ldots)}{1 + r} = 0 \qquad (13.5)$$

The *intertemporal external balance (IEB) condition* requires that countries that have negative net exports and borrow abroad today have positive net exports in the future, so that they can repay their foreign loans.

$$\left(\frac{e}{e'}\right)(1 + r_{\text{FOR}}) = 1 + r \qquad (13.9)$$

The *real interest rate parity (IRP) condition* requires that the real rates of return on domestic and foreign assets of comparable risk and liquidity be equal, when expressed in terms of either the foreign good or the domestic good. The left side of Eq. (13.9) is the real rate of return on a foreign asset measured in terms of the domestic good, and the right side is the real rate of return on a domestic asset.

Review Questions

1. Define *nominal exchange rate* and *real exchange rate*. How are changes in the real exchange rate and the nominal exchange rate related?

2. What are the two major types of exchange rate systems? Currently, which type of system determines the values of the major currencies, such as the dollar, yen, and mark?

3. What is the J curve? What explains the behavior of net exports represented by the J curve?

4. Given the real exchange rate, how are a country's net exports affected by an increase in domestic income? An increase in foreign income? Explain.

5. Why must negative net exports in the present be offset by positive net exports in the future? What does this requirement tell us about the relationship between the current and the future real exchange rates?

6. Suppose that foreign bonds pay a lower nominal interest rate than domestic bonds do, and that foreign and domestic bonds have similar risk and liquidity. Under what circumstances will financial investors prefer to buy the foreign bonds rather than the domestic bonds?

7. Discuss how a country's current real exchange rate is affected by each of the following: an increase in domestic income, an increase in foreign income, a shift in demand toward domestic goods, an increase in the domestic real interest rate, and an increase in the foreign real interest rate. Explain in terms of the supply and demand for the country's currency.

8. How does the *IS-LM* model for an open economy differ from the *IS-LM* model for a closed economy?

9. "U.S. government purchases not only crowd out investment in the United States but also reduce capital formation in other countries." Discuss.

10. What effect does expansionary monetary policy have on the nominal exchange rate in the long run? Explain.

Numerical Problems

1. West Bubble makes ordinary soap bars that are sold for 5 guilders each. East Bubble makes deluxe soap bars that are sold for 100 florins each. The real exchange rate between West and East Bubble is two ordinary soap bars per deluxe soap bar.
   a. What is the nominal exchange rate between the two countries?
   b. West Bubble has 10% domestic inflation, and East Bubble has 20% domestic inflation. Two ordinary soap bars are still traded for a deluxe soap bar. What happens to the nominal exchange rate? Which country has a nominal appreciation? Which has a nominal depreciation?

2. The number of deluxe soap bars that East Bubble can sell to West Bubble is $85 - 3e$, where e is the East Bubble real exchange rate. The number of ordinary soap bars that East Bubble imports is $90 + 12e$.
   a. Give a formula for East Bubble's net exports in terms of e.
   b. Suppose that the real exchange rate is initially $e = 1$. What is the value of East Bubble's net exports?
   c. Now suppose that the real exchange rate appreciates to $e = 5$. What is the value of East Bubble's net exports? Does the Marshall-Lerner condition apply to the change in the real exchange rate from $e = 1$ to $e = 5$?
   d. Now suppose that the real exchange rate appreciates to $e = 10$. What is the value of East Bubble's net exports? Does the Marshall-Lerner condition apply to the change in the real exchange rate from $e = 5$ to $e = 10$?

3. The United States has an inflation rate of 0.05 and a nominal interest rate of 0.10. Germany has an inflation rate of 0.03 and a nominal interest rate of 0.06. Interest rate parity holds.
   a. What is the expected rate of nominal depreciation of the dollar relative to the mark? Use the approximate interest rate parity formula, $i_{\text{FOR}} - \Delta e_{\text{nom}}/e_{\text{nom}} \simeq i$.
   b. What is the expected rate of real depreciation of the dollar relative to the mark?

4. The current yen-dollar exchange rate is 120 yen per dollar. The Japanese nominal interest rate is 10% per year. The dollar is expected to depreciate to 110 yen per dollar over the next year. According to interest rate parity, what interest rate will dollar-denominated assets (of comparable riskiness to the Japanese asset paying 10%) have to pay?

5. The current price of a German mark is 3.0 French francs. You can buy a contract today in the futures market that allows you to buy German marks three months from now for 2.94 francs per mark, payable on delivery in three months. Three-month German Treasury bills currently pay 12% nominal interest on an annual basis. (To find the return over three months, just divide by 4.) French three-month Treasury bills pay 8% nominal interest on an annual basis.

Show that interest rate parity does not hold in this problem. Find a way in which a speculator (who initially holds both German and French Treasury bills) could increase her profits without any risk.

Analytical Problems

1. Starting with the exact nominal interest rate parity condition, Eq. (13.8), derive the exact real interest rate parity condition, Eq. (13.9).

Hint: Use the definition of the real exchange rate in Eq. (13.1). To solve this problem, you need to use the exact (rather than the approximate) definition of a real interest rate, which is

$$1 + r = \frac{1 + i}{1 + \pi}.$$

A similar exact definition holds for the foreign real interest rate.

2. The application at the end of the chapter discussed the idea that the United States became a relatively more attractive place to invest in the early 1980s. Analyze this story by using the classical *IS-LM* model for two countries. Assume that because of more favorable tax laws, the user cost of capital falls in the home country, and that because of the LDC debt crisis, the expected future marginal product of capital falls in the foreign country. Show that these changes lead to an appreciation of the home country's current real exchange rate and a fall in the home country's net exports. What happens to the home country's future real exchange rate and future net exports?

3. East Bubble's main trading partner is West Bubble. In order to fight inflation, West Bubble undertakes a contractionary monetary policy.

   a. What is the effect of West Bubble's contractionary monetary policy on East Bubble's real exchange rate in the short run? In the long run? Use the Keynesian model.

   b. What is the effect of West Bubble's monetary contraction on East Bubble's *nominal* exchange rate in the short run and in the long run?

   c. Suppose that East Bubble has fixed its exchange rate with West Bubble, which means that it is committed to using its monetary policy to avoid any changes in the nominal exchange rate between the two countries. How will East Bubble have to respond to West Bubble's monetary tightening in this case? What will happen to East Bubble's output, real exchange rate, and net exports in the short run? Compare results with those of the case in which East Bubble does not respond to West Bubble's policy change.

4. Recessions often lead to calls for protectionist measures to preserve domestic jobs. This problem asks you to use the Keynesian open economy model with flexible exchange rates to analyze the macroeconomic impact of a decision by the domestic country to impose barriers to imports.

   a. The domestic country imposes restrictions on imports in the current period. These restrictions, which are generally believed to be temporary, have the effect of lowering the domestic country's demand for imports at any given level of domestic output and the real exchange rate. For given values of output and the real interest rate, what effect do these restrictions have on the current and expected future real exchange rates? (Use the *IEB-IRP* diagram.) With output and the real interest rate still held constant, what effects do the restrictions have on current and future net exports by the home country?

   b. Now analyze the effects of the import restriction on the domestic macroeconomy, assuming that the economy is initially in a recession. What effect does the policy have on domestic output, employment, the real interest rate, and the price level? According to the model, does the policy increase economic welfare in the domestic country?

   c. What effect does the import restriction have on the economies of foreign countries (including output, employment, the real interest rate, and the price level)? Assume that the effects of the policy on the domestic country's exchange rate and net exports are as you found in part a of this problem; ignore any partially offsetting feedback effects suggested by part b.

   d. Do you think import restrictions are a useful way of fighting recessions in the real world? Why or why not?

5. A country produces and exports cigarettes. As a result of dissemination of information about the hazards of smoking, both domestic and foreign residents permanently shift their demand away from cigarettes toward the good produced by the foreign country. What effects will this demand shift have on the current and future real exchange rates and on current and future net exports? Using the Keynesian model, find the effects of the demand shift on output and the real interest rate in the home country and in the foreign country. State any additional assumptions that you make.

MACROECONOMIC POLICY:
A DEEPER LOOK

14
Unemployment and Inflation

One of the most important goals of macroeconomics is to better understand how macroeconomic policy works and how it can best be used. Throughout this book we have analyzed how different policies affect the economy and discussed the policy implications of alternative theories. In this last part of the book we focus even more intensively on policy-related topics, including policymaking institutions, the trade-offs that policymakers face, and current debates about how policy should be used. We begin in this chapter by discussing unemployment and inflation, two of the most serious macroeconomic problems confronting policymakers. The next two chapters, Chapters 15 and 16, take closer looks at monetary and fiscal institutions and policy. Finally, Chapter 17 discusses the interactions of macroeconomic policy and the financial system.

Why do we study unemployment and inflation together in this chapter? As we have already suggested, these two problems are among the most difficult and politically sensitive issues that policymakers must deal with. High rates of unemployment and inflation generate public outcry because their effects are direct, visible, and immediate: Almost everyone is affected by rising prices, and few workers can be confident that they will never lose their jobs.

Another reason to study unemployment and inflation together is that there is a long-standing idea in macroeconomics that these two problems are somehow related. In a famous 1958 article A. W. Phillips examined 97 years of British unemployment and inflation data[1] and found that unemployment tended to be low when inflation was high, and high when inflation was low. This finding of a negative relationship between unemployment and inflation, now known as the Phillips

---

[1] More precisely, he studied unemployment and the rate of nominal wage inflation. See A. W. Phillips, "The Relation Between Unemployment and the Rate of Change of Money Wage Rates in the United Kingdom, 1861–1957," *Economica*, November 1958, pp. 283–299.

curve, had a major impact on the economics profession and on macroeconomic policy in the years following the publication of Phillips's article.

Initially, the Phillips curve seemed to offer policymakers a trade-off between inflation and unemployment. Many economists believed that by choosing more inflation, policymakers could help the economy achieve a lower unemployment rate. During the 1960s in the United States, the unemployment rate fell steadily and the rate of inflation rose, just as one might have guessed from the empirical relation reported by Phillips. However, in the 1970s the relation between inflation and unemployment seemed to go haywire. Instead of having low inflation when unemployment was high, the economy experienced stagflation—high inflation together with high unemployment. By 1975 unemployment had reached 8.5% of the labor force, and the annual rate of inflation was 9.1%. Although the occurrence of high unemployment together with high inflation had been foreseen by some economists, the experience of the 1970s led to major changes in macroeconomics in general[2] and to a revised interpretation of the empirical relation between inflation and unemployment.

In this chapter we study the relationship between inflation and unemployment, why it appears to have changed over time, and whether indeed policymakers face a trade-off between inflation and unemployment. To the extent that a trade-off exists, the combination of inflation and unemployment that is best for an economy depends on the relative costs of these two macroeconomic problems. In the latter part of the chapter we examine the costs of inflation and unemployment and consider the implications for macroeconomic policymaking.

14.1   UNEMPLOYMENT AND INFLATION: IS THERE A TRADE-OFF?

Does the negative relationship between inflation and unemployment reported by A. W. Phillips offer a trade-off between unemployment and inflation? To answer this question, we need to understand why such a relationship might be observed.

There are two links in the chain between unemployment and inflation. First, unemployment is linked to the level of output according to a relationship known as Okun's law. Second, the level of output is related to the rate of inflation via the price adjustment process. We discuss each of these links separately and then combine them to see how they account for the observed relationship between inflation and unemployment.

Okun's Law

How are unemployment and output related to each other over the course of the business cycle? A *qualitative* answer to this question is provided by the business cycle fact, discussed in Chapter 9, that the unemployment rate is countercyclical, rising when output is falling and falling when output is rising. A *quantitative* answer to this question is provided by Okun's law, a rule of thumb that tells how much output falls when the unemployment rate rises.

Okun's law makes use of a concept called the **natural rate of unemployment,** which is the rate of unemployment that exists when the economy's output Y is at

---

[2]We discussed some of these changes in Chapter 9, Section 9.4.

its full-employment level $\bar{Y}$. We let $\bar{u}$ stand for the natural rate of unemployment. When the economy is at full employment, with the actual unemployment rate equal to the natural rate, the people who are unemployed are without jobs because of frictional unemployment and structural unemployment. Recall from Chapter 10 that frictional unemployment arises as workers and firms search for suitable matches, whereas structural unemployment results from an imbalance between the skills, training, and locations of workers and the requirements of available jobs.

Using the concept of the natural rate of unemployment, we can express the quantitative relationship between unemployment and output as follows:

$$\frac{\bar{Y} - Y}{\bar{Y}} = 2.5(u - \bar{u}). \tag{14.1}$$

Equation (14.1) is Okun's law, first stated by Arthur Okun, chairman of the Council of Economic Advisers during the Johnson administration. The left side of this equation equals the amount by which actual output Y falls short of full-employment output $\bar{Y}$, expressed as a fraction of $\bar{Y}$. Part of the expression on the right side of Eq. (14.1) is **cyclical unemployment**, $u - \bar{u}$, which is the excess of the actual unemployment rate over the natural rate. Notice that when cyclical unemployment is zero, output equals full-employment output. When the unemployment rate increases, the level of employment falls and (as we would expect from the production function) the amount of output also falls. According to **Okun's law**, the gap between actual output and full-employment output increases by 2.5 percentage points for each percentage point the unemployment rate increases.[3,4]

To see how to apply Okun's law, suppose that the natural rate of unemployment is 6% and the full-employment level of output is $5000 billion. If the actual unemployment rate is 7%, or one percentage point above the natural rate, then cyclical unemployment $u - \bar{u}$ equals 1%. If cyclical unemployment is 1%, Okun's law predicts that actual output Y will be 2.5% (or 2.5 times 1%) lower than full-employment output $\bar{Y}$. Since $\bar{Y}$ equals $5000 billion, Okun's law says that actual output will be $125 billion below the full-employment level (2.5% times $5000 billion).

Sometimes Okun's law is expressed in a slightly different form, as

$$\frac{\Delta Y}{Y} = \frac{\Delta \bar{Y}}{\bar{Y}} - 2.5\Delta u, \tag{14.2}$$

where $\Delta Y/Y$ is the percentage growth rate of output, $\Delta \bar{Y}/\bar{Y}$ is the percentage growth rate of full-employment output, and Δu is the change in the actual unemployment rate from one year to the next. Equation (14.2) says that when unemployment is rising ($\Delta u > 0$), actual output Y is growing more slowly than full-employment output $\bar{Y}$.

The form of Okun's law given in Eq. (14.2), which is based on the assumption that the natural rate $\bar{u}$ is constant,[5] is useful for comparing changes in output and

---

[3]When the unemployment rate increases, for example, from 6% to 9%, we say that it increases by 3 *percentage points* (9% − 6%), or that it increases by 50 *percent* (3% is 50 percent of 6%).

[4]In Okun's original work ("Potential GNP: Its Measurement and Significance," reprinted in Arthur Okun, *The Political Economy of Prosperity*, Washington, D.C.: Brookings Institution, pp. 132–145), the "Okun's law coefficient" was 3.0 rather than 2.5, so that each percentage point of cyclical unemployment was associated with a difference between actual output and full-employment output of 3.0 percentage points. Current estimates put the Okun's law coefficient closer to 2.5.

[5]The Appendix to the chapter derives Eq. (14.2).

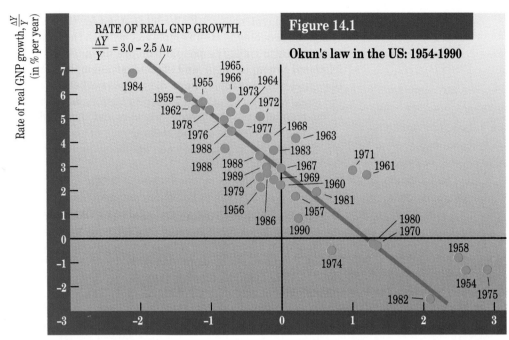

This figure shows the relation between the growth rate of real GNP (vertical axis) and the change in the unemployment rate (horizontal axis). The line in the figure is a graph of Okun's law (Eq. 14.2). The slope of this line is −2.5, indicating that a 1 percentage point increase in the unemployment rate reduces the growth rate of output by 2.5 percentage points. The line's vertical intercept, 3%, is the approximate average growth rate of full-employment output, which equals the rate at which actual output would grow if there were no change in the unemployment rate.

Source: *Economic Report of the President*, February 1991. GNP growth—Table B-2; civilian unemployment rate—Table B-40.

unemployment over time. Figure 14.1 shows the relation between the annual change in the unemployment rate (measured on the horizontal axis) and the annual growth rate of output (measured on the vertical axis) for the period 1954–1990 in the United States. The solid line in this figure represents Okun's law. Its slope is −2.5, indicating that a 1 percentage point increase in the unemployment rate is associated with a 2.5% fall in output. The vertical intercept of the relationship in Fig. 14.1 is 3%. This intercept tells us that when the change in the unemployment rate is zero, the growth rate of actual output is 3%, which is the approximate average growth rate of full-employment output in the United States.

You may find it puzzling that a 1 percentage point increase in the unemployment rate, which reduces employment by about 1%, leads (according to Okun's law) to a fall in output that is about two and a half times as large in percentage terms. The explanation is that when employment falls in a recession, other factors determining output—such as the number of hours each worker works per week and the average productivity of labor—also fall. These factors and their relation to Okun's law are discussed in more detail in the Appendix to this chapter.

Price Adjustment and the Level of Output

The second link in the chain relating unemployment and inflation is the link between the level of output—more accurately, the difference between actual output

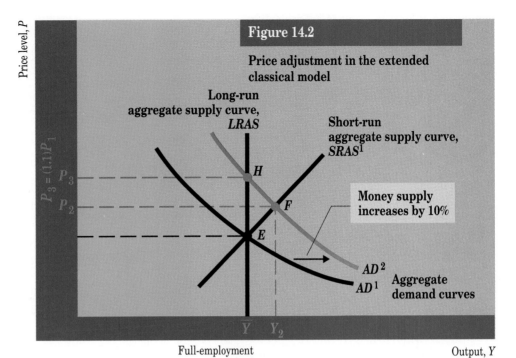

Figure 14.2

Price adjustment in the extended classical model

Periods in which output exceeds full-employment output will also be periods in which prices are rising. If we start from the initial full-employment equilibrium at point E, an unanticipated 10% increase in the money supply shifts the AD curve upward by 10%, from AD^1 to AD^2. In the short run the increase in aggregate demand raises output to Y_2 and the price level to P_2. When producers learn the true price level, the economy moves to the long-run equilibrium at point H. At point H output has returned to its full-employment level, and the price level P_3, which is 10% above its initial level P_1, stops rising.

and full-employment output—and price adjustment. In Chapters 11 and 12 we studied the determination of output and the price level by using the aggregate demand (AD) and aggregate supply (AS) curves. We review this analysis here, focusing on how inflation is related to the difference between actual output and full-employment output.

Price Adjustment in the Extended Classical Model To illustrate the relationship between price adjustment and the level of output, Fig. 14.2 shows the effects of an unanticipated increase in the money supply in the extended classical model. The extended classical model, recall, incorporates the misperceptions theory, which says that unexpected changes in the price level fool producers into supplying a level of output different from the full-employment level. In Fig. 14.2 the economy is initially at the full-employment equilibrium at point E. We assume that the money supply increases unexpectedly by 10%, shifting the aggregate demand curve upward from AD^1 to AD^2. The new short-run equilibrium is at point F in Fig. 14.2, where AD^2 intersects the initial short-run aggregate supply curve, $SRAS^1$. At point F the increase in the money supply has raised output to Y_2 and also increased the price level to P_2. Thus in the short run the economy experiences both output above the full-employment level and inflation (an increase in the price level).

According to the classical analysis, the economy does not remain very long at

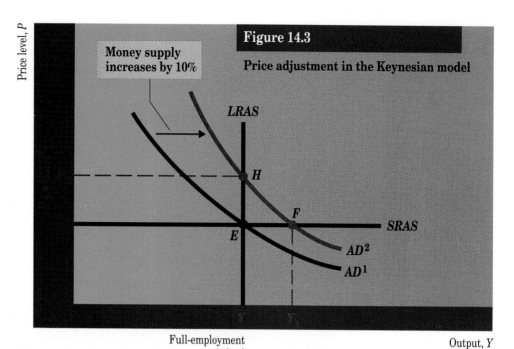

Figure 14.3

Price adjustment in the Keynesian model

As in the extended classical model, in the Keynesian model an increase in aggregate demand leads both to output above the full-employment level and rising prices. If we start from the initial full-employment equilibrium at point E, an unanticipated 10% increase in the money supply shifts the AD curve upward by 10%, from AD^1 to AD^2. At the short-run equilibrium, point F, firms raise their output to Y_1 in order to meet the demand at the initial price level P_1. Eventually, in response to aggregate demand greater than full-employment output, firms raise their prices. The economy experiences both inflation and output above full-employment output until the economy returns to the full-employment equilibrium at point H. At point H output again equals $\bar{Y}$, and prices stop rising. At point H, the price level P_2 equals 1.1 times P_1.

the short-run equilibrium represented by point F. Over time, producers learn the true price level and adjust their price level expectations, which moves the economy to its long-run equilibrium at point H in Fig. 14.2. At point H output is at its full-employment level, and the price level P_3 is 10% higher than the initial price level P_1. When the new full-employment equilibrium is reached, the rate of inflation is once again zero, and output equals its full-employment level $\bar{Y}$.

This analysis illustrates that an expansion in aggregate demand (in this case, an unanticipated increase in the money supply) leads the economy to experience a period in which output is above full-employment output $\bar{Y}$ and prices are rising. A similar analysis shows that in response to a fall in aggregate demand the economy experiences both output below $\bar{Y}$ and falling prices. This positive relationship between the change in the price level and the level of output is the second link in the chain between inflation and unemployment.

Price Adjustment in the Keynesian Model   Figure 14.2 showed the price adjustment process in the extended classical model. Price adjustment in the Keynesian model is similar, except that the price level is sticky in the Keynesian model and thus does not change in the short run. However, the subsequent price adjustment process in the Keynesian model is much like that of the extended classical model.

Figure 14.3 illustrates price adjustment in the Keynesian model. Again we assume that the economy, initially at full employment at point E, experiences an unanticipated 10% increase in the money supply. The increase in the money supply raises the aggregate demand for output at the initial price level P_1 and shifts the AD curve upward and to the right, from AD^1 to AD^2. Output rises to Y_1 in the short run (point F), as firms meet the higher demand at the unchanged price level. Although in the Keynesian model there is no immediate change in the price level, the increase in aggregate demand puts upward pressure on prices; and when firms reconsider their prices, they will raise them. Thus, as in the classical model, the economy experiences a period in which output is above $\bar{Y}$ and prices are rising. Prices stop rising only when the economy has returned to full employment, at point H in Fig. 14.3.

The Simple Phillips Curve

Now we are ready to put together the two links in the chain between unemployment and inflation. These links are summarized in Table 14.1. The left side of the table shows the link between unemployment and output given by Okun's law: When the unemployment rate u equals the natural unemployment rate $\bar{u}$, actual output Y and full-employment output $\bar{Y}$ are equal. When the unemployment rate is above the natural rate $\bar{u}$, output is less than $\bar{Y}$; and when the unemployment rate is below the natural rate, output is greater than $\bar{Y}$. The right side of the table shows the link between output and inflation that arises from price adjustment in the classical and Keynesian models. When $Y = \bar{Y}$, the rate of inflation is zero (prices do not change); when $Y < \bar{Y}$, the rate of inflation is negative; and when $Y > \bar{Y}$, the rate of inflation is positive. Putting together both links gives a negative relationship between unemployment in the first column and inflation in the third column. We can represent this negative relationship between inflation π and unemployment u algebraically as

$$\pi = -h(u - \bar{u}). \tag{14.3}$$

In Eq. (14.3) the slope coefficient h is a positive number that measures the strength of the relationship between inflation and the deviation of unemployment from the natural rate. Equation (14.3) is called the simple Phillips curve. According to the **simple Phillips curve**, inflation is positive when unemployment is below the natural rate and is negative when unemployment is above the natural rate.

Table 14.1 The Simple Phillips Curve: The Link Between Unemployment and Inflation

Okun's Law Links Unemployment and Output			Price Adjustment Links Output and Inflation	
$u = \bar{u}$	$\longleftrightarrow$	$Y = \bar{Y}$	$\longleftrightarrow$	$\pi = 0$
$u > \bar{u}$	$\longleftrightarrow$	$Y < \bar{Y}$	$\longleftrightarrow$	$\pi < 0$
$u < \bar{u}$	$\longleftrightarrow$	$Y > \bar{Y}$	$\longleftrightarrow$	$\pi > 0$

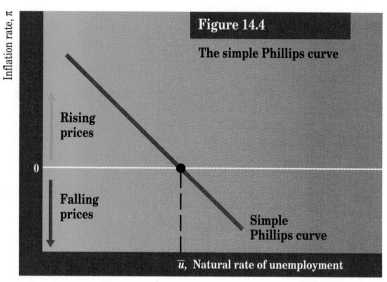

When the unemployment rate u equals the natural unemployment rate $\bar{u}$, the rate of inflation π is zero; so the simple Phillips curve crosses the horizontal axis at the natural rate of unemployment. The downward slope of the simple Phillips curve indicates that inflation falls as the unemployment rate increases. Notice that when the unemployment rate is higher than the natural rate, the simple Phillips curve implies that the rate of inflation is negative.

The simple Phillips curve is graphed in Fig. 14.4, which has the unemployment rate on the horizontal axis and the rate of inflation on the vertical axis. As implied by Eq. (14.3), the simple Phillips curve slopes downward from left to right, indicating that higher unemployment is associated with lower inflation. The simple Phillips curve crosses the horizontal axis at $u = \bar{u}$, because (as you can see from Eq. 14.3) the rate of inflation is zero when the unemployment rate equals the natural rate.

The Simple Phillips Curve in Practice

For about a dozen years after the publication of Phillips's article in 1958, the simple Phillips curve appeared to be a stable and reliable relationship. This stability is illustrated in Fig. 14.5, which shows the rates of unemployment and inflation in the United States during the 1960s. The U.S. economy expanded throughout most of the 1960s, with the unemployment rate falling and inflation rising steadily. The combination of rising inflation and falling unemployment was consistent with a stable trade-off between inflation and unemployment, and it appeared that the United States had chosen to accept higher inflation as the price of having a low unemployment rate.

Although unemployment and inflation during the 1960s seemed to conform to the simple Phillips curve, there was one important difference between actual behavior and the behavior predicted by the simple Phillips curve. Recall that the simple Phillips curve predicts not only that there will be a downward-sloping relationship between inflation and unemployment but also that inflation will be negative when the unemployment rate is higher than the natural rate. During 1961, for example, the unemployment rate was 6.7%, which was higher than the esti-

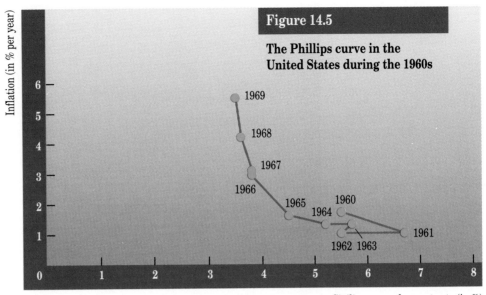

Figure 14.5

The Phillips curve in the United States during the 1960s

During the 1960s U.S. rates of inflation and unemployment seemed to lie along a simple Phillips curve. Inflation rose and unemployment fell fairly steadily during this decade, and it appeared that policymakers had chosen to live with higher inflation in order to reduce the unemployment rate.

Source: *Economic Report of the President*, February 1991: CPI inflation rate, year to year—Table B-62; civilian unemployment rate—Table B-40.

mated natural rate of 5.2%, yet the rate of inflation was positive. The simple Phillips curve cannot account for the simultaneous existence of positive inflation and an unemployment rate above the natural rate. However, an extension of the simple Phillips curve, known as the expectations-augmented Phillips curve, can explain this puzzle as well as several other problems with the simple Phillips curve that soon arose, as we see in the next section.

14.2   THE EXPECTATIONS-AUGMENTED PHILLIPS CURVE

The simple Phillips curve seemed to provide an adequate description of the relationship between unemployment and inflation in the United States during the 1960s, except for the fact that inflation was positive while the unemployment rate was higher than the natural rate during the early 1960s. However, during the second half of the 1960s a few economists, notably Milton Friedman[6] of the University of Chicago and Edmund Phelps[7] of Columbia University, questioned the logic of the simple Phillips curve. Friedman and Phelps argued that according to economic theory, the unemployment rate should be negatively associated only with *unanticipated* inflation, not with the overall rate of inflation as implied by the simple Phillips curve. As we will see, this modification of the simple Phillips curve has three important implications. First, this modification can account for

---

[6]"The Role of Monetary Policy," *American Economic Review*, March 1968, pp. 1–17.

[7]"Money Wage Dynamics and Labor Market Equilibrium," in Edmund Phelps, ed., *Microeconomic Foundations of Employment and Inflation Theory*, New York: W.W. Norton, 1970, pp. 124–166.

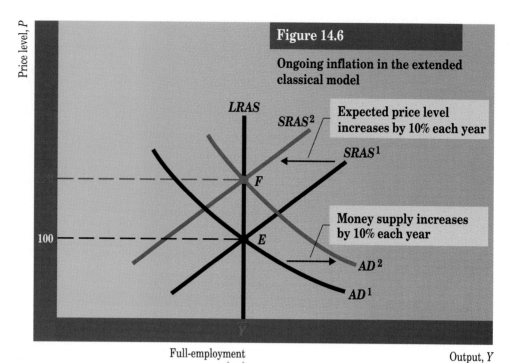

Figure 14.6

Ongoing inflation in the extended classical model

If the money supply grows by 10% every year, the *AD* curve shifts upward by 10% every year, from *AD*¹ in year 1 to *AD*² in year 2, and so on. If the money supply has been growing by 10% per year for some time and the rate of inflation has been 10% for some time, then the expected rate of inflation is also 10%. Thus the expected price level also grows by 10% each year, from 100 in year 1 to 110 in year 2, and so on. The 10% annual increase in the expected price level shifts the *SRAS* curve upward by 10% each year—for example, from *SRAS*¹ in year 1 to *SRAS*² in year 2. The economy remains in full-employment equilibrium at the intersection of the *AD* curve and the *SRAS* curve in each year (point *E* in year 1, point *F* in year 2), with output equal to $\bar{Y}$ and inflation and expected inflation both equal to 10% per year.

stagflation, the simultaneous existence of high inflation and high unemployment. Second, it implies that the simple Phillips curve relating unemployment and inflation is not a stable relation but may change over time. Third, it implies that the Phillips curve does not offer policymakers a usable trade-off between inflation and unemployment, except possibly in the very short run.

To study the importance of unexpected inflation, we use the extended classical model to examine an economy with ongoing inflation. (A similar analysis can be performed using the Keynesian model.) We consider an economy in full-employment equilibrium in which the money supply has been growing at 10% per year for many years and is expected to continue to grow at this rate indefinitely (Fig. 14.6). With the money supply growing by 10% per year, the aggregate demand curve in Fig. 14.6 shifts upward by 10% each year, moving from *AD*¹ in year 1 to *AD*² in year 2, and so on.

In Fig. 14.6 the short-run aggregate supply (*SRAS*) curve also shifts upward by 10% each year. Why? Since the growth in money is fully anticipated, there are no misperceptions. Instead, people expect the price level to rise by 10% per year, which in turn causes the *SRAS* curve to shift upward by 10% per year. With no misperceptions the economy remains at full employment. For example, when the expected price level equals 100 in year 1, the *SRAS* curve is *SRAS*¹. At point *E*

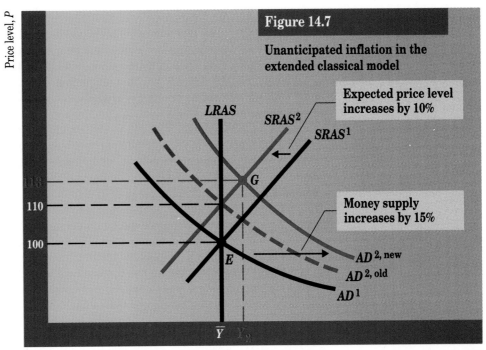

Figure 14.7

Unanticipated inflation in the extended classical model

If the money supply has been growing by 10% per year for a long time and is expected to continue growing by 10%, the expected price level increases by 10% each year. The 10% increase in the expected price level shifts the *SRAS* curve upward, from *SRAS*¹ in year 1 to *SRAS*² in year 2. If the money supply then actually increases by 15% in year 2 rather than by the expected 10%, the *AD* curve is represented by *AD*^(2,new) rather than by *AD*^(2,old). As a result of money growth being higher than expected, output increases above $\bar{Y}$ to Y_2 in year 2, and the price level increases to 113, as shown by point *G*. Because the price level rises by 13% rather than by the expected 10%, there is 3% unanticipated inflation in year 2. This unanticipated inflation is associated with output higher than $\bar{Y}$.

the price level is 100 (the same as the expected price level), and output equals $\bar{Y}$. In year 2 the expected price level is 110, and the *SRAS* curve is *SRAS*². Now the equilibrium is located at point *F*, again with output equal to $\bar{Y}$ and with the expected and actual price levels equal to each other. Each year, both the *AD* curve and the *SRAS* curve shift upward by 10%, increasing the actual price level and expected price level by 10% and maintaining output at its full-employment level.

Against this backdrop of 10% monetary growth and 10% inflation, suppose that the money supply increases by 15% in year 2 rather than by the expected 10% (Fig. 14.7). In this case, instead of being 10% higher than *AD*¹ (as shown by the curve *AD*^(2,old)), the aggregate demand curve in year 2 will be 15% higher than *AD*¹ (as shown by *AD*^(2,new)). If this increase in the rate of monetary growth is *unanticipated* as of the beginning of year 2, then the expected price level in year 2 remains 110, and the short-run aggregate supply curve is *SRAS*². The short-run equilibrium in year 2 is represented by point *G*, the intersection of *AD*^(2,new) and *SRAS*². At point *G* output is higher than the full-employment level $\bar{Y}$, and the price level is 113. Thus the actual rate of inflation in year 2 is 13%. Because the expected rate of inflation was 10%, the 13% inflation rate means that there is unanticipated inflation of 3% in year 2.

In the long run producers learn the true price level, the economy returns to full employment, and the rate of inflation again equals the expected rate of inflation, as in Fig. 14.6. In the meantime, however, as long as actual output is higher than full-employment output $\bar{Y}$, the price level must be higher than the expected price level. Indeed, according to the misperceptions theory, output can be higher than $\bar{Y}$ *only* when prices are higher than expected (and therefore when inflation is also higher than expected).

Table 14.2 shows the links in the chain that relate the unemployment rate to unanticipated inflation. The left side of the table shows the Okun's law relationship between unemployment and output, as in Table 14.1. The right side of the table shows the link between output and inflation: When output Y equals full-employment output $\bar{Y}$, the price level equals the price level that was expected and thus the inflation rate π equals the expected inflation rate π^e. When $Y < \bar{Y}$, the price level turns out to be less than expected, and so the inflation rate turns out to be less than was expected. Similarly, when $Y > \bar{Y}$, the price level and the inflation rate are higher than was expected. Putting these links together, we see that an unemployment rate lower than the natural rate is associated with an inflation rate that is higher than what was expected; and unemployment higher than the natural rate implies an inflation rate lower than what was expected. Only when unemployment equals the natural rate is the rate of inflation equal to the rate that was expected.

The relation between unemployment and inflation summarized in Table 14.2 is captured by

$$\pi = \pi^e - h(u - \bar{u}), \qquad (14.4)$$

where π^e is the expected rate of inflation, and h is again a positive number that measures the slope of the Phillips curve. Equation (14.4) is called the **expectations-augmented Phillips curve** because it is the simple Phillips curve with the expected rate of inflation added. Notice that when $\pi^e = 0$, the expectations-augmented Phillips curve of Eq. (14.4) is the same as the simple Phillips curve of Eq. (14.3).

The Short-Run Phillips Curve

Changes in the actual rate of inflation eventually cause the expected rate of inflation to change. But in the short run the expected rate of inflation remains fixed until people receive new information about inflation. The **short-run Phillips curve** shows the relation between inflation and unemployment that holds for a *given expected rate of inflation*. Holding the expected rate of inflation constant in the expectations-augmented Phillips curve equation (Eq. 14.4), we see that according to

Table 14.2 The Expectations-Augmented Phillips Curve

	Okun's Law Links Unemployment and Output			Price Adjustment Links Output and Unanticipated Inflation	
$u = \bar{u}$	$\longleftrightarrow$	$Y = \bar{Y}$	$\longleftrightarrow$	$\pi = \pi^e$
$u > \bar{u}$	$\longleftrightarrow$	$Y < \bar{Y}$	$\longleftrightarrow$	$\pi < \pi^e$
$u < \bar{u}$	$\longleftrightarrow$	$Y > \bar{Y}$	$\longleftrightarrow$	$\pi > \pi^e$

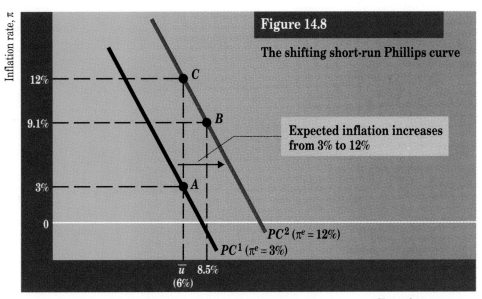

Figure 14.8

The shifting short-run Phillips curve

Expected inflation increases from 3% to 12%

$PC^2\ (\pi^e = 12\%)$

$PC^1\ (\pi^e = 3\%)$

Inflation rate, π

Unemployment rate, u

For every expected rate of inflation there is a different short-run Phillips curve. For example, PC^1 is the short-run Phillips curve when the expected rate of inflation is 3%. To see that the expected rate of inflation is 3% on PC^1, note from Eq. (14.4) that when the unemployment rate equals the natural rate $\bar{u}$, the inflation rate equals the expected rate of inflation. At point A the unemployment rate equals the natural rate and the rate of inflation equals 3% on PC^1, so the expected rate of inflation is 3% on PC^1. Similarly, the expected rate of inflation is 12% along PC^2. An increase in the expected rate of inflation shifts the short-run Phillips curve upward and to the right and can lead to both high inflation and high unemployment. For instance, at point B on PC^2 the unemployment rate is 8.5% and the inflation rate is 9.1%, the actual figures for the United States when the country experienced stagflation in 1975.

the short-run Phillips curve, an increase in the unemployment rate is associated with a decrease in the rate of inflation. The simple Phillips curve of Eq. (14.3) is an example of a short-run Phillips curve in which the constant expected rate of inflation equals zero.

Figure 14.8 shows the short-run Phillips curves corresponding to different expected rates of inflation. The curve labeled PC^1 is the short-run Phillips curve when the expected rate of inflation is 3%. How do we know that the expected rate of inflation is 3% along PC^1? Equation (14.4) tells us that when the unemployment rate equals the natural rate, the rate of inflation equals the expected rate of inflation. Thus to determine the expected rate of inflation on any given short-run Phillips curve, we find the rate of inflation at the point where the unemployment rate equals the natural rate. For instance, at point A on curve PC^1 the unemployment rate equals the natural rate, and the actual and expected rates of inflation both equal 3%. As long as the expected rate of inflation remains at 3%, the short-run Phillips curve PC^1 will describe the relationship between actual inflation and unemployment.

Now suppose that the expected rate of inflation increases from 3% to 12%. This 9 percentage point increase in the expected rate of inflation shifts the short-

The short-run Phillips curve, which was stable during the 1960s, proved to be very unstable during the 1970s and 1980s as expected inflation changed a number of times. However, the inflation and unemployment data for 1976–1979, 1980–1983, and 1986–1989 each appear to lie along a different short-run Phillips curve.

Source: *Economic Report of the President,* February 1991: CPI inflation rate, year to year—Table B-62; civilian unemployment rate—Table B-40.

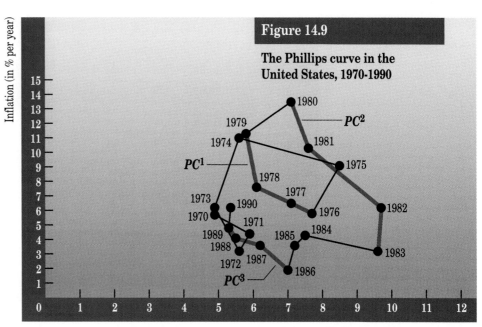

Figure 14.9

The Phillips curve in the United States, 1970-1990

Civilian unemployment rate (in %)

run Phillips curve upward by 9 percentage points at each level of the unemployment rate. The new short-run Phillips curve is PC^2 in Fig. 14.8. When the unemployment rate equals the natural rate on PC^2 (point C), the rate of inflation is 12% rather than 3% as on PC^1.

The shift of the short-run Phillips curve from PC^1 to PC^2 when the expected rate of inflation increases confirms the point made by Friedman and Phelps that the short-run Phillips curve does not represent a stable relationship between inflation and unemployment. Instead, the relationship between actual inflation and unemployment will shift over time as expected inflation changes. The short-run Phillips curve PC^2 also illustrates how inflation can be high even when the unemployment rate is higher than the natural rate. For instance, at point B on PC^2 the inflation rate is 9.1% and the unemployment rate is 8.5%, higher than the natural unemployment rate of 6%. Inflation of 9.1%, unemployment of 8.5%, and an estimated natural rate of 6% correspond to the actual situation in the American economy in 1975, a year in which the United States experienced stagflation. Thus stagflation is consistent with a short-run Phillips curve, like PC^2, for which expected inflation is high.

The instability of the actual short-run Phillips curve in the United States is illustrated in Fig. 14.9, which shows actual inflation and unemployment rates in the United States during the period 1970–1990. You can see that the apparently stable relationship of inflation and unemployment observed in the 1960s (Fig. 14.5) broke down in the two decades that followed, as changes in expected inflation caused the short-run Phillips curve to shift. Even though there is no stable relationship between inflation and unemployment in the U.S. data, a few short-run Phillips curves can be seen in Fig. 14.9. For example, the unemployment-inflation combinations for 1976–1979 seem to lie along one short-run Phillips curve (PC^1), the unemployment-inflation combinations for 1980–1983 sketch out a second Phillips curve (PC^2), and the unemployment-inflation combinations for 1986–1989 appear to lie along yet another short-run Phillips curve (PC^3). As we have seen, short-run Phillips curves are shifted by changes in expected inflation. So, for example, the downward shift of the short-run Phillips curve between the early 1980s and the late 1980s presumably reflected a fall in expected inflation over the decade. An application later in this section discusses why expected inflation changed over this period.

The Elusive Trade-Off Between Inflation and Unemployment

Does the short-run Phillips curve offer an exploitable trade-off between inflation and unemployment, one that can be used by policymakers to choose a relatively attractive combination of inflation and unemployment? For example, can policymakers choose to reduce the unemployment rate by increasing the rate of inflation, thus moving upward and to the left along the short-run Phillips curve?

According to the expectations-augmented Phillips curve, unemployment will fall below the natural rate only when there is unanticipated inflation. Classical economists argue that people quickly learn the true price level and thus the true inflation rate. When the expected inflation rate is adjusted to equal the actual inflation rate, the unemployment rate returns to the natural rate. Thus, according to classicals, policymakers cannot reduce the unemployment rate by increasing the rate of inflation, except perhaps for a very short period of time.

Classical economists also emphasize the importance of rational expectations (introduced in Chapter 11). If workers, consumers, and firms have rational expectations, they will eventually understand the pattern of behavior by policymakers (such as the Fed), and they will anticipate changes in policy. If the public correctly anticipates changes in policy, then these policy changes will not affect unemployment. Although the expectations of changes of policy will not always be right, they will be right on average, so that unanticipated inflation will be zero on average. Thus unanticipated inflation cannot be systematically created. Because any attempt to systematically affect the unemployment rate will be thwarted by the adjustment of inflation expectations, classicals conclude that the Phillips curve does not represent a usable trade-off for policymakers.

In contrast to classicals, Keynesian economists argue that the short-run Phillips curve can be exploited *temporarily* by policymakers to reduce the unemployment rate. Although many Keynesians accept the notion that people have rational expectations, they argue that the expected rate of inflation that should be included in the Phillips curve is the forecast of inflation that was made at the time that the oldest sticky prices in the economy were set. Thus if policymakers cause inflation to rise above the level that had been predicted, it takes a while for new prices to be set that incorporate the new information about the rate of inflation. In the meantime some prices in the economy are set based on older information, and the rate of inflation is higher than the expected inflation rate based on this older information. In response to increased inflation, therefore, unemployment may remain below the natural rate for a while.

Since, at best, the short-run Phillips curve can be exploited only temporarily, why would policymakers ever attempt to reduce unemployment by creating surprise inflation? One possibility is that stimulating the economy may help the incumbent political party win elections; see "The Political Environment" box, p. 568.

The Political Environment

★ ★

Presidential Elections and Macroeconomic Policy

Among the many issues affecting presidential elections in the United States, macroeconomic policy and performance are invariably among the most important. In a statistical study of presidential elections from 1916 to 1976, Ray Fair* of Yale University found that the state of the economy had a significant impact on election outcomes. In particular, he found that a declining unemployment rate and a strong growth of GNP per person during the year of the election significantly increase the reelection chances of the incumbent President or the candidate of the incumbent President's party.

According to the theory of "political business cycles" introduced by another Yale economist, William Nordhaus,† incumbent Presidents use expansionary monetary and fiscal policies to stimulate the economy during election years. The idea is to

create a temporary fall in the unemployment rate and rise in output which, according to Fair's results, increases the President's chances for reelection. There is at least anecdotal evidence to support this theory: For example, many observers claimed that President Nixon used expansionary monetary and fiscal policies to enhance his reelection prospects in 1972.‡

Despite this anecdotal evidence, this version of the political business cycle theory is not strongly supported by the data. An important problem with this theory is that it assumes that incumbents are motivated only by the prospects of reelection, which ignores the possibility that politicians have other goals such as promoting policies that they favor. For example, an implication of the political business cycle theory is that the political party to which the President belongs should not matter

for the performance of the economy, since the President will simply do what is needed to gain reelection no matter which party he belongs to. However, as shown by the overall averages in the accompanying table, economic performance under Republicans and Democrats is not the same: Unemployment falls by more and output expands by more during Democratic administrations than during Republican administrations, but inflation performance is better under Republicans.

To explain the different macroeconomic behavior during Democratic and Republican administrations, Douglas Hibbs** of Harvard University proposed a "partisan theory" of macroeconomic policy in which Democrats are assumed to care relatively more about unemployment and relatively less about inflation than Republicans do. The partisan theory accounts for the fact that unemploy-

ment is more likely to fall and inflation is more likely to rise during Democratic administrations than during Republican administrations. The partisan theory also has a problem, however: It assumes the existence of a simple Phillips curve that gives policymakers a stable trade-off between inflation and unemployment. However, as we have seen, changes in the expected rate of inflation shift the short-run Phillips curve so that poli-

*"The Effects of Economic Events on Votes for President," *The Review of Economics and Statistics,* May 1978, pp. 159–172.
†For an up-to-date survey, see William Nordhaus, "Alternative Approaches to the Political Business Cycle," *Brookings Papers on Economic Activity,* 1989:2, pp. 1–49.
‡*Ibid.,* pp. 43–45.
**"Political Parties and Macroeconomic Policy," *American Political Science Review,* December 1977, pp. 1467–1487.

Macroeconomic Performance in Democratic and Republication Administrations

Time Period	Change in Unemployment Rate		Change in Real Output		Change in Inflation	
	Democrats	Republicans	Democrats	Republicans	Democrats	Republicans
First two years of term	−0.2%	+0.7%	+4.8%	+1.3%	−0.5%	0.0%
Last two years of term	−0.2%	−0.3%	+4.1%	+3.8%	+1.0%	−0.6%
Overall average	−0.2%	+0.2%	+4.4%	+2.6%	+0.3%	−0.3%

Sources: *Economic Report of the President,* 1990; Unemployment rate is civilian unemployment rate—Table C-39; real output is real GNP—Table C-2; inflation rate is the CPI, all items, year to year—Table C-62. Democratic terms: Truman (1949–1952), Kennedy-Johnson (1961–1964), Johnson (1965–1968), and Carter (1977–1980); Republican terms: Eisenhower I (1953–1956), Eisenhower II (1957–1960), Nixon I (1969–1972), Nixon-Ford (1973–1976), Reagan I (1981–1984), and Reagan II (1985–1988). Overall average may differ from average of first two years and last two years owing to rounding.

cymakers do not face a stable trade-off between inflation and unemployment.

Recently, Alberta Alesina[*] of Harvard University has combined the partisan theory with rational expectations and an expectations-augmented Phillips curve to examine the effects of monetary policy in Democratic and Republican administrations. The importance of rational expectations and an expectations-augmented Phillips curve is that only surprises in monetary policy can affect real variables such as output and unemployment. Alesina argues that surprises can occur only at the beginning of an administration: When expectations of future inflation are formed before an election, the outcome of the election is unknown. Therefore the expected rate of inflation is an average of the higher inflation rate that would prevail under a Democratic President and the lower inflation that would occur if a Republican is elected. If a Democrat wins the election, inflation turns out to be higher than expected and unemployment falls; but if a Republican wins, inflation turns out to be lower than expected and unemployment rises. After expectations have completely adjusted to take account of the election outcome, monetary policy does not have systematically different effects for Democrats and Republicans.

The partisan theory with rational expectations and an expectations-augmented Phillips curve has four predictions:

1. Output growth should be higher in the beginning of Democratic administrations (say the first two years) than in the beginning of Republican administrations.

2. The unemployment rate should fall more in the beginning of Democratic administrations than in the beginning of Republican administrations.

3. After expectations have adjusted to the election, say in the last two years of a presidential term, there should be no systematic difference in output growth or unemployment between Democratic and Republican administrations.

4. The rate of inflation should increase more during Democratic administrations than during Republican administrations.

All four of these predictions are borne out in the accompanying table.[†]

[*]"Macroeconomics and Politics," in Stanley Fischer, ed., *NBER Macroeconomics Annual,* Cambridge, Mass.: M.I.T. Press, 1988.
[†]Inflation grows more during Democratic administrations than during Republican administrations, but it grows less during the first two years of Democratic administrations than during the first two years of Republican administrations. The inflation rate fell by more than 9 percentage points in the first year of the Truman administration. Excluding the Truman administration, the inflation rate grew by an average of 0.5% per year during the first two years and by 1.3% per year during the last two years of Democratic administrations.

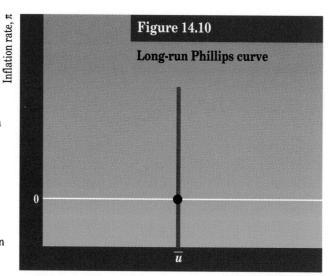

Because people will not permanently overestimate or underestimate the rate of inflation, in the long run the expected rate of inflation and the actual rate of inflation are equal, and the unemployment rate equals the natural rate. Since in the long run the unemployment rate equals the natural rate, regardless of what inflation is, the long-run Phillips curve is vertical.

Figure 14.10

Long-run Phillips curve

Inflation rate, π

Unemployment rate, u

The Long-Run Phillips Curve

Although classicals and Keynesians disagree about whether the short-run Phillips curve can be exploited to temporarily reduce unemployment, they agree that policymakers cannot keep the unemployment rate *permanently* below the natural rate by *permanently* running a high rate of inflation. Unemployment cannot be kept permanently below the natural rate because expectations about inflation will eventually adjust so that the expected rate of inflation and the actual rate of inflation are equal, $\pi^e = \pi$. The expectations-augmented Phillips curve (Eq. 14.4) implies that when $\pi^e = \pi$, the unemployment u rate equals the natural rate $\bar{u}$. Thus the unemployment rate equals the natural rate in the long run regardless of the rate of inflation that is maintained.

The long-run relationship of unemployment and inflation is captured by the **long-run Phillips curve.** Because in the long run unemployment equals the natural rate no matter what the rate of inflation, the long-run Phillips curve is a vertical line at $u = \bar{u}$, as shown in Fig. 14.10.

The fact that the long-run Phillips curve is vertical is related to the long-run neutrality of money discussed in Chapters 11 and 12. Classicals and Keynesians agree that changes in the money supply will have no long-run effects on real variables, including unemployment. The vertical long-run Phillips curve carries the notion of monetary neutrality one step further. Long-run monetary neutrality means that changes in the *level of the money supply* have no real effects in the long run. The vertical long-run Phillips curve means that changes in the *growth rate of money*, which lead to changes in the rate of inflation, have no real effects in the long run.

Supply Shocks and the Relation Between Inflation and Unemployment

So far we have been concerned with the negative relationship between inflation and unemployment that arises as a result of aggregate demand shocks. To fully understand the relationship between inflation and unemployment, we must also consider the effects of supply shocks. We have already discussed supply shocks in the classical and Keynesian models in Chapters 11 and 12; so rather than repeat those entire analyses, we focus here on the effects that pertain to inflation and unemployment.

Supply Shocks in the Classical Model When we analyzed adverse supply shocks using the basic classical model in Chapter 11, we found that a reduction in productivity reduces the full-employment levels of output and employment and increases the price level. The increase in the price level is, of course, inflation. But what happens to the unemployment rate? In the basic classical IS-LM model output falls after an adverse supply shock only because full-employment output $\bar{Y}$ falls. Because output remains equal to $\bar{Y}$ after a supply shock, the unemployment rate remains equal to the natural rate.

Although the unemployment rate always equals the natural rate in the basic classical model, unemployment can still rise after an adverse supply shock if the supply shock causes the natural rate to rise. Classicals argue that an adverse supply shock will indeed raise the natural rate of unemployment by increasing both frictional unemployment and structural unemployment. According to the classical view, frictional and structural unemployment rise because supply shocks affect the various industries and regions within the country differently, with the demand for labor increasing in some industries and some regions and falling in others. Workers in industries and regions in which labor demand is falling will be induced to search elsewhere for jobs, which raises frictional unemployment. Some of these workers will find that their skills do not match the requirements of industries with growing labor demand; these workers may become chronically unemployed, raising structural unemployment. Thus a supply shock that causes labor to be reallocated among sectors increases the natural rate of unemployment and—since in the basic classical model the actual unemployment rate always equals the natural rate—raises the actual unemployment rate as well.[8] Because an adverse supply shock increases both the rate of inflation and the unemployment rate in the classical model, it shifts the short-run Phillips curve upward and to the right.[9]

Although the actual unemployment rate always equals the natural rate in the basic classical model, in the extended classical model the actual and natural unemployment rates can diverge. This divergence occurs as a result of misperceptions about the aggregate price level arising from aggregate demand shocks. However, an adverse supply shock, such as a change in a firm's productivity or a rise in the price of energy, is usually directly observable by the firm and thus would not give rise to any misperceptions that would cause a deviation from full employment. So even in the extended version of the classical model the unemployment rate and the natural rate move together in response to supply shocks. As in the basic classical model, in the extended classical model a supply shock increases the reallocation of labor among sectors, which increases both the natural rate and the actual unemployment rate.

---

[8]The idea that supply shocks raise unemployment by leading to sectoral reallocation of labor was originated by David Lilien, "Sectoral Shifts and Sectoral Unemployment," *Journal of Political Economy*, August 1982, pp. 777–793.

[9]To be precise, in the classical model an adverse supply shock both increases the natural rate of unemployment and raises expected inflation. Both changes cause the Phillips curve to shift upward and to the right.

Supply Shocks in the Keynesian Model   In the Keynesian model with sticky prices a supply shock can cause the unemployment rate to deviate from the natural rate in the short run. Consider, for example, an oil price shock. As we discussed in Chapter 12, an increase in the price of oil is an adverse supply shock that raises the price level and reduces output in the Keynesian model. Inflation occurs despite menu costs, because firms that use a lot of oil, such as gas stations and airlines, raise their prices, even though other firms do not change prices in the short run.

As we showed in Chapter 12, the increase in the price level reduces the real money supply, which shifts the *LM* curve to the left and reduces aggregate demand. If, as we assumed, the *LM* curve shifts further to the left than the *FE* line shifts to the left, output falls below the new lower full-employment level (see Fig. 12.13). In this case the unemployment rate rises above the natural rate. Thus an increase in the price of oil increases both the rate of inflation and the unemployment rate in the short run, again shifting the short-run Phillips curve to the right.[10]

To summarize, an adverse supply shock causes the short-run Phillips curve to shift upward and to the right in both the classical and Keynesian models. In the classical model this shift occurs because the reallocation of labor from declining sectors to growing sectors raises the natural rate of unemployment at the same time that reduced supply raises prices. In the Keynesian model the natural rate of unemployment is not changed by a supply shock. Instead, the supply shock raises unemployment above the natural rate at the same time that higher costs lead firms to raise prices.

Application

Oil Price Fluctuations, Inflation, and Unemployment

The classical model and the Keynesian model predict that an adverse supply shock, such as a large increase in the price of oil, will raise both inflation and unemployment. In other words, an oil price shock leads to a shift upward and to the right of the short-run Phillips curve. Similarly, both models predict that a decrease in the price of oil shifts the short-run Phillips curve downward and to the left. In both models the shift of the short-run Phillips curve following a supply shock is the result of a change in expected inflation. In addition, classical economists argue that a supply shock will change the natural rate of unemployment, which also shifts the short-run Phillips curve.

The price of oil rose sharply in 1973 and again in 1979; then it came back down in 1986. If you refer to Fig. 14.9 on p. 566, you can see that these three changes in the price of oil had the predicted effects on the short-run Phillips curve. After the 1973 oil price increase, inflation and unemployment both increased. Rates of inflation and unemployment for 1976–1979 lie along a downward-sloping short-run Phillips curve that is to the right of the earlier values of inflation and unemploy-

---

[10]Unlike the situation in the classical case, in the Keynesian case the natural rate of unemployment does not change after a supply shock, so the shift of the Phillips curve is the result only of a higher rate of expected inflation. The temporary increase of unemployment above the natural rate caused by the supply shock may be interpreted as a movement downward and to the right along the new higher short-run Phillips curve.

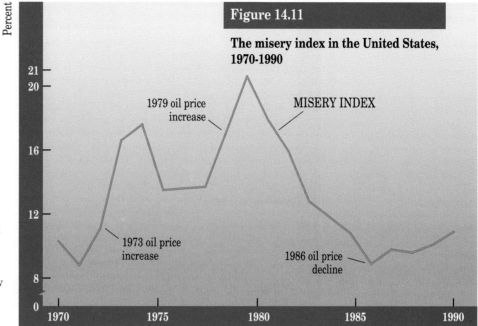

Figure 14.11

The misery index in the United States, 1970-1990

1979 oil price increase

MISERY INDEX

1973 oil price increase

1986 oil price decline

The misery index is the sum of the rates of inflation and unemployment. The oil price increases of 1973 and 1979 were followed by sharp increases in the misery index, and the misery index reached a low point in 1986 when oil prices fell sharply.

Source: Same as for Fig. 14.9.

ment. Following the sharp increase in the price of oil in 1979, the short-run Phillips curve for 1980–1983 is shifted even further to the right. Finally, in response to the decrease in oil prices in 1986, the short-run Phillips curve for 1986–1989 shifted to the left. Oil price increases following the 1990 Iraqi invasion of Kuwait were not large enough or long-lasting enough to have a major effect on the short-run Phillips curve, but you can see in Fig. 14.9 that both inflation and unemployment rose in 1990 relative to 1989.

The adverse changes in both unemployment and inflation in the 1970s led to the coining of the term *misery index*. The **misery index,** shown in Fig. 14.11, is the sum of the unemployment rate and the rate of inflation. Adding unemployment and inflation rates makes little sense from an economic point of view, since the two rates measure very different things; but the misery index caught the popular imagination as an indicator of how the economy is performing. As you can see, the misery index rose sharply in 1974 following the oil price increase in 1973, and the index rose again in 1979 and 1980 following the 1979 oil price increase. The misery index fell steadily after 1980, hitting a low point when oil prices fell in 1986.

14.3   THE LONG-RUN BEHAVIOR OF THE UNEMPLOYMENT RATE

According to both the extended classical model and the Keynesian model, the actual unemployment rate may deviate from the natural rate in the short run but returns to the natural rate in the long run. Thus the long-run behavior of the actual unemployment rate is governed by the long-run behavior of the natural rate. Unfortunately, because we cannot precisely determine when the economy is at full employment, the natural rate cannot be directly observed but must be estimated.

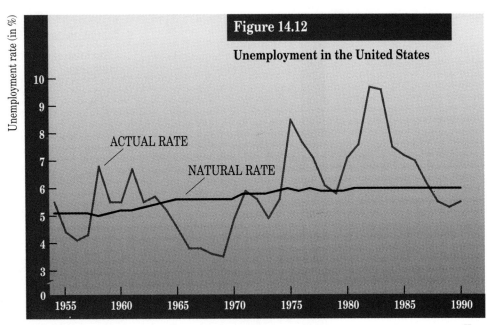

Figure 14.12

Unemployment in the United States

The figure shows the actual unemployment rate and the estimated natural rate of unemployment. According to these estimates, the natural rate of unemployment rises gradually over the period and is much smoother than the actual rate of unemployment.

Source: *Economic Report of the President*, February 1991: Civilian unemployment rate—Table B-40; natural rate of unemployment, 1954–1983—Robert J. Gordon, "Unemployment and Potential Output in the 1980s," *Brookings Papers on Economic Activity*, 1984:2, p. 563. Natural rate from 1984 onward is set equal to 6%.

There is no single, official measure of the natural rate of unemployment. Many economists believe that the natural rate was about 4% during the 1950s and increased gradually to about 6% in the 1980s. Figure 14.12 shows annual values of the natural rate of unemployment estimated by Robert J. Gordon.[11] Gordon finds that the natural rate was around 5% in the 1950s (a bit higher than other estimates) and rose to about 6% in the 1980s. Gordon's estimates also show the natural rate as a smooth series, without sharp movements up or down. Thus Gordon attributes most changes in the actual unemployment rate (also shown in Fig. 14.12) to changes in cyclical unemployment, the excess of actual unemployment over the natural rate.[12] When the actual unemployment rate is higher than the natural rate, as in 1982, there is positive cyclical unemployment. Similarly, when the actual unemployment rate is lower than the natural rate, as in 1968, there is negative cyclical unemployment.

The natural rate of unemployment estimated by Gordon and shown in Fig. 14.12 rose by 1 percentage point between the 1950s and the 1980s. If we accept the view of many economists that the natural rate was closer to 4% in the 1950s, then the natural rate rose by about 2 percentage points over this span of time. Why did the natural rate rise?

---

[11]"Unemployment and Potential Output in the 1980s," *Brookings Papers on Economics Activity*, 1984:2, p. 563. Gordon's estimates end in 1983; after 1983 the natural rate is assumed equal to 6%.

[12]Classical economists would probably argue that the natural unemployment rate tracks the actual unemployment rate much more closely than Gordon's estimates imply.

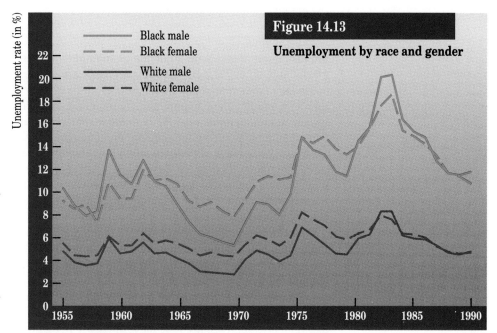

(a) Unemployment rates are shown by race and gender for the civilian labor force. Blacks have much higher unemployment rates than whites; and for much of the period females have had higher unemployment rates than males.

(a) By race and gender, civilian labor force   Year

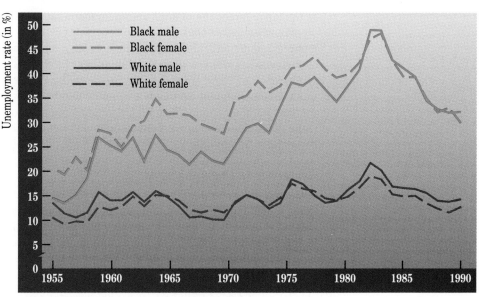

(b) Unemployment rates are shown by race and gender for the civilian labor force aged 16–19. As for adults, black teenagers have higher unemployment rates than white teenagers. Teenagers in general also have considerably higher unemployment rates than adults (compare with part a).

Source: *Economic Report of the President*, February 1991, Table B-40. Prior to 1972 black unemployment rates include unemployment of other nonwhite minorities.

(b) By race and gender, civilian labor force aged 16–19   Year

It is difficult to give a fully satisfactory explanation of the increase in the natural rate, but part of the increase seems to have been the result of demographic changes. Figures 14.13(a) and 14.13(b) show the unemployment experiences for workers within different demographic groups (based on age, gender, and race) in the United States. Notice that teenagers (aged sixteen through nineteen) have higher unemployment rates than adults (people over the age of twenty), blacks have higher unemployment rates than whites, and for much of the post–World War II period but not recently, women have had a higher unemployment rate than men.

A major reason that teenagers, blacks and other members of minority groups, and (until recently) women have higher unemployment rates is that these workers are less likely than white adult males to hold long-term stable jobs. For example, blacks and other minority group members are more likely to be trapped in the secondary labor market in which jobs often have short duration (see Chapter 10); and as a result, they experience more frequent unemployment. A cause of the higher unemployment rate for women is that traditionally they have spent more time than men in caring for children and thus have had more interruptions in their careers. For women, moving in and out of the labor force often involves periods of unemployment. Teenagers have high unemployment rates partly because they move in and out of the labor force frequently while they are in school and partly because many of them have low levels of skill or education and are likely to be in the secondary labor market.

In the period since World War II teenagers, blacks, and women have come to make up a larger share of the U.S. labor force. This shift in the composition of the labor force toward groups that have higher unemployment rates may have raised the overall unemployment rate.

The demographic explanation of the increase in the natural rate has some merit but is incomplete for two reasons. First, the changes in labor force composition by age, gender, and race account for less than 1 percentage point increase in the natural rate.[13] Second, the unemployment rate has risen *within* each demographic category.[14] Thus even if there had been no change in the demographic composition of the labor force, the overall unemployment rate would have risen.

Another factor that may have contributed to the increase in the natural rate is increased structural change in the economy, as some industries and regions have experienced significant growth while others have suffered long-term declines. The reallocation of labor from declining to growing sectors raises structural and frictional unemployment and thus the natural rate, as we discussed in the previous section. Although this effect contributed to unemployment in the 1970s when durable goods manufacturing declined and services increased, research suggests that its contribution to unemployment in the 1980s was smaller.[15]

Hysteresis in Unemployment

Although we would like to understand why the natural rate of unemployment has risen in the United States, the one or two percentage point increase in the U.S. natural rate over the past few decades probably does not represent a major change in the operation of the labor market. A more serious and puzzling change in the natural unemployment rate occurred during the 1980s in a number of countries in Western Europe.

For thirty years after World War II many Western European countries maintained low unemployment rates. Then as a result of the oil price shocks and worldwide recessions of the 1970s, unemployment rates in those countries rose quite sharply. (Unemployment rates for West Germany, France, and the United King-

---

[13]See Ellen R. Rissman, "What Is the Natural Rate of Unemployment?" *Economic Perspectives*, Federal Reserve Bank of Chicago, September/October 1986, pp. 3–17, especially p. 6.

[14]See Kevin Murphy and Robert Topel, "The Evolution of Unemployment in the United States: 1968–1985," in Stanley Fischer, ed., *NBER Macroeconomics Annual*, Cambridge, Mass.: M.I.T. Press, 1987. Murphy and Topel examined eighteen years of individual data drawn from the Annual Demographic File of the Current Population Survey. They find that "unemployment has increased in all major industries, in all age and schooling groups, and in all major regions of the country. The timing and magnitudes of changes in unemployment are very similar across identifiable groups" (p. 12).

[15]Rissman, *op. cit.*, pp. 15–16.

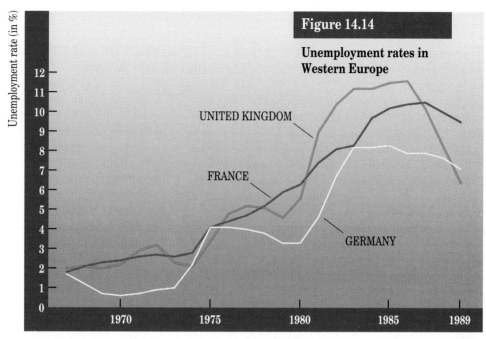

Figure 14.14

Unemployment rates in Western Europe

Western European unemployment rates rose from less than 3% in the early 1970s to 8% in the mid-1980s. The persistence of the increase in unemployment seems to indicate that the natural rate of unemployment increased. The increase in the natural rate, in response to an increase in the actual unemployment rate, is an illustration of hysteresis.

Source: *OECD Historical Statistics*, various issues; *OECD Main Economic Indicators*, various issues.

dom are shown in Fig. 14.14.) The unemployment rate in the United States also rose to high levels during the 1970s, but it fell quickly during the recovery that followed the 1981–1982 recession (see Figs. 14.12 and 14.13). In contrast, unemployment rates in Western Europe did not come down but remained at very high rates throughout most of the decade, falling only in the last few years of the eighties. This long-term increase in the Western European unemployment rate from only 1%–3% of the labor force in the early 1970s to much higher levels in the 1980s reflects an increase in the natural rate of unemployment of perhaps 5 percentage points or more, according to some estimates. How can we account for what appears to be a very large increase in the natural rate in Western Europe?

Economists have taken a term from physics, *hysteresis*, to describe the behavior of European unemployment. Applied to unemployment, **hysteresis** means that the natural rate of unemployment changes in response to the actual unemployment rate, rising if the actual unemployment rate is above the natural rate and falling if the actual unemployment rate is below the natural rate. According to the proponents of hysteresis theory, the rise in Western European unemployment in the mid-1970s, originally due to factors such as rising oil prices and contractionary macroeconomic policies, increased the natural rate of unemployment. This increase in the natural rate in turn helps account for the continued high actual unemployment rate in these countries: When these countries return to long-run equilibrium with full employment, the actual unemployment rate equals the new higher natural rate.

Most countries have unemployment insurance (UI) systems that pay workers while they are unemployed. The purpose of UI systems is to soften the economic hardship suffered by unemployed workers, but UI benefits have an additional effect: Because unemployed workers who receive UI benefits can afford to be a little more choosy when searching for a job, UI benefits tend to increase the length of unemployment spells and the unemployment rate.

Some economists have suggested that the generous UI benefits in Europe are at least partly responsible for the persistent increase in unemployment that began there during the mid-1970s (see Fig. 14.14). In a study of this issue Gary Burtless* of the Brookings Institution compared unemployment rates and the generosity of UI systems over the period 1966–1985 in Britain, France, Germany, Sweden, and the United States. To measure the generosity of UI systems, he focused on three factors:

1. The *replacement ratio*, which measures the size of unemployment benefits relative to lost wages. For example, a replacement ratio of ⅔, which characterized the French, German, and Swedish systems, means that UI benefits were equal to ⅔ of an unemployed worker's lost wages.

2. The *benefit duration*, which measures the amount of time that an unemployed worker may receive benefits.

3. *Eligibility requirements*, which specify who can collect UI benefits.

Burtless did not find much evidence that more generous UI systems lead to higher unemployment rates. For example, the UI system in the United States has a much lower replacement ratio, a substantially shorter benefit duration, and more stringent eligibility requirements than the four European UI systems in Burtless's study. If differences in generosity of UI systems are to explain the differences in unemployment rates across countries, then the United States should have a much lower unemploy-

BOX *14.1:*   THE EFFECT OF UNEMPLOYMENT INSURANCE ON UNEMPLOYMENT

ment rate than the European countries. However, prior to 1973 the U.S. unemployment rate was much *higher* than the European unemployment rates, despite the less generous system in the United States.

Similarly, according to Burtless, changes in UI benefits cannot explain increases in European unemployment rates after the mid-1970s, except possibly in France. British unemployment rose despite a reduction in the generosity of UI benefits, and German unemployment increased sharply despite the relatively constant generosity of UI benefits. Swedish unemployment remained low during the 1970s and early 1980s even though Swedish UI benefits are quite generous and became more so over the period. Only in France, where the replacement ratio increased and eligibility requirements were loosened, was a large increase in unemployment associated with increased generosity of UI benefits.

Although the generosity of UI benefits does not seem closely related to unemployment *rates*, it does appear that the *duration* of individual spells of unemployment—the length of time that an unemployed worker remains unemployed—is affected by the generosity of UI benefits. Burtless found that unemployment spells were much longer in Europe (where UI systems were much more generous) than in the United States, even during the late 1960s and early 1970s when European unemployment rates were lower than in the United States. In particular, the longer benefit duration of European systems—the fact that unemployed workers are allowed to collect UI for a longer period in Europe than in the United States—seems to account for the lengthier spells of unemployment seen in Europe.

*"Jobless Pay and High European Unemployment," in R. Lawrence and C. Schultze, eds., *Barriers to European Growth: A Transatlantic View*, Washington, D.C.: Brookings Institution, 1987.

There are two leading explanations of hysteresis in European unemployment. First, some economists have argued that the bureaucratic aspects of firms and unions, as well as government regulation, interfere with the adjustment of the labor market in Western Europe. For example, in some European countries the government severely restricts the ability of firms to fire workers. Because firms know that it is difficult to fire workers, they are reluctant to hire additional workers unless they are confident that they will not want to reduce their work force for a long time. Thus after many workers were laid off in the mid-1970s, firms were reluctant to rehire them or to hire new workers.

A second explanation of hysteresis, known as the **insider-outsider theory,** is a theory of contract negotiations between unions and firms. According to this theory, when a union negotiates a labor contract with a firm, it seeks as high a real wage (including fringe benefits) as possible without inducing the firm to reduce its employment. This union behavior is in the best interest of currently employed workers, or insiders. But think about what happens when a contract is negotiated at a time when unemployment is high: If the union negotiates the contract with the aim of benefiting only the insiders and ignores the interests of unemployed workers, or outsiders, it will attempt to get the highest wage consistent with continued employment of the insiders. If it succeeds, the wage will be set at too high a level for the firm to be willing to increase employment and hire some of the outsiders. Thus the outsiders will continue to suffer unemployment.

The insider-outsider theory applies in a unionized setting. Because European labor markets are much more highly unionized than the U.S. labor market, the insider-outsider theory predicts that hysteresis is quantitatively more important in Europe than in the United States. This prediction is consistent with the fact that during the 1980s unemployment rates in Europe (Fig. 14.14) came down much more slowly than unemployment rates in the United States (Figs. 14.12 and 14.13). Another difference between the labor markets in Europe and in the United States is that unemployment insurance is more generous in Europe than in the United States. Box 14.1 discusses the implications of this difference for the behavior of the natural rate of unemployment.

14.4 THE COSTS OF UNEMPLOYMENT AND INFLATION

In all countries the public regards high unemployment and high inflation as evils to be avoided, and policymakers devote much effort to trying to keep unemployment and inflation in check. In order to know whether this focus on inflation and unemployment is warranted, we need to have a more precise idea of the costs of these two problems to society. For Keynesians especially, who think that inflation and unemployment may be traded off in the short run, understanding the costs of inflation and unemployment is necessary in advising policymakers on how to achieve an appropriate balance between the two.

Costs of Unemployment

There are two principal costs of unemployment. The first cost is the loss in output that could have been produced if unemployed workers had been productively employed. This cost is borne partly by unemployed workers themselves and partly by the society at large. The cost to the worker is measured in terms of her lost income. Since an unemployed worker may stop paying taxes and instead receive unemployment insurance benefits or other government payments, society (in this case, the taxpayers) also bears some of the cost of unemployment.

The other major cost of unemployment is the personal or psychological cost faced by unemployed workers and their families. This cost is especially important for workers suffering long spells of unemployment and for the chronically unemployed.

We next discuss the output costs and personal costs for each of the three types of unemployment—frictional, structural, and cyclical.

Frictional Unemployment   Frictional unemployment arises from the search process in which workers and firms seek appropriate matches. Because this process promotes economic efficiency, frictional unemployment does not have any output costs. Indeed, searches that result in better matches of workers and firms may lead ultimately to higher output. Furthermore, spells of frictional unemployment are usually fairly short, so that the personal costs are generally small.

Structural Unemployment   Structural unemployment arises from imbalances in the labor market, in which the skills, training, and locations of available workers do not match the requirements of the available jobs. If structurally unemployed workers could be put to work, total output would increase, so there is an output cost associated with structural unemployment. However, putting structurally unemployed workers to work requires an expenditure of resources to train or retrain these workers and perhaps to help them relocate to areas where jobs are available. Although putting these workers to work would contribute to increased output, the resources used to get them ready for employment partly offsets the increase in output. Thus the output cost of structural unemployment may be moderate, although it is extremely difficult to get an accurate measure of this cost.

In the Keynesian model based on efficiency wages, some structural unemployment is due to the fact that the efficiency wage is set above the market-clearing real wage, with the consequence that there is an excess supply of labor. These structurally unemployed workers would be able to find work and produce output if the real wage were reduced to its market-clearing level. However, the additional output produced by these workers would be at least partly offset by the reduced productivity of existing workers, who reduce their efforts in response to a lower real wage. Thus, again, the output cost of structural unemployment is lower than it might first appear to be.

However, because structural unemployment is typically associated with long spells of unemployment, the personal costs of structural unemployment can be very high. Chronically unemployed workers and workers who endure long spells of unemployment suffer costs in terms of deterioration of job skills, reduced self-esteem, and stress. Indicating the magnitude of these costs, one study found that an increase in the unemployment rate of one percentage point maintained for six years is associated with 20,000 additional cardiovascular deaths, 920 suicides, 650 homicides, 4000 state mental hospital admissions, and 3300 state prison admissions.[16]

---

[16]The study, by Dr. Harvey Brenner of Johns Hopkins University, is cited in Barry Bluestone and Bennett Harrison, *The Deindustrialization of America*, New York: Basic Books, 1982, Chapter 3.

Cyclical Unemployment   Cyclical unemployment is the excess of the actual unemployment rate over the natural rate. The amount of output lost because of cyclical unemployment is given by Okun's law, Eq. (14.1), which says that each percentage point of cyclical unemployment lasting for one year reduces output by 2.5% of a year's GNP. If GNP is $5000 billion, then each percentage point of unemployment sustained for one year reduces output by $125 billion.

Classical economists argue that Okun's law overstates the cost of cyclical unemployment because it ignores the fact that leisure increases during a recession. As we saw in Chapter 10, in the classical model a worker supplies labor up to the point where she is indifferent between an additional hour of leisure and the after-tax income that can be earned by working an additional hour. If the worker works one hour less per week, the gain in leisure would offset the loss in after-tax income and the worker would not really suffer a loss. However, the worker's gain in leisure does not offset the lost output that would have gone to the government in the form of taxes.

The Keynesian response to this classical argument is that it does not apply to the typical situation of unemployed workers. If a firm that wanted to reduce its use of labor by 2.5% did so by having all of its workers work thirty-nine hours rather than forty hours per week, then the one hour of lost weekly wages per worker would probably be compensated for by the extra hour of leisure. However, if the firm instead laid off 2.5% of its workers, as Keynesians claim is more typically the case in a recession, these wholly unemployed workers would not feel that the increase in leisure was very adequate compensation for their lost income.

In general, the personal costs of cyclical unemployment are larger than the personal costs of frictional unemployment but are smaller than the personal costs of structural unemployment. The personal costs of cyclical unemployment are mitigated by the fact that many spells of cyclical unemployment have short durations. In addition, many workers who suffer cyclical unemployment receive unemployment insurance benefits that help to cushion the loss in income. However, if a recession is particularly deep or long, then the personal costs of cyclical unemployment can be very substantial as unemployed workers reduce their personal savings and exhaust their eligibility for unemployment insurance benefits.

Costs of Inflation

In August 1971 President Nixon instituted a set of wage and price controls in an attempt to reduce U.S. inflation. These controls made it illegal for anyone to raise wages or prices beyond amounts specified in the law. Because of the central role that wages and prices play in allocating resources, wage-price controls are a rather drastic interference with the market system. (Price controls are discussed in "The Policy Debate" box, p. 588.) However, the public and policymakers had become increasingly frustrated by the persistence of what they regarded as high inflation, which was about 5% per year at the time. From today's perspective it is somewhat surprising that an inflation rate of around 5% per year would evoke such a strong response, but many people, including policymakers, believe that inflation is very costly. What are these costs?

The costs of inflation depend in an important way on whether or not consumers, investors, workers, and firms are able to predict the inflation before it occurs. Thus we discuss two separate cases: an inflation that everyone is able to predict and an inflation that occurs as a complete surprise.

with the Macroeconomy

Price Indexes and Inflation

Inflation is the rate of change of the price level. In practice, however, there is not a single measure of "the" price level. Instead, there are many different price indexes, or price level measures, each covering a different group of goods and services and having its own rate of inflation. Two important types of price indexes are consumer price indexes and producer price indexes.

As we discussed in Chapter 2, the consumer price indexes (CPIs) measure the prices of fixed baskets of consumer goods. The Bureau of Labor Statistics (BLS) constructs consumer price indexes by using information from surveys of retail and service establishments and households, including visits by survey takers to check the prices of goods on shelves. The major consumer price index, called CPI-U, measures prices of all the goods and services, including food and energy, used by typical urban households. The BLS also releases versions of the CPI-U that exclude food prices and energy prices in order to get a picture of consumer prices that is not influenced by the sharp fluctuations that sometimes occur in the agricultural and energy sectors.

The producer price indexes (PPIs) measure the prices of various domestically produced goods, based on a mail survey of domestic producers. The three major PPIs, which cover goods at different stages of processing, are the PPI for finished goods; the PPI for intermediate materials, supplies, and components; and the PPI for crude materials for further processing.

The CPIs and the PPIs are announced by the BLS each month for prices in the preceding month, and these indexes are published in the *Monthly Labor Review* by the BLS. The CPIs and PPIs appear in numerous other sources as well, such as *Economic Indicators*, a monthly publication of the Council of Economic Advisers. In general, there are two important differences between the CPI and the PPI. First, the PPI measures the prices of goods at an earlier stage in the process of production and retailing and so may reflect changes in inflation at an earlier stage than the CPI does. Thus forecasters sometimes use the PPI as an early-warning device for future inflation in consumer prices. Second, the CPI includes the prices of domestically produced and foreign-produced goods and services, but the PPI focuses more narrowly on domestically produced goods.

Perfectly Anticipated Inflation Consider first the extreme case of an inflation that is perfectly anticipated by people in the economy. For example, imagine that you and everyone else knew that the rate of inflation would be exactly 4% per year, with the prices of all goods and services rising at the rate of 4% per year.

At first glance it is hard to see why an anticipated inflation imposes any costs at all. Although the prices you pay for groceries and movie tickets and so on would increase by 4% per year, your nominal wage or the nominal value of the goods or services that you produce would also be rising, so that your nominal income would also increase by 4% per year. Even the nominal income of retired workers would increase by 4% per year, because the nominal value of Social Security benefits is tied to the price level. Because nominal incomes are rising along with prices, no one's purchasing power is hurt by the perfectly anticipated inflation.

What about the money that you hold in your savings account? Although inflation reduces the purchasing power of money, inflation would not hurt the value of your savings account because the nominal interest rate would adjust to offset the fall in the purchasing power of money, if the inflation rate is known in advance. Suppose, for instance, that when the inflation rate is zero, the nominal interest rate on a savings account is 3%, and so the real interest rate is also 3% per year. If inflation rises to a perfectly anticipated rate of 4% per year, then the nominal interest rate will increase to 7% per year. Since savers and banks were both satisfied with a 3% real interest rate in the absence of inflation, if there is a perfectly anticipated 4% inflation, they will both be satisfied with a 7% nominal interest rate, which maintains a 3% real interest rate.[17] As long as everyone knows the rate of inflation in advance, the nominal interest rate will adjust to keep the real interest rate unchanged, and neither savers nor banks will be harmed.

This discussion suggests that perfectly anticipated inflation has no costs. This is not quite true: Inflation erodes the value of currency, which makes people try to have less currency on hand—for example, by going to the bank or the automatic teller machine to make withdrawals every week instead of twice a month. The costs in time and effort incurred by people who are trying to economize on holdings of cash are called **shoe leather costs.** Although shoe leather costs sound trivial, the shoe leather cost of a 10% perfectly anticipated inflation has been estimated to be about 0.3% of GNP, which is about $15 billion per year in the United States.[18]

A second cost of perfectly anticipated inflation arises from menu costs, the costs of changing nominal prices. When there is inflation and prices are continually rising, sellers of goods and services must use resources to change nominal prices. For instance, mail-order firms would have to print and mail catalogues frequently to report the increases in prices. Although some firms face substantial menu costs, for the economy as a whole these costs are probably small. Furthermore, technological progress, such as the introduction of electronic scanners in supermarkets, reduces the cost of changing prices.[19]

Unanticipated Inflation Much of the public's aversion to inflation is aversion to unanticipated inflation. For example, if everyone expects the rate of inflation to be 4% per year, but inflation turns out to be 6% per year, unanticipated inflation is 2% per year. More generally, **unanticipated inflation** is the actual rate of inflation minus the rate of inflation that was expected to occur.

What is the effect on you of 6% inflation if, for example, (1) you expected 4% inflation and (2) your savings account pays 7% interest? When inflation turns out to be 6% per year instead of 4% per year, the actual real interest rate on your savings account turns out to be only 1% per year (the nominal interest rate of 7% minus the inflation rate of 6%) instead of the 3% per year that you expected. By

---

[17]This argument ignores the fact that interest is taxed on a nominal basis. If the after-tax real interest rate is to be kept constant, the nominal interest rate will have to rise by somewhat more than the increase in inflation.

[18]See Stanley Fischer, "Towards an Understanding of the Costs of Inflation: II," in K. Brunner and A. Meltzer, eds., *Carnegie-Rochester Conference Series on Public Policy*, vol. 15, Autumn 1981.

[19]Many record stores mark their records, tapes, and compact discs with a letter instead of a price and then show the price associated with each letter on a chart on the wall. This practice makes the record store's menu costs small.

earning a lower actual real interest rate, you end up losing as a result of the unanticipated inflation. However, your loss is the bank's gain, since the bank pays a lower real interest rate than it expected. Note that the roles would have been reversed if the actual inflation rate had turned out to be 2% per year: In this case your savings account would have earned an actual real interest rate of 5% per year, which is 2% per year higher than you expected, and the bank would have paid a real interest rate 2% per year higher than it expected to pay.

Similarly, suppose that your nominal salary is set in advance. If inflation is higher than expected, the real value of your salary is worth less than you expected, and your loss is your employer's gain. If inflation is lower than expected, however, you benefit and your employer loses.

These examples show that a primary effect of unanticipated inflation is to transfer wealth from one person or firm to another. For the economy as a whole, a transfer of wealth from one group to another group is not a net loss of resources and hence does not represent a cost. However, from the viewpoints of individual people and firms in the economy, the *risk* of gaining or losing wealth as a result of unanticipated inflation is a cost. Because most people do not like risk, the risk of significant gains or losses arising from unexpected inflation makes people feel worse off and hence is a cost of unanticipated inflation. Furthermore, any resources that people use in forecasting inflation and in trying to protect themselves against the risks of unanticipated inflation represent an additional cost of unanticipated inflation. Some of these costs of unanticipated inflation can be eliminated by contracts that are indexed to the price level (see Box 14.2).

Another cost of unanticipated inflation arises from the fact that prices serve as signals in a market economy. For example, if wheat becomes more expensive than corn, that is a signal to consumers to switch from wheat to corn and to farmers to produce more wheat and less corn. However, the prices that act as signals in the economy are *relative* prices, such as the price of wheat relative to the price of corn. Knowing that wheat is so many dollars per bushel does not help the consumer or farmer make good economic decisions unless the price of corn is also known. When there is unanticipated inflation, particularly if it is very erratic, people may confuse changes in prices that arise because of changes in the general price level with changes in prices that arise because of shifts in the supply or demand for individual goods.[20] Because the signals provided by prices may be distorted when there is unanticipated inflation, the market economy works less efficiently. In addition, when there is a great deal of uncertainty about what the true inflation rate is, resources must be devoted to learning about different prices, by comparison shopping, for example.

The Cost of Hyperinflation   **Hyperinflation** is a situation in which the rate of inflation is extremely high for a sustained period of time.[21] The costs of hyperinflation are much greater than the costs associated with moderate inflation. For example, when prices are increasing at mind-boggling rates, there are strong incentives to minimize holdings of currency, and the resulting shoe leather costs are large. In severe hyperinflations workers are paid much more frequently—perhaps even

---

[20]This type of confusion is similar to that discussed as part of the misperceptions theory of Chapter 11.

[21]Philip Cagan ("The Monetary Dynamics of Hyperinflation," in Milton Friedman, ed., *Studies in the Quantity Theory of Money*, Chicago: University of Chicago Press, 1956) defines a hyperinflation as beginning in the month in which the rate of inflation first exceeds 50% *per month*. The Cagan article is a classic study of hyperinflation.

BOX *14.2:* INDEXED CONTRACTS

In principle, much of the risk of gains and losses associated with unanticipated inflation can be eliminated by using contracts in which payments are indexed to inflation. For instance, if a bank wanted to offer a guaranteed 3% real interest rate on savings accounts, it could index the nominal interest rate to the rate of inflation by offering to pay a nominal interest rate equal to 3% plus whatever the rate of inflation turns out to be. Then if the inflation rate turns out to be 6%, the bank would end up paying a nominal interest rate of 9%—which would give the depositor the promised 3% real interest rate. Similarly, other financial contracts, such as loans, mortgages, and bonds, can be indexed to protect the real rate of return against unanticipated inflation. Wage payments set by labor contracts can also be indexed to protect workers and employers against unanticipated inflation, as discussed in Appendix 12.A.

How widespread is indexing in practice? Most financial contracts in the United States are *not* indexed to the rate of inflation, although payments on some long-term financial contracts (adjustable-rate mortgages, for example) are indexed to nominal interest rates such as the prime rate charged by banks or the Treasury bill interest rate. Because nominal interest rates move closely with inflation, these long-term financial contracts are to some extent indexed to inflation. Many labor contracts in the United States are indexed to the rate of inflation through provisions called cost-of-living adjustments, or COLAs. COLAs provide for some increase in nominal wages if inflation is higher than expected, but usually a 1% increase in unanticipated inflation results in something less than a 1% adjustment of wages. Given the concern that the American public often expresses about inflation, it is somewhat puzzling to economists that indexed contracts are not more often employed in the United States.

In contrast, in countries that have experienced high and unpredictable inflation rates, indexed contracts are widely used. A case in point is Israel, which had a CPI inflation rate of 445% per year in 1984. At that time over 80% of liquid financial assets in Israel were indexed: For example, long-term government bonds were indexed to the CPI, and banks offered short-term deposits indexed to the exchange rate. The fraction of financial assets that were indexed decreased after Israeli inflation slowed down to a rate of 37% per year in the second half of 1985.*

*See Stanley Fischer, "Israeli Inflation and Indexation," in J. Williamson, ed., *Inflation and Indexation: Argentina, Brazil, Israel*, Institute for International Economics, 1985, reprinted in Stanley Fischer, *Indexing, Inflation, and Economic Policy*, Cambridge, Mass.: M.I.T. Press, 1986; and Zalman F. Shiffer, "Adjusting to High Inflation: The Israeli Experience," *Federal Reserve Bank of St. Louis Review*, May 1986, pp. 18–29.

more than once a day—and they rush out to spend their money (or to convert their money into some other form, such as a foreign currency) before prices rise even further. The time and energy devoted to getting rid of currency as fast as possible disrupts production.

One early casualty of hyperinflations is the government's ability to collect taxes. In a hyperinflation taxpayers have an incentive to delay paying their taxes as long as possible; because tax bills are usually set in nominal terms, the longer the taxpayer delays, the less the real value of her obligation is. The real value of taxes collected by the government falls sharply during hyperinflations, with destructive effects on the government's finances and its ability to provide public services.

Finally, the disruptive effect of inflation on market efficiency that we discussed earlier becomes most severe in the case of a hyperinflation. If prices change so often that they cease to be reliable indicators of the supply and demand for different goods and services, the invisible hand of the free market will not allocate resources efficiently.

14.5   STRATEGIES FOR REDUCING THE RATE OF INFLATION

Countries that maintain high growth rates of the money supply for sustained periods of time tend to have higher rates of inflation than countries that maintain low growth rates of the money supply (see Table 4.4, p. 140). This association between the long-run growth rate of the money supply and the long-run rate of inflation is consistent with both the classical and the Keynesian models. Furthermore, classicals and Keynesians agree that the way to reduce the long-run rate of inflation is to reduce the long-run rate of monetary growth.

Despite agreement about the long-run relationship between monetary growth and inflation, classicals and Keynesians have different views about the appropriate strategy for achieving **disinflation,** a reduction in the rate of inflation. In particular, classicals and Keynesians offer different answers to the following question: How much and how rapidly should the rate of monetary growth be reduced?

The Classical Prescription for Disinflation: Cold Turkey

Classical economists usually argue that disinflation should be implemented quickly by a rapid and decisive reduction in the growth rate of the money supply—a strategy we refer to as **cold turkey.** The cold-turkey strategy would seem to be the fastest way to a lower inflation rate, but what about the unemployment that may be created along the way? In the classical view, prices, wages, and expectations should adjust rapidly to a decisive disinflationary policy so that disinflation can be accomplished without much increase in unemployment. With rapidly adjusting prices and expectations, the actual inflation rate is lower than the expected inflation rate—with the consequence that unemployment is above the natural rate—for only a brief period of time. Remember that according to the long-run Phillips curve, changes in the rate of inflation have no effect on the unemployment rate in the long run. Essentially, the classical argument is that the long-run equilibrium—in which money growth, inflation, and expected inflation have all been reduced to lower levels, and unemployment has returned to the natural rate—is reached fairly quickly.

The Keynesian Prescription for Disinflation: Gradualism

Keynesian economists disagree with the classical argument that disinflation can be achieved without significant costs in terms of increased cyclical unemployment. Keynesians argue that menu costs that create price stickiness and labor contracts that may set nominal wages for several years into the future interfere with the rapid adjustment of prices, wages, and expected inflation. According to Keynesians, prices, wages, and expectations may take years to adjust to a disinflationary policy; in the meantime inflation is below the expected rate of inflation and the unemployment rate is above the natural rate. The basic difference between the Keynesian and the classical views is that classical economists believe that the economy's adjustment to disinflationary policies is quite rapid, and Keynesian economists believe it is more prolonged.

Because Keynesians believe that disinflation can cause substantial and prolonged unemployment, they fear the consequences of a sharp, cold-turkey reduction in monetary growth. The Keynesian prescription for disinflation is to follow a policy of **gradualism,** which involves reducing the rate of monetary growth and the rate of inflation gradually over a period of several years. Even a gradual approach to disinflation cannot avoid increasing the unemployment rate, but Keynesians believe that a gradual disinflation will cause a smaller difference between the actual and expected rates of inflation. As a result of this more gradual approach, Keynesians argue, the unemployment rate will not rise by as much as it would under cold turkey (although the period during which unemployment exceeds the natural rate may be longer).

The Importance of Credibility

Classicals and Keynesians agree that for disinflation to be achieved without high unemployment costs, it is important to reduce the public's expected inflation rate. A fall in the expected rate of inflation induces a downward shift of the short-run Phillips curve, allowing the economy to achieve a lower rate of inflation for any given rate of unemployment.

Possibly the most important factor determining how quickly expected inflation adjusts is the credibility, or believability, of the government's announced disinflationary policy. (Credibility is discussed in greater detail in Chapter 15.) If the government announces a policy to reduce the rate of inflation, and if workers, consumers, and firms believe that the policy will work and that the government will actually carry through on the policy, then expected inflation should fall fairly rapidly.

Why might people *not* believe that the government will actually carry out its announced disinflationary policy? Disinflationary policies have some undesirable side effects that make them politically unpopular. First, a reduction in the rate of inflation will increase the unemployment rate in the short run before expectations, prices, and wages can adjust. Also, as we discuss in Chapter 16, high inflation is sometimes the result of high government deficits, since the government may print money to pay for the deficit. In order to be able to stop printing money, the government must reduce its deficit, which means taking the politically unpopular measure of increasing taxes or reducing government expenditures. Because disinflationary policies have political costs, there is always the possibility that policymakers may change their minds and not carry through with disinflation. Thus inflationary expectations may fall slowly until people become convinced that the policymakers are committed to fighting inflation.

Classicals emphasize that the cold-turkey approach may be more effective than gradualism because a cold-turkey approach is more credible. A sharp decline in monetary growth and the associated reduction in the inflation rate will be very visible; the public can observe the policy and its effects, and so their expected inflation rate may drop quickly. But with a gradual disinflation the public may not see a substantial drop in the rate of inflation for a while and may begin to doubt whether the announced policy is actually being followed.

The Keynesian response to this point is that although the cold-turkey policy is more visible and dramatic, this policy also runs a greater risk of increasing unemployment to intolerable levels, which could force the government to back off from the cold-turkey approach. If, indeed, the government is forced to abandon a cold-turkey strategy, then a politically sustainable policy of gradualism may be more effective in reducing long-run inflation than cold turkey is.

THE POLICY DEBATE

Should Price Controls be Used to Fight Inflation?

Background

Policymakers are often reluctant to reduce monetary growth to fight inflation, perhaps because they fear that a slowdown of monetary growth will induce a painful and politically unpopular recession. As an alternative to reducing monetary growth, price controls—legal limits on the ability of firms to raise prices or wages—offer the possibility of a direct way to slow down or eliminate inflation.

PRO

"In the midst of public demands to do something about inflation, price controls are a direct attack on the problem of rapid price growth. By holding down the growth rate of prices, controls may help to reduce the expected rate of inflation and thus break the cycle of continued inflation."

CON

"By limiting price increases, price controls will inevitably cause shortages of some goods, disrupting the economy. Furthermore, price controls may not reduce the expected rate of inflation because people will expect sharp increases in prices as soon as price controls are lifted."

Analysis

The debate on price controls raises two analytic issues. The first issue concerns shortages and is relatively straightforward. In a free market the ever-changing forces of supply and demand lead to changes in relative prices, with the prices of some products rising more rapidly than the prices of others. If price controls prevent the price of a product from rising to the level at which quantity supplied equals quantity demanded, there will be excess demand for the product, that is, a shortage. Economic theory cannot predict which products will develop shortages, but it does predict that shortages will develop. These shortages and the disruptions they cause are a major cost of price controls.

The second analytic issue concerns the effect of controls on inflationary expectations. If, in fact, price controls reduce expected inflation, the short-run Phillips curve will shift downward, which means that a lower level of inflation can be achieved at any given unemployment rate. But do price controls reduce expected inflation? While price controls are in effect, prices rise more slowly, which may cause people to expect less inflation in the future as well. On the other hand, because price controls cause shortages and disrupt the economy, controls eventually have to be removed. Knowing that the controls are temporary, people may expect even greater inflation in the future.

One factor that may affect expectations of inflation during the period of controls is how the government handles monetary and fiscal policy. If macroeconomic policies are such that aggregate demand continues to grow quickly, people may expect renewed inflation when the controls are lifted. But if controls are accompanied by tight monetary and fiscal policy, the idea that inflation will not resume when controls are lifted is more plausible.

Evidence

On August 15, 1971, in a surprise announcement, President Nixon instituted a program of price controls in the United States. The controls began with a ninety-day price freeze, known as Phase I, that prevented any prices from increasing. The program developed haphazardly in re-

sponse to economic events, reaching Phase IV before the program was finally terminated in April 1974.

As predicted by the basic economics of supply and demand, shortages developed during the period of price controls. To try to prevent shortages, the government exempted some prices, including the prices of raw agricultural products—feed grains, for example—from controls. But prices of final products, such as "broilers" (chickens sold to consumers in grocery stores), remained subject to controls. As feed grain prices increased, broiler producers could no longer make a profit by paying for feed grain at an uncontrolled price while selling broilers at a controlled price. When, as a result of this profit squeeze, the supply of broilers nearly disappeared, broilers were reclassified as a raw agricultural product so that the price of broilers was no longer controlled. Broiler prices increased by more than 50% when they were decontrolled.* Shortages developed in

*See George P. Shultz and Kenneth W. Dam, "The Life Cycle of Wage and Price Controls," in G. Shultz and K. Dam, eds., *Economic Policy Beyond the Headlines*, Stanford, Calif.: Stanford Alumni Association, 1977.

other sectors, as well, including lumber and various steel products.

To study whether price controls succeeded in reducing inflation after the controls were lifted, Robert J. Gordon† conducted a statistical analysis of inflation in the United States during and after the period of price controls. He concluded that price controls reduced the rate of inflation during the period they were in effect (August 1971–April 1974). However, after the price controls were eliminated in April 1974, Gordon found that prices grew rapidly, so that by the third quarter of 1975 the price level had reached the same level that it would have reached had there been no controls. In other words, the reduction in the rate of inflation during the period of controls was completely offset by an acceleration of inflation after price controls were removed. A probable reason that inflation accelerated after the removal of controls is that, as mentioned in "The Political Environment" box (p. 568), the Nixon administration continued to use expansionary monetary and fiscal policy during the controls period.

†"The Impact of Aggregate Demand on Prices," *Brookings Papers on Economic Activity*, 1975:3, pp. 613–655.

The Disinflation of the Early 1980s

In the late 1970s inflation became an increasingly serious problem in the United States. The annual rate of inflation (measured by the CPI) increased steadily from 5.8% per year in 1976 to 11.3% per year in 1979, as shown in Fig. 14.15. By the time Paul Volcker became chairman of the Federal Reserve in August 1979, it was clear that the public wanted him to bring inflation under control. Volcker acted decisively. On October 6, 1979, he announced a set of policy changes intended to slow money growth and reduce the rate of inflation. As you can see in Fig. 14.15, this change in policy succeeded in bringing the rate of inflation measured by the CPI down to less than 4% per year in 1983.

The major question at the time of Volcker's announcement was whether a disinflation could be accomplished without a prolonged period of high unemployment.

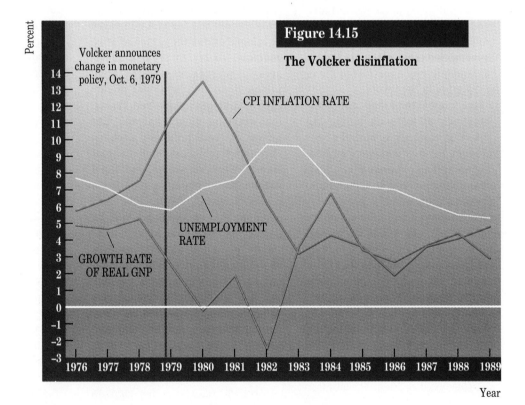

Year

To combat the rising rate of inflation in the late 1970s, Fed Chairman Paul Volcker ordered a tightening of monetary policy in 1979. The rate of inflation dropped sharply in the early 1980s. The fall in inflation was accompanied by an increase in the unemployment rate and a slowdown in the growth of real GNP.

Source: *Economic Report of the President*, February 1991: GNP growth—Table B-2; CPI inflation rate, year to year—Table B-62; civilian unemployment rate—Table B-40.

Figure 14.15 shows that the unemployment rate climbed for three years after 1979 and did not fall below 7% until 1987. The behavior of real GNP provides further evidence of a slowdown in economic activity. The first three full years of the disinflation (1980–1982) had the three lowest growth rates of GNP during the 1980s. In fact, real GNP fell during two of these years.

There is little doubt about the facts: Inflation slowed down in the first three years of the 1980s, and unemployment rose substantially during these three years. Keynesians proclaim this evidence as a victory for their theory, if not for those who suffered unemployment during this time. Classicals offer two rebuttals to the Keynesian claim.

First, classicals argue that the disinflation of the 1980s was not a true test of their theory because the announced policy was not credible. "War on inflation" had been declared several times earlier with no effect. Credibility is not easy to measure, even after the fact, so this is not a question that will be easily resolved.

Second, classicals point out that other factors besides disinflationary policy may have contributed to the slowdown in economic activity. As we discussed in Chapter 3, the price of imported oil rose dramatically following the Iranian revolution in 1979. This adverse supply shock could have caused or intensified the slowdown in aggregate economic activity.

14.6   CHAPTER SUMMARY

1. According to the simple Phillips curve, inflation is negatively related to unemployment. The relationship between inflation and unemployment has two links. One link is Okun's law, which relates unemployment to the level of output; and the other link is the price adjustment process, which relates the level of output to the rate of inflation. Inflation and unemployment in the United States seemed to conform to the simple Phillips curve during the 1960s but not during the 1970s and 1980s.

2. The simple Phillips curve has been replaced by the expectations-augmented Phillips curve, which says that unemployment is related not to the rate of inflation itself but to the difference between the actual rate of inflation and the expected rate of inflation. When the actual rate of inflation equals the expected rate of inflation, the unemployment rate equals the natural rate of unemployment. The natural rate of unemployment is the rate of unemployment that occurs when output equals full-employment output.

3. For a given expected rate of inflation, the expectations-augmented Phillips curve is a downward-sloping relation between inflation and unemployment and is called the short-run Phillips curve. If the expected rate of inflation equals zero, the short-run Phillips curve is the simple Phillips curve. An increase in the expected rate of inflation shifts the short-run Phillips curve upward. Changes in expected inflation account for the instability of the short-run Phillips curve in the 1970s and 1980s.

4. The expected and actual rates of inflation are equal in the long run, so that in the long run the unemployment rate equals the natural rate, regardless of what the rate of inflation is. Thus the long-run Phillips curve is a vertical line at the natural rate of unemployment.

5. Keynesians argue that because prices and price expectations take some time to adjust, the short-run Phillips curve offers policymakers a temporary trade-off between inflation and unemployment. For example, Keynesians believe that by increasing money growth, the Federal Reserve can increase output and reduce the unemployment rate in the short run, at the cost of increased inflation. Classicals argue that prices and expectations adjust rapidly, so that there is little or no opportunity for policymakers to trade off inflation and unemployment.

6. Supply shocks increase both unemployment and inflation and cause the short-run Phillips curve to shift upward, according to both the classical and the Keynesian models.

7. The natural rate of unemployment reflects the amount of frictional and structural unemployment in the economy. The difference between the actual unemployment rate and the natural rate of unemployment is cyclical unemployment. According to some estimates, the natural rate of unemployment in the United States has risen gradually over time.

8. The unemployment rate displays hysteresis if the natural rate increases whenever the actual rate is above the natural rate and decreases whenever the actual unemployment rate is below the natural rate. Explanations for hysteresis include bureaucratic and legal barriers to labor market adjustment and the insider-outsider theory. The insider-outsider theory is based on the idea that labor unions bargain for the highest wages consistent with continued employment of current workers and ignore those currently unemployed. These explanations are more applicable in Europe than in the United States and may account for the apparent hysteresis in European unemployment.

9. The costs of unemployment are the lost output that could be produced by unemployed workers and the personal costs suffered by unemployed workers. Both of these costs are small for frictional unemployment. The largest personal costs are associated with structural unemployment, because people out of work for structural reasons often suffer long or frequent spells of unemployment. Okun's law suggests that cyclical unemployment involves the largest output costs.

10. The costs of inflation depend on whether the inflation was anticipated or unanticipated. The costs of anticipated inflation, which (except in extreme inflations) are relatively minor, include shoe leather costs (resources used up by individuals and firms in order to reduce their holdings of currency) and menu costs (costs of changing posted prices during an inflation). Unanticipated inflation causes unpredictable transfers of wealth among individuals and firms. The risk of unpredictable gains and losses makes people worse off and causes them to use resources to try to reduce this risk. Unanticipated inflation may also reduce the efficiency of the market system by making it more difficult for people to observe relative prices.

11. Disinflation is a reduction in the rate of inflation. Classical economists argue that because prices, wages, and expectations adjust quickly, disinflation can be accomplished without large costs in terms of unemployment. They suggest the use of a cold-turkey policy, or rapid disinflation. In contrast, Keynesian economists argue that slow adjustment of prices, wages, and expectations may cause disinflation to have high unemployment costs. Keynesians argue for gradualism, or slow and gradual disinflation. The unemployment costs of any disinflation policy are reduced if the policy is credible, so that the public's expectations of inflation fall quickly.

Key Terms

cold turkey, p. 586	hysteresis, p. 577	Okun's law, p. 555
cyclical unemployment, p. 555	insider-outsider theory, p. 579	shoe leather costs, p. 583 short-run Phillips curve, p. 564
disinflation, p. 586	long-run Phillips curve, p. 570	simple Phillips curve, p. 559
expectations-augmented Phillips curve, p. 564	misery index, p. 573	unanticipated inflation, p. 583
gradualism, p. 587	natural rate of unemployment, p. 554	
hyperinflation, p. 584		

Key Equations

$$\frac{\bar{Y} - Y}{Y} = 2.5(u - \bar{u}) \qquad (14.1)$$

Okun's law states that a 1 percentage point increase in the unemployment rate u reduces output Y by 2.5% of the full-employment level of output $\bar{Y}$. When the unemployment rate equals the natural rate of unemployment $\bar{u}$, output equals its full-employment level.

$$\frac{\Delta Y}{Y} = \frac{\Delta \bar{Y}}{\bar{Y}} - 2.5 \, \Delta u \qquad (14.2)$$

An alternative way of writing Okun's law (Eq. 14.1) relates the growth rate of output $\Delta Y/Y$ to the growth rate of full-employment output $\Delta \bar{Y}/\bar{Y}$ and the change in the unemployment rate Δu. According to Eq. (14.2), output grows more slowly than full-employment output when unemployment is rising and more quickly than full-employment output when unemployment is falling. This version of Okun's law assumes that the natural rate of unemployment is constant.

$$\pi = -h(u - \bar{u}) \qquad (14.3)$$

The *simple Phillips curve* says that inflation π is negatively related to cyclical unemployment $u - \bar{u}$, where h is a positive number measuring the strength of the relationship between inflation and unemployment.

$$\pi = \pi^e - h(u - \bar{u}) \qquad (14.4)$$

The *expectations-augmented Phillips curve* says that inflation π is negatively related to cyclical unemployment $u - \bar{u}$ if the expected rate of inflation π^e is held constant. Changes in the expected rate of inflation cause the relationship between inflation and unemployment to shift.

Review Questions

1. What is Okun's law? If the unemployment rate increases by 2 percentage points between this year and next year, by how much will output change during the same period? Assume that the natural unemployment rate and full-employment output are constant.

2. How does the price adjustment process in the classical and Keynesian models lead to a link between output and the rate of inflation?

3. How does the expectations-augmented Phillips curve differ from the simple Phillips curve? Starting with the expectations-augmented Phillips curve, how do we get a short-run Phillips curve? The long-run Phillips curve?

4. How do changes in the expected rate of inflation account for the behavior of the short-run Phillips curve in the 1960s, 1970s, and 1980s in the United States? How can such changes account for stagflation?

5. Can policymakers trade more inflation for less unemployment in the short run? In the long run? Explain both the classical and Keynesian points of view.

6. Define the *natural rate of unemployment*. What factors explain the changes in the natural rate over time in the United States and in Europe?

7. What are the two principal costs of unemployment? For what type of unemployment is each of these costs the largest? The smallest?

8. Give two costs of anticipated inflation and two costs of unanticipated inflation. How is the magnitude of each of these costs affected if, instead of a moderate inflation, the economy experiences a hyperinflation?

9. Discuss the relative advantages of cold turkey and gradualism as policies for disinflation. What is the role of credibility in a disinflation?

Numerical Problems

1. Consider an economy in long-run equilibrium with an inflation rate of 12% (0.12) per year and a natural rate of unemployment $\bar{u}$ of 6% (0.06). The expectations-augmented Phillips curve is given by

$$\pi = \pi^e - 2(u - \bar{u}).$$

Assume that Okun's law holds so that a 1 percentage point increase in the unemployment rate maintained for one year reduces GNP by 2.5% of full-employment output.

a. Consider a two-year disinflation. In the first year $\pi = 0.04$ and $\pi^e = 0.08$. In the second year $\pi = 0.04$ and $\pi^e = 0.04$. In the first year, what is the unemployment rate? By what percentage does output fall short of full-employment output in the first year? In the second year, what is the unemployment rate? By what percentage does output fall short of full-employment output in the second year?

b. Now consider a four-year disinflation according to the following table:

Year	1	2	3	4
π	0.08	0.04	0.04	0.04
π^e	0.10	0.08	0.06	0.04

What is the unemployment rate in each of the four years? By what percentage does output fall short of full-employment output in each of the four years?

2. You are given the following data on the unemployment rate and output:

Year	1	2	3	4
Unemployment rate	8%	6%	7%	5%
Output	950	1030	1033.5	1127.5

a. Assuming that the natural rate of unemployment is 6% and that $(\bar{Y} - Y)/\bar{Y} = 2.5(u - \bar{u})$, find the full-employment level of output in each year.

b. Calculate the growth rate of full-employment output in years 2, 3, and 4 two different ways: First, calculate the growth rates by using the values for full-employment output that you found in part a. Then calculate the growth rate of full-employment output by using only the change in the unemployment rate, the growth rate of output, and the growth rate version of Okun's law, Eq. (14.2). Compare your answers from the two sets of calculations.

3. Consider the following extended classical economy:

AD: $Y = 300 + 10\left(\dfrac{M}{P}\right)$,

SRAS: $Y = \bar{Y} + P - P^e$,

Okun's law: $\dfrac{Y - \bar{Y}}{\bar{Y}} = -2.5(u - \bar{u})$,

$\bar{Y} = 500$,   and $\bar{u} = 0.06$.

a. Suppose that the money supply $M = 1000$ and the expected price level $P^e = 50$. What are the short-run equilibrium values of output Y, the price level P, and the unemployment rate u? What are the long-run equilibrium values of these three variables?

b. Now suppose that there is an unanticipated increase in the nominal money supply to $M = 1260$. What are the new short-run equilibrium values of output Y, the price level P, and the unemployment rate u? What are the new long-run equilibrium values of these three variables? In general, are your results consistent with the existence of an expectations-augmented Phillips curve?

4. In a certain economy the expectations-augmented Phillips curve is

$$\pi = \pi^e - 2(u - \bar{u}),$$

and the natural rate of unemployment $\bar{u}$ equals 0.06.

a. Graph the short-run Phillips curve of this economy, assuming that the expected rate of inflation equals 0.10. If the Fed chooses to keep the actual inflation rate equal to 0.10, what will be the unemployment rate?

b. A supply shock raises expected inflation to 0.12. Graph the new short-run Phillips curve, and compare this curve with the curve you drew in part a.

What happens to the unemployment rate if the Fed keeps the actual inflation rate equal to 0.10? What happens to the short-run Phillips curve and the unemployment rate if the Fed announces that it will keep inflation at 0.10 after the supply shock, and this announcement is fully believed by the public?

c. Suppose that the supply shock raises expected inflation to 0.12 and raises the natural rate of unemployment to 0.08. Repeat part b.

5. (Appendix) Consider an economy that initially has a labor force of 2000 workers. Of these workers, 1900 workers are employed, and each worker works 40 hours per week. The average product of labor is $10 per hour.

a. What is the total number of hours worked per week in the economy? What is the total output per week in the economy?

b. The economy enters a recession. Employment falls by 4%, and the number of hours per week worked by each employed worker falls by 2.5%. In addition, 0.2% of the labor force becomes discouraged at the prospect of finding a job and leaves the labor force. Finally, suppose that whenever total hours fall by 1%, total output falls by 1.4%. After the recession begins, what is the size of the labor force? How many workers are unemployed? What is the unemployment rate? What is the total number of hours worked per week in the economy? What is the total output per week in the economy? By what percentage has total output fallen relative to the initial situation? What is the value of the Okun's law coefficient relating the loss of output to the increase in the unemployment rate?

Analytical Problems

1. Some people have forecasted that someday we will live in a "cashless society" in which all businesses (including stores) and banks will be linked to a centralized accounting system. In this system you will be able to pay for purchases directly from your bank account without using cash. What are the costs of anticipated inflation in a cashless society? What are the costs of unanticipated inflation?

2. Suppose that the government institutes a program that helps unemployed workers learn new skills, find new jobs, and relocate as necessary to take the new jobs.

a. If this program reduces structural unemployment, what is the effect on the expectations-augmented Phillips curve and the long-run Phillips curve?

b. The government program is expensive, and critics argue that a cheaper way to get the unemployment rate down would be through monetary expansion. Comment.

3. Two extended classical economies (in which the misperceptions theory holds) are identical, except that in economy A money growth and inflation have been low and stable for many years, and in economy B money growth and inflation have fluctuated erratically between very low and very high levels. When producers in economy B observe changes in the prices of the goods they produce, from past experience they usually attribute these changes to fluctuations in the overall price level rather than to changes in the relative prices of their goods.

Will the slope of the short-run aggregate supply curve for economy B be flatter or steeper than the slope of the curve for economy A? How about the slope of the short-run Phillips curve?

4. To fight an ongoing 10% inflation, the government makes it illegal to raise wages or prices. However, the government continues to increase the money supply by 10% per year.

a. Using the Keynesian AD-AS framework, show the effects of the government's policies on the economy. Assume that firms meet the demand at the fixed price level up to the limits of their capacity, but that they cannot produce beyond their capacity.

b. After several years in which the controls have kept prices from rising, the government declares victory over inflation and removes the controls. What happens?

5. Consider an economy in general equilibrium with a constant money supply, zero inflation, and constant full-employment output (no real growth). Now suppose that money supply growth is increased permanently to 4% per year. What are the short-run and long-run effects on unemployment and inflation of this permanent increase in the rate of money growth? What is the long-run effect on the nominal interest rate and the real money stock? (Hint: In the long run the actual and expected rates of inflation are equal. Use the effects on the nominal interest rate and real output to determine the effect on the real demand for money.)

APPENDIX
14.A   MORE ON OKUN'S LAW

This appendix explains why the sensitivity of output to changes in unemployment, as embodied in Okun's law, is so large. The appendix also derives the growth rate form of Okun's law, Eq. (14.2).

The Sensitivity of Output to Unemployment

A 1 percentage point increase in unemployment reduces total employment by about 1%. Yet according to Okun's law, in response to a 1 percentage point increase in unemployment, output falls by about 2.5%. Why is the sensitivity of output to unemployment so large? To answer this question, we use the following symbols:

LF = the number of workers in the labor force,
u = the unemployment rate, so that
$1 - u$ is the fraction of
the labor force that is employed,
h = the number of hours per week worked by each worker,
APL = the average product of labor,
measured as the amount of output per hour of labor,
Y = total output per week.

Because a fraction $1 - u$ of the labor force is employed, the number of employed workers at any given time is $(1 - u) \times LF$. If each worker works h hours per week, the total number of hours worked per week is $(1 - u) \times LF \times h$. Total output per week equals the number of hours worked per week times the average amount produced each hour:

$$Y = (1 - u) \times LF \times h \times APL.$$

Now consider what happens when the unemployment rate increases by 1 percentage point, say from 6% to 7%. The factor $1 - u$ falls by approximately 1%, from 0.94 to 0.93. Thus if the labor force (LF), hours per week (h), and productivity per hour (APL) remained unchanged, total output Y would fall by approximately 1%. However, the labor force LF generally falls when cyclical unemployment increases, because some unemployed workers become discouraged by the poor prospect of finding a job and leave the labor force. In addition, firms usually cut back on the number of hours worked per week (h). Finally, as we documented in Chapter 9, average labor productivity APL is procyclical, rising in expansions but falling in recessions when cyclical unemployment rises. Because an increase in cyclical unemployment reduces the labor force (LF), hours per week (h), and productivity (APL), output falls by considerably more than 1% when the unemployment rate rises by 1 percentage point.

The Growth Rate Form of Okun's Law

To derive the growth rate form of Okun's law, Eq. (14.2), we start with the levels form of Okun's law, Eq. (14.1):

$$\frac{\bar{Y} - Y}{\bar{Y}} = 2.5(u - \bar{u}). \tag{14.1}$$

After multiplying by -1, we can rewrite Eq. (14.1) as

$$-1 + \frac{Y}{\bar{Y}} = -2.5u + 2.5\bar{u}.$$

Now calculate the change from the previous year to the current year of each side of this equation. Setting the change on the left side equal to the change on the right side, and assuming that $\bar{u}$ is constant (so $\Delta\bar{u} = 0$), we get

$$\Delta\left(\frac{Y}{\bar{Y}}\right) = -2.5 \, \Delta u.$$

The left side of this equation, which is the *change* in $Y/\bar{Y}$, is very close to the *growth rate* of $Y/\bar{Y}$, which is equal to $\Delta(Y/\bar{Y})/(Y/\bar{Y})$; to go from the change to the growth rate, we divide by $Y/\bar{Y}$, which is a number close to 1. Approximating the change in $Y/\bar{Y}$ by the growth rate, and using the formula that states that the growth rate of a ratio is the growth rate of the numerator minus the growth rate of the denominator,* we can rewrite the equation once more as

$$\frac{\Delta Y}{Y} - \frac{\Delta\bar{Y}}{\bar{Y}} = -2.5 \, \Delta u.$$

Rearranging this equation gives the growth rate form of Okun's law, Eq. (14.2).

15
Monetary Policy and the Federal Reserve

The government's decisions about the size and rate of growth of the nation's money supply make up its monetary policy. Along with fiscal policy, monetary policy is one of the two major tools available for affecting macroeconomic behavior. All of the macroeconomic models we have studied predict that changes in the level or growth rate of the money supply will have important effects on nominal variables such as the inflation rate and the nominal exchange rate. In addition, a number of leading macroeconomic theories (including the extended classical theory with misperceptions and the Keynesian theory) imply that in the short run monetary policy can affect real variables such as real GNP and the unemployment rate.

In this chapter we take a more detailed look at monetary policy, concentrating first on the basic question of what determines the nation's money supply. We will see that although a nation's central bank (the Federal Reserve in the United States) can exert strong influence over the level of the money supply, the money supply is also affected by the behavior of the banking system and decisions made by the public.

After discussing money supply determination, we turn to the question of how the central bank should conduct monetary policy in practice. Not surprisingly, given the differences between classical and Keynesian views about the effects of monetary policy and the desirability of trying to "smooth out" the business cycle (Chapters 11 and 12), this question is a controversial one. Keynesians usually argue that the monetary authorities should be given considerable scope to try to offset cyclical fluctuations. Opposing the Keynesian view, both classical economists and a group of economists called monetarists believe that monetary policy should not be left to the discretion of the central bank but should instead be governed by simple rules. Although establishing rules for monetary policy might seem to tie policymakers' hands unnecessarily, monetarists and classical economists argue that the use of rules would lead to a more stable and less inflationary economy in the long run. After examining the arguments for and against the use of rules, we compare the performances of rules-based monetary policies in the United States, Germany, and Japan.

PRINCIPLES OF MONEY SUPPLY DETERMINATION

How is the nation's money supply determined? Until this point in the book we have assumed that the money supply M is directly controlled by the central bank. Although this assumption is a useful simplification, it is not literally true. The central bank's control of the money supply is only indirect and depends to some extent on the institutional structure of the economy.

Most generally, three groups of actors affect the money supply: the central bank, depository institutions, and the public.

1. In nearly all countries the **central bank** is the governmental institution responsible for monetary policy.[1] Examples of central banks are the Federal Reserve in the United States, the Bundesbank in Germany, and the Bank of Japan.

2. **Depository institutions** are privately owned banks and thrift institutions (such as savings and loans) that accept deposits from and make loans directly to the public. We will refer to depository institutions as banks, for short.

3. The public includes every person or firm (except banks) that holds money, either as currency and coin or as deposits in banks—in other words, virtually the whole private economy outside of the banking system.

Before investigating how these three groups of actors interact to set the money supply in a financially sophisticated country like the United States, we begin with an example of a primitive agricultural economy, which we call Agricola. By studying the introduction of money and the development of banking in Agricola, we will get a clear view of the factors involved in the determination of the money supply. An additional benefit is that the development of the monetary and banking systems in Agricola loosely parallels the actual development of monetary and banking systems that evolved over the course of centuries in a variety of countries.

The Money Supply in an All-Currency Economy

The imaginary country of Agricola is an agricultural nation that grows a rich variety of fruits, nuts, vegetables, and grains. Initially, Agricola has no money supply, so all trading is done by barter, the direct trading of goods for goods. However, as we discussed in Chapter 4, a trading system based on barter is extremely inconvenient: Under a barter system a farmer who wants to trade some of her barley for pomegranates must find someone willing to give up pomegranates in exchange for barley, which involves a costly and time-consuming search process.

The benevolent leader of Agricola recognizes the inconvenience resulting from the barter system and resolves to create a national money to facilitate trades among Agricolan citizens. The first step in establishing a national money is to create a government agency called the Agricolan Central Bank. Once it has set up shop, the Central Bank prints paper certificates[2] and decrees the value of each

---

[1] Most industrialized countries established central banks in the nineteenth century or early twentieth century. Prior to the establishment of central banks, national Treasury Departments were often responsible for currency issue and other matters pertaining to the money supply.

[2] In most countries the actual printing of paper money is done by a separate agency, not by the central bank itself.

certificate to be one florin (abbreviated fl), which becomes the name of the national currency of Agricola. The government of Agricola prohibits anyone other than the Agricolan Central Bank from printing these certificates.

To get the florins into general circulation, the Central Bank uses them to buy some real assets from the public. In the agricultural economy of Agricola real assets are storable agricultural products such as coconuts, so the Central Bank uses newly printed florins to buy coconuts from the public. Why do people in Agricola willingly surrender valuable coconuts in exchange for paper certificates? In general, people accept paper money in payment for goods, services, or assets because they expect to be able to use it to buy other goods, services, or assets in the future. In other words, people accept paper money because they believe that other people will also accept it. The belief that money has value becomes self-justifying: If most people believe that money has value, then it has value.[3] In practice, the government helps convince the public that paper money has value, usually by decreeing that the money is **legal tender**—that is, creditors are required to accept the money in settlement of debts—and by stating its own willingness to accept money from the public in payment of taxes.

Suppose that the people of Agricola accept the new currency, and that the Central Bank trades 1 million florins to the public in exchange for 1 million coconuts. The balance sheet of the Agricolan Central Bank now looks like this:

Agricolan Central Bank			
ASSETS		LIABILITIES	
Coconuts	1,000,000 fl	Currency	1,000,000 fl

On the left side of the balance sheet are the Central Bank's assets—what it owns or is owed, in this case, the coconuts. On the right side are the bank's liabilities—what it owes to others. Since the florins are technically debt obligations of the Central Bank, they are entered as liabilities on the right side of the balance sheet.[4] The liabilities of the Central Bank that are usable as money are called the **monetary base,** or, equivalently, **high-powered money.** The monetary base of Agricola is thus 1 million florins.

Assume that initially Agricola has no banking system. With no banks and hence no bank deposits, the money supply is completely in the form of currency held by the public. That is, the paper certificates distributed by the Agricolan Central Bank are used directly as money. Thus the money supply in Agricola equals 1 million florins, which in turn equals the monetary base (the liabilities of the Agricolan Central Bank). From this example we conclude that *in an all-currency economy (one with no bank deposits) the money supply equals the monetary base.*

The Money Supply Under Fractional Reserve Banking

As the people of Agricola become financially more sophisticated, a system of private banks emerges. The banks announce their willingness to accept deposits from the public.

---

[3]Also possible is that no one believes that money has value, which would again be a self-justifying belief because no one would then accept money in payment.

[4]In some monetary systems, such as the traditional gold standard, the public was allowed to trade in the central bank's paper liabilities for real assets—for example, gold. In general, modern paper moneys are no longer backed by any real asset.

For the time being, assume that because currency is easily lost or stolen, Agricolans want to hold *all* their money in the form of bank deposits rather than as currency. After the Agricolans deposit all their currency (1 million florins) in banks, the combined, or consolidated, balance sheet of all banks taken together looks like this:

Consolidated Balance Sheet of Banks

ASSETS		LIABILITIES	
Currency	1,000,000 fl	Deposits	1,000,000 fl

The assets of the banking system are the 1,000,000 paper florins in bank vaults. The liabilities of the banking system are the deposits, which are debts or obligations that the banks owe to the public. The balance sheet of the Central Bank remains the same as it was previously.

Liquid assets held by banks to meet the demands for withdrawals by depositors or to pay the checks drawn on depositors' accounts are called **bank reserves.** In general, bank reserves consist of currency held by private banks in their vaults plus deposits held by private banks at the Central Bank. In the simple case we are describing here, all bank reserves are held as currency in the banks' vaults. Notice that in this case bank reserves equal total deposits of 1,000,000 fl. This type of banking system is called **100% reserve banking,** because banks hold reserves equal to 100% of their deposits. Under 100% reserve banking, banks are nothing more than a safekeeping service for the public's currency. Indeed, the only way banks could cover their expenses and make a profit under 100% reserve banking would be to charge depositors a fee for holding their money for them (that is, to pay negative interest on deposits).

However, one day an enterprising Agricolan banker notices that the paper florins the bank has accepted from depositors are just sitting idly in neat stacks in the bank's vault. True, a few florins flow out when a depositor writes a check to someone who banks elsewhere, or when a depositor switches his account to another bank; but this outflow is balanced by a roughly equivalent inflow, when the bank's depositors receive checks drawn on other banks or the bank attracts a depositor away from another bank. After some observation the banker calculates that keeping paper florins in the vault equal to, say, 20% of outstanding deposits would be more than enough to cover this random ebb and flow. The remaining 80% of the florins on deposit (the banker realizes in a stroke of genius) could be lent out to earn interest for the bank!

Under the Agricolan banker's scheme the reserves held by the bank will equal only a fraction of the bank's outstanding deposits. In particular, the **reserve-deposit ratio,** which is reserves divided by deposits, equals 20%. A banking system in which banks holds reserves equal to a fraction of their deposits, so that the reserve-deposit ratio is less than one, is called **fractional reserve banking.** Fractional reserve banking is profitable for banks because, instead of sitting in the vault earning no interest for the bank, a portion of the funds received from depositors can be used to make interest-earning loans. Under the alternative system of 100% reserve banking, reserves equaling deposits are always kept on hand and no loans can be made.

The insight of fractional reserve banking is quickly grasped by all the bankers of Agricola, and they all decide to keep florins in their vaults (their reserves) equal to 20% of deposits and lend out the other 80% (that is, 800,000 fl) to farmers. The farmers use the loans to buy fertilizer for their farms. The sellers of the fertilizer receive 800,000 fl in payment; and because we have assumed that everyone prefers having bank deposits to holding currency, they deposit the 800,000 fl in the banking system. After these deposits are made all of the florins are back in the banks, and the consolidated balance sheet of the banking system will look like this:

	Consolidated Balance Sheet of Banks		
ASSETS		LIABILITIES	
Currency (= reserves)	1,000,000 fl	Deposits	1,800,000 fl
Loans to farmers	800,000 fl		
Total	1,800,000 fl	Total	1,800,000 fl

The banks' assets now include the 800,000 fl in loans to farmers (since the loans are owed to the banks, they are assets of the banks). The banks' assets also include 1,000,000 paper florins: 200,000 fl originally kept in reserve plus the 800,000 fl deposited by the sellers of the fertilizer.

The banks' consolidated liabilities equal 1,800,000 fl in deposits: the 1,000,000 fl in original deposits, plus the 800,000 fl in new deposits from the fertilizer sellers.

At this point, as the bankers examine their balance sheets, they notice that their reserves (equal to holdings of paper florins) are back up to 1,000,000 fl. Their deposits equal 1,800,000 fl. On the principle that reserves need equal only 20% of deposits, their reserves of 1,000,000 fl are too high: The bankers need to hold only 360,000 fl ($0.20 \times 1,800,000$ fl). The other 640,000 fl (1,000,000 fl − 360,000 fl) can be lent out at interest again.

So the banks make additional interest-bearing loans in the amount of 640,000 fl. The banks' borrowers use the funds to make purchases. As before, these florins are eventually redeposited in the banking system. At this point the consolidated balance sheet of all the banks taken together looks like this:

	Consolidated Balance Sheet of Banks		
ASSETS		LIABILITIES	
Currency (= reserves)	1,000,000 fl	Deposits	2,440,000 fl
Loans	1,440,000 fl		
Total	2,440,000 fl	Total	2,440,000 fl

The assets of the banks now include 1,000,000 paper florins (the 360,000 fl that were kept as reserves, plus the 640,000 fl that are redeposited by the public) and 1,440,000 fl in loans (the 800,000 fl made in the first round of lending plus the 640,000 fl made in the second round). The liabilities are 2,440,000 fl in deposits (the 1,800,000 fl from earlier plus the 640,000 fl in new deposits).

The process does not stop here. Checking their balance sheets after this latest round of loans and redeposits, the bankers will find that their reserves (1,000,000 fl) *still* exceed 20% of their deposits (20% of deposits of 2,440,000 fl is 488,000 fl). So yet another round of loans and redeposits of loaned-out funds will occur.

This process of **multiple expansion of loans and deposits,** in which fractional reserve banking leads to increases in the economy's loans and deposits, will only stop when the reserves of the banking system equal 20% of its deposits. Since the reserves of the banks always equal 1,000,000 fl (the entire supply of paper florins) at the end of each round, the process can only stop when total bank deposits equal 1,000,000 fl/0.20, or 5,000,000 fl. At this final point the consolidated balance sheet of the banks will look like this:

Consolidated Balance Sheet of Banks			
ASSETS		LIABILITIES	
Currency (= reserves)	1,000,000 fl	Deposits	5,000,000 fl
Loans	4,000,000 fl		
Total	5,000,000 fl	Total	5,000,000 fl

At this final stage the ratio of reserves to deposits equals the ratio desired by banks (20%). No further expansion of loans and deposits can occur after this point, since the ratio of reserves to deposits is at its minimum acceptable level.

What is the money supply in Agricola at the end of this process? Remember that the public does not hold any currency but, instead, deposits any currency received in the banking system, where it is held in the form of bank reserves. The reserves in the banks' vaults are not available for transactions and thus are not counted as money. However, the public *is* holding deposits. Because they are very liquid and can be used for transactions, bank deposits are counted as part of the money supply.[5] Indeed, since there is no public holding of currency in this example, bank deposits *are* the money supply. Therefore in this example the money supply equals 5,000,000 fl, the total quantity of deposits.

What is the relationship between the money supply and the monetary base when there is fractional reserve banking and no holding of currency by the public? This question can be answered algebraically by using the following variables:

$$M = \text{the money supply,}$$
$$BASE = \text{the monetary base,}$$
$$DEP = \text{total bank deposits,}$$
$$res = \text{the banks' desired reserve-deposit ratio} = \frac{RES}{DEP}$$

With no currency being held by the public, the money supply equals the quantity of bank deposits:

$$M = DEP \tag{15.1}$$

For any level of deposits DEP, the amount of reserves that banks want to hold is $res \times DEP$. At the end of the multiple-expansion process, bank reserves must equal the amount of currency distributed by the Central Bank (the monetary base). Therefore we have

$$res \times DEP = BASE \tag{15.2}$$

---

[5]Remember from Chapter 4 that the most narrowly defined monetary aggregate M1 includes demand deposits and other checkable deposits. Slightly less liquid deposits, such as savings deposits and time deposits, are included in broader monetary aggregates.

Solving Eq. (15.2) for deposits yields $DEP = BASE/res$. Because the money supply equals deposits in this example (Eq. 15.1), we have

$$M = DEP = \frac{BASE}{res} \tag{15.3}$$

We conclude that *in an economy with fractional reserve banking and no currency held by the public, the money supply equals the monetary base divided by the reserve-deposit ratio.* In Agricola the monetary base is 1,000,000 fl, and the reserve-deposit ratio chosen by the banks is 0.20. The money supply is therefore 1,000,000 fl/0.20, or 5,000,000 fl, as we have already seen.

The multiple expansion of loans and deposits allows the economy to create a money supply that is much larger than the monetary base. Each unit of monetary base allows $1/res$ units of money to be created, leading to a money supply that is a multiple of the monetary base. It is because each unit of monetary base can permit the creation of several units of money supply that the base is also called *high-powered money.*

Bank Runs

Fractional reserve banking works under the assumption that outflows and inflows of reserves will be roughly balanced, and in particular that there will never be a situation in which a large fraction of a bank's depositors want to withdraw their funds at the same time. Should a large number of depositors attempt to withdraw currency simultaneously (more than 20% of the bank's deposits in the example of Agricola), the bank will run out of reserves and will not be able to meet all of its depositors' demands for cash.

Historically in the United States, there were times when rumors circulated that a particular bank had made some bad loans and was at risk of becoming bankrupt. On the principle of "better safe than sorry," the bank's depositors lined up to withdraw their money. From the depositors' perspective withdrawal avoided the risk that the bank would fail and not be able to pay off depositors in full. A large-scale, panicky withdrawal of deposits from a bank is called a **bank run.** Even if the rumors about the bank's loans proved untrue, a large enough run could exhaust the bank's reserves and force it to close.[6] We will have more to say about bank runs later in this chapter and in Chapter 17.

The Money Supply with both Public Holdings of Currency and Fractional Reserve Banking

In most economies the public holds some currency (as in our first example) and there is also a fractional reserve banking system (as in our second example). Since currency in the public's hands and bank deposits can both be used for transactions, both are forms of money. When the public holds an amount of currency equal to CU, known as currency in circulation, and bank deposits are equal to DEP, the money supply M is given by

$$M = CU + DEP \tag{15.4}$$

In this situation the monetary base has two uses: Some of the monetary base is held as currency by the public (CU), and the rest is held as reserves by banks

---

[6]To stop a run, a bank had to convince customers that it was "sound"—financially solvent—and had plenty of funds available. This was Jimmy Stewart's strategy in the movie *It's A Wonderful Life.*

(RES). Therefore the monetary base equals the sum of currency held by the public and bank reserves:

$$BASE = CU + RES \qquad (15.5)$$

As we will see, the central bank controls the amount of monetary base but does not directly control the money supply. To see how the money supply is related to the monetary base, we first divide the money supply in Eq. (15.4) by the monetary base in Eq. (15.5) to get

$$\frac{M}{BASE} = \frac{CU + DEP}{CU + RES} \qquad (15.6)$$

Next, we divide the numerator and the denominator of the ratio on the right side of Eq. (15.6) by DEP to obtain

$$\frac{M}{BASE} = \frac{CU/DEP + 1}{(CU/DEP + RES/DEP)} \qquad (15.7)$$

The right side of Eq. (15.7) contains two important ratios. The first of these is the **currency-deposit ratio,** CU/DEP, which is the ratio of the currency held by the public to the public's deposits in banks. The currency-deposit ratio is determined by the public and depends on the amount of their money that the public wants to hold in the form of currency versus the amount they choose to hold as deposits. The public can raise the currency-deposit ratio to any level that it wishes by withdrawing currency from banks (which increases currency held by the public and reduces deposits); similarly, by depositing currency in banks, the public can lower the currency-deposit ratio. We use the abbreviation cu to stand for the ratio of currency to deposits desired by the public.

The second important ratio on the right side of Eq. (15.7) is the reserve-deposit ratio, RES/DEP, which we have already discussed. The reserve-deposit ratio is determined by banks' decisions about how much of their deposits to lend out.[7] As before, we use the abbreviation res to stand for the ratio of reserves to deposits desired by the banks.

When the process of multiple expansion of loans and deposits is complete, the currency-deposit ratio equals the ratio desired by the public cu, and the reserve-deposit ratio equals the ratio desired by the banks res. Substituting cu for CU/DEP and res for RES/DEP in Eq. (15.7) and multiplying both sides of Eq. (15.7) by $BASE$, we obtain

$$M = \left(\frac{cu + 1}{cu + res}\right)BASE \qquad (15.8)$$

Equation (15.8) says that the money supply M is a multiple of the monetary base. The relation of the money supply to the monetary base depends on the currency-deposit ratio chosen by the public cu and the reserve-deposit ratio chosen by banks res. The factor $(cu + 1)/(cu + res)$, which is the number of dollars of money supply that can be created from each dollar of monetary base, is called the **money multiplier.** The money multiplier will be greater than one as long as res is less than one (that is, as long as there is fractional reserve banking). Notice that if no currency is held by the public ($cu = 0$), then the money multiplier equals $1/res$,

---

[7]As we discuss later, government regulations may set minimum levels for banks' reserve-deposit ratios.

Table 15.1 The Monetary Base, the Money Multiplier, and the Money Supply in the United States

Currency in circulation CU	$244.8 billion
Bank reserves RES	$64.5 billion
Monetary base $BASE$ $(= CU + RES)$	$309.3 billion
Deposits DEP	$577.8 billion
Money supply M $(= CU + DEP)$	$822.6 billion
Reserve-deposit ratio res $(= RES/DEP)$	0.1116
Currency-deposit ratio cu $(= CU/DEP)$	0.4237
Money multiplier $(cu + 1)/(cu + res)$	2.66
Ratio of money supply to base $M/BASE$	2.66

Source: *Federal Reserve Bulletin*, February 1991, Tables 1.12 and 1.21. Deposits are transactions deposits, and the money supply is M1. Data are for November 1990.

the same value that we saw in our earlier example when all money was held as bank deposits (Eq. 15.3).

Table 15.1 illustrates the money multiplier and the relation among currency, reserves, monetary base, and the money supply, using data from the United States. From the data on currency, reserves, and deposits given in the table, you can calculate that the currency-deposit ratio is 0.4237 and the reserve-deposit ratio is 0.1116. Thus the money multiplier, $(cu + 1)/(cu + res)$, equals 2.66. You can verify that this formula for the money multiplier gives the right answer by dividing the money supply ($822.6 billion) by the monetary base ($309.3 billion), to obtain 2.66.

It can be shown algebraically that the money multiplier decreases when either the currency-deposit ratio cu or the reserve-deposit ratio res increases.[8] To understand these results intuitively, remember that the reason that the monetary base gets "multiplied" is that under fractional reserve banking some of the money deposited in banks is used to make loans to the public. The public can either hold the money it borrows from banks as currency or redeposit its borrowings in the banking system, but in either case the result is a higher total money supply than existed before the loans were made. When the reserve-deposit ratio rises, banks lend out a smaller fraction of each dollar of deposits and so less money is created for any given amount of monetary base; thus an increase in the reserve-deposit ratio lowers the money multiplier. When the currency-deposit ratio rises, the public puts a smaller fraction of its money in banks, which means that banks have less money to use for loans. With banks lending less, less money is created from a given amount of monetary base, and so again the money multiplier is reduced.

Open-Market Operations

We have shown how the monetary base and the money multiplier determine the money supply. To change the level of the money supply, a central bank must change

---

[8]That the money multiplier decreases when cu increases is not obvious, since cu appears in both the numerator and the denominator of the money multiplier. However, as you can confirm by trying numerical examples, an increase in cu reduces the money multiplier as long as res is less than one, which must always be the case.

the amount of monetary base or change the money multiplier. Later in this chapter we discuss how the central bank can affect the money multiplier. For now we focus on the most direct and frequently used way of changing the money supply, which is by raising or lowering the monetary base. For a given value of the money multiplier Eq. (15.8) tells us that any change in the monetary base will cause a proportional change in the money supply.

Suppose the Agricolan Central Bank decides to increase the monetary base by 10%, from 1,000,000 to 1,100,000 fl. How would it go about implementing this decision? First, the Central Bank has to print the extra 100,000 fl. Then it can use the 100,000 new florins to buy assets (coconuts) from the public. After purchasing the additional coconuts, the Agricolan Central Bank's balance sheet looks like this:

Agricolan Central Bank

ASSETS		LIABILITIES	
Coconuts	1,100,000 fl	Currency	1,100,000 fl

By purchasing 100,000 fl of coconuts, the Central Bank has put 100,000 more paper certificates (florins) into circulation. The monetary base, which is the same as the total liabilities of the Central Bank, has risen to 1,100,000 fl. As we have said, assuming the money multiplier remains unchanged, the money supply will also increase by 10%.

Suppose, instead, that the Agricolan Central Bank wanted to *reduce* the monetary base by 10%. In this case the Central Bank would *sell* 100,000 fl of coconuts to the public, in exchange for 100,000 florins in cash. The 100,000 florins collected by the Central Bank are retired from circulation. (The retired florins are not treated as assets of the Central Bank; just as if you paid off a debt and retrieved your own IOU, you would not consider your IOU to be an asset of yours.) The Agricolan Central Bank's balance sheet now looks like this:

Agricolan Central Bank

ASSETS		LIABILITIES	
Coconuts	900,000 fl	Currency	900,000 fl

The Agricolan Central Bank's liabilities outstanding (the monetary base) have been reduced to 900,000. With a fixed money multiplier the money supply will fall proportionately.

As we discussed in Chapter 4, a purchase of assets by the central bank is called an **open-market purchase**.[9] An open-market purchase increases the monetary base and thus the money supply. A sale of assets to the public by the central bank is called an **open-market sale.** An open-market sale reduces the monetary base and the money supply. Open-market purchases and sales are collectively called open-market operations. Open-market operations are the most direct way for central banks to change their national money supplies.

---

[9]The term *open market* refers to the fact that the central bank's transactions with the public take place in regular asset markets that are open to and used by the public.

The Money Multiplier During the Great Depression

The money multiplier is usually relatively stable, but not always. During 1930–1933, in the early part of the Great Depression, the money multiplier fell sharply, which created serious problems for monetary policy.

The source of the instability in the money multiplier, as discussed in detail by Milton Friedman and Anna Schwartz in their *Monetary History of the United States, 1867–1960*,[10] was a series of severe banking panics. A banking panic is an episode in which many banks suffer runs by depositors, with some banks being forced to shut down. The U.S. panics resulted from both financial weakness in the banking system and the arrival of bad economic and financial news. Friedman and Schwartz emphasized the following sources of the banking panics: (1) the effects of falling agricultural prices on the economies of farm states in the autumn of 1930; (2) the failure of a large New York bank called the Bank of the United States, in December 1930 (a private bank, despite its name); (3) the failure in May 1931 of Austria's largest bank, which led to a European financial crisis; and (4) Britain's abandonment of the gold standard in September 1931. The most severe banking panic began around January 1933 and was halted only when the newly inaugurated President Roosevelt proclaimed a "bank holiday" that shut down all the banks in March 1933. By the end of this period more than a third of the banks in the United States had failed or had been taken over by other banks. Banking reforms that were passed as part of Roosevelt's New Deal legislation restored confidence in the banking system and halted bank runs after March 1933.

The banking panics affected the money multiplier in two ways. First, people became very distrustful of banks, fearing that their bank might suddenly fail and not be able to pay off its depositors. (These events occurred before deposits were insured by the Federal government, as they are today.) Instead of holding bank deposits, people felt safer holding currency, perhaps under the mattress or in coffee cans buried in the backyard. Conversion of deposits into currency caused the currency-deposit ratio to rise during the period, as shown in Fig. 15.1, with a spectacular rise in the first quarter of 1933.

Second, in anticipation of possible runs, banks began to hold more reserves (cash in the vault) to back their deposits, as shown by the behavior of the reserve-deposit ratio, also pictured in Fig. 15.1. Banks hoped to convince depositors that there was enough cash in the banks' vaults to satisfy withdrawals, so that the depositors would not be tempted to start a run.

As we discussed earlier, increases in either the currency-deposit ratio or the reserve-deposit ratio cause the money multiplier to fall. As shown in Fig.15.2(a), p. 610, as a result of the banking panics, the money multiplier fell precipitously, from 6.6 in March 1930 to 3.6 by the banking holiday in March 1933. Thus even though the monetary base grew by 20% during that three-year period, the money

[10]Princeton, N.J.: Princeton University Press for NBER, 1963.

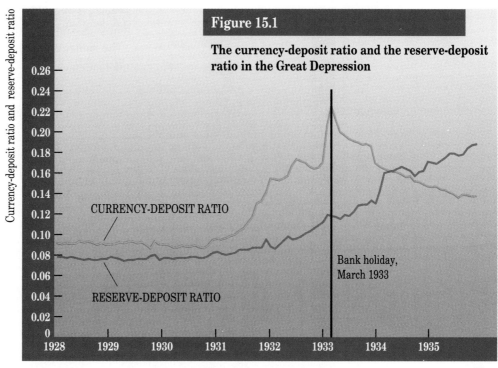

Figure 15.1

The currency-deposit ratio and the reserve-deposit ratio in the Great Depression

During the Great Depression people worried about the safety of their money in banks and so increased the ratio of currency in circulation to deposits. In anticipation of possible bank runs banks increased the ratio of reserves to deposits.

Source: Milton Friedman and Anna Schwartz, *A Monetary History of the United States, 1867–1960*: Currency—Table A-1, column (1); deposits, total commercial banks (demand and time)—Table A-1, column (4); reserves, bank reserves—Table A-2, column (3).

multiplier fell by so much that the money supply *fell* by 35%, as you can see in Fig. 15.2(b). There is some controversy about whether the fall in the money supply was a major cause of the decline in output during 1930–1933 (Friedman and Schwartz argue that it was), but there is general agreement that the drastic fall in the price level (by about a third) seen in this period was the result of the plunge in the money supply.

15.2 MONETARY CONTROL IN THE UNITED STATES

The principles of money supply determination developed in the Agricola example can be applied directly to actual economies by adding a few institutional details. In this section we link up these general principles with monetary institutions in the United States.

The Federal Reserve System

The central bank of the United States is called the Federal Reserve System, or the Fed for short. The Federal Reserve System was created by the Federal Reserve Act in 1913 and began operation in 1914. One of Congress's main motivations for establishing the Fed was the hope that a central bank would help eliminate the

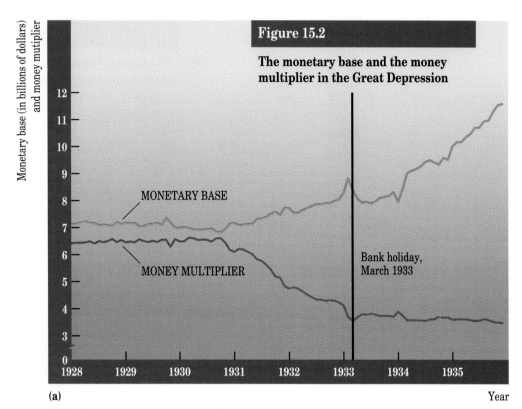

(a)   Year

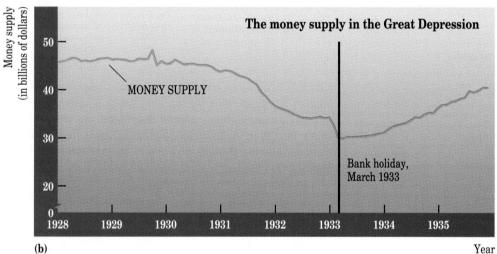

(b)   Year

(a) As a result of the increases in the currency-deposit ratio and the reserve-deposit ratio, the money multiplier fell sharply during the Great Depression. The monetary base rose during the Great Depression.

(b) The fall in the money multiplier caused a sharp decline in the money supply in the Great Depression, despite the increase in the monetary base.

Source: Milton Friedman and Anna Schwartz, *A Monetary History of the United States, 1867–1960*: Currency—Table A-1, column (1); deposits, total commercial banks (demand and time)—Table A-1, column (4); reserves, bank reserves—Table A-2, column (3); base = currency + reserves; money multiplier = (currency + deposits)/ base; money = currency + deposits.

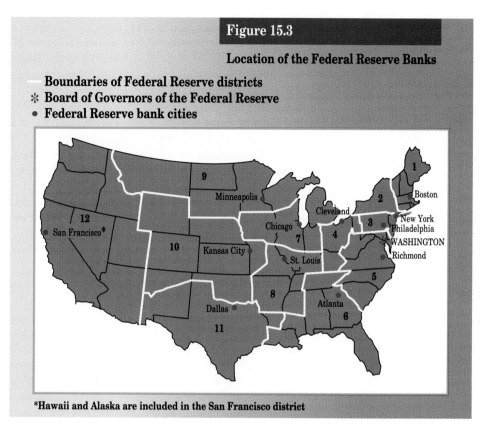

Figure 15.3

Location of the Federal Reserve Banks

— **Boundaries of Federal Reserve districts**
❋ **Board of Governors of the Federal Reserve**
● **Federal Reserve bank cities**

*Hawaii and Alaska are included in the San Francisco district

The twelve regional Federal Reserve Banks are located in twelve major cities in the United States. The Board of Governors of the Federal Reserve System is located in Washington, D.C.

severe financial crises (combinations of stock market crashes, business failures, and banking panics) that had periodically afflicted the United States before World War I. Ironically, as we have just discussed, the most severe financial crisis in U.S. history occurred in 1930–1933, barely a decade and a half after the creation of the Fed.

The Federal Reserve Act established a system of twelve regional Federal Reserve Banks, each associated with a geographical area called a Federal Reserve district. The locations of the twelve Federal Reserve Banks are given in Fig. 15.3. Technically, the regional Federal Reserve Banks are owned by the private banks within the district who are members of the Federal Reserve System. All federally chartered private banks are members of the Federal Reserve System, and state-chartered banks may elect to join. Whether an individual bank is a member of the system has ceased to mean very much, however, since Congress passed legislation in 1980 extending the responsibilities and privileges of member banks to all banks. Before 1980 member banks faced stricter regulatory requirements than nonmembers but also had access to some useful services (such as check-clearing services).[11]

The leadership of the Federal Reserve System is provided by the **Board of Governors of the Federal Reserve System** (also called the Federal Reserve Board), located in Washington, D.C. The Board consists of seven governors, appointed by the President of the United States to staggered fourteen-year terms, with one of the governors beginning a new term every other year. (See "The Po-

---

[11]Thrift institutions, such as savings and loans, are not allowed to be members of the Federal Reserve System, but they can hold deposits at the Fed and can use the check-clearing facilities of the Fed.

litical Environment" box, p. 614, for a discussion of how closely governors follow the wishes of the President who appointed them.) The President appoints one member of the Board to be the chairman of the Board of Governors, for a term of four years. Besides having a considerable influence over monetary policy, the chairman is an important figure in financial markets (the Fed has partial responsibility for regulating securities markets and the banking sector) and is often consulted by Congress and the President on matters of national economic policy.

Decisions about monetary policy are the responsibility of the **Federal Open Market Committee,** or FOMC. The FOMC consists of the seven governors, the president of the Federal Reserve Bank of New York, plus four of the presidents of the other regional Federal Reserve Banks, who serve on the FOMC on a rotating basis. The FOMC meets about eight times a year to review the state of the economy and to plan the conduct of monetary policy. (See the "In Touch with the Macroeconomy" box, p. 620.) The FOMC can meet more frequently (in person or by conference call) if developments in the economy seem to warrant discussion.

The Federal Reserve's Balance Sheet

The balance sheet of the Federal Reserve System (all of the Federal Reserve Banks taken together) is shown in Table 15.2. As you can see from the table, the Fed's largest asset by far is its holdings of U.S. Treasury securities, or government bonds. Indeed, the Fed owns about 10% of outstanding U.S. government bonds. The Fed also owns gold and makes loans to banks (depository institutions), which count as assets for the Fed. The category "Other assets" in Table 15.2 includes foreign exchange, bonds issued by Federal agencies, and other small items.

The largest liability of the Fed is currency outstanding. Some of this currency ($31.1 billion) is held in the vaults of banks and is known as **vault cash.** (Vault cash does *not* include currency in the vaults of the Federal Reserve Banks, because this

Table 15.2 The Balance Sheet of the Federal Reserve System (in Billions of Dollars)

ASSETS		LIABILITIES		
Gold	$11.1	Currency		$275.9
Loans to depository institutions	$0.1	Vault cash[a]	$31.1	
		In circulation[b]	$244.8	
U.S. Treasury securities	$245.0	Deposits of depository institutions[c]		$33.4
Other assets	$62.7	Other liabilities[d] and net worth		$9.6
Total	$318.9	Total		$318.9

Addenda

Reserves = deposits of depository institutions + vault cash = $64.5 billion

Monetary base = currency in circulation + reserves = $309.3 billion

Source: *Federal Reserve Bulletin*, February 1991, Table 1.18. Data are for November 1990.
[a]Table 1.12, line 2.
[b]Table 1.21, line 6.
[c]Table 1.12, line 1.
[d]Calculated as total minus the sum of the other figures in the column.

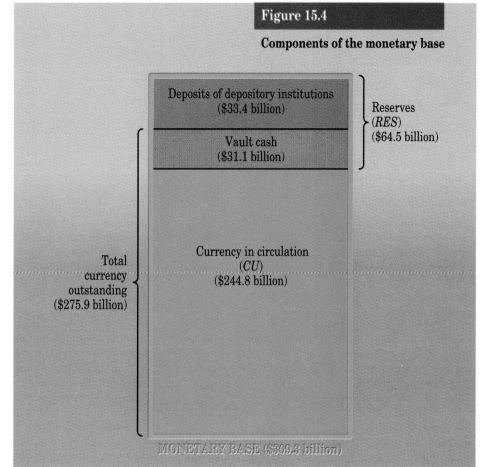

Figure 15.4

Components of the monetary base

Deposits of depository institutions
($33.4 billion)

Vault cash
($31.1 billion)

Reserves
(*RES*)
($64.5 billion)

Currency in circulation
(*CU*)
($244.8 billion)

Total
currency
outstanding
($275.9 billion)

MONETARY BASE ($309.3 billion)

The monetary base equals currency in circulation CU plus bank reserves RES. Because reserves equal vault cash plus deposits of depository institutions at the Fed, and because total currency outstanding equals currency in circulation plus vault cash, the monetary base can also be expressed as the sum of deposits of depository institutions and total currency outstanding.

currency does not represent a liability of the Fed.) The remainder of currency outstanding, $244.8 billion, is in circulation (that is, it is held by the public) and corresponds to what we have labeled CU.

The other major liability of the Fed is deposits made at the Fed by depository institutions, such as banks, savings and loans, and mutual savings banks. In accepting deposits from depository institutions, the Fed acts as the "banks' bank." Depository institutions make deposits at the Fed because it is a convenient way of holding reserves. These accounts at the Fed ($33.4 billion), together with vault cash ($31.1 billion), equal the total reserves of the banking system, what we have called RES. In Table 15.2 these reserves are shown to equal $64.5 billion.

Recall from Eq. (15.5) that the monetary base equals bank reserves ($64.5 billion) plus currency in circulation ($244.8 billion), which is $309.3 billion. As shown in Fig. 15.4, the monetary base can be calculated in an alternative but equivalent way as the sum of total currency outstanding ($275.9 billion) plus deposits of depository institutions at the Fed ($33.4 billion), which is again $309.3 billion.[12]

---

[12]The Fed has other liabilities as well, including accounts held by the U.S. Treasury and by foreign central banks. Because these accounts are not owned by the public or the U.S. banking sector, they are not counted as part of the monetary base.

The Political Environment

Reliability of Fed Governors

Although the Federal Reserve was created by an act of Congress and is ultimately responsible to Congress and the President, under normal circumstances the Fed has the authority to conduct monetary policy as it chooses without having to get the approval of other parts of the government. The most direct control that the President has over the policies of the Fed is through the appointment of Federal Reserve governors. But because governors have fourteen-year terms, they do not need to worry about pleasing the President who appointed them in order to be reappointed. Thus if the President wants the Fed to conduct monetary policy in accordance with the administration's general economic philosophy, the President will have to carefully select appointees who are "reliable"— that is, people who are loyal and persuasive and who share the President's views on economic policy.

Is there some systematic characteristic that a President can look for in trying to appoint a reliable Fed governor? To answer this question, Thomas Havrilesky of Duke University and John Gildea of Wheaton College* studied individual governors' voting records at FOMC meetings during the period 1959–1987. Although governors have different views on any given issue, the desire to present a unified stance on monetary policy leads most governors to vote with the majority most of the time. As you can see in the accompanying table, governors who were professional economists dissented only 7.6% of the time, and noneconomists dissented only 8.9% of the time. More interesting is

*"Packing the Board of Governors," *Challenge*, March/April 1990, pp. 52–55.

Like the Agricolan Central Bank, if the Fed wants to change the money supply, its primary tool is open-market operations. To increase the money supply, for example, the Fed could conduct an open-market purchase, in which it would buy U.S. Treasury securities (instead of coconuts, as in Agricola) from the public. A purchase of $1 billion in securities would increase the Fed's assets by $1 billion. To pay for these securities, the Fed would write a check on itself, redeemable by a bank either as a deposit at the Fed or as cash. In either case the monetary base would rise by $1 billion. Given the money multiplier, an increase in the monetary base translates into a proportional increase in the money supply.

To reduce the money supply, an open-market sale could be used. The Fed could sell $1 billion of Treasury securities to the public, receiving checks drawn on banks in exchange. The Fed's assets would fall by $1 billion (it owns $1 billion less in securities). The Fed would use the $1 billion in checks it receives to eliminate $1 billion in deposits of depository institutions, so that the monetary base would fall by $1 billion.

the timing of the dissenting votes: As the first row of the table shows, economists were more likely to dissent during a presidential term of the opposing party than during a presidential term of the governor's own party (a governor's own party was taken to be the party of the President that appointed that governor). For noneconomists the pattern of dissent was just the opposite: Noneconomists dissented 13.3% of the time during

their own party's presidential tenure and only 5.4% of the time during the opposing party's presidential tenure.

Consistent with the results in the table, Havrilesky and Gildea found that among ten characteristics of the governors only a Ph.D. in economics, an academic background, and experience as an economist seemed to be systematically associated with reliability. There are two explanations for the reliability of economists:

A charitable explanation is that economists are professionals with coherent and consistent viewpoints that are maintained over a long period of time. An uncharitable explanation is that they are stubborn ideologues.

If economists are systematically more reliable, then why would a President appoint noneconomists? Havrilesky and Gildea argue that noneconomists chosen as governors generally are better connected politi-

cally than are economists, and their connections may help in presidential campaigns. Thus economists bring reliability to the job of Fed governor, and noneconomists may bring political clout to the job. If so, it would make sense to appoint economists near the beginning of a presidential term to take advantage of a long period of reliability; noneconomists should be appointed near the end of a presidential term for their value in the campaign. Havrilesky and Gildea point out that this pattern holds in most administrations. An exception was President Carter, who failed to appoint a persuasive economist early in his term and, according to Havrilesky and Gildea, suffered the consequences in terms of low Fed reliability.

Fraction of Votes in Which a Governor Dissents from the Majority

Profession	Dissents During Own Party's Tenure	Dissents During Opposing Party's Tenure	Total
Economist	5.1%	9.5%	7.6%
Noneconomist	13.3%	5.4%	8.9%

Source: Based on Havrilesky and Gildea (1990), Table 1.

Other Means of Controlling the Money Supply

Although open-market operations are the main way that the Fed affects the money supply, it has two other methods available: changes in reserve requirements and discount window lending. The effects of these and other factors on the money supply are summarized in Table 15.3.

Reserve Requirements   For each type of deposit the Fed sets the minimum fraction of those deposits that banks must hold as reserves. An increase in reserve requirements forces banks to hold more reserves and increases the reserve-deposit ratio. Since a higher reserve-deposit ratio *res* reduces the money multiplier, an increase in reserve requirements reduces the money supply for any given value of the monetary base.

Over the past several years the Fed has phased out reserve requirements on many types of deposits. As of December 1990, reserve requirements had been elim-

Table 15.3 Summary

Factors Affecting the Monetary Base, the Money Multiplier, and the Money Supply

Factor	Effect on Monetary Base, $BASE$	Effect on Money Multiplier, $(cu + 1)/(cu + res)$	Effect on Money Supply, M
An increase in the reserve-deposit ratio res	Unchanged	Decrease	Decrease
An increase in the currency-deposit ratio cu	Unchanged	Decrease	Decrease
An open-market purchase	Increase	Unchanged	Increase
An open-market sale	Decrease	Unchanged	Decrease
An increase in reserve requirements	Unchanged	Decrease	Decrease
An increase in discount window borrowing	Increase	Unchanged	Increase
An increase in the discount rate	Decrease	Decrease	Decrease

Note: The relationship among the money supply, the money multiplier, and the monetary base is $M = [(cu + 1)/(cu + res)]BASE$.

inated for all types of deposits except for transactions deposits (primarily checking accounts and NOW accounts). As of December 1990, banks were required to hold reserves equal to 3% of the first $41.4 million of transactions deposits and 12% of the transactions deposits over $41.4 million.

Discount Window Lending A principal reason that the Fed was created was to try to reduce severe financial crises. The main way the Fed was supposed to accomplish this goal was by acting as a lender of last resort. As we discuss further in Chapter 17, the role of a lender of last resort is to lend reserves to banks that need cash to meet the demands of depositors or to meet reserve requirements. The Fed's lending of reserves to banks is called **discount window lending,** and the interest rate it charges for lending reserves is called the **discount rate.**

Although financial panics and bank runs are no longer common events,[13] the Fed still lends reserves to banks through the discount window. Discount window lending affects the monetary base. For example, if banks borrow $1 billion from

---

[13]See Chapter 17 for further discussion of bank runs as well as a discussion of the savings and loan crisis.

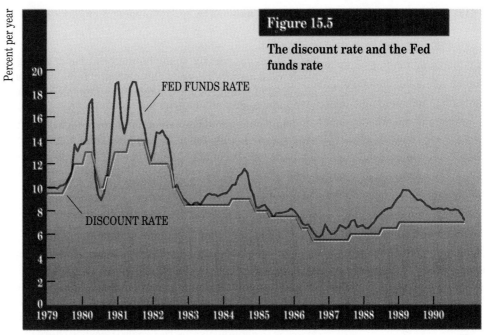

Figure 15.5

The discount rate and the Fed funds rate

FED FUNDS RATE

DISCOUNT RATE

Year

Banks can borrow reserves from the Fed at the discount window and pay the discount rate, or they can borrow reserves from other banks and pay the Fed funds rate. Because the Fed discourages borrowing at the discount window, banks are willing to pay a premium to borrow in the Fed funds market rather than to borrow from the Fed. As a result, the Fed funds rate is usually higher than the discount rate.

Source: Discount rate, end of month—*Federal Reserve Bulletin*, February 1991, Table 1.14; Fed funds rate—1991 *Economic Report of the President*, Table B-71; 1990 *Economic Report of the President*, Table C-71; 1984 *Economic Report of the President*, Table B-67; 1982 *Economic Report of the President*, Table B-67.

the Fed and deposit these borrowings in their reserve accounts at the Fed, there are two effects on the Fed's balance sheet: (1) On the asset side, loans to depository institutions rise by \$1 billion; (2) on the liability side, deposits held by depository institutions also rise by \$1 billion, which increases the monetary base by \$1 billion. Thus an increase in borrowing from the discount window raises the monetary base, and a decrease in discount window borrowing lowers the monetary base.

From time to time the Fed changes the discount rate it charges. An increase in the discount rate makes it more costly to borrow at the discount window. If banks reduce their borrowing in response to the higher discount rate, the monetary base falls. In addition, because borrowing is more costly, banks may choose a higher reserve-deposit ratio *res* to reduce the likelihood that they will have to borrow reserves in the future. The increase in the reserve-deposit ratio reduces the money multiplier. Because an increase in the discount rate reduces both the monetary base and the money multiplier, it reduces the money supply.

Although banks can borrow reserves from the Fed through the discount window, the Fed discourages banks from using the discount window frequently. Instead of borrowing from the Fed, a bank can borrow reserves from other banks that have extra reserves. These borrowed funds are called Federal funds, or Fed funds, and the interest rate charged on these loans is the **Fed funds rate.** Despite its name, the Fed funds rate is *not* an interest rate charged by the Fed; it is the interest rate charged on loans from one bank to another. Figure 15.5 shows the behavior of the Fed funds rate and the discount rate. The Fed funds rate, which is a market interest rate determined by the forces of supply and demand, changes much more frequently than the discount rate, which is set by the Fed. The Fed funds rate usually exceeds the discount rate, because banks are willing to pay a premium to avoid borrowing from the Fed, which discourages frequent use of the discount window.

The existence of the discount window does not affect the Fed's ultimate control over the monetary base. If the Fed thinks there is too much borrowing by the banks, it can discourage the borrowing by raising the discount rate or it can simply refuse to lend. Moreover, the Fed can offset any effects of bank borrowing on the monetary base through open-market operations.

Intermediate Targets

In conducting monetary policy, the Fed has certain goals, or ultimate targets, such as achieving price stability and promoting stable growth of aggregate economic activity. In trying to reach these goals, the Fed can use the monetary policy tools, or **instruments,** that we have discussed: reserve requirements, the discount rate, and especially open-market operations. The question facing the Fed is how to use the instruments that it can directly control, particularly open-market operations, in order to achieve its desired goals. Because there are several steps between open-market operations and the ultimate behavior of prices and economic activity, and because these steps are often hard to predict accurately, the Fed uses intermediate targets to help guide monetary policy. **Intermediate targets,** also sometimes called indicators, are macroeconomic variables that the Fed cannot directly control but can influence fairly predictably, and that in turn are related to the ultimate goals the Fed is trying to achieve.

The most important and frequently used intermediate targets are monetary aggregates and short-term interest rates, such as the Fed funds rate. By using open-market operations, the Fed can directly control the level of the monetary base, which influences the monetary aggregates. Fluctuations in the money supply in turn affect interest rates, at least transitorily, by causing the *LM* curve to shift. Neither monetary aggregates nor short-term interest rates are important determinants of economic welfare in and of themselves, but both influence the state of the macroeconomy. Since monetary aggregates and short-term interest rates are affected by the Fed's policies and both in turn affect the economy, they both qualify as intermediate targets.

At various times the Federal Reserve has guided monetary policy by attempting to keep either monetary growth rates or short-term interest rates at or near preestablished target ranges. Note that although the Fed may be able to stabilize one or the other of these variables, it cannot target both simultaneously. For example, suppose the Fed were trying to target both the money supply and the Fed funds rate, and the preestablished target ranges called for an increase in both the money supply and the Fed funds rate. How could the Fed meet these targets simultaneously? If it raised the monetary base in order to raise the money supply, in the short run the increased money supply would shift the *LM* curve downward and to the right, which would lower rather than raise the Fed funds rate. If, alternatively, the Fed lowered the monetary base in order to try to increase the Fed funds rate, then the money supply would fall instead of rising, as required. Thus in general, the Fed cannot simultaneously meet targets both for interest rates and for the money supply, unless those targets are set to be consistent with each other.

In recent years, as well as during much of the 1970s, the Fed's short-term monetary policies often involved attempts to stabilize the Fed funds rate at a tar-

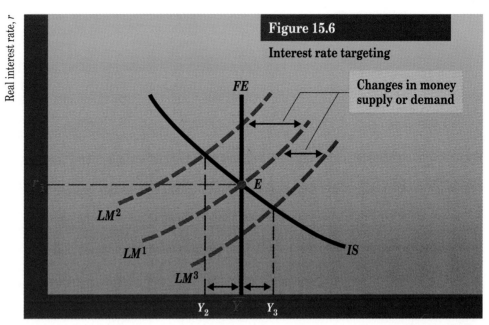

Figure 15.6

Interest rate targeting

The figure shows an economy that is buffeted by nominal shocks. Changes in money supply or money demand cause the LM curve to fluctuate between LM^2 and LM^3 and aggregate demand to move erratically between Y_2 and Y_3. A Fed policy of keeping the real interest rate at r_1, by raising the monetary base whenever the interest rate exceeds r_1 and lowering the base whenever the interest rate falls below r_1, will keep the economy at the full-employment point E.

get level. Figure 15.6 shows a situation in which this strategy is useful: In the figure, when the LM curve is LM^1, the economy is at full-employment equilibrium at point E, with output equal to $\bar{Y}$ and a real interest rate of r_1. Suppose that the main source of shocks in the economy is nominal shocks, including shocks to money supply (perhaps because of changes in the money multiplier) and to money demand. In the absence of any intervention by the Fed, these nominal shocks cause the LM curve to fluctuate between LM^2 and LM^3, which leads aggregate demand to shift erratically between Y_2 and Y_3. In either the extended classical model or the Keynesian model, random shifts in aggregate demand cause undesirable cyclical fluctuations in the economy.

A way in which the Fed could reduce the instability caused by nominal shocks is to use monetary policy to keep the real interest rate fixed at r_1.[14] In other words, whenever the LM curve shifted upward to LM^2, the Fed would increase the money supply to restore the LM curve to LM^1; similarly, shifts of the LM curve to LM^3 would be offset by reductions in the money supply, which would return the LM curve to LM^1. In this case stabilizing the intermediate target, the interest rate, would also stabilize output at its full-employment level. For interest rate targeting to be a good strategy, however, nominal shocks must be the main source of instability. As discussed in Analytical Problem 2, if other types of shocks to the economy are more important than nominal shocks, a policy of using monetary policy to stabilize the interest rate could instead be destabilizing for the output.

---

[14]In practice, the Fed targets nominal interest rates. If expected inflation is constant, targeting nominal interest rates and targeting real interest rates are the same.

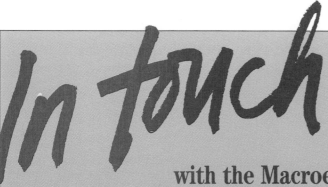

with the Macroeconomy
Decoding the Policy Directives of the FOMC

One of the most important decisions reached at Federal Open Market Committee (FOMC) meetings is whether to ease or tighten monetary policy. The FOMC transmits its decision to the Federal Reserve Bank of New York (where open-market operations are actually executed) in a domestic policy directive that guides monetary policy in the subsequent weeks. The directive and the discussion at FOMC meetings are kept confidential for several weeks, being made public three days after the *following* meeting. Then this information is published in the *Federal Reserve Bulletin* in a section called "Record of Policy Actions of the Federal Open Market Committee."

Policy directives typically contain cryptic sentences of the following form: "In the implementation of policy for the immediate future, the Committee seeks to decrease slightly the existing degree of pressure on reserve positions. Taking account of progress toward price stability, the strength of the business expansion, the behavior of the monetary aggregates, and developments in foreign exchange and domestic financial markets, slightly greater reserve restraint might or somewhat lesser reserve restraint would be acceptable in the intermeeting period." This carefully worded statement, which is taken from the domestic policy directive of the November 13, 1990, FOMC meeting,* means that the

Federal Reserve plans to ease monetary policy and probably will continue to do so until the next FOMC meeting.

The following guidelines (suggested to us by experienced Fed watchers) are helpful in decoding policy directives:

1. Increased "pressure" or "restraint" on reserves means a reduction in the growth of monetary base and thus a monetary tightening. Similarly, decreased "pressure" or "restraint" on reserves means that an easier monetary policy is planned.

2. The Fed is more likely to change reserve restraint in a direction that "would be acceptable" than in a direction that "might be acceptable."

3. The word "somewhat" refers to a larger change in reserve restraint and interest rates than the term "slightly."

Thus in the excerpted statement, "*slightly* greater reserve restraint *might* or *somewhat* lesser reserve restraint *would* be acceptable in the intermeeting period [italics added]" means that money could become either tighter or easier, but the tendency is toward easier money.

Federal Reserve Bulletin, February 1991, p. 103.

15.3

THE CONDUCT OF MONETARY POLICY: BY RULES OR DISCRETION?

There is a good deal of agreement about the broad goals of monetary policy. Ultimately, the object of monetary policy, as of economic policy in general, is to promote the economic well-being of the country's citizens. Classicals and Keynesians agree that in the long run monetary policy affects only the rate of inflation but does not have real effects. Thus they agree that monetary policy should be used to maintain a low and stable rate of inflation in the long run. As we discussed in Chapters 11 and 12, there is much less agreement about the effect of monetary policy in the short run and about whether monetary policy should be used in an attempt to smooth out business cycle fluctuations. Much of the controversy discussed in Chapters 11 and 12 focused on the issue of monetary neutrality. In this chapter we discuss another long-standing debate about the appropriate conduct of monetary policy: Should monetary policy be conducted according to fixed rules or at the discretion of the central bank?

The use of rules in monetary policy has been advocated primarily by a group of economists called monetarists (discussed shortly), as well as by classical macroeconomists. Supporters of **rules** believe that monetary policy should be essentially automatic. In particular, in its control of the money supply, the central bank should be required to follow a set of simple, prespecified, and publicly announced rules. Many such rules can be imagined: For example, the Fed might be instructed to increase the monetary base by 1% each quarter. An alternative rule, which has been used historically, is to require the central bank to conduct monetary policy to keep the price of gold at a predetermined level (this rule was the essence of the gold standard).

Although the exact form of the rule chosen is not crucial, supporters of the rules-based approach emphasize that the monetary rule should be simple; there can't be dozens of exceptions and conditions. Furthermore, the rule should be stated in terms of quantities that the Fed can control directly or nearly directly. Since the Fed can control the monetary base very precisely, a prespecified growth rate for the monetary base is acceptable as a rule. But since the Fed's control over, say, the national unemployment rate is very indirect and imperfect, an instruction to the Fed to "keep the unemployment rate at 4%" is *not* acceptable to advocates of a rules-guided monetary policy.

The opposite of the rules approach, which has been supported by most (though not all) Keynesian economists, is called **discretion.** The idea behind discretion is that the central bank should be free to conduct monetary policy in any way that it believes will advance the ultimate objectives of low and stable inflation, high economic growth, and low unemployment. In particular, the central bank should continuously monitor the economy, and using the advice of economic experts, it should change the money supply as needed to best achieve its ultimate goals. For example, if inflation is currently low and economic indicators suggest that the economy is slipping into recession, under a strategy of discretion the central bank would be free to increase the money supply to try to stimulate the economy. In contrast, under an approach based on rules the central bank would have to follow its preannounced policy and would not be free to apply such stimulus. Because a strategy of discretion involves active responses by the central bank to changes in economic circumstances, such a strategy is sometimes called *activist*.

From this description of rules and discretion, it may be hard to understand why many economists advocate the use of rules. After all, why should we arbitrarily and unnecessarily tie the hands of the central bank? The idea that it must always be better to give the central bank the option of responding to changing economic conditions—as opposed to putting monetary policy in a straitjacket dictated by rules—is the essence of the Keynesian case for discretion.

This basic argument for discretion is an important one, but there is a strong case to be made for rules as well. In the next section we discuss the traditional monetarist argument for rules. We then turn to a relatively new argument for rules, that the use of rules increases the credibility of the central bank.

The Monetarist Case for Rules

Monetarism is a school of macroeconomic thought that, as its name suggests, emphasizes the importance of monetary factors in the macroeconomy. Although the ranks of monetarists, or adherents of monetarism, have included a number of outstanding economists, the dominant figure and leader of the school is Milton Friedman. Friedman has for many years argued that monetary policy should be conducted by rules, and this idea has become an important part of the monetarist doctrine.[15]

Friedman's argument for rules can be broken down into a series of propositions.

> Proposition 1. *Monetary policy has powerful short-run effects on the real economy. In the longer run, however, changes in the money supply have their primary effect on the price level.*

As we discussed in Chapter 11, Friedman's research on U.S. monetary history (done with Anna Schwartz) provided some of the earliest and most important evidence that changes in the money supply can be nonneutral in the short run. Friedman and the monetarists believe that fluctuations in the money supply have been historically one of the most important—if not *the* most important—sources of business cycle fluctuations. On long-run neutrality, as we saw in Chapter 14, Friedman (along with Edmund Phelps) was one of the first to argue that because prices eventually adjust to changes in the money supply, the effect of money on real variables can only be temporary.

> Proposition 2. *Despite the powerful short-run effect of money on the economy, in practice there is little scope for using monetary policy actively to try to smooth out business cycles.*

Friedman backs up this proposition with several points. First, it takes a little while for the central bank and other agencies to gather and process information about the current state of the economy. Because of these information lags, it is often difficult for the central bank to tell whether the economy is in a recession and whether a change in policy is appropriate.

Second, there is considerable uncertainty about how much effect a given change in the money supply will have on the economy and how long the effect will take to occur. Friedman has emphasized that there are *long and variable lags* between monetary policy actions and their economic results. From his empirical research Friedman claims that, on average, monetary changes take about a year to have a significant impact on the economy (that is, the lag is long). Furthermore,

---

[15]Friedman's 1959 book, *A Program for Monetary Stability* (New York: Fordham University Press) presents a clear early statement of his views.

the time it takes for policy to have an effect is unpredictable and can vary from as little as six months to as much as eighteen months (the lag is variable).

Third, wage and price adjustment, while not instantaneous, is sufficiently fast that by the time the Fed recognizes that the economy is in a recession and increases the money supply, the economy may already be heading out of the recession. If the expansion in the money supply stimulates the economy with a lag of about a year, the stimulus may take effect when output has already recovered and the economy is in a boom. In this case the effect of the monetary expansion will be to cause the economy to *overshoot* full employment and to cause prices to rise. Thus the monetary increase, intended to fight the recession, may well turn out to be *destabilizing* (causing more variability of output than there would have been otherwise), as well as inflationary.

> Proposition 3. *Even if there is some scope for using monetary policy to smooth out business cycles, the Federal Reserve cannot be relied on to do this effectively.*

One reason that Friedman does not trust the Fed to manage an activist monetary policy effectively is political. He believes that despite its supposed independence, in practice the Fed is susceptible to short-run political pressures from the President and others in the administration. For example, the Fed might be pressured to stimulate the economy during an election year. If timed reasonably well, an election-year monetary expansion could expand output and employment at the time that voters go to the polls, with the inflationary effects of the policy not being felt until after the incumbents were safely reelected. (See "The Political Environment" box, p. 568 in Chapter 14, for a discussion of the political business cycle.)

More fundamentally, though, Friedman's distrust of the Fed arises from his interpretation of macroeconomic history. From his work with Anna Schwartz, Friedman concludes that for whatever reason—incompetence, shortsightedness, or bad luck—monetary policy has historically been a major source of economic *instability* rather than stability. The major example cited by Friedman is the 1929–1933 period, when, as we have seen, the Federal Reserve was unable or unwilling to stop the money supply from falling by one third in the wake of widespread runs on banks. Friedman and Schwartz's *Monetary History* argued that this monetary contraction was an important cause of the Great Depression. Thus Friedman concludes that eliminating monetary policy as a source of instability would substantially improve macroeconomic performance.

How could the Fed be removed as a source of instability? This question leads to Friedman's policy recommendation, our last proposition:

> Proposition 4. *The Federal Reserve should choose a specific monetary aggregate (such as M1 or M2) and commit itself to making that aggregate grow at a fixed percentage rate, year in and year out.*

For Friedman the critical step in eliminating the Fed as a source of instability is to get it to give up activist, or discretionary, monetary policy and to commit itself—publicly and in advance—to following some rule. Although the exact choice of a rule is not critical, Friedman believes that a constant–money-growth rule would be a good choice: First, the Fed has considerable influence, though not complete control, over the rate of money growth. Thus if money growth deviated significantly from its target, it would be hard for the Fed to blame the deviation on forces outside of its control. Second, as an empirical matter, Friedman argues that steady money growth would lead to smaller cyclical fluctuations than the supposedly "countercyclical" monetary policies that we have had historically. He concludes that a constant money growth rate would provide a "stable monetary background" that would allow economic growth to proceed without concern about monetary instability.

Friedman does not advocate a sudden shift from discretionary monetary policy to a low, constant rate of money growth. Instead, he envisions a transition period in which the Fed, by gradual preannounced steps, would steadily reduce the growth rate of money. Ultimately, the growth rate of the chosen monetary aggregate would be consistent with an inflation rate near zero. Importantly, once the constant growth rate is attained, the Fed would *not* respond to modest economic downturns by changing money growth but would continue to follow the policy of maintaining a fixed rate of money growth. However, in some of his writings Friedman appears to leave open the possibility that the monetary rule could be temporarily suspended in the face of major economic crises, such as a depression.

Rules and Central Bank Credibility

Much of the monetarist argument for rules rests on pessimism about the competence or political reliability of the Federal Reserve. Economists who are more optimistic about the ability of the government to intervene effectively in the economy (which includes many Keynesians) question the monetarist case for rules. A "policy optimist" could argue as follows: "It may be true that monetary policy has performed badly in the past. However, as time passes, we learn more about the economy, and our use of policy gets better. For example, it seems clear that U.S. monetary policy was better handled after World War II than in the Depression era. It would be foolish to impose rigid rules just as we are beginning to learn how to use activist policy properly. As to the issue of political reliability, well, that problem affects fiscal policymakers and indeed all our branches of government. We just have to trust in the democratic process to ensure that policymakers will take actions that are for the most part in the interest of the country."

For policy optimists this reply to the monetarist case for rules seems perfectly satisfactory. In the past decade and a half, however, a new argument for rules has been developed that applies even if the central bank is completely competent (it can control the money supply perfectly and knows exactly how monetary changes affect the economy) and completely public-spirited. Thus the new argument for rules is a challenge even to policy optimists. This new argument is that the use of monetary rules can affect the **credibility** of the central bank—by which we mean the degree to which the public believes central bank announcements about future policy—and that the credibility of the central bank influences how well monetary policy works.

Dad, the Kids, and the Game: Credible Threats and Commitment   To help explain what credibility is, why it may be enhanced by the existence of rules, and why it may be important in the making of monetary policy, let's look at a simple example drawn from family life. Imagine that, knowing that Mom will be going out to an important business meeting that evening, Dad has bought tickets to a baseball game for himself and the two kids, Junior and Sis. Dad likes baseball, as do the kids. Unfortunately, the kids also like to fight with each other. Dad has warned the kids: "Don't fight. If you do, we just won't go to the baseball game." It is not

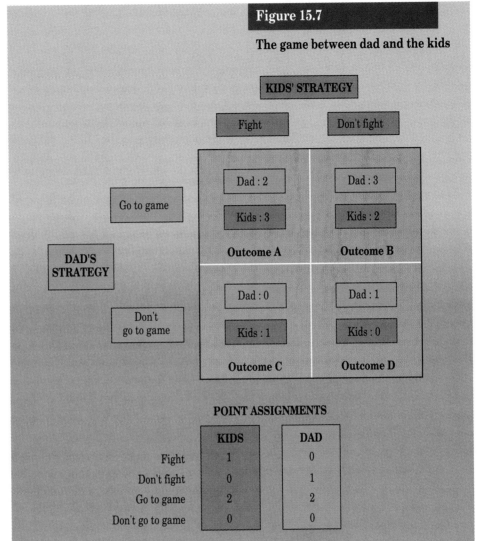

Figure 15.7

The game between dad and the kids

Each square represents a combination of an action by the kids and an action by Dad. The points assigned to each combination of actions by Dad and by the kids, shown in each square, measure how much each outcome is liked by each set of players. The kids "move" first by picking a column; then Dad "moves" by picking a row. The equilibrium is outcome A, in which the kids fight and still get to go to the game.

feasible for Dad to go to the baseball game without both kids, since Mom isn't home to baby-sit, and on such short notice he won't be able to find a baby-sitter. We are interested in the following questions about the behavior of Dad and the kids: (1) Will the kids fight? (2) Will Dad take the kids to the baseball game?

Before we analyze this situation formally, let's take a moment to discuss it intuitively. The kids know that because Dad wants to go to the game himself, he will be very reluctant to impose the punishment he has threatened. That is, Dad's threat is not credible (believable) to the kids. Therefore the kids will fight anyway, assuming that when push comes to shove, Dad won't be able to bring himself to waste the tickets and they will all get to go to the game.

The diagram in Fig. 15.7 captures this situation. The two columns of the diagram correspond to the two possible actions that the kids can take: *Fight* and *Don't fight*. The two rows correspond to the two actions that Dad can take: *Go to game* and *Don't go to game*. Each of the four squares in the diagram thus refers to a possible outcome: Square A corresponds to the outcome *Kids fight and Dad takes kids to game;* square B refers to *Kids don't fight and Dad takes kids to game;* and so on.

Dad and the kids each have preferences about the four possible outcomes shown in the figure. Let us measure preferences in terms of points: The more points someone assigns to an outcome, the more he or she likes it. Dad likes baseball, so let's assume that he assigns 2 points to going to the game. Also, he assigns 1 point to having the kids not fight. The total number of points Dad assigns to each outcome is shown in each square in Fig. 15.7. Dad's most preferred outcome (worth 3 points) is B, in which the kids don't fight and they all go to the game. Dad's worst outcome is C, in which the kids fight and no one gets to go to the game, an outcome that gets 0 points from Dad.

The kids also like baseball, and they also assign 2 points to going to the game. However, they also like to fight, and they assign 1 point to fighting. The kids' point totals for each outcome are also shown in each box in the figure. The kids' favorite outcome, worth 3 points, is A (they fight and still get to go to the game). Their least favorite outcome, worth 0 points, is D (no fight and no game).

The sequence of actions is as follows: First, the kids decide whether to fight (after hearing the warning), and then Dad decides whether to take the kids to the game. In terms of Fig. 15.7 the kids get to pick the column (*Fight* or *Don't fight*). After the kids pick the column, Dad gets to pick whether they will be in the top square (*Go to game*) or the bottom square (*Don't go to game*). Importantly, we assume that at each stage both the kids and Dad make the choices that attain the outcome that they like the most.

The kids reason as follows: "Suppose we pick *Fight* (the left column). That leaves Dad with the choice of A (*Go to game*) or C (*Don't go to game*). Outcome A is worth 2 points to Dad; C is worth 0 points. So Dad will pick A over C. Thus if we fight, we still get to go to the game.

"Now it is true that if we pick *Don't fight* (the right column) that Dad will pick B over D, so we also go to the game in that case. But since we like to fight, and we get to go to the game in either case, we might as well fight." In terms of Fig. 15.7, the kids know that once they factor in their Dad's response, they effectively have a choice between A and B. Since they prefer A to B, they pick the left column (that is, they fight).

The diagram in Fig. 15.7 is a standard tool from a branch of mathematics, much used in economics, called game theory. **Game theory** studies situations (games) in which strategy is used by individuals (players) attempting to achieve their goals, possibly at the expense of the other players. An equilibrium of a game is an outcome that occurs if all players do the best that they can for themselves.

In the particular game we are studying, the "players" are Dad and the kids. The equilibrium of the game is outcome A, in which the kids fight and still go to the game. Outcome A is the equilibrium because the kids recognize that Dad's threat isn't credible; he has a strong incentive to renege on his threat when the time comes to carry it out. Indeed, if Dad is smart enough to realize that his threat has no force, he won't bother to make it in the first place.

Is there some way for Dad to make his threat credible and thereby get the kids to behave? Yes; the key to credibility for Dad is to find some way by which he can commit himself to carrying out the threat. In other words, Dad must convince the kids that should they fight, he will have *no choice* but to keep everybody home from the game. Suppose, for example, that Dad gives the game tickets to Mom, with instructions to hide them and not to reveal their whereabouts if the kids fight. Suppose that Mom is indifferent about whether Dad and the kids go to the game and can be counted on to carry out these instructions.

How does Mom's hiding the tickets affect the equilibrium of the game in Fig. 15.7? Formally, the effect is to cross out square A (kids fight, go to game) as a possible outcome. If the kids fight, going to the game will not be a possible choice for Dad. Thus the kids know that if they choose the left column (*Fight*), Dad will be forced to choose square C (*Don't go to game*), an outcome that yields 1 point for the kids. On the other hand, if the kids choose the right column (*Don't fight*), then Dad's preferred choice between his options B and D will be B (*Go to game*). Since the kids prefer B (2 points) to C (1 point), they will pick the right column and will not fight. The key conclusion of this analysis is that by committing in advance to carry out his threat, Dad has made his threat credible. Assuming that the kids choose actions in their own best interest, Dad achieves the outcome (B) that he likes the best.

A Game Between the Central Bank and Firms   We can use game theory to think about the credibility of the central bank. Consider a situation in which the macro-economy is in general equilibrium, so that the *IS* and *LM* curves cross at the *FE* line (point *E* in Fig. 15.8a). Initially, suppose that both the money supply and the price level are growing steadily at 10% per year. Since *M* and *P* are growing at the same rate, the real money supply *M/P* is constant, and the *LM* curve, LM^1, remains fixed and passes through point *E*. Thus the economy is initially at full employment with the unemployment rate equal to the natural rate, say 6%, and the rate of inflation equal to 10% per year.

The central bank (the Fed, let us say) would like to reduce the economy's rate of inflation to zero without increasing the unemployment rate. Suppose the Fed makes the following announcement to all the firms in the economy: "There is no reason why we should be suffering from this 10% inflation. Let's make a deal. If you guys keep prices (*P*) constant this period, rather than raising them by 10%, we here at the Fed will keep the money supply (*M*) constant as well. With *M* and *P* both constant, the real money supply (*M/P*) will not change, and the *LM* curve will not shift. Thus the economy will remain at full employment, with an unemployment rate of 6%, but we will all be better off for being rid of inflation. If, on the other hand, you insist on raising prices, we will still keep the money supply constant. In this case the real money supply (*M/P*) will fall by 10%, the *LM* curve will shift upward and to the left to LM^2, and we will all suffer from both high unemployment and continued inflation (at point *F* in Fig. 15.8a)."

How will the firms respond to this statement by the Fed? As we will see, the Fed's threat to reduce the real money supply if firms raise prices is not credible, because the Fed does not want a recession. As a result, the firms will go ahead and raise prices anyway.

The game between the Fed and the firms is analyzed formally in Fig. 15.8(b). The firms' choices, *Raise P* (by 10%) and *Don't raise P*, correspond to the two columns of the diagram. The Fed's two choices, *Raise M* (by 10%) and *Don't raise M* correspond to the two rows. Square A represents the outcome *Firms raise P and Fed raises M;* square B represents the outcome *Firms don't raise P and Fed raises M;* and so on.

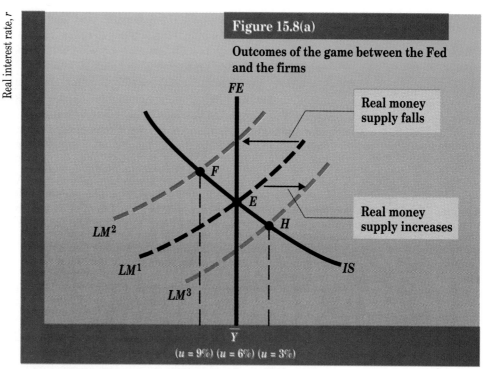

Figure 15.8(a)

Outcomes of the game between the Fed and the firms

Real money supply falls

Real money supply increases

LM^2

LM^1

LM^3

IS

FE

F

E

H

$\bar{Y}$

$(u = 9\%)$ $(u = 6\%)$ $(u = 3\%)$

Real interest rate, *r*

Initially, money growth rate = inflation rate = 10%

Output, *Y*

(a) This part of the figure shows the possible outcomes of the game between the Fed and the firms. The economy is initially at point *E* (full employment) with 10% inflation. The real money supply *M/P* depends both on the price level *P* chosen by firms and the money supply *M* chosen by the Fed. If the real money supply does not change, the economy remains at full employment (point *E*). If the real money supply falls, the *LM* curve shifts from LM^1 to LM^2, and the economy goes into a recession with 9% unemployment at point *F*. If the real money supply increases, the *LM* curve shifts from LM^1 to LM^3, and the economy goes into a boom with 3% unemployment at point *H*.

What happens to the macroeconomy in each case? Determining what happens to inflation is easy: In squares A and C, in which the firms raise prices by 10%, inflation π is 10%. In squares B and D firms don't raise prices and hence $\pi = 0$.

What about unemployment? In square A both money and prices rise by 10%, so that *M/P* is unchanged and the economy remains at full employment (point *E* in Fig. 15.8a). Similarly, in square D neither *M* nor *P* changes, so *M/P* is unchanged and the economy remains at full employment. Thus in squares A and D the unemployment rate *u* remains equal to the natural rate of 6%. In square C, *P* rises but *M* does not. Thus *M/P* falls, the *LM* curve shifts upward and to the left to LM^2, and the economy goes into recession at point *F* in Fig. 15.8(a), with the unemployment rate increasing to 9%. Finally, in square B, *M* rises but *P* does not, so *M/P* rises and the *LM* curve shifts downward and to the right to LM^3. In this case the economy goes into a boom (point *H* in Fig. 15.8a), and the unemployment rate falls to 3%.

The next step is to determine the points that each player assigns to each outcome. Start with the Fed. The Fed doesn't like inflation, so it assigns 1 point to

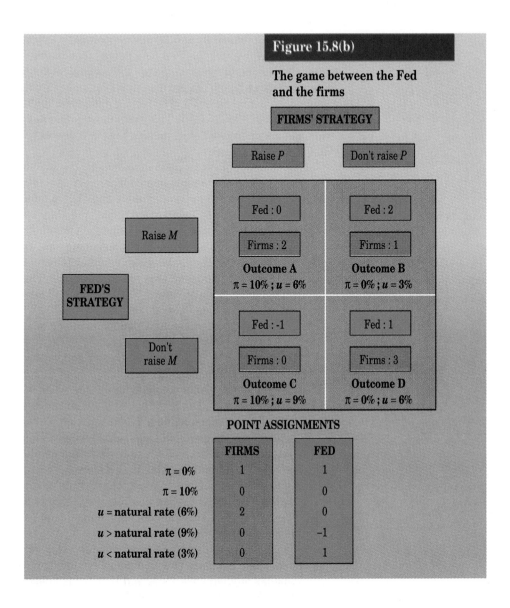

Figure 15.8(b)

The game between the Fed and the firms

(b) This diagram shows the possible moves in the game between the Fed and the firms. The firms move first by deciding whether to raise the price level P, which determines the column. Then the Fed moves by deciding whether to increase the money supply M, which determines the row. If M and P both rise (outcome A) or both stay the same (outcome D), the real money supply is unchanged, and the economy remains at full employment (point E in part a). In outcome B, M increases and P remains the same; thus the real money supply rises and unemployment falls (point H in part a). In outcome C, M remains the same and P increases, so the real money supply falls and unemployment increases (point F in part a). Point assignments show the preferences of the Fed and firms for each outcome. The equilibrium of the game is outcome A, in which the firms raise prices and the Fed increases the money supply.

having zero inflation (B and D) and no points to having a positive rate of inflation (A and C). However, the Fed also doesn't like unemployment: It assigns 0 points to having unemployment equal to the natural rate (A and D), 1 point to having unemployment below the natural rate (B), and −1 point to having unemployment above the natural rate (C). The total point scores for the Fed are shown in each of the squares in Fig. 15.8(b). The Fed's most preferred outcome is B, with no inflation and 3% unemployment, and its least favorite outcome is C, with 10% inflation and 9% unemployment.

The firms' profits are maximized when they are on the *FE* line, that is, when the economy is at full employment. Therefore the firms assign 2 points to having unemployment at the natural rate (A and D). In addition, we assume that firms prefer zero inflation to positive inflation, and they assign 1 point to having zero inflation (B and D). Total scores for firms are also shown in each box in Fig. 15.8(b).

Now let us find the equilibrium, assuming that firms first decide whether to raise prices and then the Fed decides whether to raise the money supply. The firms reason as follows: "Suppose that we raise prices. This leaves the Fed the choice between outcome A and outcome C. Since the Fed doesn't want a recession, it will choose A; that is, it will raise the money supply."

"If we don't raise prices, the Fed has a choice of B or D. The Fed prefers B to D because, given no inflation, it prefers a situation with unemployment below the natural rate to one in which unemployment equals the natural rate. So in this case it will also raise the money supply."

"Therefore (the firms reason), no matter what we do, the Fed will raise the money supply. The Fed's claim that it will maintain a constant money supply if we raise prices is just not credible. If we raise prices we get outcome A, and if we don't raise prices we get outcome B. Since we prefer A to B (we'd rather be at full employment than off the *FE* line and above full employment), we raise prices."

The equilibrium of the game is therefore outcome A, in which the firms raise prices and the Fed (failing to carry through its threat) raises the money supply. Because the Fed's threat is not credible, it is ignored by firms. Importantly, notice that *outcome D (full employment and no inflation) is preferred by both the Fed and the firms to the equilibrium outcome A.* Yet because the Fed's promise to reduce money supply is not credible, outcome D is not attained by the economy.

In contrast, suppose the Fed could credibly promise not to raise the money supply under any circumstances and that firms believed this promise. Then firms would reason: "If we raise prices, the Fed will pick outcome C (inflation and a recession). If we don't raise prices, the Fed will pick D (no inflation and no recession). Since we prefer D to C, we will not raise prices." The equilibrium in this case would be outcome D, which is preferred by everyone to the no-credibility outcome A. In outcome D disinflation has been achieved without increasing unemployment, all because the central bank is credible.

Rules, Commitment, and Credibility The formal analysis shows why central bank credibility is potentially important. If a central bank is credible, it can reduce money growth and inflation without incurring high unemployment. But how can a central bank achieve credibility?

One possibility is for the central bank to develop a reputation for carrying out its promises. Suppose that in the example just discussed firms raise their prices, fully expecting the Fed to raise the money supply. However, the Fed goes ahead and keeps the money supply steady anyway, causing a recession. Then the next time, the firms may take the Fed's promises more seriously, and the economy can attain outcome D. Analogously, if Dad crosses up the kids and refuses to take them to the game after they fight, he will improve his reputation for carrying out his threats; and the next time, the kids may take him seriously.

The problem with the strategy of achieving credibility through reputation is that it may involve serious costs during the period in which reputation is being established: The economy suffers a recession while the central bank establishes its reputation, and Dad and the kids miss the game while Dad establishes his. Is there some less costly way to achieve credibility?

Advocates of rules suggest that rules, by forcing the central bank to keep its promises, may substitute for reputation in establishing credibility. Suppose there is an ironclad rule—ideally, enforced by some outside agency—that the Fed must gradually reduce the growth of the money supply. Then observing the existence of this rule, the firms might well believe that money supply growth is going to decline no matter what, and painless disinflation (outcome D) can be achieved. Similarly, in the case with Dad and the kids, if there is an unbreakable family rule that fighting suspends all privileges—and Mom is there to help enforce it—Dad's threat not to go to the game might be more credible. Notice that if it increases credibility, a rule improves central bank performance even if the central bank is competent and public-spirited. Hence this reason for monetary policy rules is different from the monetarists' argument presented earlier.

How do advocates of discretion respond to the credibility argument for rules? Keynesians argue that there may be a trade-off between credibility and flexibility. In order for a rule to establish credibility, it must be very difficult to change—otherwise, no one will believe that the Fed will stick to the rule. In the extreme, the monetary growth rule would be added as an amendment to the Constitution, which could then only be changed at great cost and with long delays. But if a rule is completely unbreakable, what happens (ask the Keynesians) if some unexpected crisis arises—for example, a new Great Depression? Then the inability of the Fed to take corrective action—that is, its lack of flexibility—could prove disastrous. Therefore, Keynesians argue, establishing a rule ironclad enough to create credibility for the central bank would, by eliminating policy flexibility, also create unacceptable risks.

Application

Monetary Targeting in West Germany, Japan, and the United States

During the middle and late 1970s, in response to rising inflation, central banks in a number of major industrialized countries established targets for the growth rates of one or more monetary aggregates. The strategy of trying to hit predetermined monetary targets seems quite similar to Friedman's recommended strategy of a constant growth rate for money. Indeed, many observers and sometimes the central banks themselves used monetarist arguments to justify this strategy. Did monetary targeting as used in practice conform to what Friedman recommended? Did monetary targeting improve central bank credibility? And did the use of monetary targets reduce fluctuations in economic activity? To try to answer these important questions, we briefly consider the experiences of three of the major countries that experimented with monetary targeting: West Germany, Japan, and the United States.

West Germany   The Bundesbank, Germany's central bank, introduced targets for money growth in 1975 in response to a flare-up of inflation. The Bundesbank targeted only one monetary aggregate, a broad monetary measure called central bank money (CBM), which is a weighted sum of currency, checking accounts, savings accounts, and time deposits. In choosing only one aggregate to target, the Germans conformed to advice offered by Friedman, who pointed out that central banks can effectively control only one monetary aggregate at a time.[16] Target ranges, specifying minimum and maximum acceptable money growth rates, were set annually. Over time, the Bundesbank lowered the money growth targets in an attempt to squeeze inflation out of the system.

The targets and actual values for German money growth are shown in Fig. 15.9(a).[17] From 1979 to 1985 the Bundesbank did a reasonably good job of coming close to its targets. However, in the 1986–1988 period officials at the Bundesbank worried that the strength of the German mark relative to the dollar might depress the German export sector. In order to weaken the mark, the Bundesbank allowed the money growth rate to exceed its target. This deviation from the money target in order to affect short-run economic conditions is not in the spirit of the monetarist constant–growth-rate rule.

How has the German economy performed under the money-targeting strategy? As shown in Fig. 15.9(b), the inflation rate fell after the introduction of money targeting, rose temporarily at about the time of the 1979 oil price shock, then fell to low levels after 1981. The unemployment rate jumped to nearly 10% in the early 1980s and remained high for several years. External factors, such as the oil price shocks and the worldwide recession of the early 1980s, contributed to the jump in unemployment; but it is noteworthy that the major increase in unemployment was preceded by a slowdown in money growth, as the Bundesbank attempted to eradicate inflation. Thus money targeting did not seem to eliminate the unemployment associated with fighting inflation in Germany.

Japan   Like West Germany, Japan adopted monetary targeting in response to the problem of inflation. In July 1978 the Bank of Japan began to announce a quarterly target (which it called a "forecast") for M2 growth. The targeted money aggregate was expanded to include certificates of deposit (CDs) when they began to be issued in May 1979.

---

[16]Only one monetary aggregate can be targeted at a time for much the same reason that the central bank cannot simultaneously target a monetary aggregate and an interest rate: If the central bank uses open-market operations to cause one monetary aggregate to hit its target, it cannot simultaneously use open-market operations to force a different aggregate to hit a different target.

[17]See George A. Kahn and Kristina Jacobson, "Lessons from West German Monetary Policy," *Economic Review*, Federal Reserve Bank of Kansas City, April 1989, pp. 18–35.

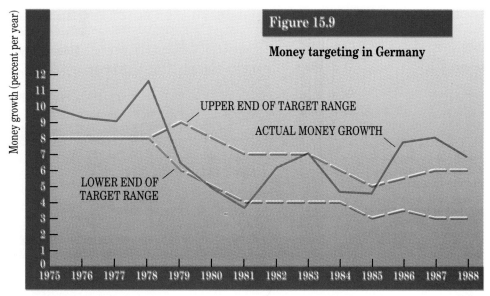

(a) Money growth and targets   Year

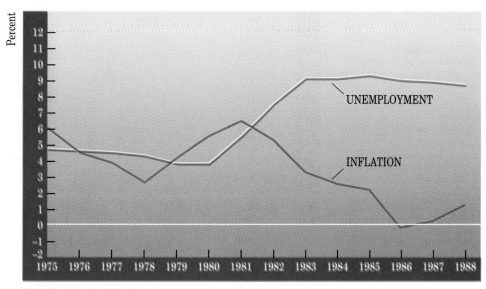

(b) Inflation and unemployment   Year

(a) Upper and lower target ranges and actual money growth rates are shown for West Germany. From 1979 to 1985 the Bundesbank came very close to its targets for monetary growth. From 1986 to 1988 concern that the mark was too strong relative to the dollar prompted the Bundesbank to allow money supply growth to exceed the target.

Source: George A. Kahn and Kristina Jacobson, "Lessons from West German Monetary Policy," *Economic Review*, Federal Reserve Bank of Kansas City, April 1989, pp. 18–35.

(b) The decline in targeted and actual money growth in Germany (part a) succeeded in bringing down the rate of inflation, but the unemployment rate increased substantially.

Source: *OECD Main Economic Indicators, 1969–88:* Unemployment—p. 378; inflation (CPI)—p. 385.

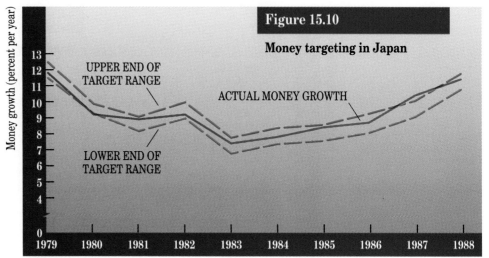

(a) Money growth and targets — Year

(a) The Bank of Japan was very successful at achieving its money growth targets.

Source: Takatoshi Ito, "Is the Bank of Japan a Closet Monetarist? Monetary Targeting in Japan, 1978–88," NBER working paper no. 2879, March 1989.

(b) The decline in Japanese inflation after the 1979–1980 oil price shock was achieved without any substantial increase in unemployment.

Source: OECD, *Main Economic Indicators, 1969–88:* Unemployment— p. 120; inflation (CPI), p. 126.

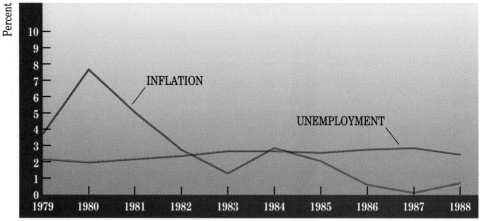

(b) Inflation and unemployment — Year

Figure 15.10(a) shows the target ranges and actual growth rates of money in Japan for the years 1979–1988.[18] You can see that the Bank of Japan was extremely successful at hitting its targets. However, although the money growth targets declined until 1983, after that year they began to rise again. As in the German case, increased money growth in Japan reflected concern about the high value of the currency, which threatened to hurt the export sector. Again, this attention to short-run factors violated the strict monetarist prescription.

Judging by the performance of the Japanese economy (Fig. 15.10b), Japanese monetary policy has been quite successful. Unlike the German case, the subduing of inflation in the early 1980s in Japan was not accompanied by a large increase in unemployment.

[18]Quarterly target ranges and actual growth rates have been averaged to give annual values. See Takatoshi Ito, "Is the Bank of Japan a Closet Monetarist? Monetary Targeting in Japan, 1978–88," National Bureau of Economic Research working paper no. 2879, March 1989.

(a) Over the period 1975–1986, M2 growth in the United States was fairly close to the upper end of the target range.

Source: Stanley Fischer, "Monetary Policy and Performance in the US, Japan, and Europe, 1973–86," NBER working paper no. 2475, December 1987.

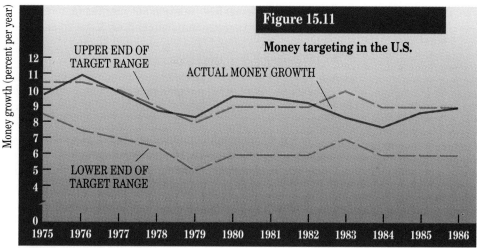

(a) Money growth and targets

Year

(b) The rate of inflation in the United States fell sharply between 1980 and 1983. The unemployment rate increased significantly during this disinflation but fell after 1983.

Source: *Economic Report of the President*, February 1991: Unemployment—Table B-40; inflation—Table B-62.

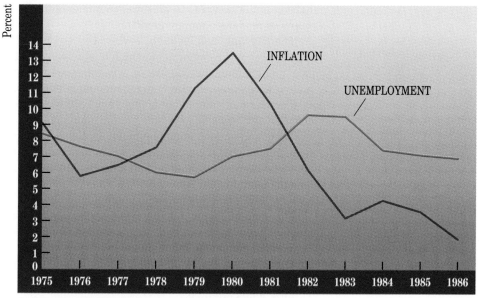

(b) Inflation and unemployment

Year

United States Unlike Germany and Japan, and counter to Friedman's advice, the United States announced target growth rates for three different monetary aggregates: M1, M2, and M3. The target and actual growth rates for M2 are shown in Fig. 15.11(a). From 1975 to 1982 the actual growth rate of M2 was fairly close to the top of target range. Although the target and actual growth rates for M2 in 1979–1981 do not appear to be particularly low, the growth rate of M2 was lower than the rate of inflation in these years. Thus the real supply of M2 (M2 divided by the price level) fell during 1979–1981, which was contractionary.

Figure 15.11(b) shows that inflation slowed dramatically in the first three years of the 1980s. This slowdown in inflation was accompanied by a severe recession and high rates of unemployment in 1981–1982. In late 1982 the Fed, having won its battle against inflation but now facing a recession, abandoned its adherence to monetary targets and switched its focus to the Fed funds rate as the primary intermediate target. The expansion following the 1981–1982 recession persisted for the remainder of the 1980s.

Lessons What do the experiences of West Germany, Japan, and the United States tell us about the use of money targets as a monetary policy rule? There are several lessons.

First, although countries are willing to try money targeting, they do not appear to be willing to tie the hands of the central bank to the degree recommended by the monetarists. Central banks value flexibility, as suggested by Keynesians. All three countries we examined modified or abandoned their monetary targets when short-run factors—rising exchange rates in Germany and Japan, rising unemployment in the United States—made a switch to a more expansionary monetary policy attractive. Thus monetarists may claim that their strict targeting strategy has never really been tried. Critics reply that if a strategy is politically infeasible, it isn't of much use no matter how appealing it is in theory.

Second, there is no doubt that concerted effort by the central bank can bring inflation under control. In all three countries inflation was sharply reduced by attempts to moderate money growth.

The key question, though, is this: Did the use of money targets (even if the targets were not as ironclad as the monetarists would have liked) have any benefits? In particular, did the use of preannounced targets reduce the amount of unemployment accompanying a given amount of disinflation?

The German central bank was very credible and had a reasonably good track record at hitting its targets, yet the German disinflation coincided with a sharp and persistent increase in unemployment. In the United States, where the credibility of the central bank was probably quite low initially, the disinflation of the early 1980s was accompanied by a shorter-lived (but severe) increase in unemployment. Thus the German and American experiences do not lend strong support to the idea that credibility helps reduce the unemployment accompanying a disinflation.

The case of Japan, on the other hand, seems to provide some evidence that rules and credibility can help. In particular, Japan was able to eliminate the inflation created by the 1979 oil shock and bring inflation to a low, steady level with virtually no increase in unemployment. This experience is what rules advocates predict would happen if the central bank's commitment to reducing money growth and inflation is credible.

What explains the differences among these cases? One rather speculative hypothesis is that there are differences among countries in the amount of cooperation that can be attained between the public and private sectors. In Japan, business leaders are used to working closely with the government, so it may be more feasible there for the central bank and the firms to strike a deal in which the central bank reduces money growth and the firms moderate price increases. In other words, the central bank and the firms in Japan may have been able to agree to achieve outcome D in Fig. 15.8(b). In Germany a similar type of deal would be complicated by the existence of powerful national labor unions, whose help in restraining wage growth would be needed to eliminate inflation but who have not traditionally cooperated with the government or with firms in that way. The United States may be an intermediate case: It has neither a tradition of public-private cooperation nor firms or unions that are large enough relative to the economy to single-handedly block disinflation by aggressively increasing prices or wages.

15.4 CHAPTER SUMMARY

1. Three sets of actors help determine the money supply: the central bank, the banks, and the public. The central bank sets the monetary base, which is the quantity of central bank liabilities that can be used as money. The monetary base equals the sum of bank reserves (deposits by banks at the central bank plus currency in the vaults of banks) and currency in circulation. The banks and the public interact to determine the money multiplier, the ratio of the money supply to the monetary base.

2. In an all-currency economy the monetary base consists entirely of currency in circulation. Therefore the money supply equals the monetary base, and the money multiplier equals 1.

3. In an economy with fractional reserve banking and no currency held by the public, the money supply is $1/res$ times the monetary base, where res is the ratio of reserves to deposits desired by banks. The money supply is greater than the monetary base in this case because banks lend out part of the deposits they receive. When the loaned-out funds are redeposited in the banking system, bank deposits and thus the money supply increase.

4. In an economy with both fractional reserve banking and currency in circulation, the money multiplier equals $(cu + 1)/(cu + res)$, where cu is the public's desired ratio of currency to deposits. The money supply equals deposits plus currency in circulation and also equals the money multiplier times the monetary base. An increase in the desired currency-deposit ratio cu or in the desired reserve-deposit ratio res reduces the money multiplier. During the Great Depression in the United States, banking crises caused both cu and res to increase, so that the money multiplier and the money supply fell sharply.

5. The central bank can affect the size of the monetary base and thus the money supply through open-market operations. An open-market sale (in which central bank assets are sold in exchange for currency or bank reserves) reduces the monetary base. An open-market purchase (in which the central bank uses money to buy assets, such as government securities, from the public) increases the monetary base.

6. The central bank of the United States is called the Federal Reserve System, or the Fed. The leadership of the Fed is the Board of Governors, which in turn is headed by the chairman of the Federal Reserve. The Federal Open Market Committee (FOMC) meets several times each year to set the course of monetary policy.

7. The Fed affects the U.S. money supply primarily through open-market operations. Discount window lending and changes in reserve requirements can also

be used to affect the money supply. The Fed often focuses on intermediate targets such as the money supply or the Fed funds rate to help guide monetary policy.

8. Monetary policy can be conducted either by rules or by discretion. Under rules the central bank is required to follow a simple predetermined rule for monetary policy, such as the requirement that money growth be kept constant, and is not allowed to respond to current economic conditions. Under discretion the central bank is expected to monitor the economy and to try to use monetary policy actively to maintain full employment and to keep inflation low.

9. Discretion for monetary policy is favored by Keynesians, who argue that it gives the Fed maximum flexibility to stabilize the economy.

10. Monetarists, led by Milton Friedman, argue that in practice, because of information problems and lags between the implementation of policy changes and their effects, the scope for using monetary policy to stabilize the economy is small. Furthermore, they argue, the Fed cannot be relied on to use active monetary policy wisely and in the public interest. Monetarists advocate a constant–growth-rate rule for the money supply in order to discipline the Fed and keep monetary fluctuations from destabilizing the economy.

11. An additional argument for rules is that they increase central bank credibility. Supporters of rules claim that the use of ironclad rules will cause the public to believe the central bank if it says (for example) that money supply growth will be reduced, with the implication that inflation can be reduced without a large increase in unemployment.

12. Empirically, the case for rules is mixed. Countries appear to be unwilling to follow strict rules without exceptions. Monetary targeting, which is a type of rule, seems to have reduced the cost of disinflation in Japan but not in West Germany.

Key Terms

bank reserves, p. 601
bank run, p. 604
Board of Governors of
    the Federal Reserve
    System, p. 611
central bank, p. 599
credibility, p. 624
currency-deposit ratio,
    p. 605
depository institutions,
    p. 599
discount rate, p. 616
discount window
    lending, p. 616

discretion, p. 621
Federal Open Market
    Committee (FOMC),
    p. 612
Fed funds rate, p. 617
fractional reserve
    banking, p. 601
game theory, p. 626
high-powered money,
    p. 600
instruments, p. 618
intermediate targets,
    p. 618
legal tender, p. 600
monetarism, p. 622

monetary base, p. 600
money multiplier, p. 605
multiple expansion of
    loans and deposits,
    p. 603
100% reserve banking,
    p. 601
open-market purchase,
    p. 607
open-market sale, p. 607
reserve-deposit ratio,
    p. 601
rules, p. 621
vault cash, p. 612

Key Equations

$$M = CU + DEP \qquad (15.4)$$

The money supply M is the sum of currency in circulation CU and deposits held by the public at banks DEP.

$$BASE = CU + RES \qquad (15.5)$$

The monetary base equals the sum of currency in circulation CU and bank reserves RES.

$$M = \left(\frac{cu + 1}{cu + res}\right) BASE \qquad (15.8)$$

The money supply M equals the monetary base times the money multiplier, $(cu + 1)/(cu + res)$, where cu is the currency-deposit ratio chosen by the public and res is the reserve-deposit ratio chosen by banks.

Review Questions

1. Define *monetary base*. What is the relationship between the monetary base and the money supply in an all-currency economy?

2. Define *money multiplier*. What is the value of the money multiplier in a system of 100% reserve banking? What is the value of the money multiplier in a system of fractional reserve banking, assuming that all money is held in the form of deposits? Why is the money multiplier higher under fractional reserve banking than under 100% reserve banking?

3. Discuss how actions of the public and of banks can cause the money multiplier to rise or fall. Does the fact that the public and banks can affect the money multiplier imply that the central bank cannot control the money supply?

4. What is the effect on the monetary base of an open-market purchase of U.S. Treasury securities? What is the effect on the money supply?

5. Who determines monetary policy in the United States? What role does the President play?

6. Besides open-market operations, what other means does the Federal Reserve have for controlling the money supply? Explain how these alternative methods work.

7. What are intermediate targets? How do they differ from the ultimate goals of monetary policy? List the two principal intermediate targets that have been used by the Fed.

8. "It is plain to see that discretion is a better way to run monetary policy than following a rule, because a policy of discretion gives the central bank the ability to react to news about the economy." What is the monetarist response to the statement? What is the more recent argument for using rules rather than discretion?

Numerical Problems

1. The Agricolan monetary base is 1,000,000 florins. The public always holds half of its money supply as currency and half as deposits. Banks hold 20% of deposits in the form of reserves. Starting with the initial creation of a monetary base that accompanies the purchase by the central bank of 1,000,000 florins' worth of coconuts from the public, show the consolidated balance sheet of the banks after they first receive deposits, after a first round of loans and redeposits, and after a second round of loans and redeposits. (*Hint:* Don't forget that the public keeps only half of its money in the form of bank deposits.)

Show the balance sheets of the central bank, the banking system, and the public at the end of the process of multiple expansion of loans and deposits. What is the final value of the money supply?

2. a. The money supply is $6,000,000, currency held by the public is $2,000,000, and the reserve-deposit ratio is 0.25. Find deposits, bank reserves, the monetary base, and the money multiplier.

b. In a different economy vault cash is $1,000,000, deposits by depository institutions at the central bank are $4,000,000, the monetary base is $10,000,000, and bank deposits are $20,000,000. Find bank reserves, the money supply, and the money multiplier.

3. When the real interest rate increases, banks have an incentive to lend out a greater portion of their deposits, which reduces the reserve-deposit ratio. In particular, suppose that

$$res = 0.4 - 2r,$$

where *res* is the reserve-deposit ratio and r is the real interest rate. The currency-deposit ratio is 0.4, the price level is fixed at 1.0, and the monetary base equals 60. The real quantity of money demanded is given by following money demand function:

$$L(Y, i) = 0.5Y - 10i,$$

where Y is real output and i is the nominal interest rate. Assume that expected inflation is zero, so that the nominal interest rate and the real interest rate are equal.

a. If $r = i = 0.10$, what are the values of the reserve-deposit ratio, the money multiplier, and the money supply? For what value of real output Y does a real interest rate of 0.10 clear the asset market?

b. Repeat part a for $r = i = 0.05$.

c. Suppose that the reserve-deposit ratio is fixed at the value you found in part a and is not affected by interest rates. If $r = i = 0.05$, for what value of output does the asset market clear in this case?

d. Is the *LM* curve flatter or steeper when the reserve-deposit ratio depends on the real interest rate, compared with the case in which the reserve-deposit ratio is fixed? Explain your answer in economic terms.

4. This question asks you to analyze a game played by two players, player I and player II. Player I can choose one of two actions, called A and B. Player II also has two actions to choose from, called a and b. Both players are affected by their own action and by the action of the other player. The points that each player assigns to each possible outcome (combination of actions) are given in the following table:

Outcome	Points for Player I	Points for Player II
(A, a)	2	2
(A, b)	5	0
(B, a)	0	5
(B, b)	3	3

In the table the first row says that if player I chooses action A and player II chooses action a, player I gets 2 points and player II gets 2 points. The more points a player gets, the happier she is with the outcome. Players don't care about how many points the other player gets.

a. If player I moves (chooses an action) first, then player II moves, what action will each player take? (Set up a game theory diagram like Fig. 15.7.) What is the outcome of the game? Does your answer change if player II moves first?

b. Suppose that player I moves first, but before player I moves, player II announces which action (a or b) he will take when it is his turn. Player II's announcement is legally binding. What is the outcome of the game now?

c. Before player I takes the first move, player II is allowed to make a *threat*, telling player I what action he will take on his turn if player I chooses A and what action he will take if player I chooses B. Player II's threats are legally binding. What is the outcome of the game now? Is player I made worse off or better off by player II's ability to threaten her?

Analytical Problems

1. How would each of the following affect the U.S. money supply? Explain.

   a. Banks decide to hold more excess reserves. (Excess reserves are reserves over and above what banks are legally required to hold against deposits.)

   b. People withdraw cash from their bank accounts for Christmas shopping.

   c. The Federal Reserve sells gold to the public.

   d. The Federal Reserve begins to pay interest on deposits of depository institutions held at the Fed (it currently does not pay interest).

   e. The introduction of automatic teller machines, which allow people to withdraw cash from the bank as needed, makes deposits relatively more convenient.

   f. The Federal government covers $20 billion of its fiscal deficit by selling bonds to the Federal Reserve. The proceeds of the sale are used to pay government employees.

   g. The Federal Reserve sells some of its government securities in Tokyo in exchange for yen.

2. Suppose that the central bank strictly followed a rule of keeping the real interest rate equal to 3% per year. The rate of 3% per year happens to be the real interest rate consistent with the economy's initial general equilibrium.

   a. Assume that the economy is hit only by money demand shocks. Under the central bank's rule, will the money supply be procyclical, countercyclical, or acyclical? Will the rule make aggregate demand more stable or less stable?

   b. Assume that the economy is hit only by *IS* shocks. What are the effects of the rule on the cyclicality of the money supply and the stability of aggregate demand? Will the central bank be able to follow its rule in the long run?

   c. Assume that the economy is hit only by aggregate supply shocks. Repeat part b.

3. In the game between the Fed and the firms shown diagrammatically in Fig. 15.8(b), what happens if the Fed does not value having the unemployment rate below the natural rate $\bar{u}$? Specifically, assume that the Fed assigns 0 points to a situation in which u equals $\bar{u}$ and assigns -1 points to a situation in which u is either above or below $\bar{u}$. How does this modification affect the outcome of the game? Assume that if the Fed is indifferent between two actions, it chooses the one that makes the firms better off.

4. Why do you think that many governments have policies against negotiating with hostage-taking terrorists? Under what conditions, if any, are such policies likely to reduce hostage taking? Discuss the analogy to monetary rules.

16
Government Spending and Its Financing

At every level of government, from the town hall to the White House, fiscal policy—the government's decisions about how much to spend, on what to spend, and how to pay for its spending—is of central importance. Politicians and the public understand that the government's fiscal choices have a direct impact on the "bread and butter" issues of how much we pay in taxes and what government benefits and services we receive. More indirect but equally important are the effects of fiscal policy on the performance of the macroeconomy. In recent years the public seems to have grown more aware of the macroeconomic effects of fiscal policy as the economic implications of government budget deficits, tax reform, and other aspects of fiscal policy have been extensively debated.

In this chapter we take a closer look at fiscal policy and its macroeconomic effects. To provide some background, we begin with definitions and facts about the government budget. We then discuss a number of important fiscal policy issues, including the role of fiscal policy in macroeconomic stabilization, the burden of the government debt, and the link between deficits and inflation.

16.1 THE GOVERNMENT BUDGET: SOME FACTS AND FIGURES

Before getting into the analytical issues of fiscal policy, we set the stage by looking at the components of the government budget and their recent trends. We discuss three major aspects of the budget: (1) spending, or outlays; (2) tax revenues, or receipts; and (3) the budget deficit. Our discussion reviews and builds on Chapter 2, which introduced the basic budget concepts.

Government Outlays

Government outlays, the total spending by the government during any given period of time, are divided into three major categories: government purchases, transfer payments, and net interest payments.

1. *Government purchases* (G) are government spending on currently produced goods and services, such as military hardware, highway repairs, and the salaries of bureaucrats and police.

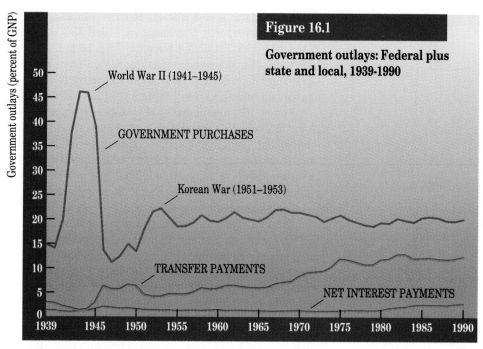

Figure 16.1

Government outlays: Federal plus state and local, 1939-1990

The figure shows the behavior since 1939 of the three major components of government outlays, for all levels of government combined and measured as a percentage of GNP. Government purchases rose most sharply during World War II (1941–1945) and the Korean War (1951–1953). Transfer payments have risen steadily as a share of GNP. Interest payments rose most sharply during World War II and in the 1980s.

Source: *Economic Report of the President*, February 1991, Tables B-1 and B-80.

2. *Transfer payments (TR)* are payments made to individuals for which the government does not receive *current* goods or services in exchange. Examples of transfers are Social Security benefit payments, military and civil service pensions, unemployment insurance, welfare payments (Aid to Families with Dependent Children), and Medicare.

3. *Net interest payments (INT)* equal the interest paid by the government to the holders of government bonds less the interest received by the government, for example, on outstanding government loans to students or farmers.

In addition to the three major categories of government outlays, there is a minor category called *subsidies less surplus of government enterprises*. Subsidies are payments made by the government that are intended to affect the production or prices of various goods. Examples are price support payments to farmers and fare subsidies for mass transit systems. The surplus of government enterprises represents the profits of government-run enterprises such as the Tennessee Valley Authority (an electricity producer). Since this category of outlays is relatively small, for simplicity we ignore it.

In the United States total outlays by the Federal, state, and local governments together are about a third of GNP. Figure 16.1 shows the behavior since 1939 of the three categories of government outlays, expressed as a percentage of GNP. The most obvious feature of Fig. 16.1 is the spike in government purchases that occurred during World War II: During 1943 and 1944, when the war effort was at its peak, government purchases exceeded 45% of GNP. The impact of the Korean War (1951–1953) is also evident in Fig. 16.1, though less dramatic: Government purchases of goods and services increased from 13.5% of GNP in 1950 to 22.3% of GNP in 1953. Since the mid-1950s, the share of GNP devoted to government purchases has remained fairly steady at around 20%.

Figure 16.1 also shows that transfer payments rose steadily as a share of GNP from the early 1950s until the early 1980s, essentially doubling their share of GNP during that thirty-year period. Transfers are currently about 12% of GNP. The long-term increase in transfer payments is the result of the creation of new social programs (such as Medicare and Medicaid in 1965), the expansion of benefits under existing programs (such as Social Security), and the increased number of people covered by the various programs.

Finally, Fig. 16.1 depicts the behavior of net interest payments—interest payments, for short. Because interest payments are much smaller than the other two categories of government outlays, their behavior appears smoother in the figure. However, interest payments rose sharply as a percentage of GNP in two periods. First, interest payments rose from 0.96% of GNP in 1941 to 1.93% of GNP in 1946, reflecting the large amount of government borrowing done in order to finance the war effort during World War II. Interest payments as a share of GNP also doubled during the 1980s, rising from 1.23% in 1979 to 2.46% in 1989. This increase reflected both higher rates of borrowing by the government and the generally high level of interest rates during the 1980s.

How does the rate of government expenditure in the United States compare with rates in other countries with similar living standards? Because official accounting rules for measuring the government budget vary widely among countries, this question is not as straightforward to answer as one might think. Nevertheless, a comparison is presented in Table 16.1, which gives the ratios of both central (Federal, in the United States) government spending and total government spending to gross domestic product for seven industrialized countries. The table shows that the United States, along with Japan, has a lower rate of government spending than the Western European countries and Canada. The principal reason for this discrepancy is that the Western European countries and Canada generally have

Table 16.1 Government Spending in Seven Industrialized Countries Percent of GDP, 1987

Country	Central Government	All Government
France	22.6%	48.4%
Italy	36.2%	45.9%
Germany (West)	13.9%	43.2%
Canada	21.7%	42.8%
United Kingdom	31.8%	42.6%
United States	18.0%	35.3%
Japan	14.5%	27.3%

Source: OECD, *National Accounts, 1975–1987*. All data are from 1987, except for United Kingdom data, which are from 1986. Note that data for the "Central government" in the United States, Japan, Germany, France, and the United Kingdom exclude social security payments, but these payments are included in the "All government" category. Data for "Central government" in Canada and Italy include some social security benefits.

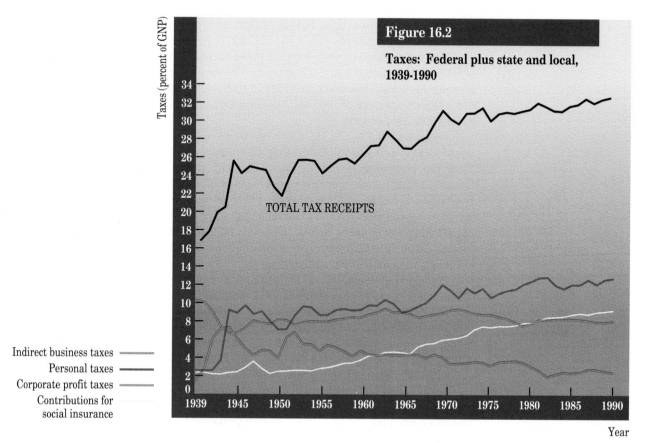

Indirect business taxes ———
Personal taxes ———
Corporate profit taxes ———
Contributions for
social insurance

Year

The figure shows the history of revenues from various types of taxes, for all levels of government combined and measured as a percentage of GNP. Total taxes have drifted upward over the past five decades. Most of the increase in taxes over this period is accounted for by the increases in contributions for social insurance and in personal taxes.

Source: *Economic Report of the President*, February 1991, Tables B-1 and B-80.

more extensive government-financed social welfare programs (such as national health insurance) than the United States.

Taxes

On the revenue side of the government's budget accounts are its tax receipts. There are four major categories of tax receipts: personal taxes, contributions for social insurance, indirect business taxes, and corporate taxes. Figure 16.2 shows the historical behavior of revenues from these four major categories of taxes in the United States, all expressed as a percentage of GNP. You can see from the figure that the share of taxes in GNP has risen steadily, nearly doubling from 16.9% of GNP in 1939 to 32.6% of GNP in 1990.

The largest category of tax receipts is *personal taxes*, which are primarily personal income taxes and property taxes. Income taxes were first introduced at the Federal level in the United States (at very low rates, and for only the richest people) during the Civil War. However, this tax faced a series of legal challenges, and eventually, the Supreme Court declared the income tax unconstitutional. In 1913 the Sixteenth Amendment to the Constitution gave Congress the right to impose an income tax. Used lightly at first, this tax is now a major source of revenue for the government.

Personal taxes took their biggest jump during World War II, rising from 2.6% of GNP in 1940 to 9.7% of GNP in 1945. The general upward drift in personal tax receipts since 1945 has been interrupted by several tax cut bills, notably the Kennedy-Johnson tax cut of 1964 and the Reagan tax cut (officially, the Economic Recovery Tax Act) of 1981.

As you can see in Fig. 16.2, a large share of the increase in tax receipts since World War II reflects the increase in the second category of taxes, *contributions for social insurance* (primarily Social Security taxes). Social insurance contributions are usually levied as a fixed percentage of a worker's salary, up to a ceiling; income above the ceiling is not taxed. The worker's contributions are in most cases matched by the employer, so that the deduction appearing on the worker's paycheck reflects only about half of the total tax levied. Increases in social insurance contributions over time are the result of both increases in the contribution rate and higher ceilings on the amount of income subject to this tax.

The third category of taxes is *indirect business taxes*, mainly sales taxes. These taxes declined as a share of GNP during World War II and have not shown any significant long-term trend during the postwar period.

The fourth and final major category of tax receipts is *corporate taxes*, particularly corporate profits taxes. Figure 16.2 shows that corporate taxes rose sharply during World War II and the Korean War, then drifted gradually downward as a share of GNP from the mid-1950s until the mid-1980s. Changes in the tax code in 1986 were intended to increase corporate tax receipts (while reducing personal income taxes collected by the Federal government), but between 1985 and 1989 corporate tax receipts as a share of GNP rose only slightly, from 2.40% to 2.45% of GNP.

The Composition of Outlays and Taxes: The Federal Government Versus State and Local Governments

The components of government spending shown in Fig. 16.1 and the components of taxes shown in Fig. 16.2 lump together Federal, state, and local governments. For most purposes of macroeconomic analysis, combining Federal together with state and local fiscal policy is the right thing to do. The macroeconomic effect of a new highway-building program, for example, shouldn't depend on whether the new highways are financed from the Federal budget or from state and local budgets. In this respect the tendency of many news stories about fiscal policy to focus exclusively on the Federal government's budget can sometimes be misleading.

Nevertheless, it is useful to know that in the United States Federal government budgets have a very different composition, on both the expenditure and the revenue side, from those of state and local governments. A summary of the major components of both the Federal and the combined state and local government budgets for 1990 is given in Table 16.2. Here are some key points to note from the table:

1. *Goods and services.* By far the largest part of state and local outlays (close to 90%) is for goods and services. In contrast, only about a third of Federal outlays is for goods and services, and three quarters of this amount is for national defense. *More than six sevenths of government spending on nondefense goods and services in the United States is done by state and local governments.*

Table 16.2 Government Outlays and Receipts, 1990 (Billions of Dollars, Annual Rates)

	Federal		State and Local	
	Billions of Dollars	% of Outlays	Billions of Dollars	% of Outlays
Outlays				
Goods and services				
National defense	*312.9*		*0*	
Nondefense	*110.6*		*674.3*	
Total goods and services	423.5	33.2	674.3	88.1
Transfer payments	511.3	40.1	162.9	21.3
Grants in aid	131.7	10.3	0	
Net interest paid	186.5	14.6	−41.6	−5.4
Subsidies less surpluses of government enterprises and less dividends received	22.8	1.8	−30.4	−4.0
Total outlays	1275.9	100.0	765.2	100.0
	Billions of Dollars	% of Receipts	Billions of Dollars	% of Receipts
Receipts				
Personal taxes	492.8	44.3	206.6	25.8
Contributions for social insurance	446.7	40.2	60.2	7.5
Indirect business taxes	61.7	5.5	378.6	47.2
Corporate taxes	110.8	10.0	24.2	3.0
Grants in aid	0		131.7	16.4
Total receipts	1112.0	100.0	801.4	100.0
Deficit (surplus, if negative) (outlays less receipts)	163.8		−36.1	
Primary deficit (surplus, if negative)	−22.7		5.5	

Source: *Survey of Current Business*, February 1991, "Federal Fiscal Programs," Table 10, p. 29; "State and Local Government Fiscal Position in 1990," Table 2, p. 31, and Table 3, p. 32.

Note: Figures may not add due to rounding.

2. *Transfer payments*. The Federal budget is much more heavily weighted toward transfer payments (particularly, benefits from Social Security and related programs) than state and local budgets are.

3. *Grants in aid*. Grants in aid are payments made by the Federal government to state and local governments to help support various education, transportation, and welfare programs. In 1990 these grants totaled $131.7 billion. Grants in aid appear as an outlay for the Federal government and as a receipt for state and local governments.

4. *Net interest paid*. For the Federal government, net interest payments are positive and quite large because of the large quantity of Federal government bonds that are outstanding. In contrast, net interest payments for state and local governments are *negative*, meaning that state and local governments (who are important holders of Federal government bonds) are net recipients of interest payments.

5. *Composition of taxes*. Nearly 85% of Federal government receipts come from personal taxes (primarily the Federal income tax) and contributions for social insurance. Only about 10% of Federal revenues are from corporate taxes and only about 5% are from indirect business taxes. In contrast, state and local governments rely heavily on indirect business taxes such as sales taxes. About a quarter of state and local revenues come from personal taxes. As we have already discussed, state and local governments also count as revenue the grants in aid that they receive from the Federal government.

Deficits

Government outlays need not equal tax revenues in each period. As we saw in Chapter 2, when government outlays exceed revenues, there is a government budget deficit (or simply a deficit); and when revenues exceed outlays, there is a government budget surplus. We write the definition of the deficit for ease of reference:

$$
\begin{aligned}
\text{deficit} &= \text{outlays} - \text{tax revenues} \\
&= \text{government purchases} + \text{transfers} \qquad\qquad (16.1) \\
&\quad + \text{net interest} - \text{tax revenues} \\
&= G + TR + INT - T.
\end{aligned}
$$

A second deficit concept, called the **primary government budget deficit**, excludes net interest from government outlays in the calculation of the deficit:

$$
\begin{aligned}
\text{primary deficit} &= \text{outlays} - \text{net interest} - \text{tax revenues} \\
&= \text{government purchases} + \text{transfers} - \text{tax revenues} \quad (16.2) \\
&= G + TR - T.
\end{aligned}
$$

The primary deficit is the amount by which government purchases and transfers exceed tax revenues. The primary deficit plus net interest payments equals the deficit. Figure 16.3 illustrates the relationship between the two deficit concepts.

Why have two deficit concepts? The reason is that each deficit concept answers a different question. The standard or overall deficit answers the question of how much the government currently has to borrow to pay for its total outlays. When measured in nominal terms, the deficit during a given year is the number of additional dollars that the government must borrow during the year.

The primary deficit answers the question of whether the government can afford its *current* programs. If the primary deficit is zero, then the government is collecting just enough tax revenue to pay for its current purchases of goods and services and its current social programs (as reflected in transfer payments). If the

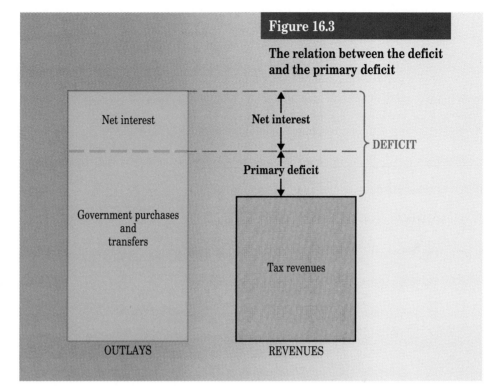

Figure 16.3

The relation between the deficit and the primary deficit

Net interest

Net interest

DEFICIT

Government purchases and transfers

Primary deficit

Tax revenues

OUTLAYS

REVENUES

The deficit is the amount by which government outlays exceed tax revenues, and the primary deficit is the amount by which government purchases plus transfers exceed tax revenues. The deficit equals the primary deficit plus net interest payments.

primary deficit is greater than zero, on the other hand, then current government purchases and social programs cost more than can be paid for out of current tax revenue. Net interest payments are ignored in the primary deficit because they represent not current program costs but costs arising from past expenditures that were financed by government borrowing. As you can see in Table 16.2, the Federal government had a *primary surplus* and an *overall deficit* in 1990, indicating that current tax revenues were large enough to cover the costs of current programs but were inadequate to fund both current programs and the interest cost of past borrowing.

Figure 16.4 shows the deficit and primary deficit for all levels of government combined as a percentage of GNP since 1940. Once again, the World War II period stands out; the government financed only part of the war effort with taxes and thus had to run large primary and overall deficits. Large deficits (using both concepts) also occurred in the middle 1970s and through much of the 1980s, although the primary deficit for all levels of government combined was eliminated in 1987, and there was a primary surplus at the end of the decade.

16.2 GOVERNMENT SPENDING, TAXES, AND THE MACROECONOMY

Fiscal policy affects the macroeconomy through three main channels: (1) aggregate demand effects, (2) government capital formation, and (3) incentive effects.

Fiscal Policy and Aggregate Demand

Fiscal policy can affect economic activity by affecting the total amount of spending in the economy, or aggregate demand. As we saw in earlier chapters, aggregate

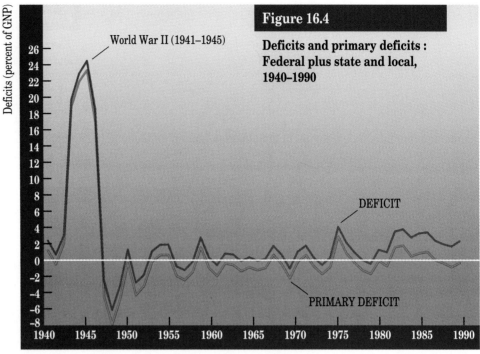

Figure 16.4

**Deficits and primary deficits :
Federal plus state and local,
1940–1990**

Year

The figure shows how deficits and primary deficits, for all levels of government combined and measured as a percentage of GNP, have evolved over time. The government sector ran large deficits during World War II. Although the overall budget deficit was large during the 1980s, the primary deficit was eliminated in 1987, and there was a primary surplus at the end of the 1980s.

Source: *Economic Report of the President*, February 1991, Tables B-1 and B-80.

demand is represented by the intersection of the *IS* and *LM* curves. In either the classical or the Keynesian *IS-LM* model, an increase in government purchases reduces desired national saving and shifts the *IS* curve upward and to the right, thereby raising aggregate demand.

Classicals and Keynesians have differing views about the effect of tax changes on aggregate demand. Classicals usually accept the Ricardian equivalence proposition, which says that lump-sum tax changes do not affect desired national saving and thus have no impact on the *IS* curve or aggregate demand. Keynesians generally disagree, arguing that (for example) a lump-sum tax cut stimulates consumption and reduces desired national saving, thereby shifting the *IS* curve upward and to the right and raising aggregate demand.[1]

Classicals and Keynesians also disagree on the question of whether fiscal policy should be used to fight the business cycle. As we saw in Chapter 11, classicals generally reject attempts to smooth out business cycles, by fiscal policy or by other means. In contrast, Keynesians argue that it is desirable to use fiscal policy to stabilize the economy and maintain full employment, for example, by cutting taxes and raising spending when the economy is in a recession.

---

[1]Ricardian equivalence was introduced in Chapter 6 and we discuss it further in Section 16.4. A summary of the issues is given in Chapter 12, Appendix 12.B.

However, even Keynesians admit that in practice it is difficult to use fiscal policy as a stabilization tool. A major problem is fiscal policy's lack of flexibility. The government's budget has many purposes besides macroeconomic stabilization, such as maintaining national security, providing income support for eligible groups, developing the nation's infrastructure (roads, bridges, public buildings), and supplying government services (such as education and public health). Much of the government's spending is committed years in advance (as in weapons development programs) or even decades in advance (as for Social Security benefits). Therefore expanding or contracting total government spending rapidly for macroeconomic stabilization purposes is difficult without either spending wastefully or compromising other fiscal policy goals. Taxes are perhaps a bit easier to change than spending, but the tax laws also have many different goals and may be the result of a fragile political compromise that is not easily altered.

Compounding the problem of low flexibility is the problem of *long time lags* resulting from the slow-moving political process by which fiscal policy is made (see Box 16.1, p. 652, on the Federal budget process). The period between the time when a spending or tax proposal is made and the time when it is put into force is rarely less than eighteen months to two years. This time lag is too long for effective countercyclical use of fiscal policy, since by the time an antirecession fiscal measure actually had an impact on the economy, the recession would probably be over.

Automatic Stabilizers and the Full-Employment Deficit A way to get around the problems of fiscal policy inflexibility and long lags that impede the use of countercyclical fiscal policies is to build automatic stabilizers into the budget. **Automatic stabilizers** are provisions in the government's budget that cause government spending to rise or taxes to fall automatically—without legislative action—when GNP falls. Similarly, when GNP rises, automatic stabilizers cause spending to fall or taxes to rise without any need for direct legislative action.

A good example of an automatic stabilizer is unemployment insurance. When the economy goes into a recession and unemployment rises, more people become eligible to receive unemployment insurance payments, which are paid out automatically without any need for action by Congress. Thus the unemployment insurance component of transfers rises during recessions, making fiscal policy automatically more expansionary.[2]

Quantitatively, the most important automatic stabilizer is the income tax system. When the economy goes into a recession, people's incomes fall, and so less income tax is paid. This "automatic tax cut" that occurs during recessions helps to cushion the fall in disposable income and (according to Keynesians) prevents aggregate demand from falling as far as it might otherwise. Similarly, when people's incomes rise during a boom, the government collects more income tax revenue, which helps restrain the increase in aggregate demand. Keynesians argue that this automatic fiscal policy is a major reason for the generally greater stability of the economy since World War II.

A side effect of automatic stabilizers is that government budget deficits tend to increase in recessions, because government spending automatically rises and taxes automatically fall when GNP declines. In order to distinguish changes in the deficit caused by recession from other sources of changes, some economists have

---

[2]This assumes that the Keynesian model is right, so that a transfer increase—which is equivalent to a reduction in taxes—is expansionary.

The enactment of a budget for the Federal government is a long and complex process, involving the executive and legislative branches of the government. The budget process has three main phases: (1) the development of a proposed budget by the President and other members of the executive branch; (2) legislative action on the budget by Congress; and (3) putting the budget into operation.

BOX *16.1:* THE FEDERAL BUDGET PROCESS

The President usually submits the proposed budget to Congress eight or nine months before the beginning of the fiscal year, which is October 1. (Thus fiscal year 1992 begins on October 1, 1991.) Since it takes about nine months to formulate the budget, this submission deadline implies that budget planning must begin a full year and a half before the beginning of the period to which the budget applies. The President is assisted in developing his budget by his staff, the Office of Management and Budget (OMB), the Treasury, the Council of Economic Advisers, and other members of the executive branch, who in turn gather information and requests for funds from the various agencies of the government.

Once it receives the President's budget, the Congress can and usually does modify it extensively. Congressional consideration of the budget begins in the House of Representatives, where spending plans are first considered by the Appropriations Committee and proposals for raising revenue are considered by the Ways and Means Committee. After the various appropriations and tax bills are approved by the House, they are sent to the Senate, which conducts its own review. Differences between the House and Senate versions of the various bills are reconciled by a conference committee, and the reconciled legislation is returned to the full memberships of the House and Senate for approval. Finally, the appropriations and revenue bills are sent to the President for approval or veto.

When some of the appropriations bills are not completed by the beginning of the fiscal year—which in recent years has happened frequently—Congress passes a *continuing resolution* to allow the government to keep operating until the new budget is finalized.

When the budget is approved, the process enters the third phase, which is the actual spending and collection of taxes. Overseeing this process is the responsibility of the President and the executive branch. The actual allocation of funds to the various government agencies is done by the director of the OMB. If more money is needed during the year, the President may approach Congress and request a supplementary appropriation.

Over the past two decades Congress has reformed the budget process several times, primarily in order to try to reduce the size of the budget deficit. In 1985 Congress adopted the Balanced Budget and Emergency Deficit Control Act (better known as the Gramm-Rudman-Hollings bill), which required a steadily decreasing deficit leading to budget balance in fiscal year 1991 (see "The Policy Debate" box, p. 670). The original bill, having failed to achieve significant deficit reduction, has been revised several times. In the 1990 revision, limits were placed on various categories of government spending. According to the law, if spending in any category exceeds its limit, then all spending items in that category will be automatically cut.

Sources: Office of Management and Budget, *The United States Budget in Brief*, and *Economic Report of the President*, February 1991, pp. 65–69.

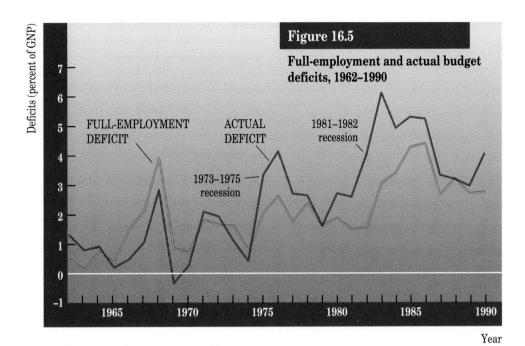

Figure 16.5

Full-employment and actual budget deficits, 1962–1990

The actual and full-employment Federal budget deficits are shown as a percentage of GNP. The actual budget deficit substantially exceeded the full-employment deficit during the 1973–1975 and 1981–1982 recessions, reflecting the importance of automatic stabilizers.

Sources: *The Economic and Budget Outlook: Fiscal Years 1992–96,* Congressional Budget Office, January 1991: Full-employment deficit—Table D-1, p. 145; actual deficit—Table D-2, p. 146; GNP— *Economic Report of the President,* February 1991, Table B-1.

advocated the use of a deficit measure called the full-employment deficit. The **full-employment deficit** tells us what the government budget deficit *would be*, given the tax and spending policies currently in force, if the economy were operating at its full-employment level. The actual budget deficit exceeds the full-employment deficit when output is below its full-employment level, with the difference between the two deficit concepts reflecting the importance of automatic stabilizers in the budget.[3]

Figure 16.5 shows the actual and full-employment budget deficits (as percentages of GNP) of the Federal government in the United States since 1962. Notice that the actual budget deficit substantially exceeded the full-employment budget deficit during the recessions of 1973–1975 and 1981–1982.

Government Capital Formation

The health of the economy depends not only on *how much* the government spends but also on *how* it spends its resources. For example, as we discussed in Chapter 8, the quantity and quality of public infrastructure—roads, schools, public hospitals, and so on—are important for the rate of economic growth. Thus the formation of **government capital**—long-lived physical assets owned by the government—is an important channel through which fiscal policy affects the macroeconomy. The government's budget affects not only the society's physical capital formation but also its human capital formation: At least some part of the government's expendi-

---

[3]In practice, the calculation of full-employment deficits uses the Keynesian assumption that recessions reflect deviations from full employment rather than the classical assumption that (in the absence of misperceptions) recessions reflect changes in full-employment output.

tures on health, nutrition, and education are an investment, in the sense that they will lead to a more productive work force in the future.

An ideal government budget accounting system would distinguish between expenditures on current items, such as the salaries of police officers or agricultural subsidies, and expenditures on capital items, such as the construction of mass transit systems or power-generating dams. Corporate financial accounts distinguish current from capital expenditures, as do the accounts of governments in some other countries, but the U.S. government's budget does not make this distinction. Some people have advocated the introduction of separate current and capital accounts into the Federal budget to allow for a better evaluation of the amount of capital formation that the government is doing. A problem is that in practice it would be hard to allocate expenditures with a partial investment component—such as those on health and nutrition—between the two accounts.

Incentive Effects of Fiscal Policy

The third channel through which fiscal policy affects the macroeconomy is its effects on incentives. Tax policies in particular, by changing the financial rewards to various activities, can affect economic behavior. We discussed the effects of taxes on the incentives to save and to invest in Chapter 6 and the effects of taxes on the incentive to work in Chapter 10.

In analyzing the incentive effects of taxes in Chapter 10, we introduced the distinction between average and marginal tax rates. The average tax rate is the total tax collected divided by the total amount of income that is being taxed. The marginal tax rate is the fraction of an *extra* unit of income that must be paid in taxes. In the context of a worker's labor supply decision, we showed in Chapter 10 that an increase in the marginal tax rate on income, with the average tax rate held constant, reduces the reward to working and thus lowers labor supply (a pure substitution effect). However, an increase in the average tax rate, with the marginal tax rate held constant, makes workers poorer and thus raises labor supply (a pure income effect). This analysis illustrated that the incentive effects of tax changes depend crucially on the distinction between average and marginal tax rates. In the belief that the substitution effects of marginal tax rate changes are generally stronger than the income effects of average tax rate changes, economists usually emphasize the incentive effects of marginal tax rates over those of average tax rates.

The Distortionary Effects of Taxes   Because tax rates affect economic incentives, they change the pattern of economic behavior from what it would be in the absence of taxes. But if the invisible hand of free markets is working properly, then the pattern of economic activity in the absence of taxes is the most efficient, and changes in behavior caused by taxes reduce economic welfare. Tax-induced deviations in economic behavior from the efficient, free-market outcome are called **distortions**.

To illustrate how distortions arise, let's revisit Prudence the golf pro, whose labor supply decision we analyzed in Chapter 10. Suppose that Prudence's fee for giving golf lessons is $20 per hour. However, because she faces a marginal tax rate of 25%, her after-tax wage is only $15 (75% of $20) per hour. Optimally trading off income and leisure, Prudence will choose to work up to the point that the value to her of an extra hour of leisure is $15, which equals the after-tax income she receives for an extra hour of work.

Now what happens if an aspiring golfer asks Prudence for a one-hour golf lesson, for which he offers to pay $19? If there were no taxes Prudence would accept the offer and give the lesson, because the $19 she would earn is greater than the $15 value she places on an hour of leisure. Indeed, by working the additional hour, Prudence would earn a surplus of $4 over the value of her forgone leisure. But because Prudence faces a marginal tax rate of 25%, her after-tax compensation for working the extra hour is only $14.25 (75% of $19), which is less than the $15 value she places on an hour of leisure. Therefore Prudence will decline the aspiring golfer's offer and will not work the additional hour.

Prudence's decision not to work the extra hour is right from her point of view, because after taxes the income she would receive from working is less than the value she places on her leisure. But from society's point of view, it would have been preferable for Prudence to work the extra hour. The aspiring golfer would have gotten at least $19 worth of benefit from the lesson (if he did not expect this much benefit, he would not have offered $19), which exceeds the $15 value that Prudence places on her forgone leisure. With no taxes this desirable economic transaction would have occurred. However, because of the 25% marginal tax, the golf lesson does not occur, which represents a distortion caused by the tax system.

Tax Rate Smoothing to Minimize Distortions A general principle is that the higher the marginal tax rate already is, the greater are the additional distortions created by raising the marginal tax rate still further. To illustrate this point, consider the effects of an increase in the marginal income tax rate on labor supply, assuming that the average tax rate is held constant. Suppose that in response to the increase in the marginal tax rate, a worker supplies one hour less labor; say he supplies 39 hours instead of 40 hours. As a result, output falls by the marginal product of labor MPN. Now suppose that the marginal tax rate is increased again, causing the worker to reduce labor supply by an additional hour, to 38 hours. Again output falls by an amount equal to the MPN. However, because of diminishing marginal returns to labor, the MPN of the worker's thirty-ninth hour is greater than that of his fortieth hour of work. Thus the output loss caused by the second increase in the marginal tax rate is greater than the loss created by the first tax increase.

A useful approximation, it turns out, is that the lost output due to tax distortions is proportional to the square of the tax rate.[4] Table 16.3 illustrates this approximation with a numerical example. In Table 16.3 if (for example) the tax rate increases by a factor of 2, from 10% to 20%, the output loss caused by the distortionary effect of taxes increases by a factor of 4 (2^2), from $100 to $400. Similarly, if the tax rate increases by a factor of 3, from 10% to 30%, the lost output increases by a factor of 9 (3^2), from $100 to $900.

How can the distortionary effects of taxes be minimized? As we can illustrate by using Table 16.3, the average amount of output lost because of distortions can be minimized by having a constant tax rate over time. To show this result, suppose that the government's spending plans require it to levy a tax rate that over a number of years averages out to 20%. The question is whether to set the tax rate equal to 20% in every year or to set the tax rate equal to 10% in half of the years and 30% in the other half of the years.

---

[4]This approximation assumes that taxes are proportional to income, so that the average and marginal tax rates are the same.

Table 16.3 Minimizing the Average Distortion by Tax Smoothing

Tax Rate	Lost Output
10%	$100
20%	$400
30%	$900

Average lost output	
If tax rate is $10% half the time and 30% half the time	$500
If tax rate is 20% all the time	$400

If the tax rate is 20% in every year, Table 16.3 shows that the cost of the distortion is $400 in every year, so that the average cost of the distortion is $400 per year. Alternatively, according to Table 16.3, when the tax rate is 10%, the cost of the distortion is only $100 per year; but when the tax rate is 30%, the cost of the distortion is $900 per year. Thus if the tax rate fluctuates between 10% and 30%, the average cost of the distortion is $500 per year (the average of $100 per year and $900 per year). This example shows that for a given average value of the tax rate the average cost of the distortion is lower when the tax rate is constant than when it fluctuates.

The result that the cost of distortions is minimized by holding the tax rate constant depends on the assumption that the government knows the average value of the tax rate needed to finance its current and future operations. However, in reality, the government's current and future spending plans change over time as a result of unforeseen developments or changes in priorities. When planned current and future government spending increases, the long-run average value of the tax rate must increase; similarly, when planned current and future spending decreases, the long-run average tax rate can be decreased. Despite this complication, the insight that tax rates should be as constant as possible still applies: The average cost of distortions will be minimized if, whenever changes in government spending require a change in tax rates, current and planned future tax rates all change by the same amount. Changing current and planned future tax rates by the same amount (essentially, requiring that all tax changes be permanent rather than temporary) makes the path of current and future tax rates as smooth as possible. A policy of maintaining a smooth path of tax rates in order to minimize average distortions is called **tax rate smoothing.**

Application

Does the Federal Government Smooth Tax Rates?

Economic theory suggests that the average distortions arising from the tax system will be minimized if the tax rate follows a smooth path over time. Has the Federal government followed this prescription for minimizing average distortions? That is, has the Federal government had a policy of tax rate smoothing?

In a study of these questions Chaipat Sahasakul[5] of Rutgers University argued that if the government is tax-smoothing, the tax rate should change only if there is a change in the long-run revenue needs of the government. The tax rate should not change in response to short-run revenue needs, since if the tax rate is rising and falling with changing short-run revenue needs, its path cannot be "smooth." However, using data on marginal tax rates from the period 1937–1982, Sahasakul found that U.S. tax rates were affected by temporary changes in defense expenditures, contrary to the implications of the tax-smoothing theory.

David Bizer of Northwestern University and Steven Durlauf of Stanford University[6] studied the behavior of the average (rather than the marginal) Federal tax rate over the period 1879–1986. Bizer and Durlauf also found evidence against the idea that the U.S. government employs tax smoothing. In particular, they found evidence of an eight-year cycle in the tax rate, which they attributed to the fact that "eight years is the most common length of time for continuous political party control of the presidency" (pp. 133–134). Bizer and Durlauf found a tendency for tax rates to be reduced two years before a successful reelection bid for President,[7] which suggests that political considerations are important determinants of tax rates in the United States. (For a discussion of the politics of setting tax rates and other tax code provisions, see the Political Environment box, p. 664.)

Although sophisticated studies have found that tax smoothing is not the only factor affecting tax rates, the idea of tax smoothing is still probably a useful one for understanding government behavior. For example, how do we explain the fact that the U.S. government ran a huge deficit during World War II (Fig. 16.4)? The alternative to deficit finance of the war would have been a large wartime increase in tax rates, coupled with a fall in tax rates when the war was over. High tax rates during the war would have distorted the economy at a time when productive efficiency was especially important. By financing the war through borrowing, the government effectively chose to spread the needed tax increase over a long period of time (as the debt was repaid) rather than to raise current taxes by a large amount. This behavior is consistent with the idea of tax smoothing.

16.3   GOVERNMENT DEFICITS AND DEBT

If there is a single number in the government's budget that is the focus of the most public debate and concern, it is the size of the Federal government budget deficit. During the 1980s a string of unprecedentedly large (for peacetime) deficits led to a barrage of claims and counterclaims about the potential impact of big deficits on the economy. In the rest of this chapter we discuss the government budget deficit and its effects.

The Government Debt

There is an important distinction between the government deficit and the government debt (also called the national debt). As we noted in Section 16.1, the govern-

---

[5]"The Evidence on Optimal Taxation over Time," *Journal of Monetary Economics*, November 1986, pp. 251–275.

[6]"Testing the Positive Theory of Government Finance," *Journal of Monetary Economics*, August 1990, pp. 123–141.

[7]A successful reelection bid means that the party of the incumbent President wins the presidential election.

ment's *deficit* (which is a flow variable) is the difference between its expenditures and its tax revenues in any given year. The **government debt** (which is a stock variable) is the total value of government bonds outstanding at any given time. Since the excess of government expenditures over revenues equals the amount of new borrowing that the government must do—that is, the amount of new government debt that it must issue—the deficit in any given year (measured in dollar, or nominal, terms) equals the change in the debt in that year. In terms of flows and stocks the deficit is the flow that corresponds to the increase in the stock of government debt.

If we let B stand for the total nominal value of government bonds outstanding (equivalently, the value of the government debt), we can express the relationship between the government debt and the government deficit by

$$\Delta B = \text{nominal deficit}. \qquad (16.3)$$

Equation (16.3) simply restates the point that the change in the nominal value of the government debt equals the nominal government deficit.

In a period of persistently large budget deficits, the nominal value of the government's debt will grow quickly. During the 1980s, for example, Federal government debt outstanding more than tripled in nominal terms, from \$909 billion in 1980 to \$3206 billion in 1990.[8] Measured in terms of 1982 dollars, the real value of government debt outstanding more than doubled, from \$1060 billion to \$2438 billion.

Since countries with a higher GNP have more resources available to pay the principal and interest on government debt, a useful measure of government indebtedness is the quantity of government debt outstanding divided by the GNP, or the **debt-GNP ratio.** Figure 16.6 shows the historical behavior of the debt-GNP ratio in the United States. The upper curve shows the debt-GNP ratio when the measure of total government debt outstanding includes both government bonds held by the public and government bonds held by government agencies and the Federal Reserve. The lower curve includes in the measure of debt outstanding only the government debt in the hands of the public.

The most striking feature of Fig. 16.6 is the large increase in the debt-GNP ratio that occurred during World War II as the government sold bonds to finance the war effort. By the end of the war the debt-GNP ratio exceeded 1.0, implying that the value of government debt outstanding was greater than a year's GNP. Over the following thirty-five years the government steadily reduced its indebtedness relative to GNP. (Even though nominal government debt grew over most of this period, nominal GNP was growing faster.) Beginning around 1980, though, increased deficits caused the debt-GNP ratio to begin rising, which it did throughout the decade. Despite this rise, at the end of the 1980s the ratio of Federal debt to GNP was still less than half of its value at the end of World War II.

The following formulas (which are derived in the Appendix at the end of the chapter) are useful for understanding the behavior of the debt-GNP ratio over time:

growth rate of debt-GNP ratio =

$$\frac{\text{primary deficit}}{B} + r - \text{growth rate of real GNP}, \qquad (16.4a)$$

---

[8]*Economic Report of the President*, February 1991, Table B–76.

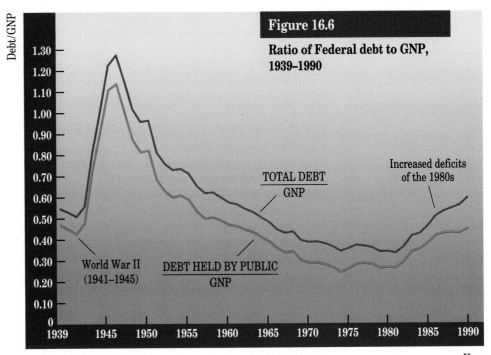

The upper curve shows the ratio of total government debt, including government bonds held by government agencies, to GNP. The lower curve shows the ratio of government bonds held by the public to GNP. The debt-GNP ratio spiked upward during World War II, fell steadily for the next thirty five years, then rose again in the 1980s.

where again B is nominal debt outstanding and r is the actual (rather than the expected) real interest rate. The primary deficit (recall) is the overall deficit less interest payments; in the formula the primary deficit is measured in nominal terms. An equivalent formula is

$$\text{growth rate of debt-GNP ratio} = \frac{\text{primary deficit}}{B} + i - \text{growth rate of nominal GNP,} \quad (16.4b)$$

where i is the nominal interest rate. To see that Eqs. (16.4a) and (16.4b) are equivalent, recall that the nominal interest rate i equals the actual real interest r plus the rate of inflation, and that the growth rate of nominal GNP equals the growth rate of real GNP plus the rate of inflation. If we make those two substitutions in Eq. (16.4b), we obtain Eq. (16.4a).

Equations (16.4a) and (16.4b) help us explain the behavior of the debt-GNP ratio shown in Fig. 16.6. The sharp increase in the debt-GNP ratio during World War II was due to the extremely large primary deficits run during the war. In contrast, for the three and a half decades after World War II, the primary deficit was small or even negative and interest rates were generally lower than GNP growth; thus the debt-GNP ratio declined. Real interest rates were especially low during the 1970s, causing the debt-GNP ratio to shrink further. The debt-GNP ratio increased during the 1980s both because the Federal government ran large primary deficits and because interest rates exceeded GNP growth rates for much of the decade.

Interestingly, there is currently a factor at work that may cause the U.S. debt-GNP ratio to fall in the not-too-distant future; see Box 16.2, p. 662.

Can the Government Roll Over Its Debt Forever?

Each year, billions of dollars of outstanding government bonds mature (that is, they come due and the original principal must be repaid). The government generally obtains the funds to pay the holders of these maturing bonds by printing and selling new bonds. This process of borrowing new funds to pay off maturing bonds is called **rolling over the debt**.[9]

Can the government roll over its debt forever without any limits? If it could, it would be able to avoid ever having to increase taxes or reduce outlays in order to repay its debt. Indeed, the government would have no need of taxes at all, since it could just borrow and then roll over these borrowings indefinitely. As you might guess, there are strong economic forces that limit the ability of the government to roll over its debt forever.

The example worked out in Table 16.4 is useful for understanding why debt rollover is limited. Suppose that prior to year 1 the government had always had a primary deficit of zero and thus had never issued any government bonds. Because the government has no debt and pays no interest, prior to year 1 the total deficit is also zero. Clearly, if it chose, the government could continue running primary and total deficits equal to zero forever. But now suppose that in year 1, and only in year 1, the government increases its purchases of goods by $100 million without increasing taxes. After this one-shot increase in spending, the primary deficit rises to $100 million in year 1 but returns to zero for every year thereafter, as shown in column (1) of Table 16.4. The government finances its deficit in year 1 by selling $100 million of government bonds, so that at the end of year 1 there are $100 million of government bonds outstanding, as shown in column (4).

Suppose that the nominal interest rate on government bonds is 8% per year. Then in year 2 the government must pay $8 million in interest on the $100 million of bonds outstanding at the end of year 1. Because the primary deficit is zero (column 1) and interest payments are $8 million (column 2), the total deficit in year 2 is $8 million (column 3). Therefore the government must borrow an additional $8 million in year 2, bringing the total value of outstanding bonds to $108 million (column 4). Notice that even though the primary deficit is zero in year 2, the stock of government debt increases during year 2 because the interest payments on government debt lead to a deficit. The remaining rows of Table 16.4 show that, because of accumulating interest payments, government debt outstanding grows by 8% per year forever, even though the primary deficit is zero. After 100 years the government debt will have grown to more than 2000 times its initial value, and after 150 years the government debt will approach 100,000 times its initial value.

Will the public be willing to hold the ever-increasing quantity of government bonds shown in Table 16.4? Possibly they will; it depends on how fast the public's

[9]The rolling over of existing bonds does not increase the total amount of government bonds outstanding, since new bonds replace old bonds of equal value. For this reason, government repayments of old maturing bonds are not counted as part of government expenditure, and borrowing done in order to roll over old bonds does not count as part of the total deficit.

Table 16.4 Rolling over the Government Debt

Nominal interest rate = 8% per year
Growth rate of nominal GNP = 4% per year

Year	(1) Primary Deficit (in Millions of Dollars)	(2) Interest Payments (in Millions of Dollars)	(3) Total Deficit (Increase in Bonds Outstanding) (in Millions of Dollars)	(4) Bonds Outstanding at End of Year (in Millions of Dollars)	(5) Nominal GNP (in Millions of Dollars)	(6) Debt-GNP Ratio (4) ÷ (5)
1	100	0	100	100	1000	0.1000
2	0	8	8	108	1040	0.1038
3	0	8.64	8.64	116.64	1081.6	0.1078
4	0	9.33	9.33	125.97	1124.9	0.1120
.	.	.	.	.	.	.
.	.	.	.	.	.	.
.	.	.	.	.	.	.
50	0	321.68	321.68	4342.74	6833.35	0.6355
100	0	15,087	15,087	203,681	48,562	4.1942
150	0	707,629	707,629	9,552,995	345,117	27.6804

wealth grows. If the public's wealth grows even more rapidly than the government's debt, then the public probably would be willing to buy the ever-increasing quantity of bonds. However, if the value of government bonds outstanding grows more rapidly than the public's wealth, then the public would have to devote a larger and larger share of their portfolios to government bonds. Eventually, the public would become unwilling (or perhaps even unable) to increase their holdings of government bonds. At this point the government's ability to borrow would be terminated. Being unable to sell additional bonds, the government would have to run a primary budget surplus (by increasing taxes or reducing purchases and transfer payments) in order to pay the interest on its outstanding debt.[10]

We have just seen that government debt cannot permanently grow more rapidly than the public's wealth. Over long periods of time the growth rate of wealth is the same as the growth rate of GNP, so we restate our result as follows: The value of outstanding government bonds cannot permanently grow faster than GNP grows; or, equivalently, *the debt-GNP ratio cannot grow forever.*

According to Eq. (16.4a), when the primary deficit is zero (as is true in our example after year 1), the growth rate of the debt-GNP ratio equals the real interest rate r minus the growth rate of real GNP. Equivalently, from Eq. (16.4b), when the primary deficit is zero, the growth rate of the debt-GNP ratio equals the nominal interest rate minus the growth rate of nominal GNP. Thus if the real interest rate is permanently higher than the growth rate of real GNP (or, equivalently, if the nominal interest rate is permanently higher than the growth rate of nominal GNP), the government debt-GNP ratio would grow forever. Eventually, the public

---

[10]The government's alternative to running primary surpluses, as we discuss later in the chapter, is to pay its debts by printing money. This strategy has the serious drawback that it may be highly inflationary.

BOX *16.2:* **THE SOCIAL SECURITY SURPLUS AND THE FEDERAL DEFICIT**

As the "baby boomers" (the generation of people born in the years immediately after World War II) age, the general American population ages as well. In 1990 there were about twenty Americans over the age of 65 for every hundred people of working age (20–64 years). Over the years 2010 to 2030, as the baby boom generation retires, this ratio will rise to about forty people over 65 for every hundred people of working age. The prospect of so many retirees raises the question of how the Social Security system will be able to pay promised retirement benefits.

Traditionally, the Social Security system was pay as you go, in that Social Security taxes collected from workers approximately equaled current benefits paid out to retirees in each year. However, under a pay-as-you-go system, the prospective bulge in the number of retirees in the twenty-first century would require very high taxes on future workers. To avoid this problem, in 1983 Congress changed the method of financing Social Security. Under the system now in effect, funds intended to pay retirement benefits in the twenty-first century are being accumulated in advance. Primarily by raising current Social Security taxes, the Social Security Amendment of 1983 provided for surpluses in the Social Security Trust Fund (the government account that keeps track of Social Security taxes and benefits) until several years after the turn of the twenty-first century. The proposed surpluses are large: According to the Congressional Budget Office, Social Security taxes will exceed benefits paid out by $129 billion by fiscal year 1996.*

Since Social Security taxes collected and benefits paid in each year are both counted as part of the current Federal government budget, the prospective Social Security surpluses will have a major impact on the overall Federal deficit. Because of the growing Social Security surpluses, the Federal budget deficit will fall significantly over the next two decades and (according to some projections) may even turn into a substantial budget surplus.

Do the large projected Social Security surpluses solve the problem of high Federal deficits? No, not really. A problem with the standard calculation of the deficit (which counts Social Security taxes and benefits as part of the current budget) is that it ignores the Federal government's obligation to pay Social Security benefits to the retiring baby boomers in the future. When the baby boomers retire, the Social Security system will pay benefits to retirees that far exceed the taxes collected from workers at that time. Thus the Social Security system itself will run large deficits during the middle third of the next century. If the Social Security surpluses over the next few decades are used simply to offset deficits in the rest of the Federal budget, then when the time comes to pay out the baby boomers' benefits, no resources will have been accumulated and a new fiscal crisis will occur.

To reduce the likelihood that Social Security surpluses will be used to offset deficits in the rest of the budget, some economists have suggested that Social Security be excluded from the official government budget. Whether or not this accounting change is made, legislators should keep in mind that if Social Security surpluses are used to pay for current government programs, then massive increases in borrowing or taxes will be necessary to pay promised Social Security benefits in the twenty-first century.

*The Economic and Budget Outlook: Fiscal Years 1992–96, Congressional Budget Office, January 1991, Table III-5, p. 72.

would not tolerate any further increase in the debt-GNP ratio, and the government would have to run a primary surplus. We conclude that *if the real interest rate is greater than the growth rate of real GNP (equivalently, if the nominal interest rate is greater than the growth rate of nominal GNP), the government cannot roll over its debt forever.*

In the example in Table 16.4 the growth rate of nominal GNP is 4% per year and the nominal interest rate is 8% per year, so the debt-GNP ratio grows at the rate of 4% per year. As shown in column (5), GNP starts at $1000 million in year 1, so that the debt-GNP ratio in year 1 (column 6) is 0.1. However, after a century of zero primary deficits the debt-GNP ratio increases to more than 4, and after 150 years the debt-GNP ratio in this example exceeds 27! Clearly, the zero primary deficits and continual debt rollover shown in Table 16.4 are not sustainable forever.

But what if the real interest rate is less than the growth rate of real GNP, as was true in the United States during much of the twentieth century (although not during the 1980s)? Then our analysis so far suggests that the government *could* roll over its debt forever. Could this be true? Have we finally discovered the proverbial "free lunch"?

Unfortunately, even if the real interest rate is below the growth rate of real GNP, the government may not be able to roll over its debt forever. The problem arises from our implicit assumption that future values of interest rates and GNP growth rates are constant and known with certainty. Suppose that the interest rate is currently below the GNP growth rate, but that there is some chance that in the future the interest rate will exceed the GNP growth rate by two percentage points. Should that actually happen, then it follows from Eq. (16.4a) or Eq. (16.4b) that in order to keep the debt-GNP ratio from rising, the government will have to run a primary surplus equal to 2% of the outstanding debt. If the government had previously accumulated a large debt, expecting never to have to repay, then running a primary surplus equal to 2% of that debt would be economically and politically very painful. Thus the possibility that future interest rates might rise or growth rates might fall should dissuade the government from trying to roll over too much debt.

16.4 THE BURDEN OF THE GOVERNMENT DEBT ON FUTURE GENERATIONS[11]

One concern that is often raised about the large Federal government budget deficits of recent years is that the accumulation of trillions of dollars of government debt will impose a crushing financial burden on our children and grandchildren. After all, future generations will be taxed in order to pay off the debts the government is incurring today. Thus, it is claimed, government borrowing amounts to "robbing the future" to pay for government spending that is too high or taxes that are too low in the present.

It may well be true that government debt is a burden on future generations (we examine some of the reasons why in this section). However, the logic underlying this conclusion is more subtle than the simple argument of the previous paragraph. The problem with the simple argument is that it ignores the fact that most government debt is owned by domestic residents. Therefore, although it is true

[11]To understand fully the latter part of this section, you will need to have covered Chapters 5 and 6.

The Political Environment

★★

Logrolling and the Tax Reform Act of 1986

From the economist's perspective there are a number of features that a nation's tax system should have: First, it should provide enough revenue to make excessive borrowing unnecessary. Second, it should be simple enough to be easily understood by taxpayers. Third, it should be fair in that each person should be asked to pay a "fair share" of the revenue raised by the government.* Finally, the tax system should be reasonably efficient; that is, it shouldn't distort incentives so that people behave in ways that are economically counter-productive.

Although these criteria for a good tax system seem straightforward, in practice, they are not systematically applied. Tax codes are typically complex, with many loopholes and special provisions that may be unfair or inefficient. One reason that tax codes may fall short of the ideal is the political practice of *logrolling*. In a system of logrolling a legislator may agree to support a particular tax law under the condition of being allowed to tack on special provisions or favors for his or her own constituents or campaign contributors. The result of logrolling may be a tax code that no one much likes—but that nevertheless musters enough votes to become law.

There have been many attempts to "reform" the U.S. tax code—that is, to try to make it simpler, fairer, and more efficient. These attempts have almost always failed, falling to the intense political pressure to add tax breaks, special provisions, and loopholes in exchange for the support of particular individuals or groups. A notable exception is the Tax Reform Act of 1986, which was passed with broad bipartisan support. This law simplified and (according to many economists) significantly improved the U.S. tax code, while raising about the same amount of revenue as the tax system it replaced. The major provisions of the Tax Reform Act included (1) a reduction in the number of personal income tax brackets from fifteen to two, and a lowering of tax rates; (2) increases in the personal exemption and the standard deduction, which relieved millions of low-income taxpayers from the obligation to pay taxes; (3) elimination of special treatment for capital gains; (4) a reduction in corporate tax rates; and (5) the closing of many loopholes both for individuals and corporations.

Why did the Tax Reform Act of 1986—which Howard E. Shuman, an expert on the Federal budget process, called a "modern political miracle"—succeed where others had failed?† The key insight here is that any individual legislator would always like to add his or her own special provisions to a tax bill; but given a choice between a bill loaded with everyone's special provisions (including the legislator's own) and a "clean" bill with no special provisions, the legislator may prefer the clean bill. The legislator will prefer the clean bill when the costs to the legislator's constituents of everyone else's special provisions outweigh the benefits of special tax breaks that the legislator's constituents get.

This discussion suggests that a tax reform bill can get through Congress *if* (1) it will bring benefits to the economy, *and* (2) the congressional leadership can keep the bill "clean" by forbidding amendments and preventing the logrolling process from getting started. Both of these factors were at work in the case of the Tax Reform Act of 1986: Intellectual leadership was provided by the staff of the Treasury Department, academic economists, and some members of Congress (notably Democrats Bill Bradley and Richard Gephardt and Republicans Jack Kemp and Robert Kasten, Jr.), each of whom made persuasive proposals for a simpler, fairer, and more efficient tax system. And the bill was kept relatively clean through the insistence of President Reagan and several congressional leaders, notably the Senate Finance Committeee Chairman Bob Packwood. Although many experienced observers predicted that the bill would fail, the final version was passed by a vote of 292 to 136 in the House and of 74 to 23 in the Senate.

*For some alternative ways of defining a taxpayer's "fair share," see Richard A. Musgrave and Peggy B. Musgrave, *Public Finance in Theory and Practice,* 4th ed., New York: McGraw-Hill, 1984, pp. 227–228.
†The discussion in this paragraph is based on Howard E. Shuman, *Politics and the Budget: The Struggle Between the President and Congress,* 2d ed., Englewood Cliffs, N.J.: Prentice-Hall, 1988. The quotation is from p. 111.

that future citizens may face heavy taxes to pay the interest and principal of the government debt, future citizens will also be the *recipients* of most of those interest and principal payments. To a substantial degree, we owe the government debt to ourselves. The debt is therefore not a burden in the same sense that it would be if it were owed entirely to outsiders.

Then in what way, if any, is the government debt a burden on the future? There are several possible arguments. First, if tax rates have to be raised substantially in the future to pay off the debt, the resulting distortions could cause the future economy to function less efficiently. These distortions would impose costs on future generations.

Second, most people hold small amounts of government bonds or no government bonds at all (except perhaps indirectly, as through pension funds). In the future people who hold few or no bonds may have to pay more in increased taxes than they receive in interest and principal payments, while people holding large quantities of bonds may receive more in interest and principal than they pay in increased taxes. Since bondholders are richer on average than nonbondholders, this would imply a transfer of resources from the relatively poor to the relatively rich. This transfer of resources could, however, be offset by other government tax and transfer policies.

The third argument that the debt is a burden is probably the most important: Many economists have claimed that government deficits reduce national saving; that is, when the government runs a deficit, the economy accumulates less domestic capital and fewer foreign assets than it would have if the deficit had been lower. If this argument is correct, then deficits will cause our children and grandchildren to have lower standards of living, both because they will inherit a smaller capital stock and because they will have to pay more interest to (or receive less interest from) foreigners than they otherwise would have. This reduction in future standards of living would constitute a true burden of the government debt.

Critical to this argument, however, is the idea that deficits reduce national saving. As we have already seen in several places in this book, the effect of deficits on national saving is a controversial issue. In the rest of this section we build on our earlier analyses to discuss this important question further.

Deficits and National Saving: Ricardian Equivalence Again

In what circumstances will an increased government deficit cause national saving to fall? Virtually all economists agree that an increase in the government deficit caused by a rise in government purchases—say to fight a war—reduces national saving and imposes a real burden on the economy (see Chapter 3). Let us restrict ourselves then to thinking about a deficit caused by a cut in current taxes (the same analysis applies to an increase in current transfers). Imagine that with its current and planned future purchases held constant, the government cuts current taxes by, say, $10 billion. To avoid discussing incentive effects, we assume that the tax cut is a lump-sum tax cut. What effect will this reduction in taxes have on national saving?

To think about this question, recall the definition of national saving from Chapter 2: National saving S equals output Y less consumption C and government purchases G (Eq. 2.7). We write this definition here for easy reference:

$$S = Y - C - G. \qquad (16.5)$$

Under the tax cut scenario we are considering, government purchases G are assumed to be held constant. Therefore, given the level of output Y, Eq. (16.5) tells us that the tax cut will reduce national saving only if it causes consumption C to rise.

The relationships among the government deficit, consumption, and national saving were discussed in Chapter 6, where we introduced the concept of Ricardian equivalence. According to the Ricardian equivalence proposition, government borrowing does *not* affect consumption and thus also does not affect national saving.

In Chapter 6 the explanation of Ricardian equivalence was presented in the context of a two-period model. We considered a government with fixed current and future purchases, denoted G and G^f, and planned current and future lump-sum tax receipts, T and T^f. The government's budget constraint in the two-period model (Eq. 6.6) is

$$G + \frac{G^f}{1 + r} = T + \frac{T^f}{1 + r}. \qquad (16.6)$$

Equation (16.6) says that the present value of the government's tax receipts must equal the present value of its purchases.[12] Thus any reduction in taxes today must be accompanied by increased taxes in the future, in order to leave the present value of taxes unchanged. For example, if current taxes T are cut by \$10 billion, then future taxes T^f must rise by \$10 billion times $(1 + r)$ in order to satisfy the government's budget constraint.

In Chapter 5 we showed that the consumption behavior of a forward-looking consumer who does not face borrowing constraints depends only on the present value of the consumer's lifetime resources. For such a consumer a decline in current taxes without a change in the expected path of government purchases will have no effect on consumption. Consumption is not affected by a current tax cut because the consumer knows that in order for the government budget constraint to be satisfied, future taxes will have to increase in a way that leaves unchanged the present value of taxes. Since the present value of taxes is unchanged by the current tax cut, the consumer is not made richer by the tax cut and so has no reason to change his consumption. This logic leads to the Ricardian equivalence proposition that current deficits will not affect consumption or national saving.

This basic argument for Ricardian equivalence assumes that current deficits will be repaid within the lifetimes of currently living consumers, so that the lower taxes we pay today are offset by the higher taxes we must pay later. But what if some of the debt the government is accumulating will be repaid not by us but by our children or our grandchildren? In an ingenious article Harvard economist Robert Barro[13] has shown that, theoretically, Ricardian equivalence can still work (so that tax cuts have no effect on current consumption) even if it is our descendants rather than ourselves who repay the government's debt.

To understand Barro's argument in its simplest form, imagine an economy in which every generation has the same number of consumers. Assume that the current generation gets a \$10 billion tax cut, which increases the government's current

---

[12]For simplicity, we set transfers equal to zero and assume that the initial government debt is also zero, so that there are no interest payments in the first period. Neither of these assumptions is necessary for our conclusions. We also ignore the possibility that the government can permanently roll over part of its debt; the previous section explained why the ability of the government to roll over its debt is limited.

[13]"Are Government Bonds Net Wealth?" *Journal of Political Economy*, November/December 1974, pp. 1095–1117.

borrowing and thus its debt outstanding by $10 billion. In order for this extra government debt to be repaid, we assume that the next generation's taxes will be raised by $10 billion times $(1 + r)$, where $1 + r$ is the real value of a dollar borrowed today at the time that the next generation is forced to repay the government's debt.

It would appear that after the tax cut the current generation of consumers should increase its consumption, because the present value of lifetime taxes paid by the current generation has been reduced. However, Barro argued that currently living consumers will not increase their consumption in response to a tax cut if they care about the well-being of the next generation. In reality, of course, people do care about the well-being of their children, which is reflected in part by the fact that they give their children economic resources. Some of these resources are transferred while the parent is alive (for example, through gifts or expenditures on the child's health and education), and some are transferred in the form of bequests when the parent dies.

How do these transfers between parents and children affect the impact of a current tax change? A member of the current generation who receives a tax cut might be inclined to increase his own consumption. But, Barro argues, the consumer should realize that for each dollar of tax cut he receives today, his children will have to pay $1 + r$ dollars of extra taxes in the future. Suppose that instead of increasing his own consumption and leaving the burden of the future tax increase to be borne by his children, the currently adult consumer were to keep his consumption unchanged and save his entire tax cut. For concreteness, imagine that he uses his tax cut to buy government bonds; and suppose that he never sells these bonds but instead leaves them to his children.

If everyone in the current generation were to follow this strategy, then the next generation would inherit a total of $10 billion in government bonds. When the time comes for the next generation to pay the extra taxes, the principal and interest on these inherited government bonds will be just enough [$10 billion times $(1 + r)$] to pay the additional taxes—without any need for the future generation to reduce its consumption. What we have shown is that if the current generation uses its entire tax cut to purchase government bonds and bequeath them to their children, then all consumers in both generations can maintain the level of consumption they would have had if the tax cut had never occurred. In this case the tax cut will have had no effect on current consumption or on national saving. Ricardian equivalence still holds, even though today's government borrowing is paid off by the future generation.

But why should the current generation of consumers bequeath *all* of the tax cut to the next generation? Why not consume at least a part of the tax cut? If a member of the current generation increases his consumption at all, he will not be able to leave enough bonds to his child to cover the extra taxes the next generation will face. As a result, the child's consumption will have to fall. But if the member of the current generation had wanted to increase his own consumption at the expense of his child's consumption, he could already have done so, by reducing his spending on his child's health and education or by cutting his planned bequest. That he did not reduce his transfers to his child indicates that he was satisfied with the division of consumption between himself and his children that was planned before the tax cut; there is no reason that the tax cut should cause this original consumption plan to change. The conclusion is that the current generation should indeed save its entire tax cut.

This analysis can be extended to allow for multiple generations and in a number of other ways. These extensions do not change the main point: If consumers are forward looking and do not face binding borrowing constraints, a cut in current taxes does not affect consumption or national saving.

Departures from Ricardian Equivalence

The arguments for Ricardian equivalence are logically sound, and this idea has had a great influence on economists' thinking about deficits. Although twenty years ago it would have been taken for granted that a tax cut would substantially increase consumption, today there is much less agreement about this claim. Empirical work on this question has been frustrating in its inconclusiveness: Although Ricardian equivalence seemed to fail spectacularly in the 1980s in the United States—a period in which high government deficits were accompanied by extremely low rates of national saving—data covering longer periods of time suggest little relation between budget deficits and national saving rates in the United States. In some other countries, such as Canada and Israel, there are episodes in which the Ricardian equivalence proposition seems to have worked quite well.[14]

Our own judgment is that tax cuts that lead to increased government borrowing probably do have some effect on consumption and national saving, although the effect is not necessarily a large one. We base this conclusion both on the experience of the United States during the 1980s and on the fact that there are some theoretical reasons to expect Ricardian equivalence not to hold exactly. The main theoretical arguments against Ricardian equivalence are the possible existence of borrowing constraints, consumers' shortsightedness, the failure of some consumers to leave bequests, and the non-lump-sum nature of most tax changes:

1. *Borrowing constraints.* As we discussed in Chapter 5, if consumers face binding borrowing constraints that prevent them from borrowing in order to increase their consumption, they will increase consumption when taxes are cut. Thus binding borrowing constraints cause the Ricardian equivalence proposition to fail.

2. *Shortsightedness.* If at least some consumers are not forward looking but instead are shortsighted, they may respond to a current tax cut by increasing consumption, even though a forward-looking consumer would not. The effects of shortsightedness on consumers' behavior may be quite similar to the effects of binding borrowing constraints: In both cases we expect consumption to depend more on current income than on the consumer's present value of lifetime resources.

3. *Failure to leave bequests.* If people do not leave bequests, perhaps because they do not care about or think about the long-run economic welfare of their children, then they will increase their consumption if their taxes are cut, and Ricardian equivalence will not hold. A more subtle reason that people may not leave bequests is that they expect their children to be richer than they themselves are and thus not in need of any bequest. If people continue to hold this belief after they receive a tax cut, then they will consume more after the tax cut, and again Ricardian equivalence will fail.

4. *Non-lump-sum taxes.* As a theoretical matter, Ricardian equivalence holds exactly only when tax changes are lump-sum, so that each person's change in taxes is a fixed amount that does not depend on the person's economic decisions, such as

---

[14]For surveys of the evidence, see Robert Barro, "The Ricardian Approach to Budget Deficits," *Journal of Economic Perspectives*, Spring 1989, pp. 37–54; B. Douglas Bernheim, "Ricardian Equivalence: An Evaluation of Theory and Evidence," in Stanley Fischer, ed., *NBER Macroeconomics Annual*, Cambridge, Mass.: M.I.T. Press, 1987.

how much to work or save. As we discussed in Section 16.2, when taxes are not lump-sum, the level and timing of taxes will affect incentives and thus economic behavior. Thus non-lump-sum tax cuts will have real effects on the economy, in contrast to the simple Ricardian view.

We emphasize, though, that with non-lump-sum taxes, the incentive effects of a tax cut on consumption and saving behavior will depend heavily on the tax structure and on which kinds of taxes are cut. For example, a temporary cut in sales taxes would be likely to stimulate consumption, but a tax break for Individual Retirement Accounts (IRAs) might increase saving. Thus we cannot always conclude that just because taxes are not lump-sum, a tax cut will raise consumption. That conclusion has to rest primarily on the other three arguments against Ricardian equivalence that we have given.

16.5 DEFICITS AND INFLATION

In this final section of the chapter we discuss one more concern that has been expressed about government budget deficits: that deficits are inflationary. We show that the principal link between deficits and inflation is that under some circumstances deficits may lead to higher rates of growth in the money supply. High rates of money growth in turn cause inflation.

The Deficit and the Money Supply

Inflation—a rising price level—results when aggregate demand increases more quickly than aggregate supply. In terms of the *AD-AS* framework, suppose, for example, that the long-run aggregate supply curve (which reflects the productive capacity of the economy) is fixed. Then for the price level to be rising, the aggregate demand curve must be rising over time.

Both the classical and Keynesian models of the economy imply that deficits can cause aggregate demand to rise more quickly than aggregate supply, leading to an increase in the price level. In both models a deficit due to increased government purchases reduces desired national saving, shifting the *IS* curve upward and causing aggregate demand to rise. This increase in aggregate demand in turn causes the price level to increase.[15] If we assume (as Keynesians usually do) that Ricardian equivalence does not hold, then a budget deficit resulting from a cut in taxes or increase in transfers also reduces desired national saving, increases aggregate demand, and raises the price level. Thus deficits resulting from expansionary fiscal policies (increased spending or reduced taxes) will be associated with inflation.

However, an increase in government purchases or a cut in taxes causes only a once-and-for-all increase in aggregate demand. Therefore, although we expect expansionary fiscal policies to lead to a one-time increase in the price level (that is, a temporary burst in inflation), we do not expect an increase in government purchases or a cut in taxes to cause a *sustained* increase in inflation. In general, the only factor that can cause aggregate demand to rise on a sustained basis, leading to continuing inflation, is sustained growth in the money supply. Indeed, as we saw in Chapter 4, very high rates of inflation are almost invariably linked to high rates of national money growth. Therefore we ask, "Can government budget deficits lead to ongoing increases in the money supply?"

---

[15]The classical analysis predicts that an increase in government purchases causes aggregate supply to rise as well, but we have assumed that the supply effect is smaller than the demand effect.

A Balanced-Budget Amendment?

Background

The large and rising Federal budget deficits of recent years have convinced many observers that the President and Congress will not willingly make the tough political decisions—the spending cuts and tax increases—needed to reduce the deficit. As a way to force action on the deficit, a number of politicians and others have advocated an amendment to the U.S. Constitution that would require a balanced Federal budget, except perhaps in very unusual circumstances such as when the country is in a state of war. Several such amendments have been proposed in Congress, and state legislatures in more than thirty states have passed resolutions calling for a Constitutional Convention for the purpose of discussing a balanced-budget amendment.

PRO

"The Federal government has run budget deficits every year since 1970, and annual deficits regularly exceed several hundred billion dollars. The Congress and the President have amply demonstrated their inability or unwillingness to balance the Federal budget. The only way that we will be able to achieve a balanced budget is to take the decision away from the Congress and the President by adding a balanced-budget amendment to the Constitution."

CON

"A constitutional amendment requiring a balanced budget would not be enforceable. Politicians can always devise clever schemes to get around a legal requirement to balance the budget. Furthermore, even if it were possible to enforce a balanced budget every year, such a limitation on the Federal budget would be bad fiscal policy."

Analysis

As shown by the debate over Ricardian equivalence, economists do not agree on whether government budget deficits represent a serious threat to the economy. However, even if we accept the premise that large deficits are harmful and should be reduced, there is still the question of whether it is desirable to have a balanced budget *in every year*.

Keynesians generally oppose a balanced-budget amendment on the grounds that requiring the budget to be balanced in every year would undo the beneficial effects of automatic stabilizers, which increase government expenditures and reduce taxes during a recession. Because automatic stabilizers tend to create deficits during recessions, under a balanced-budget amendment either automatic stabilizers would have to be eliminated or other fiscal measures to offset their effects on the budget would have to be introduced. Keynesians also worry that an effective balanced-budget amendment would eliminate any flexibility that the President and Congress have to use fiscal policy actively to fight recessions.

Classical economists also object to a balanced-budget amendment, but on different grounds. Many classicals believe that a balanced-budget amendment would divert attention from a more important issue, which is the share of the economy's total resources used by the government. Because they believe that the true burden of the government on the economy is reflected in the government's total use of resources and not in the deficit itself, these economists would prefer an amendment limiting the government spending–GNP ratio to an amendment calling for a balanced budget.

Classical economists also emphasize that tax rates should be smooth over time in order to minimize distortions in the economy. Under a balanced-budget amendment tax rates would have to rise and fall over time to offset temporary increases and declines in government spending. Year-to-year fluctuations in tax rates would increase the average distortion in the economy.

Finally, many economists of all persuasions doubt whether a balanced-budget amendment would be enforceable in practice, or whether by means of "smoke and mirrors" the Congress and the President might satisfy the letter but not the spirit of the balanced-budget law. An example of an enforcement problem is that the government cannot be required to balance the actual government budget, since tax collections and spending under some programs cannot be perfectly predicted in advance. Thus the government could be required to balance the budget only on an expected or projected basis. If policymakers want to avoid tax increases or cuts in spending while satisfying the requirement of a *projected* balanced budget, they can use very optimistic forecasts about the economy (implying, for example, that tax collections will be high) that will make the projected deficit look smaller than it might reasonably be expected to be.

Evidence

There are few cases of national governments enforcing a continuously balanced government budget, and so we have little information about the effects in practice of this fiscal strategy. We do not really know how much more volatile the economy might be if automatic stabilizers were eliminated, for example.

There is evidence available on the enforcement issue, though: Experience at both the Federal and state levels suggests that it would be quite difficult to enforce a balanced-budget amendment. At the Federal level, the 1985 Balanced Budget and Emergency Deficit Control Act (the Gramm-Rudman-Hollings bill) set legal limits on the Federal budget deficit, beginning with a limit of $172 billion in fiscal year 1986 (October 1, 1985–September 30, 1986) and ending with a requirement of budget balance in fiscal year 1991. As you can see in

Source: *Economic Report of the President,* February 1991, Table B-76; *The Economic and Budget Outlook, Fiscal Years 1992–96,* Congressional Budget Office, January 1991, summary Table, 1, 1991–1996.

the accompanying figure, the actual deficit exceeded the Gramm-Rudman-Hollings targets by a substantial amount in every fiscal year except for 1987, when it exceeded the target by only about $5 billion. In 1987, only two years after setting initial deficit targets, Congress increased the deficit targets for fiscal years 1988–1992. Nevertheless, the deficit exceeded (or was projected to exceed) even the increased target levels, with the 1990 deficit overshooting the revised target by more than $100 billion. In 1990 Congress passed the Omnibus Budget Reconciliation Act, which called for nearly $500 billion in deficit-reducing measures over the period 1991–1995. Even so, as the figure shows, projected Federal deficits for that period remain large. The experience at the Federal level gives little rea-

son to be confident that legislated limits on deficits can be enforced.

Many individual states have constitutional restrictions requiring balanced budgets, but nevertheless, a number of these states have run large deficits. For example, when Michigan rewrote its state constitution in 1963, it included a requirement that the state budget be balanced. However, between 1975 and 1982 Michigan ran budget deficits that increased its debt by $850 million.* Again, this experience is not encouraging for advocates of a balanced-budget amendment.

---

*See Daniel B. Suits and Ronald C. Fisher, "A Balanced Budget Constitutional Amendment: Economic Complexities and Uncertainties," *National Tax Journal,* December 1985, pp. 467–477.

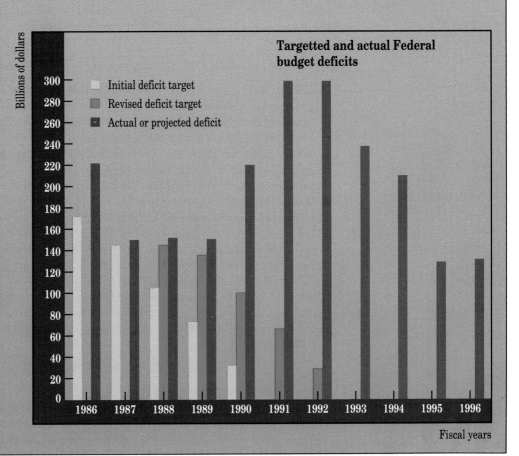

Targetted and actual Federal budget deficits

The answer is that there can indeed be a link between deficits and money growth. The link arises because printing money is a means of financing government spending that can be used when the government cannot (or does not want to) finance all of its spending by taxes or borrowing from the public. In the extreme case, imagine a government that wants to spend $10 billion (say, on submarines) but has no ability to tax or borrow from the public. One option this government has is to print $10 billion worth of currency and then use this currency to pay for the submarines. The revenue that a government raises by printing money is called **seignorage.** Any government with the authority to issue money can use seignorage; governments that do not have the authority to issue money, such as state governments in the United States, cannot use seignorage.

In practice, governments that want to finance their deficits through seignorage do not simply print new currency but use a slightly more indirect procedure. In the first step of this procedure, the Treasury authorizes government borrowing equal to the amount of the budget deficit, and a corresponding quantity of new government bonds are printed and sold. Thus the condition that the deficit equals the change in the outstanding government debt (Eq. 16.3) continues to hold. However, not all of these new government bonds are sold to the public. Instead, the Treasury asks (or requires) the central bank to purchase some of the new bonds. The central bank pays for its purchases of new bonds by issuing new currency. The purchase of bonds by the central bank increases the monetary base by the amount of the purchase, just as the monetary base increases when the central bank purchases government bonds on the open market. Equation (16.7) makes more precise the relationship between the size of the deficit and the increase in the monetary base:

$$\text{deficit} = \Delta B = \Delta B^p + \Delta B^{cb} = \Delta B^p + \Delta BASE. \tag{16.7}$$

Equation (16.7) says that the government budget deficit equals the total increase in government debt outstanding (ΔB), which can be broken down into additional government debt held by the public (ΔB^p) and the central bank (ΔB^{cb}). The increase in government debt held by the central bank in turn equals the increase in the monetary base ($\Delta BASE$). The increase in the monetary base equals the amount of seignorage collected by the government.

So far we have seen how the use of seignorage by the government to finance its deficit causes the monetary base to rise by the amount of seignorage collected. The final link between the deficit and the money supply arises because of the relationship between the money supply and the monetary base (see Chapter 15). In general, the increase in the money supply M equals the money multiplier times the increase in the monetary base (Eq. 15.8). In an all-currency economy the money supply and the monetary base are the same thing and the money multiplier equals 1. Since nothing important in this discussion depends on the value of the money multiplier, for simplicity we focus on the all-currency economy, in which the change in the money supply equals the change in the monetary base. With this assumption Eq. (16.7) implies

$$\text{deficit} = \Delta B = \Delta B^p + \Delta B^{cb} = \Delta B^p + \Delta M, \tag{16.8}$$

where we have set $\Delta BASE$ equal to ΔM.

Why would governments choose to use seignorage to finance their deficits, knowing that continued money creation will ultimately lead to higher inflation? Under normal conditions developed countries rarely rely very much on seignorage.

For example, in recent years the monetary base in the United States has typically increased about $10 billion per year, which is much less than 10% of the deficit and less than 1% of total government expenditures. Rather, a heavy reliance on seignorage usually occurs in war-torn or developing countries, in which military or social conditions dictate levels of government spending well above what the country can raise in taxes or borrow from the public.

Real Seignorage Collection and Inflation

The amount of real revenue that the government collects from seignorage is closely related to the rate of inflation in the economy. To examine the link between seignorage collection and inflation, we consider an all-currency economy in which real output and the real interest rate are fixed and there are constant rates of money growth and inflation. In such an economy the real quantity of money demanded is constant,[16] and hence, in equilibrium, the real money supply must also be constant. Because the real money supply M/P is unchanging over time, the growth rate of the nominal money supply $\Delta M/M$ must equal the growth rate of the price level, which is the rate of inflation π:

$$\pi = \frac{\Delta M}{M}.$$ (16.9)

Equation (16.9) captures the idea that there is a close link between an economy's rate of inflation and its rate of money growth.

How much seignorage is the government collecting in this economy? The *nominal* value of seignorage in any period is the increase in the amount of money in circulation ΔM. Multiplying both sides of Eq. (16.9) by M gives an equation for the nominal value of seignorage:

$$\Delta M = \pi M$$ (16.10)

Real seignorage revenue, denoted R, is the real value of the newly created money, which equals nominal seignorage revenue ΔM divided by the price level P. Dividing both sides of Eq. (16.10) by the price level P gives us

$$R = \frac{\Delta M}{P} = \pi \frac{M}{P}.$$ (16.11)

Equation (16.11) says that the government's real seignorage revenue R equals the inflation rate π times the real money supply M/P.

Equation (16.11) illustrates why economists sometimes call seignorage the **inflation tax.** In general, for any type of tax, tax revenue equals the tax rate multiplied by the tax base (whatever is being taxed). In the case of the inflation tax the tax base is the real money supply and the tax rate is the rate of inflation. Multiplying the tax base (the real money supply) by the tax rate (the rate of inflation) gives the total inflation tax revenue.

How does the government collect the inflation tax and who pays this tax? The government collects the inflation tax by printing money (or by having the central bank issue new money) and using the newly created money to purchase goods and services. The inflation tax is paid by any member of the public who holds money,

---

[16]Real money demand depends on real output and the nominal interest rate (we assume that the interest rate paid on money is fixed). Output is constant, and because the real interest rate and the inflation rate are constant, the nominal interest rate is also constant. Thus the real quantity of money demanded is constant.

674

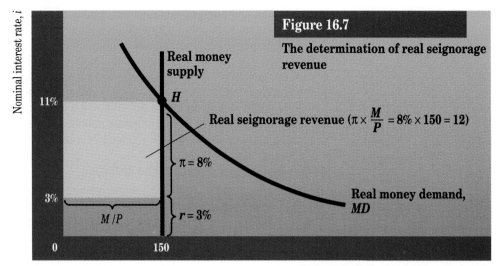

(a)

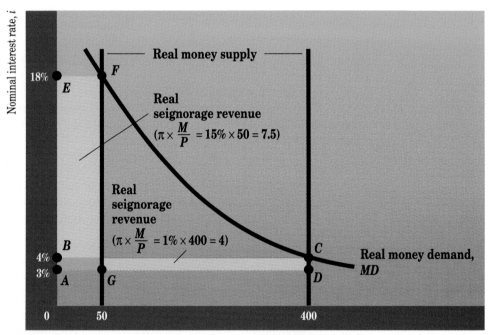

(b)

(a) The downward-sloping curve *MD* is the money demand function for a given level of real income. The real interest rate is assumed to be 3%. When the rate of inflation is 8%, the nominal interest rate is 11%; and the real quantity of money held by the public is $150 billion (point *H*). Real seignorage revenue collected by the government, represented by the area of the shaded rectangle, equals the rate of inflation (8%) times the real money stock ($150 billion), or $12 billion.

(b) The money demand function *MD* is the same as in part (a), and the real interest rate remains at 3%. When the rate of inflation is 1%, the nominal interest rate is 4%; and the real quantity of money held by the public is $400 billion. In this case real seignorage revenue equals the area of the rectangle *ABCD*, or $4 billion. When the rate of inflation is 15%, the nominal interest rate is 18%; and the real money stock held by the public is $50 billion. Real seignorage revenue in this case equals the area of the rectangle *AEFG*, or $7.5 billion.

because inflation erodes the purchasing power of money. For example, when the inflation rate is 10% per year, a person who holds currency for a year suffers a 10% loss in the purchasing power of his money and thus effectively pays a 10% tax on his real money holdings.

Suppose that a government finds that the seignorage it is collecting is not sufficient to pay for its spending, and so it begins increasing the money supply at a faster rate. Will this increase in the rate of money growth cause the real seignorage collected by the government to rise? Somewhat surprisingly, it may not: As Eq. (16.11) shows, the real seignorage collected by the government is the product of two terms, the rate of inflation (the tax rate) and the real money supply (the tax base). By raising the rate of money growth, the government can increase the rate of inflation. However, given the real interest rate, a higher rate of inflation will raise the nominal interest rate, which causes people to reduce the real quantity of money that they hold. Thus whether real seignorage revenue increases when the rate of money growth increases depends on whether the rise in inflation π outweighs the decline in real money holdings M/P.

This point is illustrated by Fig. 16.7, which shows the determination of real seignorage revenue under the assumption that the real interest rate is constant at 3%. In both parts of the figure the real quantity of money is measured along the horizontal axis, and the nominal interest rate is measured along the vertical axis. The downward-sloping curve in either part shows the real demand for money; the real money demand curve MD slopes downward, because an increase in the nominal interest rate reduces the real quantity of money demanded.

In Fig. 16.7(a) we assume that the actual and expected rate of inflation is 8%, so that (given a real interest of 3%) the nominal interest rate is 11%. When the nominal interest rate is 11%, the real quantity of money that people are willing to hold equals $150 billion (point H in Fig. 16.7a). In this case, using Eq. (16.11), we find that the real value of seignorage revenue is (8%) ($150 billion), or $12 billion. Real seignorage revenue is represented graphically by the area of the shaded rectangle in Fig. 16.7(a): The height of this rectangle equals the inflation rate (8%) and the width of the rectangle equals the real quantity of money held by the public ($150 billion).

Figure 16.7(b) shows the real amount of seignorage revenue at two different rates of inflation. The real interest rate (3%) and the money demand curve in Fig. 16.7(b) are identical to those in Fig. 16.7(a). When the rate of inflation is 1% per year, the nominal interest rate is 4%, and the real quantity of money that the public holds is $400 billion. Real seignorage revenue is (1%) ($400 billion) = $4 billion, which is the area of rectangle $ABCD$. Alternatively, when the rate of inflation is 15% per year, the nominal interest rate is 18%, and the real value of the public's money holdings is $50 billion. Real seignorage revenue in this case is $7.5 billion, which is the area of rectangle $AEFG$.

Comparing Fig. 16.7(a) and Fig. 16.7(b), we see that real seignorage revenue is higher when inflation is 8% per year than when inflation is either 1% per year or 15% per year. Figure 16.8 depicts the relation between the rate of inflation and seignorage revenue. At very low rates of inflation an increase in the rate of inflation increases real seignorage revenue. However, at very high rates of inflation an increase in the rate of inflation reduces real seignorage revenue. In Fig. 16.8 the maximum possible real seignorage revenue is $12 billion, which is achieved at an intermediate level of inflation of 8% per year.

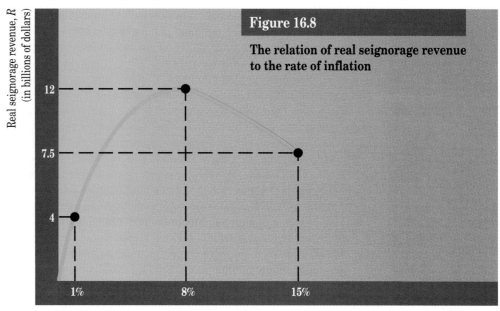

Figure 16.8

The relation of real seignorage revenue to the rate of inflation

Continuing the example of Fig. 16.7, this figure shows the relation of real seignorage revenue R, measured on the vertical axis, to the rate of inflation π, measured on the horizontal axis. From Fig. 16.7(a), when inflation is 8% per year, real seignorage revenue is $12 billion. From Fig. 16.7(b), real seignorage equals $4 billion when inflation is 1% and $7.5 billion when inflation is 15%. At low rates of inflation, an increase in inflation increases seignorage revenue. At high rates of inflation, increased inflation can cause seignorage revenue to fall.

In this example the maximum amount of seignorage revenue the government can obtain is $12 billion, which occurs when the inflation rate is 8%.

The possibility that real seignorage may fall when the inflation rate rises is related to the idea of the Laffer curve (Box 10.1, p. 377). An increase in the inflation rate raises the tax rate on real money holdings but causes the tax base (the real quantity of money held by the public) to shrink. Conceivably, as in the Laffer curve story, a higher tax rate can lead to less total revenue being collected.

What happens if the government tries to raise more seignorage revenue than the maximum possible amount? If the government attempts to increase its real revenue by printing money at an even faster rate, inflation will rise but the real value of the government's seignorage will fall as real money balances fall. If the government continues to increase the rate of money creation, the economy will experience a high rate of inflation or even hyperinflation. The inflation will continue until the government reduces the rate of money creation either by balancing its budget or by finding some means other than money creation to finance its spending.

Seignorage and the Budget Deficit in the German Hyperinflation of 1922–1923

Although there are dozens of recorded examples of hyperinflations, the hyperinflation that has been most carefully studied by economists and historians is the German hyperinflation of 1922–1923. This hyperinflation was quite dramatic: Between August 1922 and November 1923 the German price level rose by a factor of over 10 billion, while the money supply rose by a factor of over 7 billion. To appreciate the magnitude of this inflation, consider that all German mortgages together were valued at 40 billion marks in 1913, or what was about one sixth of total German wealth. By 1923 the value of 40 billion marks had fallen to less than one American cent.[17]

These huge increases in the money supply and the price level were the direct result of the German government's attempts to finance large deficits through the collection of seignorage. The German government budget deficit worsened dramatically in the aftermath of World War I both because of a reduced tax base and because of the high outlays required to make interest and reparations payments and to rebuild the war-torn country. In 1920 taxes covered only one third of German government outlays, and in the period April–October 1923 taxes covered only one eighth of outlays.[18] With a large amount of government debt already outstanding and the public unwilling to lend much more to the government, the German government resorted to money creation to finance a large part of its total deficit.

When a country embarks on a path of printing money to cover deficits, two forces threaten to drive the process out of control. First, when inflation becomes very high, the real value of tax revenues (other than revenues from the inflation tax) declines because of delays in collecting taxes. For example, consider a firm that pays sales taxes every month. If it waits until the middle of August to pay the tax on July sales, the real value of the tax on July sales will have fallen significantly because of the inflation during the intervening days. In general, during a hyperinflation taxpayers with fixed nominal tax obligations have an incentive to delay payment as long as possible, in order to pay their taxes with money that has less and less real value. The fall in the real value of government tax collections caused by hyperinflation may lead the government to try to collect more seignorage by creating money even more rapidly.

The second force leading to a higher rate of money creation is the decline in real money holdings that results from the public's response to higher inflation. As real money holdings fall, the government must create even more inflation to collect the same level of real seignorage revenue (see Eq. 16.12). This higher inflation leads to higher nominal interest rates and further declines in the public's real money holdings, in what may become a vicious circle of rising inflation and falling real money demand.

---

[17]Frank D. Graham, *Exchange, Prices, and Production in Hyperinflation: Germany, 1920–1923*, Princeton, N.J.: Princeton University Press, 1930, p. 241.

[18]See Rudiger Dornbusch and Stanley Fischer, "Stopping Hyperinflations Past and Present," *Weltwirtschaftliches Archiv*, January 1986, pp. 1–47.

We showed in Fig. 16.8 that there is a maximum amount of real seignorage revenue that can be collected by money creation. Did the German government obtain the maximum amount of real seignorage revenue? In a classic study of the German hyperinflation, Philip Cagan[19] of Columbia University calculated that in the German case the constant rate of inflation that would have maximized real seignorage revenue was 20% *per month*. The average rate of inflation during the German hyperinflation was 322% *per month*, far beyond the seignorage-maximizing rate. From this calculation it appears that the German government lost control of the situation and allowed inflation to rise well above the level that would have maximized its real seignorage.

Late in 1923 a new government took over in Germany and was given extraordinary powers to end the crisis. With help from the United States and other nations, who reduced reparation demands and provided loans, the German government brought down the budget deficit and put a stop to money creation. The hyperinflation ended almost immediately.

16.6 CHAPTER SUMMARY

1. Government outlays are made up of government purchases of goods and services, transfers, and net interest. To pay for its outlays, the government collects revenue from four major types of taxes: personal taxes, contributions for social insurance, indirect business taxes, and corporate taxes.

2. The government budget deficit equals government outlays minus tax revenues and tells us how much the government must borrow during the year. The primary government budget deficit is the government's deficit when net interest payments are excluded from government outlays. The primary deficit tells us by how much the cost of current programs (as measured by current government purchases and transfers) exceeds tax revenues during the year.

3. Fiscal policy affects the economy in three main ways: by affecting aggregate demand, by affecting government capital formation, and by affecting incentives.

4. Increases or decreases in government purchases affect aggregate demand by changing desired national saving and shifting the *IS* curve. If Ricardian equivalence does not hold, as Keynesians usually argue, then changes in taxes also affect desired national saving, the *IS* curve, and aggregate demand. Automatic stabilizers are provisions in the government's budget that allow government spending to rise or taxes to fall automatically in a recession, which helps cushion the fall in aggregate demand during a recession. The full-employment deficit is what the deficit would be, given current government-spending programs and taxes, if the economy were at full employment. Because of automatic stabilizers that increase spending and reduce taxes in recessions, the actual deficit rises above the full-employment deficit in recessions.

5. Government capital formation contributes to the productive capacity of the economy. Government capital formation includes both investment in physical capital (roads, schools) and investment in human capital (education, child nutrition).

6. Taxes generally affect economic incentives for various activities and thus distort the pattern of economic behavior relative to what it would have been in the absence of taxes. The average cost of distortions can be minimized by smoothing tax rates over time.

7. The national debt equals the value of government bonds outstanding. The behavior of the debt-GNP ratio over time depends on the ratio of the primary deficit to outstanding government debt and on whether the interest rate is greater or less than the growth rate of GNP.

8. The ability of the government to roll over its debt forever is limited. If the real interest rate exceeds the growth rate of real GNP, any borrowing the government does will eventually have to be offset by running a primary budget surplus.

9. Deficits are a burden on future generations if they cause national saving to fall, because lower national saving leads the country to have less capital and fewer foreign assets than it would have had otherwise.

10. The Ricardian equivalence proposition states that a deficit caused by a tax cut will not reduce national saving. This proposition still holds if the government debt is not repaid by the current generation, provided that the current generation cares about the well-being of its descendants. However, Ricardian equivalence does not hold if there are binding borrowing constraints, if people are short-sighted, if people fail to leave bequests, or if taxes are not lump-sum.

11. Deficits are linked to inflation when a government finances its deficits by printing money. The amount of revenue that the government raises by printing money is called seignorage.

12. The real value of seignorage equals the inflation rate times the real money supply. Increasing the inflation rate does not always increase the government's real seignorage because higher inflation causes the public to hold a smaller real quantity of money. Attempts to push the collection of seignorage above its maximum can lead to hyperinflation.

Key Terms

automatic stabilizers, p. 651	government capital, p. 653	rolling over the debt, p. 660
debt-GNP ratio, p. 658	government debt, p. 658	seignorage, p. 672
distortions, p. 654	inflation tax, p. 673	tax rate smoothing,
full-employment deficit, p. 653	primary government budget deficit, p. 648	p. 656

Key Equations

$$\Delta B = \text{nominal deficit} \qquad (16.3)$$

The change in the nominal value of the government debt equals the nominal government deficit.

growth rate of debt-GNP ratio

$$= \frac{\text{primary deficit}}{B} + r - \text{growth rate of real GNP}$$

$$(16.4a)$$

The growth rate of the ratio of government debt outstanding to GNP depends on the ratio of the primary deficit to outstanding government debt B, and on the difference between the real interest rate r and the growth rate of real GNP. An equivalent formula, Eq. (16.4b), replaces the last two terms on the right side of Eq. (16.4a) with the difference between the nominal interest rate and the growth rate of nominal GNP.

$$\text{deficit} = \Delta B = \Delta B^p + \Delta B^{cb} = \Delta B^p + \Delta M \quad (16.8)$$

The deficit equals the increase in the stock of government debt outstanding B, which in turn equals the sum of additional holdings of government debt by the public (B^p) and by the central bank (B^{cb}). The increase in debt held by the central bank equals the increase in the monetary base, which in an all-currency economy equals the increase in the money supply M.

$$R = \frac{\Delta M}{P} = \pi \frac{M}{P} \qquad (16.11)$$

Real seignorage revenue R equals the increase in the money supply M divided by the price level P. This ratio in turn equals the inflation rate (the tax rate on money) multiplied by the real money supply (the tax base).

Review Questions

1. What are the major components of government outlays? What are the major sources of government revenues? How does the Federal government differ from state and local governments in the composition of its outlays and revenues?

2. Explain the difference between the overall government budget deficit and the primary deficit. Why do we need two deficit concepts?

3. How is government debt related to the government deficit? What factors contribute to a high growth rate of the debt-GNP ratio?

4. What are the three main ways that fiscal policy affects the macroeconomy? Explain briefly how each channel of policy works.

5. Define *distortion*. How does fiscal policy cause distortions in the economy? How can fiscal policy be conducted to minimize these distortions?

6. Can the government roll over its debt forever? Why or why not? How is the government's ability to roll over debt affected by the real interest rate and the growth rate of the economy?

7. In what ways is the government debt a potential burden on future generations? What is the relationship between the Ricardian equivalence proposition and the issue of whether the government debt is a burden?

8. What is the *inflation tax* (also called *seignorage*)? How does the government collect it, and who pays it? Can the government always increase its real revenues from the inflation tax by increasing money growth and inflation?

Numerical Problems

1. You are given the following budget data from a country with both a central government and provincial governments:

central purchases of goods and services = 200
provincial purchases of goods and services = 150
central transfer payments = 100
provincial transfer payments = 50
grants in aid (central to provincial) = 100
central tax receipts = 450
provincial tax receipts = 100
interest received from private sector by central government = 10
interest received from private sector by provincial governments = 10
total central government debt = 1000
total provincial government debt = 0
central government debt held by provincial governments = 200
nominal interest rate = 10%.

Calculate the overall and primary deficits for the central government, the provincial governments, and the combined government.

2. Congress votes a special one-time $1 billion transfer to bail out the buggy whip industry. There is no change in tax collections and no change is planned for at least several years. By how much will this action increase the overall budget deficit and the primary deficit in the year that the transfer is made? In the next year? In the year after that? Assume that the nominal interest rate is constant at 10%.

3. Because of automatic stabilizers, various components of the government's budget depend on the level of output Y. Suppose that for a certain economy,

$$\text{tax revenues} = 1000 + 0.1Y,$$
$$\text{transfers} = 800 - 0.05Y,$$
$$\text{government purchases} = 1800$$
$$\text{interest payments} = 100.$$

Full-employment output is defined to be 10,000. Find the actual budget deficit and the full-employment budget deficit under the following conditions.
   a. Y equals 12,000.
   b. Y equals 10,000.
   c. Y equals 8000.

4. Suppose that all workers place a value on their leisure of 90 goods per day. The production function relating output per day Y to the number of people working per day N is

$$Y = 250N - 0.5N^2.$$

Corresponding to this production function, the marginal product of labor is

$$MPN = 250 - N.$$

   a. Assume that there are no taxes. What are the equilibrium values of the real wage, N, and Y? (*Hint:* In equilibrium the real wage will equal both the marginal product of labor and the value of a day's leisure to workers.)
   b. A 25% tax is levied on wages. What are the equilibrium values of the real wage, N, and Y? In terms of lost output, what is the cost of the distortion introduced by this tax?
   c. Suppose that the tax on wages rises to 50%. What are the equilibrium values of the real wage, N, and Y? In terms of lost output, what is the cost of the distortion introduced by this higher tax rate? Compare the distortion caused by a 50% tax rate with the distortion caused by a 25% tax rate. Is the distortion caused by a 50% tax rate twice as big, more than twice as big, or less than twice as big as the distortion caused by a 25% tax rate?

5. Find the largest nominal primary deficit that the government can run without raising the debt-to-GNP ratio, under the following assumptions:
   a. Nominal GNP growth is 10%, the nominal interest rate is 12%, and outstanding nominal debt is 1000.
   b. Nominal interest payments are 800, outstanding nominal debt is 10,000, inflation is 6%, and the economy has zero real growth.

6. Real money demand in an economy is given by

$$L = 0.2Y - 500i,$$

where Y is real income and i is the nominal interest rate. In equilibrium real money demand L equals real money supply M/P. Suppose that Y equals 1000 and the real interest rate is 0.04.
   a. Draw a graph with real seignorage revenue on the vertical axis and inflation on the horizontal axis. Show the values of seignorage for inflation equal to 0, 0.02, 0.04, 0.06, . . . , 0.30.
   b. At what rate of inflation is seignorage maximized?
   c. What is the maximum amount of seignorage revenue?
   d. Repeat parts a–c for the case in which Y equals 1000 and the real interest rate is 0.08.

7. Consider an economy in which the money supply consists of both currency and deposits. The growth rate of the monetary base, the growth rate of the money supply, inflation, and expected inflation are all constant at 10% per year. Output and the real interest rate are constant. Monetary data for this economy as of January 1, 1991, are as follows:

$$
\begin{aligned}
\text{currency in circulation} &= \$200 \\
\text{bank reserves} &= \$50 \\
\text{monetary base} &= \$250 \\
\text{deposits} &= \$600 \\
\text{money supply} &= \$800.
\end{aligned}
$$

    a. What is the nominal value of seignorage over the year? (*Hint:* How much monetary base is created during the year?)

    b. Suppose that deposits and bank reserves do not pay interest, and that banks lend out any deposits not held as reserves at the market rate of interest. Who pays the inflation tax (measured in nominal terms), and how much do they pay? (*Hint:* The inflation tax paid by banks in this example is negative.)

    c. Suppose that deposits pay a market rate of interest. Who pays the inflation tax, and how much do they pay?

Analytical Problems

1. Why do you think that some state and local spending is paid for by grants in aid from the Federal government, instead of having every state and locality pay for its spending by levying taxes on its own citizens? What are the advantages and disadvantages of a system of grants in aid?

2. Using the *Economic Report of the President*, compare the Federal government's budget in 1979, 1986, and 1991. Express the major components of Federal spending and receipts in each year as fractions of GNP. Have increased deficits since 1979 been the result more of increased spending or reductions in revenues?

3. Transfer programs as well as taxes affect incentives. Consider a program designed to help the poor that promises each aid recipient a minimum income of $10,000. That is, if the recipient earns less than $10,000, the program supplements his income by enough to bring him up to $10,000.

Explain why this program would have bad incentive effects for low-wage recipients. (*Hint:* Show that this program is equivalent to giving the recipient $10,000, then taxing his labor income at a very high marginal rate.) How might one design a transfer program with better incentive effects? Would this alternative program have any disadvantages?

4. The following conversation between the President and the Secretary of the Treasury of a faraway land was overheard:

President: I'm tired of all this talk about large deficits. They're not a problem, because we can always borrow more to cover the interest and principal on the government debt.

Treasury Secretary: You would be correct, sir, if the real interest rate were less than the growth rate of the economy. But you know the figures: Real GNP is growing at 3% a year, we are paying a 4% nominal interest rate on bonds, and the inflation rate is zero.

President: I've got it! Let's levy a 50% tax on interest income from government bonds. Then for every $100 of bonds, we will pay $4 of interest, but then we can collect $2 in taxes. We will really only be paying a 2% interest rate. Then the real interest rate will be less than the growth rate and we can roll over the government debt forever.

Treasury Secretary: It sounds too good to be true.

Comment on the President's proposal.

5. Show that if the primary deficit is zero, then the *real* stock of outstanding government debt grows at a rate equal to the real interest rate.

APPENDIX
16.A   THE PATH OF THE DEBT-GNP RATIO

This appendix derives Eqs. (16.4a) and (16.4b), which show how the debt-GNP ratio evolves over time.

Let Q be the ratio of government debt to GNP. Then by definition,

$$Q = \frac{B}{PY}, \tag{16.A.1}$$

where B is the nominal value of government bonds outstanding (the government debt), P is the price level, and Y is real GNP (so that PY is nominal GNP). A useful rule is that the percentage change in any ratio equals the percentage change in the numerator minus the percentage change in the denominator (see Appendix A, Section A.7). Applying this rule to Eq. (16.A.1) gives us

$$\frac{\Delta Q}{Q} = \frac{\Delta B}{B} - \frac{\Delta(PY)}{PY}. \tag{16.A.2}$$

The increase in the nominal value of government bonds ΔB equals the nominal value of the government budget deficit, which in turn equals the nominal value of the primary deficit plus interest payments on the government debt. Thus we have

$$\Delta B = PD^P + iB, \tag{16.A.3}$$

where D^P is the real value of the primary deficit, PD^P is the nominal value of the primary deficit, i is the nominal interest rate, and iB is the nominal value of interest payments on the government debt. Using Eq. (16.A.3) to substitute for ΔB on the right side of Eq. (16.A.2), we obtain

$$\frac{\Delta Q}{Q} = \frac{PD^P}{B} + i - \frac{\Delta(PY)}{PY}. \tag{16.A.4}$$

Observe that PD^P/B is the ratio of the primary deficit to government debt, so that Eq. (16.A.4) is equivalent to Eq. (16.4b) in the text.

The percentage growth rate of nominal GNP, PY, is

$$\frac{\Delta(PY)}{PY} = \frac{\Delta P}{P} + \frac{\Delta Y}{Y}. \tag{16.A.5}$$

Equation (16.A.5) uses the rule that the percentage growth rate of the product of any two variables is the sum of the percentage growth rates of each of the two variables (Appendix A, Section A.7). Substituting Eq. (16.A.5) into Eq. (16.A.4), and recalling that $\Delta P/P$ is the rate of inflation π, we have

$$\frac{\Delta Q}{Q} = \frac{PD^P}{B} + i - \pi - \frac{\Delta Y}{Y}. \tag{16.A.6}$$

The real interest rate r equals the nominal interest rate i minus the rate of inflation π. (Here we use r to stand for the actual rather than the expected real interest rate.) Substituting r for $i - \pi$ on the right side of Eq. (16.A.6) gives Eq. (16.4a) in the text.

17
Financial Markets and the Macroeconomy

The financial sector is perhaps the most intensely watched part of the private economy. Stock market indexes are routinely reported on the evening news, along with other financial indicators such as foreign exchange rates and the prime lending rate; sharp movements in these indicators make headlines. One reason for this close attention is that most families own some financial assets, either directly or indirectly (as through a company pension plan), and therefore have a "rooting interest" in the financial news. Others follow the financial markets for clues about what is likely to happen in the economy in general. In this latter category are the policymakers, particularly the Federal Reserve, which monitors the major financial markets nearly continuously. No major macroeconomic policy change is ever made without a discussion of "how the markets will react"; no policymaker wants to be responsible for a sharp decline in stock or bond prices.

Financial market variables have played a role in nearly all of the macroeconomic analyses of this book. For example, we have frequently discussed the determination of real and nominal interest rates and of other asset prices, such as the exchange rate. To keep things as simple as possible, however, we have generally ignored the details of financial markets and institutions in our analysis. In this chapter we look a bit more closely at those details.

We begin with a brief overview of the functions and structure of the financial sector. Some of the questions we try to answer are, "What role do financial markets play in the economy?" "How are financial markets organized?" and "Who are the participants in financial markets?"

One of the main functions of the financial system is to gather and evaluate information about potential capital investments. By providing information about potential investments, the financial system helps to ensure that savings will flow into the most productive uses. In the second part of the chapter we examine the information-gathering role of the financial system and discuss how information flows are linked to the levels of borrowing and investment in the economy. A benefit of this analysis is that it will help us understand why financial conditions, such as the health of the banking sector, matter to macroeconomic performance.

In recent years events such as the stock market crash of 1987 and the savings and loan crisis, as well as concerns about the condition of a number of other financial sectors, have made financial stability a major issue for economic policymakers.

Focusing on the banking sector and the stock market, in the last part of the chapter we discuss the causes and consequences of financial instability, some traditional solutions for this problem, and some policy alternatives for the future.

17.1 THE FINANCIAL SYSTEM: AN OVERVIEW

The world's financial system is becoming progressively more complex and sophisticated. Improved communications have allowed financial markets to link up around the globe, and computer technologies have greatly speeded transactions and made intricate new trading strategies possible. A variety of new financial instruments have become available. Despite these obvious changes, however, the basic functions and institutions of the financial markets are not really so very different from what existed fifty years ago. In this section we give a brief overview of those functions and institutions.

Functions of the Financial System

Broadly, the financial system has four principal economic functions:

1. *Consumption smoothing.* People don't necessarily want to consume precisely what they earn in each period. Instead, people usually prefer a time path of consumption that is more stable than the time path of their income. For example, although most people experience a sharp drop in income at retirement, they generally want to consume at similar rates before and after they retire. In order to consume at a relatively constant rate over their lifetimes, people must be able to save at times when their income is relatively high and borrow or draw down accumulated assets when their income is relatively low. Saving and dissaving in order to stabilize consumption over time is called consumption smoothing (see Chapter 5). Financial markets help make consumption smoothing possible by providing assets that savers can hold and by providing borrowing opportunities for those who want to consume more than their income.

2. *The allocation of savings to uses with the highest value.* The principal use of a nation's savings is to finance physical investment.[1] In the economic models presented in this book we have used the simplifying assumption that there is only one type of capital, K, that can be created. But in reality, of course, there are literally millions of ways in which current resources could be used to create capital. A shopping center in Norman, Oklahoma, a 300-passenger commercial airliner, a pizza oven, and an experimental supercomputer are very different from each other, but they are all forms of physical capital and all represent alternative ways in which a society's savings could be invested.

It is critical to the long-run health of the economy that the available pool of savings be put to the most productive uses. In a capitalist economy financial market investors and analysts compete to direct their own or their customers' savings toward the most promising investments. To find the investments with the highest return, participants in financial markets gather and evaluate massive amounts of information about new businesses, new technologies, and new markets. Thus the financial system is a central part of the mechanism by which society determines which investments will be undertaken and which will not.

---

[1]The other use of national saving is to acquire net foreign assets (see Eq. 2.9).

3. *Risk sharing.* People don't like bearing large amounts of risk. For example, except for compulsive gamblers, very few people of ordinary means would be willing to risk $10,000 "double or nothing" on a coin flip. Similarly, most homeowners are willing to pay an insurance premium so as not to have to bear the risk that a fire or hurricane will deal them a large loss.

Like insurance, financial markets can help individuals reduce the risks that they face—in particular, the risk of financial loss. One way in which financial markets reduce risk is by permitting diversification. **Diversification** is the practice of dividing one's financial wealth among a wide variety of different financial assets, each of which has its own set of risks that are related to the risks of other assets in varying degrees. The advantage of holding a diversified portfolio is that although some individual financial investments will turn out well and some poorly, it is likely that the good luck experienced by some investments will to some extent offset the back luck experienced by other investments. As a result, the overall portfolio may not be very risky at all, even though the individual investments in the portfolio are quite risky.[2]

A second way in which financial markets help in managing risk is by allowing people who strongly dislike risk to transfer risk to people who are less averse to risk. Financial investors who want to reduce their risk are called **hedgers.** Financial investors who are willing to bear more risk, usually in exchange for a higher expected return, are called **speculators.**

An example of a financial market that permits the transfer of risk from hedgers to speculators is the commodity futures market. A typical hedger in this market is someone who produces or holds inventories of some commodity (such as grain or pork bellies) and wants to protect himself from the risk that the price of his commodity may fall in the future. Using the futures market, the hedger can obtain a promise from a speculator to purchase the hedger's stock of commodities for a specified price at a specified future date. This contract effectively transfers the risk of price change from the hedger to the speculator. If the commodity's market price on the agreed-upon sale date turns out to be higher than the price specified in the futures contract, the speculator enjoys a profit equal to the difference between what she can sell the commodities for and what she promised to pay the hedger. If the commodity's market price on the sale date is lower than the price stipulated in the futures contract, the speculator loses the difference between what she must pay for the commodities and what they will bring on the market. The speculator is willing to accept this risk either because she believes the futures contract will provide a higher return than other, less risky assets or because she believes that this risk can be diversified by other assets that she holds.

4. *Liquidity provision.* In Chapter 4 we defined liquidity to be the ease and quickness with which an asset can be exchanged for goods, services, or other assets. Cash is the most liquid asset, stocks and bonds have intermediate liquidity, and a house or an automobile—which are both costly and time-consuming to sell—are examples of illiquid assets. Liquidity is a desirable feature of assets because of the flexibility it creates. For example, someone holding liquid assets is better able

---

[2]James Tobin of Yale University was awarded the Nobel Prize in economics for, among other things, his early work in the theory of diversification. When asked by reporters to summarize the research for which he had won the prize, Tobin reportedly said, "I showed that you shouldn't put all your eggs in one basket." This statement confused the reporters; but not putting all your eggs in one basket is not a bad summary of the idea of diversification.

to meet emergency expenses or to take advantage of a newly arriving investment opportunity.

Liquidity is not a property of individual assets as much as it is a property of the markets in which these assets trade. If an asset is traded in a well-organized market with large numbers of buyers and sellers and low transactions costs, then the asset will be easy to sell quickly; that is, it will be relatively liquid. Examples of assets traded in highly liquid markets are U.S. government bonds and shares of IBM stock. Assets traded in markets with small numbers of buyers and sellers and high transactions costs—shares in small, unknown companies and very specialized types of machinery, for example—will be relatively illiquid. The liquidity of an asset can change over time if there is a change in the number of buyers and sellers interested in the asset or in the organization of the market in which the asset is traded (see Box 17.1 on the changing liquidity of junk bonds). One of the functions of the financial system is to create liquidity by bringing together buyers and sellers of various financial assets and allowing them to trade with the lowest possible transactions costs.

The development during the 1980s of the market

BOX *17.1:*   LIQUIDITY IN THE MARKET FOR JUNK BONDS

for junk bonds illustrates the importance of liquidity in financial markets and also how changes in the structure of a financial market can cause the liquidity of the asset traded in that market to change. Junk bonds, more properly known as high-yield or below-investment-grade bonds, are corporate bonds that are judged by credit-rating agencies to have a relatively high risk of default. These bonds may be rated as being risky because the corporation that issued them is small, financially weak, or in a risky line of business. Because junk bonds carry a higher risk of nonrepayment than higher-graded bonds, they generally offer a higher interest rate, which is why they are sometimes called high-yield bonds.

For many corporations that want to raise funds but do not have the impeccable credit ratings of blue-chip firms, issuing junk bonds represents an alternative to borrowing from banks. However, junk bonds were not much used by corporations before the 1980s. In the earlier period a major problem was that potential purchasers of the bonds considered them to be too illiquid, or hard to resell. But during the 1980s an investment banking firm called Drexel-Burnham-Lambert undertook to increase trading activity in junk bonds. Drexel began to make the market for these bonds by matching buyers and sellers. As the

junk bond market began to function more effectively, junk bonds became perceived as more liquid and investor interest grew quickly.

Junk bonds played an important role in corporate finance in the 1980s. For example, junk bonds were used to raise funds for many start-up corporations, including, for example, the telecommunications company MCI. Junk bonds were also used in the financing of leveraged buyouts, a type of financial transaction in which a group of investors combines its own money with borrowed money in order to buy a corporation. Some leveraged buyouts were quite successful, but others left the bought-out corporation with large amounts of debt and an increased risk of bankruptcy.

In 1989 the prices of junk bonds began to fall as some companies defaulted on their bonds and investors became worried about whether outstanding bonds would be repaid. In early 1990 these problems in the junk bond market, as well as mounting legal difficulties, led Drexel-Burnham-Lambert to go out of business. With a major market maker in junk bonds no longer operating, activity in this market—and thus the liquidity of junk bonds themselves—declined.

The Structure of the Financial System

An understanding of the basic structure of the financial system requires familiarity with the major types of financial assets, markets, and financial market participants. We focus here on financial markets that are used for saving and investment because of the central role that saving and investment play in macroeconomic analysis.

Financial Assets   Financial assets, also called financial instruments, are of two general types: debt and equity.

A debt instrument is essentially an IOU. More precisely, **debt** represents a borrower's promise, given in exchange for an initial sum of money, to make a series of repayments over time. All sectors of the economy use debt: Households borrow by means of consumer loans and mortgages, firms issue corporate bonds, banks sell certificates of deposit, and all levels of government issue government bonds.

Debt instruments vary along a number of dimensions, including the risk of nonrepayment or default that they carry, the length of time until the debt is scheduled to be fully repaid, and the way in which interest payments on the debt are taxed. The interest rates that lenders charge on different types of debt depend on these various characteristics (see the "In Touch with the Macroeconomy" box, Chapter 6, p. 199). Debt instruments also differ in whether the nominal interest rate charged by the lender is fixed over the life of the loan or varies according to some formula specified in the debt contract. For example, some home mortgages carry a fixed nominal interest rate, but others—known as adjustable-rate mortgages—have interest rates that change periodically in a way that is tied to changes in a particular interest rate (such as the interest rate on one-year Treasury bills) or an index of interest rates.

The second main type of financial instrument is equity, or shares of stock. **Equity,** which is issued exclusively by corporations, gives the holder a share of ownership of the issuing firm. Firms are not legally bound to make payments to their stockholders, but many firms do make regular payments called **dividends.** In addition to earning dividends, owners of equity may earn a return in the form of a capital gain if the price of a share of stock increases. However, if the price of a share of stock falls, owners of equity suffer a capital loss.

Suppose that we let

$$i^s = \text{nominal rate of return on stocks (equity)},$$

$$D = \text{nominal dividend paid per share of stock},$$

$$P_s = \text{price of a share of stock},$$

$$\Delta P_s = \text{change in the price of a share of stock (capital}$$
$$\text{gain if positive, capital loss if negative)}.$$

Using this notation, we can write the following expression for the nominal rate of return on stocks:

$$i^s = \frac{D + \Delta P_s}{P_s}. \tag{17.1}$$

Equation (17.1) says that the nominal rate of return on an equity investment equals the sum of the dividend and the capital gain, divided by the price that was paid for the stock.

Financial Markets   Financial instruments are traded in a wide variety of financial markets. Here are some distinctions among types of financial markets that are useful to know:

1. *Primary markets versus secondary markets.* **Primary markets** are markets in which new securities are sold by their original issuers. In contrast, existing securities are traded in **secondary markets.** For example, Treasury bills (government debt of maturity of one year or less) are auctioned off by the government in the primary Treasury bill market, but holders of existing Treasury bills can trade among themselves in an active secondary market.

2. *Money markets versus capital markets.* Markets for short-term financial assets (term to maturity of one year or less) are called **money markets.** Examples of assets traded in money markets include Treasury bills and commercial paper, which is short-term debt issued by private corporations.[3] Markets for longer-term assets, such as mortgages and long-term corporate bonds, are called **capital markets.**

3. *Auction markets versus over-the-counter markets.* **Auction markets** bring large numbers of traders together in one place. Prices in auction markets are established by open competitive bidding. The best-known examples of auction markets are the stock exchanges, which are the secondary markets for the equities of major corporations. In **over-the-counter markets** there is not a single trading location. Rather, trading is done over the phone or via the computer and is organized by dealers who buy and sell for themselves and for customers. Many small company stocks are sold on over-the-counter markets.

4. *Spot markets versus futures markets and options markets.* In **spot markets,** also called cash markets, financial assets are bought and sold for "cash" (actually, payment is made by check or by a transfer between the buyer's and seller's accounts). In **financial futures markets** participants agree on a price for which financial assets will be delivered at some specified date in the future, in a way analogous to the futures markets for commodities discussed previously. In **options markets** a trader can buy the right (which he does not have to exercise) to buy or sell a financial asset at a fixed price within a certain period of time. For example, by buying the right to sell a block of stock at $100 per share, a trader can protect himself against the risk that the price of the shares he holds will fall below $100 per share over the life of the option. If the price of the stock falls to $90 per share, the issuer of the option is obligated to pay $100 per share for the shares. On the other hand, if the stock price rises to $110 per share, the purchaser of the option will not want to exercise his right to sell the stock at $100 per share, and the option becomes worthless.

Financial futures and options are examples of **derivative securities,** which are assets whose value is based on or *derived from* the value of other securities. Derivative securities provide an organized way for hedgers to reduce the risk of future price movements and for speculators to bet on their forecasts about future price movements.

---

[3]Notice that the term *money* is used here to refer to a broader set of assets than just those used in performing transactions.

Many different types of financial markets have emerged in the past few decades (and new ones continue to appear) in response to demands by financial market participants. Markets that have succeeded in attracting traders have been the ones accomplishing the four basic functions of financial markets at the lowest cost. For example, financial futures markets only began to appear in the mid-1970s. However, because they have proved very useful to financial investors attempting to manage risk, these markets are now solidly established.

Financial Market Participants   There are many participants in financial markets besides the savers, investors, hedgers, and speculators who are the ultimate demanders of financial services. For example, there are the exchanges (such as the stock exchange), which actually organize some major markets, and the brokers and dealers, who buy and sell financial instruments on behalf of their customers.

A particularly important set of participants in financial markets is a group of institutions called **financial intermediaries.** Major financial intermediaries include commercial banks, savings and loans, credit unions, insurance companies, mutual funds, and pension funds. The key characteristic of financial intermediaries is that although they borrow from the public, they do not do so in order to finance their own consumption or physical investment. Instead, financial intermediaries use the proceeds from their borrowing to purchase the debt or equity of ultimate borrowers, who do use the funds they raise for consumption or investment. For example, a commercial bank may use funds received from depositors to make a loan to a business; a mutual fund may use the funds it receives from selling shares in itself

Table 17.1 Relative Importance of Various Financial Intermediaries

Intermediary	Assets (1990) (in Billions of Dollars)	% of Total Intermediary Assets				
		1950	1960	1970	1980	1990
Commercial banks	3279	52	38	38	37	32
Life insurance companies	1378	22	20	15	12	13
Private pension funds	1194	2	6	9	12	12
Savings and loans	1159	6	12	14	15	11
State and local government pension funds	753	2	3	5	5	7
Mutual funds	588	1	3	4	2	6
Finance companies	539	3	5	5	5	5
Casualty insurance companies	507	4	5	4	4	5
Money market mutual funds	453	—	—	—	2	4
Mutual savings banks	284	8	7	6	4	3
Credit unions	213	—	1	1	2	2
Total	10,347	100	100	100	100	100

Source: George G. Kaufman, "The Incredible Shrinking S&L Industry," *Chicago Fed Letter,* Federal Reserve Bank of Chicago, December 1990.

Note: Data for 1990 pertain to the second quarter of 1990. All other data are for the fourth quarter of the year.

to invest in corporate stocks. The economic advantages of having financial intermediaries stand between ultimate savers and investors is discussed in the next
section.

Table 17.1 shows the total assets held by each type of financial intermediary
in 1990 and the percentage of total intermediary assets held by each type of intermediary at ten-year intervals since 1950. Notice that commercial banks are the
largest type of financial intermediary, though the share of commercial bank assets
has fallen from more than half of total intermediary assets in 1950 to under one
third of total intermediary assets in 1990. Intermediaries that have grown substantially in relative importance include pension funds (both private and governmental) and various types of mutual funds. Savings and loans expanded significantly between 1950 and 1980 but fell back during the 1980s.

Another major participant in financial markets is the government. First, the
government is the principal *regulator* of financial markets and intermediaries. For
example, the issuance and trading of many financial instruments, such as stocks
and bonds, is regulated by the Securities and Exchange Commission (SEC), a Federal agency. Regulation of banks and other financial intermediaries is particularly
extensive, as Section 17.3 discusses. Second, as was emphasized in Chapter 16,
Federal, state, and local governments are major *borrowers* in financial markets.
Finally, the government is also a large *lender* in financial markets, making direct
loans to farmers, small businesses, and others. Many private sector loans (such as
housing loans and student loans) are guaranteed by the Federal government or its
agencies—meaning that if the borrower defaults on a loan, the government will
make the promised payments of principal and interest.

Figure 17.1 (p. 692) summarizes the basic structure of the financial system.
Each transaction in the financial system is an exchange of funds for an asset. The
financial system facilitates the transfer of funds from lenders to borrowers, either
directly or indirectly through financial intermediaries. When lenders transfer
funds directly to borrowers, they receive financial instruments—stocks (equity)
and bonds (debt)—issued by the borrowers. When the transfer of funds goes
through financial intermediaries, lenders receive deposits or shares in the intermediaries in exchange for funds. The financial intermediaries then transfer the
funds received to ultimate borrowers in exchange for financial instruments issued
by the borrowers.

17.2   FINANCIAL MARKETS, ASYMMETRIC INFORMATION, AND INVESTMENT

The condition that desired national saving and desired investment be equal in equilibrium is a building block of the macroeconomic model we have developed in this
book. This condition is captured graphically by the familiar saving-investment diagram, in which the upward-sloping saving curve (S) represents the supply of savings and the downward-sloping investment curve (I) represents firms' demands for
funds. (See, for example, Key Diagram #2 in Chapter 3, p. 106.) The intersection
of the saving curve and the investment curve determines the real interest rate that
clears the goods market.

Underlying the basic saving-investment diagram is an assumption that the
market for saving and investment operates in a way analogous to the market for,
say, apples. In the market for apples the price of apples adjusts freely until the

Figure 17.1 The financial system

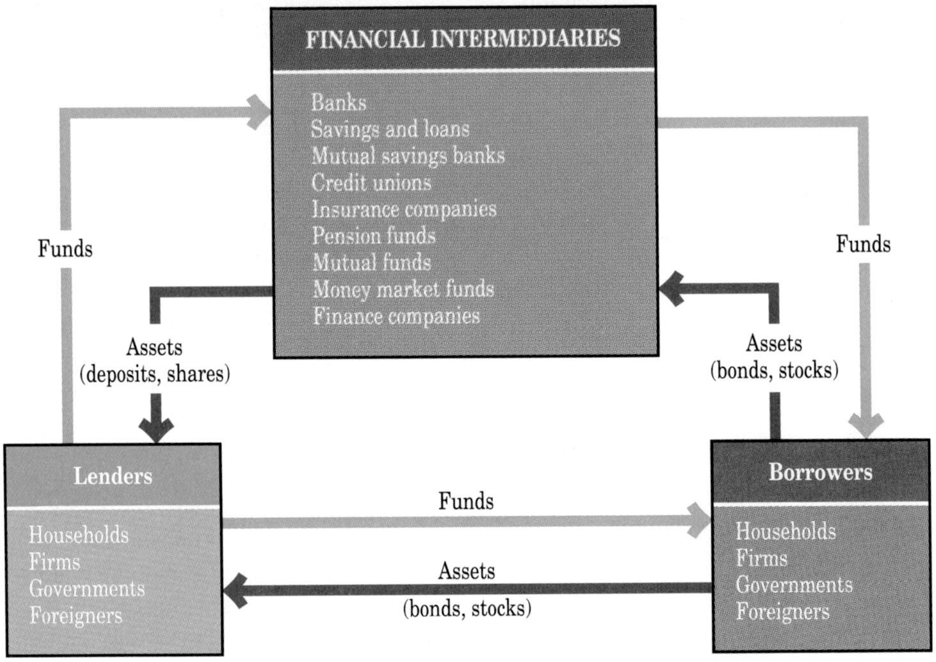

The financial system facilitates the transfer of funds from lenders to borrowers. Funds can be transferred either directly between lenders and borrowers or indirectly through financial intermediaries. In each transaction funds are traded in exchange for an asset or financial instrument issued by the recipient of the funds.

number of apples that producers want to supply equals the number of apples that consumers demand. Similarly, in the market for saving and investment we have been assuming that the "price" of savings—that is, the real interest rate—adjusts until the quantities of savings supplied and demanded are equal.

There are, however, some very important differences between the market for apples and the market for saving and investment. The apple market is a spot market, meaning that the apple and the agreed-upon monetary payment change hands simultaneously and immediately. There is no need for the apple seller to be concerned about the apple buyer's credit rating, or about whether the buyer will use the apple wisely (to make apple pie) or foolishly (to throw at someone). A transaction in the apple market can take place perfectly well between strangers who know nothing about each other.[4] Furthermore, faced with two potential buyers of the same apple, the profit-maximizing seller will always sell the apple to the buyer offering the highest price.

In contrast to the apple market, the market for saving and investment by its very nature is a credit market. A **credit market** is a market in which one party to the transaction gives up something of value today (in this case, the saver gives up current resources) in exchange for a *promise* of payment in the future. Whether the borrower in fact makes good on her promise depends on a number of factors, including her honesty, the type of investment she makes, the other resources she has available for repayment if the investment fails, and so on. In a credit market

---

[4]For purposes of the example we are assuming that the buyer has no difficulty judging the quality of the apple by looking at it, and that the seller can verify that the buyer's means of payment is good (for example, he can be sure that the buyer's cash is not counterfeit).

an intelligent lender will be concerned not just with the "price" (the interest rate) he is offered but also with the probability that the promise to repay will in fact be honored. Thus, although a credit market transaction can take place between strangers, it will only occur after a process of information gathering and perhaps with the imposition of terms and conditions beyond the interest rate itself. Furthermore, unlike the apple supplier, the supplier of credit faced with several potential borrowers will not necessarily give the loan to the borrower who offers the highest interest rate, since the very willingness to offer a high rate may indicate that the borrower does not expect (or intend) to repay.

This discussion suggests that in some fundamental ways the market for saving and investment is more complex than the market for apples. At the heart of the difference between the two markets is the much greater role for information gathering (as when the lender investigates the potential borrower) in the market for saving and investment.

Much economic research has studied the behavior of markets, such as the market for saving and investment, in which information is important. More specifically, researchers have focused on situations of asymmetric information. There is **asymmetric information** in a market when suppliers and demanders have different information about the good, service, or asset being traded. Asymmetric information is often a major factor in the market for saving and investment, because typically the potential borrower (the demander of funds) will know much more about his intended use of the funds—and the prospects for the intended use to be successful—than does the potential lender (the supplier of funds). Because the potential borrower may have incentives not to reveal all the information he has to the lender, the presence of asymmetric information can cause the market for saving and investment to function poorly. Indeed, many financial market arrangements and institutions exist primarily in order to reduce the problems created by asymmetric information.

This section of the chapter discusses some basic insights from the economic literature on asymmetric information in financial markets. We concentrate on two aspects of the financial system, the role of banking in the economy and the financing of corporate investment. Our goal is to go beyond the saving-investment diagram to a deeper understanding of how the market for saving and investment works. We then see how our conclusions affect the analysis of the macroeconomy and of macroeconomic policy.

Asymmetric Information and the Banking System

As we discussed in the previous section of this chapter, much of the saving-investment process is intermediated. Small savers in particular do not often lend directly to the ultimate borrowers. Instead, many savers lend to banks and other financial intermediaries, who in turn use the funds received from savers to purchase the debt or equity of ultimate borrowers. Among the many financial intermediaries, banks and similar institutions play the largest role in the financial system: Banks and other deposit-taking intermediaries (savings and loans, mutual savings banks, and credit unions) together account for about half of the total assets of financial intermediaries as a whole (see Table 17.1, p. 690).

How the Banking System Benefits Savers A major reason the banking system is so important as an intermediary is that there is asymmetric information about borrowers. In particular, small savers typically do not have and cannot easily obtain the information needed to evaluate a potential borrower's request for a loan. Banks reduce this problem by performing the information-gathering activities necessary for profitable lending, including checking out the borrower's credit history, determining whether the borrower's business plans are sensible, and monitoring the borrower's activities during the life of the loan. Because banks specialize in these information-gathering activities, they can perform them at much lower cost than the small saver could on her own. Banks also reduce costs of gathering information by pooling the savings of many individuals to make large loans; each large loan needs to be evaluated only once, by the bank, rather than separately by each of the hundreds of individuals whose savings are being pooled to make the loan. For these reasons the saver's return net of information costs is likely to be higher if she goes through a bank than if she tries to make loans directly.

How the Banking System Benefits Borrowers   The benefits of a well-functioning banking system are not limited to savers but extend to borrowers as well. Indeed, there are many potential borrowers who might have no access to credit at all if it were not for the banking system. Consider, for example, the owner of a small business who wants to expand but needs credit to do so. Unlike a Fortune 500 company, the small business cannot borrow by selling corporate bonds or issuing stock on the New York Stock Exchange, because bond and stock analysts and investors would not find it worth their while to investigate the prospects of a small business. The only option for the small business, then, is to borrow from a bank. Because the bank's lending officer has acquired expertise in evaluating and making small-business loans—and may even have an ongoing business relationship with the small-business owner—the bank will be able to gather the information needed to make a loan at a reasonable cost. Similarly, a consumer who wants to borrow $10,000 for home improvement would find few good alternatives to the local bank.

Credit Rationing   Earlier in this section we drew some contrasts between the market for apples and the market for loans. We have already discussed one important difference: In the market for loans, unlike the market for apples, the supplier of loans (the lender) must gather information about the demander of loans (the borrower); failing to do so would incur a great risk of not being repaid. A second difference is that the price of apples is determined by the condition that the quantities of apples demanded and supplied be equal, but the equilibrium "price" of loans (the interest rate charged) will not always be the one at which the funds demanded by borrowers equal the funds supplied by lenders. For example, in loan markets it is possible that lenders will respond to an increase in the demand for loans not by raising interest rates but instead by denying credit to some applicants. When among a group of apparently similar potential borrowers some receive credit but others do not, we say that there is **credit rationing**.[5]

To see why credit rationing might arise, imagine that a bank has a fixed quantity of funds that it has decided to lend to small-business owners. The bank's managers agree that they should charge an interest rate of 10%. However, when the

---

[5]An influential analysis of credit rationing is given in Joseph E. Stiglitz and Andrew Weiss, "Credit Rationing in Markets with Imperfect Information," *American Economic Review*, December 1983, pp. 912–927.

bank announces that loans are available, the number of potential borrowers who show up to apply for loans is five times greater than the bank expected. Even after careful screening of the applicants has eliminated the obvious bad risks, there is still a much greater demand for funds than the bank has available to lend. Suppose that the bank had not yet firmly committed to the 10% loan rate and could easily raise its interest rate without any legal problems and without losing most of its applicants. What should the bank do, assuming it wants to maximize profits?

If this were an apple market, the answer would be easy: Faced with excess demand, a profit-maximizing seller should raise the price until quantities demanded and supplied are equal. However, in a loan market with asymmetric information, the answer is not so obvious. Indeed, it is possible that if the bank raises the interest rate it charges in response to high demand, its profits could actually go down!

The reason for this seemingly paradoxical result is that the interest rate the bank charges may affect the probability that the loan is ultimately repaid. Suppose, for example, that the pool of potential borrowers consists of two different types of people: staid, conservative individuals and reckless gamblers. The conservative borrowers, if given a loan, will make an investment that pays a solid return with a high probability. The gamblers, in contrast, if given a loan will "go for broke"—stake everything on a bet almost certain to fail but with a high payoff if it succeeds. We assume that the bank would much rather lend to the conservative types, but there is asymmetric information about borrowers' types. Each borrower knows which type she is, but unfortunately, even given some investigation into their credit records and business plans, the bank can't tell for sure which potential borrowers are conservatives and which ones are gamblers.

Now suppose the bank responds to the excess demand for loans by raising its interest rate. Which potential borrowers will this drive away? Not the gamblers; they don't really expect to repay anyway. But if their gamble works out well and they do have to repay, they will still make a killing. Instead, the conservative potential borrowers, finding that their proposed investments are no longer profitable at the higher interest rate, will drop out of the pool of potential borrowers. As a result, raising the interest rate reduces the probability that the typical loan will be repaid.

Faced with the possibility that raising the interest rate may worsen the pool of loan applicants, the bank might find that it makes a higher profit by keeping the interest rate at 10% and picking qualified applicants randomly—that is, by rationing credit. The bank may also stiffen its "nonprice" terms, by asking for more collateral, for example. This type of behavior by a supplier of credit is much different from what we expect from a supplier of apples.

Banks and the Demand for Investment   We have seen that as a result of asymmetric information about borrowers, small businesses that need to acquire additional funds for investment may have no alternative but to borrow these funds from banks. To see the macroeconomic implications of this dependence on bank loans, imagine that a law were passed forbidding any new loans by banks. Such a law would prevent small firms from obtaining credit and would substantially reduce these firms' investment spending. Effectively, because small firms are excluded from borrowing, desired investment in the economy is reduced at any given real interest rate and level of output.

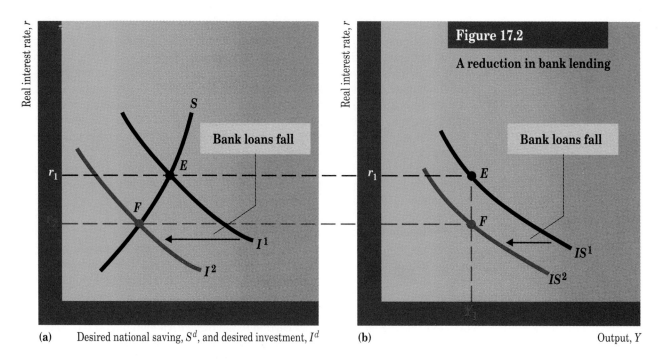

(a)   Desired national saving, S^d, and desired investment, I^d **(b)**   Output, Y

(a) A reduction in bank lending, the result of (for example) legal limits on credit extension, makes it difficult for bank-dependent borrowers to obtain credit for investment purposes. Effectively, desired investment falls. The investment curve shifts left, from I^1 to I^2. At the given level of output Y_1 the real interest rate that clears the goods market falls from r_1 to r_2, as indicated by the movement from point E to point F.

(b) At the given level of output Y_1 the fall in desired investment reduces the real interest that clears the goods market from r_1 to r_2. Thus the IS curve shifts downward and to the left, from IS^1 to IS^2.

As shown in Fig. 17.2(a), the reduction in desired investment caused by the no-lending law shifts the investment curve left, from I^1 to I^2. The saving curve S does not shift because there is no change in the desired amount of saving by ultimate savers at any given real interest rate and level of output. Given output, the real interest rate falls from r_1 at point E to r_2 at point F. Because the restriction on bank lending reduces the real interest rate that clears the goods market at any given level of output, it also shifts the IS curve downward, from IS^1 to IS^2 in Fig. 17.2(b).

Figure 17.3 shows the macroeconomic effects of a restriction on bank lending in the Keynesian IS-LM model. If we start from the initial equilibrium at point E, a restriction on bank lending shifts the IS curve downward, from IS^1 to IS^2. Because prices do not adjust immediately, the short-run behavior of the economy is represented by point G, at the intersection of the new IS curve (IS^2) and the LM curve. Comparing point G to point E, we see that a restriction on bank lending reduces output and the real interest rate in the short run in the Keynesian model.[6]

Is it realistic to imagine the enactment of a law restricting bank lending? In fact, in some countries such laws—which are called **credit controls**—are not un-

---

[6]In the basic classical model the short-run equilibrium is located at the intersection of IS^2 and the FE line (point H), so that the real interest falls and output remains unchanged.

Real interest rate, r

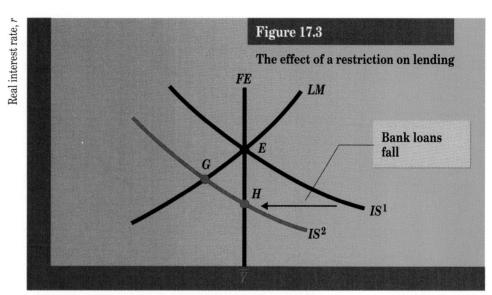

Figure 17.3

The effect of a restriction on lending

Output, Y

A reduction in bank lending reduces the ability of bank-dependent borrowers to obtain credit to finance investment. For the economy as a whole desired investment falls, causing the IS curve to move downward and to the left (as in Fig. 17.2), from IS^1 to IS^2. In the Keynesian model the short-run equilibrium moves from point E to point G, and a temporary recession results, with output and the real interest rate both falling. In the classical model, because of rapid price adjustment, the economy moves from point E to point H, so that the real interest rate falls but the level of output remains unchanged.

usual. Although credit controls have not often been used in the United States, controls on bank lending were imposed by the Carter administration early in 1980 as part of an attempt to fight inflation.[7] During the few months that the controls were in effect, bank loans, spending, and interest rates all fell, and the economy went into a brief recession, as predicted by the analysis in Fig. 17.3.

Credit controls are not the only factor that can cause banks to reduce lending. Historically, bank runs and financial panics had a similar effect on banks. During 1931–1933, as the U.S. economy plunged into the Great Depression, depositors lined up to take their money out of banks, which failed rapidly. As we saw in Chapter 15 (in the application on the money multiplier during the Great Depression), the runs on the banks reduced the money supply. This fall in the money supply shifted the LM curve upward and to the left, as shown by the shift from LM^1 to LM^2 in Fig. 17.4.

But the banking crisis also reduced the capacity of the banking system to lend: Not only did many banks close, but banks that survived—fearful of the prospect of more bank runs—reduced lending sharply in order to hold more reserves and other safe, liquid assets. As we have discussed, a reduction in bank lending effectively reduces desired investment and shifts the IS curve downward, from IS^1 to IS^2 in Fig. 17.4. Under the Keynesian assumption of price stickiness, the short-run equilibrium is located at point F in Fig. 17.4, the intersection of IS^2 and LM^2.

---

[7]The Carter credit controls actually focused more on consumer lending than on business lending, but the basic principle is the same.

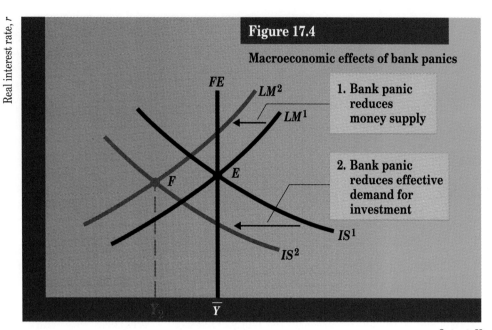

Figure 17.4

Macroeconomic effects of bank panics

1. Bank panic reduces money supply

2. Bank panic reduces effective demand for investment

Output, *Y*

If we start from the initial equilibrium at point *E*, bank runs reduce the money multiplier and the money supply, so that the *LM* curve moves upward and to the left, from *LM*¹ to *LM*². In addition, because of bank closings and the reluctance of surviving banks to lend, bank-dependent borrowers find it more difficult to obtain credit. Thus desired investment falls, and the *IS* curve shifts downward and to the left, from *IS*¹ to *IS*². In the Keynesian model the shifts in both the *IS* curve and the *LM* curve contribute to a decline in output as the short-run equilibrium moves from point *E* to point *F*.

Thus according to the Keynesian model, bank runs contributed to the severe drop in output during the 1930s both by causing the money supply to fall and by reducing bank lending.[8]

A third example of a reduction in bank lending is a **credit crunch,** a general term for a situation in which for some reason banks become unwilling or unable to supply new credit. Prior to the 1980s there was a regulation (called Regulation Q) that placed a ceiling on the interest rates that banks could pay on deposits. On several occasions—notably in 1966, 1969, and 1973–1974—open-market interest rates (as on Treasury bills) exceeded the Regulation Q ceiling on deposit rates by a significant amount. In order to be able to earn the higher yield available on Treasury bills, many depositors withdrew their funds from banks. A withdrawal of deposits from banks so that depositors can hold nonintermediary financial assets instead is called **disintermediation.** The loss of deposits caused banks and other intermediaries to sharply reduce their lending. As a result, spending declined in sectors heavily dependent on intermediary lending, such as housing, which in turn contributed to economic slowdowns.

---

[8]For further discussion of the role of bank runs in the Depression, see Ben Bernanke, "Non-Monetary Effects of the Financial Collapse in the Propagation of the Great Depression," *American Economic Review*, June 1983, pp. 257–276.

Application

The Credit Crunch of 1990

The recession that began in the summer of 1990 was accompanied by a credit crunch. Many financial intermediaries suffered losses during 1990 because of defaults on real estate loans and loans to highly leveraged firms (firms that ˅re financed with a high ratio of debt to equity). In response to these losses, a. .n an attempt to reduce the riskiness of their assets, many banks tightened their standards for making loans and reduced credit availability. The value of bank loans outstanding was lower in September, October, and November of 1990 than during August.[9] Many small firms complained that they were unable to obtain credit, even (in some cases) if they had a good credit rating and a long-term relationship with their bank.

The Federal Reserve closely monitored the credit situation and undertook several actions to counteract the credit crunch. First, in November of 1990 the Fed began to increase the money supply in an attempt to stimulate the economy and investment spending. Second, the Fed eliminated the 3% reserve requirements on nonpersonal time deposits in December 1990. This action was intended to help sagging bank profitability and to increase the quantity of funds that banks had available to lend. Third, in order to encourage banks to borrow from the Fed and to relend to bank customers, the Fed reduced the discount rate from 7.0% to 6.5% in December 1990 and to 6.0% in January 1991. Overall, the Fed's actions probably eased the credit crunch and softened the accompanying recession, although some critics have argued that the Fed delayed too long before taking action.

Asymmetric Information and Investment by Large Firms

In the previous section we discussed bank credit as a source of funds for investment by firms, and we analyzed the role of asymmetric information in bank loans. Although many firms are dependent on banks for credit, these firms are typically small. In the United States the greater part of investment spending is done by large firms. Larger firms do borrow from banks, but most of these firms are also able to finance their investments through publicly traded financial instruments, such as bonds or shares of stock. However, as this section explains, asymmetric information may be an important factor affecting desired investment even for very large firms.

Internal Versus External Funds   Our analyses of desired investment spending have related desired investment to only one financial variable, the real interest rate. The real interest rate represents the price the firm must pay for borrowed funds or, alternatively, the return that the firm could obtain by lending to someone else instead of investing. Thus the higher the real interest rate is, the less desire the firm will have to invest. In discussing the link between the cost of funds and

---

[9]Seasonally adjusted total loans and leases of commercial banks, *Federal Reserve Bulletin*, March 1991, Table 1.23, line 4.

investment, however, we have not said anything about precisely how the firm obtains the funds to finance its investment: Does it borrow? Issue new equity? Use its own undistributed profits? Implicitly, we have assumed that the source of investment funds is irrelevant to the investment decision.

In practice, though, firms seem to care about how their investments are financed, implying that the real cost of funds is not necessarily independent of how the funds are obtained. Research has generally found that *firms consider internal funds to be a cheaper source of finance than external funds*. **Internal funds** are funds that the firm has available from its own operations, including undistributed profits (profits that have not been paid out to shareholders in the form of dividends) and depreciation allowances (the portion of cash flow that corresponds to the amount of depreciation of the firm's capital stock). **External funds** are funds raised from outside investors. The main ways of raising external funds are by borrowing (either by taking a loan from a bank or by issuing corporate debt) and by issuing new stock.

Why are external funds more costly to the firm than internal funds? Asymmetric information is the basic reason. "Outsiders" who provide external finance by lending or purchasing stock know much less about the firm's planned investments than do the managers and other "insiders" such as current large stockholders. The outsiders will demand higher returns on their investment to compensate themselves for the costs of acquiring information about the firm's investment plans and for bearing the risk that the firm's managers have not revealed potential problems with those plans.

The outsiders may also try to protect themselves by attempting to exert some control over the management's actions: For outside *lenders* this control may involve the inclusion of special conditions, called covenants, in the lending terms. Outside *stockholders*, whose shares entitle them to vote at stockholder meetings, may use their votes to change company policy. From the manager's point of view this potential loss of control represents an additional cost of external finance.[10]

Because firms find external funds more costly than internal funds to use for investment, firms with more internal funds will invest more, all else being equal. This implication has been confirmed in most recent research on the topic.[11] A related finding is that the effects of internal funds on investment are strongest for young, rapidly growing firms, as opposed to more mature, stable firms. This finding makes sense: New, rapidly expanding firms will pose the most severe problems of asymmetric information to potential external investors. Thus to a greater degree than mature firms, young firms will find external financing expensive or hard to get and will be more dependent on internal financing for their investment.

Macroeconomic Implications of Internal Versus External Funds   The sensitivity of firms' investment to the availability of internal finance has several implications for the macroeconomy and macroeconomic policy, of which we discuss two of the most important.

---

[10]Although firms find internal funds to be less costly than external funds, the use of external funds may serve a useful monitoring function. The control and review by outside investors may help to ensure that the firm's managers act in the best interests of the firm's owners and do not waste the firm's resources on bad investments or overly lavish executive perks.

[11]One important study is Steven Fazzari, R. Glenn Hubbard, and Bruce Petersen, "Financing Constraints and Corporate Investment," *Brookings Papers on Economic Activity*, 1988:1, pp. 141–195.

First, this sensitivity may increase the severity of business cycles. Suppose, for example, that the economy has been driven into a recession by an adverse productivity shock. Because of the recession, firms will have lower profits and thus less internal funds. Lower internal funds, in turn, will reduce investment spending below what it otherwise might have been, further depressing aggregate demand and output. The result is a more serious recession.

Second, the dependence of investment on internal funds may be an argument against the Ricardian equivalence proposition, which states that changes in taxes without changes in government purchases have no effect. A reduction in taxes levied on corporations, for example, will increase firms' internal funds and (if investment is sensitive to internal funds) increase investment spending.[12] An increase in desired investment shifts the *IS* curve upward and is expansionary.

17.3 FINANCIAL MARKET INSTABILITY

In the nineteenth and early twentieth centuries the United States periodically experienced episodes called financial panics. A **financial panic** is a period of violent fluctuations in financial markets, typically including a sharp decline in stock prices, bankruptcies of major firms, and runs on the banks. Panics did not last very long—usually a few weeks or so—but were widely regarded as very disruptive of business and the economy. After the particularly severe Panic of 1907, Congress decided to reform the financial system to try to achieve more stability in financial markets. The principal result of this reform effort was the opening of the Federal Reserve System in 1914. A major responsibility of the new central bank was to use monetary policy and the regulatory powers conferred on it by Congress to try to eliminate financial panics, or at least to reduce their severity.

There were no financial panics between the establishment of the Fed and the onset of the Great Depression in 1929. However, during the downward phase of the Great Depression (1929–1933), the United States (along with many other countries) experienced probably the worst financial panics of its history. After the stock market crash of 1929 stock prices continued to fall until they reached a level only about one eighth of their previous peak. At the same time, waves of bank runs and loan defaults caused thousands of banks to fail or merge with other banks. By the time Franklin Delano Roosevelt was inaugurated as President in March 1933, the financial system was in shambles.

As part of the comprehensive set of New Deal reforms, President Roosevelt and the Congress introduced many strong measures designed to increase the stability of the financial system. For example, the Banking Act of 1933 (the Glass-Steagall Act) restricted banks' lending activities, put ceilings on the rates banks could pay depositors, and gave additional regulatory powers to the Federal Reserve. These measures formed the basis for a financial regulatory system that has persisted until very recently. By far the most important of the New Deal reforms, however, was the introduction of Federal deposit insurance. Under the system of deposit insurance the Federal government guarantees that depositors at insured banks will not lose their money (up to specified limits[13]), even if their bank fails.

---

[12]The effect of increased internal funds on investment spending is in addition to any effects arising from a reduction in the tax-adjusted user cost of capital. See Chapter 6.
[13]As of 1991, accounts are insured up to a limit of $100,000.

The figure shows the number of insured banks and insured thrift institutions (savings and loans, savings banks, and credit unions) that failed each year. After large numbers of failures in the 1930s, the number of failures per year subsided and remained low until the early 1980s. The number of failures shot up during the second half of the 1980s. (*Note:* Data on thrift failures in 1989 were not available.)

Source: Congressional Budget Office, *Reforming Federal Deposit Insurance*, September 1990, Appendix C, Tables C-1 and C-2.

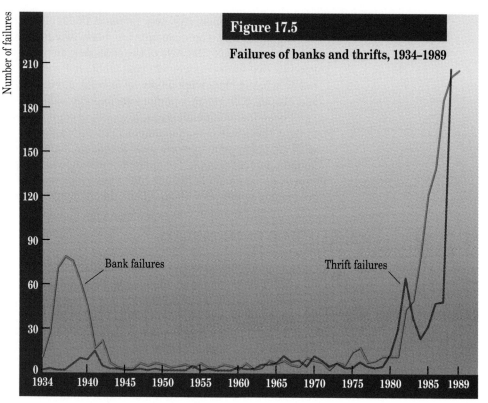

Figure 17.5

Failures of banks and thrifts, 1934–1989

Year

The New Deal reforms succeeded in helping the U.S. financial system resume operation in an orderly way. Most strikingly, deposit insurance, by protecting depositors from the effects of bank failures, virtually eliminated runs on banks. Bank failures also dropped sharply: Although more than 10,000 U.S. banks failed between 1929 and 1933, in the years between World War II and 1981 the number of banks failing per year exceeded 10 only in 1975 (13 failures) and 1976 (16 failures). The stock market had its ups and downs in the years following World War II, but it was considerably less volatile than in the period between the two World Wars.

During the 1980s, however, the New Deal solutions to the problem of financial instability began to look less and less acceptable. On the one hand, bankers complained that excessive regulation was preventing them from offering new financial services and diversifying their financial investments, which they felt they needed to do in order to meet growing international and domestic competition. On the other hand, financial instability became more of a problem than it had been at any time since the Depression. Failures of banks and thrift institutions (savings and loans, savings banks, and credit unions) increased significantly, as you can see in Fig. 17.5.[14] And particularly during the period following the dramatic stock market crash of October 1987, stock prices were often highly volatile.

In this last section of the chapter we discuss the causes of financial instability, its potential effects on the macroeconomy, and some suggested policies for dealing with this problem. Our focus is on the two parts of the financial system where,

[14]Although the numbers of bank failures and savings and loan failures were roughly equal in 1988, banks outnumbered savings and loans by more than a factor of 4. Thus the fraction of insured banks that failed in that year (1.47%) was much smaller than the fraction of insured savings and loans that failed (6.95%).

historically, the most dramatic instability has been observed: the banking system (broadly defined to include other deposit-taking institutions such as savings and loans) and the stock market.

Instability in Banking

The source of instability in banking that has historically most concerned both bankers and policymakers is the potential for bank runs and banking panics. As we discussed in Chapter 15, a bank run occurs when depositors, afraid that an imminent failure of the bank will wipe out their deposits, line up to withdraw their money. A **banking panic** occurs when bank runs spread throughout the banking system, affecting many banks simultaneously.

Two features of standard banking arrangements make bank runs possible. The first is that a large fraction of bank deposits are demandable, which means they can be withdrawn by the depositor at any time. The second is the use of fractional reserve banking (Chapter 15), under which only part of the public's deposits are held by the bank as reserves (vault cash or deposits in the central bank). Should all or most of the depositors attempt to withdraw at the same time, with only fractional reserves the bank will not be able to meet all of their demands.

Historically, most bank panics began when depositors heard rumors that one or more banks had made bad loans or financial investments. Concerned that the bank would fail (go bankrupt) and not pay off deposits, depositors hurried to be first in line to withdraw. Runs might then spread from bank to bank as other depositors, inferring from the first runs that there were problems in the banking system, began to worry about the safety of their own banks. In theory a bank run could amount to a self-fulfilling prophecy: If, for whatever reason, enough depositors think there is going to be a run and withdraw their deposits, then a run will in fact occur. In a self-fulfilling run even a bank that has made perfectly sound loans would be unable to meet the demands for withdrawals (since it holds only fractional reserves) and would have to close down. Historians disagree, however, as to whether self-fulfilling runs—as opposed to runs motivated by genuine problems with banks' loan portfolios—ever occurred in significant numbers.

Given the danger of runs, why did banks institute demandable deposits and fractional reserves? The standard view is that although bank runs are disruptive and costly, these costs are outweighed by the advantages of demandable deposits and fractional reserves during nonpanic periods. The advantage of demandable deposits is that depositors know that their funds are immediately available whenever they might need them—that is, they are very liquid. Indeed, following the advent of checking accounts in the midnineteenth century, bank deposits became useful for everyday transactions. The advantage of holding only fractional reserves is that banks are able to invest part of the deposits they receive in interest-yielding loans and securities. Interest earnings from these financial investments allow banks to pay interest to depositors, rather than having to charge depositors for check-writing and other banking services.

In addition, some economists have argued that the potential for bank runs created by demandable deposits and fractional reserve banking was not necessarily all bad.[15] In this view the threat of runs was useful in that it helped to "discipline"

---

[15]A theoretical analysis is given in Charles Calomiris and Charles Kahn, "The Role of Demandable Debt in Structuring Optimal Banking Arrangements," *American Economic Review*, June 1991, pp. 497–513.

bankers. Without the threat of runs bankers might be tempted to make risky investments, to make loans to friends and relatives, or to commit various kinds of fraud. However (this argument goes), knowing that a run can close down a bank at even a whiff of bad news about the bank's investments forces bankers to be more conservative and honest. And should a banker turn out nevertheless to be a crook, his depositors would run and shut him down before he could steal too much.

The Costs of Banking Panics   While perhaps agreeing that the threat of runs had some value as a discipline device, most economists would also agree that widespread and persistent banking panics—such as occurred during the Great Depression—are economically costly (see Box 17.2, p. 705, for some international evidence). The principal costs attributed to banking panics arise from their effects on the money supply and on bank lending and from the increased riskiness of deposits when there is a danger of panics. These costs are discussed next.

1. *The fall in the money supply.* As discussed in Chapter 15, bank runs increase the currency-deposit ratio and the reserve-deposit ratio, causing the money multiplier to fall. Without offsetting actions by the central bank, the fall in the money multiplier will cause the money supply to fall as well. If money is not neutral (as in the extended classical model with misperceptions or the Keynesian model), the decline in the money supply will depress aggregate output and employment.

2. *The loss of bank lending and other bank services.* In the previous section we noted that many borrowers, especially small firms, are dependent on the banking system as their principal or only source of credit to finance investment. If bank runs force some banks to close down and others to cut back on lending, bank-dependent borrowers will be unable to obtain credit, and investment spending will fall. The closing of banks during a banking panic also reduces the availability of other useful banking services, such as the transactions services provided by checking accounts.

3. *Increased riskiness of deposits.* In the absence of deposit insurance, deposits are not a safe asset but can be lost if a run or panic causes banks to fail. During the Depression, for example, many small depositors lost their savings or had their deposits "frozen" for an extended period as their bank went through bankruptcy proceedings.

Solutions to the Problem of Banking Instability

Given that banking panics are costly to the economy, what measures can be taken to eliminate them? We first discuss the central bank's role in controlling banking panics; then we turn to some alternative policy strategies for stabilizing the banking system.

The Central Bank as the Lender of Last Resort   Since the work of nineteenth-century British economists Henry Thornton and Walter Bagehot, economists have generally agreed that by acting as a lender of last resort, the central bank can do a great deal to reduce banking panics. As a **lender of last resort,** a central bank stands ready to supply funds to banks that need them to meet deposit withdrawals. The central bank provides these funds to banks as loans through the discount window (see Chapter 15), accepting some of the banks' commercial loans or other assets as collateral.

In the degree of financial instability experienced around the world, the year 1931 has no parallel. The world's economies and financial markets were already under extreme stress as the world depression entered its second year. The worst stage of the panic began following the unexpected collapse of the Creditanstalt, Austria's largest bank, in May 1931. An epidemic of bank runs spread to Germany, Eastern Europe, and countries as far away as South America and the Middle East. The United States also experienced severe bank runs. However, the banking systems of some countries, notably the United Kingdom and Canada, escaped serious problems.

An interesting question is why some nations' banking systems collapsed in 1931 and others survived. There are a number of explanations: Countries that had been on the losing side in World War I—Germany, Austria, and Hungary—were economically and financially unstable during the 1920s, leaving their banks in poor condition. Banking structure was also important: Countries with many small, poorly diversified banks (such as the United States and France) were more vulnerable to runs than countries with a few large, highly diversified banks (such as the United Kingdom and Canada). In certain types of banking systems, mainly in continental Europe, banks regularly held large amounts of corporate stock. These banks were severely weakened when world stock prices collapsed in 1929. Finally, banks that had large amounts of foreign deposits fared poorly, since the foreign deposits were quickly withdrawn from the bank at the first sign of trouble.

Banking panics apparently did serious damage to the economies in which they occurred. Ben Bernanke and Harold James of Princeton University* divided a sample of twenty-four countries into a group of eleven countries that experienced severe banking problems (Austria, Belgium, Estonia, France, Germany, Hungary, Italy, Latvia, Poland, Rumania, and the United States) and a group of thirteen that did not (Australia, Canada, Czechoslovakia, Denmark, Finland, Greece, Japan, the Netherlands, Norway, New Zealand, Sweden, Spain, and the United Kingdom). They showed that of the two groups the countries with the most severe banking problems went on to have greater declines in output and employment. For example, in 1932—the year following the financial crisis—the countries with banking panics experienced a 16% average decline in industrial production. In the same year the countries without panics experienced only a 2% average decline.

*"The Gold Standard, Deflation, and Financial Crisis in the Great Depression: An International Comparison," NBER working paper no. 3488, October 1990.

To see how a central bank functions as a lender of last resort, suppose that a bank called the Last National Bank has $1000 in deposits. Following the principles of fractional reserve banking, the Last keeps only $100 in the form of vault cash or deposits at the central bank. The other $900 of deposits has been lent to businesses on a long-term basis. There is no deposit insurance.

One day a rumor starts that the Last has made some bad investments, and half the depositors line up at the door to take out their money, $500 in all. What can the Last do? It only has $100 in reserves, and its loans cannot be paid back or sold to other banks on short notice. If no one helps the bank, it will have to close. However, the Last can borrow the additional $400 it needs from the central bank's discount window by giving the central bank some of its commercial loans as collateral. This loan from the lender of last resort allows the bank to pay off its depositors, which calms the panic. Eventually, deposits should come back into the bank and some of the Last's commercial loans will be repaid, allowing the Last to repay its loan from the central bank.

Historically, when central banks have acted as lenders of last resort (such as in Britain in the latter part of the nineteenth century), the frequency and severity of banking panics has been much moderated. One reason that U.S. banking panics in the 1930s were so severe and widespread was that the Fed apparently did not fully understand its responsibility to act as lender of last resort and did not act to help the banking system. The modern Fed, on the other hand, considers its lender-of-last-resort function to be very important: When the stock market crash of 1987 raised fears of a general financial crisis, for example, the Fed readily lent funds to banks.[16]

Although lender-of-last-resort activity can be very helpful in reducing panics, this approach runs into problems when many banks have made bad loans, so that the rumors that start panics turn out to be true. If the banks are in poor financial condition, the central bank runs the risk that many of the loans it makes to banks will not be repaid. There is an even greater potential problem with the lender-of-last-resort strategy: By standing ready to bail out banks that need additional funds, the central bank may encourage banks to take excessive risks in their lending, since the banks know in advance they will be helped out if things go wrong. For these reasons lender-of-last-resort activity is not by itself a complete solution to banking panics but should be supplemented by other policies.

Deposit Insurance   Government-backed deposit insurance significantly reduces the risk of bank runs by eliminating depositors' concerns that a bank failure will wipe out their accounts. With no fear for the safety of their deposits, depositors have no reason to run their bank even if they learn that the bank has made bad loans. The United States has had no significant runs on federally insured banks since the Federal Deposit Insurance Corporation (FDIC) began operating in 1934.

However, deposit insurance has problems of its own. A major drawback is that deposit insurance may lead banks to make riskier loans than they would otherwise: With no deposit insurance a bank following a strategy of making risky loans at high interest rates would also have to pay high interest rates to depositors, in order to compensate them for the significant risk that the bank will fail. In contrast, when deposit insurance is in force, depositors view their money as being equally safe in any insured bank, and the risk-taking bank can attract deposits at the same low rate that the most conservative bank must pay. Therefore the strategy of making risky loans becomes relatively more profitable—and more attractive to the bank—when there is deposit insurance.

Because deposit insurance relieves depositors of any incentive to monitor what their bank is doing with their deposits, and because it also may lead banks to make risky loans, deposit insurance creates a need for government supervision of bank-lending activities. To monitor bank lending, the U.S. government has combined two basic strategies.

The first strategy is to impose many regulations on the kinds of activities that banks can and cannot undertake. This regulatory approach has several drawbacks. One problem is that regulations can be a straitjacket that prevents banks from adapting in an economically beneficial way to a changing market environment. During the 1980s in particular, bankers complained repeatedly that regulatory limits prevented them from offering new financial services and entering profitable new lines of business. Another problem with regulation is that even if stringent rules

---

[16]For a discussion of Fed lender-of-last-resort activity in recent years, see Andrew Brimmer, "Central Banking and Systemic Risks in Capital Markets," *Journal of Economic Perspectives*, Spring 1989, pp. 3–16.

are applied, inevitably there are ways banks can satisfy the letter of the law and still make excessively risky financial investments.

The second basic strategy the government has used is to supervise bank-lending activities directly—for example, by regularly sending in bank examiners to go over each individual bank's loans. However, evaluating bank assets is a difficult and costly task, and in recent years there have not always been enough experienced examiners available to do a thorough job of supervision. Furthermore, even if an examiner finds that a bank is insolvent (its assets have lower value than its liabilities), there may be political or legal costs to shutting the bank down. Thus in practice, direct supervision has not always been effective either.

Some Alternatives for Reform Following the widely publicized savings and loan crisis (see Box 17.3, p. 708), and with the health of the banking system seeming more precarious, there has been increasing interest in reforming the deposit insurance system. We briefly discuss a few of the many specific proposals that have been suggested for reforming the deposit insurance system.

1. *Risk-based deposit insurance premiums.* Under this proposal banks with riskier loans and investments would be required to pay higher deposit insurance premiums, much as drivers with many speeding tickets have to pay higher auto insurance rates. Risk-based premiums would both penalize banks for greater risk taking and spread the costs of deposit insurance more fairly. An important weakness of this approach is that it assumes that the government can reliably measure the riskiness of bank portfolios. However, the inability of the government to evaluate bank riskiness accurately is in some sense the source of the whole problem.

2. *Risk-based capital standards.* **Bank capital** is the portion of a bank's assets that is financed by the bank's equity rather than by deposits or other forms of debt. Current regulations set a lower limit on the permitted ratio of bank capital to bank assets. Under a risk-based capital standard, banks with riskier portfolios would be required to have higher ratios of capital to assets. This policy would help reduce the risk of bank failure, since the bank remains solvent—that is, the value of its assets exceeds the value of its liabilities—as long as its capital is large enough to cover its losses on financial investments and loans. Like risk-based deposit insurance premiums, this approach also suffers from the problem that it is hard for the regulators to measure risk accurately. Nevertheless, under a recent international agreement (called the Basle Accord), by the end of 1992 U.S. banks will move part way toward a risk-based capital standard.

3. *Higher capital standards.* An alternative to risk-based capital standards would be to increase required capital-asset ratios for all banks. Higher capital requirements would induce banks to make less risky loans, since it would be shareholders' capital rather than the deposit insurance fund that would be at risk when the bank takes a gamble. Furthermore, with increased capital requirements more capital would be available to absorb any losses. A potential objection is that since equity investors typically demand a much higher return than depositors do, increased capital requirements would increase the overall cost of funds of U.S. banks and make it more difficult for them to compete internationally and with other types of lenders.

4. *Deposit coinsurance.* Under deposit coinsurance deposits would only be partly (say 90%) insured, or insured up to a much lower limit than the current level of $100,000. The purpose of deposit coinsurance would be to restore the incentive for depositors to keep an eye on bank lending, without completely eliminating

Savings and loan institutions (S&Ls) are financial intermediaries that concentrate on mortgage lending, financed by deposits. Like the deposits of banks, the deposits of S&Ls have been federally insured since 1934, when the Federal Savings and Loan Insurance Corporation (FSLIC) was established, along with the FDIC.

BOX 17.3:   THE SAVINGS AND LOAN CRISIS

During the 1980s there was a dramatic increase in the number of S&L failures (see Fig. 17.5, p. 702), as well as an overall decline in the S&Ls' share of the total assets of financial intermediaries (see Table 17.1, p. 690). For a time the seriousness of the financial problems of the S&L industry was not generally appreciated. Ultimately, though, it was revealed that the Federal government's obligation to pay off depositors of failing S&Ls—as required by deposit insurance—would amount to a tremendous sum, perhaps hundreds of billions of dollars. Although Federal insurance of S&L deposits achieved its goal of preventing runs on these institutions, it did so at the cost of creating a large financial liability for the Federal government and hence for the taxpayers.

How did this fiscal disaster come about? The initial problems of the S&Ls arose because of their practice of "lending long" (mortgages are long-term assets of S&Ls) and "borrowing short" (deposits can be withdrawn on short notice or without notice). During the 1960s and early 1970s, S&Ls made many long-term mortgage loans at the very low interest rates prevailing in those years (the mortgage rate was about 5½% in 1965, for example). When all market interest rates rose sharply in the late 1970s, S&Ls found that they were still locked into earning low interest rates on the mortgage loans they had made earlier, while at the same time they had to pay the high prevailing interest rates to attract depositors. The combination of high interest rates on S&L liabilities and low interest rates on S&L assets caused S&L profitability to fall sharply.

As the 1980s progressed, a number of other factors contributed to S&L insolvencies:

1. *Lack of diversification.* Largely because of regulatory restrictions, most S&L loans were for real estate projects within the institution's home state. This inability to diversify their assets made S&Ls very vulnerable to downturns in the local economy. For example, in oil-producing states such as Texas, Oklahoma, and Louisiana, the collapse of oil prices in the mid-1980s caused real estate prices to fall, which badly hurt S&Ls in those states.

2. *"Gambling" behavior.* When some S&Ls came to the point where it seemed sure they would become insolvent and be shut down, their owners adopted go-for-broke strategies of making very risky investments. These owners recognized that if the risky investments worked out, they would reap the benefits; but if the investments failed, the deposit insurance corporation and the taxpayers would take the loss.

3. *Deregulation and poor supervision.* The gambling strategies of S&L owners were made easier to carry out by governmental decisions that effectively lowered S&L capital requirements, greatly liberalized the rules about the types of investments S&Ls could make, raised deposit insurance from $40,000 to $100,000 per account, and made it easy for S&Ls to attract large out-of-state deposits. This deregulation of S&L activities was not accompanied by increased scrutiny from the government. On the contrary, because of accounting standards that did not reflect economic reality and also (it is alleged) because of interventions from legislators, many S&Ls that should have been closed down were allowed to continue operating.

The government's response to the S&L crisis was the Financial Institutions Reform, Recovery, and Enforcement Act (FIRREA) of 1989. This bill imposed tighter restrictions on S&L investments and increased capital requirements; created a new thrift regulator, the Office of Thrift Supervision; and created a new corporation, the Resolution Trust Corporation (RTC), to liquidate or otherwise dispose of failed S&Ls. The initial cash endowment of the RTC was $50 billion. However, it appears at this point that much more funding will be required to make good on the deposit insurance guarantee.

deposit insurance protection. A serious disadvantage of deposit coinsurance is that it would make it possible for bank runs to occur again. Supporters of the proposal argue that if the Fed performed its lender-of-last-resort role effectively, general banking panics would not occur.

5. *Required subordinated debt.* Under the required subordinated debt proposal banks would be required to finance a certain fraction of their lending by borrowing on capital markets. This debt would be subordinated in the sense that in the event that the bank fails, this debt would be repaid only after all depositors had been fully paid. Like deposit coinsurance, required subordinated debt is an attempt to create "market discipline" (as opposed to regulatory control) of banks, although under this proposal holders of the subordinated debt (rather than depositors) would have the incentive to monitor the bank. Critics of this proposal have expressed skepticism that financially weaker banks would be able to find willing buyers for the required amount of subordinated debt.

6. *More effective regulation.* Some people argue that with reform bank regulation can be made to work better. Specific suggestions for reform include (1) reorganization of the various agencies supervising the banks in order to clarify the division of regulatory responsibilities; (2) improvement of accounting procedures to reflect more accurately the true economic values of bank assets; and (3) increased powers for regulators to shut down banks that are in financial trouble but have not yet failed.

7. *Bank restructuring: the "narrow banking" idea.* An interesting suggestion for solving the problem of banking instability has been made by Robert Litan[17] of the Brookings Institution. Litan proposes that banks be broken into two separate businesses, a deposit-taking business (the "narrow bank") and a lending business. The deposit-taking business would have government deposit insurance but would be required to hold only completely safe assets (such as Treasury bills), thus eliminating the danger of excessive risk taking. Effectively, the deposit-taking business would adhere to 100% reserve banking (see Chapter 15). The lending business would make bank-type loans and would finance itself through private long-term debt and equity, not deposits. Thus its lending would be subject to market discipline. Litan's suggestion raises some hard questions: For example, would the central bank's lender-of-last-resort responsibilities extend to helping out a lending firm that was in trouble? But narrow banking may be an idea worth considering.

In summary, there are no easy or obvious solutions to the problem of banking instability. But as the costs of the savings and loan crisis become apparent, we can expect to see considerable experimentation and evolution in banking regulation in the years ahead.

Instability in the Stock Market

With bank runs a rare event in modern economies, the most dramatic remnant of the traditional financial crisis is a stock market crash, an abrupt decline in stock prices. On October 19, 1987, the Dow-Jones Industrial Average—a widely reported index of the stock market—fell 508 points, losing 23% of its total value (a record for a single day). Trading volume was about triple its normal level as panic hit Wall Street. Volatility of stock prices continued high for weeks following the crash.

---

[17]*What Should Banks Do?* Washington, D.C.: Brookings Institution, 1987.

Do large fluctuations in the stock market imply that there is something wrong with the way that market works? Ideally, stock prices should measure the true economic values of the companies whose ownership they represent. If stock prices do measure true economic values, then stock market volatility itself is not a problem but is simply a reflection of an underlying volatility in the economic fortunes of corporations. In this case the concern of policymakers should be directed at the question of why underlying economic values are fluctuating; blaming the stock market for stock price volatility would be like blaming a thermometer for changes in the weather. On the other hand, if the stock market fluctuates in a way that is disconnected from the underlying economic realities—and if these fluctuations affect people's economic decisions—then stock market volatility is indeed a problem, one that might be addressed by reforms of the market itself.

The first question to consider, therefore, is whether stock prices are somehow "disconnected" from true economic values. We begin by discussing a theory of the stock market, called the efficient markets theory, that says that stock prices *do* represent true economic values. We then consider some reasons why, contrary to the efficient markets theory, stock prices and underlying economic values might differ.

The Efficient Markets Theory According to the **efficient markets theory,** the price of a stock (or of any asset, for that matter) equals its **fundamental value,** or true economic value. According to this theory, stock prices equal fundamental values because of competition among sophisticated financial investors: If the price of a stock were lower than its fundamental value, for example, the stock would be perceived as a bargain by financial investors. Investors would rush to buy the stock, driving the price up to its fundamental value. Similarly, if the price of a stock were higher than its fundamental value, financial investors would sell the stock, forcing its price to fall.

The idea that asset prices must equal fundamental values does not imply that the expected returns on all assets are the same. Instead, expected returns may differ to reflect differences in risk and other characteristics (such as liquidity) of different assets. For example, stocks are generally riskier than bonds. To compensate financial investors who hold stocks for their greater risk, the expected nominal rate of return on stocks, i^s, will generally exceed the expected nominal rate of return on bonds, i^b. The relationship between the expected returns on stocks and bonds can be written as

$$i^s = i^b + \theta, \tag{17.2}$$

where θ is a risk premium reflecting the greater riskiness of stocks. In general, a **risk premium** is the difference in expected return between a risky asset and a safe asset.

Recall from Eq. (17.1) that the *actual* rate of return on a stock equals the dividend divided by the stock price, D/P_s, plus the percentage change in the price of the stock, $\Delta P_s/P_s$ (the capital gain or loss). The *expected* rate of return on a stock equals the dividend divided by the stock price plus the *expected* percentage change in the price of the stock. If we use the letter g to stand for investors' expectation of the risky capital gain or loss, $\Delta P_s/P_s$, we have

$$i^b + \theta = \frac{D}{P_s} + g. \tag{17.3}$$

The left side of Eq. (17.3) equals the expected rate of return on stock from Eq. (17.2), and the right side of Eq. (17.3) is the expectation of the rate of return on stock based on Eq. (17.1). Where does the expectation of the capital gain g come from? The efficient markets theory assumes that g is based on the rational expectation—or the best possible forecast using available information—of the long-term future growth rate of the dividends per share that the company will pay, which in turn depends on the future profitability of the company.[18] Because (according to the efficient markets theory) g depends only on best current estimates of the future economic value of the company, the expected return on the right side of Eq. (17.3) is tied only to fundamental values.

To find an expression for the price of the stock, subtract g from both sides of Eq. (17.3) to obtain

$$i^b + \theta - g = \frac{D}{P_s}.$$ (17.4)

Next, multiply both sides of Eq. (17.4) by P_s and divide both sides by $i^b + \theta - g$ to get

$$P_s = \frac{D}{i^b + \theta - g}.$$ (17.5)

Equation (17.5) tells us what the price of a stock will be under the efficient markets theory, which includes the assumption that investors have rational expectations about the rate of capital gains g. The stock price P_s depends on the current dividend, the interest rate on bonds, the risk premium, and the expected capital gain. As an example, suppose that the current dividend D is \$3 per share, the interest rate on bonds i^b is 0.06, the risk premium θ is 0.04, and the expected capital gain g is 0.05. Then the current price of a share of stock is \$3/(0.06 + 0.04 − 0.05) = \$3/0.05 = \$60.

The expression for the stock price in Eq. (17.5) is the fundamental value of a share of stock. Any changes in D, i^b, θ, or g will change the fundamental value and, under the efficient markets theory, will change the price of the stock accordingly. Suppose, for example, that news arrives that convinces stock market investors that the long-term rate of growth of dividends is going to be 6% per year rather than 5% per year. In this case $g = 0.06$, and from Eq. (17.5) the price of a share of stock under the efficient markets theory becomes \$3/(.04), or \$75, which is 25% higher than when $g = 0.05$! This example shows that even with efficient markets, relatively small changes in expectations about long-run dividend growth rates can cause large fluctuations in stock prices. Similarly, small changes in the interest rate i^b or the risk premium θ can cause the current price of a stock to change substantially.

Despite the fact that relatively small changes in g, i^b, and θ can cause large changes in the fundamental values of stocks, many economists remain skeptical that the efficient markets theory can explain events like the 23% drop in stock prices on October 19, 1987. They point out that there was no obvious piece of bad news that would have changed expectations on that day (or on the previous weekend), yet stock prices fell more than on days on which war was declared or Presidents were assassinated. This observation suggests that we should consider alternative explanations for the behavior of stock prices.

---

[18]The concept of rational expectations is discussed more fully in Chapter 11, Section 11.4.

Departures of Stock Prices from Fundamental Values: Bubbles and Fads Suppose that you are offered a share of stock for $100 and you know that the stock is fundamentally worthless—it will never pay a dividend. Could there be any reason for you to buy the stock? Yes, somewhat surprisingly, there is. If the expected rate of return on other stocks is 10%, you would be willing to buy the fundamentally worthless stock if you expected its price to rise by 10% per year, so that a year from now you could resell the stock for $110. By selling the stock one year from now for $110, you would earn a capital gain of 10% per year, the same rate of return that can be earned on other stocks. Why would anyone buy this stock from you? Another investor would be willing to buy the stock from you if she too thought that the stock's price would continue to rise at 10% per year, so that she can sell the stock later at an even higher price (say $121 two years from now) and also earn a rate of return of 10% per year. When the price of an asset is driven up beyond its fundamental value by the belief that it can be resold for an even higher price in the future, there is said to be a **bubble** in the price of the asset. The size of the bubble is the difference between the asset's price and its fundamental value.

Can a bubble occur if everyone understands that the fundamental value of the stock is zero—or must there be a sucker holding the bag at the end? It is theoretically possible to have a bubble, called a **rational bubble,** in which everyone has rational expectations about the fundamental value, but in which the belief that the price of the stock will rise indefinitely turns out to be self-confirming. A necessary condition for a rational bubble to exist is that the size of the bubble grow more slowly than the economy itself. Otherwise, the value of the bubble asset would eventually exceed the total wealth of the economy, and there would be no one who could afford to be the next buyer in the chain.[19]

In contrast to a rational bubble is an **irrational bubble,** in which some investors do not have rational expectations about the fundamental value of the stock. An irrational bubble corresponds to what some stock market participants call the "greater fools theory." That is, when there is an irrational bubble, even though one is a fool to buy an overvalued stock, there is always a greater fool to sell it to. For an irrational bubble, unlike a rational bubble, some investor must end up holding the bag, having paid a high price for a worthless asset that suddenly no one is willing to buy.

An irrational bubble is an example of a situation in which the price of a stock differs from its fundamental value because of a failure of rational expectations. There are any number of other ways in which, in theory, the failure of financial investors to have rational expectations could cause stock prices to differ from fundamental values. For example, some economists believe that investors overreact to news about events that affect fundamental values, with the result that stock prices rise too much in response to good news and fall too much in response to bad news. Temporary deviations of stock prices from fundamental values due to waves of investor optimism or pessimism are called **fads.**

Whether bubbles and fads are important empirically is quite controversial. Many recent studies have claimed to find important departures from the efficient markets theory. For example, one important line of research examining the efficient markets theory focuses on the volatility of stock prices. Simple versions of

---

[19]The condition for the existence of a rational bubble is very similar to the condition for permanent rollover of the government debt, discussed in Chapter 16. The fundamental logic is essentially the same in the two cases.

the efficient markets theory imply that the volatility of stock prices is determined by the volatility of dividends. Tests by Robert J. Shiller[20] of Yale University find that, given the observed volatility of dividends, stock prices are too volatile to be consistent with the efficient markets theory. Unfortunately, subtle but important statistical issues cloud the interpretation of Shiller's tests. In addition, more sophisticated versions of the efficient markets theory predict more volatility of stock prices than is predicted by the simple versions that Shiller tested. Thus the question of whether stock prices are more volatile than fundamental values is still open to debate.[21]

The Costs of Departures of Stock Prices from Fundamentals As we have said, there is considerable controversy about whether or not stock prices reflect only fundamental values. If, in fact, stock prices depart from fundamental values—for example, if the volatility of stock prices exceeds the volatility of fundamentals—what are the potential costs for the economy?

First, if stock prices were not determined by fundamental values, then the stock market would not be able to perform its basic financial functions (described in Section 17.1) as effectively as we would like. For example, if stock prices did not reflect fundamentals, then the stock market would not necessarily allocate savings to the best possible capital projects. Similarly, excessive volatility of stock prices would limit the usefulness of the stock market for diversification and risk sharing and might also reduce liquidity, if high volatility scared away potential market participants and decreased trading activity. Conceivably, if stock prices were to deviate from fundamentals, the costs arising from the impairment of the stock market's basic functions might be quite large. Unfortunately, measuring these costs is probably impossible, since doing so would require us to determine how well the stock market would perform its basic functions if stock prices *did* equal fundamentals—a task that is well beyond what can reasonably be expected from empirical research.

The second potential cost is that excessive volatility in the stock market might lead to excessive volatility in the real economy. Suppose, for example, that stock prices rose solely because of a bubble or a fad. Then consumers, made to feel wealthier by the increase in stock values, might choose to consume more even though extra consumption is not justified by fundamental conditions. When the bubble "bursts" and stock prices fell sharply, consumption spending might also abruptly fall. Similarly, if a bubble or fad allowed firms to get an artificially high price for their shares, firms might issue stock and use the proceeds to invest at a rapid rate. Again the collapse of the bubble would lead to a fall in spending, in this case investment spending. By affecting consumption and investment spending, bubbles and fads in the stock market might induce an artificial and unnecessary cycle in real economic activity.

Just as it is hard to measure the costs resulting from the impairment of the financial market functions, it is also difficult to measure the costs of economic vol-

---

[20]"Do Stock Prices Move Too Much to Be Justified by Subsequent Changes in Dividends?" *American Economic Review*, June 1981, pp. 421–436. A more comprehensive work is Robert J. Shiller, *Market Volatility*, Cambridge, Mass.: M.I.T. Press, 1989.

[21]A review and critique of this literature can be found in John H. Cochrane, "Volatility Tests and Efficient Markets: A Review Essay," *Journal of Monetary Economics*, June 1991, pp. 463–486. See also Stephen F. LeRoy, "Efficient Capital Markets and Martingales," *Journal of Economic Literature*, December 1989, pp. 1583–1621. These articles, like all those written in this area, are highly technical.

atility induced by the stock market. However, there are some reasons to think that such costs, if they exist, would not be very large. Empirical evidence suggests that consumers and investors don't pay too much attention to short-run fluctuations in the stock market but tend to concentrate on longer-term trends. Furthermore, large stock market swings have not by any means always been accompanied by fluctuations in the real economy. For example, the 1987 stock market run-up and crash did not coincide with any major fluctuations in real economic activity.

One stock market crash that *is* associated with a large movement in real output is the famous October 1929 crash, which was followed by the Great Depression. In many people's minds the 1929 crash and the Depression are almost synonymous. However, most economic research has concluded that the 1929 crash was not a principal cause of the Depression. One basis for this conclusion is that the initial decline in the economy occurred two months before the crash (indeed, the realization that the turndown had occurred may have contributed to the crash). Also, the most severe phase of the Depression did not begin until the second half of 1931, almost two years after the crash.[22]

Policies to Reduce Stock Market Instability   If the stock market is in fact excessively volatile and potentially unstable, is there anything that government policy can do to reduce this problem? Here are a few suggestions that have been made:

1. *Raise margin requirements*. Stock traders can purchase stocks partly on credit by borrowing from brokers who, in turn, usually borrow from banks. The **margin requirement,** which is set by the Federal Reserve, is the minimum fraction of the purchase price of stock paid for by the financial investor's own (nonborrowed) funds. Because buying stocks on margin yields bigger returns if the stock price rises and bigger losses if the price falls, some people have argued that margin investors are mostly risk-loving speculators. Therefore, the argument runs, raising margin requirements should eliminate some of these speculators from the market and reduce volatility.

It is possible that raising margins might be beneficial, but there are some arguments on the other side. Higher margin requirements might reduce trading activity, thereby decreasing market liquidity. Also, although margin requirements have varied historically, there is no clear evidence that the stock market was less volatile during periods with high margin requirements.

2. *Institute trading halts*. Under a trading halt rule the stock market would automatically close for a time if conditions became chaotic. Some trading halt proposals would have markets close if prices fell by a prespecified amount (say 200 points on the Dow-Jones Industrial Average). Other proposals would call a halt if trading volume got too high. Halts based on trading volume would have the benefit of reducing the confusion that occurs when high volume overloads the market's accounting systems, as occurred during the October 1987 crash. It is less clear why halts based on price declines would be helpful: One possibility is that a halt would give potential buyers of stocks time to get organized and into the market. On the

---

[22]For a detailed discussion of the links between the stock market crash and the Depression, see George P. Green, "The Economic Impact of the Stock Market Boom and Crash of 1929," in Federal Reserve Bank of Boston, *Consumer Spending and Monetary Policy: The Linkages*, 1971. An argument that the crash did contribute to the Depression, by increasing consumer and investor uncertainty, is made in Christina Romer, "The Great Crash and the Onset of the Great Depression," *Quarterly Journal of Economics*, August 1990, pp. 597–624.

other hand, opponents argue that trading halts based on price declines would only tend to create panic.

3. *Eliminate computer-based trading.* Various forms of computer-executed stock trading, or "program trading," came under fire for possibly contributing to the 1987 crash. Particularly criticized were some programs that automatically issued large sell orders each time stock prices fell. In response to this criticism, some Wall Street firms announced that they would stop using program trading.

Despite the bad press received by computer-based trading, there is not much clear evidence linking it to stock price volatility. For example, other stock markets around the world, most of which have no computer-based trading at all, were just as volatile as the U.S. market during October 1987. A possible alternative to outlawing computer trading would be to develop special rules for handling the very large buy and sell orders computer programs sometimes generate.

4. *Levy transactions taxes.* Some have suggested that if there were more "buy-and-hold" traders and fewer traders who are "churning" (constantly buying and selling), bubbles and fads would have a harder time getting started. One way to reduce churning would be to levy a tax on each stock market transaction. If the tax were high enough, churning would become an unattractive strategy.

If stock market volatility is caused by churning traders, a tax could conceivably increase stock market stability. A cost is that as trading volume fell, stocks would become less liquid assets. Another problem is that if the United States levied such a tax on its own, U.S. stock markets might lose much of their business to markets in other countries.

Generally, there remains much disagreement about whether the stock market is excessively volatile. And among people who think that there is excess volatility, there is disagreement about the causes of the excess volatility and about appropriate solutions to the problem. From the perspective of macroeconomics, it may be fortunate that the macroeconomic costs of stock market instability seem to be less than the costs of banking instability.

17.4 CHAPTER SUMMARY

1. The four main economic functions of the financial system are to allow consumption smoothing, to allocate savings to the most productive forms of capital investment, to help people share risks, and to provide liquidity.

2. The two principal types of financial assets, or financial instruments, used in borrowing and lending are debt and equity. Debt is the promise of a borrower to make a series of repayments over time. Equity gives the holder a share of ownership of the firm that issued the equity.

3. There are many different types of financial markets and market participants. Important market participants are financial institutions called financial intermediaries. Intermediaries stand between ultimate lenders and ultimate borrowers, using funds borrowed from savers to purchase the debt and equity of firms and others who need funds in order to consume or invest.

4. There is asymmetric information in the market for saving and investment when borrowers have better information than savers about how they plan to use their borrowed funds. Because of asymmetric information, savers may have a hard time assessing the creditworthiness of potential borrowers. Financial intermediaries and other financial market institutions help to reduce the problems caused by asymmetric information. For example, because banks and similar intermediaries

specialize in the information-gathering activities needed to evaluate potential loans, they can gather and analyze information more cheaply than individual savers can. By lending to the banking system, savers can earn a return net of information costs that is higher than the return from making loans directly to ultimate borrowers.

5. For many potential borrowers, especially small businesses, banks are the only source of outside funds for investment. Any factor that reduces the ability of banks to lend will reduce the amount of credit available to potential borrowers and effectively lower desired investment. Examples of factors reducing the ability of banks to lend are credit controls, banking panics, and disintermediation (withdrawals by depositors in order to invest directly in securities such as Treasury bills).

6. If the demand for loans by qualified borrowers exceeds the supply of credit that banks have available, banks may ration credit rather than increase the interest rate charged on loans. Raising the interest rate on loans in response to an excess demand for loans may not be profitable for the bank if it drives away the potential borrowers who are most likely to repay their loans.

7. Because asymmetric information raises the cost of borrowing from outsiders, firms prefer to finance their capital investment from their own internal funds. As a result, the availability of internal funds as well as the real interest rate will affect firms' willingness to invest. A dependence of investment on internal funds may worsen the severity of recessions and is also a reason that the Ricardian equivalence proposition may not hold.

8. A financial panic is a period of violent fluctuations in financial markets, usually including a stock market crash, runs on banks, and bankruptcies of major firms. Financial panics occurred in the nineteenth century but were most severe in the Great Depression. Much of the regulation of financial markets, and even the existence of the Federal Reserve itself, arose from the desire of policymakers to eliminate panics.

9. Bank runs are possible because of the combination of deposits that can be withdrawn at any time and fractional reserves. The costs to the economy of bank runs include the resulting drop in the money supply, the curtailment of bank lending and other bank services, and the increased riskiness of deposits.

10. By acting as a lender of last resort (that is, by lending cash to banks that are experiencing a run), the central bank can reduce the problem of runs. Deposit insurance prevents bank runs by assuring depositors that their deposits are safe even if the bank fails. However, the deposit insurance system may encourage excessive risk taking by banks and has imposed heavy fiscal costs in recent years (as in the S&L bailout), bringing forth many suggestions for reform.

11. There is disagreement about whether fluctuations in the stock market are "excessive" relative to changes in the underlying economic value of stocks. The efficient markets theory says that stock prices equal their fundamental values, so that fluctuations are not excessive. Alternative theories argue that because of phenomena such as bubbles and fads, stock prices can deviate from fundamental values and volatility in the stock market may be excessive.

12. If stock prices deviate from fundamental values and stock market volatility is excessive, the potential costs include less satisfactory performance of the basic functions of financial markets and increased macroeconomic instability.

13. Suggested reforms of the stock market include higher margin requirements, trading halts, reduced computer-based trading, and transactions taxes. At this point all of these suggestions remain controversial.

Key Terms

asymmetric information, p. 693

auction markets, p. 689

bank capital, p. 707

banking panic, p. 703

bubble, p. 712

capital markets, p. 689

credit controls, p. 696

credit crunch, p. 698

credit market, p. 692

credit rationing, p. 694

debt, p. 688

derivative securities, p. 689

disintermediation, p. 698

diversification, p. 686

dividends, p. 688

efficient markets theory, p. 710

equity, p. 688

external funds, p. 700

fads, p. 712

financial futures markets, p. 689

financial intermediaries, p. 690

financial panic, p. 701

fundamental value, p. 710

hedgers, p. 686

internal funds, p. 700

irrational bubble, p. 712

lender of last resort, p. 704

margin requirement, p. 714

money markets, p. 689

options markets, p. 689

over-the-counter markets, p. 689

primary markets, p. 689

rational bubble, p. 712

risk premium, p. 710

secondary markets, p. 689

speculators, p. 686

spot markets, p. 689

Key Equations

$$i^s = \frac{D + \Delta P_s}{P_s} \qquad (17.1)$$

The total nominal return on equity, or stocks, has two components: the nominal dividend D and the change in price (the capital gain or loss), ΔP_s. The nominal rate of return on equity i^s equals the total nominal return $D + \Delta P_s$ divided by the price of a share of stock P_s.

$$i^s = i^b + \theta \qquad (17.2)$$

As a compensation to financial investors for the greater riskiness of stocks, the expected return on stocks is generally higher than the expected return on bonds. The risk premium on stocks θ is the amount by which the expected nominal rate of return on stocks i^s exceeds the expected nominal rate of return on bonds i^b.

$$P_s = \frac{D}{i^b + \theta - g} \qquad (17.5)$$

According to the efficient markets theory, the stock price P_s equals the stock's fundamental value. The fundamental value of a share of stock (given by the right side of the equation) depends on the dividend D, the nominal interest rate on bonds i^b, the risk premium θ, and the expected rate of capital gain g (also equal to the rational expectation of the long-term growth rate of dividends).

Review Questions

1. List the four principal economic functions of financial markets. In each case, give an example of a financial market or institution that performs that function.

2. Define *financial intermediary*. How does the existence of financial intermediaries benefit both ultimate lenders and ultimate borrowers?

3. What is *asymmetric information*? How do banks help overcome the existence of asymmetric information in the market for saving and investment? Why does the existence of asymmetric information imply that a firm typically would rather finance a capital investment from its own profits instead of issuing debt or equity?

4. When banks are faced with an excess demand for loans by potential borrowers, why might they not increase the interest rate charged on loans?

5. What features of banking make bank runs possible? What costs do bank runs impose on the economy?

6. Explain and briefly evaluate each of the following proposed solutions to the bank run problem:
    a. Lender-of-last-resort activity
    b. Deposit insurance
    c. Risk-based capital standards
    d. Narrow banking

7. What is the *efficient markets theory?* If the efficient markets theory is true, are stock price fluctuations a problem for the economy?

8. Suppose that it is true that stock prices fluctuate excessively relative to fundamental economic values. What costs would this excessive stock price volatility impose on the economy? What policy actions to reduce stock price volatility have been proposed?

Numerical Problems

1. Suppose that you and I agree that you will buy 100 bushels of wheat from me one month from now at a price of p per bushel. The price p is called the futures price and is set today. Today's market price of wheat is $6.00 per bushel. With 50% probability the market price of wheat will be the same in one month as it is today, with 10% probability it will drop to $5.00 and with 40% probability it will rise to $7.00.
    a. You don't care about risk at all. You only care about whether on average you can expect to make a profit on this transaction. What is the maximum futures price p on which you would agree today?
    b. Suppose that you are required to put up sufficient funds today to guarantee that you will be financially able to honor your futures contract one month from now, no matter which of the three possible market prices occurs. How much money (called margin, in futures markets) should you be required to put up?
    c. Suppose that your margin requirement is fixed at the value determined in part b, and assume that no interest is paid on funds deposited on margin. To make the whole transaction worthwhile, you think you ought to earn at least 1% return over the next month on the funds you have committed. What futures price p would give you on average a 1% return on these funds? Why might I (the seller) be willing to agree to this price?
    d. Assume, as in part a, that you don't care about risk, only average expected profits. The interest rate is zero. What is the smallest amount of money you would take today to give me the option to sell you my 100 bushels of wheat for $6.00 per bushel one month from now? Assume that there is no margin requirement.

2. A bank has 100 potential borrowers, each of whom wants to borrow $10,000, and the bank has precisely $1,000,000 to lend. The bank knows the following: Ten of the borrowers are "hares," who want to use the $10,000 to make an investment that one year from now

will be worth a total of $20,000 with 50% probability and will be worthless with 50% probability. (Think of the hares' investment as gambling on a coin flip.) The other 90 borrowers are "tortoises," who want to make investments that one year from now will be worth $12,000 for sure. However, the bank can't tell which individual borrowers are hares and which are tortoises. It loans money to any potential borrower who requests it.
    a. If there is no place to borrow besides the bank, what is the highest interest rate a hare will be willing to pay? (Assume that if the hare's investment doesn't work out, he repays nothing to the bank.) What rate will a tortoise be willing to pay?
    b. How many loans will the bank make, and what will be its total profits if it charges an interest rate of 10%? 20%? 50%? 100%? 150%?
    c. What interest rate maximizes the bank's profits? (Assume that funds not lent out earn zero interest.)
    d. Suppose that the number of potential borrowers triples to 300, each of whom wants to borrow $10,000. The fraction of borrowers who are hares and tortoises is unchanged. The bank still has only $1,000,000 to lend. How should the bank respond to this increase in the demand for loans?

3. A bank can use its deposits to invest in either a risky project or a safe project (assume that investing in either requires $1,000,000). The risky project pays a 100% return with 50% probability, and with 50% probability the risky project becomes worthless (a -100% return). If the risky project becomes worthless, the bank fails and pays nothing to depositors. The safe project pays a 10% return for sure. Depositors can observe whether the bank is investing in the risky project or the safe project. Depositors don't care about risk, but on average they want to earn a 5% return on their deposits.
    a. Suppose there is no deposit insurance. If the bank invests in the risky project and therefore fails with 50% probability, what interest rate would it have to offer depositors (to be paid only if the

bank doesn't fail) to get them to lend their funds to the bank? Would the bank be willing to pay this interest rate to obtain funds to invest in the risky project?

b. If the bank invests in the safe project, what interest rate does it have to offer depositors? Would the bank be willing to pay this interest rate to obtain funds to invest in the safe project?

c. Now suppose that there is deposit insurance that guarantees depositors their full deposits plus promised interest if the bank fails. What interest rate will the bank have to offer depositors if it undertakes the risky project? If it undertakes the safe project? On average, which project yields the highest profit for the bank?

4. The current nominal yearly dividend on a stock is $4 per share, the nominal dividend and the price of the stock are both expected to grow at the rate of 6% per year, and the nominal interest rate on bonds is 8% per year.

a. If the risk premium on stocks relative to bonds is 2% per year, what is the price of a share of stock under the efficient markets theory?

b. Suppose that financial investors perceive that stocks have become relatively more risky, and as a result, the risk premium on stocks relative to bonds increases to 3% per year. By how much does the stock price change in response to the change in perceived riskiness?

c. Now suppose that the expected rate of inflation increases by three percentage points (say from 4% per year to 7% per year). If the risk premium is 2% per year, as in part a, what is the price of a share of stock? Assume that the real interest rate on bonds, the expected real rate of growth of dividends, and the current nominal dividend are unchanged. (*Hint:* What does an increase in expected inflation do to the nominal interest rate on bonds and the expected nominal growth rate of dividends?)

Analytical Problems

1. A share of IBM stock is a more liquid asset than a townhouse in San Francisco. Explain this difference in terms of the characteristics of the markets in which these two assets trade. How do you think the liquidity of these two assets has changed over time?

2. Suppose that banks are the only source of funds for consumer loans and that credit controls force banks to cut their consumer lending. How would this reduction in lending affect the *IS* curve and the economy in (a) the basic classical model, (b) the extended classical model with misperceptions, and (c) the Keynesian model? Consider both the short run and the long run. (*Hint:* What is the effect of reduced consumer lending on desired consumption and desired national saving?)

3. In this problem you are asked to show that the price of stock in Eq. (17.5) equals the present value of expected future dividends. (Present values are defined in Chapter 5.)

a. Suppose that the stock has just paid its annual dividend, so that the next dividend will be received one year from now. The dividend that will be paid one year from now equals *D*. The dividend is expected to grow at a rate *g* per year forever. (So, for example, $g = 0.10$ implies that the dividend will grow 10% per year.) Write an expression for the value of the dividend one year from now,

two years from now, and three years from now, in terms of *D* and *g*.

b. The interest rate used in finding the present values of future dividend payments is constant forever and equal to i^s, the nominal rate of return on stocks. In terms of *D*, *g*, and i^s, what is the present value of the dividend to be paid one year from now? Two years from now? Three years from now?

c. The geometric expansion formula says that for any number *x* such that $0 < x < 1$, the following is true:

$$1 + x + x^2 + x^3 + \cdots = \frac{1}{1-x}.$$

Using the formula, find an expression for the present value as of today of all future dividends (starting with the dividend to be paid one year from today). Using the fact that $i^s = i^b + \theta$, show that the expression for the fundamental value of a stock given in Eq. (17.5) is the same as the present value of future dividends.

4. Discuss how the stock market crash of October 1987 might be explained by believers in the following:

a. The efficient markets theory

b. Bubbles

c. Fads

Appendix A:
Some Useful
Analytical Tools

This appendix reviews some basic algebraic and graphical tools that are used in this book.

A.1 FUNCTIONS AND GRAPHS

A *function* is a relationship among two or more variables. For an economic illustration of a function, suppose that in a certain firm each worker that is employed can produce five units of output per day. Let

N = the number of workers employed by the firm,
Y = the total daily output of the firm.

In this example the relationship of output Y to the number of workers N is

$$Y = 5N. \qquad \text{(A.1)}$$

Equation (A.1) is an example of a function relating the variable Y to the variable N. Using this function, for any given number of workers N we can calculate the total amount of output Y that the firm can produce each day. For example, if $N = 3$, then $Y = 15$.

Functions can be described graphically as well as algebraically. The graph of the function $Y = 5N$, for values of N between 0 and 16, is shown in Fig. A.1. Output Y is shown on the vertical axis of the diagram, and the number of workers N is shown on the horizontal axis. Points on the line $0AB$ in Fig. A.1 satisfy Eq. (A.1). For example, at point A, $N = 4$ and $Y = 20$, a combination of N and Y that satisfies Eq. (A.1). Similarly, at point B in Fig. A.1, $N = 12.5$

and $Y = 62.5$, which also satisfies the relationship $Y = 5N$. Notice that (at point B, for example) the relationship between Y and N allows the variables to have values that are not whole numbers. Allowing fractional values of N and Y is economically reasonable, since workers can work part-time or overtime, and a unit of output may be only partially completed during a day.

Functions like $Y = 5N$ whose graph is a straight line are called *linear functions*. Functions whose

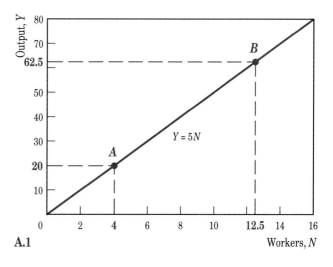

A.1

Points on the line $0AB$ satisfy the relationship $Y = 5N$. Because the graph of the function $Y = 5N$ is a straight line, this function is called a linear function.

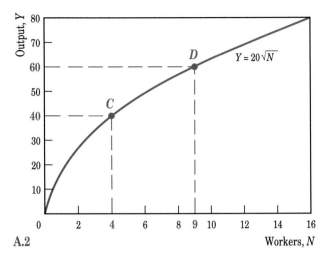

A.2

The function $Y = 20\sqrt{N}$, whose graph is shown in this figure, is an example of a nonlinear function.

graph is not a line are called *nonlinear*. An example of a nonlinear function is

$$Y = 20\sqrt{N}. \quad (A.2)$$

The graph of the nonlinear function $Y = 20\sqrt{N}$ is shown in Fig. A.2. All points on the curve in Fig. A.2 satisfy Eq. (A.2). For example, at point C in the figure, $N = 4$ and $Y = 20\sqrt{4} = 40$. At point D, $N = 9$ and $Y = 20\sqrt{9} = 60$.

Both examples of functions given so far are exact numerical relationships. We can also write functions in more general terms, using letters or symbols. For example, we might write

$$Y = G(N). \quad (A.3)$$

Equation (A.3) says that there is some general relationship between the number of workers N and the amount of output Y, which is represented by a function G. The numerical functions given in Eqs. (A.1) and (A.2) are specific examples of such a general relationship.

A.2 SLOPES OF FUNCTIONS

Suppose that two variables N and Y are related by a function $Y = G(N)$. Loosely speaking, if we start from some given combination of N and Y that satisfies the function G, the *slope* of the function G at that point tells us by how much Y changes when N changes by one unit.

To define the slope more precisely, we suppose that the current value of N is a specific number N_1, so that the current value of Y equals $G(N_1)$. Now consider what happens if N_1 is increased by an amount ΔN (ΔN is read "the change in N"). Output Y depends on N; therefore if N changes, Y must also change. Since the value of N is now $N_1 + \Delta N$, the value of Y after N increases is $G(N_1 + \Delta N)$. The *change* in Y, ΔY, is given by

$$\Delta Y = G(N_1 + \Delta N) - G(N_1).$$

The slope of the function G, for an increase in N from N_1 to $N_1 + \Delta N$, is defined by

$$\text{slope} = \frac{\Delta Y}{\Delta N} = \frac{G(N_1 + \Delta N) - G(N_1)}{(N_1 + \Delta N) - N_1}. \quad (A.4)$$

Note that if $\Delta N = 1$, then the slope equals ΔY, the change in Y.

Figures A.3 and A.4 show graphically how to determine slopes for the two functions discussed in the previous section. Figure A.3 shows the graph of the function $Y = 5N$ (as in Fig. A.1). Suppose that we start from point E in Fig. A.3, where $N = 6$ and $Y = 30$. If N is increased by 4 (for example), then

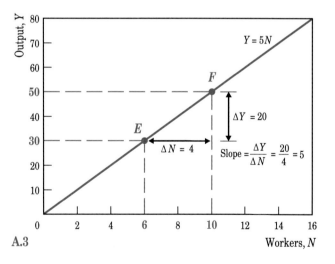

A.3

The slope of a function equals the change in the variable on the vertical axis (Y) divided by the change in the variable on the horizontal axis (N). For example, between point E and point F the increase in N, ΔN, equals 4 and the increase in Y, ΔY, equals 20. Therefore the slope of the function between points E and F, $\Delta Y/\Delta N$, equals 5. In general, the slope of a linear function is constant, so the slope of this function between any two points equals 5.

Between points G and D the change in N (ΔN) is 8 and the change in Y (ΔY) is 40, so the slope of the function between points G and D is $\Delta Y/\Delta N = 40/8 = 5$. This slope is the same as the slope of the line GD. Similarly, the slope of the function between points G and C is $\Delta Y/\Delta N = 20/3 = 6.67$. The slope of the line tangent to point G, which equals 10, approximates the slope of the function for very small changes in N. Generally, when we refer to the slope of a nonlinear function at a specific point, we mean the slope of the line tangent to the function at that point.

A.4

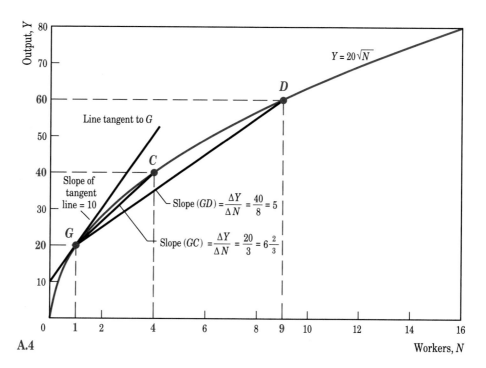

we move to point F on the graph, where $N = 10$ and $Y = 50$. Between points E and F, $\Delta N = 10 - 6 = 4$ and $\Delta Y = 50 - 30 = 20$, so the slope is $\Delta Y/\Delta N = 20/4 = 5$.

In general, the slope of a linear function is the same at all points. You can prove this result for the linear function $Y = 5N$ by showing that for any change ΔN, $\Delta Y = 5\Delta N$. So for this particular linear function, the slope $\Delta Y/\Delta N$ always equals 5, a constant number.

For a nonlinear function, like $Y = 20\sqrt{N}$, the slope is not constant but depends on both the initial value of N and the size of the change in N. These results are illustrated in Fig. A.4, which displays the graph of the function $Y = 20\sqrt{N}$ (as in Fig. A.2). Suppose that we are initially at point G in the figure, where $N = 1$ and $Y = 20$, and we increase N by 8 units. After the increase in N we are at point D, where $N = 9$ and $Y = 20\sqrt{9} = 60$. Between points G and D, $\Delta N = 9 - 1 = 8$ and $\Delta Y = 60 - 20 = 40$. Thus the slope of the function between points G and D is 40/8 = 5. Geometrically, the slope of the function between points G and D equals the slope of the straight line between G and D.

Starting once again from point G in Fig. A.4, if we instead increase N by 3 units, we come to point C, where $N = 4$ and $Y = 20\sqrt{4} = 40$. In this case

$\Delta N = 3$ and $\Delta Y = 40 - 20 = 20$, so the slope between points G and C is 20/3 = 6.67, which is not the same as the slope of 5 that we calculated when earlier we increased N by 8 units. Geometrically, you can see in Fig. A.4 that the slope of the line between points G and C is greater than the slope of the line between points G and D; that is, line GC is steeper than line GD.

In Fig. A.4 we have also drawn a line that touches but does not cross the graph of the function at point G; this line is said to be *tangent* to the graph of the function at point G. If you start from point G and find the slope of the function for different values of ΔN, you will discover that the smaller the value of ΔN is, the closer the slope will be to the slope of the tangent line. For example, if you compare the slope of the line GD (for which $\Delta N = 8$) with the slope of the line GC (for which $\Delta N = 3$) in Fig. A.4, you will see that of the two the slope of the line GC is closer to the slope of the line tangent to point G. For values of ΔN even smaller than 3, the slope would be still closer to the slope of the tangent line.

These observations lead to an important result: *For small values of ΔN the slope of a function at any point is closely approximated by the slope of the line tangent to the function at that point.* Unless specified otherwise, in this book when we refer to the slope of a nonlinear function, we mean the slope of the line tangent to the function at the specified point. Thus in Fig. A.4 the slope of the function at point G means the slope of the line tangent to the function at point G, which happens to equal 10.[1]

The numerical example illustrated in Fig. A.4 shows that the slope of a nonlinear function depends on the size of the increase in N being considered. The slope of a nonlinear function also depends on the point at which the slope is being measured. In Fig. A.4 you can see that the slope of a line drawn tangent to point D, for example, would be less than the slope of a line drawn tangent to point G. Thus the slope of this particular function (measured with respect to small changes in N) is greater at point G than at point D.

A.3 ELASTICITIES

Like slopes, elasticities provide a way of expressing how much one variable responds when a second variable changes. Suppose again that there is a function relating Y to N, so that when N changes, Y changes as well. The *elasticity* of Y with respect to N is defined to be the percentage change in Y, $\Delta Y/Y$, divided by the percentage change in N, $\Delta N/N$. Writing the formula, we have

$$\text{elasticity of } Y \text{ with respect to } N = \frac{\Delta Y/Y}{\Delta N/N}.$$

Since the slope of a function is $\Delta Y/\Delta N$, the elasticity of Y with respect to N can also be written as the slope times (N/Y).

If the elasticity of Y with respect to N is large, than a 1% change in N causes a large percentage change in Y. Thus a large elasticity of Y with respect to N means that Y is very sensitive to changes in N.

A.4 FUNCTIONS OF SEVERAL VARIABLES

A function can relate more than two variables. To continue the economic illustration of Section A.1, suppose that the firm's daily output Y depends on both the number of workers N the firm employs and

the number of machines (equivalently, the amount of capital) K the firm owns. As a specific example, the function relating Y to K and N might be

$$Y = 2\sqrt{K}\sqrt{N}. \qquad (A.5)$$

So, for example, if there are 100 machines and 9 workers, by substituting $K = 100$ and $N = 9$ into Eq. (A.5), we get the output Y: $Y = 2\sqrt{100}\sqrt{9} = 2 \times 10 \times 3 = 60$.

A function of several variables can also be written in general terms by using symbols or letters. A general way to write the relationship between output Y and the two inputs, capital K and labor N, is

$$Y = F(K, N).$$

This equation is a slight simplification of a relationship called the production function, which is introduced in Chapter 3.

The graph of a function relating three variables requires three dimensions. As a convenient way to graph such a function on a two-dimensional page, we hold one of the right-side variables constant. In order to graph the function in Eq. (A.5), for example, we might hold the number of machines K constant at a value of 100. If we substitute 100 for K, Eq. (A.5) becomes

$$Y = 2\sqrt{100}\sqrt{N} = 20\sqrt{N}. \qquad (A.6)$$

With K held constant at 100, Eq. (A.6) is identical to Eq. (A.2). Like Eq. (A.2), Eq. (A.6) is a relationship between Y and N only and thus can be graphed in two dimensions. The graph of Eq. (A.6), shown as the solid curve in Fig. A.5, is identical to the graph of Eq. (A.2) in Fig. A.2.

A.5 SHIFTS OF A CURVE

Suppose that the relationship of output Y to machines K and workers N is given by Eq. (A.5) and we hold K constant and equal to 100. As we saw in Section A.4, with K held constant at 100, Eq. (A.5) reduces to Eq. (A.6), and the solid curve in Fig. A.5 shows the relationship between workers N and output Y. At point C in Fig. A.5, for example, $N = 4$ and $Y = 20\sqrt{4} = 40$. At point D, where $N = 9$, $Y = 20\sqrt{9} = 60$.

Now suppose that the firm purchases additional machines, raising the number of machines K from 100 to 225. If we substitute this new value for K, Eq.

---

[1]Showing that the slope of the line tangent to point G equals 10 requires basic calculus. The derivative of the function $Y = 20\sqrt{N}$, which is the same as the slope, is $dY/dN = 10/\sqrt{N}$. Evaluating this derivative at $N = 1$ yields a slope of 10.

Suppose that output Y depends on capital K and workers N, according to the function in Eq. (A.5). If we hold K fixed at 100, the relationship between Y and N is shown by the solid curve. If K rises to 225, so that more output can be produced with a given number of workers, the curve showing the relationship between Y and N shifts upward, from the solid curve to the dashed curve. In general, a change in any right-side variable that does not appear on an axis of the graph causes the curve to shift.

A.5

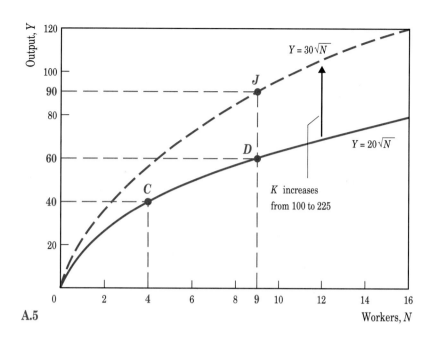

M

(A.5) becomes

$$Y = 2 \sqrt{225} \sqrt{N} = 30 \sqrt{N}. \qquad \text{(A.7)}$$

Equation (A.7) is shown graphically as the dashed curve in Fig. A.5. Notice that the increase in K has shifted the curve upward. Because of the increase in the number of machines, the amount of daily output Y that can be produced for any given number of workers N has risen. For example, initially when N equaled 9, output Y equaled 60 (point D in Fig. A.5). After the increase in K, if $N = 9$, then $Y = 30 \sqrt{9} = 90$ (point J in Fig. A.5).

This example illustrates some important general points about the graphs of functions of several variables:

1. To graph a function of several variables in two dimensions, we hold all but one of the right-side variables constant.

2. The one right-side variable that is not held constant (N in this example) appears on the horizontal axis. Changes in this variable do not shift the graph of the function. Instead, changes in the variable on the horizontal axis represent movements *along* the curve that represents the function.

3. The right-side variables that are held constant for the purpose of drawing the graph (K in this

example) do not appear on either axis of the graph. If the value of one of these variables is changed, then the whole curve shifts. In this example, for any given number of workers N the increase in machines K means that more output Y can be produced. Thus the whole curve shifts upward, from the solid curve to the dashed curve in Fig. A.5.

A.6 EXPONENTS

Powers of numbers or variables can be expressed by using superscripts called *exponents*. In the following examples 2 and 4 are the exponents:

$$5^2 = 5 \times 5 \qquad Z^4 = Z \times Z \times Z \times Z$$

For any numbers Z, a, and b, exponents obey the following rules:

$$Z^a \times Z^b = Z^{a+b} \qquad (Z^a)^b = Z^{ab}$$

To illustrate the first rule, note that $5^2 \times 5^3 = (5 \times 5) \times (5 \times 5 \times 5) = 5^5$. An illustration of the second rule is $(5^3)^2 = (5^3) \times (5^3) = (5 \times 5 \times 5) \times (5 \times 5 \times 5) = 5^6$.

Exponents do not have to be whole numbers. For example, $5^{0.5}$ is used to stand for the square root of 5. To see why it makes sense to define $5^{0.5}$ to be the square root of 5, note that by the second of our two rules for exponents, $(5^{0.5})^2 = 5^{(0.5)2} = 5^1 = 5$. That is, the square of $5^{0.5}$ is 5. Similarly, for any number Z and any whole number q, $Z^{1/q}$ is the qth root of Z. Thus $5^{0.25}$ means the fourth root of 5, for example. Using exponents, we can rewrite Eq. (A.5) as

$$Y = 2K^{0.5}N^{0.5},$$

where $K^{0.5} = \sqrt{K}$ and $N^{0.5} = \sqrt{N}$.

Most generally, consider any number that can be expressed as a ratio of two whole numbers p and q. Then using the rules of exponents, we have

$$Z^{p/q} = (Z^p)^{1/q} = q\text{th root of } Z^p.$$

Thus, for example, since 0.7 equals 7/10, $N^{0.7}$ equals the tenth root of N^7. For values of N greater than 1, $N^{0.7}$ is a number larger than the square root of N, $N^{0.5}$, but smaller than N itself.

Exponents can also be zero or negative. In general, the following two relationships hold:

$$Z^0 = 1 \qquad Z^{-a} = \frac{1}{Z^a}$$

Here is a useful fact relating exponents and elasticities: Suppose that two variables Y and N are related by a function of the form

$$Y = kN^a, \qquad (A.8)$$

where a is a number and k can be either a number or a function of variables other than N. Then the elasticity of Y with respect to N (see Section A.3) is equal to a.

A.7 GROWTH RATE FORMULAS

Let X and Z be any two variables, not necessarily related by a function, that are changing over time. Let $\Delta X/X$ and $\Delta Z/Z$ stand for the growth rates (percentage changes) of X and Z, respectively. Then the following rules provide useful approximations (proofs of the various rules are included for reference).

Rule 1. The growth rate of the product of X and Z equals the growth rate of X plus the growth rate of Z.

Proof. Suppose that X increases by ΔX and Z increases by ΔZ. Then the absolute increase in the product of X and Z is $(X + \Delta X)(Z + \Delta Z) - XZ$, and

the growth rate of the product of X and Z is given by

growth rate of (XZ) $\qquad$ (A.9)

$$= \frac{(X + \Delta X)(Z + \Delta Z) - XZ}{XZ}$$

$$= \frac{(\Delta X)Z + (\Delta Z)X + \Delta X\,\Delta Z}{XZ}$$

$$= \frac{\Delta X}{X} + \frac{\Delta Z}{Z} + \frac{\Delta X\,\Delta Z}{XZ}.$$

The last term on the right side of Eq. (A.9), $(\Delta X\,\Delta Z)/XZ$, equals the growth rate of X, $\Delta X/X$, times the growth rate of Z, $\Delta Z/Z$. This term is generally small; for example, if the growth rates of X and Z are both 5% (0.05), then the product of the two growth rates is only 0.25% (0.0025). If we assume that this last term is small enough to ignore, then Eq. (A.9) boils down to the result that the growth rate of the product XZ equals the growth rate of X, $\Delta X/X$, plus the growth rate of Z, $\Delta Z/Z$.

Rule 2. The growth rate of the ratio of X to Z is the growth rate of X minus the growth rate of Z.

Proof. Let W be the ratio of X to Z, so $W = X/Z$. Then $X = ZW$. By Rule 1, since X equals the product of Z and W, the growth rate of X equals the growth rate of Z plus the growth rate of W:

$$\frac{\Delta X}{X} = \frac{\Delta Z}{Z} + \frac{\Delta W}{W}.$$

Rearranging this equation to put $\Delta W/W$ on the left side and recalling that $\Delta W/W$ equals the growth rate of (X/Z), we have the desired result:

$$\text{growth rate of } (X/Z) = \frac{\Delta X}{X} - \frac{\Delta Z}{Z}. \quad (A.10)$$

Rule 3. Suppose that Y is a variable that is a function of two other variables X and Z. Then

$$\frac{\Delta Y}{Y} = \eta_{Y,X}\frac{\Delta X}{X} + \eta_{Y,Z}\frac{\Delta Z}{Z}, \qquad (A.11)$$

where $\eta_{Y,X}$ is the elasticity of Y with respect to X and $\eta_{Y,Z}$ is the elasticity of Y with respect to Z.

Proof (informal). Suppose that only X changes, so that $\Delta Z/Z = 0$. Then Eq. (A.11) becomes the definition of an elasticity, $\eta_{Y,X} = (\Delta Y/Y)/(\Delta X/X)$, as in Section A.3. Similarly, if only Z changes, Eq. (A.11) becomes $\eta_{Y,Z} = (\Delta Y/Y)/(\Delta Z/Z)$, which is the definition of the elasticity of Y with respect to Z. If both X and Z change, Eq. (A.11) says that the overall effect on Y is approximately equal to the sum of the individual effects on Y of the change in X and the change in Z.

Rule 4. The growth rate of X raised to the power a, or X^a, is a times the growth rate of X itself. In symbols,

$$\text{growth rate of } (X^a) = a\,\frac{\Delta X}{X}. \qquad (A.12)$$

Proof. Let $Y = X^a$. Applying the rule from Eq. (A.8) (and setting $k = 1$), we find that the elasticity of Y with respect to X equals a. Therefore by Eq. (A.11) the growth rate of Y equals a times the growth rate of X. Since $Y = X^a$, the growth rate of Y is the same as the growth rate of X^a, which proves the relationship in Eq. (A.12).

Example: The real interest rate. As an application of the growth rate formulas, we derive the equation that relates the real interest rate to the nominal interest rate and the inflation rate, Eq. (2.10).

The real value of any asset, say a checking account, equals the nominal or dollar value of the asset divided by the price level:

$$\text{real asset value} = \frac{\text{nominal asset value}}{\text{price level}}. \qquad (A.13)$$

Since the real value of an asset is the ratio of the nominal asset value to the price level, then according to Rule 2, the *growth rate* of the real asset value is approximately equal to the *growth rate* of the nominal asset value minus the *growth rate* of the price level. The growth rate of the real value of an interest-bearing asset equals the real interest rate earned by that asset; the growth rate of the nominal value of an interest-bearing asset is the nominal interest rate for that asset; and the growth rate of the price level is the inflation rate. Therefore Rule 2 implies the relationship

$$\text{real interest rate} = $$
$$\text{nominal interest rate} - \text{inflation rate}$$

which is the same relationship given in Eq. (2.10).

Problems

1. Graph the function $Y = 3X + 5$ for X such that $0 \leq X \leq 5$. What is the slope of this function?

2. Graph the function $Y = X^2 + 2$ for X such that $0 \leq X \leq 5$. Starting from the point at which $X = 1$, find the slope of the function for $\Delta X = 1$ and $\Delta X = -1$. What do you think the slope of the line tangent to the function at $X = 1$ is? (See Problem 3.)

3. For the function $Y = X^2 + 2$, use Eq. (A.4) to write a general expression for the slope. This expression for the slope will depend on the initial value of X, X_1, and on the change in X, ΔX. For values of ΔX sufficiently small that the term $(\Delta X)^2$ can be ignored, show that the slope depends only on the initial value of X, X_1. What is the slope of the function (which is the same as the slope of the tangent line) when $X_1 = 1$?

4. Suppose that the amount of output Y that a firm can produce depends on its amount of capital K and the number of workers employed N, according to the function

$$Y = K^{0.3}N^{0.7}.$$

   a. Suppose that $N = 100$. Give the function that relates Y to K and graph this relationship for $0 \leq K \leq 50$. (You need only calculate enough values of Y to get a rough idea of the shape of the function.)
   b. What happens to the function relating Y and K and to the graph of the relationship if N rises to 200? If N falls to 50? Give an economic interpretation.
   c. Given the function relating Y to K and N, find the elasticity of Y with respect to K and the elasticity of Y with respect to N.

5. Use a calculator to find each of the following.
   a. $5^{0.3}$ c. $(5^{0.25})^2$ e. $5^{0.2}/5^{0.5}$
   b. $5^{0.3}5^{0.2}$ d. $(5^{0.5}5^{0.3})^2\,5^{0.4}$ f. $5^{-0.5}$

6. a. Nominal GNP equals real GNP times the GNP deflator (see Chapter 2, Section 2.4). Suppose that nominal GNP growth is 12% and real GNP growth is 4%. What is inflation (the rate of growth of the GNP deflator)?
   b. The velocity of money V is defined by the equation

$$V = \frac{PY}{M},$$

   where P is the price level, Y is real output, and M is the money supply (see Eq. 4.3). In a particular year velocity is constant, money growth is 10%, and inflation (the rate of growth of the price level) is 7%. What is real output growth?
   c. Output Y is related to capital K and the number of workers N by the function

$$Y = 10K^{0.3}N^{0.7}.$$

In a particular year the capital stock grows by 2% and the number of workers grows by 1%. By how much does output grow?

Glossary

(The number in parentheses after the glossary term is the chapter in which that term first appears or is most extensively discussed.)

absorption: (7) total spending by domestic residents, firms, and governments, equal to $C + I + G$. (p. 247)

activist: (15) describes a policy strategy that involves active responses by the central bank to changes in economic circumstances. (p. 622)

acyclical variable: (9) a variable that is not sensitive to the business cycle. (p. 331)

aggregate demand: (4) the economywide demand for output when the goods market and the asset market are in equilibrium; the level of output corresponding to the intersection of the IS and LM curves. (p. 119)

aggregate demand (AD) curve: (11) the downward-sloping relation between the price level and the economywide demand for output. (p. 422)

aggregate demand management: (12) the use of monetary and fiscal policies, which shift the aggregate demand curve, to try to smooth out the business cycle; also known as macroeconomic stabilization or stabilization policy. (p. 476)

aggregate demand shocks: (12) shocks to the economy that shift the IS curve or the LM curve and thus affect the aggregate demand for output. (p. 477)

aggregate supply: (11) the amount of output supplied by firms in the economy at any given price level; in the long run, when prices and price expectations have adjusted to their equilibrium levels, aggregate supply equals full-employment output. (p. 426)

aggregate supply (AS) curve: (11) the relation between the price level and the total amount of output that firms supply. (p. 426)

aggregation: (1) the process of adding individual economic variables to obtain economywide totals. (p. 12)

appreciation: (13) see nominal appreciation, real appreciation. (p. 503)

asymmetric information: (17) a situation in which suppliers and demanders have different information about the good, service, or asset being traded. (p. 693)

auction markets: (17) markets with large numbers of traders in which prices are established by open competitive bidding. (p. 689)

automatic stabilizers: (16) provisions in the government's budget that automatically cause government spending to rise or taxes to fall when GNP falls. (p. 651)

average labor productivity: (1) the amount of output produced per unit of labor input (per worker or per hour of work). (p. 5)

average tax rate: (10) the total amount of taxes paid by a person divided by the person's income. (p. 373)

balance of payments: (7) the net increase (domestic less foreign) in a country's official reserve assets; equal to the official settlements balance. (p. 241)

balance of payments accounts: (7) the record of a country's international transactions. (p. 237)

bank capital: (17) the portion of a bank's assets that is financed by the bank's equity rather than by debt. (p. 707)

banking panic: (17) a situation in which bank runs spread throughout the banking system, affecting many banks simultaneously. (p. 703)

bank reserves: (15) liquid assets held by banks to meet the demands for withdrawals by depositors or to pay the checks drawn on depositors' accounts. (p. 601)

bank run: (15) a large-scale withdrawal of deposits from a bank, caused by depositors' fear that the bank may fail. (p. 604)

bequest motive: (5) the desire to leave inheritances. (p. 178)

binding borrowing constraint: (5) a restriction imposed by lenders that prevents a consumer from borrowing as much as he would choose to borrow if there were no constraint. (p. 182)

Board of Governors of the Federal Reserve System: (15) a group of seven governors, appointed by the President of the United States to staggered four-

728

teen-year terms, that provides the leadership of the Federal Reserve System. (p. 611)

boom: (9) in a business cycle, the period of time during which aggregate economic activity grows; also known as an expansion. (p. 323)

borrowing constraint: (5) a restriction imposed by lenders on the amount that someone can borrow. (p. 180)

bubble: (17) a situation in which the price of an asset is driven up higher than its fundamental value by investors' belief that the asset can be resold for an even higher price in the future. (p. 712)

budget constraint: (5) a relation that shows how much current and future consumption a consumer can afford given the consumer's initial wealth, current and future income, and the interest rate. (p. 157)

budget line: (5) the graph of the consumer's budget constraint; the budget line shows graphically how much current and future consumption a consumer can afford given the consumer's initial wealth, current and future income, and the interest rate. (p. 158)

business cycle: (9) a decline in aggregate economic activity (a contraction or recession) to a low point (a trough), followed by a recovery of activity (an expansion or boom) to a high point (a peak). A complete business cycle can be measured from peak to peak or from trough to trough. (p. 323)

business cycle chronology: (9) a history of the dates of business cycle peaks and troughs. (p. 322)

capital account: (7) the record of a country's international trade in existing assets, either real or financial. (p. 240)

capital account balance: (7) the value of capital inflows (credit items) minus the value of capital outflows (debit items) in a country's capital account. (p. 240)

capital good: (2) a good that is produced, is used to produce other goods, and—unlike an intermediate good—is not used up in the same period that it is produced. (p. 32)

capital inflow: (7) a credit (plus) item in a country's capital account that arises when a resident of the country sells an asset to someone in another country. (p. 240)

capital-labor ratio: (8) the amount of capital per worker, equal to the capital stock divided by the number of workers. (p. 292)

capital markets: (17) markets in which longer-term financial assets, such as mortgages and long-term corporate bonds, are traded. (p. 689)

capital outflow: (7) a debit (minus) item in a country's capital account that arises when a resident of the country buys an asset from abroad. (p. 240)

central bank: (15) the governmental institution respon-

sible for monetary policy, such as the Federal Reserve in the United States, the Bundesbank in Germany, and the Bank of Japan in Japan. (p. 599)

central planning: (8) an economic system in which all aspects of economic activity—including production, pricing, distribution, and investment decisions—are determined by a detailed government plan. (p. 309)

chronically unemployed: (10) workers who are unemployed a large fraction of the time. (p. 388)

classical approach: (1) an approach to macroeconomics based on the assumption that wages and prices adjust quickly to equate quantities supplied and demanded in each market. Classical economists generally argue that free markets are a good way to organize the economy and that the scope for government intervention in the economy—for example, to smooth out the business cycle—should be limited. See real business cycle theory. (p. 20)

closed economy: (1) a national economy that does not have trading or financial relationships with the rest of the world. (p. 9)

coincident variable: (9) a variable with peaks and troughs that occur at about the same time as the corresponding business cycle peaks and troughs. (p. 332)

cold turkey: (14) a rapid and decisive reduction in the growth rate of the money supply aimed at reducing the rate of inflation; in contrast with gradualism. (p. 586)

comovement: (9) the tendency of many economic variables to move together in a predictable way over the business cycle. (p. 324)

consumer price index: (2) a price index calculated as the current cost of a fixed basket of consumer goods divided by the cost of the basket in the base period. (p. 54)

consumption: (2) spending by domestic households on final goods and services. (p. 33)

consumption-smoothing motive: (5) the preference of most people for a relatively constant or stable pattern of consumption over time, as opposed to having very high consumption at some times and very low consumption at others. (p. 164)

contraction: (9) in a business cycle, the period of time during which aggregate economic activity is falling; also known as a recession. (p. 322)

contractionary fiscal policy: (6) a fiscal policy that shifts the *IS* curve downward, thereby leading to a contraction of aggregate demand. (p. 228)

contractionary monetary policy: (12) actions by the central bank that reduce the real money supply and shift the *LM* curve upward, leading to a contraction of aggregate demand. (p. 464)

convergence: (8) a tendency of living standards in different countries to become equal over time. (p. 305)

countercyclical variable: (9) a variable that tends to move in the opposite direction of aggregate economic activity over the business cycle (up in contractions, down in expansions). (p. 331)

credibility: (15) the degree to which the public believes the central bank's announcements about future policy. (p. 624)

credit controls: (17) legal restrictions on the amount of bank lending. (p. 696)

credit crunch: (17) a situation in which for some reason banks become unwilling or unable to supply additional credit. (p. 698)

credit market: (17) a market in which one party to the transaction gives up something of value today in exchange for a promise of payment in the future. (p. 692)

credit rationing: (17) a situation in which some members of a group of apparently similar potential borrowers receive credit but others do not. (p. 694)

currency: (4) paper money issued by the government; cash. (p. 111)

currency-deposit ratio: (15) the ratio of the currency held by the public to the public's deposits in banks. (p. 605)

current account: (7) the record of a country's international trade in currently produced goods and services. (p. 237)

current account balance: (7) the sum of all the credit items minus the sum of all the debit items in a country's current account. (p. 239)

cyclical unemployment: (14) the excess of the actual unemployment rate over the natural rate of unemployment; equivalently, unemployment that occurs when output is below its full-employment level. (p. 555)

debt: (17) a borrower's promise, given in exchange for an initial sum of money, to make a series of repayments over time. (p. 688)

debt-GNP ratio: (16) the quantity of government debt outstanding divided by GNP. (p. 658)

deflation: (1) a situation in which the prices of most goods and services are falling over time. (p. 9)

demand for money: (4) the quantity of monetary assets, such as cash and checking accounts, that people choose to hold in their portfolios. (p. 119)

depository institutions: (15) privately owned banks and thrift institutions (such as savings and loans) that accept deposits from and make loans directly to the public. (p. 599)

depreciation: (2) 1. the amount of capital that wears out during a given period of time. (p. 35) (13) 2. a decline in the exchange rate; see nominal depreciation, real depreciation. (pp. 503–504)

depression: (9) a particularly severe and prolonged downturn in economic activity. (p. 322)

derivative securities: (17) assets, such as financial futures and options, whose value is based on or *derived from* the values of other securities. (p. 689)

desired capital stock: (6) the amount of capital that allows a firm to earn the highest possible expected profit. (p. 203)

devaluation: (13) a reduction in the value of a currency by official government action under a fixed exchange rate system. (p. 504)

diminishing marginal returns to capital: (3) a feature of production functions that implies that the larger the capital stock already is, the less extra output can be gained by increasing the capital stock still further (with the number of workers held constant). (p. 72)

discount rate: (15) the interest rate charged by the Fed when it lends reserves to banks. (p. 616)

discount window lending: (15) the lending of reserves to banks by the Fed. (p. 616)

discouraged workers: (10) people who stop searching for jobs because they have become discouraged by lack of success at finding a job. (p. 382)

discretion: (15) the freedom of the central bank to conduct monetary policy in any way that it believes will advance the ultimate objectives of low and stable inflation, high economic growth, and low unemployment. (p. 621)

disinflation: (14) a fall in the rate of inflation. (p. 586)

disintermediation: (17) a situation in which depositors withdraw their funds from banks in order to hold nonintermediary financial assets. (p. 698)

distortion: (16) a tax-induced deviation in economic behavior from the efficient, free-market outcome. (p. 654)

diversification: (17) the practice of dividing one's financial wealth among a wide variety of different financial assets, each with its own set of risks, in order to reduce the overall riskiness of one's portfolio. (p. 686)

dividends: (17) regular payments made by firms to their shareholders. (p. 688)

dual labor market theory: (10) the theory that labor markets of advanced industrialized countries are divided into two submarkets: the primary labor market, which contains desirable long-term jobs; and the secondary labor market, which consists of undesirable short-term jobs with little opportunity for training or advancement. (p. 389)

duration (of an unemployment spell): (10) the length of time that an unemployment spell lasts. (p. 383)

economic model: (1) a simplified description of some aspect of the economy, usually expressed in mathematical form. (p. 16)

economic theory: (1) a set of ideas about the economy that have been organized in a logical framework. (p. 16)

effective labor demand curve: (12) an upward-sloping curve that shows how much labor is needed to produce any given amount of output, with productivity, the capital stock, and effort held constant. (p. 462)

effective tax rate: (6) a single measure of the tax burden on capital that summarizes the many provisions of the tax code that affect investment. (p. 212)

efficiency wage: (12) the real wage that maximizes worker effort or efficiency per dollar of real wages. (p. 451)

efficient markets theory: (17) a theory based on the assumption that asset prices equal the true economic values of the underlying assets. (p. 710)

effort curve: (12) the relation between the level of effort put forth by workers and the real wage; its positive slope indicates that a higher real wage induces workers to exert greater effort. (p. 450)

employment ratio: (10) the fraction of the adult population that is employed. (p. 382)

equilibrium: (3) a situation in which the quantities demanded and supplied in a market are equal. (p. 67)

equity: (17) assets issued by corporations that give the holder a share of ownership of the issuing firm. (p. 688)

exchange rate: (13) the number of units of foreign currency that can be purchased with one unit of the home currency; also known as the nominal exchange rate. (p. 499)

expansion: (9) in a business cycle, the period of time during which aggregate economic activity is rising; also known as a boom. (p. 323)

expansionary fiscal policy: (6) a fiscal policy that shifts the *IS* curve upward, thereby leading to an expansion of aggregate demand. (p. 227)

expansionary monetary policy: (12) actions by the central bank that increase the real money supply and shift the LM curve downward, leading to an expansion of aggregate demand. (p. 464)

expectations-augmented Phillips curve: (14) a relation that says that inflation depends, one for one, on expected inflation and negatively on the level of cyclical unemployment. (p. 564)

expected real after-tax rate of return: (6) the nominal after-tax rate of return minus the expected rate of inflation. (p. 200)

expected real interest rate: (2) the nominal interest rate minus the expected rate of inflation. (p. 57)

expected return: (4) the rate of return on an asset that financial investors expect to earn. (p. 118)

expenditure approach: (2) a procedure for measuring economic activity by adding the amount spent by all purchasers of output. (p. 28)

external funds: (17) funds raised by firms from financial investors outside the firm. (p. 700)

factors of production: (3) inputs to the production process, such as capital goods, labor, raw materials, and energy. (p. 68)

fads: (17) temporary deviations of asset prices from fundamental values that result from waves of investor optimism or pessimism. (p. 712)

FE line: (3) see full-employment line. (p. 96)

Federal Open Market Committee (FOMC): (15) a twelve-member committee (consisting of the seven governors of the Federal Reserve Board, the president of the Federal Reserve Bank of New York, plus four of the presidents of the other regional Federal Reserve Banks) that decides the course of monetary policy. (p. 612)

Fed funds rate: (15) the interest rate charged on reserves that are loaned from one bank to another. (p. 617)

final goods and services: (2) goods and services that are the end products of the productive process, in contrast to intermediate goods and services. (p. 32)

financial futures markets: (17) markets in which participants agree on a price for which specified financial assets will be delivered at some specified date in the future. (p. 689)

financial intermediaries: (17) institutions, such as banks and savings and loans, that borrow from the public and use the proceeds from their borrowing to purchase the debt or equity of ultimate borrowers. (p. 690)

financial panic: (17) a period of violent fluctuations in financial markets, typically including a sharp decline in stock prices, bankruptcies of major firms, and runs on banks. (p. 701)

fiscal policy: (1) policies concerning the level and composition of government spending and taxation. (p. 10)

fixed exchange rate system: (13) a system in which exchange rates are set at officially determined levels and are changed only by direct governmental action. (p. 500)

fixed-weight price index: (2) a price index that measures how much a fixed "basket" of goods costs in each year, relative to its cost in a base period. (p. 54)

flexible exchange rate system: (13) a system in which exchange rates are not officially fixed but are determined by conditions of supply and demand in the foreign exchange market; also known as a floating exchange rate system. (p. 500)

floating exchange rate system: (13) see flexible exchange rate system. (p. 500)

flow variable: (2) a variable that is measured per unit of time; an example is GNP, which is measured as output per year or quarter. See stock variable. (p. 47)

foreign exchange market: (13) the market in which the currencies of different nations are traded. (p. 499)

forward-looking consumer: (5) a consumer who, when making decisions, thinks about his or her future economic circumstances, such as expected future income and expected future consumption. (p. 155)

fractional reserve banking: (15) a banking system in which banks hold reserves equal to a fraction of their deposits, so that the reserve-deposit ratio is less than one. (p. 601)

frictional unemployment: (10) the unemployment that arises as the result of the matching process in which workers search for suitable jobs and firms search for suitable workers. (p. 386)

full-employment deficit: (16) what the government budget deficit *would be*, given the tax and spending policies currently in force, if the economy were operating at its full-employment level. (p. 653)

full-employment (FE) line: (3) a vertical line representing full-employment output in a diagram with output on the horizontal axis and the real interest rate on the vertical axis. (p. 96)

full-employment output: (3) the level of output that firms supply when wages and prices in the economy have fully adjusted to their equilibrium levels. (p. 80)

fundamental value: (17) the true economic value of a real or financial asset. (p. 710)

game theory: (15) the study of situations (games) in which individuals (players) use strategy in attempting to achieve their goals, possibly at the expense of the other players. (p. 626)

GDP: (2) see gross domestic product. (p. 32)

general equilibrium: (4) a situation in which all markets in an economy are simultaneously in equilibrium. (p. 135)

GNP: (2) see gross national product. (p. 30)

GNP deflator: (2) a measure of the price level, calculated as the ratio of current nominal GNP to current real GNP. (p. 53)

government budget deficit: (2) the government's outlays (spending) minus it tax receipts. (p. 41)

government budget surplus: (2) the government's tax receipts minus its outlays (spending). (p. 41)

government debt: (16) the total value of government bonds outstanding at any given time. (p. 658)

government outlays: (2) the government's purchases of goods and services plus transfers and interest payments; also known as government expenditures. (p. 40)

government purchases: (2) spending by the government on currently produced goods and services. (p. 35)

government saving: (2) the government's tax receipts minus its outlays; equal to the government budget surplus. (p. 43)

gradualism: (14) a prescription for disinflation that involves reducing the rate of monetary growth and the rate of inflation gradually over a period of several years; in contrast with cold turkey. (p. 587)

gross domestic product (GDP): (2) the value of production that takes place within a nation's borders, without regard to whether the production is done by domestic or foreign factors of production. (p. 32)

gross investment: (6) the total purchase or construction of new capital goods. (p. 214)

gross national product (GNP): (2) the market value of final goods and services newly produced by domestically owned factors of production. (p. 30)

growth accounting: (8) a method for breaking down total output growth into parts attributable to growth of capital, labor, and productivity. (p. 283)

hedgers: (17) financial investors who want to reduce their risk. (p. 686)

high-powered money: (15) the liabilities of the central bank, consisting of reserves and currency in circulation, that are usable as money; also known as the monetary base. (p. 600)

human capital: (8) the productive knowledge, skills, and training of individuals. (p. 306)

hyperinflation: (14) a situation in which the rate of inflation is extremely high for a sustained period of time. (p. 584)

hysteresis: (14) the tendency of the natural rate of unemployment to change in response to the actual unemployment rate, rising if the actual unemployment rate is above the natural rate and falling if the actual unemployment rate is below the natural rate. (p. 577)

income approach: (2) a procedure for measuring economic activity by adding all income received, including taxes and after-tax profits. (p. 28)

income effect: (5) a change in economic behavior (such as the amount a person saves or works) in response to a change in income or wealth. (pp. 194, 365)

income effect (of real interest rate on saving): (6) the tendency of savers to consume more and save less in response to an increase in the real interest rate because they are made wealthier; the tendency of borrowers to consume less and save more in response to an increase in the real interest rate because they are made less wealthy. (p. 194)

income effect (of real wage on labor supply): (10) the tendency of workers to supply less labor in response to an increase in the real wage because an increase in the real wage makes workers wealthier and leads them to want to consume more leisure. (p. 365)

index of leading indicators: (9) a weighted average of eleven economic variables, each of which leads the business cycle, used for predicting economic conditions. (p. 332)

industrial policy: (8) a strategy for economic growth in which the government, using taxes, subsidies, or regulation, attempts to influence the nation's pattern of industrial development. (p. 309)

inflation: (1) a situation in which the prices of most goods and services are rising over time. (p. 8)

inflation tax: (16) the resources raised by the government by issuing money and creating inflation; also known as seignorage. (p. 673)

insider-outsider theory: (14) a theory that attributes hysteresis of the natural unemployment rate to the supposed tendency of unions to try to obtain the highest real wage consistent with continued employment of employed members (insiders), without taking account of the interests of unemployed workers (outsiders). (p. 579)

instruments: (15) the policy tools that the Fed can use to influence the economy; these include reserve requirements, the discount rate, and, especially, open-market operations. (p. 618)

intermediate goods and services: (2) goods and services that are used up in the production of other goods and services in the same period that they themselves were produced; an example is wheat used up to make bread. (p. 31)

intermediate targets: (15) macroeconomic variables that the Fed cannot directly control but can influence fairly predictably and that, in turn, are related to the ultimate goals the Fed is trying to achieve; also known as indicators. (p. 618)

internal funds: (17) funds that the firm has available from its own operations, including undistributed profits and depreciation allowances. (p. 700)

intertemporal external balance: (13) the requirement that countries that have positive net exports and therefore lend abroad today must have negative net exports in the future; and, similarly, that countries that have negative net exports and borrow abroad today must have positive net exports in the future. (p. 512)

inventories: (2) stocks of unsold finished goods, goods in process, and production materials held by firms. (p. 32)

investment: (2) spending for new capital goods, called fixed investment, and increases in firms' inventory holdings, called inventory investment; see gross investment, net investment. (p. 34)

irrational bubble: (17) a situation in which the price of an asset is higher than its fundamental value because some investors do not have rational expectations about the asset's fundamental value. (p. 712)

IS **curve:** (3) a downward-sloping curve that shows the value of the real interest rate that clears the goods market for any given value of output. At any point on the *IS* curve, desired national saving equals desired investment. (p. 95)

J **curve:** (13) the typical time pattern of the response of net exports to a depreciation of the real exchange rate, in which net exports initially decline but then increase. (p. 508)

Keynesian approach: (1) an approach to macroeconomics based on the assumption that wages and prices may not adjust quickly to equate quantities supplied and demanded in each market. Keynesian economists are more likely than classical economists to argue that government intervention in the economy—for example, to smooth out the business cycle—may be desirable. (p. 21)

labor force: (10) the number of people willing to work, including unemployed people actively searching for work as well as employed workers. (p. 382)

labor hoarding: (12) a situation that occurs if, because of the costs of firing and hiring workers, firms continue to employ some workers in a recession that they otherwise would have laid off. (p. 482)

lagging variable: (9) a variable with peaks and troughs that tend to occur later than the corresponding peaks and troughs in the business cycle. (p. 332)

large open economy: (7) an economy that trades with other economies and is large enough to affect the world real interest rate. (p. 257)

leading variable: (9) a variable with peaks and troughs that tend to occur earlier than the corresponding peaks and troughs in the business cycle. (p. 332)

legal tender: (15) an asset that creditors are required to accept in settlement of debts. (p. 600)

leisure: (10) all off-the-job activities, including eating, sleeping, recreation, and working in the home. (p. 364)

lender of last resort: (17) a central bank that lends reserves to banks that need cash to meet the demands of depositors or to satisfy reserve requirements. (p. 704)

life cycle model: (5) a multiperiod version of the basic two-period model of consumer behavior that focuses on the patterns of income, consumption, and saving over the various stages of an individual's life. (p. 178)

liquidity: (4) the ease and quickness with which an asset can be exchanged for goods, services, or other assets. (p. 118)

LM **curve:** (4) an upward-sloping curve that shows the value of the real interest rate that clears the asset market for any given value of output. At any point on the *LM* curve, the quantities of money supplied and demanded are equal. (p. 130)

long-run aggregate supply (*LRAS***) curve:** (11) in the diagram with the price level on the vertical axis and output on the horizontal axis, a vertical line at full-employment output; indicates that in the long run the supply of output does not depend on the price level. (p. 432)

long-run Phillips curve: (14) in the diagram with inflation on the vertical axis and unemployment on the horizontal axis, a vertical line at the natural rate of unemployment; indicates that in the long run the unemployment rate equals the natural rate, independent of the rate of inflation. (p. 570)

lump-sum tax change: (6) a tax change in which each taxpayer's taxes change by a fixed amount that does not depend on the taxpayer's income, consumption, or other economic behavior. (p. 224)

M1: (4) the most narrowly defined monetary aggregate, made up of currency and travelers' checks held by the public, demand deposits (non-interest-bearing checking accounts) at commercial banks, and other checkable deposits. (p. 114)

M2: (4) a monetary aggregate that includes everything in M1 plus a number of other assets that are somewhat less moneylike, such as savings deposits, small-denomination (under $100,000) time deposits, noninstitutional holdings of money market mutual funds (MMMFs), and money market deposit accounts (MMDAs). (p. 115)

macroeconomics: (1) the study of the structure and performance of national economies and of the policies that governments use to try to affect economic performance. (p. 3)

macroeconomic stabilization: (12) the use of monetary and fiscal policies designed to promote steady economic growth without cyclical fluctuations or high inflation; also known as aggregate demand management or stabilization policy. (p. 476)

marginal cost: (12) the cost of producing an additional unit of output. (p. 461)

marginal product of capital (*MPK***):** (3) the amount of output produced per unit of additional capital. (p. 72)

marginal product of labor (*MPN***):** (3) the amount of output produced per unit of additional labor. (p. 75)

marginal revenue product of labor (*MRPN***):** (10) the benefit to a firm of employing an additional unit of labor, measured in terms of the extra revenue produced. (p. 355)

marginal tax rate: (10) the fraction of an additional dollar of income that must be paid in taxes. (p. 373)

margin requirement: (17) set by the Federal Reserve, the minimum fraction of the purchase price of stock paid for by the financial investor's own (nonborrowed) funds. (p. 714)

markup: (12) the excess of price over marginal cost. (p. 461)

Marshall-Lerner condition: (13) a technical condition that says that a depreciation of the real exchange rate will lead to an increase in net exports if exports and imports are sufficiently sensitive to changes in the real exchange rate. (p. 507)

medium of exchange: (4) an asset used in making transactions. (p. 113)

menu cost: (12) the cost of changing prices. (p. 459)

merchandise trade balance: (7) a country's merchandise exports minus its merchandise imports; also known as the trade balance. (p. 237)

misery index: (14) the sum of the unemployment rate and the rate of inflation. (p. 573)

misperceptions theory: (11) a theory, based on producers' inability to directly observe the general price level, that predicts that the aggregate quantity of output supplied rises above the full-employment level when the aggregate price level is higher than expected. (p. 429)

monetarism: (15) a school of macroeconomic thought that emphasizes the importance of monetary factors in the macroeconomy. (p. 622)

monetary aggregates: (4) the official measures of the money supply. (p. 114)

monetary base: (15) the liabilities of the central bank, consisting of reserves and currency in circulation, that are usable as money; also known as high-powered money. (p. 600)

monetary neutrality: (4) characterizes an economy in which changes in the nominal money supply change the price level proportionally but have no effect on real variables; the classical model with misperceptions and the Keynesian model predict that neutrality holds in the long run but not in the short run. (p. 139)

monetary policy: (1) policies determining the rate of

growth of the nation's money supply, which are under the control of a government institution known as the central bank (the Federal Reserve in the U.S.). (p. 10)

money: (4) assets that are widely used and accepted as payment. (p. 111)

money demand function: (4) the function that relates the real demand for money to output and interest rates on monetary and nonmonetary assets. (p. 122)

money markets: (17) markets for short-term financial assets (term to maturity of one year or less). (p. 689)

money multiplier: (15) the number of dollars of money supply that can be created from each dollar of monetary base, calculated as the ratio of the money supply to the monetary base. (p. 605)

money supply: (4) the amount of money available in an economy, consisting of currency in circulation and deposits; also known as the money stock. (p. 116)

monopolistic competition: (12) a market situation in which there is some competition but in which a relatively small number of sellers and imperfect standardization of the product allow individual producers to act as price setters. (p. 459)

multiple expansion of loans and deposits: (15) in a fractional reserve banking system, the process in which banks lend out some of their deposits, the loaned funds are ultimately redeposited in the banking system, and the new deposits are lent out again; as a result of the multiple-expansion process, the money supply can greatly exceed the monetary base. (p. 603)

national income: (2) the amount of income available to distribute among producers, measured as gross national product less depreciation and indirect business taxes. (p. 36)

national income accounts: (2) an accounting framework used in measuring current economic activity. (p. 26)

national saving: (2) the saving of the economy as a whole, including both private saving (business and household) and government saving. (p. 43)

national wealth: (2) the total wealth of the residents of a country, consisting of the country's domestic physical assets (such as its stock of capital goods and land) and its net foreign assets. (p. 47)

natural rate of unemployment: (14) the rate of unemployment that exists when the economy's output is at its full-employment level; consists of frictional unemployment and structural unemployment. (p. 554)

net exports: (2) exports of goods and services minus imports of goods and services. (p. 35)

net foreign assets: (2) a country's foreign assets (for example, foreign stocks, bonds, and factories owned by domestic residents) minus its foreign liabilities (domestic physical and financial assets owned by foreigners). (p. 47)

net investment: (6) the change in the capital stock over the year, equal to gross investment minus depreciation of existing capital. (p. 214)

net national product (NNP): (2) GNP minus depreciation. (p. 36)

nominal: (2) measured in terms of current market prices. (p. 50)

nominal after-tax rate of return: (6) the nominal rate of return earned after the payment of taxes. (p. 200)

nominal appreciation: (13) an increase in the nominal exchange rate in a flexible exchange rate system. (p. 503)

nominal depreciation: (13) a decrease in the nominal exchange rate in a flexible exchange rate system. (p. 503)

nominal exchange rate: (13) the number of units of foreign currency that can be purchased with one unit of the home currency; also known as the exchange rate. (p. 499)

nominal GNP: (2) the value of an economy's final output measured by using current market prices; also known as current-dollar GNP. (p. 51)

nominal interest rate: (2) the rate at which the nominal value of an interest-bearing asset increases over time. (p. 56)

nominal interest rate parity condition: (13) the condition that the nominal returns on foreign and domestic financial investments of identical risk and liquidity must be equal when measured in terms of a common currency. (p. 520)

nominal shocks: (11) shocks to money supply or money demand, which cause the LM curve to shift. (p. 404)

nonbinding borrowing constraint: (5) a restriction imposed by lenders on the amount that a consumer can borrow against future income, but one that does not affect actual borrowing because the consumer does not desire to borrow more than the restricted amount. (p. 182)

normative analysis: (1) an analysis of policy that tries to determine whether a certain policy should be used; involves both analysis of the consequences of the policy and value judgments about the desirability of those consequences. See positive analysis. (p. 19)

official reserve assets: (7) assets held by central banks, other than domestic money or securities, that can be used in making international payments. (p. 240)

official settlements balance: (7) the net increase (domestic less foreign) in a country's official reserve assets; equal to the balance of payments. (p. 241)

Okun's law: (14) a rule of thumb that says that output falls by 2.5% for each percentage point increase in the unemployment rate. (p. 555)

100% reserve banking: (15) a banking system in which banks hold reserves equal to 100% of their deposits. (p. 601)

open economy: (1) a national economy that has significant trading and financial relationships with other national economies. (p. 9)

open-market operation: (4) an open-market purchase or sale of assets by the central bank, used to affect the money supply. (p. 116)

open-market purchase: (15) a purchase of assets from the public by the central bank, used to increase the money supply. (p. 607)

open-market sale: (15) a sale of assets to the public by the central bank, used to reduce the money supply. (p. 607)

options markets: (17) markets in which a trader can buy the right (which she does not have to exercise) to buy or sell a financial asset at a fixed price within a certain period of time. (p. 689)

over-the-counter markets: (17) asset markets in which there is not a single trading location. (p. 689)

participation rate: (10) the fraction of adults who are in the labor force. (p. 382)

peak: (9) in a business cycle, the point at which economic activity stops increasing and begins to decline. (p. 323)

perfect competition: (12) a market situation in which there are many buyers and sellers, so that all buyers and sellers are price takers. (p. 458)

permanent income theory: (5) a theory that states that consumption depends on the present value of lifetime resources, with the implication that consumption responds much less to temporary than to permanent changes in income. (p. 170)

persistence: (9) the tendency for declines in economic activity to be followed by further declines, and for growth in economic activity to be followed by more growth. (p. 326)

personal disposable income: (2) the income of the household sector after payment of taxes and the receipt of transfer payments and interest from the government. (p. 40)

personal saving: (2) the saving of the household sector, equal to personal disposable income minus consumption; also known as household saving. (p. 43)

Phillips curve: (14) a relationship between the inflation rate and the unemployment rate; see expectations-augmented Phillips curve (p. 564), long-run Phillips curve (p. 570), short-run Phillips curve (p. 564), simple Phillips curve. (p. 559)

portfolio allocation decision: (4) the wealth holder's decision about which assets and how much of each asset to hold. (p. 118)

positive analysis: (1) an analysis of the economic consequences of a policy that doesn't address the question of whether those consequences are desirable. (p. 19)

present value: (5) the value of a future payment in today's dollars; equal to the amount of money that must be invested today at a given interest rate to be worth the specified payment at the specified date in the future. (p. 159)

present value of lifetime resources (*PVLR*): (5) the present value of current and expected future income plus initial wealth. (p. 160)

price index: (2) a measure of the average level of prices for some specified set of goods and services, relative to the prices of a specified base period. (p. 53)

price setter: (12) a market participant with some power to set prices; see monopolistic competition. (p. 458)

price stickiness: (12) in Keynesian theory, the tendency of prices to adjust only slowly to changes in the economy; also known as price rigidity. (p. 457)

price taker: (12) a market participant who takes the market price as given; see perfect competition. (p. 458)

primary government budget deficit: (16) a measure of the deficit that excludes government interest payments from total outlays; equal to government purchases of goods and services plus transfers minus tax revenues. (p. 648)

primary markets: (17) markets in which new securities are sold by their original issuers. (p. 689)

private disposable income: (2) the income of the private sector (households and businesses taken together) after payment of taxes and receipt of transfer payments and interest from the government. (p. 40)

private saving: (2) the saving of the private sector (households and businesses), equal to private disposable income minus consumption. (p. 42)

private sector: (2) the household sector and the business sector taken together. (p. 38)

procyclical variable: (9) a variable that tends to move in the same direction as aggregate economic activity over the business cycle (up in expansions, down in contractions). (p. 331)

product approach: (2) a procedure for measuring economic activity by adding the market values of goods and services produced, excluding any goods and services used up in intermediate stages of production. (p. 28)

production function: (3) a function that shows the amount of output that can be produced by using any given quantities of capital and labor. (p. 68)

productivity: (3) a measure of the overall effectiveness with which the economy uses capital and labor to produce output; also known as total factor productivity. (p. 68)

productivity shock: (11) a change in an economy's production function, that is, in the amount of output that can be produced by using given quantities of capital and labor; also known as a supply shock. (p. 404)

propagation mechanism: (11) an aspect of the economy, such as the behavior of inventories, that allows short-lived shocks to have long-term effects on the economy. (p. 436)

quantity theory of money: (4) a theory that asserts that nominal money demand is proportional to nominal GNP. (p. 125)

rational bubble: (17) a situation in which all financial investors have rational expectations and yet the price of an asset is above its fundamental value because of the self-confirming belief that its price will rise indefinitely. (p. 712)

rational expectations: (11) expectations that exist if the public's forecasts of various economic variables are based upon reasoned and intelligent examination of available economic data. (p. 435)

real: (2) measured in terms of the prices of a fixed base year. (p. 51)

real appreciation: (13) an increase in the real exchange rate, which increases the quantity of foreign goods that can be purchased with a given quantity of domestic goods. (p. 504)

real business cycle (RBC) theory: (11) a version of the classical theory that assumes that productivity shocks (supply shocks) are the primary source of cyclical fluctuations. (p. 404)

real depreciation: (13) a fall in the real exchange rate, which decreases the quantity of foreign goods that can be purchased with a given quantity of domestic goods. (p. 504)

real exchange rate: (13) the quantity of foreign goods that can be obtained in exchange for one domestic good; also known as the terms of trade. (p. 502)

real GNP: (2) the market value of an economy's final output measured in terms of the prices that prevailed during some fixed base period; also known as constant-dollar GNP. (p. 51)

real interest rate: (2) the rate at which the real value or purchasing power of an interest-bearing asset increases over time; equal to the nominal interest rate minus the rate of inflation. (p. 56)

real interest rate parity condition: (13) the condition that the expected real returns on foreign and domestic financial investments of equal risk and liquidity must be equal when measured in terms of the same good. (p. 520)

real shocks: (11) disturbances to the "real side" of the economy, such as shocks that affect the production function, the size of the labor force, the real quantity of government purchases, or the spending and saving decisions of consumers; real shocks affect the *IS* curve or the *FE* line. (p. 404)

real wage: (3) the real value of what firms must pay per unit of labor input that they employ; equal to the nominal (dollar) wage divided by the price level. (p. 77)

real-wage rigidity: (12) from the Keynesian perspective, the apparent tendency of real wages to move too little over the business cycle to keep the quantity of labor supplied equal to the quantity of labor demanded. (p. 449)

recession: (9) in a business cycle, the period of time during which aggregate economy activity is falling; also known as a contraction. (p. 322)

reserve-deposit ratio: (15) the ratio of reserves held by banks to the public's deposits in banks. (p. 601)

reserves: 1. (15) see bank reserves. (p. 601) 2. (7) see official reserve assets. (p. 240)

revaluation: (13) an increase in the value of a currency by official government action under a fixed exchange rate system. (p. 504)

reverse causation: (11) the tendency of expected future changes in output to cause changes in the current money supply in the same direction; used by real business cycle theorists to explain why the money supply leads the cycle. (p. 420)

Ricardian equivalence proposition: (6) the proposition that changes in the government budget deficit caused entirely by changes in (lump-sum) tax collections have no effect on the economy. (p. 225)

risk: (4) the possibility that the actual return received on an asset will be substantially different from the expected return. (p. 118)

risk premium: (17) the expected rate of return on a risky asset minus the expected rate of return on a safe asset. (p. 710)

rolling over the debt: (16) the borrowing of new funds by the government in order to pay off maturing government bonds. (p. 660)

rules: (15) a set of simple, prespecified, and publicly announced guidelines for conducting monetary policy. (p. 621)

saving: (2) current income minus spending on current needs. (p. 42)

secondary markets: (17) markets in which existing securities are traded. (p. 689)

seignorage: (16) government revenue raised by printing money; also known as the inflation tax. (p. 672)

shoe leather costs: (14) the costs in time and effort incurred in the process of economizing on holdings of cash. (p. 583)

short-run aggregate supply (*SRAS*) curve: (11) the relation between the price level and the amount of output supplied by firms that applies over the short period of time in which the expected price level remains unchanged. In the extended classical model the *SRAS* curve slopes upward, as producers are fooled into supplying more output when the price level is higher than expected. In the Keynesian model (12) the *SRAS* curve is horizontal, as firms meet demand at their initially set prices. (p. 432)

short-run Phillips curve: (14) the downward-sloping relation between inflation and cyclical unemployment that holds for a given expected rate of inflation. (p. 564)

simple Phillips curve: (14) the downward-sloping relation between inflation and unemployment, according to which inflation is positive when unemployment is below the natural rate and is negative when unemployment is above the natural rate; equal to the short-run Phillips curve for the case in which expected inflation equals zero. (p. 559)

small open economy: (7) an economy that trades with other economies but is too small to affect the world real interest rate. (p. 247)

speculators: (17) financial investors willing to take on risk, usually in exchange for a higher expected return. (p. 686)

spell of unemployment: (10) see unemployment spell. (p. 383)

spot markets: (17) markets in which financial assets are bought and sold for "cash" (actually, payment is made by check or by a transfer between the buyer's and seller's accounts). (p. 689)

stabilization policy: (9) monetary and fiscal policies designed to promote steady economic growth without cyclical fluctuations or high inflation; also known as macroeconomic stabilization or aggregate demand management. (p. 348)

statistical discrepancy: (7) the amount that would have to be added to the sum of the current and capital account balances for this sum to reach its theoretical value of zero. (p. 242)

steady state: (8) a situation in which the economy's output per worker, consumption per worker, and capital stock per worker are constant over time. (p. 293)

stock variable: (2) an economic quantity that is defined at a point in time; examples are wealth or the money supply. See flow variable. (p. 47)

store of value: (4) a means of holding wealth over time. (p. 113)

structural unemployment: (10) long-term and chronic unemployment arising from imbalances between the skills and other characteristics of workers in the market and the needs of employers. (p. 388)

substitution effect (of real interest rate on saving): (6) the tendency of consumers to save more, and thereby substitute future consumption for current consumption, in response to a higher reward for saving. (p. 192)

substitution effect (of real wage on labor supply): (10) the tendency of workers to substitute work for leisure in response to a higher real wage. (p. 365)

supply shock: (3) a change in an economy's production function, that is, in the amount of output that can be produced by using given quantities of capital and labor; also known as a productivity shock. (p. 75)

supply-side economics: (10) a school of economic thought based on the premise that all aspects of economic behavior—such as labor supply, saving, and investment—respond strongly to economic incentives, in particular, to incentives provided by the tax code. (p. 375)

tax-adjusted user cost of capital: (6) indicates how large the before-tax future marginal product of capital must be in order to make a proposed investment profitable. (p. 212)

tax rate smoothing: (16) a policy of maintaining constant tax rates over time (or keeping current tax rates equal to expected future tax rates) in order to minimize average distortions created by the tax code. (p. 656)

terms of trade: (13) the quantity of foreign goods that can be obtained in exchange for one domestic good; also known as the real exchange rate. (p. 502)

transfers: (2) payments by the government, excluding payments made in exchange for current goods or services; examples of transfers are Social Security and Medicare benefits, unemployment insurance, and welfare payments. (p. 35)

trough: (9) in a business cycle, the point at which economic activity stops falling and begins rising. (p. 322)

turning point: (9) a peak or a trough in the business cycle. (p. 323)

unanticipated inflation: (14) the actual rate of inflation minus the rate of inflation that was expected to occur. (p. 583)

underground economy: (2) the portion of the economy that includes both legal activities hidden from government record keepers and illegal activities. (p. 31)

unemployment: (1) the number of people who are available for work and actively seeking work but cannot find jobs. (p. 7)

unemployment rate: (10) the fraction of the labor force that is unemployed. (p. 382)

unemployment spell: (10) the period of time that an individual is continuously unemployed. (p. 383)

unilateral transfers: (7) payments made from one country to another that do not correspond to the purchase of any good, service, or asset. (p. 238)

unit of account: (4) the basic unit for measuring economic value. (p. 113)

user cost of capital: (6) the expected real cost of using a unit of capital for a specified period of time; equal to the depreciation cost plus the interest cost. (p. 206)

utility: (5) an individual's economic satisfaction or well-being. (p. 166)

variable-weight price index: (2) a price index that starts with the set of goods and services produced in the current period, then compares the cost of those goods and services today with what they would have cost in the base period. (p. 53)

vault cash: (15) currency held in the vaults of banks. (p. 612)

velocity: (4) the number of times the money stock "turns over" each period; calculated as nominal GNP divided by the nominal money supply. (p. 125)

wealth: (2) the assets minus the liabilities of an individual, firm, or country; also known as net worth. (p. 47)

world real interest rate: (7) the real interest rate that prevails in the international capital market in which individuals, businesses, and governments borrow and lend across national borders. (p. 247)

Name Index

Subject Index

KEY MACROECONOMIC DATA

Year	Nominal GNP[a] (PY)	Real GNP[b] (Y)	Consumption[b] (C)	Investment[b] (I)	Government Purchases[b] (G)	Net Exports[b] (NX)
1929	103.9	709.6	471.4	139.2	94.2	4.7
1933	56.0	498.5	378.7	22.7	98.5	−1.4
1941	125.5	909.4	531.1	138.8	235.6	3.9
1945	213.4	1354.8	592.7	76.5	704.5	−18.9
1950	288.3	1203.7	733.2	234.9	230.8	4.7
1955	405.9	1494.9	873.8	259.8	361.3	0.0
1960	515.3	1665.3	1005.1	260.5	403.7	−4.0
1961	533.8	1708.7	1025.2	259.1	427.1	−2.7
1962	574.6	1799.4	1069.0	288.6	449.4	−7.5
1963	606.9	1873.3	1108.4	307.1	459.8	−1.9
1964	649.8	1973.3	1170.6	325.9	470.8	5.9
1965	705.1	2087.6	1236.4	367.0	487.0	−2.7
1966	772.0	2208.3	1298.9	390.5	532.6	−13.7
1967	816.4	2271.4	1337.7	374.4	576.2	−16.9
1968	892.7	2365.6	1405.9	391.8	597.6	−29.7
1969	963.9	2423.3	1456.7	410.3	591.2	−34.9
1970	1015.5	2416.2	1492.0	381.5	572.6	−30.0
1971	1102.7	2484.8	1538.8	419.3	566.5	−39.8
1972	1212.8	2608.5	1621.9	465.4	570.7	−49.4
1973	1359.3	2744.1	1689.6	520.8	565.3	−31.5
1974	1472.8	2729.3	1674.0	481.3	573.2	0.8
1975	1598.4	2695.0	1711.9	383.3	580.9	18.9
1976	1782.8	2826.7	1803.9	453.5	580.3	−11.0
1977	1990.5	2958.6	1883.8	521.3	589.1	−35.5
1978	2249.7	3115.2	1961.0	576.9	604.1	−26.8
1979	2508.2	3192.4	2004.4	575.2	609.1	3.6
1980	2732.0	3187.1	2000.4	509.3	620.5	57.0
1981	3052.6	3248.8	2024.2	545.5	629.7	49.4
1982	3166.0	3166.0	2050.7	447.3	641.7	26.3
1983	3405.7	3279.1	2146.0	504.0	649.0	−19.9
1984	3772.2	3501.4	2249.3	658.4	677.7	−84.0
1985	4014.9	3618.7	2354.8	637.0	731.2	−104.3
1986	4231.6	3717.9	2446.4	639.6	761.6	−129.7
1987	4515.6	3845.3	2515.8	669.0	779.1	−118.5
1988	4873.7	4016.9	2606.5	705.7	780.5	−75.9
1989	5200.8	4117.7	2656.8	716.9	798.1	−54.1
1990	5463.6	4156.3	2682.4	689.6	820.5	−36.2